Penguin Books
Sisterhood Is Global

Robin Morgan is the author of *The Anatomy of Freedom* and *Going Too Far*, and several highly acclaimed books of poems: *Monster*, *Lady of the Beasts*, and *Depth Perception*. She has also edited two other anthologies: *Sisterhood Is Powerful* (the companion volume to this book) and *The New Woman*. A recipient of the National Endowment for the Arts Literature Grant and the Front Page Award for Distinguished Journalism, she is also a Contributing Editor to *Ms.* magazine, and for many years has been a feminist leader in the United States and an activist in the international women's movement.

RESEARCH DIRECTOR
Jane Ordway

Research and Copy
for Statistical Prefaces
Anne-christine d'Adesky
Toni Fitzpatrick
Annette Fuentes
Peggy Orenstein
Erica Romaine

Research Assistance
Pamela Abrams
Suzanna Fogel
Kenneth Pitchford
Laura Silver
Nancy Zirinsky

PRODUCTION DIRECTOR
Karen Berry

Computer Coordinator
Fran Rosen

Production
Marcia Landsman

Production Assistance
Sedef Guman
Amy Pellman
Blake Morgan Pitchford
Viv Sutherland
Mary Washburn
Anna Zeni

Translators
Magda Bogin
Carol Carl-Sime
Anne-christine d'Adesky
Cola Franzen
Annette Fuentes
Elisa Sierra Gutiérrez
Sherif Hetata
Lisa Kollisch

Edite Kroll
Agnes Liebhardt
Grace Lyu
Bobbye Ortiz
Rebecca Park
Akiko Tomii
Gloria Feiman Waldman

Interns: Joyce Chang, Nomi Itzhaik, Sandra Littell, Agnes Moses, Mercedes Suárez, Wendy Wolff, Donna Santos Yamashiro.

Extended Family: Patricia Carbine, Christiane Deschamps, Michelle Djenderedjian, Joanne Edgar, Dexter Guerrieri, Judith Helzner, Sylvia Kramer, Edite Kroll, Suzanne Braun Levine, Susan McHenry, Letty Cottin Pogrebin, Isel Rivero, Gloria Steinem, *Ms.* Magazine, The Women's Action Alliance, and the International Women's Tribune Center.*

Mascots: Ida, Grey Kitty IV, Loki.

* Also see Acknowledgments

Sisterhood Is Global

THE INTERNATIONAL WOMEN'S MOVEMENT ANTHOLOGY

Compiled, Edited, and with an Introduction by
ROBIN MORGAN

Penguin Books

The Sisterhood Is Global *Project wishes to express gratitude for the generosity of the following benefactors, without whose funding support this book would not have been possible:*

An anonymous woman donor	*Ms. Maya Miller*
The Columbia Foundation	*The Pathfinder Fund*
The Ford Foundation	*The Women's Division, General Board*
Ms. Frances Close Hart	*of Global Ministries, United Methodist*
Ms. Maria King	*Church*
Ms. Andrea Kirsch	*The World Division, Board of Global Ministries,*
Ms. Holly Lachowicz	*United Methodist Church*
The J. R. MacArthur Foundation	*The Wonder Woman Foundation*

Penguin Books Ltd, Harmondsworth, Middlesex, England
Viking Penguin Inc., 40 West 23rd Street, New York, New York 10010, U.S.A.
Penguin Books Australia Ltd, Ringwood, Victoria, Australia
Penguin Books Canada Ltd, 2801 John Street, Markham, Ontario, Canada L3R 1B4
Penguin Books (N.Z.) Ltd, 182–190 Wairau Road, Auckland 10, New Zealand

First published in the U.S.A. by Anchor Press/Doubleday 1984
Published in Great Britain by Penguin Books 1985

Printed in Great Britain by
Richard Clay (The Chaucer Press) Ltd,
Bungay, Suffolk

CONTENTS

Acknowledgments   ix

Prefatory Note and Methodology   xiii

Introduction: Planetary Feminism: The Politics of the 21st Century
by **Robin Morgan**   1

Afghanistan: Preface   38
The Silent Victims by **Sima Wali**   41

Algeria: Preface   45
The Day-to-Day Struggle by **Fatma Oussedik**   47

Argentina: Preface   50
The Fire Cannot Be Extinguished by **Leonor Calvera**   54

Australia: Preface   60
Women in a Warrior Society by **Sara Dowse and Patricia Giles**   63

Austria: Preface   69
Benevolent Depotism Versus the Contemporary Feminist Movement by **Cheryl Bernard and Edit Schlaffer**   72

Brazil: Preface   77
A Fertile but Ambiguous Feminist Terrain by **Danda Prado**   80

Britain: Preface   89
The Politics of Survival—While the Work Goes On
by **Amanda Sebestyen**   94

Canada: Preface   103
The Empowerment of Women by **Greta Hofmann Nemiroff**   107

Caribbean: Preface   114
The Dutch-Speaking Caribbean Islands: Fighting Until the End
by **Sonia M. Cuales**   117
The English-Speaking Caribbean: A Journey in the Making
by **Peggy Antrobus and Lorna Gordon**   121
The French-Speaking Caribbean: Haiti—A Vacation Paradise of Hell by **Cacos La Gonaïve**   129
The Spanish-Speaking Caribbean: We Women Aren't Sheep
by **Magaly Pineda**   134

Chile: Preface 138
Women of Smoke by **Marjorie Agosin**   141

China: Preface   145
Feudal Attitudes, Party Control, and Half the Sky
by **Xiao Lu**   154

Colombia: Preface   161
Fighting for the Right to Fight by **Luz Helena Sánchez**   163

Cuba: Preface   169
Paradise Gained, Paradise Lost—The Price of "Integration"
by **La Silenciada**   172

Denmark: Preface   **181**
Letter from a Troubled Copenhagen Redstocking   **by Tinne Vammen   184**

Ecuador: Preface   **190**
Needed—A Revolution in Attitude   **by Carola Borja   193**

Egypt: Preface   **197**
When a Woman Rebels . . .   **by Nawal El Saadawi   202**

El Salvador: Preface   **210**
"We Cannot Wait . . ."   **a collective statement by the Association of Salvadoran Women   213**

Finland: Preface   **218**
The Right to Be Oneself   **by Hilkka Pietilä   221**

France: Preface   **227**
Feminism—Alive, Well, and in Constant Danger   **by Simone de Beauvoir   232**

Germany (East): Preface   **239**
Witch Vilmma's Invention of Speech-Swallowing (A Parable) **by Irmtraud Morgner   245**

Germany (West): Preface   **248**
Fragmented Selves (A Collage)   **by Renate Berger, Ingrid Kolb, and Marielouise Janssen-Jurreit   251**

Ghana: Preface   **258**
To Be a Woman   **by Ama Ata Aidoo   261**

Greece: Preface   **269**
A Village Sisterhood   **by Margaret Papandreou   275**

Guatemala: Preface   **281**
Our Daily Bread   **by Stella Quan   285**

Hungary: Preface   **289**
The Nonexistence of "Women's Emancipation"   **by Suzanne Körösi   292**

India: Preface   **297**
A Condition Across Caste and Class   **by Devaki Jain   308**

Indonesia: Preface   **314**
Multiple Roles and Double Burdens   **by Titi Sumbung   321**

Iran: Preface   **327**
A Future in the Past—The "Prerevolutionary" Women's Movement   **by Mahnaz Afkhami   333**

Ireland(s): Preface   **342 and 346**
Coping with the Womb and the Border   **by Nell McCafferty   350**

Israel: Preface   **356**
Up the Down Escalator   **by Shulamit Aloni   363**

Italy: Preface   **368**
A Mortified Thirst for Living   **by Paola Zaccaria   373**

Japan: Preface   **379**
The Sun and the Shadow   **by Keiko Higuchi   385**

Kenya: Preface   **392**
Not Just Literacy, but Wisdom   **by Rose Adhiambo Arungu-Olende   397**

Korea (South): Preface   342
A Grandmother's Vision   by Soon Chan Park   407

Kuwait: Preface   409
God's Will—and the Process of Socialization   by Noura
Al-Falah   413

Lebanon: Preface   417
The Harem Window   by Rose Ghurayyib   421

Libya: Preface   427
The Wave of Consciousness Cannot Be Reversed   by Farida
Allaghi   432

Mexico: Preface   439
Pioneers and Promoters of Women   by Carmen Lugo   444

Morocco: Preface   447
The Merchant's Daughter and the Son of the Sultan   by
Fatima Mernissi   450

Nepal: Preface   457
Women as a Caste   by Manjula Giri   463

The Netherlands: Preface   468
In the Unions, the Parties, the Streets, and the Bedrooms
by Corrine Oudijk   472

New Zealand: Preface   479
Foreigners in Our Own Land   by Ngahuia Te Awekotuku and
Marilyn J. Waring   483

Nicaragua: Preface   488
To My Compañeras on the Planet Earth   by María Lourdes
Centeño de Zelaya   493

Nigeria: Preface   497
Not Spinning on the Axis of Maleness   by 'Molara Ogundipe-
Leslie   501

Norway: Preface   508
More Power to Women!   by Berit Ås   512

The Pacific Islands: Preface   518
All It Requires Is Ourselves   by Vanessa Griffen   520

Pakistan: Preface   528
Women—A Fractured Profile   by Miriam Habib   533

Palestine: Preface   539
Women and the Revolution   by Fawzia Fawzia   543

Peru: Preface   549
"Not Even with a Rose Petal . . ."   by Ana María
Portugal   553

Poland: Preface   558
"Let's Pull Down the Bastilles Before They Are Built"
by Anna Titkow   563

Portugal: Preface   570
Daring to Be Different   by Maria de Lourdes
Pintasilgo   574

Rumania: Preface   579
The "Right" to Be Persecuted   by Elena Chiriac   583

Saudi Arabia: Preface   585
An Emerging Social Force   by Aisha Almana   590

Senegal: Preface   **592**
Elegance Amid the Phallocracy   **by Marie-Angélique
Savané   596**

South Africa: Preface   **603**
Going Up the Mountain   **by Motlalepula Chabaku   611**
South Africa: A Bulletin from Within   **by anonymous white
South African feminists   621**

Spain: Preface   **624**
Women Are the Conscience of Our Country   **by Lidia
Falcón   629**

Sri Lanka: Preface   **635**
The Voice of Women   **by Hema Goonatilake   640**

Sudan: Preface   **647**
Women's Studies—and a New Village Stove   **by Amna Elsadik
Badri   653**

Sweden: Preface   **658**
Similarity, Singularity, and Sisterhood   **by Rita
Liljeström   664**

Thailand: Preface   **671**
We Superwomen Must Allow the Men to Grow Up
by Mallica Vajrathon   674

**The Union of Soviet
Socialist Republics:** Preface   **679**
It's Time We Began with Ourselves   **by Tatyana
Mamonova   683**

The United Nations: Preface   **693**
"Good Grief, There Are Women Here!"   **by Claire de
Hedervary   695**

The United States: Preface   **699**
Honoring the Vision of "Changing Woman"   **by Rayna
Green   708**

Venezuela: Preface   **717**
For As Long As It Takes   **by Giovanna Merola R.   719**

Vietnam: Preface   **725**
"The Braided Army"   **by Nguyen Thi Dinh   731**

Yugoslavia: Preface   **734**
Neofeminism—and Its "Six Mortal Sins"   **by Rada Iveković
and Slavenka Drakulić-Ilić   737**

Zambia: Preface   **742**
Feminist Progress—More Difficult Than Decolonization
by Gwendoline Konie   745

Zimbabwe: Preface   **749**
It Can Only Be Handled by Women   **by Olivia N.
Muchena   755**

Appendices: Cross-Cultural Rebellion—A Sampling of Feminist
Proverbs   **759**
"Sister"   **761**
Glossary   **764**
Bibliography   **770**
Index   **812**

ACKNOWLEDGMENTS

"Only she who attempts the absurd can achieve the impossible." That feminist proverb of indeterminate origin was adopted early by the *Sisterhood Is Global* staff. We did so out of desperation, since the enormity of the task we had embraced kept dawning on us anew, and could have had a highly intimidating, even paralyzing effect. But we also adopted the proverb out of a sense of good-humored self-ridicule, since each of us knew that the work was less an individual than a truly collective labor—and a labor of love, at that.

Literally thousands of women around the world (and some men of conscience as well) have helped bring this book—through more than a decade of conception and preparatory networking, plus five years of actual daily work—to completion. Some of them must remain anonymous, because they or their families still live in countries with totalitarian governments (of the Right *or* the Left), or because they are underground or in exile without proper papers, or because they face official recriminations ranging from loss of livelihood to imprisonment or loss of life. Still others should have been listed, but they helped the project without ever giving us their names; women's habit of self-effacement runs deep. Even among those who could and should have been listed, severe space limitations took their toll.

The "extended family members" on the Masthead are those specially close "chosen relatives" who kept us going over the years of this project in a variety of nurturing and creative acts—from getting us access to computers and lending us research notes to proofreading and making Chinese-food runs at 3 A.M. That "family" overlaps with some of the people named below, but in general the remarkable outpouring of encouragement and aid falls into specific categories.

The following are some of the numerous people who generously shared names and contacts in feminist international *networking:* Marta Aceredo, Sjiamsiah Achmed, Farida Allaghi, Aisha Almana, Judith Astelarra, Kathleen Barry, Magda Bogin, Charlotte Bunch, Patricia Carbine, Shirley Castley, Phyllis Chesler, Merle Goldman, Dorothea Goudart, Pat Hacker, Nancy Hafkin, Mary Heathcote, Aziza al-Hibri, Koryne Horbal, Laurel Isaacs, Kumari Jayawardena, Terry Kantai, Hala Katani, Marianne Kelling, Marta Lamas, Grace Lyu, Marcella Martinez, Fatima Mernissi, Naila Minai, Martha Moia, Marysa Navarro, Linda Ryan Nye, Andrea Pamfilis, Dunya Pastizzi-Ferencic, Amal al Rassam, Elizabeth Reid, Isel Rivero, Lala Rukh, Eileen M. Schlaeffler, Hannelore Schroeder, Alice Schwarzer, Claude Servan-Schreiber, Monica Sjoo, Hong Sookja, Diana Takieddine, Titi Memet Tanumidjaja, Raymonda Hawa Tawil, Catherine Tinker, Gaye Tuchman, Prathoomporn Vajrasthira, Valleska Van Roque, María Elena Walsh, Christa Wolf, and Joyce Yu.

The *research* aspect of this book was large in scope and complex in detail and process (see Prefatory Note and Methodology). Following are some of the people who graciously helped in innumerable ways: sharing their knowledge in conversation or correspondence, making a phone call for us in a language none of us had, bringing data personally across borders with tight security, tracking down statistics at libraries or consulates to which our research team was denied access. Without their help—and the expert aid in this area of many Contributors themselves—the Statistical Prefaces throughout this work would not have been possible: Laila Abou-Saif, Leila Abouzed, Judith Aksues, Jan Beagle, Rosemary Bell, Norma S. Chinchilla, Consul-General of India P. P. D'Souza, Joanne Edgar, Ruth Escobar, Murray Feshbach, Cathy Fitzpatrick, Laura Flanders, Gwendolyn Fortune, Manuela Franco, Myra Glazer, Alma Graham, Ellen Jamison, Amy Kesselman, Deborah Landau, Gail Lapidus, Arja Melajäervi, Mona N. Mikhail, Nesba Parisius,

Janina Rabinowitz, Diana Russell, Ani Sandstedt, Louise Shelley, Marilyn Souders, Sally Young, Jayne Werner, and Joan Hoff Wilson. In addition, the entire staff at the International Women's Tribune Center in New York deserves our special thanks; in particular, Anne Walker, Martita Midence, and Lori Ayre. They and the Center never flagged in their enthusiasm for the project, and in their hospitality to our researchers.

The following are among those who gave incalculable *general support* in myriad ways —from volunteering the use of a telex machine to giving advice on fundraising—and who offered ongoing faith in the project, and a strong, loving vision of its possibility: Bella Abzug, Mia Adjali, Kristin Anderson, Kathleen Barry, Carol Bellamy, Susan Berresford, Louise Boedeker, Alida Brill, Brenda Brimmer, Lydia Brontë, Prudence Brown, Constance Carroll, Diana Cullen, Carol Drexler, Frances T. Farenthold, Kay Fraleigh, Teresa Funiciello, Reinaldo García, Françoise Gilot, Darcy Gilpin, Kathryn Girard, Lesley Gore, Peggy Halsey, Valerie Harper, Doris Hess, Patricia Hewitt, Lucy Holland, Susan Lee Johnson, Susan Katzman, Kristina Kiehl, Roberta Kosse, Jaqueline Lapa, Laura Lederer, Suzanne Braun Levine, Bob Levine, Marilyn W. Levy, Lance Lindblom, Karin Lippert, June Makela, Catherine McKee, Judy Mello, Kathryn Mitchell, Freya Olafson, J. Stanley Pottinger, Paul Pottinger, Lucho Prugue, Rayna Rapp, Marilyn Richards, Ann R. Roberts, Avery Russell, Lois Sasson, Donna Shalala, Jill Sheffield, Bonnie Shepard, Joan Shigekawa, Susan Silk, Hugh Simon, Elinor Spalten, Lael Stegall, Catharine R. Stimpson, Margery Tabankin, Sally Tapoleski, Franklin Thomas, Amy Vance, Lindsy Van Gelder, Keith Walker, Marilyn Waring, Bill Wipfler, and Clare Woakes, and especially the staff of the Women's Action Alliance, who in patient and sisterly fashion put up with our long work hours as their sub-tenants in shared office space.

A particular debt of glad gratitude is owed to my colleagues at *Ms.* magazine, the largest and one of the oldest feminist periodical publications in the United States. The entire staff was wonderfully supportive of the *Sisterhood Is Global* project (indeed, the names of *Ms.* staff members appear in the above categories); the following people were especially helpful—with clip files, encouragement, and in a hundred other caring gestures, large and small: Jane Bosveld, Sheree Crute, Ann Hornaday, Rhoda Katerinsky, Lisa Lang, James Mitchell, Martha Nelson, Catherine O'Haire, Joan Philpott, Della Rowland, Ruth Sullivan, Mary Thom, Jane Williamson.

In addition to those internationalist US feminists whose names have already appeared in some of the above paragraphs, special mention must be made of others of my countrywomen active in the global women's movement, some of whom have been especially supportive of *Sisterhood Is Global*. The US women's movement is as non-monolithic as any other, and consequently the styles and analyses of US feminists are diverse, but any list (although regrettably non-comprehensive) of US women committed to global feminism would include: Bella Abzug, Donna Allen, Kathleen Barry, Bonnie Lee Bluh, Susan Brownmiller, Charlotte Bunch, Phyllis Chesler, Goldie Chu, Gena Corea, Mary Daly, Patricia Derian, Barbara Demming, Dana Densmore, Frances Doughty, Carol Downer, Erika Duncan, Andrea Dworkin, Ellen Frankfort, Arvonne Fraser, Betty Friedan, Leah Fritz, Gloria Greenfield, Shere Hite, Koryne Horbal, Florence Howe, Perdita Huston, Sonia Johnson, June Jordan, Sophie Keir, Mim Kelber, Audre Lorde, Congresswoman Barbara Mikulski, Kate Millett, Eleanor Holmes Norton, Grace Paley, Gracia Molina Pick, Jan Raymond, Carolyn Reed, Susan Rennie, Adrienne Rich, Faith Ringgold, Helen Rodríguez, Florence Rush, Diana Russell, Rochelle Ruthchilde, Congresswoman Patricia Schroeder, Susan Sontag, Gloria Steinem, Edith Van Horne, Carmen Delgado Votaw, Alice Walker, and Michele Wallace.

At our publisher, Anchor Press/Doubleday, my editor and friend Loretta Barrett has been a sustaining and challenging resource and has acted as midwife to the project for years; her sensitivity and commitment are deeply gratifying, as is the understanding and expertise of Paul Aron, and the cooperation of Harold Grabau, the gallant copy-editing of Gale McGovern, and, in book design, Alex Gotfryd, Doug Bergstreser, and Judith Neuman.

Last and most, there is the staff of *Sisterhood Is Global* (see the Masthead). It would require a separate book to tell that story; only the mere outlines of the work method are delineated in the Prefatory Note and Methodology, but that doesn't communicate the other side: the months and months of working until the small hours of the night (or indeed straight through until morning), the weekends and holidays spent poring over demographic yearbooks and charts, the rising at dawn to make phone calls to some country where it was midday. Believing that "the personal is political," we tried to forge a new work system that would reflect feminist vision—an approach somewhere between cheerfully anarchical self-responsibility and a practical, professional structure. We didn't always succeed; there were lively arguments, seemingly endless meetings, and not a few tears. But there was even more laughter, understanding, and teamwork. We ranged in age from adolescence to the mid-sixties, and were of an ethnic and racial composition as varied as the US women's movement itself. For some of the staff, this was the first professional job after much feminist activism; for others, it was the first *feminist* job after years of a professional career. The pay was little, the hours long, the dedication fierce—and contagious. For example, Peggy Orenstein joined us for a semester as an intern receiving academic credit for her work, reappeared after a year to work as a "recidivist" volunteer, and returned still later as a staff member. Annette Fuentes sometimes doubled as interpreter-translator for Spanish-speaking countries in addition to her research on the Statistical Prefaces. Anne d'Adesky did the same for French-speaking countries, while meeting deadline pressure on the Prefaces with energy. Toni Fitzpatrick, whose constancy and expertise earned her the responsibilities of Senior Researcher, meticulously persisted in research on a number of countries with ancient recorded histories and widely varied populations, as well as on some where the difficulty lay less in a lack than in an abundance of contemporary statistical data from which to choose (e.g., China, India, Indonesia, Sweden, USA). Fran Rosen not only organized the computer-technology aspect of the project but shared her editorial and political expertise as well. Marcia Landsman applied her considerable skills on a number of fronts—typing and word processing, proofreading, and Contributor communications. Comparable comments could be made about the devotion and the transformation of each staff member and volunteer of the *Sisterhood Is Global* team. Job functions frequently blurred—as did day and night, exhilaration and exhaustion. Pride in the audacity of our effort was matched only by a growing humility at the endurance and valor of women across the globe whose lives we were describing. We learned much—things we hadn't known but wanted to learn, and things we hadn't even known we hadn't known. We are all of us forever changed by having been part of *Sisterhood Is Global.*

It is almost impossible, however, to find words of gratitude, praise, and respect worthy of three women in particular. About Isel Rivero's voluntary and multifaceted contribution—her wisdom, courage, nurturance, wit, and love—I will try to write at greater length in a future work. Jane Ordway, who worked for two years on the project before there was any funding available for salaried staff, has consistently given inspiration, insight, and craft—not the least of which has been an eye for the finest details of research and an intrepid insistence on the highest possible standards—to this book. Karen Berry's devotion to the project has been quite literally round-the-clock, unfaltering, and always enacted with astonishing grace; her virtuosity of skills—technical, editorial, managerial, political, and interpersonal—is rivaled only by her keen intelligence and compassionate spirit. She is, in effect, Assistant Editor of *Sisterhood Is Global.*

That such women are my cherished friends I count as a mark of honor; that we passionately share a feminist vision of transforming the world I count as a sign of hope. A women's revolution, for me, consists in part of having worked with the above-named women in particular, women able to laugh at (and weep for) themselves and each other, and equally able to feel the pain and rage of women they have never met, in regions they have never seen, as intensely as if it were their own—which it is. When we had been up for two days and nights solid to meet another deadline and were still, at 5 A.M., translating cables or editing manuscripts or planning fundraising efforts or organizing bibliography cards, when we laughed together over the vagaries of politics or grieved together over the dowry murder of a thirteen-year-old bride half a world away, we were never more ourselves—and also *more* than ourselves.

Male-led revolutions, so often and so tragically mere power exchanges in a basically unaltered structure, have left dramatic accounts of their crises and heroism—of the Long March, the assault on Moncada, the taking of the Bastille, the siege of the Winter Palace. If such revolutions sometimes seem to have been based on the concept of dying for a cause, woman-conceived transformation seems more about daring to live for a cause, a heroism more difficult because it is daily—and ostensibly less dramatic. Yet I know that were I ever to find myself in a cave at Yenan or facing the gates of a Winter Palace, these are the women at whose side I would want to stand.

R.M.

PREFATORY NOTE AND METHODOLOGY

Sisterhood Is Global has been more than twelve years in conception and development and five years in its actual accomplishment. I first considered compiling and editing an international feminist anthology in 1968, shortly before the publication of *Sisterhood Is Powerful,* the first anthology of writings from the US women's movement. In fact, an internationalist perspective began to surface during my compilation of that earlier anthology, which includes articles by women of many different cultures within the United States. But much intervened in the following decade, including the great rush of US feminist activism, plus six books of my own. Most important, in 1968 a consolidated feminist network on the cross-national front did not yet exist. That was to require years of hard work, patience, travel, meetings, and changed sensibilities on the part of all of us. It was not until the late 1970's that my old dream of this book began to take shape again. Even then, and despite an awareness that the task would be far more challenging than *Sisterhood Is Powerful,* neither I nor the women who later joined me in the project had any idea of just how large, complex, and difficult an endeavor we had undertaken. Perhaps that was just as well; our naïveté served us where our courage might have failed.

The book's methodology evolved with the project. For example, the originally planned one-page "background" introductions to each country's article kept expanding. As both our knowledge and our curiosity deepened, our standards rose, and the information categories became more sophisticated. The data that came in were simply too vital and fascinating to exclude, especially since much hitherto had been unavailable and/or unpublished. Thus, the Statistical Prefaces came into being. They then necessitated a larger research staff, still more international phone calls and cables, increased office space, and, eventually, the use of word processors and computers—all of which in turn required additional fundraising. Every aspect of *Sisterhood Is Global* developed in this fashion, took more time than planned, and cost more effort than estimated—but was more rewarding than ever imagined.

The Countries

Seventy countries, plus the United Nations itself, are covered in this book. While by no means a complete list of all the world's nations, it is nonetheless, to our pride, a representative one. Every region, type of government system, and stage of "development" is here. The majority are Third World countries (as are the majority of the countries on the planet). Yet despite the wide range of nations represented, I wish that space and time limitations had permitted us to be even more inclusive.

For instance: to my regret, the women's movement in the Philippines (which has been so dynamic in opposing the sex-tourism industry) is not a presence; nor is Iceland, which has a woman president (Vigdis Finnbogadottir) and which held a day-long women's strike in 1976 to demonstrate women's importance to the economy. Although we are proud to include a distinguished and large representation from North Africa and the Arabian Peninsula, Jordan, sadly, is absent.[1] China is present, but Taiwan, unfortunately, is not; we tried but failed to gain access to feminist activists, including Lu Hsiu-Lien, the leading Taiwanese feminist writer currently serving a twelve-year prison sentence for "seditious feminist activism."

---

[1] Jordanian women won suffrage in 1974; by 1980, a woman was appointed Minister of Social Affairs; since 1965, the amount of research on women in Jordan exceeds that in any other field.

Our best efforts were also unsuccessful in obtaining articles from Angola, Bangladesh, Belgium, Bolivia, Cameroon, Chad, Czechoslovakia, Ethiopia, Guinea, Iraq, Mozambique, Paraguay, Syria, Tanzania, Tunisia, Turkey, Uruguay, the Yemens, Zaire, and Zanzibar. Sometimes the women's movement in a country was so informally structured that the most thorough networking seemed unable to locate national spokeswomen; in certain other countries, despite the existence of an established movement, a woman could not write publicly about that movement in an international forum because of censorship strictures; in still other cases, where a totalitarian government or the rise of religious fundamentalism had placed the women's movement in a totally suppressed or highly endangered state, no feminist activist could risk open communication—although many of the Contributors in this volume did manage to do so in such circumstances. Last, there were women who were forced for a variety of reasons to withdraw after already having agreed to write articles. During a five-year period, the personal and political fates of more than a hundred women all over the world change drastically: revolutions take place, people are elected to high office or forced to go underground or into exile, people feel less (or more) free to write what they believe. The country representation in *Sisterhood Is Global* was assembled, therefore, in a process kept necessarily fluid, since in many cases the life conditions—or the lives themselves—of Contributors were at stake.

There are cases of "doubling" in this book—for example, where a country has been partitioned. Both the German Democratic Republic (East Germany) and the Federal Republic of Germany (West Germany) are separately represented. We had wished to offer the same presentation of both Koreas, but despite repeated efforts to obtain a contribution from the Democratic People's Republic of Korea (North Korea), no response came back. (For those entries which have more than one article on a single country, or more than one Contributor, see the section on the Contributors below.) The United Nations seemed an important inclusion, for reasons delineated in the Editor's Note preceding that article, but mostly because as the largest world body, it often functions as a model internationally—yet it also discriminates against women. It had been our intention from the first to include Palestine as well as Israel, and we are especially heartened by the strong *feminist* voices from both, printed here.

The Contributor articles, as well as the Statistical Prefaces preceding them, vary somewhat in length. In the case of the articles, this was usually because of the Contributor's choice of approach and the breadth of issues she was engaging; in the case of the Prefaces, it was usually owing to the differing presence or absence of obtainable current data on a particular country, and/or the length of its recorded history (e.g., China, Egypt). Generally, both the Contributions from and the Prefaces on Third World countries are longer than others. *Sisterhood Is Global* is merely an opening statement to what I hope will be many such international feminist anthologies, to further the dialogue between and solidarity of women everywhere. This book is not intended to be a definitive collection of all countries (or of all the women in any given country), but is meant to be a broadly representative, energetic, and varied assemblage of facts and articles by women whose main connection to one another is a mutual commitment to worldwide freedom for female human beings.

The Contributors

The women whose articles appear in *Sisterhood Is Global* are a deliberately eclectic mix: grass-roots organizers, members of parliaments, novelists, scientists, journalists, guerrillas, scholars, poets, former heads of states, women in exile or underground, public feminist spokespersons and "closet feminists" in international diplomatic circles, activists and theorists, women never before heard from and women already known worldwide. The political spectrum embraces radical feminist, moderate/reform feminist, and socialist feminist, to show as wide as possible a world view of women's activism, and in order to see just where the differences, similarities, parallels, and overlaps really are. Each Contributor is a native of the country about which she writes; the sole exception is US-born Margaret Chant Papandreou, who has given most of her life to Greece, is a Greek citizen, and has earned the acceptance that the Greek people show her. Personally, the Contributors reflect (and reflect on) virtually every aspect of life. In their articles, they address themselves to peace, war, and development issues, agriculture and economics, sexuality and sexual preference, motherhood, nationalism, tribalism, battery, rape, contraception, religion, democracy, art, suppression, organizing techniques, youth and age, education, marriage customs, tactics, revolution, culture, spirituality—and more. A few wrote, of necessity, under pseudonyms. In several cases, authorship is collaborative, and usually so as a special sign of feminist solidarity (the Maori and European-descent co-authors of the New Zealand piece, for instance). There are a few countries represented by two-part contributions, again for specific reasons: South Africa's devastating apartheid system is movingly presented by an African feminist activist now in exile, and also by several necessarily anonymous white feminist activists still living and organizing inside the country. The reasons for other such doublings are similarly self-evident. For each Contributor, and for differing reasons, writing her article was an act of political and personal courage.

The Contributors were invited to participate in this book, and all except four of the articles (which are expanded versions of material printed earlier) were specifically assigned and appear here for the first time. The choice of whom to invite was extremely difficult. But by 1980, after years of networking in the international feminist movement, I was privileged to know many individual feminists from other countries, and the respectful trust inherent in such personal contact was a great help in gaining advice on the delicate choice of whom to invite from a particular country; further networking within that country usually confirmed the choice. In some cases (notably in the Arab world and in Latin America) women's-rights activists who already were my friends graciously suggested the names of sister activists in neighboring countries—a sort of national networking extended to the regional level—a "ripple effect."

To facilitate the onerous task of trying to depict the status of one's countrywomen in a limited space, each of the Contributors was given suggested guidelines for her own contribution, although she was urged to accept or ignore these guidelines at her own will, and many did indeed diverge from them. The guidelines included addressing such questions as: What is the basic situation of women in your country, the worst obstacle/adversary women face, the greatest strength they possess? What are the cutting-edge issues (which could range from suffrage to ending genital mutilation, from basic development issues to electing a woman prime minister)? What seem the most workable ways of uniting women in your country? Is there an organized women's movement there and, if so, what is its composition? How can other women in other countries most effectively and sensitively support their sisters in your country? Each Contributor was asked to focus her article as much as possible on present, political, and personal realities, and each was free to choose a format of her own devising. To our delight but not surprise, the Contributors embraced their responsibility with splendid creativity, managing each in her own unique fashion to depict the situation of her countrywomen with depth, inclusiveness, and fairness to the different factions of her nation's women's movement, while still maintaining the integrity of her own beliefs.

Consequently, the rich diversity in style and tone ranges from scholarly exegesis to poetry, from first-person experience to theoretical analysis, from epistolary format to journalistic reporting. Our emphasis is on *the individual voice of a woman speaking not as an official representative of her country but rather as a truth teller,* with an emphasis on *reality as opposed to rhetoric.* Thus, all but two of the articles are by women writing autonomously; despite our attempt to obtain such voices from all participating countries, the exceptions are El Salvador and Vietnam, appearing here, respectively, with articles by the official women's association of the insurgent government and by the president of the official women's federation of the incumbent government.

Each Contributor also provided a brief biography on herself and a short list of Suggested Further Reading on women in her country (both of which appear at the end of each article). Whenever possible, the Statistical Preface for her country was sent to each Contributor for her approval; in many cases, the Contributors' own research was invaluable for data in the Prefaces (see the section on Preface methodology below).

As the articles began arriving (on staggered deadlines), those requiring translation were routed to translators specially selected not only for their linguistic capabilities but also for their political sensitivity. The pieces then returned to me for editing, after which they were sent back to their authors for final approval. The translation and editing processes both were aimed at preserving the politics, flavor, imagery, and tone of each writer, while making sure that the article was easily approachable in lucid, lively, accessible prose. The cooperation with which virtually all of the Contributors responded compensated for postal delays, language barriers, and the sheer bulk of material with which we were dealing.

The Statistical Prefaces

These introductory sections to each Contributor's article are intended to perform two vital functions:

1) to free the Contributor from having to explain basic facts and background about her country, so that she can proceed directly to discussing the current status of women, central issues, indigenous needs and tactics, and strategies for change, and

2) to be of use to scholars in women's studies, international affairs, development and population issues, etc., as well as to governmental and nongovernmental women's groups, international agencies, and the general reader; to provide a wealth of data, carefully researched and sourced, some of which hitherto has been unavailable, and all of which has never before been assembled in one volume for easy reference.

Our ambitious intention quickly encountered its major obstacle: expectably but infuriatingly, most of the countries in the world have compiled very little data on their female citizens. Expectable because virtually all countries exist under patriarchal systems—not only of government but also of scholarly research—a sexism so pervasive as to become all but invisible. Women disappear. Or we do appear (statistically) as units of production or reproduction, as workers or mothers, even as daughters, sisters, and wives—but data on the "sexual politics" of our lives (battery, rape, sexual preference, incidence of sexual harassment or of incest, etc.) is scarce or nonexistent, and basic research on "what women want" has been scrupulously avoided. The United Nations itself, with characteristic understatement, recommended that each nation convene "a national conference of users and producers of the information in question . . . with a view to making recommendations concerning the desirable and possible expansion of the data base on women."[2] Meanwhile, international and national funding is not easily accessible to women social scientists—who are the obvious scholars to conduct such research, not only because they are freer of androcentric bias but also because they are likely to elicit more trust and therefore more honest responses from the female respondents of their studies. Meanwhile, too, even those nations with good intentions continue to approach "the woman question" with strategies based on questionable data gained through questionable methodology, and in many cases information that is more than a decade old (even in this epoch where change is taking place with greater rapidity than ever before).

The heartening news in all this, however, is that women scholars (and some male scholars of conscience) have persisted nonetheless in their research on the more than half the human species which is female. They are doing so more and more in independent research, and sometimes with the beginning of academic or governmental support for their invaluable contribution. Many of the Contributors to *Sisterhood Is Global* are among these scholars, and much of the material in the Statistical Prefaces is culled from studies completed only recently, or from data previously suppressed, or from sources once thought unapproachable, or from original research by the Contributors or their colleagues, or by our own research staff. Nevertheless, a new frustration settled in toward the end of the book's production: although we updated legislative and statistical data (even through galley proofs), there are cases where women's status—either progress or setback—has already altered.

Each Statistical Preface was put through a crucible of care. The research had to be conducted with as much sensitivity and as little Western ethnocentrism as possible— and had to be checked, re-checked, and edited with the same consciousness. (Indeed, we all learned much about the absence of such consciousness in a great deal of the already existing data we consulted.)

After a country had been assigned to a particular researcher, she immersed herself in various sources—the *Sisterhood Is Global* international library I had been assembling for some years, the libraries of the Women's Action Alliance, the International Women's Tribune Center, and the United Nations, public and specialty libraries, the Columbia University International Law Library (for civil and penal codes, legislation, etc.), and other published sources. She then visited or wrote UN Specialized Agencies, the country's UN mission as well as its consulate, contacted its embassy in Washington, and combed through the "country files" I had been compiling since the late 1960's—files of newspaper clippings, correspondence with women in that country, feminist media reports from the area. Again, feminist networking was invaluable here (see Acknowledgments): one could call a member of the Asian-Pacific Women's Caucus in the US, for example, for a contact who would in turn know of reliable resource people on China. On more than one occasion, we were able to find a scholar who had only recently finished the first study on a specific issue in a particular country, and who would generously make her not-yet-published findings available to us.

When the researcher had assembled as much information as she could, she drafted the Statistical Preface. It then proceeded through the staff in five routed stages of fact-checking, source evaluation, rewrites, copy editing and styling, and my final rewriting/editing. Whenever possible, it was then sent to that country's Contributor for her cri-

---

[2.] "Supplement I: Activities Designed to Improve the Data Base for Planning for Women's Participation in Development." Summary of Recommendations for Action, UNDP (G3100-1), 500–01, United Nations, Sept. 14, 1981.

tique. Even at that stage, a Preface might have information gaps; in most cases, this was because studies had not yet been done and the data simply did not exist, but sometimes it was because the information was available only in the subject country itself. Again and again, the Contributors solved the latter problem for us—going to statistical bureaus and libraries in their own countries, or to their own individual research notes, and answering what questions could be answered. In addition, they educated us further as to subtleties of possible misunderstanding that had so far escaped our editing. At every stage, updates were inserted and points clarified.

Preface Structure

All sources for data in the Statistical Prefaces, both general sources and those for specific countries, appear in the comprehensive Bibliography at the back of this book.

Each Statistical Preface begins with a brief geographical placement and area description of the country, population (and percentage female),[3] capital city, and, in the rare cases where the head of state is a woman, that fact as well.

The next section, "Demography," cites Languages, Races or Ethnic Groups, Religions, Education (broken down into primary, middle, and higher education, and with female-male differentiation), Literacy[4] (with female-male comparison rates where obtainable), and the rates of Birth, Death,[5] Infant Mortality,[6] and Life Expectancy[7] (with female-male comparison rates where obtainable). We have not always included the maternal death rate, due to space restrictions and the frequent unavailability of recent, or any, data; when such a rate is included, however, it appears further on in the Family section.

The Preface then proceeds to a "Government" paragraph, summarizing the political system of the country, and giving information on Voting (if special circumstances prevail), Women's Suffrage, Equal Rights legislation, and Women in Government.

[3] Population figures and percentage female are commonly taken from the latest available censuses, or from other sources which themselves must offer estimates based on incomplete data or rough estimates, particularly in the so-called developing countries.

[4] All adult figures dated 1977 are drawn from the *World's Women Data Sheet* of the Population Reference Bureau, Inc., which bases its information on the UNESCO *Statistical Yearbook, 1977.* (Literacy figures otherwise dated are from usually more recent sources specific to that country; "female" and "male" are used in these cases when sources do not specify age.) *World's Women Data Sheet* noted that "country definitions of 'adult' and 'literacy' vary. These data are generally based on the most recent census or survey from which an estimate can be derived." In our Prefaces, when we use the terminology "women" and "men" we are referring to adult populations only (although, again, the definition of "adult" varies from country to country).

[5] Birth and death rate figures in this book usually are sourced from the *1980 World Population Data Sheet,* whose dates are "1977 or 1978" for "developed" countries and 1975–80 for "less developed" or "developing" countries; in the latter case, the source notes that the statistics are frequently rough estimates because of less complete registration of births and deaths.

[6] Our infant mortality data refer to the number of deaths of infants under one year of age and bear the dates 1977 for developed countries and 1975–80 for less developed countries; they are based on the *World's Women Data Sheet,* which notes, "For most less developed countries, rates were derived by applying an estimated 1975–80 sex differential to the most recently available estimate of the combined infant mortality rate as shown on the *1980 World Population Data Sheet* of the Population Reference Bureau." This sheet, in turn, notes, "For many less developed countries with incomplete registration, [these] rates are the latest available estimates."

[7] If dated 1975–80, life expectancy data refer to life expectancy at birth, and are drawn from the *World's Women Data Sheet,* which notes that such estimates of life expectancy should be regarded only as rough approximations when pertaining to less developed countries.

After this, a section headed "Economy" covers the country's currency,[8] Gross National Product and Per Capita Income, Women's Wages as a Percentage of Men's, Equal Pay Policy, Production (Agricultural/Industrial), Women as a Percentage of Labor Force[9] (and a breakdown where available according to women as a percentage of agriculture,[10] industry, and the military[11]), (Employed) Women's Occupational Indicators,[12] and Unemployment[13] (with rates by sex when obtainable).

A special word is necessary about the "Economy" section of the Statistical Prefaces. Perhaps no other category shows so distressingly the confusion, lack of uniform international standards, and methodological bias—not only in terms of sex but also of age, race, class, and urban versus rural populations—as do the statistics in this area. For example, there is the general problem of having no standard definition of "unpaid family workers" (see footnote 9)—who are, in the vast majority, women. Neither is there any frequent or consistent acceptance of the fact that virtually all women *are* "economically active"; women's activity traditionally is taken for granted or is undervalued, or is even ignored totally as an economic contribution (e.g., women who work as homemakers, fuel and water gatherers, unpaid family farm laborers, etc.). Nor is there any admission that women's *reproductive* roles are central to their *productive* roles, both in personal terms of time conflict, priorities, access, and advancement, and in terms of value to the over-all national economy. In other words, the general awareness that an economy is based on production, and that production is based on its workers, seems to stop short at the next step—which is that the workers themselves are (re)produced by women, a literal labor

[8.] Exchange rates given here are as of May 31, 1983, and are from the United Nations, "Operational Rates of Exchange for United Nations Programmes" compiled by the UN Treasury, Office of Financial Services. (We had wished to avoid the ethnocentricism of giving currency rates according to the US dollar, but international rates of exchange are calculated on that standard.) Currency rates fluctuate daily, but the 1983 rate is to provide the reader with a basis for comparison with other data in our Prefaces from the comparable time period.

[9.] As a category heading, we prefer this phrase to the statistical terminology "women as a percentage of the economically active population." Definitions of such populations may vary by country and by data source, and generally refer to those both employed and unemployed; furthermore, sources themselves may vary by country and include official estimates, different types of surveys conducted in all or part of a country, and incomplete or partial censuses. Sometimes, though all too infrequently, the sources (our major source, ILO, notably) do attempt to break down the data into what percentage of the labor force is constituted by unpaid family workers—a vital distinction where women are concerned. However, the definition of who qualifies for inclusion in the "unpaid family worker" category itself differs by country.

[10.] The definition of agricultural force varies by country and by data source, and may include hunting, forestry, and fishing.

[11.] Although many feminists decry the military in all its forms, we have chosen nonetheless to include figures for women's presence (if any) and role assignment, on the basic feminist assumption that whatever one may think of a particular pursuit, female human beings must have the right to choose that pursuit as much as do males. In addition, military service in some countries is required for women, and in many countries it is the major access women have to education, skills training, travel, etc.

[12.] We use the political prefix "Employed" to specify paid labor and thus not again erase the unpaid labor of those women on whom statistics are rarely compiled, yet who are also "workers" (also see footnote 9, above).

[13.] Country definitions of "unemployment" vary (they may or may not include first-time job-seekers, workers temporarily laid off, etc.), and the age limits of those included may vary as well. The sources for our unemployment figures include the International Labour Organisation, labor force or sample household surveys, social insurance statistics, employment office statistics, and official estimates.

and means of (re)production that becomes suspiciously invisible in economic analyses and research methodology. (See, for example, the article on Spanish women by Lidia Falcón.)

The category of "unemployment" is another such saddening example of how statistics *do* lie, or at best tell an unwhole truth. Unemployment figures are usually based on those persons who have been considered part of the formal labor force to begin with, and who are now without work (see footnote 13). *Under*employment figures, which would include, for example, part-time workers (who are largely women) and seasonal agricultural workers (again, largely women—and children) are very rarely if ever considered in compiling unemployment data. In addition, the International Labour Organisation notes that "in many cases, persons engaged in agriculture and living in less populous areas are scarcely represented in the statistics, if at all." Still another group not factored in are "those seeking work," much less those who have given up the search in despair because a labor market is so restricted or a general economy so poor. There have been heartening attempts recently at international statisticians' conferences to develop a more broadly based, representative methodology and terminology, and to move toward a uniform international standard on the above issues. But progress is slow, individual governments at times resistant, and in the interim such statistics, particularly on women, must be taken with a proverbial grain of salt (a salt that may have been mined by a woman whose labor vanished in her country's incomplete definition of "economically active").

The next major section of the Statistical Prefaces is the "Gynography." This is our own coined term for sexual-politics topics. We deliberately chose not to head this section "women's issues," since *all* issues are women's issues, but we did wish to call attention to those matters that particularly affect women's lives. Indeed, the Prefaces intentionally give less space and only cursory coverage to such information categories as geography and general demography because that information is easily available elsewhere, in encyclopedias, almanacs, yearbooks, etc. What is less available—or available nowhere else—is not *demo*graphy but, precisely, *gyno*graphy.

The Gynography segment of the Preface covers Marriage, Divorce, Family,[14] Welfare,[15] Contraception, Abortion,[16] Illegitimacy,[17] Homosexuality, Incest,[18] Sexual Harassment,

---

[14.] We include single-parent and "extra-legal" families under this heading.

[15.] This category covers national insurance plans in general, plus public assistance, pensions, etc., when such plans exist in a country. We use the heading "welfare" as an over-all term, although it should be noted that in some countries the national insurance plan and the welfare plan are two separate entities.

[16.] Our Prefaces separate the categories of "contraception" and "abortion," despite various religious-fundamentalist and right-wing attempts to blur the two, and also despite the unfortunate reality that in some countries (see the USSR) where contraceptives are virtually unobtainable, women are forced to resort to frequent abortions, thus using the procedure as a contraceptive one. Nonetheless, each of these two reproductive rights—information about and access to safe, inexpensive contraceptives, and the decision of a woman to choose in safety to bear a child or to terminate an undesired pregnancy—is part of a distinct and inalienable human right: reproductive freedom.

[17.] The word "illegitimacy" heads this category because in most family or civil codes it is, regrettably, the term still used. In our informational text which follows the heading, we prefer to use the phrase "out-of-wedlock" births.

[18.] We use the word "incest" as the most clearly identifiable word to most readers and because it is the terminology which appears in penal codes, although feminist activists in some countries have been searching for a more accurate term which would not imply consent, and which would be more revealing of the worldwide statistical reality that sexual abuse of children or child rape, whether by relatives or not, is almost totally a crime committed by older males on younger females.

Rape, Battery,[19] Prostitution,[20] Traditional/Cultural Practices (see below), and Crisis Centers—each with two sub-categories: *Policy* and *Practice.* Under the former, we name[21] laws, statutes, civil and penal codes, and at times pending legislation, as well as official extra-legal government policy for the subject country. But there is inevitably a considerable gap between policy and actual daily practice, even in those countries with progressive legislation on the books; hence the sub-category "practice," which delineates the degree of success or failure of a law's implementation, the "loop-holes" by which policies are evaded, the religious or cultural override of formal legislation, and the *de facto* reality.

A special comment on the above-mentioned category "Traditional/Cultural Practices" might be helpful. This category gives the facts on those practices specifically aimed at and injurious to women, practices which have existed or still persist under the justification of "tradition" or "custom." Because all peoples are understandably defensive of their own traditions, and especially because of the past record of colonial and neocolonial imposition of cultures, as well as of Western ethnocentricity and insensitivity to any practices that seemed "foreign" to Westerners, we have taken particular care with the research and presentation of these facts. We also have striven to present such injurious practices whether or not they occur in "developed" countries: gratuitous hysterectomies or mastectomies or cesarean sections, over-prescription of tranquilizers and shock treatments to women, polygyny, female genital excision, the revival of *sati* and female infanticide, etc. We have tried to present descriptions of such practices clearly, sensitively, and in as unsensationalistic a manner as possible, both in the text of the Statistical Prefaces and in the Glossary.

In general, and following standard practice, we have rounded out percentages to one or two decimal places, which may result in totals of slightly more or less than 100 percent. In the case of contraceptive methods, totals of more than 100 percent are often due to survey respondents' use of more than one method.

The last two sections of the Statistical Preface format are "Herstory" and "Mythography." The title of the former is a popular feminist pun in English-speaking countries, and a semantic commentary on the word *"his*tory." In this section, we present a brief overview of women's activism in the subject country. Histories are, after all, easily obtainable from many other sources—although it is surely better to read a country's own view of its history than to read the version another country (especially a former colonizer or great power) propagated. Yet any history book or encyclopedia follows the format of what has been until very recently a patriarchal academic discipline: history consists of conquests, wars, dynasties, tyrannies, and revolutions—and is all too deplorably phallocentric, with power being passed from one group of men to the next or from fathers to sons. One wonders what the other (more than) half of humanity was doing all that time. This is the question the "Herstory" section attempts to answer, albeit only partially and in capsule

---

[19.] "Battery" in the gynographic section of the Prefaces carries the specific connotation of woman battery (whether that victim is a wife, lover, or cohabitational mate). We prefer the direct statement of this word to the legal phrase "spouse abuse" used in some countries (where the concept exists at all), because "spouse" inaccurately implies—against all findings—that a person of either sex is equally vulnerable, as well as covering only those who are legally married, and "abuse" is a euphemistic understatement of an act of violence.

[20.] This category is included because a vast number of women around the world are forced for economic survival to work temporarily or permanently as prostitutes, and this number is increasing due to the rural-to-urban migration phenomenon in most countries (see Introduction). Furthermore, it should be of interest that a country may factor in prostitution as an "industry" and/or as part of the Gross National Product—or may deny its existence in either category—depending on the economic or "moral" profile the country wishes to present at a given time.

[21.] When obtainable, we give the names and/or numbers as well as the dates of laws.

form, due to both space limitations and the difficulty of obtaining information from some countries. Fortunately, women scholars are unearthing these buried facts more each day, but there are still centuries of work to be done. The new social history has taught us the limitations of concentrating on individuals, especially in the study of such powerless groups as women. The statistics in the Demographic and Gynographic sections of the Prefaces are intended to address precisely that problem. The "Herstory" sections, however, may sometimes focus on individual women, for two reasons: outlines of individual lives concretize women's contributions in social movements and serve as inspiration, and also the stories of individual women are of special use in classroom research projects. Our Preface "Herstories" thus note those relatively few women who have, through sheer genius and at great cost, warranted places even in male world history: such women as Empress Wu, Marie Curie, Elizabeth Tudor, Nefertiti, Sor Juana, etc. But we also try to present lesser-known women (and women's movements), in particular those who have for centuries in every culture on the planet striven for women's freedom through politics, science, the arts, basic rebellion, and other means. Nevertheless, beyond what we have been able to present still lies a vast people of anonymous women whose lives, talents, sufferings, and contributions have in fact shaped history, but whose names have not yet been rediscovered or are lost to us forever.

In part because of such erased women, the "Mythography" section of the Prefaces is important. Although factual chronicles may be destroyed, buried, or distorted, the facts go "underground"—into legends, folk tales, myths. The work of Dr. Margaret Murray and of Robert Graves, among others, has proven that myth is usually encoded history. In this context, it is interesting that virtually every culture in the world has indigenous myths of an earlier time when women were free and powerful and civilization blossomed with less violence and fewer divisions. What was thought to be a psychological collective unconscious becomes more historically grounded with each new archeological dig. Indeed, the theme of the "Mythographies" seems to be that women were once equal human beings—and have been in continual rebellion since the gradual suppression of their freedom began millennia ago.

Preface Terminology

We have tried to break down standard patriarchal categorization and stereotyping of women, which is so pervasive that it becomes almost invisible in language itself. For example, most international and national sources for data on women use the term "unmarried woman"; we use "single woman," so as not to define a woman negatively (or positively) by her marital status. Similarly, such sources will refer to a country's policy as permitting an abortion "only to save the life of the mother," thus biasing the content of the sentence; we say "only to save the life of the *woman.*" (Regrettably, there was no comparable way to deal with the fact that many data sources factor deaths of women from illegal abortions into the "maternal" death rate.) The word "polygamy" has become synonymous with the practice of one man having multiple wives, yet it is a generic term with two distinct subdivisions—polygyny and polyandry; we use all three terms depending on which is applicable (see Glossary). On the other hand, in some cultures a woman who is a mistress or a concubine has specific legal status as such, and so we have left those terms as they are in such cases. We have adopted the term "women in union," used by some international population data sources, to cover common-law, concubinage, and cohabitational relationships between women and men as well as legal wedlock.

Throughout, we have attempted to challenge the politics of language in terms of sex and gender and also in terms of race, age, class, sexual-preference, and other stereotypes.

Undoubtedly, we have failed in some cases. But unless the attempt is made to bring the form into harmony with the content, consciousness will not change.

A Summary—and an Appeal

It is necessary to mention at least some of the issues which, to our regret, are *not* covered in this book. It was impossible to obtain consistent statistics, country by country, on the number of women incarcerated in prisons or mental institutions, or to obtain data on the conditions they endure; yet we know that in many societies women are judged criminal for behavior that is condoned in men, and the price of a woman's rebellion may be that she is declared mentally unbalanced. Similarly, we were unable to present reliable statistics on disabled women or on female suicide. We have included some information on women in trade-union movements, but volumes could be written on that activism alone—and also on the betrayal of women by male trade unionists who seized leadership and credit as soon as the unions were recognized or consolidated. (Even today, women comprise the majority of members in many free trade unions across the world, yet are almost never found in leadership positions.)

There are other such issues not engaged in these pages. At times, this was due to space and deadline considerations and the necessity to decide on which seemed priorities. But mostly it was because the information simply was not there.

When a Preface reads "No data obtainable" or "No statistics obtainable" on a given subject it means that despite intrepid efforts, we could not find or gain access to the information.[22] Those "NDOs" and "NSOs," as our staff came to call them, form a politically revealing pattern in themselves. Again and again they arise in the categories of rape, battery, sexual harassment, incest, and homosexuality; these are still the "unspeakable issues" in most parts of the globe. As long as they remain unspoken and unresearched an enormous amount of human suffering will continue to go unacknowledged and unhealed.

In a sense, this entire book is an appeal, to readers and to researchers—especially to women scholars (and to male scholars who care about documenting reality)—to continue and intensify the work in their own countries, to collect and analyze (free from patriarchal bias) the findings: to unearth the truth. It will require support and cooperation from the rest of us, as women and as feminists, and it will require pressure on national, regional, and international statistical collecting agencies to accept the findings and in turn lobby for standards that require governments to support such research.

It is my hope that by the year 2000, substantial parts of this volume may already have been surpassed by better research, legislation, and most of all attitudes about women. It is my fear that this will not be the case. Certainly it will not be the case unless we act *now*—speak to one another as women, listen to one another as women, and pass on what we have learned.

Robin Morgan
May 1984

[22.] Pains were taken always to obtain the most recent data, but in some cases no new research has been done in a distressingly long time. For instance, some of our statistics are dated 1970 or even earlier, yet those were in fact the latest obtainable. Some official sources—embassies, consulates, etc.—were extremely cooperative; others were mystified or even alarmed that our researchers were focusing their investigations on the subject of women.

INTRODUCTION
PLANETARY FEMINISM: The Politics of the 21st Century
by Robin Morgan

Sisterhood Is Global is being published in the year 1984, the year George Orwell chose, almost four decades earlier, for the title and the time period of his now classic dystopian novel. Orwell's *1984* predicted a nightmarish future: a world in chronic war, its peoples cynically manipulated by three megapowers, its societies mirror images of each other in terms of sophisticated technology, mind control, rigid job, class, racial, and ethnic classification, sentimental quasi-religiosity, literary and political censorship, total suppression of human rights including sexual and reproductive freedom, and communication through patriotic propagandistic double-talk. "War is Peace," proclaims Big Brother, the Dictator, "Freedom is Slavery," "Ignorance is Strength." To rebel is to invite torture, "attitude reprogramming," or death. Indeed, there is no rebellion that has not been anticipated and prepared against in advance through the co-optation or the crushing of those who revolt.

The year 1984 has arrived in reality. The planet is manipulated by a few superpower nations promulgating adversarial ideologies but acting in mirror-image fashion. Corporate capitalism and State capitalism between them control sophisticated technology and world markets. Propaganda—whether from government ministries, advertising agencies, or the two in league with each other—manipulates human attitudes. Religious fundamentalism breathes its hoarse condemnation across entire regions. Literary and political censorship ranges from the brutal (torture of the outspoken) to the subtle (simple erasure of the utterance). "Human rights" in any full sense has become as much an empty cliché as the double-talk phrases "pacification battle," "pre-emptive defense attack," and "armaments buildup for maintaining the peace." Wars are chronic; natural resources are being depleted or polluted rapidly and beyond revitalization; hunger and homelessness increase along with the population; revolutions become counterrevolutionary since there is no rebellion not anticipated and prepared against in advance. Big Brother smiles patriarchally from television sets in the United States and Western and Eastern Europe, from posters in Moscow and Beijing, from podiums in Africa and the Middle East, from military-review grandstands in Latin America.

But there is one factor neither Orwell nor Big Brother anticipated or prepared against: women as a world political force.

Because virtually all existing countries are structured by patriarchal mentality, the standard for being human is being male—and female human beings *per se* become "other," and invisible. This permits governments and international bodies to discuss "the world's problems"—war, poverty, refugees, hunger, disease, illiteracy, overpopulation, ecological imbalance, the abuse or exploitation of children and the elderly, etc.—without noticing that those who suffer most from "the world's problems" are *women,* who, in addition, are not consulted about possible solutions.

"While women represent half the global population and one-third of the labor force, they receive only one-tenth of the world income and own less than one percent of world property. They also are responsible for two-thirds of all working hours," said former UN Secretary General Kurt Waldheim in his "Report to the UN Commission on the Status of Women."[1] This was a diplomatic understatement of the situation.

Two out of three of the world's illiterates are now women, and while the general illiteracy rate is falling, the female illiteracy rate is rising. One third of all families in the

---

[1] Statistics from Development Issue Paper No. 12, UNDP.

world are headed by women. In the developing countries, almost half of all single women over age fifteen are mothers. Only one third of the world's women have any access to contraceptive information or devices, and more than one half have no access to trained help during pregnancy and childbirth. Women in the developing world are responsible for more than 50 percent of all food production (on the African continent women do 60 to 80 percent of all agricultural work, 50 percent of all animal husbandry, and 100 percent of all food processing). In industrialized countries, women still are paid only one half to three quarters of what men earn at the same jobs, still are ghettoized into lower-paying "female-intensive" job categories, and still are the last hired and the first fired; in Europe and North America, women constitute over 40 percent of the paid labor force, *in addition* to contributing more than 40 percent of the Gross Domestic Product in *un*paid labor in the home. As of 1982, 30 million people were unemployed in the industrialized countries and 800 million people in the Third World were living in absolute poverty; most of those affected are migrant workers and their families, youth, the disabled, and the aged—and the majority of all those categories are women. Approximately 500 million people suffer from hunger and malnutrition; the most seriously affected are children under age five and women. Twenty million persons die annually of hunger-related causes and one billion endure chronic undernourishment and other poverty deprivations; the majority are women and children.[2] And this is only part of the picture.

Not only are females most of the poor, the starving, and the illiterate, but women and children constitute more than 90 percent of all refugee populations. Women outlive men in most cultures and therefore *are* the elderly of the world, as well as being the primary caretakers of the elderly. The abuse of children is a women's problem because women must bear responsibility for children in virtually all cultures, and also because it is mostly female children who are abused—nutritionally, educationally, sexually, psychologically, etc. Since women face such physical changes as menarche, menstruation, pregnancy, childbearing, lactation, and menopause—in addition to the general health problems we share with men—the crisis in world health is a crisis of women. Toxic pesticides and herbicides, chemical warfare, leakage from nuclear wastes, acid rain, and other such deadly pollutants usually take their first toll as a rise in cancers of the female reproductive system, and in miscarriages, stillbirths, and congenital deformities. Furthermore, it is women's work which must compensate for the destruction of ecological balance, the cash benefits of which accrue to various Big Brothers: deforestation (for lumber sales as export or for construction materials) results in a lowering of the water table, which in turn causes parched grasslands and erosion of topsoil; women, as the world's principal water haulers and fuel gatherers, must walk farther to find water, to find fodder for animals, to find cooking-fire fuel.[3] This land loss, combined with the careless application of advanced technology (whether appropriate to a region or not), has created a major worldwide trend: rural migration to the cities. That, in turn, has a doubly devastating effect on women. Either they remain behind trying to support their children on unworkable land

---

[2] Statistics from the World Conference of the United Nations Decade for Women (Copenhagen, 1980), from the Oxford Committee for Famine Relief, and from the 1982 UN *Report on the World Situation.* The 1982 UN *Report* also noted that military research and development expenditures, estimated at $35 billion for 1980, surpassed all public funds spent on research and development in the fields of energy, health, pollution control, and agriculture *combined;* and amounted to at least six times the total research-and-development expenditures of all developing countries.

[3] In 1872, 14 percent of all potentially arable land was desert; in 1952, 33 percent; by 1982, almost 66 percent was dry and barren. The United Nations estimates that there will be half as much farm land per person by the year 2000 as there is now, given the rates of population growth and agricultural land loss.

while men go to urban centers in search of jobs, or they also migrate—only to find that they are considered less educable and less employable than men, their survival options being mainly domestic servitude (the job category of two out of five women in Latin America), factory work (mostly for multinational corporations at less than $2 US per day), or prostitution (which is growing rapidly in the urban centers of developing countries). Since women everywhere bear the "double job" burden of housework in addition to outside work, we are most gravely affected by the acknowledged world crisis in housing— and not only in less developed countries. In Britain, the Netherlands, and the United States, women were the founders of spontaneous squatters' movements; in Hungary, the problem is so severe that women have been pressuring to have lack of housing declared as a ground for abortion; in Portugal, Mexico, and the USSR, women have been articulating the connections between the housing crisis, overcrowding, and a rise in the incidence of wife battery and child sexual abuse.

But the overlooked—and most important—factor in the power of women as a world political force is the magnitude of suffering combined with the magnitude of women: *women constitute not an oppressed minority, but a majority—of almost all national populations, and of the entire human species.* As that species approaches critical mass and the capacity to eradicate all life on the planet, more than ever before in recorded history, that majority of humanity now is mobilizing. The goal not only is to change drastically our own powerless status worldwide, but to redefine all existing societal structures and modes of existence.

The book you hold in your hands reflects the intense network of contacts and interlocking activities the world's women have built over the past two decades. It reflects the fact that this foundation now is solid enough to support a genuine global movement of women which will have enormous political impact through the end of this century, and will create a transnational transformation in the next century. This movement will affect every aspect of life and society: reproduction and production, natural resources, political systems, nationalism, human sexuality and psychology, science and technology, youth and age and "the family," economics, religion, communication, health, and philosophy— and many other aspects we cannot yet imagine.

It is a multiplicitous movement, as befits the majority of humankind, and its styles, strategies, and theoretical approaches are as varied as its composition is and its effects will be. Just as *Sisterhood Is Global* is a cross-cultural, cross-age-group, cross-occupation/ class, cross-racial, cross-sexual-preference, and cross-ideological assemblage of women's voices, so is the movement itself. It has come into being through diverse means—informal one-to-one contacts, feminist meetings, demonstrations, solidarity actions, issue-focused networks, academic research and popular media, electoral processes and underground organizing, unofficial forums and official conferences.

A growing awareness of the vast resources of womanpower is becoming evident in a proliferation of plans of action, resolutions, legislative reforms, and other blueprints for change being put forward by national governments, international congresses and agencies, and multinational corporations. Women have served or are serving as heads of states and governments in more nations than ever before, including Belize, Bolivia, Dominica, Iceland, India, Israel, Norway, Portugal, Sri Lanka, the United Kingdom, and Yugoslavia. Yet these women still must function within systems devised and controlled by men and imbued with androcentric values. What resonates with even greater potential is what "ordinary" women all over the globe are beginning to whisper, say, and shout, to ourselves and one another, *autonomously*—and what we are proceeding to *do,* in our own countries and across their borders.

The quality of feminist political philosophy (in all its myriad forms) makes possible a totally new way of viewing international affairs, one less concerned with diplomatic postures and abstractions, but focused instead on concrete, *unifying* realities of priority importance to the survival and betterment of living beings. For example, the historical, cross-cultural opposition women express to war and our healthy skepticism of certain technological advances (by which most men seem overly impressed at first and disillusioned at last) are only two instances of shared attitudes among women which seem basic to a common world view. Nor is there anything mystical or biologically deterministic about this commonality. It is the result of a *common condition* which, despite variations in degree, is experienced by all human beings who are born female.

The Inside Agitator

No matter where she was born, no matter where she turns, a stereotype awaits her. She is a hot Latin or a cold WASP, a wholesome Dutch matron, a docile Asian or a Dragon Lady, a spoiled American, a seductive Scheherazade, a hip-swaying Pacific Island hula maiden, a Caribbean matriarch, a merry Irish colleen, a promiscuous Scandinavian, a noble-savage Native Indian, a hero-worker mother. Is it any wonder that so many articles in this book, from countries as distant as Afghanistan and Hungary, Chile and both Germanies, Pakistan and Cuba, again and again have as refrains the images of fragmentation, alienation, fractured profiles, silence, nonexistence, being "women of smoke" or, in the words of New Zealand's Ngahuia Te Awekotuku and Marilyn Waring, "foreigners in one's own land"?

But stereotypes become ineffectual unless constantly enforced. This necessitates the patriarchy's vast and varied set of rules that define not only a woman's physical appearance but her physical reality itself, from her forced enclosure in *purdah* to her forced exposure in beauty contests and pornography, from female genital mutilation to cosmetic plastic surgery, from facial scarification to carcinogenic hair dye, from the veil to the dictates of fashion. Both the Indian and the Nepalese Contributors to *Sisterhood Is Global* speak of fighting the concept of a woman's "uncleanness," her "untouchability"—and so do the Contributors from Ghana, Iran, Israel, Italy, New Zealand, and Saudi Arabia.

Still, a forced physical reality, however hideous, is not sufficient. For the power holders to be secure, it is necessary to constrain women's minds as well as our bodies. Organized religion, custom, tradition, and all the abstract patriarchal "isms" (nationalism, capitalism, communism, socialism, patriotism, etc.) are called into play, doubtless in the hope that women will not notice just *who* has dogmatized the religions, corrupted the customs, defined the traditions, and created, perpetuated, and profited by the various other "isms." The most pernicious of all patriarchal tactics to keep women a divided and subhuman world caste is the lie that "feminism is an 'outside' or alien phenomenon, not needed or desired by 'our' [local] women."[*]

This argument is wondrously chameleonic. In many Third World countries, feminists are warned that the "imported thought" of feminism is a neocolonialist plot. In Western industrialized countries, on the other hand, feminists frequently are regarded as being radical agents of communism. In the USSR and some other Eastern European nations, feminists are attacked as bourgeois agents of imperialism. (Truly, it is quite amazing how the male Right and the male Left can forge such a literal Big Brotherhood in response to the threat posed by women merely insisting on being recognized as part of humanity.)

The Contributors from the Caribbean and the Pacific Islands, among others, speak to this phenomenon. Marie-Angélique Savané (Senegal) calls the "feminism is alien" accusa-

---

[*] This is hardly a new tactic. It has been used by colonists about native populations, by slaveholders in the early American South, by management about workers trying to unionize, etc. Discontent and rebellion among the oppressed, according to those in power, is always the work of "outside agitators."

tion a "consciously maintained confusion" to divide women. Rita Liljeström (Sweden) points out that this strategy binds women to their respective men and male systems, and functions "as a protection from crosswise contacts" with women from other systems, a dangerous comparing of notes and a potentially dangerous unity. Manjula Giri (Nepal) flatly states that even if feminism in this particular period of history might have first exploded in the industrialized nations, "the universal significance of those ideas has been recognized immediately and seized upon by women all over the world." Mahnaz Afkhami (Iran) writes: "An idea's origins ought not to be the main consideration in one's judgment of its validity. . . . One need not reinvent the wheel to satisfy one's chauvinism." Ironically, Tinne Vammen (Denmark) at first seems to have fallen prey to the myth of feminism as a luxury, implying that only in industrialized nations can women dare care about feminism; as if in direct answer to Vammen's anxiety, Fatima Mernissi (Morocco) presents an impassioned exposé of the motivations behind such arguments, whether made by male supremacists in all countries or by women suffering (at times conveniently paralyzing) pangs of white, Western, Northern, or industrialized-nation guilt—which can take the form of condescension.

The strongest argument to the "feminists as outside agitators" attack is the simple truth: *an indigenous feminism has been present in every culture in the world and in every period of history since the suppression of women began.* Indeed, that has emerged as the predominant theme of *Sisterhood Is Global.* It will be difficult, I think, for anyone to finish this book and ever again believe that feminism is a geographically narrow, imported, or even for that matter recent, phenomenon, anywhere.

We know that history is written by the conquerors, with the consequent process of distortion or outright erasure of facts. As "herstory," or women's history, begins to be recovered by feminist historians and scholars, a wholly different past reappears—a past in which women never were "content with their lot." Feminists in each nation have begun to learn about their own feminist lineage, their own foremothers. In the various Herstory sections of the Statistical Prefaces (see Prefatory Note and Methodology), we have assembled such buried or ignored facts, so that we all can recognize ourselves and our sisters by seeing our foremothers—and their contexts—more clearly.

How many of us know that Gandhi's nonviolent resistance tactics were acknowledged by him to have been copied from the nineteenth-century Indian women's movement? Or that it was a woman's action which inspired the contemporary Solidarity free-trade-union movement in Poland? Or that the contemporary Women's Party in Iceland, the Feminist Party in Canada, and the Feminist Party in Spain are making crucial statements about women placing no more trust in male political parties? For that matter, how many of us know of the existence, as early as 1918, of the Argentinian National Feminist Party, or, in 1946, of the Chilean Women's Party? How many of us know the names, much less the accomplishments, of such hidden heroines as Gualberta Beccari who, in 1866, at age eighteen, founded the Italian feminist journal *Donna;* or María Jesús Alvarada Rivera, who forged a militant Peruvian feminist movement in 1900, and endured imprisonment and exile; or Me Katilili, the seventy-year-old woman who organized the Giriama uprising against the British in Kenya in 1911? Why are the triumphs of such women warriors as Yaa Asantewaa of the Ashanti people of Ghana, or of the Thai leader Thao Thepsatri, not familiar to us, and often not even to women in their own countries? What pride might women everywhere feel in learning about the waves of female rebellion in China's long history—how it was a woman, the young astronomer Wang Zhenyi (1768–97), who discovered the law of lunar eclipses; how Hong Xuanjiao led forty armies of 2500 women each, fighting for women's rights during the 1851 Taiping Rebellion; how Jiu Jin, the nineteenth-century feminist, poet, teacher, and revolutionary, dressed in men's clothing for freedom of movement, founded a girls' school, and was arrested and executed in 1908 because she refused to compromise her beliefs? What inspiration might all women draw from claiming as a foremother Raden Ajeng Kartini of Indonesia, who was forced to leave school by religious constraints at age twelve, educated herself, spoke out against polygyny, forced marriage, and colonial oppression, founded the modern Indonesian women's rights movement, started a girls' school which had an enrollment of 120 students by 1904—all before she died in childbirth at age twenty-five?

These women comprise our shared heritage, a heritage we can each affirm with emphatic pride across all male-devised borders. They are joined by the thousands of other women whose struggles illumine these pages: the first woman doctor in a country, the first woman lawyer, the first woman notary, the first woman journalist, the first woman to run for public office. Stop for a moment and imagine the hours of work, the nights of despair, the years of endured ridicule and rejection, the personal cost, the exhaustion, the stubborn vision, of just one such life.

Perhaps it becomes easier to understand why the imposition of stereotypes and the enforced silence are necessary to Big Brother. Perhaps it also becomes easier to strip off the masks, to break the silence, to examine the pervasiveness of those institutions which have buried our past and which daily bury our present.

Biological Materialism

To many feminist theorists, the patriarchal control of women's bodies as the means of reproduction is the crux of the dilemma, along with the embittering irony that this invaluable contribution of childbearing still is not regarded as such, because it is "biologically natural"—ergo unpaid, ergo not valued. Yet women do, as Savané of Senegal writes, "reproduce and maintain the work force itself," and Lidia Falcón of Spain delineates how her countrywomen virtually and consciously rebuilt the decimated Spanish population after World War II.

But the desire of mankind [sic] to define and control women's reproductive freedom is an old one. Modern history is replete with examples of governments "giving" women the right to contraceptive use and abortion access when male authority felt the nation had an overpopulation problem, then abolishing that right when male authority felt the population was dropping too low or for other political reasons "in the national interest." The point, of course, is that this is *the right of an individual woman* herself, *not a gift to be bestowed or taken back.* But until women are a major force in the political and scientific circles of the world, genuinely safe, humane, and free reproductive options will not become a priority. The United Nations Fund for Population Activities reports, "Currently, only about twenty developing countries have the capability to carry on biomedical research in family planning, and about ten more are developing these resources. A five-to-ten-year buildup is necessary for a single institution to achieve self-reliance, depending on the initial level of expertise and facilities and the national commitment and level of investment."[5]

In the meantime, women everywhere suffer from the *absence* of contraceptive information and devices and the suppression of traditional women's knowledge of them, or from the *presence* of unsafe means of preventing conception. Sterilization programs, sometimes carried out at the command of authoritarian governments or under neocolonial pressure, have for the most part focused on women, despite the fact that vasectomy for men is a simpler, quicker, and infinitely less dangerous operation than is tubal ligation or hysterectomy for women. Another highly questionable solution was proposed on July 16, 1982, when *World Health,* the magazine of the UN World Health Organization, carried a report

[5] United Nations Development Programme, UNFPA, Report of the Executive Director, DP/1983/21, Apr. 12, 1983.

on a recent WHO meeting which had concluded that Depo-Provera (DMPA) the controversial injectable contraceptive, was "an acceptable method of fertility regulation." Despite this drug's having been the target of feminist protests in numerous countries (based on research showing it to be dangerous to the hormonal system and possibly carcinogenic), representatives from drug-regulatory agencies of India, Mexico, Sweden, Thailand, the United Kingdom, and the United States—*as well as representatives of the pharmaceutical industries from those countries*—found that it "shows no additional and possibly fewer adverse effects than those found with other hormonal methods of contraception." The meeting added, "however, as DMPA has been used for a relatively short period of time, little can be said about its potential long-term effects."[6]

Meanwhile, and despite much head-shaking in international development circles over "the population issue," a semi-conscious conspiracy of Church, State, and ignorance persists in viewing "population problems" as separate from "women's problems." Population programs which at first referred to women as "targets" now have come at least as far as the terminology "acceptors"—which still connotes passivity.[7] And women everywhere continue to suffer—being forced to bear unwanted children, being kept from having wanted children, and having to bear children in desperate circumstances:

Thirty to fifty percent of all "maternal" deaths in Latin America are due to improperly performed illegal abortions or to complications following abortion attempts.

Fifty percent of all women in India gain no weight during the third trimester of pregnancy, owing to malnourishment. Every ten minutes in 1980, an Indian woman died of a septic abortion.

More than half of all live births in Venezuela are out of wedlock. Illegal abortion is the leading cause of female deaths in Caracas.

The average Soviet woman has between twelve and fourteen abortions during her lifetime, because contraceptives, although legal, are extremely difficult to obtain.

In Peru, 10 to 15 percent of all women in prison were convicted for having had illegal abortions; 60 percent of the women in one Lima prison were there for having had or performed illegal abortions.

Eighty percent of pregnant and nursing rural women in Java have anemia.

Everywhere, throughout history, an individual woman's right to reproductive freedom has been used as a political pawn. In Nazi Germany, one of Hitler's first acts on coming to power was the outlawing of contraceptive advertising and the closing of birth-control clinics; abortion became tantamount to an act of sabotage against the State. Comparably, an ultra-Right and Christian fundamentalist minority in the United States today is attempting to legislate severe restrictions on contraceptive access and to re-criminalize abortion. Reproductive freedom always is a first target of conservative, racist, and ethnocentric forces: in the USSR, it is more difficult for a "white" Russian woman to obtain contraceptives or an abortion than for a woman in one of the ethnic republics, because the government is concerned about the darker-skinned and Asiatic population's outnumbering whites; comparably, in the US, birth-control policy has at times resulted in Afro-American, Native American, and Hispanic-American women being sterilized without their informed consent. In the international arena, the same racial and ethnic bigotries are writ large in population strategies foisted by Northern countries on Southern ones, by the "developed world" on the "developing." This of course provokes racial, nationalistic,

---

[6.] Press Release, UN Department of Public Information, New York (H/2647), July 16, 1982.
[7.] See "Women, Population, and International Development in Latin America: Persistent Legacies and New Perceptions for the 1980's," by Ieda Siqueira Wiarda and Judith F. Helzner, Program in Latin American Studies Occasional Paper Series 13, International Area Studies Programs, University of Massachusetts at Amherst, 1981.

and cultural resistance against foreign interference—but the dialogue, however antagonistic, is carried on between male governments, and the women themselves are rarely consulted, if ever.

The presence of organized patriarchal religion in all this cannot be overemphasized. It shows itself in the Arab world wherever Islamic fundamentalism surfaces, in "traditionalist" Hindu practice, in the orthodox Hebrew lobby in Israel, and across the Latin world through the influence of the Roman Catholic Church. The ethical contradictions created are bizarre. For example, in Ecuador and Mexico, abortion is virtually illegal, but infanticide committed for reasons of "family honor" within the first eight days of life, or if the child is unregistered, gains a more lenient sentence or no punishment at all. Latin America today hosts a number of self-styled revolutionary regimes which have a strong pro-natalist attitude; the Roman Catholic Church has been supportive of such social revolutions and, as more than one of the Latin American Contributors notes, the Left therefore doesn't wish to alienate such a powerful ally over the question of reproduction. Thus, in Nicaragua, abortion still is illegal unless there is proven danger to the woman's life—and that proof must be ruled upon by a minimum of three doctors, *with* the consent of the woman's spouse or guardian. In the Irelands, too, this issue is central to the women's movement, as Nell McCafferty, writing here about both the Republic of Ireland and Northern Ireland, makes clear with devastating wit.

But the silence has been broken. Women are protesting, organizing, educating, lobbying. The Hungarian Contributor writes about reproductive freedom as a major issue in her country. Corrine Oudijk (the Netherlands) speaks of the 1981 Dutch women's strike for abortion rights on demand, a national strike in which 20,000 women participated. The victory gained by Italian women on this subject—at the papal heart of Roman Catholicism—is recounted by Paola Zaccaria. And in 1982, Kuwait became the first Arabian Gulf nation to legalize termination of pregnancy by choice (despite the fact that, ironically, women in Kuwait still lack the vote, although they have demonstrated by the thousands for suffrage).

The centrality of *a woman's right to choose* whether or not or how and when to bear a child is incontrovertible—and is inextricable from every other issue facing women. Because we are viewed as "reproducers" we are exploited in the labor force as secondary "producers" (even where we are primary ones). Because paternity (e.g., "ownership of issue") becomes such an obsession, our virginity assumes vital importance, clitoridectomy and infibulation persist as literal chastity belts of human flesh, "honor murders" of women are condoned. Because older women are past child-bearing age, we are discarded as useless (whatever the contrary rhetoric) in most societies: Japan, Denmark, and the United States are only three of the countries where older women's feminist activism is emerging strongly.

The tragedy within the tragedy is that because we are regarded primarily as reproductive beings rather than full human beings, we are viewed in a (male-defined) sexual context, with the consequent epidemic of rape, sexual harassment, forced prostitution, and sexual traffick in women, with transacted marriage, institutionalized family structures, and the denial of individual women's own sexual expression.

The heavy fabric suffocating women is woven so tightly from so many strands that it is impossible to examine one without encountering those intertwined with it. We can, however, summarize certain aspects of each strand, keeping in mind the *interconnections*— which emerge dramatically and cumulatively throughout this book.

The Institution of Marriage

The theory that marriage[8] has functioned as an instrument of patriarchal possession of women has been promulgated by feminists for centuries. Women in industrialized nations have confronted this reality in many ways: laws which stipulate that "the husband and wife are one, and that one is the husband," and which deny married women our own names, property rights, credit ratings, au'onomous business dealings, and child custody, and the "offstage" suffering of battery and other family violence, marital rape, sexual frustration and betrayal, personality subsumation, etc. Yet just how profoundly antagonistic this institution is to women's selfhood becomes clear only in an international, historical context.

Marriage is used to reinforce class, racial, religious, and ethnic differences, casting women literally as an exchange of "property" to strengthen group bonds (despite scientific evidence that the evolutionary gene pool of the species is enriched by exogamy). In almost all cultures, marriage (with its attendant duties of nonsalaried housewifery and child-raising) is regarded as the goal of a woman's entire life, whether such a regard is validated by local legal systems or (infrequently) challenged by them. This results in the definition of a woman as a (solely) reproductive being, which in turn restricts both her sexual and her reproductive freedom. It results in women being excluded from employment, or exploited by employers as "auxiliary income earners" and free "family laborers," and channeled into part-time, seasonal, and marginal jobs, always low in payment and prestige. It limits a woman's scope of physical and intellectual movement to the private sphere, minimizing her as a political force and eradicating her as an historical presence. It constrains her educational opportunities, since the focus of her training is on serving a husband-to-be and his family, on household skills, and on motherhood. It affects her entire life span, from childhood to old age:

Child marriage, although opposed by law in many countries, still persists: in Nepal, as of 1971, 13.36 percent of all females age 10–14 (and 2.33 percent of all females age 6–9) already were married.

The suicide rate of elderly women in Japan is higher than in any other country, because, according to the Japanese Contributor Keiko Higuchi, of the way in which society isolates widows and regards them as useless.

In the rural Punjab, the custom of a woman being given in marriage to the husband of her deceased elder sister still is observed.

In parts of China, Mexico, and Italy, kidnapping of brides (or "bridenapping") remains a tradition.

Polygyny, child marriage, forced marriage, and the right of a husband to "chastise" a wife physically are affirmed by fundamentalist interpretations of Islamic, Hindu, and various customary laws.

The concept of Patria Potestad, omnipresent in the laws of Latin American countries (with the strong support of the Roman Catholic Church), defines a husband as the supreme authority over his wife and family—in terms of choice of domicile, financial and property matters, decisions about the children's education, the wife's right to travel or go to school or seek a job outside the home, and child custody.

In the Eastern European socialist countries, legislation ensures a married woman's right to work, yet other legislation (restricting contraceptive or abortion access, re-

---

[8] I am speaking here of marriage *as an institution*, in its legalistic, religious-fundamentalist, and sexual-fundamentalist terms, not of marriage as a freely chosen and affirmed commitment between two persons (of either sex) living as sexual lovers in an emotional bond and sharing of resources.

warding large families, emphasizing and giving special benefits to homemakers and mothers) ironically manages to refocus women on the home and to perpetuate their position as second-class citizens in the labor force.

Is it then any wonder that women's-rights activists have been working for laws against wife battery and marital rape—both in the United States[9] and in all the republics of the Soviet Union?[10] Is it any surprise that indigenous feminist agitation against polygyny has been going on for decades in Indonesia, Sri Lanka, and Egypt? Is it so shocking that there were Anti-Marriage Sisterhoods in nineteenth-century China, whose members pledged to commit suicide rather than marry? Is it not natural that Argentinian, Brazilian, and other Latin American feminists have attacked Patria Potestad laws, that a Southern Italian woman who had been "bridenapped" defied tradition and went to court to accuse the man of a criminal act? Is it mere coincidence that Ama Ata Aidoo of Ghana rejects the institution of marriage with incisive humor, that 'Molara Ogundipe-Leslie, the Nigerian Contributor, speaks about the institution's deleterious effects, that Irmtraud Morgner of East Germany depicts those effects in her surrealistic parable, that Hilkka Pietilä notes the decades-long low marriage rate in her country and wonders to what extent that accounts for Finland's progressive legislation on women?

It is not then difficult to understand why the basic human right to be free of an oppressive situation is so opposed by male Church and male State, or why for most women all over the world a taken-for-granted right in some countries still is regarded as radical or unattainably miraculous: the right to divorce.

Double Standards of Divorce

The *Sisterhood Is Global* Contributors, and the statistics themselves, show us how long and onerous the battle for equal divorce rights has been—and still is. A woman's right to divorce was the single most controversial issue in the Chinese Revolution. It still is a basic right to be won in many countries where strictly interpreted Islamic jurisprudence or Roman Catholic dogma underlies or influences secular law, and in Israel, where conservative Rabbinical Courts control the issues of marriage, family, and divorce. A man's right to divorce has been a given in most societies—usually along with a woman's *lack* of rights to *contest* his decision. *Talaq,* or divorce by verbal renunciation, is solely a male right in parts of the Arab world and among Islamic communities in some other countries—a right sometimes opposed but largely affirmed in the secular laws of the relevant nations, and an issue which is the focus of much Islamic feminist activism. In countries where equal divorce laws do exist, the recriminations against the woman are still severe: economic difficulties, nonpayment of child support, family disapproval, social stigma, and sometimes automatic loss of child custody.

Nor is it only a cross-cultural sin against heaven and earth for a woman to leave a painful marriage situation. It is a sin, revealingly enough, against *property.*

Dowry—The Price of a Life (and Death)

Few institutions expose the "woman is property" concept so tragically as dowry. Whether in the form of payment in money or goods from the groom's family to the bride's (in effect, a purchase of the woman) or from the bride's family to that of the

---

[9.] As of 1983, only 10 states had enacted specific legislation against wife beating, although most other states had provisions for civil actions, protection orders, etc.; husbands could be fully prosecuted for marital rape in only 19 of the 50 states, and the severity of sentence varied from state to state.

[10.] There are no laws specifying the illegality of wife battery or marital rape in the USSR.

groom (to enhance her marriageability and ostensibly to provide her with property of her own), the bridewealth is almost never controlled by the woman herself. Masquerading as a gesture of respect or even love for the woman, this practice in fact binds her all the more to a situation she may not have chosen and may wish to leave. (Return of the dowry is one of the most frequent reasons families on either side oppose divorce.) The practice is as old as the Incans and was abolished by law in Greece as late as 1983. It still exists in most parts of the world, and is required by custom and even by statute in some countries. Furthermore, even where legislation prohibiting it has been laboriously passed, loopholes are found to get around the law, or the practice manifests itself in ingenious new ways.

Both the Kenyan and the Lebanese Contributors, Rose Adhiambo Arungu-Olende and Rose Ghurayyib, respectively, address themselves to the problem of how dowry has become more sophisticated in their countries: a woman's education, employment capability, and earning capacity now are examined by the prospective groom and put forward by the family of a prospective bride as her "modern" bridewealth. Despite repeated anti-dowry legislation in India (most recently passed in 1961) the transaction remains widespread, is growing in commercial intensity, and has reached proportions of such violence as to necessitate denunciations from the Prime Minister and new and stronger (proposed) legislation. The 1975 Report from the Indian Commission on the Status of Women declared dowry to be one of the gravest problems affecting women in the entire country. Yet in the year 1980–81, there were still 394 cases of brides burned to death reported by the police in Delhi alone; Indian women's groups claim that nationwide the police register only one out of 100 cases of dowry murder and attempted dowry murder that come to their attention, and that for each of these cases six go unreported. The practice frequently becomes a form of extortion, with the husband and his family harassing, beating, or torturing a bride to extract more money from her family. In extreme cases, she is murdered (so that the husband may marry again and receive more dowry); most dowry murders are made to look accidental (e.g., dousing the woman with kerosene, setting her afire, and claiming it was a cooking accident) or are made to appear acts of suicide. Massive anti-dowry demonstrations have been a major focus of Indian feminist activism in recent years; *Manushi,* the Indian feminist journal which publishes both in Hindi and in English, has courageously focused its coverage on dowry-murder cases and has initiated a crusade of pledges not to give or accept dowry.[11]

[11.] A few samples of *Manushi*'s coverage of hundreds of attempted and committed dowry-murder cases include the following:

"On March 9, 1981, police entered the house of Kanta Porwal's in-laws in Udaipur and found her chained on the roof, starving and on the verge of collapse. . . . Her in-laws say that she was mad and prone to violence. In fact, Kanta is a scholarship holder, but after marriage she was being harassed, tortured, and driven to madness because she had not brought enough dowry. Her four-month-old son was snatched away from her, her husband . . . sent her back to her parents many times in the last few years. Finally her in-laws tried to starve her to death by keeping her chained on the roof in the scorching sun for over two months. . . . A women's group called Udaipur Mahila Samiti is giving support to Kanta and other women like her. The police have registered a case of attempt to murder and wrongful confinement."

"Eight-year-old Savithri of Ootakalu village in Pathikonda taluk, Kurnool district of Andhra Pradesh, was married to Karuva Rayappa of Peravalli village. . . . Rayappa, his father . . . and others of the household used to abuse and beat her everyday, demanding Rs. 3000 dowry which had been promised to them. Savithri endured this cruelty for seven years. Now she is fifteen. Six months ago, her in-laws sent her to her parents' house, ordering her to come back with the money, but Savithri decided not to return . . . because she could not suffer any more. Infuriated, Savithri's husband . . . went to her village and with the help of some toughs, dragged her out of the house, overcoming her resistance. . . . They put iron rings on her feet, tied her up, put

Only by such indigenous women's activism will practices like these—whether so dramatically posed as in India or subtly preserved through "trousseau" commercialism and symbolic "giving the bride away" in the West—be eradicated, and with that eradication come the end of transacted love, and of women's marital servitude.

The Myth of "the Family"

The Peruvian Contributor, Ana María Portugal, speaks of "the sacralization of the family" in her country. The Nepalese Contributor, Manjula Giri, writes that "the family is the backbone of the authoritarian State." Miriam Habib of Pakistan notes how vast regions of her country remain in the hands of individual families who become neo-feudal powers unto themselves. La Silenciada of Cuba uncovers the "Holy Family" image promulgated by a prerevolutionary Roman Catholic ethos still venerated in the "Family Code" of postrevolutionary Cuba. Xiao Lu of China and Anna Titkow of Poland both point out how strong—and frequently, how reactionary—a force the family still is in their countries. The Japanese and Spanish Contributors expose how their own and other governments depend on the institution of the family (for which read women) for care of the sick, the young, and the elderly, thus evading the State's responsibility to provide comprehensive health insurance, childcare centers, old-age pensions, and public assistance. Magaly Pineda of the Dominican Republic deplores how firm the motherhood pedestal still is in the Spanish-speaking Caribbean, and Peggy Antrobus and Lorna Gordon of the English-speaking Caribbean remind us of the underside of "the family": that the poorest families are those which are woman-headed, in industrialized *and* developing countries.

Whether from Europe, the Middle East, Asia, Africa, or the Americas, feminist voices are synchronistically criticizing "the family"—at least in its institutionalized and patriarchal forms. In fact, one of the points women are making is that a total *redefinition of "family"* is long overdue. It has not, after all, ever been a singular or static construct; the Minankabou in Sumatra, the Ashanti in Ghana, and many peoples of the Pacific Islands are among those matrilineal and/or matrifocal societies which appear to have greater respect for women *(and* children *and* men). The prehistories of most cultures, ranging from Greece to Britain to certain Native Peoples of the Americas, show a similar pattern. Contemporary Indonesia and Sri Lanka are among the nations which include communities following matrilineal, patrilineal, and bilateral family structures. And in addition to

---

her in a bullock cart and took her back to Peravalli. Savithri says she was then locked up without food or water and not even allowed to visit the toilet. On April 8, she was forced to do the housework, with her legs still chained. On the same day, Savithri's mother . . . met a local lawyer who filed a petition with the . . . magistrate of Pathikonda, . . . [who] appointed an enquiry commission and issued a search warrant. When Savithri was finally released, she was found to be still wearing the iron rings."

"On September 5, Veena had returned to her in-laws' house, . . . having spent four days attending a wedding at her parents' house in Jullundur. A few hours later she was dead. . . . Ever since she got married, she was being harassed by her in-laws to get more things from her parents. Her life became more miserable when she gave birth to a daughter, a year ago. She was taunted with having brought a 'burden' into the family, beaten and made to work like a housemaid. . . . On September 5, at 9 P.M., the neighbors saw fire in the kitchen and ran out to help, but found the door locked. Veena's father-in-law came out and said she had committed suicide by burning herself. The neighbors suspected foul play and played a crucial role in bringing the culprits to book. . . . [Veena's] in-laws were trying hurriedly to get her body cremated, but the neighbors physically prevented them, and kept vigil round the house until the police came. The neighbors also formed an action committee, raised funds and engaged a lawyer to fight the case. It is alleged that the in-laws heavily bribed the police. . . ."

the old forms, there are the new ones: single-parent families, families of choice (cohabitational lovers, communes, cross-generational living collectives), people drawn together in a bond of shared work or politics or deep friendship.

If the real meaning of "family" is in fact the human need to establish long-term relationships of trust and closeness, then we need none of us worry about "the family" dying out. If, on the other hand, "family" is restricted to definitions of the Big Brothers— family only as a heterosexual unit of production and reproduction, family as a cell of the State—then governmental reverence for the institution becomes more grimly understandable. The irony is that, country after country, the State is hypocritical in its affirmation of "the family"—at least insofar as the daily needs of women and children are concerned.[12]

The inheritance laws of most countries by themselves suffice to expose this hypocrisy. If blood relationships are so sacred, then why are out-of-wedlock children discriminated against in most legal codes? If all members of a family are partners in that unit, then why are wives barred from inheriting property in some countries and daughters granted only half or a third of the share of sons in so many nations? Indeed, if parenting is so sacred and rewarding, why do more men not participate in this act?

The hypocrisy can be found wherever reactionary elements are trying to define "family" narrowly and androcentrically. Statements by Ayatollah Khomeini of Iran, Pope John Paul II, the Rabbinical Courts of Israel, and the ultra-Rightist spokesman Reverend Jerry Falwell in the United States are remarkably interchangeable on this subject. The harmony of such a quartet itself might make us understand why women are fighting on so many fronts to reform or transform the institution of "the family."

The War Against Female Sexuality

The brutal or subtle suppression of female sexuality is sometimes said to be a concern only of "bourgeois" or "spoiled" women in industrialized nations, since such women allegedly need not have economic issues as a priority. (It is never assumed that men in developing countries are unconcerned with sexuality just because they are, along with their sisters, faced with life-and-death economic issues, nor is it ever assumed that men in industrialized nations who are so concerned with *their* sexuality are merely "bourgeois" or "spoiled.") Yet Contributors from Australia, Brazil, Chile, China, Colombia, Cuba, Egypt, Ghana, Haiti, India, Morocco, Nepal, Palestine, and Thailand address the subject of sexuality, as do Contributors from Britain, Canada, Denmark, France, both Germanies, Hungary, Ireland, Israel, Italy, Japan, New Zealand, Sweden, the USSR, the US, and Yugoslavia. The Dutch Contributor puts it boldly as "the right to define our own sexuality," and Maria de Lourdes Pintasilgo of Portugal refers to sexuality as an articulation of the self—which can include a defiance of elaborate (for women only) virginity strictures, a woman's (as well as a man's) right to change sexual partners, the right of an older woman to her own proud sexuality, the right to erotic pleasure without compulsory pregnancy, the right to choose celibacy, and the right to a free choice of one's sexual partner, whether of the opposite or the same gender.

In fact, the issue of same-sex love, assumed to be an unspeakable subject in all but a

[12.] Witness the retention of Patria Potestad laws, the reluctance of some nations to criminalize acts of female genital mutilation, child and forced marriage, etc. Witness, too, the current (1983) "family policy" of the US, which expresses reverence for "the family" but withdraws government funding for battered women's and abused children's shelters, free lunches for schoolchildren, and medical support for women and children on public assistance. Indeed, at this moment, Sweden appears to be a rare country which actually has legislated *children's rights,* and which has dared to define "family" in a multitude of constructive forms (see the Swedish Statistical Preface).

few feminist movements in certain Western countries, emerges casually throughout this book. The human spectrum of sexuality is hardly restricted by national boundaries. It may surprise some readers to learn that Indonesia has the first homosexual-rights magazine published in any country with a large Islamic population; that the right to same-sex love is an issue in Yugoslavia, Mexico, Brazil, Cuba (tragically notorious for its postrevolutionary persecution of bisexual and homosexual persons), Spain, India, Iran (where floggings and executions of same-sex lovers are public events), Hungary (where in-name-only marriages between female and male homosexual persons are not uncommon, in order to get or keep jobs), and in the Irelands. It may unsettle some readers to find that there is a tradition of woman-to-woman marriage among various peoples in Nigeria, the northern Transvaal, parts of East Africa, and the Sudan.[13] In some cases it is purported that these woman-to-woman marriages are for convenience only, or to acquire foster children, or for inheritance reasons, amalgamation of lands, etc., yet in others the alliance seems to be for reasons of love.

Such customs were eradicated or at least distorted or suppressed by a colonial presence. It appears to be a pattern that invading cultures manage to "respect" indigenous traditions when they are patriarchal (for example, polygyny and *purdah)* but have no compunction about attacking such traditions if they happen to be in the *interests* of women (for example, matrilineal descent, female ownership of lands, etc.).

Whatever the individual choice of sexuality, however, the subject itself is of deep concern to women everywhere. There is a poverty of sexual freedom women suffer just as hideously as a poverty of economics or of education. Possibly this is because wherever genuine pleasure, affection, and the energy of erotic delight begin to flower, the State and its linear structures are in danger of exposure as being ridiculous at best and tyrannical at worst.[14]

The True "Workers of the World"

It is appalling that such questions as "Should women work?" and even "Do women work?" still are asked seriously in the twentieth century. In fact, it can be said that women do everything (see statistics on page 2 of this Introduction) but control nothing, as Hilkka Pietilä of Finland describes it. Women *are* the world's proletariat—and have no

---

[13.] Among the Yoruba, Yagoba, Akoko, Nupe, and Gana-Gana peoples of northern Nigeria; reportedly among the Iba and the Kalabari in southern Nigeria; woman-to-woman marriage also has been practiced by the Dinkas, the Barenda of the northern Transvaal, the Neurs, the Lovendu, and the Kamba in East Africa. See Laura Bohannan, "Dahomean Marriage: A Reevaluation," *Africa,* Vol. 19, No. 4, 1949; Eileen Jensen Krige, "Woman Marriage with Special Reference to the Lovendu—Its Significance for the Definition of Marriage," *Africa,* Vol. 44, No. 1, 1974; Christine Obbo, "Dominant Male Ideology and Female Options: 3 East African Case Studies," *Africa,* Vol. 46, No. 4, 1976; Audre Lorde, "Scratching the Surface: Some Notes on Barriers to Women and Loving," *Black Scholar,* Vol. 9, No. 1, Apr. 1978; Vickie M. Mays, "I Hear Voices but See No Faces," *Heresies,* 1981. Also see the Statistical Preface on the Sudan, p. 646.

[14.] Orwell's Big Brother knew this well: "It was not merely that the sex instinct created a world of its own which was outside the Party's control and which therefore had to be destroyed if possible. What was more important was that sexual privation induced hysteria *[sic]*, which was desirable because it could be transformed into war fever and leader worship." Orwell's totalitarian State also foresaw the alliance between the repressors of genuine eroticism and the purveyors of sexual degradation, a truly perverted alliance we see today in the West between right-wing legislators and a huge pornographic industry: "Pornosec, the subsection of the Fiction Department which turned out cheap pornography for distribution among the proles . . . to be bought furtively by proletarian youths under the impression that they were buying something illegal."

voice even in defining what "work" means (see the Prefatory Note and Methodology for an explanation of such terms in this book).

Women suffer from "Gross National Product Invisibility" despite our constituting 60 to 80 percent of national economies. The Kenyan Contributor speaks of this, as do Hema Goonatilake of Sri Lanka, Suzanne Körösi of Hungary, Savané of Senegal, and all of the Contributors from the Caribbean, among others. As Kathleen Newland wrote, "Of 70 developing countries surveyed by the Organization for Economic Cooperation and Development in 1973, only six counted the value of carrying water to its point of use in the GNP's. And only two assigned any economic value to housewives' services."[15] Or, as the Sri Lankan Contributor notes, a "women as 26 percent of the labor force" statistic in her country was overturned by a 1973 labor-force survey which for the first time included housewives as a component, precipitously raising the figure to 44.9 percent.

Women's "GNP invisibility" becomes all the more absurd in light of the fact that women comprise almost the totality of the world's food producers[16] and are responsible for most of the world's hand-portage of water and fuel. Amna Badri of the Sudan and Pintasilgo of Portugal both note how government definitions of the "economically active" population usually exclude women who do this valuable work, and Devaki Jain of India discusses the same invisibility factor in terms of "unemployment" and "underemployment" as terminology used instead of "those seeking employment" (see the Prefatory Note and Methodology for a further exploration of these terms). India's Chipko Movement, focused on the saving of forest land from developers, is virtually a women's movement, since it is women who gather twigs and branches for firewood and cooking fuel. As "unpaid family workers," women appear fitfully on national labor charts, although in many parts of Asia and Africa women are *the* agricultural workers on small farms; as one New Zealand farm wife phrased it, "I would assure the Government that if women entirely pulled out of farming, agriculture would suffer to an almost collapsed state in a very short time."[17]

Women comprise a large portion of tourist-industry workers, and in some countries women *are* that industry, where packaged sex-tourism is promoted (see below).

In most nations, handicrafts are largely or solely the products of female labor—mostly created as piece-work done at home for (extremely low) wage pay, with no benefits or pensions (see Chile, Haiti, and Pakistan).

"Free-zone activities" and "free-zone industry," using primarily unskilled female labor, particularly exploit women by suddenly expanding the female labor market and just as suddenly abandoning it, a phenomenon described by Sonia Cuales, from the Dutch-speaking Caribbean, and by Goonatilake from Sri Lanka; the latter also makes a basic feminist connection, noticing how the colonizer adapts the way in which he has treated his own countrywomen as a model for the way he treats the women of the country he is colonizing: "Women and children were employed as a source of cheap industrial labor in nineteenth-century Britain, and this method of exploitation was introduced into the Sri Lankan tea estates."

Carmen Lugo of Mexico is one of the many Third World Contributors who describe how Big Brother's multinational corporations rely on the sweatshop labor of women, certainly exploiting the indigenous male population as well, but at least training the men

---

[15.] Worldwatch Paper 37, "Women, Men, and the Division of Labor," by Kathleen Newland, Worldwatch Institute, Washington, D.C., 1980.

[16.] See "Women and Food: Feminist Perspectives," by Marilyn J. Waring, M.P., a paper presented at the University of New South Wales, Feb. 25, 1982.

[17.] Quoted in "Women in Agriculture: A Survey of Rural Women in New Zealand," in *Straight Furrow* (Newspaper of the Federated Farmers of New Zealand), Sept. 1981.

in some technological methods and in many cases promoting men (but never women) to middle-management or even higher positions.

The manipulation of women workers as a temporary labor force is notorious. In agrarian economies, women form the bulk of migrant-labor populations and seasonal workers; in industrialized countries, the bulk of part-time workers. Even where women form a large percentage of the employed labor force, as in such highly developed nations as Japan or the Netherlands, we are still auxiliary, marginal, or part-time workers. This in turn means that women all over the world are deprived of full work benefits and are *de facto* discriminated against in pension plans, which almost always are based on the amount of cumulative lifetime salary earned and hours worked. It also means that women's chances of promotion are reduced or eradicated, effectively keeping us out of decision-making positions which might change policy.

This vicious circle is worn as a halo around Big Brother's head: his excuse for women's part-time worker ghettoization is his solicitous concern over women's family role and responsibilities—yet those responsibilities aren't counted as "work." It is hardly coincidental that the "two-job burden" is deplored by Contributors from societies so different as China, Cuba, Egypt, Finland, Pakistan, Rumania, the Soviet Union, and the United States, to mention only a few. Sometimes the convenient male solicitude is encoded into the law itself, or into official government policies (in consolidating the Chinese Revolution, Mao Zedong urged women to pursue the Two Zeals—Family and Work). Although clear advantage is taken of women's labor in the family, that labor is not acknowledged as such. Falcón of Spain pinpoints this contradiction when she writes, "Nowadays it is no longer possible to separate the world economy from domestic work, industrial production from human reproduction, income from work (including the work of a housewife)." Yet Big Brother still tries.

Patriarchal solutions to the double-job burden have been deleterious, and at times insultingly trivial, to women. For example, special stipends or time off to reward employed women who are mothers may appear supportive, but actually can serve to keep women in the home, *unless* the same benefit is extended to male parents. The availability of part-time positions to employed mothers can compartmentalize them as such, unless, again, these jobs are available to men, *along with* education of public consciousness to ensure equal male participation in parenting and in housework. "Protective" labor legislation can militate against women being hired or promoted in many industries, *unless* that protection is extended to men in an equal way. All these supposed benefits to women can be (and have been) turned against us, and this will continue until the entire context is reevaluated and women have real decision-making power about new modes of organization and implementation. (For instance, the new employment plan and five-hour workday promulgated by the Dutch women's movement [see p. 471] is one creative solution toward equalizing and humanizing the work situation in industrialized countries.) As for trivializing solutions to the double-job burden, surely one of the most hilarious is Cuban Premier Fidel Castro's proposal that hairdressers remain open during the evening to ease the burden of the woman who is employed during the day but needs to be attractive in her housewifely role at night.

The truth is that the interest of a patriarchal State isn't served in finding genuine solutions to the double-job burden. A marginal female labor force is a highly convenient asset: cheap, always available, easily and callously disposed of. Nawal El Saadawi, the Egyptian Contributor, writes perceptively about the conspiratorial fashion in which, as the economy declines and jobs become scarcer, cries of "women should be back in the home" increase from religious fundamentalists, but with tacit State support. Titkow of Poland depicts a parallel situation. Comparably, the "Rosie the Riveter" syndrome was noted in the United States during the 1940's: when women were needed by industry because men were away at war, government propaganda lauded the patriotic woman who worked pluckily in the factory; when the men returned, the propaganda changed, implying that the employed woman was unwomanly, indifferent to her family's needs, cold, and "un-American."

But where are the trade unions in all this? And what about the New International Economic Order? What about "development" and high technology?

Sadly, most trade unions have proven ineffectual and even indifferent to the dilemmas of women workers, despite the vital part women have played in organizing unions in those countries where they exist (see especially the Caribbean, India, and Poland—both Contributor articles and Statistical Prefaces). Male trade-union leadership has been accused of "selling out" women constituents, whether from a calculated sense of brotherhood with male workers, male management, and male government, or from a more benign ignorance about the status and real problems of women workers.

The majority of employed women work in jobs not even covered by trade unions—jobs on which, nonetheless, entire economies depend: in agriculture, secretarial/clerical work, homemaking, or domestic service. This last category is hardly ever covered by insurance benefits (Ecuador, Mexico, Nicaragua, and Portugal are among the rare exceptions), and even when legislation does exist to grant domestic servants coverage, there is precious little implementation of the law to ensure it.

In the developed nations, this good-legislation-poor-implementation problem is epidemic. Even in Sweden, which can be justifiably proud of progressive legislation on women's rights, job discrimination persists (and with it the accompanying discrimination of lower pensions, etc.). Rita Liljeström demonstrates how men have entered women's (paid) jobs in greater numbers than the reverse—the result being that women are deprived of work in a previously "female-intensive" labor category but still are unable to break the gender barrier in more rewarded employment areas. Thus, even in those countries which have passed equal-pay-for-equal-work legislation, the law may have little meaning since job categorization remains in overt or covert force. For precisely this reason, the women's movements in Australia, Canada, and the United States, among others, have begun to push for the concept of "equal pay for *comparable* work" or "equal pay for work of equal *value*"—which expands the issue into hitherto uncovered areas.

If industrialized nations have such a poor record in equalizing wealth and opportunity within their own borders (whatever their political ideology), it doesn't augur well for the New International Economic Order—or, rather, it implies that the alleged redistribution and equalizing of wealth between countries will in fact take place between *men* of different countries, out of the reach of the respective women involved, in a brothers'-business-as-usual fashion. (This is neatly described by Rayna Green of the US as European men making treaties with those unauthorized to make them, e.g., what happened to the Native Americans.)

But what of "economic development"? What good—or harm—does it do when these basic connections aren't made in the minds of those who define it? Improving educational opportunities can worsen inequality if only the boys are educated. Technological advances can mean a setback if, for example, tractors shorten the working hours of men who do the plowing but lengthen the working hours of women who do the weeding. "Modernization" can mean merely more advanced feudalism for women if it disenfranchises matrilineal or matrifocal peoples, or introduces agrobusiness (and trains only men in new farming techniques) in a country where women traditionally have been the landowners, farmers, and marketers. Where is the "progress" if, as in Indonesia, rice-hulling machines cut women's income by more than $55 million and reduced half-time employment by more than 8.3 months for 1 million women, while income for men in the new mills increased by $5 million? In that same country, imports and mechanization have forced 90 percent of women weavers out of work; batik-making also has been mechanized —with men who operate the machinery earning *400–500 percent more than women* in the labor-intensive jobs (see the Indonesian Statistical Preface).

"Integrating" women into development—the new cure-all—still utterly misses the point, since women then are caught up in a pre-devised plan which still does not address our specific needs. Farida Allaghi of Libya shows just how the "trickle-down effect" of development *doesn't*—at least not to women. Vanessa Griffen of the Pacific Islands sees most development strategy as co-opting and deflecting the radical energy of indigenous feminism. La Silenciada of Cuba names "integration" a form of patriarchal neocolonialism. Giri of Nepal sees current development schemes as a boomerang; in her country, imports and mechanization resulted in a decline in the rate of employed women in the total labor force from 59.4 percent to 35.1 percent between 1952–54 and 1971. Jain of India flatly calls "development" women's worst enemy.

Most ideas of "development" and "modernization" also are among the major culprits in what could be termed the "citification of the planet"—the massive rural-to-urban migration taking place all over the world—which emerges as a major theme of *Sisterhood Is Global*. Contributors from the Caribbean, Ecuador, Kenya, Pakistan, Peru, Senegal, and Thailand are among those who refer to this phenomenon as affecting the lives of women—women who migrate *or* women who remain behind. Olivia Muchena of Zimbabwe writes about the social-emotional schizophrenia forced on a woman who must function as a capable head of household while her man is far away working in the city for long periods, and who then is expected to become a traditionally subordinate wife during his rare visits. There is also *cross-national* migration: developed countries importing women from less developed countries as cheap labor, with a resultant clash of cultures (see, for instance, the Statistical Prefaces on Kuwait and the Germanies).

At the 1980 UNITAR Seminar in Oslo on Creative Women in Changing Societies, women urged the creation of an International Commission for Alternative Development with Women, since "many development models are no longer valid, for, by omitting the female component, they not only continue to minimize the female input into production and consumption (both social and economic), but also perpetuate the exploitation, low status, and nonrecognition of women." The need for such a basic *attitudinal* change is underscored by Aisha Almana of Saudi Arabia, who explores how, even in such a wealthy and rapidly developing country as hers, women are left isolated unless the connections are made and the consciousness itself is transformed.[18]

Meanwhile, the invisible woman continues her visible work. But she has begun to fight back, whether in the manner of market-women's demonstrations in Thailand or of the Belgian flight attendant who sued Sabena Airlines over sex discrimination, lost her case in the Belgian courts, and then successfully appealed it as a discrimination case to the European Common Market Court of Justice.

To fight back in solidarity, however, as a real political force, requires that women transcend the patriarchal barriers of class and race, and furthermore transcend even the *solutions* the Big Brothers propose to problems they themselves created.

[18.] The "integration of women into development" syndrome is compounded, of course, when the issues of science and high technology are engaged: "In approximately 40 percent of developing countries, women comprise fewer than five percent of the trained human resources for science and technology." (From the Implementation of the Vienna Program of Action on Science and Technology for Development, UN General Assembly A/CN.11/38, May 3, 1983.)

Beyond Categorization

"Women," we are told, "really have nothing in common with one another, given class, race, caste, and comparable barriers." (The speaker of such Portentous Truth almost invariably is a man.) Yet Contributor after Contributor in this book contests a class analysis as at best incomplete and at worst deliberately divisive of women. Article after article attempts valiantly to not minimize the differences but to identify the similarities between and among women (with an awareness of how superbly Big Brothers of all kinds emphasize the differences).

Nor is class the only categorization invented by patriarchy to divide and conquer. As the Peruvian Contributor puts it, "class oppression often masks other oppressions." *Clanism* (as described by Habib of Pakistan), *tribalism* and *racism* both (as analyzed by Motlalepula Chabaku of Southern Africa), *the caste system* (as deplored by Jain of India), *religious bigotry* (as outlined by McCafferty of Ireland), the *rural peasant–urbanite split* (discussed by Contributors from Egypt, El Salvador, Italy, Kenya, and the Sudan), *ethnic categorization* (as in Kuwait), and the waves of *discrimination visited on Native Indian peoples* (as dealt with by, among others, Contributors from Mexico, Ecuador, Peru, Colombia, and the US)—all such compartmentalizations of human beings cause additional suffering among women—women within the various oppressed groups and women trying to build bridges between such groups.

Many of the Contributors to this book make a point of such bridge-building. Carola Borja writes of how imperative it is for an educated Ecuadoran woman to hold herself responsible to those of her sister countrywomen who are nonliterate, to speak *with* them as well as *for* them. Both the black and the white Contributors from South Africa strain toward each other across the abyss of apartheid.

It is moving to hear the impassioned desire for solidarity: the Chilean Contributor, Marjorie Agosin, dreaming of "a time when the women sitting on the sofas would join hands with the women kneeling washing the floor"; the Sudanese women's studies project in which women educated as social scientists work with village women to build a new cooking stove; the anguish of Stella Quan, the Guatemalan Contributor, writing of a massacre of her Native Indian sisters; the vibrant understanding between organizers from the Greek Women's Union and women olive-growers; the determination in the voice of an old woman who has lived her entire life by an oasis in the Libyan desert:

> I have been married for thirty years and always been an obedient wife. But when my husband and son prohibited my daughters from joining the [educational] center I became very angry and threatened to leave home. I insisted very hard that all my four daughters should be educated, and thank God I won. If I were still young, I myself would have joined the center. Educated women are more respected. . . . Their husbands will not divorce them, and will no longer treat them like they treat their animals on the farm. . . .

The anger of rural women, Native Indian women, nomad or peasant or village women—the unheard of the earth—is a feminist anger, which might surprise some readers who ethnocentrically may have thought such women untouched by feminism. *Feminism has been invented, and is continually reinvented, precisely by such women.*

It is electrifying to encounter the audacity of that feminist vision unalloyed, a radical perspective which insists on simultaneous and profound change, on freedom for all with no one waiting "until after" some promised moment, an uncompromising demand for true revolution expressed here by La Silenciada of Cuba, by Saadawi of Egypt, by Falcón of Spain (who dares affirm that women *are* a class *per se*), by Giri of Nepal (who dares define women as an oppressed *caste)* and by Tatyana Mamonova of the Soviet Union (who dares proclaim, "In our so-called classless society, women are the most oppressed class").

Rape, after all, is an omnipresent terror to all women of any class, race, or caste. Battery is a nightmare of emotional and physical pain no matter who the victim. Labor and childbirth feel the same to any woman. A human life in constraint—such suffering is not to be computed, judged, or brought into shameful competition.

Violence Against Women

Fortunately, the writing in *Sisterhood Is Global* is the work of many stubborn women of spirit, wit, and fierce goodwill. Were it not, this book would be in danger of seeming an encyclopedia of atrocities against women; the mere statistics, unretouched and unsensationalized, could suffice for that.

We are leaving aside, for the moment, such "general atrocities" as war, populations forced into refugee status, poverty, and illiteracy—all of which women suffer in greater numbers and intensity than men. Yet we must include such a basic aspect of violence against women as "health." There are specific food prohibitions against women having protein (eggs, meat, etc.) among certain peoples in North America, Nigeria, and the Sudan; there are between 65 and 75 million women genitally mutilated (see Glossary) on the planet; Titi Sumbung of Indonesia points out that women are the great majority of health workers but not the decision-makers; 97 percent of Sudanese women are anemic and 10–15 percent of women in India have toxemia, which is responsible for 15 percent of all maternal deaths in that country. The daily violence done to women in chronic ill health alone would fill a library. So it is heartening that this is a major issue of the international women's movement: traditional women's medicine being affirmed in the Pacific Islands, feminist therapists daring to announce themselves as such in Colombia and Mexico, feminist alternative health centers in Denmark, Australia, the US, and other countries, etc.[19]

The implicit violence exercised on women in terms of health is heightened by the explicit and deliberate violence committed, in culture after culture, out of direct and horrifying misogyny. The outright murder of women—attempted gynocide: the dowry murders described above (and in the Indian article and the Indian Statistical Preface); the murders of wives, sisters, and daughters which are condoned as "crimes of honor" and thus carry little or no punishment for the perpetrators in many parts of the world, including Brazilian cities and Iranian villages; the Chilean law which declares unpunishable a man who kills his wife, daughter, sister, or granddaughter claiming she was "in carnal illegitimate union"; the revival of *sati,* or widow-burning, in India and among some other Hindu populations; the persistent practice in some Islamic countries of killing (with impunity) a bride on her wedding night if she doesn't bleed as a virgin. Amanda Sebestyen describes British feminist activism in countering a morbid popular affirmation of the Yorkshire Ripper, even unto crowds cheering at the mention of his name and the

---

[19.] Interestingly, the issue of midwifery is one where ethnocentrism has oversimplified complex differences. In the industrialized countries of Europe and the Americas, the women's movement has resurrected and reaffirmed licensed midwifery as a way of women seizing control of reproductive health from the male medical establishment. But in parts of Africa, Asia, and Latin America, the women's movement is pushing for trained medical personnel to take seriously the health problems of (mostly rural) women whose needs are being met only by untrained, sometimes superstition-prey, traditionalist midwives; these midwives sometimes double as clitoridectomists, oppose contraception, and gain their sole meager prestige as "token women" by impeding indigenous feminist efforts to better the status of women.

instances of his women-murders. In 1983, the Chinese government publicly acknowledged and deplored the revival of female infanticide among its people: the new one-child-per-family policy, intended as a deterrent to overpopulation, hadn't sufficiently taken into account nor educated against a centuries-old preference for male children. Consequently, if that one child happens to be a girl, the baby may be killed; there were 130 cases of *reported* female infanticide in 1982 in Guangdong Province alone, which suggests frightful estimations for the country at large. A comparable "passive female infanticide" exists in other parts of Asia and in Latin America, where girl babies simply will be permitted to die through nutritional deprivation, since they are felt to be less of an economic asset than boys.

But even when permitted to remain alive, the female human being exists under the threat of continual violence.

Rape

In Mexico City, one rape occurs every ten minutes; in the United States, nationally, one rape occurs every six minutes.

One out of every five Canadian women is sexually assaulted.

In Iran, because of religious-fundamentalist interpretation of the *Koran,* it is illegal to execute a woman who is a virgin; therefore, women who are sentenced to death for "anti-Islamic activity" are, if virgins, first raped and then executed.

In Guatemala, specific "political rape" has been used to punish women in rebellion against government forces; in India, the women's movement has mounted protests over such "political rape" used by police as a strikebreaking terrorist tactic against women union organizers.

In the USSR, Colombia, and Hungary, a convicted rapist can gain a more lenient sentence or even go free if he agrees to marry his victim (apparently, the victim's preference is of less concern to the courts).

In Spain, a victim may "pardon" her convicted rapist, thus legally gaining for him his freedom; intense pressure and harassment by his family and friends is put upon the victim so that she will petition the court in this way.

In Egypt, the court often summarily dismisses a rape charge in order "to preserve the honor of the victim and her family."

In Colombia, there is no sentence for the crime of raping a woman thought to be a prostitute.[20]

In Argentina, rape is considered a criminal act under the heading of "offenses against honor"; in India, it is a "defilement of the husband and the family." In most countries, there is no concept of violation of a woman's own body and spirit.

The majority of nations in the world have no legislation considering rape in marriage a crime, since a woman is perceived as the property of her husband.

Everywhere, the victim is likely to be blamed as much as—or even more than—the rapist. From psychological assault on the victim's "moral character," to the admission in court of evidence on *her* sexual conduct, to the not infrequent murders of rape victims in Asia, Latin America, and the Middle East (for having "sullied the family's honor")—the violence against the rape victim doesn't end with the act of rape itself.

[20.] Nepal is unique in two respects: it is illegal to rape a prostitute, and any rape victim engaging in self-defense (even unto killing her attacker) is not punishable; see the Preface on Nepal.

Pornography

When Pintasilgo of Portugal refers in her article to a patriarchal "pornography of power" she makes a basic connection between the *propaganda* of violence against women —pornography—and the *practice* of that violence. Nor is it coincidental that feminist movements in many countries (including Australia, Britain, Canada, France, West Germany, India, Israel, Japan, the Netherlands, New Zealand, Peru, and the US) have targeted pornography as inimical to women's safety and sanity. The Cuban Contributor speaks of State-made films with pornographic images produced for export, to build tourism; the Polish government attempted to market pornographic calendars—until pressure from women made the government recall their product. International feminist networking is unearthing more facts about the enormous multinational industry of pornography and educating the public about its deadly effects—on women, on men, on children, and on any truly free and affirmative expression of human sexuality in general.

Prostitution, Sex Tourism, and the Traffick in Women

In the USSR and China, prostitution supposedly no longer exists. Yet Tatyana Mamonova exposes that Soviet untruth, and the Chinese government itself recently claimed to have cracked down on a revival of "woman-selling."

In India, the majority of women working as prostitutes are *harijans* (ironically, that lowest caste once called "untouchables").

In Libya and Mexico, great numbers of the rural women who migrate to the cities in search of work wind up as prostitutes—their only means of survival.

In Hungary, the USSR, and East Germany, feminists have made the accusation that the State arrests prostitutes and then releases them if the women agree to be used as spies and intelligence procurers.

In West Germany, the women's movement has protested the existence of so-called Eros Centers. Dutch feminists have demonstrated against the prostitution industry in Amsterdam's red-light districts, which are notorious male tourist centers.

In Brazil, France, Peru, and the US, women working as prostitutes have been trying to organize; marchers for prostitutes' rights in São Paulo, Brazil, numbered in the thousands.

In the Philippines—where the major issue of the women's movement is combatting the huge sex-tourism (see Glossary) and prostitution industry—revenues from such activities have been calculated to form a major part of the national economy.

In Egypt, a client who has been caught patronizing a prostitute can go free if he gives testimony which will suffice to jail the prostitute.

Both the Peruvian and the Iranian Contributors note how in a patriarchy all women can be defined as prostitutes: women in Peru "unescorted" in the evening are harassed by the police as if they worked in prostitution; women refusing to wear the veil in current-day Iran are attacked or arrested as prostitutes.

In Indonesia, Japan, (South) Korea, Thailand, and the Pacific Islands, as well as the Philippines, transnational women's demonstrations against sex-tourism have been organized by such groups as the Asian Women's Association, and have managed to embarrass each other's governments when it seemed impossible to affect their own.

In April of 1983, the first global meeting of the International Feminist Network Against Traffick in Women and Female Sexual Slavery took place in Rotterdam. Women from twenty-four countries attended, in an historic effort to develop world strategies for ending this cause of female suffering.[21]

Battery

Spouse abuse, woman-beating, wife battery—whatever its name, this privatized violence against women is endemic in all patriarchal cultures, and is even condoned by religious and/or secular law in some.

Battery accounts for between 70 and 80 percent of all reported crimes every day in Peru, a nation which prides itself on male gallantry, as the Peruvian Contributor notes with irony. But the institutionalized beating of women (whether seen as a form of punishment, sexual *frisson*, "duty," an outlet for a man's rage at his real oppressors, an almost inevitable accompaniment of a high rate of male alcoholism, or mere "normalcy") is also mentioned by almost every Contributor to *Sisterhood Is Global.*

We know that battery is not, as was thought, practiced only or mostly by the poor in their despair. It exists in every class and race, every nation. If "middle-class battery" is less talked about, that is only because class strictures are more effective in silencing the victim. But the victim, whatever her class or national origins, has begun to speak, and although shelters for abused and battered women still are dreadfully too few, wherever they do exist around the world, they have been begun or are run by the various women's movements in that region.

In 1976, more than two thousand women from forty countries participated in the First International Tribunal on Crimes Against Women, in Brussels. One of the organizers, Diana Russell, has noted that the conference's focus was on "crimes as personally experienced by women rather than on abstract debate." Such conferences are crucial in breaking the silence about the daily and epidemic atrocities against women.

Nationalism and Anti-Nationalism

It is by now a feminist axiom that women are fixed in the painful contradiction of being expected to fight and die (and often doing so) for national liberation struggles, yet women seem, cross-culturally, to be deeply opposed to nationalism—at least as practiced in patriarchal society. But perhaps the contradiction is lessened by the realization that women have invested entire lifetimes in the hope that national liberation would also free us as full human beings, almost inevitably to find ourselves *de jure* or *de facto* ignored, trivialized, or abandoned by the new group of men in power. Fatma Oussedik of Algeria, and the Cuban, Iranian, Israeli, Soviet, Swedish, and Venezuelan Contributors are among those who write about the central and invaluable participation of women in their respective revolutions, and about the subsequent shifting of women to the bottom of the liberation list. Ogundipe-Leslie (Nigeria) wryly wonders how men can expect to "liberate" a country and "later" turn to liberating the women of that country. Fawzia Fawzia of

[21] The International Criminal Police Organization (INTERPOL) has reported a number of international networks engaged in this trafficking: one from Latin America to southern Europe and the Middle East, one from southeast Asia to the Middle East and central and northern Europe, a regional European market in part supplied by Latin America and exporting French women to Luxembourg and the Federal Republic of Germany, one from Europe to the wealthier countries of West Africa, and a regional market in various Arab countries. See Kathleen Barry's *Female Sexual Slavery* (Englewood Cliffs, N.J.: Prentice-Hall, 1979); see also *The Report on the Suppression of Traffic in Persons and the Exploitation of the Prostitution of Others,* Economic and Social Council of the UN (E/1983/7), Mar. 1983; and the Resource Paper on Women and Tourism of the Expert Group Meeting on Women and the International Development Strategy, Vienna, Sept. 6–10, 1982 (AWB/EGM.82.1/RP/2), Aug. 13, 1982.

Palestine warns that Palestinian women—and the cause itself—can no longer endure masculine-supremacist leadership. The contributions from El Salvador and Southern Africa both express an uneasy vigilance about perfidy from male revolutions; the Portuguese Contributor points out that liberation governments seem classically to stop short of sexual-liberation issues; and the Pacific Islands article calls for women not only to gain but to *hold on to* power.

Sometimes the setback comes from within, as when the 1917 Russian Revolution failed to live up to the articulated programs of the substantial nineteenth-century prerevolutionary feminist movement (as well as to the programs of its own revolutionary women leaders). Sometimes, of course, the setback comes in the form of direct overthrow: Spanish women already had won the right to legal abortion as early as 1937, but lost it again (along with other rights) under the rule of Franco.

The "backward syndrome" is sickeningly familiar. History has repeated itself so many times in this respect that it becomes academic to wonder why Madame Nguyen Thi Binh was considered "good enough" to lead the North Vietnamese delegation (as foreign minister of the People's Revolutionary Government) at the Paris Peace Talks, but *after* peace and reunification was appointed Minister of Education and of the Young (a traditionally "female post") instead of the obvious position, Minister of State. Or why Haydée Santamaría, one of the most dedicated and charismatic leaders of the 1959 Cuban revolution, was relegated to a minor "cultural" post as head of the Casa de las Americas, instead of being made a cabinet member. Or why Teurai Ropa Nhongo, the commander of the women's detachment of the Zimbabwe National Liberation Army (at age seventeen)—a woman who led battles even during the last trimester of her pregnancy—was appointed by the new Liberation government not Minister of Defense but Minister of Youth, Sports, and Recreation.

And yet women still persist, although our attempts may be taken for granted, paid lip-service homage, discredited, ignored, or even used against us when we begin to fight for our own freedom *as women*. It is only human to believe that with enough proof of loyalty, courage, and self-sacrifice to the national cause, surely, "in time" (as we are told) our own liberation as women will be looked to. And so we try. That loyalty, that sacrifice, that hope of being accepted as true equals, rings in the voices of the Contributors from El Salvador, Nicaragua, and Guatemala. It illumines the implicit call of Gwendoline Konie (Zambia) for common sense: that women's empowerment is good for the entire nation. It informs the statement of Sonia Cuales (Spanish-speaking Caribbean) that women historically have been the strongest anticolonial force. It resonates in the words of Pintasilgo (Portugal) that women and change go hand in hand, and echoes in the words of Ghurayyib (Lebanon) when she states that the elements which stand against national unity—sectarian division and clannish family structure—are identical to those which stand for women's enslavement. (As another example, Islamic fundamentalists opposed the founding of the State of Pakistan—and today are trying to turn the clock back on Pakistani women's basic human rights.)

But this inclusive approach that women share—the perspective that freedom is the right of *all* peoples, to be won *simultaneously*—is regrettably unreflected in male-controlled politics. When we hear Nguyen Thi Dinh (Vietnam) in her official government capacity define women primarily as mothers of the population and as productive workers, or when we remember along with the three Contributors from West Germany the ominous fact that the word "Nazi" was an acronym of nationalism and socialism, then perhaps we are more open to understanding why Savané of Senegal implies that governments today are "phallocracies," and why Mernissi of Morocco asserts that nationalism repeatedly has betrayed women.

Perhaps it is that women are more interested in the potential bonds between people than in the differences (real, exaggerated, or imposed).

Perhaps it is that women have been forced to comprise the majority of refugee populations, whether as the (rare) educated refugees (from Iran, Eastern Europe, Chile, etc.) or the even more unfortunate (and more common) nonliterate and poor refugees (from Campuchea, Ethiopia, Guatemala, Palestine, Uganda, etc.)—women who have been forced by circumstances to set up new lives in utterly alien lands, often under the most ghastly of conditions. (See the article by Sima Wali, the Afghan Contributor, for a personal account.)

Perhaps it is that women are the ones who bear children, raise them, and fear for them in a war—whether a war of conquest, defense, or liberation—and who grow unspeakably weary of being those who mourn.

Perhaps it is because women are caught up in political webs not of our making which we are powerless to unravel: feminist activists who were forced to organize underground for years in Venezuela and still are doing so in South Africa, Polish women bearing the brunt of economic and political repression, Native Indian women dying in the crossfire between the Right and the Left in Nicaragua and Guatemala, women in prison (as was Nawal El Saadawi just after writing the first draft of her article for this book), women in exile (as were or still are the Contributors from Afghanistan, Brazil, Chile, Guatemala, Hungary, Iran, Libya, Rumania, South Africa, and the USSR). Perhaps women have always been so active in behalf of human rights because we hoped that men might notice we too were human.

One of the most poignant themes in this book is the cross-national reaching out of women toward one another. Danda Prado of Brazil deliberately speaks of feminism as a fortuitous "infection" of consciousness across borders; Rose Ghurayyib hypothesizes that the tradition of major women writers in Lebanon is in part owing to that country's having been a crossroads where contact with other cultures always was welcomed. Both McCafferty of Ireland and Sebestyen of Britain describe a solidarity of women across their governments' antagonisms: the Irish women who defiantly go to England for contraceptives or abortions; the English feminists who demonstrate in solidarity with imprisoned women rebels in Northern Ireland.

A desire for peace—not as Cold War competitive rhetoric but in everyday life—runs through this book like a melody of intense longing, and it is women who in fact have organized and peopled peace and disarmament movements across the world. When such superpowers as the US and the USSR now use the word "peace" in an aggressive volley, it is refreshing to encounter women making the basic connections between war and masculinism, conquest and rape, as do Sara Dowse and Patricia Giles of Australia, or women in the Pacific Islands demanding an end to nuclear testing not for abstract public-relations purposes but because it causes birth defects.

The contradiction of women's nationalism and women's anti-nationalism isn't so mystifying, after all. Wanting liberty for everyone, refusing to compartmentalize suffering or buy one's own freedom at the price of another's, trusting that one's brothers will see and understand that commitment (and also, frankly, needing their approval for mere survival's sake)—therein lies the record of heroic female altruism in national causes. Possibly the transcending of that nationalism is born only out of a growth of trust in oneself and one's own insights, shared with and validated by other women, but paid for dearly in an at least temporarily lessened trust in brothers both big and small. Possibly it is born out of a realization that until the majority of humanity is free the illusion of already existing freedom *is* slavery.

Berit Ås of Norway may have solved the mystery of women's militance versus women's pacifism by declaring that "a patriarchal state is one which is either rehabilitating from war, is presently at war, or is preparing for war."

Beyond the Right, the Left, the Center—and the Law

The consistency in this book of women's opposition to conservative Rightist forces will surprise few readers; feminism is inherently a profoundly revolutionary idea. What may be more startling is the theme of opposition also expressed in these pages to the *Left*— and to the *Center,* for that matter. This is understandable (since all three political positions of power are occupied or controlled by men as yet unable to comprehend "what women want"), but it also means that women face a truly existential tactical dilemma: there are no maps or models for the deep and all-encompassing revolution we are envisioning, and so we must invent them as we go along. This in turn means that one prerequisite for a feminist's sanity is a sense of irony.

Leonor Calvera of Argentina tells us how her countrywomen must cope with the legacy of Eva Perón, who, while shoring up her husband's dictatorship, nevertheless did manage to achieve considerable progress for women's rights, including the right to vote and to divorce. Tinne Vammen speaks of the rebellion of Danish feminists against the entrenched male supremacy of the New Left. Falcón (who spent years in prison under Franco) exposes how the Spanish Communist Party first capitalized on and then jettisoned the feminist movement. Mamonova articulates the pain of Soviet feminists caught between the KGB on one side and refusal of support by male dissidents on the other. Goonatilake describes the struggle of Sri Lankan feminists against animosity from both conservatives and progressives. Ogundipe-Leslie (Nigeria) and Savané (Senegal) warn how women's "wings" of political parties can be exploited as workers for the parties but granted no genuine political representation, and Luz Helena Sánchez (Colombia) deplores the "unfulfilled promises" of all male-controlled political parties. Sebestyen of Britain confesses the anguish of her women's movement, trapped at present between a Right-wing Prime Minister (and a woman, to boot) and an extremely sexist Left. Contributors from Cuba, Nepal, and Eastern Europe denounce the government co-optation of feminist energy into tightly controlled and conveniently ineffective official "women's federations." Aidoo of Ghana deplores that fact that "the put-downs and snobbery you may suffer from the comrades could rival any from reactionaries." Her own sense of irony well honed, Aidoo concludes that "clarity therefore becomes the only reliable companion and weapon for a fighting woman, for with such company and thus armed, she can weather sexist disillusion and betrayal, and still move on."

Such clarity is not easily achieved. What *are* Irish feminists supposed to do when caught between Britain's offer of reproductive freedom and the right to divorce, and their own people's assumption that to defy the Roman Catholic Church is to commit treason against nationalist integrity? What *are* women in Brazil to do when funding support for vitally needed feminist studies, women's centers, and contraceptives is offered at present largely by such suspect sources as the United States or the World Bank? If cultivating a cash crop turns out to be *good* for women, as Savané of Senegal points out, should women nonetheless oppose it because it may seem to some "incorrect"? What *was* a feminist in the Dominican Republic to do on seeing the dictator Trujillo co-opt the issue of motherhood with reverent hypocrisy, while insurgent forces barely noticed the issue—so far as it affected *women's* lives—at all?

The ironies proliferate. Griffen speaks of Pacific Islands women trying to plot a course between accepting needed aid from international agencies and preserving autonomy as a radical feminist force for change. Benard and Schlaffer of Austria delineate the same problem—a sense of co-optation by a liberal government (and a sense of rage at a disaffected Left which *ad nauseam* tells women to "wait until your time has come"). Afkhami describes the terrifying anti-woman alliance Leftist men in Iran made with religious fundamentalists, in order to overthrow the previous *Rightist*–religious fundamentalist alliance; the brutal lesson learned by Iranian women was that "whatever one's political preferences, the main battle for women always remains in the arena of sexual politics." According to Körösi, Morgner, Iveković, and Drakulić-Ilić, the "planned economies" of their respective nations (Hungary, East Germany, and Yugoslavia) have not solved "the woman problem" any more than corporate capitalism has; different (or identical) forms of female oppression and exploitation prosper, while the State announces to the world that the problem no longer exists—meanwhile exiling feminists (Körösi), extracting from them a "word-swallowing" silence (Morgner), or pronouncing them crazy/divisive/bourgeois/reactionary (Drakulić-Ilić and Iveković).

Ironies? What good are progressive secular laws about women's rights in Israel when, as Shulamit Aloni notes, those areas which most affect women—marriage, divorce, child custody, i.e. sexual politics—are tightly controlled by Rabbinical Courts which give less credence to a woman's testimony than to a man's? For that matter, what independence does the Palestinian Women's Union bring when its leadership is in effect chosen by men? And what accusations, harassment, and far worse must be endured from their respective sides by those Palestinian *and* Israeli feminists who have dared to open and continue a dialogue *as women* and toward genuine peace, since their lives *as women* reflect each other more than politics in the region would admit?

Socialism alone will not free women, declares Margaret Papandreou of Greece. Simone de Beauvoir, who once thought otherwise, writes here as the French Contributor, pronouncing the Left both the "chosen friend" and the "worst enemy" of a feminist movement. Contributors from Colombia, Cuba, the Dominican Republic, Egypt, the Netherlands, Spain, the Soviet Union, and the United States all add their emphasis on the imperative need for an *autonomous women's movement,* a movement which dares to put the cause of its own constituents, women, *first,* and to refuse manipulation from any quarter.

Nor do the ironies cease at some imaginary border between the male Left and the male Right, a border across which women have no visas. Until the majority of women *affect decision-making policy,* even the most enlightened of male governmental or legal structures will fail us. "Women must become income-producing citizens to gain equality," pontificate development experts—with little comprehension that women already produce income but don't control it, and with less comprehension of such complexities as those raised by the Commission on the Status of Women in India: that where women *are* considered "income-producing," polygyny can become all the more desirable, since more wives producing more income means objective economic gain for a man.

Even when (after decades of effort) the laws turn more progressive, they are empty without intrepid implementation and, even more, attitudinal change. All of the Scandinavian countries have almost model legislation vis à vis women's rights, *but* all of the Scandinavian Contributors to *Sisterhood Is Global* reveal the gap between policy and practice; Liljeström of Sweden posits the reason: the laws, the progress, the consciousness itself, were built *on male terms.* In Nepal, says Giri, women remain trapped "between the abstract law and the concrete reality." In Indonesia, writes Sumbung, women need support to become "legally literate" in order to avail themselves of what rights they do have. Ecuador, Mexico, the Netherlands, Japan—all boast of relatively progressive legislation regarding women's rights—but listen to the Contributors about the implementation. The People's Republic of China is one of those countries where the men in power feel a responsibility to implement policy even unto extreme measures, *except* where women's rights are concerned; in this area, the attitude appears to be, "The statutes proclaim you equal, so how can you complain? What more could you possibly want?" This is the kind of question calculated not to enhance female sanity.

In the Sudan, in Egypt, and recently in Kenya, various forms of ritual female genital mutilation (see Glossary) were outlawed—always a difficult step with any cultural practice, and particularly so when legal progress has been brought about by tireless work of indigenous feminist women and men of conscience, who sometimes have been dismissed as "pawns" of foreign intervention.[22] Yet the practice persists. India has repeatedly legislated against *sati* and dowry—but the practices persist. In Iran, before Khomeini, the Women's Union managed to get legislation passed allowing legal abortion—but only at the bizarre price of not publicizing that ruling, because of the government fear of riots by Islamic fundamentalists.

Ironies? If "planned economies" lock women out of planning (the socialist or communist countries); if "free-enterprise" economies exploit women's enterprise and lack of freedom (the capitalist and mixed-economy nations); if developing nations announce the eradication of poverty as their priority over "less pressing problems of women" and fail to see that women *are* the poor; if wealthy countries pour vast sums into self-development (Kuwait, Libya, Saudi Arabia), only to perpetuate a discriminatory segregated society; if international bodies and agencies drone platitudes about women while remaining firmly in the grasp of male leadership and decision-makers; if the Right murders us, the Left betrays us, the Middle ignores us, and the laws don't address our experienced reality— *what then are women to do?* How are we to invent whole new means *and* ends for change to benefit everyone, while attempting survival ourselves? How are we to fight on every level, including the most personal, intimate, and vulnerable ones? And what are we to do about our pain, our rage, our despair? Gwen Konie of Zambia wisely describes the feminist struggle as one more complex and difficult even than decolonization: "a struggle between husband and wife, brother and sister, father and mother."

One way to survive is to remind ourselves that we are not about mild reforms or "settling for a piece of the pie"; we are about revolution—and we are not settling for revolution as it has been described or practiced ever before: virtual coups d'état between brothers of different sizes. *We are formulating revolution in its most profound sense:* a complete social, political, economic, cultural, technological, sexual, and emotional transformation of human society. We are daring to redefine everything, from sexuality to power, from development to peace, from economics to psychology. We are even daring to try to free the human soul, to create a physical *and* metaphysical revolution.

God and Man

"The greatest enemy of any enlightened society, and especially of women, is the organized clergy."—Shulamit Aloni, Israel. "The Hindu sacred laws are categorical in their demands for female submission."—Manjula Giri, Nepal. "In spite of the fact that the ideological assumptions [of Church and State] are radically different, their actions cause similar results vis à vis women."—Anna Titkow, Poland. These women are joined by almost every other Contributor to *Sisterhood Is Global* in what may be the most fiery indictment of organized religion ever to sear its way across paper.

No patriarchal religion is left unconfronted. Contributors from Ireland, Italy, Spain, the whole of Latin America, and other assorted Catholic countries dissect the Roman Catholic Church: its androcentric dogma, practice, clergy, and powerful influence on secular affairs. Contributors from the Arab world and from other nations with large

---

[22.] This is particularly delicate since previous colonial foreign intervention *did* attempt to destroy ethnic integrity, and since not all international feminist support (especially from the West), however well intentioned, has been as sensitive as it should have been.

Moslem populations confront the profound misogyny inherent in fundamentalist inter-pretations of Islam (see especially Noura Al-Falah's article on Kuwait and Miriam Habib's on Pakistan, as well as the contributions from Egypt, Iran, Morocco, and Saudi Arabia). Mamonova of the USSR criticizes the Russian Orthodox Church. The Contribu-tors from India, Nepal, and neighboring countries in the Asian sub-continent engage the problem of sexism in Hindu and Buddhist theology and practice. Motlalepula Chabaku of Southern Africa (herself a Christian minister) delivers a diatribe against the past and present white and male supremacist actions of Christian churches, policies, and mission-aries on the African continent.

The anger of these women is not rhetorical; it is difficult to read through the Statistical Prefaces without encountering the influence of man's Church on man's State—and on women. Whether in the form of Protestant fundamentalists and Catholic priests in the United States using their pulpits as political soap boxes to preach against reproductive freedom, or in the form of mullahs in the Middle East using their mosques as platforms to inveigh against a woman's right to earn money, go unveiled, or hold public office, the means (and the goal) are deplorably the same. This manipulation of opinion and of legislation according to strict interpretation of papal bulls, the *Bible,* the Shari'a, the Halacha, etc., is an insult to the legislative process of a nation and even more of an insult to its spiritual integrity and to the genuine religious feelings in individual human beings, female as well as male. Yet the manipulation is real—and often extreme. Women in Iran, Ireland, and Israel must cope with survival under varying degrees of theocracy. Feminists in many African countries must pick their way through a maze of different laws tailored to the Christian and Islamic populations, as well as through male-supremacist customary laws. Women must do the same in India, Indonesia, Lebanon, and Sri Lanka, where different religious communities are governed by different legal statutes (and it is women who become the innocent victims in ongoing religious wars between those communities, as mourning mothers, widows, refugees, civilian casualties, and raped "possessions" of a rival group of men).

These miseries are intensified by their needlessness. The historical persons who were Gautama Buddha, Moses, Jesus Christ, Mohammed—among the other great philoso-pher-leaders—were remarkably progressive for their own times, a fact most of their followers have overlooked ever since. Religion may be the last resort of the patriarchal scoundrel, because the distortion of those original teachings is so drastic and pervasive. The custom of female genital excision, for instance, pre-dates Islam and is nowhere recommended in the *Koran*—yet it is fanatically defended by some as "an Islamic prac-tice." Comparably, the practice of *sati* is nowhere referred to in sacred Hindu texts, yet there are those who defend it as a holy act for a Hindu woman. The Middle Eastern religions of Islam and Judaism (so politically confrontative these days yet so strikingly similar at root) both base their theologies in daily practice guided by various laws, but both faiths claim an historical pride in the elasticity of those laws' *interpretation*—an-other fact conveniently ignored by their respective religious fundamentalists.

The most ironic aspect of the organized-religion-versus-women cathexis is that women are the ones who have taken most to heart the *original* and progressive teachings of the major world religions. Arungu-Olende of Kenya and Griffen of the Pacific Islands are only two of many Contributors who write about the activism of women's church groups in their respective regions. Women's constructive use of the churches—as meeting places, bases for female friendship and solidarity, for social and political activity and such pro-gressive community services as childcare, credit unions, and shelters—points to women's use of religion as a code for political organizing, or at least for the expression of rebellion and individuality with a modicum of safety.

Whatever the motivation, however, the authenticity of women's spiritual involvement is omnipresent. As the power of that authenticity and individual spirituality challenges the power of religious authoritarianism, then not only women but men as well will be free —in society and beyond it, free to approach the mystery of the universe with the awe it inspires.

Women and Power

Lord Acton's famous statement, "Power corrupts, and absolute power corrupts absolutely," often is quoted (by the powerful to the powerless) as a benevolently despotic warning that we should not sully ourselves with this nasty "white man's burden" of power. The powerless might do well to snap back with a quote from Adlai Stevenson: "Power corrupts, and lack of power corrupts absolutely."

But the truth is that women, bearing experiential scars from the way most men have used power, at times have seemed to want no part of power themselves. (Pineda of the Dominican Republic speaks of women's need to lose our "fear of power.") We've also been confused by relentless patriarchal propaganda informing us that we already *have* power. Contributors from the Caribbean, India, Peru, Poland, and the USSR, are among those who examine the stereotypes of women having ominous sexual power "over men" or "power in the home," or economic power (for which read a double-job burden at low pay). Mallica Vajrathon focuses much of her article on the seemingly impressive power of women in Thai life—and the reality of male dependence and female powerlessness that underlies that image.

The concept of women holding power—but using it differently from the way men have —is not new. As Ogundipe-Leslie (Nigeria) puts it, "Very often, dual-sexed political systems existed in precolonial societies. . . . Today, we behave as if it is new for women to have any political power." From Hatshepsut to Queen Christina of Sweden, we see even in most of those "token women" who have been allowed a place in male history a different use of power. In compiling the "Herstory" sections of *Sisterhood Is Global's* Statistical Prefaces, we developed a running joke about how many women rulers had been given the nickname "the Good" (Philippa the Good, Elizabeth the Good, Good Queen Katharine, etc.), and indeed women's reigns seemed marked by certain progressive characteristics: major educational reforms (Maria Theresa), special laws protecting the rights of the poor (Elizabeth Tudor), the fostering of home industry and local resources (Philippa of Lancaster), the introduction of anti-establishment religions (Nefertiti and Empress Wu Zi-Tien), and, again and again, the encouragement of art and culture, as well as a canny avoidance of war. (In our own day, we can see one such example in the person of Maria de Lourdes Pintasilgo. Read the radically feminist tone of her article here and then ask yourself if that sounds like any Prime Minister you've ever heard before!)

Most encouraging of all is the attempt in many of these articles to dare redefine power utterly: power *to,* not power *over,* the power to make things happen, much like a power plant producing energy. Nawal El Saadawi exhorts us to think, organize, and ally with other oppressed groups on specific issues of mutual interest, all with the goal of gaining a totally new kind of power. Jain of India speaks of women's power as a moral force. But each Contributor is reaching toward some redefinition of power, and urging women to seek that redefined power honestly, for the salvation of this planet.

One can glimpse women's ambivalence about the subject, and also the working through of conflict, alliances, and the learning of empowering skills, in the articles from those countries with already large and established women's movements. Here we encounter expectable schisms along predictable lines. (In nations with smaller, more beleaguered feminist movements, there seems to be less margin for factionalism. But perhaps one of the best things feminists can offer our sisters elsewhere is the chance to learn from our mistakes.) The articles on Brazil, Britain, Canada, Denmark, France, Italy, the Netherlands, Peru, and the US are among those which delineate various sectarian divisions within their respective women's movements. Liljeström of Sweden devotes her article to a fascinating theoretical analysis of the two basic tendencies underlying all these factions. McCafferty of Ireland amuses and alarms us with her humorous depiction of The Split. A restorative perspective is brought in by Zaccaria of Italy, who finds the dialectic within the movement healthy, and by Greta Nemiroff of Canada and Green of the US, who speak proudly of the difficult task of affirming both diversity and unity. It is de Beauvoir of France who wisely sums it up: "Feminism has survived all these conflicts—and it's highly probable that it will encounter a great many more. And survive them as well."

Culture—as Reaction and as Revolution

"Who controls the present controls the past" is one of Big Brother's slogans in Orwell's *1984*, and his totalitarian State accordingly and continually rewrites the past, erasing any records not in line with the Party's current version of history. It is a chillingly accurate depiction of the often-used argument against feminists in all countries—that one must not violate "tradition" or "culture." Yet the writers from India, Kuwait, Nepal, Nigeria, the Pacific Islands, and Senegal are among those Contributors who counter this argument by asking whether women had a voice in defining that defended "culture" in the first place. And Japan's Keiko Higuchi notes, "Tradition is something to be created as well as carried on."

This act of creation is alive with excitement, whether it appears as reclamation (in so many Third World nations) or as invention (in the blossoming of "feminist culture" in some Western countries). Feminists have argued that women are, in effect, a colonized people, "alienated from our own territory by a system based on exclusion, mystification, and a readiness to meet all demands for self-determination with a repertory of repression, from ridicule through tokenism to brutality. Women do not have self-determination over our own most basic 'land'—our bodies, which have been regarded as exploitable resources of sex and children. . . ."[23] Colonization also involves the deliberate distortion or eradication of indigenous culture—and as Fanon, Memmi, and other anticolonial political philosophers well knew, one of the first things the oppressed must do for their own sanity is create (or re-create) their own culture. An actual women's culture has existed all the while, but has been ignored or exploited. Sometimes it exists in collective art forms, as with the great women painters of Mithila or the *arpilleras* embroiderers of Chile, or in individual artists, as in the ancient tradition of major Arab women poets.

It is therefore hardly surprising that, country after country, education emerges as the first step in the long journey toward women's freedom. It is "the initial struggle," states Amna Badri (the Sudan); "it was my escape" writes Paola Zaccaria (Italy); and "my salvation" says Chabaku of Southern Africa; it is "the way out," according to Ogundipe-Leslie (Nigeria). It follows, then, that the founding of the first girls' school in a country, or the opening of boys' schools to female students, is a more revolutionary act than cannon exploding. It also follows that feminist activism often begins with the audacity of one woman writer—an Alaíde Foppa in Guatemala or a Goma in Nepal—daring to tell the truth about women's lives.

Because women know the centrality of education to their own freedom, they have built the literacy campaigns in most developing and postrevolutionary countries—usually with little or no credit (see the article from Cuba, for example). Now, with the revival of feminist movements in many countries, women are applying the tool of education more specifically to their own needs: women's studies programs not only in the highly industri-

---

[23.] See Robin Morgan, *The Anatomy of Freedom: Feminism, Physics, and Global Politics* (Garden City, N.Y.: Anchor Press/Doubleday, 1982).

alized nations but also in Brazil, India, the Pacific Islands, Peru, and the Sudan; "legal literacy" campaigns in Indonesia and Kuwait (to educate women about their rights under the law); concerted attempts in Zimbabwe to re-engage female students pressured to drop out of school by "tradition" or the need to earn money or to marry.

The adversary—enforced ignorance—is ugly and well entrenched. According to UNICEF, as of 1975 more than 40 percent of the world's women had no access at all to print media, with the proportion rising to 51 percent in Asia, 83 percent in Africa, and 85 percent in the Arab states. As of 1977, 78 percent of the women in India had never seen a film. Yet it is estimated that in Egypt women account for 70 percent of the audience for radio literacy courses.

Literacy itself is relative. The extremely high literacy and educational rate of Finnish women still has not consolidated their equality. And literacy is certainly not an indicator of intelligence nor a prerequisite for wisdom. As Allaghi of Libya and Arungu-Olende of Kenya both show, sharp insight and an intrepid will to be free resound in the statements and actions of nonliterate women in their respective countries.

This struggle—from learning to read and write all the way through reclaiming or inventing a new and truly humanistic culture that builds not on pain and prohibitions but on hope and expansion—is at the heart of feminist activism everywhere. If androcentric culture is one of our most reactionary adversaries, then curiosity and creativity surely are two of our most effective allies.

Strategies for the Future

In the honorable feminist tradition of shunning superficial answers, I'll attempt to connect some of the themes in Contributors' suggested strategies, and to add a few questions myself, in the belief that asking the right questions is at least as important as any right answers (if the latter exist at all), and in the hope that the more we ask of each other, the more we all will learn and invent new strategies.

Reversing the Negative

What if we were to perceive certain negative aspects of our condition as unique (temporary) tactical advantages, *if* they were turned inside out? For example, what if such separatist institutions as the all-women's branches of banks/money exchanges in Saudi Arabia, although established for segregation purposes, were gradually to be seized by those women, and the investments put to use for the *advancement* of women? What if, as the Peruvian Contributor urges, we confuse our adversaries with a deliberately affirmed "plurality of feminisms," rather than be overly concerned with which approach is "more correct" or "more feminist than thou"? What if we spent less energy being humiliated that most male power structures still consider feminism an "unserious issue" and began instead to use the temporary margin of mobility that very perception permits us tactically? (See Poland and India, for example.) What if, as Sánchez of Colombia suggests, we were to concentrate on developing a fine sense of where co-optation ended and *winning* began, ethical issue by issue, individual case by case, sharpening our instincts about just when it is necessary to consolidate our strengths in private and when it is "the right moment to emerge from the ghetto"?

Seizing the System

Domestically, we must use the ballot (where we *have* suffrage) as the potentially radical lever that it can be: daring to organize and vote as a bloc, to develop what some newspaper reporters now call "the gender gap" in voting patterns. It means more women running for public office (and fighting for the legal right to do so), and it means actively supporting those women with contributions of time, effort, organizing, and funds. (It also means making sure that those women feel an *accountability* to their constituency of women and to feminist issues.) Perhaps not all of us can accomplish the remarkable feat managed by Norwegian women, as described by Berit Ås, but since women comprise a majority of the populations in most countries of the world, where we *do* have the rights of suffrage and running for office, we ought to be using those rights more than we are, and with less fear of failure. Where we don't have these rights, winning them surely should be a priority.

Why can't we use our national and international nongovernmental traditional women's organizations more creatively and more politically than we have in the past?[24] Through these already well-organized and respected bodies, it is possible to put pressure on governments—toward, for instance, signing and ratifying the Convention On the Elimination of All Forms of Discrimination Against Women,[25] or so that women cabinet members are not inevitably assigned to such "soft politics" areas as social welfare or culture, but to positions where policy *really* is decided (ministers of state, defense, etc., and especially of economics and trade)?

What if we were to investigate, each in our own countries, just how to demystify and constructively use the vast system of the United Nations and its Specialized Agencies? (See Glossary.) How many women, for instance, know that certain of the Agencies give funding for work or study projects, need consultants on issues affecting women's lives (and sometimes claim they can find no "qualified" persons), have special women's bureaus or women's sections (often with sympathetic feminist women "inside" who are eager to be of use to women "outside")? How many women consider the bureaucracy of the United Nations *influenceable?* Yet it could be.

The conferences on International Women's Year and the UN Decade for Women may have seemed abstract and rhetorical to some feminists. Still, the Year and the Decade, and the requirement for governments to at least pay lip service to the Plan of Action and to report on implementation, have been helpful. That structure and those requirements have been put to excellent use by women organizing in certain parts of the world: see

---

[24.] Some of these organizations (the international YWCA, for example) had feminist origins and still proudly affirm those roots; others, through misunderstanding, or fear of seeming "too radical," have been less concerned with women's-rights issues than they might be—but they can be joined, convinced, and influenced. If only we will do so.

[25.] As of Feb. 1, 1984, the following countries had signed, acceded to, or ratified the Convention (official UN listing): Afghanistan, Argentina, Australia, Austria, Barbados, Belgium, Benin, Bhutan, Bolivia, Brazil, Bulgaria, Burundi, Byelorussian Soviet Socialist Republic, Cameroon, Canada, Cape Verde, Chile, China, Colombia, Congo, Costa Rica, Cuba, Czechoslovakia, Democratic Campuchea, Denmark, Dominica, Dominican Republic, Ecuador, Egypt, El Salvador, Ethiopia, Finland, France, Gabon, Gambia, German Democratic Republic, Federal Republic of Germany, Ghana, Greece, Grenada, Guatemala, Guinea, Guinea-Bissau, Guyana, Haiti, Honduras, Hungary, Iceland, India, Indonesia, Israel, Italy, Ivory Coast, Jamaica, Japan, Jordan, Laos, Lesotho, Luxembourg, Madagascar, Mexico, Mongolia, Netherlands, New Zealand, Nicaragua, Norway, Panama, Peru, Philippines, Poland, Portugal, Republic of Korea, Romania, Rwanda, Saint Lucia, Senegal, Spain, Sri Lanka, St. Vincent and the Grenadines, Sweden, Tanzania, Togo, Tunisia, Uganda, Ukrainian Soviet Socialist Republic, Union of Soviet Socialist Republics, United Kingdom, United States, Uruguay, Venezuela, Vietnam, Yugoslavia, Zaire, and Zambia. If your country has not signed, find out *why*—and begin lobbying. It is also possible that your country has signed but not yet ratified that signature; find out if this is so and, if not—begin lobbying. And if your country has signed *and* ratified, then you have excellent grounds for complaining about implementation.

especially the articles on the Caribbean and the Pacific Islands, on Venezuela, and on Nepal.

How many women know it is now possible for a women's group *or an individual woman* to register a human rights violation complaint (which can include battery, rape, job discrimination, deleterious "cultural" practices, etc.) directly by confidential or standard letter to the Secretariat of the Commission on the Status of Women (in care of the Women's Unit, United Nations Center, Vienna, Austria)—and that every complaint requires a formal investigation by the Commission, requiring in turn a response from the national government involved?

We must—and can—demystify the channels to power, in order to travel them.

Challenging the System

Whatever we do within the system, we cannot risk settling for that route as our only (or even our strongest) approach. Nor need we resign ourselves, as Liljeström of Sweden warns, to either/or thinking. On the contrary, we need to be in the legislatures *and* in the streets. And we need to preserve our *autonomy* as a movement.

But what if our demonstrations were *coordinated,* through the already existing and growing feminist network, so that we marched and picketed on each other's issues at the same time in various countries, thus beginning to show a concerted impact as a global movement? What about organizing sit-ins and rallies timed to occur simultaneously on different sides of a shared border? As the Spanish article makes clear, international pressure (a campaign of cables, letters, petitions, demonstrations at embassies, etc.) can have as much or more effect on a government as years of work done by feminists within that country. For that matter, what about more intensive *regional* networking, and the establishment of more regional alternative institutions by, of, and for women? (See the articles by Giovanna Merola R. of Venezuela and by Luz Helena Sánchez of Colombia for superb examples of such alliances.) What about national (and regional, and international) boycotts of selected products manufactured by companies notorious for exploiting women employees? (See the Indian article.)

What about considering no act of challenge too great? What if we never again apologized for emphasizing "sexual politics," but realized that, as both Jain of India and Lugo of Mexico point out, the subjects of contraception, abortion, sexual violence, and battery *are* conscious concerns of even the poorest rural woman struggling for daily survival? What if we realized that unifying on the grounds of a shared biology *is* the obvious place to begin?

What about considering no act of challenge too small? The allegedly frivolous feminist demonstrations against beauty pageants (in Britain, Venezuela, the US, Zambia, and at the UN itself, to mention only a few examples) raised public consciousness about the ways in which women are objectified, trivialized, and commercialized. "Housewives' strikes" in the Netherlands and the US had a similar educative effect on general attitudes that had regarded housework as easy, and a "petty issue."

What if (O lovely more than symbolic act!) a group of women in each country of the world held a press conference on the same day announcing our mutual request for admission to the United Nations as an autonomous people? After all, there is an ancient Turkish proverb that declares, "Women are all one nation."

Beyond the System

What if women in the developed nations realized there was no need to "teach" organizing techniques to their sisters in the developing countries, but understood that there was a great deal to learn, precisely about such techniques, *from* them? What if, for instance, Western women were to study and adopt the ancient Arab concept of *Nušuz* (women's rebellion)?

What if we were, through networking, to create an International Feminist Legal Resource Center, which would house a library of every nation's civil and penal codes with particular details on those laws specifically affecting women, and which would monitor all changes in legislation and publish a bulletin to that effect, thus informing women all over the world as to their own and other women's legal status (and alerting us about which pending legislation to demonstrate and lobby for—or against).

What if each woman (and man of conscience) reading this book were to subscribe to at least three periodicals of the international feminist media, instead of having that information filtered through Big Brother's censors?[26]

What if we were to fully comprehend that the real work of the feminist movement is accomplished less by "official" conferences attended by Big Brother's own governments than by such energizing and historic meetings as the 1972 Arab Women's Conference in Kuwait, the birth of the Feminist International in France in 1977, the 1980 First National Conference of Indian Feminists, the 1981 First Feminist Meeting of Latin American and Caribbean Women, the above-mentioned Tribunal on Crimes Against Women, and the conference of the International Feminist Network Against Traffick in Women and Female Sexual Slavery? (Think of the work—and the risk—that went into creating each of those historic meetings.)

What if we were to trust that "feminist diplomacy" often consists of simple womanly courtesy, of listening to one another at least as intensely as wanting to speak to one another, of a willingness to be vulnerable?

What if we were, for that matter, to listen to our *mothers*—and to our *grandmothers?* Heresy? Yet the grandmother's voice emerges more than once, and with great clarity, in this book. She is there in the Chilean article. She is there in the Haitian piece. She shimmers with wry wisdom in the Cuban refrains. And she speaks directly and beautifully, in her own voice, as Soon Chan Park of Korea.

What if feminist diplomacy turned out to be simply another form of the feminist aphorism "the personal is political"? Danda writes here of her own feminist epiphany, Amanda of her moments of despair, La Silenciada of personally bearing witness to the death of a revolution's ideals. Tinne confides her fears, Nawal addresses us in a voice direct from prison, Hilkka tells us about her family and childhood; Ama Ata confesses the anguish of the woman artist, Stella shares her mourning with us, Mahnaz communicates her grief (and her hope), Nell her daring balance of irony and lyricism, Paola the story of her origins and girlhood. Manjula isn't afraid to speak of pain, Corrine traces her own political evolution alongside that of her movement, Maria de Lourdes declares the

[26.] For example: *Mejane* (Australia), *Mulherio* (Brazil), *Spare Rib* or *Feminist Review* (Britain), *Broadside* or *Communiqu'elles* or *Webspinner* (Canada), *Kvinder* (Denmark), *Questions Feminists* (France), *Emma* or *Courage* (West Germany), *Manushi* (India), *The Crane Bag* (Ireland), *Effe* or *Quotidiano Donna* (Italy), *Feminist International* or *Asian Women's Liberation* or *Agora* (Japan), *Al-Raida* (Lebanon), *Fem* or *Mujer* (Mexico), *Gargi* (Nepal), *Vrouwenkrant* (Netherlands), *Broadsides* (New Zealand), *Kvinner* (Norway), *La Tortuga* (Peru), *Voice of Women* (South Africa), *Poder y Libertad* (Spain), *Voice of Women* (Sri Lanka), *Hertha* (Sweden), *ISIS* (Switzerland), *Sojourner* or *Connexions* or *Media Report to Women* (US), *Woman and Russia* (Soviet Union, now published in France), and *Woman's Exclusive* (Zambia). *ILIS* (International Lesbian Information Service) *Newsletter* is now published in Oslo, Norway. This is only a small sampling. For further information, contact the International Women's Tribune Center in New York City for their splendid current resources on feminist media, and feminist national, regional, and international networks.

personal and the political inseparable. Motlalepula still remembers the burning of a particular maroon dress, Ingrid and Renate invite us into their private correspondence, Marielouise opens herself in a poem, Elena appeals personally to us for help, Gwendoline testifies about her private life as a public figure . . .

And do we not, after all, easily recognize one another?

The Sister and the Self

Are we then really so very different? (This, Liljeström of Sweden implies, is the question men hate most for women to ask.)

Women are murdered for the sake of men's "honor" in both Latin America and the Middle East. Genital mutilation, psychological Freudian female castration, and gratuitous mastectomies and hysterectomies all are performed on women for the same purpose: male convenience masquerading as custom or even "science." Black veils shroud us in Ireland, Greece, and southern Italy, in Iran as the *chador* and in Chile as the *rebozo*. The patriarchy worships particular girl children as goddesses incarnate in Nepal and sentimentally cherishes child film stars in the West—but still evinces indifference or contempt for female children the world over in terms of mere survival, much less education, nurturance, equal opportunity. Time itself is rationed differently to women; the Cuban, Nigerian, Soviet, and Zimbabwean writers speak synchronistically of women's overfull schedules and maddening lack of time. Our perception of reality is everywhere valued at less than men's: the Halacha (religious code of Judaism) does not recognize a woman as a witness or document signatory; the Islamic Law of Evidence defines one man's testimony as being worth that of two women (see Israel and Pakistan). But is that so different from the West? The Law and Language Project of Duke University explored the difference between male ("powerful") and female ("powerless") presentation of testimony, using over 150 hours of actual courtroom tapes, and researched the effect of sexism on the perceived credibility of women witnesses—with depressing findings that women's testimony carries half the weight of men's.[27] Courts everywhere *are,* in effect, functioning under the Law of Evidence as far as women are concerned.

The underlying similarities emerge once we begin to ask *sincere* questions about differences. The *real* harem tradition included intense female friendship, solidarity, and high culture (as well as humor, bawdiness, and anti-male ridicule).[28] The *real* "belly dance" is a childbirth ritual celebrating life; the *Raqs al Sharqi* (Eastern Dance, its correct name) is meant as an exercise in preparation for labor and childbirth, and still is danced only by, for, and among women in many parts of the Middle East. The examples could go on and on.

But the most basic similarity of all is the sister in search of the self: "self identity" (Indonesia and Poland), "an articulation of selfhood" (Portugal), "self-realization" (Lebanon and Pakistan), "self-image" (Zimbabwe), "[women thirst to] see with their own eyes, think with their own minds" (Italy), "it's time to begin with ourselves" (USSR), "the right to be oneself" (Finland).

Is it any wonder that such words as daring, rebellion, journey, risk, and vision recur throughout *Sisterhood Is Global* like refrains punctuating the same basic story: one of deep suffering but also of a love—for life, children, men, other women, the land of one's birth, humanity itself—a love fierce enough to cleanse the world?

[27.] For further information on the study, contact the National Judicial Education Program, National Organization for Women Legal Defense and Education Fund, Washington, D.C., USA.

[28.] See "Western Ethnocentrism and Perceptions of the Harem" by Leila Ahmed, in *Feminist Studies* 8, No. 3, Fall 1982.

A Personal Note

The linear, patriarchal separation of thought from feeling, theory from action, is inimical to the feminist vision of wholeness. Happily, anti-compartmentalization pervades the following pages and is reflected in both content and tone. This context gives me the courage to speak personally and vulnerably.

During the years of this book's gestation, changes large and small have transformed the lives of everyone involved. Some Contributors went into exile—and some were able to return home. One Contributor survived an assassination attempt. Another triumphed over cancer. Another endured prison. Another at this moment is gravely ill awaiting a kidney transplant. Some remain underground. One got married, one got divorced, four separated from their partners. One suffered a miscarriage, one had an abortion, another gave birth to a daughter, another is at this writing pregnant. Soon Chan Park, our eldest sister, died after a lifetime of feminist and humanist service.

For myself . . . at some point during my editing of these pages, my mother died. At some point in these pages I separated from my marriage and from the home I had co-created and lived in for twenty years. At some point in these pages my son became a teenager. Somewhere in these pages there vibrates for me much personal mourning, fear, grief, celebration, and plain living. But the book continued. At times feeling like a curse of inexorable deadlines and self-chosen responsibility, it has been far more often a blessing of focused work and sanity, a demanding preoccupation which has borne me up even in moments when nothing else anymore seemed real. My personal debt of gratitude is therefore great—to every Contributor, every staff member and volunteer, every person who touched the project in any way, and to the project itself and the global women's movement which conceived and necessitated it. *Sisterhood Is Global* has functioned in my life like the rare gift of a creative obsession.

I sit now in a small room in New York City, about to send the book out into the world. As of this moment, of all the people who have worked so lovingly on different aspects of *Sisterhood Is Global,* only I have read absolutely every word you are about to encounter. I have seen in perspective the whole you are about to engage. So of course the predictable post-partum anxieties assail me: Have I been painstaking enough, respectful enough of the Contributors? Have I been sensitive enough about national, ethnic, and cultural differences? Have I been scrupulous enough about our research? One never is any of these things "enough." We have all done our utmost. The responsibility for any of our failures is mine.

So, dear reader, in the year 1984, I give this book into your hands. The voices you will hear in its pages cry out more clearly against Big Brother than any force alive on the planet. If there is hope for any of us—women, children, men, sentient life on our earth—it rings in these voices and in the whispers and even silences of the millions of women they are speaking of and for and with. Hear them. Understand them.

And understand one thing more—the most important of all. If there is to be a 1985 and beyond, it is up to you.

Robin Morgan
New York City
May 1984

AFGHANISTAN
(Democratic Republic of Afghanistan)

Located in the Persian Gulf region, bounded by Pakistan to the east and south, Iran to the west, and the USSR to the north. **Area:** 636,266 sq. km. (245,664 sq. mi.). **Population** (1980): 15,886,000, female 49%. **Capital:** Kabul.

DEMOGRAPHY. Languages: Pushtu, Dari (both official), Uzbek (Turkic). **Races or Ethnic Groups:** Pushtun 50%, Tajik 25%, Uzbek 9%, Hazara 9%, other. **Religions:** Islam (Sunni 80%, Shi'ite 20%). **Education** (% enrolled in school, 1975): Age 6–11—of all girls 5%, of all boys 26%; age 12–17—of all girls 4%, of all boys 23%; higher education— no data obtainable. **Literacy** (1977): Women 4%, men 19%. **Birth Rate** (per 1000 pop., 1975–80): 48. **Death Rate** (per 1000 pop., 1975–80): 21. **Infant Mortality** (per 1000 live births, 1975–80): Female 208, male 244. **Life Expectancy** (1975–80): Female 43 yrs., male 42 yrs.

GOVERNMENT. Soviet-backed regime (since 1979) led by President Babrak Karmal, who heads a 35-member Revolutionary Council as well as the Central Committee of the only legal party, the People's Democratic Party of Afghanistan. **Women's Suffrage:** 1965. **Equal Rights:** 1977 Afghan Constitution (Art. 27) states, "All the people of Afghanistan, both women and men, without discrimination and privilege, have equal rights and obligations before the law." **Women in Government:** Anahita Ratebzad, a member of Parliament from 1965–69, is State Ambassador. Ms. Khadija Ahrari, Ms. Roqia, and Ms. Masuma Ismati-Wardak were active parliamentarians (1965–69), Kobra Nourzai was Minister of Public Heath (1965–69), Shafiqa Ziayee Minister without portfolio (1971–72). Few women currently (1984) in higher government echelons.

ECONOMY. Currency: Afghani (May 1983: 89. = $1 US). **Gross National Product** (1979): $3.4 billion. **Per Capita Income** (1979): $225. **Women's Wages as a Percentage of Men's:** No data obtain-

able. **Equal Pay Policy:** No data obtainable. **Production** (Agricultural/Industrial): Wheat, grains, cotton, fruit; soap, furniture, textiles, coal, carpets. **Women as a Percentage of Labor Force** (1980): 19%; **of agricultural force**—no general statistics obtainable (87% of women workers are employed in agriculture, 1975); **of industrial force**—no general statistics obtainable (of manufacturing 60%, 1979); **of military**—no statistics obtainable; a few women in service sector only. **(Employed) Women's Occupational Indicators** (1979): Of administrative, managerial, and related workers 0.6%, of sales workers 1.5%, of service workers 3.9%, of clerical and related workers 8.5%, of professional, technical, and related workers 13.5%; the majority of employed women are doctors or teachers (urban) but these are not necessarily considered high-status jobs. **Unemployment** (1981): No statistics obtainable, but female rate is reportedly higher than male.

GYNOGRAPHY. Marriage. *Policy:* Based on interpretation of the Hanafi school of law in Islamic jurisprudence, the 1976 Civil Code set the legal marriage age at 16 for females (15 with paternal consent) and 18 for males. Both spouses are free to choose their marriage partner; the Civil Code allows a couple to marry despite family opposition. Dowry was legally abolished by the 1971 Marriage Law (Art. 16). Polygyny is legal; a man may marry more than 1 wife if 1) there is no injustice to any wife, 2) the husband is financially able to provide necessities for all the wives (food, clothing, housing, and health care), and 3) a lawful reason exists for the second marriage (e.g., the first wife is barren or seriously ill). In inheritance matters, 1/3 of a Moslem woman's or man's property can be controlled or disposed of as s/he wishes. The other 2/3 is distributed according to Islamic law: a female inherits 1/2 the share of a male. A widow is entitled to 1/4 of her husband's estate if he has no children; otherwise, she receives 1/8. *Practice:* Female mean age at marriage (1970–78):

18; women age 15–49 in union (1970–78): 81%. The number of polygynous marriages has decreased recently; some reports cite the high cost of living and economic provisions in the 1977 Constitution as the major deterrents. Reports indicate, however, that wives of polygynous husbands are unlikely to divorce since they would forfeit their dowry. The *touyana* or *maehr* (dowry), although legally abolished, persists, and includes money, a complete wardrobe for the bride, and jewels, which remain her property (or her family's). Among the Shi'ite Moslems, fixed-period "temporary marriages" or *mut'a (sigha* in Persian) are still practiced in some nomadic communities, although legally abolished; concubinage still is practiced in some areas. The preferred mate in Afghan society is the parallel cousin (father's brother's daughter), since this keeps dowry in the family; intrafamily marriages exist in rural and nomadic communities.

Divorce. *Policy:* Legal. The 1976 Civil Code (Art. 135, Sec. 2) allows a man to divorce his wife verbally *(talaq)* or in writing. A wife can divorce her husband only by judicial process, on the grounds that her husband has an incurable illness, if she is compromised while living with her husband, if he refuses or is unable to support her financially, or if he is imprisoned for 10 yrs. or more—whereby she can demand separation after the first 5 yrs. of his imprisonment. In addition, Art. 183 of the Code allows a wife to divorce whether or not she can prove the existence of prejudice or harm if arbitration fails to reconcile the couple. Art. 88 of the Code allows a wife to stipulate in writing (when she registers her marriage) her right to divorce if her husband takes a second wife; Art. 89 grants a woman divorce if her husband has hidden the existence of another wife. After marriage dissolution a mother receives custody of a boy up to age 7 and a girl up to age 9, after which custody rests with the father. The period may be extended by 2 yrs. for both boys and girls if it is considered to be in the child's interest. A mother who remarries or is seen to "behave immorally" forfeits custody. *Practice:* No statistics obtainable. Divorce is considered a family "dishonor"; families sometimes refuse to welcome a divorced daughter back home. **Family.** *Policy:* 1978 legislation provided a "Family Health Plan" aimed at helping the mother and child. A husband is allowed a tax exemption for a wife, and families are allowed exemptions for each of the first 5 children and for unemployed parents. In inheritance, if the father has no sons, his daughter receives 1/2 his estate; if he left more than 1 daughter, but no son, the daughters share 2/3 of his estate. If he left both daughters and sons, the daughters' shares are 1/2 the sons'. *Practice:* No data obtainable. **Welfare.** *Policy:* A limited Social Security system exists, but there is no unemployment compensation. No further data obtainable (see **Family**). *Practice:* Few people benefit from Social Security, although it does provide shelters for the homeless. Pensions are reportedly small. No further data obtainable.

Contraception. *Policy:* Legal. Government supports family planning for health and human rights reasons. *Practice:* Women age 15–49 in union using contraception (1970–80): 2%, of which modern methods 100%. Distribution of contraceptives is scarce and most (especially rural) women have little access to information or devices. **Abortion.** *Policy:* Legal only in case of danger to the woman's life, and based on a reading of Islamic law which states: "No mother shall be treated unfairly on account of her child." *Practice:* No statistics obtainable. A controversial issue because interpretations of Islamic law vary. Because children are economically vital, emphasis is put on spacing births, not reducing them. **Illegitimacy.** *Policy:* Under the 1976 Civil Code, the child of a couple in which 1 (or both) spouse(s) is under age 15 will be considered legitimate. No further data obtainable. *Practice:* No statistics obtainable. Out-of-wedlock children have low social status; reports indicate a low percentage of such births. Polygyny and "temporary" marriages produce some out-of-wedlock children: a father has the legal right to repudiate his child if he suspects his wife of "disloyalty" (even if his own parentage has been established); the wife's testimony carries little weight. **Homosexuality.** *Policy:* Illegal; punishable by imprisonment. No further data obtainable. *Practice:* No data obtainable. **Incest.** *Policy:* No data obtainable. *Practice:* No statistics obtainable (see **Marriage**). **Sexual Harassment.** *Policy:* None. *Practice:* No data obtainable. **Rape.** *Policy:* Marital rape is not recognized. No further data obtainable.

Practice: No statistics obtainable. Reportedly, rape is rare, owing in part to swift vengeance on the rapist by the victim's family. A raped woman may be repudiated by her "dishonored" husband or family. **Battery.** *Policy:* No specific data obtainable, but the Afghan Family Code gives males absolute control over female family members. Legislation (1978) supported a "change of attitude" in male domination over women. *Practice:* No statistics obtainable. Wife-beating is reportedly a common social practice. Families offer little protection, as they are afraid of losing the dowry money. **Prostitution.** *Policy:* No data obtainable on specific laws, but 1978 legislation outlawed the practice of selling young girls. *Practice:* No statistics obtainable. Afghanistan lies along the female sexual slavery traffick route from Africa and the Far East to Europe. **Traditional/Cultural Practices.** *Policy:* No data obtainable. *Practice:* Dowry murders sometimes occur (see pages 10–12) as do "bride-kidnappings," especially in rural areas. **Crisis Centers:** No data obtainable.

HERSTORY. Afghan women have been active in national liberation struggles for centuries. Malalai carried the flag at the battle of Maiwand against the British colonialists in the 19th century. Rabia Balkhi, a poet and philosopher, was also an activist. The Afghan women's movement began officially in 1921, when King Amanullah launched an "emancipation program for women." The 1921 Family Code forbade child marriages, encouraged girls' schools, and banned polygamy for government employees. Removal of the veil was part of "Islamic duty," to provide women with the prerequisites to "fully participate in the society." The King shocked Afghan society by permitting his wife, Queen Suraya, to unveil in public.

Conservative backlash followed; Is-lamic fundamentalists claimed the new code would destroy the social structure of the family and cause sexual anarchy. King Amanullah was overthrown in 1929; his successor, Nader Shah, reinstated the veil. The repressive codes lasted until 1946, when Queen Homaira, wife of Nader Shah's son and successor, Zaher Shah, created the Women's Society, the first institution for Afghan women. In 1959 the Queen supported Prime Minister Daoud Khan's call for "voluntary removal" of the veil, a measure taken up by a small percentage of educated women. Women who unveiled were accused of rejecting Islamic tradition. Eventually, as these women were seen functioning without a "loss of honor," more women unveiled and began organizing for other changes. In 1975 Daoud (then President of the New Republic) called for marriages based on "equivalence." He was killed in a coup in Apr. 1978.

The Dec. 1979 invasion of Afghanistan by Soviet troops (under the mutual defense Treaty of Friendship) drew almost universal protest by Afghan women, especially after 70 schoolchildren were killed in a brick-throwing, slogan-chanting, antigovernment demonstration on Apr. 27, 1980. A schoolgirl named Naheed led the protest, and became an instant heroine. The massacre inspired daily demonstrations by women. The Djamiat-e-Enqilabi-Zaman-e-Afghanistan (Afghanistan Women's Revolutionary League) surfaced in 1979, its purpose to organize women and girls into the national resistance struggle. Farida Ahmadi, one of the League's leaders, was imprisoned and tortured in 1981, but escaped. On Apr. 28, 1983, the Soviet-backed Afghan government announced the release of all female prisoners and some male prisoners; nearly 100,000 persons were estimated to have been imprisoned. According to UN estimates, more than 3 million Afghan refugees have fled to neighboring countries (see IRAN and PAKISTAN) since 1979; more than half of them are women.

MYTHOGRAPHY. The oral tradition of folk and fairy tales common among nomadic peoples is also to be found in

Afghanistan. The goddess Harity, represented as having suckled demons, was a remnant of a Mother Goddess figure from the ancient territory of the Gandaras. She was subsequently assimi-lated by the Buddhist (early 2nd century C.E.) and Islamic (early 7th century) cultures, but has persisted as a presence in legends.

AFGHANISTAN: The Silent Victims
by Sima Wali

Clutching at the cold prison-gate bars, Mastoora waits in the middle of a silent crowd for the posting of names of political prisoners at the Puli Charkhi jail in Kabul. The entire crowd is waiting for the list that will tell them if a brother, father, nephew, son, or grandchild is being held as a political prisoner in the deadly jail. Some have laid out their prayer rugs on the frozen ground and are offering prayers to Allah to deliver their relative from torture or execution.

A young soldier approaches with the list revealing the names of those held in this particular jail. The names of those not listed conveys dreaded news: execution. The crowd draws closer. Suddenly a young child breaks away from his mother and runs to one of the guards: "Uncle, uncle, when can I see my father?" he cries, and begs to be let in. The soldier gently pushes him away. But tears glisten in the soldier's eyes; he too is helpless in this situation. He mumbles under his breath, "I wish I could help you."

A middle-aged woman wearing the veil lets out a blood-chilling cry. A guard has risked his own life to bring news of her brother. "Sister," he tells her, "don't trouble yourself to wait here anymore. May God forgive your brother's soul." She passes out on the snowy ground. A few people rush to her aid. There is nothing the crowd can do to help ease her pain.

An old Pushtun woman has brought warm clothes and some food for her grandson. She may be the sole survivor of her family; it's uncommon for an Afghan woman to visit a prison site if there are any male relatives left to undertake this task. She draws the bundle from under her veil and pleads with the guards to take it inside the prison. Finally, out of traditional compassion for the elderly, he agrees. The rapport between the crowd and the prison guards is exceptional. The crowd knows that the guards secretly help the visitors and is grateful. But soldiers have orders from higher authorities, too, and any breach can lead to their death.

Dusk is approaching and the people gathered at Puli Charkhi silently disperse, pain in their hearts. Mastoora's husband's name is not on the list. There is no record of him anywhere. She prays that he is not being held at the Demazang dungeons. The mere name of the dungeon sends a numbing terror down her spine. Mastoora heads for home in the dark. How will she calm her children tonight when they ask for their father? She cannot erase the look that came into their eyes when soldiers came to drag their father away long after the eleven o'clock curfew.

But the next morning she will draw her veil closer to her body and return to her prison-gate vigil, despite rumors that her husband has been tortured and already killed for supposedly collaborating with those who are called imperialists and capitalists. Omar was not a political activist but was merely working with an international agency. Mastoora doesn't want to believe the rumors. For weeks she searches for a clue, a trace that will lead to the whereabouts of her husband. She reminds herself of the Afghan code of bravery. She counts her blessings, thankful that further violence hasn't crushed her family, and remembering the night when her neighbors' pleas and their daughter's screams woke her from her troubled sleep. She had heard voices shouting orders in an unfamiliar language. A few shots. Then silence. For Mastoora, safety and stability have vanished, possibly forever. She misses the sounds of children playing in the streets. An aura of fear surrounds each individual person.

Tonight, Mastoora gathers her children around her. She whispers to them that they are going to visit their uncle in Paktia. She trembles inwardly and keeps her real plans secret, not daring to breathe the word "escape" to her children: an innocent remark from one of them might have grave consequences. Just a week earlier, the parents of a child in the fourth grade were incarcerated. In school the child had responded negatively to a picture of the new head of state, and the teacher had informed the authorities that the child was reflecting the views of the parents. The parents were questioned and tortured for contradicting the "People's Party."

Mastoora visits Omar's friend at the bazaar. Perhaps he can get her in touch with the right person. After several weeks Omar's friend arranges a secret meeting with a cousin. Together they plan the perilous escape. The cousin owns a truck and has a merchant's pass to export carpets across the border. Boxes are hidden under the carpets, one box assigned to each fugitive, all of whom have been instructed that at a code word from the driver, they must retreat to the hiding spots. The driver and all the passengers have risked their lives in this escape, and they each carry messages of death and violence in their hearts.

Under the carpets, Mastoora glances at the frail woman huddled next to her. She had greeted her softly with the Islamic salutation "Peace unto you." They begin to confide in and trust each other—knowing what a woman alone without a male escort or children means. She has lost her spouse and is alone. Naheed is one of the few survivors of the Kerala village massacre, and she recounts the atrocities that occurred that night. Troops under Soviet direction had attacked in retaliation against the inhabitants of Kerala for "collaborating" with the Freedom Fighters. Every male over the age of eleven was rounded up in the village mosque and machine-gunned down.

The driver's warning cry brings Mastoora back to the present. They are approaching the border. They have been traveling at night and resting during the day to escape patrol guards and to avoid the suspicion of soldiers guarding the bridges.

Mastoora's entire life depends on these next few minutes. She grasps the hands of her children tightly for fear of losing one of them while fleeing across the border. The passengers have agreed collectively to divert the attention of the border soldiers to those among themselves who have exit permits; this will allow time for those who were unable to obtain permits their chance to flee.

The truck comes to a halt close to the border. The travelers descend. The border guards approach the truck, guns drawn. Those who have passports descend first, to keep the guards busy. A moment later the rest break into a run. The guards shout orders to stop. Then there are shots. Mastoora doesn't look back for fear of losing one second's flight. Every instant makes the difference between freedom and death.

Across the border the Pakistani official asks for identification. "Passport?" she wonders. "Identity Card?" Her existence is the sole evidence of her identification—that, and her children. The authorities offer her a refugee camp ID number.

On entering the refugee camp, she is struck by the sea of faces, all marked by the pain of loss of family, of country, of pride and dignity. Is there hope beyond all this? Her mind drifts back to the Pushtun nomad women who were accustomed for centuries to live in freedom with no restrictions on their lives. How have they come to this modern world of barbed wire, refugee camps, and iron curtains?

Mastoora is literate, young, and she has her children. Probably her chances for survival will be stronger. But what fate awaits those women who are devoid of these assets and who have learned only to survive in their own land? Who have never encountered anything foreign? How will they survive?

During her stay in the refugee camp, she sees much suffering. She sees children who have lost fingers to frostbite or limbs to bullets. But she also overhears the constant vow of those tortured or wounded: to return and fight the invaders.

The sophisticated weaponry of the superpower is not sufficient to break the will or the spirit of these brave people. They are survivors of a country often ravaged by war, resilient people who have endured countless invasions in history: Alexander the Great, Genghis Khan, the British three times in the nineteenth century, and now a superpower.

In the camps Mastoora listens to the narrations of violence in the war she has fled. Always, it seems, the women and children suffer the most, as in the slaughter of women and children on April 27, 1978, at the Palace. A soldier who has deserted the army recounts the story. "I was ordered to attack the Palace along with several others. The men, women, and children were ordered to congregate in one of the Palace rooms. Then we were instructed to fire. Any soldier who refused to shoot was executed on the spot. I will never forget the horror in the eyes of this young woman before me. Her twin boys, who had been clutching at her skirt prior to the firing, now lay in a pool of blood. Her skirt was splattered with her children's blood. She just stood there and then suddenly she collapsed."

Mastoora had known the woman the soldier was describing. They had been classmates, and later their children had gone to kindergarten together. It was only a few days before the massacre that Mastoora had seen her friend take her twin boys to the kindergarten— two beautiful boys with tousled hair and eyes like those of young deer.

The new Marxist government turned the Palace grounds into a public site a day later. Crowds were forcibly assembled to witness the victories: the blood of slaughtered women and children soaking the carpets of the Palace.

The horror of this act moved the tribes to rebellion—women as well as men. Nor was it the first time Afghan women belied their image. Malalai is the heroine of the Afghan women's movement, Malalai, the Pushtun woman who carried the Afghan flag at the battle of Maiwand against British colonialism in the nineteenth century. Rabia Balkhi is another heroine; she was a poet and philosopher. A modern heroine is a young Afghan student, Naheed, who led the schoolgirls against the Russian invaders. During their march, Russian soldiers fired at the unarmed schoolgirls and many were killed.

No, we may be suppressed, killed, or exiled, but neither by Afghan men—nor by any foreign invader—can Afghan women be easily stereotyped.

Suggested Further Reading

Dupree, Louis. *Afghanistan.* Princeton: Princeton Univ. Press, 1973.

Dupree, Nancy Hatch. *Behind the Veil in Afghanistan,* 1978; available from the Secretariat for Women in Development, New TransCentury Foundation, Washington, D.C.

Hunte, Pamela A. *Women and the Development Process in Afghanistan,* 1978; available from the Secretariat for Women in Development, New TransCentury Foundation, Washington, D.C.

Newell, R. S. and N. P. *The Struggle for Afghanistan.* Ithaca, NY: Cornell Univ. Press, 1981.

Poullada, Leon. *Reform and Rebellion in Afghanistan 1919–1929.* Ithaca, NY: Cornell Univ. Press, 1973.

Sima Wali was born in Afghanistan and attended Malalai High School and then Kabul University. Her family, the Mohammadzai clan, is the largest extended family in Afghanistan and one of the oldest; King Amanullah, a cousin of her father, was a well-loved reformer who was overthrown by Islamic-fundamentalist clergy. During the invasion of her country by the USSR in the late 1970's, Wali's immediate family was put under house arrest and many other relatives were executed—this despite the fact that no member of her family held a political position at the time. She fled the country under circumstances not unlike "Mastoora," and is living in exile in the United States, now pursuing her master's degree in the School of International Services, Washington, D.C., and working as Assistant Director of the Refugee Women's Program and Coordination Project of the Overseas Education Fund. Originally, she wished her article by-line to be pseudonymous, but since her immediate family has now escaped to join her in forced exile and thus can no longer be victimized by repercussions, she is proud to be able to sign her own name to her contribution.

ALGERIA
(Democratic and Popular Republic of Algeria)

Located in northwestern Africa, bounded by Tunisia and Libya to the east, Niger and Mali to the south, Mauritania, the Western Sahara, and Morocco to the west, and the Mediterranean Sea to the north. **Area:** 2,382,673 sq. km. (919,951 sq. mi.). **Population** (1982): 20,000,000, female 50%. **Capital:** Algiers.

DEMOGRAPHY. Languages: Arabic (official), Berber (indigenous), French. **Races or Ethnic Groups:** Arab 75%, Berber 25%. **Religions:** Islam (Sunni), Roman Catholicism, Judaism, other. **Education** (% enrolled in school, 1982): Age 6–11—of all girls 66%, of all boys 82%; age 12–17—of all girls 35%, of all boys 64%; higher education—no data obtainable. **Literacy** (1977): Women 14%, men 42%. **Birth Rate** (per 1000 pop., 1975–80): 46. **Death Rate** (per 1000 pop., 1975–80): 13. **Infant Mortality** (per 1000 live births, 1975–80): Female 134, male 150. **Life Expectancy** (1975–80): Female 57 yrs., male 55 yrs.

GOVERNMENT. National Liberation Front (FLN) is the ruling military junta and only legal party, headed by Col. Benjedid Chadli since 1979. The Political Bureau and Central Committee of the FLN and the 261-member National People's Assembly are the main legislative bodies. **Women's Suffrage:** Moslem women, 1962 (at Independence); women with French civil status, 1946. **Equal Rights:** Stipulated in the 1962 Constitution. **Women in Government:** Zhor Ounissi, Secretary of State for Social Affairs in 1982, was the first woman in government since Independence.

ECONOMY. Currency: Algerian Dinar (May 1983: 4.56 = $1 US). **Gross National Product** (1980): $36.4 billion. **Per Capita Income** (1980): $1920. **Women's Wages as a Percentage of Men's:** No data obtainable. **Equal Pay Policy:** None. In 1966, when Pres. Boumédienne declared, "Women should not be treated equally with men in employment opportunities," women protested, but the general atti-

tude today reflects his statement, despite some employment gains by women, who are concentrated in lower-paying "female-intensive" jobs. **Production** (Agricultural/Industrial): Wheat, barley, wine, olives; petroleum, fertilizers, iron, steel, textiles. **Women as a Percentage of Labor Force** (1980): 7%; **of agricultural force**—no general statistics obtainable (29% of women workers are employed in agriculture, 1975); **of industrial force** 29%; **of military**—no statistics obtainable; women have achieved the rank of captain, but no higher. **(Employed) Women's Occupational Indicators** (1981): Of doctors 25%; 73% of all employed women work in the service sector. **Unemployment:** No data obtainable.

GYNOGRAPHY. Marriage. *Policy:* Marriage age is 15 for females, 18 for males. Spouses have inheritance rights to each other's estate, following moderate interpretation of Islamic law. Under the Family Code, forced marriage and child marriage are prohibited. *Practice:* Female mean age at marriage (1970–78): 16; women age 15–49 in union (1970–78): 74%; child marriages are still not uncommon in rural areas; polygyny 2% (generally practiced south of the Sahara). Considerable emphasis is still placed on a woman's virginity at marriage; in 1978 women in rural areas and some towns were required to submit certificates of virginity before being allowed to wed. **Divorce.** *Policy:* Legal. Although men may still divorce verbally *(talaq),* reforms have permitted women judicial divorce rights, and to sue for divorce without proof of specific grounds, although a divorcing woman must forfeit her dowry and property rights and/or pay compensation. *Practice:* No statistics obtainable. Divorce usually results in a loss of economic and social status for women, and in possible loss of child custody, if they remarry. **Family.** *Policy:* National insurance covers maternity benefits for employed women: 12 weeks paid maternity leave, 1 yr. unpaid leave after childbirth, 1 hour a day for nursing, and a change of workplace to ease pregnancy whenever possible. A stated goal of the Secretary of State for Social Affairs is the creation of childcare centers in industrial areas with a high concentration of women workers. *Practice:* Childcare remains a much-needed goal; women workers usually leave their children with family members. Maternity allowances are reportedly small. **Welfare.** *Policy:* National insurance provides pension benefits to workers and maternity benefits (see **Family**); no further data obtainable. *Practice:* No data obtainable.

Contraception. *Policy:* Legal; government support of family planning, including the development of a unified national policy for contraception based on the concern "to protect the life and health of the mother and child as well as the mental and social balance of the family." *Practice:* No statistics obtainable. Reports say that contraceptive distribution is limited to urban areas and used by a small percentage of the population, primarily educated women. **Abortion.** *Policy:* Legal in cases of danger to the woman's life or health. *Practice:* No statistics obtainable, but illegal abortions are reportedly common. **Illegitimacy.** *Policy:* No data obtainable. *Practice:* No data obtainable. **Homosexuality.** *Policy:* No data obtainable. *Practice:* No statistics obtainable, but there have been rumors of lesbian women who were punished by execution. In some rural communities, women and men still live in separate areas, making male homosexuality more visible in the public sphere. **Incest.** *Policy:* No data obtainable. *Practice:* No statistics obtainable. Intra-family marriages are common custom; scattered reports indicate "consensual unions" between siblings. **Sexual Harassment.** *Policy:* No data obtainable. *Practice:* No data obtainable. **Rape.** *Policy:* No data obtainable. *Practice:* No statistics obtainable, but rape is reportedly common. The French army carried out deliberate rapes of Algerian women during the war for Independence, "to dishonor Algerian men." **Battery.** *Policy:* A woman may take an abusive husband to court, but she will lose her dowry if divorce results. *Practice:* No statistics obtainable. Social attitudes consider wife-beating customary, as

in a Jan. 1982 debate over the Family Code, when one legislator described the dimensions of the stick with which a woman should be beaten daily. **Prostitution.** *Policy:* No data obtainable. *Practice:* No statistics obtainable. Prostitution is a thriving industry in the larger urban centers; Algiers is a stop in the international sexual slavery traffick of women and children. "Courtesanship" is still practiced in some Saharan oasis towns; child prostitution is a serious problem. **Traditional/ Cultural Practices.** *Policy:* No data obtainable. *Practice:* Under the pressure of virginity strictures, some women have been known to undergo operations for hymen-reconstruction—a practice not uncommon throughout the region. **Crisis Centers:** No data obtainable.

HERSTORY. Semi-legendary women rulers (see MYTHOGRAPHY) in ancient Numidia and Carthage preceded the decline in women's status which was gradually brought about by the Roman (145 B.C.E.), Vandal (440 C.E.), and Islamic (650) invasions. The French conquest in 1830 and subsequent colonization (1848) further weakened what relative indigenous power women had, while promulgating European standards for the entire population. Algerian women actively fought in the Resistance (National Liberation Front, FLN) against the French for the entire 14-year struggle. Women political prisoners were tortured, raped, and killed by French troops. The FLN proclaimed "all sectors open to women," while the newspaper *El Moudjahid* stated in 1959, "The Algerian woman is already free because she participates in the liberation of her country." Yet, as official documents later revealed, women were not willingly accepted into the *maquis* (Resistance). Some of those who were accepted were later arrested. Others, like Djamila Bouhared and Djamila Boupacha, became famous as exceptional fighters, but most women were involved in giving moral support to male fighters, as food suppliers, etc.

After Independence (July 5, 1962), a women's wing of the FLN was founded —the National Union of Algerian Women (UNFA)—which adopted a supportive position within the Ahmed Ben

Bella-led regime. In Mar. 1966 a split occurred between moderate and radical members of UNFA over a speech by Pres. Houari Boumédienne (see **Equal Pay**), when moderates aligned themselves with the leader and militants refused. UNFA lost its base among urban progressive feminists.

In the 1960's there was a resurgence of women's movement activity. In 1962 over 12,000 women demonstrated in Harcha and Oran. Algerian feminists have fought for an end to dowry and polygyny, and for better divorce laws, legal majority at age 18, birth control, and equal pay for equal work. In Jan. 1982, women presented a 10,000-signature petition to the National Assembly and held massive demonstrations against a proposed Family Code that represented major setbacks for women. The proposal, which would have placed women under conservative interpretation of traditional Islamic law (making them permanent minors, passed from legal responsibility of father to husband to son), was defeated. The Groupe de Recherche sur les Femmes Algériennes (Research Group on Algerian Women) began publishing a quarterly bulletin, *Isis,* out of the Centre de Documentation des Sciences Humaines in Oran in 1982; the bulletin is a collective project of a group of Algerian feminist social scientists. Various writers, such as Assia Djebar, have addressed the subject of female subjugation and revolutionary betrayal. In early 1984 feminist organizing against another proposed new Family Code which would erode women's rights resulted in the jailing without formal charge of 4 women: Fattouma Ouzegane, Louiza Hannoun, Leila Souidi, and Mme. Nakkache.

MYTHOGRAPHY. The prehistoric paintings found at Tassili N'Ajjer show numerous ritual scenes of women leading processions, the most famous of which is a rock painting of a horned goddess. Astoreth, one of the major forms of the Great Goddess in the Middle East, was worshipped in the Numidia-Carthage region. Dido, the semi-legendary queen of Carthage, was immortalized in Roman literature and myth, although indigenous versions of her story depict her not as a suicide for the sake of love but as a murder victim.

ALGERIA: The Day-to-Day Struggle
by Fatma Oussedik
(Translated by Anne-christine d'Adesky)

How to understand the emergence of a movement for equal rights, a movement energized by a category of the population considered "privileged"—a group who actually enjoys material conditions that approach (at least minimally) those of the petite bourgeoisie in European countries?

This question in turn exposes at least two underlying issues: that of the dubious importance of material conditions in modifying the position of women in a patriarchally dominated society, and that of the degree of suppression of women (even women of the bourgeoisie and petite bourgeoisie) *by* the ruling power.

For a long time, the small fringe of qualified women working in the Algerian public services internalized the concept of privilege as having a paid skilled job.[1] To a large degree, this was an unconscious reference to the model set for women in Europe and also

[1] In 1977, only 138,000 women worked in the labor force; 73% work in the service sector despite the fact that 46% of working women have diplomas versus 15% of the men workers.

by the realistic expansion of areas in which the new generation was expected to move ahead.

If the hour of our demand for equal rights as women has arrived, it is precisely with reference to this "privilege" and this "progress" that reveal themselves to be at the same time instruments of oppression and of resistance.

We do have access to jobs—but only on the bases of guilt and anxiety. The State invests little in social services or childcare centers. School schedules are incompatible with a professional life. Public transportation is impractical. The result: we are made to feel like monstrous mothers, delivering our children to the streets, to the grandmother, to the neighbor, maid, or nanny. Not valued as workers (being privileged), we are also not valued as mothers.[2]

A single woman states, "I must arrive at my parents' home with a smooth, relaxed, facial expression. My brother can say he is tired, but not me. Because I am supposedly so lucky, I am 'allowed' to go out to work at my job. Yet on my days off, if I want to go out to see a woman friend, they say, 'But you *are* out, all week long.' " Only over the years, as prices continued to rise, did we realize how much our salaries were vital to the daily life of the whole family. So this possibility of personal freedom that so few of us possess, why *not* make it an area in which to struggle?

For a long time, we were reproached for answering this question from a woman's point of view. If food prices have risen, it is said, the same is true for the whole population; if women have no voice in politics the same is true for the majority of the population; if there is no government investment in social services, this is but an index of class politics.

But it *is* certain that we women are: those who must raise our children *and* work; those who must manage the tour de force of feeding the entire family with those vegetables that *are* available—and at the prices they cost.[3] We are also the daughters of those women who were the last to eat—and who then ate the men's leftovers; the daughters of those women who waged a liberation war and whose only liberation was to return to their kitchens—all of this to remember that *we know where we come from:* a history of women marked by an oppression that certain people still don't see or believe.

But we also are daughters and sisters, and even a little bit those who harbor the illusion of eventual happiness by conforming as much as possible to the type of person society orders us to be. Thus we are also the mothers who taught our daughters to walk in the shadows of the walls, to lower their heads in front of men, to tuck in their shoulders to conceal their breasts. And out of all these women, will we be able to live? And anyway, what is it all about? *It's about women who, while challenging the oppression under which they live, necessarily challenge all forms of oppression.*

Why necessarily? Because the "sexual" variable poses the basic question of society's hierarchical organization, not only as an abstract categorical sample but as a constant in everyday life—everyday life marked by oppression but also by resistance. And it is this resistance that renders oppression visible and unites women *with* resistance as part of an over-all social movement.

Is this a rearguard, undermining struggle, or does it have its own historic place specific to Algerian society? All feminist issues are viewed, in Algeria as in many other developing countries, as an alignment with occidental Europe—that is, viewed as "undermining" the nationalistic movement.

The only true response to such accusations is to restate the desire of all human beings for a peaceful world and for happiness. It's obvious that men and women must fight for

---

[2] The average number of children borne by a woman is seven.

[3] There are no vegetables on the market selling for less than D. 5. The lowest-priced meat sells for D. 60.

more social justice everywhere on earth. In addition, any examination of how painful and alienating daily life is constitutes a strong enough argument to convince one of the impossibility of living in silence. Consequently, it is false to try to answer the question of "undermining" or of "historic place." The resurgence in everyday life of a demand for women's empowerment is the very sign that all movements which internalize power and repress others' claims to share it are condemned to see those claims resurrect themselves again and again, day after day.

Suggested Further Reading

Center of Documentation and Research in Human Sciences (CDSH). *Acts of the Days of Study and Reflection on the Situation of the Woman in Algeria.* Oran, May 1980.
————. *Acts of the Day of Information and Reflection on Contraception.* Oran, Nov. 10, 1982.

Fatma Oussedik is an assistant professor of sociology at the University of Algiers, and researcher at the Center of Research and Applied Economics in Algeria. Her work focuses on the body and sexual morality in Algeria, "in an attempt to express the point of view of women in the face of both the symbolic and actual manipulations that confront us."

ARGENTINA
(Argentine Republic)

Located in southern South America, bounded by Chile to the west, Bolivia and Paraguay to the north, Uruguay to the northeast, the Atlantic Ocean to the east, and Chile and the South Atlantic Ocean to the south. **Area:** 2,808,602 sq. km. (1,084,120 sq. mi.). **Population** (1980): 27,085,000, female 50%. **Capital:** Buenos Aires.

DEMOGRAPHY. Languages: Spanish (official), English, Italian, German, French. **Races or Ethnic Groups:** European (Spanish, Italian) descent 97%, Indian, Mestizo, Arab. **Religions:** Roman Catholicism 92%, other. **Education** (% enrolled in school, 1975): Age 6–11—of all girls 100%, of all boys 100%; age 12–17—of all girls 66%, of all boys 61%; higher education—no data obtainable. **Literacy** (1977): Women 92%, men 94%. **Birth Rate** (per 1000 pop., 1975–80): 26. **Death Rate** (per 1000 pop., 1975–80): 9. **Infant Mortality** (per 1000 live births, 1975–80): Female 42, male 48. **Life Expectancy** (1975–80): Female 73 yrs., male 66 yrs.

GOVERNMENT. Military junta headed by Gen. Reynaldo Bignone, who assumed power in July 1982, pledged to democratize Argentina by Mar. 1984 and lifted a 6-yr. ban on political parties and an 8-yr. ban on political meetings.* **Voting:** General elections were suspended from 1976–1983. **Women's Suffrage:** 1947. **Equal Rights:** 1947 law granted women equal rights with men. **Women in Government:** None in cabinet; 1 Supreme Court judge. Vice-President María Estela (Isabel) Perón became the first woman head of state in 1975 after her husband, President Juan Domingo Perón, died. Perón's first wife, Eva, had shared power with him in the 1940's and early 1950's—but unofficially; her attempt to hold formal office herself failed.

ECONOMY. Currency: Argentine Peso (May 1983: 69,000. = $1 US). **Gross National Product** (1980): $66.4 billion. **Per Capita Income** (1980): $2390. **Women's Wages as a Percentage of Men's:** No statistics obtainable, but women reportedly make less than their male counterparts in general and are concentrated in lower-paying, "female-intensive" service-sector jobs. **Equal Pay Policy:** Required under labor laws, but with rare compliance. **Production** (Agricultural/Industrial): Grains, oil, linseed, livestock products, sugar cane; petrochemicals, motor vehicles, processed foods, oil. **Women as a Percentage of Labor Force** (1980): 26%; **of agricultural force**—no general statistics obtainable (4% of women workers are employed in agriculture, 1975); **of industrial force**—no data obtainable; **of military** (1983) 40 women in each branch as "auxiliary personnel"; marines accepted women cadets in 1979, infantry and air force in 1982. **(Employed) Women's Occupational Indicators** (1980–81): No general statistics obtainable. Most women work in the service sector; 2 out of every 5 employed women work as domestic servants for below-minimum-wage pay. **Unemployment** (Mar. 1983): 5% (official), 15% (unofficial); no rates by sex obtainable**; underemployment 40% (unofficial).

GYNOGRAPHY. Marriage. *Policy:* Law of Patria Potestad gives husbands complete authority over family—education of children, finances, property matters, and domicile location. Women need their husbands' signatures for most legal matters. Laws governing marriage are based on strict interpretation of Roman Catholic doctrine. *Practice:* Female mean

---

* In Oct. 1983, free elections took place; Raúl Alfonsin of the Radical Civic Union was elected president.

** The latest national census (as of 1983) did not factor in female unemployment because of an official government assumption that all women who "leave" their jobs do so by choice in order to return to their "primary occupation"—the home.

age at marriage (1970–78): 23; women age 15–49 in union (1970–78): 59.8%; married women are subjugated in terms of legal decision-making, and are expected to assume a passive role. It is a tolerated cultural practice for a husband to have a mistress. **Divorce.** *Policy:* Legal but without the right to remarry (thus functioning as a legal separation rather than a divorce). Earlier (1954) "dissolution of marriage" had been legalized by Juan Perón. *Practice:* Middle- and upper-class Argentines go to Uruguay, Mexico, and Bolivia for divorces (which are not recognized under Argentine law). Prior to 1970, approx. 57% of women were divorced. In cases of legal separation or annulment (sometimes granted), women generally receive custody of children, while men are responsible for children's education and financial support; women also can claim a subsidy under social security, although the sum is low and often received by the father, who does not necessarily pass it along to the dependents. Alimony is rare.

Family. *Policy:* Government support of "pro-family" legislation includes State-plus-industry childcare, where employers of more than 50 workers must provide childcare facilities. Government employees receive special stipends for large families, and for children's schooling (paid to males as "heads of households"). Maternity Commission regulations provide employed women with 8–12 weeks paid maternity leave before childbirth, 6 weeks after childbirth, and a total of 2 hours per day for nursing for 1 yr. No woman can be fired for pregnancy. *Practice:* Childcare benefits do not pertain to the majority of employed women (those in the service sector, and especially in domestic service), who themselves often provide childcare for middle- and upper-income women. Reports say that pregnant women are fired "for other reasons" and that recently (1983) employers are hiring men to replace them. **Welfare.** *Policy:* National insurance covers certain family and maternity stipends (see **Family**),

housing credits, and provides certain workers with a small monthly pension after retirement***; domestic workers are eligible for these benefits but must rely on the cooperation of their employers. Widows receive (a reduced portion of) spouses' pensions; widowers do not. Medical assistance is available to all persons at minimal or no cost (this covers only basic medical services in State hospitals, which are too few to meet the needs). *Practice:* No statistics obtainable. The majority of the poor receive no government assistance. In the cities, domestic workers have won court cases against employers for nonreceipt of pension benefits; in the provinces, such recourse is rarely available. Homemakers seldom receive pensions because, not having their own monies, they rarely can contribute to pension funds. Housing credits invariably are reserved for (legal) families, never awarded to single women or men.

Contraception. *Policy:* Pro-natalist; family-planning services are limited. A 1971 decree forbade distribution and open sale of contraceptives, although the State let lapse a 1974 decree further restricting contraceptive use. Recent amendments forbade prescription of devices to single women by doctors. *Practice:* No statistics obtainable; distribution of birth-control devices is tightly controlled. Information about contraception is scarce and most rural women are uninformed of modern methods. **Abortion.** *Policy:* Legal only in cases of danger to a woman's life, or if pregnancy resulted from rape or incest; punishable by 1–4 yrs. imprisonment for the woman, 1–10 yrs. for the practitioner. *Practice:* Current estimates show 1 out of 4 women has an abortion, mostly illegal; reportedly, a high number of maternal deaths are due to improperly performed illegal abortions and/or complications following abortion attempts. Many rural women use the *sonda,* a rubber stick-like instrument, to abort. In 1970 the number of abortions almost equaled the number of live births. **Illegitimacy.** *Policy:* Government sources

---

*** Women age 60 and men age 65 with over 15 yrs. of employment and "voluntary contribution" to pension fund; the age and work-yrs. requirements vary in different fields but all such standards are State-controlled. Homemakers can claim such a pension if they have contributed to the appropriate fund earlier.

state that children born in or out of wedlock are given equal treatment under the
law. Fathers may repudiate children or
refuse parentage on grounds of suspected
"infidelity" or adultery; in this case, the
mother assumes full legal responsibility
for her child. In inheritance cases, out-of-
wedlock children receive 1/4 of the
amount received by children born in
wedlock. The law requires parents to educate their ("legitimate") children in accordance with family social position and
to provide food for them until age 21, but
requires education for out-of-wedlock issue only through primary school and
food provision only until age 18. A single
mother is regarded as having committed
a sexual crime. *Practice:* No statistics obtainable, but unofficial estimates report
many "illegitimate" births. Common-law
marriages are not legally sanctioned,
which produces a high number of "illegitimate" children among the poor and
rural populations.

Homosexuality. *Policy:* Not illegal unless "as an offense against public morality" (see **Prostitution**), in which case it is
punishable by a fine and imprisonment
varying in severity from months to several yrs. No further data obtainable.
Practice: No statistics obtainable. Severe
institutionalized repression of homosexual men and women, reportedly including torture and murder. Any person
picked up by the police for any reason
may be asked to sign an "H-2 Form" on
penalty of not being released; H-2, a declaration of one's homosexuality, is a formal record which is used in discriminatory hiring practice by both government
and private sector employers. After the
1976 coup, a wave of terror began when
Dept. of Morality police patrolled streets
for signs of "homosexual behavior":
clothing, gestures, or speech could result
in arrest, loss of job, or imprisonment.
Earlier (1940–60), police had regularly
raided parks, public bathrooms, and hotels arresting suspected homosexuals and
lesbians. In 1970 a brief period of tolerance allowed a few homosexual bars to
operate discreetly, and the Federation for
the Liberation of Homosexuals (an underground organization) was founded.
Under the new (1983) government, there
is discussion of abolishing the H-2 Form

as an invasion of privacy, but no legislation yet has been proposed.

Incest. *Policy:* Not defined as a crime
unless committed with a minor, in which
case it falls under rape or "corruption of
a minor" statutes. If victim is under age
12 the penalty is 4–15 yrs. imprisonment,
if victim is age 12–15 penalty is 8–20 yrs.,
if victim is age 15–18 penalty is 3–10 yrs.,
if victim is age 18–21 penalty is 2–6 yrs.
Penalties are more severe if perpetrator is
a relative, priest, teacher, or guardian,
and/or if deceit, threat, violence, or
abuse of authority is employed. *Practice:*
No statistics obtainable, but a strong social tabu against incest exists. Incidence
is nevertheless reportedly high in all societal levels, but particularly in rural areas.
Sexual Harassment. *Policy:* None. *Practice:* No statistics obtainable. While labor
laws prohibit sexual discrimination, sexual harassment is a severe problem for
women, who have no grievance measures
against harassment. Rape. *Policy:* Illegal.
Defined as carnal access with a person of
either sex if victim is a minor, sick, or
unable to defend her/himself, or when
force or intimidation is used; punishable
by 6–15 yrs. imprisonment in cases of
rape with "no serious injuries," 8–20 yrs.
if accompanied by serious injuries, 5–25
yrs. if death results. Rape falls under the
category of "offenses against honor"
(also see **Incest**). *Practice:* No statistics
obtainable. Marital rape is rarely recognized by law; single women who are rape
victims often are viewed as having incited
the attack. There is common use of domestic servants to initiate young boys
sexually; domestics have no measure of
protest against rape for fear of loss of job,
beatings, etc. Many women have been
raped by military junta security forces,
particularly women political prisoners.
Battery. *Policy:* No specific laws govern
wife-beating; general laws on assault may
apply. *Practice:* No statistics obtainable.
Wife-beating is a commonly tolerated
practice. Women have no real measure of
grievance against battery, since Patria
Potestad legally gives husbands complete
authority over their wives. **Prostitution.**
Policy: Not a crime according to Art. 19
of the Constitution: "private actions that
in no way offend order and public morals
or do damage to a third party are re-

served to be judged by God and fall outside the competence of judges." It is, however, illegal to solicit, aid, or abet a prostitute, operate a hotel for prostitution purposes, or live off a prostitute's earnings; the penalty for pimping ranges from a fine to 1–3 yrs. imprisonment. *Practice:* No statistics obtainable, but prostitution is a thriving industry in urban centers. Prostitutes are arrested and fined or jailed for 21 days under "police edicts" which permit their arrest for having "offended public morals." The average arrest record of a prostitute is 70–80 jailings. Prostitutes have little control over their own earnings, and have no State protection. **Traditional/Cultural Practices:** No data obtainable. **Crisis Centers.** *Policy:* None. *Practice:* Argentine feminists are organizing rape-crisis and battery centers in urban areas.

HERSTORY. The indigenous population was an agricultural people when Juan Díaz de Solís "discovered" Argentina in 1516; it became a Spanish colony in 1580. In 1823 a benevolent society of wealthy women organized in protest of discriminatory laws regarding women. *La Argentina,* the first women's paper, was published in 1830 and *La Camelia,* a tract subtitled "Equality Between the Sexes," in 1852. The Socialist Feminist Center was started in 1900 by women fighting for protective labor legislation in textile and tobacco industries; Alicia Moreau, a member and active feminist, pressured Congress to change the Civil Code, which denied women equal rights. Cecilia Grierson became the first woman doctor and founded the National Council of Argentine Women, a charity organization devoted to cultural and social gains for women. Grierson and Juliet Lanteri also established the Organization of University Women.

In 1910 the First International Feminist Congress was held in Buenos Aires, linking Latin American women with other suffrage movements. Their goals included civil equality for married women, equal pay for equal work, education, and legalized divorce. In 1918 Lanteri became president of the newly founded National Feminist Party and ran as a congressional candidate. Elvira Rawson de Dellepiane established the Women's Rights Organization (1919), which claimed 11,000 members and fought for the right to vote. In 1924 maternity laws were passed for employed women; in 1926 Congress gave women equal civil status with men (married women were no longer "permanent minors," though men remained "heads of households"). In 1932 the Argentine Assoc. for Women's Suffrage had over 80,000 members; in 1936 the Argentine Union of Women used the term "women's liberation." With Eva Perón (popularly called Evita) as an ally, women won the right to vote in 1947 and took to the streets in celebration. In 1951 Eva set up the Feminist Party, albeit as one of the Peronist Party's 3 branches (with men's and workers' branches), and threw her power toward legalization of divorce. Although everything Eva Perón (a former actress and charismatic public presence) did was bent on keeping her husband in power, she nonetheless used her extraordinary influence with him and her almost cult image with the masses to further certain aspects of women's equality. Under that influence, Juan Perón named 7 women to the Senate and 24 women as deputies, the government turned a more permissive eye on contraceptive use, and women in general began to be viewed as a political force. Eva Perón died in 1952. In 1954 the new Family Code included the right to divorce (see **Divorce**).

Perón himself did not enjoy the same popularity among women as did his late wife, and many women participated in the massive procession in Corpus Christi to protest against him before his fall. A 20–year transition period followed (a succession of military dictatorships and short–lived constitutional governments), marked by repression of women's rights, until 1970, when the creation of the Feminist Union signaled a renewed spirit. Abortion became a political issue. In 1974 Juan Perón returned to power, together with his third wife, María Estela (Isabel); they were elected president and vice–president, respectively. The following year, when Perón died at age 78, Isabel Perón became the first Argentinian woman head of state. Re–elected president of the Peronist Party in Aug. 1975,

she faced in–party opposition to her policies, a staggering 330% inflation rate,
and mass labor strikes; in Mar. 1976 a 3–
man military junta deposed and arrested
her; she later lived in exile in Spain.

The 1976 military coup was a setback
for women's rights; women activists were
tortured, raped, killed, or "disappeared"
and continue to suffer persecution as of
1983 (see following article). Feminist
groups went "underground," although
beloved national figures like the poet-
folksinger María Elena Walsh wrote and
sang of both feminism and civil liberties
under the cover of their art. In Mar.
1977, 14 women whose children had disappeared began weekly vigils in the Plaza
de Mayo; they were arrested, imprisoned,
and threatened by security forces, yet
2500 other women joined them. These
women—the *Madres* (Mothers) and
Abuelas (Grandmothers) or "Crazy Ladies," as they've been called—have
launched international appeals about the
tortures and disappearances (est. at approx. 30,000 since 1976) in Argentina. In
1982 Argentine feminists denounced the
Malvinas conflict and issued joint statements in solidarity with British feminists.
Multisectorial de Mujeres, a national coalition of women in political parties and
autonomous feminist groups, was formed
in Dec. 1983; the women plan to pressure
for reforms promised by the new government—the creation of a Women's Affairs
Ministry, legalized divorce, revision of
Patria Potestad, etc.

MYTHOGRAPHY. In the territory of
Tierra del Fuego, the Ona tribe (presently
in the process of assimilation and extinction) believes that women once governed
the tribe's destiny. Men rebelled and demanded the women's secret knowledge;
they then killed the adult women, leaving
alive only females age 6 or younger—
who grew up under the institution of
male power.

ARGENTINA: The Fire Cannot Be Extinguished
by Leonor Calvera
(Translated by Gloria Feiman Waldman
and Elisa Sierra Gutiérrez)

As in most other countries, twentieth-century feminism in Argentina suffered a decline
that lasted more or less fifty years; the 1970's marked the hour of a resurrection that
many had thought would never come. It started this time with small consciousness-
raising groups of women united by impatience about their condition and a desire to
analyze it. The new expression of feminism by North American women was studied, and
books were re-examined from this new perspective. The end result was the creation of
UFA, the Feminist Union of Argentina, a name chosen in part to honor the "unions" of
feminist groups from the end of the last century, and also as a play on the colloquial
interjection *ufa*—which expresses a state of being fed up.

Coincidentally, Argentinian society was passing through a phase of great excitement,
of changes and questions. An unusual permissiveness in the discussion of different political ideologies allowed women to explore topics that, up until then, had been practically
tabu. Nevertheless, hopes were focused, ironically, on the return of Juan Perón. Defeated
in 1955 by the Liberation Revolution, deprived of his military hierarchy, he still managed
from his exile in Spain to become the factotum of the intellectual as well as the popular
movements. And next to him floated the resurrected image of Eva Perón—Evita, around
whose phantom the liberation movement was to fight a battle still unfinished.

Within UFA, the original group advanced rapidly in consciousness-raising and in feelings of sisterhood. Avidly we read material from other countries, works that told us of the

same pain, the same fury, the same desperation, and the same desires for change that we as women felt here in Argentina.

Caught between admiration and doubt, we put into practice what appeared to be crucial for personal development and women's solidarity: the techniques of consciousness-raising. Up to a point, the results were excellent. Nevertheless, the dominant note of the plan—the emotional-existential level as a means to understand and, eventually, to act —was unadaptable to the needs of our group. It was clear that women were capable of an emotional outpouring, a sentimental catharsis on a particular theme, but they would return again and again to the same themes without making headway toward a common cause of oppression, much less an *action* that might bring change. The words would remain floating in a haze of compassion for their own miseries—perhaps because of the old habit of our people to delight in verbal expression without giving it much value, or because of the extensive effect of psychoanalysis that has strengthened the human tendency to justify the status quo on a personal basis.

The truth is that with the urgency to find answers, it was necessary to improvise partial hypotheses and analyses. But it wasn't long before this hurried speculation revealed itself to be insufficient, especially when it came to moving the group to action. The urgency to act resulted in many cases of dramatic *individual* change. Yet without ideological clarification or sufficient reflection, these experiences had no hope of general impact. The group was then held responsible for these disappointments—which of course diminished its support base and credibility.

Feminism everywhere is born in the bosom of patriarchy, upon whose threshold of tolerance it of necessity depends in order to develop. This threshold was rather limited in our country, which made the diffusion of ideas extremely difficult. Not only was it necessary to confront male reactions when men felt themselves affected (the foreseeable counteroffensives of mockery, indifference, ridicule, distortion, etc.), but the feminist counterattack had to link itself to the *assimilation* of feminism by subversive and guerrilla groups —with the consequent repression that this implied. For a society whose values are based on a hierarchy of God, country, and home, the questioning of such institutions, implicit in the espousal of feminism, constitutes an assault on the power of the State. And the State wastes no time in punishing it.

Consequently, we became very cautious, even about using the term "feminism." Finding it impossible to gain access to the mass media, with scarce economic resources, and fighting our own fears and doubts, the advances we realized were neither rapid nor explosive. Nevertheless, some of the issues of the movement slowly filtered into public opinion. The press began to ask who we were. (Of course, it did not direct itself to *us* to ask the question, nor allow us to explain our pain and our hopes.)

The minor political parties on the Left included some publicity on the women's movement in their platforms. The circle of silence around us began to crumble thanks to small campaigns revolving around such topics as the right to abortion and the demythification of Mother's Day, but fundamentally thanks to word of mouth. When we no longer thought it possible, certain ideas suddenly reached the press. Along the way, to be sure, they lost their bite and their potential for change and were transformed into sexual rhetoric.

Unfortunately, this fragmentation corresponds to a certain degree to reality. Lacking an all-encompassing theory, the movement found it difficult to avoid arbitrary polarizations—the inherited patrimony of patriarchy. To the traditional dichotomies, new ones were added: lesbian women versus heterosexual women (and vice versa), "intellectual" women versus "emotional" women, women from the cities versus women from the provinces, radical women versus reformists. To these antagonisms were added still another, the problem of leadership, which resulted in horizontal decision-making in an attempt to avoid those questions which were unavoidable. This in turn led to a kind of paralysis in our public evolution, for fear of criticism by our own sisters. Each time, the dilemma threatened to explode with greater force—whether to move forward with generalized answers, or to completely put to one side introspection and analysis in order to concentrate on concrete problems. For the moment, neither one road nor the other could be taken.

Around us, the union between the Left and the Right was beginning to fall apart. Expectations of Perón's return had brought a unity whose contrivance didn't take long in exposing itself. Divided again, the country was thrown into another search for elusive Argentinian democracy.

That period—of awakening to political life, to the play of words and seductions, where what stood out most were desires for power and self-interest—had as a corollary the night of authoritarianism. The darkness had begun to make itself visible toward the end of 1974, but it was not until 1976 that the curtain finally fell. Then—persecutions, police raids, imprisonments, deaths. The air itself was heavy with suspicion. Any and all activities associated with free expression were stopped. It became necessary to get rid of all material that might be considered compromising; books and papers were burned for fear of a surprise police search. The past was being brought to a close, sacrificed on the altars of a newly established order. Many women, alarmed by the gravity of the circumstances, chose to follow a husband, brother, or son into exile. Others of us preferred a worse exile —to be a foreigner in one's own country. We were like strangers, and we were afraid. But we stayed to endure whatever might come.

Within the limited possibilities allowed, we continued sporadic contacts with the early militants in exile. As optimists, some of us thought in terms of the future and prepared for a new resurgence of feminism. With no groundwork, statistics, or financial resources, and with only a few books to consult, we nevertheless had, after all, managed to explore an ideology that we had tried and tested, albeit one that left too many blank spaces and divided the universe in a somewhat Manichaean way. Now that strategy had to be revised for the bitter times upon us.

But by 1981 we were again in the fray.

Even while Argentine law (on the books) reveals little discrimination against women, there still remain such problems as a six-month jail sentence for adultery (although it is almost never imposed), the unresolved issue of abortion, and the matter of *patria potestad* (parental authority over minor children), always decided in favor of the father. Given these issues, the topic with which we chose to open this feminist wave was that of judicial reform. In search of a change in public opinion, and wanting acceptance rather than debate, we decided on a change in the law of *patria potestad* as our rallying point. In the appalling Roman tradition, *patria potestad* in Argentina meant that the father has all the rights regarding the child, while the mother has the obligation for the child's care. With justice as our criterion, we asked that in all cases the *patria potestad* be shared.

The campaign (which initially we did not even identify as feminist), was launched. The people were wary when we asked them for signatures needed to strengthen our petition to the Ministry of Justice. It was "inopportune" to address the issue with a *de facto* government. We responded that the moment is *never* "opportune" for a woman. Surprisingly, the mass media became the campaign's echo. To our amazement, it was considered a feminist proposition—and signs of agreement even appeared.

Feminism had come back on its own. On a reduced scale, its basic points were analyzed. Almost without cultural exchanges, it crossed barriers—and managed this despite a strong censorship that even prohibits the use of the word "couple" on television (astonishing because feminism favors the legitimizing of extramarital unions), and despite the lack of general information. Apparently, in the intervening years, feminism had achieved a certain respectability. This made us believe in miracles. However, in analyzing this phenomenon, we find that a cause might be attributable to one of the oldest exchanges in the world: that of travel. But the fact remains that in spite of repression, jailings, and so many barriers placed on knowledge, feminist ideology has saturated the Argentinian public conscience.

Nevertheless, it is a feminism heavily indebted to reformism. For example, it is understood that women advocate total equality under the law, better education, and improvements in the area of labor; but it is considered inconvenient that we concern ourselves with control over our own bodies. Attempting to debate these perceptions is fruitless, because even today there is complete and enforced prohibition of the sale and distribution of contraceptives, and abortion (or even its mere mention) is still virtually illegal. In this, Roman Catholic ecclesiastical pressure wields a strong and negative influence, because the clergy continues to view maternity as the permanent and cohesive factor in the family and society. With respect to control over our own bodies, then, women's consciousness has only gone backward since the beginning of the 1970's—in no small part owing, pitifully, to the despicable effects of censorship.

Besides the censorship obstacle, we feminists find ourselves facing another barrier in our work with women. In a country unaccustomed to political self-expression, women have not had time to make the journey through political party rhetoric. This is especially damaging because the example is still alive of how one woman—Eva Perón—was able to overcome the "restrictions of her sex" in order to reach the second highest position in the country (from which she resigned in the early 1950's). All of this the legendary Evita managed, without neglecting to obtain for women legislation that would help them in work, a five-year social and economic plan that took them into consideration, and a massive women's political organization that came into existence for the first time. Of course, the lack of feminist consciousness makes it impossible for many Argentinian women to see just how much emotional subjugation there was in this "true leader" who found it reasonable to move in the shadow of the "just man" whose name she constantly evoked.

That example was to appear re-authenticated, twenty years later, with the ascent of another woman—Isabel Perón—to the office of the presidency. All things considered, the image of Evita still greatly exceeds that of Isabel, her sentimental imitator and successor, especially since the original has almost been converted into the saintly focus of a popular cult. It is difficult—even for feminists—to do battle with a myth.

As for the rest, the obstacles we encounter today are depressingly similar to those of ten years ago: the lack of information, the impossibility of holding public demonstrations without official permission, the curtailment of individual civil liberties, the lack of funds. And a new misunderstanding of feminism recently has been added to the old ones. Instead of going to the militants of the women's movement for an explanation of feminism, the press has substituted in our stead members of the Association of Catholic Women or the Mothers of the Plaza de Mayo (the "Crazy Ladies")—supposedly to speak in the name of the women's liberation movement. This in turn has made it necessary for us, when speaking to a new woman, to help her divest herself not only of old ideas but also of new and more subtle ones that make her see herself and feminism in a distorted light.

But no matter how much the erroneous interpretations grow, or how difficult the diffusion of ideas becomes, we will continue to go forward. In our search to widen the parameters of public consciousness about women, we have planned and organized a Women's Congress, which will serve a dual purpose: to examine immediate concerns and conflicts and to study the level of self-awareness women have attained as well as their willingness to express it. In addition, in a nation under almost permanent military law, such a congress will provide an excellent occasion to unite women so that we can meet each other and share ideas and experiences. We already know the revolutionary strength that can be tapped in a feminist gathering, even when liberal, fortuitous reasons have motivated it. Imagine, then. . . . It can be said that the congress will respond to the intellectual necessity of examining the present condition of the female sex in our country, the causes for its oppression, and the possible roads to improve women's integration into the male world—*or to transform that male world.*

Study and information, as fundamental concepts, would be basic rallying points for the development and furthering of a new Argentinian women's movement. Nevertheless, it's unthinkable at present that such rallying points might complement another level of convergence: concrete tasks. It is impossible to articulate a coherent plan to attract masses of women if one *doesn't* heed the imperative for concrete changes—especially in a country sick of promises and deferred basic needs. Nevertheless, during this period of gestation in which we find ourselves, that aspect is less available to us than we would wish.

We foresee that in future feminist organizing, our limited resources will constitute a powerful drawback. Big plans are out of our reach currently; the breadth of our actions must be modest. Furthermore, the time that can be dedicated to these approaches is severely limited, because of the disproportionate amount of our hours devoted to the struggle for survival and to minimal albeit active militancy. Nor can we help but resent the *quality* of our own activities, because of our lack of materials that would contribute to the investigations—no scholarships or subsidies. And, finally, we have at the moment no place of our own to lend cohesiveness to our group, no place from which to orchestrate future actions.

Given the fact that feminism must both create and rely on certain historical conditions of probability in order to advance, we have the hope that eventually a new era will be born—one in which the exercise of the right to freedom will be tolerated (even if only minimally), thus giving us more than a mere margin in which to express ourselves. If this does happen, then perhaps Argentina—against all adversities and negation—will be able to carry the news of a successful advance of its women's movement to the UN Conference for the Decade of Woman, to be celebrated in 1985.

Still, whatever does or doesn't happen "officially," we will do whatever is necessary (and even more) in order to achieve female autonomy—which in turn will lead to the discovery of broader horizons for all of humanity.

The tide cannot be drained. The fire cannot be extinguished.

Suggested Further Reading

Arana, Alberto Meyer. *Matronas y maestras* (Matrons and Teachers). Buenos Aires: Imprenta de Gerónimo Peace, 1923.

De Newton, Lilly Sosa. *Diccionario biográfico de mujeres Argentinas* (Biographical Dictionary of Argentinian Women). Buenos Aires: Editorial plus Utra, 1981.

Mercader, Marta. *Juanamanuela, Mucha Mujer* (Juanamanuela, Great Woman). Buenos Aires: Editorial Sudamericana, 1980.

Moreau de Justo, Alícia. *La mujer en la democracia* (Women in Democracy). Buenos Aires: El Ateneo, 1945.

Sebreli, Juan José. *Eva Perón, ¿aventurera o militante?* (Eva Perón, Adventurer or Militant?). Buenos Aires: Siglo XX, 1966.

Leonor Calvera is a poet, writer, translator, and specialist in oriental religions. Her book *El Género Mujer* (The Woman Gender) was published in 1982 by Editorial de

Belgrano. In it she evaluates history from the Paleolithic Age to the present time and delineates a strategy for the future. She has been a militant feminist since the resurgence of the women's movement in Argentina in the 1970's, because she believes that "the transformation of the planet will be achieved by women."

AUSTRALIA
(Commonwealth of Australia)

The Australian continent and its territories lie in the southern hemisphere, south of Indonesia, bordered by the Coral Sea, Pacific Ocean, and Tasman Sea to the east, the Indian Ocean to the south and west, and Timor and Arafura Seas to the north; the island state of Tasmania is south of New South Wales. **Area:** 7,686,843 sq. km. (2,967,909 sq. mi.). **Population** (1982): 15,100,000, female 50%. **Capital:** Canberra. **Titular Head of State:** Queen Elizabeth II.

DEMOGRAPHY. Languages: English (official), indigenous Aboriginal. **Races or Ethnic Groups:** European (primarily Anglo descent), Aborigine 1.2%. **Religions:** Anglican 36%, Roman Catholicism 33%, Methodist 7%, Presbyterian 7%, indigenous faiths. **Education** (% enrolled in school, 1975): Age 6–11—of all girls 99%, of all boys 99%; age 12–17— of all girls 80%, of all boys 82%; higher education—in 1980 women were 41.8% of university students and 32% of postgraduate degree-earners; as of 1975, 25% of Aborigines (female and male) had never attended school, and only 2% had finished secondary school. **Literacy** (1977): Women 100%, men 100% (Euroaustralian only). **Birth Rate** (per 1000 pop., 1977–78): 16. **Death Rate** (per 1000 pop., 1977–78): 8. **Infant Mortality** (per 1000 live births, 1977): Female 12, male 16; Aborigine children comprise 50% of all deaths under age 5. **Life Expectancy** (1975–80): (Euroaustralian) female 76 yrs., male 70 yrs.; (Aborigine) female and male average 52 yrs.

GOVERNMENT. Constitution is the basis of a bicameral parliamentary system consisting of an elected 125-member House of Representatives and a 64-seat Senate. A coalition of parties forms the federal government headed by a prime minister and ministry. The governor-general represents the Queen of England and is appointed by the ruling government (Labor Party as of 1983). The 6 states and 2 territories each have a governing body and are represented in the Federal Parliament. Commonwealth Status links the country to Great Britain. **Women's Suffrage:** (Euroaustralian) in federal elections, 1902; on state level, won over a period from 1894 to 1908. Aborigines of both sexes won citizenship and suffrage in 1967. **Equal Rights:** 3 states already had anti-discrimination laws: New South Wales, Victoria, South Australia, and in 1984 the Labor Party-sponsored federal Anti-Sex-Discrimination Bill passed Parliament. **Women in Government:** There are 19 women in the Parliament, 13 in the Senate and 6 in the House of Representatives; Susan Ryan is Minister for Education and Youth Affairs (1983); Dame Margaret Guilfoyle (former Minister for Foreign Affairs) is a leader of the Liberal Party; Justice Dame Roma Mitchell is chair of the Human Rights Commission. A National Women's Advisory Council (formed 1978) advises the Minister for Home Affairs and Environment.

ECONOMY. Currency: Australian Dollar (May 1983: 1.15 = $1 US). **Gross National Product** (1980): $142.2 billion. **Per Capita Income** (1980): $9820. **Women's Wages as a Percentage of Men's** (1979): 76%. **Equal Pay Policy:** In 1972 the government's Conciliation and Arbitration Commission adopted equal pay for equal work or work of equal value. **Production** (Agricultural/Industrial): Wool, meat; machinery, iron, steel, textiles. **Women as a Percentage of Labor Force** (1980): 40%; **of agricultural force** (1979) 21%; **of industrial force**—no general statistics obtainable (of manufacturing 25%, 1979); **of military** (1982) 6.4%, noncombat roles only. **(Employed) Women's Occupational Indicators:** Of administrative and managerial workers 14.6%, of professional and technical workers 46%, of sales workers 53.4%, of service workers 63%, of clerical workers 70% (1980); of teachers 60%, of nurses 93% (1979). **Unemployment** (mid-1982): 6.5%, female 8.2%, male 5.5%.

GYNOGRAPHY. Marriage. *Policy:* Regulated under the Commonwealth Marriage Act (1961); for the territories of Christmas Island and the Cocos (Keeling) Islands, marriage is governed by the Christian Marriage Ordinance, Civil Marriage Ordinance, Muslim Ordinance, etc. Legal marriage age is 16 for females, 18 for males; marriage is by mutual consent and rights and responsibilities are equal. The choice of a married woman's domicile is independent from that of her spouse. Tribal marriage among the Aborigines, if arranged without mutual consent, is not recognized under law (except for estate and child-status rights). In 1981 the Australian Law Reform Commission began examining the applicability of partial or whole Aboriginal customary law where relevant. *Practice:* Female mean age at marriage (1970–78): 22; women age 15–49 in union (1970–78): 68.2%. In 1982, 4.7% of heterosexual couples chose cohabitation instead of marriage. A pending (1982) *De Facto* Relationships Act would improve women's situation in such circumstances as *de facto* divorce. **Divorce.** *Policy:* Under the 1976 Family Law Act (amended 1981), "irretrievable breakdown of marriage" is the only grounds for divorce; couple must be separated for 1 yr. before court accepts petition. Either parent may be awarded custody of children or it may be jointly granted; property divided by court, in case of nonagreement, in accordance with need. In common-law marriage, mother is given sole custody of children but cannot collect alimony. *Practice:* Divorces (per 1000 pop., 1978): 2.87.

Family. *Policy:* Child Care Act (1972) added federal funds to state funds for day care. In 1979 maternity leave was granted to all employed women, married or single, comprising 12 weeks without pay and guaranteed reinstatement, with full pay for certain government workers, and up to 1 yr. unpaid leave. Paternity leave had been available under the 1973 Maternity Leave (Australian Government Employees) Act, but was abolished in 1978. *Practice:* Federal subsidies to childcare centers are $34 million annually, but are currently threatened by cutbacks (1983). Lack of centers caused an increase in women doing piecework at home—particularly among women with young children, and among migrants from Greece, Turkey, and Italy. In 1980, 27.4% of women in the labor force had childcare responsibilities, while centers provided 21.7% of needed care. **Welfare.** *Policy:* Social security system consists of pensions for the aged, invalids, and widows, plus unemployment compensation, sickness benefits, child endowment and maternity allowances (see **Family**), and health insurance. *Practice:* Most benefits are in the form of direct payments and are not based on contributions to a fund. Men age 65 and women age 60 are eligible for pensions which are determined by income and assets. Women's average lifetime earnings are much lower than men's. Single mothers and fathers with dependent children receive benefits, as do deserted wives. Women constitute 75% of those living below the official poverty line.

Contraception. *Policy:* Legal; federal subsidies of family-planning programs (since 1973); services available at private and State clinics. *Practice:* Women age 15–49 in union using contraception (1970–80): 72%, of which traditional methods 34.7%, modern 65.3%. Depo-Provera, a controversial injected contraceptive, has been given by government agencies to Aboriginal women, but rarely to women of Anglo descent. **Abortion.** *Policy:* Legal on broad health grounds in the states of Queensland and Western Australia, on health and eugenic grounds in the Northern Territory, and on health, eugenic, and social grounds in Victoria, New South Wales, and South Australia; in Tasmania, the procedure may be done only where "reasonable with regard to the woman's state of mind and the circumstances of the case." National Health Insurance funds 80% of fees in nonprofit clinics. *Practice:* Abortions (per 1000 women age 15–44, 1977): 22; 200 abortions for every 1000 known pregnancies. **Illegitimacy.** *Policy:* 1977 Child (Equality of Status) Act gives out-of-wedlock children full rights; Superannuation Act amended to provide benefits to out-of-wedlock children of eligible women. *Practice:* No data obtainable. **Homosexuality.** *Policy:* Victorian Crimes Act

(1958) provides for punishing male homosexual acts by up to 20 yrs. imprisonment. The law does not recognize the existence of same-sex relations between women. *Practice:* Lesbianism can be interpreted as grounds for divorce and for granting the husband child custody; discrimination against female and male homosexuals is common, especially against teachers. A landmark South Australian court decision in 1974 granted child custody to a lesbian mother. The laws are infrequently and selectively enforced; prosecutions under various state public ordinances for "offensive behavior" have included women holding hands and men embracing in public. At least 10% of Australians are homosexual, according to an active gay-rights movement which is working for reform of discriminatory laws. **Incest.** *Policy:* Illegal in New South Wales as of 1924, but not in Australian Capital Territory; law defines it as parent-child and brother-sister sexual relations. *Practice:* No statistics obtainable, but incidence is reportedly not uncommon.

Sexual Harassment. *Policy:* Victoria and South Australia amended anti-discrimination legislation in 1982 to cover sexual harassment. Under the new Sex Discrimination Bill (see **Equal Rights**) sexual harassment is specified as illegal. *Practice:* No statistics obtainable. Women's centers and the Women's Advisory Council are focusing attention on the problem, and some unions are taking up the issue at the workplace. **Rape.** *Policy:* Illegal, punishable by a maximum penalty of life imprisonment. Marital rape is recognized in the state of South Australia only. A pending (1982) law would make rape a crime of sexual assault to include forced oral and anal penetration as well as marital rape. *Practice:* No statistics obtainable (see following article). **Battery.** *Policy:* 1981 Amendment to Family Law Act extends court protection to married women and children who are victims of domestic abuse. Limited funding of shelters for women by federal and state government is available but unreliable. *Practice:* No statistics obtainable, but the incidence of battery is reportedly high. **Prostitution.** *Policy:* Illegal in all states. *Practice:* In many cities prostitution operates openly while officials appear to ignore it. Women who are arrested for soliciting serve 2–3 weeks in jail. **Traditional/Cultural Practices:** No data obtainable. **Crisis Centers.** *Policy:* Some limited government support. *Practice:* In 1977 there were 72 refuges for battered women, funded in part by state and federal aid through community health programs. There are centers for rape victims at some hospitals. In 1974 the first rape-crisis center opened in Sydney as a result of women's movement pressure.

HERSTORY. Little is known about the status of Aboriginal women within their own culture for the approx. 20,000 years since the Aborigines are thought to have come to Australia from Southeast Asia, although it is certain that this status was disrupted by the imposition of European culture in the 17th century C.E. British convicts and other "undesirables" were sent to "settle" the country; in the early settlements, 15% of the 150,000 convicts were women, and a balance of the sex ratio was not achieved until the 1850's. Settler women faced a harsh existence on the periphery of a male culture.

The women's movement developed in the late 1800's, focusing on citizen rights and on strengthening women's position in the family. Louise Lawson founded *Dawn,* a feminist newspaper, in the 1890's. The Women's Political Assoc. was formed in 1909 to educate women in the use of the vote; it included a platform of equal pay for equal work, equal rights in marriage and divorce, international suffrage, and international peace and arbitration. Eleanor Glencross organized the Australian Federation of Housewives in 1923 (her motto: "If you've got a battle to fight, my dear, put on your best bonnet"). For Aboriginal women, the *jilimi* was (and still is) the center of solidarity; a camp for single women, widows, and women who leave their husbands, the *jilimi* is tabu to men and offers refuge and freedom from the restrictions of male society. Aboriginal women in recent years have spearheaded movements for land rights, health care, and housing for Aborigines. In Nov. 1983 women held a peace encampment for 2 weeks in Pine Gap, the location of a major US intelligence base; the protest focused on peace and protection of Aboriginal land rights. (For further information on the contemporary women's movement, see following article.)

MYTHOGRAPHY. Ancient Aborigine religious beliefs centered on the First Mother or Divine Ancestress. Caves were thought to be routes to the spirit, and the entering of a cave was an entry into the womb of the First Mother. At the time of death, the spirit of the deceased entered the cave to reunite with the First Mother until its next birth.

AUSTRALIA: Women in a Warrior Society
by Sara Dowse and Patricia Giles

Symbols are powerful. They can stimulate the intellect and open perceptions onto the connections between people, ideas, and events. When asked to write this article about women in Australia, we conceived the notion of focusing on Anzac Day, that peculiarly Australian celebration of patriotism. To us it was a potent symbol, a commemoration of a rite of passage: the blood sacrifice of 60,000 Australian men in the 1914–18 war—our contribution to the survival of the British Empire seen, paradoxically, as our coming of age as a nation. Needless to say, it was an exclusively male initiation ceremony.

Most Australian schoolchildren are taught about the courage and sacrifice of men in wartime: they learn the Anzac legend, about the Diggers,[1] those "tall, bronzed Anzacs," the heroes of our national day; about the landing on April 25, 1915, of Australian and New Zealand troops on the shores of Gallipoli; about the thousands of soldiers who died, making "men" of them all and turning Australia—then only fourteen years old—into a "proper nation." Every year on April 25 the country comes to a standstill. Veterans march in each of the state capitals and in the national capital. Wreaths are laid on "shrines of remembrance."

It wasn't until the 1950's that the legend began to be debunked. We heard the truth about Gallipoli—that it was an appalling waste of life, an offering to please the British War Ministry; that young men volunteered to fight because they couldn't get jobs and were primed to fight by propaganda. By the 1950's, the pressure on young men to conform to the male ethos was so strong that many began to react against it. The bronze was showing signs of tarnish.

So it is interesting that in the last few years there has been a kind of restoration. The new interest is critical. There is a strong connection between its emergence and the search for national identity that has preoccupied Australians over the last decade.

The reality, of course, is something else. After the wreath-laying and speech-making and flag-waving, the veterans all go off and get thoroughly drunk with their "mates." For many people, the true meaning of Anzac Day is a public holiday on which a lot of old soldiers drink too much alcohol—a peculiarly graceless Dionysian ritual, but one which has nonetheless firmly established Australian masculinity in a bellicose mold and provided the ideological bulwark for the most powerful lobby in the country: the Returned Servicemen's League (RSL). Until quite recently this was the only national organization to have an audience with the government each year before the national budget was

---

[1]. Originally, the term "digger" referred to a miner on the Australian goldfields, but then it took on an additional meaning as a soldier from the digging of trenches in the 1914–18 war.

decided. Since Vietnam, however, its influence has dwindled, and for its own part, the RSL has mellowed a bit. Vietnam contributed to changing Australian attitudes to war: Vietnam veterans are seen as more pathetic than heroic.

Australia has not known war on its own soil—that is, apart from the attempted genocide of the Aboriginal Australians, mob violence against the Chinese on the goldfields, and the bombing of remote northern cities in 1942. For most Australians war happens "over there," in crusades during which manhood can be tested in exotic places. The need to test it may indeed have something to do with feelings of inferiority, for the lives of most Australian men bear the thinnest resemblance to their myths. From the beginning of the twentieth century the majority have lived in cities; more specifically, in vast suburbanized cities. Neither fighting wars nor driving sheep is a major occupation, yet Australian masculinity has been significantly shaped by two dominating archetypes: the Digger and the Drover. Australia is a deeply patriarchal society, perhaps all the more so because of this discrepancy between fact and fantasy.

Yet much has happened to challenge both the form and the content of Australian patriarchy. First, mass post-war immigration has turned a predominantly Anglo-Saxon population with strong allegiances to the United Kingdom into a highly cosmopolitan society in which those allegiances are ineluctably weakened. Second, there has been a growing awareness of the tragic injustice perpetrated against the Aboriginal people, an increased appreciation of the intricacies of their culture and of their ability to come to terms with the unique Australian environment.

Finally, and most tellingly, the women's movement has reasserted itself. As a result, enormous changes have occurred: in ideas about women's roles; in relations between men and women (in groups and as individuals); and in the cultural expression of the emerging consciousness. Inevitably, there has been resistance to these changes, which may be a measure of their effect. Change never happens without conflict . . .

Picture an Anzac Day parade. It is 1975. After the dawn service, veterans of all the wars in which Australians have taken part—starting with the one against the Boers—gather in mid-morning and form into the remnants of their battalions. The march begins, one by one the battalions pass the cenotaph and lay wreaths for their fallen companions. Drums roll and pipes play, honoring the dead. Contingents of uniformed servicemen follow the veterans, who are dressed in civilian clothes but strew themselves with medals. There are women, too, conspicuous by their small numbers; nurses and a few soldiers, no pilots or sailors. Families stand on the sidelines; children wave tiny Australian flags. Down at the cenotaph, politicians, generals, and the British monarch's viceroy officiate. In Canberra, the capital, the Governor-General officiates, soon to exercise his constitutional power to "dismiss" the democratically elected government. In his morning suit he looks deceptively anachronistic: a figurehead. The sun is warm but there is a chill in the air and a light wind roils the fallen leaves.

The same scene, two years later. The nation has been riven by the "dismissal" of the Labor government and the election of a conservative Liberal–National Country Party coalition, our very own bloodless coup. The marches continue, much as before, but now there is a deep bitterness toward the Queen's representatives. The Governor-General feels the chill in the wind and is visibly discomposed. Around the country, groups of women march to protest against rape in war but, in the circumstance, draw little comment.

The following year their numbers increase. There is a new Governor-General. In Canberra, twenty women raise a banner—"Women Against Rape"—over the heads of passing Boy Scouts and Girl Guides, pipe bands, and returned soldiers. A gesture which, again, appears to attract little notice. The next year no banner is raised.

But then, in 1980, sixteen women marched. Fourteen were arrested. The women had to be bailed out and sustained during their court cases, and out of this a campaign grew, centering round Anzac Day.

By autumn 1981, the campaign had drawn large numbers of women. The RSL got wind of their plans and from there all sorts of wild rumors were circulated. The women were going to spray paint over the soldiers, they were going to pour porridge down the marching tubas and slash the drums; they were going to throw themselves down in front of the marchers, "forcing" them to commit symbolic rape. In truth, the women took great pains to ensure that they would provoke no violent confrontation; they wanted their protest to be a dignified remembrance of the *forgotten* victims of war: women. Nevertheless, the Minister for the Australian Capital Territory (ACT) announced that he was amending the local traffic ordinance so that anyone "likely to give offense or cause insult" to people taking part in an Anzac observance would be guilty of an offense.

As might have been expected, the Minister's action produced its response. Now, instead of being solely a matter of protesting against the rape of women in war, to march was to demonstrate for the *right* to march. On the day, about five hundred people gathered in a small park off a side street at right angles to the Anzac Parade, out of sight of the official marchers. Most of the protesters were women, but there were some men who agreed not to march but to support the women. Under a single black banner with white letters reading *"In memory of all women of all countries raped in all wars,"* the women began marching up the side street. In a matter of minutes they faced some seventy police, blocking access to the Parade. The women sat down in the middle of the road. The arrests began. Sixty-one women were arrested. To have seen the television coverage one would have thought the Minister's action perfectly justified, when the truth was that any confrontation that occurred was provoked by the police. Yet even allowing for the fact that the police had a difficult task trying to operate under the vague provisions of the ordinance, it is hard to take their brutality as anything other than an extreme expression of hostility toward the protesting women. All the afternoon and into the evening the women were processed and released, two by two, to be greeted by women standing outside waiting for them. Inside, the women sang in their cells and could be heard by the women outside, who began to sing too. Back and forth the voices rang, the women inside and the women outside singing to each other. Then at one point two cops came out of the station, grabbed one of the waiting women, and stripped her to the waist. For no apparent reason, except to humiliate her.

Still, when the official ceremony was over and the crowds had dispersed, the black-and-white banner reappeared and the women, joined by many women onlookers, laid their flowers on the Stone of Remembrance with a ceremony of their own. A triumph, but not without its costs.

A year passed. Not surprisingly, the movement continued to grow. This time they had buttons: "Women Against Rape—Canberra, We're Marching Anzac Day 1982"—the first in a series of "medals" struck for veteran marchers. The organizers ran workshops to foster quick decision-making and nonviolent defense.

The publicity surrounding the 1981 march had awakened consciousness in the community with some interesting results. An assistant police commissioner stated publicly that he had told his daughters that if they were raped he would not want them to report it "under the present system of law and the trauma they would have to go through in the witness box." Twenty-one women rang up a rape-crisis center to tell of their wartime rapes. Three men rang up to admit that they had raped in war and had had official encouragement to do so.

Moreover, the implications of marching widened. The local Civil Liberties Council, lapsed since Vietnam Moratorium days, was re-established. And the government's Human Rights Commission noted that the lack of self-government in the ACT could be an instance of Australian noncompliance with the International Covenant on Civil and Political Rights.

For his part, the Minister brought in yet another piece of legislation—the Public Assemblies Ordinance of 1982—which the local Law Society decried as having "far-reaching effects on the rights of any person whose presence somewhere may be deemed likely to cause a breach of peace." However, the Minister's tactic seemed to have backfired. In the first place, the women, who were the target of his ordinance, decided *not* to march during the official ceremony, and therefore sidestepped the requirement that they apply for permission to the Commissioner of Police. Instead, a number of new groups applied, and three were approved, on the grounds that their expressed intentions in marching were similar to those of the RSL.

The community was in an uproar, deeply polarized between those who felt it their right to participate in a national ceremony and those who wanted to exclude any group that would not limit itself to honoring men fallen in battle. But everyone (including by this time the RSL) was opposed to the Minister's ordinance, for varying reasons.

Some of the groups that had received permission to march decided, having made their point, to pull out; others who previously had pulled out decided to march. The Naval Association, for example, was happy to march once it was established that the Ex-Servicemen for Peace and Disarmament were withdrawing; while the Council for Civil Liberties announced that, instead of marching, they would stand on the sidelines and monitor any arrests. The director of the Australian War Memorial formally applied for permission to conduct the official ceremony, raising the question as to whether the Stone of Remembrance was private or public property. He claimed to be particularly worried about the women, who by then had caught everyone off guard by announcing that *their* march would take place *before* rather than after the official one. Meanwhile, the president of the Vietnam Veterans Association accused the women of being "guilty of the very act they are protesting against. Their action is nothing less than an act of symbolic rape."

On the morning, 750 women met at the end of Anzac Parade, then marched up to the Stone of Remembrance. There a wreath was laid while the assembled crowd listened to a speaker draw the connections between rape and war and express the desire of every woman present to remember the unsung victims of mankind's savagery. When the ceremony was over and the official march about to begin, the women took their banners and posters (written in twenty-five different languages this time) and stood on the hill overlooking the cenotaph. And there they remained, throughout the official wreath-laying, with *"In memory of all women of all countries raped in all wars"* in full view of everyone.

This time, there were no arrests.

How well do symbols work? If they do work at all it is because they successfully embody a number of related but often contradictory impulses. If Anzac Day is the noble expression of the "mateship" between comrades, it also stands for the harsh exclusion of over half the population from that comradeship—the racism and sexism that forged Australian patriotism. And while to some the commemoration of the slaughter at Gallipoli nearly three quarters of a century ago is a solemn pledge to uphold values ascendant at that time, to others it is becoming a sign of determination never to submit to such slaughter again. There is indeed a world of difference between patriotism and genuine national pride. As simple yet as intangible as vision, it may be something called a feminist perspective.

The struggle over who will march on Anzac Day brings into high relief the fundamental opposition between the women's movement and the patriarchal state. In a way, this is salutary, since in recent years this opposition has been somewhat disguised. The Labor government which took office in 1972 introduced, if grudgingly, a number of measures that benefited women. Several state governments followed suit. But since 1975 the conservative federal government has been systematically whittling back these gains. Women's services such as childcare centers, health centers, refuges, and rape-crisis centers have been fighting for survival as government funding dries up. Policies encouraging the replacement of the traditional manufacturing base with capital-intensive mineral extraction and the rapid introduction of new technology in the service sector have made large dents in women's employment. And while women have been fighting back, most of the activity has been invisible. The Anzac Day movement is one of the really obvious *public* confrontations with the patriarchy.

That it has broad implications can be seen in the beginning of the protest against nuclear weapons. There are three essential American nuclear bases here—at Pine Gap, Nurrangar, and North West Cape—and Australians are becoming increasingly uneasy about their presence, about the very real possibility of nuclear war *and* the Australian contribution to it, through both the sale of Australian uranium and Australia's integration in the US missile system.

The clear-cut association between feminism and nonviolent protest has not gone unnoticed. Nor has feminist opposition to the values that have produced past wars. Women's pacifism is not a new thing; women have always played an important part in movements for peace. But there has been a risk for women in this, for it has been far too easy to mistake pacifism for passivity. Will it be so easy this time to dismiss women's concern about the waste of human life as further evidence that we are just "soft," or as the "mere" extension of our roles as mothers?

The implications for feminism are enormous.

The impact of the Women Against Rape campaign on the Canberra community and the publicity it received nationwide excited interest beyond the specific question of rape. There seems little doubt that the women's campaign has changed the nature of Anzac Day, activating a growing number of people opposed to the glorification of war and the ideology expressed in the traditional celebrations. There is also little doubt that the wider involvement threatened to swamp the issue of women raped in war.

There are many within the movement who would argue that it would be a mistake to let feminism be subsumed into the movement for disarmament, or the protest against the mining or sale of Australian uranium, or the demand for the removal of US bases. They would contend that the women's movement would be taken over as it was in the past and that women, once again, would be putting their demands aside in favor of other, seemingly more relevant or popular, causes.

Yet it seems to us that the challenge for the women in Canberra parallels the challenge to the women's movement at large. *Without sacrificing our own demands* for the just recognition of women's suffering and contributions, we can demonstrate the connections between a feminist world view and a brighter future for human society—indeed any future at all. This may well mean being prepared to put ourselves forward as leaders in the antinuclear movement—*as* feminists, *because* we are feminists.

We can see the beginnings of a new kind of Anzac Day, one that celebrates life instead of death and a comradeship crossing the barriers of sex, race, and nation. A change we women made possible . . .

Suggested Further Reading

Bell, Diane, and Pam Ditton. *Law: The Old and the New; Aboriginal Women in Central Australia Speak Out.* Published for Central Australian Aboriginal Legal Aid Service by Aboriginal History, Canberra, ACT, 1980.

Bettison, Margaret, and Anne Summers, eds. *Her Story: Australian Women in Print 1788–1975.* Sydney: Hale & Iremonger, 1980; an annotated bibliography.

"But I Wouldn't Want My Wife to Work Here . . .": A Study of Migrant Women in

Melbourne Industry. Research Report for International Women's Year by the Centre for Urban Research and Action, Fitzroy, 1976.

Daniels, Kay, and Mary Murnane, eds. *Uphill All the Way: A Documentary History of Women in Australia.* St. Lucia: Univ. of Queensland Press, 1980.

Dixson, Miriam. *The Real Matilda: Woman and Identity in Australia 1788 to 1975.* Ringwood: Penguin, 1976.

Summers, Anne. *Damned Whores and God's Police: The Colonization of Women in Australia.* Ringwood: Penguin, 1975.

Sara Dowse was born in 1938 and was one of the first members of Women's Liberation in the Australian Capital Territory when it began in 1970. She worked for the Minister for Labor on several aspects of women and employment, including the extension of the adult minimum wage to women. In 1974 she was appointed to head the Department of the Prime Minister and Cabinet's newly established Women's Affairs Section, and steered it through three stormy years and several upgradings (it became in 1977 the Office of Women's Affairs)—until its transfer to a junior department after the December 1977 elections forced her resignation. In 1975 she was an alternate delegate to the World Conference on International Women's Year in Mexico City. She obtained a university degree while looking after her children, and before joining the government service held numerous odd jobs to keep them, including a short stint in publishing. She has published articles, poetry and fiction, and has scripted and directed a short film. At present she is on the editorial board of Sisters Publishing Pty. Ltd.

Patricia Giles, born in 1928, is a feminist/activist and the mother of four feminist/activists. She was elected Labor Senator for Western Australia in 1980. She became a "foundation" member in 1972 of Western Australia's Women's Liberation, was inaugural convener of that state's Women's Electoral Lobby in 1973, and in 1975 was a member of the Australian Government-sponsored delegation to the International Women's Year Tribune in Mexico City. She has been active in union affairs, from 1978 to 1982 chairing the first women's committee of the Australian Council of Trade Unions, and from 1974 to 1976 chairing the Western Australian Committee on Discrimination in Employment and Occupation. In 1980 she argued the case for maternity leave before the Western Australian Industrial Commission. Currently she represents Western Australia on the ALP National Status of Women Committee, as well as being a member of Senate standing committees on Social Welfare and Education and the Arts, and a Senate select committee inquiring into private hospitals and nursing homes. Trained as a nurse, she took a mature-age university degree while in her forties, majoring in politics and industrial relations.

AUSTRIA
(Republic of Austria)

Located in central Europe, bordered by Hungary to the east, Yugoslavia and Italy to the south, Switzerland and Liechtenstein to the west, and West Germany (FRD) and Czechoslovakia to the north. **Area:** 83,851 sq. km. (32,375 sq. mi.). **Population** (1980): 7,497,000, female 52.5%. **Capital:** Vienna.

DEMOGRAPHY. Languages: German (official), Slovene, Croat, Hungarian. **Races or Ethnic Groups:** German 99%, Slovene, Croat, and Hungarian 1%. **Religions:** Roman Catholicism 90%, Protestant 6%, Judaism, other. (Before WW II, Vienna's Jewish pop. numbered 115,000; by the war's end, only 6000 Jews survived.) **Education** (% enrolled in school, 1975): Age 6–11—of all girls 93%, of all boys 93%; age 12–17—of all girls 72%, of all boys 70%; higher education—in 1978–79 women were 32% of vocational students (almost 90% of female apprentices are concentrated in 10 professions and trades, e.g., dressmaker, hairdresser, office clerk, etc.), 39% of university students, 43% of arts college, 75% of academy, and 95% of medico-technical students. A 1980 amendment eliminated most sex-specific and sex-segregated teaching in public schools. **Literacy** (1977): Women 99%, men 99%. **Birth Rate** (per 1000 pop., 1977–78): 11. **Death Rate** (per 1000 pop., 1977–78): 12. **Infant Mortality** (per 1000 live births, 1977): Female 16, male 20. **Life Expectancy** (1975–80): Female 75 yrs., male 68 yrs.

GOVERNMENT. Parliamentary system based on the 1920 Constitution. Executive power rests with an elected president and chancellor who appoint a cabinet. The bicameral legislative body consists of the elected Bundesrat (upper house) and National Assembly (lower house). **Women's Suffrage:** 1919. Women first elected to the National Assembly in 1920. **Equal Rights:** Constitution states that all citizens are equal before the law and bars discrimination on the basis of sex, race, religion, or creed. **Women in Government:** In 1980, 12 out of 58 Bundesrat members, 10 out of 57 National Assembly members, and 21 out of 100 provincial government leaders were female. There are 3 cabinet ministers as of 1983 —Elfriede Karl (Minister for Family Affairs), Johanna Dohnal (Minister for Women's Affairs), and Beatrix Eypeltauer (Minister for Construction)— and 2 women mayors.

ECONOMY. Currency: Austrian Schilling (May 1983: 17.3 = $1 US). **Gross National Product** (1980): $76.5 billion. **Per Capita Income** (1980): $10,230. **Women's Wages as a Percentage of Men's** (1978): 72%. **Equal Pay Policy:** 1977 federal law requires wage equality in most sectors, except agriculture and the public sector. **Production** (Agricultural/Industrial): Grains, livestock, forest products; iron, steel, oil, electrical and optical equipment. **Women as a Percentage of Labor Force** (1980): 38.5%; **of agricultural force** 49%; **of industrial force** —no general statistics obtainable (of manufacturing 29%, 1980); **of military—** no statistics obtainable, but women in support roles (i.e., medical, clerical) only, not combat. **(Employed) Women's Occupational Indicators:** Of professional/technical workers 7%, of administrative/managerial workers 49.4%, of sales workers 58%, of service workers 68.3% (1980); of unskilled workers 50% (1978–80). **Unemployment** (mid-1982): 2.3%, female 2.4%, male 2.2%.

GYNOGRAPHY. Marriage. *Policy:* Marriage legislation of 1975 and 1978 eliminated the concept of the man as sole head of household. Both spouses have equal rights and duties in housework, childcare, and financial support of the family. Women have the right to work outside the home, and housework should be shared if both spouses are employed. A couple may choose either husband's or wife's surname at marriage. Government grant of 7500 Schillings to each person upon first marriage. *Practice:* Female mean age at marriage (1970–78): 22;

women age 15–49 in union (1970–78): 68%. **Divorce:** *Policy:* Law reformed in 1978 to allow divorce by mutual consent and dissolution of marriages in which spouses had already been separated for many years. Person who is responsible for grounds of divorce is obligated to support the other, based on their respective financial resources. Housework and childcare are regarded as economic contributions, to be considered in division of property. *Practice:* Divorces (per 1000 pop., 1977): 1.55.

Family. *Policy:* The 1957 Maternity Protection Act gives women 8 weeks pre- and 8 weeks post-delivery paid leave from work, with guaranteed reinstatement, plus a maximum 1-yr. unpaid leave option (with unemployment benefits in certain circumstances). Birth allowance of 16,000 Schillings is paid after the birth of a child, and supplementary family allowances are available, including a monthly family allowance for children up to age 19. Nursing breaks of up to 90 minutes per 8-hour working day are permitted. A father legally continues to exercise his paternal rights for all decisions concerning his (legitimate) children, even in the case of divorce and when the mother has been granted child custody. Government-sponsored childcare centers are a priority of the State. *Practice:* No statistics obtainable. The Austrian feminist movement claims that existing creches and childcare centers are not sufficient to meet the need. **Welfare.** *Policy:* Comprehensive social security programs include insurance for health, accidents, unemployment, and retirement, and are paid for by both employers and employees. Pension age for women is 60, for men 65. Both men and women can collect on the basis of spouse's contributions if they have no income. *Practice:* Women's pensions average 1/3 less than men's because of lower income. **Contraception.** *Policy:* Legal; family planning is promoted by a 1974 law that established agencies (funded by federal grants) to provide services for everyone regardless of age, sex, or marital status. *Practice:* According to selling figures of the pharmaceutical industry, "at least 22% of this [15–45] age group were taking the pill." Other recent data revealed that 11% of Austrian

women use the rhythm method, 9% use coitus interruptus, and 11% used no contraceptives. No further data obtainable. **Abortion.** *Policy:* A 1975 reform legalized termination of pregnancy within the first trimester, by a physician, with parental consent if the woman is a minor. *Practice:* Before legalization, some 100,000 illegal abortions were performed each yr., with limited prosecutions and imprisonments. A woman who self-aborts or has unauthorized assistance is subject to 1 yr. imprisonment. **Illegitimacy.** *Policy:* A 1970 law reformed the Civil Code, enaing discrimination against children born out of wedlock. Child takes mother's surname and citizenship. Mother has sole custody and can obtain support from father by court action. *Practice:* Out-of-wedlock births have been increasing since 1966, comprising 16.5% of all births in 1978. **Homosexuality.** *Policy:* Criminal Law Amending Act of 1974 ends illegality of homosexual acts between adults, although discriminatory legislation is reportedly pending (1983). *Practice:* There has been some homosexual-rights activism, and in 1983 a new Lesbian Center and Social Club opened in Vienna.

Incest. *Policy:* No data obtainable. *Practice:* No data obtainable. **Sexual Harassment.** *Policy:* None. *Practice:* No data obtainable. **Rape.** *Policy:* Penal Code reform includes prosecution in cases of rape, indecent assault, and seduction; sexual intercourse with a female under age 16 is illegal. *Practice:* No data obtainable. **Battery.** *Policy:* No specific spouse-abuse law; considered a general crime of assault, and dealt with under the Penal Code. *Practice:* The first refuge for battered women and their children opened in Vienna in 1978. A second opened in 1980, housing an average of 25 women and 35 children. Refuges are planned for other provinces. **Prostitution.** *Policy:* Legal. Prostitutes are registered with the local authorities, carry identification cards, and attend medical check-ups once a week. Unregistered prostitution is a minor offense dealt with at the municipal level. *Practice:* In 1983 the number of registered prostitutes in Vienna was 1000, with an est. equal number of women working as unregistered prostitutes. **Traditional/Cultural Practices:** No data obtainable. **Crisis Centers.** *Policy:* None. *Practice:* See **Battery**.

HERSTORY. At the time of the Roman conquest (15 B.C.E.–10 C.E.), the area now known as Austria was occupied by the Celtic and Suebi peoples, and women leaders and warriors were not uncommon. With Charlemagne's conquest (788) and the consolidation of Christianity, women's status declined.

Margaret of Austria (1480–1530), the daughter of Hapsburg Emperor Maximilian I, became regent of the Netherlands in 1507, co-founded the League of Cambrai in 1508, and established the "Ladies' Peace" (between France and the Holy Roman Empire) in 1529 with Louise of Savoy. Archduchess Maria Theresa succeeded her father (Holy Roman Emperor Charles VI) in 1740, owing to a special inheritance law (the "Pragmatic Sanction"). Her reign was memorable for many reforms: the army and every branch of government was restructured toward centralization, tax reforms were begun, the educational system reorganized (and made accessible for all), and the concept of multiple dwellings (the first "apartment houses") developed.

A women's movement began in the late 18th century for equal education, equal rights, and better working conditions. The Women Writers and Artists Organization was founded in 1885. Austrian women were very active in the late 1800's in the International Socialist Movement: Louise Kautsky, who delivered a paper on the protection of women workers in Zürich (1893) at the International Socialist Workers Congress; Amalie Seidl, who organized the first strike among women textile workers in Vienna; the eloquent political agitator Anna Boschek; the founders and leaders of the General Austrian Women's Assoc.

—Auguste Fickert, Marie Lang, Therese Schlesinger-Eckstein, and Rosa Mayreder (author of a critique of femininity). Bertha von Suttner (1843–1914) was a pacifist, a novelist, and a friend of Alfred Nobel, and was indirectly responsible for the creation of the Nobel Prizes. She herself received the Nobel Peace Prize in 1905.

The first women's strike (1893) was started by 600 workers in 4 different factories; the goals were better pay and working conditions. In 1897 women had been admitted to universities for liberal arts; by 1919 all universities were opened to women. The Federation of Austrian Women's Associations was founded by Marianne Hainisch in 1902, encompassing 100 organizations. Activist Adelheid Popp edited a newspaper, *Working Women,* and campaigned for women's political equality, for an 8-hour workday, and for the vote. In 1918 women were permitted to participate in political organizations for the first time. In 1938, when Hitler annexed Austria, all independent women's organizations were outlawed and could not reconstitute themselves until 1945. (For information on the contemporary women's movement, see following article.)

MYTHOGRAPHY. The oldest religious artifact ever found, a tiny statue of a human female, was discovered near a small town a few miles outside of Vienna, and so came to be called the Venus of Villendorf; goddess worship was prevalent in the Rhine valley and in the Danube regions for centuries before the Roman conquest. The Danube itself is named for Dana, one of the deities of the Celtic peoples. Teutonic deities—Freya, Fricka, and Erde (a Mother Goddess figure)—were revered in the region now known as Austria.

AUSTRIA: Benevolent Despotism Versus
the Contemporary Feminist Movement
by Cheryl Benard and Edit Schlaffer

Political change is always a reflection of the society in which it occurs, and the paradoxes of contemporary Austria are mirrored in its women's movement. The combination of antique tradition, a conservative and Roman Catholic population, an urbane history as a multinational empire, and the present socialist government*—all these elements have brought about a situation in which the women's movement *per se* is weak while, ironically, general public awareness of the issues, government willingness to initiate reforms, and the actual facts of women's status compare favorably with other Western industrial nations.

Austria is a country still very much determined by its monarchic past; more has remained of the imperial bureaucracy than the baroque angels that decorate all government buildings. One legacy is that reforms traditionally come from above, from enlightened rulers in the capital city who impose their ideas on recalcitrant provinces. This was true of Maria Theresa, the Empress who reformed the school system, and true today on such an issue as abortion, where legislation is among the most progressive in Europe—but is sabotaged by Catholic doctors and nurses outside of Vienna who refuse to perform the procedure. Austria is a country where women, left to survive two world wars on their own as their men were drafted, have always performed traditional "men's work"; a country that quietly included an Equal Rights Amendment in its constitution at the turn of the century but whose universities nevertheless managed to bar women (the last bastion of male academic exclusivity was not broken until Hitler, in a gesture of vengeance against the Catholic Church, ordered the theological faculty to admit females—yet another irony).

The mix of authoritarianism, repression, and rigidity on the one hand, and progressive liberalism, socialism, and innovation on the other, is still typical of Austria today. Things that are difficult elsewhere can happen overnight with no one's having agitated for them. Contrarily, political activism *outside* the existing structures incites severe disapproval. For example, an advertisement for stockings showing a man chasing a woman through a deserted subway station was willingly changed by the company responsible into a sequence showing the woman chasing the man (hardly the ideal feminist solution, to be sure, but still . . .). All it took was a phone call from the Ministry of Consumer Affairs: original version would encourage crime on Austria's peaceful subways. Yet a group of feminists caught defacing billboards showing sexist advertisements were arrested, prosecuted, and charged punitive fines.

The benevolent attitude of Austrian governments to the needs of the downtrodden (so long as these needs are presented as humble petitions and not radical demands) has traditionally moderated the condition of women; its continuation into the present tends gently to suffocate any signs of radicalization. Another fateful development has been the early linkage of "women's issues" with social democracy in Austria. Constituted around the turn of the century and associated with such women as the factory worker and later

* In 1983, a coalition government came into power.—Ed.

ideologue Adelheid Popp,[1] the Austrian women's movement was closely allied with the workers' movement. As everywhere in the world, this association operated on the basis of one-sided solidarity: women supported the "common cause," which was "common" only as long as it emphasized the rights of men. Even such famous socialist agitators and theorists as Viktor Adler urged the women, in the name of this "common cause," to subordinate the question of their own rights, including the right to vote—promising that in return for their "self-discipline, understanding, sacrifice, and devotion" the movement would fight for women's rights with the utmost vigor *as soon as the time was right.* First the general franchise had to be won for men, and *then* the enfranchised progressive men would liberate their sisters. After the initial part of this "common struggle" had been achieved, of course, the comrades disappeared, leaving the women to struggle for their own vote under serious handicaps, including a law that prohibited "women, national minors, and foreign nationals from belonging to a party or attending any kind of political gathering." Women finally received the vote in 1919. There are barely more women in Parliament[2] today than there were then, just as if the political parties were still acting on the statement made by the Liberal Party at the turn of the century that "the man represents the State, and Parliament must not become feminized, but should on the contrary become stronger and more masculine."[3]

The parallel careers of the workers' movement and the women's movement in Austria have culminated, in the 1980's, in a similar mix of passivity and progressiveness. The unions don't strike: the women rarely agitate. Instead, they petition, send delegations to explain the problem to the Chancellor personally, or simply wait for the government to copy whatever innovations are currently modern or fashionable. On the other hand, the basic conservatism of the population can be misleading. They elect and re-elect socialist governments, and women vote disproportionately for the Socialist Party (the Socialist majority is due to 5% more women's than men's votes).

The tendency to operate within feudalistic structures has another typically Austrian feature: it tends to produce radical individuals in high positions. Empress Elisabeth wrote pacifist poetry and attended secret gatherings of the anarchists. Princess Erzsi, (the daughter of Crown Prince Rudolf of Mayerling fame), was known as the Red Princess after joining the Socialist Party in 1922. Some of Austria's most famous dissidents have been treated very badly—Freud, for example; others, however, continue in the tradition of rebellion from above. One such personality has been the seventy-two-year-old feminist Minister of Science and Research Hertha Firnberg. The baroque environment of her ministry and her stately appearance have stood in such contrast to the radicalism of her utterances that it took a few moments for them to sink in. This is an effect she employed to best benefit when she addressed gatherings of university professors, since these are traditionally conservative antisocialist strongholds. (At such occasions, she introduced her remarks with the observation, "Science has always been the faithful servant of the powerful," and fixed the professors with a significant look.) A few years ago she caused turmoil within the Party when a move was made to reduce the proportion of women candidates. In that case, she threatened, she would leave the Socialists and organize an independent women's party. "Fortunately," she recalls, "it was not necessary to follow through on this threat. It wouldn't have been a good idea, because the organized women were not so weak that they had to withdraw, and they were not so strong that it would have been a success. But as a threat it was effective."

As an organization, the present-day Austrian women's movement is in a somewhat

[1] Adelheid Popp, *Die Dugend einer Arbeiterin* (Vienna: Dietz Verlag, 1980).
[2] In 1980 women comprised 19% of all delegates.
[3] Agnat Seipel, *Der Kampf und die Österreichische Verfassung* (Vienna: n.p., 1925).

sorry state. Party discipline still prevents many activist women from pursuing women's issues in a systematic fashion, and most changes tend to come about through the desire of one of the political parties to appear more progressive than the others. (Many of the major changes in the past few years were initiatives of the Socialist Party: the reform of marriage and divorce law, the liberalization of property law, and the funding of a number of women's cultural, educational, and work training programs.)

The feminist groups seem to be composed largely of students and often demonstrate tendencies typical of student-based movements—to factionalize, and to remain at roughly the same point of development because the membership is always changing. The Austrian movement has the additional problem of being derivative. Initiatives tried and tested in the German, French, or Italian movements are modified and copied. However, there is a great deal of diffuse support for feminist issues, and feminists tend to be active in the context of other movements, especially the peace movement, the environmentalist movement, and the antinuclear movement (in which some successes were achieved even in opposition to the government's wishes, such as the referendum rejecting nuclear power for Austria).

Visitors to Austria tend to see the cities and the cathedrals and to form an idyllic Alpine image. The situation of the population in many rural areas, however, is characterized by poverty and underdevelopment—and women bear the heaviest burden. In agricultural areas, the men usually commute to the nearest city to work in construction, coming home only on weekends. The women are left behind to run the farm, manage a family which often includes elderly relatives, and work an eight-hour day in the nearby textile factory for minimum wage. Battery is common. Working conditions in the factories often resemble the early days of manufacture, with fifteen-year-old girls providing the cheapest labor and with frequent occupational injuries because safety measures required by the law are not met (they slow productivity). The chance to escape this situation is slim for girls, because educational opportunities are heavily weighted in favor of boys and men. A rural educator recently commented that regarding attitudes toward daughters, parts of Austria "resemble the Orient."

In Austria's version of benevolent (socialist) despotism, Chancellor Bruno Kreisky** has distinguished himself by developing a new approach to the woman question—something we might term "paternalistic feminism." Shocking the press with the remarkable sentence, "The people are reactionary on two issues, capital punishment and women's rights," and the statement that reforms were necessary whether the public wanted them or not, he refused to moderate this statement when criticized for it. In fact, he added that the Party leadership was not much more enlightened, and that in order to get them to accept his introduction of a "Secretary of State for Women's Affairs" he had to threaten to resign as Party chair.

Bruno Kreisky, controversial defender of liberation movements the world over, gave some tactical advice to the women's movement in an interview with us in 1981:

BENARD AND SCHLAFFER: In the past, the Social Democrats have required their women members to subordinate their own goals to the "common struggle"; women were told that feminism was bourgeois separatism and that they should "wait for the revolution." Would you comment on that?
KREISKY: No, I think that today one must say that every kind of emancipation advances the emancipation of society. The more women's emancipation there is, the more emancipation there is in the sum of society.
B. AND S.: Do you think this is the consensus in the Left today?

** Kreisky resigned and retired in 1983.—Ed.

K.: Oh, the Left. Nothing annoys me more about the Left than the way in which these groups treat women as a kind of fashion accessory.

B. AND S.: Compared to other political leaders, your public support for the women's movement is somewhat atypical . . .

K.: Well, out of vanity, I hope so. Of course politicians always swear that they are not against women's equality. They all say, "We believe in women's rights, *but* . . ." That's the same as saying, "I have nothing against Jews, *but* . . . ; I have nothing against black people, *but* . . ." We all know what comes after that "but."

B. AND S.: Such initiatives as your legal reforms provoke ambivalent responses from feminists. The reforms *are* good, yet a political movement shouldn't be dependent on arbitrary gestures of goodwill from above. After all, what's "given" instead of won can also be taken away.

K.: Well, if the women's movement were to consult me, I would advise a somewhat different strategy from the current one. In politics, you know, every means is justified. I would round up all the men who are willing to be intelligent about this issue and send them out to do something. Of course, one would have to keep an eye on them to make sure they weren't getting off too easily.

B. AND S.: But men have a stake in keeping things the way they are. How can they be involved in this movement?

K.: I always say that it makes no difference, historically, *why* somebody does something. Never ask too many questions about purity of motive. As long as someone can be pressured or embarrassed into supporting their cause, women must learn not to care. Take my example. After all, my party won the majority in the last elections *because* of the votes of women. And against the interests of my own party, let me tell you: it's a better strategy to play the candidates and parties off against each other. Party loyalty is better for the parties, but it's certainly not better for the cause.

The above-mentioned structural weaknesses of the Austrian women's movement are compensated for by some important advantages. Austrian feminists, like European feminists in general, tend to feel ideologically superior to US feminism, although they admire its strength and follow its lead on a great many issues. Still, Austrians consider US feminism insufficiently "political," or too "bourgeois." Initiatives like networking and affirmative action aimed at putting more women in top-level positions are rejected with the argument that this strategy will change the individual women more than it will change society. This somewhat puritanical attitude to power as a corrupting agent that must be avoided at all costs obviously paralyzes Austrian women's groups in many ways: it causes unending ideological fights over whether a particular demand is too "individualistic" or whether it will further "the revolution"; it continually saps leadership potential in the movement, as women who distinguish themselves by unusual activism are accused of ego-tripping; in many ways it is a continuation of the age-old dictum that women should work for others, but never for themselves.

Connected with this is yet another problem, the eternal question of men. Conferences on feminist issues in Austria invariably degenerate, at some point, into a civil war between four factions: women who stand up to announce self-righteously, "We are not fighting against the men, after all" (and that they are distressed at the generalizations about men which have maligned their own little emancipated Theodore); women who, in the interests of keeping the movement intact, launch into conciliatory apologetics about fighting shoulder-to-shoulder with our brothers against capitalist patriarchy; women who point out that whenever it comes to women's rights, all these hypothetical emancipated male comrades-in-arms are conspicuously absent; and a radical wing of women who argue that one can neither fight alongside men, nor live with them, nor put them to any constructive use whatsoever, and why should one want to anyway, and when will the panel/conference/movement finally address itself to the real issue, which is to declare that feminism and lesbianism are identical?

From all this it can be seen that Austrian men (like their French and German brothers) have developed a subtle line of defense: subversion. Referring to themselves by the generic term "softies" (as opposed to the hard-liners or "chauvies," derived from "chauvinism") they can be seen in the first row at all feminist events, frequently knitting and monopolizing the subsequent discussion with comments on the "failings of the women's movement." They are also to be found in labor rooms, where they become indignant if the woman decides to have an anesthetic after all because "we agreed" that "we believed in natural childbirth." They generally attend consciousness-raising groups whose members decide, after eight months of weekly meetings, that to "find their identity" and become "equal partners" they must "accept their sexuality" and "face the fact" that what they "honestly feel" is an aggressive and violent desire to sexually objectify women. The corresponding women's group is at this point generally requested to incorporate the question of men's naturally aggressive sexuality into their agenda, which it usually refuses to do—at which point the men's group dissolves.

Writing as Austrians, we do feel an impulse to conclude with some redeeming features, some optimistic note. Yet an honest conclusion would have to be that the emancipatory attitude taken by the Socialist government has genuinely improved women's status but had the effect both of co-opting activist women and of reducing the incentive for grassroots agitation. The real remaining problems are the insidious, corrosive attitudes that make a woman's contribution less important than a man's, a woman's deviance more reprehensible, a woman's voice less weighty; that continue, in other words, to make gender into class. Alongside all the flaws, weaknesses, and sometimes trivial preoccupations of the Austrian women's movement, it has one decisive strength: its recognition that to fight the tyranny of gender, you have to fight the tyranny of gender-*class*—and that women's liberation is part of global revolution.

Suggested Further Reading

Benard, Cheryl, and Edit Schlaffer. *Liebesgeschichten aus dem Patriarchat.* Reinbek: Rowohlt, 1981.

Frauenbericht der Österreichischen Bundesregierung. Vienna: Chancellor's Office, 1975.

Mid Decade 1980: Review and Evaluation of Progress. Vienna: Austrian State Printing Office, 1980; collection of statistics and programs in connection with the UN Decade for Women.

Mitterauer, M., and R. Sieder. *Vom Patriarchat zur Partnerschaft.* Munich: Beck, 1979.

Weinzierl, Erika. *Emanzipation? Frauen in Österreich.* Vienna and Munich: Jugend und Volk, 1980.

Cheryl Benard and Edit Schlaffer are social scientists and have published widely on the subject of women's rights. They initiated the first refuge for battered women in Austria and founded the international human-rights organization Amnesty for Women, based in Vienna.

BRAZIL
(Federative Republic of Brazil)

The largest South American country, occupying nearly half of the continent, bordered by the Atlantic Ocean to the northeast and east and by every other South American country except Ecuador and Chile. **Area:** 8,511,957 sq. km. (3,286,470 sq. mi.). **Population** (1980): 121,967,000, female 50%. **Capital:** Brasilia.

DEMOGRAPHY. Languages: Portuguese (official). **Races or Ethnic Groups:** European (primarily Portuguese) descent 60%, Mestizo 26%, African descent 11%, indigenous Indian; Italian, German, Japanese, Arab immigrants. **Religions:** Roman Catholicism 91%, Candomble, Macumba, Umbanda (religions syncretizing indigenous, African, and Roman Catholic rituals), Protestant, Judaism. **Education** (% enrolled in school, 1975): Age 6–11—of all girls 71%, of all boys 69%; age 12–17—of all girls 52%, of all boys 54%; higher education—no data obtainable. **Literacy** (1977): Women 63%, men 69%. **Birth Rate** (per 1000 pop., 1975–80): 36. **Death Rate** (per 1000 pop., 1975–80): 8. **Infant Mortality** (per 1000 live births, 1975–80): Female 103, male 115. **Life Expectancy** (1975–80): Female 67 yrs., male 61 yrs.

GOVERNMENT. Brazil is a confederation of 22 states, 4 territories, and 1 federal district. Current government (1983) consists of a military junta, led by Gen. João Baptista de Oliveira Figueiredo, and a bicameral legislature. **Women's Suffrage:** 1932; integrated into the Constitution in 1934. **Equal Rights:** Stipulated in a 1962 constitutional amendment. **Women in Government:** 5 out of 421-member Chamber of Deputies, none in 72-member Senate; 4 mayors; Ester Figueiredo Ferraz is Minister of Federal Culture and Education (1983).

ECONOMY. Currency: Cruzeiro (May 1983: 515. = $1 US). **Gross National Product** (1980): $243.2 billion. **Per Capita Income** (1980): $2050. **Women's Wages as a Percentage of Men's** (1982):

A São Paulo Economic Research Institute survey shows that the mean individual wage of women is 57% less than that of men. **Equal Pay Policy:** Equal salary for equal work mandated by law, although 1976 Labor Ministry research found women's salaries lower than men's nationwide. **Production** (Agricultural/Industrial): Coffee, beef, rice, sugar cane, corn; steel, chemicals, machinery, motor vehicles, lumber. **Women as a Percentage of Labor Force** (1980): 23%; **of agricultural force**—no general statistics obtainable (17% of women workers are employed in agriculture, 1975); **of industrial force**—no general statistics obtainable (of manufacturing 22%, 1975); **of military** (1980)—less than 1% and only in unarmed service divisions. The 1970 Census figures showed 29.6% of females over age 10 in the labor force (when adjusted to include domestic service, the statistic rose to 75.5%). **(Employed) Women's Occupational Indicators** (1981): Women are concentrated in nursing, teaching, and service sectors; over 80% of the female labor force is concentrated in 10 female–intensive and low–status professions, e.g., 27% are domestic servants, 18% are rural workers (61% of whom earn 1/2 of the minimum wage), 9% are elementary school teachers, 8% are office workers, 6% are seamstresses; 12.8% of employed women are in the industrial work force. **Unemployment:** No general statistics or rates by sex obtainable; 10% in Rio de Janeiro, 9% in São Paulo (1982 official figures); national underemployment est. at 23% (1983).

GYNOGRAPHY. Marriage. *Policy:* Under "Patrio Poder," husband is legal "head of the marital union" (Civil Code, Art. 380), in authority over children and general family matters. Prior to 1962 (Law 4121) married women were considered permanent minors. Wife assumes husband's surname, but can control her own earnings and property gained before marriage; she can administer common goods only with husband's permission or in his formal absence, although he can dispose of communal goods or her property without her permission (Civil Code, Art. 274). Married women by law cannot be discriminated against in employment. Widows are entitled to 1/2 of husband's estate. *Practice:* Female mean age at marriage (1970–78): 23; women age 15–49 in union (1970–78): 56%. Women have little control over family decision-making beyond household management, and difficulty overcoming discrimination that requires a husband's signature in most financial and legal matters. **Divorce.** *Policy:* Legalized in 1977 after opposition from Roman Catholic Church. One divorce permitted per person and only after 3 yrs. legal or 5 yrs. *de facto* separation. Child custody is based on "friendly separation," innocent party gains custody or mother gains custody if both parties are guilty (of adultery); father pays for child support and educational costs. Widowed or divorced women (but not men) must wait 270 days before remarrying. *Practice:* No statistics obtainable. Divorces are hard to obtain but separations are common. Alimony is hard to obtain, and child-support payments difficult to enforce.

Family. *Policy:* "Salario Familial" (family salary) gives financial support to the head of household (by law the husband) amounting to approx. 5% of minimum wage per child. Financial aid is proportionate to number of children, indirectly encouraging larger families as a means of supplementing income. Law of "Maternity Salary" gives government support to pregnant women, and includes measures "to safeguard the health of the mother and child." Women employees are entitled to 4 weeks paid maternity leave before childbirth and 8 weeks after, and by law cannot be fired for pregnancy. *Practice:* No statistics obtainable. Husbands (legally the heads of households) often spend the Salario Familial as they wish; male alcoholism and gambling are culturally tolerated. Women employees frequently are fired or not hired when pregnant. Existing laws covering maternity salaries are hard to enforce, and the amount of maternity pay is small. There is widespread discrimination against domestic workers, who are rarely covered by maternity legislation. Lack of day care

and family opposition to women working outside the home were major concerns of women metalworkers during 1980–81 labor strikes. **Welfare.** *Policy:* The INPS (National Insurance Program) covers employees, and includes "Maternity Salary" and benefits (see **Family),** accident benefits, and retirement pensions. Women are eligible for pensions after 30 yrs. employment, men after 35 yrs.; in general, pension is 75–80% of prior salary, although 100% for civil servants (women and men). *Practice:* No statistics obtainable. Although eligible, in practice domestic servants rarely receive benefits.

Contraception. *Policy:* Legal; the government is developing a policy under pressure from the World Bank regarding future economic aid tied to family planning; in 1984 the Health Minister announced plans for a national program. In the northeast, family-planning services are available, although controversial. All advertising of process, substance, or objects to prevent conception or bring about abortion is prohibited and punishable by a fine of 500–5000 Crz. *Practice:* In 1980 official São Paulo state sources reported 6 million women using contraceptives. A 1978 São Paulo study found that of 2789 women age 15–19, 62% of those married used contraceptives; of these, primary methods used (1978) pill 25% (access through pharmacies, where a doctor's prescription frequently is not required), sterilization 16.9% (chosen, not forced, although illegal except for certain pilot projects in specific clinics), interrupted coitus 7.5%, condom 6.1%, rhythm method 5.2%. While a program of voluntary female sterilization exists, reports indicate that some women living in rural areas or in *favelas* (slums) are sterilized by tubal ligation without their consent. **Abortion.** *Policy:* Legal only in extreme cases of danger to the woman's life or if pregnancy resulted from rape or incest. All other procedures are punishable under the Penal Code (Arts. 124–27) as a "Crime of Feticide," by 1–3 yrs. imprisonment for the woman, practitioner, or anyone who refers her to a practitioner (doctor, nurse, midwife, etc.). *Practice:* Illegal abortions number approx. 3 million annually; 25% of all hospital beds (1980) were filled by women whose illegal abortion attempts had failed. Self-induced abortion methods include jumping from heights, using hot water to "scald the uterus," and drinking poisonous herbs sold on the open market. Wealthier women reportedly pay for expensive operations sometimes performed under unsanitary conditions and without proper anesthesia. **Illegitimacy.** *Policy:* No longer a concept in the law. *Practice:* No statistics obtainable. Single mothers have difficulty in gaining employment but face no discrimination regarding social benefits once they are employed. **Homosexuality.** *Policy:* Illegal if the act is judged to be obscene under rules governing "Offenses Against the Public Morality." *Practice:* There are many groups, centers, and social places for lesbian women and homosexual men in the major urban centers. Repression of homosexuality occurs through strong social tabus and police raids and arrests. The Lesbian Feminist Action Group (GALF) is active, and there is a lesbian journal, *Chana com Chana.*

Incest. *Policy:* Illegal, punishable by imprisonment. No further data obtainable. *Practice:* No statistics obtainable, but incest reportedly is common in rural areas. Its frequent appearance as a theme in Brazilian literature suggests that incest is more recognized than socially admitted. Feminist groups are organizing on the issue. **Sexual Harassment.** *Policy:* No specific law, but could be punishable under "acts against public morality and decency." A proposed antisexist employment law is pending (1983). *Practice:* No statistics obtainable, but reports indicate that women working in previously "male" sectors encounter ridicule, attempted rape, etc., and have few grievance measures against such attacks. **Rape.** *Policy:* Illegal, punishable by imprisonment. Marital rape is not legally recognized. *Practice:* No statistics obtainable. The burden of proof is on the rape victim. A single woman who is raped is often socially repudiated; few rapists are convicted, some are fined. Feminists are campaigning actively for more effective rape legislation. **Battery.** *Policy:* No specific laws; under general assault laws, a wife can prosecute her husband for battery. Under a legal "defense of honor"

plea, husbands who murder their wives are very rarely convicted. *Practice:* No general statistics obtainable. In 1980 feminists reported 772 cases of São Paulo women who were murdered by their husbands, victims of "crimes of passion"; the men still are free. On Nov. 6, 1981, feminist groups won a major victory when Doca Street, a wealthy playboy, was convicted for murdering his live-in companion, Angela Diniz. Street originally had been acquitted in 1979 under the "defense of honor" plea (see HERSTORY).

Prostitution. *Policy:* It is illegal to induce a person into prostitution, or prevent one from abandoning it; both are punishable by fines and/or imprisonment. *Practice:* No statistics obtainable. Prostitution is a thriving industry in Rio de Janeiro, São Paulo, and other urban centers, particularly in the north, and is controlled by international traffickers and individual pimps. Prostitutes regularly are harassed by police; they spend a few nights in jail and are released after paying a fine. Reportedly informal arrangements exist between police and pimps whereby sex with a prostitute is exchanged for the police officer's willful ignorance. Prostitutes have begun organizing for their civil rights (see HERSTORY). **Traditional/Cultural Practices.** *Policy:* No data obtainable. *Practice:* Some researchers have cited evidence of female genital mutilation (see Glossary) practiced as a puberty rite in rural areas. **Crisis Centers.** *Policy:* No government centers. *Practice:* Feminists have organized centers for battered and raped women in São Paulo, Rio de Janeiro, Minas Gerais, and Pernambuco (Recife), and an SOS hot-line in São Paulo and Minas Gerais. In 1980 feminists set up the Center for the Defense of the Rights of Women after 2 women were killed by their husbands.

HERSTORY. Many of the indigenous peoples of Brazil were matrilineal peoples (see MYTHOGRAPHY). The status of women declined with the Portuguese conquest (1500–1549 C.E.); much native culture was crushed and European and Roman Catholic mores were imposed. In 1888 Isabel, daughter of Pedro II (Emperor of the by then independent kingdom of Brazil), abolished slavery while she was regent during her father's absence in Europe.

The Brazilian women's movement began in the late 19th century with the publication by Joana Manso of *O Jornal das Senhoras* (The Journal for Ladies), which called for the "moral emancipation of women" and civil rights. In 1910 Ernestina Lesina published *Anima Vita* (Life Force) calling for women to organize; a league for the "intellectual emancipation of women" was formed in 1919. In 1922 the Brazilian Federation for the Advancement of Women (founded by Bertha Lutz) fought for women's political and economic gains, resulting in women's suffrage (1932). The first woman deputy, Dr. Carlotta Pereira de Queiroz, was elected to the National Assembly in 1933. The Women's Union united women workers and intellectuals in 1934; many were later arrested for opposing the Getulio Vargas regime. The Federation of Brazilian Women organized the Latin American Congress in 1949; in the 1950's–60's, women actively protested the Korean War. In 1964 middle-class women organized the march "for God and Country" protesting Pres. João Goulart; 800,000 people participated.

A new wave of feminism began in 1975. Women lawyers set up the first feminist law firm, the Brazil Women's Center opened in Rio de Janeiro, and 2 feminist newspapers began: *Brazil Mulher* (Brazil Woman) and *Nos Mulheres* (We Women). The Brazilian Women's Movement for Amnesty— which later was to claim 14,000 members —published a bulletin, *Maria Quiteria*,

and in 1977 wrote the Brazilian Women's Manifesto, which was signed by 12,000 women and presented to the National Assembly. The First Congress of São Paulo Women was held in 1979, marking the start of the day-care movement. Feminists also held massive demonstrations protesting the acquittal of Doca Street and the "defense of honor" plea which had in effect allowed husbands to kill their wives (see **Battery**). In Jan. 1980 women demonstrated for abortion rights. International Women's Day 1980 united 3000 women from feminist groups, women's clubs, church, and labor organizations. The first women metalworkers' strike occurred. In June–July 1980, mass demonstrations by São Paulo prostitutes demanding their civil rights won international feminist support. In 1981 "TV Mulher," the first women's program (by and for women) drew 8 million viewers. *Mulherio* is a feminist journal published by Fundação Carolos Chagas. In May 1983 feminist demonstrations again erupted over the 2-year suspended sentence given to a man pleading "defense of honor" for wife-murder in Belo Horizonte; the same week, a Brasilia woman had been sentenced to 14 years imprisonment for a comparable crime.

MYTHOGRAPHY. Among the Amazon tribes, the Tukano Indian women are warriors, live together, and meet with men primarily for procreation; the women keep the female children with them. Legends of women warriors and/ or of an ancient gynocracy still exist among most of the indigenous peoples.

BRAZIL: A Fertile but Ambiguous Feminist Terrain
by Danda Prado
(Translated by Magda Bogin)

I sometimes think that ideas spread as if composed of microbes. These microbes "contaminate" the predisposed for any one of a thousand reasons; they may pass some people by completely one day, only to possess them from head to toe the next. Others, metaphorically vaccinated into immunity by societally determined "certainties," spend their lives untouched . . .

It's amusing for me to trace the process by which these microbes linked my life with contemporary Brazilian feminism. I realize that just as others, both at home and abroad, gave me their "germs"—through books, conversations, and life example—so I was and am in turn a communicator. The only way to trace this process is to view my own experience within a broader historical context.

Early Symptoms

Just as the virus of libertarian thought lived in the sweat of immigrant Italian and Spanish workers at the turn of the century, so contact with European and North American women demanding the right to vote became a major influence on the lives of many Brazilian women. But it was Dr. Bertha Lutz (a scientist of Anglo-German origin) who, applying her ability to catalyze people around a shared goal, led the battle to obtain female suffrage in Brazil in 1932. Twenty years later, the young lawyer Romy Medeiros da Fonseca challenged the Civil Code, having discovered that the Code equated women with minors, savages, and the insane. Ten years of battle—in Parliament and the press—would pass before reforms were approved.

In 1960, Simone de Beauvoir visited Brazil. Her book *The Second Sex* had been published in Portuguese in 1949 and had served as a major consciousness-raiser for generations of Brazilians. I experienced her impact personally at the University of Brazil in Rio de Janeiro, and I vividly remember our impassioned discussions about her condemnation of male privilege. At that point, however, de Beauvoir still believed that socialist regimes would solve the problems between the sexes. Her words most featured in the press were: "Women should fight alongside men to reorganize the world's productive forces and for social justice, not to uphold the equality of the sexes but rather the parity of men and women."[1] Many Brazilian women were beginning at that time to question the extreme socioeconomic injustice in our country, and some had found a solution through a Marxist analysis. Thus, while part of her book excited us by verbalizing the oppression we felt as women, our combativeness in that very direction was diverted by the other part and by her speeches, in which she pointed to class struggle as the priority.

It was perhaps de Beauvoir's ideas that inspired an editor of the most widely read monthly women's magazine—*Claudia*—to inaugurate a section called "The Art of Being a Woman" in 1963. This series became the province of Carmem da Silva, the Brazilian writer and psychotherapist, who had just returned from a number of years in Argentina, where she had written articles that were revolutionary for those days, denouncing the inferior status of married women—the so-called *rainhas do lar* (queens of the hearth). Carmem still runs this section, which has considerable influence on middle-class married women. For myself, I feel certain that these articles, along with de Beauvoir's influence, reinforced my own latent wish for a divorce, which I eventually obtained (my three children being then fourteen, twelve, and five years old).

I too had my period of preconceptions about feminism. In 1965 Carmem suggested that I start a magazine to denounce sexism on a more sophisticated level than was being done in any then-existing publication. I rejected the idea as "unimportant" and "outmoded"! At the time, I was head of the editorial department at Editorial Brasiliense, and already had planned a collection called "A New Woman," which eventually brought out works by Alba de Cespedes, Sarah Pinheiro de Las Casas, and others. Still later, in 1967–68, I lived in the US while studying at Columbia—and I remained unaffected by the just-

[1]. L. G. Ribeiro, "Simone de Beauvoir and Women," *Diário de Notícias,* Rio de Janeiro, Aug. 9, 1960.

then-exploding new women's movement, despite my involvement with the anti-Vietnam War crusade and the civil-rights movement.

Years later, in 1970, de Beauvoir revised her earlier stand. Disillusioned by the socialist countries' silence on the whole issue of women, she took up a militant position alongside radical feminists and supported the formation of an autonomous movement unconnected to any of the parties of the French Left. (Her new stand went unnoticed in Brazilian papers.) The conflict between these two approaches to "the woman issue" is still strong in Brazil. One approach, besides coinciding with the patriarchal ideological vision of the Left, does not ask men to make any effort to overcome their *machismo*—neither in their private lives nor within their parties, unions, etc. The other has, as one of its consequences, the exodus of women from political activity in the infrastructure of the parties of the Left.

I arrived in Paris in 1970, in a self-exile which would later become forced exile when the Brazilian consulate refused to renew my passport. I arranged for a personal interview with de Beauvoir, and she advised me not to make contact with the women's liberation movement there until I had spoken with a left-wing feminist[2] who would understand not only my curiosity about the radical ideas of French feminists but also my conviction that for Brazil the priority was still class struggle and anti-imperialist struggle. It seemed impossible to me that there could be any reconciliation between the extreme poverty of our population and feminist activism. (And it would take many discussions before I would be able to see the basic patriarchal structure of society as a fundamental obstacle to social justice for *all* human beings.) At the time I was preparing a dissertation on the condition of women for a doctorate in social psychology at Paris VII University. After rereading Christine Delphy's *L'Ennemi principal* (The Primary Enemy), which I had vehemently rejected the first time around, I was forced to rewrite my thesis two years later. Delphy placed men as the oppressors, at the head of the capitalist structure *within* the over-all plan of patriarchy.

Meanwhile, also in 1970, Betty Friedan came to Brazil to promote the Brazilian translation of her book. In interviews she talked about family planning and abortion, matters which greatly upset both the Right and the Left. The press reacted by linking her "criminal" lack of beauty with all "the American feminists who burn bras in public," in contrast to the "ultra-feminine" women of Brazil.[3] Yet less than two years later, in 1972, women professionals and intellectuals of various political tendencies from all over Brazil accepted a personal invitation from Romy Medeiros da Fonseca, president of the Conselho Nacional de Mulheres (National Council of Women), to attend a meeting at the Hotel Serrador. There was a right-wing "label" associated with both the Council and its president, which evoked the distrust of many opposition women. However, attracted by her unusual initiative, many opposition intellectuals did attend, since there were no restrictions on participation. There were debates on reforming the Civil Code, and even on family planning and abortion. Furthermore, the formation of a female civil service was proposed.

It was not until 1975, however, that a collective voice of women identifiable as "feminist" was heard. In Rio de Janeiro the first national seminar was held in the offices of the Associação Brasileira de Imprensa (ABI, Brazilian Press Assoc.). This event had tremen-

---

[2] De Beauvoir gave me the name of a friend of hers, Anne Tristan, who had been in Cuba and had written, under that pseudonym, *Maternité esclave* (Enslaved Motherhood), *Histoires du MLF* (Stories from the MLF), and *Histoires d'amour* (Love Stories). I'm grateful to her to this day for her support during the years I spent in France (1970–80).

[3] Friedan came at the invitation of Rosemarie Muraro, director of the publishing house Vozes and a journalist.

dous social impact even though it was downplayed by the media. It was an opportunity for women from different fields to meet, and also to attract women from a broad range of political tendencies. In this respect, the "legitimizing" umbrella of the UN and International Women's Year was extremely important; this was the only way to maneuver in a period of severe repression against anyone who tried to organize in Brazil.

At the 1972 meeting, the Centro da Mulher Brasileira (Brazilian Women's Center) was set up, with an elected board of governors.[4] It still exists, despite the departures of most of its founding members through successive critiques of their political positions. The schisms within this group gave rise to the women's organizations active in Brazil today. (I was not in Brazil at that time, but I did take part later in the International Women's Year Mexico City meeting, as an observer from the UNDP–UN Development Program, for which I was working as a consultant. At both the official and the alternative Mexico City meetings, I saw first-hand the confrontations between women of the Latin American Left, particularly Chilean, Argentine, and Uruguayan exiles, and feminists of the industrialized nations—including Friedan. I saw scenes of near-violence between various "political" and "autonomous" factions, but the over-all experience was positive for me, because I finally began to understand the "whys" of these two positions.)

The 1972 women's meeting back in Brazil took place in a specific context. Since 1964 we had been living under a fierce military dictatorship, and in such a situation no one was prepared for the convergence of so many women from all regions of the country. To understand the development of Brazilian feminism after this memorable meeting, it's helpful to study the relationship between the authoritarian State and the social movements that arose during the 1970's: "The great majority of these movements, including those composed of women, bore the stamp of resistance to the military dictatorship. They used *every* possible avenue at a time when the institutional channels of popular representation were either blocked or weakened by repression."[5]

During this time, a small group of eight or ten women had been meeting regularly (since 1974). Of this nucleus, four had spent time in the United States and two in France, where they had taken part in feminist events; others had been awakened to these ideas by the international literature. Many of them subscribed to *Nosotras,* a bi-monthly newspaper put out in Paris by Latin American feminists, including myself, who felt the need for a publication that would serve as a bridge between France and Latin America during a period of silence and rigorous censorship in many nations of that continent.

Meanwhile, in the Rest of the Country . . .

In contrast to this effervescent beginning of feminism, in October 1978 in Pernambuco, a state in northeast Brazil, the Tribunal de Justiça rejected the applications of ninety-one women candidates for judge on the grounds that, in the President's words, "women do not possess the aptitudes necessary for judgeship." At the same time, in the north, a woman was elected to the identical office in Pará—in accordance with the Federal Constitution, which grants equal rights to all citizens. This is a clear example of the contradictions we live with in Brazil, and of the weakness of the written law before the force of tradition.

[4] Among them Branca Moreira Alves, Leila Barsted, Moema Toscano, Berenice and Mariska Ribeiro, Maria do Espírito Santo (Santinha) Tavares, etc.

[5] Velasco (Anette Goldberg), "Os movimentos de liberação da mulher na Franca e na Itália (1970–80)" (Women's Liberation Movements in France and Italy [1970–80]); unpublished paper presented at a seminar on Oct. 10, 1981.

The Evolution of Feminist/Feminine Groups

A new national meeting was held in 1981, also in Rio de Janeiro. Having recently returned to Brazil, I was able to attend. This time it was not an open seminar but an opportunity to take stock of women's groups' activities throughout the country. Numerous short films by women were shown (something that in 1975 had not been possible because such films hadn't existed). Many books, magazines, and newspapers also were presented. Fifty-four groups participated, many of them rejecting the word "feminist" and describing themselves simply as "working with women." These groups can be divided *grosso modo* into three broad categories, with frequent overlap:

1) Militant Feminist Autonomous Organizations, including *grupos de reflexão* (reflection groups), an ambiguous term that could mean reflection on any theme. Perhaps the name was chosen instead of *grupos de autoconsciência* (consciousness-raising groups) to avoid the criticism that these were "group therapy gatherings without a therapist" and thus spare participants a degree of ridicule.[6] It is certainly important to note that, while before 1979 there was a theoretical and literary awareness of the international movement, there had been very little personal experience of a new *practice.* (This is why so many feminists still laugh when they tell about the time in 1979 that Gilda Grillo, a member of the group Nosotras in Paris, began to clear up dishes, cups, and ashtrays at a meeting of twenty-five women in a private house. The idea that other people are always "guests" and never help the hostess is immutably engraved in every Brazilian social class. It was Gilda who first explained to them how a consciousness-raising group actually functions.) The autonomous feminist groups include: *Work Groups*—small groups meeting with the objective of a specific form of action, such as self-help groups *(autoajuda de corpo),* groups working for changes in sexist education, hot-lines for women who are the object of violence (SOS *violência),* a tribunal to denounce discrimination against women, an updated taped telephone message giving information on the movement,[7] feminist lawyers' groups, women's radio programs, the national newspaper *Mulherio,* lesbian women's groups, etc. (Unlike the first two Brazilian feminist groups in exile, *in* Brazil lesbian women felt totally ignored at the beginning, if not overtly discriminated against. Today there is more than one lesbian group active in the Brazilian women's movement.)

With regard to violence against women, there have been several actions with nationwide repercussions. In 1979, for the first time, a journalist was denounced for sexually harassing a receptionist who worked at his newspaper. There were also actions in support of women who wanted to sit alone or in groups of two or three in bars—and in support of prostitutes' human rights as well. Most important was the beginning of a campaign that questioned the innocence of men who killed their wives or lovers *em defesa da honra* (in defense of their honor). "Honor" is understood to mean a woman's "fidelity." The killer is exonerated and the personal life of the victim dissected in court, re-emphasizing the traditional code: women must dress in a "non-seductive" manner, not involve themselves in social issues, avoid "advanced" television programs, and so on. Feminists took to the streets and appeared on radio and television to denounce this. But it was in 1980 that the whole country was shaken by the news that Belo Horizonte (the capital of Minas Gerais, the most traditional state in Brazil), had awakened to a blanket of graffiti saying: HE WHO LOVES DOES NOT KILL—DOWN WITH THE FARCE OF HONOR—HOW MANY MORE CORPSES UNTIL WOMEN'S OPPRESSION IS ACKNOWLEDGED? From that moment, there were demonstrations after each new case, and by 1981 feminist pressure had forced a reconsideration of the legal assumptions used to judge these crimes.

2) Feminist Groups with Ties to Political Parties. This second category consists of

---

[6.] Velasco (A.G.).

[7.] The number in Rio de Janeiro is 274 0905 (as of 1983).

groups linked directly or indirectly to political parties or organizations. Generally, they are concerned with questions similar to those of groups in the first category, except for the *focus* of their action—and their priorities. Instead of rejecting a central organization and a leadership, and instead of emphasizing solidarity and respect for spontaneous initiatives, these groups tend to replicate the traditional forms of vertical, hierarchical organizations. Within the "new Brazilian feminism" it is groups of this tendency that articulate the need for greater participation by women in the so-called specific struggles, *in order* for women to "move on" from those struggles into the "more general societal ones."[8] These groups hold congresses and manipulate the voting in plenary sessions, de-emphasizing such issues as abortion, sexual repression, and sexist education, while stressing the priority of day-care facilities, better wages, maternity benefits, etc.—all of which are certainly issues of great urgency, but ones which should not be bought at the expense of raising women's consciousness about their specific oppression *as women.* Yet these organizations are closer to feminists than are women's groups of the extreme Left, which try to take over congresses and use them for extranational ends; who attack feminist book tables in public squares, even wielding metal chains against women whose ideas they oppose. Curiously, as of this writing, there have been no incidents of Brazilian feminists being attacked by extreme *right*-wing groups, as has occurred in France and the US, for example.

The ranks of all these Leftward organizations grew after the change in the political situation that followed the amnesty law of 1979, and the subsequent return to Brazil of many women exiles who had experienced foreign women's liberation movements. Some Leftist women who had stayed in Brazil began to examine their position vis à vis "the woman question," and, influenced by the feminist groups that were forming here, they began to pressure their own parties to support either specific women's groups within their existing structure or groups founded under other names but retaining links to the parties. At the end of 1979, with the return of a female former member of the Central Committee of the Brazilian Communist Party, there was a fierce public debate in which the two positions were articulated. There was clear-cut support for the beliefs of the autonomous feminist movement. However, the majority was still afraid to detach itself from the existing parties, and opted for a double activism.

3) The "Intellectuals." This third major category of women's groups is composed of social scientists, whether working independently or in associations. The character of women's studies and research in Latin America contrasts sharply with that of its counterpart in the industrialized world. Here the funding for research projects is provided by international foundations (private, religious, UN agencies, etc.). In the industrialized countries, women had to fight to overcome the prejudice that kept women's studies from being taught in universities and research centers; here in Brazil, on the contrary, a whole job market opened up for women who were not necessarily involved in a radical examination of sex roles, creating a certain elitism that separates the "intellectuals" from movement activists. Some of their academic publications overtly disavow a connection to the women's movement, while others present analyses diametrically opposed to those of feminist researchers in other countries. (Of course, many women have overcome these attitudes. But some seem as if they don't want even to try to overcome them.) I attribute this situation in great measure to the fact that those in charge of grants from abroad were not involved in the women's movements in their *own* countries, and consequently had difficulty recognizing it in Brazil. This is particularly true of such countries as Germany, France, and the US, all of which use grants to export their own culture (but not real feminism) to Brazil. Yet despite these obstacles to genuine *feminists'* entry into academia,

[8] Velasco (A.G.).

the doors were opened at the thirty-second annual meeting of the SBPC (Brazilian Society for the Advancement of Science), held in Rio de Janeiro in 1980. For the first time, erudite exhibits on the situation of women gave way to the live voice of feminist activists (in an auditorium of a thousand people); even lesbian women took the microphone.[9] Although this did not happen again the following year in the official meetings of the SBPC, it did set in motion an annual tradition for feminists from all over Brazil to gather and meet parallel to the SBPC meetings, albeit in improvised headquarters. Nevertheless, there still is a gap between "academics" and "feminists"—and women's studies are still excluded from the basic university curricula, except in isolated cases, and then usually with funding from abroad.

Issues in Themselves: Abortion and Contraception

The fight for full control over one's own body, for the right to choose abortion, and for a free sexuality—these are certainly among the great catalyzing themes of the contemporary women's movement all over the world. Not so—yet—in Brazil.

Several years ago, some Brazilian women—both within party-linked organizations and in separate feminist groups—began to wage a broad campaign for the decriminalization of abortion. They were surreptitiously derailed or blatantly ignored. There already had been several mobilizations around individual cases of women imprisoned for practicing abortion, or even for distributing pamphlets. There even had been a few public debates with members of the Roman Catholic Church. But there was no continuity to these actions. There are several hypotheses that might explain the lack of intense organizing on this issue (which *is* one of the fundamental problems facing women in Brazil today). I would reduce them to two:

First, the Catholic Church's influence. In Brazil, certain sectors of the Church have taken progressive positions in recent decades, condemning the abuse of the masses by the dominant class. Many such clergy were imprisoned and tortured, beginning with the military coup [1964] until the so-called opening in 1979. Leftist groups count on the support of such progressive clergy in elections and don't want to lose these powerful allies by taking a position on reproductive or sexual-preference freedom that goes against established dogma. The Left itself, for that matter, has never taken a clear stand in support of the decriminalization of abortion; on the contrary, it has stepped up criticism of sterilization and family-planning programs. The Left claims that women should have financial support so they can *have* children they want, but places no emphasis on women's also having the means to *stop* having children they *don't* want. It should be noted that even feminist candidates for elective office, while they may personally support abortion rights, are reluctant to take a public stand, preferring to campaign for the creation of day-care facilities, an immediate objective they feel links them to the voters.

Second, there is undeniable pressure from the World Bank, which has made loans to the government conditional on family planning. The experience of other countries has shown clearly that a change in the rate of population growth is closely tied to a change in women's attitudes, not just to economic stimuli, penalties for those who have too many children, etc. Funding for women's studies courses, women's centers, films, and publications are thus linked to this international politics that wants population growth slowed. But the linkage is often for manipulative power-politics reasons, not out of any idealistic or genuinely feminist motivation, thus complicating the Brazilian woman's reaction to it even further.

As of this writing, a number of independent feminists and autonomous groups are launching a broader campaign for the decriminalization of abortion. This campaign will

---

[9.] *Veja* magazine, July 16, 1980.

have to face the profound antagonism of the Catholic Church, of the spiritists and other religious groups, of the traditional Right, and of the Left as well. Ironically, it will have the veiled support of the highest echelons of government and of certain financial circles. We believe that this campaign could set in motion an autonomous women's movement whose concerns go beyond the single issue of abortion. Its potential is to reach a broader range of social strata, since there is no doubt about the dramatic situation of poor women, especially regarding reproduction and the tyranny of biological fatalism.

Postscript

In writing this article, I found myself doing a great deal of personal introspection. I combed through the correspondence I had kept up with Brazilian feminists during my exile in Paris; I reminisced with some of those women who lived through those years here in Brazil. I remembered, relived, and realized many things. I can only add that while attempting to be objective about the politics involved, I was surprised to discover much about myself and my own feminist odyssey in the process. That, of course, is what feminism is all about.

(The following women collaborated on the research and writing of this article: Eunice Gutman [filmmaker], Maria José de Lima "Zezé" [nurse]. The following women were consulted in conversation: Diva Mucio Teixeira [journalist], Leni Silverstein [sociologist], Romy Medeiros da Fonseca [jurist], Carmem da Silva [journalist].)

Suggested Further Reading

Barroso, Carmen. *Mulher, Sociedade e Estado no Brasil.* São Paulo: UNICEF and Ed. Brasiliense, 1982.

Costa, Albertina O., *et al. Memórias das mulheres do Exílio.* Río de Janeiro: Ed. Paz e Terra, 1980.

Goldberg, Anette. "Feminismo em regime autoritário: a experiência do movimento de mulheres no Río de Janeiro." Paper presented at the XII Congress of IPSA (International Political Science Assoc.), Río de Janeiro, Aug. 9–14, 1982; mimeo.

Hahner, June. *Women in Latin American History—Their Lives and Views.* Los Angeles: UCLA Latin America Center Publications, 1976.

Piza, Clelia, and Maryvonne Lapouge. *As Brasileiras.* Paris: Ed. des Femmes, 1977.

Danda Prado was born in São Paulo, Brazil, in 1929. Her parents divorced; the father was a historian and member of Parliament for the Communist Party, the mother a businesswoman. She graduated in psychology from São Paulo University during marriage, while becoming a mother to Claudia, Nelson, and Carla. Prado was divorced, exiled for political reasons, and lived in Paris (1970–80), obtaining her doctorate at the University of Paris VII in psychology with research on the psychosocial aspects of married women's behavior. While in Paris, she co-founded the Latin American women's group, and co-edited the Spanish and Portuguese newsletter *Nosotras.* She also worked as a consultant for UNDP in Mexico, Guatemala, and Peru, and researched women-headed families in Colombia (1977). On her return to Brazil, she became an active member of the Coletivo de Mulheres do Río de Janeiro, was involved in the national abortion-rights campaign, and became correspondent for the ISIS international feminist network. Among her published books are: *Ser esposa, a mais antiga profissão* (To Be a Wife, the Oldest Profession), Ed. Brasiliense; *Cicera, um destino de mulher* (Cicera, a Woman's Destiny), Ed. Brasiliense (the life history of a Northeastern migrant worker, who signs as co-author, whose personal drama was divulged through the Río press in 1980, and whose thirteen-year-old daughter was prohibited from legally interrupting the pregnancy resulting from rape by her stepfather); *O que é Familia* (A Family—What Is It), Ed. Brasiliense. Prado lives in Río, working as a writer and a social researcher, teaching courses in women's studies, and organizing feminist actions and conferences.

BRITAIN
(United Kingdom of Great Britain and Northern Ireland)*

The UK (comprised of England, Scotland, Wales, and Northern Ireland) is located off the northwest coast of Europe, with the North Sea to the east, the English Channel to the south, and the Atlantic Ocean to the west and north. **Area:** 244,108 sq. km. (94,250 sq. mi.). **Population** (1980): 55,759,000, female 51%. **Capital:** London, England. **Head of state:** Queen Elizabeth II; **head of government:** Prime Minister Margaret Thatcher.

DEMOGRAPHY. Languages: English, Gaelic, Welsh. **Races or Ethnic Groups:** English, Irish, Welsh, Scots; West Indian, Indian, Pakistani, African immigrants. **Religions:** Church of England (official, Episcopal), Church of Wales (official), Church of Scotland (official, Presbyterian), Methodist, Calvinistic Methodist, Wesleyan Reform Union, other Protestant, Church of Ireland (official), Roman Catholicism, Judaism. **Education** (% enrolled in school, 1975): Age 6–11—of all girls 98%, of all boys 98%; age 12–17—of all girls 85%, of all boys 85%; higher education—(England only) in 1978–79 women were 37% of undergraduates, 33% of postgraduates. **Literacy** (1977): Women 99%, men 99%. **Birth Rate** (per 1000 pop., 1977–78): 12. **Death Rate** (per 1000 pop., 1977–78): 12. **Infant Mortality** (per 1000 live births, 1977): Female 12, male 16. **Life Expectancy** (1975–80): Female 75 yrs., male 69 yrs.

GOVERNMENT. Constitutional monarchy with a bicameral legislative parliament consisting of a popularly elected 635-member House of Commons and a non-elected House of Lords of over 1000 members. Executive power is the purvey of the prime minister, who is chosen from the majority party to head a cabinet. Major political parties include Conservative, Labour, and Liberal. **Women's Suffrage:** 1918 (for women over age 30). In 1928 this right was extended to women over age 18. **Equal Rights:** Sex Discrimination Act (1975) bans sex-discrimination in employment, education, and housing. The Employment Equality Act (1977) makes discrimination on the basis of sex or marital status in employment or training illegal (except in the military). **Women in Government:** Margaret Thatcher of the Conservative Party became the first woman British Prime Minister (in 1979); Shirley Williams, former Secretary of State for Education, was re-elected to the Commons (1981) on the Social Democratic and Liberal Alliance ticket. There are 23 women MPs in the House of Commons and 46 women (28 marquesses and 18 peeresses in their own right) in the House of Lords; Baroness Young is Keeper of the Privy Seal and Leader of the House of Lords (1983). Mary Donaldson is the first woman to be Lord Mayor of London in 800 yrs.; she assumed office Nov. 11, 1983. Juvenile and domestic courts in England and Wales normally sit with 3 justices—including 1 woman—presiding.

ECONOMY. Currency: British Pound (May 1983: 0.62 = $1 US). **Gross National Product** (1980): $442.8 billion. **Per Capita Income** (1980): $7920. **Women's Wages as a Percentage of Men's** (1981): 73%. **Equal Pay Policy:** Equal Pay Act of 1970 became effective in 1975 and mandates equal pay for equal work, although most employed women remain in less remunerative, female-intensive labor sectors. **Production** (Agricultural/Industrial): Cereal, livestock, livestock products; steel, metal, motor vehicles, electronics, chemicals. **Women as a Percentage of Labor Force** (1982): 42.4%; **of agricultural force** (1979) 19%; **of industrial force** (1980) 48% of semi-skilled, 45% of unskilled; **of military** (Great Britain, 1982) 4.7%—air force 5.6% (370 officers, 4453 airmen *[sic]*), army 3% (497 officers, 6400 soldiers), navy 5% (280 officers, 3000 seamen *[sic]*); largely in service sector (see **Equal Rights**). **(Employed) Women's Occupational Indicators** (1980): Of professional and scientific

* All statistics refer to the UK unless otherwise specified. See also IRELAND(S), p. 340–53.

employees 11%, of employers and managers 13%, of personal services workers 82%. **Unemployment** (mid-1982): 12.7%, female 8.75%, male 15.3%; from 1975–80 the number of registered unemployed men rose 50% compared to 150% for women.

GYNOGRAPHY. Marriage. *Policy:* The 1949 Marriage Act derives from common law, and established spousal equality in marriage; the 1960 Marriage (Enabling) Act lists the requirements for marriage to include: both parties over age 16 and not blood-related; it stipulates complete reciprocity in the obligations of spouses to support each other during marriage. The 1960 Matrimonial Proceedings Act increased the courts' authority to enforce maintenance and custody of children in the family. The 1973 Domicile and Matrimonial Proceedings Act established that a wife's domicile is ascertained independently from her husband's. *Practice:* Female mean age at marriage (1970–78): 21; women age 15–49 in union (1970–78): 70%. **Divorce.** *Policy:* The Divorce Reform Act of 1969 made irretrievable breakdown of marriage the sole grounds for divorce; this was amended by the 1970 Matrimonial Proceedings and Property Act, which concerned maintenance of spouses and children in cases of divorce. Both were consolidated into the 1973 Matrimonial Causes Act, which extended the grounds for divorce to include adultery, bad behavior, desertion over a continuous 2-yr. period, and separation for 2 yrs. (if by mutual consent). Divorce will not be granted on the grounds of bad behavior or adultery if s/he did not seek divorce during the 6-month period following the discovery of misconduct or adultery. If a couple has been separated more than 2 but less than 5 yrs., the respondent must consent to the divorce. Divorce will not be granted during the first 3 yrs. of marriage except in cases of special hardship or "exceptional depravity." A divorce will not be granted unless the welfare of any "children of the family" have been provided for, and only if 1 partner is domiciled in England when the divorce proceedings begin. Extensive legislation covers alimony payments, child custody, and maintenance payments.

Practice: In 1980 there were 12 divorces per 1000 married couples (England and Wales); in 1980 there were 170,000 divorce petitions and 148,000 divorce decrees made absolute in Great Britain. The proportion of divorces granted to women in 1980 was 70%. The average age at divorce in 1980 was 37–38 for men and 35–36 for women.

Family. *Policy:* Employment Protection Act (1955) guarantees maternity leave of 29 weeks including 6 weeks pay at 90% of weekly wages. National insurance pays weekly allowance for 18 weeks to mothers who have been employed and paid sufficient contributions. Government pays maternity grant of £25 at birth of each child. There is no "absolute prohibition" against dismissal of a pregnant employee, although such employees are entitled to "protection against dismissal" by the Employment Protection Act. Day care is supported both by State subsidies and private funding. *Practice:* Labor legislation does not protect part-time workers from discrimination; nor do benefits apply to them. The majority of employed married women work part time. In 1979 there were 121,000 day-care centers in England and Wales (40 places for every 1000 children under age 5). In "sessional" (½ day) day-care centers, there were 140 places for every 1000 children under age 5. **Welfare.** *Policy:* Social Security (1975) includes national insurance, income supplements, workers' compensation, retirement and war pensions, some maternity benefits, child benefits, widows' benefits. National Health Service Act (1946) enables anyone "normally resident" in England and Wales to avail her/himself of all health services with no insurance qualification. Low-income persons can receive legal aid, rent rebates, allowances, health care, and free school meals. Social Security Pension Act (1975) bans discrimination against married women in collecting benefits. Full-time heads of households with at least 1 dependent can receive supplements of money, school meals, milk, and reduced fees for medical/dental care. *Practice:* Social Security System is ¼ public spending.

Contraception. *Policy:* Government-supported family planning. Contraceptives are easily available.** *Practice:* Women under age 45 in union using contraception (England and Wales only, 1976): 77%; methods used (Great Britain, 1976) pill 36%, condom 23%, male sterilization 11%, female sterilization 10%, IUD 9%, withdrawal 6%, diaphragm 3%, rhythm 1%; using inefficient methods 7%. In Dec. 1979 there were 1743 family-planning centers dispensing contraceptives in England for National Health Service patients. The visit and "diagnosis" are for a small fee or are free; there is no fee for the contraceptives themselves, as with other prescription items. In Apr. 1981 it was estimated that women in Great Britain were being sterilized at a rate of as many as 54,000 a yr. Half of all sterilizatio..s are conducted at childbirth or during abortions, sometimes without the women's consent. **Abortion.** *Policy:* Legal in England, Scotland, and Wales (Abortion Act, 1967) if 2 doctors certify a physical or mental risk to the woman or to her "existing" children, or if there is a risk of severe fetal abnormality. Abortions are performed in National Health Service hospitals or approved private premises; doctors can refuse participation on "moral" grounds. *Practice:* Abortions in England and Wales (per 1000 resident women age 15–44, 1981): 12.6; approx. 21% of all abortions were performed on nonresidents in 1981. **Illegitimacy.** *Policy:* In English law, the inheritance rights of out-of-wedlock children were improved by the Family Law Reform Act (1969) but still are unequal to those of children born in wedlock. The father has no duty to maintain the child, but the court may order maintenance until the child is age 16, and the 1966 Social Security Act extended the liability of 1 spouse to maintain the other as well as "their children" to include out-of-wedlock children. In Scots law, comparable legislation has somewhat improved the status of out-of-wedlock children. A proposed bill would allow men to "legitimize" their children by establishing paternity, and would give such fathers child-custody and visitation rights. *Practice:* In 1979 almost 1 out of 9 children was born out of

wedlock. Out-of-wedlock children are still discriminated against under both English and Scots laws in the areas of custody, inheritance, child support, and guardianship. **Homosexuality.** *Policy:* The 1967 Amendment to the Sexual Offences Act legalized homosexuality between 2 consenting male adults over age 21. The statute names male homosexuality only, not lesbianism. *Practice:* No statistics obtainable. There are numerous lesbian and male-homosexual support groups, clubs, and hot-lines. A 1980 landmark Court of Appeals decision in England awarded child custody to a lesbian mother. Harassment reportedly is common; from 1978 to 1982, there were several cases of homosexual women and men being discharged from the military.

Incest. *Policy:* Sexual Offences Act (1956) makes intercourse with one's sister, daughter, or granddaughter illegal; punishable by life imprisonment if victim is under age 13 or 7 yrs. imprisonment if victim is older. *Practice:* No statistics obtainable. Feminist groups have taken up the issue. **Sexual Harassment.** *Policy:* Sex Discrimination Act (1975) makes employment discrimination on the basis of sex illegal. No legislation specific to sexual harassment. *Practice:* Sexual harassment usually goes unpunished. A 1982 survey revealed that more than 1 out of 10 women polled experienced sexual harassment at their jobs (the percentages among women age 25–34, and divorced women, were even higher). Some trade unions issue pamphlets on how to deal with the problem. **Rape.** *Policy:* Illegal; rape is punishable by a maximum sentence of life imprisonment, attempted rape by a maximum 7-yr. sentence. A 1976 statute defined rape as "unlawful sexual intercourse with a woman who at the time of intercourse does not consent to it"; jury must decide whether the rapist had grounds to believe the woman had consented and penetration must be proven. Marital rape, sexual assault without intercourse, and anal rape are not legally recognized as rape. *Practice:* London police records show 1 rape reported every 30 hours in 1978. In Dec. 1982, a Crown Court judge's sentence of 12

** See IRELAND(S), p. 340–53.

months imprisonment with 8 months suspended sentence for a man convicted of raping a 6-yr.-old girl resulted in public outcry for more stringent sentences in actual practice. Feminist groups have been active in confronting issues of sexual violence, organizing Take Back the Night marches, establishing refuges, etc. (see following article). **Battery.** *Policy:* The Domestic Violence and Matrimonial Proceedings Act (1976) allows a judge to order the arrest of an abusive husband and require him to stay away from his wife's home; the husband must be brought to court within 24 hours of his arrest and cannot be released without a court order. *Practice:* No statistics obtainable, but battery is a common problem. Feminists have been organizing on this issue, and established some of the first refuges for battery victims in the world (see **Crisis Centers).**

Prostitution. *Policy:* It is illegal to procure a woman for prostitution (2 witnesses needed), to live off the earnings of prostitution, to detain a woman in a brothel against her will, or to own or lease a building as a brothel.

Practice: No statistics obtainable. Prostitutes are arrested for loitering or soliciting, jailed for short periods, and fined. Prostitutes in England have been organizing since the mid-1970's for control of their business and for legal protection (see HERSTORY), as they are frequently beaten and raped and have no legal recourse. **Traditional/Cultural Practices.** *Policy:* No data obtainable. *Practice:* Gratuitous over-prescription of tranquilizers for women. No further data obtainable. **Crisis Centers.** *Policy:* No data obtainable. *Practice:* There are over 200 branches of Women's Aid, feminist refuges for battered women, in England; there are rape-crisis centers and hot-lines in London and most urban centers.

HERSTORY. The British Isles have a long record of women leaders, rulers, intellectuals, and artists. Camilla was queen of Latium in the 13th century B.C.E. Queen Eire and Queen Scota (for whom Ireland and Scotland are named, respectively) were pre-Romanic warrior queens. As early as the 5th century B.C.E., Herodotus wrote respectfully of the Celtic queen Tomyris who slew the Persian king Cyrus the Great in battle. In the 3rd century B.C.E., Martia Proba, a Celtic queen, ruled in Britain and devised the basics of what was to become British common law. Julius Caesar noted that the Celts were most formidable because of their fierce female generals. The warrior queen Boadicea (died 60 C.E.) led an uprising in which 70,000 Romans were slain. Cartimandua, ruler of the Brigantes, also rose up against the Romans, and it was not until 71 C.E. that the Brigantes finally were subdued.

(St.) Hilda (614–80 C.E.) was thought "the most learned woman in all Europe," and founded Whitby Abbey, a double house for nuns and monks, and a center of scholarship. Bridget (5th century) was so legendary for her erudition that she became a quasi-religious figure, merging in the popular concept with the Celtic goddess of the same name (see MYTHOGRAPHY) and, later, with St. Bridget (also see IRELAND[S]). In 853 an Englishwoman named Joan, who had risen through Roman Catholic Church ranks disguised as a man, was elected Pope by her colleague cardinals in Rome. She sat on the papal throne for 2 years, 4 months, and 8 days, when she was discovered to be a woman and was stoned to death.

The "Old Religion" of the British Isles, one of goddess worship in various forms, persisted underground throughout the consolidation of Christianity. So strong and widespread was this resistance that hundreds of persons, usually female, were accused, tried, and sometimes executed for witchcraft—the first such formal accusation is thought to have been made in 1209, the last such execution in 1682. Yet fewer people were persecuted for being witches in the British Isles than in any other European country during what has been called "the Burning Time" (see MYTHOGRAPHY; also see, for example, GERMANY, ITALY, and SPAIN).

In the 10th century, the Anglo-Saxon queen Aethelflaed of Mercia (reigned 911–918) successfully fought off the Danes. Britain in the 12th century was dominated by the figure of Eleanor of Aquitaine (1122?–1204), duchess in her own right of the richest province in France and former Queen of France, who married Henry II (son of the regnant Queen Matilda) and co-founded the Plantagenet line. During her earlier marriage to Louis VII of France, she had led a battalion of women garbed as Amazons to the 2nd Crusade. After surviving years of imprisonment by Henry for her periodic rebellions, she endured to govern outright or to influence throughout the reigns of her sons Richard I and John; a literary patron, she brought the concept of courtly love (see FRANCE) to Britain. In the 14th century, "Good Queen Philippa" of Hainault became Edward III's English queen; she founded the wool industry at Norwich and made innovations in social welfare. Philippa founded Queen's College, Oxford, and was a major patron of the arts—influencing Philippa Roet, who married Geoffrey Chaucer and is said to have collaborated with him in the writing of *The Canterbury Tales.* Juliana of Norwich (c. 1343–c. 1416) was revered for her mystical writings.

The 6 queens of Henry VIII included women of intellect and courage. Katharine of Aragon was a theologian, Anne Boleyn a musician, Anne of Cleves a respected diplomat, and Catherine Parr a leading intellectual and religious reformer of her day. Lady Jane Grey, briefly queen before the ascension of Mary I, was a brilliant scholar and an expert in Greek, as were the writer Lady Mary Sidney (sister of the poet Sir Phillip Sidney), and Margaret Roper, the daughter of Sir Thomas More. Elizabeth I, herself a poet, intellectual, and musician, has been called one of the greatest political geniuses of all time. Her liberal religious policies and audacious diplomatic and military ones, together with her stabilization of trade and domestic economy, poverty-curbing "Poor Laws," and labor and judicial reforms, brought about England's greatest age. Mary, Queen of Scots, executed for fostering repeated Roman Catholic uprisings, was also a woman of learning, despite her apparent

vulnerability to manipulation by individual men and various foreign powers.

Emilia Bassano, a musician thought to be the Dark Lady of Shakespeare's *Sonnets,* was herself a sonneteer. Katherine Fowler Philips, "the matchless Orinda" (1631–64), was at the center of the group of writers who produced the great body of 17th-century English literature. Aphra Behn (1640–89), known as the first English professional woman writer, worked as a British spy in the Dutch Wars. Under Queen Anne (reigned 1702–14) the 1707 Act of Union merged the kingdoms of England and Scotland. Lady Mary Wortley Montague (1689–1762) was an author and crusading feminist. Mary Astell wrote *Reflections on Marriage* in 1706. In 1792 Mary Wollstonecraft published *Vindication of the Rights of Women,* and 2 years later gave birth to a daughter, also Mary, who wrote the novel *Frankenstein* and married the poet Shelley. The feminist literary tradition persisted into the 19th century—with Emily, Anne, and Charlotte Brontë, Jane Austen, and Mary Ann Evans (George Eliot); Harriet Taylor and her husband John Stuart Mill published *On the Subjection of Women* in 1869.

Queen Victoria, while frequently denouncing feminism, nonetheless left her mark on an entire epoch while presiding over the by then British Empire; she did set a precedent by accepting the use of anesthetics during childbirth—a radical step in a time when it was still thought that women should suffer during labor. Florence Nightingale (1820–1910) created the concept of health nursing as a profession for women.

The 19th-century women's suffrage movement was large and militant. Lydia Baker, Emmeline Pankhurst and her daughters Sylvia, Adela, and Christabel, Constance George Lytton, Keir Hardie, and Emmeline Pethick-Lawrence were among the leaders. From 1893 to 1918 they disrupted Parliament sessions to present their demands, suffering repeated arrests and imprisonment. The first suffragette*** to begin a hunger strike was Wallace Dunlop; others took up the tac-

---

*** "Suffragette" was the name popularly given to—and accepted by—the militant activists in Britain, in differentiation from "suffragist," a more generic name.

tic and the government ordered force-feeding. Women defaced property, bombed men's clubs, and sent snuff and red-pepper letters to politicians; over 1000 suffragists were imprisoned in the long struggle. Early 20th century British feminism had a literary tone, in the writings of Virginia Woolf, Katharine Mansfield, Vita Sackville-West, and other "Bluestocking" intellectuals.

The contemporary wave of the women's movement began in the late 1960's when Hull fishermen's wives and sewing machinists in Dagenham protested women's poor labor conditions. In 1969 the National Joint Action Committee for Equal Rights began, and women demonstrated against the Miss World beauty pageant. In 1971 Erin Pizzey, a housewife, formed Women's Aid, the first battered-women's shelter in the UK. The Oxford Conference (1971) gave birth to local chapters focusing on such issues as rape, battery, prostitution, and improved labor laws. In 1973 the Isle of Man, birthplace of E. Pankhurst, was selected as the site of the first World Festival of the Women's Liberation Movement. The Women's Aid Federation (an expansion of the early Erin Pizzey group) was formed in 1975. In 1976 the Working Women's Charter Campaign won support for equal pay, with 10,000 women taking part in a women's support march. Trade unions called for massive demonstrations to protest MP John Corrie's proposed antiabortion bill in 1979, and the Asian Women's Movement (AWAZ) protested immigration tests. On Mar. 8 in both 1979 and 1980, English feminists held demonstrations in solidarity with the vigils outside the Armagh jail in Northern Ireland, where Irish women political prisoners were being held (see IRELAND[S]). In June 1981, the English Collective of Prostitutes together with Sheffield feminists demonstrated during the trial of "Yorkshire Ripper" Suttcliffe, who killed 13 women (see following article). In May 1982, nurses struck for better wages; on Dec. 11, 20,000 women formed a 9-mile human chain around the Greenham Common military base to protest the planned deployment of Cruise and Pershing missiles. Current feminist activism is diverse and persistent (see following article).

MYTHOGRAPHY. The British Isles have a legacy rich with legends of supernatural female figures. The Celts worshipped Danu (or Tana, sometimes called Tabiti), an ancient Mother Goddess (see USSR: MYTHOGRAPHY). Other Great Goddess personifications were the Welsh Cerridwen and the Irish Brigid; less numinous but powerful supernatural figures included the faerie queen–sorceress Morgan Le Fay, Queen Maeve, Diedre, Eathne, Oestre, and Guinevere, among many others. The word "witch" has its etymological origins in Anglo-Saxon *wicce;* the *Wicce,* or Wise Ones, were the remnants of goddess-followers who practiced midwifery and herbal medicine from pre-Roman times through the Middle Ages. Practicing Wicceans still exist today in Britain, reviving great festivals on sites considered holy since pre-history.

BRITAIN: The Politics of Survival—While the Work Goes On
by Amanda Sebestyen

Three years have gone by since I wrote what is now Part One of this piece. I've resisted the temptation to alter anything in that section; by cleaning up my past I'd lose the chance for all of us to learn from it. So I won't disown a single high-strung word, nor the particularly paranoid moment of British history when those words were written. War was in the air, and perhaps we feminists felt as immobilized as anyone, faced with that threat.

And yet we moved! And I'm so pleased to have the chance to say what we've gained since then. You'll have to wait until Part Two for that, however. Meanwhile, here's my original report.

Part One

In one of the earliest issues of our first women's liberation paper *Shrew* ("Cost, sixpence to women, a shilling to men, till we get equal pay"), a feminist from Spain wrote: "Whenever I have tried to talk politics with an English person, I have bored her or him. In the country I come from this situation is quite unthinkable."

Marilyn French's *The Bleeding Heart* gives the same view from the other side of the Atlantic. In this scene, Englishwoman Mary is telling American Dolores about her marriage—how her husband, a successful academic, beat her almost to death, turned her friends against her, and took her children away:

> She told her tale calmly, often smiling, her face impassive when she told the worst parts.
> And there were lots of worst parts.
> Finally Dolores burst out: "How can you sit there smiling?"
> She was enraged, she wanted to break crockery, or a head; she wanted to leap up, to *do* something, *something!*
> "It doesn't do to get angry in this country. People hold it against you."

Imagine a small country facing imminent war (apart from the one in Ireland that's going on already), with mass unemployment following on ten years of inflation and the wreck of the social services; where street riots are becoming expectable, and the fire-bombing of black families is too routine to even rate a mention—where *it doesn't do to get angry.*

"Oh well, mustn't grumble" carries the force of law. Anyone who disobeys deserves rubber truncheons, plastic bullets—or more usually a cold, blank stare.

English patriarchy has a hooded face: fewer street rapes, more wife-beating behind locked doors. Less abuse, more dismissal. Which brings us of course to women's libbers. Shrill and humorless. Unappealing, forbidding. Dungareed and bovver-booted. Silly cows. *Angry.*

Also isolated. Imagine again: the whole ex-imperial shambles apparently headed by two women, the Queen and the Prime Minister. Then imagine the nature of the Left opposition: a radical play is entitled *Ditch the Bitch*, a *Socialist Worker* headline goes one better with "Ditch the Witch." Imagine football crowds of many hundreds of thousands cheering the Yorkshire Ripper with his score of thirteen women dead . . .

One Week in Leeds, Yorkshire

14 November 1980: Douglas Cole up at Leeds Crown Court; *charge:* manslaughter of wife, Ethel; *mitigation:* she nagged and was neurotic; *sentence:* two years' probation and psychiatric treatment.

17 November 1980: Charlene and Annette Maw up at Leeds Crown Court; *charge:* manslaughter of father; *mitigation:* he was drunken, violent, battered them and their mother all their lives, tortured and killed family pets, they killed in self-defense; *sentence:* three years' imprisonment.

17 November 1980: Jacqueline Hill leaves a meeting, walks from the bus stop to her student hostel and becomes the thirteenth victim of the Yorkshire Ripper.

Five hundred women came to the Sexual Violence Conference. We decided action be taken around 12 December in the name of Angry Women. All over Britain, sex and porn shops were picketed, cinema queues leafleted, public meetings planned, self-defense groups started. Women have given interviews and written articles for local and national press, appeared on television and radio, and taken direct action against media lies. Postering and spray-painting have transformed the face of British cities. In Leeds, direct action has included: gluing up sex-shop door-locks, disrupting sadistic woman-hating films by throwing paint and oil at the screens, smashing windows of strip-clubs, removing about £400-worth of porn from an ordinary bookshop, and sending the resulting ashes out with press releases locally and nationally.

—Some Women in Leeds, *Spare Rib*
February 1980

Reading about all this magnificent public action, it would be hard to guess that for much of the last ten years our movement has conducted itself with truly British reticence. The mass marches of women in Italy, the United States, and Ireland never happened here. Our strengths have been barely visible, networks of small groups burrowing deep. Like the numberless women squatters, leaving men or parents (or just isolation) behind to occupy and rebuild deserted houses and build communities in the inner cities. Or like the houses of refuge for battered women, which began in England and have spread over Europe and North America. They now cover the British Isles, in small towns as well as large cities, with autonomous federations for Wales, Scotland, Northern Ireland, and England. They are currently enduring the sudden cut-off of local government grants gained with such effort over the years; they are finding new ways to raise money; they will survive.

The quiet approach has had its weaknesses as well. The movement here has spent too many years apologizing for itself and seeking a niche in the male-dominated socialist movement. Early British feminist writing exhausted its theoretical energy attributing all sexism to capitalism, stressing that men were Not the Enemy, and waving away the twin specters of "bourgeois" women's rights and sexual separatism. By the mid-1970's many socialist feminists were reacting to the structurelessness of small women's groups by joining the mixed Leninist organizations that women's liberationists all over the world had rejected. Suddenly civil rights were O K and *campaigns* were the thing—anything with a familiar structure of resolutions to be argued through trade-union branches or with recommendations to be maneuvered into law. As these initiatives petered out, the tendency was to turn inward: to therapy, to refinements of linguistic and psychoanalytic theory, to religion, even back to the family and motherhood. For radical feminists, the temptation was to create a small separate world with its own special code of dress and manners: women's discos, poetry, motorcycle maintenance, and matriarchy. Sometimes it felt like decorating the walls of a ghetto.

By 1977 the movement has such a low profile that even the word "liberation" was being dropped. Then, from several directions and for a number of reasons, came revival. Consciousness-raising groups started gaining on academic study groups; the National Abortion Campaign's patient petitioning and lobbying gave way to a women's takeover of the Roman Catholic Westminster Cathedral; a new grouping calling itself Revolutionary Feminists emerged to counter "the liberal takeover of the Women's Liberation Movement" and to start direct action against male violence; black and working-class feminists started challenging the quiet elitism that had grown in our language and organizations.

We are still in ferment, but some of the new priorities for struggle have emerged clearly: rape, pornography, compulsory heterosexuality, racism, and imperialism. I admire the new militancy, but am worried by the new orthodoxies that so quickly have taken shape alongside. Perhaps a revivalist movement must always be more orthodox than the original. The "new" anti-imperialism certainly seems to hark back to Mao and Trotsky—and once again to discredit the sexual politics of women, especially white women. While the "new" Revolutionary Feminism goes back to selected quotes from the radical writing I personally most admire—Shulamith Firestone, the original US Red-stockings, the pioneers of women's-liberation theory—it's nonetheless depressing to see those fiery words dwindle into cliché. Instead of the German-Latin of Marxist jargon or "Franglish" Althusserianism, we now have a string of 1960's Americanisms: "house nigger," "piece of ass"—phrases equally far from the words we ourselves would normally use.

When times get bad, people turn to a hard line because it seems to offer protection. As Britain gets poorer and more violent and its future more frightening, I get the feeling that feminists are starting to go for conformity and get a thrill from "leadership." Rhetoric becomes harder. Dialogue becomes harder, too. Most of the feminists I respect are ceasing to write; many have even stopped reading the movement's journals and newsletters.

Internal debate is restricted by a series of compulsory ordinances. You Must Be Angry. You Must Not Speak About Sexual Pleasure. You Must Not Speak About Living with Men. You Must Not Speak to a Transsexual. Women Must Not Look After Boy Children. Men Must Not Look After Girl Children. The kernel of truth in any of these statements has shriveled away under a thick crust of totalitarianism. Sometimes, too, there are unexplained and absolute changes of line: at one time, Sexual Choice Is Irrelevant; then, suddenly, Every Woman Must Be a Lesbian. At one moment, Making Demands on Men is a Waste of Time; then, suddenly, We Must All Make Demands on Men (as Loudly as Possible) . . .

All this has happened before, of course. As we enter a new cold war, I find myself superstitiously turning to writing from that earlier time, muttering as I add little bits of my own in brackets to passages like this:

A modern [feminist] intellectual lives and writes in constant dread—not, indeed, of public opinion in the wider sense, but of public opinion within [her] own group. As a rule, luckily, there is more than one group, but also at any given moment there is a dominant orthodoxy, to offend against which needs a thick skin. . . . As soon as certain topics are raised, the concrete melts into the abstract and no one seems able to think of turns of speech that are not hackneyed . . . Political writing in our time consists almost entirely of prefabricated phrases bolted together like the pieces of a child's Meccano set. It is the unavoidable result of self-censorship.

—George Orwell, *Writers and
Leviathan, Politics and the
English Language, The Prevention
of Literature*

Yes, yes, yes. Oh, the burned-over districts of inner-city theoretical debate have such an endless fascination even when things are going wrong!

But one thing I know.

The *work* of the movement goes on. That is the important thing. When I get off the duplicator belt and look around, I can see how we're growing. Last year there were half a dozen rape-crisis help-lines, this year the list would cover a page. Small initiatives continue to flourish: The Women's Tape-Over, recording feminist writing for blind sisters, is one of the latest. At the same time, we are learning to think bigger and bolder—one group has just put in for a grant of half a million pounds for Safe Women's Transport, a nighttime bus and car network for all of us out after dark; the group backed up their fundraising with an appeal on television. A few years ago this simply wouldn't have happened.

Looking toward the future, Women Oppose the Nuclear Threat are saying W O N T to the ultimate male violence. And Women for Life on Earth last summer walked a hundred and twenty-five miles to camp outside the U S airbase in Greenham Common. These women are friendly, they have children, the local people feed them during their sit-in, the media are prepared to listen (at the moment). *But most important, the women will not go away* until the Cruise missiles threatening Europe with extinction are scrapped. They face the winter in tents: "We'll show we can endure."

It will be hard for us all to win, different as we are. There's a poem by a feminist named Janet Dubé which describes the many ways I feel about the movement better than I can myself:

the joy
that gets lost
in the struggle

that is hidden
in the saying

that no one understands
except ourselves;

the joy
because we choose
because we have chosen
to struggle:

the struggle

something is winning
even while we are losing

the witches were winning
even while they were burned

our mothers were winning
while they worked endured and died:

the poet was winning
even while she put her head
in the oven.

even we are winning
we feel it in the joy;

all this struggle
so that something
may win that was winning
all along. a woman's

right to choose.
women's right to choose.
a woman's right to choose.

all this.[1]

[1] From a poem by Janet Dubé, first published in *Housewife's Choice* (Abernawmor, Pencader, Dyfed, Wales: Mustardseeds, n.d.). Excerpted with permission.

Part Two

It is fitting that the poem I chose to console me in a burned-out moment was written by a supporter of the first Greenham Common marchers. The small, stubborn peace camp they started grew within one year to an immense gathering of women, which encircled the entire nuclear base three times over and left as a lasting protest thousands of pictures, textiles, personal treasures, slogans, poems, and children's toys literally woven into the miles of barbed-wire fence. Last Hallowe'en another two thousand women mobilized secretly by word of mouth, arrived with cutters, and astonished the police and the army by downing the fence all over the place and cheerfully walking in. There's an ongoing opera of Ministerial panic, Parliamentary uproar, "shoot-to-kill" scares, versus spectacular and hilarious acts by disorderly females: like occupying the control tower, or accidentally picking out to paint a prize U S spy plane (the Blackbird, only two in the world, unique anti-radar coating . . . one can of paint equals a quarter of a million pounds' worth of damage). In the background, the endless courage of women filling the jails, resisting repeated evictions, surviving our cold winters under the plastic-covered branches that are now the only shelters allowed to stand.

The relation of your actual Women's Liberation Movement to all this has been problematical. Like the Women's Aid Movement before it, the Women's Peace Movement has run parallel with smaller groups of long-term feminists. Some participate ardently. Others are critical: "The protest is the traditional voice of the poor woman left at home who can only use emotional appeals (on *others'* behalf) to influence those who do have power. . . . It goes along with some biological notion that we inherit our behavior with our genitals or that we are protectors of life because we bear children." [2] Yet others, feminists from within the peace movement, fear the Greenham camp may have become too separatist to get local support or mobilize enough bodies to cope with the new situation of airlifted missiles. One thing seems clear: Greenham Common has been an opening for many *thousands* of women, from very different classes and ages, who never went near our movement before. Never again can I say that mass women's actions don't happen here!

The old rocky face of established British culture does actually seem to be softening, too. It's true that the archaic behavior of the native male still has the power to amaze visitors, and sexual politics often continue to be viewed as an automatic joke. But while this country changes slowly, its changes tend to *last*. Women's art, for instance, gathering momentum after a decade and more of lonely persistence, now sends flowing into the galleries works of astonishing verve and quality, from richly textured mythological canvases to cool linguistic critiques. I'd take seriously, too, the phenomenon of women militants in the churches—suppressed deaconnesses claiming their rights, overflow audiences for the lectures of female theologians, even a radical feminist rabbi— all of which counterpoints the network of covens witching away at their psychic healing, and the researchers whose work on past matriarchies is a most fascinating growth area in scholarship. Women's Studies in general have taken a decade to get off the ground, but are now hopping with their own celebrities, new magazines, and a range of books from all the main publishers—sheer numbers meaning a far wider range than the rather cloistered Marxist-academic audience of earlier years.

And now we have a feminist best-seller of our very own! Zoe Fairbairns' historical saga *Stand We At Last* spans the suffragette movement and contemporary Women's Liberation; the novel takes in the pernicious Contagious Diseases Act which allowed suspect prostitutes to be arrested without trial and subjected to what Victorian feminists

---

[2] From an article by Lynn Alderson published in *Breaching the Peace* (London: Onlywomen Press). Excerpted with permission.

justly described (and the novel frighteningly conveys) as "instrumental rape." Strong stuff for a Top Ten paperback.

Then there was the 1984 Feminist Book Fair, which astonished even its organizers, who dreamed (and we allowed ourselves BIG dreams) of a Fair that would not only affect Britain but would achieve worldwide attention. Exhibition Hall, Town Halls, theaters, libraries—they were all packed to bursting. Writers, publishers, and readers came from every continent, and from almost as many countries as are represented in *Sisterhood Is Global*. Guest speakers visited forty-two towns all over Britain and Ireland. The largest stationery chain held a national promotion, so women's books were publicized up and down the country. (It does sometime seem as if we read more about feminism than we talk! There's been no national Women's Liberation conference since 1978; and while my heroines from abroad flew in to speak at Paris, Sydney, or Auckland, somehow we didn't manage those international exchanges in London.) I still find it surprising that in the midst of financial crisis it turned out to be a *commercial* venture that created such a great coming together. What an irony, too, when feminism provides a boom for publishing, that archetypal gentleman's profession! Still, a high score for the Fair's first aim: to put feminism "squarely and firmly in the mainstream market place, into the educational curriculum, and on library shelves." The second, the organizers continued in their catalogue, "was to move the spotlight of attention from Europe and North America, to search out and draw in feminists from around the world, particularly in the developing countries."

A sign of the times. The last three years have seen intense debate over race and imperialism. At first these seemed subjects almost nobody could talk or write about with honesty (the kind of hack language I grumble about in Part One of this report has laid waste to the pages of most feminist journals at some time or other). But now some corner has been turned, and suddenly there are: many more black and Third World women in every part of the women's movement; many more varieties of lively personal writing; many more projects, performances, papers, and books by and for black women themselves. Some similar deliverance may be at hand from the confrontation between Palestine and Israel, a confrontation that's been dividing our movement, and one which has carried particular upset for me, as the child of a middle-European Jewish father and a gentile mother. Gassable on the one side, excluded by Israel's racial Law of Return on the other, I felt equal fear for a fairly evident British anti-semitism *and* for Zionist nationalism. (Zionism perhaps I feared as a counterpart to my own past separatism, now rejected: e.g., were we cornering ourselves into a *female* nationalism, with its own siege mentality, its own internal elites, its own belief that the road to liberation lay over the face of the enemy?) There's been change here, too. A great blossoming of Jewish feminist writing (books, pamphlets, a journal), and delayed justice to the Palestinian cause in *Spare Rib* magazine, which had formerly excluded it. *Spare Rib* is opening out just now; so I live in hope that the pages will next include Jewish Feminist groups' responses, and slogans will be replaced by that exchange of experience which for me lies at the heart of feminism.

Still more news. Sisters Against Disablement are now an active network, fighting for the rights of disabled women. Incest survivors have emerged among the most militant against pornography and rape. A majority of the National Abortion Campaign have moved on from single-issue organizing to found the Women's Reproductive Rights Campaign and work on such issues as infertility, *in vitro* fertilization, and post-abortion workshops, as well as on contraception, abortion, and forced sterilization. Denise Flowers took up a one-woman campaign for Free Sanitary Protection (an end to value-added tax on tampons or sanitary towels), and gathered 110,000 signatures for its petition to Parliament. My own favorite tendency, the radical feminists—less strong in numbers here than the socialist, revolutionary, or cultural feminists (though *not*, I maintain, in clarity, insight, or wit)—have put on a spurt of influence with the new quarterly *Trouble and Strife*, to join that lively irregular periodical *Catcall*.

Another new (and highly unusual) thing is happening. Feminists are temporarily getting access to money. The Greater London Council, that little "red republic" scheduled for demolition by an increasingly embarrassed and unpopular government, has been the fairy godperson. Other Labour Party councils in Sheffield, Liverpool, Leeds, and Bristol have followed with women's committees and training workshops, often funded by the Common Market. Socialist feminists are now at work in the belly of London's County Hall, and I've a feeling that a layer of trained progressive women administrators will survive, as they did the fall of Australia's Labor government, to become a lasting presence in national life. The GLC has so far funded 140 childcare projects, laundries on council housing estates, campaigns around low pay, homeworking and benefit claims, training courses, and free cancer screening for the Council's employees. Every job plan and every project applying for funds has to take in the implications for women and the care of children and dependents. The Council also is using its purchasing power—£700 million a year on 20,000 companies—to insist those companies meet equal opportunity requirements for all women, ethnic minorities, and gays. The influence of a Women's Liberation organizing approach comes out in the stated ideal of popular planning: not bestowing a blueprint from above, but trying to give local people money *for their own choices*.

The effects inside the movement itself have been odd. Lots of properly paid workers and comfortable premises certainly make a nice change for those groups who do go for Council funding. Nonetheless, many feminists prefer to do without. They notice "Save the GLC" stickers and the petitions all over the funded offices, and suspect a *quid pro quo* of lining up with the Labour Party; they see a gap between the new paid workers and the volunteers; and they fear more energy going into grant applications or conditions of work, away from the purposes of the projects themselves. But the research done and the networks created will always be useful, and if nothing else, life in the Labour-governed cities has become a lot more fun. Festivals and performances of all kinds create a culture that resists the depression.

I'd liked to finish with just one occasion, one of those gifts the movement so beautifully makes when you're not really looking. A hot June evening, a crammed Sisterwrite bookshop, a reading of black women's poetry: the quality of the writing, the power and style of the readers, the listeners' sharp attention, the sisterhood inspired by Fatima-Zarah Salah from Morocco speaking about her own very different movement growing by unexpected leaps and bounds, the sense of *focus* for hour after hour ... they were all magnificent. Writing about it now, I notice something: the last fifteen years of my life have been spent in the best possible company! What a piece of luck.

Suggested Further Reading

Burford, Barbara, Grace Nichols, *et al. A Dangerous Knowing*. London: Sheba Feminist Publishers, 1984; poetry by Black British women.

Campling, Jo, ed. *Images of Ourselves*. London: Routledge & Kegan Paul, 1981; women with disabilities speaking out.

Cockburn, Cynthia. *Brothers: Male Dominance and Technological Change in the Print Industry*. London: Pluto Press, 1983; union patriarchs exposed.

Dowrick, Stephanie, and Sibyl Grundberg, eds. *Why Children?* London: The Women's Press, 1980; to have or have not.

Fairbairns, Zoe. *Benefits*. London: Virago, 1979; acute science-fiction picture of its times.

Friedman, Scarlet, and Elizabeth Sarah, eds. *On the Problem of Men*. London: The Women's Press, 1982; conference papers.

Holland, Joy, ed. *Feminist Action*. London: Battleaxe Books-Wildwood House, 1984; wide range of campaigns and tendencies.

Mohin, Lilian, ed. *One Foot on the Mountain*. London: Onlywomen Press, 1979; lesbian feminist poetry anthology.

Owen, Ursula, ed. *Fathers*. London: Virago, 1982; some well-known British feminist daughters.

Rowbotham, Sheila. *Hidden from History*. London: Pluto Press, 1973; three hundred years of women's oppression and the fight against it.

The periodicals and pamphlets mentioned may be ordered from Sisterwrite Bookshop, 190 Upper Street, London N1.

Amanda Sebestyen, a longtime activist in this wave of British feminism, writes of herself: "Radical feminist. Born 1946; mother Irish, father Hungarian. A series of schools that didn't fit. Escaped to one of the New Universities of the 1960's—where all my friends were men. Five years later, in 1969, I staggered into the Women's Liberation Movement and have been there ever since. Some of the groups that I've learned from: celibacy, factory working, squatting, feminist theory, and HOWL (History of Women's Liberation). I've also written: for conferences, for the first English radical feminist collection (*Thoughts on Feminism*, 1972), for the movement magazines *Shrew*, *Catcall*, and *Spare Rib*, where I worked for three years. In 1977 I helped organize a conference and write a controversial pamphlet, 'Feminist Practice.' More recently I've co-edited an anthology covering the last five years of the British movement (*No Turning Back*, published by the Women's Press, 1981). And one day I'd like to write a full-length history of British Women's Liberation. But not yet.

P.S.: I've since spent a year going round the world, landing up in Sydney. Now back in London, I write reviews for *City Limits* magazine. I still haven't written that history; but in the summer of 1984 a new Women's Liberation Oral History conference created an impressive exhibition, and brought together movement 'oldies' for a weekend of taping our early experiences. An idea (and hopefully a future book) whose time has come!"

CANADA

A North American country covering most of the northern part of the continent, bordered by the continental United States and Alaska to the south and west, by numerous seas, bays, and straits extending from the Pacific and Atlantic Oceans to the west and east, respectively, and by the Arctic Ocean to the north. **Area:** 9,976,139 sq. km. (3,851,809 sq. mi.). **Population** (1982): 24,625,000, female 52%. **Capital:** Ottawa. **Titular Head of State:** Queen Elizabeth II.

DEMOGRAPHY. Languages: English, French, indigenous. **Races or Ethnic Groups:** European (French and English) descent, Native Indian and Inuit, Caribbean, East Indian, Pakistani, Japanese; Toronto's pop. is 51% recent immigrants. **Religions:** Roman Catholicism, United Church of Canada, Anglican. **Education** (% enrolled in school, 1975): Age 6–11—of all girls 100%, of all boys 100%; age 12–17—of all girls 90%, of all boys 89%; higher education—in 1980–81 women comprised 46% of fulltime university students, 60% of part-time university students, 36% of fulltime and 39% of part-time graduate students, 51% of fulltime community college students, 97% of nursing, 54% of art, 38% of science, 16% of education, 11% of business administration, and were 30.8% of students in adult education government and industrial training programs. **Literacy** (1977): Women 98%, men 98%. However, the 1976 Census reported that 28.4% of all Canadians age 15 and over have completed less than 9th-grade education, and World Literacy Canada found that approx. 28% of the Canadian adult pop. is functionally illiterate (1975–76); 25.5% of women age 15 and over are functionally illiterate, and the rate is higher in rural areas (1976). **Birth Rate** (per 1000 pop., 1977–78): 15. **Death Rate** (per 1000 pop., 1977–78): 7. **Infant Mortality** (per 1000 live births, 1977): Female 13, male 16. **Life Expectancy** (1975–80): Female 77 yrs., male 70 yrs.

GOVERNMENT. A federal union (created by the 1867 British North America Act) of 10 provinces, plus the territories of Yukon and the Northwest. The Act established a government similar to Britain's with a bicameral parliament consisting of a 282-member (elected) House of Commons and a 104-member Senate (appointed for life). A prime minister from the majority party heads the government. A governor-general is the Queen's representative. **Women's Suffrage:** Vote won by Euroamerican women in Alberta, Manitoba, and Saskatchewan (1916), Nova Scotia (1918), New Brunswick and Ontario (1919), British Columbia (1920), Prince Edward Island (1922), Newfoundland (1925), and Quebec (1940). Federal vote won by Euroamerican women over age 21 in all provinces in 1918. In 1949 "universal" suffrage, excluding Native peoples, granted throughout Canada; in 1960 Native Indians (male and female) won the vote. **Equal Rights:** 1977 Canadian Human Rights Act prohibits discrimination in employment on grounds of sex, age, marital status, race, religion; each province has a similar code or ordinance. **Women in Government:** First woman Supreme Court judge (Bertha Wilson) appointed in spring 1982. As of 1983, women constitute 5.7% of Parliament, and the 3 female cabinet ministers are Monique Begin (Minister of Health and Welfare), Judy Erola (Minister Responsible for the Status of Women), and Celine Hervieux-Payette (Minister of State for Youth); Jeanne Sauvé is the first woman governor-general (1984).

ECONOMY. Currency: Canadian Dollar (May 1983: 1.23 = $1 US). **Gross National Product** (1981): $331.3 billion. **Per Capita Income** (1981): $11,520. **Women's Wages as a Percentage of Men's** (1978–79): 66% in clerical and transportation, 50% in sales and service sector. **Equal Pay Policy:** Human Rights Act prohibits discriminatory pay differentials between men and women for work of equal value, but affects public employees only. **Production** (Agricultural/Industrial): Wheat, fish, livestock, dairy; iron, steel, forest products. **Women as a**

Percentage of Labor Force (1981): 40.7%; **of agricultural force** 2.3%; **of industrial force** 27%; **of military** (1979) 5.9%; 2/3 of non-combat classifications open to women; in 1979 a 3–5 yr. trial program of women in near-combat positions was initiated. **(Employed) Women's Occupational Indicators** (1981–83): Of managerial workers 5%, of teachers 57.2%, of clerical workers 75%. **Unemployment** (mid–1982): 10.2%, female 9.95%, male 10.4%.

GYNOGRAPHY. Marriage. *Policy:* All marriage laws are under provincial jurisdiction; minimum age varies between provinces with the factor of parental consent for those under age 18. Under the 1951 Indian Act, Indian women who marry non-Indians legally cease to be Indians; their children are not considered Indian and must forfeit property rights and access to Indian reservations; Indian men bear no such penalty. *Practice:* Female mean age at marriage (1970–78): 22; women age 15–49 in union (1970–78): 66%. From 1970–79 there was a 25% decline in marriages. **Divorce.** *Policy:* Legal under the 1968 Federal Divorce Act; universal-divorce grounds (excluding Quebec) include sodomy, rape, adultery, bestiality, homosexual acts, bigamy, mental or physical cruelty, or "marriage breakdown" (separation due to imprisonment, drug addiction, desertion, or no conjugal relations for 1 yr.). Varying provincial legislation controls alimony, separation, and annulment. Under provincial law, goods bought by each spouse are privately owned. Until 1973 a homemaker's contribution was disregarded in property division; that yr. *Murdoch* vs. *Murdoch* in Alberta brought the problem to public attention. As of 1978, divorcing spouses can divide equally the pension credits accumulated in their Canadian Pension Plan (aiding homemakers in getting pension credit for their contributions). *Practice:* 1 in 3 marriages end in divorce (1981). The average length of marriage is 9 yrs. From 1969 to 1979, 95.7% of the mothers requesting custody received it. **Family.** *Policy:* Maternity leave for employed women is 18 weeks in Quebec, Saskatchewan, and Alberta; Prince Edward Island and the Territories have no maternity leave; in other provinces, leave is 17 weeks. There is no federal requirement for mandatory leave. Childcare provisions vary under provincial jurisdiction. *Practice:* Women in unionized jobs can go on unemployment insurance for maternity leave with no loss of job security or time accrued for seniority; only 25% of Canadian women are in unionized jobs. In 1979, 5.7% of children under age 2 and 12.6% of those 2–6 were enrolled in day care. **Welfare.** *Policy:* Old Age Security Pension (OAS) is a fixed, monthly payment made to every Canadian over 65. A guaranteed income supplement is paid to those over 65 with no income other than OAS. A spouse allowance is paid to a low-income married person whose spouse already receives other pensions, but widows are not eligible. Canadian Pension Plan is "contributory" (deducted from salaries of all employees). *Practice:* System discriminates against women who leave the work force to raise children, and the women's movement is working to have homemakers' contributions go toward homemakers' pensions. Fewer women than men are in private (company) pension plans. Average annual pension for women is $2112, for men $3331; 59.5% of single or widowed women 65 and over live at poverty level (1979).

Contraception. *Policy:* Legal; services vary between provinces. Advertising of contraceptives was illegal until 1969, and a province still can outlaw the packaging or sale (but not the use) of contraceptives. *Practice:* No national statistics obtainable. Methods used (Quebec only, 1976) tubal ligation 27.7%, pill 24.8%, periodic abstinence 9.1%, vasectomy 8.6%, IUD 7.3%, condom 7%, body temperature 4.2%, withdrawal 3.6%, other methods 7.7%. In areas with strong Roman Catholic influence such as Newfoundland, and in rural areas, contraceptives are almost unobtainable. Federal funds to family-planning centers were cut by more than 60% in 1982. **Abortion.** *Policy:* Decriminalized in 1969 to permit abortions in cases where a woman's life or health is endangered. Procedures can be performed only in hospitals by doctors with the approval of a 3-physician committee appointed by the hospital board. *Practice:* Hospital abortions (per 1000 women age 15–44, 1980): 11.5. By 1980 only 3 out of 10 public hospitals had established approval committees, and 19% of those reported no abortions that yr. Most Roman Catholic hospitals, especially in Quebec, refuse to perform abortions. **Illegitimacy.** *Policy:* Ontario (in 1978) and New Brunswick (in 1981) eliminated distinctions between in- and out-of-wedlock children. In other provinces legislation allows for "legitimization" of out-of-wedlock children and guarantees them the right to economic support and to inheritance under a parent's will or intestacy. *Practice:* No statistics obtainable. Out-of-wedlock children are generally accepted, and the number of women who choose to become single mothers is increasing. **Homosexuality.** *Policy:* Legal as of 1969, when the law was changed to permit acts of "gross indecency," which include homosexual practices, between consenting adults over age 21, in private. Law refers to both women and men. *Practice:* There is substantial activism over homosexual rights, and a sizable lesbian-feminist activist presence in the Canadian women's movement.

Incest. *Policy:* Illegal, punishable by 14 yrs. maximum imprisonment. *Practice:* No statistics obtainable. Father-on-daughter rape most prevalent. Incest-survivor groups exist in large cities. **Sexual Harassment.** *Policy:* Human Rights Act had been interpreted to include federal prohibition of sexual harassment. Legislation varies by province. Victims can sue under Criminal Code or file a civil action suit for damages. *Practice:* A 1982 survey of 2500 women by the YWCA Feminist Action Group (Quebec) showed that 64% experienced sexual harassment at work and 70% experienced sexual harassment in general. The Human Rights Commission, on the federal and provincial level, handles complaints based on varied legislation. There is a general 2 1/2-yr. backlog of cases. **Rape.** *Policy:* A Dec. 1982 law changed the definition to one of sexual assault/violence and made marital, anal, and oral rape illegal, as well as forced penetration with a foreign object, amending the previous definition (vaginal penetration by a penis without a

woman's consent); victim's prior sexual conduct is no longer admissible as evidence. The 3 categories are sexual assault (pinching, unwanted fondling, etc.) at a maximum penalty of 10 yrs. imprisonment, sexual assault with a weapon or threats to a third party at a maximum of 14 yrs., and aggravated sexual assault (accompanied by wounding, maiming, etc.) at a maximum life sentence. *Practice:* In 1974, 1827 rapes were reported; 1 in 8 rapes is reported to the police; 1 in every 17 Canadian women is raped, 1 in every 5 sexually assaulted. A rape occurs every 29 minutes, an assault every 6 minutes. In practice, defendants under category 1 (see above) are discharged or given suspended sentences.

Battery. *Policy:* Under federal law a woman may charge her husband with assault, apply for a peace bond, or divorce him on grounds of cruelty. Under provincial laws, women may apply for an injunction if it is accompanied by a petition for divorce or separation, or a short-term court order of protection. *Practice:* Laws offer little protection because of police refusal to arrest husbands, as well as demands of proof and legal delays. Wife-beating is common across race, class, and ethnic lines. In 1978, 9688 women stayed in 47 refuges; 60% were physically battered. An est. 12,000 women requested help from refuges because of battery, while 40,000–50,000 women suffered physical and mental abuse and sought help through refuges or divorce (see **Crisis Centers**). One in 10 women married or living with a man was battered; 8 in 10 women seeking refuge had been beaten while pregnant. **Prostitution.** *Policy:* Not an offense *per se* in the Criminal Code. In 1972 the law (which had applied only to women) was replaced by one applying to anyone "persistently" soliciting in a public place for the purposes of prostitution; pimping and brothel-keeping are illegal under federal law. Transactions in private are legal. Sentences vary under municipal ordinances. *Practice:* No statistics obtainable. Some cities use municipal by-laws relating to loitering, public nuisance, etc., against prostitutes. Women activists have been pressing to make the customer liable for prosecution. **Traditional/Cultural Practices.** *Policy:* No data obtainable.

Practice: Nationally, tranquilizers are prescribed to twice as many women as men, increasing with age. A health study found that 23.7% of all hysterectomies performed in Saskatchewan from 1970 to 1975 were unnecessary (the number has since declined). In Quebec, 63.8% of all electroshock treatments were administered to women age 25–55 (1976). Feminists have been organizing on behalf of victims of DES (diethylstilbestrol). **Crisis Centers.** *Policy:* Funding is available from provincial and local welfare funds, federal grants, and private donations. *Practice:* In 1972 the first transition houses opened in British Columbia and Alberta to house battered women. There are 71 transition houses or hostels in the 10 provinces, 2/3 of them in Ontario and Quebec; as of 1980, 12 more were planned. There are 35 rape-crisis centers in Canada, supported by various sources.

HERSTORY. The indigenous peoples of the country included a wide range of Native American tribes and nations. A Euroamerican record began with 16th-century conquest and settlement. A women's movement emerged in the 1870's in Ontario as an effort to open educational opportunities. The Women's Christian Temperance Movement was a key element. Dr. Emily Howard Stowe, the first female doctor in Canada, began the Toronto Literary Club, which focused on suffrage. Nellie McClung, Judge Emily Murphy, and Agnes MacPhail were leaders in the growing women's suffrage movement. A major event in the early women's movement was the so-called Person's Case of 1928. Five women—Judge Emily Murphy, Nellie McClung, Irene Parlby, Louise McKinney, and Henrietta Muir Edwards—petitioned the governor-general for a judicial interpretation of the word "persons" which appeared in a statute referring to Senate appointments. The court found that "persons" did not include women. A year later, these women brought the issue before the Privy Council, which reversed the previous ruling.

In 1945 Quebec women, under the leadership of Mme. Casgrain, forced the federal government to pay the new family allowance directly to them instead of their husbands. The Royal Commission on the Status of Women was established in 1967 to ensure equal opportunities; its 1970 report was an important tool for the women's movement, but in 1979 an update reported that only 1/3 of the recommendations had been fully implemented. Native Indian and Inuit women have been extremely active in movements to reclaim tribal lands. Organizing separately from the men, they have fought to improve health and educational opportunities for their people and to preserve their cultural heritage. Women united to force the government to include women's and Native people's rights in the new (1982) Constitution, but the "notwithstanding" clause may permit provincial governments to abrogate these hard-won gains.

MYTHOGRAPHY. Among the Inuit (Eskimo), the Three Kadlu Sisters are said to cause thunder and lightning by rubbing their bodies together. Sedna is the goddess of the dead and sovereign of the ocean. Among the Athabascan peoples of the northwest, there is the legend of Asintmah, the first woman, who helped Mother Earth create the world. They also tell of Changing Woman, who tends the cycles of life. Other indigenous peoples tell of Tsonoquah (or Dash-Kayah, or At'at'lia), who is the personification of beauty and of sometimes terrifying power.

CANADA: The Empowerment of Women
by *Greta Hofmann Nemiroff*[1]

Introduction

Canada is a vast and variegated country, rich in natural resources and in regional and individual disparities. We are one of the "democratic nations," run by a patriarchy (with the token inclusion of a few select women) which represents the interests of a limited number of men. Women in Canada are poor and underrepresented, our issues often rendered invisible by the State and the communications media. We are a fragmented group with differing languages and cultural heritages, issues and regional priorities: Native Indian and Inuit women, immigrant women, oriental, and black women bear the double burden of sexism and racism; French-speaking Canadian women are often torn between the causes of French nationalism and feminism; lesbian women face the special discrimination of homophobia. All of us, though, face the issue of sexism. There are both women's groups and feminist groups in Canada, and often their stated ideologies differ. However, all these groups address women's issues and often join forces in the ongoing struggle for women's rights. Because of the size of the country, it is costly for women to travel and meet together. Our groups, both locally and nationally, often keep afloat on meager funds and in isolation, sometimes duplicating efforts which are expensive in both human and material costs.

Women's Situation

Women and Work

Canada is undergoing an economic crisis; there is massive unemployment. Half of all women are in the paid labor force, and they are found disproportionately in minimum-wage and part-time jobs. The latter means that they are less likely to be eligible for sick pay, paid vacation, pension and unemployment benefits, or job security—the rights enjoyed by most fulltime workers. Although their participation rate in the labor force has

[1] In undertaking this article, I became aware of the many lacunae in my knowledge of my own country. For this reason, I solicited and received information from over fifty feminists throughout Canada. Through interviews and written exchange, they made inestimable contributions to my knowledge and this project. I thank them all for their generosity of spirit and time and their support: *British Columbia:* Eleanor Wachtel; *Manitoba:* Martha Colquhoun, Jan D'Arcy; *New Brunswick:* Marie Patrick; *Newfoundland:* Gerry Rogers; *Nova Scotia:* Mairi Macdonald; *Ontario:* Lisa Avedon, Varda Burstyn, Amy Gottlieb, Margrit Eichler, Pat Hacker, Jennifer Newstrom, Mary O'Brien, Bette Pié, Linda Ryan-Nye, Marylee Stephenson, Susan Vander Voet, Pamela Walker, Carol Zavitz; *Québec:* Irene Angelico, Hugh Armstrong, Pat Armstrong, Gloria Demers, Laurette Deschamps, Fleurette Duchamp, Mary Two-Axe Early, Mona Forrest, Michèle Fortin, Françoise Guenette, Gisèle Guilbault, Dorothy Hénaut, Susan Hyde, Signe Johansson, Joy Johnson, Bonnie Klein, Nicole Laverdure, Cerise Morris, Jaquie Manthorne, Jackie Newell, Francine Pelletier, Donna Read, Terry Richmond, Dorothy Rosenberg, Vicky Schmolka, Ruth Selwyn, Beverly Shaffer, Kathleen Shannon, Eileen Shea, Nell Tenhaaf, Ann Usher, Carole Wallace; *Saskatchewan:* Agnes Ananichuk, Jean Buchanan, Gloria Geller, Lenore Rogers, Sue Smee, Kathy Stedwill; *Yukon Territories:* Suzanne Cowan.

doubled in the last thirty years, women's *un*employment rate has tripled. Women provide the service of a reserve army of labor for the lowest-paid jobs, hired last and fired first in numbers convenient to maintaining a desirable margin of profit for industry. The disparity between men's and women's average wages extends ultimately to lesser unemployment and pension benefits, since these are relative to earnings. Almost 60 percent of all widows and single women over the age of 65 live below the official poverty line.

Women are ghettoized in virtually the same occupational categories as in 1900: clerical, sales, and services account for 62.2 percent of their jobs. (But not for long: it's estimated that by 1990, one third of these jobs will disappear, owing to the introduction of microcomputer technology.) Teaching and health-related jobs account for another 16.6 percent of women's work: these areas too are suffering major cutbacks, and it's unlikely that many new jobs will open to replace them. A short time ago, women were beginning to enter trades not traditionally open to them. Now, with numerous men being let go from these jobs, this recent access, too, is closed to women.

Only 25 percent of working women (as opposed to 40 percent of working men) are protected by unions, many of which have active women's committees. The concessions won by unions, however, apply only to their own membership, although the visibility of their struggle has great social impact, encouraging other women to press for their rights. Though there is equal-minimum-wage legislation for men and women in each province, there has been little headway in the struggle for affirmative action or equal pay for work of equal value. Many of the least advantaged women are forced to sell their labor well below minimum wage in order to survive. They often work under dangerous and barely tolerable conditions, both physically and psychologically. There are frequent reports of sexual harassment on the job, but this is not a complaining group: they need the money too much.

Single and married mothers who hold jobs carry the load of the double day, maintaining both job and home. In some cases, husbands might "help" their wives, but housework and childcare are widely regarded as women's domain. It is difficult to find good, inexpensive day care, and 75 percent of day-care costs are shouldered by the parent(s).

Women who stay at home still experience the impact of the economy through their effort to make the family wage work. They themselves are not paid for their labor (except for small governmental monthly child allowances), nor do they receive pension benefits for years of hard work in isolation, often under poor conditions with inferior equipment and long hours. The negligible amount of discretionary money they have gives them little power. They depend on the goodwill of the men who bring home the money. Many women are indispensable to their husbands' work: Inuit and other coastal women are vital to the fishing economy; farmers' wives and other rural women contribute to their family resources; the wives of wage workers maintain their husbands' health and ability to work, and crucial support during strikes.

One in three marriages ends in divorce in Canada. Even women who "take time off" from the paid labor force to raise families can expect to spend five times as long in the paid labor force as at home. When they do go out to work, they find that rearing children and managing the family economy on limited resources are not considered skills in the workplace. Women head 83 percent of all single-parent families; 44.1 percent of these live below the poverty line. A very small percentage of Canadian women "make it" in our economy—and most of these more privileged women also experience sexism in their professional and personal lives.

While there is a need for better legislation about working conditions, retraining, wages, and affirmative action, that still would not solve our problems. The universal application of women's right to earn wages can only be realized through a radical restructuring of society. Such a restructuring is overdue when we look at the future impact of technology, not to speak of the unfair allocation of wealth and resources in Canada. Some feminists claim that in these hard times we must be especially militant, fighting men for every job. Others counsel alliance with males in the same situation. Everyone agrees, though, that such coalitions must be made on women's terms and monitored with extreme vigilance; we must not let our issues be co-opted.

Health

The best news about women's health in Canada is the dramatic decrease in the infant and maternal mortality rate. Yet Indian women and children have a significantly higher mortality rate than others.

Birth-control information and measures are not universally available. Although there are no legal obstacles, access cannot be taken for granted in small towns and villages, especially for unmarried women. In Newfoundland, access is denied to all women through the social control of the Catholic Church, which makes it difficult for doctors and pharmacists to provide birth-control information or means.

Canadian abortion laws were "liberalized" in 1969—and have been undermined by various factors ever since. The initiative for abortion availability must come from local hospitals, which are supposed to form special committees to recommend abortion if the pregnancy is considered deleterious to the mother. Some hospitals don't even form these committees; in others the committees are infiltrated by the so-called Right-to-Lifers; still other hospitals cut back on the number of abortions allowed; in many cases delays make the procedure impossible. In some areas where doctors are allowed to charge over the national health plan for their services, the expense is beyond the means of most women.

Canadian women are over-medicated for symptoms of depression and anger that have a legitimate base in our oppression. Pregnancy and parturition are still treated as illnesses rather than natural conditions. On the other hand, women throughout the country are taking matters more into our own hands. There is an increasing awareness of fitness and nutrition. Women-run women's health centers exist in many major cities, and these provide a variety of services: contraceptive and abortion counseling; feminist therapy; rape counseling; cancer self-examination groups; pre-natal care; general gynecological care; nutrition and hygiene.

Violence Against Women

The general violence of the economic order is further commodified through pornography—in films, cassettes, print, and even store-window displays. Its prevalence is symptomatic of a generalized acceptance of women's oppression. The Women's Studio D of the National Film Board of Canada has documented this in its movie *Not a Love Story,* which has alerted many people to the issue. So far, though, despite the pressures of many women's groups, the lucrative pornography industry persists in Canada.

There have been numerous "Take Back the Night" demonstrations staged by women all over Canada in protest against the continual possibility of violence faced by women when we go out at night. Self-defense classes also are popular. It is estimated that one in ten married women is so severely beaten by her husband as to require medical attention. For this reason, women have set up transition houses all over Canada for battered women and children. (There seems to be a high incidence of this phenomenon in the north, where the climate causes great isolation.) The attitudes underlying this brutality were exhibited recently by our male parliamentarians, when they met the tabling of a report on wife abuse with inane jokes and laughter. They apologized only under duress.

We still have a long way to go. While recent rape legislation is an improvement, further action is still required. There is improved family law in many provinces, but its application is too often in the discretion of unsympathetic police and courts. Many advances for which Canadian women have struggled end up as only parts of what should always have been ours.

Women, Education, and Scholarship

"We have moved from being invisible to being utterly negligible."
—Martha Colquhoun, Winnipeg

In the twelve years since the first major feminist critiques of education in Canada, there has been little fundamental change. Some textbooks have been replaced and others revised, and individual professors in teacher-training programs have made some concessions to feminism, but there has been no systemic change in teaching or curriculum criteria.

There *is* a steady increase in the participation rate of women in community colleges and universities. However, they are still concentrated in the traditional fields of the arts and the helping professions—which have the lowest pay and status and the fewest job opportunities. Commerce, engineering, and the sciences show a low percentage of women at all levels. While there is an appreciable increase in the number of women training in law and medicine, these make up a very small percentage of the total of women students. Women professors are few, mostly low in the academic hierarchy, and thus not very visible role models. Canadian government training courses in the trades also militate against women. In these areas of highest priority to the government, where jobs are most likely, there are dominant male prejudices in student selection as well as in hiring.

Academic institutions in Canada are patriarchal in structure and attitude. The accepted theory of knowledge is androcentric and women's issues virtually subsumed under the notion of "man." While there are excellent women's studies courses and programs in many colleges and universities, their presence does not necessarily change the structures or assumptions of these institutions. The ghettoization of women's studies might even serve patriarchal interests by localizing "women's issues" and maintaining the sexist *status quo* within traditional disciplines. Women's studies and research still face a problem of validation as a legitimate field of study; in order to receive necessary funding, women scholars are often forced into serious ideological or methodological compromises. But there is good news: the Canadian Research Institute for the Advancement of Women (CRIAW) brings together researchers for annual meetings, prints a newsletter, and is establishing a resource bank of feminist researchers. Its aim is to create a national norm that only nonsexist research will be funded. There are also excellent feminist research journals and newsletters from academic women's organizations and governmental agencies.

Sexism is so prevalent in our society that women are touched by it in all the academic disciplines. Women scholars have, after all, been educated by patriarchal institutions. We all came to women's studies through a process of consciousness-raising, and we should never forget this. Consciousness-raising is the alphabet of feminist education and should be a factor in curriculum planning and methodology at all levels of teaching.

Women and the Arts

What would I say to male curators? I'd say, "I've got a good product which has the additional attraction over yours that it's politically more meaningful."

—Nell Tenhaaf, Powerhouse
Gallery, Montreal

Women form a large percentage of students taking music, fine arts, theater, cinema, and writing in Canadian universities and special schools. When we emerge into the "real world," however, we become invisible. We get few grants and are underrepresented in mainstream productions, exhibits, and collections. Our works receive little publicity or critical attention outside the feminist press. We know that the presence of women on juries and boards of selection does increase the percentage of women chosen for those particular events; often the preoccupations of women's work are deemed "uninteresting" by men who attribute universality to their own interests.

Consequently, there are "alternative" projects in all media for women. We have three feminist art galleries, several feminist journals and publishing houses, theaters, musical groups, and film companies. Television and radio are controlled by big private money or by the government, and their most consistent attention to women is in the spheres of beauty and homemaking. As long as patriarchal institutions (partially supported by women's taxes) establish the criteria and make the decisions about who will receive funding, it is dubious that these obstacles can be overcome. Women clearly must infiltrate the arts establishment, but we must simultaneously keep alive those alternative situations where we can be most true to ourselves.

The Struggle

A Cautionary Tale

A group of women from a national organization were against a proposed federal bill which would militate against the most disadvantaged women in the country. For months, we each traveled about 350 km. to meet midpoint between our four cities. After much research, we wrote a detailed report on the disastrous effects of this legislation. One brisk autumn day we met with the cabinet minister responsible in the incumbent Conservative government. Armed with our document, we sallied forth to meet with this most "sympathique" gentleman and his two female assistants. It turned out that they had access to even more up-to-date statistics than we did. They commiserated with us: yes, it was terrible, and even the Prime Minister and his wife were concerned with these issues. Before we knew it, twenty-five minutes of our precious half-hour audience had passed. It was only as we were entering the "easing-out amenities" that I miraculously broke out of my stupor: "David," I said to the Minister (we were all on first-name terms by then), "I can see that you're informed and your heart's in the right place. What I want to know is: whatcha goin' to do about it?"

The Minister gazed at me with ingenuous blue eyes and responded in reasonable expository tones: "I hope you're aware that in order to change women's situation in Canada, there would have to be radical change in the entire society."

"Yes," I rejoined, "but I can't help wondering how dedicated the Conservative Party is to radical change."

To his credit, the Minister joined in the laughter.

The Women's Movement

All the major political parties in Canada have women's caucuses. Provincial and federal governments have advisory groups which churn out reports and recommendations with extraordinary patience. There are also several national women's groups: the National Action Committee (NAC) is a coalition of 220 groups representing 2 million women. The Fédération des Femmes du Québec represents 34 associations and over 100,000 women. There are also groups representing the rights of Native women: Indian

Rights for Indian Women, and the Assoc. of Inuit Women of Canada. (Indian women actually lost many of their traditional rights under the white man's rule and are now struggling to regain greater equality.) NAC was responsible for mobilizing Canadian women's input into our Constitution in 1981; it has now begun a watchdog committee to make sure that important legislation for women is being enforced. In some cities and provinces there are local networks which meet on a regular basis, and throughout the country there is a network of women who know or know of one another and who can be mobilized quickly on important issues. The active regeneration of the peace movement in Canada is largely owing to sustained efforts over decades by Voice of Women.

The most immediate impact of the women's movement is experienced by the majority of women through services delivered by grass-roots organizations throughout the country. Women's information and social centers, local publications which advise women of their resources, health centers, programs for re-entry women, abortion-referral groups, transition houses, and advocacy groups often provide the first step toward self-determination. Once this step is taken, women rarely turn back; more Canadian women than ever before are aware of their rights. But both grass-roots and larger pressure groups are usually dependent on governmental or politically based funding, although some also have their own fundraising schemes. They must all tread a thin line if they want to survive without being co-opted.

The struggle for women's rights is recognized as valid by most Canadian women as long as it is not labeled "feminism." There is a prevalent fear, especially among women in smaller communities, of alienating men. Some women are frightened of being identified with lesbianism. These fears are divisive *within* the women's movement. Heterosexual women with strong affective ties to men fear antagonizing men; lesbian women often feel prejudged by compulsory heterosexuality and forced to compromise their own beliefs for relationships they do not endorse. A toxic process of defensiveness then takes place: stances of the "politically correct" are struck, unstated dress and behavioral codes emerge, and accusations of elitism fly from all directions. Clearly our shared cause is too urgent for such divisions. We still have much to learn about shared power—as well as empowering some women to go on ahead and prepare the way. Many of us who have worked without respite since the 1960's sometimes feel exhausted. Yet we cannot afford to be tired in these hard times when our vigilance is doubly important. We must welcome new ranks of supporters from the young as well as from the so far uncommitted.

Canada was built on the backs of strong women: the Europeans who colonized it and the Native Indians who resisted that colonization. All over the country there are powerful women who know how to "make do" in their private domains. It is urgent that the women's movement implicate more women in our struggle and welcome the specific strengths and ingenuities passed along from mother to daughter in our history.

There is no doubt that all questions about the cause of our oppression lead to patriarchy. Men have most of the wealth, own most of the land and means of production, and have all of the armaments. They also have a culture of centuries of dominance. The women's movement in this country is less than a hundred years old. It is unlikely that Canadian women want to or could meet men's institutionalized violence with violence of the same sort. The notion of "power over" others is not embedded in our shared ideology. *Our concept is one of "empowerment," of taking back what is rightfully ours.* We now face the dilemma that women's fullest rights to self-determination cannot be attained without the kind of radical change that will be resisted by men. We must develop a forceful strategy that stops short of the violence which has plagued male-dominated revolutions.

We have no models to follow. We join women everywhere, then, in the journey of discovering our own strengths and determining the course of our own lives. In that process, we might even manage to keep this planet alive.

Suggested Further Reading

Armstrong, Pat, and Hugh Armstrong. *The Double Ghetto: Canadian Women and their Segregated Work.* Toronto: McClelland and Stewart Limited, 1978.

Conseil de Statut de la Femme. *Pour les Québécoises: Egalité et Indépendance.* Québec: Gouvernement de Québec, 1978.

Fitzgerald, Maureen, Connie Guberman, and Margie Wolfe, eds. *Still Ain't Satisfied! Canadian Feminism Today.* Toronto: The Women's Press, 1982.

Luxton, Meg. *More Than a Labour of Love: Three Generations of Women's Work in the House.* Toronto: The Women's Press, 1980.

Réd: Véronique O'Leary et Louise Toupin. *Québecoises Deboutte!,* Tome 1. Montréal: Editions du Remue-Ménage, 1982.

Greta Hofmann Nemiroff lives in Montreal, where she was born in 1937. She is Director of the New School of Dawson College, where she teaches English and Women's Studies, and is on the boards and a member of various Canadian feminist organizations. She is a writer of articles and fiction whose work has been published in Canada and the United States. Married, she is mother to three children.

THE CARIBBEAN

Editor's Note: The decision to include four separate contributions from the Caribbean region (in addition to Cuba*) was based on two factors. First, it is possible to trace what international-development experts call a "laboratory effect" in many of the island nations in the region, which is to say that the area in a given country is relatively so small and the rate of change potentially so swift that development strategies operate as if in a laboratory: planning errors can be detected, or successful strategies can bear fruit, within 10–25 years, as opposed to the 50–100-year period in larger countries. This of course is vitally important in learning what are helpful tactics for application elsewhere, what the impact of various strategies is, how (or how not) to approach certain similar situations. Second, the Caribbean nations function together in many ways as a microcosm—of colonialization and decolonialization; of cultures unique in their triple mixture of indigenous, African, and European influences; of disparate language groups, religions, etc.

The ethnic populations, for example, include African, Creole, East Indian, European, Maroon, Mayan, and Mulatto—to name only a sampling. In addition, there are sizable immigrant populations of Chinese, Cubans, Indonesians, Lebanese, Portuguese, Syrians, and others. The language range is considerable, including not only the four major language groups (a legacy from colonial times) represented by our Caribbean Contributors—Dutch, English, French, and Spanish—but also such indigenous tongues or mixed languages as Papiamentu and Patois. The religious spectrum covers Rastafarianism, Voudon, Hinduism, and Islam, in addition to Christianity (mostly Roman Catholicism but with an active Protestant population on many islands), Judaism, and various ancient religions still practiced by Native Indian peoples in different areas.

Similar variation** is to be seen in social structures: some matrilineal peoples, such as the Djuka Maroons of Suriname, persist in their traditional ways, although patrilineage—another colonial legacy—is more the rule. Common-law marriage is legally recognized on many islands, and "visiting relationships" are practiced, as well as, in some communities, polygyny. Governmental systems range from those countries which have "territorial" status or are considered "possessions" or "protectorates" of other nations (such as the Commonwealth of Puerto Rico and the US Virgin Islands), to those still under direct colonial control; from those who are "semi-dependencies" (usually meaning internal self-rule but with foreign relations conducted through the colonial power), to those with full Independence. Women's presence in government also differs widely—from the Prime Minister of (Independent) Dominica, Mary Eugenia Charles, to countries which have few or no women in their governments, to indigenous Native councils which—depending on their traditions—have a large or small representation of women, or no representation at all. Although most of the island nations are engaged in the dual struggles of democracy and development, at least two have housed dictatorships infamous for their one-man or one-family rule: former leader Rafael Trujillo in the

---

* Because of its size (largest of all Caribbean islands) and its emergence as a considerable political influence in Latin America, Cuba is dealt with separately in this anthology; see the Cuban feminist contribution on p. 166–77.

** This wide and rich diversity clearly necessitated a divergence from the usual structure of our Statistical Prefaces. Space limitations—and the unavailability of data on women for many of the islands—would have forced us to offer a superficial and statistically uneven assemblage of material, thus doing a disservice both to the women of the Caribbean and to the reader. For further in-depth reading on the region, however, the reader is urged to pursue not only the "Suggested Further Reading" lists at the end of the four following articles, but also the listings under "Caribbean" in the Bibliography.

Dominican Republic and the Duvaliers (first father and now son) in Haiti.

What they do all share, however, is a history of colonialism, slavery, racism and the fight against it, and, in recent times, the problems of economic neocolonialism and of tourism. All of these naturally have a particular impact on women. Caribbean women have had to bear the above-mentioned burdens in addition to the weight of colonially imposed (and sometimes indigenous) patriarchal and sexist traditions and structures. That they have done so and still managed to survive with extraordinary creative energy has merely won for them the reputation of being "powerful" or even "matriarchs"—a conveniently imposed stereotype which is movingly exposed as such by the four articles in this section. On the contrary, perhaps the primary means by which Caribbean women have accomplished their survival and that of their children lies in what the Caribbean Contributors refer to repeatedly: the tradition of women helping one another, both within and across blood and generational lines. This strategy may have originated out of necessity, but it has been developed into a high art from which women everywhere can learn.

The following short general HERSTORY and MYTHOGRAPHY (for the primary language-group countries) are intended to provide a basic although cursory background for the Dutch- , English- , French- , and Spanish-speaking Caribbean contributions. Although two of the Contributors (Dutch- and English-speaking) discuss the status of women in all the countries of their own language group, the other two have chosen to focus on individual island-nations (Haiti and the Dominican Republic). None of the four is meant as a representative voice for Caribbean women. Rather, they are, as are the other Contributors in this book, speaking clearly and courageously from their own experience—both as individual women and as dedicated activists in various Caribbean women's movements. As a quartet, their voices are at once as distinct and harmonious as the islands from which they speak.

HERSTORY. Four groups of women were used to build what are now the nations of the Caribbean: the Amerindian women whose people (primarily Siboney, Arawak, and Carib) had inhabited the islands before conquest; the European women who were uprooted from their homelands and sent by (usually) arranged marriage to settle in far-off colonial provinces, or who were shipped there as indentured servants; the African women who were kidnapped, sold into slavery, packed into the suffocating holds of slave-ships, and brought to the islands; and the Asian women who were brought forcibly as indentured labor. All four groups have a hidden record of rebellion.

Women were active in the 1791 slave revolt led by Toussaint L'Ouverture and Cristope (themselves slaves) on St. Dominique (now Haiti); among these women was Marie Jeanne à-la-Crete-a-Pierrot, Victoria (nicknamed "Toya"), a commander, and Henriette St. Marc, who was publicly executed by the French in 1802. Similar slave rebellions occurred later—with similar female participation—in El Español (later the Dominican Republic), and in Martinique and Guadeloupe. In 1750 and 1795, Maroon women participated in the rebellions on Jamaica. Nanny of the Maroons, a Jamaican fugitive slave, was a military guerrilla leader who helped bring about Independence in 1739; she was a powerful spiritual and civic leader and was named one of Jamaica's National Heroines in 1975. In the 1880's, indentured workers were imported from East India to work on the plantations; many Indian women committed suicide as their sole option for protest.

In the late 18th and early 19th centuries, women of European descent formed organizations aimed at literacy campaigns, social reform, legislative changes, and education for women. During the American occupation of Haiti (1915–34), women guerrillas were among the "cacos," the peasant army led by Charlemagne Perraulte. In 1934, the League Feminine d'Action Sociale (Women's Social Action League), a forerunner of the modern feminist movement in Haiti, pressed for better labor, marriage, and family laws, as well as the right to education, and edited *La Voix des Femmes* (Voice of Women) a book about Haitian women. In Port-of-Spain, Trinidad, women activists took part in the 1937 strike at the APEX oilfields. In 1939 Alice Duries, a writer, published *One Jamaica Gal,* a book about Jamaican women. In the 1950's several hundred "Gonaïves," women from the island of Gonaïves and other areas in Haiti, demonstrated for the vote, which was granted in 1957. Many women's groups were formed in the 1950's: the YWCA, Red Cross, Soroptimist, church federations, etc.

Women workers began organizing for better wages and working conditions in the 1950's; English- and Spanish-speaking Caribbean women helped found unions. Seamstresses in Haiti won a battle against the introduction of electric sewing-machines (to ensure continued production of handicrafts), but the Duvalier regime stamped out the movement, arresting Mme. Guttierez, Mme. Leroy, and others active in the trade-union movement. One of the most brutal examples of Duvalier's torture methods was to use whips to cut off the breasts of Casserne Dessalines, a young member of the antigovernment group Femmes Patriots, in 1965. Yanick Rigaud and Tata Alphonse were famous activists who were executed by his firing squad.

In 1970 CARIWA, the Caribbean Women's Association, was launched to serve as an umbrella for a number of national organizations and councils. Family-planning programs began; many of the pioneers in family planning in the region were women. Although women's branches of political parties already had been active, in the mid-1970's more independent women's political groups were formed: the Organization of Surinamese Women, working to establish crisis centers for women in need; the United Antillean Women's organization, pressing for independence in Curaçao and for better labor legislation for working women; several women's groups in Aruba and the other Dutch-speaking islands. In the English-speaking islands, important laws were passed: minimum wage, maternity leave, a single legal status for all children, etc. The SISTREN women's theater collective and the Women's Bureau in Jamaica (by 1975), plus, soon after, women's bureaus/ministries/commissions on almost every island, signaled the beginning of an autonomous women's movement in the region.

In May 1980, 187 women died in a fire in the Kingston Alms House women's ward. Feminist activity intensified, and organizations began uniting Caribbean women with Latin American women. In Oct. of that year, Marie France Claude, vice-president of the Haitian Christian Democratic Party, was arrested and sentenced to 15 yrs. imprisonment. In Barbados, a symposium on Women and Culture was held (1981) as part of the Caribbean Festival of the Arts—CARIFESTA —a major showcase and convocation for artists, poets, dancers, and musicians from all the different language and cultural groupings of the Caribbean. The Women and Development Unit (WAND) at the University of the West Indies is a major resource center, catalyst, and focal point for women's activities throughout the Caribbean. Popular reggae singer Rita Marley is one of a group of women who represent the strong emerging voice of Jamaican and other island women. Among important women writers in the English-speaking Caribbean are Sylvia Wynter, Erna Brodber, and Louise Bennett (Jamaica), Paule Marshall and Elizabeth Clarke (Barbados), Merle Hodge and Marian Jones (Trinidad and Tobago), Jean Rhys and Phyllis Allfrey (Dominica), and Janice Shinebourne (Guyana). Spanish-speaking women's activism includes many groups: Acción Femenina Incorporado (Women's Action Incorporated); CIPAF (Center for Investigation of Women's Action); CEF (Women's Studies Circle); UMD (Union of Dominican Women), which organizes domestic and factory workers, among others; the "Promotion of Women of the South," the Women's Social Movement; CIFEPAD, a government center for the Integration of Women in Development (created in 1975 to help women enter the agro-industrial and technical industries), and El Club Mencia, a radio program in the southeast region of the Dominican Republic directed at rural and peasant women. Exiled Haitian women's groups in the US include Van Yan, named after a courageous anti-Duvalier woman activist; Femina is the official government women's group in Haiti, headed by founder Marie-Carmel Lafontant, and Centre Haitien Pour la Promotion Feminine (Haitian Center for the Promotion of Women) is also based in Haiti. Well-known Haitian women writers include Marie Chauvet, Marie-Thérèse Colimon, and Nadine Macloire.

MYTHOGRAPHY. Etu is an African ritual celebration of the dead currently practiced only in western Jamaica; its participants are usually female, and a queen presides over the ceremonies. Winti is an African dance religion in which some Dutch-speaking Caribbean women are active celebrants; in Winti, women are thought to be prophets and keepers of the spirit. Djuka Maroon women are respected for their special knowledge of natural medicine, herbs, and roots. Women play an important role in Haitian Voudon, an African-origin religion in which women are high priestesses and female gods are vested with great powers.

THE DUTCH-SPEAKING CARIBBEAN ISLANDS:
Fighting Until the End
by Sonia M. Cuales[1]

An old song goes like this:

Katibu ta galiña, Mama	A slave is a chicken, Mama
Katibu ta galiña	A slave is a chicken
Shon ta bende nos, Mama	Massa sells us, Mama
At'e shon ta bende nos, Mama	Look how Massa sells us, Mama
Ku plaka na man	Through down payment

This song reveals the essence of female slavery. First, the woman owns nothing, not even her own children. Second, there is a strong emotional tie between the woman and her child; the father is absent. External economic forces of the system crudely and openly determine the very existence of the slave family.

In the course of time, *galiña* (chicken) acquired the meaning of girl or young woman. This reveals something of the perceptions about and reality of women today. A closer look at some historical facts may throw light upon the character of this patriarchal, dependent society, which has been under Dutch rule for over three hundred years.

The history of the raids in Africa and the horrors of the so-called Middle Passage tells us about the acquisition procedures and the transfer of Africans, packed like herrings into Dutch ships which took them as slaves to the New World. Selection and separation on arrival implied disruption of slave unions and slave families. This marked any kind of social relation that the woman could develop. And separation from partner or nearest kin could even happen repeatedly to the same slave.

Black slavery in the Caribbean was experienced in different ways. The Dutch islands were not only different from the rest, they were also different among themselves. Planta-

[1.] I am grateful to many women and a few men who participated in my reflections and contributed with their ideas and analyses. Particular mention should be made of Gladys Dorego, Ettienne Goilo, and Lelia Peternella. However, the responsibility remains exclusively mine.

tion economies were developed in the three Windward Islands—St. Maarten, St. Eustatius, and Saba—while Curaçao was the slave-trade center, and Aruba and Bonaire were reserved primarily for cattle raising.

The criteria applied by slave traders and owners for selecting and separating slaves introduced the need for competition among the slaves themselves. The shade of skin would, for instance, determine one's category as domestic slave or field slave. Female slaves in either category were expected to satisfy their master's sexual ambitions, in addition to their work in the field and domestic chores. Because children who had been procreated by a white master would usually be somewhat privileged by their father, female slaves competed for his attention, toward the relative benefit of their children.[2] Thus, in addition to open coercion in terms of production, women had to endure the humiliation of being upgraded as attractive trade objects. Contradictorily, they often found themselves upholstering their physical charms to compete for the delight of the master.

From the time of slavery to the present, Caribbean women never accepted their lot. There are numerous examples of women who committed suicide or infanticide, underwent abortion, or simply ran away. Others resorted to poison brews, theft, or less violent though effective actions: gossip, protest songs, and proverbs. In the eighteenth and nineteenth centuries, women were engaged in various spheres of paid domestic work, petty production, and home industry for the local market. Again they developed many forms of resistance. Washerwomen, for example, were said to deliberately damage the laundry, for which they usually received a miserable pay.[3] Through these manifest though silent forms of rebellion, women continuously struggled against their oppression.

What then is the character of the present-day society in which women live, and in which the twentieth-century women's movement has developed? The Netherlands Antilles consist of six islands. Aruba, Bonaire, and Curaçao are close to the Venezuelan coast and are referred to as the Leeward Islands, while St. Maarten (half of which is under French administration), St. Eustatius, and Saba are part of the Windward Islands. The total area covers 993 square kilometers. Total population is 246,500. Aruba and Curaçao are the main islands, with populations of 63,000 and 159,100 respectively. The native tongue is Papiamentu, while the Windward Islands are basically English-speaking. Dutch is the official language in all islands. People are generally familiar with English and Spanish. Our strategic (and thus dependent) geographic position in the region and our colonial history largely explain this phenomenon.

In the middle of the twentieth century, the decolonization policy of the Dutch, plus liberation movements in Aruba and Curaçao—however weak in their conceptions—resulted in a reformulation of the colonial status. The Netherlands Antilles obtained the so-called Autonomy, but remained fully integrated *within* the Kingdom of the Netherlands: its citizens continued to be Dutch citizens; even today, Holland is in charge of the country's National Defense and external relations. The islands are ruled by a Central Government, headed by the Governor, who is appointed by the Queen of the Netherlands. There are a Central Parliament and distinct Island Parliaments, elected by the people. The Ministers and the members of the Advisory Board are appointed and presided over by the Governor.

If the Netherlands Antilles are dependent politically, they are even more dependent economically. First, because they are an important link within the network of international capitalism. Second, because there is very little agricultural production and almost

[2.] Nolda Kenepa, "Vrouwenleven op Curaçao Laat Achttiende en Vroeg Negentiende Eeuw," Oct. 1980, p. 25; mimeo.
[3.] Kenepa, p. 31.

all consumer goods have to come from abroad. Food imports represent 25 percent of the total merchandise imports.[4] Third, in all sectors of the economy, foreign-owned (mainly Dutch) companies dominate—and their incomes leave the country. Financial institutions, for example, invest up to 75 percent of their funds abroad.[5] The major sectors of our economy are industry and services.

Ship repair is an important activity, carried out by a large drydock company. Employment generated here is highly skilled and almost exclusively male. Manufacturing activity concerns consumer goods and simple intermediate goods. This sector is limited, owing to the geographic fragmentation of the economy, the small domestic market which limits the scope for import substitution, and the lack of indigenous raw materials. Construction activities accounted for a relatively important source of male employment in the 1970's. (This sector is subject to erratic changes, though.) In the service sector, tourism and trade constitute relatively important sources of employment—to which women do have access. Offshore and free-zone activities have a relatively small employment-generating capacity.[6] These activities started in the 1950's and increased considerably since the late 1970's, because of the accommodating attitude of the government and its lenient foreign-exchange policy. But it seems that they failed to turn the Netherlands Antilles into a staple market, as it was for centuries.[7] The free-zone activities consist of transit trade to Latin American importers and should not be confused with free-zone *industry*. The latter was experienced in Curaçao in the late 1960's and the 1970's, employing mainly unskilled female labor. The increased rates of female unemployment, appearing in the National Statistics, should be understood in the light of the sudden expansion of the female labor market during the operation period of free-zone industry, and the absence of alternative employment for women when the companies "ran away." Women, who are usually heads of households in this matrifocal society, reverted more and more toward commercial self-help, buying and selling consumer goods and engaging in a variety of economic activities which might be referred to as the informal sector. In general they do not earn much from this, nor do they make significant profits. Still, these activities provide for a continuous circulation of cash, which helps them solve their recurrent and urgent needs.

The above characterization of the society is by no means complete. Nevertheless, it allows us to understand that women in the Dutch-speaking Caribbean today experience three levels of domination: colonial, class, and sexual domination.

The type of economy developed under neocolonial rule excluded woman from significant participation in the economy. Colonial domination distorted her mind, stripped away her cultural identity, and imposed misconceptions of her own reality.

As members of the dominated classes, women are not owners of means of production. They can sell their labor only when it suits the system. Women are the first to fill the ranks of the reserve army of labor. While actual heads of households, lower-class women have less access to employment opportunities and qualify for only minimum wages. If some of these women own means of production at all—as is the case of petty producers and petty traders—this does not guarantee a sufficient and autonomous subsistence. Moreover, lower-class women have no access to real power. As members of the dominated classes, their interests are shaped by patron-client relationships which have institutionalized corruption rather than serving the interests of the poor.

Sexual domination is experienced in a very crude way. Men, who are generally passen-

[4] IMF Report, Kingdom of the Netherlands, Netherlands Antilles, Recent Economic Developments, Mar. 21, 1980, p. 58.

[5] IMF Report, p. 52.

[6] IMF Report, p. 8.

[7] Jaap van Soest, *Trustees of the Netherlands Antilles* (Curaçao: n.p., 1978), pp. 294–95.

gers through the lives of women, actually control more than a superficial perception would admit. Women have no control over their own bodies. Be it for economic aspirations or for romantic love convictions, pregnancies follow upon pregnancies. Again and again a woman is left alone to manage her survival and that of her children—and often of her mother and other close kin too. The performance of her supposed duties is controlled by violence, as is her adherence-to expected behavior. She is solely responsible for the reproductive tasks of the family and is discriminated against with respect to economic activities she must be able to develop. Her participation in political life is minimal and passive, while she is discriminated against by legislation.

There is an image of Caribbean women as exceptionally strong and powerful. They rule the household alone, combine this with work outside the domestic sphere, make all decisions, are apparently dominant, and manage to maintain psychological strength and physical attraction for men. This view fails to understand that Caribbean women have been *conditioned* in this way, and furthermore have no alternative. They have to develop defense mechanisms in order to survive in a male-dominated world in which, paradoxically, the male is invisible. This hidden presence, controlling all spheres of life, makes his power all the more present.

The international women's movement has not escaped women in the Netherlands Antilles, thank God. Although women organized themselves long ago around traditional women's activities, an increasing number of women have realized that they have to struggle politically against subordination. This level of consciousness can by no means be generalized for all women's organizations in the Dutch-speaking Caribbean, but the need to advance and the knowledge that such advancement will occur only through struggle is generally felt.

There are about eighty women's organizations, with an average membership of thirty women each, in Curaçao. Aruba counts a few smaller groups, and the other islands one or two. The deeply internalized values emanating from the historical forms of oppression suffered in the Dutch islands, the effectiveness of capitalist ideology in a "better-off" developing country, the dependency relations sowed and maintained by Dutch colonialism—all these, among other factors, constitute a major handicap to the movement as a whole. This is realized by very few groups in Curaçao and Aruba. In Curaçao, the work of at least one group is geared precisely toward destroying these barriers.

Most of the groups, though calling themselves women's organizations, represent nothing more than service clubs, charity organizations, or the women's arm of political parties. Although they do not carry "struggle" in their banner, still it has been possible to mobilize and unite a number of groups in Curaçao around hot economic issues (problems of housing and legal limitations for employment of married women and unmarried mothers, for example). The most active group in this regard, UMA (United Antillian Women), in Curaçao, deserves credit for this. The fighting spirit of UMA also paved the way for the coordinating Steering Committee to unite and mobilize organizations with diverse objectives and conceptions into one front vis à vis issues related to women.

United action is not confined to issues in the society at large, but also takes place within organizations. Recent action by the united women's organizations to support the struggle of women within a labor union had spectacular results. It was the time for election of the Union Board. Many women are members of the union and there is a specific women's arm of that organization, but there were no women candidates: they felt they shouldn't register themselves as candidates since they wouldn't be elected anyway. The women's movement from *outside* stimulated and encouraged female union members to register as candidates. Action was organized to educate both male and female members of that union for the need to have female members on the Board. The struggle of women from outside achieved the election of three women. (Among the postelection analyses of their victory are: the innovative character of the proceedings, the motivation of the female candidates in their speeches explaining why it was important to be elected, and the convincing power of the analyses made by the women. No male candidate had explained why he should be elected.)

The struggle is carried out on various fronts. Independence is the *leitmotiv* for the activities of UMA, for example. It is felt that substantial improvement in the situation of women in the Dutch islands will not be achieved without suspension of colonial relations. From a broader perspective, the movement has grown into the strongest social movement in Curaçao. Policy-makers increasingly take women seriously. They know now that when the women take up an issue they fight until the end.

Women's views no longer can be bypassed. And if nothing else, this for sure is a major advance in Netherlands Antilles society.

Suggested Further Reading

Abraham Van Der Mark, Eva Elisabeth. "Wives and Mistresses of a White Caribbean Elite." Paper prepared for the Fifth Annual Conference of the Society for Caribbean Studies, held at High Leigh, Hoddesdon, Herts., England, May 26–28, 1981.

————. *Yu'i Mama* (Mother's Child). Willemstad: n.p., 1969; some aspects of family structure in Curaçao.

Cuales, Sonia M. "Women, Reproduction and Foreign Capital in Curaçao." *Caraibisch Forum,* No. 2, The Hague, 1980.

Hoetink, H. *Het Patroon van de Oude Curaçaose Samenleving* (The Pattern of Ancient Curaçao Society). Aruba: n.p., 1974.

Marks, A. F. *Male and Female in the Afro-Curaçaoan Household.* The Hague: n.p., 1976.

Sonia M. Cuales was born in Curaçao in 1941. She studied anthropology and development sociology at Leiden University, the Netherlands, doing field research in Curaçao on women and export-oriented electronics industries, and in Colombia on women and export-oriented flower industries. She has actively participated in the women's movement, especially the Antillian Women's Organizations in the Netherlands, has lectured on women at the University of the Netherlands Antilles, attended the Women in the Caribbean Project Conference in Barbados in 1982, and published numerous articles on the subject of women in the Caribbean. She is a Project Officer, UNICEF Regional Office in Latin America and the Caribbean in Bogotá, Colombia, in charge of UNICEF assistance to Guyana and Suriname.

THE ENGLISH-SPEAKING CARIBBEAN:
A Journey in the Making
by Peggy Antrobus and Lorna Gordon

The fourteen countries in the English-speaking Caribbean[1] form an identifiable sub-regional group within the geographic region of Latin America. Each island is like a member of a family with its own unique characteristics, but all are recognizable by their common

[1] These include the island states of Jamaica, Trinidad and Tobago, Barbados, Grenada, St. Vincent, St. Lucia, Dominica, St. Kitts/Nevis, Antigua, Anguilla and Montserrat, and the English-speaking countries of Guyana and Belize, which border the Caribbean Sea.

history of slavery, racism, and colonialism from which evolved the social, cultural, political, and economic foundations of today's society.

What we refer to as the Caribbean was, as one sociologist put it: "One of the rare cases of human society being artificially created for the satisfaction of one clearly defined goal: making money through the production of sugar."[2]

The advent of adult suffrage, mass worker organizations, and political "flag" independence has had minimal effect on the essential power patterns within and outside of Caribbean society, or on the attitudinal variant of the colonial mind. Caribbean governments predominantly comprise members of a black middle-class bourgeoisie who have benefited from the democratization of a Eurocentric educational system, but who have not yet evolved an indigenous political consciousness to revolutionize the legacies of the plantation society. It is their fundamental assumption (with few but notable exceptions) that economic development depends on metropolitan control of the means of production, which have tended to reinforce the characteristics of plantation society.

This strategy of development assumes that a climate of auspicious material conditions will be created over time, bringing, in turn, political independence, social equality, and social justice. Such a history of allegiance to different metropolitan countries has served to keep the Caribbean countries apart, has mystified the root cause of underdevelopment, and has kept the peoples of the region in the grip of persistent poverty.[3]

Choose any point of reference in the Caribbean and you will observe the ongoing problems of unemployment, unequal distribution of incomes, illiteracy, growing populations, widening inequalities, and deepening dependencies. It has become evident that the cultural, political, and socioeconomic institutions adapted from Western models and imposed on the Caribbean society to guarantee reproduction of the labor force and domestication of a predominantly black race continue to determine the structure, experiences, values, concerns, and loyalties of the members of the Caribbean family.

The Role of Women in Caribbean Society

From the time of slavery, women in the Caribbean have played active roles in social/political movements which led to emancipation, adult suffrage, independence, and the movement for closer integration.[4] Individually and collectively, they have contributed to the development of social services through their pioneering work in family planning, education, youth work, social welfare, and rural development.

Despite the production of bauxite in Jamaica and Guyana, oil in Trinidad, and the omnipresent tourist industry, the islands of the Caribbean are predominantly agricultural; approximately 31 percent of the labor force in these countries is engaged in agriculture.[5] Between 30 and 40 percent of the agricultural labor force in the Caribbean is female.[6] Women perform the lowest-paid and most back-breaking jobs, including cultivation and marketing, without the training or technology which could ease their burden.

[2] Orlando Patterson, *The Sociology of Slavery* (East Brunswick, NJ: Fairleigh Dickinson Univ. Press, 1970).

[3] George L. Beckford, *Persistent Poverty: Underdevelopment in Plantations of the Third World* (Oxford: Oxford Univ. Press, 1972).

[4] Lucille Mathurin, "A Historical Study of Women in Jamaica from 1655–1844," Diss., n.p., n.d.; also Peggy Antrobus, *Promoting and Accelerating Women's Participation in Development Programmes in the Caribbean Through Technical Co-operation Among Developing Countries*, UNDP Paper TCDC/2/13 (New York: United Nations, Mar. 1981).

[5] See Norma Abdulla, "Human Resources: Labour Force in the Commonwealth Caribbean—A Statistical Analysis," *ISER Occasional Papers*, UWI, St. Augustine, June 1977. This figure is based on the 1970 Census.

[6] Figures quoted in USAID *Caribbean Agriculture Planning*.

Failure to give official recognition to women's contribution to agriculture is reflected in their limited access to land, credit, and training. Consequently, few women achieve managerial positions in agriculture: women account for only 17 percent of all farm managers, supervisors, and farmers.[7]

While women do have access to senior positions in both traditional and nontraditional sectors, such access is owing more to the relative shortage of skills in the society than to an absence of sex discrimination. Furthermore, although the Caribbean female population is estimated at roughly 51 percent of the total adult population, the positions of leadership within the major political parties, the trade unions, the security forces, the civil service, and the key economic, industrial, and financial sectors are held by men.

A 1981 regional conference, Women and Decision-Making in the Caribbean, noted the virtual absence of women from the ranks of such influential developmental institutions as the Caribbean Development Bank and the Caribbean Broadcasting Union, whose member organizations reach an audience population of 5.8 million. Notwithstanding the "visibly" increasing numbers of women in such professions as medicine, the media, the arts, education, etc., there is still a yawning gap between the number of men and the number of women in critical decision-making positions.

The pyramidal structure of Caribbean society places the mass of women, "the invisible majority," at the base of the socioeconomic structure. The burden of poverty weighs heavily on their power to use even the minimal concessions wrung from the system on their behalf. Poor living conditions, inadequate social services, malnutrition, limited opportunities to acquire marketable skills, and unemployment (the rate is 6.77 percent for men and 10.66 percent for women, and for every age category of unemployed, female rates exceed the male[8]) are all experienced more intensely by women than by men.

In the lower economic strata, where legal marriages coexist with common-law marriages and visiting relationships, the number of households headed by women (22 percent in Guyana, 33.3 percent in Jamaica, 46 percent in St. Kitts) has given birth to the "myth" of a Caribbean matriarchal society. The rationale is, if so many women are heading the primary social institutions, without or with men, and affecting development of future generations, then they have *power.* The fact that the existence of nontraditional (Western) households is derived in part from such historical factors as slavery—which rendered the male powerless as father-husband and forced the Caribbean woman to cling to her matrifocal orientation for survival and, in contemporary society, for economic survival—this is never considered. Meanwhile, wife-beating, child-beating, sexual violence, verbal violence, and other forms of abuse and sexual exploitation are constant reminders of "who really wears the pants."

Moreover, the violence of Caribbean society is hardly reflective of values traditionally ascribed to women. There is little evidence of the sort of caring society which could come into being if the influence of women were truly felt.

The expressions of insecurity in Caribbean men who continue to bear a deep-rooted resentment against the strength of their women are much more pronounced and combative than is the so-called green-eyed monster of jealousy and bitching one is told to expect of females. This resentment is evidenced in the sexual imagery of songs in the popular idioms (reggae in Jamaica, calypso in most eastern Caribbean islands); in mass-media advertising images which persist in degrading and belittling womenfolk; in pro-white biases which influence Caribbean women to acquire "straight hair" and cosmetic adornments to produce Caucasoid features. The Caribbean male's racial predilections are

---

[7.] *Caribbean Agriculture Planning.*

[8.] IBRD Report No. 5668, *Caribbean Regional Study,* Vol. 7, "Population and Employment" (June 1975).

deeply motivated by his class status and reinforced by socialized sexist biases. In the context of unequal power fostered by inherent inequalities plus the competition of a free market system, the power derived from one social sphere is used to lever benefits or impose deprivations in another. Caribbean women, already marginalized by sex-role stereotyping which defines the nature and content of their education and the nature and value of their productive labor, find themselves at the mercy of the male power broker when driven into the work force by necessity. Their mobility is a struggle against a host of structural factors: differential wage scales, occupational segregation, infractions of protective-labor legislation, non-unionization, lack of security, minimal if any support for their domestic role and functions.

It is to the lasting credit of the strength gained from her experience heavy with its history of pain, deprivation, and oppression that today's Caribbean woman comes far nearer to occupying an "equal status" with men in her society than do women in many parts of the world.

To capture the essence of Caribbean women and avoid stereotyping, a few representative women can be described. Each is at a different level in the socioeconomic and educational scale, but together they give a better picture of Caribbean women than the profile offered by official statistics. There is one important omission: the women of East Indian origin. The East Indian communities in Guyana and Trinidad and Tobago represent about 50 percent of the population of these countries. They form a separate cultural group, and the status of women in this subculture is very different from that of women in the rest of the Caribbean society.

However, the coauthors of this article do not know enough about this group to make any statements about their condition. Apart from this omission, the women described below can be encountered in any Caribbean island.

The Market-Woman/Higgler/Vendor

She is the mainstay of Caribbean agricultural production. She was introduced to agriculture at a tender age, when she helped in the family "garden," often a small plot of land on the slope of a nearby hill or mountain. Her mother would work the land and sell its produce in the marketplace of the nearest town. She would travel by bus to the town on a Thursday, laden with baskets of fruits and vegetables. Sometimes the younger children went along with her. Now her daughter performs the same duties, barely making a living for herself and her children.

The buses, roads, and marketplace have not changed a great deal over the sixteen years from childhood to adulthood, except that they are more in need of repair. It is a rough life, but one which enables the family to survive and, in her village, she has the authority and independence of a person who knows she can survive with dignity.

The Domestic Helper

She is in her early twenties—a bright girl, her mother's "hope for the future" until she got pregnant and had to leave school without completing her education. Thereafter, the absence of steady employment (for someone with limited skills and the need to provide for her children) led her through a series of "visiting" relationships, each resulting in a new child, each building greater dependency. The only job for which she is equipped is domestic work, which exposes her to exploitation from a woman this time, her employer. The employer's preoccupation with her own status usually makes her insensitive to the fact that she owes the possibility of being "superwoman" to her helper's endurance of long hours and low wages. The domestic worker is not eligible for unionization and has no association to which she can air her grievances. Her job can be terminated at any time with minimal or no penalties to her employer.

The Shop Assistant

She is just out of school with a good certificate, and lucky to find work in a shop. Most of her classmates remain unemployed. She wants to go to evening classes to learn shorthand and typing but is under constant pressure from her supervisor, who threatens to fire her unless she is "friendly" to him.

The Nurse

She went to secondary school and was recruited to work in the public hospital, which has a training program. She can get her qualifications there and perhaps save enough money to go to England or the United States. If she marries, she will have children, but will continue to work at the hospital, taking minimum leave and giving her children to the care of her mother or a member of her extended family.

The Doctor

She got high grades at school and won a scholarship to the university and medical school. She is married and has two children but can continue to work since she has domestic help and flexible hours. She leads a comfortable and satisfying life, enjoying the comforts and privileges which attend her social status. She often cannot understand what "this woman's lib" is all about.

The Housewife

She has a temporary status: as soon as the children start school, she will return to her job as a teacher. There are few fulltime "housewives" among Caribbean women with secondary education. The high cost of living, the shortage of skills, the possibilities for employment (and for domestic help), as well as the tradition of "working mothers," all make it likely that women educated to this level will work. Yet while education has been the key to socioeconomic mobility for women (and men), enabling those with secondary and tertiary education to gain access to professional, executive, and administrative positions of their choice, nevertheless sex stereotyping in school curricula restrict the career options of female students.

Women with secondary educations are still mainly in the traditional fields: nursing, teaching, and commerce. With the exception of nursing, in all of these fields they remain in just below the top positions.

The life of the low-income Caribbean woman is a constant struggle for survival—a "feminist struggle," although the term is never used because it is not a part of the vocabulary. These women work largely in service and low-skilled areas and are the main victims of low wages, poor working conditions, and sexual harassment.

An important feature of society among this group of women is the extent to which they help each other in their struggle for survival. The word "family" goes beyond kinship. Neighbors, close friends, the children who have been raised together in a single household, all become "family" to each other. Women feed and care for each other in hard times. They look after each other's children when the cycle of unemployment is broken or when they are abandoned by their male partners. (Countless women are mothers forced to "father" the total upbringing of their children without any assistance from the male.

Men boast about the number of children they have, without apparently being concerned with their ability to support them. The women manage somehow.)

"Educated" middle-class women, on the other hand, may have secure incomes, but their lifestyle is determined by their husbands' status and they are often trapped by its false security. The relative ease with which the middle-class professional woman manages her double day makes her generally insensitive to feminist issues. Interestingly, while displaying a general lack of concern about the everyday condition of the majority of women in the society, because of her visibility she is usually the first to be coopted into the leadership ranks of government-sponsored agencies for "Women's Affairs"—which are, ironically, welfare-oriented.

In addition, the class consciousness of the plantation society continues to inhibit the development of a sense of solidarity among Caribbean women which can nourish a cohesive, feminist movement. The tendency of the middle-class woman is to equate "feminism" with the most negative media-projected manifestations of the North American women's liberation movement.[9]

However, the battle for single-issue reforms within the system *has* been waged by middle-class-led working-class women's groups affiliated in the main parties and trade unions, with support from the national women's units established by governments. Advocacy for equal pay, maternity leave, a minimum wage for domestic workers, and legislation to remove the stigma of bastardy from children born out of "wedlock"—all have resulted from such cooperative action.

While Caribbean women lack a politically defined consciousness of their oppression, many can pinpoint an individual source of discrimination and take personal or group action against a specific infraction. However, their socialization as an oppressed class has induced an inability to identify the real source of oppression—and to challenge that source from a nascent feminist perspective.

Toward a New Consciousness

During the 1960's, the black American struggle reinforced the growing Caribbean awareness that liberation meant breaking the bondage imposed by an economic system which is symptomatically patriarchal, racist, and sexist. While securing the political right to define their sovereignty and the model of development which could address equal rights and justice for all, the peoples of the Caribbean questioned the inherited socioeconomic premises of their existence. At the same time, vocalization of the scope and nature of female oppression by an emerging international feminist movement added fuel to the momentum of Caribbean *female* self-discovery.

By the 1970's, Caribbean women began to propound both reformist and radical strategies to guarantee their inclusion and participation in developmental goals and processes. Under the rubric of the principles articulated by the United Nations for the observance of International Women's Year in 1975, Caribbean women advocated and secured the establishment of women's desks and bureaus as part of the national machinery. At the regional level, the Caribbean Community (CARICOM) Secretariat is the equivalent of these units. These agencies, together with various departments of the University of the West Indies (UWI)[10] and the University of Guyana, and assisted by international funding agencies (ILO, FAO, UNESCO, and UNDP, etc.), have pursued research on all aspects of women's lives which can provide the framework for analysis and affirmative, appropriate

---

[9.] Within Caribbean society "feminism" is a buzzword.

[10.] Most notable is the regional research project on the Role and Status of Caribbean Women being conducted by the Barbados branch of the Institute of Social and Economic Research (ISER) of the UWI.

action. It is now obvious, however, that while such agencies can secure significant concessions and serve as an intercessionary force between governments and the mass of women in the society, they do not have the autonomy or administrative capability for promoting structural changes in the status of women.

This role is more appropriate to the nongovernmental women's organizations. Many of these organizations are affiliated at the regional level with the Caribbean Women's Association (CARIWA) and the Caribbean Church Women (CCW). However, it is uncertain that these more traditional organizations have the authority or revolutionary consciousness to challenge the status quo. The onus of this task must be placed on the women within organized "progressive" political parties who can influence policy-making, and on independent, self-supporting, and quasi-independent women's groups and agencies which have a feminist perspective and can survive through judicious multiple funding.

One such agency which falls in the latter category (and which, as a consequence, has enjoyed relative freedom to innovate and promote a feminist bias to developmental efforts) is the Women and Development Unit (WAND) of the Extra-Mural Department of the University of the West Indies. This Unit, the first within a major regional institution, designed *by* women *for* women, has succeeded in:

(a) raising the level of consciousness of both women and men to a heightened awareness of the nature and scope of discrimination against women;

(b) promoting and providing short-term technical assistance to groups wishing to assert control over their lives;

(c) designing and implementing the models and methodologies for integrating women in the development process; and

(d) encouraging and supporting a new spirit of participatory democracy.[11]

At the political level, groups such as the Marxist-oriented Committee of Women for Progress (CWP) in Jamaica and the Socialist National Women's Organisation of Grenada provide the necessary social and political analysis for feminist action. In Guyana, two groups of women with different political affiliations are involved in programs which address the issue of poverty. The Women's Revolutionary Socialist Movement (WRSM) within the ruling party has been engaged in developing economic projects and appropriate technologies for rural women. The Women Against Terrorism (WAT) group has been waging a public campaign against various forms of politically inspired terror including "economic terror," which in their view institutionalizes mass poverty and suppresses human dignity. In each country, women's involvement in political parties and trade unions presents possibilities for the development of a feminist consciousness and programs within these structures. The path has been charted by the Women's Movement within the People's National Party of Jamaica—a group which consciously chose to move from the status of an auxiliary to that of a movement.

At the educational level, SISTREN, a Jamaican working-class theater collective, has succeeded in articulating the plight of women in Caribbean society through stage productions, consciousness-raising sessions, and education-through-drama workshops. The group uses the personal experiences of its members in an improvisational format which synthesizes modern drama techniques and traditional folk theater from Jamaica's rich cultural heritage.

The work of all these groups is representative of the complex strategies, both reformist and radical, which Caribbean women must necessarily use to achieve social transformation. Each sector—the bureaucracy, the political, and the nongovernmental—has its own unique contribution to make to the process of change. If each can subscribe to a common

---

[11.] A Pilot Project on the Integration of Women in Rural Development in St. Vincent is an example of this.

goal, understanding and respecting the different routes each must take, the journey will be easier for all.

Both sexes are engaged in a search for solutions to the most basic of human needs: survival with dignity. Undoubtedly, Caribbean women have a specific place in the vanguard of revolutionary politics. Over time, they have come to acknowledge that being supportive of their men to the detriment of their own self-definition and personhood will neither guarantee "equality" with men nor make them contributors to and beneficiaries of male-determined developmental goals.

The wind of social change which has been blowing through the Caribbean in recent years has given fresh impetus to the need for Caribbean women to share and analyze their common experiences, and to define the bottom line of their desired existence, if they are not to be left out of a "new society" or relegated once again to a subordinate role. The level of consciousness is rising individually and collectively. The rallying cry is for a unifying force, a feminist framework, through which Caribbean women can identify the rationale for short-term and long-term action.

If we succeed in creating feminist politics out of the collectivization of our mutual experiences, instead of imitating the structures of the patriarchy, then Caribbean women may have established a "new feminist" model for the rest of the world. For, in the words of a Jamaican poet, Christine Craig:

> ". . . man's truth is an empty yabba . . ."

CODA
by Christine Craig (1981)

Poor woman, the man's truth
is an empty yabba* for you.
Vainly you try to fill it
with a whirling, shifting
liquid of your own.
Where can we meet, my brother,
my lover, my friend,
to make something new together.

I will meet you on the road
for I have done with waiting.
I will help you with your load
and welcome your greeting.
I will meet you on the road
for I have shaped my journey.

Suggested Further Reading

Antrobus, Peggy. *Promoting and Accelerating Women's Participation in Development Programmes in the Caribbean Through Technical Co-operation Among Developing Countries.* UNDP Paper TCDC/2/13. New York: United Nations, Mar. 1981.

Marshall, Paule. *The Chosen Place, the Timeless People.* New York: Avon Books, 1976.

Massiah, Joycelin. *Women in the Caribbean: An Annotated Bibliography.* Occasional Bibliography Series, No. 5, ISER (Eastern Caribbean), Apr. 1979.

Mathurin, Lucille. *The Rebel Woman in the British West Indies During Slavery.* Kingston: Institute of Jamaica, 1975.

---

* Yabba: a container used in the preparation of food.—Ed.

Roberts, G. W., and Sonja Sinclair. *Women in Jamaica: Patterns of Reproduction.* New York: KTO Press, 1978.

Peggy Antrobus is Tutor/Co-ordinator of the Barbados-based Women and Development Unit (WAND) of the Extra-Mural Department of the University of the West Indies. She is the former Director of the Jamaican Women's Bureau. Up to the time of her appointment in Jamaica (1975), she had "never been involved in women's organizations or taken a great deal of interest in women's issues." Born in Grenada and educated in St. Lucia, St. Vincent, and England, she found her background in economics, social work, community development, and administration useful to "what became a voyage of discovery and self-discovery which has led to a feminist commitment." After an "uncritical acceptance of official 'Women and Development' programs," she came to understand "the necessity for the establishment of a feminist vision of a humane and caring society." She is married and the mother of two children.

Lorna Gordon is a mass-communications consultant in private practice in Jamaica. She became a radical feminist through her personal experiences of sexual abuse and violence in her first marriage and her indoctrination into revolutionary politics at the age of fifteen. Since then, she has worked consistently with feminist groups in the Caribbean and with women engaged in liberation struggles in various parts of the world. She writes frequently on the politics of female oppression. She is married and the mother of one child.

HAITI: A Vacation Paradise of Hell
by Cacos La Gonaïve
(Translated by Anne-christine d'Adesky)

"Cé Pou Fi Guin Droits Tou"

Fi travail tou patou
Cé pou you quin atou
Pou défen'n intérè
—Et san gadé dèyè—
Toutt fi qui nan souffrance
Toutt moun' cap passé transe
Cé pou'n guin libèté . . .

"For Women to Have Equal Rights"

Woman works everywhere
To try to move ahead
To defend her interests
—Without looking back—
All women who are suffering
All those who have known hardship
It's to gain liberty . . .

—Lyrics to a Haitian Creole folksong.

I have returned to the land of my foremothers, rooted as I am to childhood memories of home: the low-hanging flamboyant tree, or poinciana, with its brilliant bursts of red flowers and graceful saber-shaped pods, the mango and the kumquat trees, the dusky, pungent smell of young husked corn thrown onto an open fire and baked until the kernels turn black. Along with that memory comes another: the specter of poverty that cobbles shadows on the sunny streets. In Haiti, cool, hilltop verandas brood over the slums of tin-roofed shanties below. From the window of my grandmother's house, nothing appears to have changed; the crush of humanity suffers its way into the city at dawn and back out again to the villages at night.

In the crowded markets of Port-au-Prince, women traders spread their goods on the open pavement: fruits, baskets of different-colored beans, stalks of sugar cane, and the sweet, sticky peanut clusters wrapped in wax paper. A pregnant mulatta woman pushes her naked child toward me. *"S'il vous plaît, madame. . . ."* Before I can reach into my pocket for a coin, the childhood warning has already surfaced: "Don't give them a *centime* . . . give one of them money and they'll all want some. You'll only cause a fight."

Driving the air-conditioned car along the newly built airport road, my businessman uncle points to a row of concrete buildings on the outskirts of town. "New plants, new factories . . . we even have a Club Med now. . . ." He doesn't mention the thirteen-year-old girl rethreading a needle at two in the morning, her heavy eyelids and fingers guided by an instinct to survive. In an average twelve-hour day, she will stitch twenty-four American-type baseballs, earning eight *gourdes* ($1.68 US). Now, in the middle of the night, her young girl's breasts ache with the need to nurse. She thinks of her far-off village, of her hungry baby, of her new man . . . will he be drunk, beat her, run off with another woman? "There is talk of oil in the bay," my uncle remarks.

"Vacation Paradise": the picture of Haiti offered to tourists is one of sun and beaches, charming gingerbread houses and tableaux of primitive art, the rhythms of meringue music and the wild carnival of dance during Mardi Gras. A travel brochure shows smiling "native washerwomen" posing like exotic birds on the balcony of a Pétionville hotel.

The real picture is very different. To live there, especially as a woman, is to experience sharp divisions—and odd similarities—in the lives of poor, black, rural women, middle-class mulatta women, and white, upper-class women; distinctions based on pigmentation and wealth, similarities based on gender. In addition, the tyranny of Jean-Claude ("Baby Doc") Duvalier's regime adds to women's particular oppression. No woman can refuse the demands of the brutal "Tontons Macoutes" ("bogeymen"), or the Volunteer National Security forces—not without risking imprisonment or even death. Racism, classism, sexism; in Haiti, they are the entwined roots of a patriarchy that effectively strangles women.

In the night, they drove me to the National Penitentiary with a group of prisoners, some of them later sent to Ft. Dimanche, nicknamed "Hell's Jaw." I was taken to a cell two and a half meters wide and three meters long, with a small grilled opening ringed with sharp tips. On the dirty, damp walls, the names of women were engraved: Gladys Jean François, Gertrude, Jacqueline (Tata Alphonse), and Madame Faustin Charlot, mother of eight-month-old twins, who had been arrested because the police were searching for her husband. . . .[1]

There are no statistics documenting the thousands of women who disappeared and died during François ("Papa Doc") Duvalier's thirty-year reign of terror. Today, a decade after his son inherited the post of "president for life," a shroud of silence hangs over the lives of women who remain locked inside the walls of Haiti's prisons. For other women, a different silence, one of deliberately trained passivity, is the response to years of social training; a specific code of female behavior that is male-defined and male-controlled. There are two roles assigned to women in Haiti: sexual object and wife/mother. Within, above, and across all categories of race and class, a Haitian woman's primary social identity centers around a man. (Even the feared Mme. Duvalier herself has for decades wielded her enormous power "invisibly"—first from behind her husband, "Papa Doc," then as regent for, and later behind, her son. It is unthinkable that she might ever have been permitted to exercise power openly or in her own name.)

[1.] Testimony of Elizabeth Philibert, excerpt reprinted in *Femmes Haïtiennes,* published by the Collective of Haitian Women, Montreal, Canada, 1980.

A visit with Sabine, my cousin who is the same age as me. Her tiger eyes, long blonde hair, an easy smile; she is our beauty queen, the family pride, "la belle." Sabine, at age five, showing me how to walk, balancing a book on her head as she sways her hips from side to side. Teaching me how to meringue, how to be light on my feet and guide the boy along without letting him know. When we begin dating, escorted at the age of seven by boys our family has selected, Sabine is my guide. "Yes," she nods to the boys who are the right color, handsome, and from good families—meaning rich. "No" to all the others. "We have to keep the line pure"; she echoes our parents' logic. Blessed with a beautiful daughter, my uncle is careful to protect Sabine, keeping her for the highest bidder. From the age of thirteen on, we are escorted everywhere by our brothers who "hold" our money for us and are the only ones allowed to drive the family car. "A good girl doesn't walk alone in the streets," my grandmother admonishes; "les autres, c'est toutes des putes." At the same age, mulatta girls find themselves barred from certain (white) social clubs—but are forbidden by their families to date boys of their own color.

I did not attend Sabine's wedding, the crowning point of her seventeen-year-old life, an extravaganza attended by wealthy Haitians. Her husband is white, European, handsome, and rich. Her first child (born when she was eighteen) is a boy. Sabine is a "success," her social mission as wife and mother fulfilled. No one protested when she dropped out of college. Now no one asks if she is happy, or if she cries when her husband sleeps with his mistress.

For Sabine, like most of her Haitian sisters, white, black, and brown, education merely has been a side route on the way to life's ultimate goal: marriage. The slogan of a well-known vocational school reads: "A woman who possesses her ten fingers is a treasure for her husband."

Sabine has followed all the rules, been a "good" girl, her dreams sacrificed for those of her father, her brother, her husband, and now, her son. Today, at twenty-five, she is an old woman, shrunken, lost inside her beautiful house and her "perfect" marriage, a silent shadow gliding at her husband's side.

My child grew up in the darkness of the cell. At the time, she was the only child in the political ward, but the ward of the common prisoners was a veritable nursery of skeletal, starving children. Children deprived of all health care or schooling. Children always dirty, eaten away by parasites and vermin. The rats entered the common cells—as they did the health supplies. It was only in 1971, to give a new face to the J. C. Duvalier regime, that they began to remove the children. But later, they started locking the children in the cells with their mothers. We have not been able to liberate the children. . . .[2]

After the death of "Papa Doc" in 1971, his son opened up the country to foreign investment after years of isolation. American and European capital began to flow into Haiti, along with economic aid and international relief programs to boost the economy and overcome the staggering poverty and unemployment. Tourism, beach resorts, new businesses . . . in Port-au-Prince, the sleek, glass-fronted Banque Internationale de Paris rises above pastel archways under which beggars sleep. While the face of the capital is changing, the basic structures remain intact.

Moving across the countryside, we repeatedly encounter the guards who signal our car to stop. Seeing our white faces, each guard waves us on. Behind us at one checkpoint, a woman on a donkey is forced to dismount. One by one, she removes the contents of her basket: vegetables, chicken, laundry, cigarettes . . . the guard seizes the cigarettes. "Go

[2] Elizabeth Philibert.

on, get out of here, hurry up." The woman trader whips the animal into a trot, crossing herself in a prayer of thanks. They will not arrest her or rape her. They did not ask for any papers. They let her keep the food. Such is the presence of the Tontons Macoutes, who extract their wages from a terrified population. Poor women are the most vulnerable. They have no bribery money to offer the guards; they must often pay the price of survival with their own bodies.

Those female bodies are also the vehicles for another presence on the island—religion —which exerts its tremendous influence in two different ways. While the dominant Roman Catholic doctrine constricts women, *Voudon,* the mix of African, indigenous, and Catholic beliefs, provides women with an avenue of resistance and even power. In Haiti, the Catholic Church has played an active role in opposing birth control and abortion and in supporting traditional institutions of marriage and the family in which women have inferior status to men.

By contrast, *Voudon* has a matriarchal focus, with such powerful female gods as Ezili and Dambala-Yeda. Women play an important role, participating in the ritual songs and dances even more than men, and going into states of ecstatic "possession" wherein they act as visionaries. The woman priestess or *hougan* (sorcerer) is both revered and feared for her special knowledge of herbs that can cure—or kill. *Hougans* are spiritual advisers and physical healers: more than one husband has been "advised" by a *hougan* to give his wife money or to never dare beat her again. The *hougan* also acts as a midwife, and offers women natural means of birth control and abortion through the use of certain herbs and roots.

Marie is a "restavek" (reste avec—"stay with"). Brought to our house when she was a baby, she is my grandmother's personal servant, her nanny. They are almost the same age, Grandmother with her coppery skin lightened by powder and her hair dyed an odd gray-blue; Marie with her skin black as coal and a pipe clenched between her teeth. I watch them, Grandmother lying on her bed, Marie sitting by her side, and wonder: How have you lived like this for so long? When did you stop playing together as children and become mistress and servant? How is it that you can claim to love each other? I want to know, as I accompany Grandmother on a special trip to buy Marie her favorite tobacco.

Marie receives a small wage, plus room and board. While Grandmother eats, she stands in the kitchen or in the shadows, waiting to fetch milk or butter, to climb the narrow stairs at Grandmother's whim. At night, after Grandmother is asleep, she herself sleeps on a cot in the hall, or if she is lucky, retires to her own room, a small concrete square covered with corrugated tin. Inside, her personal belongings are carefully arranged: bed, wooden chair, plastic washbasin, rosary beads, and a crucifix on the wall. Sunday is her only morning off. She will accompany Grandmother to church, as always.

"What about women's groups, the official Ministry for Women's Affairs?" My question is met with silence by recently arrived refugee women seeking exile in the US. Two words sum up their attitude: Tontons Macoutes. To them, anything connected with the government is suspect, and anyone who is living in Haiti—and can afford not to—is a tacit accomplice.

Up to now, the struggle of women in Haiti has been carried out by women of different classes whose goals have differed sharply. On the one hand, there are the many traditional women's clubs and social/charity groups, religious organizations, and government agencies whose campaigns center around such issues as health care, infant mortality, and education. These groups are composed of middle- and upper-class women whose views reflect their own enforced traditional role: women as mothers. On the other hand, there are the masses of poor, black, lower-class and rural women, whose daily existence is a struggle merely to survive.

Political parties are outlawed, yet women have been active leaders in the underground democratic movement. Recently, however, the government escalated its repression. In 1980, Marie-France Claude, vice-president of the illegal Christian Democratic Party, was sentenced to fifteen years imprisonment.

Since 1972, thousands have braved the dangerous Atlantic crossing in leaky boats to seek exile in the United States—only to be "welcomed" into detention camps. Of these immigrants, women have borne the brunt of the suffering: gang rapes, murders, their children thrown overboard by the profiteering male boatmen. This is their testimony. . . .

> Dear readers, judge for yourselves. No one who has a human heart, no one who knows what it is like to keep a home would act this way: to imprison more than a hundred women of different ages. . . . We have had terrible examples among the women . . . a girl of twenty-two who swallowed pieces of glass; another, aged twenty, who did the same; a third who drank a bottle of shampoo. How can a human being accept such crimes on his conscience! Who can we compare such a being with, who ignores the suffering of his neighbors?[3]

Today, I can visit Haiti only in my memory. I have left, unable to accept my own silence and fear. I do not condemn my cousin Sabine for surviving in the only way she could, but I deplore the society that fueled her racism and class privilege, and now sends her off to a living death. I wait for the day when women like Marie and my grandmother can join hands in the love they claim to feel for one another, and expose the common root of their false power and true powerlessness: sexism. Only then will they understand that we have all been victims of a patriarchy that denies our existence, and that as women we must free each other to free ourselves. I take courage from the actions of Marie-France Claude and my other Haitian sisters locked today in yet another prison—a US immigration detention center.

Woman of Haiti. She has survived. Her testimony begins to emerge. From the vacation paradise of hell, she is beginning to speak.

Suggested Further Reading

Détachement Féminin Vertières et Union Fanm Ayisyèn Patriyot (UFAP). *Femmes Haïtiennes ou La Moitié d'une Population* (Haitian Women or One Half The Population). Montreal: Maison d'Haïti, n.d.

Rasanbleman Fanm Ayisyèn (RAFA). *Femmes Haïtiennes.* Montreal: Maison d'Haïti, Inc., 1980.

Sylvain, Jeanne. "Notes sur la Famille" (Notes on the Family). *Conjonction,* No. 124, Aug., 1974.

Sylvain-Comhaire, Suzanne. "La Paysanne de Kenscoff" (The Peasant Women of Kenscoff). *La Femme de Couleur en Amérique Latine.* Ed. Roger Bastide. Paris: Anthropus, 1974.

Trouillot-Pascal, Ertha. "Droits et Privilèges de la Femme dans la Législation Civile et Sociale d'Haïti" (Rights and Privileges of the Woman in Civil and Social Legislation in Haiti). *Conjonction,* No. 124, Aug. 1974.

[3.] Open letter to the President of the United States, signed Feb. 25, 1982, by thirty-eight Haitian women; received and translated by the office of the Inter Regional Council for Haitian Refugees, Baldrich, Hato Rey.

Cacos La Gonaïve is a pseudonym for a writer whose family has lived in Haiti for three generations. She is a feminist activist "deeply involved in the struggle to create a world where women have a voice." She views the need to use a pseudonym for her above article as "a perfect example of the oppression a woman faces from the Duvalier regime."

THE SPANISH-SPEAKING CARIBBEAN:
"We Women Aren't Sheep"
by Magaly Pineda
(Translated by Magda Bogin)

"Those women who say they can't be at this meeting because of their 'responsibilities' aren't telling the truth. The truth is that their men don't want them here, because they don't want them finding out that women have rights. Because once we know those rights exist, we fight for them."

The speaker is a withered, prematurely aged woman, like most of the women in this isolated rural area near the border that separates the Dominican Republic from Haiti.

As in many other Third World countries, rural women of the Dominican Republic feel the weight of patriarchal ideology most strongly. The authority of father and husband is unquestioned, and submission even to one's own sons is simply not debatable. Nevertheless, on this half-island in the heart of the Caribbean, gateway to the conquest of the New World and three times overrun in this century by invading troops from the United States, an original and impressive phenomenon has begun to take hold: the active participation and struggle of women.

> We women aren't sheep
> you can lead to the fold,
> We will fight for our rights
> despite what we're told.

This *decima*, a peasant song that is invented or re-created in the exhausting hours in the fields, or at parties, or at the fiesta of the village patron saint, expresses the new, intense feeling of women being reborn. The birth, however, has been a painful one.

Background

Under the Trujillo dictatorship which turned our country into a jail for more than thirty years, patriarchal ideology and the exaltation of motherhood were used as pillars to support his iron rule. There were pensions for prolific mothers, special subsidies for women who bore twins, the deification of the dictator's own mother, and the exaltation of Catholic virgins. All this, along with demagogic concessions to "women's issues"—such as women's suffrage and the enactment of a protective labor code—plus the climate of general repression, made it virtually impossible for any major women's movement to develop prior to 1961. Neither did a deformed, underdeveloped capitalism contribute to the development of women's struggle.

Nonetheless, it's important to point out that the struggle of three women—against a dictatorship that attempted to silence them, tried to rape one, and finally had all three killed by paid thugs in 1960—helped speed the fall of the tyrant Trujillo.[1] Beginning in

[1] Minerva, Patria, and María Teresa Mirabal, along with the rest of their families (parents, husbands, and children), maintained a militant opposition to the Trujillo regime for more than twenty

1961, the country entered a period of accelerated confrontation and struggle during which women were, ironically, manipulated by the conservatives.

Balaguer, or the Return to the Past

With the North American military invasion of April 1965, 30,000 marines cut short the liberation struggle of an entire people. Not only did this action leave a profound scar in the national conscience of the Dominican Republic; it left wounds that are still bleeding.[2] Women, particularly younger women and those of the middle class, joined the struggle for sovereignty, though not in large numbers. The nature of their participation—which was led by the Federación de Mujeres Dominicanas (Dominican Women's Federation), a group formed in 1961—reflected the as yet undeveloped image of women, who were seen not as a social force in their own right but as a moral-support auxiliary for the struggles of men.

In July 1966, the North American troops withdrew, leaving behind as company stooge the recently elected President, Dr. Joaquín Balaguer. Nothing had changed since 1930. Woman-mother was again called on by the conservatives as keeper of the family: she was requested to contribute to the restoration of "order."

For twelve years, the government made sure to win women's support so as to keep itself in power. This was by demagogic appointments (we wound up with women in all of the twenty-six provincial governments), liberalization of various laws (elimination of discriminatory sections of the civil code, etc.), and an intense campaign to get women to vote. Furthermore, an enormous scaffolding of donations—*La Cruzada de Amor* (The Crusade of Love)—supported by the treasury and by forced contributions from merchants, was lavished for years on women from the poorest urban neighborhoods and rural areas. Bags of rice, oil, chickens, clothing and shoes, toys for children and candy at Christmas—these bought the vote and the consciousness of hundreds of thousands of women in need throughout the country. The bachelor president, surrounded by his sisters and depicted as a loyal, loving son, boasted, "While there are women and peasants I'll stay in power."

But the suffocating political climate, the lack of basic freedoms, and the economic recession were sapping the regime. Especially after 1975, women who had begun to learn words like discrimination and sexism began a process of change.

In the presidential campaign of 1978, women turned furiously against those who tried to use their poverty as a political weapon: "We want work, not charity" was the slogan women sang, particularly in urban areas, which were more accessible to opposition literature, and which were also more severely repressed. That year marked the first democratic moment in more than a century in the Dominican Republic. Political prisoners and exiles were granted amnesty. The ban on printing and dissemination of socialist ideas was lifted, inaugurating a political era marked by the people's enormous hunger to organize.

"Ever since my husband joined he really changed a lot. He's not so rough with the children and he pays more attention to the house and all of us. That's why the women here have started to think about joining, too. It's good to work together. You have more strength for the struggle." This sort of understanding about organization doesn't get born in a day. It is the result of patient, tenacious work—often at the cost of their own lives—

years. They were all imprisoned in 1960 and the three women, later liberated, were killed on a solitary road while returning from visiting their jailed husbands.

[2.] In 1965 a popular insurrection led by army colonel Francisco Caamaño defeated the government that had taken power in 1963 as a result of a coup. Pretending to "protect the lives of the US citizens living in the Dominican Republic," President L. B. Johnson ordered the landing of US troops in Santo Domingo and occupied the country for eighteen months.

by men and women who went out among workers, peasants, grass-roots organizations, students, and women throughout the country.

There have been several key factors which help to explain the increase of women's organizations: the greater numbers of females in higher education, the intensification of the economic crisis in rural areas, and the deplorable job conditions in the cities. And the growing international feminist movement has also had a vital impact.

However distorted and/or minimized, news of "crazy" women demanding freedom, equality, and participation in countries all around the world did not fail to reach the ears of Dominican women. The "officialization" of the theme of women through the declaration of International Women's Year extended the radius of influence. There is a broad radio-communications network in our country, as well as an able and generally progressive press corps, both of which saw to it that echoes of International Women's Year reached even the most isolated regions of the country.

Those of us who, as militant feminists, spent that year speaking all over the country— both in cities and in the countryside—were astonished at women's receptivity to the idea of their oppression. But we were distressed by the question most frequently asked at the end of each conference, no matter where it was, whether in the bare headquarters of a peasant group four hours from the capital or in a community center: *"We understand that we're oppressed, [but] what can we do about it?"*

This latent question now began to seek out answers. Even under repression, several organizations had been working patiently for years, but it was really in 1978 that these and others began to flourish. The increase and/or strengthening of women's groups was most impressive in the countryside, less so in poor or "marginal" urban neighborhoods, and weakest, though qualitatively important, within the so-called critical Left.

Unlike many developed countries and some Third World nations with a strong French or British influence, in the Dominican Republic the women's movement has not taken hold within the middle class. Such professional women as social scientists and professors are generally outside the movement and in many cases constitute a serious resistance to it. As a result, there has been scant development in such areas as feminist theory, the discussion of specific women's issues, or the raising of demands considered crucial to our liberation: abortion, sex education, etc. Only a very small number of women from these sectors (the professions) has articulated a clear feminist position. Beaten by the Right and criticized by the Left, misunderstood by women of the middle class, some have succumbed to the anguish of being standard bearers for the feminist heresy and have dropped out of the movement.

But there is good reason to expect new perspectives, in light of the creation of new nuclei of women in the past few years. Many women still linked emotionally and officially to traditional political parties have nonetheless begun to believe in feminist ideas and to join together, creating important connections between the Dominican Republic's women's movement and the women's movement in the rest of the world.

A Feminism with Popular Roots

For feminists with close ties to the lives of poor women, organizing women in our country is a challenge that revolves around the following questions:

How can we broaden, strengthen, and deepen the organized participation of poor women?

How can we attract women from the middle class (intellectuals, professionals, state employees, workers from the private sector) and ensure their participation?

Which demands should be central to organizing, not only to draw women in but broaden their political awareness and ensure their participation in social change?

What forms and modalities should we develop in our propaganda, and in meetings, to ensure that our work, study, and mobilization efforts are carried out not only democratically but with the full participation of poor women—and to make that participation critical, creative, and dynamic?

These are the questions we are trying to answer and about which we are sharing information and reflections with other women of Latin America and the Caribbean. The challenge for Latin American feminists is to build a women's movement that makes central the struggle to be free as a gender and at the same time is rooted in the social forces historically engaged in social change—to build, in other words, a feminist movement with genuine popular roots.

It is true that we have no model or successful frame of reference for this feminism. It is also true that we can see in our own practice certain similarities with old forms of struggle we still need to overcome. Nonetheless, the most important thing is to study our own errors, learn from our successes, continue to develop our theoretical level, and maintain a systematic critique of our methodology.

We also believe that women must lose our fear of power if we want to become a serious political force. This is vital if we want to build a clearly *feminist* women's movement with the strong support of those women who feel the most social and personal oppression, and if we want to build a new society while simultaneously confronting the system of values and prejudices that allows exploitation and oppression to flourish. For us there can be no difference. We cannot say, "Today the people are breaking their chains, tomorrow will be women's turn." No. We believe that the dual relationship of patriarchy and capitalism can only be destroyed by combatting both of them *at once* through a feminist socialist struggle against the bases of sex and class power.

Suggested Further Reading

[Practically speaking, only one book exists on the situation of women in the Dominican Republic; published in 1976, it contains the works of the Seminario Hermanas Mirabal (Mirabal Sisters Seminar) done in 1975 by the University Committee of Women. The majority of the works on women have appeared as articles in newspapers and magazines, and some research works or theses from universities, most focusing on specific aspects: fertility, health, etc.—M. Pineda.]

Seminario Hermanas Mirabal, eds. *La Mujer Dominicana.* Santo Domingo: Universidad Autónoma de Santo Domingo, 1976.

Magaly Pineda was born in Santo Domingo in 1943. In 1960 her parents left to live in Puerto Rico because of the dictatorial regime of Rafael Trujillo; there she entered the University of Puerto Rico and obtained a bachelor of political science degree in 1964. She returned to her own country in 1965, several months before the armed conflict which resulted in the intervention of the US on April 28 of that year. During the foreign occupation she participated in defensive actions against it, organized by the Federation of Dominican Women. After 1970, she worked to publicize feminist ideas through alternative education projects, while a professor in the department of sociology at the Autonomous University of Santo Domingo—dividing her time between feminist work, classes, raising her three children, and working with the Committee of Relatives of Political Prisoners and Missing Persons, since her husband was one of hundreds detained by the Balaguer regime. She founded the Center of Investigation for Women's Action (CIPAF), and is general coordinator of the Center. She is also involved in developing the Women's Studies Association of Latin America and the Caribbean (ALACEM), and has written for various newspapers and magazines on women.

CHILE
(Republic of Chile)

Chile is located in southwestern South America, bordered by Peru to the north, Bolivia and Argentina to the east, and the Pacific Ocean to the south and west. **Area:** 741,766 sq. km. (286,396 sq. mi.). **Population** (1980): 11,487,100, 50.5% female. **Capital:** Santiago.

DEMOGRAPHY. Languages: Spanish, indigenous languages. **Races or Ethnic Groups:** Mestizo 66%, Spanish 25%, Native Indian (Fuegians, Araucanians, Changas) 5%, other. **Religions:** Roman Catholicism 90%, Protestant, Judaism. **Education** (% enrolled in school, 1975): Age 6–11—of all girls 100%, of all boys 100%; age 12–17—of all girls 85%, of all boys 85%; higher education—in 1977 women were 39% of all university students. **Literacy** (1977): Women 87%, men 89%. **Birth Rate** (per 1000 pop., 1975–80): 21. **Death Rate** (per 1000 pop., 1975–80): 7. **Infant Mortality** (per 1000 live births, 1975–80): Female 38, male 42. **Life Expectancy** (1975–80): Female 69 yrs., male 62 yrs.

GOVERNMENT. A military junta led by Gen. Augusto Pinochet (now President) came to power by an army-led coup in 1973; the National Congress was dissolved and all political activities banned. A 1980 Constitution stipulates a return to democracy after a minimum of 8 yrs. **Women's Suffrage:** National, 1949; municipal elections, 1934. Federal elections currently (1983) suspended for all voters. **Equal Rights:** Discrimination based on sex, religion, race, etc., is prohibited by the Constitution. **Women in Government:** As of 1983, the Minister of the Department of Justice is a woman; approx. 28% of family court judges are women (a less well-paid job avoided by most male lawyers). In Apr. 1982 the President created a Ministry of the Family headed by Carmen Grez, who opposes divorce, contraception, and abortion.

ECONOMY. Currency: Chilean Peso (May 1983: 74. = $1 US). **Gross National Product** (1980): $24 billion. **Per Capita Income** (1980): $2160; 38% of the population lives in poverty. **Women's Wages as a Percentage of Men's:** No data obtainable. **Equal Pay Policy:** None. **Production** (Agricultural/Industrial): Fish, grains, fruit; iron, steel, machinery, paper, pulp. **Women as a Percentage of Labor Force** (1980): 36%; **of agricultural force**—no general statistics obtainable (2% of women workers are employed in agriculture, 1975); **of industrial force**—no general statistics obtainable (of manufacturing 25%, 1970); **of military**—women are not subject to a draft, although some are in the armed forces in civilian jobs, and in the auxiliary branch of the army, in the *carabineros,* civil police, and the investigation service. **(Employed) Women's Occupational Indicators** (1980): Of professionals 50% (80% of whom are concentrated in nursing and primary education); the majority of women are employed in domestic service. **Unemployment** (1980): 12%, female 11.1%, male 12.2%.

GYNOGRAPHY. Marriage. *Policy:* Governed by the Acts on Civil Marriage. Marriage is by mutual consent. Property generally comes under joint ownership *(sociedad conyugal)* which is managed by the husband; if both spouses agree, property can be owned separately. *Practice:* Female mean age at marriage (1970–78): 23; women age 15–49 in union (1970–78): 53.4%; marriages (per 1000 pop., 1980): 7.7. In recent decades there has been a great increase in common-law unions. A woman has no rights as a common-law wife and cannot demand support for herself or her children if a man refuses to recognize them. **Divorce.** *Policy:* There are no provisions for divorce. *Practice:* Extra-legal dissolution of marriages is reportedly common. **Family.** *Policy:* Employed women are entitled to a 6-week pre- and 12-week post-delivery paid maternity leave. Decree Law No. 2200 restricted maternity leave by allowing employers to hire women for short- or fixed-term contracts without maternity benefits. The Civil Code requires employers of more than 20 women to provide day-care services; employed women have the right to take 2 nursing breaks per day. *Practice:* No data obtainable. **Welfare.** *Policy:* A national system of health services and a social security system have been established. An emergency public works program is run by the State and is the principal aid for unemployment. *Practice:* In 1977 approx. 1.5 million employees were covered under the national health service. In 1983 the emergency public works program employed almost 13% of the Chilean labor force. The majority of the employees are women who work 27.5 hours a week and earn $27 per month with an additional $5.50 for each child under age 8. Another program pays heads-of-households $110 per month. Both programs are filled.

Contraception. *Policy:* Legal; sterilization illegal. The government has stated that it will not restrict family-planning services but opposes their "indiscriminate use." The State's goal to encourage population growth "plays a basic role in national security." *Practice:* Women age 15–44 in union using contraception (1981): 43%, of which modern methods 100% (primarily IUD). Pressure from the Roman Catholic Church impedes contraceptive use. **Abortion.** *Policy:* Legal only in cases of risk to the woman's life; the performing physician must have the written approval of 2 other physicians. Other procedures are punishable under the Penal Code (Arts. 342–45) by 3–5 yrs. imprisonment for the woman and 540 days–3 yrs. for the practitioner (physicians are subject to harsher penalties). The Civil Code gives courts authority to take any steps to protect the fetus; if a pregnant woman is convicted of a crime, any punishment which could threaten the life or health of the fetus must wait until after delivery; under the Penal Code (Art. 85), "the death penalty shall not be carried out against a pregnant woman, nor shall she be informed of the sentence imposed upon her, until 40 days after the birth." *Practice:* Illegal abortions (per 1000 women of fertile age, 1974): 17.9. Abortions account for 38% of all maternal deaths in Chile; hospitalization rates for complications from abortion averaged 40 per 1000 women

(reproductive age) in Santiago (1975). **Illegitimacy.** *Policy:* A Reform of the Civil Code improves the legal status of "natural children" who are voluntarily accepted by 1 or both parents. *Practice:* In 1980 out-of-wedlock births accounted for 26.8% of total births; among females under age 20 the rate was 44.1% (the rate of infant mortality was 3 times as high among the latter group as children born to women age 20–29). **Homosexuality.** *Policy:* Under the Penal Code (Art. 373), any person who offends "good customs or modesty" and/or "provokes serious scandal" is subject to a minimum–medium punishment. *Practice:* No statistics obtainable. Harassment of lesbian women and homosexual men is reportedly common.

Incest. *Policy:* Illegal; sexual relations between persons with knowledge of blood relation, whether ascendant or descendant or "legitimate" or "illegitimate," through blood or marriage (even if the person is over age 20), is punishable under the Penal Code (Art. 364). *Practice:* No data obtainable. **Sexual Harassment.** *Policy:* None. *Practice:* No data obtainable. **Rape.** *Policy:* Illegal under the Penal Code (Arts. 358–62) "if force or intimidation are used," if the female is without her senses or reason, or if she is under age 12; punishable by up to the maximum penalty. A convicted rapist can get a suspended sentence if he agrees to marry his victim (Art. 369) or pay her or her family financial compensation (Art. 370). *Practice:* No statistics obtainable (see HERSTORY). Rape as a form of torture inflicted by police on female political prisoners has been documented as common. **Battery.** *Policy:* No specific legislation concerning wife-beating; covered under general assault laws. *Practice:* No data obtainable. **Prostitution.** *Policy:* Illegal under the Penal Code (Art. 367). A person who promotes prostitution of minors is punishable by a fine and the maximum penalty. *Practice:* No statistics obtainable. Prostitution is reportedly rising among young girls who have been forced to drop out of school by the economic crisis (1983). **Traditional/Cultural Practices:** No data obtainable. **Crisis Centers.** *Policy:* None. *Practice:* None.

HERSTORY. Pre-Columbian Chile was inhabited by the Incas (see PERU) in the north and the Araucanians in the south. Spanish colonization took place in the mid-1500's; Independence was won in 1818. The beginnings of a women's movement in the late 1800's focused on the entrance of women into higher education and the professions. Paulina Starr was the first woman dentist (1884) and Ernestina Pérez and Eloisa Díaz were the first 2 women to receive medical degrees (1887). Gabriela Mistral, one of Latin America's greatest poets, was born in 1889. Amanda Labarca, a prominent early feminist, set up a Círculo de Lectura (Women's Reading Circle) in 1915. The President appointed her director of the girls' Liceo Rosario Orrego of Santiago in 1916, despite conservative charges that this created a "threat to Catholic precepts and practices in Chile" and the resignation of the cabinet. She created the Chilean Federation of Women's Institutions, which worked for suffrage but dissolved when the vote was achieved. In 1919 the National Council of Women was founded to pursue the civil and political rights of women. In 1928 the Feminine Union of Chile was founded and in 1935, the Pro-Woman's Emancipation movement formed to organize all women to fight for social, economic, and legal liberation. The first National Congress of Women was held in 1944. María de la Cruz founded the Chilean Women's Party in 1946 and helped build a women's movement that was instrumental in electing Carlos Ibáñez president in 1952. In 1973 many housewives of the middle class were mobilized for food-shortage protest demonstrations, their own genuine needs manipulated by reactionary forces in the military coup that overthrew the socialist government of Salvador Allende Gossens.

Since the coup, the situation of women has deteriorated, and women of all social strata have suffered extreme repression by the government. Many women have organized for the first time to combat the dictatorship, forming resistance committees to carry out acts of sabotage and setting up kitchens in the slums with revenues produced by *arpilleras*—embroideries with political themes that are smuggled out of the country for sale. Gladys Díaz, a prominent journalist member of MIR, an outlawed party, was one of thousands of women political prisoners taken by the secret police in 1975; she was tortured repeatedly with electric shock and beatings to force her to divulge information about her activities. The assassination of Orlando Letelier, a former Allende cabinet member, and an American woman, Randy Moffitt, caused strong international protest in 1978. In 1982 Letelier's widow, Isabel, founded the Chile Committee for Human Rights, to compile information on violations in additions to those already documented by Amnesty International and the OAS Human Rights Commission.

Women are also organizing specifically against male domination and abuse. In Antofagasta, north of Santiago, a group of karate-trained women are operating a "hit squad" to take revenge on male adulterers, rapists, and batterers. Their stated purpose: "We are determined to make it known here in northern Chile that women are no longer abused."

MYTHOGRAPHY. Auchimalgen was the moon goddess and special protector of the Araucanians, who shared pre-conquest Chile with the Incas. There still exists a tradition of fortune-telling and sorcery, practiced primarily by women, among but not exclusive to the indigenous peoples of Chile.

CHILE: Women of Smoke
by Marjorie Agosin
(Translated by Cola Franzen)

And even though they keep me blindfolded forever, I will always be able to find my way back to Chile, my country, set between the Cordillera of the Andes and the sea, between a dialectic of landscapes, between the malevolent Pacific and the untamable Andes. Between these opposing confines I grew up, among things proper for little girls, beside my grandmothers who predicted a tranquil future for me, and also beside marvelous wise old women dressed in black, *rebozos* around their shoulders, who bewitched me with their native wisdom and their universe of signs and symbols.

From an early age, I understood the inequality between social classes in Chile. I felt—and later learned for a fact—that social mobility in Chile is completely imaginary, and that the servant who bathed us and perfumed us with the odor of her skin would remain a servant, a marginal person, living in the back room in houses of "good families." A girl fortunate enough to be born in a house made of cement and not of adobe will enjoy some privileges, such as going to school and being able to enter the university. But this privilege will be chilled during adolescence into something ambivalent, doubtful, and limited. The girl who grows up in this bourgeois home and continues her studies will rarely be able to acquire meaningful work or an important position. Regardless of intelligence or ability, she will remain subordinate to men.

The Roman Catholic religion which functions as a dominant ideology in Latin American society seeks to ensure that women from the middle and upper classes stay at home and devote themselves solely to the care of their children and households. Women of the lower classes, perhaps less bound by the morality of the Church, nonetheless procreate for two other reasons: ignorance of birth-control methods and the hope that children born to them will somehow remedy their situation as marginal beings. As a consequence, women of all classes are relegated to do the minor chores of the society.

I find myself remembering two cases. I think of you, María J.—you who have from childhood worked in a beauty shop in order to contribute to the upkeep of your family. You sweep up hair with a macabre broom, lank hair, faded and abandoned on the floor. You spend years subjected to that broom, until suddenly it is transformed in your hand. You begin to paint with it on pieces of newspaper, to paint with the broom instead of with a paintbrush. You are reborn as an inspired artist, and your broom is no longer fetter but flight. But this was all ephemeral. You have seven children, and must go with your husband and children to the north. You are returned to the broom. You turn into a woman insubstantial as smoke.

And you, Emma S., born into a wealthy household, your father an owner of tin mines. You lacked for nothing—except for the only thing you really wanted: to be allowed to learn to take photographs. But first your father and then your husband told you that girls never could learn to use complicated gadgets, and you never managed to get near a camera. And now, Emma, with no father, no husband, and no country, how will you picture and develop your story of solitude?

Oppositions and conflicts. Duality of classes. I close my eyes and fly back in memory to the patio of my childhood home. I find there the sky-blue eyes of my grandmother, her dark-skinned servant by her side, both women watching life go by from behind the grillwork of the fence, both of them strangers sidelined from the flow of history.

But there have always been stories of exceptions. I must, I have to, believe that it wasn't always this way, that somewhere, in some place, the exceptions bloomed: that the women sitting on the sofas joined hands with the women kneeling washing the floor.

Something like this has indeed occurred in Chilean history, most recently at the end of the 1960's during the government of the Christian Democratic Party and, following their term in office, during the government of Salvador Allende, 1970–73. This was a period when we all experienced an intense reconstruction of our lives as women.

It cannot be overemphasized that the emancipation and liberation of women in Chile has always been tied to the political situation. Women's liberation is not a separate, isolated action, but an integral part of political events. Progress in the status of women in Chile has historically been associated with political movements of the Left.

In the 1960's, then, it was the express policy of the Christian Democrats to reform the values accorded to women by the dominant society. This policy broke with the past and started to build a new structure. Organizations were set up, such organizations as the Mothers' Centers, places where working women and women from the middle class could come together and work together for the common good.

One of the most successful projects to come out of the Mothers' Centers was to start a sort of country-wide communal cottage industry where women came together to make embroidery-paintings called *arpilleras*. They are an authentic popular art form, appreciated not only all over Chile but throughout the world. They show everyday scenes—the church, the school, a woman kneading bread—and are embroidered in brilliant colors with wool yarn on ordinary fabrics. But for women, their significance goes far beyond their esthetic qualities, though these qualities are impressive. It is the collective nature of their creation which is so important to women. Antonia Pérez from Isla Negra, a small fishing village south of Santiago, tells how she and other fishermen's wives began to make the *arpilleras:* one was assigned to buy the yarn, she says, another to choose the colors, another to pick designs, others to do the selling; then, amid the noise of the Pacific and the hiss of the braziers, they came together to tell stories and to embroider.

During the government of Allende, the Mothers' Centers multiplied. More than ever before, women became a powerful work force in the country, working alongside the men. For the first time, women were in the midst of history, until then forbidden territory.

So in spite of the various economic and political problems that developed during the government of Allende, it was a period of renaissance for women and for popular culture. We were reborn out of an iron silence. The Marías could again begin to paint, the Emmas could learn to take photographs. My nana Delfina, round as a fish, learned to knit and to read.

But not all women were happy with the new order. I remember very well the demonstrations with empty pots during Allende's time. Housewives of the middle class, manipulated and organized by the Right, began to march every evening at the same time, banging empty pots to protest food scarcities. (For the poorer classes, of course, food scarcity has always been a way of life.) And the only thing accomplished by that famous march of the empty pots was to forge another link which led to the violence in the soccer stadiums where approximately 5000 political prisoners were taken by the fascist junta. And now the pots are full only for some . . . and who will bring our dead sisters back to life? Perhaps some nights the pots will sleepwalk and fill themselves with guts, viscera, and nipples from the garbage cans.

And so the old aristocratic, bourgeois ideology reappears. The traditional values which have been the sole lot of women for so long—order, family, religion—are reimposed. The insurgence of working-class women is dissipated; the enthusiasm of one of the most humane revolutions in our history is extinguished.

Today, in 1982, women in Chile are still divided. More than ever I see my grandmother behind the grillwork, her dark-skinned servant by her side. And I see my mother yearning to return to the country she left but never left. I see them hidden behind their *rebozos,* black, white, and gray, each one enclosed in her own silence, speaking only in gestures.

In Chile today the possibilities for social change and for women's liberation seem farther away than ever, because of economic and political factors. Social mobility continues to be completely illusory. I see shopwindows filled with imported perfumes and clothes priced within the reach of very few. I see blonde, thin models on the covers of slick magazines, reinforcing the old restricting values.

The group suffering most since the events of 1973 are the women of the lower class. Unemployment and widowhood affects them in particular, and we once again see their children barefoot in the snow, their skin blue with cold, just as they were described so many years ago by our Nobel Prize-winning poet Gabriela Mistral. We see girl-women, women-girls, who, instead of being able to learn to read, to sing, and to embroider, must become prostitutes in order to survive: Cecilia, who wonders if she should buy a coat made of animal skins with money earned through the sale of her own skin; Jacqueline, hiding in her pocket the fifty pesos earned from a disgusting old man; María Elena, her belly swollen with a child from an unknown father, washing the sheets of her *patrón* in the bathtub, and walking alone down the hill to the charity ward where Carlitos was born. Nobody went to see you, María Elena; the father had already disappeared, and you asked me if I could give you a diaper. My radiant country has been dulled into a place where everybody is a suspicious stranger. Silence and memory closes over all of us women.

But out of the silence come voices which will become hands and histories. There is now a Center of Women's Studies in Chile, where groups of women, especially from the middle class, meet to study and to think about their lives. Perhaps this will be a first step in freeing ourselves from the prevailing ideology. There is also the work of CENECA (Center of Cultural and Artistic Investigation), which is directed mostly by men but which claims to be interested in reviving the Mothers' Centers and in promoting popular culture. *Arpilleras* are still being made in Chile, though they are not as luminous as before. They show empty pots, empty tables, the door and name of the agency that gives aid to the unemployed. But in spite of the silence that envelops and overwhelms us, the *arpilleras* fly like doves through the world, telling our story. And I found Antonia Pérez recently, surrounded by her children, embroidering a tree just leafing out in spring.

In Santiago, my city, I ask at the bookstore, "Where are the women poets, the women novelists?" Nobody answers me. But I know that we exist, here and abroad. I think of Ester, who was allowed by her editors to sign her articles in one of the leading newspapers only with her initials. But we knew they were *her* initials. And I cannot forget the all-women's poetry readings to which women came from far and near, even from the distant southern island of Chiloé. But the poets of the oligarchy didn't come to listen to the "Muses"—which was what they called us. And my uncle didn't come either. He stayed drinking scotch with his friends. . . . And what did their absence matter, after all? We listened to each other and grew and gave life to our unknown giants. And blind Mila, our splendid poet, came to see us.

So the hope green in earlier years is not destroyed, only dormant—and not because we want to sleep, but because once again the political situation of the country dictates our position as women. We are women without papers, without power. We are sleepwalkers searching for bread and for injured children and for drunken husbands. . . .

Chile is my beloved country and even though they keep me blindfolded forever, I will always live nestled in her slender waist, with her mountains like breasts and the southern rains falling like the tears I shed now as I write. And somehow we must continue to ask ourselves: *How can we live and die in peace? How can we escape the violation of our bodies?*

I would tell the powerful nations to stop building Holiday Inns when they build no schools, to stop sending airplanes and to send pencils and books instead. Keep the bottles of perfume in your own countries, I would say, and let the odor of our solitary southern *araucaria*[1] flowers cover our country.

Our liberty as women will come from our own efforts. And it will come with the help of others strong enough to help us, those who will want to know and understand us, who will want to learn from those of us who have not forgotten how to live and how to sing. Bullets cannot kill us, bonds cannot bind the strength of our hands, blindfolds cannot imprison our vision. We hold in our own palms our ultimate truths.

Suggested Further Reading

Andreas, Carol. *Nothing Is as It Should Be.* Cambridge, MA: Schenkman, 1976; a North American feminist tells of her life in Chile before and after the coup.

Castells, Manuel. *Lucha de Clases en Chile.* México: Siglo XXI Editores, 1974.

Klimpel, Felicitas. *La Mujer Chilena.* Santiago: Editorial Andres Bello, 1962.

Mattelart, Michelle and Armand. *La Mujer Chilena en una Nueva Sociedad.* Santiago: Editorial del Pacífico, 1968.

Parra, Violeta. *Poésie Populaire des Andes.* Paris: Maspero, 1964.

Marjorie Agosin, poet and literary critic, was born in Chile in 1955. She is the author of two volumes of poetry, *Chile: Gemidos y Cantares* (Editorial El Observador, Santiago, Chile, 1977) and *Conchali* (Senda Nueva de Ediciones, 1980). She has published several articles dealing with contemporary Latin American women writers and her latest book-length work of criticism is devoted to the Chilean author, María Luisa Bombal (New York: Senda Nueva de Ediciones, 1983). Presently she is an assistant professor of Latin American literature at Wellesley College in Massachusetts.

[1.] *Araucaria araucana,* named for the Araucano Indians who lived in the region where the flower flourishes.

China
(People's Republic of China)

China occupies the bulk of the habitable mainland of East Asia. Bordered to the north by the USSR, to the east by North and South Korea, the Yellow Sea, and the East China Sea, to the south by Vietnam, Laos, Burma, India, Bhutan, and Nepal, and to the west by India, Pakistan, and the USSR. **Area:** 9,597,000 sq. km. (3,704,400 sq. mi.). **Population** (1982): 1,031,882,511, female 48.5%. **Capital:** Beijing.

DEMOGRAPHY. Languages: Modern Standard Chinese (official, based on Mandarin), Canton, Shanghai, Fukien, and Hakka dialects, Tibetan, Vigus (Turkic). **Races or Ethnic Groups:** Han Chinese 93.3%, 55 national minorities (including Manchu, Mongol, Korean, Turkic groups) 6.7%. **Religions:** Confucianism, Taoism, Buddhism (traditional), Islam 5%, Roman Catholicism 0.2%, Protestant. Constitution guarantees right to practice religion or not, and to propagate atheism. **Education** (% enrolled in school, 1980): Age 6–11—93%; national education level (1982)—primary school 35.7%, junior middle school 17.8%, senior middle school 6.6%, university 0.6%; in 1981 females comprised 43.9% of primary school, 39.6% of middle school, and 24.4% of university; higher education—(Beijing University only, 1982) women were 25% of all students, 20% of science students, 9% of physics; in 1982 women were 27% of students in workers' vocational schools and part-time universities, and 30% of students in short-term training courses in factories, mines, and other enterprises. **Literacy** (1982): 76.5%; 70% of the illiterate and semi-literate pop. is women (government est., 1983). The Women's Federation organizes special literacy programs for women. **Birth Rate** (per 1000 pop., 1982): 20.9. **Death Rate** (per 1000 pop., 1982): 6.3. **Infant Mortality** (per 1000 live births, 1975–80): Female 49, male 53. **Life Expectancy** (1975–80): Female 70 yrs., male 66 yrs.

GOVERNMENT. There are 22 provinces (including Tawian),* 5 autonomous regions (Inner Mongolia, Xinjiang-Uygur, Guangxi-Zhuang, Ningxia-Hui, and Tibet), and 3 municipalities (Beijing, Shanghai, Tienjin), with various forms of local government; affiliation with the central government ranges from semi-autonomy to direct administration. Deputies to the National People's Congress (NPC) are elected indirectly from local and provincial congresses for 5-yr. terms. The NPC chooses the Premier of the State Council at the recommendation of the Central Committee of the Communist Party, and chooses the State Council's other members at the recommendation of the Premier. The State Council, or administrative branch, is composed of 40 ministries and 13 commissions. The Communist Party: Party members are admitted at the local level (currently 39 million members, 3.8% of total pop.). Members choose delegates to the Central Party Congress, which elects a Central Committee; it in turn appoints a Standing Committee and Politburo. The Politburo has a 7-member Standing Committee and is the center of political power. There are 8 other political parties, all under the leadership of the Communist Party. **Women's Suffrage:** 1921 in Hunan Province; full political rights stipulated nationally for women in 1949 by the "Common Program" (prelude to the Constitution). **Equal Rights:** The 1952 Constitution stipulated women's equality in all spheres of political, economic, cultural, social, and family life, as does the 1982 Constitution (Art. 48). **Women in Government:** 21.2% of the delegates to the Sixth National People's Congress, 9% of the Standing Committee of the NPC, and 1 out of 13 members of the State Council, Vice-Premier Chen Muhua, are women (1983). There are 4

* The People's Republic of China defines Taiwan as 1 of its provinces (see pp. xiii of Prefatory Note).

women ministers out of 40 (Minister of Foreign Economic Relations, Minister of the Nuclear Industry, Minister of the Textile Industry, and Minister of Water Conservancy and Electric Power), and no women in the Standing Committee of the Politburo (1982). There are 11 women out of 210 members (5.2%) of the Central Committee of the Communist Party, and 13 out of 138 (9.4%) alternate members (1983). There is 1 woman out of 26 members of the Politburo, Deng Yingchao, and 1 woman alternate, Chen Muhua. The actual number of individual women holding high government positions is lower than statistics indicate since most women hold more than 1 title at the same time. The number of women in official positions increases at the local level.

ECONOMY. Currency: Yuan (May 1983: 1.96 = $1 US). Gross National Product (1980): $283.3 billion (in 1983 China reported a marked GNP increase to $495 billion). Per Capita Income (1980): $290. Women's Wages as a Percentage of Men's: No data obtainable. Equal Pay Policy: In effect since 1949; in actuality, wages are determined by the number of work points assigned to a job, and industries with a high concentration of women are assigned fewer work points. On rural communes men typically earn 10 points per day while women are restricted to a ceiling of 8 points not based on work performed, but because of the belief that women are weaker. Production (Agricultural/Industrial): Rice, wheat, grains, cotton; iron and steel, textiles, farm implements, plastics, petroleum, trucks. Women as a Percentage of Labor Force (1980): 38%; of agricultural force 40–50%; of industrial force—no general statistics obtainable (of factory and office workers 33%, 1982); of military—no data obtainable. (Employed) Women's Occupational Indicators: Of University faculties 25%, of scientists and technicians approx. 33% (1983); of metallurgy 14%, of medicine 58%, of textiles 60%, of childcare and early childhood education 100% (1982). Unemployment (1979): 20 million; no total rate or rates by sex obtainable, but most of those who remain unemployed are

women, because women are seen as problem workers: pregnancy, childcare, etc.

GYNOGRAPHY. Marriage. *Policy:* Violation of freedom of marriage is prohibited by the Constitution (since 1952) and by the Marriage Law (1950 and 1980). Interference by force is prosecuted only upon complaint and is punishable by imprisonment for not more than 2 yrs. or, if death results from the force, 2–7 yrs. Bigamy is punishable by imprisonment for not more than 2 yrs. Mercenary marriage (selling brides) and the exaction of money or gifts is prohibited. The Marriage Law stipulates that both partners enjoy equal status in the home, property is jointly owned and managed, a woman has the right to use her birth-name, children can choose their father's or mother's name, husbands and wives can inherit each other's property. The legal marriage age is 20 for women and 22 for men. *Practice:* Female mean age at marriage (Shanghai Area sample only, 1980): 26.8 urban, 24.2 suburban; women age 15–49 in union (Shanghai Area sample only, 1980): 46% urban, 66% suburban; no national data obtainable. Very few women remain single for life or marry before age 20. Traditionally, marriages were contracted by parents with the help of a go-between. Often girls were betrothed as children and sent to live with their future in-laws. Girls also were sold as concubines or as second wives. They had no status in the family except through their sons. Second wives were often taken when a first wife failed to produce a son. Widows were not allowed to remarry, and girls who had been betrothed or married as children were considered widows if their husbands died before the girls reached maturity. Widows were expected to enter Buddhist convents, serve their parents-in-law, or commit suicide. Widows in poor families were often sold by their parents-in-law, who kept their children; marriage to a widow was inauspicious, so they were usually sold as concubines or slaves. An adulterous woman legally could be killed by her husband.

Free marriage without the aid of a go-between is still relatively rare, and largely an urban occurrence. A 1979 sample study in Anhui Province showed that of

14,586 marriages 15% were free choice, 75% were arranged but agreed to, and 10% were arranged against the will of the couple. Women are still sold occasionally in marriage or as concubines, either by their parents or through kidnapping.** Women for sale have been reported in at least 7 provinces from 1980 to 1982. In 1981 a man in Guangdong was convicted of kidnapping and selling 115 women for a total of $14,000 US. (Traffickers are sentenced to 5 or more yrs. in prison.) Despite a public policy of shared housework, in practice women shoulder the double burden. Women almost always move in with their husbands' families, where they occupy a relatively subordinate position. It is difficult for a woman to assert her legal rights, especially in rural areas. Avenues of recourse do include the local women's committee.

Divorce. *Policy:* Legal under the 1980 Marriage Law when both husband and wife desire it. When 1 party insists on divorce, the court (or commune, factory, neighborhood committee) try to effect a reconciliation. The husband is not allowed to apply for divorce when the wife is pregnant, or within 1 yr. after the birth of a child (unless there are extenuating circumstances). Infertility and infirmity are not acceptable grounds. *Practice:* No national divorce-rate data obtainable. For Beijing (divorces as % of marriages, 1980): 2.66%; for Shanghai Area Sample (divorced women as % of total married women of child-bearing age, 1980): 0.5%. Divorce rates are even lower in the countryside. In dynastic China divorce was solely a male privilege. The 1930 Civil Code gave women the right to divorce under limited circumstances. The Communists' attempt to implement an equal divorce law created more controversy than any other issue in their base areas. During the Marriage Law campaigns of 1950 and 1953, the pending law became known as the "divorce law" and

the "women's law" because so many women sought divorces. Between 70,000 and 80,000 suicides were reported for each yr. from 1950 to 1953—the majority (many of which were murders) over the issue of divorce. Divorces became much more difficult to obtain after 1957. Despite liberalization of the law (1980), divorce remains difficult to obtain unless both parties petition for it. Since many cases involve battery and the husband refuses to co-petition, mediation often locks women into abusive marriages. **Family.** *Policy:* Owing to tremendous population pressures, the State Family Policy is "1 couple, 1 child." Incentives (instituted in 1980) for having 1 child include preferential housing, employment, childcare, free education and medical benefits for the child, and a monthly cash bonus for as long as 14 yrs. in some places. In 1982 penalties for having more than 1 child came into effect. These may include taxes of up to 15% of a family's income from the time a woman becomes pregnant with her second child until that child is age 7; penalties become harsher with additional children. Neither incentives nor disincentives are uniform nationwide. Parents are legally responsible for the support of their children, and adults for the support of their parents and grandparents. Abandoning a dependent is punishable by imprisonment for not more than 5 yrs., detention, or surveillance. Pregnant women receive free pre- and post-natal care and free delivery either at home with an attendant midwife (rural) or in a hospital (urban).*** In cities, women factory and staff workers are entitled to 8 weeks paid maternity leave, and 1 hour nursing time during workdays for 1 yr. (1950 Labor Insurance Law). On rural communes maternity leave is not paid and lasts from 1 to 2 months, depending on location. The government encourages the development of nurseries and kindergartens.

Practice: 40% of couples followed the 1-child-per-family policy in 1983. De-

---

** In 1977 Gao Yanfang was sold in marriage to a family in a neighboring village for 1100 Yuan. She was married against her will before indifferent Party officials. After trying to escape, she was returned to her owner, beaten, raped, tortured, and locked up. It was not until she was almost killed that Party officials took any interest in the case. To obtain a divorce she was eventually required to pay compensation of 250 Yuan to her husband's family.

*** Episiotomies are routinely performed on all women giving birth in hospitals.

spite recent attempts to legislate greater equality for women, preference for sons remains strong. Some families continue to produce children until a son is born. Female infanticide, although illegal, is once again becoming a problem.† Childcare is inexpensive but in great demand: 990,000 nurseries and kindergartens enroll 25% of pre-school-age children (1982). Most children are cared for by mothers and female relatives. Childcare still is considered women's work.

Welfare. *Policy:* Constitution stipulates that family members are legally obligated to provide mutual support and that livelihood of retired persons is ensured by the society, as is the right to material assistance from the State when old, ill, or disabled, and the right to receive education (1982). Since 1950, childless senior citizens have been guaranteed 5 basic necessities—food, clothing, housing, medical care, and burial. *Practice:* Main source of support is from family members. Factories and communes have social-welfare funds from which workers can draw in emergencies. Education is free through university and advanced levels. Medical plans at factories, communes, and offices provide health care free or for 1 Yuan per yr. Children are given annual check-ups and innoculations free at school. Age of retirement: factory workers—men age 55, women age 50; staff and office workers—men age 60, women age 55. Factories and offices pay pensions of 60–90% of salary, depending on number of yrs. worked. Women, responsible for childcare, retire earlier and consequently receive smaller pensions. Pensions (including free medical care) are paid to only 8 million workers and staff members. **Contraception.** *Policy:* All forms legal; family planning is mandated by the Constitution. Government actively researches new forms of contraception, notably a male pill. Contraceptives available only

to married people, cost subsidized by the government. *Practice:* The pill is the most popular urban contraceptive. Couples of child–bearing age using contraception (1977): 84%; of these, methods included IUD 14.6%, induced abortion 5.9%, tubal ligation 3.1%, vasectomy 2.9%. Contraception was an issue of concern as early as the May 4th Movement (1919) and was much discussed in the early 1920's when Margaret Sanger visited China. In the early 1950's the debate revived. The Women's Federation lobbied for birth control as a prerequisite for women entering the public sector. The government began to promote birth control in 1955. Abortion was discouraged as a contraceptive method and sterilization considered only in exceptional cases. Today contraceptives are free and available; pills, jellies, and condoms are distributed at pharmacies, clinics, and workplaces. Diaphragms are not widely used and are manufactured in only 1 size. Tubal ligation is often performed after the birth of a second child. (It is difficult for childless young women to get tubal ligations.) In 1983, cases of forced sterilization were reported in rural areas. Vasectomy is not popular with men, who fear it will affect their virility.

Abortion. *Policy:* Abortion on request is free and legal (since 1955). *Practice:* Abortions (per 1000 women age 15–44, 1978 est.): 25; abortions (per 1000 known pregnancies, 1978 est.): 250; due to the 1-child-per-family policy, rates as high as 500 per 1000 known pregnancies were reported in some cities, but may include procedures performed on nonresidents (1980). **Illegitimacy.** *Policy:* Children born out of wedlock have equal rights (Marriage Law 1950 and 1980). *Practice:* No national statistics obtainable. According to a Shanghai sample study of 3968 women married in 1970, 85 had their first child before they were married.

---

† In 1983, China's daily newspapers reported an alarming rise in female infanticide over the previous 2 yrs., resulting in a serious nationwide outnumbering of female infants by males. The most affected provinces are Anhui, Liaoning, Shandong, Hebei, Guangdong, and Sichuan. According to the *People's Daily* (Mar. 3, 1983), "The phenomenon of butchering, drowning, and leaving to die female infants and maltreating women who give birth to female infants is a grave social problem." In 1982, according to the paper, "196 women in a 9-city sample reported [such] maltreatment to the Chinese Women's Association." On Nov. 30, 1982, in a statement to the People's National Assembly, Premier Zhao Ziyang specifically condemned the "murder by drowning" of infant girls.

Bearing a child out of wedlock still subjects a woman to severe criticism and possible violence. Children born out of wedlock are not accepted into State orphanages, to discourage women from having them. **Homosexuality.** *Policy:* Official position is that homosexuality is a product of bourgeois decadent morality and does not exist in China. *Practice:* No data obtainable.

Incest. *Policy:* Illegal. Rape or seduction of a minor (under age 14) under "odious circumstances" is punishable by 10 yrs.–life imprisonment. The penalty for mistreating a family member under "odious circumstances" is from detention or surveillance to not more than 2 yrs. imprisonment. If serious injury or death results, the penalty is 2–7 yrs. Mistreatment of a family member is tried only upon complaint. *Practice:* No data obtainable. **Sexual Harassment.** *Policy:* Acts of "hooliganism," including molesting women, are punishable by imprisonment for not more than 7 yrs. Women who experience sexual harassment are encouraged to bring complaints to the attention of co-workers or Party organs in criticism sessions. *Practice:* No statistics obtainable, but sexual harassment of women entering male-dominated professions is common. The practice of male cadres abusing their power also has a long history, dating from pre-liberation cadres who would not grant a woman a divorce without raping her first, to cadres raping women graduates in the countryside (1978). **Rape.** *Policy:* Illegal. Rape "by threat or force" is punishable by 7–10 yrs. imprisonment. If the rape "results in serious injury or death," the penalty is 10 yrs.–life imprisonment or the death penalty. *Practice:* No statistics obtainable. **Battery.** *Policy:* Laws against abuse of a family member apply to wife-beating (see **Incest**). Government condemns battery as a remnant of feudal thinking. Batterers are portrayed as misguided bullies and are "re-educated" by neighbors and cadres. Yet penalties for intentionally injuring or accidentally killing a stranger are more serious than for the same crimes within the family. *Practice:* No statistics obtainable, but domestic violence remains a common problem and must become extreme before there is any intervention.

Prostitution. *Policy:* Illegal (1979 Criminal Code, Art. 140); penalty for forcing a woman into prostitution is 3–10 yrs. imprisonment. Luring a woman into prostitution or housing prostitutes for personal gain is punishable by fines, confiscation of property, and prison terms of 5 yrs. or more. *Practice:* No statistics obtainable. In 1949 the new government closed down all houses of prostitution in major ports and cities, including 237 in Beijing. Prostitutes were retrained, educated, and relocated to begin new lives. But there have been recent cases of women being sold into prostitution and in 1982–83 a crackdown on a 6-province-wide abduction ring that had kidnapped, raped, and sold 150 women resulted in 1 death sentence, 1 life imprisonment, and 30 other prison terms (also see **Marriage**). Prostitution is on the rise in such large cities as Beijing, Shanghai, and Guangdong, where unemployment is high. **Traditional/Cultural Practices.** *Policy:* During the reign of Shunzhi (1644–61), a court edict declared it unlawful for a woman to cut off a piece of her flesh to feed to her parents; a piece of flesh from a filial daughter was believed to cure sick parents. Footbinding, a traditional practice which arose in the 10th-century Sung court, entailed binding the feet of young girls (age 5–7) until the arch broke under pressure and the toes folded under permanently. The practice gradually spread to the lower classes, until all but the poorest women were crippled by it. Ideal bound feet were only 3 inches long and would fit in the palm of a man's hand. The custom was supposedly erotic, but men never actually saw the bare foot, which was always bound, slippered, and scented to cover the smell of rotting flesh. Mothers bound their daughters' feet despite the torture, because a woman with unbound feet would never find a husband. The actual purpose of breaking women's feet was to prevent freedom of movement. Footbinding was outlawed by the Ching Emperor Kangxi in 1662, but the ban was ineffective and rescinded in 1668. A number of men agitated for a ban on the practice including the poet Yuan Mei (1716–97), and writer

Li Zhujen (1763–1830), whose fantasy, *Kingdom of Women,* reversed all gender roles and portrayed men with bound feet. By the 1890's footbinding was attacked as an embarrassment before foreigners and as the cause of weak mothers producing weak sons. Kang Yuwei wrote a petition to the Empress Dowager Zi Xi in 1898 advocating a ban on footbinding, and started the first Anti-Footbinding Society in Guangdong and Shanghai in 1892. The Empress finally denounced footbinding in 1902. Members of Natural Foot Societies pledged not to marry women with bound feet, not to bind their own or their daughters' feet, and to marry their sons to women with natural feet. The custom died slowly in rural areas and in the 1940's women cadres were still explaining and enforcing the ban in some areas. Manchu women, Hakka women, and the Boat-women of Guangdong rarely bound their feet.

Infanticide has long been practiced in parts of China, and girls have been the main, if not the exclusive, victims. In one 19th-century study women admitted to killing 30% of their daughters at birth, and none of their sons; 60% of the boys and only 38% of the girls lived past age 10. Suicide as a cultural practice has been required of women under many circumstances in the past, including rape or dishonor, divorce, and widowhood. It was also an act of protest which women took in the face of extreme oppression and nonexistent alternatives. At the end of the 19th century in some southern provinces, women silk-workers of independent income formed anti-marriage sisterhoods; 10 young women would live together and swear to kill themselves if any of their number was forced to marry. *Practice:* The feet of Chinese women are no longer bound. Female infanticide, though illegal, is on the rise (see Family). Suicide is still used by women as a means of drawing attention to the wrongs committed against them, and they often write letters to newspapers before they kill themselves. Cultural values are expressed in the pictographic structure of Chinese characters themselves. The word for "good" is a woman with a child; for "peace," a woman enclosed in a house; for "quarreling and mutual slander," 2

women together; for "chaotic and traitorous," 3 women together; for "slave," a woman under the hand of a master. **Crisis Centers.** *Policy:* Domestic problems are the community's concern. *Practice:* No independent crisis centers. Local Women's Federation branches often are a source of emergency aid for women, providing protection and mediation.

HERSTORY. The earliest civilizations in China showed signs of matriarchal influence. The first Chinese dynasty, the Shang, dates from 1600 B.C.E. The ancient concept of *yin-yang* originally symbolized the interaction of dynamic principles in the universe. Eventually their associations changed, *yin* becoming equated with passivity, darkness, degeneration, femaleness, *yang* with activity, creativity, light, and maleness. This philosophy, expanded by Confucius in the 5th century B.C.E. formed the foundation for the intensely patriarchal culture of traditional China. Women were subject to the Three Obediences (to fathers, husbands, and sons) and to the Four Virtues (to be humble, silent, clean and adorned to please the husband, and hard-working).

While the vast majority of women lived in ignorance and seclusion, there are some notable exceptions. Ban Zhao, the author of the *Precepts for Women,* assumed the position of court historian at the end of the Han Dynasty (206 B.C.E.–220 C.E.). The poet and court adviser Cai Wenji is also of this period. The Yellow Turban Uprising which occurred at the end of the Han Dynasty (200 C.E.) called for an assertion of women's rights. The Tang Dynasty (618–906) saw the reign of Wu Zi-tien, the only woman ever to be Emperor of China. She ruled from 665 to 705 as a brilliant politician and military strategist, conquered Korea and negotiated treaties with the Tibetans and Turks, patronized Buddhism (making it the State religion), and extended the period of mourning for mothers to equal that of fathers. The Tang Dynasty was a liberal period for women, but the intensely conservative Sung Dynasties (960–1234) reemphasized Confucianism and introduced footbinding.

The tradition of women-warriors is an

old one. Mulan, the most famous, served as a general in her father's place during the Tang Dynasty; she led an army for 12 years and was honored by the Emperor without her sex being discovered. During the Sung Dynasty, Yo Fei fought to prevent the Tartars from invading China. Chin Liangyu led troops in support of the Ming Dynasty (1368–1644). Women fought in bands in the White Lotus Rebellion (1790's), calling for women's rights. Legends and stories are still told of heroic women-warriors, expert at fencing and acrobatics, who often championed the poor.

The Qing Dynasty (1644–1911) saw the rise of many women artists and writers. The young astronomer Wang Zhenyi (1768–97) discovered the law of lunar eclipses.

A reform movement—to eradicate footbinding and educate women after China's defeat in the Opium Wars (1842) —was not aimed to benefit women *per se* but to make them better mothers for the benefit of their sons. The Taiping Rebellion (1851) had as a primary principle equal rights for women, and Hong Xuanjiao led 40 armies of 2500 women each. Widow Pai was another military leader. Women were allowed to sit for Taiping examinations and serve in the government. Footbinding was outlawed.

During the Boxer Rebellion (1899–1901), women formed their own peasant and military associations. The Green, Blue, and Red Lanterns were all women's groups. (The Red Lanterns, whose members were young women under 18, were reputed to be able to walk on water and loosen the screws of their enemies' cannons from miles away.)

The first girls' schools were opened by missionaries between 1844 and 1873; the first Chinese girls' school in 1897; the first government-run girls' school in 1907. The girls' schools soon became centers of radicalism: they published the first women's magazines and trained girls in military exercises under the guise of physical education classes. Some of the leading women activists during the republican period leading up to the 1911 revolution were teachers. Jiu Jin is the most famous: she was a nationalist, a feminist, poet, writer, teacher, and one of the first women to join Sun Yatsen's Revolutionary League. She studied in Tokyo, dressed in a man's suit, and became the principal of a girls' school. Her poems were used as evidence of treason, and she was arrested and executed by beheading in 1907, at age 28.

Other women leaders in the republican revolution were He Xiangning, Sophia Chang, Soumay Cheng, and Xu Zihua. The actress Jin Jilan was executed in 1911 for her activities. Many women smuggled arms and planted explosives. Some fought at the front in all-woman units, including the Women's National Army, the Women's Murder Squad, and the Amazon Corps of the famous Dare to Die Soldiers. After the abdication of the Qing court, the women's militias became groups fighting for equal rights and suffrage. Tang Junying founded the Chinese Suffragette Society in Beijing in 1911. She led women to the first meetings of the National Assembly, and when they were refused the vote they launched an attack; by the third day the Assembly had to send for troops for protection. In Guangdong the Provisional Government had promised women the vote but retracted it, and women invaded the legislature. In 1913, when Yuan Shikai, a former warlord, became president, women's activities were crushed and Tang Junying was arrested.

There was a resurgence in the women's movement during the post-WWI nationalist May 4th Movement of 1919. Many of the future women leaders became active during this time: Cai Zhang, Deng Yingzhao, Ding Ling, and Xiang Jingyu. In 1920 women were first admitted to colleges. The graduates formed alumnae and businesswomen's clubs. In Guangdong 40 factories were owned and operated by women. In Nanchang women owned and operated both the city's electric light and telephone companies. In 1921 Hunan Province became the first province to grant women the right to vote and stand for office, and equal rights in work, education, property inheritance, and free marriage. The Chinese Women's Banks in Beijing and in Shanghai were opened in 1922.

In 1924, during Sun Yatsen's National Congress to establish a permanent constitution, women were not invited to participate and were denied the vote. They organized street demonstrations which were suppressed by the police and the military. The women formed a National Women's Rights Assoc. to coordinate their activities. The Communist Party of China (CPC), which had been founded in Shanghai in 1921 with 50 members, supported the full emancipation of women as one of its first policy platforms. Xiang Jingyu, a May 4th activist who had studied in Paris, returned to China in 1922 and joined the rapidly growing CPC. She was elected to the Central Committee and headed the Party's Women's Dept. The Women's Depts. of the CPC and the GMD (Sun Yatsen's Guomindang, or National Party) worked together during the first united front (1923–27). He Xiangning, head of the GMD Women's Dept., and Song Qingling, an active feminist and the wife of Sun Yatsen, were elected to the Central Committee of the GMD.

During the Northern Expedition, 300–400 women students and propagandists followed the Nationalist armies, organizing women in the areas through which the army passed, founding independent women's unions, and informing women of the footbinding ban. A women's political school was set up in Hankou in 1926. The women's unions sheltered runaway slaves and prostitutes, granted divorces on their own authority, and intimidated wife batterers. More than 1.5 million women were involved in these unions at the height of the Nationalist Revolution.

In the GMD purge of Communists by Chiang Kaishek (1927–30) some of the most famous women leaders of the Communist Party were killed. These included Yang Kaihui (Mao's first wife), Xiang Jingyu, and Zhang Jianzhen. The Communists were accused of sexual license and free love. Young women in the Nationalist cause were identified by their short hair and killed; many were wrapped in cotton wadding, doused with oil, and burned. Women found in men's uniforms were stripped publicly and executed.

After the conservative backlash, the women of the GMD and the CPC took different paths. The GMD women pursued welfare work, literacy classes, and education. A 1930 Civil Code, which Soumay Cheng had helped draft, granted women free marriage, the right to divorce under similar circumstances as men, property inheritance, and the rights of ownership. Adultery became punishable for men. The patriarchal family was still assumed, and the husband retained managerial rights to common property. In 1931 the Factory Law granted women equal pay for equal work in some instances. With these laws many GMD women's leaders declared women's emancipation complete, although there was no attempt to publicize or implement the laws. Song Qingling disassociated herself from the GMD and left the country.

In 1934 the New Life Movement was launched by Chiang Kaishek and his wife Song Meiling, advocating a return to Confucian values. Work in the rural areas stressed sanitation and literacy, not women's legal rights.

Communist Party women worked either in the local base areas to which the purge had forced their retreat or in urban trade unions organizing women. In the first constitution of the Jiangxi Soviet (base area), women were granted thorough emancipation, and women cadres organized local women to take advantage of their new rights. In 1931 the Japanese had occupied northeast China; when they attacked Shanghai, Chiang Kaishek deserted Shanghai to concentrate on fighting the Communists, who were forced to flee and in Oct. 1934 began the year-long 7775 mile Long March to northern Shanxi. Fifty women participated in the Long March, forming a special women's detachment. In 1936 the Communists and Nationalists formed a second united front for the War of Resistance against Japan, and the GMD and CPC women's organizations again worked together. By 1941 more than 317 women's organizations in 21 provinces were doing war work. The Communists organized women into production cooperatives and taught spinning and weaving classes and modern farming techniques. The Yunnan Women's Battlefield Service Unit marched 2000 miles to the front in central China. The Guangxi Women's Battalion was made up of 500 students.

Again women's energies were directed into a nationalist war. Both Ding Ling and Xu Guang were censured for their feminist views. In her article "Thoughts on March 8th" (1942) Ding Ling proclaimed that sexism ran high within the CPC, and Xu Guang favored direct struggle with men for rights in the family. Both were brought back to the Party line: war effort first, women's rights second.

During the third civil war (post WWII), women again organized on their own issues in the Communist bases and became active in local politics.†† The CPC emphasized that the struggle for women's rights was not an antagonistic contradiction, as was the class struggle, but an internal contradiction among the people. By 1948 there were 20 million members of women's associations across the country. On Oct. 1, 1949, the People's Republic of China was founded in Beijing; Chiang Kaishek and the remnants of the GMD retreated to Taiwan.

In 1949 the All China Democratic Women's Federation (ACDWF) was founded as the central organizing body of the women's movement. The ACDWF was in contact with 76 million women through its network; by 1952 there were branches in 80% of the counties in the country. Local congresses and meetings are frequent, and National Congresses have been held in 1949, 1953, 1957, and 1978. The ACDWF publishes the magazine *Women in China*. It undertakes to explain Party policies to women, and to lobby for women's rights within the Party. Local branches pressure to achieve equal pay for equal work, protection for women in danger from husbands, family members, or supervisors, and for expanded childcare facilities. The ACDWF and *Women in China* were disbanded during the Cultural Revolution (1966–69)—accused of mouthing a conservative Party line and advocating economic solutions to cultural problems—and reconstituted in 1978.

Women were urged by Mao himself to excel in the Two Zeals: taking care of their families and building a socialist economic base. More or less emphasis has been placed on one or the other "zeal" to manipulate women as a surplus labor force. During the period of land redistribution (first Five Year Plan), millions of women gained at least a theoretical right to a share of land. During the Great Leap Forward (1957–60), communal dining-halls, laundries, service and day-care centers created work for women and also freed them for other jobs. Many housewives started small-scale shops and industries, earning their own money for the first time. However, on rural communes women were routinely paid half as much as men, and all wages were paid to the husband. Women were concentrated in low-paying, low-skilled jobs.

The Cultural Revolution brought confusion for women. They were encouraged to join fully in the socialist revolution on an equal basis, but their women's associations were disbanded, day care was no longer a priority, and although women were encouraged to enter men's fields, men were never expected to enter women's. Jiang Qing, Mao Zedong's wife, gained power in Shanghai and led the most radical faction of the Cultural Revolution. In 1976 Mao died, and the fall of Jiang Qing and the "Gang of Four" was accompanied by an outpouring of sexism; she was disparaged for being a woman seeking power more than for her political beliefs. The opportunity was seized to castigate any view of feminism seeking independence from Party policies.

Since 1977 the women's movement has returned, but in a moderated version. In a time of rising unemployment, the family has again been made the basic unit of production. Once-protective regulations affording women relief during pregnancy and menstruation are being used to encourage women to work at home and care for their children.

†† In 1 village where they were denied voting rights the Women's Assoc. refused to recognize the new village head. Women were urged not to sleep with their husbands. A second election was held and a woman was elected deputy village head.

MYTHOGRAPHY. In the *Tao De Jing,* Lao Ze's Taoist classic, the Female Principle is expressed as inexhaustible, the Tao itself as "the mother of all things." A form of tantric yoga was developed in Taoism where women's sexual energy and essence was thought to be inexhaustible while men's was limited; the Queen of Heaven ascended to her position by sexually exhausting 1000 young men and balancing her *yin* essence with their *yang* essence. The Buddhist goddess of mercy, Guanyin, is one of the most popular of all deities. One of China's creation myths involves the goddess Nu Kua as the mother of the cosmic order. Tien Hou is a popular goddess in the south, where she is worshipped as the Queen of the Sea and the Protectress of Fisherfolk. Belief in the legendary prehistoric matriarchy persists. Local goddesses and female water spirits are numerous, and female fox-spirits (who bewitch men) and women-warriors (who rescue them) are part of folklore.

CHINA: Feudal Attitudes, Party Control, and Half the Sky
by Xiao Lu

In comparison with the state of women before 1949, women's situation in the People's Republic of China (PRC) today is much improved. However, despite constitutional guarantees and official pronouncements of the Chinese Communist Party, equality between the sexes has yet to be achieved. The situation is worse in the countryside than in urban areas, but even in large cities women do not have the same access to opportunities as men do. Traditional attitudes toward women are still widespread, and the consciousness of people at every level of society, including cadres and Party members, remains low. While most people recognize that no government can undo 3000 years of history in 30 years, they are uncertain about the government's commitment and determination to make women's rights a priority—without which the extent and scope of equality are likely to be limited.

Although women are of course found in virtually every area of society and are 34 percent of the nation's work force, the number of women in central decision-making positions is still extremely low. For example, of the 210 members of the Central Committee of the Party, only 11 are women; and of the 253 members of the Chairpersons Committee of the Fifth National People's Congress (Fifth Plenary Session), only 39 are women. Not everyone agrees that the lack of representation at the national policy-making level is a serious problem of sex inequality. Some common rationalizations are: "This is only a remnant of the past. Not many women were trained, therefore not many now qualify," and "Women are both physically and mentally unsuited for these demanding and responsible jobs." These responses are given by both men and women, although much more often by those over age thirty. For those who feel that such statistics are an indication of sex inequality and that women's situation needs to become a national priority, the areas of education, employment, family, and self-concept are highlighted.

Education

One of the most serious problems the PRC faces in achieving its goal of modernization is the generally low level of development of its humanpower. Because of political disruptions, universities virtually ceased operation for about a decade, and during the same period the quality of high-school education plummeted. In 1977, competitive entrance examinations were administered nationwide to select the most qualified students for college education. Owing to the lack of economic resources and qualified instructors, the number of spaces has been severely limited. Currently about 25–30 percent of college students are women. While during the early years no explicit consideration was given to the gender of the applicant, beginning in 1982, officials decided to raise women's admission score by two points. In other words, while a male applicant can get into the university with, say, 360 points, a female applicant will not be admitted unless she has scored *362* points or even higher. Some universities are instituting a quota system designed to limit the number of female students on their campuses or in selected departments.

One must ask why it is that while the government officially promotes sexual equality it chooses to adopt such a blatantly discriminatory practice. The explanations given by administrators are: 1) it is less economical to train women than men and, 2) women are not suitable for certain work. It is pointed out that women after graduation will get married and have children; even under the current policy of one child per family this will mean that a woman will need at least one maternity leave. Then, since the care of children is still the major responsibility of women, she will have to spend time at home even with the provision of nurseries and childcare facilities. In addition, household work, though gradually being shared by men and women, is still mainly the burden of women and will occupy a large share of her time. All of this means that the return on her college education is likely to be less than that of her male counterpart. Furthermore, it is still widely believed that while girls do better than boys in elementary and middle schools and therefore tend to pass college entrance exams in larger numbers, after they reach their sophomore year they tend to become concerned with marriage and family and consequently will not do as well.

In China, human-resource development is by central planning. The reason why women have to score at least five points higher than men for admission to the foreign-languages department of some universities is that "the government feels that we must train people for diplomatic services and certain work that requires the knowledge of foreign languages, such as tourist guides. But these jobs are best carried out by men. Sending women abroad tends to create unnecessary problems. If they were unmarried, we have to be concerned about their marital future: whom are they likely to meet and how are they going to find suitable mates. It will be very unfortunate if as a result they do not find happiness in marriage. If they were married, who would take care of their husbands and children and parents or parents-in-law? Even if these problems are taken care of, sending a married woman abroad without her husband is likely to create problems. The government prefers to send men abroad. If we send any women, they would be sent with their husbands. For these reasons, and because currently there are just too many female students in foreign-languages departments, we decided to encourage men to get into these departments by making it easier for them."

In 1981 the Academia Sinica, the most prestigious body of scientists, held an election. Before the election there was only one woman member. After the election, of the more than four hundred members, there were fourteen women! If current university admissions policy persists this situation is unlikely to change.

Employment

Young women are complaining that many of the most desirable jobs are not open to them. The more prestigious the unit, the more unlikely that it will accept a woman as an employee. Unit heads give the same reasons for discriminating against women as those given in the case of university admissions: the need for maternity leave, time pressure for childcare and housework, physical and mental "limitations," etc. Even those men and women who see themselves as pro women's liberation claim that there are natural distinctions between the sexes that must be reflected in job training and assignment. "The mistake that the Western women's movement made, and which was also evident during the Cultural Revolution, was the disregard for women's special condition. Women are more patient, more gentle, less decisive, and physically weaker. They should be in jobs that fit these characteristics and not in jobs that require other qualities." It is strongly believed by almost all pro-liberation individuals interviewed that the "correct" view of sexual equality is not that men and women should have the same opportunities to obtain the same jobs but that "feminine jobs" and "masculine jobs" should be compensated equally. This is apparently the goal.

In the countryside, despite numerous campaigns for "equal work, equal pay," peasant women still receive fewer workpoints than their male counterparts generally and even when they do the same tasks. Since the implementation of a new system of responsibility in production in 1982, it is reported that the situation of peasant women has greatly improved—because they can engage in occupations that were previously considered subsidiary or secondary (such as silkworm-raising and herb-growing), and because they are given the responsibility of managing whatever productive activities they have organized. However, it is revealing that one of the claimed advantages of this new policy is the "flexibility" women now have so that they can better reduce the conflict between *collective production, family sideline activities,* and *household work.* Articles[1] describing improvements on rural women's situation often refer to the mechanization of housework—such as the gradually widespread use of electric irons, sewing machines, flour grinders, rice thrashers, etc.—as great inventions to help ease the housework burden of peasant women. These articles rarely mention the concept of men sharing that burden. The prevalent view among the rural masses is still that women's main responsibility is housework and men's main responsibility is income-producing work. If women can produce income *and* manage the household well, that is most desirable; but if women's income-producing activities lead men to have to share housework responsibility that would not be desirable.

Sexuality, Marriage and Family

Female sexuality is still not a subject of public discussion. Among the intellectuals, "sexual revolution" is more a sign of decadence than a progressive and liberating force. Among the younger generations, especially college students, there is a growing interest in understanding female sexuality and sexual fulfillment in marriage.

In the PRC one's personal and public lives are intertwined to such an extent that an undesirable personal style (usually referring to sexual behavior) is often detrimental to one's career and lifelong development. The loss of virginity before marriage or an extramarital affair is cause enough for social ostracism, job dismissal, or denial of promotion. Although it applies to both men and women, the effect is usually much more serious for the women.

Despite what is stated in the marriage law, parental and kin interference in marriage is not uncommon, especially among peasant families. In 1982 almost every issue of the *Zhongguo Funu* included at least one report of such interference in rural areas. Feudal attitudes toward women and the general ignorance of the legal system have led to the beating and severe mistreatment of peasant women. Officials who come to the rescue of women are often met with angry local residents. The recent "one-child" policy has resulted in widespread resistance by both men and women, and in a number of tragedies. Since women are considered responsible for the gender of the child in rural areas, giving birth to a baby girl has led to ridicule and resulted in suicides and female infanticides.

The life of urban women is much better. However, family and social pressures on

[1.] The *Zhongguo Funu,* the official organ of the All-China Federation of Women.

women to marry as soon as they reach the legal marriageable age, once married to stay married regardless, and to have a male child to carry on the family name—these are still formidable. The recent rise in the divorce rate has prompted a great deal of public discussion and studies on the disintegration of the family and the adverse effect on women, even though a large proportion of the divorces were initiated by women. Although some men are sharing housework with their wives, it is still mainly women's burden, and girls are asked to help with household chores more than boys.

In China, housing is allocated by the work unit. The allocation policy is determined by the city where the unit is located and the administration of the policy is left to the unit. Typically, units entrust the actual allocation work to a committee made of worker representatives. Since workers in most of the units are male, the committee is usually male-dominated and is insensitive to women workers' needs. To make matters worse, municipal policy is often blatantly discriminatory, stipulating that male workers should as a rule have priority in obtaining housing over female workers because "they have families to take care of." Under the current stringent economic situation, there is not enough housing for everybody, and female workers have to wait much longer than male workers to obtain housing (and even then only under very special circumstances). Since housing is priority-allocated to the male worker, it's always close to where the man works. This means that married women often find themselves living far from their own workplace, spending a much longer time in travel. In addition, since they are responsible for the housework, they often have to get up much earlier than their husbands and go to bed much later. Young married women complain bitterly about this. A woman who sits on one of these allocation committees said that whenever she complains, her co-members, all of whom are male, nod politely but in the end give the available housing to males just the same.

Organized Efforts

The root of the problem lies in the persistence of feudal attitudes and the total control of political life by the Communist Party—which does not allow an independent women's movement to exist. The Constitution of the PRC, the Marriage Law, and the Party platform all proclaim equality between the sexes, yet feudal attitudes die hard and, given the social organization of China, these attitudes seep through every sphere of life, consciously and unconsciously affecting the making of administrative policies and their implementation.

The All-China Federation of Women, with its regional branches, is the only national mass organization which has as its purpose the promotion of women's interests. Like other mass organizations in China, it is subordinate to the leadership of the Chinese Communist Party and has no authority over any government units. Its work is education, propaganda, persuasion, and recommendation. Most Chinese women believe that the existence of the Federation is useful and often bring their complaints to the organization. But they also believe that it is too limited. In cases of severe physical abuse or clear infringement of women's constitutional rights, the Federation is helpful. But it cannot function independently or separately from the direction and the scope set by the Party. Meanwhile, as women are being actively recruited into the labor force, they are also asked to shoulder the responsibility of nurturing the next generation, caring for the aged, and providing a comfortable environment for the family—the notorious "multiple-job" burden of women.

Future Prospects

The new Constitution promulgated in December 1982 contains a number of articles pertaining to women's rights. Article 34 stipulates, "All citizens of the People's Republic of China who have reached the age of eighteen have the right to vote and stand for election, regardless of nationality, race, sex, occupation, family background, religious belief, education, property status, or length of residence, except persons deprived of political rights according to law." Article 48: "Women in the People's Republic of China enjoy equal rights with men in all spheres of life—political, economic, cultural, and social, including family life. The State protects the rights and interests of women, applies the principle of equal pay for equal work for men and women alike, and trains and selects cadres from among women." And Article 49 states: "Marriage, the family, and the mother and child are protected by the State. Both husband and wife have the duty to practice family planning. Parents have the duty to rear and educate their minor children, and children who have come of age have the duty to support and assist their parents. Violation of the freedom of marriage is prohibited." In comparison with the Constitution of 1978, these provisions are both more inclusive and more specific and reach both the domestic and the public spheres of life.

The increasing participation of women in the labor force has clearly begun to push certain issues of equality to the level of consciousness. The one-child-per-family policy, coupled with the availability of more labor-saving mechanical devices, will help relieve the housework burden on women, making them freer to compete with men for more demanding and responsible jobs. As women begin to have more responsible jobs, their self-concept will also change. Newspaper reports proliferate about women who were surprised at their own abilities once they were given more responsibility. The government's commitment to recruit more women for cadre positions (as stipulated in the Constitution) is likely to put more women into policy implementation or even policy-making positions. The existence of women's organizations at every level may become a decided advantage to channel women's concerns to various levels of government. The traditional and continuous confinement of sexuality to the private sphere of life in China might possibly make it more likely for women in high-status positions to command respect and compliance than is the case in the West. Finally, given the political structure of China, and the ruling ideology, it will be less difficult to effect change if the government is determined to do so. The educational institutions, the neighborhood organizations, the work units, the media, etc., all can become agencies to educate the public as well as to implement policies.

In other words, if the apparatus of Party control can be convinced to truly engage the feudal attitudes, then, perhaps, it will be possible for women not only to—in Mao Zedong's words—"hold up half the sky" but to do so with respect, compensation, and on their own terms.

Suggested Further Reading

Broyelle, Claudine. *Women's Liberation in China.* Sussex: Harvester Press, 1977.

Croll, Elisabeth. *Feminism and Socialism in China.* London: Schocken Books, 1978.

Davin, Delia. *Woman-Work: Women and the Party in Revolutionary China.* Oxford: Clarendon Press, 1976.

Sidel, Ruth. *Women and Childcare in China.* Baltimore: Penguin Books, 1972.

Women of China, an official publication of the All-China Women's Federation; issued monthly, it contains translated selections from its Chinese version, *Zhongguo Funu,* Beijing.

Xiao Lu (a pseudonym) was born in China in 1939. She is a professor at a major university. She based her above article on interviews she conducted recently with fifty-two Chinese women in Guangzhou, Shanghai, and Beijing, as well as twenty Chinese women in the West, supplemented by Chinese newspaper and magazine reports, and personal observations.

COLOMBIA
(Republic of Colombia)

Located in northwestern South America with the Caribbean Sea and Panama to the north, Venezuela and Brazil to the east, Peru and Ecuador to the south, and the Pacific Ocean to the west. **Area:** 1,179,369 sq. km. (455,355 sq. mi.). **Population** (1982): 28,000,000, female 47.5%. **Capital:** Bogotá.

DEMOGRAPHY. Languages: Spanish. **Races or Ethnic Groups:** Mestizo 68%, European descent 20%, Native Indian 7%, African descent 5%. **Religions:** Roman Catholicism (official) 96%, Protestant. **Education** (% enrolled in school, 1975): Age 6–11—of all girls 67%, of all boys 62%; age 12–17—of all girls 56%, of all boys 54%; higher education—no data obtainable. **Literacy** (1977): Women 80%, men 82%. **Birth Rate** (per 1000 pop., 1975–80): 29. **Death Rate** (per 1000 pop., 1975–80): 8. **Infant Mortality** (per 1000 live births, 1975–80): Female 71, male 84. **Life Expectancy** (1975–80): Female 64 yrs., male 61 yrs.

GOVERNMENT. A republic with executive power held by a president and legislative power held by an elected bicameral congress consisting of a 112-member Senate and 199-member Chamber of Deputies; cabinet is appointed by the president. Major parties are Liberal, Conservative, and National Opposition Union (a Leftist coalition). **Women's Suffrage:** 1954. **Equal Rights:** Constitutional Decree 2820 (1974) states, "The rights, obligations and legal status of women are defined on the basis of equality with men." **Women in Government:** Doña Berta Hernández de Ospina is Senator and Conservative Party leader (1983). María Eugenia Rojas de Moreno was a presidential candidate in 1974.

ECONOMY. Currency: Colombian Peso (May 1983: 73. = $1 US). **Gross National Product** (1980): $31.6 billion. **Per Capita Income** (1980): $1180. **Women's Wages as a Percentage of Men's:** No data obtainable. **Equal Pay Policy:** No data obtainable. **Production** (Agricultural/In-dustrial): Coffee, bananas, rice, corn, sugar cane; textiles, clothing, processed food, chemicals. **Women as a Percentage of Labor Force** (1980): 25%; **of agricultural force** 14.3%; **of industrial force**—no general statistics obtainable (of manufacturing 36.7%); **of military**—no statistics obtainable; women are not permitted in combat but are in the service sector. **(Employed) Women's Occupational Indicators** (1973): Over 50% of employed women are in the service sector, 75% of whom are domestic servants who work 12–15 hours per day for an average of $25 per month plus room and board (see **Rape**). **Unemployment** (1980): 9.9%, female 12.3%, male 8.3%.

GYNOGRAPHY. Marriage. *Policy:* A Concordat between the Church and the government of Colombia (1974) established the right to civil marriage without renunciation of Roman Catholicism; civil marriage now has equal status with Roman Catholic wedlock. The Civil Code (amended 1974) established the marriageable age as 18 for both women and men, but within the framework of a Catholic marriage, the minimum female age is 14, male 16. Women have full legal status in marriage (1974) and can retain their birth-names (1982); they can retain control of property acquired before marriage, and widows who remarry can retain control of property from a previous marriage. Both husband and wife may determine the family's place of residence; if there is a disagreement, it will be decided by the court (Art. 179, Civil Code, amended by Art. 12, Decree 2820, 1974). The Penal Code (1936, amended by Contravention Code, 1970) stipulates acquittal of a husband who kills a wife if he is "beside himself with anger and despair" after discovering her in adultery; the wife has no such right. *Practice:* Female mean age at marriage (1970–78): 22; women age 15–49 in union (1970–78): 52%. No further data obtainable. **Divorce.** *Policy:* A 1976 law legalized divorce for civil marriage; Roman Catholic marriage remains indissoluble. Adultery by either spouse is grounds for legal separation; previously a woman could obtain a separation only if her husband lived openly with another woman. *Practice:* No statistics obtainable. The possibility of divorce exists only for a small percentage of the population (primarily middle and upper classes). Couples who separated before the 1976 law became effective must go abroad to remarry. Alimony is awarded on the basis of "good conduct" by the woman. Women generally must wait 270 days before remarrying.

Family. *Policy:* Under the Civil Code (Art. 288, 1974 reform), both parents share responsibility for education of children, financial matters, choice of residence, and domestic tasks. The Substantive Labor Code (Art. 236) prescribes 8 weeks paid maternity leave to all salaried employees who are pregnant; if the work has been part time or interrupted, the leave is based on a percentage of the yr.'s earnings. Social Security (Clause 536 of 1974) grants medical assistance, obstetrical care, dental treatment, and paramedical help during pregnancy, birth, and nursing, as well as a financial subsidy for 8 weeks (equivalent to a percentage of the base salary of the last 12 weeks worked before maternity leave); this benefit is available only to women employed by firms associated with the program. The government supports childcare through the Institute of Colombia, which has offices in every city. *Practice:* No statistics obtainable. Many aspects of family legislation are difficult to enforce; under the 1974 Concordat, the State "considers the Apostolic, Roman and Catholic religion as a fundamental element in the common well-being and in the integral development of the community." The Church is guaranteed the right to veto decisions by the government when "integral development" is threatened. Women continue to bear the main responsibility for work in the home. Pregnant employees, including domestic servants, are often fired; many work until the day of delivery and return to their jobs the following day. Most women do not receive maternity leave or benefits. **Welfare.** *Policy:* Social Security schemes cover limited employee categories; those in domestic service or part-time employment are not included. Bene-

fits are provided for medical service, maternity leave (see **Family** and **Illegitimacy**), disability, and funeral service. Law 90 (1946) prevents homemakers from insuring themselves directly and only permits coverage through an insured husband. There is no unemployment insurance. Social Security provides pensions for retired employees over age 60 if they have worked for the government or a business for at least 20 yrs. *Practice:* No statistics obtainable. The majority of women either are employed part time, as domestic servants, or are homemakers; consequently they are not eligible for Social Security benefits. Domestic servants can enroll in voluntary insurance programs.

Contraception. *Policy:* Legal; sterilization is also legal. The government has initiated family planning as part of a population-control program. *Practice:* Women age 15–49 in union using contraception (1977): 46%; methods used (1977) pill 31%, IUD 20%, rhythm 12%, withdrawal 11%, female sterilization 9%, diaphragm 6%, condom 4%, abstinence 2%, douche 1%, injectables 1%, other methods 2%; using inefficient methods 28%. Distribution and services limited, largely because of the Roman Catholic Church's opposition to birth control. **Abortion.** *Policy:* Legal only to save the life of the woman; illegal abortions are punishable by imprisonment. Yet infanticide, if motivated by "family honor" and committed within 8 days of birth, is a crime "to be judged with leniency" (Penal Code, Art. 369). *Practice:* In 1980, 280,000 illegal abortions were performed. In 1971, 2 women died each week in hospitals in Bogotá from ill-performed abortions; an est. 2 illegal abortions were performed for every 4 births; 66% of abortions requiring hospitalization were performed by practitioners with no medical training. In 1970 more women died from unsanitary illegal abortions than in delivery complications. Abortionists perform 54% of procedures, nurses 15%, women themselves 8%, doctors 4%, midwives 3%, druggists 2%, others 14%. The majority of women seeking abortions are married, Roman Catholic, and have at least 3 children; abortion of a first pregnancy is rare. **Illegitimacy.** *Policy:* A

1982 law accords children born out of wedlock equal rights, including inheritance rights. Both parents are legally responsible. A single woman is eligible for a 56-day maternity leave, if the father is insured. A single parent who lives with a child has guardianship rights. *Practice:* No data obtainable. **Homosexuality.** *Policy:* Illegal; punishable by 1–3 yrs. imprisonment. *Practice:* No statistics obtainable. A strong tabu against homosexuality is exacerbated by the Roman Catholic Church. Colombian feminists support the protection and civil rights of lesbian women and homosexual men.

Incest. *Policy:* Illegal under the Penal Code as a "Crime Against the Family"; punishable by 6 months–4 yrs. imprisonment. *Practice:* No data obtainable. **Sexual Harassment.** *Policy:* No data obtainable. *Practice:* No data obtainable. **Rape.** *Policy:* Illegal; punishable by 2–8 yrs. imprisonment or 3–12 yrs. if the victim dies. If the victim is under age 14, the penalty is 1–6 yrs. imprisonment; if venereal disease is transmitted, the sentence is increased by 1/4. A rapist can be freed if he agrees to marry the rape victim. *Practice:* No statistics obtainable. Reportedly, domestic servants frequently are raped by their employers, and are assumed available to initiate employers' adolescent sons sexually. A single woman who is raped can be considered to have a damaged reputation; a married woman who is raped can be considered a willing participant in "adultery" and a husband can use this charge as grounds for divorce. Legal action is rarely taken against a rapist, and cases are difficult to prove (see **Prostitution**). **Battery.** *Policy:* No general legislation. Under the Penal Code, "physical injury" resulting in loss of employment is punishable by 2 months–4 yrs. imprisonment if more than 1 month of work is missed; permanent injury or disfigurement is punishable by a fine and 1–6 yrs. *Practice:* No statistics obtainable. Battery is a major problem. Most women have no legal recourse or State protection, as the majority of them are not in the labor force and therefore are not protected by the law of "physical injury." Feminists have been pressing for legal reforms to protect battered women and have begun to establish refuge shelters (see **Crisis Centers**). **Prostitution.** *Policy:* Illegal; defined as an offense against public morality. Procuring is not legislated as a crime, although promoting prostitution of minors is punishable by a fine and imprisonment. *Practice:* No statistics obtainable. Adult and child prostitution is not uncommon. Adolescent girls who "lose" their virginity are often rejected by their families, and prostitution becomes one of their few economic options. Rape is excused when the victim works as a prostitute (Penal Code, Art. 317). **Traditional/Cultural Practices:** No data obtainable. **Crisis Centers.** *Policy:* No data obtainable. *Practice:* The Bogotá Women's Center opened Mar. 1981.

HERSTORY. The indigenous Chibcha peoples had a matrilineal system of succession to office and a patrilineal system of inheritance. The Chibchas developed a highly evolved culture, including mining of emeralds, casting of gold, agriculture, pottery, and weaving. In the late 14th and early 15th centuries, Spain conquered the Chibchas and other indigenous peoples, and instituted slavery, to work the gold and mineral mines. Women participated as leaders of the slave revolts in 1795 and in Gual-Espina in 1797; Joaquina España and Isabel Gómez were imprisoned for distributing revolutionary literature. In the early 1800's, upper-class women participated in discussions of the revolution in such literary circles as *El Buen Gusto* (The Good Taste), and radicals Camila Torres and Josefa Palacios helped launch the Independence movement (1809). Women fought in the Wars for Independence (1810–22), sometimes disguising themselves as male soldiers. In the Battle of Boyaco (1819), Evangelista Tamoya served as a captain under Simón Bolívar. Women organized such batteries as "Las Mujeres," which defended cities, and women from the island of Margarita were famous fighters. The spy Policarpa Salvarrieta, who was arrested and executed by the Spanish authorities, became a national heroine.

After the Revolution (1819), women were excluded from political participation, but did win the right to university education in 1821. Independence was declared in 1824.

Civil and political unrest marked much of the 19th century, and it was not until 1930 that Georgina Fletcher organized the IV International Women's Congress, which was attended by regional male political delegates but which represented the first public voice for women. The next 6 years marked a period of legislative reform; Lucrecia Oardo Espinal became treasurer in Choachi, the first woman in an official position. Uribe de Acosta organized conferences to study the need for suffrage and the social conditions of women. Ofelia and Inés G. Rojas formed *TUNJA, La Hora Feminista* (YOURS, The Feminist Hour). Rosa María Aguilera and Ilde Carriazo founded the women's university and presented Congress with a petition for suffrage signed by 500 women. The journal *Agitación Femenina* (Feminine Action) was started. Dr. Zea Hernández fought for suffrage (1946) and later was imprisoned for opposing dictator Gustavo Rojas Pinilla.

In 1954 women's suffrage was won; 79% of registered women voted in 1957 elections. In the early 1970's, the First Feminist Meeting of Latin America and the Caribbean was held, out of which ALACEM (Asociación Latino-Americana y del Caribe de Estudios de la Mujer) was created. In 1974 the system of secondary education which had limited women *de facto* to teaching and nursing professions was abolished, and Decree 2820 eliminated legal sex-discrimination. In 1976 women employees at the Vanitex textile factory struck for better wages (they were earning $1–1.50 per day) and better working conditions. In Dec. 1978 a National Women's Congress was held in Medellín, uniting 19 women's groups to discuss abortion and sterilization abuse. Domestic workers (Chicas de Servicio) began organizing to form a union. Cine Mujer, a women's film group, and the Corporación Mujer y Familia (Corporation of Women and Family) were formed in 1980. On Mar. 8, 1981, the Women's Center opened in Bogotá. Mujeres en la Lucha (Women in the Struggle) began studies on sex and health, and in July, the first All Latin American Women's Conference was held in Bogotá, with 250 participants from 25 countries. On Aug. 6, 1982, 8 women were named vice-ministers of education, development, health, labor, communications, energy, justice, and public works. Beatriz de Londano was named head of the Dept. of Caldas against the wishes of the regional Roman Catholic authority.

MYTHOGRAPHY. The Chibcha peoples believe that the creator of human life was a divine woman who appeared at Lake Iguaque, carrying a child in her arms; later, both she and the child transformed themselves into snakes and disappeared into the lake. Chia, the moon goddess of central Colombia, was responsible for the great flood: in a quarrel with her husband, the god Bochica, she caused the river Funzha to overflow with her rage, and she then escaped to the mountains and finally to the sky. Lake Guatavita is the still existent remnant of that flood.

COLOMBIA: Fighting for the Right to Fight
by Luz Helena Sánchez
(Translated by Lisa Kollisch)

"A *macho* bourgeois is a redundancy. A *macho* revolutionary is an obscenity."
One man!

"A new woman and man in a new society: this is what feminism is seeking. This feminism is creative in its actions and not in speeches. It teaches us that certain hierarchical conceptions in our ideology and our struggle fit all too well with the existing structures of society."

Another man!!

Discrimination against women is a reality in our country, equally visible in the public and the private (domestic) sector.

Women are at the bottom of the occupational pyramid, where there are not only more of them but where they also receive less pay.

In education, women are still "tracked" into programs that could be termed auxiliary, which make them directly dependent on men on the professional level: careers in social work, psychology, the field of education itself, and the auxiliary branches of medicine (nursing, technicians, etc.). Colombian women have a higher drop-out rate in high school than do men, and as a result, more men than women complete professional studies.

From that point on, work experience is the determining factor for the best salaries. Studies reveal that the need for work experience discriminates against women: time out for reproduction—which is fundamental for the maintenance of society—nonetheless makes it difficult for women to develop a continuous work history. Furthermore, women approach salaried work as auxiliary income, as a way of adding to the family's funds: this is how employers perceive it, and also how women sometimes describe it. Not only are women discriminated against in the abstract because they reproduce; in many cases they are forced to sign away their right to maternity benefits or even to present a certificate of nonpregnancy before being hired for a job.

This situation is the result of deeper problems that in turn indicate structural problems: the whole basis of the present system—the patriarchal ideology that supports power, hierarchy, and domination among classes, ages, sexes, and nations.

An extraordinary woman* of this century said: "Women are not born, they're made." I would like us to ask ourselves: "How do they make us into women?" and, even more important, "How do we make women?"

As feminists, we call for a complete and implacable break with the social order that makes us into "women." Because of the oppressed nature of the "feminine subculture," this break must be produced without the blessing of male power as represented by the father, husband, political party, or State.

I believe that a period of autonomy is absolutely necessary and that it must involve a break with and a temporal/spatial distancing from any power structure, call it what we will. At this time I don't see how the same power we want to destroy could devise a theory and practice that would allow us to re-create our identity on the level of body-mind-sex, and to see ourselves genuinely in a new light.

At the individual level, some of us have already achieved this in our daily relationships with the men we call our friends. But we need to confront the same contradictions on a societal level by taking on all situations in which patriarchal power is exercised. We must create small groups of women, small autonomous organizations, and a social process of rehabilitation that seeks a new definition of women. I am referring to the absolute neces-. sity for long-term work which on a short-term basis would probably not produce results that would be classically viewed as "political."

We are pursuing a new course, trying to turn every situation we are in, and every women's meeting, into an opportunity for subverting the order. We are creating a split *in* the system—and generating change. Arguments to the contrary are tediously familiar and unacceptable, and can generally be classed into two categories:

1) "A feminist movement is unnecessary because it diminishes the strength of the class

* Simone de Beauvoir—Ed.

struggle." This position weakens more every day on a theoretical level. Nevertheless, on a practical level it continues to ridicule and stereotype those of us who have accepted feminism as a total form of action at this time in history.

2) "The 'feminist' struggle is necessary, but should be *subordinate* to the 'revolutionary' struggle for transformation of socioeconomic structures. The woman question should be resolved within the context of the socialist movement." This position does recognize the "feminine" struggle. Nevertheless, as much in practice as in theory, it does not approve of feminism as a viable alternative to the ideology of domination that existed *prior* to capitalist forms of exploitation. This ideology constitutes a dehumanizing view of the existing relationships between men and women, adults and children, the young and the old—and is the prototype of all forms of domination.

Women must put forward a practical-theoretical analysis that, while drawing on some elements of historical materialism, should improve on it, allowing us to account for the questions that we ask ourselves as feminists. The work has already begun. Timidly at first, feminists have been creating a theoretical corpus that confronts not just the positivist academic world (which produces partial and subjective explanations) but also the world of Marxist intellectuals (who have not looked favorably on our work, viewing as they do the question of women as secondary to that of class).

Yet new interpretations can be adapted by a wide range of women's groups only if the theoretical discussion of the need to break down the distinction between "intellectual and ignorant" approaches a practical plan of action. In Europe and (to a lesser extent) in North America, small groups of women have begun to articulate important new proposals. In addition, there have been some successful attempts to get closer to the feminists of the Third World: the solidarity of women participating in the Alternative Conference at Copenhagen in 1980; the international meeting on Women and Health held in Geneva in 1981 at the initiative of a European feminist group; the presence of American and European women at the Encuentro Feminista de América Latina y del Caribe in 1981 (Feminist Meeting of Latin America and the Caribbean).

The Situation in Latin America

With some variations in timing (attributable to differences in the social organization of various Latin American countries), the rise of the "New Feminism" occurred in the 1970's. It involved: 1) a struggle for autonomy vis à vis the structures of patriarchal power—political parties and the State; and 2) the fact that the first women to form autonomous groups came from student, trade-union, syndicalist, or human-rights groups generally led by organizations with ties to political parties. Other common elements were that many of these women, for political or academic reasons, had gone to North America and Europe, where they had experienced the rise of the women's movement of the 1960's; almost all of them belonged to the petite bourgeoisie; they all had worked with women from different sectors: workers, housewives, domestic servants, peasants, students, and professional women.

The gap between militancy and academia has been narrowed, and there has been a conscious effort to find new ways to do research on women: on the female body, sexuality, and pleasure, and the forms of social production carried out by a reproductive body. At the same time, there has been a search for new forms of creative artistic expression and denunciation of different forms of violence against women.

These goals came together at the Primer Encuentro Feminista de América Latina y del Caribe. The meeting dealt with the need for creating continent-wide organizations, first as a loose network of information and support, and then as a formal structure that would articulate a common politics. This in turn has led to the provisional formation of ALACEM: Asociación Latino-Americana y del Caribe de Estudios de la Mujer (Latin

American and Caribbean Association for the Study of Women) in Brazil in late 1981. It was the realization of a dream that many of us have cherished for a long time.

We women of the Latin American continent have lived through the struggle to gain new spaces in the humanities, in graphic and visual arts, in research; for the right to feel desire and pleasure, for a totally changed position in politics. We have fought sexual discrimination in union and political organizations. In different geographical areas and cultural contexts, timidly or openly, *we have fought for the right to fight.*

The Situation in Colombia

Because so little is known about the foremothers who fought for women's rights from colonial times through independence and the first half of this century, I will limit myself to a brief overview of the "new feminism" in our country.

Since the first autonomous feminist groups in Medellín and Bogotá began in 1975, we have seen major progress: the publication of the magazine *Cuéntame tu vida* (Tell Me Your Life) in the city of Cali; the call for the first Encuentro Nacional de Mujeres (National Meeting of Women) with the goal of joining the international campaign for abortion and against forced sterilization; work collaboration with women from different class sectors; the success of the First Feminist Meeting of Latin America and the Caribbean; demonstrations against violence toward women; the creation of such formal groups as Cine Mujer (Movies About Women) with the aim of seeking new images; new research on women—Corporación Mujer y Familia (Association for Women and the Family); the development of theory, both in universities and in research centers; the opening of La Casa de la Mujer (Woman's House) on March 8, 1982; and continued references to feminism in the patriarchal press.

In terms of established parties, it's important to recognize the attempts of the Trotskyist organization to explore the question of women and their efforts, not always successful, to organize women. Recent reports in *Voz Proletaria* (Proletarian Voice, a publication of the Colombian Communist Party) have been interesting, particularly since they came after press releases issued by the late CPC (Communist Party of Colombia) leader Yira Castro at the end of 1980, asserting that feminism, along with the bourgeoisie, was the enemy of the proletariat. Furthermore, many of us who have witnessed the stubborn antifeminist position of the Maoist organization have been pleasantly surprised by a recently published issue of *Tribuna Roja* (Red Tribune), with an extensive editorial and a conversation with women of the Party concerning the situation of women in Colombia.

We are well aware that these expressions have not appeared in a political-ideological vacuum. They are a response, on the one hand, to the brave struggle for autonomy some of us have waged, and on the other hand to the important work carried out by women from various sectors. Also deserving of mention is the pioneering work of the group Mujeres en la Lucha (Women in the Struggle) in the areas of health and sexuality: their work will have a strong influence on Colombian feminism for a long time to come, as well as the internal ideological fight being waged (with fury) by some women activists within the parties. Thus, feminism can no longer be ignored. I feel that it will begin to be faced with different options. We must defend what we have won and be careful not to fall into the trap of co-optation. In addition, we must know when is the right moment to emerge from the ghetto.

Autonomous Feminism

Those of us already familiar with unfulfilled promises and alliances broken by party activists know that a joint effort between party members and autonomous feminists will be possible only if there are profound changes in the party structure. This is especially true if, as I believe, the parties do not firmly believe that the struggle against patriarchal ideology should begin *here* and *now*. Their theory expresses an eagerness to attract "masses" of women around demands that would convince them to join in specific strategies—but it also allows them to ignore the issue of the party's own domination, of domination by revolutionary men, of women's exclusion from discussions on the revolution—all this at the same time as they mistreat and prostitute their women, and maintain the inferiority of women activists through the perpetuation of a sexual division of work, both at party headquarters and in the guerrilla camps (see the writings of Ana María Araujo, an exiled Tupamaru guerrilla).

Why is autonomy necessary?

We have become women within the family unit, where our model has been woman-as-mother—victimized, dominated, sacrificing her creativity for the sake of her husband and children; where we have not had the right or the time to explore the continual changes in the world. Women have had to sacrifice their careers for the sake of a brother, since, according to the logic of a *macho* world, the salary of a man is higher. We have been denied the opportunity of exploring the world of movement, of relationships, of breadth. The discussions they have allowed us to hold have always tended to be childish, at times even showing in our tone of voice. Our bodies, "castrated" by the *macho* culture, have been forced to conform to codes alien to us. Our sexuality, controlled by the alienated masculine image, is nevertheless the object of consumption in a society that seems to produce without end and calls for the mishandling and mistreatment of women's bodies. Our reproductive capacity and our motherhood are fully embedded in the interests of the State.

Since we don't know what we want, since we have been kept from learning how to think abstractly or solve problems efficiently, and since we are the objects of continual violence, we gave ourselves up to the only thing that remained: passive resistance within the four walls of a room, a house, or a palace. Because of this we are poor leaders, "frigid," "hysterical," mothers of eleven (or none, because of sterilization without informed consent), and victims of birth-control hormones that the "doctors" describe as protective. Raped, mistreated, and finally crazy, we fill the asylums or pay their stand-ins —psychiatrists, psychologists, and psychotherapists—to help us.

This is the world that has been created for us and for which we call ourselves "unsuited." We no longer want to surrender our physical and mental health in exchange for companionship or the possibility of material survival. This is why, at this time, we defend our right to pull away and organize ourselves separately.

Separate from whom? From the patriarchal organizations where they forgot to sing to liberty in order to arrive at insurrection-revolution set up beforehand as a party strategy? Strategy that now seems to take women into account, of course, women from the "popular" sectors—long live the revolution!

It is precisely because we do not want to be passive, dumb, frigid, hysterical, vehicles of reproduction according to someone else's definition, objects of the violence of the medical institution and raped "by consent" or because we have gone crazy, that we are forced to turn toward an essential period of autonomy. We must join together, not only to seek a new individual identity for women, but also to create a new identity for all women, for "us." We women are not part of "the masses." We have the right to search for new ways, and we are searching. We welcome all men who understand the vitality of our undertaking and the hope that the values traditionally assigned to women (the ones that now place us in an unequal situation) will be the very ones through which to build a new democratic society.

Only by confronting the contradictions and breaking free from the rigid, antiquated discourse that allows the perpetuation of hierarchies, domination, and violence in daily life; only by defining the process as a struggle for happiness and by destroying the death figures we have internalized, can we succeed in establishing a coherent political strategy for change. Autonomous feminism will not turn back. No one can ask it to do so, nor does anyone have the right to say that it is not clearly on the path of such a strategy for society's transformation.

Suggested Further Reading

Asociación Colombiana de Estudios de Población. "Debate sobre la Mujer y la familia en América Latina y el Caribe," n.p., n.d.; a compilation of articles on different aspects of women's situation in Latin America.

García-Márquez, Gabriel. *Crónica de una Muerte Anunciada.* Bogotá: Edit. Oveja Negra, 1982; the latest novel by the author of *One Hundred Years of Solitude.* It is based on recollections of what happened in a small Atlantic-coast town when a husband discovers that his bride is not a virgin.

Grupo Mujeres en la Lucha. "La Mujer y la Salud en Colombia," 1980 (mimeo); a diagnosis of the women's health situation in Colombia.

Rey de Marulanda Nohora. "La Mujer y el Trabajo." Monografías Cede, Universidad de los Andes, 1981.

Luz Helena Sánchez is a founding member of the oldest feminist group in Colombia (Mujeres en la Lucha), and also a founding member of Corporación Mujer y Familia, a private nonprofit feminist institution whose main objective is to conduct research and action programs for and by women. She is also a founding member of the International Feminist Collective Inc. She writes of herself: "I had never felt discriminated against until I was seventeen. My classmates asked about my plans. 'Getting married very soon and going to the University,' was my reply—followed by a chorus-laugh from them. I didn't understand. In fact, I did marry soon thereafter, had a baby boy 18 months later, started medical school when he was one year old, and began to feel the victim of a conspiracy from other women because I was a "nonloving" mother—I had a career. In the middle of that career we had a second son (1972), and later, our first and only daughter (1978). I have lived on and off with the same person; it has not always been easy, but our relationship has lasted 17 years. After I finished medical school, I went abroad to get a master's degree in public health. I have also been trained as a psychotherapist. My interests now are: 1) to go deeper into the problems women face in terms of our own identity and develop creative, "deprofessionalized" ways of dealing with them; 2) to contribute to defining Latin American feminism, for I see feminism in our continent as the most important political project; 3) to contribute to and strengthen the struggle for the autonomy of the women's movement."

CUBA
(Republic of Cuba)

Largest of the West Indies islands situated at the mouth of the Gulf of Mexico, east of Mexico and south of the United States in the Caribbean Sea. **Area:** 114,524 sq. km. (44,218 sq. mi.). **Population** (1980): 9,961,000, female 50%. **Capital:** Havana.

DEMOGRAPHY. Languages: Spanish. **Races or Ethnic Groups:** European (Spanish) descent, African descent, Mestizo, Chinese, Native Indian. **Religions:** Roman Catholicism 90%, Protestant, mixed-faith Afro-Cuban, Judaism. **Education** (% enrolled in school, 1975): Age 6–11—of all girls 100%, of all boys 100%; age 12–17—of all girls 63%, of all boys 67%; higher education—in 1980 women comprised 41.7% of post-secondary students. **Literacy** (1977): Female 80%, male 76%. **Birth Rate** (per 1000 pop., 1975–80): 18. **Death Rate** (per 1000 pop., 1975–80): 6. **Infant Mortality** (per 1000 live births, 1975–80): Female 22, male 21. **Life Expectancy** (1975–80): Female 74 yrs., male 70 yrs.

GOVERNMENT. Centralized 1-party government under the aegis of Cuban Communist Party, with a National Assembly and provincial governing bodies chosen by national elections. Fidel Castro is President of the Republic, the Council of Estate, the Council of Ministers, and the National Assembly, Commander-in-Chief of the Armed Forces, and First Secretary of the Central Committee of the Communist Party; his brother, Raúl Castro, is the Second Secretary of the Central Committee and Deputy Commander-in-Chief of the Armed Forces. **Women's Suffrage:** 1934. **Equal Rights:** Women's equality in marriage, employment, salaries, education, and all spheres of life is stipulated in the 1976 Constitution. Discrimination on the basis of sex is punishable by a fine of 200–500 quotas (ration points) and 6 months–3 yrs. imprisonment. **Women in Government** (1978–80): Less than 10% of each of the commissions of construction, transportation, and agriculture;

22.2% of National Assembly; 20% of judges in the People's Supreme Court; 19% of Communist Party membership; none as full members in Central Committee, or currently on Council of Ministers.

ECONOMY. Currency: Cuban Peso (May 1983: 0.86 = $1 US) **Gross National Product** (1980): $14 billion. **Per Capita Income** (1980): $1407. **Women's Wages as a Percentage of Men's:** No data obtainable. **Equal Pay Policy:** Equal pay for equal work stipulated by 1934 protective labor legislation and restated in the 1976 Constitution. Practice follows the government-stated (revised Marxist) principle "From each one according to his [sic] capacity, to each one according to his [sic] work." **Production** (Agricultural/Industrial): Sugar, tobacco, coffee; refined oil products, textiles, chemicals. **Women as a Percentage of Labor Force** (1980): 31%; **of agricultural force** 14.8%; **of industrial force** 24.8% (of manual laborers in light industry 81%, of manual laborers in Cubatabaco—nationalized tobacco industry—93%); **of military**—no statistics obtainable. Women age 17–35 may volunteer for 2 yr. service but are not subject to the draft. Women were prominent in the militias during the early 1960's; a 1980 campaign aims to put more women in territorial militias. **(Employed) Women's Occupational Indicators** (1981): Of public health workers 34.3%, of commerce workers 43%, of administrative workers 48%. **Unemployment:** No data obtainable.

GYNOGRAPHY. Marriage. *Policy:* The 1975 Family Code recognizes the equality of partners in marriage, the economic value of domestic tasks, and the duty of both spouses to cooperate in them. Property and income acquired during marriage is jointly owned; both partners are responsible for financial support of their home. *Practice:* Female mean age at marriage (1970–78): 20; women age 15–49 in union (1970–78): 67%. Women still perform majority of household tasks. **Divorce.** *Policy:* Legal. Family Code establishes divorce by judicial decree in cases where marriage "loses meaning for the couple, their children, and society as a whole." The Code recommends equal division of jointly owned property, and alimony (for 6 months if no children or 1 yr. if children) for the spouse who has no job. *Practice:* Divorces (per 1000 pop., 1980): 2.5; no further data obtainable.

Family. *Policy:* 1974 Maternity Law grants employed women 16 weeks paid leave and up to 1 yr. without pay, ensuring medical care. Care of children is the responsibility of both parents. The 1976 Constitution (Art. 43) provides for creation of day-care centers. *Practice:* In 1978, 782 day-care centers throughout Cuba provided meals, care, and medical/dental services to 86,000 children age 2 months–5 yrs. There are also boarding and semi-boarding schools for children of working parents. Parents pay for these services. **Welfare.** *Policy:* Government provision for the basic needs of all citizens, including free medical and dental care, subsidized housing, food allotments, education, and employment. *Practice:* No statistics obtainable. Food, clothing, and certain electrical appliances are rationed according to what the government calls "equitable distribution." One's employment or worker-identity card plays a classifying role in rationing, as well as indicating special needs (milk, eggs, fruit, and meat for persons who are infants, diabetic, pregnant, elderly, etc.). When individuals lose their employment, their worker-identity status changes; they can be considered "social undesirables" and thus forfeit part of their food and other allotments. A black market exists in terms of rationing, as when diabetics sell samples of their urine so that nondiabetics can qualify for special-needs status. Preventive dental care is free; medicines must be purchased. **Contraception.** *Policy:* Legal. Government-sponsored family-planning services have been made part of the Ministry of Health. Sterilization is legal without conditions. *Practice:* No statistics obtainable, but IUD is most widely used method. **Abortion.** *Policy:* Legal. Available free and on request in government hospitals on broad

medical grounds during first 12 weeks of pregnancy; for minors, parental consent is required. *Practice:* Abortions (per 1000 women age 15–44, 1980): 55.3. Abortion is free and easily obtainable only if the woman is a minor or already has more than 3 children. Otherwise, she must apply for permission to the Ministry of Health and, if permission is granted, then she must pay for the procedure. **Illegitimacy.** *Policy:* Family Code establishes equality of all children regardless of parents' marital status. *Practice:* No data obtainable. **Homosexuality.** *Policy:* Up until 1978, lesbianism was considered a sickness to be treated in mental institutions, not punishable by prison (as was male homosexuality). The 1978 Law of Endangerment makes homosexuality a threat to public morality punishable by 4 yrs. imprisonment, now applying to both women and men. *Practice:* In the 1960's homosexuals were sent to labor camps* along with other such "undesirable elements" as Jehovah's Witnesses. In 1980 many homosexuals were among the 125,000 people who immigrated to the US during a mass exodus from the port of Mariel (see HERSTORY).

Incest. *Policy:* Illegal. If the victim is under age 16, punishable by 6 months–1 yr. imprisonment as statutory rape; if both parties are over age 16, both are punishable. *Practice:* No data obtainable. **Sexual Harassment.** *Policy:* See **Equal Rights;** also punishable under the 1938 Social Defense Code (Arts. 484–87) by 1–6 yrs. imprisonment. *Practice:* No statistics obtainable. Reportedly, sexual harassment is still prevalent and complaint procedures are complex and slow, discouraging women from availing themselves of their rights of grievance. **Rape.** *Policy:* Illegal; Social Defense Code makes frontal or anal rape by force or intimidation punishable by 4–12 yrs. imprisonment. Gang rape and rape in which victim is "injured" or killed is punishable by 15–30 yrs. imprisonment or by death. Rape of a minor is punishable by up to 30 yrs. imprisonment or by death, as is homosexual rape of a male under age 16. Testimony of the victim is sufficient evidence for conviction. *Prac-*

---

* UMAP (Military Units of Assistance to Production) camps.

tice: No data obtainable. **Battery.** *Policy:* No data obtainable. *Practice:* No data obtainable. **Prostitution.** *Policy:* Illegal, and prohibited by the Penal Code as a "state of danger." Prostitution and pimping are punishable by 1–6 yrs. imprisonment. Clients are not prosecuted. *Practice:* No statistics obtainable. Before the 1959 Revolution, prostitution was rife in Havana. Currently, street prostitution and brothels seem to have been eradicated, but reportedly the elite have access to "call-girls." Women working as prostitutes are dealt with by "therapy, rehabilitation, and preventive detention." **Traditional/Cultural Practices:** *Policy:* No data obtainable. *Practice:* Residual versions of dowry contracts still exist in trousseau and "bridewealth" practices. **Crisis Centers:** No data obtainable.

HERSTORY. Cubanacán, as it was known by the indigenous peoples, was "discovered" by Columbus in 1492 and remained under Spanish colonial rule until 1898. In 1811 a women's magazine, *El Correo de las Damas* (The Women's Post), published information regarding women's sexuality. The Archbishop of Havana issued a pastoral letter attacking the magazine. Gertrudis Gómez de Avellaneda (1814–73) was a brilliant writer in many different genres, including drama. "La Avellaneda's" abolitionist novel *El Mulato Sab* was published 10 years before Harriet Beecher Stowe's *Uncle Tom's Cabin* in the US. Emilia Casanova and Ana Betancourt were well-known anticolonial fighters. The former was forced to leave Cuba in 1832 because of her politics. In New York she formed the League of Cuban Daughters, which organized women in exile to continue fighting Spanish colonialism. Ana Betancourt demanded rights for women at the Revolutionary Assembly held at Guaimaro (1869) during the Ten Year War. In the 1850's and 1860's, Luz Vázquez (La

Bayamesa) provided her house as a center for anticolonial conspiracy; her daughter, Adriana, was a courier for the Liberation Army.

Cuba adopted its first constitution in 1901, fought off US occupation, and suffered through 3 dictatorships. Because of pressure from women's organizations, on July 18, 1917, 2 laws were passed granting women the right to child custody regardless of their marital status, the right to divorce, and to administer their property, including dowry. Graciella Barinaga y Ponce de León's book, *Feminism and the Home* was published in 1931, paving the way in 1932 for the First National Congress of Women in Havana, followed by the founding of the Feminist National Alliance. After the overthrow of dictator Gen. Machado (1933) women won the vote, and progressive labor legislation was passed. A 1934 decree provided for the protection of Cuban women employees, including equal pay, regulation of night employment, medical examinations conducted by industry, and social security for domestic workers. Maternity legislation was passed in 1934. In 1936, women first occupied positions in the House of Representatives. A new Social Defense Code was established (1938) that made pimping and rape (but also abortion and prostitution) crimes.

During WW II, Fulgencio Batista organized the Feminine Service of Civil Defense (1942) to prepare women for civilian tasks. In the early 1950's, Haydée Santamaría (who committed suicide in 1980**), Celia Sánchez, María Antonia Figueroa, and Melba Hernández joined the underground movement against the Batista dictatorship. The movement was composed of members of the July 26 Movement (led by Fidel Castro) and the Student Directorate (led by Fauré Chomón after the assassination of José Antonio Echeverría). Such women as

---

** The official reason given out was that she was emotionally disturbed; the gossip was that she had been depressed by marital problems. Yet Professor Carlos Ripoll claims that, as early as the mid-1950's, Elena Maderos was among those liberal leaders who had witnessed Santamaría's impassioned statement that the only valid political act when all else had failed was suicide (said by Santamaría to Cosme de La Torriente, a revered republican statesman who had not succeeded in persuading Batista to leave power voluntarily). Santamaría killed herself on July 26—the 21st anniversary of the Revolution.

Carmen Castro Porta, of the José Martí Civic Front of Women, helped Castro in the organization of the underground while he was exiled in Mexico, residing at the home of another woman collaborator —María Antonia González. Batista was overthrown in 1959.

The Federation of Cuban Women was created by the government in 1960 and its first president was—and still is— Vilma Espín, the wife of Raúl Castro and sister-in-law of Fidel Castro. She is an alternate member in the Political Bureau of the Central Committee of the Cuban Communist Party. Women mobilized during the US-backed attempted invasion by anti-Castro Cubans at the Bay of Pigs (1961) and the subsequent partial export embargo that became a total trade blockade by 1962; women also mobilized during the USSR's attempt to establish nu-

clear missile warheads on the island. In 1980, 500,000 Cubans attempted to leave via the port of Mariel; of these, 125,000 did emigrate—approx. one-quarter of them women.

MYTHOGRAPHY. Small carved-stone female idols pre-dating Columbus's landing have been found recently in the Banes region. Goddess worship was carried to Cuba by the African (Yoruba) population who were brought as slaves, and who later combined their own deities with Roman Catholic saints. Yemayá, Oshún, Oyá, and Obatalá-Yemmu are the better-known goddesses. Women officiate as *santeras,* predict the future, and receive the *santo* (saint's spirit). The patron saint of Cuba is the Virgin of Charity from El Cobre. Mariolatry is still prevalent.

CUBA: Paradise Gained, Paradise Lost— The Price of "Integration"
by La Silenciada

Wherever she looked she saw women working, she saw women organizing the neighborhood committees, the committees for the defense of the revolution, she saw women carrying guns and women carrying alphabetization manuals, she saw women working in their homes and in the factories, women doing voluntary work, women nursing and teaching, women at the laboratories and women sitting at desks taking and transcribing dictation, women at popular meetings, at political meetings. And yet the national hero, the national director, the national leader, the national army chief, the national ideologist, the national eye to survey the State—all were male.

Why did I have to explain to a Cuban woman official—after she had participated in twenty-five years of socialist-communist government—that the search to provide input for women in national development plans, in the diverse projects which involved every sector of the economic life of a country, was not an imperialist plot but a necessary step to secure the training and *real* integration of women in any society? What, I asked, is the Women's Federation doing regarding women's input in bilateral and multilateral arrangements? She confessed that she knew very little about economic-planning activity in the country. Then again, I asked myself, why, if women are so organized at all levels, is it that integration ends up by being double exploitation? Why was Vilma Espín, the president of the Federation of Cuban Women, careful never to call herself a feminist? What seemed to be such a contradiction between a communist-Marxist-Leninist consciousness and feminism? Was it at all possible to bridge the gap? Or was it that loyalty is sworn first to the Party which, being controlled by men, refuses to recognize that women remain an oppressed class? How many times had I heard that the question of women's equality had already been solved in countries with centrally planned economies? And yet why, after twenty-five years, did the Central Committee not include even one woman as a full member? The usual excuses—no qualified women, or blaming the US economic blockade for poor or slow performance in the productive sectors (where women are concentrated) —could not explain the lack of visibility of women in top positions in the country's leadership. With the mobilization of power that the government has, and with the sustained and loyal effort of the Women's Federation, why wasn't even Vilma Espín a Minister? I recalled my enormous disappointment when Haydée Santamaría was given directorship of only the Casa de las Américas[1] and not even the Ministry of Education. Haydée had been a hero on even standing with Ché Guevara, Camilo Cienfuegos, Fauré Chomón, or the man who was to become her husband, Armando Hart.

The Grandmother, daughter of patricians who had fought against the Spanish colonialists in 1840 and 1898, leads her horse peacefully, with me following close by, across what had been her father's land, now all partitioned among her brothers and sister. The Grandmother leaves her husband and flees to the capital with my father; she buys a house in the old part of Havana and earns extra money by sewing. The Grandmother smokes cigars in a Havana salon, much to the surprise of the male guests. The Grandmother tries to teach me to gallop while riding sidesaddle. The Grandmother takes me to church three times until the priest consents to baptize me with an un-Christian name.

Women are still receiving orders and still have no real power, no advancement; perhaps, even, they have *lost* ground. (One must not forget that Cuban women had won the right to work and to equal pay for equal work back in 1934.)

Every able-bodied person was needed to defend the revolution.[2]

The government needed women in the early 1960's and then, having realized women's enormous productive potential, continued calling for their massive participation in the work force, simply because the government had to survive; it had its economic targets, its production goals—and it needed hands to execute the program. So was launched the 1973–74 campaign to boost to 100,000 the number of women working outside the home. When the Women's Federation had to answer for its failure in not meeting this target, it became known that pressure from the family was one main factor, as was lack of services or support by the government, lack of economic incentive, lack of minimal conditions of hygiene and protection in the workplace, and lack of understanding about women's role in society. It was obvious that husbands, fathers, and the State were the ones who lacked understanding, because women are seldom consulted before *major* decisions are taken concerning their lives and well-being.

The Grandmother says: This new leader, he talks too much, who is he trying to convince, himself?

Thereafter, improvements were introduced. Women who were employed would not have to wait on line for a long time at the grocery store since a "shopping-bag action"[3]

[1.] A cultural institution geared to establish links with the Spanish-speaking world.

[2.] Said, at various times and in similar circumstances, by Lenin, Mao, Fanon, Ho Chi Minh, Fidel Castro, Col. Qaddafi, etc.

[3.] This consisted of the following: having secured a ration card, an employed woman could leave a list of desired items at the store in the morning and on her way home, she could pick up the shopping bag. (Men—husbands, brothers, fathers—apparently could not pick them up.)

was initiated. To minimize serious absenteeism, electrical appliances were earmarked for such women, but it was still assumed that a woman had to do the housework as well as her production job.

Discussion of the Family Code began in the mid-1970's. Through the Code the unity of the State and family became codified not unlike that union of the Church and the family, or the Trinity and the Church. True, the Church Fathers stipulated the wife's obedience to the husband while the Code Fathers stipulated the husband's obligation to share housework with the wife. But having encoded the nuclear family as the cornerstone of the State, it follows that anything which does not fit into that pattern might be highly suspicious.

The Grandmother says Cubans are like the Phoenicians or the Jews, we are all very restless. Should we blame the Jesuits for what is happening in Cuba? The Grandmother says that nothing good could be expected from a revolutionary trained in Loyola's school of thought —which Fidel was, after all.

> Woman is nature's workshop where life is forged.
>
> —Fidel Castro

The Family Code has not reformed the sexual division of labor. Women are in fact made responsible for the future of the State—as mothers *and* wives *and* workers. The Code's version of the family remains strictly based on a masculine way of organizing sexual activity; it established, for example, a reformed version of the Church's vision of heterosexual pairing as a production unit where women continue to manufacture the species but do not determine its—or their own—destiny.

> It wouldn't be possible to write the history of our revolution in the last twenty years without mentioning the Federation of Cuban Women.
>
> —Fidel Castro

The Federation was created in the summer of 1960 to serve as the basis of organization, indoctrination, education, and mobilization of women. It has played a leading role in the campaign against illiteracy and the raising of educational standards for all, and it continues to be substantially involved in the upgrading of education for rural women.[4] The Federation has 2,363,559 women members and is self-supporting through a dues-paying process (it is not subsidized by the Party or the State). According to the Federation's Report to the Third Congress (1980), the majority of its members are housewives.

The Grandmother insists that men can't help being weaklings, they can't stand pain, they don't know how to govern without stealing, they don't know how to love, they all need women to lead them, teach them, civilize them.

One of the Federation's main objectives is the promotion of Marxist-Leninist political-ideological development; study groups are in charge of this activity and women assigned to this task are specially trained. At the Third Congress, however, it emerged that 16 percent of the organizations affiliated with the Federation did not hold ideological study-group meetings at all and that 35 percent of the Federation members did not attend such meetings regularly. One reason for this apathy, obviously, is lack of time: study groups

---

[4] One of its offshoots, the contingency Militant Mothers for Education, has a membership of 1.4 million and is supposed to assist in upgrading education of all workers to the sixth-grade level.

meet "after work," when housewives are still working (or have returned from their jobs—in order to do housework—or are already engaged in volunteer labor as well).

The Federation has at its disposal the facilities of the different government departments and ministries. It has access to mass media, the power to call for mass meetings, and all the prerogatives given to it by the Party apparatus. The Federation's 41,891 agitator-and-propaganda groups, made up of 221,780 Federation members, constitute not only a fundamental instrument but an impressive body of leaders. Yet despite this fact, the Federation had to complain in its report to the Third Congress that the media were giving an image of woman "which did not support our goals." As early as 1975, the problem of the media and the entertainment industry (including the Queen of Carnival Pageant) had been raised. Tropicana, a cabaret which had been prominently featured in the "old, pseudo-republic days" had been kept open with the same type of choreography and dance of the 1950's—namely, women (mulattas and whites) feathered and emplumed, half naked, parading under the stars. Several tourist films released outside Cuba featured mulattas as sex objects, concentrating on close-ups of buttocks and breasts. The Third Congress took place in 1980. Now, four years later, still no progress had been achieved in the "image of woman."

I join the militia; The Grandmother says she never liked uniforms. I say, Fidel says no one will have any other grade in the military above Commandante. Later she points out to me he has a newly designed uniform and that there are other military grades being handed out.

I volunteer for a labor census and see a woman in the slaughterhouse—the only woman slaughterer. I do my work in a state of shock.

I go looking for a job in the new Ministry of Transport and a certain Commandante Marrero sexually assaults me. I tell The Grandmother I am beginning to be less impressed with the new government elite. She says, What made you expect them to be any different?

The Federation's activities also extend to 12,754 social workers and administrators of 782 day-care centers. The social workers concentrate on crime prevention and work hand in hand with the Ministry of the Interior, which is also the Ministry for State Security. Since 1967 they have worked through rehabilitation institutions—on minors with police records and on adult women in penal institutions. They are also instrumental in determining "social deviance": homosexuality, vagrancy, etc. The support brigades for public health comprise a total of 61,071 women committed to assisting the Ministry of Public Health in such matters as vaccinations, cancer detection, pre-natal and post-natal control. It may be concluded that the government would be literally paralyzed without the widespread support activities of the Federation. Considering the immense importance of this organizational tool for mass mobilization, it is surprising that better results for the rights of women *as* women have not been achieved. Or is that not a priority?

Pastorita Nuñez loses her job in the Ministry of Housing. Nobody hears about her again. She was a revolutionary of her time, later discredited. Sad fate of women revolutionaries, I say. Haydée Santamaría commits suicide in 1980.

The Report of the Third Congress, as well as Fidel Castro's closing speech, identifies a major area of concern which will affect women's employment in the coming years:

In 1979, 800,000 women were employed (30 percent) compared with 590,000 women (25.3 percent) in 1974. This high rate of growth cannot be sustained permanently because it is the result not only of correct Party policy but also of the country's economic needs during that period under review. The mobilization of additional supporters was needed in a transitional productive period. The Federation is therefore being called to raise the technical skills of women workers and improve the information network on job opportunities so that women are not driven out of the job market by young graduates newly competing for jobs. [No resources seem to have been allocated to this end.]

The Federation's report to the Third Congress also shows housework/childcare plus the voluntary work one is compelled to perform to be integrated in the construction of a truly socialist society. In 1979 the Federation created the Third Congress Detachments which called for the contributions of women to various voluntary, after-work agricultural activities, i.e., social and manual work. One might well be puzzled by Vilma Espín's stated disappointment that women in the Federation do not attend cultural events organized by it. How could they? Is there any time left?

Fidel Castro, of course, did address the problem in his concluding remarks to the Third Congress. Women would be accommodated in a highly competitive labor market by the introduction of new jobs—such as electric-bill collector, and operator in the textile industry.[5] In passing, the Prime Minister also suggested solving the problem by the creation of a night shift for hairdressers and laundries.[6]

I say they have offered me a scholarship to go to China. Who has offered that to you? asks The Grandmother. The mistress of Ramiro Valdés, I reply. What are you going to do there if you don't speak Chinese? I don't go to China. Later I realize that the government has begun to send "political undesirables" who are nevertheless still acknowledged as revolutionaries to the People's Republic of China.

> The intensification of counterrevolutionary attacks led (in September 1960) to the formation of the Committees for the Defense of the Revolution (CDRs). Even larger numbers of women joined the CDRs, which were organized on a block-by-block basis. They guarded public buildings, watched for suspicious activities in the

[5.] In the first instance energy has become more expensive, and so rather than pay quarterly on the basis of an average, bills are to be collected monthly; this will require monthly meter readings and the immediate collection of charges incurred; this job, Fidel said, can largely be done by women. He also said that textile-industry factories, which had been operating an average of 280 days a year, could operate 355 days a year, requiring an additional shift—for women.

[6.] "What constitutes an unfair burden for women? . . . I really have my doubts as to whether we are going about things in the right way. When the hairdressers close at such and such an hour, that's that. And then the working woman can't go to the hairdresser. [Applause] . . . And of course what Vilma said in the report I've heard too: that absenteeism, authorization to receive those services during work hours, has practically been legalized. . . . Because the point is that if they don't go to the hairdressers they'll be doing their hair at home, and if they do go to the hairdressers they'll be paying for the service they receive. And not all the employees have to be there at, say, during peak hours. The whole staff doesn't have to be around at 8:00 or 9:00 at night. There can be just one or two. That'll have to be studied. And why can't the laundries be working at night, if it's a service that's being paid for? [Applause] People are going to pay for that service; they're going to pay for it! . . . I haven't heard a single man, let me tell you, protest about that. [Laughter] Not a single one! [Applause] And there must be some reason! Despite the [family] code! [Laughter]" (From the transcript of Fidel Castro's speech to the Third Congress, as translated in *Women and the Cuban Revolution,* ed. Elizabeth Stone, New York: Pathfinder Press, 1981.)

neighborhoods, and carried out other important tasks of the Revolution.

—Vilma Espín

The establishment of the CDRs was an important step toward mobilization and surveillance. The CDRs are still in operation and women constitute the majority of their members but are not the leadership. They monitor public and private behavior, sexual preferences, and black-market activity, and are responsible for preserving the canons of "proletarian morality."

There is another mass demonstration in support of the Trials against former petty administrators of the Batista regime. Since these are open trials they are televised. But these people are irrelevant since the big fish have all fled, including Batista's master torturers. Grandmother, I say, the world is going into black and white, either/or; why, why? She laughs and replies, They feel they must show us that justice takes its course. The Firing Squad begins to work.

The Grandmother comes to my room and tells me nothing good ever comes from killings. She says, Study, no one is going to take that away from you. In her seventies she goes into exile—to work in New York as a seamstress.

On the international front, there are also women who have volunteered as teachers: 600 women went to Nicaragua, out of a total of 1200 volunteers; women went as part of the Ché Guevara Internationalist Detachment to Angola. The official unstated policy, however, is to be found in the following remark of Fidel Castro: "If there are openings for the nation to be engaged in overseas work . . . we can use our reserve of men—without excluding the women, of course, without excluding them; but we are aware that when women must leave the family behind, the human sacrifice is greater than when a man leaves." What does that mean? It may be noted that certain opportunities for overseas employment may involve better-remunerated and more prestigious work, which can lead to a better career in a ministry, and eventually to a position of leadership in government departments.

Before 1959, the Catholic Church had the last word on women's reproductive freedom. Legalized abortion and contraception, divorce and remarriage, have indeed been opened to women as options by the government, together with a program of health, and day-care centers—to "facilitate the utilization of women's labor potential." Yet when Castro spoke of the difficulties in accommodating women in the labor market, he also warned of the population increase. In other words, contraception and abortion are all part of an unstated State policy—not motivated by a desire to give *women* options, but rather as economic remedies in the demographic life of the country. Male sterilization has not been mentioned in any of the Federation's discussions, nor are there vasectomy centers.

Marx and Engels were philosophers in the context of their time—the so-called decadent world of nineteenth-century Europe. Lenin's adaptation of their thoughts to the reality of a feudal Russia—and subsequent Stalinization—provided, after all, little genuinely original thinking in the organization of government structures. One patriarchal monolith was replaced by another. (Bureaucracy is not a twentieth-century invention; from the Pharaohs through dynastic China, from the Roman Empire up to the Austro-Hungarian empire, such a system had functioned for millennia.)

Before 1959, Cuba had a republican system of government which followed the model of the Enlightenment: it had a constitution, two legislative houses, presidential elections, independent trade unions, a multi-party system, and an independent apolitical university

—where, in fact, most of the political opposition and critical thought was forged. It is tragic that after fifty-odd years of existence this structure was not respected or honored, but rather fell prey—owing to economic neocolonialism and domestic greed—to the tyranny of the Batista dictatorship. It is tragic, too, that Batista was overthrown *not only* because he was a corrupt dictator, but also because he was a (powerful) mulatto man *(Este es "El Hombre")* in a white racist society.

The flexibility of the Republic had permitted all incipient freedoms—including even corruption in a country perhaps too young and naïve to understand neocolonialism, and whose anticolonial fighters, including its major thinker, José Martí, had all died in the struggle. The monolithic structure of the present system, on the other hand, leads to stratification and rigidity (also not excluding corruption). Both systems reflect patriarchal organization of power in a pyramidal shape. One (the so-called democratic or parliamentarian) is rooted in patriarchal Greece; the other, possibly, in *theocracy.* Both structures hold only meager and ancillary rewards for women.

In Paris I ask for an appointment with Alejo Carpentier, then Cuban cultural attaché, to inquire about the fate of two friends who had been committed to an asylum for reasons having nothing to do with sanity. I ask him, too, about other friends who had disappeared into the concentration camps—the Camps of the UMAP (Military Units for Production Assistance). He denies their existence. He does not look in my eyes. I write The Grandmother about the incident. She replies, What do you expect of an opportunist. But he is a novelist, I reply. She writes back, Perhaps, but an opportunist.

Slowly friends are allowed to leave, monies go through Canada; corruption saves lives. The Grandmother says, It happened in the war of 1898, and in the European war; it always happens; thank god for the human frailty for money, thank god for human imperfection. I say, But Fidel says the Revolution wants to create the New Man who will be incorruptible. She laughs, and asks about the New Woman.

Fidel Castro is aware that women are essential in keeping the State afloat, at least while he is consolidating the present structure. His speeches to the Women's Federation, which read like biblical elocutions, are very apologetic, but contrition is not an excuse—though it does provide (and feed on) hope. The fact remains that women have made the literacy campaign a reality; that they have won the health and hygiene campaigns, the productivity drives, the total surveillance of the population through the CDRs, and that this is being advertised as an international model for women in the developing world—especially in Latin America. But it is unforgivable that the Haydée Santamarías, the Mirta Aguirres (Aguirre was a respected communist leader relegated to a professorial post until her death), the Pastorita Nuñezes (already forgotten by the revolutionaries), the Celia Sánchezes, and the Vilma Espíns, were never given the chance, say, of a Ché Guevara—who was placed at the head of the National Bank and then at the head of the Ministry of Industry with no experience, background, or technical competence for either post. If it was said that trust was essential at the beginning, why couldn't these women have been trusted equally? (Ché was just a medical doctor, after all.) Furthermore, it is abysmal that the situation has not changed. The Vilmas, Haydées, Mirtas, Celias, will continue to do the grass-roots organizing and the volunteering, but nothing higher. Perhaps a textile-mill managership, or the coordinator of a district's hairdressers, or the deputy to the head of the Communist Youth, or a judge of a people's court.

The Head of Government is a man. The Head of the Army is his brother, another man. And so on with the ministries. No illusions.

Early in 1959 we all went and signed the Declaration of Habana. We thought we had gained, conquered, reconquered, our own paradise. After all, Columbus had hailed Cuba as the most beautiful land he had ever seen. Women wanted to share in the triumph we had so courageously fought for, both in the mountains and in the underground. Yet what we saw coming on January 1, 1959, were many, many bearded men, and on the jeep with a white dove and peace signs, two men: the co-leaders, Camilo Cienfuegos (dead soon after in a mysterious plane crash) and Fidel Castro. The real transformation never took place. And it will not take place as long as the bearded men cling to power.

The Grandmother was never a cynic. Yet she will die in exile—away from her ancestors, from her family—as an unknown, after generations of great national pride, blood, and civic honesty.

What then of the women? *Our* liberation has to be fought for again, this time not in correspondence with or in the service of the State but on our own terms. And for that we need more courage to go further and deeper. We must organize outside of male-conceived and male-controlled master plans of development. We must define what *our* development is and means. We must plot our own course. And above all, we must seize the freedom to do so.

(The preceding article drew statistics, information, and quotes from the following sources: "Cuban Women, 1975–1979," Report on the Review and Appraisal of the World Plan of Action of the United Nations, Havana, June 1980; "Report of the High-Level Experts of Non-Aligned and Other Developing Countries Concerned with the Role of Women in Development," Havana, May 25–27, 1981; *Boletín FMC,* which includes the Central Report rendered by Comrade Vilma Espín, president of the Federation of Women at the Third Congress, and the speech delivered by Commander-in-Chief Fidel Castro at the close of the Federation's Third Congress, and the Solidarity Declaration adopted by the delegates to the Third Congress of the Federation, 1980; *Thesis: On the Full Exercise of Women's Equality,* paper presented to the First Congress of the Communist Party of Cuba, 1975; Family Code, Law No. 1289 of Feb. 14, 1975, published in the *Official Gazette,* Feb. 15, 1975, Havana; "Memories, Second Congress of the Cuban Women's Federation," Editorial Orbe, Havana, 1975; Social Code, Reform of Article 25 in the Social Defense Code, as printed by *Juventud Rebelde,* Jan. 29 and 31, 1973; "La Influencia de los Medios de Comunicación de Masas en la Mujer, La Niñez y la Familia," Cuban paper to the International Seminar held in Panama, June 10–13, 1980; Elisabeth J. Croll, *Socialist Development Experience: Women in Rural Production and Reproduction in the Soviet Union, China, Cuba and Tanzania,* Institute of Development Studies, Univ. of Sussex, Brighton, England, 1979; several articles published in the *Journal of the World International Democratic Federation.*)

Suggested Further Reading

Franqui, Carlos. *Diario de la Revolución* (Diary of the Revolution). Paris: Ruedo Ibérico, 1976. (English ed., *Diary of The Cuban Revolution.* New York: Viking Press, 1980.)
Stone, Elizabeth, ed. *Women and the Cuban Revolution.* New York: Pathfinder Press, 1981.
Tharn, Nathaniel, ed. *Con Cuba* (With Cuba). London: Cape Golliard, 1969. (In English and Spanish; an anthology of contemporary Cuban poetry.)

La Silenciada ("The Silenced One") is an artist who actively participated in the 1959 revolution. She writes that she "came to feminism first through Virginia Woolf's *A Room of One's Own,*" and that her feminism "solidified under the literary influence of Herma Briffault, Louise Labé, Colette, and Sor Juana Inés de la Cruz." She further adds, "Article 38(d) of the Cuban Constitution stipulates that artistic expression is free if its contents are not contrary to the revolution. (Who decides what is contrary?) Thus the need for a pseudonym. I am an author whose desire for freedom of expression coincides with that of

Rosa Luxemburg—who argued with Lenin on this matter. I wish there were enlightened world leaders who, rather than resort to bombs, would parachute instead over this island the writings of Luxemburg, as well as those of Kafka, Sartre, and others whose works are either heavily restricted or simply not permitted at all. Women have no chance of attaining and holding on to power in the Latin American continent until the question of sexual politics—as eloquently discussed by Lidia Falcón, Nawal El Saadawi, and Kate Millett—is taught openly in the classrooms and until the totality of novels written by Latin American male authors is critically exposed for what they make of women: concubines, whores, saints, fallen women, and decorative accessories."

DENMARK
(Kingdom of Denmark)

A Nordic European country bordered to the north by Sweden and Norway (across the Skagerrak), to the east by the Kattegat Sea and Øresund Strait, to the south by West Germany, and to the west by the North Sea. (Includes the Faroe Islands in the Norwegian Sea, and Greenland.) **Area:** 43,075 sq. km. (16,631 sq. mi.). **Population** (1980): 5,136,000, female 50.6%. **Capital:** Copenhagen. **Head of State:** Queen Margrethe II.

DEMOGRAPHY. Languages: Danish. **Races or Ethnic Groups:** Scandinavian 98%, other. **Religions:** Lutheran, Roman Catholicism, other Protestant, Judaism. **Education** (% enrolled in school, 1975): Age 6–11—of all girls 99%, of all boys 99%; age 12–17—of all girls 76%, of all boys 87%; higher education—in 1978 women comprised 48% of post–secondary students and were concentrated in liberal arts. **Literacy** (1977): Women 99%, men 99%. **Birth Rate** (per 1000 pop., 1977–78): 12. **Death Rate** (per 1000 pop., 1977–78): 10. **Infant Mortality** (per 1000 live births, 1979): Female 7, male 10.4. **Life Expectancy** (1975–80): Female 77 yrs., male 71 yrs.

GOVERNMENT. Constitutional monarchy based on 1953 Constitution, with legislative power jointly held by the sovereign (who appoints the prime minister) and a unicameral elected 179-member parliament (the Folketing). Queen Margrethe II (ascended 1972) is Denmark's first regnant queen since the 15th century. Faroe Islands and Greenland are self-governing regions. **Women's Suffrage:** 1915. **Equal Rights:** No constitutional provision, but much specific legislation, and the 1978 Equal Treatment Act (see ECONOMY). **Women in Government:** In 1979 there were 49 women in the Folketing; in 1980 there were 3 women in the Social Democratic minority government (the Ministers of Education, of Social Affairs, and of Cultural Affairs); women were 16% of representatives in local governments.

ECONOMY. Currency: Danish Krone (May 1983: 8.7 = $1 US). **Gross National Product** (1980): $66.4 billion. **Per Capita Income** (1980): $12,950. **Women's Wages as a Percentage of Men's:** 72% in public sector (1981), 84% in nonagricultural activities (1980). **Equal Pay Policy:** 1976 Equal Pay Act. **Production** (Agricultural/Industrial): Meat, dairy, fish, fur; industrial equipment, electronics, textiles, furniture. **Women as a Percentage of Labor Force** (1980): 38%; **of agricultural force** (1979) 28.3% (81% of whom are unpaid family workers); **of industrial force**—no general statistics obtainable (of manufacturing 29.7%, of textile and garment production 69%, 1979); **of military** (1982) 2%—army 408, navy 59, air force 223. The Equal Treatment Act (1978) prohibits discrimination in hiring, promoting, or re-educating employees, and stipulates the same workplace conditions for both sexes; pregnancy is not legal grounds for dismissal; no distinctions can be made in job advertising. **(Employed) Women's Occupational Indicators** (1980): Of university professors 4%, of skilled workers 4%; 70% of women workers are concentrated in "female intensive jobs." **Unemployment** (average Jan.–May 1982): 10.5%, female 10.4%, male 10.6%.

GYNOGRAPHY. Marriage. *Policy:* Under 1970 Marriage Act, both wife and husband are obliged to support each other and contribute to family needs; work in the home is considered equivalent to outside employment, and salary earner must share income with non-paid partner; any item purchased during marriage belongs to person who paid for it; parents may decide which surname child will bear; woman may use her birth-name after marriage; husband may take wife's birth-name. *Practice:* Female mean age at marriage (1970–78): 23; women age 15–49 in union (1970–78): 64%; marriages (per 1000 pop., 1979): 5.4. Generally, 1 in 8 couples (and at least 1 in 4 couples age 20–29) living together are unmarried (1980). **Divorce.** *Policy:* Legal. In cases of mutual consent, separation and divorce can be obtained by applying to provincial authorities, but parties must agree on child custody, allowances, and disposition of family dwelling; divorce can be granted unconditionally after a 1-yr. separation. In cases where separation is not mutually desired, grounds include neglect of maintenance, adultery, intemperance, desertion, and depravity; cessation of marital relations plus a 1-yr. separation are necessary. Either parent may have child custody. Alimony is based on earning potential and either spouse may be required to pay. *Practice:* Divorces (per 1000 pop., 1979): 2.55; almost 1 in 3 marriages ends in divorce (1980). More than 90% of separations and divorces are granted without contest.

Family. *Policy:* Tax-free Family Allowance payments initiated in 1970 include benefits for all children under age 16, augmented allowance for children of single parents, allowance for single parents, and a special allowance for children of widows, widowers, or pensioners. Maternity benefits, under the Social Insurance scheme (see **Welfare**), are a 5-month leave with half pay for salaried workers and a daily benefit for up to 14 weeks for hourly wage earners. Homemakers are entitled to a daily benefit if they pay for insurance. Social Assistance Act (1974) instructs municipal authorities to provide day-care and recreation centers for children and young people. Cost is subsidized by public funds, with parents paying 35% for pre-school children, 25% for school-age children, and 20% for youth clubs. *Practice:* In 1980 there were 21,000 children in day care, 54,000 in registered "child-minding," 102,000 in nursery schools, and 50,000 in private homes under municipal supervision; about 50,000 are awaiting vacancies. **Welfare.** *Policy:* Social Insurance system is composed of various acts of legislation, financed by public funds, and covers all citizens. Benefits include sickness, maternity (see **Family**), unemployment (a "contributory" fund subsidized by the State, which pays 90% of wage), retirement pensions for those over age 67, pensions for single women over age 62, and national health service, which provides free medical and hospital care for all. *Practice:* 1/3 of the national budget is spent on the Social Insurance system.

Contraception. *Policy:* Legal. Social Security Act covers doctor and hospital visits (but not prescriptions) for contraceptives. A 1978 bill before the Folketing proposed free birth control but was halted by a bad economy; 1973 law made sterilization available to anyone over age 25; 1970 amendment to the Primary Schools Act calls for sex education in schools' curricula. *Practice:* Women age 15–49 in union using contraception (1970–80): 67%, of which traditional methods 19.4%, modern 80.6%; sterilization 15,000 per yr. (mostly men). In 1976 some counties established birth-control-advice clinics; by 1979 clinics throughout the country began giving free advice and often free contraceptives. **Abortion.** *Policy:* The 1973 Termination of Pregnancy Act made abortion on request legal during the first 12 weeks. *Practice:* Abortions (per 1000 known pregnancies, 1981): 300. **Illegitimacy.** *Policy:* 1938 law gives out-of-wedlock children the right to claim paternal inheritance and paternal name. Both parents are responsible for maintaining child for 18 yrs.; father's financial contribution required according to his means. *Practice:* In 1979, 30.7% of all births were out of wedlock. Such children rarely face discrimination. **Homosexuality.** *Policy:* Legal since 1933. Age of consent is 15 (the same as for heterosexuals). *Practice:* There were 28 convictions of "homosexual offenses" in 1978. The Lesbian Movement has existed since 1974 as an activist and support group. **Incest.** *Policy:* 1978 Penal Code (Art. 210) prohibits sexual relations between siblings (if over age 18) or relatives in lineal ascent or descent; marriages are legal between uncle/niece, aunt/nephew, or cousins. *Practice:* 11 convictions in 1978. The Joan Sisters (see **Crisis Centers**) have been organizing on this issue. **Sexual Harassment.** *Policy:* Penal Code (Art. 220) states that persons who "grossly misuse another person's occupational and economic dependency sexually outside marriage" are liable for a maximum 1 yr. imprisonment; if victim is under age 21, the penalty can be raised to 2 yrs. *Practice:* No data obtainable. **Rape.** *Policy:* Illegal; Penal Code (Art.

216, amended 1981) stipulates that use of violence or threat of violence to force sexual intercourse is punishable by maximum 6 yrs. imprisonment; if the rape has an "especially dangerous character" penalty may be raised to 10 yrs. imprisonment. Other sexual acts involving violence/force or threat are punishable by up to 4 yrs. *Practice:* Reported rapes (per 100,000 pop., 1978): 14.1; 99 convictions. **Battery.** *Policy:* No specific law pertaining to spouse abuse. *Practice:* No statistics obtainable. The Danish women's movement has focused attention on the issue in recent yrs. and is pressuring the Folketing to introduce special legislation. (See **Crisis Centers**.)

Prostitution. *Policy:* Illegal; Penal Code (Arts. 232–233) prohibits prostitution, pimping, and brothel-keeping; penalties range from fines to maximum 4 yrs. imprisonment. *Practice:* No statistics obtainable. Certain sections of cities (e.g., Vesterbro in Copenhagen) are known prostitution centers. **Traditional/Cultural Practices:** No data obtainable. **Crisis Centers.** *Policy:* Some centers for raped and battered women receive partial government funding. *Practice:* The Joan Sisters, a women's group, offers counseling for rape victims; Danner House in Copenhagen, built in 1800 as a shelter for homeless women, was renovated in 1979 as a battered-women's refuge; women intervened to prevent its demolition and launched a national campaign for funds to restore it. Other battery refuges exist in Randers, Roskilde, Silkeborg, and Nørre Sundby.

HERSTORY. In 1397 Queen Margrethe I, jointly elected by Denmark, Norway, and Sweden, united all 3 countries under her rule; Sweden left the union in 1523 but a series of Danish-Swedish wars spanned the next 2 centuries (see SWEDEN and NORWAY). The earliest Danish feminist movement in modern times was pioneered by Mathilde Fibiger, a young writer inspired by liberal ideas of the mid-1800's, and Pauline Worm, a private schoolteacher. Fibiger's book *Twelve Letters* raised a controversy over women's place in society. The Women's Social Union was created to develop trade unions for women but it soon became a support group and fund raiser for general labor efforts. In 1886 Mathilde Bajer became the first president of the Women's Union for Progress, which focused on such issues as reduced military spending, and published a paper, *What We Want*, edited by Johanne Meyer; it became the organ of the newly formed Confederation of Women's Unions. Also in 1886, 200 women weavers staged a walkout over pay rates and won a small increase. The General Union of Working Women, under Olivia Nielsen, organized women at the Tuborg Breweries. When she died in 1910, the union had 2000 members with branches all over Denmark. In 1871 the Danish Women's Society was founded to assert women's moral, economic, and intellectual rights. The Danish Women's Union Suffrage Committee, an alliance of groups, was formed in 1898 to work for the vote. The following year, the Danish Women's National Council linked 7 women's organizations to work with international women's groups on such issues as peace, suffrage, women's legal status, and occupations; still active, the council now consists of over 40 groups and has representatives on government commissions. In 1908 a law gave female taxpayers over age 25, or wives of male taxpayers, suffrage in local elections.

The new Constitution of 1915 incorporated women's suffrage for all citizens over age 21. During the WWII German occupation, women were intensely active in the Danish effort to shelter many fugitive European Jews. The contemporary women's movement is widespread, various, and active (see following article).

MYTHOGRAPHY. The goddess legends of Scandinavia are a synthesis of

Nordic and Finnish cultures.* The Nordic people believed the sun to be female, the moon male. Icelandic lore tells of the divine cow Audhumla, who created the first human. Freyja, known as the Queen of the Vanir deities, is a frequent image. In the *Kalevala,* the great Finnish epic poem, Ilmatar (Sky Mother) is the force who created the earth. Mielikki, goddess of the forest, nurtures the young bear, a symbol of reverence across parts of the Arctic.

DENMARK: Letter from a Troubled Copenhagen Redstocking
by Tinne Vammen

Dear Unknown Women,

It is not all that easy for me to write to you. *Sisterhood Is Global* is the title of this anthology you now hold in your hands. But can I address you as my sisters? Sisterhood! The word strikes a note of intimacy, solidarity, and common hopes. Yet here I am, sitting in front of my electric typewriter in my spacious rented flat. My refrigerator is fairly well stocked. If I need a pint of milk, shampoo, a fresh loaf of bread, or a soft avocado, I just have to take a short walk to one of the supermarkets. True, my bank account is somewhat meager and will soon become even slimmer, as I am joining the army of the unemployed next month. But as a trade-union member, my unemployment insurance will help me muddle through until some other job turns up, or else I shall pass into the ranks of the growing numbers living on social aid. My little daughter plays with other children in a public kindergarten every day from 8 A.M. until 4 P.M. My teenage son is a private-school pupil and says he wants to go to the grammar school[1] next year. Both kids are bright, well fed, and healthy. So all in all, what is the problem, living as I do, almost forty years of age, not so differently from other Danish feminists of my generation and wider groups of women with a good education?

Indeed, I am rather overwhelmed by the fact that I write from a comparatively privileged position, when I think of who you now reading this letter may be. Sisterhood! What a wonderful, appealing, utopian idea—so detached from the realities of women's past and present lives in this country and in a world ridden by differences of class and creed, race and ethnicity, and battling economic and political systems. I am keenly aware that I am a citizen in a society belonging to the small elite of nations as to living standards, social benefits, educational standards, and average life expectancy. All of which are privileges that may well be bought at the expense of the very countries and peoples that you are part of. Opponents of the Danish representative democracy are not jailed, exiled, or tortured for their political beliefs. Trade unions are allowed; we have a long tradition both of labor conflicts and of peaceful bargaining between labor, capital, and State. Political organizations are not forbidden, and every now and then free elections are held. How then am I to contend in an honest way that something is really rotten in the State of Denmark?

As you probably know, looking at the lives of women from the inside and leaving external comparisons aside does make a difference. My belief that something *is* rotten in

---

* The Finns at one time inhabited parts of Norway and Sweden as well as all of Finland. Later, they were pushed farther north by Germanic tribes from central Europe. As a result, there was a merging of myths and legends of all Nordic peoples.

[1.] In Denmark, the grammar school is an "advanced" school form beyond the obligatory "folk-school" level.

the State of Denmark is bred by recent developments, both political and cultural. I feel that the feminist movement is now more on the defensive than the offensive, as the very conditions of feminist politics have changed radically in recent years.

During the 1950's and 1960's the traditional life prospects of many Danish women changed in a number of important ways. Increasing numbers of (especially married) women entered the labor market on an unprecedented scale, changing the patterns of wage labor of women and weakening their traditional economic dependence on husbands. Since the onset, around 1975, of the current economic crisis both national and international in scale, un- and underemployment have again raised their ugly heads and spelled out the message: women's possibilities of individual economic independence are closely related to the shifting demands of capital and State. Working-class women in industries producing footwear, textiles, clothing, and other consumer goods have been hit severely. Unemployment is also spreading rapidly within the very sectors—private and public— that absorbed most female labor power which earlier was so crucial in creating the economic wealth and social welfare of this nation. Getting a foothold outside the family, despite the double work burden, also introduced a wider sphere of activities to many women of my own generation. I am not the only one who now and then feels overwhelmed by the thought that we may in fact become a kind of parenthesis in modern Danish history!

The changes in women's relationship to the labor market and family situation were a major force in creating a new feminist wave in the early 1970's. Much of the initial protest grew out of our experiences of wide gaps between the dominant ideology of equal rights/opportunities and the facts of the sexual division of labor inside and outside of families, of wage differentials, different advancement possibilities, and the lacking female presence and voice in trade-union and party politics. New feminism did not, however, start from scratch. It arose at a time when the centennial of feminist struggle in Denmark was about to be celebrated. It was nourished by the flowering of the "New Left" movement, highly critical of both orthodox communism and reformist social democratic traditions. Many new feminists brought with them a left-wing distrust of the capitalist economy, a disbelief in the State as a neutral benefactor of the working class and other salaried workers, and a critical outlook on trade-union structures as necessarily favorable to furthering initiatives coming from ordinary members.

The anticapitalist ideology of the new feminism showed its connection to the New Left and set it apart from the moderate and reformist old feminism of Dansk Kvindesamfund (Danish Women's Society) and it's parliamentary traditions and tactics. At the same time, the antipatriarchal emphasis of new feminists closed the rising movement to male activists and cut it off from forming permanent and formal links to left-wing organizations. "We won't any longer make tea for the revolution" was a popular slogan, signifying a widespread wish to spell out what a revolution *might* mean—in those days of optimism and somewhat youthful naïveté as to the possibilities of revolution in Western Europe.

A couple of weeks ago I joined Annie and Anse, Elisabeth, Annelise, and other members from the editorial collective of *Kvinder* (Women), the bimonthly journal of Rødstrømpebevaegelsen (the Redstockings movement) in Copenhagen. We went to the annual Women's Festival, held at Faelleden (the Common) to sell our latest issue—an issue on women's relations with men, apparently an inexhaustible subject! Colorful tents and stalls dotted the vast lawn. An all-female band was playing, a hundred people or so listening. Scattered clusters were sitting on the grass or walking around to collect pamphlets and literature from the many groups which had organized this event. Other people were eating health foods or dancing in small circles. I was struck by the contrast between this festival and earlier ones. Gone are the days of huge crowds of euphoric women raising their arms into the air victoriously or listening to Angela Davis talking about racism.

Yet on my return home, my discomfort was modified. I took out some of the latest issues of *Kvinder*. More than fifty women's groups inside and outside the capital were listed, plus women's houses as an established part of townscapes. While memberships of older feminist organizations seem to have dwindled, the new feminist movement has taken hold of the minds and energies of women, not only in the big urban centers of Copenhagen and Aarhus but north and south, east and west, to such provincial towns as Esbjerg and Frederikshavn, Helsingør and Nykøping Falster. The new feminism is still very much alive, not always presenting itself as the Redstockings movement, but choosing neutral names locally; sometimes, in fact, being critical of the Redstockings and claiming to emphasize more the interests of working-class women.

It is true that the Redstockings, as the up-to-now main trend in Danish new feminism, have not mobilized working-class women to any great extent. Our movement is composed mainly of students and academic women, of folk-school teachers and women working in the media, of artists and social counselors, nurses and a fringe of white-collar office workers. Ad hoc alliances between the Redstockings and working-class female trade unions are not untried: such an alliance did, for instance, take place during the 1970's fight for equal pay, and several feminists supported strike activities and other labor conflicts, where a new militancy was showing among women both in working-class trade unions and in some of the professional organizations.

"No feminist struggle without class struggle; no class struggle without feminist struggle" ran a now rather old and cherished slogan of the Redstockings. Exactly what this meant has been a matter of debate within the movement over the years, as has the problem of the relationship between socialism and feminism. I don't think that any clear-cut answers have been produced. Many feminists feel that such general questions are difficult to discuss in a meaningful way without being too abstract and theoretical, or that the current models of socialist societies do not form examples to be followed, just as— from a Danish feminist point of view—those same models have not guaranteed women's liberation. How a Danish socialist society may be brought about, and the role of feminism in such a transformation—a feminism revolutionary in its content and aims—these are not, however, unanswered questions only within the Redstockings or other new feminist organizations, but a problem of the entire New Left movement, which is now defensive and in a stage of internal crisis. Meanwhile, growing disillusion as to the ability of political parties to solve the problems of present society has in recent years given rise to new grass-roots movements mobilizing many people, men and women both, against the lunatic rearmament race and for international peace, against the introduction of atomic energy and the exploitation of nature generally, and for better uses of natural energy resources.

Questions such as these will, I think, be taken up by the feminist movement, and signs of this are visible. But one of the striking features on the feminist scene today is the growth of what might be termed "social feminism," organizing around specific needs and single issues: in a number of towns, feminists give psychological, legal, or other practical advice to women newly divorced or suffering from mental illness, to battered wives and rape victims. One group, the Joan Sisters, tries to bring about changes in the practice of police and court treatment of rape victims. "Women Over Forty," founded in 1974, is a group within the Redstockings movement, trying to deal with sexuality, the prospects of the "empty nest," and similar questions. The Woman's House in Gothersgade (first seized and occupied illegally by the Redstockings, but since accepted by authorities as feminist domain in the Copenhagen area), is the base for a number of groups not formally attached to the Redstockings, including the Lesbian Movement, founded in 1974 as a reaction against what was felt as the intolerance or direct hostility of heterosexual feminists against lesbian feminists. As they have stated, "In the Redstockings, we experienced having to explain ourselves all the time and were made to feel that we ought to keep out mouths shut to further *the cause,* to avoid people thinking that everyone in the movement was a lesbian." It should not be overlooked, however, that lesbian and heterosexual women do in fact work well together in a number of contexts; Redstockings, lesbians, and a number of new and old feminist organizations—twenty-three in all—cooperated during recent years to open a big Women's Center in the capital.

Consciousness-raising groups, so-called function and activity groups (those dealing, for example, with the administrative running of the movement, selling books in the book café, running courses and lectures inside and outside the Women's House, or arranging the annual summer camp at Femø)—these are basic organizational models of the Red-stockings. The structure is very much one of direct democracy and no leadership, the style an anti-bureaucratic, almost anarchist one which has given women the feeling that *their* problems, points of view, and aspirations should be taken seriously—and are, in fact, what politics ought to consist of. When it comes to influencing parliament or politi-cal parties *directly,* however, the model has some limits.

It has been the old feminist organizations, Dansk Kvindesamfund and Danske Kvinders Nationalraad (the Danish Women's National Council)—an umbrella coalition of about forty organizations with a membership of around half a million members from various housewives' and/or religious and professional groups—some trade unions, tem-perance societies, and charitable organizations that have comprised the forces most di-rectly involved in pushing parliamentary commissions, etc. "Old-style" feminism also marks the composition of the Ligestillingsraadet (the Equal Status Council) set up by government initiative in 1975, International Women's Year.

New feminism has had a more widespread ideological influence than a political one, if politics in this context means direct participation in the policy-making processes of par-liament and party organizations. Yet it is also thanks to the new feminist movement that no political party these days dares not pay at least some lip service to the various prob-lems of women. The new feminists, much more than party organizations generally, have kept the "women's question" alive over the years. And the new feminist movement, by altering the very concepts of what politics is about—the totality of our lives, not frag-ments of them—and by its insistence that the very methods we use *now* must reflect what we hope to bring about, has been more truly democratic and closer to the real needs of women than most other organizations.

Politics is not only a question of the right organization, it is also very much an educa-tional and ideological process. What in the early 1970's started in fragmented and modest ways in universities—where committed feminists began teaching and research within such departments as law, sociology, history, language, literature, or anthropology—has grown into something much bigger. In our attempts to change traditions of patriarchal intellectual dominance and to make women visible in the content of higher education, networks and groups, increasingly transcending old departmental lines, have been created and are now very much alive. Within other fields of adult education, such as the Univer-sity Extramural Department, women's studies have made an impact and attracted wide audiences all over the country. Courses on various aspects of women's lives are now put in the curricula of many folk high schools. Kvindehøjskolen (Women's School) in the southern part of Jutland has now had its doors open for around five years; it is run entirely by women and is the result of joint Scandinavian efforts by feminists from Den-mark, Norway, and Sweden, teaching courses wide in scope, ranging from how to mend a car and build houses to lesbianism, feminist astrology, the history of matriarchy, feminist theory, and alternative energy resources. In 1982 an information/documentation center called Kvinfo, formally a branch of the Royal Library of Copenhagen, was established.

The journal published by the staff of Kvinfo is one of the first attempts to popularize research on women in a form more accessible to an unacademic readership.

In bringing out feminist ideas and dealing with present female dilemmas, art has played an important role as well. Numerous novels, short stories, and poems have reached women who might not dream of joining a feminist organization. In recent years, where the new feminist movement seems to be in a process of transformation as evidenced by the spread of single-issue groups and in evident need of adjusting its politics in the context of both the political backlash of the left wing and the growing material and social difficulties experienced by many women, it is very much in the cultural field that feminism is flourishing. The diversity of women's artistic abilities was clear at the tremendous women's exhibition in Copenhagen in 1975. I was very much struck by its heterogeneity rather than homogeneity, by well-known artistic styles that contrasted with more experimental ones. Since then, women's art galleries have opened both in and outside of the capital, trying to bring together professionals and amateurs. How difficult but also how important it is to try to break down such divisions between women who write, sculpt, paint, or do graphics, and women learning these skills! This is also a problem in the editorial collective of *Kvinder*. How are we to avoid divisions into "big girls" and "little girls" and find a common process?

Culture is of course more than the fine arts, academic work, or journalism; it is a whole way of life. The setting up of communes and collectives in both agrarian and urban settings has been a (minority) aspect of change in Danish social life of recent decades. Its supporters tend to be within the middle strata of society, critical of the isolation of the nuclear family or of single living, of traditional sex roles and traditional childrearing. Feminists have taken part in this movement, becoming members of sexually mixed or of segregated collectives and similar living arrangements. The reality of most women's lives today is, however, still the nuclear family and single living. The rather drastic fall in the birth rate during recent decades has given family life a somewhat new flavor, as have soaring divorce rates, now dissolving about a third of every newly formed marriage, at least in urban areas.

Free abortion on demand was introduced by law in Denmark in the mid-1970's. The easy availability of contraceptives, together with free abortion, has brought about a situation that does give women much better chances of splitting sexuality from biological reproduction. What has been termed the unofficial birth strike by women is, I think, a reaction of many women against having to bear the main responsibility in childrearing, plus the problems of day-care facilities. In Denmark the day-care situation may seem favorable compared with many other industrial societies, yet it still does not cover the need for public childcare.

Feminists have not concerned themselves very much with the quantity of children, discussing rather the quality and conditions of modern motherhood. Pre- and post-natal courses are held at the Woman's House in Copenhagen; the experiences of motherhood, children, and female sexuality are discussed in consciousness groups, and problems of mental and physical health and of making the public-health service more open to patients' needs.

Talking of children! I must end this letter now, as I have to pick up my daughter and do my daily round of shopping. I started writing this in a somewhat dejected mood. But by writing it, and thinking about all the activities I am *not* able to mention in such a short space, my spirits have risen. So I shall end by saying: Feminism is here to stay. It faces a backlash, as reactionary winds are blowing in this part of the world. Still, we have some foothold from which to fight back and from which to move further someday—to get beyond the now acute problems so inherent in the structure of this society, a corner of which you have now heard from, dear unknown women.

Sincerely yours
Tinne Vammen

Suggested Further Reading

Arnfred, S., *et al. Nichts fallt vom Himmel. Frauen streiken. Berichte, Analysen, Ehrfahrungen aus Europa und USA 1970–76.* Munich: Frauenbuchverlag, 1977; readers who know German may gain some useful information about Danish women in labor conflicts during the 1970's.

Dahlsgaard, Inga. *Women in Denmark: Yesterday and Today.* Copenhagen: Danish Institute for Information about Denmark and Cultural Cooperation with Other Nations, 1980.

Further information on the Danish feminist movement may be obtained from "Kvinfo" (Women's Research), Laederstraede 15, 2, 1201 Copenhagen K.

Tinne Vammen was born in 1942. She is a divorced mother of two children, and a historian who has taught family and women's history, contributed articles to anthologies and periodicals, done free-lance journalism, and been active in the Redstockings movement. She is currently a member of the editorial board of *Kvinder.*

ECUADOR
(Republic of Ecuador)

Located in northwest South America, bounded by Peru to the east and south, the Pacific Ocean to the west, and Colombia to the north. **Area:** 270,670 sq. km. (103,906 sq. mi.). **Population** (1980): 8,021,000, female 49.9%. **Capital:** Quito.

DEMOGRAPHY. Languages: Spanish (official), Quechuan, Jivaroan. **Races or Ethnic Groups:** Mestizo 40%, Native Indian 40%, African descent, European descent, Asian descent, other. **Religions:** Predominantly Roman Catholicism. **Education** (% enrolled in school, 1975): Age 6–11—of all girls 79%, of all boys 79%; age 12–17—of all girls 52%, of all boys 56%; higher education—women constitute 34% of university students (1983). **Literacy** (1977): Women 70%, men 78%. **Birth Rate** (per 1000 pop., 1975–80): 42. **Death Rate** (per 1000 pop., 1975–80): 10. **Infant Mortality** (per 1000 live births, 1975–80): Female 66, male 74; under-registration of infant deaths is est. to be substantial, and deaths of children under age 5 account for approx. 1/2 of the country's deaths. **Life Expectancy** (1975–80): Female 62 yrs., male 58 yrs.

GOVERNMENT. Consists of a president and a 69-member Chamber of Representatives, and a 1978 Constitution (adopted 1979, after nearly a decade of military rule). **Women's Suffrage:** 1929. **Equal Rights:** Stipulated by the 1978 Constitution. **Women in Government:** There are no women cabinet members or full delegates, and only 3 women are substitute delegates in the Chamber of Representatives (1983).

ECONOMY. Currency: Sucre (May 1983: 84.4 = $1 US). **Gross National Product** (1980): $10.2 billion. **Per Capita Income** (1980): $1220. **Women's Wages as a Percentage of Men's:** No general statistics obtainable, but women migrant workers are paid a daily wage equal to 1/2 men's wages (1981). **Equal Pay Policy:** Equal pay for equal work is ratified in the Labor Code. **Production** (Agricultural/Industrial): Bananas, coffee, cocoa, sugar cane, fruits, corn; processed foods, textiles, chemicals, petroleum, fishing. **Women as a Percentage of Labor Force** (1980): 26.6% (only 18% of those trained by the Ecuadoran Service of Professional Training were women, 1977); **of agricultural force** (1974) 4.5% (in 1975, 16% of women workers were employed in agriculture); **of industrial force** 18% (official est.); **of military**—none. **(Employed) Women's Occupational Indicators** (1974): Of management 12%, of craftspersons 20.6%, of commerce 27%, of office workers 36%, of professions 43%, of personal-service workers 59.7%. The majority of employed urban women work as domestics, as washerwomen, or in retail trade; the majority of peasant women are migrant workers on cash-crop plantations, hired as temporary or part-time workers with no job security or benefits. Labor law (Art. 138) forbids the employment of women (and minors under age 18) at night, with the exception of household workers. **Unemployment:** (1981): 19%; no rates by sex obtainable.

GYNOGRAPHY. Marriage. *Policy:* Both civil and religious marriages are recognized by the State; legal marriage age is 16 for females and males. Title II of the 1978 Constitution sets forth rules for marriage founded on principles of "equal rights, obligations, and legal capacities of both parties," yet the Civil Code requests a wife's obedience (Art. 134) and stipulates a husband's right to force his wife to live with and follow him (Art. 135). A married woman has rights only over property acquired before marriage; she may not dispose of or administer goods that are part of the "conjugal society," including her salary or pension(s), unless given legal permission to do so by her husband, who is technical owner and administrator (Civil Code, Arts. 139, 140, 157). Bigamy is a crime punishable by 2–5 yrs. imprisonment; adultery is illegal, with both partners subject to 6 months–2 yrs. imprisonment. Murder committed by either sex on grounds of adultery is not punishable;

neither is murder punishable if committed on finding a daughter, granddaughter, or sister in "carnal illegitimate union" (Penal Code, Arts. 22, 27). *Practice:* Female mean age at marriage (1970–79): 21; women age 15–44 in union (1970–79): 57.8%. According to the 1974 Census, 62% of unions were legal marriages and 25% were consensual marriages (the latter were as high as 72% in some coastal provinces). **Divorce.** *Policy:* Legal; grounds are mutual consent, or in cases of alcoholism, drug abuse, serious contagious disease, or separation for more than 3 yrs. A woman must wait 1 yr. to remarry (Civil Code, Art. 105). *Practice:* No data obtainable.

Family. *Policy:* The Labor Code forbids work for employed pregnant women 2 weeks before and 6 weeks after birth. Factory workers have no paid maternity leave and must find a worker to replace them; teachers are entitled to 4 weeks paid leave, public employees 7 weeks (Art. 153). Firing a woman because of maternity or post-delivery illness is prohibited (Art. 154). Labor Code Art. 156 stipulates nursing breaks for 15 minutes every 3 hours for the 9 months after birth. Employers with more than 50 employees are required to provide day care. Infanticide within the first 3 days of birth is seen with clemency (Penal Code, Arts. 153, 453). *Practice:* No statistics obtainable; reports indicate widespread discrimination against employed women who become pregnant—in hiring, firing, lack of childcare facilities, and nursing breaks. **Welfare.** *Policy:* Social Security (to which every citizen has a right by law) provides unemployment benefits and pensions and has as a goal the protection of the insured and her/his family in cases of sickness or maternity, including women in rural areas (Constitution, Section IV, Arts. 29, 30). Women are entitled to retirement, regardless of age, after 25 yrs. of contribution; 1964 legislation extended coverage to domestic workers. Migrant workers, temporary workers, and part-time workers are not covered by the program [see **(Employed) Women's Occupational Indicators**]. *Practice:* No statistics obtainable; reports indicate employers attempt to hire women as part-time workers in order to avoid giving benefits or setting up childcare facilities.

Contraception. *Policy:* Legal, except for sterilization; 1978 Constitution supports "responsible parenthood" and guarantees the right of parents to have the number of children they can support and educate. *Practice:* Women age 15–49 in union using contraception (1970–80): 6%, of which modern methods 100%. International agencies have established family-planning programs including voluntary female sterilization, but reports say that some women have been sterilized unknowingly and that contraception distribution is limited, particularly in rural areas. In 1969 a "malaria control" program resulted in the mass sterilization of peasant women. **Abortion.** *Policy:* Illegal, but sometimes tolerated without penalty if performed "to guard honor" (Penal Code, Art. 444), and sometimes permitted for therapeutic reasons (Art. 447), or in cases of rape or danger to woman's life (see **Family**). *Practice:* In 1978 there were an est. 26 illegal abortions per 1000 women. Illegal abortions are usually very expensive and are performed by midwives, country medical practitioners, and doctors, often in unsanitary surroundings. Rural and peasant women attempt self-induced abortions through various folk methods. **Illegitimacy.** *Policy:* Children born in or out of wedlock have equal rights to education and inheritance. Civil registration of births is obligatory. *Practice:* No statistics obtainable; illegitimacy is still considered a social stigma. **Homosexuality.** *Policy:* Adult male homosexuality is a criminal offense punishable by 4–8 yrs. imprisonment, under the Penal Code category "Offenses Against the Public Morality." There are no specific laws dealing with lesbianism. *Practice:* No statistics obtainable. Reports say that the social tabu against homosexuals is strong. **Incest.** *Policy:* Illegal; punishable by a fine and a maximum penalty (usually 8–12 yrs. imprisonment); fathers found guilty of incest with their children lose their civil rights. "Concubinage" between relatives carries a sentence of 12–16 months imprisonment. *Practice:* No statistics obtainable; reportedly common in rural areas. **Sexual Harassment.** *Policy:* No specific laws against sexual harassment, but complaints could be registered under a general category of "offenses against a woman's honesty." *Practice:* No statistics obtainable. Harassment is reportedly a severe problem and women have little or no legal recourse. **Rape.** *Policy:* "Seduction" of an honest woman through deceptive means is punishable by fines and prison sentences varying from months to several yrs. under "Offenses Against the Public Morality." Seduction of a minor (female) age 12–18 is illegal as a sexual offense (Penal Code, Arts. 509–11). *Practice:* No statistics obtainable; reports indicate that rape is a grave problem, that the majority go unreported, and that few rapists are prosecuted. **Battery.** *Policy:* No laws specific to wife-beating. *Practice:* No statistics obtainable; reportedly wife-beating is common and women have little or no legal recourse.

Prostitution. *Policy:* Procuring and soliciting for prostitution are crimes under "Offenses Against the Public Morality," with varying penalties. Corruption of a minor or running of a brothel are punishable by 2–5 yrs. imprisonment. *Practice:* No statistics obtainable. Prostitution is reportedly common, often being the only economic means available to poor and uneducated girls. Prostitutes are typically arrested for "disturbing the peace," given a light prison sentence, and fined. **Traditional/Cultural Practices:** No data obtainable. **Crisis Centers:** No data obtainable.

HERSTORY. The northern highlands of what is now Ecuador were inhabited by Amerindians who formed the Kingdom of Quito (c. 1000 C.E.), which was eventually subsumed into the Incan Empire. Lorenza Avemanay and Baltazar Chiaza led the Guano and Guamote revolts against the Spanish colonialists in 1778 and 1803, and later were executed by Spanish troops. Manuela León was second in command to Fernando Daquilema, leader of the most important indigenous revolt of the colonial era. Hundreds of peasant women fought in Ecuador's Independence Wars (1802–22), but no change in their status followed Independence. In 1895 the Liberal Revolution brought women into the ranks of the

popular army; Joaquina Galalzo de Larrea was named a colonel for her role in the battles of Apr. 9 and Aug. 6, 1895.

A period of reform followed; women made gains in university education, election to public office, and new marriage laws that defied the Church's monopoly and later allowed divorce. Other laws protected married women's civil rights. Women were active in the Nov. 1929 railroad labor strikes; Tomasa Garcés lay across the tracks to prevent trains from leaving the station. In 1944 women participated in the May Revolution against dictator Arroyo del Río. The 1945 Constitution (under Velasco Ibarra) stipulated equality between men and women in marriage and improved women's civil rights. Dolores Cacuango became the first woman General Secretary of the Federation of Indigenous Ecuadoreans. Women became leaders of the Ecuadorean Workers Confederation, one of the country's largest trade unions.

An autonomous feminist movement began in the mid-1970's, out of the organizing done by working-class women in their demands for livelihood, food, health care and childcare, especially in rural areas. In 1975 women organized the Women's Committee in Solidarity with Labor Conflicts and published the journal *Pachacama,* after a woman textile worker was killed in the Dec. 1974 labor strikes. In June 1976 a Women's University Brigade was formed to work with women in construction, retail trade, service sectors, and textiles. In 1980 the Grupo Autonomode de Mujeres (Autonomous Women's Group) in Quito helped produce the journal *Eva de la Manzina.* The Union of Women Workers (UMT) held its first congress, focusing on daycare centers in factories, time off for nursing, and equal opportunities. The National Union of Ecuadorean Women works for the rights of women in education and for information about family planning. In Nov. 1981 the Oficina Nacional de la Mujer (National Office on Women) and the Asociación Jurídica Femenina de Guayaquil (Assoc. of Women Lawyers of Guayaquil) held a national workshop which proposed new legislation to be submitted to the government subsequent to its ratification of the

UN's International Convention Against All Forms of Discrimination Against Women.

MYTHOGRAPHY. One ancient myth of the region is that all Canari Indian people are descended from an immortal macaw bird who transformed herself into a human female and, as such, mated with one of the great Twins—survivors of the devastating flood in Huanyan (or Huaca-yan); their progeny were the Canari peoples.

ECUADOR: Needed—A Revolution in Attitude
by Carola Borja

The Andes traverse Ecuador from north to south in a chain. Snow-capped mountains and deep green valleys alternate through the eastern and western *cordilleras,* yet ironically it is this beauty that has been a tremendous obstacle for socioeconomic development in this second smallest republic in South America, inhabited by about 8¼ million people. Owing to its topography, regional differences, and social stratification, one finds an insurmountable breach between rich and poor, between upper and lower social classes—the major cause of the nation's disunity.

Throughout its history, Ecuador has had very progressive laws. We were the first country in South America to permit divorce, the first country in South America granting suffrage to women (in 1929), and as recently as December 1981, legislation was passed by the President to ratify and implement the Convention Against All Forms of Discrimination Against Women as resolved by the General Assembly 34/180 of 18 December 1979.

Our Constitution, under Title II, "Civil Rights, Duties, and Guarantees," prohibits any kind of discrimination by sex and verifies that a "woman, whatever her civil status, has the same rights and opportunities as a man in all aspects of public, private, and family life, especially in civil, political, economic, social, and cultural aspects."[1] Under the Family Heading it provides for protection of the family as the fundamental unit of society and stresses the importance of assuring moral, cultural, and economic conditions to work toward this end. It provides protection of marriage, maternity, and family assets, emphasizes that marriage is founded on the "principle of equal rights, obligations, and legal capacities of both parties," and goes on to say that "children within the same family are given equal rights before the law, with no preference given according to sex or birth order."[2] A relevant article points out that the State supports responsible parenthood and appropriate education for the advancement of the family, including the guarantee of the right of parents to have the number of children they can support and educate.[3] Parents are protected in the exercise of their authority in compliance with the reciprocal obligations present between parents and children.

Yet inequalities persist. In order to comprehend the spectrum of the society in Ecuador one must first understand the breakdown of its population and rigorous geographic divisions between the two main regions: *coast* and *sierra.* Of the total population of Ecuador,

---

[*NOTE:* The views expressed in this article are those of the author and not of the United Nations, where she is presently employed.]

[1] Constitution of Ecuador, Section I, Art. 19, No. 4.

[2] Constitution, Section II, Art. 22.

[3] Constitution, Art. 24.

40 percent are Indians, the majority of whom are concentrated in the Andes Mountain areas called the sierra. Here illiteracy is extremely high. Large segments of the Indian population speak Quechua either exclusively or as their first language. These Highland Indians are the poorest of the poor, extremely humble and almost totally marginal, the latter partly because of their own tradition: it is very difficult for them to leave the soil of their elders—in the land they concentrate their emotions, love, misery, and whatever happiness they know. Another 40 percent are the peasant Mestizos, who are in a much better position than the Indians. The remaining 20 percent can be called "white folk." (Percentages based on the 1974 Census.) The peasants of the coast of Ecuador are called *montuvios*. These people are outgoing, with entrepreneurial qualities which make them very active: they have a fairly balanced diet since they sustain their livelihood from the sea and also eat a variety of tropical fruits. Sometimes they are even considered arrogant since they love their freedom, the seeming contrast of their cousins of the sierra, the Highland Indians, whose staple consists of corn and potatoes and whose attitudes appear subservient.

At a first glance, anyone going to the three major cities of Ecuador, Quito (the capital), Guayaquil (a port and the most powerful commercial center), and Cuenca (the third largest city), comes away feeling that economic growth has benefited the country. But what one is seeing is the product of a fragmented development where economic growth has benefited the developed centers, favoring only a small segment of the population where the elite, upper, and middle classes are usually concentrated (those who have the purchasing power to take advantage of the domestic imported goods offered in these centers). This fragmented development has sharpened the inequalities of the country where the mass, or at least a large percentage, of the people still live in abject poverty. Within this context it is safe to say that in many developing countries the question of equal rights is less emphasized because the basic needs of the majority of both men and women have not yet been met. It becomes very difficult to demand equal rights when malnutrition, disease, unemployment, and all the other ills of poverty seem equally widespread among men and women.

By illustrating the roles of women in Ecuadorean society it's easy to show the social disparities of the country. Women account for 52.7 percent of the total rural-to-urban migration: they constitute 49.6 percent of Ecuador's population, 51.2 percent of the urban population, and 48.4 percent of the rural population.[4] The conditions in which women live vary enormously according to the socioeconomic strata in which they find themselves. It is safe to say that through the entire country an aristocracy in name still exists, albeit with weak economic power. The "elite" women of the above-mentioned developed centers seem content with their lot: they draw power through their husbands' positions, travel a great deal, have homes abroad in Miami or in Europe, and appear in no way eager to change the system. The few who are employed can generally get high-level positions. There is a similar group—the rich upper class—which has a comparable lifestyle. Still a third group is formed by the high rich "bourgeoisie." In all of these groups an amelioration of the social ills which fall on the rest of the women of Ecuador is not necessarily a priority.

The middle-class woman is the one who has taken advantage of the increased educational opportunities women have gained in recent years. This middle-class professional has become more and more the working class of the country; she has the advantage of still-cheap, readily available household help, and therefore is less handicapped in working after marriage and motherhood. However, this newly independent woman is only able to maintain her status *through* the help of other women—mainly the domestic servant,

[4] JUNAPLA, "Migraciones hacia la ciudad de Quito y Proyecciones de la Población" (Quito, 1975).

which of course perpetuates class differences. A by-product of this situation is the lack of interest of middle-class women toward their servants, the terrible opposition to public or private initiatives for upgrading the position of domestic employment.

Over Latin America as a whole, two of every five women are domestic servants,[5] and most come from rural areas. In the case of Ecuador, with all the economic and social consequences brought about by migration, it must be said that given the lack of options in the rural areas, migration by these women to the cities is in itself a prerequisite first step in the socioeconomic ladder which in turn gives them both hope and upward mobility. This change from a provincial to a metropolitan setting exposes them to different environments and incentives to try something new and different, once they have been domestic workers for a couple of years. By law in Ecuador a domestic worker is entitled to social security benefits, unemployment compensation, and all the extra salaries decreed. Many domestics in Ecuador look for employment in foreign households, though, and not only because of higher salaries, but more importantly because they claim that in a foreign household they are not as exploited as in an Ecuadorean household, that their integrity of character is not so scrutinized as in an Ecuadorean household, where everything is kept locked up and if something is missing the maid is blamed. The maid is also considered "irrational" due to her social condition—and yet ironically this very maid is entrusted with the lives of the children of these households. The domestic worker has high expectations for her own children. When asked what occupations they want for their children most of them will say schoolteachers, nurses, etc. These women who work as servants see the acquisition of a profession as social respectability.

We come now to the Highland Indian woman of Ecuador—by far the most neglected and invisible of all. In 1964 the government initiated agrarian reform, requiring landowners to cultivate 80 percent of their farmlands or face expropriation. Land reform is such a potentially explosive issue that neither government officials nor wealthy people in developing countries like to discuss it. In Ecuador, needless to say, the pace of reform has not proceeded according to plan. In the last eighteen years less than 20 percent of land distribution has actually taken place. In the majority of the cases only small portions of land were expropriated and turned over to the land-starved Indians. There has been no significant effect, for example, felt in Canton Colta, a beautiful valley in the shadow of snowcapped Mount Chimborazo, where about thirty thousand Quechua-speaking Indians live; they are extremely poor and some of them live in inhuman conditions, with the highest incidence of malnutrition and exposure to diseases in the whole country, as well as a high infant mortality rate and low life expectancy.[6]

The burdens of the Indian woman start in childhood, and the physical aspects are devastating. By the time she is five or six years old she already helps do chores around the home. Her work enables her parents to take jobs outside the home. She minds younger brothers and sisters, carries them wrapped in a square piece of cloth slung over her young shoulders, collects firewood, tends the animals, helps to fetch water, and often walks miles carrying meals to her parents in the fields. She also cooks and washes clothes. Those little girls who attend school do so only for one or two years, and by the time they reach adulthood they've forgotten what they learned. As adults, they often head households because of male migration to the cities. By the time the Indian woman is in her mid-twenties, more than likely she will look twice her age and have borne at least four children—of whom only one or two will survive. She is also vulnerable to physical abuse from her husband and other male members of her family; the Highland Indian male of Ecuador tends to get drunk quite often. She owns no farming land, usually no more than

[5] Ester Boserup, *Woman's Role in Economic Development* (New York: St. Martin's Press, 1970).
[6] National Nutrition Institute.

the plot where her hut stands. She works long hours every day of the year simply to survive, and the result of her labor is pitifully small. Without land, livestock, or capital, she is economically weak and marginal. Without organizations to defend her interests, she is politically powerless.

The conditions of women in Ecuador are a social fact. More than ever before, Ecuador needs the common effort of both men and women to liberate themselves. We need a change of attitudes in women about women, and in each class about class—but most importantly in men about women. We need to support women in *all* aspects of their lives and in *all* their roles. This fundamental change requires organization at all levels, from institution-building at grass-roots levels with indigenous methods to rural or urban institutions and international agencies.

In Ecuador there has been a gradual awakening among women. I am happy to say that there are a number of women's organizations working toward the improvement of women's status. Yet even if there are government initiatives as well as feminist agitation, the problems of most of these women are compounded by class oppression. Deep attitudinal change—consciousness—and common participation are fundamental for the goal of a just society, of individual dignity, and of development in the best sense of the word.

Suggested Further Reading
[The Contributor regretfully cannot recommend any books on Ecuadorean women.]

Carola Borja was born in Quito, Ecuador. She received her post-secondary education in the United States. Before joining the UNFPA in 1974, she worked for four years for FAO in a World Food Program Project in Ecuador. Since 1975 she has been a Member of the Ad Hoc Group on Equal Rights for Women in the United Nations, and served as co-editor of a publication by the Ad Hoc Group entitled *Equal Time*. She is also a member of the Women's Action Group of the United Nations Development Program and a contributor to an analytical paper for a report on the Status of Women in UNDP/UNFPA.

EGYPT
(Arab Republic of Egypt)

Egypt is located in northeastern Africa, bordered to the east by the Red Sea and Israel, to the south by the Sudan, to the north by the Mediterranean Sea, and to the west by Libya. **Area:** 1,001,998 sq. km. (386,872 sq. mi.). **Population** (1980): 42,116,000, female 49.5%. **Capital:** Cairo.

DEMOGRAPHY. Languages: Arabic (official). **Races or Ethnic Groups:** Egyptian, Bedouin, Nubian majority, minority of Greeks and Turks. **Religions:** Islam (predominantly Hanafi school of Sunni Islam) 93%, Coptic Christian (primarily Greek and Syrian Orthodox). **Education** (% enrolled in school, 1975): Age 6–11— of all girls 52%, of all boys 80%; age 12–17—of all girls 27%, of all boys 49%; in 1979 female students were 40% of primary school enrollment, 37% of intermediary, and 36.1% of secondary; higher education—in 1982–83 women were approx. 34% of master's and doctorate students; in 1979 women were 46.7% of university students, 13.5% of technical industrial students, 54.6% of technical commercial students. **Literacy** (1977): Women 29%, men 57%; from 1966–76, illiteracy dropped from 84% to 70% for the female pop. but as of 1980 the majority of women were nonliterate. **Birth Rate** (per 1000 pop., 1975–80): 38. **Death Rate** (per 1000 pop., 1975–80): 10. **Infant Mortality** (per 1000 live births, 1975–80): Female 85, male 95. **Life Expectancy** (1975–80): Female 56 yrs., male 54 yrs.

GOVERNMENT. Under the 1971 Constitution, Egypt is officially a "democratic socialist state" with a president and a prime minister. A 360-member People's Assembly is elected by universal suffrage. There are 4 legal political parties. **Voting:** Compulsory for men but not women. **Women's Suffrage:** 1956. **Equal Rights:** 1962 National Charter called for the liberation of women to ensure complete equality; the 1971 Constitution (Art. 40) proclaimed all citizens equal before the law, but with a qualifying clause (see following article). **Women in Government:** At cabinet level women have occupied only the position of Minister of Social Affairs; Amal Osman holds the post (1983). From 1980 to Apr. 83, 30 Assemblywomen had been elected. Women are prevented from holding certain high-level positions, such as provincial governor; because of a reading of Islamic law, a woman's testimony is considered worth half of a man's, which prevents women from holding judgeships (also see HERSTORY).

ECONOMY. Currency: Egyptian Pound (May 1983: 0.82 = $1 US). **Gross National Product** (1980): $23.1 billion. **Per Capita Income** (1980): $580. **Women's Wages as a Percentage of Men's** (1980): 63% in nonagricultural activities. **Equal Pay Policy:** Legislation in 1933, 1959, and 1978 promoted better wages and working conditions for women and stipulated the principle of equal pay for equal work for public-sector and government employees only. **Production** (Agricultural/Industrial): Cotton, wheat, rice, sugar cane, corn; textiles, processed foods, chemicals, tobacco manufactures. **Women as a Percentage of Labor Force** (1980): 8%; **of agricultural force** (1976) 3% (in 1982 unofficial indicators put the figure closer to 45% including unpaid family workers); **of industrial force**—no general statistics obtainable (of manufacturing 6.6%, 1976); **of military**—no statistics obtainable, women in service sectors only. **(Employed) Women's Occupational Indicators:** 80% of women employed by the government are in health and educational services (1983); of transport workers 0.9%, of public administration 9.2%, of service workers (including domestic service) 16%, of professional workers 22.6% (1977). In 1974, 250 of the thousand-odd members of the Journalists Union in Egypt were women. **Unemployment** (1979): 4.6%, female 18.2%, male 3.4%.

GYNOGRAPHY. Marriage. *Policy:* Egyptian law is largely based on the Hanafi school of Sunni Islam's interpretation of the Shari'a. Egyptians are required to register their marriages, meet minimum-age standards (16 for females, 18 for males), and marry with mutual consent. Under Hanafi law, the *mahar* (dowry) accompanies the marriage contract and is paid either in full when the contract is drawn or in part at that time and then in deferred payments. The *mahar* belongs to the wife, to control and dispose of as she wishes, only by the marriage act. If the engagement has not been solemnized in marriage, the full *mahar* must be returned to the fiancé (in case of full payment at engagement) no matter who is at fault. If the marriage has been solemnized but unconsummated, half the *mahar* must be returned to the groom. In case of either spouse's death, the wife (or her family) keeps the full *mahar;* the wife is also entitled to all of the furnishings in her husband's house. Polygyny is legal for Moslem men, with a 4-wife limit. Decree Law 44 (1979) stated that a wife's duty was to obey her husband or else legally be in a "state of infringement"; she could be forced to submit to her husband's demands under Art. 345. A married woman can retain her birth-name and has the right to own and control her own property. Marriage between a Moslem woman and a non-Moslem man is forbidden, but a Moslem man can marry a Christian or Jewish woman. A Moslem woman has the legal right to bring criminal charges against her husband for personal injuries (see **Battery**); if a wife leaves her husband (even for reasons of battery) he has the legal right to obtain a court decision to force his wife's return.

In inheritance matters, 1/3 of a Moslem woman or man's property can be controlled or disposed of as s/he wishes; the other 2/3 is distributed according to Islamic law, which says that a female inherits 1/2 the share of a male, although a female has the right of "testamentary disposition" which can give her a larger share. A widow is entitled to 1/4 of her husband's estate if he has no children; otherwise, she receives 1/8. Married persons of different religions cannot inherit from each other. Christian minors under age 21 must have the consent of legal guardians to marry. Any Egyptian married woman who wishes to work outside the home needs her husband's authorization. A woman who does so against her husband's wishes, or a married woman who refuses to live with her husband, forfeits the right to financial support by him. *Practice:* Female mean age at marriage (1970–79): 22; women age 15–44 in union (1970–79): 63.4%; arranged marriages are common and child marriages still frequent. The use of family identification cards at registration of marriage is promoted as a measure to deter polygyny; in 1979 plural marriages were 3% of total Egyptian marriages.

Divorce. *Policy:* Legal. A man is allowed unilateral divorce *(talaq).** Law 25 (1920 and 1924) established broader grounds for divorce: mutual consent, and divorce by judicial decree through annulment or dissolution. A man has a right to 3 divorces. If a woman tolerates battery or adultery by her husband early in their marriage without seeking an immediate divorce, she cannot obtain it later. In the case of revocable divorce, a woman cannot remarry during the period of *idda* (see Glossary), remains under her husband's control for that duration, and can be taken back anytime during *idda.* After *idda,* if his divorced wife remarries, the divorce is not applied to his 3-divorce quota. A divorced woman receives alimony during *idda;* in the case of deferred payment of the *mahar,* she receives the remaining share on divorce. Under divorce by mutual consent *(khole),* a wife pays her husband to obtain a divorce or forfeits her deferred dowry. Furthermore, a woman can be granted the right to divorce if her husband is incurably sick or disabled. Divorce by judicial decree may be granted if the husband fails to support his wife financially, is seriously ill or disabled, physically maltreats or damages the wife "on moral or social grounds," and if he has been absent for at least 5 yrs, with whereabouts unknown or imprisoned on a long sentence. Child maintenance is the father's responsibility; if he is unable to do so, responsibility passes to his male next of kin. Children/dependents are defined as male minors and un-

---

* The *Koran* itself, however, says, "Repudiation is the most hateful to God of all the permitted acts."

married, widowed, and divorced daughters. Child custody is given to the mother until age 7 for boys and age 9 for girls (may be extended by the courts to 9 for boys and 11 for girls). *Practice:* A 1980 study showed that divorce rates were 2.9% (of the married pop. that yr.) in Cairo and Alexandria, and had dropped to under 2% in the different provinces of north and south Egypt. The divorce rate was higher among women in the labor force. It is still easy for a man to divorce at will, force his wife to return if she has left him or he has conditionally divorced her, and to by-pass the limits of polygyny through loopholes in the law. It is common for men to refuse to pay alimony, and a woman has little recourse for enforcement. Despite the law, it is mothers who raise and support their children. **Family.** *Policy:* A Moslem man's children automatically assume his religion. If a woman is a non-Moslem, her children cannot inherit her property. If the father has no son, his daughter receives 1/2 his estate; if he left more than 1 daughter, but no son, they share 2/3 of his estate. If he left daughters and sons, the daughters' shares are 1/2 the sons'. A 1977 clause allows an orphaned child to inherit from grandparents. Labor laws of 1959 established maternity leave for married women at 50 days post–delivery with pay equivalent to 70% regular wage; the laws were revised substantially in 1978 (see following article). The 1959 laws contained provisions prohibiting women from jobs deemed harmful to their physical health or "morals" (e.g., underground work, some night employment). The Ministry of Social Affairs has established 71 family guidance offices, set up 2341 childcare nurseries (176 of which are for girls), and created 25 institutions to care for girls "exposed to moral danger" (1983). *Practice:* Single pregnant women are not entitled to maternity leave. Religious courts refer approx. 8500 cases to family guidance offices each yr. (1983). A 1983 report stated that because of male migration for employment, there were no adult males in some villages of Upper Egypt and the Nile Delta. **Welfare.** *Policy:* A comprehensive national insurance program exists; no further data obtainable. *Practice:* No data obtainable.

Contraception. *Policy:* The Supreme Council of Family Planning was established in 1956; in 1962 the National Charter made family planning a government priority. Government centers were operated under the auspices of the Ministry of Public Health and the Ministry of Social Affairs; the latter supervises privately run agencies. While Egyptian law does not outlaw sterilization, some interpretations of Islamic doctrine prohibit sterilization except in the case of proven risk of "hereditary disease, physical deformity, or mental illness." *Practice:* Women age 15–49 in union using contraception (1970–80): 20%, of which traditional methods 5%, modern 95%. In 1977 there were 3030 family–planning centers operated by the Ministry of Public Health (mostly in rural areas) and 418 by the Ministry of Social Affairs. Withdrawal is favored as a traditional means of birth control; pills are the preferred modern method. **Abortion.** *Policy:* The 1937 Penal Code (Arts. 260, 261, 263) outlawed abortion except in case of danger to a woman's health or life or if "it is proven that the child will be physically deformed or congenitally abnormal." A woman who agrees to an abortion in any other circumstances is subject to punishment (Art. 262). Under strict Islamic law, abortion is prohibited except in case of danger to a woman's life; a more liberal (but rarely followed) reading allows abortion through the first 120 days of pregnancy whether or not there is danger to the woman's life. *Practice:* In 1980, 1 out of 4 pregnancies ended in illegal abortion performed under unsanitary conditions with inferior health care; wealthy women who abort outnumber poor women 3–1; 90% of abortion cases are married women age 25–35, 80% of whom have had 2 children. **Illegitimacy.** *Policy:* Largely because of interpretation of Islamic law, any child born within 6 months of marriage is considered the "legitimate" offspring of the husband unless specifically disclaimed; if the marriage is voided, legitimacy is established on proof of consummation. Paternity may be challenged by a husband if he can prove he and his wife were physically apart since their marriage, or if the wife gives birth after the couple has been apart at least 1 yr., or 1 yr. after divorce. A man can legally repudiate his acknowledged child through *la'am*. *Practice:* No statistics obtainable; out-of-wedlock children have inferior legal rights and carry a social stigma. **Homosexuality.** *Policy:* Illegal; no further data obtainable. *Practice:* No data obtainable.

Incest. *Policy:* Illegal; punishable by severe sentence (varies depending on circumstances); the union of a stepmother and a stepson is forbidden as being "odious marriage." *Practice:* No statistics obtainable. Reportedly, sexual assaults on young women and female children are common. Cases have been reported in which male family members who molested a young female family member killed her before she could "dishonor" the family by revealing that she was not a virgin on her wedding night. In ancient Egypt, marriage by consanguinity (especially brother-sister) was the rule among royalty and nobility. **Sexual Harassment.** *Policy:* No data obtainable. *Practice:* Prevalent; a 1973 study of 160 Egyptian females of all ages and social classes found harassment to be common, as high as 45% in noneducated families and 33.7% in educated families. **Rape.** *Policy:* Illegal; maximum sentence 15–25 yrs., punishable by capital sentence when accompanied by murder or attempted murder of the woman. Marital rape is not recognized by law. *Practice:* No statistics obtainable. Rape is reportedly common and women have little protection against it because the social emphasis on virginity causes silence about rape. Rape victims who were virgins often attempt reconstruction of their hymens so that they will bleed at marriage and can retain their *mahar* (see **Traditional/Cultural Practices**). It is common for the court to dismiss a rape case to "protect the reputation" of the raped woman and her family, thus permitting the rapist to go free. In some cases, the rapist is freed if he agrees to marry the woman he raped. **Battery.** *Policy:* Under Islamic law, a woman can bring charges against her husband for "personal injuries"; other laws cover general assault and battery (see **Marriage**). *Practice:* No statistics ob-

tainable, but reports indicate that wife-beating is common; a woman who registers a complaint risks immediate divorce.

Prostitution. *Policy:* Illegal as of 1951; punishable by imprisonment with varying sentences. Egyptian law states that a man who is "caught with a prostitute" is not imprisoned; instead, his testimony is used to convict and imprison the prostitute. *Practice:* No statistics obtainable, but prostitution is prevalent, particularly in major urban centers. Prostitutes are socially ostracized. Reports indicate that some divorced women are forced to turn to prostitution as a means of economic survival, particularly if their families refuse to support them. In ancient Egypt, daughters of noble families would be offered to the temple priests (in Thebes) to become "sacred prostitutes" or "high priestesses" referred to as "Harem of the God Amoun." **Traditional/Cultural Practices.** *Policy:* The Egyptian government passed legislation in the 1970's that opposes "female circumcision"**; some interpretations of Islamic law officially support the practice as "an Islamic tradition of the prophet" (although it is mentioned nowhere in the *Koran)* and sanction it "in view of its effect on attenuating the sexual desire of women and directing it to desirable moderation." Other Islamic interpretations oppose the practice. *Practice:* A 1973 study of 160 women of all ages and social classes in Egypt indicated that 97.5% of noneducated families and 66.2% of educated families maintain the practice; the operation is carried out on girls before they have reached puberty, usually by a *daya* (midwife), who makes her living performing "female circumcisions" and reconstruction of the hymen, as well as general midwifery. While "female circumcision" is not obligatory, most women either are unaware of laws opposing the practice or face such strong social pressure that they agree to have their daughters "circumcised." Egyptian feminists are campaigning about the deleterious effects of this practice. Other reports indicate that the beating and even murder of women who are not virgins (including women who are, but have naturally elastic hymens) by

** See Glossary.

husbands or families still occur. **Crisis Centers:** No data obtainable.

HERSTORY. Ancient Egypt's history was divided into 3 periods, referred to as the Old (3110–c. 2000 B.C.E.), Middle (2000–c. 1786 B.C.E.), and New (1570–c. 332 B.C.E.) Kingdoms. The 18th dynasty (in the New Kingdom) is considered the most important; among the rulers were the great queens Hatshepsut (reigned 1486–1468 B.C.E.) and Nefertiti, co-ruler (1372–1350 B.C.E.) with Pharoah Ikhnaton. Hatshepsut, the daughter of Thutmose I, maintained a peaceful reign, overseeing the development of mining in the Sinai and the construction of the great temple at Deir el Bahari in West Thebes. Queen Nefertiti was a brilliant stateswoman and influenced Ikhnaton to introduce the concept of monotheism. During the Ptolemy dynasty, Queen Cleopatra (69–30 B.C.E.) overthrew her husband (her younger brother, Ptolemy XII) with the aid of Julius Caesar. Later, she influenced Marc Anthony to further empower Egypt. The Arab conquest of Egypt took place from 639–642 C.E.; Nassiba Bint Kaab and Om Solayem Bint Malhan were famous warrior women who fought alongside the prophet Mohammad in the battle of Ahad. Mohammad's first wife, Khadija, was a strong-willed woman sometimes credited with having introduced him to his religious vocation; his third wife, Aisha, was an accomplished theologian, medical healer, and poet; his only child, Fatima, was followed by many as his religious and philosophical heir. Successive waves of conquest, the Crusades, and the invasion of Napoleon, followed, and in 1805 Mohammed Ali was named Egyptian pasha by the Ottoman emperor. Under Mohammed Ali, veiled women were allowed to work alongside men in national factories; he also established a school of midwifery in 1842.

In 1873 El Soyovfia, the first primary school for girls, was established. British troops occupied Egypt in 1882; by 1914 Egypt was a British Protectorate. Secondary-school education for women began in the 1900's; during that time, 1000 veiled women led by the al-Ghazali sisters (Communist Party members Hikmat and Zaynab, head of the Moslem Sisters faction of the Resistance) staged a protest against British occupation. In 1923 the Egyptian Feminist Union (or Federation) was organized by middle-class women pressing for social reform. In 1933 the first protective legislation for working women was passed. Hoda Shaarawi (1879–1947) was a pioneer of the Egyptian feminist movement, working to raise the minimum marriage age for girls to 16, for the reform of marriage laws, and better health standards.

In Feb. 1943, Ruz al-Yusuf, a woman activist, played an important role in anti-British demonstrations. Egyptian delegates attended the First World Congress of Women in Paris (1945). In 1946, the 2 main feminist parties were Ittihad Bint al Nil (Doria Shafiq, president) and Fatmah Nirmat Rashid's party. Inji Efflatoun wrote and published *80 Million* (1948), and *Women with Us* (1949), both books about women in Egyptian society. In 1954 Col. Gamal Abdal Nasser became president and expelled the last of the British; new labor laws brought better conditions for working women.

At the start of the 1956 war with Britain over the Suez Canal, the Popular Committee of Women's Resistance taught women to fight with weapons and to serve in paramedical units. In 1958 the attempts of Efflatoun and other women to organize a general women's party (Itihad al-nisa-al-gunmi) were thwarted by the government; Efflatoun was imprisoned for 4 years. In the 1960's Sallama Shaker became the first woman accepted into the Foreign Service; she is currently (1983) the First Secretary of the Egyptian Embassy in Turkey. The 1962 National Charter was a progressive document supporting women's equality.

The 1960's saw general development in the status of women, followed by a wave of religious fundamentalism in the early 1970's that called for, among other things, a return to the veil. Assiza Hussein initiated the first village family-planning programs during this time, and was elected president of International Planned Parenthood in 1977.

In 1982 Nawal El Saadawi announced the formation of a major pan-Arab women's-rights organization, based in Egypt.

Its provisional name is Jam'iyyat-Tadhamun-el-Mar'a (Assoc. of Women's Solidarity); men are permitted in the membership. In Aug. 1983 the Assoc. was refused registration as an organization by the Egyptian government; the Assoc. plans an appeal.

MYTHOGRAPHY. In 3000 B.C.E. Upper Egypt was called the land of the goddess Nekhebt; Lower Egypt was called the land of Ua Zit, the Cobra goddess. Ua Zit was worshipped on the Nile Delta as the Eye of Wisdom. The Egyptian pantheon was rich with goddesses. Isis, or Au Set, the Great Goddess of Divine Wisdom, was a virgin/mother/crone presence with wide influence, especially over natural phenomena, agriculture, healing, and childbirth. Other goddesses include Maat (moral judgment), the Lady of Amenta or "Holy Hidden Mother" (who welcomed the dead into the underworld), Bastet (the cat goddess of cleverness), Seshat (goddess of the written word, credited with inventing the hieroglyphs), Hathor (the cow goddess who breathed life through her nostrils and nourished with her milk), and Nut or Neit (mistress of the heavens who ruled the earth and sun).

EGYPT: When a Woman Rebels . . .
by Nawal El Saadawi
(Translated by Sherif Hetata)

Visitors on a Sunday Afternoon

I am writing this article on women in Egypt for the second time. I had promised Robin Morgan that she would receive the manuscript by September 15, 1981. I handed it to a friend of mine, ready for typing, on September 1, and we agreed that she would drop in at my place on September 7 with the typed manuscript. This would give me time to correct the typescript and send it to New York by express mail.

But on Sunday afternoon there was a sudden burst of violent knocking at the front door of my apartment. I opened the glass frame and looked out. To my astonishment, I found a group of armed policemen standing on the threshold. Since they were not carrying a warrant with them, I refused to open the door. They broke it down, charged into my flat, searched my desk and library, confiscated some of my books and papers, and carried me away to prison.

On September 7, my typist friend saw my photograph in the newspapers and read my name included in a long list of political personalities who had been detained by the authorities. The charge brought against the 1536 men and women on this list was: "Participation in stirring up sectarian (religious) strife."

Immediately the word went around that the homes of my relatives and friends would be searched. If any person was found to have assisted me with my writings he or she would be arrested. My friend was seized with panic. She tore up the original article as well as the typed manuscript.

As for me, I spent eighty days and nights in the Women's Prison at Kanatir El Khaireya, a suburb of Cairo. The "Socialist Prosecutor" interrogated me twice. The official charge brought against me was "Publishing articles critical of President Sadat's Policies." Article 74 of the new Constitution promulgated under the Sadat regime authorized the President to take whatever measures he saw fit against those whose activities or ideas disturbed "social peace," undermined "national unity," or were contrary to the "traditions and spiritual values" of the country.

On October 6, Sadat was assassinated by three Islamic fundamentalists. One was an officer of the army and two were young trainees of the reserve army. The assassination took place during an army march celebrating the anniversary of the October war against Israel. On November 25, 1981, I was released by order of Hosni Mubarak, who succeeded Sadat as President. I, among thirty-one detainees, was in the first batch of accused set free because the charges brought against us were found to be without substance.

I was taken from my prison directly to Kasr El Ourouba (the Palace of the Arabs) and there we met with President Hosni Mubarak. During this meeting I emphasized that I was a writer and had never carried a gun or a sword; my pen was my only weapon. If we wished to achieve true democracy and real freedom in Egypt, it was essential that people like me, who were trying to develop their thought and express their views openly, be protected by the law.

I recount this incident to illustrate the fact that democracy and freedom are necessary conditions if the women of Egypt are to achieve liberation. The cause of women is closely interwoven with the total political and social development of society.

Women like me—who rebel against the many-sided oppression exercised by society against us—can easily end up in jail, even if they are not members of any political party. This oppression is most ferocious where the poorer working-class and peasant categories of women are concerned. An obvious conclusion is that the conceptions and aims of women's liberation must perforce be a serious threat to the very roots of patriarchal society—mainly because they do *not* recognize separation among political, social, economic, cultural, psychological, and sexual oppressions.

Egyptian Women's Struggle for Emancipation

Women of ancient Egypt enjoyed an elevated status in the various areas related to political, economic, administrative, religious, and cultural activities. The thrones of the gods were not the monopoly of men, nor were ruling secular positions held only by representatives of the masculine sex. Women's status, however, declined with the advent of private property and with the social system built on slavery and later on feudalism (2420–2140 B.C.E.).

Women in ancient Greece had been looked down upon by Greek men, but during the Egyptian civilization there were continual up-and-down shifts in the status of women, which tended to change in harmony with political and social developments. When the Greeks occupied Egypt in the year 332 B.C.E., women lost their relatively favored position.

Matters grew even worse under the Romans. According to Roman law, a father was entitled to sell his daughter as a slave—or even kill her if he so desired. Yet despite the diminished status of Egyptian women under the Roman Empire, the remnants of tradition from ancient times permitted a woman like Cleopatra to ascend the throne and to be the last of the king/queen emperors of Egypt. Nevertheless, under the reign of Cleopatra, average women were still victims of a cruel discrimination enforced by the tyranny of class and patriarchy.

With the advent of Christianity, a humanitarian moral and spiritual revival was announced, related to the birth of the new faith. Polygamy, for example, was opposed as being evil. But the Church gradually linked up with the system and itself became a central pillar of tyranny exercised by feudalism against the common man—but particularly against the common woman. Religious teaching and practice advocated and accentuated differentiation according to class, and the status of women retreated to its lowest ebb. Woman became synonymous with the Devil under Byzantine rule.

The Arabs invaded Egypt in 640 C.E. Islam became the religion of the State, and Islamic jurisprudence the basis of the legal system. But men still continued to exercise total supremacy over women, and the feudal system prevalent at the time continued to enforce patriarchal and class discrimination. Egypt remained under Arab Islamic domination for many centuries. At the end of the Fatimid reign a woman named Shagaret el Dur ruled the country, but women were still exposed to the same discrimination, and their status declined even further under the Mamelukes, and later under the Turks. From 1517 onward, poor women were driven to work in cultivating the land, and middle- and upper-class women were imprisoned in their homes and forced to wear the veil.

In 1882 the British occupied Egypt and transformed it into a colony. Men and women became a source of cheap labor; cotton was the product of their field-work. But resentment mounted and in 1919 the national movement exploded in a revolution which left no part of the country untouched. When British troops opened fire on the massive demonstrations and popular insurrections, scores of women were killed.

With the birth of the 20th century, women writers (side by side with a small number of enlightened men) enlisted their pens in the cause of women's freedom. Notable among such women were Aisha El Taymoureya, Zeinab Fawaz, and Malak Hefni Nassif, as well as Mai Ziada, who founded a literary salon in 1915 but subsequently died young, alone, and suffering from a mental breakdown.

Through their participation in the revolution of 1919, women obtained the right to create a federation—which was founded in 1923 by Hoda Shaarawi. The Federation defended the right of women to education and advocated raising the age of marriage for females to sixteen, improving the laws of marriage and divorce to women's advantage, franchise rights for women, and abolition of the veil. But the Federation failed to achieve its full potential, partly because it was composed exclusively of upper-class women and had no links with the poorer sectors of the female population.

After the establishment of the Egyptian Federation of Women, charitable and social-welfare associations were created in increasing number by women. Their activities expanded, especially after 1940, and included various forms of assistance to victims of the war or epidemics, as well as to orphans, invalids, and the sick. There are around five thousand of these associations at present, but only a few hundred are active. They are placed under the supervision of the Ministry for Social Affairs and are composed mainly of housewives from the middle and upper classes. Their activities remain limited to the confines of social welfare.

Popular discontent with the regime and opposition to the British reached a peak in July 1952. On the night of July 23, the system was overthrown by a movement of patriotic officers; this is known as the July Revolution. After the nationalization of the Suez Canal in 1956, Britain, France, and Israel launched a concerted attack on Egypt. In the ensuing military and populist resistance to the attack, women played an active role against the triple aggression: a Women's Committee for Popular Resistance was constituted. In the Constitution of 1956 (promulgated after the withdrawal of the foreign troops), women obtained the right to vote, to present themselves as candidates in the national and local elections, and to hold public office in many areas previously closed to them. During the elections of 1957 five women won seats in the National Assembly, and the National Charter (issued in 1962) dealt with the situation of women in the following terms: "It is essential that women be rid of those chains which hinder their free movement, so that they be enabled to participate actively and profoundly in the remouldings of our life."

The first woman minister in Egypt was appointed in 1962. After the nationalizations of 1961, Egypt set itself a course which in certain areas was characterized by a "socialist" orientation aiming at accelerating socioeconomic development and reducing the differences among social classes.

But the defeat suffered by Egypt in 1967 in the face of Israeli aggression led to a retreat in all areas of socioeconomic development and affected the socialist orientation of the country by strengthening right-wing forces and aggravating economic difficulties. As a consequence, the women's struggle also suffered a reverse. After Nasser's death, and throughout the 1970's, the so-called "open-door" economic policy liquidated the remains of socialist orientation and accelerated the development of an economy based on capitalist speculation, black-market activities, currency manipulations, and other forms of nonproductive activity which led to a rapid widening of the gap between a small, rich minority and the vast majority of urban and rural poor. There was a rising clamor of voices enjoining women to "return to the house" and to "the veil." Wealth and power became more and more concentrated in the hands of a few, while the number of unemployed youth and university graduates increased. Greater sections of the population found it more and more difficult to make ends meet.

Developments in Women's Education and in Employment of Women Outside the Home.
At the beginning of the 19th century, tradition required that Egyptian women belonging to middle- and upper-class families remain at home. Poor women, whether urban or rural, continued to work in the fields or as domestic servants. Official primary education for girls was begun only in 1873 and was meant as a form of training for poor girls, orphans, and slaves so that they could perform certain functions more effectively. In 1979 the number of females in primary education was around 1.7 million and constituted about 40 percent of total primary-school enrollment. In the same year, the corresponding proportion for girls in intermediary schooling jumps to 37 percent, but in secondary-school education it does not rise above 36.1 percent. If we move to other areas we find the percentage in technical industrial schooling only 13.5 percent for the same year, but it rises to 54.6 percent[1] in technical commercial schools.

A private university was established in 1908—but its students were all male. In 1929 women were admitted to the university for the first time: 17 female students. However, in 1979 there were 138,052 female students in the university (now public) and they constituted 46.7 percent of the total number of students.[2]

In the last official population census (1976) illiteracy among females was shown to have dropped by 14 percent (i.e., from 84 percent to 70 percent) since the previous census carried out ten years earlier.

I have already mentioned that women's progress was held back and even turned into a retreat during the 1970's. The Constitution of 1971 reflected this setback in many of its articles. As an example:

The state is responsible for ensuring that the duties of women toward their families are appropriately harmonized with their work in society and the equal rights they enjoy with men in the fields of political, social, and cultural activity, in such a way that no infringement of Islamic jurisprudence be permitted.

This stipulation means that women are obliged to combine employment outside the home *with* their family duties. It also maintains the unjust marriage and divorce laws so as to avoid any "infringement of Islamic jurisprudence."

The first law for the protection of employed women was issued in 1933; the first comprehensive Labor Law saw the light in 1959 and was remodeled in 1978. This 1978 remodeling includes stipulations related to employed women. For example, all enterprises employing 100 or more women must provide their employees with a nursery for children.

[1] *Women and Education in the Arab Republic of Egypt.* The National Institute for Pedagogical Research, May 1980, pp. 42, 82.
[2] *Women and Education,* p. 76.

Lactating mothers are allowed two breaks a day (half an hour each) in order to nurse their infants—this for a period extending to eighteen months after childbirth. Employed women also are allowed three months fully paid leave after childbirth, repeated to a maximum of three times during their working life (recently reduced to two times, ostensibly as a family-planning measure). Employed women may also be allowed unpaid leave for a period of two years in order to care for their newborn children; this may be repeated up to a maximum of three times during the woman's working lifetime.

Despite the fact that women were permitted to become ministers for the first time in 1962, in actual practice the only ministerial post opened to women so far has been that of Social Affairs. In addition there still remain many areas of activity which are completely closed to women: the judiciary, the police, the army, and certain high posts like that of provincial governor.

Male Domination in the Marriage Law

Where matters of marriage and divorce are concerned, Egyptian women are still governed by a law issued in 1920 and amended in 1929. In 1979 a new law was passed by the "People's Assembly" which maintains the essentials of what already existed albeit with some minor, insignificant changes.[3] This law draws its inspiration from Islamic jurisprudence and has in no way lightened the injustices suffered by wives and mothers at the hands of the male heads of families. The husband still has an absolute right to divorce at any time; the wife has no such right. She can call upon the judge to grant her a divorce only if her husband suffers from an incurable disease or disability. The law stipulates that the husband should try, to the best of his capacity, to reach agreement with his wife. But on the other hand, the duty of a wife is to obey her husband, and if she does not, she is considered legally to be "in a state of infringement" and can be obliged by force of law to submit herself to her husband's requirements (Art. 345). According to other legal provisions, a woman is entitled to only half the inheritance her brother receives on the death of their father, and before the courts a man's testimony is equivalent to that of two women. Finally, responsibility for the children (tutelage) is wholly in the hands of the father, despite the fact that children are allowed to remain with the mother up to a certain age in case of divorce (nine for boys and eleven for girls).

As an example of tutelage, I would like to share one of my own experiences. In 1976, my daughter, then nineteen years old, was invited to Algeria to participate in a tennis tournament. I had divorced her father a few months after she was born, and by mutual agreement he allowed her to live with me. Throughout the years I remained solely responsible for her livelihood and for everything concerning her. Nevertheless, the passport authorities refused to allow her to travel without her father's permission. Since he was working in Saudi Arabia as a medical doctor I was unable to obtain an official document from him in time for her departure, and so she missed the opportunity to visit Algeria and participate in the tournament.

Even today, a husband continues to exercise full tutelage over his wife, and she cannot obtain a passport without his permission. In addition, the legal stipulations related to marriage and divorce are couched in terms so ambiguous that they permit husbands to detain their wives from going to work. The usual excuse is the harm caused by the absence of the wife to the smooth running of the household, family affairs, and the rearing of the children. The one who decides such matters, of course, remains the man.

Economic Problems and the Egyptian Woman

The majority of women in Egypt belong to working-class or peasant families and are exhausted by the strain of working outside the home *and* the time taking care of the

---

[3.] Decree Law 44, 1979, published in the *Lawyers Journal,* Nos. 3 and 4.

household and rearing their children. The problems of such women have been aggravated by the "open-door" economic policy practiced since the early 1970's. This policy has led to increased inflation,[4] a rapid escalation of prices, a continued drop in production where the public sector and national industries are concerned, and a flow of consumer goods and luxury items imported from the West which saps already meager resources required for investment in important development projects.

Egyptian working women who go to the market to buy their provisions can no longer find locally produced macaroni or the popular white cheese or cheap soap produced in Egypt. But they can always find expensive shampoos, imported foods and cheeses, and other items mostly out of their budgetary reach. The mass media are replete with advertisements about cosmetics, perfumes, imported articles for house decoration, electrical gadgets and so on—despite the fact that the vast majority of women are no longer able to buy the essentials of everyday life.

With the "open-door" policy, important development projects get pushed into the background and comprehensive plans for the total socioeconomic development of the country get dropped. This has led inevitably to increased (open and masked) unemployment which affects young men and women and recent graduates. Investment companies established during the past years are out for quick profit, and are not prepared to risk the big capital required in substantive developmental projects. Opportunities for employment of young women are the first to decrease—except in certain areas where their sex is considered an asset: hotels, tourism, secretarial work, etc., and where being pretty is the most important quality required. Here a female becomes an object for attracting clients rather than a human being performing a task. As a result of the shrinking market, more and more voices are being raised insisting on a "return of women to the home, where they belong."[5] Yet at one time in the mid-1960's such voices had fallen almost completely silent. Parallel to this development is the attempt to mask the situation by a revival of traditional morality based on religious precepts advocating the need to hold fast to the purity and values of Islam. In sum, we are assailed by the vociferous clamor for a return to Islamic jurisprudence, the veil for girls and women, and segregation of the sexes.

The authorities responsible for these "open-door" policies insist on blaming the disastrous economic situation on the "population explosion," and the growing unemployment on a lack of resources. The Vice-Prime Minister for Economic Affairs in the late 1970's (he who was considered the "brain" behind the new economic policies) stated that "the labor of women is an additional burden to the economy."[6] Thus the women who in the 1960's were encouraged to seek employment outside the home have become, in the late 1970's, a liability to the State.

Other economists—who believe in the independent, self-reliant development of the economy and oppose the "open-door" policy which has led to the subjugation of our national interests to capitalist circles and the giant multinationals—have continued to defend different views, different solutions. To them, we must mobilize our national energies and resources in national production on a planned basis and break with policies that

[4.] According to the estimates of the Central Administration for Mobilization and Statistics, by 1980 the price of fruit had increased 5 1/3 times, that of vegetables 5 times, milk products 4 times, cereals 4 1/3 times since 1967. The price of certain consumer goods increased over 10 times. It is to be noted that official statistics very often do not reflect the real situation. Nevertheless, officially the rate of inflation is estimated at 30 percent per annum.

[5.] *El Akhbar* daily newspaper, July 27, 1981, p. 3; an investigation into the problems of working women.

[6.] *Al Ahram* daily, June 28, 1981, p. 9.

favor foreign interests against those of the country, serve the rich at the expense of the poor, cause increased unemployment, and build up the very atmosphere which permits Islamic fundamentalism to prosper.

Clearly, economic problems have not only made life more difficult for women as a result of inflation, the escalation of prices, and reduced employment opportunities, but have also brought with them a multiplicity of negative influences in the social, moral, and cultural aspects of life. They have reinforced the chains (some of the vital links of which women had succeeded in breaking) and aggravated an already difficult and complex situation.

Women and Population Problem

In the year 1800 the population of Egypt was only 2.5 million. By 1900 it had reached 10 million, and today it has topped the 44 million mark (estimates built on the 1976 census). In 1966 the national program for family planning was launched, aiming at achieving a drop in the crude birth rate from 42 to 24 in 1982. It succeeded only in reducing this rate to 38 per thousand, and the annual increase of Egypt's population therefore has continued to fluctuate around 2.8 percent. The reason for this failure is that concentrating on distributing contraceptives and convincing mothers to reduce the number of births constitutes a hopelessly inadequate program. Among the important influences which must be taken into consideration are those exerted by the socioeconomic situation: how can we forget that infant mortality is still very high (close to 100 per 1000 live births) and that repeated pregnancies are a compensating mechanism; that children and later youths are a source of income and security to families, especially in rural areas and among the poorer urban dwellers; that wives tend to tie their husbands to wedlock by having many children? Over 99 percent of the population is still crowded on 3.5 percent of the total land area. If desert land is cultivated, if the technical revolution in agriculture becomes a fact (on condition that it is coupled with land reform), if industrialization is intensified—then the standard of living and the needs of people can change. Only when women no longer fear divorce, become more equal to men, work outside the home, and develop other interests will they cease to believe in and need repeated births and many children.

Contradiction and struggle are at the heart of societies where people live in dire need, deprived of both justice and freedom. Thus in Egypt we have a situation where the national family-planning program calls on women to seek education and gainful employment outside the home as a means of reducing the birth rate, while other authorities in the economic, cultural, and religious fields advocate a return to the home—since women's labor has become a liability to the State!

Egyptian Women and the Future

Since the death of Anwar Sadat and the nomination of Hosni Mubarak as head of state the new President has concentrated his efforts on the two major problems which face our country: the economic situation and the question of democratic freedom. Yet both these problems cannot adequately be dealt with if the female half of the population remains neglected and unresponsive. Democracy requires that people organize everywhere and work together to change their lives. It requires a free expression of opinion, an examination of options, an exchange of ideas, a continuous debate, and a genuine search for solutions.

Women are a great potential force. They must participate and organize—form their own associations, groups, political parties—and become a real and constructive force. There are still many obstacles which stand in the way, and which hold women back not only in the political but in the economic field. But the future will surely be better than the present, just as the present is an improvement on the past.

The liberation of women is above all based on their capacity to think their own problems through and to link them to the total progress of the society and the world in which they live, to their capacity to develop a political and cultural consciousness. Only then can they become an organized political and cultural *power,* capable of contributing effectively to changing societies based on patriarchy and class, capable of abolishing the values, traditions, and ideas based on discrimination between one human being and another, between men and women.

Nowhere has this aim yet been achieved.

But women have begun the long, hard road to liberation, and everywhere—in all countries—we will continue.

Suggested Further Reading

Abdul, Ibrahim, and Doria Shafik. *Tatawour El Nahda El Nissaiya min Ahd Mohammed Ali Ila Farouk* (Progress of Women's Status from Mohammed Ali to King Farouk in Egypt). Cairo: Al Aadab, 1945.

Farid, Zeinab. *Tatawour Ta'aleem El Bint fi Misr fil Asr El Hadith* (Progress of Women's Education in Contemporary Egypt). Cairo: n.p., 1961.

Khairat, Ahmed. *Markaz El Mara'a Fil Islam* (History of Arab Women at the Beginning of Islam). Cairo: Dar El Maaref, 1975.

Saad, Mohammed Ebn. *El Tabakat El Kobra* (Layer Upon Layer of Greatness). Cairo: Dar El Tahrir, 1970.

El Saadawi, Nawal. *The Hidden Face of Eve.* London: Zed Press, 1980; Boston: Beacon Press, 1982.

Nawal El Saadawi is a medical doctor, novelist, and nonfiction writer on Arab women's problems and their struggle for liberation. She has published six novels, five collections of short stories, five nonfiction books, and numerous articles on women's problems. Her works are widely distributed in the Arab world, and when censorship made it impossible for her to publish in Egypt she shifted to publishing in Beirut. In 1972 she lost her post in the Egyptian Ministry of Health, and in 1981 she was imprisoned in Cairo because of her writings. Her feminist, democratic, and socialist stands, and her writing, have gained her wide recognition in Arab countries and many other parts of the world as well.

EL SALVADOR
(Republic of El Salvador)

Located in Central America, bordered by Honduras to the north and east, the Pacific Ocean to the south, and Guatemala to the west. **Area:** 21,393 sq. km. (8,260 sq. mi.). **Population** (1980): 4,500,000, female 53%. **Capital:** San Salvador.

DEMOGRAPHY. Languages: Spanish (official), Native Indian languages. **Races or Ethnic Groups:** Mestizo 89%, Native Indian 10%, European descent 1%. **Religions:** Roman Catholicism. **Education** (% enrolled in school, 1975): Age 6–11— of all girls 63%, of all boys 62%; age 12– 17—of all girls 49%, of all boys 56%; higher education—in 1977 women were 25% of all students. **Literacy** (1982 est.): 50% total; illiteracy twice as high for women as for men. **Birth Rate** (per 1000 pop., 1975–80): 40. **Death Rate** (per 1000 pop., 1975–80): 7. **Infant Mortality** (per 1000 live births, 1975–80): Female 45, male 56. **Life Expectancy** (1975–80): Female 64 yrs., male 60 yrs.

GOVERNMENT. Current (1983) military junta came to power by coup in 1979. In 1982 a 60-member Constituent Assembly was elected with a right-wing coalition majority.* The opposition Democratic Revolutionary Front (FDR), also a coalition of organizations, is recognized as the representative of the people of El Salvador by the governments of Mexico, Venezuela, France, and Denmark. **Women's Suffrage:** 1946, but with higher age requirement than men; vote on equal terms won in 1950. **Equal Rights:** No legislation. **Women in Government:** None in the governing junta; women comprise 40% of the Revolutionary Council, the leading body of the FDR/FMLN (see HERSTORY); Ana María Gómez was Secretary of Information in the Popular Revolutionary Bloc, but was arrested in 1981. Ana Guadelupe Martinez is a leader of the People's Revolutionary Army and the only woman in the FDR leadership; Mélida Anaya Montes ("Ana María"), a professor and lawyer, was second in command of the Popular Liberation Forces until assassinated by government forces in Nicaragua in 1983.

ECONOMY. Currency: Colón (May 1983: 3.9 = $1 US). **Gross National Product** (1980): $2.7 billion. **Per Capita Income** (1980): $590; 60% of the pop. receives less than $180 per yr. **Women's Wages as a Percentage of Men's** (1980): 40% in agriculture, 78% in industry. **Equal Pay Policy:** None. **Production** (Agricultural/Industrial): Coffee, cotton, livestock, fruits; clothing, textiles, petroleum products. **Women as a Percentage of Labor Force** (1979): 33.4%; **of agricultural force** 17.6% (15% of whom are unpaid family workers); **of industrial force** —no general statistics obtainable (of manufacturing 47%, of whom half are self-employed); **of military** 40% of the commanders in the People's Revolutionary Army are women, as are a large portion of the guerrilla forces and local militias; none in the government forces. **(Employed) Women's Occupational Indicators:** Of teachers 70%, of domestic servants 70% (1982); of administrative/ managerial workers 16%, of clerical workers 40.6%, of professional/technical workers 42.8%, of sales workers 69%, of service workers 73% (1979). Many rural women who migrate to cities become street vendors and face fines and harassment from police. **Unemployment:** No data obtainable.

GYNOGRAPHY. Marriage. *Policy:* According to the Civil Code, a husband owes a wife protection, a wife owes a husband obedience; he has right of decision regarding domicile. Each spouse retains exclusive property rights to anything acquired individually before or during marriage. A married woman under age 18 must be represented by her husband in legal matters. *Practice:* Female mean age

---

* In May 1984, José Napoleón Duarte (Christian Democrat) was elected president in contested elections.

at marriage (1970–78): 19; women age 15–49 in union (1970–78): 57.4%. **Divorce.** *Policy:* Grounds for divorce include pregnancy of wife from illicit relations, adultery by wife, adultery by husband accompanied by public scandal, desertion of wife, attempt against life of one spouse by the other, serious abuse or physical maltreatment, habitual drunkenness, willful desertion for 6 months, attempt to corrupt children or wife, or 1-yr. separation. Mutual-consent divorce is permitted under certain conditions. Custody of children under age 5 goes to the mother unless she was found guilty of adultery. The father receives custody of male children over age 5 unless he is "morally or legally incapacitated." Each spouse receives property acquired individually before or during marriage, and the balance is divided equally. No alimony. Child maintenance is paid if spouse with custody is destitute. *Practice:* Divorces (per 1000 pop., 1978): 0.35 (includes annulments and separations).

Family. *Policy:* Maternity-leave benefits equal 1/2 of wages for 12 weeks if the employed woman has had 12 weeks of employment in the preceding 12 months. No childcare policy. *Practice:* Women employed in manufacturing are often laid off when they become pregnant. Children frequently work alongside their mothers in the market or in the countryside. Daycare facilities are virtually nonexistent for the majority of women in the work force. **Welfare.** *Policy:* Social security system includes workers' compensation and old-age pension for women over age 60 and men over 65 who have worked 750 weeks, and is financed by workers, employers, and the State. Widows' or widowers' pension equals 60% of insured person's earnings; there are "temporary pensions" for widows under 60. *Practice:* No statistics obtainable, but rural women in agriculture are often unpaid family workers and receive no benefits; the same is true for women in the informal labor market—street vendors, market-women, and domestic servants.

Contraception. *Policy:* Government is pro-population reduction and sponsors family-planning programs; sterilization is legal without conditions. *Practice:* Women age 15–49 in union using contraception (1970–80): 34%, of which traditional methods 9%, modern 38%, sterilization 53% (frequently practiced on peasant and working-class women—sometimes with uninformed or no consent); contraceptives are available primarily in the cities. Women still have an average of 6–8 children and often twice as many pregnancies. The Salvador Population Assoc. has 150 family-planning centers, which dispense contraceptives liberally. **Abortion.** *Policy:* Legal only to save the life of the woman, in case of grave deformity of the fetus, or pregnancy as a result of rape. Other procedures are punishable under the Penal Code by 1–3 yrs. imprisonment for the woman and 2–4 yrs. for the practitioner. If the woman can claim that the procedure was necessary to "save her honor," the penalty may be less severe. *Practice:* Abortion is common. Approx. 20% of all El Salvadoran women have reportedly had abortions. **Illegitimacy.** *Policy:* The Constitution stipulates that children born out of wedlock shall have equal rights to education, assistance, and parental care. Unless a man voluntarily acknowledges paternity, a woman must rely on the court to declare him the father. *Practice:* No statistics obtainable, but there is a high incidence of single mothers. **Homosexuality.** *Policy:* Homosexual acts between men, or those performed with a minor, are considered a crime against the public morals. No specific mention of women. *Practice:* No statistics obtainable; both the "official culture" and the "revolutionary culture" reportedly express extreme negativity to same-sex preference.

Incest. *Policy:* Sexual relations between siblings or ascendant and descendant relatives of any age are punishable by 3 yrs. imprisonment. *Practice:* No data obtainable. **Sexual Harassment.** *Policy:* None. *Practice:* No statistics obtainable, but women working as domestic servants commonly face abuse from male employers, and are then fired if they become pregnant, as do women working in factories (90% of which are foreign-owned multinationals in the free trade zones). **Rape.** *Policy:* Considered a crime "if rapist uses force," if victim is without reason or sanity or under age 12; punishable by up to 9 yrs. imprisonment. Marital rape is not recognized as a legal concept. *Practice:* No statistics obtainable. Rape, and torture of female political prisoners by the introduction of rodents into their vaginas, has been reported. **Battery.** *Policy:* Husbands who abuse wives, are subject to a fine and 21 days imprisonment. *Practice:* No data obtainable. **Prostitution.** *Policy:* Illegal. No further data obtainable. *Practice:* No statistics obtainable, but many rural women who migrate to the cities for work turn to prostitution as a last resort. **Traditional/Cultural Practices.** *Policy:* None. *Practice:* By some reports, an old peasant custom is to carve a cross with a razor blade on the clitoris of a newborn female, so that later "she will work harder and stay away from men." **Crisis Centers:** No data obtainable.

HERSTORY. Women always have played a role in popular political El Salvadoran movements. In 1922 market women led a mass protest against the Melendez government, demanding freedom for political prisoners. Women organized part of the peasant insurrection for land reform in 1932—a revolt which the government suppressed, killing 30,000 people, largely Native Indians. In 1944 women were active in the Brazos Caídos strike which helped depose Gen. Martinez. In the 1940's Rosa Ochoa, one of the first women's movement activists, began to organize women of all classes against discrimination at the job and in the family. Her work evolved into the Sisterhood of Salvadoran Women, which in the 1960's focused on literacy programs for rural women and campaigned successfully to remove the President, Col. Lemus, from power. Many women from this movement became pioneers in the trade-union movements of teachers and bakers. ANDES, the militant teachers' union begun in the 1960's, has an 85% female membership.

In 1970 rural women workers joined mass organizations on a large scale to combat government repression. In 1977 women created the Committee of Mothers of Political Prisoners and the Committee for the Liberty of Political Prisoners and the Disappeared. That same year, the Frente Femenino (Women's Front) was formed; it is now an 150,000-member national organization spanning classes from market-women to middle-class, professional women, and works to promote democratic elections. In 1979 AMES (see following article) was founded and began to incorporate women from all sectors of society, including housewives, into the liberation movement. Azutramez, an organization of women market vendors, successfully organized strikes in 1980. On Dec. 4, 1980, 4 US Roman Catholic nuns active in the insurgent revolutionary movement were killed by government forces. As the conflict between government troops (aided by US advisers and paramilitary troops from Honduras) and popular forces has intensified, growing numbers of women have joined the ranks of the Democratic Federal Front and the National Military Liberation Front. The current (1983) number of displaced Salvadorans is more than 20% of the entire population (500,000 displaced internally, 330,000 as refugees in other countries); the majority are women and children.

In Mar. 1983 Marianela García Villas was assassinated; she, together with María Magdalena Henriquez (killed in 1980) had co-founded the human rights group Comisión de Derechos Humanos de El Salvador.

MYTHOGRAPHY. A creation legend common to the indigenous peoples is that the moon, a white goddess, came down and built a great palace. A triangular stone was placed in the center of the palace, as her talisman weapon against all enemies. Although a virgin, she bore 3 children, and divided her realm (the world) among them when she grew old. As her death came near, she had her bed carried to the highest tower in the palace; when she died, an exquisite great bird ascended to the heavens again.

EL SALVADOR: "We Cannot Wait . . ."
by the Association of Salvadoran Women*
(Translated by Bobbye Ortiz)

Traditionally the mode of development of the Latin American economies has been structured around the production of raw materials and oriented toward satisfying the demands of the foreign market and the interests of the bourgeoisie. Concomitant with this was high concentration of income, large foreign debt, inflation, and military dictatorship. Permanent economic, political, and social crisis is therefore characteristic of the great majority of the countries of the continent; and in its wake, poverty, super-exploitation, and repression.

Latin American women, who face double oppression, have not been exempt from this dramatic reality. Although the principal source of our subjection is capitalism, even before its advent feudal society had already assigned a subordinate role to women. The oppression of women is a suffocating cultural heritage, and, as Simone de Beauvoir has pointed out, "One is not born, but rather learns to be, a woman." We Latin American women have undoubtedly been learning: learning *not* to be accomplices of the myth of Cinderella, who waited for Prince Charming to free her from misery and convert her into the happy mother of numerous little princes; learning to take to the streets to fight for the elimination of poverty; learning to be active protagonists in the forging of our social destiny.

To be a member of the working class is not the same as being a member of the upper class; to be a North American or a European is not the same as being a Chilean or a Salvadoran. . . . For women of low-income sectors, joining the labor force is linked with a survival strategy similar to that of men of the same class and obeying the same necessities. However, for the women of the middle and higher strata, incorporation into production is determined by the number and age of their children, by their level of education, by the gap between the family wage and their consumer expectations.

There are also differences arising from the degree of development of a region, or from the pattern of urban and rural zones. Our struggle as Latin American women is different from that of women in developed countries. Like us, the latter play a fundamental role as reproducers of labor power and ideology, but . . . while in the developed countries there is a struggle for contraception and abortion, in Latin America we must also fight against forced sterilization and certain birth-control projects agreed to under pressure from the United States. For us, it is not a question of demanding such collective services as day-care centers or laundries, but rather of demanding general community services: water, light, housing, and health care.

Our "double day" has another dimension which converts "wages for housework" into

* This is an excerpted translation of a paper presented by a representative of AMES (Association of Salvadoran Women) at the First Latin American Research Seminar on women in San José, Costa Rica in Nov. 1981, and printed in the June 1982 issue of *Monthly Review*. AMES is an affiliate of the FDR (Democratic Revolutionary Front), the coalition of parties and popular organizations which together with the Farabundo Martí National Liberation Front (FMLN) leads the struggle for national liberation in El Salvador. The full paper from which the following article is excerpted is available from WIRE (Women's International Resource Exchange), 2700 Broadway, New York, NY 10025.

a remote goal; our short-term goals are related to employment and job opportunities, to the exploitation of the principal wage earner, and the impossibility of survival with starvation wages. It makes no sense to struggle against the consumerism of one part of society if we are faced with poverty and the impossibility of consuming. . . .

In sum, we are fighting for a thoroughgoing change which will include women in the production process, which will free both women and men from exploitation and poverty. At the same time the search for solutions to the specific problems of women must not be neglected.

Invisible Work

Man's work in capitalist society is carried out at the cost of women's work within the home, which saves him the extra hours required for the reproduction of his labor power: hence the higher level of masculine skill and the male monopoly of political power. Both factors are characteristic of class society and are due to an enormous amount of invisible labor done by women and appropriated by men through the mechanism of the family as an economic unit. . . .

In other words, the fundamental aspect of women's problem, exploitation, is the direct result of capitalist relations of production. However, there exists another dimension, *oppression,* which is useful to the system and whose cultural and social roots go back to the dawn of civilization: female subordination to the male and the division of labor (along gender lines), which pre-date capitalist society. They are found in most societies known to the history of humanity. So we can conclude that the problem of women is a fundamental social and cultural reality.

In the 19th century, socialist thinkers assumed that the cause of women was identical with the cause of the working class. Although these thinkers acknowledged that women's subordination pre-dated capitalism, they thought that the abolition of that social system would simultaneously abolish both workers' exploitation and commercialized human relations, freeing women from economic dependence on men and consequently from subordination. However, we think that to achieve our total emancipation such a change is a necessary—but not sufficient—condition.

It is indispensable that we also transform the ideological superstructures that perpetuate a male-female relationship based on domination-subjection and reproduced fundamentally in the family. The family nucleus is the locus where models and values useful to the system are transmitted through the sexual division of labor; on the legal level, through inheritance through the male line; on the economic level, as a unit of production and consumption and a mediator between needs and resources; and on the social plane, by relegating women to the "private" domestic sphere and hampering our social and political participation. . . .

We are conscious of the fact that the alleged separation beween the "private" and the "public" is merely a sophism. The private is directly political because patriarchal ideology permeates the individual lives of men and women. It is important to recognize the link between the two areas and understand that although women will not be liberated without a change in society, it is equally true that there can be no genuine social transformation without women's emancipation. . . .

Changes That Don't Change Anything

There is a daily growing contingent of women who question our passive role, the defense of the status quo, and our being distanced from political activity on our continent; there is a daily growing number of women who question why we work as much as eighty hours a week on the "double shift," which prevents us from participating in the social process and in decision-making.

In the light of this situation, many ruling regimes promulgate paternalistic legislation which establishes "equality before the law," even "no sex discrimination," including certain measures in favor of mothers and children. These are formal measures which do not affect the daily reality of the great majority of people. Such is the case with education, access to which is limited for the majority of both men and women of the lower classes, but especially women. Six out of ten Salvadorans are illiterate; well over half are women. In the cities twice as many women as men are illiterate.

In order to avert the threat of a genuine change in the specific role of women and our active participation in the liberation processes which would follow upon a massive increase of female consciousness, many governments have promoted modernist or developmental solutions. They point to the betterment of general living conditions in capitalist countries and to the introduction of new technology; they claim that this economic prosperity offers women the possibility of participating in the labor market and, consequently, of having "access to and participation in social life."

These seductive conceptions of women's liberation . . . provide a basis for exalting the role of women within the family as an institution which creates consensus and continuity of a culture, and which is an outgrowth of the capitalist system—*macho,* repressive, and based on the commercialization of human relations.

We think that the integration of women into capitalist society . . . does not constitute liberation. . . . Nor can our problem be solved by the "insertion" (the very word implies passivity) of women into such a system, without our full participation as subject, not object. . . . To postulate our insertion into development, without determining what kind of development, resolves nothing.

First Steps Toward Liberation

The struggle of Latin American women to transcend the domestic takes place on several levels. . . .

The condition of the *mujer del pueblo* [literally, woman of the people] on our continent during the last decade has been affected in two different ways. In terms of repression, thousands of women have been harassed and tortured, and have disappeared or been assassinated by the dictatorships. We have also been affected in our specific roles as mother, wife, or daughter of an unemployed, persecuted, or assassinated man. We have had to face the sudden destruction of our families and the need to find a way to manage without our *compañeros,* who had frequently been the only wage earners in the household.

Then, as a result of the unpopular economic policies of the dictatorships, we women began to organize in *frentes*—of shantytown dwellers and housewives affected by economic, social, and political repression; of factory workers, peasants, and professionals who organized to defend the gains won through long years of struggle. The *frentista* format has become one of the principal responses utilized by Latin American women for dealing with specific demands. . . .

When the domestic realm is altered from the outside, Latin American women come out of their homes and take to the streets. In strikes of miners, industrial workers, and building workers, women have pounded at the doors of ministries and parliaments, pressured the authorities and employers to demand wage increases or jobs for their male family members, or to demand their release from prison. . . . That is to say, their demands are not their own, but are rather familial. . . . Historically, however, both the strength and the weakness of such movements have resided in their spontaneity. Arising as support groups for male struggles, many of these groups dissolve when the conflicts that gave rise to them are ended; when husbands, fathers, sons, return to center stage, we women retreat to our homes, leaving to the men, once again, the sphere of public activity.

Perhaps that is why in Latin American history threats to traditional roles have frequently been converted into factors of women's mobilization. However, many of us, as a result of this experience, have recognized the implications of this dynamic, which opens up a terrain bordering on the political and gives to us objective possibilities of losing the "fear of power," of transcending our traditional condition, of beginning to open up our political space.

The Difficult Task of Being Members of an Organized Movement

If men have, for centuries, devoted themselves to political work and fulfilled themselves in it, it is because they have always had the support of one or several women who have provided them with children, affection, domestic services; to these women are diverted all psychological tensions, freeing men from the problems of domestic life.

We women do not have such support systems available to us, and in order to utilize our intellectual potential must organize ourselves so that the private sphere does not interfere with our specific political work. It is indeed dramatic to organize ourselves physically and psychologically to exercise this role without experiencing guilt vis à vis the "neglected" roles of mother and wife which relegate us to the domestic sphere.

For a woman to be active in sociopolitical organizations implies the assumption of a definitive commitment, a commitment which, she feels, will have repercussions on her activities as woman, wife, mother, and, in some cases, as paid worker. This situation is aggravated by the fact that until now it has not appeared that men have the intention of truly assuming some of the responsibility which for centuries has been delegated to women, . . . to raise their consciousness concerning the privileges conveyed by masculinity and to relinquish their role as the star members of the cast, becoming instead comrades who share daily life and struggle. . . .

The parties and movements of the democratic Left have, in general, not dealt with the problems of women with the same consistency with which they confront other social problems. Their pronouncements in this regard are limited to the realm of class struggle and thus appear to be detached from political discourse. . . . Women's liberation . . . is, for the moment, conceived of as technical and private, becoming collective and social only *after* the exploited sectors have won their liberation, that is to say, in some distant and unpredictable future. . . . A change in the relations of production is advocated, but not in the relations of reproduction; society is to be overturned economically and ideologically, but nothing is said of changes in the family, the sphere not only of consumption but of reproduction of labor power. . . .

Will the people's organizations be capable of focusing on the specifics of daily life, or will they leave this to the mercy of the dominant ideology? . . .

Participation of Women in the Process of National Liberation

The political-military organizations currently offering a new alternative for people's struggle . . . arose early in the 1970's. At the beginning, women's participation was minimal, limited primarily to students and teachers. But with the advent of revolutionary peasant-workers' organizations, peasant women have also joined the struggle in large numbers. Children are participating together with their parents, since they also experience exploitation and repression.

In the mid-1970's, the mass struggle reached new, qualitatively higher, levels of struggle; there were qualitative leaps in respect to combativity, and there was an acceleration in the process of self-defense in mass political actions. Salvadoran women are participating in diverse and exemplary ways—in tasks of agitation, propaganda, and organization, as well as in the military struggle of our people.

In 1977, organizations arose, composed primarily of women, which demanded the freedom of the many captured and disappeared prisoners taken by the government. . . . At the same time the class struggle, which had been characterized by legalistic thinking since 1967, underwent a transformation. With the advent of the revolutionary trade-union movement, women workers also joined the struggle.

In 1978 the first steps were taken toward forming the organization that was to become AMES (the Association of Salvadoran Women) as a way of incorporating into political life those sectors of women (housewives, professionals, teachers, secretaries, shantytown dwellers, students, etc.) who, because of their special circumstances, had not yet joined the people's struggle. The year 1978 saw also the organizing of market and street vendors. AUTRAMES (the Association of Market Vendors and Workers) and the Luz Dillian Arévalo Coordinating Committee of Market Vendors led spirited struggles, occupying markets and demonstrating. . . .

Salvadoran women also have been joining mass organizations which today form part of the Democratic Revolutionary Front (FDR). Concurrently women have been joining the political-military organizations and armed units of the people. Thousands of women fight with weapons in the militia, the guerrilla forces, and the popular army of liberation, participating at the rank-and-file level and in the leadership.

Our revolutionary struggle is a political and military war of the entire people against a minority supported by US imperialism. Salvadoran women constitute half the population and we are participating in this effort on a massive scale. . . .

We think that in a revolutionary organization there can be no contradictions between professed ideas and behavior. There must be consistency between the choices made, the values affirmed, and daily life—with no exceptions, no ambiguity.

No real change in society is ever brought about painlessly, nor will the problem of women's organized participation be resolved by the insertion of stipulated quotas of women in the leadership. It is necessary to face seriously and self-critically the male-female relationship with all its implications and to understand the gravity of our exclusion from, or relegation to a minor role in, the process of change. We constitute half of humanity and we constitute an objectively exploited and oppressed social group with enormous revolutionary potential.

Keeping clearly in mind that the struggle for women's liberation must be immersed in the struggle for the liberation of our peoples, it is also necessary to point out that we women are a group defined by our own conditions and specific demands and that we cannot wait for socialism or a change of structures to solve tomorrow the very problems that are today the source of our limitations, of our backwardness as integral human beings, as agents of change.

A woman's conscious decision to join in organized struggle implies a transition much longer and more arduous than that of men, inasmuch as we must overcome an endless number of hurdles. If we evaluate these hurdles, we see that, qualitatively speaking, a dual leap has been taken. Obviously this does not mean that we have solved our specific problems of "being women," nor is organized participation a panacea that will permit us to achieve our full identity. However, we think that the hallmark of revolutionary feminism is that it locates itself within a context of total transformation of society. We also know that the liberation of women requires a level of generalized collective consciousness which is the result of a development of a new ideology. And that new ideology must be the result of a project for a new structuring of society—a society without private property and without exploitation of one human being by another.

Suggested Further Reading
[See Bibliography.—Ed.]

FINLAND
(Republic of Finland)

Located on the Scandinavian peninsula, bordered by Norway to the north, the USSR to the east, the Gulf of Finland to the south, and Sweden and the Gulf of Bothnia to the west. **Area:** 337,009 sq. km. (130,119 sq. mi.). **Population** (1980): 4,774,000, female 52%. **Capital:** Helsinki.

DEMOGRAPHY. Languages: Finnish, Swedish (first and second official, respectively), Lappish. **Races or Ethnic Groups:** Finn, Swedish, Lapp, other. **Religions:** Lutheran 93%, Greek Orthodox 1%, other. **Education** (% enrolled in school, 1975): Age 6–11—of all girls 90%, of all boys 86%; age 12–17—of all girls 87%, of all boys 82%; higher education—in 1980 women earned 48.9% of vocational education degrees broken down as follows: 92.3% of humanities and fine and applied arts, 92.3% of nursing, 74.3% of commerce and office work, 67.3% of teacher education, 48.3% of general education, 15.2% of industrial trades and engineering; women also earned 54% of masters' degrees, 22.9% of licentiates, and 23.7% of doctoral degrees. **Literacy** (1977): Women 100%, men 100%. **Birth Rate** (per 1000 pop., 1977–78): 14. **Death Rate** (per 1000 pop., 1977–78): 9. **Infant Mortality** (per 1000 live births, 1981): Female 6.5, slightly lower than male. **Life Expectancy** (1975–80): Female 76 yrs., male 68 yrs.

GOVERNMENT. The president is head of state and appoints a cabinet which is headed by the prime minister (head of government). Legislative power resides in the elected 200-member unicameral Eduskunta (parliament). **Women's Suffrage:** 1906; Finland was the second country in the world to grant women's suffrage, and the first country to elect women to parliament (1907). **Equal Rights:** The Constitution (Art. 5) states, "All Finnish citizens shall be equal before the law." **Women in Government:** Approx. 60 women are members of Parliament, and 3 women are cabinet ministers (1983).

ECONOMY. Currency: Markka (May 1983: 5.45 = $1 US). **Gross National Product** (1980): $47.3 billion. **Per Capita Income** (1980): $9720. **Women's Wages as a Percentage of Men's:** 61% (1981); 75% in industry (1977–80). **Equal Pay Policy:** Legislation is currently (1983) pending. **Production** (Agricultural/Industrial): Grains, potatoes; machinery, textiles, paper and other forest products. **Women as a Percentage of Labor Force** (1980): 47.1%; **of agricultural force** 40.7% (20.4% of which are unpaid family workers); **of industrial force**—no general statistics obtainable (of manufacturing 36.3%); **of military** (1975) 1.3%. **(Employed) Women's Occupational Indicators:** Of executive positions in the private sector 4%, and public sector 10%, of lawyers 15%, of dentists 70% (1977–78); of physicists 5.1%, of physicians 29.5%, of textile workers 76.6%, of social workers 77.4%, of clerical workers 94%, of nurses 98% (1975). **Unemployment** (first quarter, 1982): 7%, female 6.5%, male 7.3%.

GYNOGRAPHY. Marriage. *Policy:* The minimum marriage age is 17 for females with parental consent, and 18 for both without parental consent. Marriage is based on the concept of spousal equality and the right to own individual property. *Practice:* Female mean age at marriage (1970–78): 23; women age 15–49 in union (1970–78): 60%; marriages (per 1000 pop., 1979): 6.5. **Divorce.** *Policy:* Legal. Divorce is granted upon joint petition if the couple has lived separately for 2 yrs. Other grounds include adultery, desertion for 1 yr., venereal disease, attempted homicide or grave bodily harm caused by 1 spouse, imprisonment of a spouse for a minimum of 3 yrs., drug addiction, insanity, or 3-yr. absence if there is no reason to believe spouse is alive. A judicial separation releases the spouses from married life, but does not dissolve the legal bond. After divorce, property is divided according to individual ownership; joint property is divided to compensate both partners equally. Custody of children is determined by the court. *Practice:* Divorces (per 1000 pop., 1979): 2.14. In Helsinki, 25% of marriages ended in divorce (1978). Women-initiated divorces are increasing.

Family. *Policy:* Women are entitled to an 11-month maternity leave and an allowance, paid by the State, regardless of employment. Plans for 1982 included a 100-day paternity allowance, and a parental leave which can be divided after the child is 4 months old. A family allowance is paid on the birth of the first child; the amount increases up to the fourth child, with larger allowances paid for children under age 3. The 1973 Day Care Act stipulates a place for all children who need services; the Act included a 5-yr. plan to develop day-care centers; municipalities are required by law to provide adequate care and receive State aid to do so. Single-parent families are given priority in obtaining day care. Parents pay sliding-scale fees for day-care centers and for care in private homes. *Practice:* A maternal and childcare clinic has been established in every municipality. In 1981, 76% of women with children under school age were employed; single-parent families were 15% of all families, and 90% of these were headed by women. The Council for Equality Between Men and Women reported that women do twice as much housework as men, regardless of employment, and that girls do twice as much as boys (1981). In 1977 only 43.2% of the demand for day care was filled. **Welfare.** *Policy:* Social security is comprised of 3 sections: social insurance, transfer of income, and social welfare. Social insurance includes benefits for sickness, employee accidents, disability, unemployment, and old age. Pensions for employees are based on income and length of employment (1962 Employee Pension Act); persons over age 65 who have not been employed receive pensions from the Social Insurance Institute. Income transfers include maternity and children allowances (see **Family**), and payments to families of the conscripts. Social welfare covers individuals in extreme need, regardless of employment. *Practice:* In 1977 social expenditure accounted for 1/5 of the GNP. No further data obtainable.

Contraception. *Policy:* Legal. In the 1970's the government supported a policy to reduce "unwanted" births through family-planning education and an increase in contraceptive availability. However, government concern over the low birth rate also resulted in an official pro-natalist policy. Family-planning counseling and contraceptive devices are still available in public and private clinics. *Practice:* Women under age 45 in union using contraceptives (1977): 80%; methods used (1977) condom 40%, IUD 36%, pill 14%, female sterilization 5%, withdrawal 3%, diaphragm 1%, male sterilization 1%, rhythm 1%; using inefficient methods 4%. **Abortion.** *Policy:* Abortion was legalized after WWII and the law was liberalized in 1970. A 1978 amendment lowered the limit on abortion from the first 16 weeks to the first 12 weeks of pregnancy, in conjunction with the new government policy. Requests for abortion must be approved by 2 physicians or the State Medical Board. *Practice:* Abortions (per 1000 women age 15–44, 1981): 11.9; abortions (per 1000 known pregnancies, 1981): 170. The rate of abortions has been declining since 1974. Requests for the procedure are rarely refused. **Illegitimacy.** *Policy:* Under the law, out-of-wedlock children receive equal treatment. If paternity is confirmed, a legal kinship is created between the child and the father, and the father's heirs (1975 Paternity Act); the child is entitled to maintenance from the father until age 18 and becomes his heir. A mother has custody unless otherwise decided by the court. *Practice:* In 1979, 11.4% of live births were out-of-wedlock. In Helsinki, the rate of out-of-wedlock births doubled from 1968 to 1978, reflecting a change in attitudes regarding the family and marriage. **Homosexuality.** *Policy:* Legal for both women and men since 1971. Publicly instigating the commission of a homosexual act is punishable by a fine or a maximum 6 months imprisonment. *Practice:* There are several organizations, including the Organization for Sexual Equality (SETA, founded in 1973), which has both female and male members, and an autonomous lesbian group, Akanat, which publishes the magazine *Torajyva.* In 1981 lesbian women and homosexual men protested a law that prohibits any "propaganda" or incitement to homosexuality.

Incest. *Policy:* Sexual intercourse between a parent and a child is punishable by a maximum 4 yrs. imprisonment; sexual intercourse between siblings by a maximum 2 yrs. Sexual relations between other relatives, as between an uncle and a niece, are not penalized. *Practice:* No data obtainable. **Sexual Harassment.** *Policy:* No specific policy, but may be considered a crime under sections of the Penal Code that cover taking advantage of a person's position of dependence or "distressed situation" for sexual purposes; the perpetrator may be subject to same punishment imposed for rape. *Practice:* No data obtainable. **Rape.** *Policy:* Illegal. Sexual intercourse by force or threat of bodily harm is punishable by a maximum 10 yrs. imprisonment. Attempted rape is also punishable. Marital rape is not recognized but may be prosecuted as assault and battery. *Practice:* In 1980 there were 367 reported rapes, a rate of 10.9 per 100,000 pop. **Battery.** *Policy:* Legislation regarding wife-beating is pending in Parliament (1983). *Practice:* No data obtainable. **Prostitution.** *Policy:* Prostitution is not illegal. Procurement of women for the purpose of prostitution is a felony and punishable by a maximum 4 yrs. imprisonment. *Practice:* No data obtainable. **Traditional/Cultural Practices:** No data obtainable. **Crisis Centers.** *Policy:* No data obtainable. *Practice:* Refuges for battered women have been established in some cities.

HERSTORY. Tacitus described the early Finns (the Feuni Tribe) as being nomadic peoples, whose women as well as men were skilled hunters. As Finland became an agrarian society, labor was divided into women's tasks and men's tasks. This division led to legislation that benefited men as the farmers and discriminated against women. Property laws gave men title to the farm lands and inheritance laws gave sons twice as much as daughters in dividing family estates. In eastern Finland daughters were not permitted to inherit until 1878 (less than 15% of Finland's farm holdings are owned by women even today).

Suffrage was the first issue around which women began to organize, in the late 1800's. Unioni, one of the largest and first women's organizations, was a leader in the fight for electoral rights. Lucina Hagman (1853–1946) was a pioneer in coeducation; Miina Sillanpää (1866–1952) began by working as a housemaid, but she eventually ran for and won a seat in Parliament, where her focus was on legislation to improve the status of domestic servants and to help single mothers; Wivi Lönn (1872–1966) was the first woman architect in Finland; Laimi Leidenius (1877–1938) was the first woman to be appointed full professor at Helsinki University and the first president of the Finnish Federation of University Women. In 1906 women's right to vote was won and 1 year later 19 women were elected to Parliament. The first woman cabinet minister (Miina Sillanpää) was appointed in 1926.

The contemporary women's movement, which began in the 1970's, is small and centered in Helsinki. Unioni is the oldest and largest organization. Members focus on women's right to work, to take part in decision-making, and to have quality childcare. Feministerna is a newer, smaller, and more radical-feminist group. Women for Peace in Finland is a sizeable movement for disarmament.

Helvi Sipilä was appointed Asst. Secretary General to the UN in 1972. She was the first woman to hold such a high UN post and subsequently became Asst. Secretary General for Social Development and Humanitarian Affairs.

The Finnish Council for Equality Between Men and Women, which functions as a consulting organ, was established in 1972. Finnish women continue to be active in politics (see following article), and in the peace and antinuclear movements.

MYTHOGRAPHY. The *Kalevala,* the great Finnish epic poem, as well as a collection of chants called *Magic Songs,* provide fragments of ancient Finnish lore that emphasizes goddess worship. Maa Ema was the Earth Goddess of the peoples of Estonia; the Votyaks of Siberia knew her as Muzjem Mumi. Ilmatar (Sky Mother or Water Mother, as she is referred to in *Kalevala)* had created the earth as she moved about in the ocean. Mielikki, goddess of the forest, is the protector of animals, especially the sacred bear. The Forest Mother, Rauni, was represented by the rowan tree, whose orange berries were used by women during childbirth. The rowan (also known as the mountain ash) was sacred to those rituals celebrated on Rowan Witch Day, May 1, of each year. Goddess images were also revered as Divine Mother, Queen of the Witches, and Queen of the Elves.

FINLAND: The Right to Be Oneself
by Hilkka Pietilä

Yesterday I was present at the most powerful gathering in Finland, the country's economic elite coming together at their annual meeting to review and foresee the nation's economic prospects. The composition of the invitees was typical, about 350 men and 15 women. Many of the women were there more or less by chance, like myself—not because they fit the subtle qualifications of holding economic power.

One of the gentlemen, rector of a university, called for us in Finland to follow the Japanese model, where research and development resources permit every second male to obtain academic training. Somehow he omitted that in Finland almost *half* of the *whole* generation—not only of the males—nowadays obtains the examination which qualifies for academic studies. The difference is that *in Finland two thirds of the students are women*, i.e., only every *third* male youth obtains this qualification. Among young women, two of every three becomes qualified. But that doesn't seem to count—or maybe that is exactly the point!

The picture reflected the situation of women in Finland: we run the society as laborers in industry and administration, as low-paid nurses in such welfare institutions as child-care centers, hospitals, health centers, and homes for the aged, as mothers and wives in families—but we are not present among those who set the goals for the society's development and thereby decide the material setting of our lives.

This picture is typical for technologically and materially well-developed countries. The rules of the game in the public family, i.e., in the economic and political arena of society, are formulated according to the visions of men. Women shuttle between the private family, the home, and the public family—and work as servants in both.

Finland could stand as a perfect illustration of how industrial development in the form it has taken in market-economy countries can in fact *obstruct* the possibilities for women to make a genuine female impact on the development of society and culture, even where they are formally rather well represented in economic and political life.

Political Rights

Finland was the second country in the world (after New Zealand) to give political rights to women (1906) and the first country where women were elected to a parliament (1907). In Finland women were given both political rights—the voting franchise *and* electoral eligibility, at the same time; this differed from many other countries—New Zealand, for example, where eligibility was given later. The degree of the political participation of women in those years was demonstrated by the fact that in the first parliament in Finland there already were 9.5 percent women, 19 of 200 members—a ratio which, in most countries using the British parliamentary system, has not yet been achieved even today. The effect of the forces of obstruction, on the other hand, can be demonstrated by the fact that today the proportion of women in the Finnish parliament still is not more than 26 percent.

Economic Rights

The story of women's economic participation in Finland is equally pioneering and impressive. For example, in Helsinki, the capital, 55 percent of all women of working age already were employed in the year 1900. This, however, must be viewed in relation to the fact that in traditional agrarian societies women are always economically active—although it usually is not recognized in the statistics. Thus the economic activity of women is not a phenomenon first appearing within the process of industrialization and urbanization. The specific characteristic of Finland in this respect is that women were economically active very early in urban areas as well as rural ones.

The number of working women in cities has been partly explained by the fairly high proportion of single women—i.e., the low marriage rate in Finland through the decades. Finnish women have not relied on marriage as the means of livelihood in cities to the same degree as women in many other countries. Neither did the economic activity of women decrease in Finland in certain phases of industrialization, as it did in many countries due to increased male wages and a promulgated and consequently desired pattern of family life which implied that the wife stayed home and provided services for the man and children. The proportion of genuinely bourgeois families—the classic middle class, with a typical housewife role for women—was never high in Finland and did not have as much impact on social patterns as it did in many other European countries.

Education

The history of Finnish girls in education stands in marked contrast to many other countries. In my grandparents' family in a remote farming village of Finland in the 1920's, it was the youngest daughters who went to secondary school, not the boys. The boys were badly needed to work on the farm. But as there were about ten children, some of the daughters could as well be in school, especially since there was enough female labor on the farm anyway.

This example was not unusual. Already in the school year 1910–11, 50.6 percent of secondary-school pupils were girls, and the proportion has slowly increased ever since. In the 1930's it was over 54 percent, went down to under 53 percent during the economic recession, but rose to 57 percent in the first years of peace after World War II in 1945–46. The proportion of girls among student examinees was 52.6 percent in 1947 and has increased steadily to almost two thirds, 63.8 percent, in 1981, as I mentioned above.

So, Are There Any Problems with Women in Finland?

Women seem to have received all the opportunities in Finland very early. What are the problems then? Are there any?

Yes, there are, many. Some are easy to define: inequality of wages, difficulties of promotion in working life, inadequate social security as a housewife, discrimination in employment due to actual or potential motherhood, double burden of paid labor and housekeeping, etc. But why do these problems still exist even though women seemingly have had both political and economic opportunities to influence the society? This is the crucial question.

If we look back on the women's liberation movement in Finland (or in most other countries), we find the following stages:

The first stage is the struggle for the right to education, access to all forms and levels of schooling. This was achieved in Finland early and substantially.

The second stage is the right to a profession and to remunerative employment. This also was reached early in Finland, but often at the price of not having a family. Most working women in the early decades were not married.

The third stage is the right to both remunerative work *and* family—as men always have had. This is being achieved lately, but on condition that the woman manage the family duties as well—at the cost of double work *and* discrimination in employment due, in turn, to the double burden.

And wasn't this all gained anyway on terms which already were decided before we came in? By those who already had all these rights? By those who never became pregnant, never fed anybody with their breasts, never left their heart behind with a sick child when coming to a job? Never had unwashed dishes and clothes or an untidy house waiting for them at home? Never even thought through the human implications of the production they ran, but only its productivity and profit capacity?

Therefore these pre-set conditions were unfit for us as women. Therefore we found many things very strange. Like the ever-growing competition in status and salaries, the insidious race for power and higher positions. Like indiscriminate mechanization even in the treatment of human beings, a subdivision of labor at the cost of human capabilities. And therefore the struggle for equality has not brought us the opportunities to realize ourselves as full human beings.

The Swedish sociologist Rita Liljeström* has said it precisely in her book *Kultur och arbete (Culture and Work)*:

If industrial capitalism's first historical offense was to sever hand and brain, theory and practice, intellectual and manual, its second is no less serious: here reason dispels feeling, brain and heart are disengaged, two knowledge processes are kept from fertilizing each other. And at accelerated speed we are heading for a separation of hand and heart, a disintegration of qualifications. We organize and divide labor so that systematically it destroys and squanders the most valuable combinations of human life resources.

Now it is time for *the fourth stage* in the struggle: *To gain the right to be an indigenous female human being and to be recognized as an equal member in the human family—both private and public—on one's own terms.* From the point of view of the prevailing economic and political systems this will imply virtually a revolution, a revolution in values and attitudes, a reconstruction of the basic patterns of production and the basic structures of the entire society.

How to Find Ourselves

But before we can launch that struggle we have to recognize ourselves, to discover our own nature as female human beings, genuinely and profoundly. Aren't we then aware of ourselves? If not, why not?

Most of Western science, history, philosophy, theology, economics, technology, social science, and even human science (psychology, for instance) reflects male thinking, images, and values. These have been developed by men for centuries and have grown to dominate the whole of Western culture. They represent, however, the visions and experience of only half of humankind, although they have been put forward as the full picture, the whole and only truth of life and society. Male thinking has defined *us,* ourselves, has told us who we are as women and how we are.

Therefore we are confused. What we have been taught doesn't seem to fit. Now we

* Rita Liljeström is the Swedish Contributor to this anthology. See her article on women in Sweden on p. 662.—Ed.

actually dare to realize that it really does *not* fit. This is the beginning of change. But we have a long way to go and very few signposts. The nature of our societies themselves—the schools, the academic studies, the economy, the politics—imposes an image of women which is not our own. They program us to adapt rather than allowing us to be ourselves. They transform a female child into a male woman, mentally and intellectually if not physically and emotionally. This transformation is all the more profound the higher the education we receive and the more successfully we perform in a male society. On the other hand, the entertainment, social life, and general expectations of men amplify the physical sexuality and emotionality of women to a distorted degree. In work and public life women are expected to be like males; in private life like (sometimes excessively) sensual and sexual creatures. There is no space for women to be themselves as *distinct and dignified female human beings.*

This is the greatest problem for women in industrialized countries; it is the primary obstacle to more humane development in these countries altogether: it obstructs women from emerging into society and it blocks our influence in development. At these cross-roads, we must decide whether we will live as reflections of the male world or as manifestations of our own world, whether we wish to build our own identity as women even at the risk of being confronted by men.

The question is: do we choose to be the subjects or the objects of our own lives?

Sex Roles in the Parliament

A recent study in Finland has been surveying the initiatives of women in Parliament from 1907 to 1977. It is the first such study of its kind, observing the *substance* of women's political initiatives, not only women's numerical presence. It confirms the feminist assumption that women give priority to different things than do men. Women concentrate on social, cultural, and educational issues, and lately also on such issues as protection of minorities and the handicapped, and preservation of the environment.

Women have made very few initiatives in the fields of economics, foreign policy, national security, or transport and public works, which seem to be the favorite areas of men. Does this distribution of interest merely demonstrate a genuine inclination of women to those fields close to human life, following the traditional distribution of roles even in the politics? Or is it just a reflection of society's expectations of women? In any case, it means that women do not seem to make specific contributions in "important" fields in the society, such as shaping the goals of economic development, industry and trade, priorities in the field of national security and foreign policy, and the policies of transportation and public works, all of which create the infrastructure of our societies. Perhaps these sex roles in politics partly answer why the influence of women is lacking in the most important fields of development.

Personal Experiences

"There is no case for gradual means if more forthright ones will serve. But if belief is the source of power, the attack must be on belief. Law cannot anticipate understanding." This quote is from John Kenneth Galbraith's book *Economics and Public Purpose,* in which he discusses the power of economics. But it also pertains to us, since the power against women's liberation is based in beliefs, strong beliefs planted even in the minds of many of our sisters. Law cannot anticipate understanding and therefore real liberty has not dawned on women even in the Nordic countries, although the laws carefully have been rectified and new laws prohibiting sex discrimination are on the way. Our attack must go deeper, and be on beliefs.

"Belief that is inconvenient . . . is not suppressed; it is either ignored or stigmatized as eccentric, unscientific, lacking in scholarly precision or repute or otherwise unworthy."

Here Galbraith describes a strategy tediously familiar to many of us who have tried to speak with a woman's voice in politics, economics, or development affairs. Personally, I have experienced it for years, when, for example, intervening in the public discussion on economic policies and development. The discussion goes on between the male partners of the game as if I had not said anything, although my comments have been printed in the same media. The deafness is like a wall. So far the female voices have been far too few; a scream in the desert is easy to ignore. We must multiply; more women's voices speaking out in spite of being ridiculed or unacknowledged. This is the way we can support each other within countries and across borders. Even the walls of Jericho fell when there were enough trumpets blowing!

My own life story reflects the phenomenon I mentioned above: that short, thin tradition of an urban, educated, middle class in Finland. The transformation of the society from an agrarian to an industrial, urban economy took place rapidly. Consequently the female role as a fulltime housewife never has been well established; it was passed over—to the advantage or disadvantage of women. I was born in a farming family in the Finnish countryside and received my basic views on life, work, and society in that agrarian setting. The farming family traditionally had ideals of self-reliance, independence, and a comprehensive grip on the necessities of life. Although patriarchal, it gave due credit to female work and contributions in providing for the family's livelihood. Everybody's work was needed: even the contributions of children were desired, according to their growing capabilities.

From this background I came directly to urban academic surroundings. I seem to have retained a need for independence and self-reliance as an individual as well as a strong desire for freedom and the longing for an over-all comprehension of life. This, combined with the awareness and affirmation of being a woman, has led me to try to formulate and implement a dignified female role in society. So far it has led me

—to demonstrate against the society's prevailing norm in which everyone is supposed to compete for positions, salaries, and power;

—to demonstrate the satisfaction of work *as such,* work which is meaningful for both oneself and society, irrespective of its formal status in the societal hierarchy;

—to struggle toward influence and change in society on grounds other than those of money, power, or academic authority;

—to realize all this in spite of—or because of—being a woman.

I think there are millions of sisters in developing countries which are making a still shorter cut from the agrarian to the industrialized, technologically advanced society. I hope they can retain their life-affirming base and their indigenously female approach and bring these directly to the more advanced society. I hope that the new, emerging societies will learn from our experience and *not* follow the same road which has brought Western societies to this stage of male-dominated mal-development. On the contrary, they could then emerge directly to a more harmonious humane society where the visions of women and men have been recognized equally in designing and shaping life and development.

Suggested Further Reading

Haavio-Mannila, Elina. "Women in the Economic, Political and Cultural Elites in Finland." *Access to Power: Cross-National Studies of Women and Elites.* Eds. Cynthia F. Epstein and Rosa L. Coser. London: Allen & Unwin, 1981.

———. "Essay on Finland." *The Politics of the Second Electorate: Women and Public Participation.* Eds. Joni Lovenduski and Jill Hill. London: Routledge & Kegan Paul, 1981.

———. "The Position of Women." *Nordic Democracy.* Eds. Erik, *et al.* København: Det Danske Selskab, 1981.

Sinkkonen, Sirkka. "Women's Increased Political Participation in Finland: Real Influence or Pseudodemocracy?" Paper delivered to the ECPR (European Consortium for Political Research) Workshop on Women in Politics, Berlin, Mar. 27–Apr. 2, 1977; available from Univ. of Essex, Central Services, Dept. of Political Science, Wivenhoe Park, Colchester, CO4 3SQ Essex, United Kingdom.

————, and Elina Haavio-Mannila. "The Impact of the Women's Movement and Legislative Activity of Women MPs on Social Development." *Women, Power and Political Systems*. Ed. Margherita Rendel. London: Croom Helm, 1981.

A Woman in Finland. A booklet produced by the Finnish Council for Equality Between Men and Women, 1981; available from Korkeavuorenkatu 47 B, 00130 Helsinki 13.

Hilkka Pietilä was born in 1931 in Kiikka, Finland. She took her master of science degree in nutrition at the University of Helsinki in 1956, was president of the Finnish Assoc. of Home Economists (1960–62), has been a member of the Finnish National Commission for UNESCO since 1971 (and vice-president since 1975), and stood as a candidate in parliamentary elections in 1966, 1979, and 1983. Her books include *Syo Elaaksesi* [Eat to Your Health] (Otava, Helsinki, 1963) and *Ihmisen Poulustus* [In Defense of Human Dignity], and she has written numerous articles and lectured on women's issues, world food problems, and development issues. She was an advisory member of the Finnish Delegation to the UN General Assembly in 1965, 1966, 1967, 1970, 1972, 1974, and 1975, and a member of the Finnish delegations to the UN Conferences on Human Environment (1972), on World Population (1974), on International Women's Year (1975), on Science and Technology for Development (1979), and was a Finnish delegate to the General Conferences of UNESCO in 1976, 1978, and 1980. She also has been an active member of the Finnish Women for Peace group since 1980, and since 1963 has been the Secretary-General of the Finnish UN Association and editor-in-chief of its magazine.

FRANCE
(French Republic)

Located in western Europe, bordered by Switzerland and Italy to the east, the Mediterranean Sea, Spain, and Andorra to the south, the Atlantic Ocean to the west, the English Channel, Belgium, and Luxembourg to the north, and West Germany to the northeast. **Area:** 551,600 sq. km. (212,973 sq. mi.). **Population** (1980): 53,634,000, female 51%. **Capital:** Paris.

DEMOGRAPHY. Languages: French, Breton, Alsatian German, Flemish, Italian, Basque, Catalan. **Races or Ethnic Groups:** French, immigrant pop. from Europe, Asia, and the African continent. **Religions:** Roman Catholicism 90%, Protestant, Judaism, Islam. **Education** (% enrolled in school, 1975): Age 6–11—of all girls 100%, of all boys 97%; age 12–17—of all girls 85%, of all boys 79%; higher education—in 1980–81 women were 33.2% of science students, 35.5% of dental, 41% of economics, 43% of medicine, 51.5% of law, and 67.4% of humanities. **Literacy** (1977): Female 97%, male 97%. **Birth Rate** (per 1000 pop., 1977–78): 14. **Death Rate** (per 1000 pop., 1977–78): 10. **Infant Mortality** (per 1000 live births, 1977): Female 10, male 14. **Life Expectancy** (1975–80): Female 77 yrs., male 69 yrs.

GOVERNMENT. The 1958 Constitution established the Fifth Republic. A bicameral parliamentary system comprises an elected 491-member National Assembly and a 304-member Senate; an elected president appoints a prime minister and a cabinet. Major political parties include the Socialist Party, Rally for the Republic, Union for French Democracy, and the Communist Party; Choisir, a women's party, has been formed. **Women's Suffrage:** 1945. **Equal Rights:** The 1958 Constitution incorporated the provision of equal rights "in all domains" from the 1946 Constitution. In Mar. 1983, legislation (modeled on a 1972 law against racism) was introduced making illegal any images deemed degrading to women through incitement to discrimination, hatred, violence, insult, or defamation; the

offense would be punishable by fine (up to $44,000) or maximum 1 yr. imprisonment. Bill is still pending. **Women in Government:** Women comprise 5.7% of the National Assembly, 3% of the Senate, and 14% of municipal councillors; 6 women ministers include Yvette Roudy, Minister for Women's Rights (1983). In 1982 women were 2.3% of mayors and 21% of French representatives in the European Parliament.

ECONOMY. Currency: French Franc (May 1983: 7.4 = $1 US). **Gross National Product** (1980): $627.7 billion. **Per Capita Income** (1980): $11,730. **Women's Wages as a Percentage of Men's** (1980): 69%. **Equal Pay Policy:** Legislation was enacted in 1972 and 1975 but remained inadequate; 1983 legislation makes employers subject to a $300–400 fine or 2 months–2 yrs. imprisonment if they fail to comply with equal pay laws. Legislation does not cover part-time workers, who make up 6.5% of the total labor force and are 82% women. **Production** (Agricultural/Industrial): Cereals, feed grains, livestock, dairy products, wine; chemicals, autos, processed foods, iron, steel, textiles. **Women as a Percentage of Labor Force** (1980): 44%; **of agricultural force** (1975) 30% (60% of whom were unpaid family workers); **of industrial force** (1977) 25%; **of military** 14,080 (including paramedical corps); women volunteers have been admitted into unarmed divisions since 1938. **(Employed) Women's Occupational Indicators:** Of doctors 30%, of lawyers 33% (1980–82); of administrative/managerial 16.4%, of professional/technical 44%, of sales 50%, of clerical 66%, of services 67% (1975). **Unemployment:** In July 1982, 950,000 women were unemployed; no total rates or rates by sex obtainable; in Mar. 1980, 60% of unemployed persons under age 25 were women.

GYNOGRAPHY. Marriage. *Policy:* Minimum marriage age for females is 15 with parental consent, 18 without consent; for males, 18 with or without consent. A 1970 Civil Code abolished the legal status of "head of household," making women and men equal partners in marriage, with equal parental authority. However, according to fiscal law, a woman's husband's signature is required for her to obtain credit and negotiate financial arrangements, as well as for social security payments, family allocation, creches, schools, and medical payments. Since 1982 a married woman's signature is required on tax forms; previously she could be kept uninformed of a husband's income even though a wife can be required to pay debts accrued by a husband. Previously, married women assumed control over their own property and earnings (1804) and gained full legal status (no longer permanent minors) in 1904. *Practice:* Female mean age at marriage (1970–78): 23; women age 15–49 in union (1970–78): 64%. **Divorce.** *Policy:* Legal; 1975 law permits divorce on grounds of mutual consent, breakdown of marriage (after a 6-yr. separation or in case of mental illness), or divorce with fault (1 partner has committed a serious crime or is guilty of misconduct). *Practice:* Divorces (per 1000 pop., 1979): 1.3; in 1975 there were 512,440 divorced men living singly versus 740,915 divorced women living singly. Women receive custody of children in 80% of cases; as of 1983, 56% of maintenance payments are paid irregularly (25% of which are not paid at all).

Family. *Policy:* An employed pregnant woman is entitled to 18 weeks paid maternity leave (10 of which are compulsory); she must have been employed for at least 200 hours prior to leave and have been registered for at least 10 months before delivery. Fathers are entitled to a 3-day paid parental leave. Medical costs relating to pregnancy are also covered for a woman who has personal social security insurance or whose husband is insured, or who is a dependent daughter of an insured person. Post-natal benefits are available, if certain requirements are met, for 2 yrs. after delivery. A woman cannot be fired for pregnancy. A family allowance includes benefits for 2 or more dependent children or children under age 3; benefits also are available to any single parent with 1 or more children under age 3, and to a single woman during a first pregnancy if she fulfills certain requirements. Government-supported childcare is available for children over age 3. *Practice:* According to a 1982 survey, 17% of husbands participate in housecleaning, 20% in cooking, and 30% in childcare. As of 1983, 10% of families (representing more than 1 million children) are supported by the mother alone; in 1977–83 the rate of single mothers rose 150%, forming a new group in the "poverty ranks." In 1978 approx. 6 million families received family allowances. Few fathers take parental leave. Current laws rarely apply to part-time workers. There are places for 11% of children in creches; 60% have places in additional preschooling.

Welfare. *Policy:* A comprehensive social security system includes health insurance and benefits for unemployment, disability, old age, and death; maternity benefits and family allowances are also covered (see **Family**). Those who are not covered by compulsory programs are entitled to join contributory insurance plans. A welfare program provides for those who have insufficient resources. A 1983 law provides partial reimbursements for abortions (see **Abortion**). *Practice:* No statistics obtainable. Pensions are quite small and eligibility requirements for supplements limit the number of women who receive them. **Contraception.** *Policy:* Legalized in 1967. A government-sponsored commercial supporting birth control appeared on television in 1981. *Practice:* Women age 15–50 using contraception (1980): 30%, of which 23.5% use the pill and 7% use IUDs; in 1981, of 1413 family-planning centers, 755 offered consultations, examinations, and contraceptives. Birth-control use has decreased since 1978.

Abortion. *Policy:* Legalized in 1979 (after a 5-yr. trial period); available on request if the woman is in a "distress situation" up to the 10th week of pregnancy; she must consult an approved counseling center and wait 1 week after the request. The procedure is also legal if there is risk to the life or physical/mental health of the woman or of the fetus. Abortions can be performed in public or authorized private hospitals although private hospitals can refuse to perform the procedure; elective abortions cannot exceed 25% of all procedures in any hospital. Physicians must provide women seeking abortions with a list of clinics that perform the procedure, but must warn them of potential risks, and may themselves invoke a "clause of conscience," thus refusing to perform the procedure. Despite opposition from antichoice groups, a 1983 bill to provide State reimbursement for 70% of the cost of all abortions passed under the Mitterrand government. *Practice:* Reported abortions (per 1000 women age 15–44, 1980): 15.3; abortions (per 1000 known pregnancies, 1980): 176. In 1976 the reported number of legal abortions was only 53% of the est. number. Many doctors refuse to perform abortions and neglect to give proper referrals. As of 1980, only 14 out of 29 State hospitals were performing the procedure. In 1979, 95% of abortions were performed in private clinics for approx. $625–$750. Choisir, formed in the early 1970's, was and is a major feminist movement focused on the right to reproductive freedom. **Illegitimacy.** *Policy:* 1972 legislation permits a mother to "legitimize" her child by placing her own name on the birth certificate. If the child is the issue of extra-marital relations, the mother may have the child "legally recognized" by the father without a paternity disavowal from her husband. *Practice:* 1 in 9 births is out of wedlock. **Homosexuality.** *Policy:* Decriminalized in 1982; previously decriminalized under Napoleon in 1789, but declared an "indecent assault" by the Vichy government under German occupation, later a criminal offense again under de Gaulle. *Practice:* No statistics obtainable. The new law is part of a platform of campaign promises pledged by Pres. Mitterrand in 1979 after he won the majority of the homosexual-bloc vote. In 1983 a lesbian woman who had been refused a job won the first court case against a "morality" clause covering civil servants. There are many active lesbian-rights groups in Paris and most urban centers.

Incest. *Policy:* Illegal; punishable by severe fines and sentences; no further data obtainable. *Practice:* No data obtainable.

Sexual Harassment. *Policy:* Under the Mitterrand government, 1982–83 legislation forbids any form of discrimination against employed women and can be used to cover sexual harassment; a newly created task force to help victims of sexual harassment and an active antisexism campaign are part of the government's program. Any woman or her labor union can file a suit charging sexual harassment against her employers, and a special commission will represent her in court. *Practice:* No statistics obtainable, but application of the new laws is difficult; few women have won cases of sexual discrimination. **Rape.** *Policy:* Illegal; a 1980 law defines rape as an act of sexual penetration "of whatever nature," committed against another person by violence, constraint, or surprise; punishable by 10–20 yrs. imprisonment; attempted rape by 5–10 yrs. Rape of a minor under age 15 or by a person with authority (teacher, cult leader, etc.) is subject to the maximum sentence. *Practice:* As of 1983, approx. 2000 cases of rape are reported each yr.; government estimates the actual incidence of rape at 20,000 per yr. There are approx. 300 prosecutions for rape annually, but a majority of those convicted are given suspended sentences as first-time offenders, and only 1 or 2 of those found guilty receive maximum sentences; the remainder receive under 5–10 yrs. **Battery.** *Policy:* No specific laws on wife-beating; general assault laws make wife-beating a criminal offense punishable by imprisonment. Penalties vary according to injuries sustained by the victim. *Practice:* 95% of battery victims are women; 78% of cases take place in the home; 51% of batterers are husbands, 31% are acquaintances (see **Crisis Centers**). **Prostitution.** *Policy:* It is illegal under the Penal Code to aid, abet, or live off the earnings of a prostitute; punishable by a fine of FF. 10,000–100,000 and 6 months–3 yrs. imprisonment. *Practice:* As of 1983, approx. 12,000 pimps are prosecuted each yr. There are an est. 400,000 "regular" prostitutes and an equal number of "occasional" prostitutes; prostitution rings exist in Paris and most urban centers. As of 1978, the Ministry of the Interior declared pimping and procuring the third largest business in France, with a $7 billion annual profit. Current (1983) government policies focus on prosecuting large traffickers and pimps and helping prostitutes prepare for new careers by setting up aid centers which offer counseling, education, and job referrals. Such groups as NID (Association of National Action and Defense of Prostitutes) and the CRI movement fight for prostitutes' rights. **Traditional/Cultural Practices:** No data obtainable. **Crisis Centers.** *Policy:* A government program assists victims of battery, rape, etc., through the Office of Health and Social Action. *Practice:* As of 1983, 18 battered women's shelters exist.

HERSTORY. France's Mediterranean coast, c. 600 B.C.E., was the location of Greek and Phoenician settlements. The population included Celts, Basques, and Germanic tribes, some of which followed female leadership (see MYTHOGRAPHY). The grave of a Celtic woman—most likely a chief or queen—was discovered at Vix near Châtillon-sur-Seine; the grave was filled with gold objects, including the royal torque necklace, and the grave sides had been lined with oak, a procedure not followed in the Celtic burial of men.

Frankish rule in the 5th century C.E. was dominated by Roman Catholic doctrine and the Salic Law, which gave women inferior social status with no right to own property, inherit, or succeed to the throne. Eighth-century feudalism, the 11th-century Crusades, and the persecution of witches (13th–18th centuries) firmly established patriarchal domination over women.

Héloïse (d. c. 1164) was the leading philosophical mind of her day, although she is now known primarily for her relationship with Peter Abelard (1079–1142), the theologian. After Abelard's maiming by her uncle in revenge for their secret marriage, Héloïse joined a convent at her husband's insistence but rose to become abbess and to found other convents in turn, creating a religious community of learning for women.

In 1170 Eleanor of Aquitaine and her daughter, Marie de France (a poet), established the Court of Love, holding secular trials of men for crimes ranging from minor misgallantries to such major offenses as rape and abduction; under Eleanor's hegemony, the arts flourished and women troubadors and tapestry weavers established centuries-long traditions. Eleanor accompanied her first husband, Louis VII of France, on the 2nd Crusade, leading her own troops of women fighters dressed as Amazons (also see BRITAIN).

In 1208 the Roman Catholic papacy conducted the 100-years-long Albigensian Crusade, literally wiping out "heretical" Catharism, a Provençal-region religion committed to equality for women. In 1339 Christine de Pisan wrote *Le Livre de la Cité des Dames* (Book of the City of Ladies), considered the first European feminist tract.

Anne of Brittany (1477–1514), forcibly married into the French ruling House of Valois, unwillingly began the annexation of Brittany by France. In 1429, at the Battle of Orléans, Jeanne d'Arc (c. 1412–31) became the military heroine of the Hundred Years' War against England and Burgundy; she was later accused of witchcraft and burned alive at Rouen. The Roman Catholic Church, which had condemned her in 1431, canonized her in 1920.

Marguerite de Navarre (1492–1549), sister of Francis I, was a supporter of religious freedom and moderate church reforms; her court was renowned for its brilliance. A patron of artists and intellectuals, she was herself a writer, best known for her *Heptameron* (1558), a collection of roisterous tales, and for her plays and poetry. Francis I's official mistress, Anne de Pisseleu (1508–80) was notable for her patronage of the arts. Catherine de Médicis (1519–89; see ITALY) married the duc d'Orléans (later Henri II) but was less powerful during his reign than was his official mistress, Diane de Poitiers (1499–1566), who exerted great political influence. In 1560, however, Catherine came to power as regent for her son Charles IX; she attempted a moderate policy toward the French Protestant movement (the Huguenots), but the onset of the Religious Wars led to her collaboration in the

St. Bartholomew's Day Massacre of Protestants (1572).

During the persecution of the Huguenots in the 16th century, women began to fight for the right to education: Louise Labé, Marie de Gournay, and Magdeleine de Scudéry wrote in defense of women's rights. The "Précieuses" (Precious Ones) and "Femmes Savantes" (Learned Ladies), most notably Mme. de Sévigné (1626–96), were intellectuals and liberals; the *Journal des Dames* (Ladies' Journal) was published in 1754.

Marie Antoinette (1755–93), daughter of Maria Theresa (see AUSTRIA), was the unhappy pawn in an arranged marriage with Louis XVI of France; her loyalty to Austria heightened her unpopularity with the French and, although the phrase "Let them eat cake" is unfairly and inaccurately ascribed to her, she was perceived as the symbol of the decadence indulged by Louis's court. She was arrested during the French Revolution, tried as "the Widow Capet" after the execution of Louis, and guillotined on Oct. 16.

The 1789 Revolution provided a stage for women's political action: 800 marketwomen marched to Versailles to present their grievances to the King; 6000–10,000 others joined them. Some took up arms: Marie Charpentier, recognized as a "conqueror of the Bastille," was one of the 73 wounded; Théroigne de Méricourt, a former prostitute, was the first to gain entrance to the prison. She and Etta Palm d'Aelders organized the first women's clubs and urged women to form "Amazon battalions." Women were active in the 1792 Paris Commune; at Creuil, women from a company of the National Guard used javelins as weapons; at Valence, women fought with swords.

Olympe de Gouges (1748–93) published the *Declaration of the Rights of Women* in 1790; she was later beheaded for "having forgotten the virtues of her sex." Other republican revolutionaries were Pauline Léon, Claire Lacombe, and Charlotte Corday (who assassinated Marat). Mme. de Staël (1766–1817) was the focus of literary and political ferment at her famous salon.

Marie Joséphine Rose Tascher de la Pagerie, better known as Joséphine (1763–1814), survived her own imprisonment and the execution of her first (aristocratic) husband during the French Revolution and in 1796 married Napoleon Bonaparte, later becoming his first empress. She was highly influential in political circles, and was Napoleon's declared "great love" until his own death, despite the fact that he had the marriage annulled on the grounds of her supposed barrenness; Marie Louise (1791–1847) became his second wife and bore him the requisite children.

In the early 19th century, the Napoleonic Code abolished divorce. George Sand (Aurore Dupin) wrote many novels, including *Indiana,* an attack on marriage, and, as well as being a major literary and intellectual figure, played a role in political affairs and dared live an independent life. The political philosopher Alexis de Tocqueville was a male supporter of women's rights. Union Ouvrière (Women Workers Union) was created.

The 1871 Paris Commune, at the end of the Franco-Prussian War, involved many women; it embraced radical republicans as well as followers of the Marxist First International; reprisals by Versailles troops were intense, and almost 18,000 people, including many women and children, were executed.

Women were active in the war effort in WW I and strongly involved in the underground resistance during WW II. Edmée de la Rochefoucauld, a novelist, mathematician, artist, and member of the Royal Academy of Belgium, was extremely active in the fight for Frenchwomen's suffrage. In 1935, Irène Joliot-Curie (the daughter of Marie Curie; see POLAND) won the Nobel Prize in chemistry, together with her husband. The 1946 Constitution established gender equality in many spheres, but *The Second Sex* (by Simone de Beauvoir) was the first contemporary work to expose women's inferior status. The Movement for Family Planning began in 1956 to counter a 1920 ban on the sale of contraceptives.

Many women participated in the May 1968 student-and-worker strikes which initiated the contemporary women's liberation movement (see following article). Women's groups began to organize on such issues as abortion, divorce, battery, and rape. *F.* magazine was founded. Prostitutes in major cities demanded legislation to improve their rights, staging sit-ins in cathedrals and city halls in 1976.

In 1980 novelist Marguerite Yourcenar became the first woman to be elected to the "Immortals" of the French Academy. Other important writers in French history include Colette, Nathalie Sarraute, Violette Le Duc, Françoise Mallet-Joris, Françoise Sagan, and Monique Wittig.

MYTHOGRAPHY. The Dordogne valley in southwest France is a major site of Paleolithic art, including several sculptural goddess or "Venus" fertility figures, some carrying the sacred matriarchal labyris, or double ax. The cave paintings at Lascaux, discovered in 1940, are perhaps the greatest record of Cro-Magnon sensibility; the handprints accompanying the paintings are small, and it has been suggested by some scholars that the highly sophisticated art was the work of women.

During the period of the Celts and other Germanic tribal peoples (see HERSTORY) the Celtic pantheon of female divinities (see EAST/WEST GERMANY, IRELANDS) was worshipped throughout the area. With the entrenchment of Christianity, the reverence of Mary became primary, and during the Middle Ages French heretics were accused of Mariolatry.

One French legend pertaining to Mary refers to her having traveled from Palestine after the death of her son and settling in Marseilles until her own death. The town of Lourdes, at the foot of the Pyrenees in southwest France, is the shrine site of an alleged visitation in Feb. 1858 by Mary to a peasant girl who eventually became St. Bernadette of Lourdes. Each year, hundreds of thousands of Roman Catholics make pilgrimages to Lourdes, where, they believe, they will be miraculously cured of ill health and even terminal disease.

FRANCE: Feminism—Alive, Well, and in Constant Danger
by Simone de Beauvoir
(Translated by Magda Bogin and Robin Morgan)

The French Feminist Movement 1970–82

After World War I, French feminism fell into an abrupt decline and disappeared completely from the political scene for half a century.

During the 1940's and 1950's, a number of works written by women on the situation of women were published: *La situation des femmes françaises aujourd'hui* (The Situation of Frenchwomen Today), by Andrée Michel and Geneviève Texier; *Demain les femmes* (Tomorrow the Women), by Evelyne Sullerot; and, earlier, *Le deuxième sexe (The Second Sex)*. But these analyses appeared in the absence of any political action. Many women's organizations existed, but were affiliated with the three main political parties; their goal was less to defend the rights of women than to "bring women to politics"—in other words, to recruit women into the parties' memberships.

In the heady intellectual climate of May 1968, various women began to discuss their own situation, and in so doing made use of the above-mentioned analytical works. But the militant feminist past, French and foreign, was neither recalled nor evoked; only the derogatory image it had endured remained, including the word "suffragette," with its deliberately trivialized connotations that evoked derision and hysteria.

After the euphoria of the May–June 1968 "revolution" (a revolution more hoped for than achieved), the ensuing period of normalization decimated the few women's groups that had been formed. Nonetheless, several, however weakened, managed to survive the loss of momentum. These groups were unaware of each other's existence—but within two years they had reinvented feminism.

In 1969 we first heard of the American women's liberation movement, and this exciting news bolstered the few scattered French feminists in their determination that it was possible to build a movement of their own. In the French political climate of that time, such an idea was anathema to all men and even to most women. For the vast majority of self-defined progressives the idea of a feminist organization, especially one that excluded men, was simply unthinkable. Those on the Left were in fact its staunchest opponents: any struggle not led from "the heart of the working class"—or from the heart of those organizations claiming dedication to defending working-class interests—was viewed as counterrevolutionary and divisive. Furthermore, for many of these revolutionaries "the woman question" was at the least a "petit-bourgeois problem," or at best something socialism would resolve—*after* its triumph, of course.

Nevertheless, in 1970, one of these women's groups managed to publish an article entitled *"Pour la libération des femmes"* (For Women's Liberation) in a Leftist monthly which has since ceased publication.[1] At last the silence was broken. Isolated feminists discovered they each were not alone—and they began to meet.

The first meeting, attended by forty women, led to the forming of an embryonic women's liberation movement. What is now considered the beginning of the contemporary French feminist movement was a demonstration in solidarity with the strike organized by American women, on August 26, 1970,[*] at which the term "women's liberation" made its first public appearance in France. Nine women bore a banner with the words "More Unknown Than the Unknown Soldier: His Wife" to the Arc de Triomphe; the next day this symbolic action made front-page headlines in all the major Paris dailies.

From its debut, this wave of the French feminist movement situated itself within a militant left-wing perspective. Whether they were Trotskyists or Maoists, whether they had bolted these parties or never been part of them formally, all the women who helped found the original MLF (Mouvement de Libération des Femmes) felt themselves to be in an ongoing dialogue with the extreme Left, which was both their chosen friend and their worst enemy. And this has remained true until quite recently.

From its inception, however, the MLF organized on an innovative platform that did break both with the platforms of the political parties and with other women's organizations. Its major principles were clear from the start:

—It would be a single-sex movement; this was its most striking feature, and the one most contested by outsiders.

—It would be an extra-parliamentary movement inspired by the tradition of "direct action"; it was thus at odds with the traditional political parties which seek power through the vote, and also with the parties of the extreme Left which use the elections as an opportunity to make their views known to the general public.

—It would be a movement, not a party or an organization; it would reject the hierarchical, pyramidal structure of traditional political groups, as well as the concepts of

---

[1.] *L'Idiot internationale.*

[*] A one-day strike sometimes referred to as Alice Doesn't Day, with large demonstrations and marches in major US cities; the demands embraced all the basic issues: reproductive freedom and freedom of sexual choice, equal pay for (and access to) comparable work, equality in education, childcare centers, the Equal Rights Amendment, an end to the daily violence against women—rape, battery, sexual harassment, pornography, etc.—and an end to discrimination based on race, sexual preference, age, and class distinctions among women.—Ed.

representation and delegation of power, and would function instead as a "direct democracy."

—Finally, the women's movement would be totally independent of any existing parties or organizations; on this point there was no unanimity, and the matter would, in fact, lead to numerous debates, ultimately bringing about a split between radical feminists and socialist feminists.

The Different Tendencies

The Split Between
"Radical Feminists" and "Socialist Feminists"

The need for and desirability of a women's movement was not obvious to many women who had been active in the Left, and at first they fought against its emergence. When the movement took root despite their opposition, some of them decided to participate after all, but with goals that radical feminists did not share: to make their own organizations accept feminism, and (in the name of the structural relationship between class struggle and gender struggle) to place the women's movement, in effect, *under* the tutelage of their own respective organizations.

The tension between women who remained active in the Left and feminists who had broken with it was expressed early by their organizing into separate groups. Beginning in 1971, the socialist women clustered under the banner *Libération des femmes, tendence lutte de classes* ("Women's Liberation, Class-Struggle Tendency"). They held separate meetings which were attended by all the groups that were part of the Coordination des Groupes-Femmes de Paris (Coordinating Committee of Parisian Women's Groups), who were subsequently joined by women belonging to the Groupes-Femmes d'Entreprises (Salaried Women's Groups). From 1973 to 1976 these groups worked together toward the supposed goal of creating an "autonomous women's movement." Since the MLF already was autonomous, this meant in reality the creation of a second movement distinct from the MLF, which was viewed by the Leftist-loyalist groups as "sexist" and "petit bourgeois." The autonomy of this second movement would in actual fact be relative and merely organizational in nature. The attempt ended in failure, but in 1976 the same coalition created the Coordination Nationale des Groupes-Femmes (National Coordinating Committee of Women's Groups), which functioned as a representative body. However, between 1978 and 1982 it was gradually reabsorbed by the MLF.

The Radical Feminist Tendency

The "radical" wing never created a formal organizational structure at all. Strongly influenced by US "consciousness-raising groups," French radical feminists attempted to encourage a similar practice. While American-style CR groups did not take hold in France, small discussion groups based on shared interests—rather than on geographic proximity like those of the socialist tendency—remain the dominant model. The radical-feminist vision of the movement allows for the juxtaposition of many small, spontaneously created groups, each completely autonomous in relation to the others, but ideally sharing some form of communication. However, since they rejected any formal delegation of power or structure, radical feminists failed to establish an information network, with the result that their groups have little way of contacting each other. This makes the whole radical-feminist tendency—as well as its specific groups—virtually invisible: newcomers can rarely find them. Socialist groups, on the other hand, are organized by neighborhood and are easily accessible to women from "outside"; consequently, they receive the majority of newcomers.

The problem of radical-feminist invisibility became particularly acute after 1972, when the open meetings in Paris, which had been infiltrated and all but taken over by "Psych. et Po." [see below], were gradually abandoned. The problem was partially solved by women's centers, which functioned as places where women could gather and share information. But these centers have usually been short-lived, and there have been intervals when a large portion of the movement simply could not be located by others—or even, at times, by its own members.

"Psych. et Po."

In 1972 a third tendency emerged: the group Psychanalyse et Politique (Psychoanalysis and Politics), abbreviated as Psych. et Po. Its political line was unclear at its inception—and remains unclear to this day.

Radical feminists lost no time in calling it reactionary because of its early denunciation of feminism in general and its subsequent espousal of the ideology of neo-femininity. Psych. et Po. possessed an immense fortune of unknown origin, which it used to create a publishing house (Des Femmes) and a number of bookstores of the same name—all of them most luxurious—both in France and abroad. Not content with having appropriated the generic name "Des Femmes" for its business enterprises and then its weekly magazine *Des Femmes-hebdo,* in 1979 this group managed to register the words Mouvement de Libération des Femmes—MLF ("Women's Liberation Movement") as a copyrighted trademark.

From that moment, all the other tendencies united against Psych. et Po. The socialist feminists—who until then had viewed the conflict between radical feminists and Psych. et Po. as a mere internal conflict within the "sexist, petit-bourgeois MLF"—now realized that this group posed a grave threat to the entire women's movement. Furthermore, that same year (1979), socialist feminists abandoned their previously relentless attempts to build an alternate women's movement, and once they again defined themselves as active participants in the already existing women's liberation movement, they suddenly became concerned about its appropriation.

Analyses and Actions

Each of the three major tendencies—and it must be noted that many feminists active in the French women's movement don't identify with any one of the three—differs not only in structure but also in an analysis of women's oppression. These analyses—and the differences between them—are not fundamentally different from comparable variations found in the women's movements of other Western countries. Perhaps the specificity of French socialist feminists in relation to their English and American counterparts lies in their greater allegiance to mixed groups (men and women) of the extreme Left. The socialist-feminist position has, of course, evolved over the years—toward a more radical political line.

The specificity of French radical feminists may lie in their fuller theoretical development of the international radical-feminist position. Like radical feminists elsewhere, those in France believe that women constitute an oppressed class within a particular system, patriarchy, and they therefore insist on the absolute autonomy of the feminist struggle. From this perspective they argue a less "biological" line than their Anglo-Saxon counterparts, perhaps because in France those analyses which accord biology a significant role in shaping women's oppression are linked to such politically reactionary positions as those of the group Psych. et Po., which believes that women, rather than being "oppressed,"

are *"re*pressed," that the female self has been denied expression by men, and that liberation should be sought in the reaffirmation of women's uniquely "female nature." This so-
called profound womanly nature bears a curious resemblance to the image of femininity
constructed by the patriarchy. The political consequence of this analysis in practice is
that it isn't necessary for women to fight against the material conditions of their oppression. In fact, according to Psych. et Po., there is no material basis to women's oppression;
rather, the struggle must be "to change our own heads." They call for a "symbolic
revolution."

This doubtless explains why the celebration of traditional feminine values is so very
suspect in France: it has been linked to a rejection of the need to fight for social change.
In the United States, on the other hand, such a celebration seems able to inspire and
parallel activism, but in France the "cult of femaleness" is inseparable from precisely the
attitude most American feminists oppose: "cultural feminism"—namely, the renunciation of political action.

The major feminist campaigns have followed the same course in France as in other
countries, beginning in 1970 with the demand for the right to abortion and then expanding into the struggle against rape. The anti-rape movement in other countries led to
a broad campaign against all forms of violence against women (England) and to the anti-
sexual harassment and anti-pornography campaigns (USA). In France the struggle
against pornography was defused early,** and at the moment there is no single issue
around which women are mobilized.

All of the major campaigns and debates—particularly that on heterosexuality and
homosexuality—were launched by radical feminists. This does not mean that socialist
feminists played no role; from the beginning they mobilized around such themes as equal
pay and the defense of a woman's right to work, which radical feminists called "reformist" because these issues did not explore the roots of women's oppression. Yet today it can
be seen that these are important rights for which to fight in a period of recession, when
women are sent back into their homes and the movement is forced into a defensive rather
than an offensive position. In addition, even if the socialist-feminist faction did not initiate any major campaigns (and even if it fought against them at first, as it did, for instance,
with the anti-rape campaign), it did lend its eventual and sustained support. On abortion,
for example, socialist feminists continued to work toward changing the public consciousness and to struggle as well within their own institutions long after radical feminists had
virtually quit that terrain, moving on to other issues.

Thus, with a certain hindsight, one can hypothesize that while they each brought
sharply differing analyses to the struggle, these two tendencies operated with a certain
complementarity; radical feminists—paradoxically, because they are opposed to the idea
—functioned as the vanguard, while socialist feminists provided the base. The specific
character of the relationship between these two groups, compared with that in other
countries, lies partly in this relationship and partly in the fact that in France, theory has
emanated almost exclusively from radical feminists.

The Present Status of the French Women's Movement

In its twelve years of existence, the feminist movement has had an impact on French
society disproportionate to the number of its active members, its limited means, and
above all its limited media access. The distortion of feminist ideas, the disdain and the
ridicule which have characterized media coverage of the women's movement, have been
painful irritants to militant French feminists. French society is suffused with feminist

** See Statistical Preface preceding this article for description of new anti-discriminatory images bill.
    —Ed.

thought, but in the process the ideas are, with or without malice, devitalized to the point of being unrecognizable. Feminists themselves, even though they conceived the ideas which have for the most part been met with acceptance, are still viewed with defiance (to say the least) in all circles. This two-faced process constitutes the co-optation that has become a quasi obsession of French feminists.

The media, along with other institutions, have played their part in this process. As early as 1974, for example, the press happily announced the death of the movement. Beginning in 1976, feminists themselves began to worry about the existence of their movement. There seemed a reduction in numbers and a lack of central mobilizing issues; "Where Have the Feminists Gone?" was the cover story of a magazine in 1981. Instead of the movement's demise, however, it is the movement's transformation we should be discussing.

Over the past several years the French women's movement has followed the same course observable in other countries: the radical-feminist discussion groups and the socialist-feminist neighborhood groups have gradually given way to groups organized around specific themes or projects: groups in support of battered women, groups that organize seminars, publish a journal or magazine, run a bookstore or café, etc. This practical side is extremely underdeveloped in France compared with such countries as Germany, England, or the United States; certainly the number of concrete projects is much smaller. The total amount of services offered to women by women is laughable compared with those offered, for example, in the United States. No French city has more than two women's centers, and many lack even one. Certain projects, such as women's savings banks, don't exist at all. This may be due partly to the fact that in France private groups in general and feminist groups in particular do not usually obtain official funding from either the federal or the municipal governments. With the election of the socialist government in 1981, a few new openings seem possible, but they are still very narrow ones. (The Paris Women's Center receives no cash funding, for example, yet must pay a monthly rent of $1,500 US.)

Obviously, material difficulties constrict the development of alternative institutions for women, just as they do for other social groups. Nevertheless, a recent guide to feminist resources lists no fewer than two hundred women's groups throughout France. And one of these groups publishes a yearly agenda which lists the main groups under the following headings:

—libraries and information centers (more than 20, for the most part officially run)
—cafés/restaurants (16)
—women's bookstores (10)
—women's centers (16)
—miscellaneous projects (anti-rape groups, theater groups, audio-visual groups, lesbian groups, groups organizing against sexual mutilation, etc.)
—battered-women's shelters
—groups of Third World women (blacks, Algerians, etc.)
—neighborhood and regional groups
—presses and publishers (19 national publications, 8 regional ones)

The French women's movement thus is alive and well. But it is in constant danger, because of the existence of such groups as Psych. et Po. which pass themselves off as *the* women's movement and exert considerable influence, thanks to the unfortunately all-too-warm reception the general public has given their ideology—a convenient neo-femininity developed by such women writers as Hélène Cixous, Annie Leclerc, and Luce Irigaray, most of whom are not feminists, and some of whom are blatantly *anti*-feminist. Unfortunately this is also the aspect of the French women's movement best known in the United States. Such books as Elaine Marks's *New French Feminisms* give a totally distorted image of French feminism by presenting it, on the one hand, as if it existed only in theory and not in action and, on the other, as if the sum of that theory emanated from the school of neo-femininity—which celebrates women's cycles, rhythms, and bodily fluids, along with "writing of the body" *(écriture du corps)* and women's "circular thinking." On the contrary, one of the most interesting contributions to real French feminist theory is the radical-feminist critique of neo-femininity which has surfaced, particularly in *Questions Féministes* (now *Nouvelles Questions Féministes)*. [2]

Yet other dangers threaten. One has for a long time been aimed by the Left at the women's movement—an attempt to divide it; in 1981, a lesbian-separatist tendency also contributed to schism; finally, after the socialist government came to power, a difficult debate began on the relation of the women's movement to national institutions *(la question des institutions),* i.e., on the advisability of opening a dialogue with those in power. This issue, too, runs the risk of dividing the movement, because the French feminist movement, unlike its American counterpart, does not have the option of delegating comparable negotiations to such a large reformist group as NOW (National Organization for Women) in the United States.

Still, so far, French feminism has survived all these conflicts—and it's highly probable that it will encounter a great many more. And survive them as well.

Suggested Further Reading

Coquillat, Michelle. *La poétique du mâle.* Paris: Gallimard (Collection Idées), 1982.
Le Sexisme Ordinaire (monthly periodical). Paris: Les Temps Modernes, 1974–83.
Tristan, Anne, and Annie de Pisan. *Histoires du MLF.* Paris: Calmann-Lévy, 1977.
Questions Féministes (Issues I–VIII). Paris: Editions Tierce, Nov. 1977–May 1980.
Wittig, Monique. *Les Guérillères.* Paris: Minuit, 1969; English trans., New York: Viking Penguin, 1971.

Simone de Beauvoir was born in Paris in 1908. She was one of the founders of French existentialism and has published philosophical writings (essays and books) as well as authoring novels, memoirs, and political works, including *Pour une morale de l'ambiguité (The Ethics of Ambiguity)* in 1947, the classic *Le deuxième sexe (The Second Sex)* in 1949, *Les mandarins (The Mandarins)* in 1954, *Mémoires d'une jeune fille rangée (Memoirs of a Dutiful Daughter)* in 1958, *La force de l'âge (The Prime of Life)* in 1960, *Une mort très douce (A Very Easy Death)* in 1964, *Djamila Boupacha* in 1967, *La femme rompue (The Woman Destroyed)* in 1967, *La vieillesse (The Coming of Age)* in 1970 and *Tout compte fait (All Said and Done)* in 1972. A political activist as well as theorist all her life, she was a founder of *Les Temps Modernes* in 1945 and worked actively against the Vichy government in WW II and against the French and the US wars in Vietnam in the 1950's and 1960's, and marched in demonstrations on behalf of and with students in the May 1968 French uprisings. She is a founder of numerous French feminist organizations including Choisir (To Choose) in 1970—a group devoted to women's reproductive freedom, which sponsored demonstrations and the first famous abortion petition; Ligue du droit des femmes (League for the Rights of Women), in 1974; the newspaper *Nouvelles Féministes* (The New Feminists) which published from 1974 to 1977; and the journal *Questions Féministes (Feminist Issues)* in 1977.

[2] A periodical of feminist essays edited by Simone de Beauvoir.

GERMANY (EAST)
(German Democratic Republic)

Located in central Europe, bordered by Poland to the east, Czechoslovakia to the south, West Germany to the south and west, and the Baltic Sea to the north. **Area:** 108,000 sq. km. (41,800 sq. mi.). **Population** (1980): 16,726,000, female 53%. **Capital:** East Berlin.

DEMOGRAPHY. Languages: German. **Races or Ethnic Groups:** German, Lusatian Sorb (the only ethnic minority). **Religions:** Protestant (Lutheran) 80.5%, Roman Catholicism 11%, Judaism. **Education** (% enrolled in school, 1975): Age 6–11—of all girls 100%, of all boys 99%; age 12–17—of all girls 84%, of all boys 84%; higher education—in 1982 women were 52.5% of university students and 72% of engineering and technical college students. Official government booklets (1981) refer to a woman's education as her "most valuable dowry." **Literacy** (1981): 99%; no rates by sex obtainable. **Birth Rate** (per 1000 pop., 1977–78): 14. **Death Rate** (per 1000 pop., 1977–78): 14. **Infant Mortality** (per 1000 live births, 1977): Female 14, male 18. **Life Expectancy** (1975–80): Female 75 yrs., male 69 yrs.

GOVERNMENT. The 1968 Constitution invests 1-party governing and legislative power in the elected 500-member People's Chamber; the Chamber elects a Council of State, Council of Ministers, National Defense Council, and Supreme Court judges. Political power is concentrated in the Socialist Unity Party and its State organ, the Politburo. **Women's Suffrage:** In (unified) Germany, 1919; continued under the East German government in 1949. **Equal Rights:** Constitution (Art. 20) stipulates equal rights for women and men and the same legal status in all spheres of social, State, and private life. **Women in Government:** In 1982 women were 33.6% of the People's Chamber, 20% of the Council of State, and 33% of the Socialist Unity Party; a woman was Minister of Education; no women in the Politburo.

ECONOMY. Currency: GDR Mark (May 1983: 2.45 = $1 US). **Gross National Product** (1980): $120.9 billion. **Per Capita Income** (1980): $7180. **Women's Wages as a Percentage of Men's:** No general statistics obtainable, but women earn M. 200–300 per month less than men, owing to household duties which cause women to forgo extended training. **Equal Pay Policy:** Constitution (Art. 24) establishes principle of equal pay for equal work. **Production** (Agricultural/Industrial): Grains, potatoes, sugar beets; steel, chemicals, machinery, textiles. **Women as a Percentage of Labor Force** (1982): 50.2%; **of agricultural force** 43%; **of industrial force** 44%; **of military**—no statistics obtainable, but women have been admitted to all ranks since 1956, training is not as severe as for men, and women are not permitted in combat duty. In 1982, 87% of females age 15–60 were employed or attending school. **(Employed) Women's Occupational Indicators:** Of managerial positions in industry and agriculture 17%, of managerial positions in higher education 33%, of doctors 50.8% (1982); of supervisory and skilled workers 57.4% (1979–80); government placement generally channels women into such low-paid jobs as sales, sewing, and textile or chemical production. **Unemployment:** No statistics obtainable; officially, there is no unemployment.

GYNOGRAPHY. Marriage. *Policy:* Under the 1965 Family Code, minimum marriage age is 18 for both females and males, and marital partners have equal rights and responsibilities. Income earned by spouses is considered common property. Newlywed couples who are under age 26, are marrying for the first time, and have a minimum income may receive a government loan which is canceled in part with the birth of their first child and completely canceled after the birth of the third child. The question of whether men should be penalized legally if they do not share housework has been debated by the People's Chamber, but it was decided that the State could not intervene. *Practice:* Female mean age at marriage (1970–78): 21; women age 15–49 in union (1970–78): 68%; marriages (per 1000 pop., 1979): 8.2. Women average 37 hours of housework per week compared to 5.5 hours by men. The DFD (Democratic Women's League), the official women's organization, runs over 210 consultation centers that promote marriage and family life. **Divorce.** *Policy:* Legal (1965 Family Code, Sec. 24); either spouse can apply for divorce; a court must establish that the marriage has "lost all meaning" for the spouses, the children, and society. Either parent can have legal prerogative of child custody; property is divided equally. *Practice:* Divorces (per 1000 pop., 1979): 2.67; 10% of divorces were filed because of brutality, alcoholism, and sexual problems; the majority of all applications are made by women. The divorce rate is increasing.

Family. *Policy:* The 1965 Family Code is based on the concept of the family as the most important cell of society. The 1950 Maternal and Childcare and Rights of Women Act extends State protection to mother, children, and "family life." Employed pregnant women are entitled to a fully paid maternity leave of 6 weeks pre- and 20 weeks post-delivery and up to 1 yr. unpaid leave after birth of the first child, with guaranteed reinstatement; for every child thereafter, the woman is entitled to a full yr. of partially paid leave. These benefits apply to both single and married women. A birth allowance of M. 1000 is granted for each child. Monthly family allowances increase with the number of children. Employed women with 2 or more children under age 16 work 40 hours per week instead of the standard 43¾ hours, without reduction in pay. Employed mothers are given 1 day off with pay per month "for their household chores." Establishment of creches and kindergartens is a priority of the government; parents are charged a flat fee for childcare. State-run after-school centers care for primary-school children free of charge. *Practice:* In 1979 the State allocated M. 259.8 million for maternity leaves. In 1982 family allowances were M. 20 each for the first and second child, M. 50 for the third, 60 for the fourth, and 70 for the fifth and subsequent children.

In 1981, 61% of children under age 3 were in creches, and 95% of under-school-age children had places in kindergartens. There is still a great shortage of places in childcare centers. From 1978–81, 370,000 women chose a year's leave. The government emphasizes the nuclear family through financial incentives, maternity and work policies, and housing allotments—which are State-controlled and which favor married couples. Maternity benefits, reduced work week, and the paid 1 day a month at home reinforce women's role in the family, as these benefits are not offered to male parents.

Welfare. *Policy:* A social insurance system is composed of 2 plans: the State plan and the trade-union plan. Participation in 1 of them is mandatory; nonworkers are covered under the State plan. They are financed by employee, State, and employer contributions. Insurance pays for all medical and hospital care, as well as workers' compensation. A portion of the federal budget is distributed through such social funds as allowances and benefits (see **Family**), income supplements, and subsidies for rent, utilities, education, health, etc. Pensions for women over age 60 and men over 65 are based on lifetime earnings; pensioners pay no taxes or social insurance contributions and receive free medical care and full insurance. The State runs homes for the aged. *Practice:* Approx. 80% of the pop. is insured by the trade-union plan, 20% by the State plan; 18% of the pop. is pensioners. The average retirement pay is 30% of an employee's average gross earnings. As of 1980 there were places for approx. 120,000 people in homes for the aged. In the 1970's government housing settlements for young families were built (called the "storks' nest"). **Contraception.** *Policy:* Legal. Birth control is considered indispensable to women's equality; however, the government is pronatalist and encourages population growth through material incentives for having large families. The pill is the most available method and is free, with a doctor's prescription. *Practice:* No data obtainable. **Abortion.** *Policy:* Legal and free on request during the first trimester in State clinics since 1972. The procedure is generally not permitted within 6 months of a previous abortion. Because the Socialist Unity Party feared a declining birth rate and with it a shrinking labor force, from 1950 to 1965 abortion was permitted only on medical or eugenic grounds; after 1965 a women's social environment could be considered. *Practice:* Abortions (per 1000 women age 15–44, 1977): 22.5; abortions (per 1000 known pregnancies, 1977): 260. **Illegitimacy.** *Policy:* Under the Civil Code, single mothers and their children have equal rights. The father of a child born out of wedlock pays support as directed by the court; if he fails to pay, the money is deducted from his salary and paid to the mother. Children of single mothers are given priority for placement in creches or kindergartens. Mothers are paid a monthly benefit if no places are available and are granted up to 13 weeks per yr. of paid sick leave to care for sick children. *Practice:* No data obtainable. **Homosexuality.** *Policy:* Under the Penal Code (1871, amended 1950), same-sex relationships are punishable by up to 3 yrs. imprisonment; women are not mentioned specifically. Laws against "sexual slander" or "inciting to sexual exhibitionism," punishable by up to 2 yrs., also may be applied. *Practice:* Considered an "abnormality and incompatible with socialist morality." Homosexual-rights associations and a few specifically lesbian-rights groups exist covertly, because of government opposition.

Incest. *Policy:* Illegal under the Penal Code (1871, amended 1950); ascendant relatives convicted of incest are punishable by up to 5 yrs. imprisonment, descendant by up to 2 yrs., brother/sister by up to 2 yrs.; loss of civil rights may also be imposed. Persons under age 18 are not subject to punishment. *Practice:* No data obtainable. **Sexual Harassment.** *Policy:* None. *Practice:* No data obtainable. **Rape.** *Policy:* Illegal under the Penal Code (1871, amended 1950); anyone who by force, threat, or immediate bodily harm forces a woman to submit to extramarital sexual intercourse is subject to imprisonment; marital rape is not recognized by law. Rape of a female under age 16, gang rape, or rape with "major physical violence" is subject to a more severe punishment. If (undefined) extenuating

circumstances exist, the crime is punishable by not less than 1 yr. *Practice:* No data obtainable. **Battery.** *Policy:* No data obtainable. *Practice:* No data obtainable. **Prostitution.** *Policy:* Illegal (1871 Penal Code, amended 1950, Sec. 123); the practice of prostitution is punishable under laws pertaining to "parasites of society" by a maximum 2 yrs. imprisonment; a male who derives his livelihood wholly or partially from a female prostitute by exploiting her "immoral" trade, or who habitually or for gain renders protection or otherwise furthers the exercise of her illicit trade is punishable by maximum 5 yrs. imprisonment; traffick in girls or women for the purpose of prostitution is punishable by up to 8 yrs. *Practice:* No data obtainable. **Traditional/Cultural Practices:** No data obtainable. **Crisis Centers.** *Policy:* No data obtainable. *Practice:* None.

HERSTORY. Germany has been divided into 2 countries, East and West, since 1949, a result of WW II. East Germany (the German Democratic Republic) thus shares a 2-millennium past with West Germany (the Federal Republic of Germany). In the 6th–4th centuries B.C.E., Germany was populated by tribes from central Asia. They were influenced by and in time overran the Roman Empire, which at its height had advanced into Germany as far as the Rhine. One of the Germanic tribes, the Franks, prevailed and ruled western Europe under Charlemagne, who was crowned in 800 C.E.

Early Germanic and Celtic tribes ranged in structure from patriarchal to matriarchal, but even the more androcentric of them surprised Roman chroniclers (Tacitus, Hesiod, and Julius Caesar) by the presence in battle of women, often leading raids. In 1954 the grave of a 4th-century B.C.E. Celtic woman was discovered at Reinheim near Saarbrücken; it is thought that she was a chief, as she was buried with gold treasure signifying leadership rank.

After Christianization (under Charlemagne), women were more confined to the private sphere, but there were exceptions—notable German scholars and religious figures, such as Hrotsvitha (Roswitha von Gandersheim, 10th century), the poet, playwright, and nun; Hildegarde of Bingen (1098–1179), a composer and religious mystic called "the Sibyl of the Rhine"; and the mystical religious writers Mechtilde of Hackeborn (c. 1241–1298), Mechtilde of Magdeburg, and Gertrude of Helfta (c. 1256–1302).

In "the Burning Time," approx. 9 million women and girls were killed as witches over a 300-yr. period (c. 1400–1700) in central Europe, primarily in the area now known as Germany. Wurzburg, Mannheim, and Eichstadt were only 3 of the many centers of trials, torture, and execution (usually by burning) of women accused of witchcraft. Many Christian female leaders and some entire convents (which had functioned as centers of learning for women) were accused and executed; 1 major trial was of Sister Maria Renata Sanger, the sub-prioress of the Premonstratensian Convent at Unter-Zell, who was accused of lesbianism and was tortured and killed.

Margaret Moultash (1318–69) was Countess of Tyrol. Historically depicted as an evil woman, she was a rebellious political figure of her time. She expelled her husband, John Henry of Luxembourg, from the Tyrol, defied the Pope (Benedict XII) by obtaining a secular annulment, and married Louis of Brandenburg; although her subjects remained loyal to her, the nobility denounced her.

Katharina Zell-Schützin (14th century) wrote major theological treatises, and her contemporary, Katharina von Bora, was a Cistercian nun in Leipzig who fled the convent and later (1523) married Martin Luther, the religious reformer. "Proud and arrogant," as Luther termed her, Katharina often intervened in his scholarly discussions with other theologians.

Anna Magdalena Wülken married Johann Sebastian Bach in 1721 after the death of his first wife, Maria Barbara; Anna Magdalena bore 13 children (Maria Barbara had borne 7), and was thought to have inspired the *Anna Magdalena Bachbüch* of musical pieces, until it was realized that the work—and some of Bach's other works, including parts of the B Minor Mass, the Passions, and many of the Cantati—may have been composed by her, since she was herself a notable musician and composer. In addition to the Bach sons, a daughter, Elisabeth, authored many works as part of the Bach family atelier.

The observation of the Salic Law in most of Prussia and surrounding areas meant that women were barred from ruling, although the ascension of Maria Theresa (see AUSTRIA and HUNGARY) to the Hapsburg throne in the 18th century was a notable exception. In 1851 the Prussian Law of Association prohibited women from engaging in politics, joining political parties, and even attending political meetings; only in the states of Baden, Bremen, Hamburg, and Württemberg were women permitted any political rights.

Nineteenth-century feminist activism included the German Women's Assoc. (1865), which worked for reform of the Civil Code to grant women more power within the family. Under the leadership of Louise Otto-Peters, a novelist, the group also focused on women's education and entrance to medical schools. Otto-Peters published the *Women's Newspaper* in 1849. The Women's Educational Assoc. in Leipzig, founded in 1866, was notably democratic in structure—unusual among the hierarchical forms of most German organizations of the period. In 1878, at the suggestion of the Crown Princess, select segments of the Civil Service (such as the Telegraph Center) were opened to women applicants. That year, 3-week unpaid maternity leaves were enacted, in response to the campaign by the Society for the Protection of Motherhood and Sexual Reform; paid leaves were not introduced until 1882.

In 1894 the Federation of German Women's Associations (BDF) united 34 women's groups with social-welfare orientations. Minna Cauer founded a feminist magazine, *The Women's Movement*, in 1895. Cauer, Anita Augspurg, and Marie Stritt, feminists with a radical stance, influenced the direction of the BDF, leading another Civil Code reform effort in 1896. A specifically Jewish feminist movement emerged at the turn of the century, called Judischer Frauenbund. Founded by Bertha Popenheim, the group had 50,000 members who worked for suffrage for the entire Jewish community, to end the practice of female sexual-slave traffick, and to increase jobs for women. Prostitution and morality dominated discussions in the movement in the early 1900's, led by the Abolitionists.

By 1902 attention turned to suffrage, and the German Union for Women's Suffrage was founded, led by Anita Augspurg and influenced by English suffragists and suffragettes (see BRITAIN). In 1905 Paula Mueller organized a school of social work for women. The 1908 Law of Association allowed women to join political parties for the first time; the German Alliance for Women's Suffrage was created in 1911. Helene Stöcker, a leader in the (prostitution-) Abolitionist movement, was also a founder of the "New Morality" school, advocating free love and moral libertarianism, and criticizing the institution of marriage. The League for Mutterschutz (motherhood) was founded in 1904 by Ruth Bré, who called for restoration of matriarchy and the establishment of communes where single mothers and their children would live and work; the League fought a ban on the sale and advertisement of contraceptives. Minna Cauer, Adele Schreiber, and Helene Stöcker, some of whom were leaders of the Union of Progressive Women's Associations, were supportive of the League. The New Moralists wanted legal equality between husband and wife, easier divorce, recognition of "free marriages," and equal rights for out-of-wedlock children.

During WW I, the BDF set up the National Women's Service to do support work with government agencies. Nationalist, pro-war sentiments caused a split in the movement, with such radical feminists as Anita Augspurg and Lida Heymann calling for German participation in the international peace movement. Authorities in the government, suspicious of feminist pacifists, demanded an end to all feminist activities during the war, for "public security" reasons. Augspurg led a delegation of feminists to the 1915 Hague Congress, demanding international arbitration and democratic control of foreign policy. After Germany's defeat in the war, constitutional reforms were introduced, including "universal" suffrage but excluding women. Women finally won the vote in 1919.

Major figures in terms of both feminism and left-wing politics between the wars included Clara Zetkin (1857–1933; see USSR), founder of the Socialist Women's Movement and of the newspaper *Equality,* and lifelong friend of Rosa Luxemburg (see POLAND); the artist Kaethe Kollwitz was a political activist, following in the tradition of such painters as Paula Modersohn-Becker.

Under the Weimar Republic, women's professional and white-collar-work associations proliferated, as well as unions and societies representing women postal workers, government employees, and kindergarten teachers. The German Housewives' Assoc. had a membership of almost 100,000 and was an active economic pressure group. A lesbian women's subculture flourished in Berlin. By 1926 German feminists had elected 32 women to the Reichstag. They had also begun organizing against "protective" labor legislation (which served to keep women out of certain jobs), on international pacifist issues, and on decriminalization of prostitution and abortion.

In the 1930's and 1940's the women's movement was an early and primary target for attack by the rising National Socialist Party. With the rise in unemployment and inflation, propaganda put the blame on women in the work force as well as on Jews and Marxists, and the entrenchment of Nazi Party power was due in no small part to the male backlash against feminist achievements. (As early as 1912, this backlash had begun in the founding of the League for the Prevention of the Emancipation of Women.) The National Socialist Movement and Party agitated against contraception and abortion, homosexuality, and employed women, and revived the *Kinde, Kirche, Kuche* (Children, Church, and Kitchen) ideal for German womanhood. Most religious groups backed Hitler's view of the family and of women; the working coalition served long enough to solidify Hitler's aims.

Feminist groups and publications and contraceptive clinics were closed down. Hitler became chancellor in 1933; that year feminists, along with "non-Aryans," were forced out of their jobs in teaching and other public positions. Women were barred from political office in the Reichstag and from the judicial bench. Single women were punitively taxed; loans were given to young married couples, with extra allowances for those who had children. By 1934 Hitler was president and chancellor. Abortion was banned and made a criminal offense punishable by hard labor for the woman and death for the practitioner. Feminist and family-planning books were banned and then publicly burned.

The Nuremberg Laws of 1935 stripped Jews in Germany of their citizenship, outlawed marriage between Jew and Gentiles, and eliminated Jews from professional life. A systematic attempt began to exterminate the Jewish population of Germany and later of German-occupied countries—the "Final Solution" to the "Jewish Problem." In 1936 Hitler remilitarized the Rhineland, annexed Austria and the Sudetenland, and in 1939 invaded Poland. Germany allied with Italy and Japan; these 3, together with Spain, constituted the major Axis Powers. In the early years of the war, Germany conquered Poland, Denmark, Norway, Belgium, the Netherlands, Luxembourg, France, the Balkan States, and Greece.

During the war, official Nazi women's organizations furthered the anti-feminist propaganda and reality. German women staffed factories. Women and children, as the bulk of the civilian population, suffered from food shortages and from bombing devastation by the Allied Forces in such cities as Dresden and Cologne. Jewish women were imprisoned in forced-labor and concentration camps along with Jewish men and children, and in some all-woman camps such as Ravensbrück—which were used as brothels for German soldiers or as the sites of medical experimentation at the level of torture; they were also gassed by the hundreds of thousands. Many women fought back inside the death camps, including Sala Lerner at Sachsenhausen, and Olga Benario and Charlotte Eisenbletter, who organized the Women's Resistance at Ravensbrück. The "death camps" facilitated the murder of 6 million Jews and

approx. 6 million other "undesirables": partisans, Christians, radicals, homosexuals, Gypsies, and Slavs. Some German women were active in the underground resistance movement, and some hid fugitive Jews or political partisans.

After Germany's defeat and partition by the 4 major allied powers, the USSR clashed with France, the US, and Britain, resulting in a blockade between Berlin and western zones of Germany and the eventual creation of Communist East Germany (GDR). The 3 Western powers merged zones, creating West Germany (see WEST GERMANY, FRD). Hope of any resurgence of an autonomous women's movement was co-opted by official women's federations of the East German State. Abortion regulations were tightened, as an immigrant labor force was imported (largely from Turkey) to compensate for a declining birth rate. In 1953 workers' riots in East Berlin and other cities erupted in an atmosphere of political repression and economic hardship; Soviet troops put down the riots with force. In 1955 East Germany joined other Soviet-allied countries in the Warsaw Treaty Organization and built the Berlin Wall in 1961, separating the east and west sectors. A new constitution was adopted in 1968, based on 1-party rule.

Nonetheless, women continued to be active, especially in the (official) trade unions and in the more autonomous albeit constricted arts. The Trade Union Commission of Women in Industry claims that more than 1/2 of its 9 million members are women, and the official WIDF (Women's International Democratic Federation) publishes a magazine, Women of the Whole World, in a number of languages. Gisela Mauritz, a chemist, was imprisoned in 1974 for "illegal crossing of the border"; released in 1978, she formally applied for emigration and was re-arrested; she is 1 of 160 people currently imprisoned for trying to leave the country. As of Feb. 1984, Barbel Bohley and Ulricke Poppe remain in custody after a 1983 arrest for peace and nuclear disarmament activism. Of contemporary East German women writers, Christa Wolf and Irmtraud Morgner (see following article) are the best known.

MYTHOGRAPHY. The Teutonic peoples have a long record of religious-cultural reverence of female deities and heroic figures, including those in the Niebelung Legend (Norse goddesses Erda, Freya, Fricka, etc., and the warrior Brunhilde and her Valkyrie sisters). Respect for and fear of "witchcraft" was so prevalent in the Middle Ages that it became manipulated by Church and State into the most extensive witch purge in European history (see East German HERSTORY).

GERMANY (EAST; GDR): Witch Vilmma's Invention of Speech-Swallowing (A Parable*)

by Irmtraud Morgner
(Translated by Edite Kroll)

"It annoys me," Diderot says in his philosophical writing, "that passions are regarded only negatively. People must think they are insulting reason if they say anything in favor of passion. Yet only passions, and intense passions for that matter, can elevate the soul to greatness. Without passions nothing noble can exist in morals or in works of art; without passions the beautiful arts would sink back to the stage of childhood, and without passions virtue becomes petty."

My husband Konrad is distinguished by great passions. His historical archive is, to him, no collection of documents. He does not guard a mere scientific treasure. To him, history is the queen of all the social sciences, and he treats it as a person of his character would: royally. His associates are aware that he loves and reveres history in a personified way; no one smirks when Dr. Tenner talks about "Her Majesty." His conceit is accepted even in official speeches. Employees of the Institute for History gratefully pick up every hint of a new Tenner oddity and spread it by gossip. They have come to demand eccentricity from their boss. And Tenner knows what he owes himself and his people. He obliges them by expressing what he is, and occasionally going even further than that, so as not to disappoint his troops. Acquiring five television sets, all of which he either turns off at once or keeps on at once—this does not strike me as a natural eccentricity but an artificial one. It was spread around the Institute with such speed and so much pleasure that only respectable folk could be surprised at Tenner's sudden election to his union's executive committee. The others like their contact with quality, and he invigorates, he propels. The majority knows that intellectual power manifests itself as originality, in thought processes that abandon normal channels—which results in eccentricity. Only passion can transport one out of those normal channels. These thought processes are consequently not merely exercises for the brain. The whole personality is affected by it. When Konrad lingers with his queen, History, his eyes shine and his face appears frozen and enraptured. He usually lingers with Her Majesty. I of course behave accordingly: any interruption of concentration results in gestures of physical pain—and inflicts some, as I know from experience. My children all learned very early when their father was unapproachable, and to behave accordingly. If they didn't, Konrad would throw whatever was

---

* Excerpted with permission from *Amanda: A Witch Novel* (Aufbau-Verlag in East Germany and Luchterhand in West Germany, publication 1983), Vol. 2 in a projected trilogy by Irmtraud Morgner which began with *Leben und Abenteuer der Trobadora Beatriz nach Zeugnissen Ihrer Spielfrau Laura* (Copyright © 1974).

closest at hand. He had adopted this habit from Newton. Konrad argued, "If even a genius like Isaac Newton could not work without uninterrupted concentration, a poor body like me must *insist* on it in order to produce anything useful." A good argument, this. Lovely, passionate determination, which officially honors any man—and which officially ruins any woman. Because passion is permitted us women only in love. In all other areas, the scourge of good behavior keeps us down. Konrad and the world at large expect me to be relaxed, even-tempered, retiring, adaptable. Any woman who regarded herself as Konrad does, as unapproachable by her children, would be considered a cruel mother. I would have been remiss in my duty if I had not swallowed the pain which results from having one's concentration disrupted. The children would have felt rejected. And over a period of time they would have become psychologically sick as well, if they had not known someone was there for them. Somebody had to be there. Every human being needs a refuge. I am the refuge for Konrad and the other children. And where is my refuge? Where could I go with my passions? "Management of a household is almost as taxing as management of an entire country," Montaigne said, "Everything demands total attention; consequently, less important matters are no less burdensome."

A woman who would anthropomorphize or personify science would be considered sick. She would be called crazy. Then again, I would have trouble regarding history as a queen in any case, since written history has historically expropriated women. And the history that's not considered worthy of being written down is a history of crimes committed against the female sex.

Unwritten philosophy is my queen, though I had to keep this secret for several reasons. To keep passions secret—how come? Occasionally I fled to the bathroom to delay being interrupted in my unofficial work. There I often suppressed my pain at being interrupted in order to fulfill my duties—that is, to satisfy moral expectations.

Konrad has accepted great sacrifices in order to develop his basic abilities. I had to expend most of my energy on adapting as demanded of me. But I swallowed no pills, took no so-called tranquilizers which every modern woman carries in her pocketbook next to the birth-control pill. In the past, witches were destroyed at the stake, today they are destroyed with I-don't-give-a-shit pills.

My discovery dates back to my student days, when my secret philosophical studies had not progressed very far. Sometimes I thought I was going in the right direction. At other times I had doubts. Sometimes I pursued sources with passion. At other times I was forced to passionately disagree. How? And where?

"Extinguished passions diminish a person," said Diderot. "Nothing extraordinary is created in poetry or painting whenever the tendency to pettiness has the same effect on temperament as that of old age."

The best discoveries are born out of need. "One has to try to wind one's way with clever tricks if it proves impossible to lead a beautifully delineated life," said Kafka.

The art of swallowing food is considered natural.

I invented the art of swallowing words.

This art eases all women's sufferings. It liberates many powers that would otherwise have to be expanded on adaptation. It qualifies.

Whenever Konrad had or has an idea, he had or has the unquenchable need to communicate it. If the idea strikes him at home, he tells it to me immediately through the kitchen window. If it occurs in the archive, an associate is forced to receive it; if it comes to him in the course of a séance, it is communicated to a friend. Such communications are eruptions of enjoyment: shared pleasure, doubled pleasure. And pleasure is healthy. Successful experiences produce new strengths.

Mostly, of course, it is not a successful experience. Because it wasn't an idea. Real ideas occur seldom. Some ideas are revealed as counterfeit ones as they are uttered by their conceiver, others are recognized as such by those who hear them. Konrad needs the communication so as to rid himself of false riches. He calls unspoken thoughts "false riches" or "headclouds." And he doesn't allow storage space for headclouds. He makes sure that his brain is used rationally, pointing out that Schiller could not write poems without communicating with his friends.

I have become an inventor, because my need to communicate is as great as Konrad's. The invention of body speech permits me, as well as all women, to satisfy our need to communicate. No more amassing of false riches, no headclouds. But also no side effects of abstaining because of censorship, because society permits women ideas only when they do not burden anyone.

Whenever I have formed a philosophical idea, I say it aloud—and swallow it. The technique of ingesting speech is easy to learn: swallowed speech equals examined speech. Self-examination may not be able to replace examination by strangers or intellectual stimulation, but it can help one keep one's reason.

Without the art of swallowing speech I would never have reached my twenty-fourth year without having lost my reason.

Without speech ingestion I would have become a suicide.

Consequently, my thesis is: Speech-swallowing by women is a stabilizing factor of our worker and farmer republic.

Suggested Further Reading

Wander, Maxie. *Guten Morgen, Du Schöne: Frauen in der DDR*. East Berlin: Der Morgen, 1978; Darmstadt: Luchterhand, 1978.

Wolf, Christa. *A Model Childhood*. New York: Farrar, Straus & Giroux, 1980.

———. *The Quest for Christa T.* New York: Farrar, Straus & Giroux, 1970.

———. *The Reader and the Writer*. New York: International Publishers, 1978.

Irmtraud Morgner was born in 1933 in Chemnitz, and studied German literature, philosophy, and linguistics in Leipzig. Since 1958 she has been a free-lance writer. She lives in East Berlin and has written four novels: *Hochzeit in Konstantinopel* (Wedding in Constantinople), 1959, *Gauklerlegende* (A Tall Tale), 1971, *Die wundersamen Reisen Gustav des Weltfahrers* (The Awesome Travels of Gustav the World Traveler), 1972, *Leben und Abenteuer der Trobadora Beatriz nach Zeugnissen Ihrer Spielfrau Laura* (Life and Adventures of the Troubador Beatrice as Chronicled by Her Playmate Laura), 1974. She is published by Aufbau-Verlag in East Germany and by Luchterhand in West Germany.

GERMANY (WEST)
(Federal Republic of Germany)

Located in central Europe, bordered by East Germany and Czechoslovakia to the east, Austria and Switzerland to the south, France, Luxembourg, Belgium, and the Netherlands to the west, and the North Sea, Denmark, and the Baltic Sea to the north. **Area:** 248,161 sq. km. (95,815 sq. mi.). **Population** (1980): 61,132,000, female 52%. **Capital:** Bonn.

DEMOGRAPHY. Languages: German. **Races or Ethnic Groups:** German, immigrant pop. from Spain, Yugoslavia, Italy, and Turkey, other. **Religions:** Protestant 49%, Roman Catholicism 44%, Judaism 1%, other. **Education** (% enrolled in school, 1975): Age 6–11—of all girls 96%, of all boys 96%; age 12–17—of all girls 93%, of all boys 90%; higher education—in 1979–80 women were 36% of university students, 28% of technical college, and 27% of theological college. **Literacy** (1977): 99%; no rates by sex obtainable. **Birth Rate** (per 1000 pop., 1977–78): 9. **Death Rate** (per 1000 pop., 1977–78): 12. **Infant Mortality** (per 1000 live births, 1977): Female 17, male 22. **Life Expectancy** (1975–80): Female 75 yrs., male 69 yrs.

GOVERNMENT. The 1949 Basic Law (constitution, since amended) established a republic which gained full independence and sovereignty in 1955. A bicameral parliament consists of the 45-member Bundesrat (upper house), appointed from 10 Laender (states) plus West Berlin, and the elected 520-member Bundestag (lower house); representatives from West Berlin are nonvoting. The entire parliament elects a president who appoints a cabinet; the Bundestag elects a chancellor. **Women's Suffrage:** In (unified) Germany, 1919; continued under West German government in 1949. **Equal Rights:** 1949 Basic Law (Art. 3) stipulates equal rights for men and women and prohibits discrimination on the basis of sex, race, creed, etc. **Women in Government:** In 1983 women comprise 22% of the Bundesrat and 10% of the Bundestag; Dorothee Wilms is Minister

of Education and Science and Annemarie Renger is vice-president of the Bundestag. Petra Kelly heads the Green Party (1983). Fewer than 10% of city and state parliament members are women.

ECONOMY. Currency: Deutsche Mark (May 1983: 2.45 = $1 US). **Gross National Product** (1980): $827.8 billion. **Per Capita Income** (1980): $13,590. **Women's Wages as a Percentage of Men's:** No general statistics obtainable (in nonagricultural activities 72%, 1981; in agricultural force 78.5%, 1975). **Equal Pay Policy:** 1980 law stipulates equal pay for equal work and equal status in employment, and prohibits discrimination in hiring, promotions, and firing. In practice, men but not women are often given "labor market allowances" for hard-to-fill jobs, and different wage rates evade the law. **Production** (Agricultural/Industrial): Grains, potatoes, sugar beets; iron, steel, coal, machinery, motor vehicles. **Women as a Percentage of Labor Force** (1980): 38%; **of agricultural force** 51% (of whom 81% are unpaid family workers); **of industrial force**—no general statistics obtainable (of manufacturing 31%, 1980); **of military** (1982) 48,895 women are employed by the Federal Ministry of Defense; of these 21,053 are in civilian jobs in the armed forces; since 1975, women physicians can become medical officers. Women are prohibited from bearing arms. In 1982 the Defense Minister proposed a plan to recruit 30,000 women because of the acute shortage of draft-age men. **(Employed) Women's Occupational Indicators** (1980): Of administrative and managerial workers 16.5%, of technical and professional workers 38%, of sales workers 56%, of service workers 56%, of clerical workers 58%. **Unemployment** (mid-1982): 6.8%, female 8%, male 6%.

GYNOGRAPHY. Marriage. *Policy:* Minimum marriage age is 16 for females and males with parental consent and 18 for both without consent. The 1977 Marriage and Family Law eliminated the concept of male as head of household. Both partners are jointly responsible for family income, household work, and children's welfare; women now have the right to work outside the home without obtaining husbands' permission. *Practice:* Female mean age at marriage (1970–78): 22; women age 15–49 in union (1970–78): 67%. According to a 1983 government report, women still do the majority of housework; 1 survey revealed that 70% of employed women with at least 1 child received no help at all from their husbands. **Divorce.** *Policy:* A 1979 law replaced the principle of "guilty party" with "irreparable breakdown." Marriage can be dissolved after a 1-yr. separation if there is mutual consent or a 3-yr. separation without consent. Each partner is responsible for her/his own maintenance after divorce unless 1 partner has custody of children, cannot find employment, could not complete study/training because of marriage, or is disabled. All pensions and other entitlements acquired during marriage are divided, benefiting women who work as homemakers. *Practice:* Divorces (per 1000 pop., 1978): 0.53. In 1978 only 29% of all divorced women were entitled to alimony, and average payments were DM. 420 per month.

Family. *Policy:* Employed pregnant women are entitled to paid maternity leave 6 weeks pre- and 8 weeks post-delivery; in addition, an optional 4-month leave is available with monthly payments up to DM. 750; a woman cannot be dismissed during pregnancy or for up to 2 months after leave. Child allowances are paid regardless of parents' income and increase with the number of children. The government subsidizes childcare centers. *Practice:* There are approx. 23,000 day-care centers in the country, but many areas have no facilities. In 1979 monthly child allowances were DM. 50 for the first child, 100 for the second, and 200 for the third and subsequent children. In 1976, 1.25 million single (never married, divorced, separated, or widowed) mothers lived alone with children. **Welfare.** *Policy:* The social security system, financed by employee, employer, and State contributions, includes maternity benefits and child allowances (see

Family), and health, unemployment, disability, and old-age insurance. A welfare program assists persons with insufficient income or in special circumstances. *Practice:* In 1980, 1/3 of the GNP was spent on social services. In 1982, 92% of the pop. was covered under compulsory health insurance. A proposed law would compensate for the differential between men's and women's pensions, which stems from women's generally lower earnings.

Contraception. *Policy:* Legal, including voluntary sterilization. The State funds some family-planning centers and subsidizes Pro-Familia, a private organization. *Practice:* No statistics obtainable. Highest number of birth-control users choose the pill and the IUD, with a very small percentage using sterilization. **Abortion.** *Policy:* Legal (Penal Code). Abortion was made legal on request in 1974, but the law was struck down by a court decision; 1976 revised legislation permits the procedure up to the 22nd week if, according to medical findings, the life or physical/mental health of the woman or the health of the fetus is endangered, taking into account the current and future living conditions of the woman, and up to the 12th week if pregnancy is a result of rape or other sexual abuse, or would cause such grave consequences that the woman cannot be expected to continue pregnancy, or that cannot be averted by other means. In other than health- or life-threatening situations, the woman must obtain counseling and wait 3 days, and the physician authorizing the abortion cannot perform the procedure. Other procedures are punishable by a fine or up to 5 yrs. imprisonment for the practitioner, and a fine or up to 1 yr. for the woman (though the court can refrain from punishing her). Social health insurance assists in the cost of legal abortion. *Practice:* Reported abortions (per 1000 women age 15–44, 1981): 6.5 (in FRD). In addition to 87,500 procedures in West Germany, residents obtained 21,400 abortions abroad (incomplete 1981 est.); actual number est. at 200,000. As of 1983 an abortion cost DM. 200–300 in public clinics and DM. 800–1200 in private clinics. Many physicians and hospitals refuse to perform the procedure. The law is under attack by churches and conservatives. **Illegitimacy.** *Policy:* According to Basic Law (Art. 6.5), "children born out of wedlock are to be granted the same chances as legitimate children with regard to their physical and mental development and position in society." Mothers exercise full parental authority. Fathers are required to pay maintenance if paternity has been established; if they fail to do so, the State assists in child support. Since 1969, out-of-wedlock children have had equal inheritance rights. *Practice:* In 1979, 7% of births were out of wedlock. In 1976 there were 116,000 single mothers with 135,000 children. **Homosexuality.** *Policy:* Legal between consenting adults since 1975. *Practice:* No statistics obtainable. There is a sizable homosexual-and-lesbian-rights movement in West Germany.

Incest. *Policy.* Illegal (Penal Code); ascendant relatives convicted of incest are punishable by a fine or up to 3 yrs. imprisonment, descendant relatives by a fine or up to 2 yrs.; descendants or siblings under age 18 are not punishable. *Practice:* No data obtainable. **Sexual Harassment.** *Policy:* None. *Practice:* No data obtainable. **Rape.** *Policy:* Illegal (Penal Code). A man who forces a woman by violence or threat with a dangerous weapon to have extra-marital sexual relations with him or a third person is punishable by not less than 2 yrs. imprisonment; if "premeditation or malicious intent" is involved the punishment is up to 10 yrs.; in other cases (if the woman had been sexually involved with the man previously, for example), rape is punishable by 6 months–5 yrs. Marital rape is not recognized by law. *Practice:* In 1977, 9000 cases of rape were reported, 7000 were filed via the police, and 850 led to convictions. **Battery.** *Policy:* No specific laws covering wife-beating. If a woman files a complaint of bodily injury, general assault laws can apply. *Practice:* A 1977 Federal Family Report stated that battery occurs in approx. 5 million families. The Munich-based National Congress on Violence Against Women is 1 of several groups working against the problem (see **Crisis Centers**).

Prostitution. *Policy:* Legal; prostitutes are required to have health check-ups. Brothels must be located in designated areas and operate only between certain hours. The Penal Code (Sec. 181) makes traffick in children punishable by up to 10 yrs. imprisonment. *Practice:* No statistics obtainable. In the tourist section of Hamburg, "Eros Centers"—State-sanctioned prostitution hotels—began flourishing in the mid-1960's. Such places are charged high taxes and bring in large revenues for the State. Organized trafficking of women from other countries into prostitution (est. in the thousands) has been uncovered. **Traditional/Cultural Practices:** No data obtainable. **Crisis Centers.** *Policy:* The Women's House, supported by 80% federal and 20% city funds, opened in Berlin in 1976 as a 3-yr. model project. Limited government support has been extended to other projects. *Practice:* During 1976–79, 2500 women and approx. as many children found refuge in the Women's House in Berlin. The government's general attitude has been that already existing social agencies can absorb the problem, and so it rarely gives financial assistance to other centers. Feminists contend that autonomous shelters which offer safety, medical and legal advice, skills training, and self-help skills— not resocialization into a former abusive environment—are needed desperately. As of 1982, 120 shelters had been established by women's groups. The Working Group of Women's Houses, a coalition of feminist groups and shelters in North-Rhine Westphalia, coordinates regional and national meetings and recently was granted DM. 1.5 million from the State.

HERSTORY. See GERMANY (EAST) for data prior to 1949. West Germany became the Federal Republic of Germany in 1949.

The current wave of feminism, rising out of the student movement of the late 1960's, spearheaded the campaign for legalized abortion. In 1970 journalist Alice Schwarzer organized a campaign for abortion by stating publicly, "I have had an abortion." Success was achieved in 1974 (see **Abortion**).

The first women's movement congress was held in 1971 and every year thereafter through 1976. In the 1970's Ulrike Meinhof co-led the "Bader-Meinhof Gang" of left-wing urban terrorists; she died in prison, allegedly a suicide; by 1977, 10 of the 16 terrorists "most wanted" by West German police were women. In 1979 the German Housewives Union was revived (see EAST GERMANY HERSTORY) to improve social security, health insurance, and protection of mothers. Feminist publications blossomed in the 1970's: *Courage,* founded in 1976 in Berlin by a socialist-feminist collective, and *Emma,* founded by Alice Schwarzer, the largest feminist magazine in West Germany. Frauenoffensive is a major feminist book-publishing company. Women's cafés, centers, and bookstores, lesbian collectives and feminist activist groups organizing against pornography and violence-against-women issues

have proliferated. "Take Back the Night" marches have become an annual event, with thousands of women participating in candlelight demonstrations in cities all across West Germany. Women's leadership is also active in the large antinuclear and peace movements, and in the Green Party, a pacifist-ecologist political party. In 1983 Klaus Hecker, a newly elected Green Party member of parliament, was asked by women deputies to resign, on charges of sexual harassment; women Green Party members confirmed his behavior as physically assaultive.

MYTHOGRAPHY. See EAST GERMANY.

GERMANY (WEST; FRD): Fragmented Selves (A Collage)
by Renate Berger, Ingrid Kolb, and Marielouise Janssen-Jurreit

A Correspondence
(Translated by Carol Carl-Sime)

A day in May 1982. The mail on my desk includes an invitation to the Second Congress of the "Women's Initiative of 6th October," a letter from a rapist inquiring from prison whether I would be interested in writing about his case, and an essay by my friend Renate Berger on sexist tendencies in modern art. I shall go to the Congress. I know the women who launched this initiative the day after the last West German general election, as an expression of the anger and disappointment they felt toward the patriarchal politics of the established parties. It is an important conference; more than ever before we must demonstrate the threat we pose to the ruling classes. In our cities we now have women's centers, women's pubs and cafés, women's publishing houses, women's bookshops, women's refuges. But we continue to live in a man's world. The contemporary independent women's movement in West Germany has been in existence for some ten years. When I came to Hamburg in 1973 I heard that women were getting together to fight for their rights. I decided to join them; nothing in my life ever seemed more natural. It was in the women's group that I met Renate Berger. She was still a student at the time; now she's involved in teaching and research as an art historian. I've been working as a journalist for almost twenty years. (At *Stern,* where I have been since 1977, women writing for the magazine are in a minority, feminists a positive rarity.) When Renate went abroad for a while in 1976 we decided to write to each other. We have kept up our correspondence ever since. We hope that the extracts we have chosen reflect something of the country in which we live; something of ourselves; something of the women and the women's movement in West Germany.

—Ingrid Kolb

To Ingrid from Renate
31st March 1977

In our discussions yesterday I was struck by how backward most men are on issues with which we women have been concerning ourselves for years. Their naïveté, the blind faith they choose to place in the expert—this behavior is really very strange. They are obviously preoccupied with other problems, fighting their battles on a planet where women do not appear to exist. This is just an observation on my part; it is not intended to be a moral judgment.

To Renate from Ingrid
19th May 1977

Think back to our conversation about body language, and imagine an old woman with heavy legs (all bloated and lined with varicose veins) sitting on a bench: her skirt has risen to reveal too much of those poor thighs and that alleyway leading up to her genitals. It looks obscene since we all know that no one would want to go up there (nor do we wish to be reminded of what we may be like one day). One can see this picture quite clearly and dismiss it as unesthetic. But one can visualize the same scene and understand it as an "unesthetic" challenge to a world based on some false esthetic ideal, one which subjugates and represses women. We shouldn't be afraid of taking a closer look if it helps us to become angry and assume the attack.

To Renate from Ingrid
17th August 1977

What do you think of the German writer Günter Grass, who, when explaining his latest novel, *The Flounder,* said: "Originally, I set out to write about the history of nutrition. It's ended up as a history of women"? I mentioned this to a colleague. She couldn't understand my anger.

To Ingrid from Renate
5th May 1978, Vienna

Yesterday, Ascension Day, I took part in a meeting organized by the Austrian support committee of the Russell Tribunal. I heard that the Hamburg police had let loose Alsatian dogs on women during a Walpurgis Night demonstration and had some of them arrested. We were also told that policemen, after consulting with the leaders of the trade-union movement (of all people), had divided off the "mixed bag" at the end of the procession (the non-trade-union members of the march, the women, etc.) and roughed up some of them pretty badly. Am I overreacting to say that soon I feel the only option left to us is to become exiles or go down fighting like heroines?

I am frightened, not so much for myself, but in a rather diffuse sense. The causes of what is happening in Germany have not fully come to light. Contemporary circumstances force us to admit how little we really know to this day, for instance, about the causes and development of fascism—i.e., National Socialism. Can one really only become aware of the significance of such a phenomenon in a political period such as the one we are living through at this moment?

It is strange how close Germany is to me when I am abroad. We are becoming a nation of petty bourgeoisie, aspiring working-class and white-collar social climbers who, growing fat and increasingly more self-assured, push aside everything of secondary importance if it does not seem dynamic enough. The omissions of our intellectuals, if they have not since fled into more fruitful areas, are steeped in pathos—the degree of pathos depending on the measure of the desperation.

To Renate from Ingrid
19th May 1978

This morning I distributed leaflets at the weekly market. Our women journalists' group is organizing an election meeting in which Hamburg politicians are due to take part. What struck me particularly was the impregnability of those young mothers pushing their way through the crowds, laden down by children they are holding by the hand or pushing in the pram. They are unapproachable, silent, apathetic. If they would at least vent their aggressions! They are closed like oysters—but no pearl is being formed inside that shell.

To Renate from Ingrid
21st July 1978

Things are coming to a head in a strange way. Ever since I wrote a commentary supporting the ten women who took *Stern* to court over the issue of sexism on its front pages, I am considered by many of my *Stern* colleagues to be an intolerant, prejudiced (?!), humorless spinster. The question now is whether I can still become section editor.

Of course, all the wheeling and dealing goes on among the men on the top floor. I am the last person to be told anything. From the few scraps of information that have reached me from the negotiating table, I gather that the editor in chief doesn't want me for the job (or is at least reluctant to support me), but that the other lords presiding over my fate are anxious to find a quick, easy (cheap?) solution. For my part I am relaxed about the whole matter, knowing that if worse comes to worst, alliances of convenience will be forged, but that I cannot count on any genuine male allies. Men will not support women because they don't wish to be identified with weakness.

To Ingrid from Renate
22nd April 1979

I dreamed about having to live in a matchbox. What does that mean? (It was terrible, between you and me, although the box was empty.) You see, your friend wants to be pitied. Last winter, the gardeners cut back the high bushes in front of my window right to their stumps. It will take years for them to begin to recover from such radical surgery. They are showing no attempts to bud. Next autumn I shall lay poison for those gardeners —in keeping with the traditional role of the devious woman.

To Renate from Ingrid
26th May 1980

I would love to lead a double life like the Greek gods, and approach my chosen ones in varying guises. . . . And woe betide anyone who dares to ask me if I'm enjoying it. To hell with sexual perfectionism which turns off the erogenous zones.

To Ingrid from Renate
24th September 1981

I now get involved in everything: on the street (where I am particularly scared), at the fair, etc. You have to act or speak out when some youth tries to trip a pregnant woman or when an old man tells crude jokes about his "old girl." You have to be on the offensive the whole time and never give in—because it's the sum total of all these "trivial" incidents that will one day utterly overwhelm us. I'm losing faith in systems; instead, I concentrate my energies and attention exclusively on ideas and people. Every utopia feeds on those few remaining areas of humanity which are still meaningful in a personal way.

To Ingrid from Renate
20th October 1981

It's occurred to me that any State-paid torturer has more imagination than certain artists who still regard themselves as avant-garde because they haven't yet understood that there are no more tabus to break where women are concerned.

The final tabu is man, his dignity, offended by women.

* * *

A Poem

(Translated by Agnes Liebhardt)

When I wrote "Poem for My Mother" in 1970, the contemporary women's movement was just beginning in the Federal Republic of Germany. Feminist ideas were fresh and exciting. My mother had wanted to condemn me to live the same type of life she had lived: the life of an order-loving housewife corseted by her own conception of sexual morals, of the proper way for a woman to live and behave. I have always wanted freedom but have acknowledged from the very beginning that my freedom had its roots in the bondage and hopelessness of my mother's generation. Moreover, joining the women's movement meant to me that daughters were obliged to avenge their mother's deplorable life in post-war Germany. It was in this mood that the poem for my mother was written.

It is now almost fifteen years later—years of struggle by women against the patriarchal structure of parties, trade unions, big businesses, and the mass media. The result of those years is depressing, compared to what I had expected and deemed feasible. There is no doubt that there is increased consciousness in many women (and men). But in reality the situation of German women has deteriorated. Discrimination in the labor market continues. Such reforms as anti-discrimination acts or other legislation were not, after all, initiated. Programs to promote women in fields where they are underrepresented or not represented at all do not exist—except for the alibi of some pilot schemes to train a few dozen girls in technical vocations, which doesn't guarantee them jobs afterward anyway.

Furthermore, I am unavoidably aware that I live in a divided country whose population on both sides would be caught inextricably in the missile trap, should there ever be war. Many formerly feminist-focused activist women in Germany now concentrate their activities on peace and ecological movements.

I am prey to feelings of resignation, painful affection, and contemptuous mockery for my country. Law, order, and economic expansion were the fetishes of this nation in which I grew up. To all that, I opposed the world of women, the powerlessness of those who had not shaped it so.

Not before this powerlessness has been transformed into *refusal* shall we as women have a change—and no small change, I believe.

—Marielouise Janssen-Jurreit

A Poem

for my mother,
to bid farewell to her unhappy
ovaries and the tyranny
of the full moon
above her house,
I know she still
loves Russian basses and has dedicated
her menopause to them,

(sunset glow in the throat
of the Don Cossacks,
   who, except for her,
    sees it shine?)
for whom "who" does not exist,
does she clean windows,
whom does she expect
hourly—
with nostrils
of the violence of two vacuum cleaners
she hangs above the rug
and vomits dust
into an empty giant Tide box,
in order to stamp out
the mysterious spots
that keep forming in the bedroom,
she presents herself
in newspapers,
wife available,
cancer-free and ready-for-work,
known for her creative
Sunday goulashes,
her Pizza Primavera and her very special herring,
who adores her divine flour perspirations
who wants her?

for my 65-year-old aunt who is hard of hearing,
still trembling
over the man
under the bed,
hated for her hand-crocheted wedding presents,
humorless foliage plants
and marriage-making pot holders—
at night she dreams of the Führer
who visits her bed
with a special detachment
and sends her
a parachute of roses
and whips—
never
will she forgive us,
that she never was a widow, isn't a widow and never will be a
widow.

a poem

for my dead grandmother
and her rubbing alcohol
which she used to fight venereal disease,
which she never contracted,
unfortunately
she bequeathed me

her mistrust
and her ugly dreams of
freedom, rape, and syphilis,

for my great-aunt
in an asylum in Westphalia,
there's this old man there,
who follows her around
with his sagging pumpkin-belly,
an old man, soft like mull, he
loves all that's sour, sour pickles, sour lentil,
sour sperm, sour aspirin, sauerkraut,
an old man who masturbates
on time three times a week,
he hates women and
female dogs and is afraid of
women's rooms, where used
sanitary napkins stare at him,
there's this old man there,
who follows her around and demands
that she climb into the white enamel bucket
in the women's room
at his feet,

for my cousin from my mother's side,
a row house, lawnmower, dishwasher,
three-week-vacation-in-Italy, Saturday and Sunday
intercourse, every evening
the pill, news, and weather,
Mondays very early
she puts her orgasms
into the washing machine,
in order to reach that white for her sheets,
which lies beyond all names for white,

for my daughter,
who brings confusion to the street
with her intense Mama-cries
I shall have to
tell her the truth
about me—

a poem

for my mother
who cannot live
without a man
a poem
for her uterus-German,
that I cannot translate
into German
without destroying

> her life
> and my German.

Suggested Further Reading

Krechel, Ursula. *Selbsterfahrung und Fremdbestimmung* (Paths Toward the Self and the Alien). Darmstadt: Luchterhand Verlag, 1975.

Kuhn, Annette, and Valentine Rothe. *Frauen im Deutschen Faschismus—zwei Bände* (Women in Nazi Germany, 2 vols.). Düsseldorf: Schwann Verlag, 1982.

Schwarzer, Alice. *Der "kleine Unterschied" und seine grossen Folgen* (Fine Distinctions and Great Consequences). Frankfurt: S. Fischer Verlag, 1975.

————. *So fing es an! 10 Jahre Frauenbewegung* (So It Began! Ten Years of the Women's Movement). Cologne: Emma Verlag, 1982.

Stefan, Verena. *Häutungen.* Munich: Frauenoffensive, 1976; an autobiographical account of the contemporary German women's movement. (English trans., *Shedding,* Trans. Beth Weckmueller and Johanna Moore. New York: Daughters, Inc., 1978.)

Twellmann, Margrit. *Die Deutsche Frauenbewegung: Ihre Anfänge und erste Entwicklung, 1843–1889, Quellen* (The German Women's Movement: Its Beginning and Development 1843–1889; its Origin). Meisenheim am Glan: Anton Hain Verlag, 1972.

Dr. Renate Berger is an art historian living in Hamburg. Her doctoral thesis was "Women Artists on Their Way into the Twentieth Century: Art History as Social History." This work appeared in a book in West Germany in 1982. Her current research is involved with the presentation of suicide in the fine arts.

Ingrid Kolb is a journalist living in Hamburg, working for the magazine *Stern.* The series she wrote for it, "The Myth of Sexual Liberation," has since appeared as a book. Her particular areas of interest include emancipation, sexuality, and psychology.

Marielouise Janssen-Jurreit was born in 1941 in Dortmund, West Germany. From 1965 to 1971 she was editor of and reporter for the German magazine *Twen* and a correspondent on the war in Vietnam. In 1979 she edited an anthology on sex-discrimination legislation, *Frauenprogramm* (Women's Program), published by Rowohlt Verlag, Hamburg. Her book *Sexism* was published in 1976 (US edition: *Sexism,* New York: Farrar, Straus & Giroux, 1981). She is married, and has one daughter.

GHANA
(Republic of Ghana)

Located in West Africa, bordered by Togo to the east, the Atlantic Ocean to the south, Ivory Coast to the west, and Upper Volta to the north. **Area:** 238,537 sq. km. (92,100 sq. mi.). **Population** (1980): 11,679,000, female 50.6%. **Capital:** Accra.

DEMOGRAPHY. Languages: English (official), Twi, Fanti, Ga, Ewe, Dagbani. **Races or Ethnic Groups:** Akan (Ashanti, Fanti) 44%, Moshi–Dagomba 16%, Ewe 13%, Ga 8%, other. **Religions:** Christian 43%, indigenous faiths 38%, Islam (Maliki school of Sunni Islam) 12%. **Education** (% enrolled in school, 1975): Age 6–11—of all girls 47%, of all boys 56%; age 12–17—of all girls 38%, of all boys 56%; higher education—no data obtainable. **Literacy** (1977): Women 18%, men 43%. **Birth Rate** (per 1000 pop., 1975–80): 48. **Death Rate** (per 1000 pop., 1975–80): 17. **Infant Mortality** (per 1000 live births, 1975–80): Female 105, male 124. **Life Expectancy** (1975–80): Female 50 yrs., male 47 yrs.

GOVERNMENT. Present (1983) government installed by coup in 1981, led by Flight Lt. Jerry Rawlings, replacing civilian president Hilla Limann. Rawlings is Chair of the Provisional National Defense Council and rules by decree. The Constitution is suspended and no elections are held. **Women's Suffrage:** Universal suffrage granted in 1950 during colonial period, and confirmed in the 1957 Constitution after Independence. **Equal Rights:** No data obtainable. **Women in Government:** 6.5% of boards and councils at national and local levels (1975–78); Annie Jiagge is a Supreme Court justice and Chair of the National Council on the Status of Women (1983). As of 1979, only 1 woman had held a cabinet position, under Nkrumah, and few had ever been elected to Parliament, but in 1982 Ama Ata Aidoo (see following article) became Secretary of Education and Joyce Aryee Secretary for Information—both cabinet-level posts.

ECONOMY. Currency: Cedi (May 1983: 2.75 = $1 US). **Gross National Product** (1980): $4.9 billion. **Per Capita Income** (1980): $420. **Women's Wages as a Percentage of Men's** (1980): No general statistics obtainable; in agriculture 50%. **Equal Pay Policy:** None. **Production** (Agricultural/Industrial): Cocoa, coffee, palm products; timber, aluminum, light manufactures. **Women as a Percentage of Labor Force** (1980): 42%; **of agricultural force**—no general statistics obtainable (52% of women workers were employed in agriculture, 1975); **of industrial force**—no data obtainable; **of military**—no data obtainable. In 1971, 54% of all women were economically active. **(Employed) Women's Occupational Indicators:** No general statistics obtainable. Women are traditionally active in the economy, especially in food distribution. The market-women have great control over food trade and internal retail trade and are involved in real estate and transport. In 1960 women were 80% of the trade labor force. Women own and work farms for cash crops and subsistence farming. There is a small percentage of educated professional women. **Unemployment** (1980): 1.2%, female 0.8%, male 1.5% (official); unofficial reports indicate a high rate of unemployment in areas other than government employment.

GYNOGRAPHY. Marriage. *Policy:* Dualistic legal system composed of British colonial laws still influencing current Ghanaian statutory law, and customary laws of the people. There are 3 marriage systems recognized in Ghanaian law: the Marriage Ordinance (1886, revised 1971) follows British law based on monogamy and the nuclear family. Customary marriage is an alliance between 2 families and requiries parental consent as well as that of the spouses; Islamic marriage is also recognized; polygyny is considered valid. A dowry is usually paid by the husband's family to the wife's as a pledge of commitment and to compensate the woman's family for their loss of a daughter. Widows are usually not permitted to remarry under customary law. Property is considered separate. In such matrilineal groups as the Ashanti, a woman's status is not affected by marriage; children are part of her lineage, though the husband has certain rights and duties toward them, including their naming. Polygyny is common in the form of a man having a wife and several "girlfriends" with whom he may have children. In Ghanaian Islamic marriage, a man contracts with a woman's guardian to marry her, pays a dowry to the wife, may marry up to 4 wives at a time, and is entitled to unlimited concubines. The woman, as under customary law, may have only 1 husband and no other men. *Practice:* Female mean age at marriage (1981): 17.7; 97.7% of all females are married by age 25; as of 1960, 86% were customary marriages, 5.1% Islamic marriages, 2% Church and Ordinance marriages. Ordinance marriage is preferred by the Ghanaian elite. Social distinctions between wife and girlfriend in polygynous arrangements are often blurred. Problems exist with men not fulfilling responsibilities toward children from various unions. In 1956 the Federation of Ghana Women campaigned for legislation to strengthen customary marriage. A law to ban polygamy was proposed in 1968. Courts give women few rights to hold property jointly under customary marriage.

Divorce. *Policy:* Legal. Under customary and Islamic jurisprudence, divorce is the reverse of the marriage ceremony and involves negotiations between families of both spouses. Property is divided by arbitration. Among such patrilineal groups as the Ewe and the Ga, children go to the father; among matrilineal peoples, to the mother. There is no obligation to support an ex-wife. Marriages contracted under the Ordinance are subject to provisions of the Matrimonial Causes Act, which permits divorce on the grounds of "irretrievable breakdown of marriage" and requires a formal hearing before the court and a 2-yr. waiting period to receive a decree. *Practice:* No statistics obtainable. Women married under the Ordinance have more legal protection from arbitrary divorce by their husbands and greater economic security in receiving mainte-

nance. **Family.** *Policy:* Under customary law, parental obligations vary among the diverse ethnic groups. Fathers' responsibilities are less defined in such matrilineal societies as the Ashanti. Women are often heads of household, and among most groups the extended family is common. Family is the source of identity, status, and support for the elderly. The 1967 Labor Decree made maternity benefits available to employed women: 6 weeks pre– and 6 weeks post–delivery leave at 50% salary, guaranteed reinstatement, and nursing breaks during the workday. The State's family-planning program (see **Contraception**) includes such disincentives as limitations of maternity benefits and child allowances after 3 births for civil servants. The 1965 Maintenance of Children Act makes fathers legally responsible for child support. *Practice:* Breakdown of traditional patterns of familial obligation means women are not getting usual support from kin in maintaining children. Few women go to court for child support and most men default on court-ordered payments. There is a great demand for day nurseries in urban areas to aid employed women. Government and private agencies give minimal funding. **Welfare.** *Policy.* Social Security system pays benefits to employees and their families, including pensions (at age 50 for women), coverage for invalid widows, the sick, and the unemployed. Women are also eligible for workers' compensation. *Practice:* No data obtainable.

Contraception. *Policy:* Legal. Population control was part of the government's 5-yr. program (1975–80) to reduce the birth rate and improve health conditions. The Ghana Family Planning Program has been assisted by UNIDO in producing oral contraceptives at local factories since 1975. Manufacture and sale of most contraceptives is not regulated by law. Condoms and sometimes IUDs are sold in pharmacies and supermarkets; the pill is controlled by prescription; sterilization is legal, with conditions. In the late 1970's, a program of free or low-cost sterilization was proposed. *Practice:* Women age 15–49 in union using contraception (1970–80): 4%, of which traditional methods 25%, modern 75%.

Abortion. *Policy:* Legal to save the life of the woman and on health grounds. Under the Criminal Code, illegal abortions are punishable by a fine and 10 yrs. maximum imprisonment. *Practice:* No statistics obtainable, but illegal abortions are common in urban areas. In rural areas abortions are rare, due to the acceptance of out-of-wedlock children and large families. **Illegitimacy.** *Policy:* In customary law, concept of illegitimacy doesn't exist. In matrilineal cultures, all children's care and maintenance are assured by the mothers' kin. In such patrilineal cultures as the Ewe, children are under the protection of the father and his kin. A child socially recognized by its father is not considered illegitimate, regardless of parents' marital status, since polygyny and concubinage are common. Under the British-influenced Maintenance of Children Act, a mother may report a man who doesn't support her and their child. *Practice:* No statistics obtainable. Law lacks force of penalization. Most women don't have the funds for a court battle which would force a man to pay support under the Maintenance of Children Act. **Homosexuality.** *Policy:* Statutory law considers "unnatural carnal knowledge" of one man by another without his consent to be a first-degree felony; a homosexual act between consenting males is a misdemeanor. No policy exists regarding lesbianism. *Practice:* No data obtainable. **Incest.** *Policy:* Under statutory law, no data obtainable. Under customary law, marriage or sexual relations between people related by blood is tabu in both matrilineal and patrilineal societies. *Practice:* No data obtainable. **Sexual Harassment.** *Policy:* None. *Practice:* No data obtainable. **Rape.** *Policy:* Illegal. A first-degree felony, defined as "carnal knowledge of a female of any age by a man without her consent." Proof of vaginal penetration is necessary. "Carnal knowledge without rape" of a woman who is insane or "without reason" is a misdemeanor. *Practice:* No data obtainable. **Battery** *Policy:* No data obtainable. *Practice:* No data obtainable. **Prostitution.** *Policy:* Illegal. Prostitution, soliciting a female for unlawful carnal purposes, or living off a

prostitute's earnings, are all considered misdemeanors. *Practice:* No data obtainable. **Traditional/Cultural Practices.** *Policy:* No data obtainable. *Practice:* Clitoral excision* is commonly practiced in the western African region, including Ghana. **Crisis Centers.** *Policy:* None. *Practice:* No data obtainable.

HERSTORY. West African women of the matrilineal peoples have always had high status within their communities. The Queen Mother, usually the King's sister or aunt, is the one who traditionally possesses the genealogical knowledge for selecting the new king. *Abusua,* the matrilineal line of descent, places a high value on female babies. Roles of women in precolonial Ghana varied among the ethnic groups, but generally women were independent and integral to the economy as traders and cultivators. Social mores did not limit women's sexuality by overvaluing virginity. Women held important political positions and were highly respected. Among the Akan, women served as chiefs. Yaa Asantewaa was an Ashanti woman who led her people into battle during the Anglo-Ashanti War in 1900. Certain high religious positions were reserved for Ga women. Colonization contributed to the decline in status of all Ghanaian women.

In 1915, 1 girl was educated for every 6 boys. The Ghanaian elite began to adopt British names, clothing, and values promoted by Christian missionaries that emphasized the nuclear family, replacing the traditional extended family in which women had been respected and relatively powerful. Many women were active in the nationalist movement. In 1957 Ghana became the first of Britain's African colonies to win Independence.

Several women's organizations have developed to protect women's interests. The Federation of Ghana Women, founded (1953) by Dr. Evelyn Amartiefio, was composed of women in trading and business. The Women's League for Social Advancement, formed by Hannah Cudjoe during nationalist leader Kwame Nkrumah's presidency, began with or-

---

* See Glossary.

ganizing day nurseries. It soon became more politically oriented.

Nkrumah and his CPP (Convention Peoples Party) had a limited commitment to incorporating women into governing positions. The Party advocated equality of sexes, and proposed rewriting the marriage laws in 1962, but the proposals encountered resistance. Nkrumah replaced the Federation of Ghana Women with the National Council of Ghana Women as a section of the CPP, to neutralize the political nature of the former group, which had ties to an opposition party.

Some women's organizations have attained relative power, but not through being affiliates of male-dominated groups. Market-women's associations are stronger than the small groups of educated women. Delegates from the market-women's groups were sent to the Constitutional Convention of the Second Republic. Nanemei Akpee (Society of Friends) is a market-women's organization with chapters in many towns. It provides financial assistance to members and helps form trading businesses as well as administering funds, based on members' contributions, to women in need. The National Council on Women and Development was created in 1975 in response to the UN's International Woman's Year. The Council is involved in research for appropriate technology and such labor-saving devices as mechanical graters for producing *gari* (a staple made of roasted cassava meal).

MYTHOGRAPHY. The concept of Goddess Creator, mother of all people, is common throughout Africa, though her names vary. In Ghana, the Ashanti revere the goddess Nyame, and the goddess Ngame is sacred to the Akan.

GHANA: To Be a Woman
by Ama Ata Aidoo

I had sensed vaguely as a child living among adult females that everything which had to do exclusively with being a woman was regarded as dirty. At definite traditional landmarks in a woman's life cycle, she was regarded literally as untouchable. The scope and frequency of the restrictions depended on such factors as the family's mode of ancestral worship and the propinquity of the woman's domicile to private and public shrines. These landmarks included the first menstruation and (for some) all other menstruations; all of the post-partum forty days for the firstborn and subsequent births; a whole year of widowhood (compare forty days at most for a widower), and dying pregnant—in which latter case, it was the corpse of the woman which was exposed to ostracism and humiliation.

A girl's first menstrual flow was celebrated after a whole week of confinement. Put "celebrated" in quotation marks. Because we know now that the "celebration" was really a broadcasting of the fact that she was ready for procreation. And once you, the young man, had been bold enough to go forward and take her off her mother's back, you could also take it for granted that you had acquired

a sexual aid;

This article is based on an essay of Ama Ata Aidoo's, originally written for the UNITAR Seminar Creative Women in Changing Societies, July 9–13, 1980, and printed in *Creative Women in Changing Societies: A Quest for Alternatives* (Dobbs Ferry, N.Y.: Transnational Publishers, Inc.). Copyright © 1982 by UNITAR. Reprinted by permission.

a wet-nurse and a nursemaid for your children;

a cook-steward and general housekeeper;

a listening post;

an economic and general consultant;

a field-hand and,

if you are that way inclined,

a punch-ball.

No, the position of a woman in Ghana is no less ridiculous than anywhere else. The few details that differ are interesting only in terms of local color and family needs.

I was lucky or unlucky enough to have been born into one of those families that could see alternative lives for children other than the one the adults were already living. For instance, by the time I was born, my father had come to consider formal Western education the answer to the limitations of the untrained mind, and to the definite waste that was the sum of female lives.[1] An aunt who had learned to read only enough of our language to be a member of the church choir once told me, "My child, get as far as you can into this education. Go until you yourself know you are tired. As for marriage, it is something a woman picks up along the way."

Is it any wonder that I get plainly confused now if, in associating with both female and male undergraduates, graduates, lecturers, and professors, I learn that they believe basically that marriage is what a woman was created for? And that higher education for a woman is an unfortunate postponement of her self-fulfillment? That any successful career outside the home is naturally for men—and a few rather "ugly" women? That the only way for a woman to be and remain in the academic world is for her also to be married? And if she does not marry, and yet is quite obviously an attractive person in other respects, then she is just making other people feel uncomfortable?

Dialogue, June 1976; with a female colleague:

COLLEAGUE: My sister, could I caution you to be careful of how you interact with these male lecturers?

ME: Why?

COLLEAGUE: Because I'm a married woman. And I know that sometimes their wives feel so uneasy when they see you with their husbands.

ME: Too bad I don't feel attracted to anyone on this campus sufficiently to steal him from his wife.

To myself I wondered how people could allow themselves to lead such insecure lives. But poor me, too. As a writer, I not only can *cope* with aloneness; I have to actively *seek* it in order to produce. Yet as an academic, can I maintain a vibrant intellect, condemned as I am to ostracism because I refuse to consider marriage the only way to live? Male colleagues resent your professional standing and punish your presumption in mean little ways. They blame your *femininity* for what one would have thought was evidence of regular *human* frailty: ill health, laziness, and other excuses for poor productivity. Yet rather than avail themselves of your expertise, they consult other male colleagues, however mediocre. If they do not find you physically repulsive, they take your continued single state as an insult to their manhood. If you remain single into your thirties, then you have no right to look well: to wit, well dressed with a slight plumpness, a good skin, a smiling face. Because scholarly spinsters should be normally sour with discontent and wizened for lack of semen in their system! Sure, we are looking for an African version of the blue-stocking! Besides, any proper woman's seeming well-being should always be

[1] It was from my father I first heard the rather famous quotation from Dr. Kwegyir Aggrey: "If you educate a man, you educate an individual. If you educate a woman, you educate a nation."

recognized for what it is: a direct product of some man's affection and *his* successful career.

It goes without saying, therefore, that being married to the worst of men—read: vicious, mean, brutal, stupid—is better than being unmarried at all.

Dialogue, November 1975; with a female colleague who is in a crumbling marriage:
COLLEAGUE: . . . their [her children's] father has sent them so many things from London: clothes, money, toys . . . Hmm; Sissie, even a bad husband is better than no husband!

The real puzzle is that, you, a woman, should be encroaching on male territory. Married or unmarried, you are unwanted, period. And insulting you publicly is nothing if they can get away with it.

Vignette, 1971; from a rather young lecturer to a crowded Senior Common Room— among those present, me!
. . . really, these independent academic bitches? They are incapable of love or affection. They realize their need for men only when they want babies.

Certainly it is a little easier on the nerves of your high-minded colleagues if, with the unmarried state, you are childless. For then they just put you down for being a bitter old maid. Definitely, it is not fair to anybody that together with the outrage of your unmarried state, you should also insist, shamelessly, on being a single parent.

In any case, as a woman, your persistence in staying in the academic field is a total waste of time, since articulateness and other manifestations of intelligence are all masculine. Therefore it is unseemly in a female to get passionate and vocal about public issues, or engage in any abstract speculations.[2]

Dialogue, 1972; after participating in a televised discussion on how much help this country should give to the liberation struggle in southern Africa, I meet a male colleague:
COLLEAGUE: My sister, *hei,* I heard you on TV.
ME: You did? And what did you think of the discussion?
COLLEAGUE: Well, well. Actually, my sister, I wish I could find a man to marry you . . . you know, a man tough enough to soften your tongue somewhat.

Even on the campus, within the so-called ivy-covered walls, no one expects a woman to perform well in areas apart from cooking, sewing, and other so-called traditional feminine activities.

Dialogue, May 1980; after a hard morning of lectures and tutorials, I go to the senior common room for my one-bottle ration of beer. A mature, final-year student rushes to me, eyes shining and full of smiles:
STUDENT: *Hei* you. Shake my hand. (I take his extended right hand, all the while wondering why.)
STUDENT: It's all over the halls of residence that you gave two super lectures this morning. (I smile, beginning to be pleased.) But you know we like your lectures: except

---

[2.] "She . . . enjoyed talking . . . with Christian, but somehow she felt she should not be enjoying it that much. It was not right for a woman to talk so much even with a family friend."—And with that, I.N.C. Aniebo crushes the intellectual flowering of Ejiaka, a rather charming character he himself has created in *The Journey Within* (London: Heinemann, 1978), p. 224. The image of woman which emerges from contemporary African novels indicates not only that the writers are aware of her traditional stereotypes, but that they are quite happy to leave things that way.

that we hear you outdid yourself this morning. They say your English was absolutely masculine . . .

And I fold back into myself—I who am yet to find me on the graph of "speakers of English as a second language" or where I stand as a "nonnative" user of the English language. At least once in the lifetime of a colonial or, in fact, any person who operates in a language other than the mother tongue, there is a confrontation with the remark: "But you speak English (French, German, etc.) like an Englishman (Frenchman, German, etc.)." One's feelings at such times are ambivalent enough. Now I speak English like a man? And they intend it for a compliment. Yes.

They had always told me I wrote like a man. Read: a bold and legible script. They had always told me I drove like a man. Read: relaxed steering, near-perfect reflexes, a predilection for speed. . . . Now I speak English like a man? Read: an over-all confident handling of the language, perhaps? (The real irony is that there is not a single man—or woman—on the campus of the University of Cape Coast who handles English the way I do, if for no other reason than personal idiosyncrasies.)

So, the list of areas covered by female incompetence grows to include linguistic aptitude? And while you are about it, include political awareness, sensitivity to social issues, and vulnerability to mental and physical pain.

Dialogue, May 31, 1980; at the end of a symposium organized by the Students' Representative Council and the local branch of the National Students' Union; the panel and chair comprised of three members of the faculty and a recent head of state. The topic is: Violence—Its Structure and Uses. When all the major speeches have been given (by males), the chair calls a female student to the stage. And that of course, strictly in accordance with bourgeois intellectual practices; it is now fitting that a girl should "grace" the occasion by giving "the vote of thanks"! On impulse, I comment on this to my nearest neighbor to the right, also a university teacher:
COLLEAGUE: Yes, yes . . . Now that you mention it . . . But it is a-l-l r-i-g-h-t.
ME: Is it?
COLLEAGUE: Sure . . . what's wrong if the four main speakers are all men?
ME: Nothing. If they had not asked a girl to go and give a vote of thanks.
COLLEAGUE: Hmm. I see what you mean. But really, my sister, what do women know about violence?

And I wonder how I could have imagined that I was being petty, bringing up the issue. Obviously, my colleague had never heard of the all-female battalion in the armies of the Abomé kings of Dahomey; of the Celtic Boadicia; of Yaa Asantewaa of the Ashantis; of Joan of Arc of France; of Rosa Luxemburg; of Fannie Lou Hamer; of Deolinda Rodrigues Francisco de Almeida of Angola . . . But if this colleague had not always struck me as a gentle type of human being, this remark alone would have automatically betrayed him as a secret wife-basher!

Since doing anything "like-a-man" implies that you are doing whatever it is impressively, it should be submitted that not only aptitude and skill but also expertise, professionalism, diligence, perfection, talent, genius—are all masculine.

And it should further be submitted that since these are also precisely the criteria for measuring and judging human accomplishments, if they are exclusively masculine, then only men are human beings. Women are *not* human.

What is completely bewildering, though, is that once we have been reduced to nonpersons, our efforts to prove ourselves human by entering fields of human endeavor should go so totally unappreciated. In fact, worse than that, our attempts to do well in these fields almost inevitably provoke resentments, both overt and covert.[3]

And perhaps this should not have surprised us so much if we were ourselves human or knew anything about human beings.

Once in a while I catch myself wondering whether I would have found the courage to write if I had not started to write when I was too young to know what was good for me. (Frankly, I am glad the question is purely hypothetical now.)

For instance, in an argument on a national issue, some professors from another Ghanaian university shouted that I was not fit to speak about public matters—that I should leave politics to those best qualified to handle it, and concentrate on doing what I do best, which is writing plays and fiction.[4]

Most certainly, my trials as a woman writer are heavier and more painful than any I have to go through as a university teacher. It is a condition so delicate that it almost cannot be handled. Like an internal wound and therefore immeasurably dangerous, it also causes a ceaseless emotional hemorrhage.

You feel awful for seeing the situation the way you do, and terrible when you try to speak about it. Because this kind of resentment never even comes out in jokes. Yet you have to speak out since your pain is also real, and in fact the wound bleeds more profusely when you are upset by people you care for, those you respect.

So it is with the unreception given my latest book.[5]

Dialogue, January 1980: My head of department (a good friend and a well-known writer himself) and I are discussing the latest edition of the book which had just then come out in New York. We are both going on about how well laid out it is, the beautiful type used, etc. Then I remark that unfortunately, my impression is that the publishers don't seem to care much whether they sell it or not.

"What a shame," says he, "because there are all these women's-studies programs springing up in universities all over the United States. Surely *they* would be interested in it . . ."

And I bled internally. Because although the protagonist of the story is a young woman, anybody who reads the book would realize that her concerns are only partially feminist, if at all. In any case, what if they are? Feminism is about half of the human inhabitants of this earth!

I am convinced that if *Killjoy* or anything like it had been written by a man, as we say in these parts, no one would have been able to sleep a wink these last couple of years, for all the noise that would have been made about it. If *Killjoy* has received recognition elsewhere, it is gratifying. But that is no salve for the hurt received because my own house has put a freeze on it. For surely my brothers know that the only important question is the critical recognition of a book's existence—not necessarily approbation. Writers, artists, and all who create, thrive on controversy. When a critic refuses to talk about your work, that is violence; he is willing you to die as a creative person. And when someone you consider a friend refuses to talk to you because of a book you've written, he is trying to drive you insane with speculation. For: 1) Is he angry with you for daring to write that

[3.] The existence and ever-increasing popularity of a magazine like *Ms.* proves that even in the highly technologically advanced societies of the world, women do not have it easy.

[4.] "LSNA Statement: To Our Detractors," *The Legon Observer,* July 14, 1972. Rereading the relevant papers on the controversy for the purpose of this reference, I am appalled by the vulgarity and venom with which they met an ordinary intellectual challenge.

[5.] *Our Sister Killjoy or Reflection From a Blackeyed Squint* (Harlow: Longman, 1977).

book? Or, 2) Is he ashamed of you because you wrote that book? Or, 3) Is he jealous because he wished he had written that book?

This was not meant to be a catalogue of slights suffered and bitterly stored over the years. Nothing in my background had prepared me for them. Indeed, I must confess to having taken many of the remarks either for jokes or even compliments at the time they were made—the way we all help other people laugh at us or even insult us because of our ethnic origins, race, sex, physical peculiarities, and such. Because subconsciously, we want to believe that people mean no harm. Then, a change occurs in our consciousness, and we acquire a new eye, a new ear; we look around, and we listen. The discoveries are incredible.

For me, the shock has been truly rude. Because I had grown to adolescence among a people whose reduction of females to non-persons I had not thought I should take seriously, since I thought it was articulated only informally; the degree of the reduction left to individual households. (I remember, on more than one occasion when I was growing up in the village, hearing a mature man ask another whose wife had just had a new baby if the infant was "a girl or a human being"!) But I have realized that in the long run, the cumulative effect of this smooth operation on adults of both sexes is as stupefying and degrading as any more aggressively articulated sexist tradition.

An inquiry of this nature runs the risk of getting charged with pettiness. Yet petty or not, it is legitimate. The ancients have said that if you assume indifference at a meat-sharing, you end up with the bones.

And we all know that with not only our indifference but also our acquiescence (and even connivance), women have ended up with very much less than bones. Primarily resting on women's fears of physical (and economic) insecurity, but tightly encased in the myth of male superiority and moral blackmail, marriage has proved singularly effective as an instrument of suppression. It has put half (or often more than half) of humanity through mutations that are thoroughly humiliating and at best ridiculous. In an economically embattled environment like present-day Ghana, it is believed that the average urban housewife is not only busy peddling something or other but also teaching, nursing, etc.— *plus* she also has to secretly or openly whore around to keep her family and husband well fed.

As the very foundation of the family, marriage has maintained a chameleon-like capacity to change its nature in time and space and to serve the ignominious aims of every society: slave-owning, feudal, or modern bourgeois. Throughout history and among all peoples, marriage has made it possible for women to be owned like property, abused and brutalized like serfs, privately corrected and, like children, publicly scolded, overworked, underpaid, and much more thoroughly exploited than the lowest male worker on any payroll.[6]

To date, nobody—least of all women themselves—can remotely visualize a world in which the position of women has been revolutionized.[7]

And you know the solution does not lie with you, the individual woman, married or

[6.] If the African-American woman is ambivalent about the movement to liberate women, who can blame her? Knowing as she does that during slavery "Miz Ann" (your average white wife of the plantation owner) often actively collaborated in the degradation and brutalization of the black female.

[7.] Her Vitriolic Highness, Phyllis Schlafly, of US notoriety, knows she can get away with her vicious campaign against women's liberation. Because she also knows that she speaks to a great number of people's deep-seated fears of a world in which women are really free. In this regard, compare the psychology of racism in the rise of Hitler of Germany, and the continued existence of the fascist South African State.

unmarried, no matter how keenly aware you are of the problems in your environment. Naturally, to keep up some kind of sanity through the working day, you may have to adopt a position of combative protest of your own against the continuous and veiled insults. On the other hand, over-personalizing the issue exposes you to the growth of some rather dangerous convictions:

—That somehow you are alone in this world with such problems.

—That either there is something terribly wrong with your individual self or

—That you are unique, and therefore you excite the envy of the people around, who,

—Meanwhile, are more immature than other people of similar environments anywhere else.

It is obvious that for a long-term answer, if one is at all possible, only collective action would be meaningful. We must organize.

Because you are not alone. Out there are all the women from all sorts of economic and social backgrounds struggling with different levels of consciousness.

As a university teacher and a writer, one already belongs to a rare enough category without rarefying oneself further. Rather, one has to keep reminding oneself that whatever one goes through is nothing compared with the humiliation other women suffer daily, as a result of belonging to politically more violent or economically more depressed backgrounds. In all such situations being a man is terrible enough. Being a woman is intolerable. (In war, for instance, men are normally beaten and killed, women are normally beaten, *raped,* and killed.)

One must also resist any attempts at being persuaded to think that the woman question has to be superseded by the struggle against any local exploitative system, the nationalist struggle or the struggle against imperialism and global monopoly capital.[8] For what is becoming clear is that in the long run, none of these fronts is either of greater relevance than the rest or even separate from them. They all explain the past, define the present, and predict the future of the contemporary imperialist world order and especially its genocidal technology, territorial expansionism, and militarism. (On the morning of June 18, 1980, the BBC quoted UN Secretary-General Kurt Waldheim as saying that the arms race is costing one million dollars every minute!)

And the only way to halt the orchestrated rush of humanity into global anarchy and annihilation is to clearly delineate all the possible areas of the struggle, and pick any part of it that is within our reach. We cannot afford to limit ourselves by shelving any aspect of our consciousness.

In any case, if, as a woman, you also try to flex your muscles as a revolutionary cadre where your comrades are predominantly male, you can hit the concrete wall with such force that you might never recover your original self. Clarity therefore becomes the only reliable companion and weapon for a fighting woman. For with such company and thus armed, she can weather sexist disillusion and betrayal, and still move on. Otherwise how could Deolinda Rodrigues, 1939–67, have survived until the enemy murdered her? In the poem "Christmas Feast," she tells how, at a preliminary meeting with a male comrade who was to help her and five other female comrades to cross some particularly dangerous territory, the male comrade declared:

". . . if they find you are gone it's me they'll shoot,

What's the reward in that?"

She asks:

[8] Again a case in point is the African-American woman whose dilemma is whether to opt for the dragon of the class struggle, the Scylla of black liberation, or the Charybdis of women's liberation! See Michele Wallace on Angela Davis: *Black Macho and the Myth of the Superwoman* (New York: Dial Press, 1978), pp. 160–67.

"The signal
Are we ready to go?"
He replies:
". . . Not quite. But soon enough,
first my reward—
I'll take you here in the grass."
Silence from her.
He: "You don't agree?
        You are choosy?"

Of course, she refuses. And he does *not* turn up for the rendez-vous. The poet and her other comrades are betrayed. They are captured, imprisoned, tortured, and, yes, finally killed. And "as the precise dates of death are not known, March 2, the anniversary of their internment, is observed as Angolan Women's Day." *(Poems from ANGOLA,* selected and translated by Michael Wolfers, London: Heinemann, 1979, pp. 67–68, 106–07).

To date, the fact that a comrade understands the finer points of Marxism or is the most fearless fighter in the bush does not automatically mean that he has the haziest notions of those contradictions bedeviling the struggle, which are occasioned by the dangerously anomalous position of women in history. Or, even more important, how that fact influences your group's notions of a woman's capabilities. To be noticed at all, you would have to be extra-special in all respects. Ask Rosa Luxemburg.

Otherwise, the put-downs and the snobbery you may suffer from the comrades could rival any from reactionaries.

And don't be shocked if—when victory is won—they return you to the veil as part of the process for consolidating the gains of the revolution.

But all of that is another story.

Suggested Further Reading

Boserup, Ester. *Woman's Role in Economic Development.* London: Allen & Unwin, 1970.

Bukh, Jette. *The Village Woman in Ghana.* Uppsala: The Scandinavian Institute of African Studies, 1979.

Hafkin, Nancy. *Ghanaian Women in Development.* Washington, D.C.: USAID, n.d.

National Council on Women and Development. Proceedings of the Seminar of Ghanaian Women in Development, Sept. 4–6, 1978.

Pellow, Deborah. *Woman in Accra—Options for Autonomy.* Algonac, MI: Reference Publications, 1977.

Ama Ata Aidoo was born at Abeadzi Kyiakor in the Central Region of Ghana, attended Wesley Girls School, Cape Coast, and graduated from the University of Ghana. She is the mother of one child, a fourteen-year-old daughter. Beginning in September 1970, she was based at the University of Cape Coast as a lecturer in the English department, and she has traveled widely in Africa, Europe, and North America on matters concerned with being an African woman, a university teacher, and a writer. In January of 1982, she was appointed Secretary for Education in Ghana. Her publications include *The Dilemma of a Ghost,* a play (Harlow: Longman, 1965); *Anowa,* a play (Harlow: Longman, 1970); *No Sweetness Here,* a collection of short stories (Harlow: Longman, 1970, New York: Doubleday, 1972); *Our Sister Killjoy or Reflection From a Blackeyed Squint,* fiction in four episodes (Harlow: Longman, 1977; New York: NOK, 1979). She has also published other short stories, poems, reviews, and critical essays in many anthologies and journals, including *Black Orpheus, The New African, New Society, Okyeame, Zuka, etc.*

GREECE
(Hellenic Republic)

Located in Eastern Europe on the Balkan Peninsula, bordered by Turkey and the Aegean Sea to the east, the Mediterranean Sea to the south, the Ionian Sea to the west, and Albania, Yugoslavia, and Bulgaria to the north, with islands off all coasts. **Area:** 131,986 sq. km. (50,960 sq. mi.). **Population** (1980): 9,551,000, female 50.9%. **Capital:** Athens.

DEMOGRAPHY. Languages: Greek (official), Turkish. **Races or Ethnic Groups:** Greek, Turkish, Pomak, Armenian. **Religions:** Greek Orthodox 98%, Roman Catholicism. **Education** (% enrolled in school, 1975): Age 6–11—of all girls 99%, of all boys 100%; age 12–17—of all girls 64%, of all boys 76%; higher education—in 1977–78 women were 38.7% of university students and 31.2% of higher technical and vocational education students. **Literacy** (1977): Women 76%, men 93%. **Birth Rate** (per 1000 pop., 1975–80): 16. **Death Rate** (per 1000 pop., 1975–80): 9. **Infant Mortality** (per 1000 live births, 1975–80): Female 21, male 26. **Life Expectancy** (1975–80): Female 75 yrs., male 71 yrs.

GOVERNMENT. Constitution (adopted in 1975 after the 1974 collapse of a military dictatorship) provides for an elected president, a presidentially appointed prime minister who is of the majority party in Parliament, an elected 300-member Parliament, and a government, consisting of the prime minister and other ministers. Pres. Constantinos Karamanlis is head of state and Andreas Papandreou is prime minister and head of PASOK, the Panhellenic Socialist Movement (1983). Other major political parties are the New Democratic Party and the Communist Party. **Women's Suffrage:** 1929 in local elections with higher age requirement than men; 1952 full suffrage. **Equal Rights:** The 1975 Constitution states that women and men have equal rights and responsibilities (Art. 4) and requires the revision or abolition of existing laws that conflict with that principle (Art. 116). **Women in Government** (1983): Women

are 4% of Parliament deputies, 2 under-secretaries (Maria Kypriotaki, Deputy Minister of Health and Social Services, and Roula Kakla Manakis, Deputy Minister of Social Insurance), the Minister of Culture (Melina Mercouri), and the Chair of the Prime Minister's Council for the Equality of the Sexes (Chryssanthi Laion-Antoniou); 33% of the 170 Women's Union of Greece (EGE) members who were candidates in local elections won.

ECONOMY. Currency: Drachma (May 1983: 83.7 = $1 US). **Gross National Product** (1980): $42.2 billion. **Per Capita Income** (1980): $4520. **Women's Wages as a Percentage of Men's:** No general statistics obtainable; women earn 67.2% of male wages in manufacturing and 58.3% of clerks' average monthly salary (1981). **Equal Pay Policy:** "All working people, irrespective of sex . . . have a right to equal pay for equal work" (1975 Constitution, Art. 22). A 1975 national collective agreement provided for equalization of minimum daily wages for unskilled women and men workers within 3 yrs. **Production** (Agricultural/Industrial): Grains, fruits, olives, olive oil, tobacco; textiles, metals, chemicals. **Women as a Percentage of Labor Force** (1980): 33%; **of agricultural force** (1979) 27.9% (over 50% of "economically active" women were in agriculture, 80% of whom were unpaid family workers, 1971); **of industrial force**—no general statistics obtainable (17% of employed women work in industry, 1982); **of military** (1980) 9.5% army, 5% navy; 300 women officers out of 184,000 troops. In Jan. 1979, the first 1500 female volunteers enlisted in the previously all-male military; most are in noncombat roles, although all receive combat training. (**Employed) Women's Occupational Indicators:** Of public- or private-sector executives 5% (1982); 47% of employed women work in nonagricultural activities: of managers and administrators 0.4%, of commerce workers 10%, of professional or related workers 15%, of office workers 19%, of service workers 20%, of laborers and craftspeople 33% (1971). The number of women in agriculture has decreased since the 1960's while on the whole increasing numbers of women are employed; social acceptance of women in nonmanual jobs is growing in urban areas. **Unemployment** (1983): 8%; no rates by sex obtainable. From 1974–79 the number of unemployed women in urban/semi-urban areas increased by 98%, compared to 11% for men.

GYNOGRAPHY. Marriage. *Policy:* Civil marriages were legalized in 1982 (Law 1250). Under the landmark 1983 Family Law spouses must make joint decisions in all areas of their common life, thus abolishing a husband's previous authority; a woman may keep her birthname at marriage; the traditional institution of dowry was prohibited. Property brought to and acquired during marriage is separately owned by each spouse, unless otherwise contracted. Adultery is no longer a criminal offense (1982). *Practice:* Female mean age at marriage (1970–78): 25; women age 15–49 in union (1970–78): 66%; marriages (per 1000 pop., 1979): 7.6. Despite current prohibitions and the fact that dowries are frequently an economic burden to the bride's family, dowries are still sometimes given at marriage. Wives are generally expected to be subordinate to their husbands. **Divorce.** *Policy:* The 1983 Family Law legalized no-fault divorce based on mutual consent. Divorce is allowed in cases of nonagreement, on grounds of incompatibility, and after a 4-yr. separation. At separation, the "disfavored" party is entitled to a minimum of ⅓ the family property unless it is proven that the spouse had made no contribution to the family wealth. *Practice:* Divorces (per 1000 pop., 1979): 0.49. Prior to 1983, a woman's refusal to obey her husband or her seeking a job without his consent was among grounds for his obtaining a divorce; in settlements, the courts traditionally acted against women who defied their husbands' authority. **Family.** *Policy:* Equal status is stipulated for women by the 1983 Family Law reform, and the con-

cept of husband and father as head of household was abolished. All family matters, including domicile, must be decided jointly. A woman no longer need obtain her husband's permission to start a business, take their children out of the country, or place them in a school. Maternity leave and benefits for civil servants and employees of public legal entities are 2 months pre- and post-delivery (1962 Civil Service Code). A 1912 law mandated that women employed under a private law contract receive 12 weeks leave for certain manual and nonmanual work. For women not covered by either law (such as agricultural and private hospital workers) there is no maternity leave. Maternity benefits are paid by the Social Insurance Foundation to insured workers; employers pay leave wages. Day-care centers are State-subsidized and built by both government and voluntary agencies. *Practice:* In rural areas, family status is increased if it is not economically necessary for the female family members to work in the fields. Extended families are common in rural areas, while nuclear families are characteristic of the cities. In 1981 the Ministry of Social Welfare counted 738 totally State-run, 66 partially State-run, 41 voluntary, and 181 privately owned day-care centers, serving 60,000 children. The demand for day-care places is est. to be twice that of those available, and there is a great deficiency in trained personnel and equipment in already existing facilities (1982).

Welfare. *Policy:* The Ministry of Social Insurance, created in 1981, directs various insurance and pension programs such as the Social Insurance Foundation (IKA), which provides pensions to handicapped persons and to persons at age 60 based on contributions from earnings, and the Farmers Insurance Fund (OGA), which now provides equal pensions to both female and male farmers, and separate pensions to wives of farmers. The Ministry of Health and Welfare established a Central Health Council to formulate a national health plan (1982). The government operates 1700 health advisory centers for women and children, with free laboratory tests for low-income women. State maternity hospitals offer free childbirth and hospitalization services for low-income, uninsured women (see **Family**). *Practice:* In 1982, 2.1% of women over age 60 lived alone; almost 75% of them lived below the poverty line. Of women over age 65, 41% derive their main income from pensions, compared to 75% of men; for 55% of women over age 65, families were the main financial support. The majority of aging people depend on the extended family network for support.

Contraception. *Policy:* Legal with a physician's prescription. Legislation calls for the creation of a network of family-planning centers and staff training (Law 1036/80). *Practice:* Approx. 2% of women of reproductive age use the pill (1982); no further statistics obtainable. Prior to 1979, only 2 privately run family-planning centers existed; an additional 5 centers opened in 1979. Church influence against modern birth-control methods remains strong. **Abortion.** *Policy:* Legal in cases of pregnancy resulting from rape or incest, serious threat to the woman's life or health, or risk of fetal defect (1950 Penal Code, amended 1978). Obtaining or self-inducing an illegal abortion is punishable by 3 yrs. imprisonment; the practitioner is liable to a minimum 6 months imprisonment. In Jan. 1984, the government announced a bill further liberalizing abortion law and making the procedure coverable by State and private insurance plans. *Practice:* 45 legal abortions were performed in 1978, yet an est. 78,000 married and single women in the Athens area had abortions that same yr. The annual number of illegal abortions performed nationwide is est. at 500,000, with the repeat rate among married women reportedly high. **Illegitimacy.** *Policy:* Children born out of wedlock now have equal rights (1983 Family Law). The mother is automatically the guardian. *Practice:* In 1978, 13% of all births were out of wedlock; in 1982, the rate had dropped to 1.4%. **Homosexuality.** *Policy:* No data obtainable. *Practice:* No statistics obtainable. A bill pertaining to venereal disease which could have been used to prosecute homosexuals and prostitutes was defeated in 1978, in large part by lesbian women and homosexual men who mobilized against it. Homosexual- and lesbian-rights groups exist, including the Autonomous Group of Homosexual Women. In 1981 lesbian women founded *Labyris,* the first lesbian-feminist magazine in Athens.

Incest. *Policy:* Sexual relations between lineal blood relatives, siblings, or parents and children, is illegal. *Practice:* No statistics obtainable. Rapes of young girls by older male relatives, particularly fathers and uncles, are reportedly common and are increasingly being denounced publicly. **Sexual Harassment.** *Policy:* "Unchaste acts" committed by a person in authority with an employee are punishable by 1 yr. imprisonment; this applies to civil servants and public institutions only (Penal Code, Art. 343). *Practice:* No data obtainable. **Rape.** *Policy:* Illegal; defined in the Penal Code as extra-marital intercourse forced on a woman by threat of bodily injury or serious danger; punishable by up to 10 yrs. imprisonment. Sexual abuse of a female or male who is "incompetent" is punishable by 6 months imprisonment. *Practice:* No statistics obtainable; rape is reportedly common and the incidence of rape charges is increasing. Rape is usually blamed on the woman; courts sometimes attempt to persuade women to marry the rapists, or to obtain a financial settlement. A woman who wounded a man attempting to rape her was imprisoned for 3 yrs., while the attacker received a 5½-month sentence (1980). **Battery.** *Policy:* No data obtainable. *Practice:* No statistics obtainable. Battery is common; the Democratic Women's Center for Battering and Rape Victims in Athens receives dozens of women weekly. **Prostitution.** *Policy:* Soliciting is not illegal; exploiting a prostitute's income, inducing a woman to commit prostitution, and trafficking in women are all illegal and punishable by 6 months–3 yrs. imprisonment. *Practice:* No general statistics obtainable. A 1983 Athens police study reported 600 women working as prostitutes. **Traditional/Cultural Practices:** No data obtainable. **Crisis Centers.** *Policy:* No data obtainable. *Practice:* See **Battery.**

HERSTORY. The earliest archaeological finds from the Greek world are female idols of the Cycladic Islands, dating to

3000 B.C.E. Evidence of matriarchal cultures (Pelasgian, Cretan, and Mycenaean) includes the frescoes at Thera, seals and statues at Knossos on Crete, and pottery, carved stone, and ivories at Phaestos, Pylos, and Mycenae.

The name Athene-Potinija appears in one of the tablets discovered at Knossos. The colossal statue of Athene built by the Lydians at Mount Sipylus was called Potnia-Tiamat, and for the Ionians she was the Great Goddess. Herodotus wrote of Lycia, a city founded by the Ionians, as being matriarchal: the Lycians traced descent by the mother, and if a male slave wed a free woman he and their children would become free.

Contemporary scholars now theorize that Helen, Clytemnaestra, and Medea were in fact historical and not merely mythical figures—and were regnant queens, not consorts of kings. The famous warrior Hiera, for example, thought to have been a mythical being, now is believed to have fought in the Trojan War and was praised by the chronicler Philostratus.

The persistence of goddess worship in the Greek pantheon left an indication that the importance of women in ancient Greece survived the Dorian influence and patriarchal domination through the "code" of religion—and that religion was central to Greek unity. During the wars against the Persians (ending in 449 B.C.E.) and other invaders, the sole means by which the different city-states found unity was through religious festivals, games (such as the Panathenaic), and celebrations of the Mysteries; of these last, the most sacred were established at Eleusis and Delphi, and women presided at both. Theoclea was chief priestess at Delphi and a disciple of Pythagoras, and Theano became head of the Pythagorean Order (c. 800 B.C.E.). Because of Hippodaemeia, an alternative was created to the all-male Olympic games in 600 B.C.E. Although there are theories that Homer's *Odyssey* was really written by a woman bard, no certain proof exists. But there is no doubt about the existence of Sappho (6th century B.C.E.), acknowledged to have been one of the greatest poets who ever lived. Later, Pindar's only rival in

poetry was said to have been Corinna (500–400 B.C.E.).

In the 5th century B.C.E., Queen Artemisia of Halicarnassus assumed the throne after the death of her husband and allied her forces with those of Xerxes I against the Greeks, in revenge for an insult. Of a Cretan mother, Artemisia was famous for her battle spirit. A later successor, Queen Artemisia of Caria, conquered Rhodes; a patron of the arts, she memorialized her dead brother-husband Mausolus by building the famous mausoleum which depicts Amazons in combat; the remainder of the ruined mausoleum is to be seen in the British Museum. Although the Amazons and certain of their leaders (Penthesilea, Hippolyta, Antiope) are thought of as mythical, not only the poet Homer but the historian Herodotus referred to them as real.

The city-state Sparta is known today primarily for its interest in the martial arts and self-discipline. But Sparta was known throughout the ancient world for an additional reason: its education was completely egalitarian, and Spartan women enjoyed independence and power. Herodotus claimed that Gorgo, daughter of Cleomenes I of Sparta, was consulted on all political issues; she deciphered a secret message on wax tablets from a Greek spy and so was able to warn of an impending Persian invasion.

During the Periclean Age (495–429 B.C.E.), women still enjoyed many rights: a woman could obtain a divorce easily, and she could be fully educated and participate at symposia; women would be seen at the Agora among the disciples and students of philosophy, rhetoric, and oratory. Pericles' closest friend and chief adviser was Aspasia, who devised his famous funeral oration on the occasion of the Peloponnesian War. Socrates (469–399 B.C.E.) claimed, according to Plato, that his own wisdom was small compared to that of Diotima; his mother, Phaenarete, was known for her genius in midwifery and herbal medicine and also was a respected mathematician; his wife, the much-maligned Xanthippe, is thought to have been a midwife as well. A tradition of women herbalists already existed, since healing, drama, and religion were thought interrelated. This threefold tradition was kept alive at Epidaurus under the aegis of the deities Artemis, Hygiaea, and Asclepius.

The conquest of Greece by Rome (146–30 B.C.E.) was almost symbiotic, and Roman women adopted many of the habits and canons of Greek women (see ITALY).

Greek women also were visible during the Byzantine period. In 421 C.E., Emperor Theodosius II married a pagan Athenian woman, Athenais; after baptism she became Eudocia. She was conversant with all the arts and sciences of her day and influenced her husband in founding the university at Constantinople in 425. She was brilliant at theological argument and championed the heresy of Nestorius, the Patriarch of Constantinople. Of all Byzantine empresses, the most famous is Theodora, Justinian's wife (also see ITALY). Of Cyprian descent, she was a keen politician and skilled diplomat. An imperial edict reputed to be hers shows concern with the issue of rape: "We have set up magistrates to punish robbers and thieves; are we not even more straitly bound to prosecute the robbers of honor and the thieves of chastity?"

In 768 another Athenian woman, Irene, married Emperor Leo IV; she became regent in 780 and initiated a vigorous campaign to consolidate her power, stabilize the region, make peace with the Arabs, and reconcile Byzantium with the papacy. She restored religious tolerance and free speech and called for ecumenical councils—in 786 in Constantinople and 787 in Nicea. She assumed the title of Emperor [sic] after the death of her son (799), protected the monastic orders, and introduced financial reforms. She was deposed at the time of her negotiating an alliance with Charlemagne and died in exile at Lesbos in 803.

The Empresses Theofano, Zoë the Porphyrogenita, and her sister Theodora, were all of Macedonian origin. Anna Commena (1090–1120) has been described as the fourth muse; she was the daughter of Irene Ducas, a devout empress whose treatise *Typikon* set the tone for the foundation and organization of convents. Like her mother, Anna Commena was a writer—a historian—and was founder of and lecturer at the medical school of Constantinople. Eudocia, a woman described as "another Theano" and "another Hypatia," was sought in marriage by Constantine, son of Andronicus II. During the reign of Anna of Savoy in the last years of the Byzantine Empire, Theodora Paleologus (1320) and Irene Asan were known for their diplomatic skills.

With the conquest of Byzantium (1453) by the Ottoman Turks after centuries of intermittent siege, a long period of reaction against women set in.

A heroine of the 1821 Greek War for Independence was Bouboulina, a sea pirate who won many victories against the Turks. At the end of the 1800's, numerous women's groups were founded, with goals ranging from charitable works to social and educational reform. One of the first, the Union of Greek Women, was founded in 1879. The *Ladies' Daily* was the first women's journal (1888). The National Council of Greek Women's Organizations, created in 1907, encompassed 50 different women's societies 1 year after its founding. These early groups did not identify themselves openly with women's emancipation, but in time many did forge links with the International Alliance of Women, an association of feminist movements in many countries.

The experiences women enjoyed in these societies increased their skills in organizing and social activism and moved them into public life. From 1922 to 1944, Greece suffered wars and foreign occupation, and women came out of the domestic sphere to enter the fields of production and education. The League for Women's Rights and the Assoc. of University Women appeared during this period, focusing on women's equal status and opportunities. In 1924, 6 women's organizations joined as the Cooperating Women's Associations, to lobby for women's rights. During the 1930's, Lilika Nakos wrote controversial novels about women's lives.

After WW II, women's entrance into the public sphere increased further. Women won suffrage rights in 1952, and 1 year later the first woman was elected to Parliament. Compulsory 6-year schooling for both girls and boys increased educational opportunities.

For 7 years (1967–74), during a military dictatorship, all political activity was banned. With the overthrow of the regime, and a new government publicly committed to improving women's status, women have reactivated their campaigns for legal and economic rights, and new groups have emerged.

Since the 1975 Constitution guaranteed the elimination of discriminatory laws, women began pressing for the adoption of provisions for equality, social rights, and protection of maternity, youth, and old age; they offered draft proposals to the Parliament. A committee of 12 was created to reform the Family Code in 7 years' time, but since only 2 women were chosen, the Women's Union of Greece (founded 1976) insisted on equal representation. As a result, the final committee had 8 women and 7 men. The WUG, the largest Greek women's organization, was begun by 20 women, many with connections to PASOK (see GOVERNMENT), although they espouse an independent feminist line (see following article). As of 1982, over 10,000 women were WUG members.

That same year, Parliament passed a bill to create the Council of Equality—9 members to advise the prime minister on "women's issues," investigate legal inequities, survey mass media for offensive images of women, and check educational institutions for unequal policies and practices in teaching. The council reviews cases brought to its attention and establishes State machinery to make changes. The first woman named manager of the Bank of Greece, K. Kokkta, was appointed in the fall of 1982, several months after Alice Guitopoulos-Narankopoulos became the first woman appointed to the bank's administrative council. The Movement of Democratic Women, another national organization, was active in supporting a northern Greek woman during a 1982 rape trial; the woman was successful in prosecuting the rapist, who was sentenced to 8 years imprisonment. The League for Women's Rights opened a research and information center in Athens in 1982. The Center of Research Studies on Mediterranean Women was established as a result of a Plan of Action adopted by women's organizations at the First Conference of Mediterranean Women in Athens (1980), and is presently conducting a study on immigrant women. While most of the larger women's organizations have connections to various political parties, autonomous feminist groups, including some civil-rights groups founded by lesbian women, have been emerging. The focus of these groups tends to be less on legal reform than on public education and activism about such issues as sexuality.

In 1983, in response to pressure from Greek women's groups, the landmark Family Law was passed (see **Marriage and Family**), and was celebrated as a major triumph for Greek women.

MYTHOGRAPHY. The peoples of Minoan Crete, as well as those of the Argolis, Asia Minor, and the Peloponnese, all venerated one or another form of the Great Goddess. She had different names and often became tripartite in her manifestations. According to Hesiod, the pre-Olympian goddess Gaia was the creator, while Cronus, the devouring father, was the destroyer. The correlation of Greek history and Greek religion and the change from goddess worship to god worship is interpreted by some scholars as a record of the shift from a matriarchal to a patriarchal society (see HERSTORY).

At first, the female deity had been singular—as the Assyrian Astarte or the Babylonian Ishtar; then she became three, as the Horae, the Erinnyes, the Graeae, the Gorgons. In the triad form, as virgin/mother/crone, she had both benevolence and power. Cities were consecrated to her—among them Ephesus (to Artemis) and Athens (namesake of Athene); she was the Ancient Mother Rhea, the creatrix; she held the secrets of procreation and regeneration as Demeter and Kore in Eleusis; she was all wisdom as the Pythia at Delphi; she was invincible warrior as Athene-Parthenos; she was inspiration as the Muse, abandon as the Bacchante, victory as Nike; guardian against all evil as the Gorgon, keeper of the hearth as Hera, and eternally renewing love as Aphrodite. As Ariadne, she held the threads of Greek identity, and as Psyche she personified the Greek soul.

The Olympian gods appeared with the Heroic Age, and the wars of the Greeks reflected on their gods. Patriarchal versions were overlaid on the original images, and the goddesses were reduced to being counselors of the heroes—Athene guiding Perseus' hand, Amphitrite giving Theseus a crown.

To this day, in small mountain villages in Greece, women observe a festival once a year for a single day: they seize the towns in celebration and abandon, and the men hide at home in fear—although no one can quite say why, and despite the fact that the feast of the Maenads is ostensibly forgotten.

GREECE: A Village Sisterhood
by Margaret Papandreou

The dirt road wound through a narrow gorge, sprang free to lace a precipice, and kept losing itself in the scrubbrush—but it provided a slow if torturous passageway to the village of Fourkas, which we could glimpse from time to time perched on the mountain peak, beseeching us to hurry.

We were four women, members of the Rural Organizing Committee of the Women's Union of Greece, and it was one of our weekend forays into the countryside to meet with village women: to talk, to listen, to proselytize, to persuade—to organize.

In addition to me at the wheel, there was Anna, thirty-five, divorced, remarried, and financially comfortable from the profits of her father's business, which she shared with her brother. There was Maria, twenty-four, a secretary at odds with her mother, who felt that her daughter's association with the WUG (Women's Union of Greece) was sinful and dangerous and would be her undoing. There was Sophia, forty-five, the philosopher-theorist of the group, mother of two grown daughters, at one time a unionist, a widow. There was me, an American-Greek president of the union—and wife of the Prime Minister of Greece. Whatever one could say about our personal lives, we were all fervently dedicated to the struggle against discrimination toward women and for social change that would bring about a socialist society.

As an organization we were still young, having been incorporated (or legally recognized) in 1976, two years after the fall of the junta which had terrorized Greece for seven years. During that period, the dictators had abolished all women's organizations along with political parties. The only positive element in this act was the silent acknowledgment of the power of women, a fact which sustained us in some of our darker and more difficult hours.

Because of the dissolving of women's organizations and the known intimidation of women activists by the Colonels' security apparatus during the years of the dictatorship, women were reluctant—and fearful—of joining a women's organization in the early years of return to democratic rule, and organizing was difficult.

Now, in 1982–83, we were inundated with requests for contact with the WUG from all corners of Greece, invitations actually beyond our capacity to meet. In addition to our own group's foray on the summer weekend I'm describing, there were three other teams in action: one had gone to the islands of Cos and Leros, one to villages in central Thessaly, and one to Myteline, the island of Sappho. Still, it was not enough.

As we reached the village outskirts, we saw a gathering of twenty or more women along with some men—the president of the community and his council. Several young girls were in local costumes, and a small child was holding a bouquet of flowers, waiting for me to descend from the car and walk toward the group.

(This is where the roles get confused—my role as president of the Women's Union of Greece and my role as the wife of the Prime Minister. The way it works is this: I maintain my role as the P.M.'s wife during the initial ceremonies, whatever they may be. Then we all roll up our sleeves, enter the space where other women are waiting—be that the elementary school, a room in the community building, or the village café—and get down to the main business, a long discussion with the women. A café is the most unlikely place to meet, since for time memorial it has been considered men's province, and few village women have ever even been inside. I remember seeing women walk in with an air of awe and trepidation, looking around as if they were trespassing on holy ground. Others entered with a look of triumph on their faces: at last a barrier broken.)

After introductions were made, we started the dialogue by telling them a bit about us as an organization—what our goals were, what our activities were, how we were organized. This was standard to give a framework to the ensuing conversation. We told them that our slogan was "There can be no women's liberation without social liberation, and no social liberation without women's liberation." We believe, we said, that women suffer from two types of oppression—one from the capitalist system and the other from a patriarchal mentality, each of which feeds the other—but that these were formal and theoretical concepts and what we really wanted to know was how they felt *as women,* how they were treated as women, and what were the issues they, as women, felt to be most critical and burning in their village life.

We asked one woman, undoubtedly in her fifties, but looking ten to fifteen years older (as did most of the rural women) how she spent her day.

"Work, work, work," was her answer.

"All day?"

"All day, from five in the morning to midnight."

"And you?" pointing to another woman.

"The same."

"And your husband?"

"He works in the fields, too."

"Until what time?"

"Until three o'clock."

"And then?"

"After lunch and a rest, he goes to the *kafenion.* He has his friends. They talk politics, or they play *tavli.*"[1]

"And you?"

"I have the house to look after. Dinner. The children."

At this point Anna cut in: "In a few months it will be olive-picking time. Do any of you pick olives?"

"Most of us," was the response.

"How much do you earn?"

"When we're not picking our own olives, about a thousand drachmas a day" (US$13).

"And the men?"

"Fifteen hundred" (US$20).

"Why the difference?"

Some silence and some thinking.

[1.] A checkers game with dice.

"Do the men pick more than you a day?"

"No, the same. But . . . well, they go up in the trees and shake the branches."

"And you do the bending and picking below."

"Right."

Here I chimed in. "When I was a kid I rather liked climbing trees. I think I would prefer to shake the branches. Is it hard?"

"No."

"But it pays more. Why?"

"I think," said a younger woman, "it is dangerous."

"And that's why it pays more?"

"No," said another woman adamantly, "it's not dangerous."

"Then can you explain to me why the man gets more pay for a job that is easier—and not dangerous?"

A new hand went up. "Because he's a man."

There was a certain amount of laughter and nodding of heads—and a sense of relief. The key had been found.

"Is that just?"

"No, but that's the way it is."

"Let's turn to something else before we try to analyze that reality. Did any of you women here today run into difficulties in coming to the meeting? That is, did your husbands, or other members of the family, object?"

The general response was in the negative.

"Are there any women not here who wanted to come? And what are the reasons?"

"Koutsombolio," was the answer. Meaning "Gossip."

"Could you explain that a little bit?"

"Well, in a village people talk. They say that if you join a women's organization you are a loose woman. Or that you've gotten big ideas, trying something political. Next thing you know, they say, you'll be running for Parliament."

Sophia picked up the questioning at this point. The four of us were lined up at a small table in an elementary-school classroom, along with the local woman who had set up the meeting and who was presiding. The women were squeezed into chairs behind desks designed for ten-year-olds, a group of all ages, most of the older women in the traditional black clothing with black headscarf which is put on at the time of a husband's death and worn for the rest of life. (The status of widow is revered, but the clothing is a warning that other men should stay away, that she is re-wedded to the man who died and must remain faithful to him. That would seem to me the ultimate in patriarchal demands— fidelity after death.) Others in the audience were dressed in their best clothes for the occasion. Young teenagers, more aware of the worldwide feminist movement, were listening eagerly to hear something that concerned them specifically. The windows were open and a soft breeze brought in the delicate smell of mountain herbs and wild flowers that were rainbowing the countryside. A woman of about twenty-five with the mentality of a six-year-old came up and hugged me, then pulled up a chair behind me, took my hand and held on to it. We were sisters.

We returned to the discussion.

"Are you afraid of criticism?" said Sophia.

"We don't like it."

"And it stops you from acting sometimes?"

"Yes. You don't know about village tongues."

"I do know," replied Sophia, "because I come from a village, too. In fact, many women now living in Athens come from villages. But I want us to look at this phenomenon a little more closely. Do men stop their activities because of gossip, of criticism?"

The women laughed. "No!"

"Why do we, then?"

"We're more sensitive, maybe," was a tentative response from a middle-aged, bright-eyed woman.

"Or less sure of ourselves," Sophia offered. "Perhaps we don't have a strong sense of identity. We don't stand on our own, but try to behave the way other people expect us to behave, or want us to behave. A man knows who he is and what he wants, and goes after it. Is this a correct picture?"

There was silence and reflection, and heads nodded in affirmation here and there.

"But what about the woman who wants to come but is blocked by her husband, not by gossip. Does he have a right to hold her on a leash? Is she an animal?"

"Well, no, of course she's not an animal," piped up one of the teenagers. "But she's scared."

"Scared of what? Physical violence? Will he beat her?"

"No, no," most of the women responded.

"Women don't get beaten in this village?"

With rather too much protest, the women continued to proclaim "No."

The teenager blurted out. "That's not true, and you know it. There are men who beat their wives here."

There was an embarrassed silence, as if we had discovered a skeleton in the closet, as if we had torn off the emperor's clothes and were exposing the village. Eyes were averted, although several women glared at the girl who had made the revelation. Sophia told them that this was not uncommon in most villages; even in Athens—that mecca of civilization and advanced ideas—such beatings took place. She said that of course this was an unacceptable act, a form of tyranny which naturally bullied a woman into submission as long as she tolerated it. "But," Sophia went on, "what about the woman whose husband does not use violence, and still she does not demand her right to attend a meeting if she so desires?"

"There are the children," volunteered another participant.

"Let's say she has arranged for the children, that they are no obstacle."

"She doesn't want to hear 'gavgas.'"

"You mean her husband will shout at her. Sure, that's no fun. Does she have, by any chance, a deeper fear? That he may leave her?"

There was tittering and murmuring, but the initial consensus was that this was not the case.

"Suppose that he does decide to leave her. How can she live? Or let's say he simply decides not to give her any money for things she needs if she disobeys him. Could he do that? Or do you have your own money?"

"Ha!" was the spontaneous ejaculation.

"But at the beginning you said you worked all day. Don't people who work get paid?"

"Not us."

"And why?"

"Because we're women." We had now come full circle.

"But you get wages when you pick olives. What do you do with that? Give it to your husbands?"

There was a sheepish nodding of the heads.

"Tell me, ladies," Sophia smiled, "isn't that just a little crazy? Unless you have a common cash pot with equal freedom to withdraw, aren't you giving away something precious? A form of independence? And isn't that a major source of freedom and dignity, your economic independence? We believe, as a women's organization, that a lot of the fear and lack of self-assurance that a woman has is a result of her dependent status. She is obliged to perform according to someone else's wishes. She does not have complete control over her actions."

It was Maria's turn now. The women had warmed up to the subject and hands were being raised. Even more than that, everyone was finally talking—but at once. This phenomenon we run into all the time, and it is one of the worst hurdles to bringing about an understandable dialogue. We try pounding the table; we shout "one at a time"; we explain the rules for group functioning. To no avail. I find the most effective way is for me to stand up and simply stare at them. Slowly, one starts shushing the other, or a talker is hit on the arm and a finger pointed to me. I wait like a statue, until I can hear the proverbial pin drop. Then we have order again. For a while.

Maria starts. "The WUG believes that a lot of these things we are describing here are a part of the capitalist system; that is, it is in the interests of the system to keep women in an inferior position, to use them as surplus labor, as cheap labor. We believe also that men are victims in this system as well, except for the upper-class man, the capitalist himself, who exploits the working man. Farmers, for instance, contribute 14 percent of our national income—that is, they contribute in goods to all of the country that percentage—yet they receive only a small percentage in return. Where does the rest go? To the middleman, to the profiteers at the end of the line, to the retail sellers, to the loan sharks."

The middle-aged woman, whose name was Eleftheria, spoke up. "We received five drachmas a kilo for our tomatoes this summer. When I traveled to Yannena one day I found them selling in the grocery store for fifty-five drachmas a kilo."

"Apart from the need to change the system where there will be a more equitable division of income and a society with social services for the working man *and* woman, we need to change the *attitudes* toward women. Our organization does not believe that socialism will automatically bring equality between the sexes. Changing the economic factors breaks down class barriers, but not necessarily gender barriers."

Maria stopped for a moment to let this seep in.

A woman of sixty spoke up, her Greek tinged with an accent. "I lived in Bulgaria for over thirty years, as a refugee. And I know that the Bulgarian woman still does double duty, at her job and at her home. What is true is that she has more opportunities for work, and there are many childcare centers that do a good job of tending children. But household work and child-raising are still considered women's work."

Sophia took over. "This is what we are trying to say. That even in societies where supposedly there are equal opportunities to work and a more equitable division of income, the woman is still expected to maintain her traditional role of housewife and mother. That's what we mean, in simple terms, when we talk about patriarchy."

We had been talking for over an hour, and no one had stirred or indicated a need to leave. It appeared that this was one time Sunday dinners might be late—and no one seemed to care.

During the second hour we touched on many subjects: childcare centers, contraception, cultural activities, civil marriage (a new institution established by the socialist government), abortion, female and male roles, agricultural cooperatives—we covered the waterfront. The four of us did less talking ourselves, encouraging the village women to speak, trying to make every woman say *some*thing, no matter how timid she might feel.

"Dear friends," said Anna, "we could go on forever. The problems are endless. The big question is, what do we do about it? How are we going to tackle these problems?"

"With a socialist government," Aliki replied. (By now we knew all of their names.)

"We have one, and that helps. But is that enough?"

Elsa, the teenager, answered. "We know of course why you are here. You are members of the WUG and you do organizational work in the villages. Earlier, I was unconvinced about separate women's organizations, but I think after hearing the discussion today, it's essential that we organize a chapter here. Only when we women develop power through-out Greece will our demands be listened to. I am unsure, however, as to how many women here would join."

"That we can quickly determine. How many of you would like to become members of the WUG?"

Several hands went up, then more, and still more. Three fourths of the women were ready.

"Among the women whose hands are up, we want a five-member coordinating com-mittee, as a start: the women who will take responsibility for calling meetings, for devel-oping a plan of action, for adding to the membership, for being in touch with central offices . . ."

"You, you, you, you, and you," pointed out Sophia. (At this point, I confess, we swerve from democratic procedures and choose the most dynamic and committed among the participants.)

The room was bristling with excitement, appreciation—and definitely, undeniably, *sisterhood*. A new chapter of the Women's Union of Greece had been born.

Suggested Further Reading

Kaklamanaki, Roula. *"Η θέση της Ελληνίδας στην Οικογένεια"* (The Position of the Greek Woman in the Family). Athens: Pedia, 1979.

Kara, Maria. *"Προβλήματα της εργαζόμενης γυναίκας"* (The Problem of the Working Woman). Athens: Maria Kara, 1977.

Nikolaidou, Magda. *"Η γυναίκα στην Ελλάδα"* (The Woman in Greece). Athens: Kastaniotis, 1979.

Takari, Dina. *"Η κοινωνική και επαγγελματική θέση της σημερινής γυναίκας"* (The Social and Professional Position of Today's Woman). Athens: Dina Takari, 1978.

"Γυναίκες στην Αντίσταση—Μαρτυρίες" (Women in the Resistance—Witnesses). Compiled by the Movement of Greek Women in Resistance. Athens: Amnesty International, 1982.

Margaret Chant Papandreou was born in 1923 in Oak Park, Illinois (USA). She at-tended the University of Minnesota, gaining her B.A. in journalism in 1946 and her master's degree in public health in 1956. She married Andreas G. Papandreou in 1951 and they subsequently had three sons and a daughter. Margaret Papandreou's political activities began at the age of twelve when she participated in her grandfather's state Senate campaign; he was running on the Socialist ticket. At the university she became editor of the Agricultural Campus news for the University of Minnesota *Daily*. Later she joined the Democratic-Farm-Labor Party in Minnesota and was sent as an official dele-gate to several state conventions. She was a founding member of the Stevenson Forum Board, which worked after 1952 to see that the Democratic party re-nominated Adlai Stevenson as their candidate in 1956. When her husband ran for Parliament in Greece from the district of Ahaia, she was again on the campaign trail. During the dictatorship and after the family left Greece, she produced a book, *Nightmare in Athens,* which described her experiences under the junta. She was a founding member of the Panhellenic Liberation Movement, a resistance group. Since her return to Greece in 1974, she has been active in the Panhellenic Socialist Movement and is a member of the International Relations Committee. In addition, she helped found the Women's Union of Greece and was elected president in March 1982. Recently she has written two children's books, illustrated by Sophia Zarambouka. The first, called *Imper the Giant,* concerns the strug-gle of the people against imperialism; the second, called *Lightning and Her Three Broth-ers,* concerns the struggle against the oppression of women.

GUATEMALA
(Republic of Guatemala)

A Central American country, bordered by Belize, the Caribbean Sea, Honduras, and El Salvador to the east, the Pacific Ocean to the south, and Mexico to the west and north. **Area:** 108,889 sq. km. (42,042 sq. mi.). **Population** (1980): 7,007,000, female 49.3%. **Capital:** Guatemala City.

DEMOGRAPHY. Languages: Spanish, Quiché, Mam, Kekchi, Kakchiquel. **Races or Ethnic Groups:** Native Indian 54%, Mestizo 42%, European descent 4%. **Religions:** Roman Catholicism 88%, indigenous faiths. **Education** (% enrolled in school, 1975): Age 6–11—of all girls 49%, of all boys 51%; age 12–17—of all girls 24%, of all boys 32%; higher education—no data obtainable. **Literacy** (1977): Women 38%, men 54%. **Birth Rate** (per 1000 pop., 1975–80): 43. **Death Rate** (per 1000 pop., 1975–80): 12. **Infant Mortality** (per 1000 live births, 1975–80): Female 71, male 81. **Life Expectancy** (1975–80): Female 59 yrs., male 57 yrs.

GOVERNMENT. On Aug. 8, 1983, Gen. Oscar Humberto Mejia Victores overthrew José Efraín Ríos Montt, who had taken sole power in June 1982, after being one of 3 members of a military junta which had seized control in a Mar. 1982 coup. There is no constitution currently (1983) in effect; the "Estatuto Fundamental" (Basic Statute) regulates the country. **Voting:** The most recent presidential election was in 1978. The 1974 election results were disputed. **Women's Suffrage:** Guatemalan Constitutions of 1851, 1879, 1945, and 1965 each have different regulations regarding women's suffrage (see HERSTORY). The 1965 Constitution expressly gave women the right to citizenship and voting. **Equal Rights:** The 1965 Constitution (Art. 43) prohibited discrimination because of race, sex, religion, birth, political opinion, etc. **Women in Government:** Only a few women have served in the Guatemalan government as elected or appointed officials. Reportedly, women are participating in the opposition leadership, espe-

cially since its change in recent years from a guerrilla-focused effort to the GPR, the Guerra Popular Revolucionaria (Popular Revolutionary War); Rigoberta Menchu, a Quiché Indian woman, is the GPR spokesperson for women.

ECONOMY. Currency: Quetzal (May 1983: 1. = $1 US). **Gross National Product** (1980): $6.9 billion. **Per Capita Income** (1980): $1110. **Women's Wages as a Percentage of Men's** (1973): In industry, skilled women workers receive 57%, unskilled 87% (absolute wage amounts are very small: $0.63 per hour for skilled, $0.33 per hour for unskilled). **Equal Pay Policy:** Discrimination on grounds of sex is expressly prohibited by law in the work place. The 1965 Constitution (Art. 114) required "equal pay for equal work under equal conditions, efficiency, and seniority." **Production** (Agricultural/Industrial): Coffee, cotton, bananas, cattle, sugar; textiles, prepared foods, construction materials. **Women as a Percentage of Labor Force** (1979): 13.8%; **of agricultural force** 1.4% (of whom 22% are unpaid family workers); **of industrial force** —no general statistics obtainable (of manufacturing 21.8%); **of military**—no statistics obtainable; women serve in the government's military forces and are reportedly active in the country's opposition movement. **(Employed) Women's Occupational Indicators** (1979): Of administrative/managerial workers 18.5%, of clerical workers 34%, of sales workers 35%, of professional/technical workers 40%, of service workers 60%. Many peasant workers (mostly Indian) migrate seasonally to large cotton, coffee, and sugar cane plantations to earn cash income. Reports indicate that women are paid less for the same hours as men for work on the plantations, and that 16-hour days in the fields are not uncommon. Domestic servants also work extremely long hours; the only protection technically given them by the law is that they should be allowed "to sleep for 8 hours" and have 1 day off per week, although reportedly labor legislation for domestics stipulates vacation, a Christmas bonus, and a lump-sum payment on dismissal. However, these benefits are almost never granted, and salaries may be as low as $15–$25 per month. Weaving is an important part of Mayan culture and of women's economic activity. In addition to the textile industry, there is much home-working of handmade woven products. Most benefits of such tourist purchases go to non-Indian intermediaries and institutions (shops and hotels) rather than to the Indians. **Unemployment:** No total rate or rates by sex obtainable; females are 25% of total unemployed (official est.).

GYNOGRAPHY. Marriage. *Policy:* Legal marriage age for both females and males is 18 (majority); 14 for females and 16 for males with parental consent (Civil Code, Art. 81). Marital domicile is determined by mutual agreement (Art. 109). A husband is obliged to protect a wife and provide for maintenance; a wife has the obligation to care for minor children and domestic affairs and must contribute equitably to the maintenance of the household if she has her own source of income (Arts. 110, 111). Upon marriage, a couple may choose 1 of 3 different economic systems: absolute separation of all properties *(separación absoluta),* joint holding of all properties *(comunidad absoluta,* in which the husband has the legal responsibility to administer all properties, Art. 131), or *comunidad de gananciales* (wherein each retains ownership of property held at the time of the marriage but divides equally everything acquired during marriage). If no system is specified, this last option is in effect. Common-law marriages may be recognized by law and recorded in the civil register after proof that the couple has lived together for 5 yrs. *Practice:* Female mean age at marriage (1970–78): 20; women age 15–49 in union (1970–78): 65%. In rural Indian villages, women often marry at age 15. They usually keep separate accounts from their husbands and have strong community ties to sustain them. Middle- or upper-class *ladino* (Spanish-heritage) women in the cities may marry later. **Divorce.** *Policy:* Di-

vorce and separation are legal, and either can be by mutual consent or contested. A mutual-consent divorce is possible only after 1 yr. of marriage. A legal judicial separation may be converted to a full divorce after 1 yr. upon application to the court. These options are for both legal marriages and registered common-law marriages. Adultery charges against a married woman, or against a man not her husband who knows she is married, may be brought only by the woman's husband; this carries a penalty of 6 months– 2 yrs. imprisonment. If a married man has a lover within the marriage domicile, he is subject to a prison term of 4 months–1 yr.; the woman involved is subject to a fine of $50–$100. (Penal Code, Arts. 232–35.) *Practice:* No statistics obtainable. Divorce has become more of an option for *ladino* urban women in the last 2 decades, since economic growth (triggered by the formation of the Central American Common Market in 1960) has created employment for middle-class women in banks and commercial enterprises.

Family. *Policy:* Joint parental authority is given to mother and father in both marriages and common-law unions (Civil Code, Art. 252). In a divorce case, girls remain with the mother, custody of boys over age 7 may be awarded to the father. Maternity policies mandate a leave (30 days pre- and 45 days post-delivery) with 100% pay, plus 2 short rest periods per day for nursing mothers during the first yr. A woman may not be fired because of pregnancy. *Practice:* Custody of children in a divorce case is generally awarded to the mother unless she rejects it. In the private sector, despite the law, women are often fired when they become pregnant. In rural Indian villages, pregnancy and childbirth are exclusively within women's realm; traditional midwives attend most rural births. **Welfare.** *Policy:* There is no unemployment insurance program or welfare system for those who are not working. Government employees have a contributory retirement plan. The law mandates that the social security system cover retirement for private employers as well. Social security laws provide pensions for wives and children of disabled or deceased men. "Indemnization" policies require that men and women who resign or are fired receive 1 month's salary for each yr. worked, to be paid in a lump sum. *Practice:* The law requiring retirement payments for private-sector employers has not been enforced. A few private companies have retirement plans. "Indemnization" payments are often not made even to a worker who has been with a company for many yrs., or who has been disabled in a job-related accident. Some reports indicate that efforts at labor organization within factories have resulted in advances, though such organizing is often suppressed.

Contraception. *Policy:* Legal; sales and advertisements of products are allowed. *Practice:* Women age 15–44 in union using contraception (1981): 18%, of which traditional methods 17%, modern 50%, sterilization 33%. The government has made some efforts to train nurses and traditional midwives in family-planning methods. A private association (APROFAM, Asociación Pro-Bienestar de la Familia), based in Guatemala City, carries out a variety of programs, including offering vasectomy. In 1978 among couples who elected sterilization, 1 in 15 chose vasectomy rather than tubal ligation; the over-all numbers involved in this ratio are small (0.4% of men and 6% of women choosing sterilization). The majority of the Indian pop. in rural areas has little or no access to contraceptive information or methods, though some attempts have been made to translate materials into their native languages. **Abortion.** *Policy:* Legal, with declarations by 3 certified doctors, only if the life of the woman is in danger. Performing an illegal abortion is subject to criminal punishment. *Practice:* No statistics obtainable, although illegal abortions are reportedly more common than legal ones. **Illegitimacy.** *Policy:* Children born in and out of wedlock have the same rights and obligations; the law prohibits mention of the legal status of parents on the birth certificate. *Practice:* A woman who bears an out-of-wedlock child suffers loss of status, and the child may not be socially accepted. **Homosexuality.** *Policy:* Homosexuality is not explicitly mentioned in the Penal Code. *Practice:* No data obtainable.

Incest. *Policy:* Illegal. Punishment ranges from 2–4 yrs. imprisonment, or 3–6 yrs. if the victim is under age 18 (see **Rape**). *Practice:* No data obtainable. **Sexual Harassment.** *Policy:* None. *Practice:* Some reports state that factory security forces use their authority to molest women workers on the pretext of searching for anything concealed under their clothing. Domestic servants are sometimes used for sexual purposes by males in the household; if they become pregnant, they are generally fired or must have the child raised somewhere else in order to retain their job. **Rape.** *Policy:* Illegal; if the woman is asleep, unconscious, or insane, the punishment is 6–12 yrs. imprisonment for the rapist. Aggravated rape, involving 2 or more people, a relative or guardian, or a victim who suffers "grave damage" carries a prison term of 8–20 yrs., or 20–30 yrs. if the victim dies; if the victim is under age 10, the death penalty can be applied. *Estupro* or "carnal access" to a female under age 18 by using deceit, false promises of marriage, or taking advantage of her inexperience, is punishable by 1–2 yrs. if the victim is under age 14, or 6 months–1 yr. if she is age 14–18. If the accused is a relative or guardian of the victim, imprisonment can be increased by 2/3. *Practice:* No statistics obtainable. Thousands of women, mostly Indian, have reportedly been raped by members of the military. **Battery.** *Policy:* No data obtainable. *Practice:* No statistics obtainable. Wife-beating is common, and linked to male alcoholism. **Prostitution.** *Policy:* Promoting or facilitating prostitution is punishable by a fine of $500–$1000; practicing prostitution carries a fine of $300–$1000. These fines may be increased by 1/3 if the promoter is a relative or guardian, if the victim is under age 18, or if violence or deceit are used. Transporting a person to another country for prostitution purposes is punishable by 1–3 yrs. imprisonment plus a fine of $500–$3000; if the victim is under age 12, the penalties may be increased by 2/3 (1973 Penal Code, Arts. 193–94). *Practice:* No statistics obtainable. Prostitution is prevalent in cities. In recent yrs. it is reported to have spread to rural areas, in direct proportion to the influx of government military forces in the countryside. **Traditional/Cultural Practices.** *Policy:* None. *Practice:* There have been some reports of bride-selling in Native Indian areas. **Crisis Centers:** No data obtainable.

HERSTORY. The Mayan civilization had 3 major epochs: *pre-classic* (1500 B.C.E.–300 C.E.), during which time the cultivation of maize (or corn, still important in the Guatemalan economy) began, *classic* (300–900), when such cultural advances were made as the development of 2 calendars and a base-20 system of mathematics, sculpture, and architecture (see MYTHOGRAPHY), and *post-classic* (900–1697). Spanish conquistador Pedro de Alvarado conquered Guatemala in 1523–24, and women have been participating in the fight for liberation since colonial days. Felipa Soc fought in the Indian revolt of 1820 against tribute imposed by Spain on the population of Totonicapán. The 1851 Constitution stated that men and women could be recognized as citizens if they were economically independent (a condition which posed a *de facto* obstacle to most women's political participation). The 1879 Constitution contained more explicit legal discrimination: only men age 18 or over, literate, and with income were recognized as citizens.

Women were active in the battle against the dictatorship of Jorge Ubico (1930–44); María Chinchilla was a teacher who was assassinated in one of the demonstrations that led to his fall. The 1945 Constitution (Art. 9) recognized all men of age 18 as citizens, but only those women over 18 who were literate. The Alianza Femenina Guatemalteca (Guatemalan Women's Alliance) was founded in 1944 but was dissolved by governmental decree in 1954 after the coup resulted in the downfall of Pres. Jacobo Arbenz Guzmán. In 1954 women participated in the many protests against the government of Castillo Armas. The Constitution of 1965 was the first to give men and women equal right to citizenship, without literacy or income requirements.

Much of the information that exists about Guatemalan women today is in the form of *testimonios* (verbatim accounts) of the political torture and general exploitation women face daily. Mama Maquín, an Achí Indian woman, led hundreds of peasants in an attempt to regain their lands in Panzos and was killed with over 100 others in May 1978. In Jan. 1980 a group of people from Quiché took over the Spanish Embassy to try to make their concerns heard; the government burned down the building with the demonstrators inside, and Regine Pul Juy, María Ramírez Anay, María Pinula Lux, and Sonia Magaly Welchez Valdéz were among those who died. In Mar. 1980, UNAM—the Unión Nacional de Mujeres de Guatemala (National Union of Guatemalan Women) was formed. On Aug. 30 of that year, a young lawyer named Guadelupe Navas was killed. On Dec. 19, the feminist Alaíde Foppa disappeared in Guatemala while on a visit to her mother (see following article); Foppa's daughter, Silvia Solorzano Foppa, is a leader of the Ejército Guerrillero de los Pobres (EGP; Guerrilla Army of the Poor). In Mar. 1983, América Yolanda Urízar, an attorney, returned to Guatemala in accordance with the government's declared amnesty for dissenters; she has "disappeared"; her daughter, Yolanda de la Luz, was imprisoned and tortured.

MYTHOGRAPHY. The sacred Mayan books describe the different periods which pre-date the Spanish invasion. The second of these eras included the creation of a cult of goddesses: Ixmucane (moon and agricultural goddess), Ixquic (earth mother and fertility goddess), and Ixchel or Ixchebel Yax (goddess of weaving and embroidery). In Indian villages today, traditional midwives are still believed to serve as the intermediary between the pregnant woman and the supernatural female guardian of childbirth. They perform religious rites and ceremonies before and after the birth, as well as giving physical care.

GUATEMALA: Our Daily Bread
by Stella Quan
(Translated by Gloria Feiman Waldman
and Elisa Sierra Gutiérrez)

> What most impressed us in speaking with the people, in reading
> documents and in reflecting upon our own experiences in Guate-
> mala, was the ability of its people to continue their battle sur-
> rounded by terror; and even more so, the ability of the
> Guatemalans to strengthen and enrich the most profoundly human
> qualities in the face of such brutality. This project is dedicated to
> those qualities in the Guatemalan people that allow them to trans-
> form the horror into hope.
>
> *Concerned Guatemalan Scholars*[1]

The women of this anthology project, *Sisterhood Is Global,* did well in asking me specifically not to exclude personal experiences—my own and other women's—when writing
this article. This allows me to establish from the outset that it should not be me who
writes this piece, or at least I should not be doing it alone; this article should be written
by—among so many other women, especially Native Guatemalan women—Alaíde
Foppa.*

But it happens that just as with thousands of other Guatemalan women and men
(eighty thousand since 1954, the date of the counterrevolution), Alaíde is no longer with
us. Alaíde was kidnapped in December of 1980 by the army of those who wield power in
Guatemala. Now, years after her abduction, we still know nothing of her whereabouts.
We can deduce (from daily evidence) what surely must have happened: Alaíde was raped
and tortured, as happens to thousands of Guatemalan women, especially to our Native
sisters. And at sixty-seven years of age, Alaíde was not able to survive. Nevertheless, the
Guatemalans who dare to fight—following the example of millions of Latin Americans
who refuse to accept the deaths of relatives and friends until the guilty governments
assume responsibility for them—will not accept the probable fact that Alaíde and all our
sisters and brothers kidnapped there have died.

We will continue to demand from the military an explanation as to what they have
done with Alaíde, and with the hundreds of Guatemalans who disappear each day. The
mothers of the Plaza de Mayo** in Argentina have shown us the way. This was agreed
upon at the First Latin American Congress for the relatives of those who have disappeared, held in Costa Rica in January of 1981.

In spite of my longing for Alaíde to be here with me, writing this manuscript, I can no
longer count on her. Alaíde was a friend, sister, mother, *compañera*—and she is no longer

---

[1] Concerned Guatemalan Scholars. *Dare to Struggle, Dare to Win,* Oct. 1981; P.O. Box 270, Wyckoff
Heights Station, Brooklyn, NY 11237.

* Among her many other activities (see preceding Preface, HERSTORY), Alaíde Foppa was one of
the founders of *Fem,* the Latin American feminist journal based in Mexico, where it is still being
published.—Ed.

** The mothers of Plaza de Mayo are women who have for years kept up perpetual vigils and
  demonstrations in Buenos Aires, demanding of the Argentine government the whereabouts of
  their "missing" relatives. See Leonor Calvera's article on Argentinian women, p. 54.—Ed.

with me. Many are missing, many have been amputated from us by death or exile, many have ceased to be. As is true for the majority of Guatemalans, not only do I miss Alaíde, I miss her two sons, Juan Pablo and Mario, and I also miss her husband, Alfonso, leader of the Democratic-Nationalist Revolution of 1944. In only that one Guatemalan family, I miss four members.

This terrifying drama, that abominable reality—that a family of seven in one year changes to a family of three—this is our daily bread in my country. A mother kidnapped, two sons murdered, a father dead in an "accident" because he could not tolerate the death of his sons—our daily bread.

This is true above all, and in mass numbers, among the poorest of the poor in Guatemala: the 60 percent of the population which is indigenous. The rest of us are a little less Indian. But it is these Native Indians who are being herded into certain "strategic villages" as was done in Vietnam, who are bombed daily with napalm, who are being annihilated. I repeat: our daily bread in Guatemala.

I have said that I miss Alaíde, her sons, and her husband. All Guatemalans are missing someone. But the Native Guatemalans, the peasants, are missing everything: the relative or relatives murdered, the house burned, the cornfields destroyed. And thousands of them (150,000 in Mexico alone, according to the Mexican press, in addition to those who arrive day after day) are also missing a country. They arrive daily in the border countries, fleeing massacres and seeking refuge.

In response to so much sadism, to the irrationality and stupidity which installed itself in power twenty-nine years ago, the Guatemalan woman is fighting, as she has done for the last decades, with arms in her hand, or by helping those who make the arms, aware as she is that any other road is now closed to Guatemalans.

She also realizes that it is an entire people who struggle against the madness, avarice, and savagery of those who have unsurped power. This explains why our Native sisters have abandoned their butterfly dresses—as Luís Cardoza y Aragón would say—for boots and a rifle.

The following excerpt vividly documents how the Guatemalan woman is treated by the government, and the reasons why hundreds of them, along with their families, are leaving their country. In *El Gallo Ilustrado,* the weekly supplement of the newspaper *El Día,* on May 23, 1982, México, D.F., this story appeared:

> *I can tell you a little about what I lived through in a village of Chichi Castenango.*
> It must have been 11 A.M. when we believed that we were safe hiding in the mountain. All of a sudden, the helicopters began to arrive, and we saw that they were surrounding us, enclosing us in a circle. The children, like all children, could not stay still.
>
> In five minutes the army started to bomb us, to open machine-gun fire. I do not know where the planes came from, but they flew very low and dropped many bombs. We all began to hide as best we could in the mountain. The children began to scream; many women called for their children because they were losing them. It was a race—run, run, run, fall down into a cloud of earth. We would yell to the women, "Don't stop. Throw yourselves on the ground because you can get hit by a bullet," but many didn't understand Spanish and there were those of us who couldn't communicate with them in their native language.
>
> We saw many women get hit by bullets. Others went back when they realized that their children weren't with them. They would call, and the children would scream back, searching for their mothers. Only those the mothers carried on their backs were safe. The worst were the four-, five-, and six-year-olds who were able to run by themselves—they were the ones left behind.

That's why many women returned for them in desperation. The infantry had been able to enter and they were running and hurling grenades and firing machine guns. Many of the women who went back were hit. We couldn't go back to see if they were dead or only wounded; it was impossible. Hundreds of people ran and ran in desperation. We ran for almost six hours. We saw people running with their heads opened, with their hands missing. Often we were unable to identify the children because their faces were covered with blood. I saw a woman who had given birth fifteen days earlier, and who had her infant on her back and carried another child in her arms, fall on her back. She crushed her newborn baby. When she was able to look back at him, she saw him bleeding from his ears, mouth, and nose, and she screamed, totally inconsolable.

Another day many women set out to return to their villages to look for the children they had lost. These women could not sleep, eat, or hear any warnings. They could only think about their babies, and weep. Many of them would say, "Just to know what is happening to them. To know if they are crying. To know if they are hurt or lying in a river or on a mountain with no one to help them." This is how we lost many women—because they went back to look for their children.

This is the daily bread of most Guatemalan women. Only within this context is it possible to understand why women have taken up arms in Guatemala.

How can you, the women of other countries, help us? Our *compañeros* in *Concerned Guatemalan Scholars* answer:

It is vital to develop international solidarity. This task can be realized in different ways, from denouncing the repression and rejecting any military or political intervention that would support the regime now in power to providing real help to the national liberation movement. It is also important to recognize the role played by those governments and political organizations . . . that have taken a stance independent of the United States in recognizing the right of the people of Guatemala to rebel against unjust social structures and illegitimate regimes.

The task of effective solidarity requires that people understand the role played by their own country when it supports such regimes. . . . And, of course, solidarity also demands a true knowledge of the people of Guatemala, their history, and their quest for liberation.

And I would personally add: Help us by seeing to it that those peasants who find themselves forced to emigrate *not be deported back to Guatemala.* Help us by demanding in national and international forums that Guatemalan emigrants be granted legal status in the countries to which they flee. Help us eliminate savagery and death as ingredients in our daily bread. Realize that only with worldwide solidarity will we, the people of Guatemala, be able to transform horror into hope.

We want work, peace, and happiness to be our daily bread. We—the women of Guatemala—ask that you help us to reach this goal.

Suggested Further Reading

Galeano, Eduardo. *Guatemala: Occupied Country.* New York: Monthly Review Press, 1969.

Jonas, S., and D. Tobis, eds. *Guatemala: And So Victory Is Born.* New York: NACLA, 1974; Re-edition, 1981.

Guatemala: A Government Program of Political Murder. London: Amnesty International, 1981.

Melville, Thomas and Marjorie. *Guatemala: The Politics of Land Ownership.* New York: Free Press, 1971.

Stella Quan has lived in Mexico since 1963, when she had to emigrate from Guatemala. She married by proxy the father of her two children. Her husband, an archeologist and professor at the Universidad de San Carlos, was jailed in Guatemala and later expelled. She is divorced. She is an anthropologist (M.A. in ethnology; specialty, ethnohistory) and a Ph.D. candidate in anthropology at the Universidad Nacional Autónoma de México. In January of 1980 she, Alaíde Foppa, and other Latin American and European women founded AIMUR (International Agrupation of Women Against Repression in Guatemala). Since Foppa's kidnapping on December 19, 1980, AIMUR has been an active member of CWAF (the International Committee for the Life of Alaíde Foppa). Stella Quan is presently a member of ATCG (Assoc. of Workers for Guatemalan Culture), Alaíde Foppa Brigade. Their *Declaration of Principles,* issued in Mexico City in April 1982, reads: "The Association has chosen the name Alaíde Foppa in homage to a prestigious woman, cultural worker, and possessor of one of the most brilliant artistic and intellectual careers of our time, impeccable in her moral and ethical behavior and committed until the end to our country's cause. . . ."

HUNGARY
(Hungarian People's Republic)

Located in east central Europe, bounded by Rumania to the east, Yugoslavia to the south, Austria to the west, and Czechoslovakia and the USSR to the north. **Area:** 93,030 sq. km. (35,919 sq. mi.). **Population** (1980): 10,752,000, female 51.3%. **Capital:** Budapest.

DEMOGRAPHY. Languages: Magyar (Hungarian, official), German, Slavic, Croatian. **Races or Ethnic Groups:** Magyar 98%, German 0.5%; Slovak, Croatian; Hungary's 400,000–person Gypsy pop. is a distinct and discriminated against ethnic minority. **Religions:** Roman Catholicism 60%, Protestant (Calvinist). **Education** (% enrolled in school, 1975): Age 6–11—of all girls 97%, of all boys 96%; age 12–17—of all girls 71%, of all boys 77%; higher education—in 1982 women were 49.8% of college students; in 1970–72, 0.8% of art and music students, 1.4% of communications, 1.9% of agriculture, 4% of commerce, 6.9% of industrial professional school, 16.4% of economics. **Literacy** (1977): Women 98%, men 98%. **Birth Rate** (per 1000 pop., 1977–78): 16. **Death Rate** (per 1000 pop., 1977–78): 13. **Infant Mortality** (per 1000 live births, 1977): Female 26, male 33. **Life Expectancy** (1975–80): Female 73 yrs., male 67 yrs. (Gypsy women and men have a 15-yr. lower life expectancy, respectively.)

GOVERNMENT. An elected 352-member National Assembly holds legislative power and elects a 21-member Presidium, the highest State body. A premier heads a council of ministers, the main administrative body. The Hungarian Socialist Workers' Party (Communist), is the only legal political party; the Party's Politburo holds supreme *de facto* power. **Women's Suffrage:** 1945. **Equal Rights:** The 1949 Constitution (Art. 62) states that "men and women in the Hungarian People's Republic shall enjoy equal rights." **Women in Government:** Women are 27% of the National Assembly and Ms. Cservenka is a Deputy Chairperson (1983). In 1975, 23.5% of the Hungarian Socialist Workers' Party, over 40% of union representatives, and the Minister of Industry, Secretary of Health, and president of the Central Council of Trade Unions were women.

ECONOMY. Currency: Forint (May 1983: 35.58 = $1 US). **Gross National Product** (1980): $45 billion. **Per Capita Income** (1980): $4180. **Women's Wages as a Percentage of Men's** (1983): Women earned an average 20–30% less than men in the same jobs. **Equal Pay Policy:** The Council of Ministers' Resolution No. 1013 (1970) reinforced the existing principle of "equal pay for equal work"; 1970 reports showed noncompliance in many areas. **Production** (Agricultural/Industrial): Corn, wheat, potatoes, sugar beets, vegetables, wine grapes, fruits; measuring equipment, pharmaceuticals, textiles, transport equipment. **Women as a Percentage of Labor Force** (Jan. 1980): 44.8%; **of agricultural force** 39.1% (28.7% of whom are unpaid family workers); **of industrial force**—no general statistics obtainable (of mining/quarrying, manufacturing, electricity and gas 44.8%); **of military**—no statistics obtainable; women are permitted in the military only as service workers (clerical, etc.). **(Employed) Women's Occupational Indicators:** Of construction 17.8%, of transport, storage, and communication 24.7%, of wholesale/retail trade, restaurants, hotels 64.2% (Jan. 1980); of physicians 40.8%, of teachers 85%; of industrial designers 85%; of tailors and seamstresses 90%, of paramedical professionals 92% (1975); women were the majority of industrial workers doing spinning-mill work, and assembly-line work producing TV tubing (1975). Labor legislation prohibits women from doing approx. 40 types of work, including night employment, underground work, certain industrial jobs, moving and trucking jobs. **Unemployment** (1983): Officials report no unemployment.

GYNOGRAPHY. Marriage. *Policy:* The 1949 Constitution (amended 1972) gives

State protection to the institution of marriage; men and women have equal spousal rights. Legal marriage age is 16 for females, 18 for males; it may be lowered to 14 and 16 respectively in exceptional cases, and with parental or guardian's consent. A 30-day waiting period after obtaining a marriage certificate and prior marriage counseling are both required; these measures were enacted to counter the high divorce rate (see **Divorce**). A married woman may take her husband's name followed by the possessive prefix "ne" (meaning "wife of," in this context) and then her birth-name, assume both her own and her husband's family names, or keep her birth-name. She can own and administer her own property. Bigamy is illegal (as an "Offense Against the Family"), with a maximum penalty of 3 yrs. imprisonment. *Practice:* Female mean age at marriage (1970–78): 21; women age 15–49 in union (1970–78): 71.9%. Registered marriages (per 1000 mid-yr. pop., 1979): 8.1. While the law grants spousal equality, the majority of married women occupy a social position inferior to that of their husbands, who make final decisions in legal and financial matters. **Divorce.** *Policy:* Legal by mutual consent or by judicial decree. The welfare and education of any children must be considered before a couple will be granted a divorce. Child custody and alimony payments are court-determined. *Practice:* Final divorces (per 1000 pop., mid-1979): 2.62, a relatively high divorce rate (see **Marriage**); no further data obtainable. **Family.** *Policy:* The 1949 Constitution (amended 1972) gives State protection (maternity benefits, family allowances, etc.) to the family. The father is the legal head of household in most legal and financial affairs. Pronatalist maternity legislation (1967 and 1973) by the Council of Ministers (Decision 1040) gives employed married women a cash benefit paid at childbirth and a maternity leave with full salary and guaranteed job security for up to 20 weeks, 45 days of which are pre-delivery. Employed mothers are entitled to a childcare allowance for up to 31 months after the end of the paid maternity-leave period if the woman remains out of the labor force to care for her child; as of 1982, the same benefit applies to single fathers. In 1975 the allowance was approx. 850 Forints for first child, 950 for second, 1050 for third. Employed mothers are entitled to 45-minute nursing breaks twice daily, a 60-day paid sick leave for each child age 1–3, 30 days for each child age 3–6. There are government-run childcare centers. *Practice:* According to a 1980 report, 254,110 employed mothers received childcare allowances. The same report indicated that only 10% of children under age 3 are in nurseries. Reports indicate that the burden of day care frequently rests on grandmothers. In 1982 the average employed woman spent over 4 hours a day on housework while the average employed man spent 1.

Welfare. *Policy:* Employees are eligible for national social insurance; benefits cover sickness and old-age pensions at age 55 for women, age 60 for men (also see **Family**). Medical care is free for everyone, but patients pay 15% of the cost of medicines. *Practice:* Benefit payments totaled 65 million Ft. in 1978; no further data obtainable. **Contraception.** *Policy:* Legal although government policy is pronatalist; sale of contraceptives is legal and they are available from private family-planning programs. As of 1980, oral contraceptives were forbidden to females under age 16; women who had not given birth were prohibited from obtaining IUDs. *Practice:* Women age 15–49 in union using contraception (1970–80): 73%, of which traditional methods 30%, modern 70%. **Abortion.** *Policy:* Legal on request from 1956–73; 1974 Decree 1040 restricted abortion on request to pregnant (single) teenagers, single, divorced, separated, or widowed women, married women over age 35, or those who have undergone 3 births or who have 2 children and have undergone an additional "obstetrical event"; in other cases, abortion is permitted on grounds of health, eugenic reasons, pregnancy resulting from cases of rape or incest, and possibly in cases of inadequate housing. No current (1983) penalties for abortion obtainable. The 1962 Criminal Code made performing an illegal abortion punishable by a maximum sentence of 3 yrs., or 5 yrs. if the operation was performed without the woman's consent or if the practitioner was a professional abortionist; if the woman's death resulted, the practitioner was subject to 2–8 yrs. imprisonment. A woman who procured an abortion was punishable by a maximum 6 months imprisonment. *Practice:* Abortions (per 1000 women age 15–44): 35.3 in 1981, compared to 90.6 in 1969. The 1969 rate of 20.1 abortions per 1000 pop. was greater than the birth rate (15 per 1000 pop.), a figure that led to pro-natalist laws in the 1970's. In the summer of 1973, feminists petitioned local representatives and the president of the Parliament in protest against the pending restrictive legislation. Subsequent legislation was less restrictive than anticipated, but abortion cost increased approx. fivefold.

Illegitimacy. *Policy:* No data obtainable. *Practice:* No data obtainable. **Homosexuality.** *Policy:* Illegal as an "Offense Against the Family and Youth." Homosexual acts (by male or female) accompanied by "force or threat" are punishable by 6 months–5 yrs. imprisonment, 2–8 yrs. if one is the guardian or in legal authority over the other. *Practice:* No statistics obtainable; there are no publicly known homosexual-rights groups; Egyetem in Budapest is one of the few male homosexual bars. Lesbianism is even more hidden; reports indicate that some lesbian women and homosexual men marry because of strong social and State pressure, and because marital status is considered crucial to some jobs.

Incest. *Policy:* Illegal, punishable by 6 months–5 yrs. imprisonment. Sibling incest is punishable by up to 3 yrs. imprisonment. A descendant relative under age 18 cannot be punished for incest. *Practice:* No data obtainable. **Sexual Harassment.** *Policy:* No data obtainable on specific legislation; indecent assault is considered an "Offense Against the Family and Youth" and punishable by 6 months–5 yrs. imprisonment. *Practice:* No data obtainable. **Rape.** *Policy:* Illegal; if "force or threat" is used, or if a woman is unable to defend herself or express her will, the penalty is 2–8 yrs. imprisonment. If the rapist is the victim's guardian or authority in charge, the penalty is 5–12 yrs. imprisonment; the same penalty is ap-

plied in the case of 2 or more attackers. If the accused rapist marries the victim before sentencing, the punishment may be more lenient. Marital rape is not recognized by law. *Practice:* No data obtainable. **Prostitution.** *Policy:* "Professional prostitution" is illegal, punishable by up to 1 yr. imprisonment, or up to 3 yrs. for repeating offenders. Inducing a person into professional prostitution is punishable by 6 months–5 yrs. imprisonment. Managing a brothel, aiding a person to enter prostitution, and living off the earnings of a professional prostitute are punishable by up to 3 yrs. imprisonment, with increases of 6 months–5 yrs. for recidivists. Procuring is punishable by up to 3 yrs., professional procuring by 6 months–5 yrs. *Practice:* No statistics obtainable; reports indicate that there are many prostitutes in urban centers, and that some are employed by the State's intelligence network (see following article). **Battery.** *Policy:* No data obtainable specific to wife-beating; general assault laws make battery illegal and punishable by up to 1 yr. imprisonment if the injured party recovers in 8 days, or up to 3 yrs. imprisonment if the injured party suffers longer. In the case of particular cruelty, if the person is a recidivist, or if grievous bodily harm was inflicted "for a base motive," the penalty is 6 months–5 yrs. imprisonment. *Practice:* No statistics obtainable; reports indicate that the high rate of male alcoholism results in much battery. **Traditional/Cultural Practices:** No data obtainable. **Crisis Centers:** No data obtainable.

HERSTORY. Legends such as the Nibelungenlied imply that women, during the early periods of repeated invasions throughout central Europe, commanded power. Nevertheless, illiteracy, even among the aristocracy, was widespread, and few names of women, even the consorts to Hungarian Kings, have been adequately chronicled.

The second canonized Hungarian (after St. Stefan who, as King Stefan, unified Hungary and reigned 1001–38 C.E.) was Elisabeth (1207–1231), daughter of King Andrew II and wife of Louis II of Thuringia; she devoted herself to care of the sick and poor and retired to Marburg (1227), where she died at age 23.

The eldest daughter of Louis I (reigned 1342–82), Maria of Anjou was selected to succeed her father on the Hungarian throne. She died young (1395), but nevertheless managed to initiate policies protecting the arts and the organization of trade.

Considerable injustice has been done to Elisabeth Bathory, who in the late 15th–early 16th centuries attempted to escape the suffocation of a provincial noblewoman's life by notorious sexual escapades, primarily with other women. She was accused of being a "female dracula," and imprisoned in 1610 on the charge of having murdered women and bathed in their blood to "preserve her youth"; she died in 1614.

The Hungarians accepted the "Pragmatic Sanction" (see AUSTRIA) in 1723; under this ruling, Empress Maria Theresa of Austria was allowed to succeed her father to the throne of Hungary. Her famous appeal to the Hungarian Diet for military assistance was delivered in their native tongue and has been acknowledged as one of her most brilliant diplomatic coups. She opposed the "Germanization of Hungary" policies of her son (later Josef II), and was held in great esteem by the nobles.

Queen Elisabeth of Austria (Queen of Hungary by marriage to Emperor Franz Josef), although of Bavarian descent,

supported her son's conspiracy for Hungarian independence; a woman who detested the conventions of her day and prized her own autonomy above the crown, she was assassinated by an Italian anarchist in Geneva in 1898.

Hungarian women were active in the 19th-century national movement and the European suffrage movement. Women labor organizers in the early 20th century worked for better conditions and equal treatment of women workers. Women were also very active in the peace movement. Rosita Schwimmer distinguished herself during WW I as a major pacifist organizer in Europe. In 1915 she was appointed the first Hungarian woman ambassador and posted to Switzerland; she also worked with (US activist) Jane Addams in the Woman's Peace Party. Ditta Bartók, second wife of the composer Béla Bartók, was herself an important composer as well as a major concert pianist in the 1920's and 1930's.

Women played a central role in the rebellion of 1956 against the Soviet-backed regime, and also in the mid-1970's student rebellions, out of which grew contemporary feminist activism on reproductive freedom (see following article). Well-known contemporary writers include Agnes Heller and Mari Hegedvës.

MYTHOGRAPHY. Many of the traditional folk tales, in which Hungary is rich, speak of Gypsy queens and fairies.

HUNGARY: The Nonexistence of "Women's Emancipation"
by Suzanne Körösi

A few years ago, I read an unpublished interview with a first-class prostitute living in Budapest. She had a select clientele made up of members of the political elite and top-ranking visitors to the People's Democracy of Hungary. Well educated and intelligent, she related her rise from being a poor suburban kid to becoming one of the most appreciated courtesans of Hungarian high society. With surprising sincerity and detachment, she explained that a girl like herself, born into a *lumpen* family, had no other choice than to become a prostitute if she wanted to have her own two-bedroom apartment or enough money and time for traveling and reading—if she wanted to *feel free*. Although atypical, this woman's case somehow symbolizes Hungary today: whoever is born working-class and poor has every chance of remaining so. Exceptions are as rare as this woman's beauty.

In *Makoldi csalad* (The Makoldi Family), a brilliant book published in the 1970's by Katalin Fabian, a journalist, ten members of a poor shantytown family talked about their lives, memories, and desires. The parents were jobbers, and none of the children could rise higher than unskilled positions. A twenty-six-year-old daughter recounted her mother's life, which is much less atypical than our courtesan's career.

> Then we went to Monor, to the cooperative. We didn't know anybody there. Mother looked around there first because she wanted to get away from Father. She found a place but couldn't take it unless Father was in the cooperative. She plumped pigs and crammed chickens with half the income going back to the cooperative. But Father kept drinking. . . . There were seven of us in such a small place. After divorce, Mother applied to the council for an apartment. She wanted to save the family from Father, who sold and broke everything. . . . When Mother came home, the apartment was empty. She asked the council to do something. They said she must separate off one of the two rooms for him. When he came home, he found a wall where the door between the two rooms had been. . . . He tore down the wall, came into our room, kicked us, slapped us . . . and it's still going on. . . .

Western tourists and journalists frequently have the impression that women are emancipated in Hungary, or at least more so than in their own countries. This misapprehension of women's situation results basically from the complexity of female labor under communist regimes. In Hungary, since women constitute nearly half the labor force, and approximately three quarters of women between the ages of fifteen and fifty-four work, foreigners instantly imagine that women are emancipated. A stay longer than a few weeks is necessary in order to hear and believe what a young woman in Budapest recently told a French visitor, "Male chauvinism is so pervasive that we do not even have a word for it."

Sexual discrimination is, in fact, a quite banal feature of Hungarian society. A few basic statistics prove this. Between 1949 and 1979, the proportion of skilled women workers in industry has decreased, whereas that of unskilled women workers has increased. Among men, the trend was just the opposite. The same is true in agriculture and the service sector. In the 1970's, female industrial workers earned about 30 percent less than male workers in the same job categories. In agriculture, the difference was even bigger. In so-called intellectual jobs (a category denoting non-workers and non-peasants) it was slightly larger than in industry but smaller than in agriculture. (Statisticians explain this discrimination as "the effect of a retard.")

Accordingly, women entered production jobs later, thus replacing men under less favorable conditions. This late entry automatically marked out those activities available to women—namely less skilled and less prestigious positions in both intellectual and manual occupations.

The flow of peasants into industry around the turn of the century provides a comparison with women's late entry during recent decades. The contradiction of this point of communist regimes is striking. The free-enterprise ideology of classical capitalism with supposed open competition did not imply governmental interventions but entailed possibilities for even more pronounced inequalities in the labor market. However, in a society *with* a meticulously planned economy *and* a radically egalitarian ideology, women still found no legal or other protection against systematic discrimination. Until the late 1960's, the extensive phase of East European economies demanded mostly cheap and unskilled labor. Unqualified in their jobs and unexperienced in trade unionism, women formed the cheapest pool of labor.

Official propaganda launched slogans of emancipation that vigorously encouraged women to work, but they were mainly *forced* to work because of general pauperization in the 1950's and the decimation of male breadwinners during the war and later purges. Not only were women pushed into taking jobs but they also had to subordinate their fertility to an absurd economic policy that had the aim of pursuing extensive growth for decades: a 1951 law forbade abortion and contraception.

Fifteen years later, the whole system of economic planning turned out to be a fiasco. The accumulated mass of unskilled labor was hindering economic growth; it had to be reduced. Another problem had arisen. Since 1956, when the antiabortion law was repealed, the birth rate had been declining. One child per family had become the dominant ideal in Hungarian households.

State economic planners changed strategies. They no longer sought to reconcile the incompatible, as they had fifteen years earlier. They tried to eliminate part of the unskilled labor force—women—and to stimulate birth rates without the investments (daycare centers, kindergartens, or municipal laundries) that a baby boom would have demanded. Official propaganda insisted much less upon emancipation; rather, it concentrated on the pleasures of rearing children. (Nationalist writers eagerly joined the establishment on this latter point.)

In 1967, a system of maternity allowances was introduced to ensure a three-year leave for women after each childbirth. Payments were slightly lower than the salaries of the less paid, approximately 10 percent of working-class women. This measure met with instant success: three quarters of eligible working-class women took advantage of it during the following two years. With the help of this allowance, they could temporarily abandon jobs that brought little satisfaction and no emancipation. In fact, *working-class women's reaction to maternity allowances shows more clearly than anything else the failure of, or more simply the nonexistence of, women's emancipation through integration into the work force.* Although this measure reduced the number of unskilled workers, it did not affect the birth rate, which remained stationary until 1973. In that year, the fertile age group swelled with young women who had been born during the "artificial" baby boom in the first half of the 1950's (under the law forbidding abortion and contraception).

Given these results, an important lobby of economists, nationalist writers, and journalists devoted themselves to fighting the liberalized abortion law. The abortion rate in Hungary was undeniably higher than in other European countries. Ironically, in a planned society, these "radicals" obtained a hearing in 1973, when the birth rate was going up all by itself. The Law on Population Policy included a restriction on abortions, though a much milder one than its protagonists had wanted. However, it did not significantly affect the rate of officially registered abortions except during the first two years: from 63 percent to 38 percent and then 36 percent. Whether these data account for all actual abortions is a matter of doubt. In the following years, the number of abortions increased again as women and doctors resisted the suppression. This restriction symbolized the darkest years of Stalinism. Hungarians had thought Stalinism was past for all times, and their resistance made it seem so.

From the point of view of women, an appropriate conclusion to Hungarian history during the last thirty years is that, in the words of one woman statistician-sociologist: the inequality between women and men has been defined

not only by professional and general education, by childbirth and its concomitants, such as childcare and the assignment of roles within households, but also by a general opinion held by both men and women according to which the man is—naturally—the family's principal breadwinner, whereas the woman merely brings in a salary that supplements family income. *All social and economic policy measures that have dealt with the situations of women in general and of employed women have been—consciously or unconsciously—based upon this tradition.* Therefore, the female work force has been more mobile than the male one, more easily absorbed into or eliminated from the labor force.

It is consequently all the more of a surprising anachronism that the official women's organization—the National Alliance of Hungarian Women—which has supported all government measures, sometimes initiated them, and "fought" for application of the principle "equal pay for equal work," has done so without ever questioning the basis of sexual discrimination. *Nok Lapja,* the only national women's paper, has regularly published complaints from women paid less than men, but has never proposed solving this problem at its roots (introducing anti-discriminatory legislation, for example). This weekly paper often presents examples of husbands who help (or don't help) with housework, but never sponsored bills for recognizing the right of women (married or single) to be heads of family, or for transforming maternity allowances into parental allowances so that fathers could also take care of children. Anyway, pages about real women with real difficulties are outnumbered by those on fashion, handiwork, recipes, stars, sight-seeing tours in foreign countries, children's stories, and third-rate entertainment literature.

No other women's organization and no other women's paper has ever been authorized in communist Hungary. Once, however, in the summer of 1973, when Parliament was to vote the clause restricting abortions, a group of young women, mostly students (I among them), did try to raise our voices and organize public opinion against this measure. We wrote a letter to the members of Parliament about the disastrous effects of such a restriction upon women and the entire population. In a petition, we argued that this clause would only increase the number of illegal abortions or else lead to unwanted births, as had happened in the 1950's. The psychological effects of that earlier law were still painfully alive. Of course, we did not defend abortion as a preferred means of birth control, but we did insist that outlawing such procedures certainly would not make women and men want to have children. If the government wanted to stimulate birth rates, we declared, then it should create favorable conditions by resolving the housing shortage, building day-care centers and kindergartens, guaranteeing the rights of women as full-fledged members of society, and making men legally responsible for sharing the burdens of childcare.

Collecting signatures in the capital and the provinces turned out to be as important as writing the petition itself—because then we had the chance to discuss the issues with very different people: young workers, rock singers, major writers, and persons who had been participants in the 1956 revolution. Organizers were particularly efficient in finding places for collecting new signatures, typing up the right numbers of petitions, and distributing them. Having collected 1553 signatures (an unprecedented number in communist Hungary), we presented the petition to members of Parliament and asked them to oppose the pending restrictive bill.

Nevertheless, the law was voted in September of that year, and the secret police soon identified the signers. The organizers dispersed without the possibility of any further plans.

An incipient feminist movement had sprouted out of contacts and discussions during that summer of 1973, but it soon withered. However, it retains a privileged place in the history of Hungarian rebellion against all tyrannies: this ephemeral feminist movement was the first manifestation of new, *active,* democratic opposition.

Suggested Further Reading

(No general work free of the above-mentioned "influences" has been published in Hungary. Nevertheless, sociologists have described significant aspects of Hungarian sexual inequalities, cited below.—S.K.)

Ferge, Zsuzsa. "Social Policy and Women." *Studies on the Status of Women,* Budapest, 1972 (in Hungarian).

Vajda, Agnes. "Women in Occupational Structure 1949–1970." *Statisztikai Szemle,* n.p., July 1976 (in Hungarian).

Publications in France and the USA:

Körösi, Suzanne. "Une petition pour l'avortement en Hongrie." *Les Temps Modernes,* Paris, Nov. 1976.

Rindt, Anita. *Etre femme à l'est.* Paris: Editions Stock, 1980.

Scott, Hilda. *Does Socialism Liberate Women? Experiences from Eastern Europe.* Boston: Beacon Press, 1974.

Suzanne Körösi was born in 1950 in Budapest. She studied at the University Eotvos Lorand, Budapest, the Sorbonne, Paris, and Columbia University, New York, taking her master's degree in history at Columbia. She became interested in questions of feminism in the beginning of the 1970's, and took part in a 1973 campaign organized by women to defend reproductive freedom in Hungary; for this activity she was excluded "forever from all universities of Hungary" and prevented from working in her profession. She emigrated and settled in France in 1975, and is now a free-lance journalist and translator based in Paris.

INDIA
(Republic of India)

Located in southern Asia, India is bordered by Pakistan to the northwest, China, Tibet, Nepal, and Bhutan to the north, Burma to the east, and the Indian Ocean to the southeast, south, and southwest. The far eastern states and territories are almost separated from the rest of the country by Bangladesh. **Area:** 3,185,019 sq. km. (1,229,737 sq. mi.). **Population** (1982): 700,000,000, female 46.7%; 80% of the pop. lives in rural areas. **Capital:** New Delhi. **Head of State:** Prime Minister Indira Gandhi.

DEMOGRAPHY. Languages: Hindi (official), English (associate official); 15 languages listed in the Constitution: Assamese, Bengali, Gujarati, Hindi, Kannada, Kashmiri, Malayalam, Marathi, Oriya, Punjabi, Sanskrit, Sindhi, Tamil, Telugu, Urdu; over 122 languages are spoken. **Races or Ethnic Groups:** Indo-Aryan 72%, Dravidian 25%, Mongolic 3%. Aryan tribes invaded Dravidian civilization in 1500 B.C.E. and instituted a racial/religious hierarchy preserved in the Hindu caste system. Racial discrimination, while banned by the Constitution, is omnipresent. The scheduled (recognized) tribal groups receive special assistance from the government, and are protected by the Constitution. **Religions:** Hinduism 83%, Islam 11%, Christianity 3%, Sikh 2%, Buddhism. Animosity between some Hindus and some Moslems persists today. Riots and resultant deaths are not uncommon. The caste system was repudiated by Mahatma Gandhi and outlawed by the Constitution in 1950. The classification of "untouchable" *(dalit)** was especially prohibited, yet these legislative proscriptions have not been able to eradicate the caste system. **Education** (% enrolled in school, 1975): Age 6–11—of all girls 49%, of all boys 73%; in 1978–79, age 11–14—of all girls 28%, of all boys 52%; in 1975, age 12–17—of all girls 19%, of all boys 36%; higher education—in 1971, 246 women per 1000 men obtained college or higher degrees. In 1972 women comprised 1% of engineering students, 5% of business students, 21% of medical students, and 38% of students in teacher-training programs. In 1978–79 an est. 2/3 of the total non-enrolled children age 6–14 were girls. **Literacy** (1977): Women 19%, men 47%; female literacy (1971) 13.2% rural, 42.3% urban. The female literacy rate for scheduled castes was 6.44%, and for scheduled tribes 4.85%. Female literacy rates vary widely: 3.58% in Arunachal Pradesh, 4.8% in Rajasthan, 7.2% in Bihar, 61% in Kerala. **Birth Rate** (per 1000 pop., 1975–80): 34. **Death Rate** (per 1000 pop., 1975–80): 15. Females have a higher death rate than males from the age 0–4, mostly owing to neglect and lower food allotment, and from age 20–39, when work is most intense and pregnancies most frequent (see **Family**). **Infant Mortality** (per 1000 live births, 1978): Female 131, male 120. Many female babies are neglected from birth; 2/3 of the children who die before age 4 are girls. **Life Expectancy** (1981): Female 51.6 yrs., male 52.6 yrs. India is one of the only countries where women have a shorter life expectancy than men.

GOVERNMENT. India is a democratic union of states, comprised of 22 states and 9 union territories. There is a bicameral parliament consisting of the Council of States and the House of the People. Representatives to the House are elected directly by universal suffrage from state constituencies; 17 parliamentary representatives are elected or appointed from the union territories. The president is elected by the Parliament and the various state legislatures for a 5-yr. term and appoints a prime minister who oversees the cabinet. (Seats are reserved for scheduled castes and tribes in the House of the People and in the Legislative Assemblies of the states.) **Women's Suffrage:** Madras was the first province to accord women the vote in statewide elections (1921). In 1926 women were granted the right to be

* Renamed by Mahatma Gandhi *harijans,* or "children of God."

elected as legislative councillors. A limited number of women were allowed to vote in national elections as of 1935, and universal suffrage for adults over 21 was enacted by the 1950 Constitution. **Equal Rights:** The Constitution states that all citizens shall be equal before the law (Art. 14), prohibits discrimination on the basis of sex (Art. 15.1), and permits affirmative-action legislation to benefit women (Art. 15.3).

Women in Government: Indira Gandhi served as prime minister from 1966 to 1977, and was elected again in 1980. As of Jan. 1982, there were 2 women ministers of state and 2 women deputy ministers. In 1980, there were 23 women in the Council of States (9.2%) and 22 women in the House of the People (4%). Women never have comprised more than 17% of the candidates for a national election. Theoretically, 1 seat in every *panchayati* (village council) is reserved for a woman, but women comprise only 1–2% of local decision-making bodies. Government apparatus for addressing women's concerns includes a National Committee on Women, a Steering Committee, and a Women's Welfare and Development Bureau under the Central Ministry of Social Welfare. The Women's Bureau introduced a policy and program for the employment and welfare of women into the 1980–85 National Plan. It also distributes funds to voluntary organizations and collects statistics pertaining to women. In 1971 the National Commission on the Status of Women in India was constituted; 24 state governments have created committees on the status of women.

ECONOMY. Currency: Indian Rupee (May 1983: 9.81 = $1 US). **Gross National Product** (1980): $159.4 billion. **Per Capita Income** (1980): $240. More than 1/2 the pop. lives on less than $100 per person per yr. **Women's Wages as a Percentage of Men's:** No national data obtainable. In the mining industry women earn 33% of men's minimum and 20% of their maximum total pay (1975). In a Bombay sample, women earned 41.4% of men's wages (1977). **Equal Pay Policy:** Mandated by the Constitution (Art. 39.d); the Equal Remuneration Act (1975) was passed to re-enforce the equal-pay provision and to ban discrimination against women, but no charges were brought under the Act from 1978 to 1980. Hiring women as perpetually "temporary" workers serves to exempt them from most labor legislation. Only 4% of all employed women are in trade unions; in agriculture, where the Equal Remuneration Act does not apply, only 2% of women laborers are organized (1981). The government, which legislates equal-pay policies, has set sex-differential wages for the same job: female sowers at 69.8% of the male wage in Madhya, 62.2% in Tamil Nadu (1977). Women are frequently fired from their jobs upon marriage or pregnancy, although this constitutes illegal discrimination. Married women's right to work is protected by the courts. **Production** (Agricultural/Industrial): Cardamom, rice, wheat, oilseeds, cotton, tea, opium; jute, processed foods, steel, machinery, textiles and clothing, cement.

Women as a Percentage of Labor Force (1980): 32%; **of agricultural force** 80% (32% of waged); **of industrial force** —no general statistics obtainable (of manufacturing 9.8%, of the "organized" sector 12.4%, 1979); 6% of the female labor force was employed in the over-all organized economic sectors in 1979; **of military**—no statistics obtainable, but women serve as doctors and nurses. **(Employed) Women's Occupational Indicators:** 79% of employed women are in agriculture (1981); of the cashew industry 80%, of marginal workers 75.3% (1981); of mining and quarrying 9.4% (1980); of doctors and surgeons 19.25% (1979); of teachers 30% (71% of women teachers are in primary education, 8% in higher education, 1971); 40–49% of the female labor force is termed "unpaid family labor" (1971 Census). The 1948 Factories Act and 1952 Factories and Mines Act prohibit women's employment in fields considered dangerous to their health or safety; the 1951 Plantations Labor Act, the 1952 Mines Act, and the 1966 Bidi and Cigar Workers Act, prohibit women from working between 7 P.M. to 6 A.M. **Unemployment** (1980): 66.8%, female 73.6%, male 65.8%; 60% of the rural unemployed are women; 95% of all educated women are unemployed. With increased mechanization of agriculture and industry, traditionally female occupations are being eliminated. (In 1983 the theme of International Women's Day demonstrations in India was women and employment—the marginalization of women workers and their exclusion from the new technologies.) Off-season, many temporary agricultural women workers migrate to urban areas seeking construction or domestic-service.

GYNOGRAPHY. Marriage. *Policy:* The 1954 Special Marriage Act established monogamy for Christian, Parsi, and civil marriages. The 1955 Hindu Marriage Act outlawed polygyny for Hindus. Moslem men are still allowed to marry as many as 4 women. A small number of polyandrous peoples still exist, mostly in the Himalayan region. Scheduled tribes are governed by their own marriage customs, and Hindu law does not apply to them. There are 2 offenses against marriage covered by the 1972 Indian Penal Code: under the adultery clause, a husband may press charges against his wife's male lover, although the wife may not be prosecuted since she is not considered responsible for her own actions (comparably, a wife cannot press charges against her husband's female lover); the second offense, "taking and enticing a married woman with the intent that she have illicit intercourse with another person," is considered to deprive the husband of "his custody and proper control over his wife." In 1978 the legal ages for civil marriage were raised to 18 for females and 21 for males, remaining at 14 and 18 respectively in religious marriage, although the 1929 Child Bride Restraint Act prohibits sexual intercourse with a bride under age 15. The payment of dowry, most recently banned by the 1961 Dowry Prohibition Act, is punishable by a Rs. 5000 fine and 6 months in jail. In 1980 Indira Gandhi's government proposed legislation requiring a Rs. 10,000 fine and 2 yrs. hard labor for anyone demanding gifts or cash from a bride's family; as of 1983, the bill is still pending. The practice of *sati* (see HERSTORY), wherein widows were voluntarily or forcibly burned alive on their husband's funeral pyres, was banned by the British in

1829, and the 1856 Widow Remarriage Act allowed widows to remarry, but it was necessary for the Indian government to outlaw *sati* yet again in 1956. Under Hindu, Christian, and Parsi laws a widow may be disinherited by her husband in his will; under Islamic law a man cannot will his property away from his wife and daughters, but daughters receive ½ the share of sons. Both policies and practice regarding women's inheritance rights vary among different scheduled tribal groups, but all of the complex variations are in effect discriminatory against widows and/or daughters. Under the 1956 Hindu Minority and Guardianship Act, the 1890 Guardian and Wards Act, and Islamic law, children belong to their fathers, although Hindu fathers can no longer will their children away from their wives when they die.

Practice: Female mean age at marriage (1971): 17; women age 15–49 in union (1970–78): 81.2%. Some Moslem middle- and upper-class women are still subjected to the stringent restrictions of *purdah* (see Glossary). According to the 1971 Census, 5.8% of Hindu marriages and 5.7% of Moslem marriages were polygynous. Child marriage persists. According to census data, 17.5% of girls age 10–14 were married, and 56% of females 15–19 were married (1970–78). The penalty for violating the Child Bride Restraint Act is a maximum 2 yrs. imprisonment, but it is rarely enforced. A majority of the marriages in India are still arranged by the couple's parents, and Hindu marriages are usually arranged within caste and class boundaries.

Dowry (in the form of cash, clothes, furniture, and appliances) is paid by the bride's family to the groom. The cost of a dowry has risen drastically, from Rs. 200 in 1909 to as much as Rs. 100,000 (approx. $10,000) in 1982. The practice of dowry payment is a primary reason for prejudice against daughters. The 1975 Indian Commission on the Status of Women report stated that dowry had been found to be one of the gravest problems affecting women in almost every Indian state. But the Dowry Prohibition Act is easily evaded because gifts made at the time of the wedding are not included in the legal definition of dowry. From

1961 to 1977 only 30 cases of violation of the Act were brought to court, with 1 conviction as of 1981. The practice often becomes a form of extortion, with the husband and his family harassing, beating, or torturing a bride to extract more money from her family. In extreme cases, the bride is killed (see Introduction, pp. 10–12). These cases are extremely difficult to prosecute: witnesses and police are frequently bribed, and even the woman's own family is sometimes reluctant to press charges for reasons of "family honor." Dowry murders have been committed by men in all castes; 394 cases of young brides burned to death were recorded by the police in Delhi in 1980–81. Women's groups claim that the police register 1 out of 100 cases brought to their attention. In some scheduled tribes, bride-price is paid by the groom to the bride's family. In effect, the woman is sold, but there is the advantage of her not being pressed for more dowry. A special form of marriage, *chaddardalna,* in which a younger sister is married to the husband of an older sister who has died, is prevalent in certain areas, including rural Punjab. Patrilocal marriage is the norm and is cited as a reason why women rarely inherit land. Traditionally, widows —including child widows who had never become sexually active—were not allowed to remarry. Widows have been allowed to remarry as of 1856 but rarely do; there were 23 million widows in 1971. The practice of *sati* has a 1000-yr. history and is thought to help the dead husband atone for his sins; a revival of *sati* began in 1981, and a case in Rajasthan was portrayed by the media as "elevating the entire state to sainthood" (see HERSTORY and **Traditional/Cultural Practices**).

Divorce. *Policy:* Legal. The 1955 Hindu Marriage Act permitted both women and men to sue for divorce if either had committed adultery, deserted for 2 yrs., subjected the partner to physical or mental cruelty, ceased to be Hindu by conversion, was incurably insane, had leprosy or venereal disease, entered a religious order, had been missing and presumed dead for 7 yrs., or had withdrawn "conjugal rights" without a reasonable excuse for more than 1 yr. after a court

had ordered them restored. In addition, a wife could sue for divorce from a husband who was found guilty of rape, sodomy, or bestiality. If a woman had married before age 15 and repudiated the marriage before age 18, she could be granted a divorce—if the marriage never had been consummated. In 1976 the Hindu Marriage Act and the Special Marriage Act were amended to permit divorce by mutual consent after the couple had been legally separated and living apart 1 yr.; a clause covering mandatory and prior guarantee of support for dependent children and wives is new in divorce law, although acknowledged to be unenforceable. Under Islamic laws, the husband has unilateral rights to divorce a wife. Parsis have equal rights to divorce under the 1936 Parsi Marriage and Divorce Act on a fault basis. The wife has 1 additional ground: if her husband forces her into prostitution. Christians are governed under the 1869 Indian Divorce Act, which permits divorce only in case of adultery. The husband need prove simple adultery, but the wife must prove an additional ground: incestuous adultery, bigamy, or cruelty. *Practice:* According to the 1971 Census, 0.5% of the total female pop. was divorced or separated. The divorce rate among educated, middle-class women is rising. In Bombay (1975–76) there were 1000 court-ordered divorces, triple the 1968 number. Traditionally, it is men who seek divorces, but recently more women have been braving the social stigma of seeking a divorce. An est. 81% of all divorces are *de facto* and not registered by any court. Hindu men may also convert to Islam and divorce their wives by pronouncing a verbal repudiation. Moslem women may obtain a divorce by paying their husbands to divorce them, or through a prenuptial agreement whereby the husband delegates his right to divorce to his wife under certain specified circumstances (e.g., if he should take another wife). Many Moslem women are tricked or forced into renouncing their rights to *mahar.*

Family. *Policy:* Women receive maternity benefits if they have worked 160 days per yr. under the Employees' State Insurance Plan or the 1961 Maternity Benefits Act, which apply in mines, plantations, and factories employing more than 30 women. These women receive 6 weeks pre- and 6 weeks post-childbirth leave and are paid either their daily wage or Rs. 1 per day by their employers; dismissal is prohibited during the leave; 2 unpaid nursing breaks per day are allowed until a child is 15 months old. The 1948 Factory Law required factories employing more than 50 women to maintain creches for children under age 6; in 1975 it was extended to factories employing more than 30 women. A special nutrition program was started in 1971 to provide nutritional supplements to pregnant and nursing women and to children age 0–5. The government intends to train village midwives *(dais)* in hygienic methods of delivery and post-natal care and to train additional Auxilliary Nurse Midwives to meet the requirements of local clinics (1980–85 Development Plan).

Practice: On average, pregnant women consume only 60% of what their nutritional requirements demand and 30–50% of these women have iron and folic-acid deficiency anemia, the direct or indirect cause of 20% of maternal deaths; 10–15% of all women have toxemia, which is responsible for 15% of maternal deaths; 80% of pre-partum and post-partum hemorrhages could be avoided by proper care and blood transfusions (1981). Obstructed labor, often related to calcium deficiency, causes 15% of maternal deaths. One government-paid Auxiliary Nurse Midwife is assigned to a pop. of 10,000; 90% of all deliveries are assisted by *dais.* The incidence of tetanus and sepsis is very high, as are maternal mortality rates: 370 per 10,000 births. In some areas it is reportedly as high as 1800 per 10,000. For each woman who dies in pregnancy or childbirth, a minimum of 20 suffer damaged health; approx. 90% of all women have no pre-natal care at all; 50% of them experience no weight gain in their final trimester. Between age 15 and 45, the average woman becomes pregnant 8 times (1981). Very few women are covered by the Maternity Benefits Act, yet the cost of creches and benefits is used as an excuse to retrench women workers. In 1977 only 507,754 women were covered by the Act, and only 36,755 claims were filed (of these,

84% were paid). Creches are often located far from the workplace or are poorly staffed. Most children are cared for by relatives, and girls are often kept out of school to care for younger children. One program, Mobile Creches for Working Mothers' Children (founded 1980), runs a chain of centers in Delhi, Bombay, and Pune which provide on-site, integrated day care for children (age 0–12) of low-income working women. Women do virtually all of the housework, which often involves their having to haul water long distances, gather fuel, clean and grind grain, shop, prepare food, wash, and clean, all with the most rudimentary tools. Time spent in housework averages 6–10 hours per day for women who work outside the home, and 12–14 hours for those who do not. Many women eat after their men, and frequently eat the leftovers, receiving an average of 2/3 of the male calorie intake.

Welfare. *Policy:* The government reserves a number of places in schools at all levels for *harijan (dalit)* students and other scheduled tribes and castes. Some stipends and scholarships are available. Scheduled tribe and caste members are issued cards which entitle them to limited economic and food subsidies. Twenty-four state governments and union territories have some form of cash assistance plans for the elderly (1979–80). The government of Uttar Pradesh provides lifetime pensions to the widows of government workers. The Social Welfare Dept. funds literacy classes for women, hostels for working women and students, and aid for destitute women and children. The Training of Rural Youth for Self-Employment Program is placing special emphasis on training women. *Practice:* Government welfare programs reach only a fraction of those in need. Women of scheduled tribes and castes are especially vulnerable to corrupt officials; there have been cases of their having been forced to submit to rape to obtain benefits cards. As of 1980 there were 248 hostels for working women and children at reasonable rates, government funded and organized by volunteer social welfare organizations. There is not a large pop. over age 65, and most of the elderly live with their children's families. Very few receive pensions of any kind. **Contraception.** *Policy:* Legal. The government actively supports and subsidizes family planning. In 1982 a massive campaign was launched which involved media, the subsidized distribution of pills and condoms, and an emphasis on female sterilization. Family planning is a major concern of the 1980–85 Development Plan. Women are paid $22 to be sterilized, men $15. *Practice:* Women age 15–49 in union using contraceptives (1970–80): 16%, of which traditional methods 6.3%, modern 62.5%, sterilization 31.2%. During the state of emergency (1975–77), Indira Gandhi's government pursued a vigorous policy of sterilization in an attempt to control pop. growth. The program was directed mainly toward men and by 1977 the government was performing almost 1 million vasectomies per month. Resistance to this program is cited as one of the primary reasons for the ousting of Ms. Gandhi and the Congress Party. The subsequent Desai government avoided the issue; during its first yr. in office the sterilization rate averaged 20,000 per month, the lowest level since 1963. An est. 3.5 million sterilizations of women are done each yr. (1981). Hysterectomies are being prescribed for women with irregular bleeding, post-coital bleeding, white discharge, and pains in the abdomen; they cost from Rs. 250–1000 and are the main source of support for some clinics. Increasingly, women are sterilized by laparoscopy, a procedure that does not require hospitalization. The government is trying to popularize use of oral contraceptives.

Abortion. *Policy:* Prior to 1972, abortions were permitted only to save the woman's life. The 1972 Medical Termination of Pregnancy Act also permitted abortions in consideration of present or potential mental anguish caused by pregnancy resulting from rape or failure of a contraceptive method. The law was liberalized further (1975) to permit abortions "when a child resulting from a pregnancy that will cause mental anguish or physical torture is not desirable"; this amounts to abortion on request through the 20th week of pregnancy and permits a woman to obtain an abortion even if her husband objects. Abortions must be performed by

a registered doctor in an authorized facility. *Practice:* Authorized abortions (per 1000 women age 15–44, 1981): 2.6 (385,700). Legal and illegal abortions together approximate 2–9 million per yr. (1980). It is est. that millions of abortions are performed in rural areas without medical facilities, and a woman dies of a septic abortion every 10 minutes (1980). Uterine surgery is a popular method; in 1978, 25% of all abortions also involved the sterilization of the woman. Some hospitals force women to accept insertion of IUDs in order to obtain an abortion. Amniocentesis is currently being used to detect and abort unwanted girl children. The All India Institute of Medical Sciences had used the test in 1974–75, but stopped when it discovered that it was being used to abort female fetuses. A forum of women's organizations has called for a ban on the tests and disciplinary action against doctors who perform it. In addition to induced abortions, the rate of miscarriage and stillbirths is 15–25%, owing to overwork and malnutrition.

Illegitimacy. *Policy:* The 1956 Hindu Minority and Guardianship Act recognized the right of the mother in the case of children born out of wedlock. Children born to single women are legally termed "bastards," and the result of "unlawful sexual intercourse." *Practice:* No statistics obtainable. As a result of rape, prostitution, and "friendship contracts" (in which a man draws up an unenforceable contract with an unsuspecting woman to act as his wife), the number of children born out of wedlock is increasing. The Suicide Enquiry Commission of 1960–64 noted that the primary cause of suicide among women was pregnancy outside of marriage. After the 1972 Termination of Pregnancy Act, gynecologists reported a high number of abortions sought by single women. Children who use their mothers' names are deprived of the special services and educational opportunities provided for scheduled tribe and caste members. The Commission on the Status of Women called for "rehabilitation" opportunities for single mothers, care for their children, and counseling for their families to increase tolerance. **Homosexuality.** *Policy:* The Unnatural Offenses Law prohibits "carnal intercourse against the order of nature"; punishable by 10 yrs. to life imprisonment. The law specifies male homosexuality and anal rape (a Hindu woman can seek divorce from a husband "guilty of sodomy"). No data obtainable on laws concerning lesbianism. *Practice:* No data obtainable. There is a long myth-history of ancient Indian civilizations of women, some of which were characterized by lesbian relationships (see HERSTORY). The harems of traditional India were reputedly centers of lesbian love and women poets dating back to 100 B.C.E. write of the subject as a noncontroversial topic. Buddhist rules of discipline, developed in India, contain a number of precepts designed to discourage lover-relationships between the nuns.

Incest. *Policy:* Sexual intercourse is illegal between parties "within certain degrees of consanguinity or affinity." No further data obtainable. *Practice:* No statistics obtainable. Incest appears to be one of the most common forms of rape. A 1983 psychiatric study found incest prevalent in extended-family households. **Sexual Harassment.** *Policy:* Insulting the "modesty" of a woman by word, gesture, or act is a punishable offense (1972 Penal Code, 509). Originally it could only be pursued upon complaint, but it has been made a cognizable offense, so that the police can interfere and press charges. Two laws cover assault and the use of criminal force with intent to "outrage the modesty" of a woman, and criminal intimidation with a threat to impute unchastity to a woman (Penal Code, 354, 509). These are serious offenses punishable by heavy fines, imprisonment, or both. *Practice:* No statistics obtainable. "Eve-teasing" is the local name for sexual harassment. Women organized a demonstration at the Delhi Transport Corp. to demand more women-only buses to protect themselves from the increasing harassment (1982).

Rape. *Policy:* Illegal; defined as vaginal penetration against a woman's will, with-out her consent, if consent is obtained through direct threat to her life, if she is led to believe the man is her husband, or regardless of her consent if she is under age 16 (Penal Code, 376).** The rape survivor must prove that she did not consent. If she consented under threat to the life or safety of her child, parents, or husband, her consent is deemed voluntary. A man may rape his wife without penalty unless she is under age 15, in which case he may be subject to a maximum of 2 yrs. in prison. If a man forces a wife from whom he is legally separated to have sexual intercourse, he is guilty of rape. The Penal Code suggests life imprisonment as punishment but sets no minimum sentence. A 1983 amendment shifts the burden of proof from the woman to the accused (in custodial rape), sets a minimum sentence of 7–10 yrs. imprisonment in such cases, and prohibits publication of a victim's identity without her consent. *Practice:* In 1979, 4000 rape cases were reported nationally. In Bombay, an est. 12 rapes are unreported for every rape reported. Employers and police are often accused of raping poor and lower-caste women who have no protection.*** A consortium of women's organizations demanded a law to prohibit women from being forced to go to a police station between 8 P.M. and 6 A.M. and, if necessary, to be placed under house arrest instead (1980). Women who kill their attackers in self-defense have been imprisoned for murder. Rape is also a frequent tactic employed to terrorize politically active women, and to break *dalit* movements and peasant land-reform movements. Women who have been raped may be ostracized, deserted, or driven to suicide. In some tribes a woman who has been raped by a nontribe member immediately loses all inheritance and property rights and may be divorced; in some regions it is customary practice that water and food may not be passed to or taken from the hands of a rape survivor. The Bombay

---

** The Penal Code states: "The offense [rape] owes its enormity to the defilement and dishonor it reflects on the whole family. For, if they prize anything above all others, it is the honor of their women, and their forcible ravishment arouses all those feelings of retaliation and revenge which have accounted for so much bloodshed in history."

*** In Feb. 1982, a 15-yr.-old *harijan* girl was raped by constables in a village near Bilaspur, Faridkot, according to a local doctor. The case is still pending at the time of this writing.

Forum Against Oppression, among other women's groups, is demanding reform of the rape laws. **Battery.** *Policy:* No data obtainable. *Practice:* No statistics obtainable. In 1982 a group of Bombay women textile workers gave their description of the ideal husband as one who did not beat his wife, did not drink, and held a regular job; they could think of no single example of such a man. Police often refuse to interfere, calling battery "an internal family matter." Battery is frequently associated with male alcoholism or opium addiction.

Prostitution. *Policy:* The 1956 Suppression of Immoral Traffick in Women and Girls Act does not outlaw prostitution but states that no one can be forced into prostitution and that brothels cannot be run for gain. Kidnapping a woman to force her into prostitution, procuring a minor, importing women, selling or buying a minor for the purposes of prostitution, are all punishable by a 10-yr. prison term (Penal Code). No laws prohibit solicitation or protect prostitutes. The 1934 Devdasi Abolition Act banned the consecration of girls to the goddess Yellamma, in whose service they were forced to become temple prostitutes. *Practice:* No general statistics obtainable. Many prostitutes in large cities are young Nepalese or Bengali women who were abducted and sold into sexual slavery. In 1981 a prostitution ring specializing in abducting and selling women was exposed in Madhya Pradesh, Rajasthan, and Uttar Pradesh. A 16-yr.-old girl, expected to service 10 men per day 250 days per yr. for 3 yrs., is commonly sold for Rs. 6000. Women are sold far from their native homes, and resold every few yrs. at decreasing prices, so that they can never develop a support base. The Devdasi Abolition Act has never been enforced, and as of 1982 not a single case had been filed by the government under it, despite the fact that thousands of young girls still are being dedicated to temple service. These girls usually are born of rape or out of wedlock, or born to mothers who cannot afford to feed them. In June 1980, the Devdasi Rehabilitation Conference took place in Nipani; 550 *devdasis* attended and demanded enforcement of the Abolition Act, government pensions, and paternal inheritance for their children, as well as training and rehabilitation facilities. Many *harijan* women are forced into prostitution from financial desperation (see following article).

Traditional/Cultural Practices. *Policy:* Child marriage, dowry, female infanticide, and *sati* are all illegal (see **Marriage**). *Practice:* All of the above institutions still exist (see **Marriage** and HERSTORY). Female genital mutilation is also practiced in some communities (see Glossary). **Crisis Centers.** *Policy:* The government recognizes the need for hostels for battered and abandoned women and their children (see **Welfare**). *Practice:* There is 1 independent women's shelter in New Delhi, founded 1980. The members of Manushi Trust have helped battered women retrieve their property from their husbands' houses. Women's organizations have demanded special hostels for women separated from their husbands, services to find them jobs, counseling groups for battered and harassed wives, and a task force to investigate suspicious suicides (see HERSTORY).

HERSTORY. Before the Aryan invasions (c. 1750 B.C.E.) the status of women in the Indus civilization was reportedly very high. In the 4th century B.C.E., a civilization of women, Strirajya, supposedly existed in various parts of India. Men were excluded, and mutual relations between the women were reported to be primarily lesbian. There are stories of many warrior queens (also see PAKISTAN): Sultana Razia, who succeeded her father to the throne of Delhi and led her troops in battle (13th century C.E.), Nur Jehan, the real power behind her husband Emperor Jehangir (early 17th century); Lakshmi Bai, known as the Rani of Jhansi, led her troops against the British colonists (1857) and died in combat. Such women as Opala, Ghosha, Viswabara, and Indrani were among the composers of the sacred Hindu texts, the *Vedas*. Leelavati, a female mathematician, is thought to have invented algebra.

Sati may actually pre-date the Aryan invasions; few examples exist in ancient Hindu mythology. It seems to have arisen and become most prevalent in central India. A number of Mogul emperors tried to curtail or abolish it. Emperor Jehangir, backed by Nur Jehan, declared *sati* murder and illegal within the borders of his empire. In 1510, early Portuguese colonists tried to ban the practice in areas under their control, as did the French and the Dutch later on. The British refused to interfere with "religious practices," despite pressure from Christian missionaries. In 1813, after consultations with the Hindu *pandits* (judges), regulations were issued prohibiting use of drugs and coercion to force a woman into *sati*. With the appearance of government recognition conveyed by the regulations, figures rose from 378 reported cases in 1815 to 840 in 1818. Orthodox Hindus sent a petition to the government seeking the repeal of all regulations, and Raja Ram Mohan Roy, a devoted reformer, sent a counterpetition demanding a ban on *sati* and pointing out that the practice was sanctioned by neither the *Sastras* nor the *Laws of Manu*. His campaign greatly affected public opinion, and, with the help of the British Governor General, William Bentinick, *sati* was outlawed in the Bengal Presidency (1829) and in Bombay and Calcutta (1930). Yet as late as 1981 there was an increase in the number of cases reported; one, in the Nagaur district of Rajasthan, was passively witnessed by the local police constable. Independent feminist organizations staged demonstrations, and Prime Minister Indira Gandhi denounced the glorification of widow-burning.

The question of widow remarriage was a topic of progressive reform in the 19th century. There were provisions for widow remarriage in ancient Hindu law, but in the medieval period the higher castes forbade it. Reformers between 1830 and 1856 included Iswar Chandra Vidyasagar, who published *Marriage of Hindu Widows* (1856) and wrote a petition to the government, and Debendranath Tagore, who formed an organization to improve widows' rights and improving the status of women. With support from the British and the press, widow remarriage was legalized in 1856. Child marriage was more difficult to eradicate, since it was widespread among all classes and castes. The most famous reformers were Keshab Chandra Sen and

Vidyasagar. The 1872 Marriage Act set the minimum marriage age at 14 for females and 18 for males. Further reform led to the 1891 Age of Consent Bill, which raised the age of consent to sexual intercourse from 10 to 12 years for females.

Education for women was supported by both orthodox and progressive forces, for different reasons. Conservatives believed that education for women would elevate their skills as mothers and wives, producing better-quality sons. The first girls' schools were started in Calcutta (1820), and in Bombay (1848). Radicals, including Jotirao Phule, opened schools for girls and *harijans* in the 1850's which taught equality of the sexes and introduced the use of nonsexist language. The Bethune Girls' School, which became the first women's college, was founded in Calcutta in 1851. Vidyasagar founded 40 girls' schools in Bengal between 1855–58. The first women's teacher-training college was opened in 1870. By 1882 there were 2700 (mostly primary level) girls' schools with 127,000 students, 82 secondary schools, 15 teacher-training schools, and 1 college. In 1916 the Indian Women's University in Bombay, and Benares Hindu University, with an affiliated women's college, were founded. Education was restricted to a tiny minority of upper-class urban women, but it did lead to new employment opportunities. These women became doctors, teachers, nurses, and midwives. Many became social and political leaders and activists. These included Anandibai Joshi, Kadambini Ganguli, and Rukmabai—who left her husband to work in a women's hospital in Rajkot. She was sentenced to 6 months in prison for leaving him and could avoid serving the term only by paying a huge sum to ransom herself from her husband and by agreeing not to remarry.

The most famous feminist of her time was Pandita Ramabai (1858–1922). She was a Sanskrit scholar who used her knowledge to counter conservative interpretations of Hindu law and to raise the status of women. Widowed in 1882 with an infant daughter, she founded a series of Mahila Samaj (women's organizations) across the country, wrote *Women's Religious Law* (advocating women's emancipation), traveled widely, and founded schools, orphanages, and widows' homes. In 1889 she was one of ten women delegates to the Indian National Congress.

Other major activists included Ramabai Renade, who held free classes for women in sewing and health care and who co-formed the Indian National Social Conference in 1887, and Swarnakumari Devi (sister of Rabindranath Tagore), a Bengali writer and activist who co-edited the progressive magazine *Bharati,* founded the Ladies Theosophical Society (1882) and a women's organization, Sakhi Samiti (1886), attended the Indian National Congress, and was a novelist.

Moslem reforms also took place in the late 19th century. Male reformer Syed Ahmed Khan advocated modern education for women and challenged the religious validity of *purdah* and polygyny. Syed Imam financed Moslem girls' schools in Patna. Women activists included Amina Tyabji, who started a girls' school in 1895, and Begum Abdullah, who managed a girls' school in Aligarh (1906) which later became a women's college affiliated with Aligarh Moslem University. In 1905 Rokeya Sakhawat Hossain published a short story, "Sultana's Dream," about a country run by women where men were kept in seclusion; she argued that if men were the source of danger to women, then *men* should be restricted. In 1916 the Begum family of Bhopal founded the All India Women's Conference, which in 1917 passed a resolution that polygyny be abolished.

In the nationalist movement, English-educated middle-class women occupied some leadership roles, and masses of women participated in the *swadeshi* movement to boycott foreign goods and in nonviolent civil-disobedience actions. Annie Besant, a theosophist activist, birth-control advocate, Fabian socialist, and labor organizer who was active in the Home Rule League in India, became the first woman president of the National Congress in 1917. Sarojini Naidu, a poet and politician, was the best-known woman leader of the time, one of the main figures in the Congress in the 1920's and 1930's, and its president in 1925.

Sarala Devi, daughter of feminist Swarnakumari, was the most well-known woman leader in the *swadeshi* movement. Kamaladevi Chattopadhyay was a Congress activist and militant. Many Moslem women also joined the *satyagraha* and noncooperation movements. Their participation was tolerated by Moslem men, but their legal status did not change within their own community. Mahatma Gandhi saw and used the potential of women in the national liberation movement and confessed that his tactics were derived from women-suffragist struggles in India and England.

There were women in other factions of the nationalist struggle. In the late 1920's in Delhi, Roopvati Jain, a 17-year-old, was in charge of a chemical factory manufacturing bombs. In 1928, in Calcutta, a women's student group, Chhatri Sangha, recruited and trained women revolutionaries. Members included Kalpana Dutt (who often wore male attire and was deported for her role in the Chittagong Armory raid), 2 young girls, Santi and Suniti (who shot the District Magistrate of Comilla and were imprisoned for life), and Kamala Das Gupta (a courier who carried bombs in Calcutta). Many of these women were inspired by Subhas Chandra Bose, a socialist leader in the National Congress in the 1930's. He formed an Indian National Army to fight the British, made a special appeal to women to join the struggle, and formed a women's regiment called the Rani of Jhansi, which was led by Lakshmi Sahgal, a woman who achieved the rank of captain. Most of these women were branded terrorists, and later were to join the Indian Communist Party in frustration at National Congress policies.

Independent women's organizations were formed early in the 20th century. Annie Besant, Margaret Cousins (an Irish feminist and suffragist), and Dorothy Jinarajadasa formed the Women's Indian Assoc. in 1917, and middle-class women's organizations waged a concerted lobbying effort for women's suffrage. Margaret Cousins, Sarojini Naidoo, and a deputation of women met with the British Viceroy to demand the vote, and a delegation of 4 women went to Britain to lobby. In 1918 the Indian

National Congress supported the vote for women, and constitutional reforms in 1919 allowed state legislatures to decide the question. The All India Women's Conference led the women's movement in the 1930's and 1940's in campaigns for better education and equality in marriage, divorce, and property rights. At present it has 94 main branches and 500 sub-branches and is involved in legislative lobbying and social welfare work.

Other major women's organizations currently active include: Bharatiya Grammen Mahila Sangh (founded 1955) with 18 state branches covering 7000 villages and organizing maternity care and childcare, crafts and skills training centers, family planning, and training in agricultural methods; the Indian Federation of Women Lawyers (1962), which provides legal aid to women, legislative review, and education on legislation; the National Federation of Indian Women (1954), a broad-based national group organizing demonstrations, conferences, and seminars on an extensive feminist program; and Shramik Stree Mukti Parishad (1980), comprised of working-class *adivasi* (indigenous) women, focusing on villages, with programs on sexual oppression, economic exploitation, wife-beating, and tribal oppression. SEWA (Self-Employed Women's Assoc.), formed in 1973, represents thousands of women who work as cart-pullers, pieceworkers, manual laborers, vendors, etc., and has formed production and marketing cooperatives all over India. There are many other women's groups throughout the country, active in protest against rape, battery, dowry murder, *sati,* sexual harassment, pornography, and sexist advertising. Women were a major force in price-control demonstrations during the state of emergency and are also beginning to organize unions as domestic workers and in factories. Women working as prostitutes in Ujjain have organized an association to work toward their rights as women, to give literacy courses to themselves, their children, and other women, and to affirm religious freedom. Women are militant activists in land reform and peasant movements; they began and sustain the *chipko* movement, which protects fuel trees and works on afforestation.

Indira Gandhi (the daughter of former Prime Minister Jawaharlal Nehru) became the third prime minister of India in 1966. In 1969 the Congress Party split into the Old Congress Party and the New Congress Party, led by Ms. Gandhi. In 1975 she was accused of election fraud, and evoked a state of national emergency, suspending some civil liberties and electoral politics; measures to control price rises, protect small farmers, and improve productivity were enacted, as was a radical birth-control program (see **Contraception).** The New Congress Party and Indira Gandhi fell from power in 1977, and the Janata (People's) Party under Prime Minister Desai gained control. Facing parliamentary censure, Desai resigned in 1979, and Ms. Gandhi again became prime minister in 1980.

MYTHOGRAPHY. In Vedic mythology, the male Aryan god Indra killed Danu, the Great Mother Goddess of the conquered Harappan people. Ancient goddess beliefs persisted among non-Aryan peoples and emerged in the *Tantras* and *Puranas* around the 6th century C.E. These works gradually were incorporated into the Hindu canon. On the Malabar coast, worship of the Ammas (Mothers) is still the primary religious theme, and for centuries the people of the area had a matrilineal, matrilocal, and polyandrous culture. Tantric groups in Bengal and Assam worship the goddess Devi as the greatest power, allow women into the highest religious positions, and were the first to object to the practice of *sati.* There are hundreds of Indian goddesses. Some of the most powerful and popular are: Shakti (cosmic energy), Devi (supreme intelligence and pure mind), Kali and Durga (the forces of destruction which makes way for new creation), Sarasvati (mother of the written word), Ushas (dawn), Chamundi (the demon slayer), Annapurna ("She of the Abundant Food"), and Jagad Amba ("World Mother"). In the early 1980's, a cult developed around a new goddess, Satoshi Ma, who is said to have emerged from a cave in the Himalayas to bring peace to the victims of modern industrial civilization; she is a divine mother figure to whom one cannot pray for negative favors or revenge, but only for positive ben-

efits, and her est. 5 million worshippers are mostly northern Indian women age 18–50.

INDIA: A Condition Across Caste and Class
by Devaki Jain

Far more questions than answers confront the women's movement in India today. Political instability, economic confusion, and social unrest fill the air—at times making those sensitive women who are fighting for women's rights feel stereotypically "trivial." Yet in all this chaos, it may well be that women—who suffer most among the suffering—uniquely can supply and embody entirely new and visionary solutions.

Women from the masses as well as from the educated elite are becoming politicized with a certain innocent sincerity that is both startling and beautiful. Now is the turning point—whether we can transform society or whether it will seduce, corrupt, and negatively transform us. There is an added problem: the popular belief that Indian women are really powerful. It is said that a woman wields invisible power within the home, wields power as the mother of sons and therefore through them, and wields power because of her special sexual characteristics. References are made to the goddesses in the Indian pantheon—Saraswati, Lakshmi, Durga—and to such great female scholars as Gargi. But it is false logic to assume that just because women play certain motherhood and home-making roles and have certain intellectual and spiritual capabilities that they therefore already have operational power and that nothing needs to be done in terms of giving them more power.

The truth is that women are powerless in Indian society; worse, the value given to them even as physical beings is particularly low.

The statistics on women in India tell a poignant story.* From birth almost until the age of sixty, female mortality is greater than male mortality. The usual pattern around the world is that more males are born than females. However, males are more vulnerable to disease and death in the first seven days and even in the first twelve months; many male infants die and the sex ratio evens out. India breaks this universal pattern. Female infants die in greater numbers than male infants, even during the first week. And this pattern of death continues through their lives. Research shows that Indian women systematically get less nutrition. There are certain presumptions that they need less food since their metabolism supposedly makes more efficient use of energy, and their work requires less energy than men's work.

But the reality is that Indian women are caught between a heavy drain on energy *and* inadequate nutrition. The discrepancy between male and female mortality at all ages persists even now—the divergence increasing with poverty—and provides unassailable evidence of this cruelty.

Half as literate as men, the women cluster in monotonous, low-paid occupations. Every trend-statistic indicates further deterioration: more women "seeking work," more women among the destitute, much more rape and sexual humiliation—as if the troubled society released itself through a desire for obscenity.

---

* See the Statistical Preface preceding this article for details.—Ed.

Economic development, that magic formula, devised sincerely to move poor nations out of poverty, has become women's worst enemy. Roads bring machine-made ersatz goods, take away young girls and food and traditional art and culture; technologies replace women, leaving families even further impoverished. Manufacturing cuts into natural resources (especially trees), pushing fuel and fodder sources farther away, bringing home-destroying floods or life-destroying drought, and adding all the time to women's work burdens.

Other, relatively new information is related to women's economic roles—but impinges on their roles as reproducers and housekeepers. For example, a close association has been noticed between the age of intensive reproduction and the age of intensive *pro*duction, or economic participation. Approximately 15–35 percent of the poorest families are usually headed by women or have women as sole supporters. (This pattern—that destitute families usually have no adult males—is not limited to India. The poorest households in the black ghettos of the US and in Malaysia are also headed by women.)

Studies of the time-disposition of members in, for instance, rural dairying families, have shown that among the assetless, the acquisition of an asset (a cow, buffalo, loom, or spinning wheel) in order to improve household income invariably leads to an *addition* in the hours of work for women, albeit the additional income.

An average Indian woman's day is one long stretch of toiling for survival—only to be interrupted by violence generated by liquor or social attitudes. Yet these women struggle for a microcosm grouping called "the family"—struggle to keep it alive and, if possible, happy and healthy. They work, go hungry, even offer their bodies for the sake of providing this survival kit. The female-headed household, the acceptance by women of minimal reward for hard work rather than no income at all, the reluctance of women to join unions and strike, the willingness to be dubbed passive—all seem consequences of this dedication.

Nonetheless, women are beginning to overcome their reluctance to organize. They have started, sometimes within a political party framework, sometimes on class or religious platforms, but increasingly across all conventional stratifications: women in India are organizing on the basis of biological boundaries. The more the attack on female sexuality, the greater the consolidation of solidarity based on sex.

These women represent such different ideologies as the Communist Party of India (Marxist), the Community Party of India, Janata (People), Rashtriya Swayamsevak Sangh (Voluntary Helpers' Union), different networks like the All India Women's Conference, and the National Federation of Indian Women, as well as such theater and literary groups as the magazine *Manushi,* Stree Sangharsh (Women and Conflict), students from the universities, and so on.

Apart from biological issues, price is the main issue on which women have chosen to be active across ideological variations. Yet the protests of middle-class housewives against a rise in the price of cylindered domestic gas or bus fares can seem superficial in a context of the urban or rural poorest, whose consumption capacity lies far beneath cylinder gas, sugar, oil, or the bus.

The question then arises as to whether uniting on biological grounds provides an effective basis for the generation of women's power in society. So long as women cling to demands which are based on their sex, while they may be protecting themselves from being vulnerable (which is an important activity), they are doing no more than limiting their power *to* the weakness of their sex. Rape, which is a function of women's sexual powerlessness—and dowry—which is also the consequence of the low value given to women by society, are only evidence of women's powerlessness, and not of women's power.

United actions protesting these crimes are, of course, women's effort to overcome such powerlessness through collective energy. But this does not become an expression of women's *positive* power as a *revolutionary force* playing upon other forces operative in the environment. In other words, it draws still more attention to their sexuality—and preempts them from "hard-core" political issues. Still, these alignments—demonstrations against dowry, processions denouncing rape—*are* giving women a place in the political process and building confidence and leadership among them. These can be the first steps toward women's wider political participation. A women's movement which wishes to assert that women are a political force and can revolutionize society because of their historical *as well as* biological experience must expand from sex-based issues to all social issues.

Most of the political or economic systems operating on the globe today are spent forces. They have not been able to contend with inequality, inflation, or the threat of war. They have shaken natural formations violently and introduced distortions which are compelling the planet toward destruction. No global organization (such as the United Nations) or global ideology (such as Marxism) is able to deflect the world from this path since they are all parties to the existing system. Women, however, can generate these new energies—because women are not parties to the system. But how can this be accomplished? In organic ways.

During the freedom struggle in India, women were in the vanguard of all public meetings and processions—a visual counterpoint to female seclusion. In the economic arena, there was the famous boycott of foreign goods and the *swadeshi* movement to use only Indian-made goods. Today's Indian women can reflect this Gandhian[1] methodology by a commitment to simplicity in consumption further directed to and directly providing incomes to the poor. This would lead to a certain austerity, as the options for consumption are limited. It would mean buying hand-pounded rice, buying pickles and processed foods only from small cooperatives. (It would have an indirect impact on conservation, in itself a critical global problem.) If all the women's organizations unite to use their purchasing power through select producing organizations, there can be a dramatic change in the distribution of economic power.

Another issue on which Indian women have always displayed solidarity is prohibition. Alcohol consumption hits the poverty and laboring household in urban and rural areas hardest. It is true that poor women—especially tribal and scheduled-caste women—participate in the trading of liquor. But women's identification with prohibition can have a healing effect on society. Between March 1975 and June 1976, women from all over Manipur[2] state, rural and urban, mobilized themselves into what are popularly known as the Night Patrollers. Groups of thirty to fifty women with long bamboo poles in their hands and kerosene lanterns held high patrolled the alleys at sundown. They surrounded any inebriated men returning home after an evening at the wine shop, extorted a fine of Rs. 50, and took him to the police station for creating "a public nuisance." (There is no legal provision for committing a person to custody specifically for misbehavior under the influence of intoxicants.) If the offense was repeated, the men were beaten up by the women. The Patrollers were sometimes accompanied by policemen or a few young men. But the extent of protection they got from the law varied with the political climate of the state. The movement had spread to almost all parts of the state by 1976, and although it

[1] Gandhi himself claimed that he had learned the basic concept of *satyagraha* (militant, nonviolent resistance) from Kasturba, his wife, and he had been sensitized to women's oppression and capabilities by such women leaders as Kamaladevi Chattopadhayay and Sarojini Naidu.

[2] Manipur is a small northeastern state landlocked and wedged between Burma and three other Indian states. Except for a picturesque and fertile valley covering less than 10 percent of the area, the rest of the state is mountainous.

has since waned, patrol groups were still found at the end of 1978 in areas of the larger towns. As a consequence of this campaign, alcohol consumption fell dramatically in the state and the state government was forced to introduce a prohibition bill.

What makes Manipuri women so strong and well organized? They play a critical role in all operations related to rice-paddy production: cultivation, harvesting, intermediate processing (which includes husking, pounding, and parboiling), and in the marketing of rice. In addition to the retail trade in rice, women control a large proportion of the trade in such other essential commodities as hand-loom cloth. Catering and the food industry is also dominated by women, who run tea stalls, snack shops, and hotels. Just as men socialize in public places in most societies, the women do in Manipur. Researchers point out how the "market-women" led Manipuri women in mass movements earlier in the century, against rice export and unjust systems in wage payment of contract labor.

However, the Manipuri case also provides an important illustration of the complexities of women's struggle. Manipuri women are still subject to traditional hierarchies: men are still the heads of households, often marry more than once, drink, beat women, and so on. Analyzing this apparent contradiction between a high economic contribution made by women and their retarded social status (as evidenced in polygyny), the Committee on the Status of Women in India observed:

> An important motivation for polygamy *[sic]* is economic gain. Where women are not a burden but are self-supporting and contribute substantially to productive activity like cultivation and handicrafts, they are real assets and a man can gain by having more than one wife.

So it seems, after all, that in order for the experience of being a woman to be fulfilling, *more* than political and economic participation would be necessary—even if that was in greater proportion than men. *It would require a new evaluation of the basic biological role of women as well as a re-evaluation of many other aspects of society and the environment.*

Yet another issue which is critical for the Indian women's movement to address is the scar of untouchability—the "curse" of the *harijans.***

What are the priorities for *harijan* women? What are their social issues? their house-bound issues? their economic issues? their sexual issues? How can *harijan* women articulate their voices as a group? Nobody knows. It is women from these castes, as well as the tribals, who are the majority of those entering the prostitution market. It is common knowledge that their entry into this market is not only because of the corruption in the society but because of the compulsion of poverty. What should constitute a comprehensive program for these women? Is it only a question of providing employment? Why is this not a priority of women's organizations?

These are the kinds of issues which could be the platform for a new ideological formation of women, issues which can extend across national boundaries and yet be effective. For example, a boycott of products of multinationals, a purchase of handmade goods by women of the "North," can have its ripples in the "South." These actions can influence the choice of technologies. Reduction of wasteful expenditure on food and energy can relieve the pressure on resources and thereby on prices. A solidarity of women across color, caste, religion, national boundary, and economic disparity can shake the world political system more than the so-called NIEO (New International Economic Order). Furthermore, its impact would not be merely negative resistance to existing systems but could deflect the present direction of forces to re-create new systems—if women can

---

** See the article on Nepalese women by Manjula Giri (pp. 461–65), in which the author contends that women themselves constitute a cross-class caste (and an "untouchable" caste at that) in the view of the patriarchy.—Ed.

unite. The basis of their solidarity would be sex: they are women who believe in women and have biology-based connections. But their platform would be about all the wounds of society. And their methods would be organic.

One example, from Assam, might be the experience of the women of Kumarikatta. Some tribals had long occupied land in Kumarikatta and were cultivating it. Periodically, the legality of their action was questioned and initiatives were taken to evict them. Each time, somebody intervened on their behalf. But finally the authorities gave notice that they would bring a herd of elephants to trample down the huts. The elephants came. The village people gathered outside the huts. There was tense silence. The social workers who had been advocates of the tribals could see no further way of protecting the "squatters." The finale seemed to have its own momentum.

Suddenly, with no discussion and without the advice of any so-called organizers, village women rushed out of the crowd and started to embrace the elephants' trunks and legs, chanting the prayers that they usually sang on a particular *pooja* [sacred] day. This *pooja* was devoted to the elephant god and it was customary for these women to stroke the elephants and rub sandal paste, *kumkum,* and flowers on them with devotion and love. These women started to imitate the same ritual, with full devotion. The elephants responded in turn by accepting this with their conventional grace. They refused to move further. No one—the authorities, the social workers, or even the men squatters—could do anything. The elephants turned back—and the women, men, and children returned to their huts.

The ability of women to identify their common problem and perceive a solution that requires steel-like courage and great risk to life but still is a *nonviolent* method is well illustrated by this true story. All that seems to be needed is a link to some source of self-confidence. Women may need someone to help them to recognize their own inner strength, but they do not need to be told "how to organize."

Nor need the women of Manipur or Kumarikatta be isolated in their efforts.

This, then, is my appeal to my sisters: the opportunity is there; will we have the energy to reach out for it?

Suggested Further Reading

Chattopadhayay, Kamaladevi. *Indian Women's Battle for Freedom*. New Delhi: Abhinav Publications, 1983.
Jain, D., ed. *Indian Women*. Publications Division, Ministry of Information and Broadcasting, Government of India, 1975.
————, assisted by Nalini Singh and Malini Chaud. *Women's Quest for Power*. Vikas Publishing House Pvt. Ltd., Vikas House, 20/4, Industrial Area, Sahibabad, Ghaziabad, 1980.
Sixth Five Year Plan: 1980–85. New Delhi: Planning Commission, Government of India, 1980; chapter 27.
Towards Equality. Report of the Committee on the Status of Women in India. Ministry of Education and Social Welfare, Government of India, 1975.
Women in India—A Statistical Profile. Ministry of Education and Social Welfare, Government of India, 1978.
Women in the Indian Labour Force. Report of a seminar held in Trivandrum, 1980 (ARTEP/ILO, Bangkdi).

Devaki Jain was born Mandyam Ananth Devaki, one of seven children. Her father was a civil servant in the Karnataka government and her grandparents and ancestors, both maternal and paternal, were in the service of temples associated with Sri Vaishnavism. She took a diploma in economics and political science at the Labour College (Ruskin) in

Oxford and became research assistant at the Indian Cooperative Union and later assistant to Gunnar Myrdal while he was writing *Asian Dilemma*. She returned to Oxford to complete her master's degree in economics and statistics and was awarded a prize for her performance in moral philosophy, which was being taught by Iris Murdoch. Returning to India in 1959, she joined a women's college at Delhi University as a lecturer in economics, leaving the university ten years later to be fulltime housewife and mother of two sons, born 1967 and 1969. Currently she is associated with the Institute of Social Studies, a registered Trust for research and education on underprivileged groups, especially women. Her publications include books (see Suggested Further Reading) as well as many research reports and articles published in India and in international journals.

INDONESIA
(Republic of Indonesia)

Indonesia is in Southeast Asia and consists of 13,677 islands (6000 inhabited), including Java, Bali, Sumatra, Madura, Sulawesi, Kalimantan (most of Borneo), Irian Jaya (western half of New Guinea), and Timor; it is part of the Malay archipelago with Malaysia to the north, Papua New Guinea and various seas to the east, Australia off the southern islands, and the Indian Ocean to the west. **Area:** 1,904,344 sq. km. (735,268 sq. mi.). **Population:** (1980): 147,383,075, female 50.3%. **Capital:** Jakarta.

DEMOGRAPHY. Languages: Bahasa Indonesian (official), almost 300 local languages and dialects, Dutch, English. **Races or Ethnic Groups:** Javanese, Sumatran, Sundanese, Chinese, other, including approx. 300 indigenous groups. **Religions:** Islam (primarily Sunni) 87.5%, Protestant 5.2%, Roman Catholicism 2.2%, Hinduism 1.7%, Buddhism 1.07%, indigenous faiths 2.03%. **Education** (% enrolled in school, 1975): Age 6–11—of all girls 58%, of all boys 66%; age 12–17—of all girls 32%, of all boys 42%; age 20–24 (1976)—of all women 2.8% (rural 1.2%), of all men 7.4% (rural 4.4%); higher education—(University of Indonesia only) in 1973 women were 35.9% of all students, 9.2% of technology students, 27.9% of medical students, 49% of law, 68.1% of dentistry, 69.3% of literature, 72.8% of psychology; in 1971, 16% of agricultural training, 59% of teacher education; in 1978, 0.6% of jr. technical school students, 1.5% of sr. technical, 99.92% of jr. "family life education,"* 99.85% of sr. "family life education"; in 1979, 28% of academy and university students. As of 1976 only 9.7% of females over age 10 completed primary school, 1% of women completed vocational, and 0.2% completed university education. The Constitution stipulates that all citizens have a right to education, but because of the shortage of schools, teachers, and materials, it is not compulsory. Though primary school is free, entrance fees, costs of supplies, etc., prevent many children from attending. Government schools are co-ed; 18% of primary schools are Moslem and sex-segregated. Sons are generally given preference over daughters for the limited available places; government plans include places for all children in primary schools by 1984–85. **Literacy:** 60% (1981); female 49%, male 70.9% (1979); 75.8% of nonliterates age 10–45 were female (1978). **Birth Rate** (per 1000 pop., 1983): 33. **Death Rate** (per 1000 pop., 1983): 13. **Infant Mortality** (per 1000 live births, 1976): Female 128.9 (urban 104.3, rural 137.4), male 152.2 (urban 123.3, rural 161.8); infant mortality (per 1000 live births, urban/rural 1971)—educated mothers 57–74, noneducated mothers 156–75; deaths of children under age 5 accounted for 44% of the mortality rate for the total pop. (1971). **Life Expectancy** (1983): Female 52 yrs., male 50 yrs.

GOVERNMENT. A republic with a prime minister (head of government) and a president (head of state)—both offices currently held by Gen. Suharto (1983). The 920-member People's Consultative Assembly holds supreme power; half of this body constitutes the 460-member (360 elected, 100 appointed) House of Representatives, which holds legislative power. The 27 provinces have elected assemblies and appointed governors; village heads, clan elders, and local *rukun kampung* and *rukun tetanggo* (groups of 10–20 families) are highly influential at the local level. Major political parties in 1980 were Sekber Golkar (Functional Group), Partai Persatuan Pembangunan (United Development Party), and Partai Demokrasi Indonesia (Indonesian Democracy Party); the Communist Party was outlawed in 1966. **Voting:** Literate citizens over age 17 are eligible to vote; consequently, most women are disenfranchised (see **Literacy**). **Women's Suffrage:** 1941, granted by colonial Dutch government; granted by the 1945 Consti-

* Courses in nutrition, hygiene, family planning, etc.

tution upon national Independence. **Equal Rights:** 1945 Constitution stipulates equal status before the law. **Women in Government:** 6.2% of the Assembly, 7.2% of the House, and 9–10% of provincial councils (1977); approx. 40% of local *rukun kampung* and *rukun tetanggo* were women. In 1983 there were 2 women cabinet ministers, Minister of Social Affairs Nani Soedarsono, and the Director General for Culture in the Ministry of Education, Ms. Haryati; there are 2 women (Rusiah Sardjono and S. Salyo) on the 79-member Supreme Advisory Council, 1 woman (Sri Widoyati Wiratmo Soekito) on the Supreme Court, and 2 women ambassadors—to Denmark and Switzerland. An Associate Minister for the Role of Women, L. Soetanto, was appointed in 1978 and is still serving (1983). In 1975 women were 16% of judges and were permitted on Islamic religious courts from 1975–78; 12 women had been appointed by 1978. Few women are in leadership positions in political parties.

ECONOMY. Currency: Rupiah (May 1983: 970. = $1 US). **Gross National Product** (1980): $61.8 billion. **Per Capita Income** (1980): $420. **Women's Wages as a Percentage of Men's:** No general statistics obtainable; 50% of women employees and 10% of male employees earned less than Rp. 3000 per month, 6% of women and 25% of men made over Rp. 15,000 per month (1976). **Equal Pay Policy:** Sex discrimination in implementing the General Labor Law was prohibited by 1969 Law 14 (Art. 2); lack of minimum-wage laws and inadequate enforcement of existing labor laws render equal pay laws ineffectual in all sectors but the civil service. **Production** (Agricultural/Industrial): Rice, cassava, soybeans, rubber, copra, coffee, tea, palm oil, timber; textiles, processed foods, light manufac-

tures, cement, oil, gas, tin, copper, bauxite. **Women as a Percentage of Labor Force** (1977): 33.7%; **of agricultural force** 32.6% (58% of whom are unpaid family workers; in 1975, 61% of women workers were employed in agriculture); **of industrial force**—no general statistics obtainable (of manufacturing 47.3%, 21.7% of which are unpaid family workers, 1977); **of military**—no statistics obtainable; women are permitted in noncombat roles, including as paratroopers, and a few have reached the rank of colonel. In 1976 the labor force participation rate was 40–50% for rural women (depending on the season) and 25% for urban women; in 1978, 75% of widowed and divorced women were in the labor force.

(Employed) Women's Occupational Indicators: Of civil-service workers 32%, but women are only 5% of those in decision-making positions (1983); of agricultural extension workers 16.5% (1978); of administrators and managers 8.3%, of clerical and related workers 10.6%, of employers and self-employed 22.8% (in agriculture 25%, in sales 50%), of government university teachers 25.8%, of sales workers 46.1%, of unpaid family workers 56.7%, of kindergarten teachers 100% (1977). Traditionally, most women in Indonesia have been economically independent in the subsistence agricultural economy. Such traditional women's occupations as harvesting, rice-pounding, weaving and batik, handicraft manufacturing, and small-scale marketing and trade have been marginalized rapidly and critically by industrialization and imports.** Unemployment and poverty have forced women to work at extremely low wages in domestic manufacturing (which grew by 225% from 1961 to 1977) or in "free trade zones" for multinational electronics companies. "Protective" labor laws, granting 2 days per

** Rice-hulling machines have cut women's income by $55 million and reduced half-time employment by more than 8.3 months for 1 million women; yet income for men who work in the new mills has increased by $5 million. From 1971 to 1973, hand-pounding of rice in Java was reduced by 65–70%. Rural women lost their major source of income when high-yield rice was introduced (1972); men working with scythes for wages replaced women working with *ani-ani* knives for a portion of their harvest. Imports and mechanizations have forced 90% of women weavers (over 1 million women) out of work. Batik-making has been mechanized, with men who operate machinery earning 400–500% more than women in the labor-intensive jobs.

month paid menstrual leave and 3 months paid maternity leave, or restricting women from night employment, underground mine work, and lifting of more than 25 kgs., are frequently disregarded or cited as reasons for hiring men. In 1978, 8000 women were working for multinational companies for $0.17 per hour. Young women, hired mostly on a daily or probationary basis, earned Rp. 200–350 per day; women were paid 30% less than men for comparable work. Cost of in-factory food and transportation (Rp. 250) is often deducted from wages, and consequently a woman takes home approx. $0.25 per day. Women are 65% of the tobacco industry, doing piece-work at home for extremely low pay. Women hand-loom operators earn approx. Rp. 50 per day. Many women have turned to construction work, tailoring, tourism, plantation work, domestic service, and prostitution for employment. Some women landowners (Minankabau) and women in labor-scarce areas (South Sulawesi) have benefited from new technologies. **Unemployment** (1973): Female urban 3.2%, rural 1.1%; male urban 5.8%, rural 2.2% (see following article). Underemployment (rural, 1973): Female 48.7%, male 29.7%.

GYNOGRAPHY. Marriage. *Policy:* The 1974 Marriage Law established some uniformity between customary or *adat* (19 distinct systems), civil, and Islamic jurisprudence; variance is still permitted in accordance with religious laws. Minimum marriage age is 16 for females and 19 for males, with parental consent, or 21 for both without parental consent; exemptions for minimum age can be granted by the court. Consent of both parties is required unless a conflict exists in religious law. The 1974 law stipulates that "rights and obligations of the wife are proportionate to those of the husband" (Art. 31) and that "the husband has an obligation to protect and support his wife, while the wife has an obligation to take care of the household" (Art. 34). Polygyny is permitted among Moslems; however, the 1974 law tightened rules concerning polygyny, which is regulated by religious courts. A request for a polygynous marriage can be granted when a wife is unable to "fulfill her duties as a wife" or is disabled, terminally ill, or unable to have children; a man must have the consent of his first wife/wives and prove ability to support and to provide equal treatment for all wives and children. The Indonesian Islamic wedding-contract ceremony takes place between a groom and *wali* (male representative of the bride). In monogamous marriages, women and men can be punished for adultery; in polygynous marriages, women can be punished, but men can be prosecuted only as "accomplices" to adultery. Inheritance laws have not been standardized; in *adat* marriages, surviving spouses may inherit 1/2 of common property; in Moslem marriages, a widow inherits 1/4 of a husband's estate if there are no children or 1/8 if there are children; in civil marriages, a widow inherits an equal share with children. All wives of polygynous civil servants receive widows' pensions.

Practice: 66% of females and 5% of males marry before age 17 (1980); among Moslems, many females are married before menarche (23% in rural areas, 1973) and 75% are married before age 18 (1982); 98% of women marry before age 49 (1980). The majority of the pop. is Moslem, and many Islamic legal concepts have been absorbed into *adat* laws. Arranged, child, and forced marriages still exist; in a 1974 survey near Yogyakarta, 69% of marriages were arranged. The incidence of such marriages is reportedly decreasing, as is the rate of polygyny: only 5% of all marriages were polygynous (1978). The clan system is predominate in many parts of Indonesia. In patrilineal groups (TobaBateak, Balinese, Buginese, Timorese, Ambonese) a bride-price, *jujer*, is paid to the bride's family to release her from her clan, and she brings a dowry to the husband's clan. In Moslem marriages, a gift of *mahar* is often presented directly to the bride. In matrilineal groups (Minankabau and Rebangan of Sumatra, and some groups in Eastern Indonesia) a husband lives with, or visits, the wife's family, and women retain their birth-names. Bilateral groups (Javanese, Sundanese, Madurese) are the most common kinship system; both husband and wife remain members of their own clans. In 1971, 13.2% of all women were widows; widow remarriage is common.

Divorce. *Policy:* A divorce can be granted only after an unsuccessful attempt at reconciliation by the court; grounds include adultery, addiction (to alcohol, drugs, or gambling), 2-yr. desertion, 5-yr. imprisonment, cruelty which endangers the life of a spouse, disease or disability preventing the fulfillment of spousal duties, and constant incompatibility; a divorce can be granted to husband or wife. The 1974 Marriage Law restricted divorce through *talaq* (repudiation); a Moslem man must now notify a religious court of his intention to divorce and state his grounds, and a general court must confirm the religious court's decision. If either party requests, courts determine alimony, property settlements, child support, and child custody. Both parents are responsible for the care and education of children; the father is generally responsible for financial support. *Practice:* Divorces (per 100 marriages, 1974): 27. The 1974 law (see above) does not provide sanctions for enforcement against arbitrary *talaq*, which is still practiced frequently among Moslems. The divorce rate is highest among Moslems and the poor. Many forced marriages end in divorce. Child custody is generally awarded to the mother. Remarriage by divorced women is common.

Family. *Policy:* In urban and many rural areas men are *de jure* family heads, and a son age 15 is considered a family head in his father's absence. The government mandates that employed women (formal sector) are entitled to paid maternity leave 6 weeks before and after delivery or miscarriage, and nursing breaks during work. Both parents are responsible for the care and education of their children, and children are legally bound to support elderly parents. The government is urging couples to have only 2 children and has reduced dependents' allowances for civil servants and tax deductions for numerous children. The State supports 19 model kindergartens (1978). Under some *adat* laws, children inherit instead of spouses. In patrilineal groups, fathers have rights to the children, and sons inherit from their father's estate but

must support sisters and other female relatives. In matrilineal groups, the eldest brother of the senior woman or (less frequently) the woman herself, is clan head; children are members of the mother's clan, and the father's main responsibility is to his sister's children. Sons and daughters inherit equally from the mother and the maternal uncle's estates. In bilateral groups, children are members of both parental clans, and sons and daughters inherit equally from their mother and father. In Islamic communities children inherit from both parents, but daughters receive ½ the share of sons. Communal property returns to the clan of the deceased. *Practice:* In 1978, 23.3% of all household heads were women, 78% of whom were widows. Large families are valued, since children contribute to family income. There is little preference for sons and in bilateral families mother-daughter ties are usually strongest. Children under age 15 are 44% of the pop., creating a high dependency rate. In many areas food tabus prevent pregnant or nursing women and small girls from receiving the necessary protein; 80% of pregnant and nursing women in rural Java, and 46% in Bali, have anemia (1978). The maternal death rate is 80–100 per 10,000 live births (1977); the rate is 206.3 per 10,000 births in Yogyakarta (1970–75), and varies with hospital accessibility. *Dukun bayi* (midwife healers) assisted at 95% of births for women with little education, 40% with primary education, and 10% with secondary education (1973). Some *dukuns* are trained in sanitary and modern techniques, but most use traditional methods. In 1978 there were 5698 Maternal and Child Health Centers staffed by *bidans* (professional midwives), but these were not easily accessible. In 1978, 9000 kindergartens were run by women's religious organizations. An est. 60% of male migrants who seek work in cities leave their families permanently. Rural women spend approx. 46% of their time in childcare, food preparation, housework, shopping, and fuel collection. Women work a total average of 11.1 hours per day and men work 9.2 hours per day, but women spend 5.9 hours and men spend 7.9 hours in direct economically productive activities.

Welfare. *Policy:* No social security system exists for the general pop., although the government has been studying the need since 1978. Government and military employees receive raises upon marriage, child allowances, and pensions. Companies with 100 employees or Rp. 5 million per month payrolls must provide an employees' social insurance plan covering workers' compensation, a provident fund (pension), and death benefit (1977). The government's development program is focused on expanding basic health, education, nutrition, water, and sanitation services to the entire pop. Care of destitute children and orphans is shared by the State and the community. *Practice:* An est. 1 million private-sector employees were covered by social insurance (1978). In 1979, 299 orphanages were run by women's organizations. Real PCI on Java has been decreasing since the 1930's, and landlessness is an immediate and growing problem; 81% of rural households had no land or had less than the minimum 0.2 hectares necessary for subsistence; 57% of rural and 54% of urban families on Java were living below the poverty line (1970). The government is attempting to resettle people from overcrowded areas to the outer islands, but job-seekers continue to migrate to Jakarta. Only 6% of the pop. had access to safe water, 80% of the rural pop. had no latrines, and 61% had no electricity (1976). In an attempt to provide low-cost clinics, mass immunizations, and disease control, all medical and health personnel must serve for 3 yrs. after graduation in exchange for free education and training (1961 Law 8 and 1964 Law 18). In 1980 there were more than 3251 Public Health Clinics, at least 1 in each sub-district, but they were accessible to only 25% of their assigned populations. There are hospitals at the district level.

Contraception. *Policy:* Legal and free. The government vigorously promotes family-planning information and services, based on voluntary use. In 1967 family planning was declared a basic right and is stressed in schools. Distribution of contraceptives to the young, open displays, and unsolicited distribution are illegal under the Penal Code. Sterilization with spousal consent is legal, and the government is now recommending it after the second child. *Practice:* 3,885,000 couples are using contraceptives; approx. 50% of couples in the eligible age group use some form of birth control continuously; 90% of the use is by women (1982–83). Methods used (1982–83) pill 52.9%, IUD 23%, injectables 17%, condom 4.2%, other methods 2.4%. The Indonesia Planned Parenthood Assoc. was founded privately in 1957 and began receiving government support in 1968. The National Family-Planning Coordinating Board was created by the government in 1970, in a major policy move to seriously promote contraceptive use. In 1973 groups of village women began sending representatives on long trips to bring back contraceptive supplies; by 1980, 20,000 supply depots were distributing to 55,000 women's groups nationally. Some "mothers' groups" are demanding roads, water, and comparable services in return for their participation in family-planning programs. The Assoc. for Voluntary Sterilization was founded in 1974; 42,000 partners in married couples had been sterilized by 1977. Sterilization is not viewed as a solution to family-planning problems, and most Moslems oppose it.

Abortion. *Policy:* Illegal; punishable by a maximum of 4 yrs. imprisonment for the woman and 5½ yrs. for the practitioner (Penal Code). Medical use of "menstrual regulator" devices was so restricted as to be made virtually illegal in 1976. *Practice:* No statistics obtainable. Abortions have been performed without resulting in prosecution in circumstances when the woman's life was endangered. Medical and women's groups are working to liberalize the law, but religious groups oppose this; Moslems would permit abortion only to save the life of the woman.

Illegitimacy. *Policy:* Children born out of wedlock have civil (legal) relationships only with their mothers and maternal relatives (1974 Marriage Law, Art. 33). *Practice:* No statistics obtainable. In general, out-of-wedlock children are less accepted, and in some communities they are believed to bring bad luck. Pressure is exerted to force a pregnant single woman to marry before the child is born. **Homo-**

sexuality. *Policy:* Penal Code does not prohibit homosexual acts between adults. *Practice:* No general statistics obtainable. In 1981, 2 young women in Java were sentenced to 8 months imprisonment and 20 months probation for "committing indecent acts with each other"; 1 of the women was diagnosed as having "too many male hormones," and a doctor attempted to "cure" her medicinally and surgically. Within a week, 2 other young women in Java openly acknowledged their lesbian relationship with a wedding ceremony; 100 guests were present and their parents expressed acceptance, although the marriage was not legally valid. Lesbian women and homosexual men have published the first same-sex preference newspaper in a country with a major Moslem population, *G Gaya Hidup Ceria.* **Incest.** *Policy:* Sexual relations with an under-age-15 relative, a child in one's care, or a young employee are illegal and punishable under the Penal Code (Art. 294). *Practice:* No data obtainable. **Sexual Harassment.** *Policy:* None. *Practice:* No data obtainable. **Rape.** *Policy:* It is illegal to use force or threat of force to compel a woman to have sexual intercourse out of wedlock (Penal Code, Art. 285). Sexual intercourse with a girl age 15 or younger is considered statutory rape. Both are punishable by a maximum 12 yrs. imprisonment. *Practice:* Reported rapes (1980) 2000; the number of reported rapes drastically understates actual incidence. Rape is sometimes tried as "adultery"; rapists are rarely sentenced to more than 1 yr. imprisonment. **Battery.** *Policy:* No specific laws on spouse abuse; covered under general assault laws. Battery is a ground for divorce. *Practice:* No data obtainable.

Prostitution. *Policy:* Illegal. The Penal Code prohibits a person, by profession or habit, from deliberately giving the opportunity or encouragement to another person to commit fornication (Art. 296); it also prohibits traffick in women and male minors (Art. 297), acting as an agent for a prostitute, or living off profits from prostitution (Art. 506). *Practice:* No general statistics obtainable. Although prostitution is illegal, the government registers prostitutes and issues work-permits to them in certain areas; they are required to have regular medical exams and are offered some rehabilitation and training programs. Approx. 20% of the nonagricultural female labor force is classified in the category "activities not adequately defined," which includes prostitution. Most prostitutes are young, many under age 14, from rural Central and East Java. They migrate to such big cities as Jakarta, Surabaya, Medan, and Yung Pandang in search of work, and often are economically forced into prostitution. Jakarta has been a popular stop on the "sex tourism" route in Southeast Asia. **Traditional/Cultural Practices:** No data obtainable. **Crisis Centers.** *Policy:* None. *Practice:* No data obtainable.

HERSTORY. Indian traders and Hindu and Buddhist monks spread their influence among the indigenous peoples of Indonesia in the first century C.E. Kingdoms allied with India came to power in Java and Sumatra (7th–8th centuries), and the Buddhist state of Sri Vijaya was centered in Sumatra from the 7th–13th centuries. The Hindu state of Majapahit on Java (13th century) dominated most of the Malaysian peninsula for 200 years. Moslem traders propagated Islam in the 14th century.

In precolonial times Javanese women were royal leaders of powerful queendoms. When the Dutch arrived in the 17th century they encountered Cut Nyak Dien, a woman who had ruled Aceh for 50 years. Women also led armies in Aceh, were chiefs in the Buginese parts of South Sulawesi and in Kalimantan, and royal leaders of the Balinese (19th century). In the 19th century the Minankabau in Western Sumatra fought the Pandrie War to protect their matrilineal system from the influence of Islam. Lingga clans of Northeast Borneo were ruled for many years by 2 noble women. Dyak women of North Borneo have fought in battle, hunted, and proven great strength and endurance. The Dutch colonization disrupted most local patterns of leadership by investing only men with hereditary authority. Such Christian Ambonese women as Christina Tiahahu, Buginese women in South Sulawesi, and Dyak women, however, maintained some positions of authority, although in diminishing numbers.

Raden Ajeng Kartini, the daughter of a high civil official, became the founder of the modern women's-rights movement and provided inspiration to the nationalist cause. She attended a Dutch private school until age 12, when Islamic constraints forced her to discontinue her education. She wrote for *De Hollandsche Lelie,* a socialist women's magazine, and corresponded with the militant Dutch feminist Stella Zeehandelaar. Kartini spoke out against polygyny, forced marriage, and colonial oppression. She argued for women's emancipation through education, and started a girls' school which had an enrollment of 120 students by 1904, when Kartini died in childbirth at age 25.

Christian missions established the first local girls' schools in Ambon, Minahassa, and the Batak highlands. Dewi Sartika founded 9 girls' schools, Maria Walanda Maramis crusaded for women's education in North Sulawesi, and the Dutch government opened a limited number of girls' schools after 1912. The Kartini Foundation founded more schools after 1916. Some women, including Taman Siswa, opened coeducational schools in their homes, stressing equality of the sexes. The first modernist Islamic girls' vocational school was founded (1909) by Dr. St. Mahardja of the Minankabau. Schools were also opened by such progressive Minankabau women as Sitti Rohanda, who began the first feminist magazine in Sumatra (1912), and Rahma El Jausia, the founder of the first modernist religious girls' school (1922). Despite these efforts, educational opportunities remained extremely limited, and by Indonesia's Independence, of the literate 7% of the pop., only 14–25% was female. The first women to receive higher education became teachers, midwives, and lawyers.

In the 1920's and 1930's women were deeply involved in the nationalist movement, and some male nationalist leaders supported women's struggle for equal rights. Women were imprisoned for their political writings. The Indonesian Women's Congress (KOWANI) was formed in 1928. The Dutch adopted a policy of gradual expansion of political rights and women were allowed to stand for office but could not vote; a few women were elected to municipal councils. Women won the right to vote under the Dutch in 1941, and this right was confirmed by the 1945 Constitution at Independence. In 1946, 28 women members (5.2%) of the national government were appointed. Extensive support and participation of women in the war against the Dutch led to greater acceptance of women in public life after Independence.

Since the first voluntary women's organization (1912), women have played an increasingly important role in the provision and delivery of social welfare services throughout the country. Middle- and upper-class women are very active in numerous social welfare organizations, which are often attached to religious and/or political groups and run kindergartens, schools, clinics, and literacy, sanitation, domestic science, and skills-training classes, family-planning services, orphanages, nursing homes, and women's hostels.

The struggle for equal rights, led by KOWANI and its member organizations, has focused largely on the passage of a more uniform marriage law, an end to child marriage, polygyny, arbitrary male-initiated divorce, forced marriage, and unequal inheritance laws. After many attempts at legislation and an interim campaign to inform women of the rights already won, some success was achieved with the passage of the National Marriage Law in 1974. The focus has now turned to equalizing inheritance laws for women and, for a few women's groups, reforming abortion laws. The central concerns of urban women are enforcement of equal pay laws and employment opportunities, while rural women continue to focus on safe water, food, and income-generation projects. KOWANI's 52 member organizations represent a spectrum of more than 10 million women.

MYTHOGRAPHY. In Java, Srikandi is a legendary figure of a woman warrior, fearless in battle; a brave or militant woman even today is referred to as "a Srikandi." Matrilineal clans generally trace descent from a common legendary mother ancestor. Among the Sea Dyak culture of Southern Borneo, this ancestor is Fire Woman. It is believed that a great flood was sent to punish the killing of a sacred serpent, and only 1 woman and her infant son survived. She discovered how to make fires and cook food. The Sea Dyak are enjoined by this mother ancestor never to kill or eat the sacred serpent. Women shamans, healers, and priestesses are powerful in many Indonesian cultures.

INDONESIA: Multiple Roles and Double Burdens
by Titi Sumbung

Indonesia proclaimed its independence on August 17, 1945, after almost 350 years under Dutch occupation. The country with the fifth largest population in the world, Indonesia contains more than three hundred ethnic groups, each with its own traditions and culture.* However, these differences are subordinate to a common identity, which is reflected in the motto *"Bhineka Tunggal Eka"* ("Unity in Diversity"), which unifies Indonesia as one nation.

Life in the Indonesian community is controlled by norms based on *adat* (customary law) and on religious and indigenous beliefs. These norms control all ceremonies and rituals and govern the relationship of an individual to the community. They also define the roles and positions of community members and the status of women within the family *and* the community. As part of the Indonesian legal system, *adat* regulates ownership, inheritance rights, marriage, and family kinship.[1]

From studies conducted in rural areas (in which 80 percent of the population lives), problems encountered by women are as follows:

—Low level of education;

—Low income (Per Capita Income [1983] is estimated at about $520 US);

—A large proportion of time is consumed by fulfilling duties as homemaker, as well as earning extra family income;

—Existing social and cultural values that do not act in favor of women;

—Inadequate knowledge of health, nutrition, and sanitation, causing a high death rate among infants and children as a result of conception by malnourished mothers.

—Lack of opportunity for women to engage in the planning/managing of programs that directly affect them, and in decision-making positions at all levels.

Because of the above problems, women are left behind by their male counterparts with the impact of continuing male-dominated patterns in all sectors of life.

Government Policy on the Improvement of Women's Roles

History has proven that Indonesian women, along with their male compatriots, have played an important role in the nation's struggle for independence. The highest acknowledgment of their participation is manifest in Art. 27 of the 1945 Indonesian Constitution, which guarantees equal rights for men and women. These rights are emphasized in the Guidelines of State Policy put forward by the People's Consultative Assembly in 1978:

---

* See Statistical Preface to this article for a general religious/ethnic breakdown.—Ed.

[1.] Tapi Omas Ihromi, *et al.,* "Study on the Status of Women in Family Planning," Jakarta, 1973; unpublished document.

1) Over-all development requires the maximum participation of men and women in all fields. Therefore women have the same rights, responsibilities, and opportunities as men to engage fully in all development activities.

2) The role of women in development does not diminish their role in fostering a happy family and in guiding the younger generation, and in the development of the Indonesian people in all aspects of life.

3) In order to give women a greater role and more responsibility in development, it is necessary to increase their skills in various fields according to their needs.

To enhance the role of women, the government has appointed an Associate Minister for the Role of Women in the Development Cabinet III, announced in 1978. The office of the Associate Minister is a national center for the integration of women in development, and the Associate Minister is in charge of coordination, supervision, monitoring, and evaluation of various women's programs implemented by different ministries in the government, women's organizations, and society as a whole.

The Indonesian Women's Movement

Pioneered by Raden Ajeng Kartini, Dewi Sartika, Walanda Maramis, and a small number of other outstanding women from various regions [see HERSTORY] of the archipelago, the Indonesian women's movement was started in the late 1800's, with the aim of promoting equal opportunity for women in education and improvement of rights and status in marriage. These efforts took about twenty years to reach the point where the needs of women could be discussed and developed in a public forum.

The first recorded women's organization was the Putri Mardiko (Independent Women), founded in 1912 in Yogyakarta and soon followed by many others. In 1928, activist women took more assertive steps by calling on all existing women's organizations to combine efforts in a federation called Perikatan Perkumpulan Perempuan Indonesia, which was convened on December 22, 1928, in Yogyakarta, marking the starting point of the contemporary Indonesian women's movement. This federation now has a membership of more than fifty organizations and is known as the Indonesian Women's Congress (KOWANI).

In 1964 another coalition, for the wives of members of the Armed Forces, Dharma Pertiwi, was founded—followed in 1974 by the organization of wives of civil servants, Dharma Wanita. To enhance the promotion of the status of women, a National Commission on the Status of Women (NCSW) was established in July of 1968—a semi-governmental body which has the task of conducting surveys on issues concerning women. The data obtained form the basis of project proposals and recommendations to the government and to women's organizations.

The most effective type of activities, from the provincial down to the village level, is the Family Welfare Development Movement (PKK), which aims to carry out various development activities to promote family welfare in the community. The ten programs of PKK are civics, mutual self-help, food, clothing, housing and household management, education, health, family planning, human environment, and cooperatives. The mechanism for the execution of these programs is through the existing administration in the respective location, while the leadership of PKK is in the hand of the wife of the highest local government official. As a village base movement, PKK accommodates and carries out the aspirations and initiatives of the community—and the implementation of programs is done by the members (mostly women) of the village.

Since the 1970's, the PKK movement has been intensified throughout Indonesia and recently has been promoted by the President as a model and channel of rural development programs.

The Current Profile of Women in Indonesia.

One of the ways of measuring the advancement of a nation is by observing the status and level of progress of women in the context of the family, community, and country in general.[2] Indicators among others are the level of education, employment opportunity, decision-making position, role in politics and government, etc.

In almost all communities and cultures in Indonesia, it is the husband who holds the position of "family head" and who is responsible for the family's welfare. This places him in the decision-making position in the family and community. From several studies, it can be said that women have "domestic" roles and "informal" power, while men have "extra-domestic" and "formal" power to function in the community. However, the process of decision-making is not going on in any absolute manner only by men or women; it varies according to access to productive resources, the background of socialization, and the pattern of community (rural, urban, or semi-urban).[3] Sometimes, in the case of production, the last decision by the husband is only a formality, because the wife's suggestion is accepted and implemented. In other words, the husband "gives the authority" to his wife and the wife "makes the decision" without consulting her husband.

In matters of health and nutrition in the family, the wife is predominant—except that in determining the daily menu it must be admitted that the husband's favorite food is given priority.[4] In family planning it is the husband (and/or his parents) who decide the number of desired children.

In Indonesia marriage is based mainly on customary law and religion. These include views that may be counterproductive for the active involvement of women in the community and in implementing development activities. For example: the pre-literate woman normally takes marriage, pregnancy, lactation, childcare, and hard work in her stride; marriage is considered a necessity for the continuation of the family and for maintaining good relationships between families, groups, or communities; being unmarried is considered a shortcoming or exception; having children is thought to be good fortune (the more the better).

The basic issues concerning women and marriage rights have been child marriage, forced marriage, polygamy, and easy divorce (by the husband). It was only in 1974 that a Marriage Act was promulgated—and that was due to the untiring struggle of the Indonesian women's movement. And even though the law now contributes to and accelerates the improving status of women, in *practice* there still are many difficulties in implementation and many discrepancies in real life. To overcome this situation, KOWANI has launched a "legal literacy" project to elevate legal awareness among the people, especially among women in rural and poor urban areas.

Women and Education

Since Independence, the Indonesian education system has undergone a considerable improvement, particularly with regard to women. In 1961 the literacy rate was 46.7 percent; of this figure 34.1 percent were women and 59.8 percent men. After ten years,

[2] Titi Sumbung, *Women in Health and Development*, Country Statement, WHO SEARO Meeting on Women in Health Development, New Delhi (Jakarta: National Family Planning Coordinating Board Monograph, 1980).

[3] Pudjiwati Sayogyo, "Rural Household Economics and the Role of Women," Diss. Univ. of Indonesia, 1981.

[4] Mely Giok Tan *et al.*, "Social and Cultural Aspects of Food Patterns and Food Habits in Five Rural Areas in Indonesia," Jakarta, 1970; unpublished document.

the 1971 census showed a literacy rate of 61.2 percent (50.3 percent for women and 72.1 percent for men).**

Although the government provides equal rights and opportunities for boys and girls in education, cultural values and family circumstances remain unsupportive to females in education. There are still more illiterate women (50 percent) than men (30 percent), and the higher the level of education the less girls are enrolled in school. The drop-out rate is high, particularly in primary education in rural areas. In 1971 it was approximately 60 percent cumulative, of which 70 percent were girls.

In order to support the government's programs in education, all women's organizations have educational activities, formal as well as informal. In pre-school education the contribution of the women's organizations is enormous—99 percent of the kindergartens (about 25,000) are run by them. In addition, literacy programs are now being implemented by women's organizations, for school drop-outs and adults.

Women and Employment

According to the Central Bureau of Statistics in 1978, 36 million males and 20 million females between the ages of ten and sixty-five were employed. Of the latter, 60 percent of the total women employed had never been exposed to formal education, and only 4 percent had enjoyed education higher than primary school.

Traditionally Indonesian women have been active economic participants, especially in the agricultural sector, which forms 67.3 percent of the total female labor force. Currently, with an increasing number of educated women, the opportunity for professional and skilled female workers capable of finding work outside the homes is increasing. (The motive of many working women is to earn an extra income for the family, or to develop a career or fulfill a personal satisfaction to do some good for the community. Another factor inspiring married women to work outside the home is that many households have "domestic help"—either relatives and/or paid servants.) Yet confronting the dilemma of being working women, Indonesian women still find it difficult to change their traditional role. However high a woman's career position, her place and primary responsibility is still considered to be the family.

Women in Politics and Government

The rights to vote and to be elected have not been major issues since Independence. During the second general election in 1971, 80 percent of eligible women voted. A sizable number of women stood for election; however, fewer than 7 percent at the national level and 9–10 percent at the provincial and sub-district level were elected.

The number of women civil servants, according to 1979 data, is 454,295 (or 23.3 percent) compared with 1,498,936 (or 76.7 percent) male civil servants. But if we look at their *rank,* the higher the position the scarcer the women. There are only about 3–5 percent women holding decision-making positions. This number is quite small in relation to the number of women graduated from the university: 30–40 percent.

As yet another example, the majority of health workers are women, but at the decision-making level women's presence drops to only 13 percent.[5] The rest are in the lower administration or health-skill category considered "women's work" (nurses and midwives). This discrepancy between the skills of women health workers and their low decision-making power characterizes the modern health-care system (not only in Indonesia) as one of the most discriminatory areas involving women.

** But see Statistical Preface.—Ed.
[5.] Titi Sumbung, *Women's Participation in Decision Making on Policy Concerning Health Services* (Geneva: WHO Multinational Studies on Women as Providers of Health Care, 1981).

The main obstacles to women holding high positions are the persistent attitudes about women's "biological function" and the sociocultural values that stereotype women as "holder" of household responsibilities. On top of those responsibilities, women are now expected to engage in development activities *and* to conduct all of their multiple roles equally well—and without disturbing the men's role or comfort. In general, there is no objection to a woman working, *but* with the reservation that her tasks at home must not be neglected. It is of course impossible for women to perform all these roles without some goodwill from men in sharing the household responsibilities in an effort to lighten the double burden.

Conclusion

From the current profile of Indonesian women, we can conclude that development efforts have *not* fully included women as part of the community and as a potential human resource, and the results of development have not been equitably distributed to all—rural women in particular. In fact, the modernization process, which does bring changes to better the quality of life, at the same time also causes negative side effects. A study on women's employment in rural Java, for example, illustrated the ways in which many fields of employment traditionally dominated by women are being altered or eliminated as new technology is applied (especially in agriculture).[6]

For the above reasons, attempts to improve the role of women should focus on changing the public *attitude* and *perception* of women as a human resource, on raising public consciousness to the truth that women must have the opportunity to develop their abilities, skills, and self-identity, on changing women's tacit acceptance of their inferior status, and on better equipping them to perform their roles as *equal* partners with their menfolk in a proposed new—and refreshing—style of family life.

Suggested Further Reading

Milone, Pauline. *A Preliminary Study in Three Countries: Indonesia Report.* Washington, D.C.: Federation of Organizations for Professional Women, International Center for Research on Women, Sept., 1978; mimeograph.

Papanek, Hanna. "Jakarta Middle Class Women: Modernization, Employment and Family Life." *What Is Modern Indonesian Culture?* Ed. Gloria Davis. Athens: Ohio Univ. Press, 1979.

———, Mely G. Tan, T. Omas Ichromi, Yulfita Rahardjo, Ann Way, and Pauline R. Hendrata. *Women in Indonesia: Family Life and Family Planning.* Jakarta: Univ. of Indonesia, 1976.

Oey, Mayling. "Rising Expectations but Limited Opportunities for Women in Indonesia." *Women and Development: Perspectives from South and Southeast Asia.* Eds. Jahan and Papanek. Dacca: University Press, 1979.

Soewondo, Nani. "Law and the Status of Women in Indonesia." *Law and the Status of Women.* Ed. *Columbia Human Rights Law Review.* New York: Centre for Social Development and Humanitarian Affairs, United Nations, 1977.

Titi Sumbung was born in 1938, in Surabaya, East Java, Indonesia. She graduated from law school and has a master's degree in public administration from the Harvard University Kennedy School of Government. She has practiced law, worked as a government civil servant for five years, and was Assistant to the Deputy Prime Minister of Indonesia (1965–67), heading the Research Bureau of the Supreme Advisory Council (1967–70).

[6.] Nancy Lee Peluso, "Collecting Data on Women's Employment in Rural Java," *Family Planning Studies* (Washington, D.C.: Population Council, 1979).

She was involved in drafting the Marriage Act in a Working Committee of the Ministry of Justice (1966–68), was a member of the Advisory Board to the National Family Planning Coordinating Board (1970–72), and was on the Research Team on the Status of Women and Family Planning (1971–73) and the Research Team on Law and Population (1972–74). She worked with the WHO (South East Asia Region) Focal Point to Indonesia on Women in Health and Development, and conducted research on Women's Participation in Decision-Making of Policies Concerning Health Services, as requested by WHO Geneva. Since 1967 she has been involved in the Indonesian women's movement—on the board of the Indonesian Council of Women (KOWANI), as a member of the National Commission on the Status of Women, a council member of ASEAN*** Confederation of Women's Organizations, and a board member of Dharma Wanita (Women's Civil Servant Association). She is married and has three children.

*** The Association of Southeast Asian Nations, established on Aug. 8, 1967, with the member countries Indonesia, Malaysia, Philippines, Singapore, and Thailand.—Ed.

the Aryan population had divided into Medes and Persians. Cyrus the Great (d. 529 B.C.E.) founded the Persian Empire. The Greeks and Parthians occupied Persia until the early 3rd century C.E., when the Sassinids began their 400-year rule. During the Sassanid dynasty (c. 224–c. 640 C.E.), Pourandokut and Azarmidokht were powerful queens; Gordafarid was a woman warrior who led the Persians against a Turkish invasion. In 636 C.E., Arab invaders defeated the Sassinids and introduced Islam; a Shi'ite community was created.

Babism, a religion that advocated social reforms, higher status for women, limits on polygyny, and prohibition of violence against women, developed in the 1840's; Qurrat Ul Ayn was a Babi leader, poet, and warrior who appeared unveiled in 1844, when women first began protesting the code of Islamic dress. An educational movement began in the 1870's; Khanum Azmodeh started the Namus school for girls. Among outspoken women in the royal harem, Anis Ud Daula, the Shah Nasir Ud Din's third wife, helped topple the Persian Prime Minister in 1872; he was accused of putting Britain's colonial interests above Persia's. In 1890 royal harem women organized a successful tobacco strike against the British, who had monopolized Persian tobacco production. Women participated in the nationalist "constitutional revolution" of 1905, demonstrating in the streets and appearing unveiled, for which they were denounced by male crowds as "prostitutes."

Although the Persian Constitution of 1906 and the formation of a parliament that same year did little to aid women, several women's secret societies formed; members included Malikiya-yi Iran, Safia Yazdi, Sadiqa Daulatabadi, and Badri Tundari, all related in some way to the constitutionalist leaders. *Danish* (Knowledge) was a secret society publication—written by and for women. A literacy campaign for women was launched in 1908. In 1911, during the Russian invasion of northern Iran, the Persian Women's Society appealed to British suffragists for support and held protests separate from men. When the Persian Parliament was about to concede to Russian demands, 300 women holding pistols under their skirts threatened to kill their husbands, their sons, and themselves if the deputies conceded.

The *Messenger of Happiness,* a magazine for women, was published in 1921, the year in which a military coup brought Gen. Reza Khan to power; he became Shah Reza Pahlavi in 1925, founding the Pahlavi dynasty. Sadiqa Daulatabadi opened a girls' school in Isfahan; as a child, she had attended her brother's school disguised as a boy. Women's groups in the 1920's included the Patriotic Women's League, which published the journal *Nesvane Vatankhah,* and the Higher Council of Women's Organizations in Iran, a federation of 17 women's groups. The Second Congress of Oriental Women in 1932 supported women's rights.

In 1934 Shah Reza Khan ordered women teachers and students to unveil, as part of the modern dress code for women. The *chador* was made illegal in 1936; some men ripped veils off women in response to the decision (whether the women concurred or not), although most men opposed it; the Queen and Princesses appeared unveiled. During the Shah's reign, there was a decline in upper-class polygyny and a rise in salaried work for women.

In 1941 the Shah abdicated in favor of his son, Mohammed Reza. That same year, women textile workers organized. Throughout the 1940's and 1950's, the Organization of Revolutionary Women fought for equal rights. Women won the right to vote in 1963, when the first elections were held, but few women benefited from the Shah's land-reform program, since only men were given land grants. The Shah's twin sister, Princess Ashraf, and his third wife, Farah Diba, are credited by some with having influenced his pro-women's-rights policies. Fundamentalist religious groups opposed the reforms, joined by political and democratic groups who opposed the Shah's autocratic rule.

Forough Farrukhzad, the most celebrated woman poet of modern Iran, died in 1967. In 1968 women were admitted to the Revolutionary Corps. Women also joined the political underground and anti-Shah nationalist guerrilla groups, despite the risk of arrest and torture. Ashraf Deghan was a guerrilla leader who escaped from SAVAK, the Shah's dreaded secret intelligence force. In the 1970's, the Women's Organization of Iran (WOI) provided educational and vocational training for women; the Literacy Corps and Health Corps admitted women (see following article).

In 1978 massive anti-Shah demonstrations broke out and escalated until Jan. 1979, when the Shah and his family went into exile.

In Mar. 1979, 100,000 women gathered at the University of Teheran to celebrate the Shah's fall. A few days later, these women were protesting the fundamentalist policies of the new leader, the Ayatollah Khomeini. "In the dawn of freedom, there is no freedom" was the slogan shouted by 6000 women in a Teheran march on Mar. 8; 2 days later, 15,000 women seized the Palace of Justice, demanding their rights. Women's marches in major Iranian cities were the target of attacks and stoning by male onlookers, but support demonstrations were held by feminists in cities all over the world. On Mar. 13, 2 Iranian women attacked Sadegh Ghotbzadeh (Khomeini's spokesperson), one with a gun, the other with a knife.

Khomeini's government abolished virtually all previous legislation favoring women's rights. In June 1981, 50 schoolgirls were shot and thousands of girls and women arrested (for "counter-revolutionary" or "anti-Islamic" activity) without trials; reports to date (1983) indicate that more than 20,000 women have been executed, including pregnant and elderly women, and young girls. Many women have joined rural guerrilla forces; in 1981, women who supported the opposition Mujahideen-i-Khalq movement attacked armed guards; 2 women were killed and 2 injured. The Moslem Mothers' Society united 20,000 women who protested the slaughter. In Mar. 1982, the legal minimum age of execution was set at 10 yrs. (or puberty) for girls and 16 yrs. for boys.

In June of that year, the government banned women from most sports events, and initiated a new wave of arrests;

15,000 people were executed. In Apr. 1983, veiling was made compulsory for women; a group of Khomeini supporters called the Zeinab Sisters monitor conformance to the new law; since 1979, they have harassed and spied on women, causing many arrests and subsequent deaths.

In 1982 and 1983, government persecution of religious minorities—in particular Jews and Baha'is—increased, and the UN Commission on Human Rights began an investigation into reported mass violations of human rights. On June 18, 1983, 10 women, including 3 teenagers, were hanged in Shiraz, sentenced by order of the Islamic Revolutionary Court for having been members of the Baha'i religion who had refused to convert to Islam; the executed included Iran's first woman physicist, a concert pianist, the former personnel director for Iran Television, a nurse, and college students; most of the women had been active in Baha'i Women's Committees which promulgated equal rights for women. Reports in late 1983 est. that 50,000 children who had been recruited to "clean minefields" had been killed during the 4 years of border war between Iran and Iraq.

The National Movement of Resistance, an anti-Khomeini organization, has adopted women's rights as part of its platform. The People's Mujahideen Organization of Iran has among its supporters the Women's National Alliance, Moslem Women's Assoc. in South Teheran, Groups of Women Workers, and Moslem Iranian Students' Society (in Britain)— all in opposition to the Khomeini government.

MYTHOGRAPHY. A major culture of goddess worship developed among the Sumerians in areas close to the Persian Gulf around 3500 B.C.E. Nammu was the goddess of heaven and earth; Nina was a fish-tailed goddess whose cult centered near the juncture of the Tigris and Euphrates rivers and the Persian Gulf. Nidaba was the goddess and inventor of writing, Inanna a fertility goddess whose symbol was the serpent winding around a stick. Similar goddess worship was practiced throughout ancient Persia.

The Themodontines, or Amazons,

were semi-legendary women-warriors in the area who fought the Persians, Tatars, and Kalmucks during the Homeric period. Among the Iranian people of the Sigyns—a matriarchal culture of women-warriors—a woman was forbidden to marry until she had killed 3 male enemies.

IRAN: A Future in the Past—
The "Prerevolutionary" Women's Movement
by Mahnaz Afkhami

In December of 1979, Ms. Farrokhrou Parsa, the first woman to serve in the Iranian cabinet, was executed after a trial by hooded judges—a trial at which no defense attorney was permitted, no appeal possible, and the defendant had been officially declared guilty before the proceedings began. She was charged with "expansion of prostitution, corruption on earth, and warring against God." Aware of the hopelessness of her case, she delivered a reasoned, courageous defense of her career decisions, among them a directive to free female schoolchildren from having to be veiled and the establishment of a commission for revising textbooks to present a nonsexist image of women. A few hours after sentence was pronounced she was wrapped in a dark sack and machine-gunned.

Ms. Parsa, whose mother had been exiled for *her* stance on women's rights (especially her opposition to the veil), had been educated as a medical doctor but chose to serve as a teacher and, later, as principal of a girls' high school. In 1964 she was one of the first six women elected to Parliament. In 1968 she was appointed Minister of Education. At the time of her death she had been retired for four years.

She was not a heroic figure but a hard-working, disciplined woman who struggled to achieve her position in government. She was a practical, level-headed feminist. The significance of her position for the Iranian women's movement rested not so much in her considerable personal achievements but in that *she was one of hundreds of thousands.* Those who executed her also understood this and staged the event as a symbolic attempt to reduce her—and through her the type of woman she represented—to an insignificant, lifeless shape in a dark sack. In the year following her death, many women marched against the tyranny of the mullahs. Many were beaten, stabbed, imprisoned. Some of the very young were tried and executed without ever identifying themselves as other than "fighters, daughters of Iran." No further identification was necessary. It was a type of woman the regime meant to destroy.

History has shown that execution of people who are committed to an idea seldom destroys the idea. At this moment the regime of the mullahs shows signs of crumbling. Whatever form of government replaces it must come to terms with feminism in Iran. The struggle of Iranian women during and after the "revolution," and their presence in all social and political movements, means that what they have gained in terms of awareness, organizational experience, and political consciousness must be taken into account. The future must begin at the point when persecution drove the feminist movement underground. It is with this belief that, although I must discuss the Iranian women's movement in the past tense, I speak of it not as a thing of the past, but as a strong foundation for the enormous work lying ahead.

The single most important factor to keep in mind about the movement is that its most spectacular achievements took place within a time span of *less than two decades.* As late as 1962, Iranian law regarded women as being in the same class as minors, criminals, and the insane. They could not vote or stand for public office, were not allowed the guardianship of their own children, could not work or marry without permission of their male "benefactors," could be divorced at any moment (with or without their prior knowledge, through the utterance of a simple sentence by the husband), and could be faced with the presence of a second, third, or fourth wife in their home at any moment—with no legal, financial, or emotional recourse.

At the beginning of the 1960's, feminists had two points of strength. One was the existence of a national leadership which, although by *no* means feminist in orientation, at least was committed to modernization and change. But the second and greatest strength was the existence of an increasing number of educated women with an already respectable history of feminist endeavors—beginning with the establishment of the Patriotic Women's League and the publication of its organ *Nesvane Vatankhah* in 1923, leading in turn to the creation of organizations throughout the country, and culminating in the establishment of a federation of fifteen organizations called the High Council of Women's Organizations of Iran, which concentrated its efforts on the achievement of women's suffrage. The national referendum of 1963 reflected general support for the six-point reform program, which included land reform and the franchise for women.

The first serious victory brought about a wave of reaction from the fanatic religious opposition. Riots were organized under the leadership of the (then scarcely known) Ayatollah Khomeini, whose earlier petition to the Shah against land reform *and* women's franchise had been ignored. Marching mobs demonstrated against the new role of women. The Ayatollah's activities were temporarily curtailed when he was exiled to Turkey. Feminists, however, became even more conscious of the extent of opposition to their ideas and of the need for unification of their own forces. In 1964, fifty-one women representing diverse groups and interests came together to study various ways of achieving a more viable organizational structure for women's activities. In 1966 the draft constitution of the Women's Organization of Iran (WOI) was presented to an assembly of representatives from across the nation. The constitution of the new organization envisaged a grass-roots, nationwide movement whose officers would be elected from among the members in each branch. These officers would in turn elect an eleven-member central council which would provide guidelines and set goals. Princess Ashraf, the twin sister of the Shah and by far the most powerful woman in the country, was asked to act as honorary president; her patronage was to assure the organization political leverage in the battle against its fanatic enemies. The organization's initial efforts were based on a few simple, agreed-upon concepts: that every individual in society must be encouraged to learn, work, grow, and contribute to nation-building; that this goal could be achieved within the spirit of Islam and the cultural traditions of the nation; that full participation of women must be achieved by women themselves through methods which they choose; that education in the broadest sense is the most important vehicle to bring about change; that economic independence is one of the first priorities and the basis for achievement of other rights; and that the acquisition of power, through the infiltration of feminists in various institutions and mobilization of groups from various strata of society, is a prerequisite for gaining the means to achieve these goals.

Feminism was thought to be a Western phenomenon. But an idea's origins, it was agreed, ought not to be the main consideration in one's judgment of its validity; Christianity came from the Middle East, while democracy was of Western origin. One need not reinvent the wheel to satisfy one's chauvinism. Yet the organization stressed the importance of reinterpreting each concept within the cultural framework of the Iranian people. The movement's immediate audience was the growing urban, educated, middle class, but ways had to be found to reach the rural and urban masses, and communication had to be devised in terms relevant to their lives. As one literacy-corps woman pointed out, "It was fruitless to discuss the finer points of human rights with a pregnant, illiterate, village woman who was doing her chores as she breast-fed one baby, tried to extricate her skirts from the clutches of another child, and kept a worried eye on her two other children fighting and screaming nearby. The ideas were not only alien to her life, but worse, they were irrelevant."

It was imperative for the movement to gain access to decision-making at the national level in order to redirect the entire developmental process to include women. It was crucial to create awareness that *women are the most significant element in the solution of these problems.* Thus, the movement was faced with the tasks of gaining support among the decision-makers on the one hand, and mobilizing mass support among women on the other.

Mass mobilization had to begin pragmatically, by offering useful services in order to gain trust and support. Accordingly, a main category of functions included the provision of vocational training and literacy classes, childcare, legal and professional counseling, family planning, and a wide range of cultural and sport activities for the young (depending on the expressed preference, talent, and know-how of each group in each area; recitation of the *Koran,* for example, would be chosen by women in one area and organization of a soccer team or a self-defense class in another).

In order to mobilize support among the decision-makers, however, goals of the movement had to be disguised in terms palatable to power groups who were not feminist but who might be persuaded to back ideas in tune with some of their own goals. Thus, special programs to combat illiteracy among rural women were not demanded solely on the basis of women's right to education, but as a necessary means of modernization. Special vocational training for women was sought not only on the grounds of their rightful access to better-paying jobs, but for the sake of eliminating sociocultural problems inherent in large-scale importation of foreign labor.

Legal action usually followed years of discussion within the movement in order to transform vague feelings of injustice into coherent and well-reasoned demands for change. Thorough research was carried out in terms of the socioeconomic background of each proposal, as well as the cultural and religious factors to which the proposal would relate. Then there followed publication of works on various levels of complexity for women with different levels of education.

Each legislative proposal was brought to the attention of the more enlightened senior religious authorities, and their views were incorporated into the body of the laws. Often they provided valuable advice on ways of preparing legislative texts which would embody feminist ideas in language which avoided conflict with religious dictates, especially the text of the *Koran.* Their approval, however, did not bring immunity from attack by the more fanatic leaders, who were fully aware that the rapidly changing status of women presented a threat to their world view, power, and prestige. (The Family Protection Law, for example, not only presented a view of women which approached the concept of equality within the family but brought family disputes within the realm of *secular* law and thus outside clerical jurisdiction.)

The proposals would then be subject for discussion at a high-level committee of the women's organization to which senators, judges, and various other high officials would be invited as participants. Endless hours of decorous discussions on the sacred role of motherhood and the "special but decidedly different" intellectual and emotional make-up of women would be patiently tolerated. Diplomatic presentation by some feminists would be juxtaposed against more radical statements by other feminists. Slowly the discussions began to have an effect, producing surprising changes among the male participants. What finally emerged was often couched in terms which were not our ideal (customary introductory slogans regarding respect for religion and the sanctity of the family became a necessary part of each document). But the sacrifices were considered well worth the results.

One phase of legal action always involved convincing the Monarch—whose national role was the essence and symbol of patriarchy. Since he was regularly briefed by the Queen and Princess Ashraf (both intelligent, active, professional women), constantly exposed to international opinion and attitudes, and possessed by a vision of Iran as a "progressive" nation, it would sometimes suffice to demonstrate to him the importance of the proposal to national development. On issues which were in apparent conflict with the text of the *Koran,* he took a very rigid stance. On the eve of a legal seminar, the Minister of Court informed me of His Majesty's concern over our proposed stance on inheritance laws. This was both a personal concern and an indication of mounting pressure from the fundamentalists. One long legal campaign had produced the 1975 far-from-ideal but still significant revision of the Family Protection Law. We had supported the compromise as a step forward, but as soon as the law passed we began to prepare the next revision proposals. It was hopeless at the time of the 1975 revision to try to achieve equal powers for partners within the family during the husband's lifetime. But we managed to secure the right of women to legal guardianship of their children after the death of the father. (In the majority of Islamic countries guardianship of children after the father's death is given to the male members of the father's family.) In the same law, although we were not able to strike out the right of the husband to prevent his wife from engaging in a profession "repugnant to his family honor," we *were* able to include the same prerogative for the wife. Practically speaking, neither provision is enforceable, but the revision is significant: for the first time women were legally considered to possess "honor" in their own right.

The Passport Law and Article 179 of the Penal Code were cases where negative publicity and great controversy forced us to put aside our proposals for a time. The Passport Law required a woman to present the written permission of her husband in order to be issued a passport to travel. Senator Manouchehrian, president of the Women Lawyers' Association, made a speech arguing for freedom of travel, basing her argument on the Koranic dictum that no one has the right to detain another from pilgrimage to Mecca. An avalanche of attacks ensued and we were portrayed as advocates of "travel by honest Moslem womenfolk to the West to shop and gamble." Ms. Manouchehrian's next speech was curtly interrupted by the President of the Senate, who publicly accused her of misrepresenting Islam. The publication of a pamphlet called "Legalized Wife-killing" by the WOI also brought a backlash. Article 179 of the Penal Code states, "If a man witnesses his wife in the act of intercourse or a situation which could be construed as being engaged in intercourse with a man other than her husband and injures or murders one or both of them, he is immune from punishment." The cases which occurred with frequency involved murder of the woman, seldom the other man, and were rarely the result of a spontaneous reaction. As late as 1974 an absurdly broad interpretation by a fanatic judge had extended this immunity to a brother who had murdered his sister because he had seen her get out of a taxi accompanied by a stranger. The opposition to our pamphlet, however, began with a wave of propaganda implying that feminists supported adultery and wished to "expand prostitution." We were forced into tactical retreat on this issue also. It was extremely difficult to fight implications of sexual immorality on the relatively sophisticated grounds of the human rights of women. It took us five years of quiet negotiation and a low-key but extensive media campaign to be able to relaunch the effort to change these laws.

There were times when we *were* successful in implementing legal change without arousing much public attention. Such was the case of abortion, which was made legal by removing the penalty for performing the operation embodied in a law dealing with medical malpractice. Ministry of Health officials agreed to cooperate, mostly because of the added impetus for the unsuccessful birth-control campaign. It was agreed that to minimize organized attacks by the opposition, publicity would be avoided, so legalization was announced through internal memos of the Ministry of Health, Ministry of Justice, and the WOI. We were fully aware of the limited impact of the law under these circumstances, but we agreed because even under these conditions the law would save tens of thousands of women from disability or death.

Legal changes were only the beginning; implementation was even more complicated and difficult. Important as it was to gain the right to sue for divorce, it would be useless to a woman who had no means of financial support. Raising the legal age of marriage was of limited value since in some outlying villages, records of birth were scribbled on the front page of the *Koran* and one child's birth date could be given as another's. The problem of implementation was related to the general problems of education and socioeconomic development—which brought us back to our primary goal: full integration of women in the process of development. Nevertheless, legal change is of tremendous value. As a reflection of what a society thinks about the role of women, the laws affect a woman's self-appraisal as well as the attitude of men.

In every area of women's-movement activity, we faced potential or actual opposition from fundamentalist religious figures who enjoyed influence among the people, had access to the masses through the network of mosques, and used established religious events as occasions to affect public opinion. Their claim to monopoly on the interpretation of the sacred texts, their presumed communion with God, prophets, and Imams, and their mastery of the vehicle of oral communication were strong means of reaching the illiterate masses. However, the fundamentalists would have had little impact among the urban intelligentsia and middle classes were it not for the vital assistance they received from the radical Left.

The Left saw class struggle as the only legitimate one and viewed any "revisionist" attempt to bring about progress within the system as detrimental to the success of revolution: once the class struggle was won and the proletariat achieved victory, *then* the problem of women (a by-product of the class system, of course), would automatically disappear. Accordingly, the growing influence of the women's organization among the people was seen as a threat to be counteracted. The radical Left, however, enjoyed very little mass support, owing to the antireligious stance of Marxism as well as a deep-rooted fear of the Soviet Union's threatening presence along the 1200 miles of shared border with Iran. So, learning from past mistakes, the Left shrewdly chose to join forces *with* the religious fundamentalists, bringing political know-how to the latter's activities. Indeed, considerable sophistication (as well as a lack of political scruples) was necessary to be able to choose the feminist repugnance to the objectification of women as a battle cry for a movement whose entire philosophy was based on the negation of women's social existence. Thus, Leftist university women suddenly put aside their jeans to don black *chadors*. They sometimes zealously exceeded the mullahs' mandate by wearing gloves to cover their hands. The controversial issue of abortion, which had been handled with such extreme caution, suddenly became the subject of front-page headlines one year after actual legalization and on the day of the first fundamentalist demonstrations. In the hysterical media campaign just before and after the revolution, feminists who could see beyond particular political posturings could recognize the antifeminist techniques: allegations of immorality, of weakening family ties, and of sexual misconduct were spread through the media, fanned by revolutionary zeal and with astounding power and success. Pictures of women in bathing suits were used to support charges of prostitution against women working in the government bureaucracy. No holds were barred in the smear campaign to belittle and discredit women leaders. Khomeini repeatedly called any unveiled woman "naked," and any woman who had normal professional contact with men "a prostitute."

Yet despite the power of the opposition, by 1978—only twelve years after its establishment—the Women's Organization of Iran had grown into a network of 400 branches and 118 centers, with 51 affiliated organizations, including religious minorities, professional associations, and other special-interest groups.[1] And we had accomplished the following:

—During the first half of the 1970's the number of girls attending elementary school rose from 80,020 to 1,508,387; the number of girls attending vocational training schools rose tenfold; the number of women candidates for the universities rose seven times. By 1978, 33 percent of all university students were women and they began to choose fields other than traditionally female occupations. Further encouragement was provided through a quota system which gave preferential treatment to eligible girls who volunteered to enter technical schools. In 1978, the number of women who took the entrance examination for the School of Medicine was *higher* than that of men.

—Three years of research, experimental teaching, and discussion by an ad hoc committee of members of WOI and the faculties of Tehran and National Universities established an accredited program of women's studies at these universities.

—In employment, priority was given to training women for semiskilled and skilled work. All laws and regulations were revised to eliminate sex discrimination, and equal pay for equal work was incorporated into the body of all government rules. All regulations regarding housing, loans, and other job benefits were adjusted to eliminate discrimination.[2]

—In 1979 there were 2 million Iranian women in the labor force and 187,928 enrolled in academic and specialized fields; 146,604 worked as civil servants, and of these 1666 were managers or directors. There were 1803 women university professors. Women worked in the army, in the police force, as judges, pilots, engineers—in every field except religious activities. Schools of theology were the only academic institutions closed to women.

—Women were encouraged to run for political office. In 1978 a vigorous mobilization campaign resulted in the election of 333 of 1660 candidates to local councils. Twenty-two women were elected to Parliament and two served in the Senate. There were one cabinet minister, three sub-cabinet under-secretaries (including the second highest position in the Ministries of Labour and Mines and Industries), one governor, an ambassador, and five mayors.[3]

[1.] The centers provided vocational training, literacy classes, childcare, legal and professional counseling, and family planning through a professional staff of two thousand and a volunteer staff of seventy thousand to approximately a million women each year. The WOI School of Social Work selected potential staff members from among village women and trained them for two years to return and work in their own environment.

[2.] A legislative package supportive of women's employment was prepared and approved by Parliament. It contained provisions for a working mother to work half time, up to her child's third year of age. The three years would be considered *equivalent to fulltime work* in terms of seniority and retirement benefits. It also provided for up to seven months maternity leave with full pay. Most important, it contained a provision which made the establishment of childcare facilities on the premises of factories and offices *obligatory*. These centers were supervised by an elected committee of the mothers who were allowed paid time off to perform this function.

[3.] The degree of political awareness reached by the masses of Iranian women became strikingly apparent during the antigovernment marches of 1978–79. In a meeting of the secretaries of WOI we asked the Secretary of Kerman Province about the veiled women who had taken part in a recent demonstration. "Who were they?" we asked. "Our own members," she said. "You kept saying 'Mobilize them.' Now they are mobilized, and they shout 'Long Live Khomeini.'" Yet to

—Perhaps the most important accomplishment was the formulation of the National Plan of Action—based on the results of more than 700 seminars, informal gatherings, and conferences throughout Iran. It was presented to the cabinet and approved in May 1978. This event was significant not only because of the enormous task of achieving consensus among women on all major issues, but also because cabinet approval included approval of the machinery for *implementation,* through the designation of a special committee in each of twelve ministries to plan, implement, and monitor efforts toward full integration of women in society.

—The movement considered international action on feminist issues one of the most important means of achieving its goals. Exchange of information, pooling of research resources, and mutual assistance between women's groups in different nations (especially in times of political and social tension) is vital in terms of both pressuring governments and bringing crucial moral support. The WOI was successful in channeling substantial financial aid to UN programs for International Women's Year. The Iranian delegation introduced the idea *and* the funds for the creation of the Regional Center for Research and Development for Asia and the Pacific, *and* for the International Center for Research on Women. The beginning of the 1980's was to have been the birth of a new phase in the history of Iranian women and a significant era for women of all Third World Moslem nations.

Within a few months, the entire picture changed. The convulsions within the nation turned to upheaval and finally revolution. In February 1979, Khomeini returned to Iran. Within a few months, a systematic and vigorous attempt began to reverse all the changes we had achieved. Women were eliminated from all decision-making positions within the government. Those who remained at low levels were required to wear the veil. The President (considered moderate as compared to other leaders), stated, "It is an obligation of the female to cover her head because women's hair exudes vibrations which arouse, mislead, and corrupt men." The Family Protection Law was set aside. Childcare centers were closed. Abortion became illegal under all circumstances. Women were ruled unfit to serve as judges. Adultery became punishable by stoning. The Women's Organization was declared a den of corruption and its goals conducive to the expansion of prostitution. University women were segregated in cafeterias and on buses. Women who demonstrated against these oppressive rules were slandered, accused of immoral behavior, attacked, and imprisoned. Opposition grew. Executions became a daily occurrence.

But the regime held within its reactionary philosophy and oppressive style the seeds of its own destruction. Disillusioned with the incompetence and inhumanity of the mullahs, the Iranian people (both inside the country and in the West, where millions have fled to escape the tyrannical theocracy) have organized themselves to overthrow the regime and install a government respectful of Iranian national and cultural traditions as well as those of law and reason. Women have had an active role in every opposition political group. We have learned a lesson, though: we know now that whatever one's political preference, *the main battle for women always remains in the arena of sexual politics.*

The years ahead will be difficult. To unite a torn and battered nation and rebuild what had been destroyed is a monumental task. But as I contemplate the future of Iran, a reassuring image gives me hope. I recall a young woman I met in the southern village of Zovieh. She had finished her military service in the literacy corps to return to her home and establish a school in which she taught all subjects to all four grades. On the day I saw her, she was walking out of a village meeting in her faded uniform, flushed and proud,

---

this day we are all still in agreement that what is important is that they marched and shouted their will. That it was in support of a destructive force came from political naiveté which only time and experience can correct.

followed by the old men who had just selected her *Kadkhoda,* or "elderman," of the village.

Those who have struggled and those who have died sacrificed so that women like her may exist.

She is the future.

Suggested Further Reading

Azari, Farah. *Women of Iran.* London: Ithaca Press, 1983.

Bamdad, Badr al-Muluk. *From Darkness into Light: Women's Emancipation in Iran.* Trans. F. R. C. Bagley. Hicksville, NY: Exposition Press, 1977.

Farman-Farmaian, Sattareh. "Women and Decision-Making: With Special Reference to Iran and other Developing Countries." *Labour and Society,* Geneva, Apr. 1976.

Henderson, Behjat. "The Effect of Modernization on the Roles of Iranian Women." *Occasional Papers in Anthropology,* Buffalo, 1979.

Nashat, Guitty, ed. *Women and Revolution in Iran.* Boulder, CO: Westview Press, 1983.

Population and Family Planning in Iran. United Nations Mission Report. New York: United Nations, 1971.

Rachlin, Nahid. *Foreigner, A Novel of an Iranian Woman Caught Between Two Cultures.* New York: W. W. Norton, 1978.

Tabari, Azar, *et al,* eds. *In the Shadow of Islam: The Women's Movement in Iran.* London: Zed Press, 1982.

(Among the publications of the Women's Organization of Iran are a series of Comparative Studies on the Laws of Iran and international conventions and declarations on the role of women. These are in Persian. The only copies in existence after the revolution are, I believe, those I have donated to the library of the Foundation for Iranian Studies in Washington. They will photocopy and at times translate segments for the use of serious scholars. Publications of the Women's Organization of Iran's Research Center available in English are the following.—M.A.)

Afkhami, Mahnaz. *The National Plan of Action for the Improvement of the Status of Women in Iran: Ideology, Structure, and Implementation.* This was to have been published by Ziba Press, Tehran, 1979.

Moser-Khalili, Moira. *Urban Design and Women's Lives.* Tehran: Women's Organization of Iran, 1976.

Iranian Women, Past, Present and Future. Tehran: Women's Organization of Iran, 1976.

Sources in Persian:

Karnameye Sazemaneh Zanane Iran. Tehran: Ziba Press, 1978.

Naqshe Zan Dar Farhang va Tamadone Iran. Tehran: Bisto Panje Shahrivar Press, 1971.

Mahnaz Afkhami was born in Kerman, Iran, in 1941. She taught at the National University of Iran and in 1968 became chair of the English department. She is the founder of the Association of Iranian University Women and served as the secretary-general of the Women's Organization of Iran from 1970 until the revolution of 1979. She was Minister of State for Women's Affairs from 1976 to 1978, when the position was eliminated on the eve of the religious upheaval. She has written and lectured extensively on the women's movement and headed the Iranian delegation to the conferences of the International Council of Women in 1972 (in Lima) and again in 1973 (in Vienna). She headed the Iranian delegation on visits to the USSR (1974) and the People's Republic of China (1974), on the invitation of the women's organizations of those nations. She also headed the Iranian delegation to the UN Consultative Committee for the World Conference of the International Women's Year in New York (1975), and the Iranian delegation to the Commission on the Status of Women's 1978 session. She served as a member of the High Council of Family Planning and Welfare, the board of trustees of Kerman University, and the board of trustees of Farah University for Women. Among her writings are *Notes on the Curriculum and Materials for the Women's Studies Program for Iranian University Women.* She is presently the executive director of the Foundation for Iranian Studies in the US and is preparing a *History of the Iranian Women's Movement in the Twentieth Century.* She is married and has a son, Babak.

IRELAND
(Republic of Ireland)

Comprised of 26 out of 32 counties on the western British Isle, located in the Atlantic Ocean, with Northern Ireland to the north and east, the Irish Sea and St. George's Channel to the east, and the Atlantic Ocean to the south, west, and north. **Area:** 68,894 sq. km. (26,600 sq. mi.). **Population** (1980): 3,292,000, female 50%. **Capital:** Dublin.

DEMOGRAPHY. Languages: Irish (Gaelic), English (first and second official, respectively). **Races or Ethnic Groups:** Irish (Celtic origin), English, Scots, other. **Religions:** Roman Catholicism 95%, Protestant (Church of Ireland, Presbyterian, Methodist) 5%. **Education** (% enrolled in school, 1975): Age 6–11—of all girls 97%, of all boys 96%; age 12–17—of all girls 85%, of all boys 81%; higher education—in 1977–78 women were 43% of university students, 22% of medical students, 25.2% of technical school, 74.9% of teacher-training. Elementary education is compulsory and free; most secondary schools are privately owned, primarily by religious orders but with State support. **Literacy** (1977): Women 98%, men 98%. **Birth Rate** (per 1000 pop., 1977–78): 22. **Death Rate** (per 1000 pop., 1977–78): 10. **Infant Mortality** (per 1000 live births, 1977): Female 15, male 21. **Life Expectancy** (1975–80): Female 75 yrs., male 70 yrs.

GOVERNMENT. National Parliament (Oireachtas) consists of a 166-member House of Representatives (Dáil Éireann) elected by proportional representation, a 60-member Senate (Seanad Éireann) partially nominated by the prime minister and partially elected by borough councils representing various interest groups and party affiliations; a president elected by direct vote, and a 7-15 member government appointed by the president from the House and Senate, hold executive powers. The government must resign if it loses majority support in the House of Representatives. The major political parties are Fianna Fáil, Fine Gael, the Labour Party, the Workers' Party, and In-

dependents. **Women's Suffrage:** 1918 (limited suffrage, women over age 30) under British hegemony; 1922 full suffrage (at Independence). **Equal Rights:** No data obtainable. **Women in Government:** There are 14 women in the National Parliament, including the Minister for Education (Gemma Hussey) and Junior Minister for Women's Affairs (Nuala Fennell). Tras Honan is Chair of the Senate, which has 5 women members (1983). Fennell, Honan, and Hussey are major figures in the (opposition) Fianna Fáil Party; Hussey is Ireland's first woman Minister for Education, under the current (1983) coalition government, and also a founder member of the Women's Political Assoc.

ECONOMY. Currency: Punt [Irish Pound] (May 1983: 0.79 = $1 US). **Gross National Product** (1980): $16.1 billion. **Per Capita Income** (1980): $4880. **Women's Wages as a Percentage of Men's** (1979): 57.6%. **Equal Pay Policy:** The 1974 Equal Pay Act (Anti-Discrimination) stipulates equal pay for equal work and work of equal value; women who file wage discrimination suits in court cannot be fired on those grounds. It is illegal to "discriminate on the grounds of sex or marital status" in recruitment, access to training, and general employment opportunities, and illegal to fire a woman who files such a case in court (1977 Employment Equality Act). Reports indicate the principle of equal pay is often ignored by employers; in addition, Protestant women (and men) face discrimination (in Northern Ireland, Catholics face religious discrimination in employment and other areas). **Production** (Agricultural/Industrial): Potatoes, barley, sugar beets, hay, silage, wheat, cattle and dairy products; processed food, beverages, textiles, chemicals, pharmaceuticals, machinery. **Women as a Percentage of Labor Force** (1980): 28%; **of agricultural force** (1979) 9.6% (53.2% of whom are unpaid family workers, 1979; 6.9% of employed women work in agriculture, 1977); **of industrial force**

(1977) 19.8% (24.4% of employed women work in industry); **of military** (1979) 300 women are in all the armed forces, and can rise to ranked positions; the military forces are explicitly excluded from the Employment Equality Act. **(Employed) Women's Occupational Indicators:** Of administrative and managerial 12.1%, of sales workers 34.4%, of professional, technical, and related workers 46.6%, of service workers 56%, of clerical and related workers 71% (1979). In 1977 employed married women were 13.6% of the total female labor force, the lowest % in the Western European community. As of Mar. 1983, a new law permitted employed women who were previously prohibited from engaging in night employment to do so at their employers' request, and with the approval of their workers' representative organizations. **Unemployment** (Apr. 1983): 14.5%; women were 48.7% of the total unemployed in 1981.

GYNOGRAPHY. Marriage. *Policy:* Minimum marriage age for women and men is 21, or 16 with parental consent. Bigamy and forced marriage are illegal (1960 Matrimonial Proceedings Act and 1870 Matrimonial Causes Act). The husband is considered legal head of household; he is required to maintain his wife and dependent children (1976 Maintenance of Spouses and Children Act). A married woman or man may control and dispose of her/his own property as s/he wishes. *Practice:* Female mean age at marriage (1970–78): 24; women age 15–49 in union (1970–78): 41.9%. Prior to 1975, the minimum marriage age with parental consent was 12 for females and 14 for males. **Divorce.** *Policy:* Divorce is constitutionally prohibited. A "judicial separation" which does not permit remarriage is obtainable through the High Courts on narrow grounds which render the marriage "void" or "voidable": "lack of capacity" (i.e., if one already is married), non-observance of marriage-procedure formalities, impotence, absence of consent at the time of marriage owing to insanity or intoxication, or marriage by duress or fraud (1870 Matrimonial Causes Act). Divorces obtained in other countries are recognized only if 1 spouse

has been domiciled there. Remarriage is legal only for those married and divorced in another country. A couple may separate by mutual consent if a lawyer draws up a separation contract governing child custody, alimony, and division of property. In cases of nonagreement, judicial separation may be granted on grounds of adultery or physical cruelty, with the court determining the terms (Matrimonial Causes Act). *Practice:* Judicial separation (sometimes called "divorce by bed and board") is extremely expensive and difficult to obtain. Reports indicate that sometimes it is easier for a Roman Catholic couple to obtain an annulment, and that upon remarriage the State will not necessarily prosecute for bigamy. It is common practice for a spouse to live in England for 6 months, obtain a divorce, and return to Ireland, where it is then recognized. Ireland was convicted by the European Court of Justice for violating the 1950 Human Rights Convention by not providing Irish women with affordable judicial separation (1980). A strong Roman Catholic stand against divorce is shared by many. Reports indicate that a considerable number of women are deserted by their husbands (1980).

Family. *Policy:* The husband is legal head of household. The Constitution (Art. 41) recognizes that "by her life in the home, woman gives to the State a support without which the common good cannot be achieved. The State shall endeavor to ensure that mothers shall not be obliged by economic necessity to engage in labor to the neglect of their duties in the home." If a maintained spouse is adulterous, maintenance may be forfeited, although the court may decide to enforce maintenance after examining the circumstances (1976 Maintenance of Spouses and Children Act). Maternity leave and benefits are available to employed women (also see **Welfare**). *Practice:* No data obtainable.

Welfare. *Policy:* A social-welfare system provides both flat-rate and pay-scale-related insurance and assistance benefits, with the cost supported by employers, employees, and the State. Benefits include disability, widow's pension, unemployment, maternity benefit, deserted wife's benefit, retirement pension (payable at age 60 for women, or 65 in special cases, and age 65 for men), old-age pension at age 66, and death grant. A free, comprehensive health service, including maternity and infant-welfare services, is available to persons unable to afford general practitioners' fees; persons earning under I£.7000 annually receive State assistance toward the cost of drugs and prescriptions, free hospital services, and specialist medical services, but must make a contribution of I£.24 a yr. to help pay for the services. All insured persons are entitled to State assistance toward the cost of prescriptions, which limits a family's expenses in this area to I£.6.50 per month. Persons suffering from long-term medical conditions may receive a free supply of medicines. There are special allowances for single mothers, single women age 58–66, prisoners' wives, and deserted wives under age 66, and a supplementary allowance for those with insufficient resources to meet their needs. Unemployment assistance is given to persons not entitled to receive unemployment benefits under the State social insurance program. *Practice:* 1982 reports indicated that 1 million persons were covered by the State social insurance program; 1983 reports indicate that the pension for a single mother was $63 a week (for herself and her child) and that she was not entitled to food stamps or eligible for rent subsidies. In a landmark 1982 ruling the Labour Court upheld the right of a woman journalist to work until age 65, setting a precedent for a future extension of the retirement age for women.

Contraception. *Policy:* Legalized (Nov. 1980) under the Family Planning Act, which requires all contraceptive agencies to be registered and contraceptives to be sold only by authorized pharmacists to married couples with a prescription; illegal sale is punishable by a $12,500 fine and/or up to 1 yr. imprisonment. Doctors and pharmacists may refuse to prescribe or sell contraceptives by invoking a "clause of conscience." *Practice:* Women age 15–44 in union using contraception (1981): 60%, of which traditional methods 76.7%, modern 23.3%. A 1981 survey reported that 50–80% of pharmacists were refusing to stock contraceptives (see HERSTORY and following article). Fa-

vored "traditional" methods of birth control are those acceptable to the Roman Catholic Church—the rhythm method and the mucous method (the latter a daily examination of the odor and color of vaginal discharge to indicate phase of menstrual cycle and fertility). **Abortion.** *Policy:* Illegal. In Apr. 1983 a proposed antiabortion amendment to the Constitution which proclaims "the equal right to life of the unborn" was passed in the National Parliament by 87 votes to 13 (with massive government abstentions); the amendment was passed by national referendum on Sept. 7, 1983 by 841,233 votes to 416,136, with 46% of the electorate not voting; the issue will now be contested in the courts (see following article). *Practice:* An Apr. 1983 report indicates that an est. 5000 Irish women obtain abortions in England annually. Feminists in the Republic of Ireland argue that termination of pregnancy is authorized there by the Roman Catholic Church under the double-effect principle of indirect killing, where the woman's life is directly at risk, and that such authorization and practice have not been subjected to legal scrutiny.

Illegitimacy. *Policy:* Defined as a child born either to a single woman or to a married woman whose husband is not the father. A child can be "legitimized" only if her/his natural parents marry (1931 Legitimacy Act). A single mother may sue the father for paternity maintenance; a woman who was married (to a man who was not the father) at the time of conception may sue the father only if she is separated from her husband (1930 Illegitimacy Child Affiliation Act). Out-of-wedlock children may inherit only from the mother, and have no legal recourse against their father for maintenance (1931 Legitimacy Act), whereas "legitimized" children may sue their parents if they have been inadequately provided for (1935 Succession Act). *Practice:* An est. 10% of children are born out of wedlock (1980). The lack of easily accessible divorce and abortion, plus the restricted availability of contraceptives, contribute to the rate. **Homosexuality.** *Policy:* Sodomy and "gross acts of indecency" between men are illegal (1861 Offenses Against the Person Act and 1885 Criminal Law Act) and punishable by penal labor; there are no laws specifically prohibiting same-sex relationships between women. *Practice:* No statistics obtainable. There is a strong social tabu against homosexuality and reports indicate that lesbian women and homosexual men are frequently harassed. In early 1983 the Norris Case challenged the 1861 Offenses Against the Person Act, contending it was invalid on grounds of invasion of privacy. The Supreme Court ruled against Norris, upholding the Act. Currently (1983) there are active civil-rights groups—2 for lesbian women and 2 for homosexual men—in Dublin.

Incest. *Policy:* Illegal; defined as carnal knowledge with or without consent between full-blood and half-blood relatives (1908 Punishment of Incest Act). *Practice:* No data obtainable (see Editor's Note on Northern Ireland). **Sexual Harassment.** *Policy:* No data obtainable. *Practice:* No statistics obtainable. Employed women report a high degree of sexual harassment. **Rape.** *Policy:* Sexual intercourse with a female of any age without her consent is illegal (1981 Criminal Law Rape Act). Marital rape is not recognized by law. *Practice:* In 1977, 222 sexual-offense cases were reported, 153 of which underwent prosecution; no data

obtainable on convictions. Irish feminists estimate that an extremely small % of rapes are ever reported. **Battery.** *Policy:* A battered wife can have her husband excluded from the family home if it is determined that her safety or her dependent child's welfare requires it (1976 Irish Act). *Practice:* No statistics obtainable; reports indicate that wife-beating is a grave and common problem, aggravated by a high rate of male alcoholism.

Prostitution. *Policy:* Soliciting is illegal, punishable by 2–6 months imprisonment. It is also illegal to procure the services of a person for the purpose of prostitution and to own or operate a brothel. *Practice:* No statistics obtainable. Feminist groups are working for enforcement that would penalize pimps and customers rather than women working as prostitutes. **Traditional/Cultural Practices:** No data obtainable. **Crisis Centers.** *Policy:* No data obtainable. *Practice:* Ireland's Women's Aid, a privately run organization, opened the first battered-women's shelter in the mid-1970's. A privately run rape-crisis center was opened in 1979.

See joint HERSTORY and MYTHOGRAPHY following Preface for Northern Ireland.

NORTHERN IRELAND

Editor's Note: The standard format for our Statistical Prefaces is not applicable to the northeastern 6 counties* which comprise Northern Ireland (an area of 14,121 sq. km./5452 sq. mi.), for a variety of reasons. The laws of the region are similar or identical to those of the United Kingdom, of which it is titularly a part—an issue which has been the cause of militant debate and recurrent warfare for approx. 800 yrs. The notable exception to this legal similarity is the issue of abortion—which is legal elsewhere in the United Kingdom (see BRITAIN) but illegal in Northern Ireland, except insofar as it may—rarely—be authorized only to save the woman's life. (In 1980, women launched the Northern Ireland Abortion Campaign in an effort to have the UK's 1967 Abortion Act extended to cover Northern Ireland.) In addition to jurisprudence being entangled with that of the UK, many statistics for Northern Ireland are included (without specification) under general UK statistics.

It is, however, possible to offer the following information. Northern Ireland's religions, for some time functioning as warring religio-politico-nationalist factions, include: Roman Catholicism 35%, Protestant (including Presbyterian) 29%, Church of Ireland 24%, Methodist (specific) 5%, and other. The races/ethnic groups, and the languages as well, are the same as for the Republic of Ireland. Under the Northern Ireland Act of 1974, the 6 counties are governed by 12 members (all male, as of 1983) in the British House of Commons, with a secretary of state accountable to the (British) Parliament. A Central Secretariat coordinates the departments of agriculture, education, etc., as well as interdepartmental groups, and serves as the liaison with the Northern Ireland office; local services are administered by 26 district councils. Major political parties with elected representatives include the Official Unionist Party

(Protestant), the Democratic Unionist Party (Protestant), the Social Democratic and Labour Party (Roman Catholic), the Alliance Party, and Provisional Sinn Fein (allied to the IRA—Irish Republican Army). Reports (1982) indicate that unemployment is high, and that approx. 1/3 of the total labor force earns less than the official minimum wage; women comprised 42% of the labor force (1982), 29% being fulltime and 13% part-time workers. They are concentrated in the expectable "female-intensive" job areas: service sectors and manufacturing/factory work. Married women reportedly receive a reduced insurance rate which can disqualify them from receiving such major social insurance benefits as unemployment, sickness, and invalid benefits.

As in other countries, the problems of rape, battery, educational discrimination, lack of day-care facilities, sexual harassment, incest, and homophobia** are tragically common, although few statistics are obtainable and the only reliable data are those emerging from the testimonies of Northern Irish women themselves, as individuals and as members of the women's movement. In the late 1970's, Northern Irish feminists led an international feminist campaign to protest the sentencing of 19-year-old Noreen Winchester to 7 yrs. imprisonment after she killed her father, who had been raping her since she was 11 yrs. old, and who had molested her younger siblings and heavily abused their mother. Battery is an especially severe problem, since the rate of male alcoholism is high; as of the late 1970's, Belfast police and hospital officials said they kept no records of the large numbers of raped and battered women who approached them for aid; at that time, assault of a wife by a husband in their home was not a crime unless the woman was murdered. The Northern Ireland Women's Rights Movement operates a center in Belfast which aids bat-

---

* Antrim, Armagh, Down, Fermanagh, Derry, and Tyrone.

** In 1981 the European Court ruled that the British government had violated the Council of Europe's Human Rights Treaty by a British law in Northern Ireland banning homosexuality; the suit had been filed by Irish homosexual-rights activists.

tered women, and Women's Aid networks (see BRITAIN) also provide refuges for the victims of wife-beating. Despite the painful and complex predicament of Irish women past and present (which is movingly and wittily delineated in the following article), the women of Northern Ireland, like their sisters in the Republic, have a heritage of valiant women—from ancient warrior queens through revolutionary leaders to contemporary women who have dared to organize on the grounds of insurrection—or of peace—often at the cost of their lives. The following joint HERSTORY and MYTHOGRAPHY of Northern Ireland and the Republic of Ireland indicate, albeit in outline form, the depth of women's suffering and bravery. Caught between Church and State, foreign patriarchal rule and domestic patriarchal control, different systems of economic inequality, and extremist religious factions engaging in what some consider a "holy war," the women of Ireland(s) have fought, buried their dead, borne their children, mourned, rebelled. Still, somehow, these women have managed to sing and even to laugh. Had *they* control of the State(s), the entire populace might learn better how to do both.

HERSTORY (of the Republic of Ireland and of Northern Ireland). During the Stone and Bronze Ages, Ireland was occupied by the Picts in the north and the Erainn in the south, peoples believed to have then inhabited all of the British Isles. Celtic tribes began invading Ireland around 400 B.C.E.; the Firbolgs, the Tuatha de Danann, and the Milesians invaded and settled there.

Ancient Hibernian pre-Celtic Ireland was a land rich in women poets, sages, leaders, and warriors (see MYTHOGRAPHY). There were many important Irish Celtic warrior-queens: Éire, leader of the Tuatha de Danaan (People of the Goddess Dana), who led her armies against the Milesians, and after whom Ireland is named; Scota (after whom Scotland is named), Éire's adversary, who led the Milesians; and Queen Maedb of Connaught, a historical figure on whom the Faerie Queen Mab is based. By the 3rd century B.C.E., these matrilineal

and goddess-worshipping Hibernian peoples had developed a sophisticated culture: they revered the environment (trees were held sacred), used not one but a variety of alphabets for different purposes, devised crop rotation, rejected capital punishment, and explored astronomy. The later Celtic peoples, whose religion was Druidism, still consulted Druid priestesses and sybils.

Dierdre was a mytho-historical princess said to have been instrumental in bringing Christianity to Ireland, although St. Patrick usually is credited with this act in the 5th century C.E. Celtic women were scholars and educators at the great Irish centers of learning (Tara, Kells, etc.); (St.) Bridget (5th–6th centuries C.E.) founded a monastery at Killdare and was known for her skill in the classics and in law. Liadan (7th century C.E.) and Lady Uallach (died 932) are among the great Irish poets. Norse invasions began in 795 C.E., and in the 12th century Henry II of England was given lordship over Ireland by Pope Adrian IV; the English conquest of Ireland began. With the consolidation of the Roman Catholic Church in Ireland, the "Old Religion" of goddess worship (see MYTHOGRAPHY) was driven underground, but persisted for centuries as the Craft of the Wicce (Wise), declared by the Church to be witchcraft and heresy. In 1324 the Bishop of Ossory accused Dame Alice Kyteler of witchery—the first Irish woman to be tried by the Church for witchcraft. Kyteler escaped, but one of her Coven, Petronilla de Meath, was caught, tortured, and burned—the first woman to be executed for witchcraft in the British Isles. Yet despite persecutions, the belief system persisted and was widespread up through the 18th century.

Irish women fought in the rebellions against the Tudors, James I, Charles I, and Cromwell, and were active in political and intellectual circles in the 19th and early 20th centuries. Women also suffered during the Great Potato Famine (1845–49) and in the mass emigration to the US which ensued. Lady Augusta Persse Gregory was a playwright, literary scholar, and a founder, manager, and director of the Irish National Theatre Society (1902) and the Abbey Theatre in Dublin, Republic of Ireland. Constance Gore-Booth Markievicz and her sister Eva Gore-Booth were both prominent in the nationalist struggle. Constance joined Maude Gonne's Daughters of Erin, a national anti-British organization, and published a newspaper for women; she organized the Women Workers' Union, and later was imprisoned as a leader in the 1916 Easter Rebellion. She was the first woman to be elected to the British House of Commons (in 1918) but she chose instead to sit in the Dáil Éireann (an independent assembly which proclaimed an independent Irish republic). She became the Republic of Ireland's Minister of Labour in 1922 when the Irish Free State was declared with Dominion status to Great Britain. Eva Gore-Booth was a prominent suffragist and a labor organizer who helped form the Women's Trade Union Council. A new constitution was drafted in 1937; the sovereign nation of Ireland, or Éire, within the British Commonwealth, was declared. After WW II, during which Éire remained neutral, Éire's goal of total independence from Britain and of a United Ireland led to its withdrawing from the Commonwealth, proclaiming the Republic of Ireland in 1949.

Women began a new wave of political activity in the 1960's, protesting poor economic conditions and the continuing religious-political conflict. In Dec. 1967 Brigid Bond sat-in in the mayor's chambers at Derry City, Northern Ireland, to protest poor housing, and in 1968 women helped organize the civil-rights march from Coalisland to Dungannon. In 1969 Bernadette Devlin, a Roman Catholic civil-rights leader of Northern Ireland, became the youngest member elected to the British Parliament (at age 22). That same year, factory women in Derry marched to protest a ban on marching imposed by the Minister of Foreign Affairs. In 1970 women on Fall Road in Belfast broke a curfew imposed by British troops by marching through the streets at night. Devlin received a 6-month prison sentence for having led an insurrection against the police, in the 1969 Battle of Bogside, following which the British Army had been brought onto

the streets for the first time. Women in Ardoyne picketed the courts, protesting the arrest of 6 IRA suspects as a "frame-up."

In the early 1970's the women's movement began in the Republic of Ireland; *Irish Women—Chains or Change* was published in 1971 (see following article). Women joined the IRA and other militant groups in the North; in 1971 Margaret O'Connor and Susan Loughran were the first women prisoners at Armagh, receiving 9- and 12-year sentences, respectively, for car bombings.

The Catholic-Protestant conflict affected women on all sides of the issue: in 1971 Martha Doherty was tarred and feathered for her engagement to a British soldier; Anne Ogilby was stoned to death by 3 Loyalist women for her relations with a married imprisoned Loyalist. In May 1971, 50 members of the Irish Women's Liberation Movement (IWLM) protested the ban on contraceptive distribution (see following article). By 1973 women civil-rights activists in Northern Ireland had become known as the "Petticoat Brigades."

During the early 1970's, feminists published *Banshee,* a magazine for women. Women IRA members faced stiff sentences and harsh treatment at Armagh prison. In 1973 Marian and Dolours Price went on a hunger strike at a London jail; in response, British officials re-enacted the notorious Cat and Mouse Act (previously used against British suffragettes), force-feeding the 2 sisters for 206 days. Both were released at the end of the decade due to frail physical and psychological health. The Wages for Housework movement began on the island; feminists protested such issues as rape, battery, abortion, and contraception restrictions; a refuge for battered women opened in Belfast. Bernadette Devlin lost her parliamentary seat in 1974.

The Northern Ireland Women's Rights Movement (NIWRM) began on International Women's Day, 1975, and wrote the Charter of Women's Rights. Gemma Hussey won election to the Republic of Ireland's Senate that year, and worked for a reform of rape laws.

In Aug. 1976 the Peace People's Movement began in Northern Ireland after the 3 children of Anne Maguire were killed during British-IRA fighting. In Sept., Oct., and Nov., peace rallies took place in Belfast, Dublin, and London, some attracting up to 25,000 Catholic and Protestant followers. In Dec. the Nobel Prize was awarded to the organizers of the movement, Betty Williams and Mairead Corrigan, aunt of the dead children. In Jan. 1977 the organizers differed publicly and the movement foundered. Many demonstrators had suffered attacks by hostile crowds and IRA supporters.

The war continued to produce tragedies in the late 1970's: Marie Drumm, acting president of the Sinn Fein, was shot dead by Loyalists; Emily Jones, a Belfast mother, was blinded when British soldiers fired rubber bullets at her; Agnes Jean Wallace was shot dead by provisional IRA members. Anne Maguire, the death of whose children had led to the founding of the Peace Movement, died of suicide in Jan. 1980. In Feb. of that year, women in Armagh jail began a "dirt strike" after being locked in for 23 days without sunlight; the women spread urine, excrement, and menstrual blood on the walls of their cells. In 1981 Pauline McLaughlin was released from Armagh, weighing 70 lbs., due to anorexia and the dirt strike. That Feb., Bernadette Devlin McAliskey and her husband were shot and critically injured by 3 Loyalist gunmen. The Northern Ireland Abortion Campaign (NIAC) waged a battle with the UK Parliament to have the 1967 Abortion Act extended to Northern Ireland.

In the early 1980's, the active women's groups in the Republic included the Irish Countrywomen's Organization, Women's Refuges (for battered women), Cherish (which provides emergency help for single mothers), 2 lesbian-rights groups, AIM (family-law-reform group), Irish Feminist Information, the Rape Crisis Centre, the National Assoc. of Widows, and the Campaign Against Sexual Exploitation.

MYTHOGRAPHY. Few peoples have as rich, preserved, and recorded a tradition of gynocratic myths, legends, and religio-philosophical beliefs as do the Irish. From the earliest known inhabitants (see HERSTORY) through the Tuatha de Danaan (People of the Goddess Dana), a strong goddess-worshipping culture prevailed. Sometimes called simply the Lady, the One, the Great Mother, or the Great Goddess, the female deity was also celebrated under the names of Dana and Tailtiu (related to Danu, Anu, Diana, Tana, Thama, Danae, and similar Great Goddess appellations in other Celtic regions), Oestre, Cerridwen (a Welsh-origin name), Fand, Morgan (or Morrigen or Morgana—"child of the sea"), Macha (goddess of horses), Dichtire (mother of the mythic hero king Cuchulain), Aiffe (a seeress-witch), Emir, (a personification of Aiffe and Cuchulain's lover), Moina, Éire, and Bride, Bridget, or Brigit. Bridget was a triple goddess (virgin/ mother/crone figure) who brought the power of healing, poetry, and fire. Her worship was so strong among the Irish that the Roman Catholic hierarchy finally ceased their attempt to dismiss her as a pagan figure and co-opted the name by canonizing an historical Bridget (see HERSTORY); to this day, the Irish make more devotions to St. Bridget than to any other figure in the Christian pantheon.

Irish folklore is a dense tapestry of faerie figures (such as the goddess faerie Niamh and the magic witch Scatbach, Queen of Darkness), legends, and spells which encoded political and religious records of reverence for the female.

IRELAND(S): Coping with the Womb and the Border
by Nell McCafferty

First the good news. Fifty-one percent of the total population of this island is female.
Now the bad news.

The island has been divided in two for the last eight hundred years, with six northern counties under the control of Britain and twenty-six counties under the control of the Irish government. This has led to intermittent and permanent hostility, with many outbreaks of quarrelsome peace.

And that's only among the women.

The men kill each other.

Ireland, in short, has two sets of laws—one for the North and one for the South. At the time of this writing, Northern Ireland is under the effective control of two women, Queen Elizabeth II and Prime Minister Margaret Thatcher of the Conservative Party of Great Britain. Under their dual regime, women in Northern Ireland can have equal pay, equal educational opportunity, contraception, divorce, abortion, and gay rights. Because Northern Ireland is the poor relation of the British Isles, they cannot in reality have jobs, may avail themselves of the other facilities only if they have escaped the rigid influence of both the conservative Roman Catholic and the Protestant churches, and can expect to be regularly killed, maimed, or imprisoned by any one of the many legal and extra-legal groups that constitute an effective armed patriarchy within that small area.

For all of that—and it is much, and dreadful—the cauldron of Northern Ireland has forged many women of fine temper. Northern Ireland has produced Bernadette Devlin McAliskey.

What of the South?

Divorce is constitutionally forbidden. Abortion is illegal. Homosexuality is punishable by penal labor. Contraception is officially available to married couples only, and then only if the doctors and pharmacists agree to prescribe and sell them. If their consciences forbid them from doing such things, tough luck. Children born outside marriage are of course considered in law to be illegitimate.

What are our female politicians doing about such things?

First the good news.

In the South of Ireland there are fourteen elected female politicians, of whom two hold government posts—as Minister for Education and Junior Minister for Women's Affairs, a newly created portfolio.

That is the end of the good news.

Now the bad news.

There are fourteen women versus over 200 men in the National Parliament; the women are opposed to each other across the spectrum of three different political parties, and not one of them has dared speak publicly in support of abortion, even in the case of pregnancy through rape or incest. Officially, all these women oppose abortion.

In Northern Ireland, no women have been elected to the national parliament. Before cries of "Sexism!" ignite the air, it must be pointed out that no men have been elected there either. That is because Northern Ireland has no national parliament, elected or otherwise. It was abolished in 1972 (its name was Stormont) when the British government, speaking from across the Irish Sea, decided that the people of Northern Ireland weren't fit to govern themselves. They fought too much and couldn't agree on anything, the British government said. There was absolutely no connection between the abolition of Stormont and the massacre of thirteen unarmed civil-rights demonstrators in the city of Derry three months beforehand. They were shot dead by the British Army in a day known throughout the world as Bloody Sunday.

The reader will have assumed by now that it is absolutely impossible to discuss feminism in Ireland without first referring to the more urgent political problems—which in turn means that feminism is relegated to the back seat. That has not necessarily been so. Like women all over the globe we have found ways round our difficulty; equally, like women all over the globe, including in Iran, South Africa, and Palestine, we have found that we cannot deny our history and it keeps coming back to haunt and divide us.

What the hell.

Since the women's movement was launched (in Dublin, in 1970), there has been profound, mainly personal, sometimes political, startling social change. Sometimes it has been great fun. We have managed to confront the absurd without ourselves becoming too absurd in the process. The situation of Irishwomen was ludicrous when the movement for women's liberation was first set up by a founding group of twelve women who were mostly journalists, mostly left-wing, and mostly Roman Catholic by birth and culture. The situation of the group was rather ludicrous too. Brendan Behan once said, reflecting on the over-all division of Ireland, that the first item on the agenda of any new political group was The Split. Which side, North or South, did the group favor, and what approach to which side did the group as a whole take. Thus—The Split.

Our founding group was not like that.

We decided not to split, not to take sides, and not even to take any notice of the division of the country. This was in 1970, mind you, in the midst of the latest outbreak of war. We decided to ignore it. We decided, indeed, to ignore Northern Ireland, which was just fifty miles up the road. We decided to concentrate on the South. Some people might say now that this in effect constituted a split of the first order, particularly since two of the founding members were born in Northern Ireland on either side of the cultural divide up there, and were now being asked to ignore their birthright.

However, it seemed to all of us at the time only right and proper to ignore divisions. The group had been founded because one of the women had read the newly published *Sisterhood Is Powerful* and we thought in the first flush of enthusiasm that sisterhood could overcome all obstacles.

It very nearly did.

Historians will have to take into account, of course, the fact that the obstacles were sitting targets, and it was comparatively easy for us to evoke justice on our side. In the South of Ireland, in 1970, for example, contraception was forbidden even for married couples, as were references to it in print. There was no equal pay. There was no official State assistance for the woman known as the unmarried mother. There was no unemployment assistance for the female school-leaver looking for her first job—though there was for her brother. Women were obliged to resign from the Civil Service on the day of marriage.

The only break we got was that a single woman was allowed to have one illegitimate child before being obliged to resign from the Civil Service, and the quota was raised to two illegitimate children in times of war. That is assuming, of course, that she survived public censure on the trip from the maternity ward to the government desk: in 1970, in some parishes, the names of women who became pregnant outside of marriage were announced from the pulpit by priests.

So we had a riotously joyful time rectifying those wrongs, especially given our trumpeting access to the pages of national newspapers, and the common sense of a public who were, as usual and as always, two steps ahead of the State and the ninety-eight-percent-majority Roman Catholic Church. Even then, in 1970, it was possible for three members of the founding group to stand before a cheering public meeting and describe their liabilities as perceived by Big Brother:

"I am a bastard," said one.

"I am a lesbian," said the second.

"I am a nun," said the third.

Boo to Church and State, said the audience.

The first real *frisson* occurred when the women's movement challenged the ban on birth control in the South. It was decided to take a train to Northern Ireland, buy contraceptives there, and import them across the border in defiance of Southern law. This action posed several problems, containing in a nutshell the problems of feminism, then as now, in an intimate and divided country like Ireland.

First, if contraception was available in Northern Ireland, should one advocate that the whole country would be better off, in feminist terms, under the colonial rule of Great Britain? Second, if national unity was more beneficial than colonial rule, should one admit that women's affairs were by definition of secondary importance? Third, if contraception was available in Northern Ireland because the majority population there was Protestant like that of Britain, should one therefore attack the domination of the Roman Catholic Church in the South? Fourth, if we did, would we get the famous belt of the bishop's crozier and never survive to tell the tale? Fifth, would we all lose our jobs or prospect of promotion in a country where the State bowed to the influence of the Church? Sixth, if we bought contraceptives publicly in Northern Ireland, would we be called upon by the media to give our opinion of the political state of affairs there, and would our movement therefore be plunged into the classical Split? Finally, and most important: in a country which can be crossed in a good car in no more than four hours, what would our mothers say? And whatever they said, would our fathers blame our mothers?

It was the fervent hope of those who embarked on that Pill Train that the Irish government would arrest us on our return, making us instant martyrs and obliterating all our sins. If you want to progress socially in colonized Ireland, we told ourselves, the first thing you have to do is go to jail. Look at Eamon De Valera. Look at Countess Markievicz, who came out of jail to become the first woman ever elected to the British Parliament of Westminster, the first woman Minister (of Labour) in an independent Irish Parliament, the first female commandant of the IRA . . . (and her Polish and aristocratic by marriage, at a time when neither Poles nor aristocrats were fashionable or popular).

It is a commentary on Irishwomen that we came off the Pill Train only thirteen years ago, walked into pharmacies in Northern Ireland, and demanded coils, loops, and pills AT ONCE. Most of us knew nothing of medical consultation beforehand, or size, or fittings. We were informed coolly of our ignorance by the pharmacists, and were obliged to settle for condoms, lubricating jellies—and aspirin. Yes, aspirin. We had worked out a plan.

On our return to Dublin we were met at the ticket barrier by customs officials, railway officials, and police officers. We refused to hand over our condoms. We tossed the loose aspirin, which looked remarkably like pills, to our sisters waiting beyond the barrier. We waved our creams aloft. We read aloud articles on birth control from forbidden British magazines. We burst through the barrier and marched to a police station where we declared, in the full glare of national and international television, that we were in illegal possession of birth-control devices and that we were consciously breaking the law. We challenged the authorities to come out and get us.

God love our wit.

They refused to come out. Two days later the Prime Minister declared coldly to his parliament that all contraceptives had been seized and the law had been upheld. His cohorts and opposition males were quick to agree. The matter was solved, by men, by ignoring it.

Among women in the movement, and feminists in the closet, the fall-out was vastly different. The Pill Train was the last cohesive, radical, officially sanctioned gesture of a united women's movement in Ireland. Women took seriously the issues raised by the Pill Train—nationalism, control of fertility, pluralism, and even capitalism (because contraception was available to the bourgeoisie, regardless of legalities, and what did that tell us about class politics?).

In the wake of the Pill Train, splits, resignations, and realignments followed in abundance. During the ensuing decade we stumbled about, looking for feminism, winning many reforms. We resolutely disregarded the historical fact and fate of Bernadette, who had been elected to the British Parliament, was a left-wing militant opposed to the British presence, had refused an abortion, had become an unmarried mother, and had lost her seat. Was that because of her socialism, her resistance to the British army, or the circumstances of the birth of her first child? Was it because of all three? Was it because she refused to take one step at a time and took on all causes at once? Did it matter to us in the South, because she worked, after all, in the North? Did we have anything in common with her anyway since she had never—ever—espoused the primary cause of feminism?

We refused to think about it, couldn't afford to think about it, because the country was coming down, North and South, with single mothers, battered wives, underpaid women, deserted wives, married women with no legal right to the family home or the husband's income. We concentrated, painstakingly, on moderate public reform, and underwent personal revolution.

And yet, like the death of Kennedy, the killing of Lennon, Irishpeople of whatever religious and political persuasion remember where they were and what they were doing on the morning that the news came through of the attempted assassination of Bernadette. That was in 1981. The wheel of history had just then turned a full swift circle. The hunger strikes had started in jails in Northern Ireland and women members of the IRA were smearing menstrual blood on the prison walls. Bernadette was at death's door. In the South, the government of the day and the opposition had agreed to support a referendum enshrining the absolute constitutional right to life of a fetus over that of a woman, regardless of the circumstances of the pregnancy.*

What was the feminist position at that awful turning of the decade, when feminism was once more confronted head-on with nationalism and control of fertility?

We split.

We wished Bernadette well, hoped she would live, and didn't want to know about the issues raised by the assassination attempt. The men convicted of trying to kill her were politically pro-British, culturally of the Protestant faith. What were feminists supposed to do about war? Were we supposed to take sides in the killing? Were we supposed to take sides at all? What were feminists supposed to do about abortion? Did that involve, literally, killing also? Would it be possible to avoid the issue of the border and the womb, and keep some fragile unity on the other issues?

What, indeed, about the other issues? It was time now, surely, having identified them *ad nauseam,* to identify the solution. Did that mean taking on capitalism?

And what, oh what, did men have to do with all this? It is difficult to keep honed the cutting edge of feminism in a closely knit community such as little Ireland represents,

---

* See Statistical Preface preceding this article.—Ed.

where the Prime Minister is practically on first-name terms with every single constituent, and you can trace blood kinship with hundreds of people within a small radius, and intimacy is the order of the day. It is impossible within Ireland to run away and start a whole new life after an argument. The alternative is a purist feminist ghetto. Membership in the European Economic Community has allowed some small winds of change to blow our way and shed light into the ghetto. The sight of sisters beyond these shores is a continual comfort.

Meanwhile, North and South, the outward political structure, as defined by the ballot box, has been severely destabilized. No parliament in Northern Ireland, but a part-time Assembly, elected in October 1982, to which Britain promises devolved powers if the members can agree on power-sharing. This has proved impossible.

The only parties which have agreed to attend the Assembly are those who support the link with Britain, and they have agreed that they will not share power with parties which seek to break the link with Britain. The latter, which refuse to attend the Assembly because of this, include the newly elected Provisional Sinn Fein, political arm of the IRA. And even if they did agree to attend, no one would share power with them—not those who do attend nor those others who refuse to attend. The British government, which would share power with Sinn Fein, is also officially at war with them.

This is a true story.

I am tempted to explain the destabilization of the South, which has had three general elections since June 1981, but I prefer to tantalize readers into doing their homework. Suffice it to say that besides the country going broke, the government and the opposition are united in a campaign to so amend the Constitution as to prohibit the introduction of abortion through appeals to it, which was done in the US; that they cannot agree on the wording of the amendment; that the government wording is reluctantly supported by the Protestant churches; that the opposition wording is thunderously supported by the Catholic Church; that many members of the government have defected to the (Catholic) opposition on the issue; that the country will suffer the religious reverberations for years to come; and that thank God we won't end up like those countries which slaughter the unborn. It is of course perfectly legal for our women to go yearly, by the thousands, over to England for such abortions. It used to be, in the words of an Irish proverb, that "all our wars were merry, and all our songs were sad." Consciousness in the last thirteen years, which has seen the simultaneous outbreak of war and feminism, has turned the problem somewhat on its head. Our war is sad, and our women are a lot merrier.

There is also, of course, the cloud of worldwide recession, which has cast a very heavy shadow on our open free-market economy. Must Irish feminism ponder the problem of worldwide capitalism?

If it is a problem.

That is for future discussion. In the meantime, in Ireland, we are still coping with the womb and the border. The Pope tried to solve both when he came to Ireland in 1979 and concentrated his speeches on women and the North. He spoke, of course, from south of the Border, condemning the IRA and advising women not to use the Pill. He was much loved and much ignored. Sure he has his own problems with Solidarity and communism.

And now for the final bit of good news.

Ireland has an official policy, supported by its women and men, of international neutrality. We absolutely refuse to fight with anyone beyond our territorial waters.

Suggested Further Reading
Evanson, Eileen. *Hidden Violence: A Study of Battered Women in Northern Ireland.* Belfast, Northern Ireland: Farset Cooperative Press, 1982.

Levine, June. *Sisters: The Personal History of an Irish Feminist.* Dublin: Ward River Press, 1982.

O'Brien, Edna. *The Country Girls.* Harmondsworth, England: Penguin, 1970.

Women in Modern Irish Society, Vol. 4, No. 1. Greystones, Co. Wicklow, Ireland: The Crane Bag, 1980.

Wynne, Andrew. *Abortion: The Irish Question.* Dublin: Ward River Press, 1982.

Nell McCafferty was born in March 1944 in Derry City, Northern Ireland. She was a civil-rights supporter there until 1970, when she came to Dublin to work as a journalist and help found the Irishwomen's Liberation Movement. She witnessed Bloody Sunday in Derry in 1972. She has published two books, *The Armagh Women* (about female members of the IRA on "dirty protest" for recognition as political prisoners, and "the relationship, if any, of feminists to them"), and *The Eyes of the Law* (about court trials in the Republic of Ireland).

ISRAEL
(State of Israel)

Located in southwest Asia, bordered* by Syria and Jordan to the east, the Gulf of Aqaba to the south, Egypt to the southwest, the Mediterranean Sea to the west, and Lebanon and Syria to the north. **Area:** 20,699 sq. km. (7,992 sq. mi.). **Population** (1980): 3,881,000, female 50%. **Capital:** Jerusalem.*

DEMOGRAPHY. Languages: Hebrew, Arabic (both official), Yiddish, Ladino (Jewish-Spanish), English. **Races or Ethnic Groups:** Majority Sephardic (Semitic) and minority Ashkenazic (European) Jews 83% total, Arab (including Bedouin, Circassian, other) 16%, Druze,** Samaritan, other. **Religions:** Judaism (Sephardic/Oriental rite and Ashkenazic/European rite) 83%, Islam (Sunni), Christianity (including Greek Orthodox and Greek Catholic or Melkite, Roman Catholic, Maronite, Chaldean Catholic, Syrian Catholic, Armenian Catholic, Episcopal, and other Protestant), Druze, Baha'i, Samaritan, other. **Education** (% enrolled in school, 1978–79): At primary level—of all Ashkenazic girls 98%, of all non-Ashkenazic girls 90%, of all Ashkenazic boys 98%, of all non-Ashkenazic boys 95%; at secondary level—of all Ashkenazic girls 72%, of all non-Ashkenazic girls 37%, of all Ashkenazic boys 58%, of all non-Ashkenazic boys 53%; higher education —in 1979 women were 45% of university degree-earners. Education is free and compulsory at primary level. There has been steady increase in the number of female Arab and Druze pupils. Still, the drop-out rate in elementary school is much higher in the Arab and Druze than in the Jewish sectors—and is many times greater for girls than for boys. As of 1978 the drop-out rate at elementary school level was 38% among Arabs and Druze

(80% of whom were female). The dropout rate for girls increases through the upper grades of elementary school and junior high school. Reasons include overcrowding and classroom shortage, parental objection to co-education, parental demand that girls help with housework and childcare, the need of low-income families for extra income gained by early employment, and cultural traditions that favor education for sons rather than daughters. In 1975 approx. 40% of the entire adult pop. in Israel had less than 8 yrs. of education. In 1978 the % of Jewish (both Ashkenazic and Sephardic) women with no education was 11.1% (men 5%); among Arabs, 36.9% of women have had no education (9.7% of men). **Literacy** (1977): Women 83%, men 93%; literacy rate for Arab pop. is considerably lower, but there are no statistics obtainable. (In 1982 there were 125 literacy centers in refugee camps in West Bank and Gaza.) **Birth Rate** (per 1000 pop., 1977–78): 25. **Death Rate** (per 1000 pop., 1977–78): 7. **Infant Mortality** (per 1000 live births, 1977): Female 14, male 16. **Life Expectancy** (1975–80): Female 73 yrs., male 71 yrs.

GOVERNMENT. Israel was established as a Republic in 1948. The elected 120-member unicameral Knesset (parliament) holds legislative power and elects a president (head of state). The president appoints a prime minister (head of government) who in turn appoints a cabinet. The Labour Party is the largest of over a dozen political and religious parties which often form coalitions within the Knesset. Israel has no constitution, but the Knesset enacts Foundation Laws which have the status of secular constitutional law. Separate religious courts of Christian, Druze, Jewish, and Moslem

---

* Israel's borders have been contested and altered repeatedly by both Israel and its adversaries through both hostilities and negotiation, making even a description of its physical location and capital city seem to be a geopolitical stand. The above border descriptions and capital designation are official ones from the Israeli Consulate in New York as of June 1983.

** The Druzes are an Arabic-speaking people with a distinct religious belief-system originating in the Fatamid branch of Islam.

communities have autonomous parallel authority with civil courts and maintain jurisdiction over most matters concerning marriage, divorce, family, and personal status, except in areas where secular law has primary jurisdiction (see **Marriage, Divorce,** and **Family); women** are not permitted to sit on Hebrew Rabbinical or Islamic Kadi courts. **Voting:** All citizens, including the Arab minority, have the right to vote; Arabs have been elected to the Knesset. **Women's Suffrage:** 1948, at formation of the State. **Equal Rights:** The 1951 Women's Equal Rights Law stipulates equal standing before the law regardless of sex, and that any provision of law which discriminates with regard to any legal act against women shall be of no effect; however, the 1951 law is not a Foundation Law (see GOVERNMENT) and can be superseded by other legislation. A proposed Foundation Law on Equality of Men and Women was under review by the Justice Ministry in Jan. 1983; this bill includes a clause which states that "relevant distinctions" would not constitute discrimination, but the law would provide a basis for testing existing discriminatory legislation (see following article). Women, classed with children, the mentally deficient, the insane, and criminals, are not permitted to testify in the Rabbinical Courts. **Women in Government:** 8 women are in the Knesset; Sarah Doron is the 1 woman cabinet member (1983). Golda Meir was prime minister from 1969–74. A women's party was formed in 1977. Various government bureaus and a Commission on the Status of Women were set up after International Women's Year in 1975.

ECONOMY. Currency: Shekel (May 1983: 45.3 = $1 US). **Gross National Product** (1980): $17.4 billion. **Per Capita Income** (1980): $4500. **Women's Wages as a Percentage of Men's** (1980): 78%. **Equal Pay Policy:** A 1964 Equal Pay Law (amended 1973) stipulates equal pay for equal or substantially equal work. **Production** (Agricultural/Industrial): Citrus and other fruits, vegetables, beef; processed food, cut diamonds, clothing and textiles, chemicals, metal products, transport and electrical equipment, plas-

tics; ¼ of all Israeli produce is sold in West Bank and Gaza.

Women as a Percentage of Labor Force (1980): 36%; **of agricultural force** 23.4% (41.7% of whom are unpaid family workers); **of industrial force**—no general statistics obtainable (of manufacturing 22%); **of military**—no general statistics obtainable; the 1959 Defense Service Law (Consolidated Version) makes military service compulsory for women age 18–26 (18–34 for reserves) unless they are married, pregnant, or receive conscientious or religious exemptions. In 1976–77 approx. 51.5% of women who were eligible for recruitment were accepted; a large % of women failed educational requirements which are reportedly more rigorous than those for men. Women are barred from combat roles. In 1980 women participated in 270 of 850 military categories, of which approx. 50% were clerical; typing and parachute folding are reserved for women. Women's basic training includes a course in cosmetics; the women's corps are called *chen*—an acronym which translates into "charm." Twelve thousand women serve in the 100,000-member Civil Guard. Approx. 8.5% (12,000) of Arab and Druze women are employed as paid labor—in agriculture, the services, and industry. An est. 70,000 Arab workers from West Bank and Gaza are employed in Israel, largely in construction and service sectors. The number of employed Arab women is low because unpaid (largely agricultural) labor is not factored into the work statistic, but also because for Arab and Druze women there is no employment close to home and no occupational training. The intervention of a "contractor" as a condition for the employment of Arab women is often a source of exploitation (also see PALESTINE). **(Employed) Women's Occupational Indicators:** Of managerial 9%, of sales 28%, of scientific and academic 34%, of services 56%, of clerical 57% (1979); of professional and technical 61% (1978). In 1978 women were 44% of all Civil Service employees (but only 19% of senior positions). An Equal Employment Opportunity Law was passed in 1981. The 1954 Employment of Women Law (amended 1972, 1973, 1974, and 1976) prohibits women from hazardous occupations and night employment, except in hospitals, managerial positions, State services, and newspaper offices, or where conditions are not "prejudicial to health" and a permit has been issued by the Minister of Labour and Social Welfare. Although women comprise nearly 50% of the Histadrut (umbrella organization of trade unions) membership, they are only 14% of the central committee and 8% of the executive council. **Unemployment** (1981): 5%, female 6.3%, male 4.3%.

GYNOGRAPHY. Marriage. *Policy:* Different religious courts of the various ethnic communities govern most matters regarding marriage (see GOVERNMENT and see following article).*** Secular law has primary jurisdiction on certain issues: female minimum marriage age is 17 unless a female has borne a child, is pregnant by her prospective husband, or is age 16 with special conditions justifying her marriage (1950 Marriage Age Law); polygyny is prohibited; a woman may keep her birth-name, add her husband's name to her birth-name, or adopt her husband's surname (1956 Names Law); if a man dies intestate, his widow is entitled to household goods, the family car, and 50% of his estate if she has had children by him, or 25% if he had children from another marriage (1965 Succession Law). Interfaith marriages are not performed by either Rabbinical or civil courts but, if performed abroad, are recognized in the civil courts (although not in the Rabbinical). *Practice:* Female mean age at marriage (1970–78): 23; women age 15–49 in union (1970–78): 66% (see following article). **Divorce.** *Policy:* Legal. Secular law grants divorce only by mutual consent (see following article) and makes provisions for secular litigation of property division and alimony. The different religious courts adjudicate divorce according to their respective codes. Under the 1972 Maintenance (Assurance of Payment) Law, a woman who has been awarded alimony or maintenance payments by a religious or secular court will receive payment from the National Insurance Institute if her husband refuses to pay. Under the 1973 Spouse (Property Relations) Law, if the couple does not agree otherwise, property acquired during marriage must be divided equally upon dissolution of the marriage. *Practice:* Divorces (per 1000 pop., 1979): 1.11 (see following article). Women's organizations that work in the field report that many women are sued by their husbands for waiver of alimony and relinquishment of communal property claims.

Family. *Policy:* Secular law has primary jurisdiction in terms of the following: a husband is responsible for the housing, clothing, and "daily needs" of a wife, who is entitled to live in a comparable standard as before marriage, and equal to that of her husband (1959 Family Law Amendment [Maintenance] Law). Both parents are guardians of their children and responsible for their educational and vocational needs (1962 Capacity and Guardianship Law). The 1954 Employment of Women Law (amended 1972, 1973, 1974, and 1976) provides protection from dismissal during pregnancy, except by permission of the Minister of Labour and Social Welfare for non-pregnancy-related reasons, provided the woman has been employed in the same place for at least 6 months prior to pregnancy; a 12-week paid maternity leave post-delivery; a daily 1-hour nursing break. Paternity leave is not provided. The 1968 National Insurance Law (Consolidated Version) provides a 1-time maternity grant to both employed women and homemakers, allowances for each child under age 18, or up to age 21 if child is in school or the army. A woman

*** Because of space limitations, it is impossible even to summarize the variations among these many religious courts and codes. There are considerable differences, for example, even between Ashkenazic and Sephardic approaches to the legal code of the Rabbinate, the orthodox Halacha as summarized in the *Shulkan Aruch,* a 17th-century code, and there are comparable variances among the numerous Eastern- and Western-rite Christian communities. In general, Islamic jurisprudence in Israel, as elsewhere, is based on concepts in the *Koran* and precepts in the Shari'a codes (see, for example, the Statistical Preface for EGYPT or Prefaces for other neighboring Islamic countries).

is entitled to severance pay if she resigns within 9 months of delivery to care for a baby, resigns because she marries a man who lives more than 40 km. away, or must care for a sick child or husband (1963 Severance Pay Law). The government subsidizes some day-care centers.

Practice: There are approx. 20,000 single-parent families in Israel, 80% of which are headed by women. Approx. 630 day-care centers, including 40–50 at workplaces, existed as of 1980; facilities are insufficient—approx. 1/5 of children of employed women received day-care services (1977); 90% of day-care centers are run by women's organizations. In some rural areas, family life is centered in the *kibbutzim* or the *moshav.* The *kibbutz* is a collective (living community) whose (usually Jewish-only) members equally share food, clothing, education, production, and work; adult members form the General Assembly, the authoritative body. In the *moshav,* non-Jewish members are admitted; there is private home ownership but land and supplies are communally shared; the family is the basic production unit. Approx. 3% of Israel's pop. lives in the *kibbutzim.* Although members are given equal rights to production and work, a traditional sexual division of labor exists (see following article). Another 4% of the pop. lives in the *moshav,* where a similar sexual division of labor persists. Many women of Asian and North African descent form a large part of the *moshav* community (Moslem and Christian Arabs, Druze, Bedouin).

Welfare. *Policy:* The 1968 National Insurance Law (Consolidated Version) provides maternity and family allowances (see **Family**), benefits to homemakers and survivors, and pensions. A homemaker receives invalid's benefits if her performance of household duties is curtailed by 50% or more; she can insure herself by paying a premium based on her husband's income and become eligible for pensions. Most employed women receive pensions at age 60, men at 65. A woman with minor children receives survivor's benefits; if she is under age 45 and does not have children, she receives a monthly benefit only if she cannot work. Widows who remarry lose their survivor's benefits but are entitled to a 1-time grant. Women who are widowed or divorced or whose husbands have deserted for 2 yrs. are insured for a small premium. Persons in common-law unions are entitled to the same benefits as legally married couples. Arab workers from the occupied territories are entitled to some of the social benefits that Israelis receive, but most are not entitled to large family bonuses or disability pensions. *Practice:* The conditions on both optional old-age insurance and disability benefits are discriminatory because of restrictions. Optional insurance is the most expensive; consequently, of hundreds of thousands of Israeli women who are housewives, only 3000 have insured themselves (1978). Many women are not covered for disability because while in general a 35% physiological disability is sufficient entitlement to claim benefits, a homemaker must show 50%. Homemakers have been covered by disability insurance since Apr. 1977; only 50 women were recognized as disabled during the first yr. of coverage.

Contraception. *Policy:* Legal, although official government policy is pro-natalist. *Practice:* No statistics obtainable; family planning is available from private sources. **Abortion.** *Policy:* Legal (since 1976) if continuance of the pregnancy would endanger the woman's life or physical or mental health, if the pregnancy resulted from incest, or if the woman was under age 17 or over age 40. Requests for abortions must be approved by a 3-member committee, and the woman must be warned of "physical risk and mental anguish" before approval is granted. *Practice:* No statistics obtainable. The number of illegal abortions performed in Israel is reportedly in the tens of thousands, and their high cost drives poor women to more dangerous methods. A women's campaign against the 1979 repeal of social-economic reasons as grounds for abortion—under which most abortions had been granted—received international support. **Illegitimacy.** *Policy:* Effective Apr. 1, 1977, single mothers who gave birth after Oct. 1, 1970, are entitled to inclusion in the assistance program for young couples, and to receive either low-rental apartments or mortgage benefits, according to the program's criteria. In the Rabbinical Courts, the only form of illegitimacy is that of a *mamzer*, a child born of incestuous or of adulterous union, which can include a child born to a remarried woman who has not been divorced by her first husband in a Rabbinical Court (see **Divorce** and also see following article). *Practice:* No data obtainable. **Homosexuality.** *Policy:* Male homosexual acts are punishable by 10 yrs. imprisonment; there is no specific legislation regarding lesbianism. *Practice:* Discrimination against lesbian women in employment, etc. has been reported. Some lesbian women's organizations exist. No further data obtainable.

Incest. *Policy:* Sexual intercourse with a minor is punishable by 5 yrs. imprisonment. Marriage with a near relative is prohibited by secular law (see **Illegitimacy**), overruling Mosaic law. *Practice:* No data obtainable. **Sexual Harassment.** *Policy:* No data obtainable. *Practice:* No data obtainable. **Rape.** *Policy:* Rape is punishable by 5–14 yrs. imprisonment; if a weapon (specifically a knife or gun) has been used to threaten the victim, the penalty is 20 yrs. Recent (1982) legislation permits conviction of a person accused of a sexual offense solely on the victim's testimony; previously, corroborative evidence had been required. As of 1978, a victim's prior sexual history was admissible evidence in court. *Practice:* An est. 7000–10,000 sexual assaults occurred in 1980; 2000 sexual assaults and 1500 rapes are reported each year. Approx. 10% of all rape victims report the crime. **Battery.** *Policy:* Under secular law, personal assault is punishable by 15 yrs. imprisonment, but legal complaints against a spouse can be deferred to a religious court, which has a limited authority of punishment. *Practice:* In 1978 approx. 60,000 cases of wife-beating were reported; only 2 men were imprisoned on this charge. Women do not receive protection during the filing process and thus rarely register complaints. If a Jewish woman leaves her home without Rabbinical Court permission she can be deemed a *moredet* (rebellious wife) and lose such rights as financial support and custody of children. The Rabbinical Court requires proof of serious injury; since a woman's testimony is not considered acceptable evidence in these courts, she must have police records and a hospital or physician's certificate as proof (see **Crisis Centers**). **Prostitution.** *Policy:* Illegal. Soliciting is punishable by 3 months imprisonment; living off the earnings of a prostitute is punishable by 5 yrs. imprisonment. *Practice:* No statistics obtainable; reportedly, ultra-orthodox religious men are among the steadiest customers of Israeli prostitutes, due in part to Talmudic rituals of marital celibacy during certain time periods.

Traditional/Cultural Practices. *Policy:* Child marriage is illegal (see **Marriage**), as are bride-kidnapping and "family honor" killings (of unmarried women who become pregnant). *Practice:* In some rural areas, child marriage (unregistered) as permitted in some Talmudic interpretation, and bride-kidnapping still occur. "Family honor" murders occur in the West Bank on an est. average of 1 per week; since 1980 an anonymous group of Arab, Christian, and Jewish women's-rights activists have been running an "underground railway" to rescue young women so endangered by their families and to smuggle them out of the country, either to obtain an abortion or to give birth, and then resettle into new lives. Orthodox Jewish practices include ritual "cleansing" which must be performed by a woman after menstruation, shaving of a married woman's hair so as not to attract in a lascivious fashion (strict orthodox Jewish women wear *sheitls* or wigs to cover the cropped hair), and kosher food rituals, including the keeping of separate kitchen and dining utensils for dairy products. A divorce granted by the Rabbinical Court requires that the woman be present to receive the decree, and that she back out of her former husband's presence. A childless widow, who may not remarry until her husband's brother has an opportunity to claim her, makes use of *halitza*, an ancient custom whereby the two exchange phrases and spit on the floor, and the woman kneels to take the shoe off the brother-in-law's foot—releasing him from his obligation (see following article). **Crisis Centers.** *Policy:* The government subsidizes some crisis centers. *Practice:* In 1983 there were 3 battered women's shelters (Jerusalem, Herzlia, and Haifa) and 4 rape-crisis centers

(Haifa, Jerusalem, Rehovath, and Tel Aviv) operated by women's groups.

HERSTORY. The State of Israel was proclaimed at Tel Aviv on May 14, 1948, after a decades-long Zionist campaign waged by many Jews around the world for a national homeland. Prior to 1948, Jewish Semitic inhabitants had occupied the region dating back to the 2nd millennium B.C.E. (see PALESTINE); Ashkenazic (European) Jews had repeatedly settled and resettled all over the world, enduring persecution, ghettoization, pogroms, and expulsions.

In ancient Palestine there were powerful queens and semi-legendary women tribal leaders until the shift from matriarchy to patriarchy, which took place, it is thought, during the hegemony of the Canaanites (see MYTHOGRAPHY). The Old Testament of the *Bible* gives clues to women's status in the time of the first Heberu (Hebrew) kingdom (c.1000 B.C.E.): the influence of Miriam over her brothers Moses and Aaron, the bond between Ruth and Naomi, the wisdom of Devorah and her high position as a judge, the political maneuverings of Bathsheba. In the Book of Esther, Queen Vashti, the first wife of Ahaseurus, refuses the king his wish to display her beauty before his male guests and is sent into exile for her rebellion; when he takes Esther as his new queen, she manages to gain from him a pledge of safety for her people, the Jews. The story of Susannah and the Elders is one of the most ancient reportings of sexual harassment on record, while that of Judith killing the enemy Holofernes in his war tent implies a high level of militance on the part of women in ancient Judea. That the Hebrews practiced polygyny is clear from the story of Abraham and his wives Sarah and the tragic Hagar. That early blood sacrifice of children was sometimes observed seems implied both in the story of Abraham and Isaac and in that of Jephthah's daughter, who, unlike Isaac, was not saved at the last moment.

In addition to the Biblical mytho-historical clues, it appears that a real Queen Jezebel built a temple to the goddess Asherah in Samaria (9th century B.C.E.), a real Queen Alexandra reigned in 142 B.C.E., and a real Queen Maacah did reign in Judah, and that it was under the influence of his possibly Sidonite queen (by legend, Sheba) that Solomon tried to re-introduce goddess worship in his kingdom.

Through the hundreds of generations that lived and died during the Diaspora (exile) of the Jews, we know about the women as citizens of the countries in which they lived, rather than by their religious or ethnic affiliation (but see AUSTRIA, POLAND, and EAST/WEST GERMANY). Before the establishment of modern Israel, Jewish women in Palestine lived in ways not that different from their Palestinian sisters (see PALESTINE).

The first modern wave of European immigration contained no formal policy of equality in its ideology. Women unsuccessfully fought for suffrage in 1886. In the second wave (1904–14), female equality was a basic tenet and many educated women were attracted to the rebellious, egalitarian state; 1911 saw the opening of a training settlement for girls, begun by Hannah Meisel. As early as 1914, a 3-day conference was held on women in agriculture.

World War I slowed the growing women's movement, but the third wave of immigrants following the war showed renewed interest in women's rights. The ratio of women to men in the *Yishuv* (pre-1948 Jewish community in Palestine) was 1:2 and as low as 1:5 in the first *kibbutz* (community settlement) and work brigades. In spite of opposition, some of the women formed female construction groups. The founding of the Jewish Federation of Labor in Palestine weakened the women's movement somewhat, as more women placed their allegiance and political energy there. The Working Women's Council was absorbed by the Histadrut labor organization and became a group defined by male leadership. (Na'amat is the current women's section of the Histadrut; as well as functioning as the largest "autonomous" women's organization.) The underground nationalist volunteer defense force, Haganah, was 20% women, although most did guard duty. Women also served in the elite Palmach battalion, although in separate sections from the men. During WW II, many women served in a military capacity, a change from WW I.

The Women's Corps was created soon after the establishment of the nation. Women had voted in internal/local governmental elections since 1925 and were granted suffrage in 1948, on the declaration of Statehood.

The long-standing anti-Semitic policies of many European countries intensified during WW II, when Hitler's Nazi forces mass-exterminated the bulk of the German Jewish population, as well as hundreds of thousands of Jews from other European countries, forcing millions to flee Europe for the US, South America, and the Middle East region (see EAST/WEST GERMANY). After WW II women's organizations turned to social welfare work, integrating refugees into society. Women worked to educate the new immigrants, to keep up standards of hygiene, and to provide day care. WIZO (Women's International Zionist Organization), founded in 1921, has as its primary focus social work and community action programs, but has become involved in educating about and lobbying for improvements in women's status. In 1969 Golda Meir became Israel's third (and first woman) prime minister (1969–74). From pre-Statehood to the present, women have been active in various ways (as non-combat military, medical personnel, *kibbutz* guards, etc.) in the hostilities surrounding Israel's existence, from full-scale wars (in 1948, 1956, 1967, 1973) to offensive raids and defensive maneuvers, in contested settlements, and in the recent (1982) Israeli invasion of Lebanon.

Israeli feminist activity began in the early 1970's. In 1971 a feminist group, Nilachem (We Shall Fight)—an acronym for "Women for a Renewed Society"—began in Haifa. The first national feminist conference was held in 1978. In 1982 a group formally registered as The Israeli Feminist Movement opened a center in Tel Aviv. Various feminist groups around the country meet regularly, some working on women's studies, some with the "underground railway" (see **Traditional/Cultural Practices**), others on legislative reforms; the groups convene annually. In May 1983 feminists organized a National Anti-Violence Against Women Week, focusing on abusive images of women in pornography and the general media. The Beer-Sheva Women's Health Collective issues critical studies of women's pre- and post-natal services and works to bring about change in these areas. A feminist publishing house in Tel Aviv is called "The Second Sex," and *Noga* is an Israeli feminist quarterly journal. Women also have been intensely active in the Israeli peace movement since the 1970's, and were highly visible in anti-government demonstrations following the invasion of Lebanon. Women Against Occupation, composed primarily of Jewish women but with the participation of some Palestinian women, was formed after the invasion. The group calls for Israel's withdrawal from Lebanon and the occupied territories and for self-determination for the Palestinians; it also educates about connections between militarism and patriarchy, and recently supported the strike by 26 Palestinian women political prisoners in Neveh-Tirtsa prison (see PALESTINE).

MYTHOGRAPHY. The Levant—the ancient area encompassing what is now Israel, Lebanon, and Syria—was one of the centers of matriarchal religion in the pre-historic world. Asherah, the Great Goddess of the Canaanites, later became Astarte—and the battle between a polytheistic matriarchal religious system and a monotheistic one devoted to the patriarchal Yaweh was protracted and fierce. Some of the Heberu (Hebrew) peoples worshipped Asherah so devotedly that the Yawhists burned and destroyed the sites of goddess worship in order to suppress the practice. Yet the theme went underground, surfacing in Jewish mystical theology. The *Kabbalah* describes the Sabbath Bride who personifies peace, joy, and holy pleasures and is ushered in at Friday sundown each week. Kabbalistic texts are filled with esoteric references to female godhead (the Shekinah), as are the Sepheroth and Qliphoth Mysteries. Apocrypha and folklore recount the myth of Lilith, Adam's first wife, who refused to lie beneath him and so was rejected in favor of the more passive Eve; Lilith was exiled and came to be viewed as demonic. Folk legends also refer to Sarah, Abraham's wife, as being "Laughing Sarah" who was both wiser and more powerful than he, and could perform magic as if she were a witch. Sarah, possibly a diminuative form of Asherah, was likely a fertility-goddess figure; her ability to bear a child in her old age seems only one indication.

The decline in women's secular status coincided with the crushing of goddess belief, so much so that in the Old Testament King Saul's great sin against his god is his visit to the Witch of Endor for prophecy and advice; the *Bible* personifies all evil as Jezebel—an historical figure (see HERSTORY) and also thought to be a variant of one of the many names of the Levantine goddess.

ISRAEL: Up the Down Escalator
by Shulamit Aloni*

I grew up in a society where there seemed to be no sexist discrimination. During the War of Liberation in 1948 I was in the battle for the Old City of Jerusalem—and men and women, girls and boys, fought side by side.

Throughout my childhood and adolescence we were too involved in rescuing the hapless remnants of the Holocaust to think about whether they were women or men. Six million people had died; the survivors were *people* to be helped return to life.

Again, during Israel's struggle for independence there was virtual total equality. Our goal was to build a nation, and differentiations and antagonisms had no place in the common struggle for survival. I did not realize then that this was a feature common to all revolutions. Upon the establishment of the State we took it for granted that we would have a modern, liberal state. Our Declaration of Independence stated unequivocally that there would be no discrimination—not of race, sex, religion, or any other kind. Unfortunately, this declaration was not translated into action.

The lack of a written constitution was largely responsible for this failure—and also the absence of a democratic tradition. During the first years of the State, thousands of people were brought in and "absorbed." The great majority of them came from Eastern Europe and the Middle East—areas not notable for egalitarian values. This opened the door to political pressures and the beginning of the power game, especially the pressure of the established organized clergy as part of the religious parties.

In 1951, Rachel Kagan, a leading figure in the Women's International Zionist Organization (WIZO), proposed the introduction of an equal-rights law for women, and the first obstacle came out openly and brutally. The religious sector of the population was against it, and the Labour Party needed the support of the religious bloc to maintain its Knesset [parliament] majority. The bill had certain positive elements: equal political rights for women, the right of women to own property, the recognition of joint parental guardianship. However, Article 5, introduced at the behest of the religious bloc, undermined the over-all purpose of the legislation. It left all aspects of personal status, and especially marriage and divorce, under the aegis of the religious courts, enacted according to the Halacha, the religious code of Judaism. Any possible loopholes were stopped up by the passage in 1953 of a special law specifically directing *all* Jews to the Rabbinical Court, which has sole jurisdiction over personal status. Ever since then, the status of women in

* This article is based on an interview done with Shulamit Aloni by Cynthia Bellon.

Israel has traveled two roads—parallel to be sure, but different—secular and religious. Israeli society and Israeli women have become "schizophrenic." On the one hand, women have every freedom—education, choice of work, lifestyle. On the other, every aspect of a woman's personal status is controlled by a code laid down some three thousand years ago for a nomadic desert tribe.

The inhibition becomes clearer when it is pointed out that most people have little association with the civil or criminal courts. After all, how many of us get involved in big commercial deals? And most of us, women and men both, are relatively law-abiding. But 99 percent of people have some association with the *religious* courts: they are born, they get married, sometimes they get divorced, and they die. (Why only 99 percent? Because 1 percent die outside Israel—and some still stay single.)

How then can we explain the image that Israel has projected ever since its establishment; of an ultra-modern, ultra-democratic society? Up to the mid-1970's we lived under this illusion because women seemed to move side by side with men; they were drafted into the armed services, they had the right to vote and be elected to all representative bodies. We had a woman in our first cabinet who later became prime minister. The *kibbutz*—that concept so unique to and so symbolic of Israel—fostered the illusion. Women and men equally drove tractors and did kitchen duty. But the myth which goes back to pioneering times has been proved hollow.

A woman can indeed become a member of the Knesset, a judge (and we accepted a woman justice of the Supreme Court—Miriam Ben Porath—before and with much less fanfare than did the United States on the appointment of Sandra Day O'Connor), but a woman in Israel cannot sit on the bench in a family court which adjudicates on marriage and divorce, although it is lower than the Supreme Court; she cannot be a witness because the Halacha does not acknowledge her right to sign a document.

Even our fabled woman prime minister had to go through the sieve of religious law. The latter does not permit a woman to become a judge, a mayor, or a head of state, so that when Golda Meir was appointed prime minister by the Labour Party, the religious members of the Knesset, whose support was essential for the continued existence of the coalition, were asked if they would accept her in this role. They came up with various reasons to justify their acceptance (because, after all, they wanted to remain in the government).

Most bizarre of all was the verdict given by certain learned rabbis. They pontificated that she had not been elected as such, but inspired by God—which made her acceptable, even as Deborah had been *(Judges LV)*. So we had a prime minister who was a prophetess—and Golda loved it (although later she had to pay heavily for this to the religious parties).

I think that the illusion of equality became dispelled because the development of the feminist movement throughout the world made us wake up and really look at ourselves. There was no real equality in the armed services: women conscripts not only did not fight in the front line, they were even debarred from training and maintenance; they were shunted into clerical work. In *kibbutzim* men and women reverted to their traditional roles: the men worked the fields and the women worked in the kitchens and laundries. In the commercial area, the principle of equal pay for equal work is easily sidestepped by changing the job description. In the free professions, the sky is not the limit, except for a few rare exceptions. Equal opportunity does not exist because a working mother has to adjust her working hours to school hours—and we have only half-day, not full-day, schools.

Furthermore, in practice, the religious coercion turns a woman into a second-class citizen. Because God has enjoined "Be fruitful and multiply" *(Genesis* I;28), the first duty of any woman in Judaism is regarded as getting married and having as many children as possible. Thus we have many wretched women with large families they are not capable of caring for, physically, materially, or emotionally. Observation of the Tenth Commandment makes the woman, quite simply, the chattel of a man: "Neither shalt thou covet thy neighbor's house nor thy neighbor's wife, nor his manservant, his maidservant, his ox, his ass, or any *thing* that is thy neighbor's" *(Deuteronomy* 20). She is the husband's property. She ceases to be the master of her own body. He masters her—and only he can divorce her.

The most painful results of this injunction are manifested in Israel's marriage law. Here are some examples:

—Sarah married twelve years ago as a young bride of twenty. The marriage did not go well and her husband deserted her and went overseas. She lost all trace of him. No one could find out where he was but no court of law could loosen the bond between her and the deserter whose wife she was and who was her husband. So long as he could not be found and no bill of divorcement was received from him, and so long as there were no witnesses that he was dead, his wife Sarah was not allowed to marry another man. This means that she is compelled to remain alone all her life. Neither can she become a common-law wife of another man since she is already a wife and an act of this kind would not be acceptable from "a member of the Jewish community." As for non-Jews, the law in Israel provides that after seven years of desertion the woman is free to marry.

—Esther is today a woman of thirty-five. She has two children. For the last eight years her husband has been in a mental home and is not even in a condition to divorce and release her. The doctors see no hope of any cure. This means that so long as her husband is alive, Esther is condemned to being alone. Although everyone pities her and the bitterness of her fate (including those rabbis to whom she has turned for an annulment of her marriage), no one can help her. She is her husband's property. And since a woman can buy her freedom only in two ways—with a divorce or by the death of her husband—all she can look forward to is her husband's death. That, and to proclaiming to all who might care to listen that the laws of Israel are worse than those of India, where the custom was to bury a living wife with her dead husband, though in that case the agony is at least not prolonged for years.

—Miriam has been separated from her husband for thirteen years. In the sentence given by the Rabbinical Court ten years ago, it was ruled that the two could not live together and that they could not be reconciled with each other. However, since the husband claims that he is ready to take his wife back at any time, it was decided that there is not sufficient reason to compel him to give her a divorce. And so long as he is not willing to give the divorce, Miriam remains his wife and cannot marry another man—and this despite the fact that the Rabbinical Court ruled that the two cannot live together.

A married man may enter into any number of adulterous relationships without being stigmatized. A woman may not—and any children resulting from such a union are stigmatized as *mamzerim* and excommunicated, which means that they are forbidden from marrying other Jews.

Another iniquitous anachronism is the prohibition of marriage between a man who is a "Cohen" (the priest clan of antiquity) and a divorced woman. This applies not only to bearers of the name Cohen but also to those of the officially accepted *derivatives*—such as Cagan, Kaplan, Adler, Rappaport, etc. Although this injunction places no stigma upon the children other than forbidding them to join the priesthood, no rabbi in Israel would perform such a marriage, and since no one other than a rabbi is a marriage officer, the couple would be forced to marry by civil contract outside Israel.

Then we have the Levirate Law, whereby a widow without children becomes the property of her husband's brother, unless he carries out *halitza*,** which would free her. Today, the least that the refusal of *halitza* entails is that the woman is not free to remarry. Blackmail is implicit in this state too, because the dead husband's brother is his heir, and can refuse *halitza* unless he receives a share of the widow's property, including pension and any other compensation she may receive.

And as for the single woman? Unmarried women do have rights. But traditional Jewish society does not respect those rights because these women have not carried out the injunction to "be fruitful and multiply."

Yet there *is* a feminist movement in Israel. We have two women's organizations which are large and could wield power—the Pioneer Women and WIZO—and a third, smaller one, the Mizrachi Women. All three are strong and have a long history, but unfortunately they are all equally conservative. They concentrate largely on philanthropic activities, and while I would not dismiss the importance of their work, they too have fallen victim to the power game and political party pressures. Consequently they will not risk tackling the real problems for fear of rocking the boat. In fact, they often act as an impediment to any initiatives toward improving the situation.

They have, however, made considerable progress in terms of day-care centers and other issues which do not clash with the establishment. But they actually opposed the modern feminist movement. When their insidious effect is demonstrated, they fall back on an excuse that is almost impossible to counter in Israel: more important priorities, e.g., the national security situation. It is an infallible excuse because *every* family in Israel has someone in the armed forces, and no Jewish mother or wife would do anything that might remotely harm her man.

As for the newer, less traditional feminist movement in Israel, I have sometimes felt those groups to be *too* strident—although their initial shock tactics certainly were useful. I have never been a member of any of them, but I did work with them from the beginning. Still . . . forming woman-only groups to fight for women's rights—it's not comparable to other units formed to support such rights as farmers, or blacks, or teachers, I don't think. Men are part of our lives, we have to live with them, don't we?

Today, despite my years in public service and my long struggle for women's rights, I feel that things are only really beginning. It's rather like running up a down escalator, though—a very unequal battle because the speed of the escalator keeps increasing!

The greatest enemy of any enlightened society and of freedom for all human beings— and especially women—is the organized clergy. Particularly when it holds political power. We have seen this happen brutally in Iran. In Israel, the clerical establishment is becoming stronger; violence isn't necessary because they achieve their ends by legislation.

Nevertheless, I am optimistic. Women in Israel have started becoming aware of their rights (or their lack of them). Our whole world has become smaller and more open. We know what is happening almost everywhere. The fight should be *for all human rights*— religious, ethnic, sexual . . . We have to stop grouping people; they aren't pickle bottles and you can't stick labels onto them. We still have a long way to go, as long as religion and politics continue hand in hand. I'm afraid that I don't see any separation in the near future, which means that women will continue to suffer.

But I do feel that if we continue working steadily, particularly at the populist level, we will gradually slow that escalator down, and eventually even make it match our pace— *and* our direction.

** See Statistical Preface preceding this article.—Ed.

Suggested Further Reading

Friedman, Ariela, Ruth Shrift, and Dafna X. Israeli. *The Double Bind—Women in Israel.* Tel Aviv: Hakibutz Hameuchad Publishing House, 1982.

Glazer, Myra, ed. *Burning Air and a Clear Mind: Contemporary Israeli Women Poets.* Akron: Ohio Univ. Press, 1981.

Hazelton, Lesley. *Israeli Women: The Reality Behind the Myth.* New York: Simon & Schuster, 1977.

The Interim Report of the Prime Minister's Commission on the Status of Women. Jerusalem: The Knesset, Dec. 1976 (in Hebrew only).

Lahav, P. "The Status of Women in Israel—Myth and Reality." *The American Journal of Comparative Law,* Vol. 24, 1974.

Stern, Geraldine. *Israeli Women Speak Out.* Philadelphia: Lippincott, 1979.

Shulamit (Adler) Aloni was born in Tel-Aviv. She grew together with the State, joining the Palmach (the pre-State Defense Force). She graduated from Teacher's Training College in 1948 and took her law degree at the Hebrew University of Jerusalem in 1956. She ran a radio program, "After Office Hours," where she became an unofficial ombudsman for average citizens' problems. In 1965 she was elected to the Knesset (Labour Party); in 1966 she was elected chair of the Israeli Council for Consumers' Rights; in 1973 she established the Citizens' Rights Movement and was elected to the Eighth Knesset. From June to Oct. 1974, she was Minister without Portfolio under Prime Minister Yitzhak Rabin. She was re-elected to the Ninth Knesset in 1977, and is a member of the Knesset Committee for Constitutional Law and Legislation. She also writes a weekly political column for the paper *Yediot Aharonot,* and another column for the weekly tabloid *La Isha* (Woman). Her books include *The Rights of the Child in Israel, The Arrangement: A State of Law as Against a State of Religion,* and *Women as Human Beings.* She is married and has three children.

ITALY
(Republic of Italy)

Southern European country bordered by Yugoslavia and the Adriatic Sea to the east, the Mediterranean Sea to the south, the Tyrrhenian Sea and France to the west, and Switzerland, Liechtenstein, and Austria to the north. **Area:** 301,225 sq. km. (116,304 sq. mi.). **Population** (1980): 57,182,000, female 51%.* **Capital:** Rome.

DEMOGRAPHY. Languages: Italian. **Races or Ethnic Groups:** Italian, Slovene, Albanian, French, Greek, Filipino. **Religions:** Roman Catholicism, Protestant, Judaism. **Education** (% enrolled in school, 1975): Age 6–11—of all girls 100%, of all boys 100%; age 12–17—of all girls 70%, of all boys 77%; higher education—in 1977–78 women comprised 41% of all students, 66.2% of teacher training, 84.6% of medical professions training. **Literacy** (1977): Women 93%, men 95%. **Birth Rate** (per 1000 pop., 1977–78): 12. **Death Rate** (per 1000 pop., 1977–78): 9. **Infant Mortality** (per 1000 live births, 1977): Female 20, male 25. **Life Expectancy** (1975–80): Female 76 yrs., male 70 yrs..

GOVERNMENT. Bicameral parliamentary system consisting of an appointed and elected 315-member Senate and an elected 630-member Chamber of Deputies. Parliament elects a president (head of state) who nominates a premier (head of government) and a cabinet. Government operates by coalition of the major political parties—Christian Democrats, Socialists, Social Democrats, Liberals, and Communists. The Constitution prohibits reorganization of the Fascist Party. **Women's Suffrage:** 1945. **Equal Rights:** Stipulated in the 1947 Constitution (Art. 3). **Women in Government:** 7% of Parliament (1983); 2 out of the 15-member Consiglio Superiore della Magistratura, the highest judicial body (1981). In Apr. 1983, Elda Pucci, a Christian Democrat and pediatrician, was elected mayor of Palermo, Sicily—the first woman mayor

of a major Italian city. ANDE (Associazone Nazionale Donne Elettrici— National Assoc. of Women Voters) is organizing toward more political activism for women.

ECONOMY. Currency: Italian Lire (May 1983: 1480. = $1 US). **Gross National Product** (1980): $369 billion. **Per Capita Income** (1980): $6480. **Women's Wages as a Percentage of Men's:** In agriculture 91.8% (1975); in industry 74% (1978). **Equal Pay Policy:** None as of 1983. The National Committee for Achieving the Principle of Equal Treatment and Opportunity for Women Workers was instituted in 1982 to propose legislative changes aimed at ending all forms of employment discrimination against women. **Production** (Agricultural/Industrial): Grapes, olives, citrus fruits, wheat; automobiles, textiles, shoes, machinery, chemicals. **Women as a Percentage of Labor Force** (1980): 29%; **of agricultural force** 36% (29% of whom are unpaid family workers); **of industrial force**—no general statistics obtainable (of manufacturing 31.6%); **of military**—no statistics obtainable; a 1981 court decision to exclude women from military service was in response to Diadora Bissani's attempt to enroll in the Naval Academy; despite a 1982 bill initiated by the Minister of Defense to accept women into military service on a voluntary basis, they are presently (1983) permitted only in civilian roles. **(Employed) Women's Occupational Indicators:** Of teachers in higher education 47.5%, in primary and secondary education 66% (1982); of service sector workers 33.7%, this last comprising 55.6% of all employed women (1977). **Unemployment** (Jan. 1981): 7.7%, female 12.9%, male 5%.

GYNOGRAPHY. Marriage. *Policy:* 1975 family legislation brought about major changes in the legal status of married women. Minimum marriage age is 16 for females, 18 for males. Marriage by

---

* Area and population statistics do not include Sardinia, Sicily, and small offshore islands.

religious and/or civil ceremony is now recognized and requires mutual consent. Spouses have equal rights and responsibilities for moral and material support, fidelity, and family maintenance, through either paid employment or housework. A woman may keep her birth-name only if she adds her husband's. Property is jointly owned except for that acquired before marriage. Dowries are illegal. *Practice:* Female mean age at marriage (1970–78): 23; women age 15–49 in union (1970–78): 64.2%. In 1965 the landmark case of Sicilian Franca Viola (who refused to marry a man who had kidnapped and raped her to force her into marriage) set a precedent; she pressed charges, and the rapist was sent to jail. Since then, fewer cases of kidnapping and forced marriage have occurred. Incidence of child marriage and dowry payment has diminished. **Divorce.** *Policy:* Legalized in 1970. Under 1975 family legislation a wife now receives 1/2 of the assets acquired during marriage. The court determines child custody. Separations are obtainable when continuation of marriage is intolerable to one or both parties. Whether consensual or contested, separations must always be court-approved. *Practice:* Divorces (per 1000 marriages, 1982): 0.2. More than half of all divorces are pronounced in northern Italy; in the south, *de facto* separation is more common. In 1971 more than 17,000 divorce decrees were pronounced; in 1972 when long-standing disputes were legalized, the number rose to 32,600 decrees; since 1973 the number of decrees has been falling.

Family. *Policy:* 1975 family legislation makes both parents equally responsible for educating and maintaining their children, "within their respective capacities." Childcare centers receive limited funding from the government and voluntary (largely Church) agencies. Employed women are entitled to paid maternity leave (at 80% of salary—paid by insurance) for 2 months before and 3 months after childbirth, 1-yr. voluntary leave after birth (at 30% of salary, insurance-paid), and cash benefits for maternity care paid by employer. Reinstatement is stipulated. *Practice:* Parental equality is not yet a reality; fathers still exercise au-

thority. In 1982, 2.4% of families were headed by a single parent. **Welfare.** *Policy:* A National Social Security System financed by mandatory contributions from members, employers, and government, offers disability benefits, maternity benefits (see **Family**), survivors' benefits to widows, widowers, and children of deceased parents, and retirement insurance to women over age 55 and men over 60 with a 15-yr. employment record. National Health Insurance Institute provides free health services including drugs, maternity care, and hospital treatment to all employees and pensioners who are members. *Practice:* No data obtainable.

Contraception. *Policy:* Legal. Before 1971 information on contraceptives was not legally available. Government supports some family-planning clinics and the concept of birth control, and the Italian Assoc. for Voluntary Sterilization has been conducting a campaign to encourage men to have vasectomies; nonetheless, Roman Catholic Church prohibitions against any but "natural" methods are still influential. *Practice:* Women under age 45 in union using contraception (1979): 78%; methods used (1979) withdrawal 46%, pill 18%, condom 17%, rhythm 11%, IUD 3%, diaphragm 3%, female sterilization 1%, other methods 1%; using inefficient methods 58%. **Abortion.** *Policy:* In 1978 Law 194 legalized abortion for women over age 18 during first trimester for "economic, medical, psychological, and social reasons," with or without a doctor's authorization, and thereafter only if a woman's health is endangered or in cases of fetal abnormality. The law permits hospital personnel to refuse to comply as "conscientious objectors." *Practice:* Abortions (per 1000 women age 15–44, 1980): 18.5. Within the first 6 months after legalization, 3009 abortions were performed in Sicily. Prior to 1978, abortion was punishable by 2–5 yrs. imprisonment; there were an est. 3 million illegal abortions annually, from which approx. 20,000 women died per yr. Abortion had been prevalent when contraceptives were unobtainable, and "unofficial abortion" is still common among poor women who are less informed both about birth control and about their rights in obtaining legal abortions; ironically, this means that they often pay for what they could obtain for free. Since legalization, the number of women hospitalized after abortions has decreased by 60%. A 1981 public referendum showed 70% in favor of keeping abortion legal. The functioning of the 1978 law is dependent on a system of family-planning clinics, and the law allocated government funds to establish them. The money often goes, however, to Roman Catholic clinics (owing to a powerful Church lobby) or is unaccounted for. Six months after abortion was legalized, 72% of all doctors claimed to be "conscientious objectors," refusing to perform the procedure. Hospital facilities cannot handle the high volume of requests for legal abortions (see HERSTORY).

Illegitimacy. *Policy:* The 1975 family law grants children born out of wedlock equal rights (including inheritance). Recognition of paternity can be through court action if it is not voluntary. *Practice:* No data obtainable. **Homosexuality.** *Policy:* A homosexual act is considered an "offense against the common sense of decency" in the Criminal Code, punishable by 3 months–3 yrs. imprisonment. *Practice:* No statistics obtainable. In 1980 a man who shot a lesbian woman was acquitted on the grounds that she inherently threatened him and that he acted in self-defense. Lesbian-support and civil-rights groups exist in Rome, Milan, and Florence. *CLI* (the Italian Lesbian Connection) is a bimonthly Roman newsletter. **Incest.** *Policy:* Illegal. A 1982 sexual offenses bill categorizes incest as a crime of sexual violence. Incest between adults is punishable by 1–5 yrs. imprisonment; sexual abuse of a minor by a relative or guardian is punished more severely. "If force is used" the penalty increases. *Practice:* No data obtainable. **Sexual Harassment.** *Policy:* None. *Practice:* No statistics obtainable. Italian feminists have begun organizing on the issue. **Rape.** *Policy:* Illegal. A new bill (1982) amended the Criminal Code to make sexual offenses, including rape, a crime against individuals and their freedom. Previously these were considered crimes against public morals. Rape is now punishable by 3–8 yrs. imprisonment; penalty increases if the victim is "physically or psychologi-

cally debilitated" and if the crime is committed by 2 or more people. The bill establishes automatic prosecution of sexual offenses, but married women or common-law wives must file a complaint. A rape victim's sexual history is not admissible evidence, but she must prove she resisted. *Practice:* No statistics obtainable. The 1982 law was brought about by feminist agitation, which began in 1977. Women's groups had organized in support of a southern Italian woman who was raped by 2 men, then rejected by her family and village for causing "disgrace," and subsequently raped again—this time by 20 men. **Battery.** *Policy:* Personal injury to the body or mind of another is punishable by 3 months–3 yrs. imprisonment. Penalty increases if injury is severe, life-threatening, if the victim is pregnant and miscarries, or if loss of one of the senses results. *Practice:* No statistics obtainable; government recognizes wife abuse as a common problem with victims deserving of State support (see **Crisis Centers**).

Prostitution. *Policy:* A 1958 law abolished brothels, previously regulated by the State. It is illegal to live off the earnings of a prostitute and punishable by 2–6 yrs. imprisonment; prostitutes are required to make periodic security and health checks with the authorities. Inducing a minor or a physically or psychologically unsound person into prostitution is punishable by a fine of 24,000–80,000 Lire and 1–5 yrs. imprisonment. *Practice:* No statistics obtainable; however, in 1976 it was est. that prostitution was the second largest Italian industry after Fiat. **Traditional/Cultural Practices.** *Policy:* See **Marriage;** no further data obtainable. *Practice:* Bride-kidnapping (see **Marriage**), arranged marriages, dowry, and jealousy "crime of honor" murders still persist in certain rural areas and in parts of southern Italy and the islands, where such residual customs as the public showing of stained bridal sheets (in proof of the bride's virginity) are sometimes still practiced. **Crisis Centers.** *Policy:* A 1975 bill provides for the establishment of government-financed centers offering psychological assistance to families and economic aid to battered wives and rape victims. *Practice:* Government centers are few and offer limited services;

feminists run a rape-crisis center in Rome. In 1982 the Dept. of Social Services for the province of Rome was planning a refuge for battered and sexually abused women.

HERSTORY. Italy's indigenous peoples are thought to have been Ligurians, Latins, and Sabines. In the 8th century B.C.E. Etruscans invaded the north, in turn being driven out by Celts and Samnites (4th century B.C.E.). Herodotus wrote that the Etruscans charted their lineage from the mother, and 19th-century archeological unearthings of Etruscan tombs revealed the special respect accorded women: only the women's names were on the tombs and the female bodies had been buried in sarcophagi, unlike the bodies of males. In the Umbrian frescoes women are depicted as being socially active and powerful. According to both Livy and Virgil, Lavinia was the hereditary ruler of Latium and continued reigning after her husband Aeneas' death. Livy further claimed that the 2 greatest families of (subsequent) Rome—the Julians and the Claudians—were named for Etruscan women leaders Julia and Claudia, and Tacitus confirmed that Claudia Quinta, an early Claudian, was held in semi-divine reverence. Rhea Silvia, an Etruscan princess, was thought to be the mother of Romulus, founder of Rome.

In the 5th century B.C.E., Romans established the Republic. Roman women were highly visible in social, political, and even athletic spheres; Juvenal (1st–2nd centuries C.E.), railed against "unfeminine" sportswomen. Martial (c. 40–c. 104 C.E.) implied that Roman women practiced birth control and (legal) abortion. Divorce was a woman's right as well as a man's. Aurelia (Julius Caesar's mother), Atia (Augustus' mother) and Livia (Augustus' wife and Empress) all wielded great political influence and outright power in their time, as did the leaders of the Vestal Virgins. Plotina went to the Parthian Wars (117 C.E.) with her husband, the Emperor Trajan. After the murder of Caracalla in 217, Julia Maesa placed her grandson Heliogabalus on the throne; during his reign she held the office of consul and sat in the Senate. The Roman reign of Julia Mammaea (222–

35) was a strongly democratic one, during which senatorial power increased.

There were notable women among the early Christians, not only those who were martyred, but also such activists as Thecla (one of the first missionary-apostles and a colleague of Paul) and Fabiola, Marcella, and Paula, who established the first hospitals in Rome. One reason for the spread of Christianity was its preaching of the equality of all—including women and slaves.

Amalasuntha (reigned 534–35) was an Ostrogothic queen in Italy, and daughter of Theodoric the Great. Her friendship with the Byzantine Empress Theodora caused her own people to overthrow, exile, and murder her; Justinian and Theodora (reigned 527–65) used her murder as an excuse for attacking and reclaiming Italy for the Byzantine Empire. From 853 to 855 Joan (see BRITAIN) was pope. Adelaide (931–999) was the empress consort of the first Holy Roman Emperor, Otto I; she ruled the Empire (991–94) as regent for her grandson, Otto III, and was a patron of religious houses. In the 11th century, Matilda, Countess of Tuscany (1046–1115), ruled Tuscany and parts of Emilia-Romagna and Umbria, controlling the most powerful feudal state in central Italy.

Trotula, a medical doctor and university lecturer at the University of Salerno (c. 1050), is considered the mother of gynecology. (St.) Clare of Assisi (1194–1253) was a great medieval contemplative and founded the order of the Poor Clares; (St.) Katherine of Siena (1347?–80), philosopher, mystic, and papal ambassador to Florence, is 1 of the only 2 women Doctors of the Roman Catholic Church.

Isabella d'Este (1474–1539) and her sister Beatrice (1475–97) were 2 of the most renowned intellects of the Italian Renaissance. Lucrezia Borgia (1480–1519), maligned as an (unproven) poisoner, was the daughter of Pope Alexander VI and married into both the Sforza and the d'Este dynasties; her court at Ferrara was famous for the artists and thinkers she attracted there. Vittoria Colonna (1492–1547), was a poet and friend of Michelangelo.

The Inquisition raging through Europe

was felt heavily in Italy, since the seat of the Church was there. Como, in particular, was zealous in its persecution of women accused of being witches; in 1485 the Inquisitor of Como burned 41 women, and the Dominican hierarchy in the Diocese of Como boasted that between the years 1500 and 1525, 1000 women in Como and the surrounding area had been tried for witchcraft, and 100 burned to death.

Catherine de Médici (1519–89), Lorenzo de Médici's daughter, became Queen of France by her marriage to Henry II (see FRANCE). She was regent for her son Charles IX in 1560 and exerted enormous power until her death.

In the 18th and early 19th centuries, women were active as organizers and armed participants during the Risorgimento (unification movement). Sara Nathan and Carlotta Benettini were dedicated nationalists, and Ismene Sormani Castelli raised money for the wounded and started the first day-care center in Milan. After unification, women continued fighting to improve women's status, protesting inequalities in the Civil Code. The Casati Law of 1859 mandated the training of women teachers for public schools, opening the way for legions of young women who became the foundation of Italy's education system. Teachers' associations to improve conditions and wages were formed, and teaching became the most accessible career for women. In 1866 Cristina di Belgiojoso, a feminist and patriot of the Risorgimento, wrote *Scritto sulla condizione delle donne* (Writings on the Condition of Women). Gualberta Beccari founded the journal *Donna,* in 1868, when she was age 18; her feminist ideas stimulated a national women's network. In the 1880's secondary-education opportunities for women increased: technical and preparatory schools were opened to women (1883) and then universities. The first Feminist Congress (1911) was held by Per la Donna; women pressed for divorce rights and nonreligious schools.

In 1919 the National Fascist Party emerged, led by Benito Mussolini; in 1922 he assumed power. During Mussolini's era, feminists were active in the resistance against the Fascists. After WW

II, feminists began the bulletin *Noi Donne;* it became the magazine of the Unione Donne Italiane (Union of Italian Women), an organization of women of the Communist and Socialist parties. By the 1970's the political parties had withdrawn their support and the magazine became independent and feminist-oriented.

In 1970 the Women's Liberation Movement (MLD) was founded in Rome, and wages for housework became an important early issue. Women in Torino formed a decision-making assembly that organized an occupation of a housing project in 1972. In Naples, cashiers in a department store held a "smile strike," refusing to be pleasing to customers until salaries and work conditions improved. In 1973 a collective began publishing *Effe,* a monthly magazine that covers a spectrum of feminist issues. Legislators Maria Eletta Martini and Nilde Jotti spearheaded reform of the family law in 1975. That year feminists opened clandestine abortion clinics in Florence, and 30,000 women marched in Rome for abortion rights. CISA (Italian Center for Sterilization and Abortion) was established by feminists of the MLD during 1975–76; smaller groups set up abortion services, and dispersed information on birth control.

In 1977, 10,000 women demonstrated in Rome against rape; this was the start of a large and visible national campaign which finally brought about a change in the rape law in 1982 (see **Rape).** Early in 1978, Catanian women on Sicily—who had been organizing since the early 1970's—staged a pro-abortion-rights march, during which many women were beaten, stoned, and arrested. The Catanian women establishing a feminist birth-control and abortion clinic as soon as the procedure was legalized in 1978. In 1979 they opened a feminist "consultory" or women's service center, with family welfare advice, some medical services, child-care, and skill-teaching aimed at support for poorer women in the slum areas of Catania.

In 1978 some women became involved with the Leftist terrorist Red Brigade, an urban guerrilla group dedicated to insurgency against the government. In Apr.

1979 Maria Rosa Dalla Costa, one of the theorists of the "wages for housework" groups, was arrested and charged with writing subversive material. That year, Radio Donna of Rome, the only women's radio station in Italy, was attacked and bombed by neo-Fascist extremists; all 5 staff women were hospitalized. Subsequently, a feminist bookstore and a women's center were bombed. The National Assoc. of Housewives was founded in 1981 by Teresita De Angelis; they proposed a national pension for homemakers over age 55. In 1982 Mafia widows in Sicily and Calabria formed an organization to oppose the culture of "male violence and female submissiveness." In Jan. 1983, 20 women successfully blockaded the entrance to the proposed missile base in Comiso, Sicily, as part of an international women's peace action. There are more than 60 feminist organizations throughout the country and feminist bookstores and libraries in the major cities (see following article).

MYTHOGRAPHY. The Italian peninsula appears to have been inhabited by goddess-worshipping peoples both before and after the Etruscan invasion (see HERSTORY). In the 1st century B.C.E., Strabo wrote of a Lucanian temple in southern Italy which had been founded 12 or 13 centuries earlier and dedicated to a goddess; he referred to this as the Heraion (Hera temple) of Silaris. After the colonization of Greece, and particularly after the intensification of Greek cultural influence in the 1st century B.C.E., the Greek pantheon of divinities was adopted and modified by the Romans; Hera became Juno, Artemis Diana, Aphrodite Venus, etc.—although these imported deities were mixed with such local ones as Lucia (later absorbed by the Roman Catholic Church as St. Lucia) in southern Italy, and the various *strega* (witch) traditions throughout the country. Diana of the Witches was revered as queen and founder of an indigenous affiliation of women allied by their spiritual powers and knowledge of medicinal herbs. In rural areas belief in the powers of the *strega* persists, and some midwives refer to themselves or are called by that title, which still inspires a mixture of fear and respect.

ITALY: A Mortified Thirst for Living
by Paola Zaccaria

Born a female child to countrypeople in a square white little farmhouse in a forgotten place (the school we walked to was three kilometers away) in the forgotten South of Italy only just starting to recover from the war; born female to a couple already the parents of three other daughters in a rural environment where the birth of a male is a highly blessed event because it means extra work force, while a daughter means only dowry and no income.

The awareness that for my mother I represented the fourth seal of disgrace: to be fertile yet unable to give birth to a son is almost the equivalent of being barren. The feeling of refusal I breathed ever since I was two or three, the brand of the inadequacy of my sex, these must have been the causes of my determination to escape as much as of my personal difficulties in accepting myself as a being with a body endowed with genitals—female in this case.

My mother, though the "owner" of the small estate, worked in the fields together with the female farm laborers who were, and still are today, subject to a system called the *caporalato*: a man, the "corporal," a kind of ruffian, enlists the required number of women and drives them to the fields—ten or more to a truck authorized to carry only six,

a truck usually the worse for wear. Frequent fatal road accidents arouse temporary
indignation, but once the sight of the women's corpses disappears from the TV screen, the
problem is again forgotten. The "corporal" takes a considerable rake-off from the money
his employer gives him to pay the women.

I grew up in an all-woman environment—mother, sisters, great-aunts, my friends'
mothers, and the female farm laborers who were often young and dear to us. They sang a
song in dialect which ran:

> I don't mind being a peasant
> I don't mind my heavy daily toil . . .
> I only care for my looks
> I only care for my love.

This reality is inescapable: nowadays women in the South still work as peasants—some in
their own fields, others at home, often a form of illegal and underpaid labor.

I cannot date the begining of my revolt. I feel as if it has always been there, boiling
inside me together with the perception that the lifeline came from education (two of my
sisters had to leave school at age eleven). I knew, though in an obscure way, that education meant knowledge—and that it would provide me with the means of escape.

Inevitably, I got involved in the politics of the New Left at the university. Then, at the
beginning of the 1970's, that great discovery: the budding flower of feminism. From the
North, Milan and Rome particularly, through Naples, the movement spread to the heel
of the Italian boot. After 1975, feminist issues had reached almost every small center,
where groups of women started consciousness-raising sessions and cried out for advisory
boards, nursery schools, contraceptive information.

The intellectual Southern woman felt it her duty to refuse to emigrate, unlike the
working classes and some of the male intellectuals who were forced to leave, especially in
the years 1951–71. Yet as time passes she has had to face reality: notwithstanding the
laws (family-planning guidance, equality of the sexes as regards working conditions—
1977; abortion—1978), "man is always man." Most women still practice illegal abortion
(to go to the local hospital would bring shame and dishonor upon the family, namely the
pater); most women do not go to the advisory boards for contraception (actually, these
are usually run by Catholic staff or people whose minds have been distorted by Catholic-
oriented education). And female workers are still greatly discriminated against.

The hemorrhage which dooms the South to intellectual anemia bleeds on: some women
feel they are being choked to death by this stifling land where the hand which moves over
everything and keeps things still is always black and hairy, connoting its sex as definitely
male. The procession of the daughters of the South moves North.

And yet, when an earthquake (as in November 1980) destroys hundreds of villages and
towns south of Naples, many of our mournful sisters come back. They actively participate in the first drive toward reconstruction. Together with their stricken sisters, organizing, promoting, rebuilding, refusing to delegate this task to the notorious inefficiency of
bureaucracy, that monster of governmental (dis)organization and corruption. And so
again, both the returned daughters and those who never left have to surrender. And now
the most restless are thinking of emigrating again for the second time—or have already
left. (I, luckily not from the earthquake area, remain—though I am often tempted to
escape. My work gives me the impression I can pass something on to other young women
and help to create a network of resident rebels.)

As for the women's movement at that national level, abortion is the issue over which
the main struggles have been fought. Contemporary Italian feminist history has also
marked the passage from consciousness-raising practices and the refusal of politics as

conceived in the world of patriarchy, to civil-rights-for-women battles. On the abortion issue, the MLD (Movement for the Liberation of Women), allied with the Radical Party, organizes women coming from the extra-parliamentary Left: they cry out for a referendum. In September 1973, the CISA (Italian Center for Sterilization and Abortion), linked to MLD, starts its activities. The center has repeatedly been investigated, and the medical personnel and their patients jailed even while some of the latter were still under anesthesia. In June 1975, the CRAC (Roman Committee for Abortion and Contraception) is founded by all the Roman feminist groups, together with women of the New Left. In the meantime, the political parties start the race to present bills regulating abortion—whereas women were asking for *decriminalization.* On April 3, 1976, the UDI (Union of Italian Women), a group founded mainly from the files of the PCI (Italian Communist Party), and one which had always fought for the emancipation of women but never sided with the feminist movement, joins in a demonstration of fifty thousand women protesting against the Christian-Democratic and the extreme-Right MSI (Italian Socialist Movement) parties, which had re-established penalization for abortion. From then on, the UDI begins to differentiate its positions from those of the PCI and moves toward feminist issues.[1]

Undoubtedly, the turning point for Italian feminism is the year 1977, when the movement realizes its failure in coming to terms with the status quo—i.e., how to influence institutions without being involved *in* the institutions. It reorganizes itself mainly in cultural centers. (In passing, it is worth remembering that 1977 also sees the last regurgitation of attempts at radical changes, which failed because of the omnivorous capacity of Italian politics to ingest morsels of liberalization and then spit them up munched and mangled in the form of a "law.") So it was in 1978 when Law 194 on abortion appears, a law which the patriarchy declares "the most advanced in Europe"— and which compels a woman to undergo a long miserable journey among doctors before finding one willing to provide her with a certificate enabling her to be hospitalized. And of course the doctors often assert themselves as "conscientious objectors" and refuse to operate. So the journey continues from hospital to hospital until the deadline (abortion must be performed within the first twelve weeks) is reached. But the arms of the male *partitocrazia* and of its main ally, the Catholic Church, still reach out for us. In 1981 they compel women to take sides with the law we have fought against because two further referendums demand the abrogation of even Law 194. One bill, supported by the Pope, asks for a drastic restriction of the law; the other, called by the Radical Party, wants its liberalization, although still allowing doctors the possibility of refusing to operate *and* insisting that abortion be practiced also in private clinics under payment—meaning that almost all the State hospitals would opt for conscientious objection and the private clinics would grow fat.

Meanwhile, feminist groups seem to have been folding all over the place; only here and there fragments remain of what once was a network of activity. The splits seem mostly due to two major tendencies: there is one faction which believes it's time to enter the institutions and fight by any means offered; the other faction refuses to accept any instruments offered by male-ordered society (including cooperation with the political parties).

On the theme of sexual violence, this painful division has reasserted itself. Groups organized around MLD, UDI, MFR (Roman Feminist Movement), and the feminist publications *Effe, Quotidiano Donna,* and *Noi Donne,*[2] have proposed a bill which a

---

[1.] For more detailed information, cf. *La Politica del femminismo (1973–76),* ed. B. Frabotta (Rome: Savelli, 1976), pp. 91–151.

[2.] Other feminist publications include the journals *Orsa minore, Donnawomanfemme,* and *Memoria;* there are also two publishing houses, Edizioni Delle Donne, and La Tartaruga, and the "Women's

smaller (more "intellectual" and, to some, more "radical") group opposes. Their opposition to the bill is based on the legislation's provision for the *procedibilità d'ufficio* (which means that though the raped woman may not want to face a trial, she would have to), and also on its provision for severe penalties for the rapist (i.e., the bill is in conflict with women's opposition to the penitentiary institution as a whole). In general, however, Italian women support such legislation, out of a justified rage fed by such shameful episodes as a judge's refusing to accept the request of the raped woman to be considered plaintiff because the woman was handicapped, and also refusing to accept her parents' complaint because "they were not really injured, since the girl was *already* disabled."

Again, and again, on the theme of rape, everything seems to slip out of our hands. Various political parties are working toward reviving a law which declares rape "an offense against public decency." But what the male establishment is not willing to admit is a *woman's* right to exist as a subject, not an object—her right to autonomy as a physical being. The word "auto-determination" used by Italian feminists in the battle for abortion and against rape is threatening to men because it means men can neither decide nor control the continuation of the species. They resort to the old defensive offenses: playing on the stereotypes of motherhood as sacred and abortion as assassination, and trying to divide women—though many Catholic women secretly voted pro-divorce and a consistent number of them voted pro-abortion; groups of women from the dissident Catholic movement publicly declared their decision to vote in favor of the civil laws.[3] Through careful use of the mass media, the Catholic "Movimento per la vita" ("Pro-life movement") celebrated the "culture of life" as opposed to the "culture of death." The Pope, in his countless speeches, goes on linking terrorism, the arms race, and abortion with the destruction of the institution of the family. Salvation can only come from the woman who maintains the sacredness of family through her subordination.

So: the Italian woman lives confused and disturbed by the male-*pater* figure of Pope John Paul II, the roaring voices of the bishops, and the ambiguous, mystifying words of the politicians. Every now and then she switches off all outside voices in an attempt to listen to her own interior voice. Sometimes she succeeds. In fact, if it is true that feminism as a formal movement sometimes seems no longer to exist in Italy, it is even more true that feminism is alive in the "common woman" who has recognized as her own the needs for freedom and sexual dignity—as well as the feminist yearning for inclusiveness, namely the capacity of embracing the *conjunction (. . . and . . . and . . . :* body *and* spirit *and* head *and* heart *and* rationality *and* emotionality *and . . .).* If the male mind seems usually to work along bipolar oppositions, the female brings into the world contradiction, dialectics, inclusiveness; she is not even afraid of dialectics inside the movement itself.

As for that inclusiveness, Italian feminist culture has been able to "conjugate" different influences, American and French above all. Especially over the last four or five years, French theory (in part linked to the psychoanalytical work of Jacques Lacan), has influenced our theoretical elaboration. Though positive at the beginning *(Speculum* by Luce Irigaray has represented the "moment of being" to many women), the French tendency

University," the Centro Culturale "Virginia Woolf," in Rome. In addition, the following major women's organizations and resource centers are focuses for Italian feminist activism: Centro Studi Storici Sul Movimento Di Liberazione Della Donna In Italia, in Milan; Centro Donna, in Venice; Udi—Centro Studi "Sibilla Àleramo," in Milan; Isis—Centro Di Documentazione Internazionale Sul Movimento Di Libera Zione Della Donna, in Rome; Centro Studi "Donnawomanfemme," in Rome; Biblioteca Delle Donne e Centro Documentazione Effe, in Rome; Centro Spazio Donna, in Naples; and Centro Studi Ricerche e Documentazione "Sara Heiz," in Naples.

[3.] For more detailed information on the Church politics *re* women, cf. No. 16, 1981, of *Donnawomanfemme* which bears the title of "In hoc signo . . . Ideologia e Politica della Chiesa."

toward dilution, its liking for *de*-arrangement, and its cult of the abstract has often produced in Italy work "without a tail." Yet the debate on the themes of mother-daughter relationships, separatism, and lesbianism has contributed to the individual growth and the rise of all women's consciousness.

The first National Meeting of Lesbian Women (December 1981), was preceded and followed by a wide debate in the feminist papers. I have my personal opinion about the delay with which Italian feminists engaged the issue. In this land of saints and madonnas but also of "hot sex," up to only a few decades ago in the North and often still today in the South, a woman may only go out with another woman; a girl can go for a walk or to the cinema or stay overnight only with female friends. Up to the age of fifteen I went around hand in hand with my girlfriends. I slept with them, and we often kissed. I was completely ignorant of the word "lesbianism"; otherwise most probably I would have lived through the experience without the sunny radiant innocence of my years. The passage to male-orientated sexuality put an end to a natural—although exacerbated by the social *mores*—preference.

What I want to stress is that in this land of virgin martyrs, it is very likely that lesbianism has been allowed or even, ironically, promulgated precisely by those who condemn it. Even within the movement, debate on separatism has smothered the real issue; feminists themselves often regard separatism as being more abstract ideology, since few women practice it in real life.

But despite all the attacks from without and confusion within what has been called the Italian feminist movement, I dare say that although my sisters are a bit short of breath on ideological issues, they are desperate for a deep breath of life. They have for so long felt in their throats a mortified thirst for the savor of living that once having begun to taste it, they are not willing to do without it. Stubbornly we go, I go, women go—through the world and against it—not only to rediscover ancient truths, but also to discover their own time "seen with their own eyes, spoken in their own language, thought with their own minds"[4]—and the visions they discover and invent are *womanist,* fresh, and true.

Suggested Further Reading

Collettivo "Vivere Lesbica," ed. "Atti del convegno di donne lesbiche" (Proceedings from the First Lesbian Conference). Dec. 26–28, 1981. *Differenze,* No. 12. Rome: Via Pompeo Magno 94, 1982.

Frabotta, Biancamaria, ed. *Femminismo e lotta di classe* (Feminism and Class Struggle). Rome: Savelli, 1975.

————. *La politica del femminismo 1973–1976* (The Politics of Feminism 1973–1976). Rome: Savelli, 1978.

Grasso, Laura. *Madre amore donna* (Mother/Love/Woman). Firenze: Guaraldi, 1977.

AA.VV.* *Lessico politico delle donne* (Political Lexicon of Women). Milan: Gulliver, 1979.

AA.VV.* *Luna e l'altro: rappresentazione e autorappresentazione del femminile* (The One and the Other: Images and Self-Images of the Feminine). Supplement to *Nuova Donnawomanfemme,* No. 16, Rome, 1981.

Paola Zaccaria was born thirty-three years ago in the South of Italy (Monopoli). While active in a small feminist group in her town, she graduated in foreign languages at the University of Bari, where she now teaches English literature and language. She lives with her husband (who works in the field of ecological energy and "with whom the relation-

---

4. In the words of Biancamaria Frabotta, poet and essayist.

* AA.VV. is the Italian formula to quote volumes which collect articles by several authors.—Ed.

ship is continuously under discussion"), and with her four-year-old son, Daniele—with whom she is "shamelessly continuously in love." She has written articles on applied linguistics, James Joyce, Christina Rossetti, Tillie Olsen, Katherine Mansfield, and Karen Blixen, and a book on Virginia Woolf: *Trama e Ordito di una Scrittura* (The Web of Writing), and she has translated poetry.

An archipelago in the Pacific Ocean, separated from the eastern coasts of the USSR, North Korea, South Korea, and China by the Sea of Japan; the 4 main islands are Honshu, Hokkaido, Kyushu, and Shikoku. **Area:** 371,857 sq. km. (143,574 sq. mi.). **Population** (1980): 116,850,000, female 50.7%. **Capital:** Tokyo.

DEMOGRAPHY. Languages: Japanese. **Races or Ethnic Groups:** Japanese 99.4%, Korean 0.5%, Ainu, Buraku. **Religions:** Shinto and Buddhism are practiced syncretically by the majority, Christianity 0.8%. **Education** (% enrolled in school, 1975): Age 6–11—of all girls 100%, of all boys 100%; age 12–17—of all girls 95%, of all boys 95%; higher education—in 1980 women were 22% of college and university students, 88.1% of jr. college students; in 1978, 13.2% of post-graduate, 1.2% of engineering, 13.9% of medical students. Adult-education classes are attended by 2.5 million women (in clerical skills, health, consumer protection, women's history, and hobbies). **Literacy** (1977): Women 97%, men 99%. **Birth Rate** (per 1000 pop., 1977–78): 15. **Death Rate** (per 1000 pop., 1977–78): 6. **Infant Mortality** (per 1000 live births, 1977): Female 7, male 9. **Life Expectancy** (1979): Female 78.9 yrs., male 73.4 yrs; average life expectancy for a *hibakusha* (direct or generational atomic bomb radiation victim) is 66 yrs.

GOVERNMENT. Emperor Hirohito is symbolic head of state. Legislative power is held by an elected bicameral Diet (parliament), consisting of a 511-member House of Representatives, and a 252-member House of Councillors. Executive power is held by a 20-member cabinet appointed and headed by the prime minister. Forty-seven prefectures and 4 municipalities administer local affairs through elected assemblies and local councils. Major political parties include the ruling Liberal Democratic Party, Japan Socialist Party, Komei Party, Democratic Socialist Party, and Japan Communist Party. **Women's Suffrage:** After a 60-yr. campaign, full voting rights were won in 1945. **Equal Rights:** The 1947 Constitution (Art. 14.17) states, "All people are equal under the law and there shall be no discrimination in political, economic or social relations because of . . . sex. . . ." **Women in Government:** Women were 1.8% of the House of Representatives, 7.2% of the House of Councillors (1983), and 1.3% of local and prefectural governments (1979). The first woman cabinet minister was appointed as Minister of Health and Welfare in 1960; only 1 other woman (early 1960's) has ever held a cabinet position; 54.8% of national Advisory Councils to the government had no women members (1979).

ECONOMY. Currency: Yen (May 1983: 235. = $1 US). **Gross National Product** (1980): $1152.9 billion. **Per Capita Income** (1980): $9890. **Women's Wages as a Percentage of Men's:** 53% (1983); in metals industries 53.8%, in textiles 43.1%, in cottage industries 45% (1979). **Equal Pay Policy:** The 1947 Labor Standards Act states, "The employer shall not discriminate against women concerning wages by reason of the worker being female." No laws specifically prohibit discrimination in hiring, training, promotions, conditions, or benefits. Prior to 1976, it was common for firms to have separate salary scales for men and women; after a court ruled this illegal, corporations downgraded the titles of women's jobs without changing the tasks. In 1978, 91% of companies had jobs which were closed to women, 73% had different starting salaries for women, 52% did not promote women, 77% had different retirement systems, and only 19.4% offered equal training. In effect, there is no enforceable policy, since there is such extensive sex-segregation in employment. The Ministry of Labor's plan to propose an Equal Opportunity bill has met strong opposition from business (1984). **Production** (Agricultural/Industrial): Rice, vegetables, fruit, meat, natural silk; fishing, machinery and equipment, steel, textiles, autos, chemicals, electrical and electronic equipment.

Women as a Percentage of Labor Force (1981): 38.7% (80.7% of the unpaid labor force); **of agricultural force** 47.6% (16.5% of paid, and 81.1% of unpaid force); **of industrial force** 36%; **of military**—no statistics obtainable; women are not admitted to the Defense Academy but play a limited noncombat role in the military. **(Employed) Women's Occupational Indicators:** Of clerical workers 52.3%, of service workers 54.4% (1981); 23.6% of women in the labor force are unpaid family workers (1981); of managerial 0.3%, of judges 2.6%, of lawyers 3.3%, of professors and asst. professors—in 4-yr. colleges 9.9%, in junior colleges 58.3% (1977–81); 20% of all employed women are in part-time jobs. The New Economic Social 7-yr. Plan for Achievement of Full Employment specifies preferential employment to household heads, most of whom are male. In 1980 there were still 6 Civil Service job categories closed to women. Women are concentrated in smaller enterprises and in industries with low product value (women are 10% of steel, machinery, and tools workers, but 50–90% of rubber and textile workers, 1979). Women clerical workers are given special etiquette booklets to help them become ideal *shokuba-no-hana* (office flowers); instructions include offering to work overtime, smiling continuously, and not refusing to date a prospective marriage partner suggested by the boss. Higher education often becomes a liability for women seeking employment, because university graduates are considered over-qualified for "women's" jobs; 78% of companies did not hire female university graduates (1978), and between 1970–80 employment of female university graduates dropped by 22%. It is illegal to have different retirement ages, but 99.7% of companies retire men at 55 yrs. or older, and 55% retire women at 40–55 yrs.; regarding women, some companies have a "30 and out" rule. Women forced to "retire" may be rehired immediately as part-time workers at the lowest possible salary grade (that of a starting middle-school graduate), with a loss in pensionable income and fringe benefits. "Protective" provisions (Labor Standards Act) prohibit women from working between 10 P.M. and 5 A.M., more than 2 hours per day and 6 hours per week overtime, in "heavy" work, or in "dangerous jobs" (in mines). Women are also allowed paid monthly menstrual leave. In 1978 a report by the Labor Standards Law Research Committee to the Labor Minister stirred controversy by suggesting the removal of "protective" provisions in the law. The consensus was that factory workers must remain ensured of protection against increased exploitation, but that equal employment legislation must be drafted to prohibit sex-discrimination. Only 25% of female employees are unionized; they rarely hold union offices, and unions are reluctant to back women in cases of sex-discrimination. **Unemployment** (1981): 2.2%, female 2.19%, male 2.3%. Women in marginal "temporary" or "contract" positions are frequently fired during recessions, while most men are hired/protected by a system which ensures lifetime employment. The unemployment rate for *hibakusha* (see DEMOGRAPHY) is triple the national average.

GYNOGRAPHY. Marriage. *Policy:* According to the Constitution (Art. 24), "Marriage shall be based only on the mutual consent of both sexes and maintained through mutual cooperation with the equal rights of the husband and wife as its basis." The legal age for marriage is 16 for females and 18 for males; minors must have the consent of 1 parent. The couple can take either the husband's or the wife's surname. Marriage partners are jointly responsible for household expenses and debts and have the right to acquire and retain individual property. Spouses inherit ½ of each other's property if there are children. Common-law marriages are recognized, but the husband and wife do not have the same surname, their children are considered "illegitimate," and they do not have mutual rights to succession of property. A woman cannot remarry for 6 months after the end of a previous marriage (to guarantee knowledge of paternity). *Practice:* Female mean age at marriage (1977): 25; women age 15–49 in union (1970–78): 51.9%; approx. 40% of marriages were arranged (1982), sometimes by corporate employers; 10% of women never marry. Because of the attitude that regards marriage and the home as a woman's primary occupation, the 45% of married women who were in the labor force in 1977 work predominantly in part-time jobs.

Divorce. *Policy:* Divorce by mutual consent was legalized in 1898; property settlements, child custody and support, and alimony are agreed upon, or either spouse can apply to Family Court within 2 yrs. If consent is lacking, the case goes to conciliation in the family court system; a court determination is made if no agreement is reached, and this decision can be appealed to the Supreme Court for a final judgment. Contested divorces are awarded on grounds of adultery, malicious desertion, if a spouse is not known to be dead or alive for 3 yrs., severe mental disease, or "some other grave reason which makes it difficult to continue the marriage." *Practice:* Divorces (per 1000 pop., 1979): 1.17; 90% of divorces are by mutual consent, and 9% through the conciliation process. Women initiated 55% of divorces (1978), and wife battery was cited as the second most frequent reason (1977). In 1979 only 50.7% of wives received financial settlements, and in 55% of these cases the amount was below 1 million Yen. Mothers gained custody of children in 48% of mutual-consent divorces (1979); average monthly child-support awarded by the courts was only Y. 33,000 (1978).

Family. *Policy:* Lineal relatives by blood, and siblings, are legally responsible for mutual support (Civil Code, Art. 877). Abandonment of a dependent family member is punishable by a maximum 1-yr. imprisonment, or 3 months–7 yrs. if death results (Penal Code, Arts. 217–19). Pregnant employed women are entitled to 6-weeks pre- and 6-weeks post-delivery leave, paid at 60% of insured wage by social insurance; they may not be fired during, or 1 month following, leave. Local governments provide limited childcare facilities. *Practice:* For centuries the 3-generation Confucian family was the model; the first-born male was (after the father) legal head and exercised control over joint property and family members. After 1946 the legal support for this sys-

tem was withdrawn and there has been an increase in nuclear families. Elderly parents often still live with their eldest son; sometimes a daughter is expected not to marry so that she can care for her parents. The 1979 Liberal Democratic Party plan, "Outline of Measures Related to Fulfillment of the Family Basis," signals a return to the family as the unit responsible for providing social welfare services to its members. Care for the elderly, disabled, sick, and young devolves primarily upon the shoulders of women. Women over age 15 average 26.3 hours per week on work in the home, while men average only 1.5 hours (1976). The average maternity leave was 36.6 days pre- and 48.3 days post-delivery; 24% of mothers claimed hourly (unpaid) leave for baby care (1978); 39% of pregnant employed women were "retired" from their jobs (1976). Female agricultural workers rarely receive maternity leave. Only 1.7% of companies had childcare facilities (1978). In 1979, 20,000 nursery schools enrolled 1.9 million children, but 1 million remained on waiting lists; 3000 day-care centers enrolled 90,000 school-aged children in 110 cities. Childcare fees are increasing. **Welfare.** *Policy:* Company health-insurance plans cover almost 100% of employees' and 70% of dependents' health-care costs. Since 1961 National Health Insurance has been available to all citizens and covers 70% of medical costs. Programs include workers' compensation, unemployment insurance, and "livelihood assistance." Company pension plans are based on income and length of employment. The National Pension Plan can be joined on a voluntary basis, and government Welfare Pensions are provided to those over age 70, widows with children, and the disabled, if they are not covered by any other plan. *Hibakusha* (after official designation as such) receive a special cash allowance and free medical care. *Practice:* 12.2 people per 1000 pop. received welfare (1979); women age 20–40 received 84.7% of men's welfare allowances (1980). Since women generally receive lower wages or are not employed, they receive inadequate or no unemployment benefits and pensions. In 1983, 56% of older women receive pensions, but only 20% could live adequately on the sum. A widow receives 50% of her husband's pension. The cash allowance for *hibakusha* is $80 monthly, so small an amount that some of these atomic radiation sufferers have turned to crime as a means of survival.

Contraception. *Policy:* The Ministry of Health considers the pill "potentially dangerous" and prohibits its use (1983). The IUD was approved in 1974. Midwives are permitted to administer barrier-method contraceptives. The government supports family planning for other than demographic reasons (e.g., human rights). *Practice:* Women age 15–49 in union using contraception (1970–80): 67%; 81% of couples using birth control rely on condoms, and 1.1% of women use diaphragms (1983). Contraceptives are difficult to obtain, and distribution of diaphragms is very limited. **Abortion.** *Policy:* Legal in cases of certain hereditary diseases, when pregnancy is the result of rape, or endangers the woman for health or economic reasons. If the woman is married, her husband must give consent (1948 Eugenic Protection Law). In 1976 the time limit for abortions was changed from 28 to 24 weeks. Other abortions are illegal and punishable by a maximum 1 yr. imprisonment for the woman, and 3 months–7 yrs. imprisonment for the practitioner (Penal Code, Art. 212). *Practice:* Abortions (per 1000 known pregnancies): 274 (reported, 1980), 547 (actual est., 1975); abortions (per 1000 women age 15–44): 22.5 (reported, 1980), 84.2, (actual est., 1975). Liberal interpretation of the law almost made abortion available upon request. In 1972 and 1974, legislation to limit abortion access by removing the "economic" provision was introduced unsuccessfully. In 1982 restrictive legislation was re-introduced, and a coalition of feminists and family-planning groups held pro-choice demonstrations in protest. **Illegitimacy.** *Policy:* A child conceived during marriage or born 200 days after the marriage begins, or 300 days after divorce or death of the husband, is considered to be the "legitimate" child of the husband. A husband can deny paternity for up to 1 yr. after he learns of the birth (Civil Code, Art. 772). Out-of-wedlock children have equal rights with "legitimate" children,

except that they receive 1/2 share of inheritance (Civil Code, Arts. 900–4). *Practice:* No data obtainable. **Homosexuality.** *Policy:* Legal. *Practice:* In 1975, 12 women formed the first openly lesbian group in contemporary Japan and published a magazine, *Wonderful Women.* Two other groups, Mainichi Daiku and Hikari Guruma, merged in 1979 to form the Lesbian Feminist Center in Tokyo. A Lesbian Feminist Alliance was founded in Kansai (1979).

Incest. *Policy:* No data obtainable. *Practice:* No data obtainable. **Sexual Harassment.** *Policy:* Physical sexual harassment is illegal under the Penal Code (Art. 176) heading "Indecent Liberty" and is punishable by 6 months–7 yrs. imprisonment. *Practice:* No statistics obtainable. Women are beginning to combat sexual harassment in public places, especially on city trains, by making citizens' arrests. **Rape.** *Policy:* Illegal. "Sexual relations with a female person by use of force or intimidation without her consent" is punishable by 2 yrs.–life imprisonment, or 3 yrs.–life imprisonment if it causes "serious injury" or death; sexual intercourse with a woman who is physically or mentally incapable of resisting or with a female under age 13 is also considered rape. A woman is required to resist until resistance becomes dangerous or useless, but not to the limit of her capacity, to prove nonconsent. Marital rape is not recognized. Rape is prosecuted only upon complaint (Penal Code, Arts. 177–81.) *Practice:* Arrests for rape (1976): 2970. Self-defense classes and therapy groups for rape victims exist, and the Tokyo Lesbian Feminist Center has shown an anti-violence-against-women slide show in more than 80 local forums. **Battery.** *Policy:* None. *Practice:* No statistics obtainable (see **Divorce**, and **Crisis Centers**).

Prostitution. *Policy:* Illegal for both prostitute and client, but only the prostitute is punishable under the Prostitution Prevention Law. It is illegal to solicit in public, to advertise, to use physical, economic, or family pressure to force a woman into prostitution, to procure clients, to provide a place for a prostitute to work, or to live off the gains from prostitution. *Practice:* No general statistics obtainable. Prostitution is a huge industry. Youth prostitution and the importation of women from other Asian countries are on the rise. Japanese men have made group "sex tours" to South Korea, Taiwan, the Philippines, and Indonesia a billion-dollar industry. The Asian Women's Assoc., founded in 1977, is focusing on the effects of Japanese sex tourism on the status of women in other Asian nations. Co-ordinated campaigns by women in Japan, the Philippines, and Korea forced Prime Minister Suzuki to curtail sex tourism to some extent (1981). **Traditional/Cultural Practices:** No data obtainable. **Crisis Centers.** *Policy:* The Women's Counseling Center was opened in 1977 by the Tokyo Metropolitan Government in response to women's demands. It can house 30 battered women and their children. *Practice:* In its first year the shelter housed only 919 out of 6000 women who sought refuge. A Kyoto welfare organization opened the Yamanouchi Home for Mothers and Children to shelter women beaten by alcoholic and violent husbands (1981).

HERSTORY. The Ainu were one of the earliest peoples to migrate from the Asian continent to Japan in prehistoric times; this indigenous group lives today in Hokkaido. The first recorded ruler of Japan was Himiko, the Queen of Wa (4th century C.E.). She united 30 warring tribal and clan territories, sent emissaries to the Chinese court, and was succeeded by her 13-yr.-old female relative, Toyo. Some scholars believe that Queen Himiko was mythologized as Amaterasu, the Sun Goddess. The Yamato clan settled in the Kyoto area in the late 5th century. A succession of 6 empresses ruled for 2 centuries, beginning with Empress Suiko (598). Society was influenced by Tang Dynasty China in the 6th–8th centuries; government became more centralized, Buddhism was introduced, and the arts developed. After the reign of Empress Koken, who remained single, the Taika Reforms barred women from succession to the throne (8th century).

Following the Heian period (794–1185 C.E.), there was an emergence of female literary genius. Lady Murasaki Shikibu (970–1040) wrote *The Tale of Genji,* one of the world's first novels, and Sei-Shonagon (10th century) wrote *The Pillow Book.* In the Kamakura period (1185–1333) women maintained property rights, but lost them with the rise of feudalism and Samurai values. Women of Samurai families were given physical and weapons training, and were expected to be as loyal to family and *daimyo* (lords) as their brothers. In the early 17th century, the priestess Okuni developed ceremonial dance forms into Kabuki, with women playing both male and female roles. During the Tokugawa Shogunate (1603-1854), the government prohibited women's Kabuki. In 1630 an all-male form of Kabuki, Wakushu, was introduced. The enforcement of Confucian values entailed a progressive decline in women's status.

Feudalism was abolished in 1871, and education for women was introduced in 1872, although it was intended to produce *ryosai kembo* (good wives and mothers). Tokyo Women's Normal School was established to train primary-school teachers in 1876. The Emperor authorized a constitution and a parliamentary form of government in 1889, but the 1889 Peace Preservation Law prohibited female participation in any political groups. The Meiji Code upheld the traditional family: parental consent was required for marriage, and adultery by women was made a crime; women did gain divorce rights (but husbands kept custody of children) and limited property rights (but husbands remained managers).

The Girls' High School Ordinance (1899) opened the way for public middle schools for girls. In 1900 a private Women's Medical College was started and other women's colleges opened in 1901. Though Tokyo and Kyoto universities denied entrance to women, a few were admitted to imperial universities in 1913. (By WW II, 30,000 men but only 40 women were attending imperial universities.) Education improved job opportunities for some women, but the majority of employed women were nonliterate rural women engaged in virtually forced labor in the textile industry. Kishida Toshiko (1863–1901) campaigned for women's rights, especially suffrage.

Many educated women gained prominence in the literary field. Contemporary feminist activism evolved from literary circles in the early 20th century. In 1911 Raicho Hiratsuka formed Seitoscha (Blue Stockings Society), which published the journal Seito, a forum for feminist issues ranging from marriage to suffrage. Seito was often censored and banned by the government and ceased publication in 1916. Kimura Komako catalyzed the first suffrage meeting and organization (1917). Yosano Akiko, a poet and radical feminist, and Raicho Hiratsuka, a socialist feminist, engaged in public debate over the issue of government-funded welfare and maternity benefits. Raicho Hiratsuka and Fusae Ichikawa formed the Assoc. of New Women (1919) to work for equal rights, women's labor unions, and repeal of repressive legislation. In 1921 the Peace Preservation Law was repealed. Margaret Sanger was prevented from lecturing on birth control by Japanese police (1922), but Shidzue Ishimoto carried on a birth-control campaign which generated public debate. Fusae Ichikawa met with US women's rights leaders, including Carrie Chapman Catt and Alice Paul, while studying in the US, and she formed the Women's Suffrage Alliance (1924) upon her return to Japan. Women's suffrage campaigns in the 1920's failed, though universal manhood suffrage was instituted in 1925. A group of feminist anarchists, including Takamure Itsue, Kanno Suga, Ito Noe, Kaneka Fumiko, and Yaki Akiko, were imprisoned for their deviation from conservative norms. Yaki Akiko edited 2 radical women's magazines, Women and Art and Women's Front.

With the rise of militarism and totalitarianism, feminist activities were suppressed, and women were drafted into the war effort. In 1932 the Third National Women's Suffrage Conference denounced the rise of fascism, but by 1937 such opposition was considered treason and the Fourth Suffrage Conference was the last. The government formed the Greater Japanese Women's Assoc., with emphasis on patriotic goals. Women were encouraged to marry young and were awarded for having many sons. Former members of the Women's Suffrage League formed the Motherhood Protection League (1934) and worked to pass the Motherhood Protection Law (1937), which gave assistance to mothers with young children.

In WW II, women and children comprised the majority of victims in the devastation of Hiroshima and Nagasaki by atomic bombs dropped by the United States in 1945. More than 70,000 persons were burned alive in a less-than-2-mile radius; in the following months the number of people who were exposed to thermal and radioactive rays rose to 140,000; in 1983, almost 40 years after the bombings, there are 370,000 persons in Japan still suffering and dying from the effects. The hibakusha (atomic bomb victims) are largely female, and suffer from myriad diseases resulting from radiation; they endure a high incidence of miscarriage and birth-defect offspring, and they and their children suffer from leukemia and other cancers, decalcification, retardation, tumor growth, cataracts, etc., and die early and painful deaths. Disfigured hibakusha women were abandoned by their husbands in the thousands, and are often ostracized (see Unemployment and Welfare). Since WW II, Japanese women have been extremely active in national and international peace movements; the Mushroom Club, a national organization of mothers and their affected children—atomic holocaust survivors or generational victims—was formed after WW II and still exists.

In 1946 Fusae Ichikawa influenced Gen. MacArthur's promotion of women's suffrage. She was criticized later for cooperation with the occupation government but nonetheless founded the Women's Suffrage Center (1946) and served in the Diet; she was re-elected (1980) with more votes than any other candidate.

In the early 1970's, the feminist movement re-emerged. In 1972 Enoki Misako led Chupiren (Pink Panthers), which held militant feminist demonstrations against violent husbands and in support of abortion rights, legalization of the pill, and equal hiring. The group had 4000 members (1977) but disbanded when Misako made an unsuccessful bid for election to the Diet. Many active feminist organizations have been founded, including Agora (Forum, 1964), the International Women's Year Action Group (1975), Feminist (1977), the Women's Studies Assoc. of Japan (1979), and International Feminists of Japan (1978). In 1975 almost 25% of women over age 20 belonged to at least 1 women's organization; the National Council of the Federation of Regional Women's Clubs had over 6 million members. Junko Tabei, member of an all-woman Japanese expedition, became the first woman to scale Mt. Everest, on May 16, 1975. In 1977 the government proposed a Plan for Women, but since no women had participated in its formation, 48 nongovernmental women's organizations held a (1980) conference and put forth their own proposals. Since 1978 feminists in the Group to Frame an Employment Equality Law have been lobbying for legislative action, and the first case against discrimination in promotion was brought to court in 1978. The Group also held a hunger strike (1981). Women's Liberation Communication Networks formed in Osaka and Kyoto in 1979. In 1981 a group of women refused to load rice at the port of Uotsu in protest of soaring prices; the act touched off national riots.

MYTHOGRAPHY. Izanami is believed to be the creatrix of all the world's rivers, mountains, and plants, of 33 gods, and of Japan itself. She is the mother of Amaterasu, the goddess of the sun and ancestor of the Japanese people, founder of the imperial line (see HERSTORY). The most sacred temple in Japan is her shrine at Ise, built in 260 C.E. The goddess Ukemochi was the source of plenty, especially food and silk, and the male moon god was banished from the heavens by his sister Amaterasu, for killing her. Kwannon is a version of the Chinese goddess of mercy, Guan Yin, and is still honored today. There also is a legendary figure, Yakami, who slew a sea serpent to which young women had been sacrificed. In early Japanese religious ritual, *mikos* (priestesses) played an extensive and powerful part both in worship and politics. Fuji, the goddess of fire, was worshipped by the Ainu; her sacred place is volcanic Mt. Fuji.

JAPAN: The Sun and the Shadow
By Keiko Higuchi
(Translated by Akiko Tomii)

Ms. K. was a sixth-grade teacher in Odawara. She anticipated that this might be her last year of teaching, and she was especially determined that her students would finish school both mentally and physically strong. Putting up a huge map of Japan, she said to the students, "Let's run the equivalent of the distance to Kyushu [about a thousand kilometers] during this year, every one of us!" At first the children were eager to run every day. But as time passed they became tired and began to lose interest. Undaunted, the fifty-year-old former physical education major inspired her students to persevere, she herself daily running at the head of the class. She worked hard to encourage and praise them, even calling the race a "marathon." In that year every one of her students succeeded in running the thousand kilometers and through this "marathon" learned the great joy of achieving a difficult goal.

One of the students, a little girl, wrote about her experience of the "whole class marathon." Her composition was published in a collection of schoolchildren's works and included as a student's composition in the most widely used reader for Japanese sixth-graders. When Ms. K. heard the news she was overjoyed. Her colleagues showered her with congratulations; even the local newspapers reported the event.

When she got a sample copy of the textbook, she proudly and eagerly began reading her student's essay. But as she read, her joy turned into deep disappointment. She had been obliterated: a young male teacher was leading the class marathon. "This is not me," she thought to herself. "Even if I insisted, no one would believe that this composition is about what I have accomplished in my class." Did the textbook editors believe that difficult marathon training would be better conducted by a man teacher? With such questions in mind she retired from teaching, her profession for thirty years, and was elected a member of the municipal assembly.

In late 1979 I visited Odawara and met Ms. K. She told me her story. "If it were a fiction," she said, "a man teacher would be all right. But it was *me*, a *woman*, who led the class in long-distance running. None of the men teachers ever tried such a thing."

How could the woman teacher vanish? The Japanese Constitution says, "There shall be no discrimination in political, economic, or social relations because of race, creed, sex, social status, or family origin." Still, the teacher had been erased. Let us see, then, how this happened—through a series of anecdotes on what it is to be a woman of Japan from birth through old age.

In modern Japan a baby boy is still more welcomed than a baby girl—just as in feudal times when an illegitimate son preceded a legitimate daughter in inheritance. Recently I heard three men in different positions utter the same remark: "It is as if a girl were born when we were expecting a boy!" One was a politician who failed to attain the result he anticipated in negotiations with another country. The second was a farmer who used the expression when the price of rice fell short of his expectation. In the third case, a labor-union staff member made the analogy when his demand for higher wages was not satisfied.

There *are* cases where a baby girl is welcomed. A family that has had boys successively would like a girl; in such a case either the girl tends to be loved and spoiled much like a pet or she is valued as the one who will take care of her parents in old age. A woman who had four sons was overjoyed when she had a baby girl—but then she was stunned to hear her eldest son, while changing the baby's diaper, say, "There, there! Dear baby, you will have a hard time. You are born to take care of Mommy in her old age." The mother was shocked because her son correctly guessed her own unconscious expectation for her daughter.

Thus women either are valued below men from the moment they are born or are valued for the docile services expected of them.

Parents love their sons and daughters equally. However, their expectations for them are quite different. Pre-school girls and their mothers in Kumamoto interviewed on the TV program *Women Today* said:

"I am often told to help Mother. My brother watches TV without helping her at all."

"Girls are different from boys. They must learn early to take care of other people."

"A girl will become a member of another family by marriage. So I discipline a girl more strictly than a boy."[1]

Regarding higher education, there remains a great sex-role difference in the minds of parents. Seventy-four percent of boys' parents want their sons to go to the university, while only 25 percent want university educations for their daughters.

And what happens when school begins? In elementary-school social-study textbooks,

[1] One change is that many mothers *have* come to agree that boys should be taught homemaking at school. According to recent research by Tokyo Municipal Office, 24 percent of mothers think that only girls should study home economics, while 30 percent think both boys and girls should study it and another 30 percent think both should be able to choose whether to study it or not. The traditional idea that boys should not enter the kitchen is changing.

father and mother are given stereotyped roles: father the breadwinner and mother the housewife. In the chapter describing farming, those who work machines in the illustrations are all men; women are tending the vegetables in the greenhouse or picking fruit. (In fact, according to the Prime Minister's Office, 62 percent of Japanese farmers are women, and two thirds of them are the main hands in farming and handling big farming machines.) In junior high school there is a course called "technology and home economics." This means that boys study technology and girls home economics. In senior high school girls study homemaking and boys physical training. It is an obvious violation of the Pact to Abolish All Forms of Discrimination Against Women (which Japanese government representatives signed in Copenhagen in 1980) to make only girls study home economics. Many groups, including the Federation of Lawyers' Organizations, insist that boys should also study the subject, but the Ministry of Education continues to argue that their policy is not discriminatory.

Girls are generally encouraged to go to junior college rather than a four-year university. At present the percentage of female students in universities is only 20 percent, which is the lowest of the developed countries. Moreover, most of them are in departments of education, literature, or home economics; very few female students are to be found in the fields of law, economics, and engineering.

What is the future for this 20 percent? Even though the unemployment rate is very low in Japan, female university graduates find it nearly impossible to secure a job which uses their education and skills. A new tendency is that female students are increasing in the departments of medicine, dentistry, and pharmacy because in these fields they are qualified as specialists through the State examination. So the woman who managed to overcome the handicaps of the stereotyped educational system now must face the hurdles of the work world.

There *is* some good news. Early in 1980 a woman [Nobuko Takahashi] was appointed ambassador [to Denmark] for the first time in Japanese history. Women gradually began to occupy some top positions: a woman as vice-president of a political party, a woman chief in a research institute of Tokyo University, a woman stationmaster, etc. The Imperial Household Agency and the national Tax Administration Agency employed women in positions previously occupied only by men. Tokyo Mercantile Marine University admitted female students to train as first officers. The women employees who had sued the Municipal Office of Suzuka for sexual discrimination in wages won the case. It is a cause for rejoicing that there are a number of government offices opening the door to women and making promotions available to female employees.

To this sunny side, however, there is a shadowy side. According to the Labor Ministry's current statistics on women's work conditions, the number of women who work is the largest in history, and yet the difference in wages between male and female workers has *increased* by 1.3 percent compared with the previous year.*

For female high school or two-year-college graduates it is easier to find a job. But beyond the age of twenty-five there are few chances of promotion. If a woman quits her job in order to get married or to raise children, it is virtually impossible for her to find a job again, other than a part-time one, even if she is as young as thirty.

One restriction put only on female applicants is that private enterprises do not employ women unless they can commute from their parents' home. The reason is not necessarily derived from the traditional concept that a young woman should not live by herself. The personnel manager of a business firm says, "The employees of a business company must work very hard. Women are no exception. During the busy time they have to work overtime almost every night. We have a dormitory for men, but not for women. So if a

* See Statistical Preface preceding this article for additional labor statistics.—Ed.

woman employee goes home very late at night and has to cook or wash for herself, she is tired and cannot work as efficiently as the others the next day."

"Women are no exception" *sounds* like the equality of sexes. As a matter of course, however, his words suggest the sexual division of roles: an employee should devote himself to the work of the company, not take care of his own food, clothing, and shelter. Those should be left to (the free labor of) the woman who stays home as housewife.

Consequently, most Japanese enterprises depend on women workers, whatever schooling they have had, only for temporary supplementary labor. But in truth women's labor as a whole is far from supplementary in Japanese business and industry. Without women's labor many enterprises in the distribution, food, and manufacturing industries would be ruined. Women actually are the cornerstone of the Japanese economy, and yet they are patently ignored except in the lowest-paid, temporary, unskilled positions. Decision-making women are virtually unheard of. (When I worked for a company some years ago and answered a telephone, I was often asked, "Isn't anybody there?" Although I was the manager of that department and was answering the telephone, they asked simply because I was a woman. Their next question was "Is there any *man* there?")

It is said that the Japanese people are enjoying affluence and freedom. But Japanese *women* are not "enjoying" their guaranteed rights. Women are not granted the right to work; they are supposed to stay home and care for the children. But women *are* working, and under poorer conditions than men. In accordance with the United Nations Decade for Women, the government has established offices to deal with women's "problems." Yet there is an increasing imbalance in pay, and a decreasing availability of skilled-work positions and decision-making responsibility for women.

Even in community life, women are subordinate to men. A housewife who was recommended by a women's group to stand as a candidate for the presidency of the local community self-government was rejected on the grounds that only the head of a household could become president. Mothers in a Parent-Teachers' Association who tried to nominate a woman as a candidate for president were strongly opposed by teachers and fathers—even though mothers, not fathers, usually work in the PTA.

Why, in the face of all this, don't more Japanese women get angry?

There seem to be a number of reasons. They are not treated as cruelly as their female ancestors of pre-war days. (This is because men and women have become legally "equal" and the economy of Japan has grown remarkably.) Since the idea of "men at work and women in the home" is deep-rooted, women in Japan have more rights and freedom *in* "their own area," the home, than women in many other countries: the husband usually hands his monthly salary to his wife and she takes charge of the household money. He never checks housekeeping expenses. (Traveling in Europe, I was shocked to see a middle-aged American woman asking her husband for money to buy picture postcards.)

"Sazae-san" is a popular comic-strip series which newspapers published daily from 1946 to 1979. Sazae-san is a housewife in a middle-class white-collar family. She still appears in a weekly TV cartoon series. Looking into Sazae-san's life I find some aspects which are not entirely in keeping with Japanese traditions. Although she is married, has taken her husband's surname, and has a child, contrary to tradition she lives with her parents, not her husband's parents. In her home she is respected. Her husband wishes he could spend his salary to choose his own shoes without Sazae-san's permission. In reality the status of wives may not be so high as in the comic, but the fact that Sazae-san is accepted and loved by so many people shows that the status of wifehood has been somewhat elevated. Therefore, if a woman is satisfied being a housewife, she can live a fairly comfortable life.

To be a housewife in Japan, however, also involves problems. Home is the *only* place where women are recognized and have (relative) management responsibility. Therefore, if children do anything which the culture views negatively, the whole community blames only the mothers. If a woman with young children has a job, people blame her for neglecting her children. If she stays home and her children do something wrong, people blame her for overprotection.

It is true that overprotected children have a lot of problems. But since married women are shut out of society, they cannot help devoting themselves to children; a parent can educate children properly only when that parent has a place in society her/himself. These mothers who don't work outside the family can spend their energy only in educating children. Yet people look down upon such a mother as "an education mamma." A middle-aged woman who found her purpose in life in helping her children through the severe school "entrance examination war," says, "My friends aren't around anymore. There is a distance between my children and me because of my strict attitude toward them during the 'examination war.' I no longer know who I'm going to be friends with and what my purpose in life is. What shall I do until the age of seventy-something? A long, lonely, bitter old age seems to be awaiting me. I am, as it were, an 'entrance examination war' widow who was deprived of everything during my children's school years."

A Japanese woman's perspective on her own life is always very short. In her youth she cannot plan her life beyond the age of twenty-three. After that she follows her husband, and then her children. (When a man proposes marriage to a woman, even today he uses stereotyped words: "Will you follow me?"—and she answers, "I'll follow you.") During her married life a woman is totally dependent on her husband economically and her children psychologically. By her mid-forties she already does not know what to do with the rest of her life. If she should lose or be divorced from her husband, she will most probably have to go on relief, because she has had no income of her own. This is the life of a Japanese middle-class woman.

One woman, who fully realized the great difference between the status of wives in the household and the status of women in society at large, said, "People claim that women and stockings became stronger after the war. That is true in a sense. But it is only one aspect of women—wifehood—that has become stronger. Women outside the household are by no means strong."

There is much to be improved in the Japanese laws. Part of the Law of Inheritance was amended in 1980, so that the spouse's portion became one half (formerly one third) of the inheritance when there is a child. Although the wife's status is thus elevated, the government is not eager to improve the conditions of women in jobs. On the contrary, they are encouraging people to make much of home so that both young children and old parents can be taken care of by their own families. The underlying motive is to save social-welfare expenses by capitalizing on the family. *But who will bear the responsibility of caring for the children and aged people in the home? Women, of course.* This is why Japan's Executive Committee to promote the United Nations' Decade for Women is opposed to the government's suggestion to strengthen family unity.[2] Some women are already aware that making much of "home" does not necessarily make much of women as human beings.

As I mentioned before, Sazae-san is the best-loved woman character in Japan since the war. But I find a problem in that comic strip. Sazae-san has managed to be a pretty

[2] The Committee has made the following statement: "Because of the slowdown of economic growth, depression, and high prices of commodities, labor conditions of women are rapidly worsening. Both national and local governments are reconsidering their welfare policies owing to budget deficits. As a result, social welfare is already suffering deterioration. The suggestion of the Liberal Party to 'strengthen the family unit' intends to force all childcare responsibility as well as tending aged and disabled people onto the family—that is, on women."

housewife for thirty years because a character in a comic strip never gets old. Old age (now thirty years longer than it was for the previous generation) is perhaps the biggest of all women's problems in Japan. When a woman has finished her career as a mother, she loses status in being a woman. Only women who have been "accused" of having a job have their own pension, property, and friends. Yet even for those, the pension is smaller than that of men because women occupy lower job positions than men.

According to research on the conditions of aged people done by the Ministry of Welfare, 70 percent of the aged have some income (84 percent of the men and 56 percent of the women). But this means that *nearly half of the women have no income.* A survey done by a gerontological research institute in Japan shows that more older women become senile than men. Yet if a woman is prohibited from taking an interest in anything but her family, how can she help becoming senile after her husband has died and her children (and even her grandchildren) have grown up? Senility in old women reflects the history of Japanese women who have been hindered from cultivating their own minds and characters.

A young friend of mine asked her grandmother, "What do we live for?" She was shocked at the answer: "Women live in order to care for men." It may be natural that this traditional idea should still be alive in this country, for Japan was in the feudal age until one hundred years ago. Japanese women have faithfully performed their duty. What is the result? What is the fate of old women? Recently an old woman was killed by her grandson because she was too meddlesome. Moreover, *the suicide rate of old women in Japan is higher than in any other country.*

From birth through old age, women in Japan live in shadow. Still, how was Ms. K.—our example back at the beginning—erased from her own story? It is one thing to be required to serve others; it is another to be totally obliterated.

I decided to follow up on Ms. K.'s story by visiting the company who was publishing the school reader. As I had expected, they admitted that they had changed the sex of the teacher on purpose. The first reason was that since many women teachers appeared in lower-grade readers, they wanted a man teacher in the sixth-grade reader "for balance." The second reason was that a marathon was traditionally a men's race, so they thought a man teacher would be more "natural." As for the issue of balance, I found that as many men teachers as women appeared in lower-grade readers. Since 57 percent of the elementary-school teachers are now actually women, 50 percent representation was by no means too high. (Furthermore, if balance was so important I would have liked to question the sexual "imbalance" of the editors. The editorial staff for the book consisted of twenty-two men and one woman.) The second reason—"tradition"—is utterly beside the point. Tradition is something to be created as well as carried on. Now we have the Tokyo International Women's Marathon. By the time the student's story was "rewritten" into sexist terms it had already been decided that the women's marathon would be included in the Olympic Games.

The editorial staff could not substantiate their claims. They agreed to rewrite the marathon story because the proposed version "was substantially different from the student's original composition." Ms. K. was resurrected in the reader.

This can give us hope. History and today's reality have cast a long night over the lives of Japanese women. The day can come when the women of this "land of the rising sun" will bask instead in its light.

Suggested Further Reading

Higuchi, Keiko. *Omnanoko no Sodatekata (Bringing Up Girls).* Tokyo: Bunka Shuppankyoku Publishing Co., 1978. Complete English translation available on request to Keiko Higuchi c/o publisher in Japan.

Komashaku, Kimi. *Majo no Ronri* (Witch's Logic—Thirst for Eros). Tokyo: Epona Publishing Co., 1978.

Mizuta, Tamae. *Josei Kaiho Shisoshi* (History of Feminism). Tokyo: Chikuma Shobo Publishing Co., 1979.

Shufa to Onna (Housewives and Women). Record of Citizens' Seminar at Kunitachi Community Center. Tokyo: Mirai Publishing Co., 1973.

Tanaka, Sumiko, ed. *Josei Kaiho no Shiso to Kodo* (Ideas and Movements of the Emancipation of Women; Vol. 1, Prewar Days, Vol. 2, Postwar Days). Tokyo: Jifi Press, 1975.

Keiko Higuchi was born and raised in Tokyo and graduated from Tokyo University in 1956, majoring in art history and journalism. She has worked as an editor and a housewife, and has written articles on childrearing, education, old age, and other women's issues for newspapers and magazines. Currently she is a free-lance writer and lecturer. She belongs to the Women's Problem Discussion Group and is an active committee member of the Tokyo Municipal Child Welfare Council and the Tokyo Municipal Vocational Training Council. In the Central Social Welfare Council of the national government she specializes in old-age problems. She is author of a number of books, including *Jobs Fit for Women, To Think About the Distance Between Parent and Child, Bringing Up Girls, Women, You Have Only One Life, Toward Tomorrow's Women,* and *Dear Old Age: Aged Characters in Literary Works.* She has one daughter and lives in Tokyo.

KENYA
(Republic of Kenya)

Located in east Africa, bordered by Somalia and the Indian Ocean to the east, Tanzania to the south, Uganda to the west, and the Sudan and Ethiopia to the north. **Area:** 582,646 sq. km. (224,960 sq. mi.). **Population** (1980): 16,466,000, female 50.6%. **Capital:** Nairobi.

DEMOGRAPHY. Languages: Swahili (official), Bantu, Kikuyu, English, other. **Races or Ethnic Groups:** Kikuyu 20%, Luo 15%, Luhya 14%, Balhya 13%, Kamba 11%, Asian, Arab, European, other. **Religions:** Protestant 33%, Islam 24%, Roman Catholicism 17%, indigenous faiths, Hinduism. **Education** (% enrolled in school, 1975): Age 6–11—of all girls 91%, of all boys 98%; age 12–17—of all girls 40%, of all boys 58%; higher education—in 1978 women were 22% of university students, of which 66% were concentrated in education and liberal arts; in 1977 women were fewer than 3% of engineering students. In 1976 there were 54 boys' schools, 31 girls' schools, and 15 sex-integrated schools at the secondary level; sex-integrated schools have higher male enrollments. Fees for secondary school limit girls' enrollment since parents give male children priority if their income is limited. As of 1974–75, 65% of rural women age 20–29 had never attended school. **Literacy** (1977): Women 10%, men 30%. **Birth Rate** (per 1000 pop., 1975–80): 53. **Death Rate** (per 1000 pop., 1975–80): 14. **Infant Mortality** (per 1000 live births, 1975–80): Female 76, male 90. **Life Expectancy** (1975–80): Female 58 yrs., male 54 yrs.

GOVERNMENT. A constitution was established in 1963 upon full Independence. The legislature is a unicameral parliamentary system with an elected and appointed 172-member National Assembly; an elected president appoints a cabinet. The Kenya African National Union is the sole political party. **Women's Suffrage:** 1963, at Independence. **Equal Rights:** The Constitution (Sec. 82) prohibits discriminatory legislation according to race, tribe, political opinion, etc.;

sex-discrimination is not mentioned, and in fact the provision explicitly excludes the areas of marriage, divorce, inheritance, and matters of personal law, in which women face unequal treatment. **Women in Government:** There are 3 (1 elected, 2 appointed) women in the National Assembly (1983). From 1978 to 1983, 4 women were in the National Assembly; in 1974 Dr. Julia Ojiambo was elected to Parliament and became Assistant Minister for Housing and Social Services. No women have served as full cabinet ministers or high-level government administrators.

ECONOMY. Currency: Kenyan Shilling (May 1983: 12.9 = $1 US). **Gross National Product** (1980): $6.6 billion. **Per Capita Income** (1980): $420. **Women's Wages as a Percentage of Men's:** 63% in urban areas (1977); the average monthly wage for women was 69.2% of men's in the private sector, and 90.5% of men's in the public sector (1976); less than 13% of all employee monetary benefits were paid to women (1975). **Equal Pay Policy:** None. **Production** (Agricultural/Industrial): Coffee, tea, sisal, cotton; plastic goods, textiles, paper products, tourism. **Women as a Percentage of Labor Force** (1980): 33%; **of agricultural force** (1979) 18% (in 1975 women were 31% of unpaid family workers); **of industrial force** —no general statistics obtainable (of manufacturing 8.4%, 1979); **of military** —no statistics obtainable, but women are admitted to service on equal terms with men; only a few women are in the military. In 1980, 85% of women on small farms worked their own land and provided 60–80% of all labor for food production; in 1976–77, 75% of all females over age 17 were economically active, although the majority of women employees are "casual" labor (see **Welfare**). **(Employed) Women's Occupational Indicators** (1976): Of lawyers, physicians, and engineers less than 5%, of primary and secondary teachers 30%, of secretarial workers and nurses 90%; 84% of employed women in the private sector were unskilled workers. **Unemployment:** No data obtainable.

GYNOGRAPHY. Marriage. *Policy.* Marriage is governed by customary laws of the different ethnic peoples, various religious laws, and laws based on British jurisprudence during the colonial period. The 1975 Marriage Act, Christian Marriage and Divorce Act, and Hindu Marriage and Divorce Act stipulate monogamy and the free consent of both partners. Under the Marriage Act, minimum marriage age is 18 for females and males*; under the Hindu Marriage and Divorce Act, age 16 for females with a guardian's consent, 18 without consent, and 18 for males regardless of consent. Under statutory law, spouses have equal rights and duties with the exception that a husband is required to provide a wife with all necessities; if he does not, she has a right to sue for separation and maintenance, and he is subject to up to 3 yrs. imprisonment. A widow who has no children is entitled to all of her husband's household and personal property, a portion of the estate, and a life interest in the remainder; a widow with children inherits equally with them. In both customary and Islamic marriages a female is marriageable at puberty and polygyny is permitted; free consent of both parties is stipulated. Customary unions may vary, but generally they are contracted between 2 families of different lineage. A man must pay a bride-price to the female's family to compensate for the loss of her labor. A widow has no right to inherit her husband's property but is entitled to maintenance unless she returns to her family or marries her deceased husband's brother. Islamic marriages allow a man up to 4 wives, and a woman 1 husband, who must be Moslem. The groom must pay *mahar* to the bride. A widow receives 1/8 of a husband's property (including land or livestock) if she has children, or 1/4 if she has no children. The 1970 Married Women's Property Act, which (it has been argued) applies to all marriage systems, entitles a woman to legal control over her property and the right to sue to protect it; however, this applies only to court actions against someone other than her husband, unless he has broken a contract. The Act grants the right to benefit from the assets a husband lists in an insurance policy; a husband also has this right regarding a wife.

Practice: Female mean age at marriage (1970–78): 20; women age 15–49 in union (1970–78): 70%. Since the 1970's there has been an increase in polygynous unions in which a man married under statutory law marries a second woman under customary law; although legally bigamous, these unions are rarely prosecuted. Although free consent is stipulated in all systems, arranged marriages are common in Islamic and customary communities, and early marriages are increasing. In 1982 Dr. Alex Kabugua, the District Officer for the North Division of Kiligi District, began an investigation based on the absence of girl children from school and exposed the cases of 40 girls age 10–13 who had been married to elderly, wealthy men by their parents. Payment of *mahar* and bride-price is still practiced frequently and is becoming more expensive and commercialized, with women valued according to level of education, etc. An average of 21% of male heads of household were in polygynous unions, 34% in the Nyanza and Coast provinces (1974–75). Many argue that the Married Women's Property Act should be amended so that it does not depend solely on an insurance policy and takes deserted spouses into account. In addition, most agricultural land is registered in a husband's name and is not covered by an insurance policy; thus a wife frequently does not benefit regardless of her contribution. Women are often required to obtain their husbands' signatures for loans, limiting their own ability to purchase land. Proposed family-law reforms in 1976 and 1977 were designed to establish a degree of uniformity among the various legal systems; the to date unsuccessful reforms would have granted married women the right to veto additional wives and to hold joint control of family property, made dowries and bride-price nonmandatory for customary unions, abolished marriages arranged

* A deviation from this age limit is permitted by law through "special contracts" of marriage.

without the female's consent, permitted a woman to sue her husband to protect her property, made adultery a criminal offense punishable by 6 months imprisonment, and entitled widows to inherit their husbands' property.

Divorce. *Policy:* Statutory marriages may be dissolved through court action only. Under the Matrimonial Causes Act a woman may seek divorce if her husband is convicted of rape, sodomy, or bestiality; she may seek a judicial separation—a quicker, less expensive method—under the Subordinate Courts Act, if her husband is a chronic drug or alcohol user, has subjected her to prostitution, has venereal disease, has been convicted of causing her bodily harm, or fails to provide maintenance for her and her children, or on the same 3 grounds as for divorce. A court can order a husband to pay maintenance after divorce or separation. Customary marriages are generally ended by negotiations between families and clan elders. Islamic marriages can be ended unilaterally by a husband—*talaq* divorce (repudiation). The wife has no such recourse, nor does she receive maintenance payment under local interpretation of either Islamic or customary law. Custody of children under age 18 is determined in all cases by courts according to a child's best interests. *Practice:* No statistics obtainable. The divorce rate is increasing in urban areas among people married under statutory law. Custody of young children is usually given to the mother. An unsuccessful 1976 proposed reform would have outlawed *talaq* divorce.

Family. *Policy:* Among customary groups, the family unit is a basic part of the clan or unified lineage. Young people and women are considered legally incompetent as clan members in religious and business matters. A woman retains her lineage after marriage, while children are considered part of the lineage of the father and his kin. Parents have equal responsibilities to maintain children according to the Children and Young Persons Act and the Guardianship of Infants Act. The 1972 Law of Succession codified discriminatory inheritance rights. In Hindu communities, only sons could inherit; single daughters were entitled to

maintenance. In Islamic communities, a daughter inherited 1/2 the amount of a son. Under statutory law children inherited equally with a wife. A 1981 amendment to the law established equal inheritance rights for all children. There is no official policy on childcare, but in 1980 the Women's Bureau began a project to build day-care centers in 4 urban areas. Since 1976, maternity leave for employed women is 2 months with full pay but entails forfeiting the annual vacation. *Practice:* Profound changes have shaken the family as the growth of a cash-based economy forces men and women to work for wages; a large % of men migrate to cities for work, fulfilling less of a traditional support role and leaving women to maintain the family. Rural women produce much of the family's food, are responsible for getting water and firewood (often walking 10 miles to do so), as well as performing childcare and household chores. In urban areas, women lack the familial support system for housework and childcare. There are some day-care centers, mostly in Nairobi, founded by women's groups. In 1980, 40% of households in the sub-regions were headed by women. Despite the change in inheritance laws (see above), some communities persist in following traditional inheritance practices.

Welfare. *Policy:* The National Social Security Fund (NSSF) and the Pension Trust Fund provide retirement (age 60), sickness, and disability benefits to employed persons, based on their contributions. Since 1975, employers are required to register female employees with the NSSF; however, female workers are not required to contribute to the fund. The National Security Fund Act (Sec. 7) does not apply to "casual" workers—those who are paid at the end of each day and who are employed for less than 1 month (see **Women as a Percentage of Labor Force**). The National Hospital Health Insurance Act (1966) established a mandatory contributory health plan for employed people with a minimum salary of SH. 1000 per month. A man can designate only 1 wife as beneficiary; additional wives can be covered only if he makes special contributions. An employed woman's compulsory membership may be waived if her income is "commingled" with her husband's and considered his earnings for tax purposes; however, she is covered only if he names her as beneficiary. *Practice:* Most employed women are not covered by the NSSF since the highest % of women employees are "casual" workers; many others who are eligible do not receive benefits because they have not made the noncompulsory contributions. Few people qualify for the national health plan; in 1973 in urban areas, 40% of employed women who were heads of households earned less than SH. 20 per month, opposed to 14% of men. The traditional family network is still the main support for old age and sickness.

Contraception. *Policy:* Legal; the population growth rate is a State concern. The government supports family-planning clinics and programs. Information and free IUDs, pills, and condoms are available in clinics at government hospitals and health centers. *Practice:* Women age 15–49 in union using contraception (1977): 8%; methods used (1977) pill 30%, rhythm 16%, abstinence 16%, female sterilization 13%, IUD 10%, injectables 8%, condom 2%, male sterilization 1%, other methods 3%; using inefficient methods 35%; 88% of married women know of modern contraceptive methods, 42% know where to obtain them. **Abortion.** *Policy:* Legal only to preserve the woman's life (Penal Code); the law specifies that the procedure must be a surgical operation performed with reasonable care and skill. Illegal abortions are punishable by a maximum of 14 yrs. imprisonment for the practitioner, 7 yrs. for the woman, and 3 yrs. for the supplier of abortifacients. *Practice:* No statistics obtainable. Illegal abortions in both rural and urban areas are common. A few women with the financial means to do so go to countries with less restrictive legislation to obtain abortions; poorer women sometimes resort to such means as puncturing their wombs with sharp objects when they cannot obtain legal abortions. The law is unclear as to whether the practitioner must be a physician; courts differ on how broadly "preservation of the woman's life" can be interpreted. **Illegitimacy.** *Policy:* A woman is responsible for her children born out of wedlock.

The Affiliation Act—which required men to provide financial support for their children born out of union—was repealed in 1969 by an all-male Assembly. *Practice:* No statistics obtainable. Pregnancies among single teenage girls are increasing. While social prohibitions against out-of-wedlock pregnancies still exist, there has been an increased acceptance of children born to single mothers. One provision of the unsuccessful 1976 law reform would have made a father responsible for part of the maintenance and education of his out-of-wedlock children. **Homosexuality.** *Policy:* It is illegal under the Penal Code (Sec. 162) to have carnal knowledge of any person "against the order of nature" and is punishable by 14 yrs. imprisonment; the law does not specifically mention lesbianism. It is specifically illegal for 2 men to commit an act of "gross indecency" in public or private, and is punishable by 5 yrs. imprisonment. *Practice:* No data obtainable.

Incest. *Policy:* Illegal (Penal Code); a male who is convicted of incest with his sister, granddaughter, daughter, or mother is subject to 5 yrs. imprisonment; if the victim is under age 13 the sentence is life imprisonment. A female over age 16 who consents to incestuous relations with her brother, grandfather, son, or father is subject to 5 yrs. imprisonment. *Practice:* No data obtainable. **Sexual Harassment.** *Policy:* None. *Practice:* No data obtainable. **Rape.** *Policy:* Illegal (Penal Code, Sec. 14); rape is defined as sexual intercourse with a woman without her free consent. The moment of vaginal penetration is considered the key point of either consent or refusal. "Defilement" is rape of a girl under age 14, regardless of consent, who is not the wife of the perpetrator; the law does not recognize marital rape. *Practice:* No statistics obtainable. Very few cases of rape are reported. It is a crime generally dealt with at the community level without involving the police. **Battery.** *Policy:* None. *Practice:* 1976 marriage law reform included the criminalization of wife-beating, but the bill was defeated by male parliamentarians, one of whom reportedly stated, "If you do not slap a woman her behavior will not appeal to you. Just slap her and she will know you love her." The only woman assistant cabinet minister, Dr. Julia Ojiambo, had supported the legislation and urged women not to vote for those in favor of wife-beating.

Prostitution. *Policy:* There is no legal definition of prostitution in the Penal Code or prohibition against practicing prostitution; however, it is illegal for a person to live off the earnings of prostitution. *Practice:* No statistics obtainable. Prostitution is increasing in urban areas, as many rural migrant women fail to find other employment in the cities. Police regularly harass prostitutes under sections of the Penal Code that deal with disorderly persons and vagrancy. **Traditional/Cultural Practices.** *Policy:* On July 26, 1982, President Daniel arap Moi issued a decree banning the custom of female genital excision, instructing the police to arrest and prosecute those who perform clitoridectomies** and excisions. Moi issued his ban after the deaths of 14 girls in the Rift Valley from these operations. On Aug. 12, Dr. Karuga Koinange, director of medical services for the country, ordered all health officials to cease performing the operations. *Practice:* Excision of the clitoris, although declining as a practice, still is widely performed throughout Kenya among the Kikuyu, Masai, Kisii, Meru, and Kalenjin peoples. Infibulation*** is practiced to a limited degree in the northeast. Nutritional tabus exist among certain groups, prohibiting women from eating chicken or eggs; the belief is that such foods in women produce deformed children. **Crisis Centers.** *Policy:* None. *Practice:* No data obtainable.

HERSTORY. Farming and herding peoples lived in the Kenyan highlands as early as 1000 B.C.E. On the coast, trade with the Arabs led to the establishment of Arab settlements and the city-states at Mombassa, Pate, and Malindi in the 8th century C.E. Bantu people migrated to the interior c. 1000. The first Europeans to arrive in the region (1498) were the Portuguese, who dominated Mombassa and the coast until 1729. German and English explorers traveled the interior in

the mid-1800's, and Britain claimed present-day Kenya in 1886 by agreement with Germany.

Women in precolonial Kenya generally enjoyed respect in their communities as farmers and traders as well as domestic laborers; Masai and Kikuyu women dominated trading. British control altered women's position dramatically. Europeans took women from the east coast as slaves and concubines, the household productive unit was overshadowed by the growth of industry, and women were left with home production and farming as men entered paid employment in the towns and cities. Colonial land policies favored white settlers and overturned traditional tribal ownership and inheritance rights, giving African men an advantage over women in the new system. Women's status fell as the importance of the rural subsistence farm economy decreased; they could not gain entrance to cooperatives or obtain credit to buy farm machinery or land, and so were left to farm on ever shrinking amounts of land. Vocational and farming courses catered to men, as did regular education instituted by the colonial government.

Me Katilili, a 70-year-old Giriama woman, organized her people against the British in the Giriama uprising of 1911–14. Campaigning from settlement to settlement, she incited the people with fiery speeches, and built solidarity among the Giriama, who pledged refusal to pay taxes and do forced labor, and to keep colonial settlers from their lands. When the resistance fighters set several administration offices on fire, the British sent soldiers in to arrest Me Katilili; she was sent to Kisililand, but escaped by cutting through the prison bars. The British accused her of being a witch who was deceiving her people. She was again captured and sent to Kismayu Island, and then disappeared from colonial records.

In the early 1920's, a Luo woman gained notoriety of another sort. Loye Elizabeth, from Kowe, was famous in her clan for her talents as singer, dancer, and farmer; her granaries were overflowing.

** See Glossary.
*** See Glossary.

She bought cattle with her surplus crops. She was the first woman of Kowe to embrace Christianity, burning the *chieno*-fiber tassel, which marked her married status, and adopting European dress. For these actions her husband forced her out of the house, but she continued to farm successfully, experimenting with new crops and techniques that she shared with other women.

Women participated in the independence struggle of the 1950's, acting as couriers with food, arms, and intelligence about the British soldiers. Moslem women of the coast were politically active in that region's struggle; 100 Mombassa women organized against colonial policies that denied them the vote while enfranchising women of other groups. They succeeded and began registering Moslem women from house to house. After Independence (1963) women organized in the Maendeleo ya Wanawake (Progress of Women), which had been created a short while earlier by a coalition of Kenyan and European women.

In 1975 the Women's Bureau was formed as part of the Ministry of Culture and Social Services, to increase women's involvement in development. From 1971 to 1977 women's groups multiplied rapidly, numbering 6800 by 1977. Many of these groups work on income-generating projects for women, teach literacy classes, and offer information on new farming techniques.

A court trial which received wide media attention in 1980 involved Prof. Wangari Muta Mathai, who was found guilty of adultery in a divorce suit brought by her husband, a member of the National Assembly. Although she protested her innocence and the prosecution offered no evidence, Prof. Mathai's reputation was destroyed and she lost her position as chair of the National Council of Women. She gave a critical interview to the Kenyan women's magazine *Viva,* in which she called the court and judges incompetent or corrupt. She was subsequently sued for contempt and sentenced to 6 months in jail for refusing to recant her criticisms. She was finally released upon giving an apology to the court.

In 1983 the Kenyan Women Finance Trust, Ltd., was formed by women professionals; the new bank/credit assoc. aims, through membership fees, to give loans to female-owned business ventures and compensate for the way in which businesswomen are excluded from the credit market.

MYTHOGRAPHY. Among the Masai, it is believed that once men and women were equal; there were no village elders, and women were *ilpongolo* (warriors) while men were *moran* (living outside the villages, guarding them, and raiding neighboring peoples). The *moran* accompanied the *ilpongolo* to war one day, and that night, the *moran* surprised the *ilpongolo,* producing a weapon that was unknown to the *ilpongolo,* the bow and arrow. The *moran* took the arrows and pierced the *ilpongolo's* bodies, creating vaginas. The *ilpongolo* lay with the men and in the morning, the men said, "These are just women after all," and took them in marriage. Women lost their equal status and their warrior bravery, and fertility began.

KENYA: Not Just Literacy, but Wisdom
By Rose Adhiambo Arungu-Olende

The woman in Kenya today is hardly different from the one I knew yesterday. She is, however, struggling desperately to acquire the means by which to meet her basic human needs as well as to improve her social status. To her it may have little to do with the women's liberation movement; in fact, she has barely heard of contemporary feminism.

To her it is simply a "development process." Perhaps tomorrow (if that finds her still alive), when her minimum basic needs have been met, she might find time to articulate her feminism.

This is a woman who has no easy access to water—much less clear tap water—to drink, cook, and wash; a woman who has no decent house in which to live; a woman who as yet has no gas or electricity. Her needs are many and immediate, and she has no energy for anything but the task of feeding her family and trying to keep her children alive. This is the situation of the majority of Kenyan women. More than 88 percent of them face a life in the rural areas, where what matters is food, water, shelter, and good health (the latter if you are blessed or can afford occasional clinic visits). They depend on agricultural produce, through subsistence farming, for their families' livelihoods.

These women do not rely on their husbands or anybody else to provide their food. It is through their own hard work and sweat that they survive. In fact, the crucial role they play in food production has been accorded public acclaim—especially in the light of the limited facilities at their disposal. In farming, women's tasks continue the whole year round, from tilling the ground and sowing seeds through weeding to harvesting. The work-load varies only with the seasons. After harvest, any extra food crops (after putting aside enough for feeding the family) are sold for small sums or exchanged for other products. The farms these women work are usually less than two acres.

Such a woman must always be organized in order to meet the enormous demands put on her. And most of these women are just that highly organized. The lack of modern equipment has made their work tedious and their hours long, especially in cases where they are also the *de facto* heads of households—their male partners having migrated to urban centers in search of salaried employment.

These women perform a crucial developmental role. If what I have described above does not constitute an important economic contribution, then I for one do not know what else to call it. They are basically self-supporting. They somehow managed to accomplish this in previous years and they will continue to do so tomorrow. In terms of "tomorrow," however, the government could make their lives easier through a real commitment to rural development strategies—and to the *implementation* of these strategies in action, rather than in words only.

I do, nevertheless, already see a slight change, a difference in the situation of women who yesterday were in the villages and now are living in urban centers. The majority of the urban poor population is female. To survive, they involve themselves in all sorts of jobs and trades. They would like to lead a decent life, but at the moment many have no opportunities to do so in the cities. They would actually be better off rejoining their hard-working sisters in the villages. How many times have I heard this said? Yet they are not moving anywhere. They moved once before, *from* the rural areas, and they are determined to stay put whatever the personal cost.

This determination to stay in urban centers has made their lives—and the lives of some other (especially married) women quite precarious. Prostitution has increased; it is one means of survival. Many married women now basically accept being second or third wives. In fact, since they have no other means of survival, they depend on men who can afford to support them under whatever arrangements the men choose—sometimes at the expense of their own families. But, as the women say, who is to blame? If we can both survive, let us survive. The over-all existing economic *and* social situations have constructed the lifestyle of these women.

Of course there are women—about 10 percent—for whom life has changed for the better. Among these are educated women, women holding well-paying jobs, and, to an extent, those women for whom husbands comfortably can provide. Their standards of living will vary only according to their own means or those of their husbands.

They are slightly better off because they have some independence in their decisions and some form of identity on which to build. Yet they too do not speak out much or demand improvement on their traditional roles. They do demand equal treatment at work, equal pay for equal work, and fair consideration in general—both indirect and direct. However, they must still struggle against negative attitudes by men (and by some women). They still face blatant discrimination in some issues; for example, there is no automatic housing allowance for married women who are civil servants (while there is for men), except under very special conditions. They as yet have no recourse to demanding an equal sharing of household responsibilities.

Records in Kenya show that there has been great increase in young girls getting pregnant, leading to school drop-outs and at times to very early marriages. Despite all the well-known methods of contraception, only a small percentage of Kenyan women use them. The figure is actually less than 10 percent. The reasons are in part cultural, although values are changing. When I was growing up, the society would shun a woman who had a child outside marriage. At present, one gets the feeling that out-of-wedlock birth has almost become an accepted way of life, which in turn has led to Kenya's population boom.

But this means that many young girls have had to interrupt their education. Few get the chance to go back and finish some level of learning; the majority end up roaming the streets or becoming second or third wives.* And the number continues to grow. Polygynous marriages are on the increase.

Even the few women who do continue their education still tend to stick to traditional fields, those fields from which women in other parts of the world are trying to break free. There are indeed equal opportunities in Kenyan education, regardless of sex—except that the underlying *attitudes* have not changed much. For example, we have no visible women senior engineers or scientists. There has been an increase of women lawyers, yet there are not many known *practicing* lawyers and there are only two women judges (although we have many women lawyers capable of serving on the bench). There are women teachers at all levels, yet very few women head schools (other than all-women schools); in fact, to get elected head of a school a woman must use all the political machinery she knows. We have a number of qualified businesswomen, yet hardly any are executive heads of business enterprises, or even directors. The country is full of capable women civil servants, yet no women are in the highest posts. Over half the registered voters in Kenya are women, but only four out of 172 seats in Parliament are held by women. Numerous other examples could be quoted.

Whose fault is it, one well might ask. What is the obstacle to women's progress in Kenya? We ask ourselves this, too, and I can find only one answer: there has been no positive government policy—social or otherwise—to promote women.

Kenyan women on their own have shown great capacity to organize themselves (religious groups, service clubs, etc.). They have more organizations than the men do. I do not believe that women organize these groups merely because they "have more time on their hands than men do"; as I already noted, women are the busybodies in Kenya. No, on the contrary, I believe it is because they too have realized that only through their own autonomous and united strength, strong commitment, and determination can they improve their status. Furthermore, these organizations also provide the means for women to contact and meet each other; they have hardly any other ways of meeting alone as women —certainly nothing comparable to men's clubs and bars. Many women who do *not* belong to these organizations hardly know who is who among themselves.

There are over forty registered national women's organizations, and over six thousand

* See Statistical Preface preceding this article for details.—Ed.

local women's groups in Kenya. Some of the best-known are National Council of Kenyan Women, Maendeleo ya Wanawake (Progress of Women), YWCA, International Federation of Business and Professional Women, International Council of Women, Church International Women's Organizations, and the Salvation Army.

Maendeleo ya Wanawake, an organization known by all Kenyans (and one I grew up always hearing about), encompasses the widest membership throughout the country. It grew out of the government's community development department in the early 1950's and became a nongovernmental organization. Through its multi-purpose centers, it has concentrated mostly on teaching women simple home economics, primary health care, and nutrition. But it has also worked to give women self-confidence and taught them to discuss issues and articulate their needs. As do many of the other women's organizations in Kenya, Maendeleo ya Wanawake realizes the need to train women for leadership roles right up from the local grass-root level.

What has been lacking in such an organization as Maendeleo ya Wanawake is the participation of many educated women *alongside* less-educated ones, including women who can barely read. Many of us have shared the belief that such organizations are for the uneducated, and that educated women only need go there to teach the others what to do. But having had the opportunity to work on women's issues for more than five years now, I have come to realize how much we can gain *from each other*, by coming and working *together*. How we could enhance the activities and programs of such organizations through introducing diverse topics that cover *all* issues that affect us! Instead of concentrating only on areas such as home economics, we could broaden our activities to include public affairs, politics, legal issues, understanding of our legal rights, and national issues—meaningful subjects that have hitherto been left to men.

Many women in Kenya, whether they can read or not, are still ignorant of their legal rights. There are also forms of discrimination that persist despite the laws. Issues of inheritance are still very complicated because of our customary traditions. In practice, women do not inherit equally with men notwithstanding the 1981 Law of Succession which (on the face of it) gave equal rights of inheritance to all, irrespective of sex.

Such customs as the paying of bride-price still persist in Kenya. In fact, this custom is getting even more expensive and becoming very commercialized; it is a big trade for men, at the expense and to the disadvantage of women. Women themselves never have a say on the subject of bride-price being levied on them. This was once a noble custom of which women actually could be proud, since it was meant as a symbolic gesture of respect. At present it has lost this meaning. Today, bride-price makes the intended bride look like a chattel for sale. She is "paid for" according to her level of education and her ability to produce or to earn money. There have been cases where the bride herself has assisted her husband in completing the payment of dowry, leaving both of them struggling to set up their new home against economic odds. So far, women's groups have not taken any firm stand on the subject. It is a subject intricately woven into various tribal customs and so would be difficult to outlaw, though it would not be impossible to regulate the proceedings, taking into account the changing society.

Some legal rights women enjoy in Kenya today have been achieved without an activist feminist movement. True, pressure has come from women's groups, but the initiatives have come from different sources, men and women alike. I have felt that failure to incorporate officially and fully women's well-known participation in social issues, economic development, and food production, and failure to comprehend the magnitude and complexity of their roles (either socially or economically), has led to the simplistic portrayal of them as dependent consumers and not producers. It cannot be forgotten that a great many women in Kenya have learned not to depend on men for their survival. Some of them may get defeated because they lack education, skills, or financial security; like women all over the world, they still have these limitations.

But Kenyan women are more and more strongly demanding recognition, consideration, and understanding of their real situations—*and* demanding a change of attitudes. Many women in Kenya may not be formally educated. But they are, as I have discovered, far from ignorant about their own lives. They may be illiterate in the strict sense of being unable to read—but they are highly literate in terms of knowing what they need. And they are beginning to organize themselves together to learn how to achieve those needs.

That is not just literacy, but wisdom.

Suggested Further Reading

Boserup, Ester. *Woman's Role in Economic Development.* London: Allen & Unwin, 1970.

Employment, Income and Equality: A Strategy for Increasing Productive Employment in Kenya. Geneva: ILO, 1972.

Pala, Dr. Achola. *Preliminary Survey of the Avenues for and Constraint of Women in the Development Process in Kenya.* Discussion Paper No. 213, Institute of Development Studies, Univ. of Nairobi, June 1975.

Strobel, Margaret. "Lele Mama to Lobbying." *Women in Africa, Studies in Social and Economic Change.* Eds. Nancy J. Hafkin and Edna G. Bay. Stanford, CA: Stanford Univ. Press, 1976.

Women's Bureau. *Kenya Country Report for the UN Mid-Decade for Women Review Conference.* July 1980. Nairobi: Ministry of Culture and Social Services, 1980.

Rose Adhiambo Arungu-Olende was born and educated in Kenya. She graduated from the University of Nairobi in 1973 with an L.L.B. Hons., is married, and has three children. She works for the Kenya Mission to the United Nations as Chief Advisor on Social and Humanitarian Affairs and is in charge of relations with Non-Governmental Organizations.

KOREA (SOUTH)
(Republic of Korea)

Located in east Asia, bordered to the east by the Sea of Japan, to the south by the Korea Strait, to the west by the Yellow Sea, and to the north by North Korea (Democratic People's Republic of Korea). **Area:** 98,500 sq. km. (38,031 sq. mi.). **Population** (1980): 38,205,000, female 49.6%. **Capital:** Seoul.

DEMOGRAPHY. Languages: Korean. **Races or Ethnic Groups:** Korean. **Religions:** Buddhism 39%, Christianity (primarily Protestant) 19%, Confucianism 13%, Chondokyo. **Education** (% enrolled in school, 1975): Age 6–11—of all girls 100%, of all boys 100%; age 12–17 —of all girls 56%, of all boys 70%; higher education—in 1978 women were 30% of university and college students and 16% of graduate students. In 1980, 3% of women age 15–49 ever-married, had university/higher education; in 1974, 53% of women age 45 and older had no education. **Literacy** (1977): Women 81%, men 94%. **Birth Rate** (per 1000 pop., 1975–80): 23. **Death Rate** (per 1000 pop., 1975–80): 7. **Infant Mortality** (per 1000 live births, 1975–80): Female 34, male 42. **Life Expectancy** (1975–80): Female 65 yrs., male 60 yrs.

GOVERNMENT. The 1980 Constitution established an elected 7-yr., 1-term presidency. The National Assembly, a unicameral legislature, has 184 elected members and 92 members appointed according to party strength. The Democratic Justice Party and the Democratic Korea Party are the main political parties. **Women's Suffrage:** 1948. **Equal Rights:** The Constitution (Art. 9) states that all citizens are equal before the law and that there shall be no discrimination in political, economic, social, or cultural life on account of sex, religion, or social status. **Women in Government:** 9 women in the National Assembly and a woman Minister of Health and Social Affairs, Jung-Lei Kim, the fourth woman Minister ever to serve (1982); 45 women served in the National Assembly from 1948 to 1982.

ECONOMY. Currency: Won (May 1983: 762. = $1 US). **Gross National Product** (1980): $58.6 billion. **Per Capita Income** (1980): $1520. **Women's Wages as a Percentage of Men's:** Average monthly earnings of women in manufacturing were 45% of men's (1980); in agriculture, hourly earnings were 74.2% of male wage (1979). **Equal Pay Policy:** None. **Production** (Agricultural/Industrial): Rice, barley, vegetables; textiles and garments, electronics, processed foods. **Women as a Percentage of Labor Force** (1980): 37.6% (of whom 36% are unpaid family workers); **of agricultural force** 43.8% (of whom 69.3% are unpaid family workers); **of industrial force**—no general statistics obtainable (of manufacturing 39.3%, 1980, of whom 7% are unpaid family workers); **of military**—no data obtainable. Of women age 15–49 ever in union, 49.1% are employed (1974); women age 16–25 constitute 30% of the entire industrial work force (1980). **(Employed) Women's Occupational Indicators** (1980): Of administrative/managerial workers 4.9%, of doctors 13.6%, of university professors 15.2%, of teachers 28.7%, of professional/technical workers 32%, of clerical and related workers 32.7%, of service workers 58%, of health and medical services 75.7%; women comprise 70–90% of workers in garment/textile, toys, and electronics manufacture for export, earning approx. $0.63 per hour (see HERSTORY). **Unemployment** (1981): 4.6%, female 2.5%, male 5.7%.

GYNOGRAPHY. Marriage. *Policy:* The 1958 Civil Code incorporates aspects of customary law and makes marriage a union between a female and a male at least age 16 and 18 respectively, based on monogamy, requiring mutual agreement and registration with the authorities. A woman enters into the family register of her husband, unless she is the head or successor to headship of a family herself (Arts. 826, 876). Both spouses keep their own family names and places of lineage origin. People with the same surname and patrilineal clan origin are forbidden to marry. Spouses are bound to cohabit and mutually support each other. Property brought to marriage or acquired during marriage by each spouse is owned by her/him unless otherwise contracted before marriage. Property of dubious ownership is considered the husband's (Art. 830). Bigamy and polygamy are illegal (Art. 810). *De facto* or common-law marriages are recognized and accorded certain rights under the Code: a common-law spouse may have the right to receive certain benefits or collect compensation if the other spouse ends the relationship, but has no rights if another (legal) spouse exists. *Practice:* Female mean age at marriage (1970–78): 23; women age 15–49 in union (1970–78): 59.8%. *De facto* marriages and concubine relationships are still not uncommon. Half of all marriages are arranged by families. Until 1979 parental consent had been required for women under age 23 and men under age 27 (Civil Code, Art. 808-1).

Divorce. *Policy:* Legal; obtainable either by mutual consent between spouses or by court action on 5 grounds: unchastity of a spouse, malicious abandonment including neglect of support, extreme maltreatment of a spouse by the other or her/his lineal ascendants, disappearance of a spouse for 3 yrs., and any other cogent cause for marital breakdown (including drug or alcohol abuse, impotence, or lack of affection). Action for divorce must proceed no longer than 6 months after learning of cause or 2 yrs. after a particular event which is cause. Fathers retain child custody and authority over children's education unless otherwise agreed. Spouse can claim award for damages, but no alimony or property. A woman's name is removed from her husband's family register and returned to her father's. *Practice:* No statistics obtainable. Women have few rights in divorce, often lose their children and have no economic support, and find that remarriage is usually difficult. Men take concubines frequently, with no need to obtain formal divorce from their legal wives. **Family.** *Policy:* The 1953 Labor Standards Law provides for a maternity leave of 60 days pre- and post-delivery on full pay for employed women. Childcare centers are funded by the government and women's organizations. Family law is a complex system defining kinship and lineage, based on customary law. Paternal lineage is the family's basis. The *hojok* (family register) must contain the names, domiciles, birth dates, and relations of all family members. Children take the surname and family origin of the father. Persons not related by blood may legally join a family if enrolled on its register (Civil Code, Art. 784). The head of the family, generally the eldest male who is a lineal descendant of the head, is obliged to support the family members, may choose domicile, may apply to courts for convening a family council to settle disputes, and is entitled to family lands and increased inheritance when succeeding to headship (Civil Code, Arts. 790, 984). Members of the family must obey the head. *Practice:* There is growing pressure to abolish the system of family headship as being discriminatory against women and the other members of the family who must be subservient to the eldest male. The traditional preference for sons over daughters still exists and the government has instituted educational measures to decrease it. The majority of young people live with their families until marriage. Women maintain their traditional role of wife and mother despite their increasing participation in the paid work force. In 1980 the government subsidized 606 day-care centers; women's groups and agricultural cooperatives funded 10,304 centers in rural regions.

Welfare. *Policy:* National Welfare Pension System (1973) provides pensions for persons at age 60 and establishes a compensation fund for workers and their families; a compulsory system for employed persons earning over 15,000 Won annually is funded by wage deductions. Pensions are 40% of the average monthly salary. Free medical service is provided by the government plan for those on social relief—mostly widows and families of deceased soldiers or police—and low-cost health care is available for low-income earners. Wage earners buy health insurance through government-subsidized insurance plans. *Practice:* No data obtainable.

Contraception. *Policy:* Legal. Since 1976 the government's population policy includes direct support of family-planning programs to decrease fertility rate, and accepts aid from UNFPA and WHO in research and education. A goal of the 1976 policy was to sterilize 700,000 women and men of child-bearing age and to increase the number of government-subsidized birth-control clinics from 1747 to 5036 by 1981. *Practice:* Women age 15–49 in union using contraception (1974): 35%; methods used (1974) pill 24%, IUD 23%, condom 15%, rhythm 13%, male sterilization 10%, withdrawal 7%, female sterilization 5%, diaphragm 1%, douche 1%, injectables 1%, abstinence 1%; using inefficient methods 22%. In 1980, 86% of married women knew of an outlet for contraceptives, 39% used contraception. **Abortion.** *Policy:* Legal; 1973 law permits abortion within 28 weeks in cases of life or health risk to a woman, or fetal defects, or pregnancy caused by rape or incest. Penalties for illegal abortions are a fine or up to 1 yr. imprisonment for the woman, up to 1 yr. for the practitioner, with harsher penalties for medical personnel. *Practice:* Abortions (per 1000 women age 15–44, 1977–78, Seoul only): 235; in 1977–78 a total of 480,000 abortions were performed in hospitals and private clinics in Seoul. In 1960–71 the rate increased 180%. Before 1973 a more restrictive law was in force, but abortions were routinely performed in private clinics. In 1971, 2/3 of people surveyed were unaware that abortion was illegal. The current law is widely ignored by both the public and the government, which subsidizes abortions if sterilization is included or pregnancy occurs while an IUD is in use. **Illegitimacy.** *Policy:* According to the Civil Code (amended 1964) children born out of wedlock may be "legitimated" by or during the marriage of their parents. If the parents do not marry, legitimation may occur through the voluntary acknowledgment of paternity or through a court action to determine paternity. Out-of-wedlock children take their mother's surname and are subject to maternal authority unless the father recognizes them; they are entitled to inherit equally with legitimate children. *Practice:* No statis-

tics obtainable, but there is a high incidence of out-of-wedlock births due to the prevalence of concubinage and unregistered marriages. **Homosexuality.** *Policy:* No data obtainable. *Practice:* No data obtainable.

Incest. *Policy:* No data obtainable. *Practice:* No data obtainable. **Sexual Harassment.** *Policy:* Criminal Code makes sexual intercourse with an employee by force or threat of force a crime punishable by up to 5 yrs. imprisonment. *Practice:* No statistics obtainable, but sexual harassment and intimidation of women working in factories is prevalent. Male supervisors (often non-Koreans in multinational factories) exploit culturally enforced women's obedience to male authority and the women's fear of losing their jobs. **Rape.** *Policy:* Illegal. A person who commits an act of sexual intercourse with a female by means of violence or intimidation is punishable by a minimum of 3 yrs. imprisonment; if "injury" or death results, 5 yrs. *Practice:* No data obtainable. **Battery.** *Policy:* Illegal. According to the Criminal Code, cruelty to a spouse or lineal descendant is punishable by a maximum of 5 yrs. imprisonment. *Practice:* No data obtainable. **Prostitution.** *Policy:* Illegal; 1962 law prohibits "decadent acts," including prostitution, and penalizes both the prostitute and clients. Nevertheless, the government tourist associations issue ID cards to women who work in the tourist industry, ostensibly as "hostesses" and in fact as prostitutes. *Practice: Kisaeng,* traditionally entertainers who might engage in sex, are today integral to the tourist industry. *Kisaeng* tourism is promoted by travel agencies which publicize South Korea as a male paradise. Tour packages often include the price of a *kisaeng* as well as sightseeing and accommodations. The *kisaeng* women themselves earn only 1/6 of their fee, which is split among guides, hotel owners, travel agents, and officials. Japanese males are a majority of the customers, numbering 400,000 a yr. from 1965 to 1978 and spending an annual amount equal to 60% of the country's total circulating currency. The Japanese male use of Korean women as prostitutes during WW II remains an old antagonism (see HERSTORY). Today's *kisaeng* are usually rural women who have migrated to the cities in search of employment but found no other options. Cross-national women's groups (see JAPAN), now active throughout Asia, have begun to organize against sex tourism. In Dec. 1973, students of EWHA Women's University in South Korea, together with Church Women United, demonstrated at the Seoul airport against *kisaeng* tourism. A Japanese group, Women Against *Kisaeng* Tourism, started their own publicity campaign at Haneda Airport in Japan. A conference on *kisaeng* tourism was held in Feb. 1974, demanding action from the government and the travel agencies.

Traditional/Cultural Practices. *Policy:* The government is attempting through legal reform and educational campaigns to change the traditional cultural preference for male children. *Practice:* Sons are still preferred over daughters. **Crisis Centers.** *Policy:* None. *Practice:* No data obtainable.

HERSTORY. Koreans are descendants of Tungustic tribes who originated in Siberia. One of the first settlements was founded by Chinese scholar Ki-tze in Pyongyang in the 12th century B.C.E. The first Korean state, Koguryo, evolved in the north in the 1st century C.E. Two other Korean kingdoms, Paekche and Silla, emerged in the south in c. 250 and c. 350 respectively. Aided by the Chinese, Silla engulfed Paekche and Koguryo in the 7th century, establishing a unified rule of the peninsula.

In the Silla Kingdom before unification, 3 women were monarchs and women in general occupied a strong position in society. The first woman on the throne was chosen when there was no male heir. Women also exerted influence as advisers, queen dowagers, and regents. Both matrilineal and patrilineal lines of descent existed in the Silla era. Women could head a family, and their vital statistics were recorded on the official register, indications that their status was relatively high. After the merging of the 3 kingdoms, patrilineage came to dominate kinship systems and eroded women's previous positions of autonomy. Wang Gon toppled Silla in 935 and founded the

Koryo Dynasty, during which Confucianism became the main influence in government. In the Koryo era, the king took 29 wives to improve his political position and unify divided factions. By that time, women could gain status only through marriage.

When the Mongols invaded (1231), they conscripted Korean women to marry members of their court as well as soldiers on the China mainland. Families hid their daughters, forcing the government to decree that no one could marry without familial consent. The establishment of Confucianism as the official religion during the Yi Dynasty (begun by Yi Songgye in 1392), institutionalized the subjugation of women. One of the tenets of Confucianism demands the 3 obediences of women: to the father when young, to the husband when married, and to the son in old age. Widows who remarried were punished. Wives required their husbands' consent to leave home during the day. Houses were segregated into male and female quarters.

When Korea opened to the West in the late 1800's, women missionaries were instrumental in reviving women's rights activism. Education for women was an important issue by the end of the 1800's, and the first women's school was opened in 1886; 4 years later the first woman doctor was educated abroad and returned to Korea to practice. During the Japanese colonial period (1905–40) women's societies for improving attitudes about women flourished, and women were also active in various revolts against the Japanese.

WW II was a setback in the drive to increase educational opportunities for women. During the war, Japanese troops recruited or conscripted Korean women to be prostitutes, supplementing the 70,000 Japanese women they used as camp followers; there were approx. 80,000 Korean women used as prostitutes by the Japanese army during that period. After WW II, the country was divided, with the primarily agricultural south under US control and the more industrial north controlled by USSR troops, which led to the 1948 creation of separate States. From 1950 to 1953 the Korean War between north and south claimed 54,000 casualties; in 1972 the 2 Koreas formulated an accord to work toward unification.

In 1957 Lee Tai Young, the first woman lawyer, opened a law practice that served poor women. Still functioning and now called the Korean Legal Aid Center for Family Relations, the center's clients are 70% women with marital and divorce problems. Lee's political ideas made her an enemy of Pres. Park Chung Hee, who had her arrested. In 1977 she was given a 3-year suspended sentence and 7-year disbarment.

During the 1960's and 1970's, the growth of export manufacturing industries, often owned or controlled by multinational corporations, has radically changed women's lives. South Korean women comprise a huge segment of the labor force in export industries [see (**Employed**) **Women's Occupational Indicators**]. The growth of industry in urban areas, paralleling the rise of agrobusiness and the decline of traditional agriculture in the rural areas, has brought young women into paid employment; many families send their young daughters to work in factories as a main source of income; the majority of women contribute over 1/2 their salaries to their families. The conditions and wages—usually under $0.70 per hour—are significantly worse than those in Western factories and are the main reasons multinationals choose to relocate or subcontract their jobs in South Korea. Textile manufacturing, toys, and computers/electronics production are among the major employers. In 1 electronics plant, 95% of the work force developed severe eye problems within the first year of employment. But women have become militant labor activists in many factories.

In 1971 and again in 1975, workers at Dong-il, a major textile company, elected a female union president; almost a decade of intense union organizing and protest plus strong company attempts to break the union resulted in a 1980 victory by management: 126 activist women employees were blacklisted. At the YH Textile plant in Seoul, 200 women workers staged a vigil and fast in Aug. 1979, protesting the company's plan to close and move elsewhere. After the fifth day, over 1000 riot police armed with steel shields and clubs broke into the union office building where the women were staying and forced them out. Kim Kyong Suk, a 21-year-old woman, was killed during the struggle; it was her death that caused public outrage and the subsequent rioting that ended in the assassination of Pres. Park that year. At Korea Control Data of Seoul (headquartered in Minneapolis, Minnesota), women workers organized to increase salaries from $3.87 a day during contract renewal in 1981. Although the company had record profits, it refused to concede wage increases and in Mar. 1982 fired the women's union president and 5 workers; 300 women staged a work slowdown to protest and 100 women disrupted a negotiating session involving the dismissed workers and company and government representatives. In July 1982 Control Data closed the plant for reasons of "technology changes and labor problems." Later that year Lee Tae-Hi, Park Young-Son, and Cho Sang-Hi were jailed for holding a sit-in of 50 workers at the Ministry of Labor.

Feminist activism has also focused on abolition of *kisaeng* tourism (see **Prostitution**) and on legislative reforms.

MYTHOGRAPHY. In ancient Korea, female *shammans*/religious leaders were prominent. Up until the 7th century C.E., the word *shamman*, in Korean, was assumed to apply to women. A *shamman* was an intermediary between god and humans. As *shammans*, women presided over national ceremonies, performed healings and exorcisms, and acted as prophetic sibyls.

KOREA: A Grandmother's Vision
by Soon Chan Park
(Translated by Grace Lyu [Eun Hi Lyu])

When I go out these days, Korean young people recognize me and greet me with the affectionate name "Grandmother."

When I was young and could not understand the reason of life, I knew even then that nothing will change its shape and nature. A grandmother, for example, will always take sides with the grandchildren. She will be kind and gentle to them. But the reason of life seems to have changed, and the old grandmothers have gone. Yet now I, who am still *myself*, somehow have become a grandmother. *I* am now being called "the grandmother" by my young people.

And the strange truth is that I would rather be called grandmother with warmth and affection than be known as a woman of great achievement, as I had so hoped to be when I was still young.

But then I wonder, have I fulfilled my role of grandmother for young people? With this hand, the hand of a grandmother, the caressing hand of all remedies for the suffering and pain in the minds of our young people: I find myself reflecting whether I have, after all, given much hope and courage to the young.

Some things I know. I know that I want to live the rest of my life with intensity and earnestness. I want to continue my struggle for women, but I also hope to be the grandmother who contributes to the total guarantee of human rights in this world, so that all young people can grow freely.

I find myself thinking that among women, a grandmother is the doctor for everybody, the protector of all. A grandmother is the supreme essence of women. She carries the majesty of all women. Men may rule and control the world. But it is women who love and raise all human beings—including men. It is the woman who is the personification of love, who creates happiness and peace.

Korean history has not lacked for many great women. One, still revered, is Shin, Sa-im Dang, the mother of the great scholar Lee, Yul Gok, during the Yi (Lee) Dynasty. Comparably, in America, Helen Keller, although blind, deaf and mute, was the primary humanitarian of the twentieth century. Shin, Sa-im Dang of Korea raised, educated, and challenged her son to become a great scholar who made many contributions to Korean culture. Helen Keller conquered her disabilities and as an adult went on to make great contributions for the rights of disabled people. Both women symbolize the first and the highest spirit of humanity. These women gave children and disabled people patience, perseverance, and courage. They also bequeathed to us the spirit of love for all persons committed to justice.

This is the power of women. Wherever we work—at home or out in society—women tend toward love and helping others. It is as if Shin, Sa-im Dang and Helen Keller were the grandmothers of all Koreans and all Americans.

Because I am a Korean woman, I have introduced myself as a Korean grandmother. But human nature is the same all around the world—so Korean women, Asian women, American women, European women, *every* woman has in herself her own version of truth, virtue, and inner beauty. Such a woman will forever be called a warm-hearted grandmother when she becomes old.

Young people who received the values of their mothers and other women will grow to work for their motherland and love their people. They will also be committed to world peace and the protection of human rights. They will not compromise with the strong but will love the weak and poor. They will take care of the unhappiness of others as if it were their own. They will be truly human.

Throughout my more than eighty years of life in Korea, I had certain hopes. One was for the independence of Korea—which we have achieved. But we have not achieved the unification of Korea—which will lead us to the protection of human rights. My only wish now is to be a grandmother who can raise the children and the youth with a caressing hand to cure all pain.

So it is that Korean young people greet me with the title of "grandmother." But I want also to be the grandmother of young people all around the globe. I wish to be remembered as an average warm-hearted grandmother, forever.

Suggested Further Reading

Lee, Hoyo-Chai. "Patterns of Change Observed in the Korean Marriage Institution." *Journal of Sciences and Humanities,* No. 26, Seoul, n.d.

———. "The Changing Family in Korea." *Journal of Sciences and Humanities,* No. 29, Seoul, n.d.

Kim, Yung-Chung. *Women of Korea—A History from Ancient Times to 1945.* Seoul: EWHA Women's Univ. Press, 1976.

Soon Chan Park was born on September 10, 1898, in Dong-Nai, Korea. She graduated from the Japanese Women's College where she majored in sociology. She married a professor of law and bore six children—three daughters and three sons. In 1948 she founded the Korean National Women's Association and was elected its first president. She also founded the first Korean women's newspaper and became its editor. In 1955 she was elected to the National Assembly as one of the first women members. She once filibustered for three days and nights (resting, at times, on a silk quilt brought from home) in the Assembly, for women's inheritance and property rights. From 1961 to 1968 she was re-elected to the National Assembly for two terms, and in 1967 she was elected to be the only woman member of the National Advisory Council of the Democratic Party. In 1970 she became the Secretary-General of the Democratic Party (the first woman in the world to hold such a post), and a member of the Supreme Council of the Democratic Party.

When she wrote the above article, Soon Chan Park was a member of the Consulting and Advisory Council of National Policy for the Republic of Korea. It was the last article she ever wrote. One month later, on Monday, January 10, 1983, at age eighty-four, Soon Chan Park died in Seoul. To many Asian women, she was an inspiration equivalent to what a Simone de Beauvoir or an Eleanor Roosevelt has been for Western women. Her death is a loss to women everywhere—but her life was an even greater gift, to women and all humanity.

KUWAIT
(State of Kuwait)

Kuwait is located on the Arabian Peninsula and is bordered by Saudi Arabia to the south, Iraq to the west and north, and the Persian Gulf to the east. **Area:** 20,150 sq. km. (7780 sq. mi.). **Population** (1980): 1,357,952, female 42.8%; Kuwaiti 565,613, female 50.38%; non-Kuwaiti 792,339, female 37.4%* **Capital:** Kuwait.

DEMOGRAPHY. Languages: Arabic, English, other. **Races or Ethnic Groups:** Arab 72.5%, Asian 25.76%, African 0.2%, European 1.26%, other. **Religions:** Islam (official—predominantly Sunni) 91.5%, Christian 6.4%, other 2.1%. **Education** (% enrolled in school, 1975): Age 6–11—of all girls 62%, of all boys 67%; age 12–17—of all girls 59%, of all boys 67%; higher education (Kuwait University graduates only, 1980–81)— 58% women, of whom 33% were non-K (the high % of female students is because most male university students study abroad); 226 K women and 2010 K men studied abroad on government scholarships (1981–82). Nationally, 28.91% of all women over age 20 held university degrees in 1980, 81.09% of whom were non-K; in education 45.79% of students were women (80.7% of whom were non-K), in natural sciences 39.16% (of whom 83.49% were non-K), in medicine 30.06% (of whom 84.77% were non-K), in engineering 4.08% (of whom 88% were non-K). Education is sex-segregated from kindergarten through university; it is free through post-graduate level and compulsory through intermediate level. **Literacy** (1980): Female 64.3% (K 50.4%, non-K 77.1%), male 75.8% (K 77.39%, non-K 75%). **Birth Rate** (per 1000 pop., 1980): 39.7 (K 47.6, non-K 33.5). **Death Rate** (per 1000 pop., 1980): 4.1 (K 5.4, non-K 3). **Infant Mortality** (per 1000 live births, 1981): K 27.9 (female 26.5, male 29.3), non-K 19.8 (female 16.6, male 22.8). **Life Expectancy** (1975–80): Female 72 yrs., male 67 yrs.

GOVERNMENT. Constitutional hereditary monarchy with executive power held by the Amir (head of state), prime minister (head of government, appointed by the Amir), and a 17-member cabinet; legislative power is held by the elected 50-member National Assembly, which can be dissolved by the Amir. Legislation and court jurisprudence are based on the Islamic Shari'a, as stipulated in the 1962 Constitution. There are no political parties which are recognized by the government. **Voting:** Literate male Kuwaitis over age 21 who are "first-class citizens" (related to pre-1920 residents) have the right to vote; 3.2% of the total population were "qualified" voters in 1981 elections. **Women's Suffrage:** None (see HERSTORY). **Equal Rights:** The 1962 Constitution mandates equality before the law for all citizens, but Shari'a jurisprudence stipulates that women are "under the protection" of men (see **Education, Marriage,** etc.). Kuwaiti society is almost entirely sex-segregated, including schools, the work force, hospitals, and the home. **Women in Government:** Fadda al Khaled was Under-Secretary of the Ministry of Education (1981) and is currently (1983) Assistant of Social Services. Women hold important posts in the Ministries of Health, Social Affairs, and Foreign Affairs—although they are rarely sent abroad in diplomatic service (1982).

ECONOMY. Currency: Kuwaiti Dinar (May 1983: 0.30 = $1 US). **Gross National Product** (1980): $30.9 billion. **Per Capita Income** (1980): $22,840 (highest PCI in the world). **Women's Wages as a Percentage of Men's:** No data obtainable. **Equal Pay Policy:** Constitution stipulates equal pay for comparable work. **Production** (Agricultural/Industrial): Livestock, produce; oil, fish, petro-

---

* Kuwaitis are relatives of pre-1920 residents; non-Kuwaitis are all post-1920 immigrants and compose 58.5% of the total pop. Because of space limitations, "Kuwaiti" and "non-Kuwaiti" have been shortened to K and non-K in the statistical sections of this Preface.—Ed.

chemicals. **Women as a Percentage of Labor Force** (1980): 12.9% (77.6% of all employed women are non-K); **of agricultural force**—no general statistics obtainable (22 [K 13, non-K 9] individual women were employed in agriculture, hunting, and fishing); **of industrial force**—no general statistics obtainable (341 [K 21, non-K 320] individual women were employed in industries); **of military**—women are not permitted in the military. **(Employed) Women's Occupational Indicators:** Of government physicians 23.6%, of whom 73.7% are non-K (1981); of administrative and managerial workers 2.04%, of whom 46% are non-K, of clerical and related service workers 17.7%, of whom 54.4% are non-K (1980); 22.5% of employed women, of whom 94% are non-K, are in the service sector (1980). In the service sector, most K women are employed by the government as teachers in girls' schools, in the Ministry of Education, or in health and social services; most non-K women are employed as teachers, governesses, or domestic servants. In 1975, 53 (K 16, non-K 37) individual women were employers, 118 (K 25, non-K 93) were self-employed, and 898 (K 30, non-K 868) were in wholesale and retail trade. Many employed non-K women are recent immigrants, recruited from poorer Asian and Arab countries, who seek higher wages in Kuwait; of this pop., 51% are semi- or nonliterate. Generally, women are hired at the lower-paid levels, receive fewer promotions than men, are excluded from formal/informal decision-making, and rarely reach administrative levels. **Unemployment** (1980): 1.81% (K 4.92%, non-K 0.14%), female 1.95% (K 2.55%, non-K 1.78%), male 1.79% (K 5.27%, non-K 0.81%). The government guarantees employment and training to any citizen, male or female, who is "willing and able" to work.

GYNOGRAPHY. Marriage. *Policy:* There is no minimum-age law for marriage. Polygyny is legal (up to 4 wives). All sexual relations outside of marriage are classified as "sex crimes" and are punishable as felonies by 5–15 yrs. imprisonment. It is illegal to kill a daughter or wife who has pre- or extra-marital sex.

Kuwaiti women who don't marry by age 18 receive a monthly government stipend. *Practice:* Marriages (per 1000 pop. age 15 and older, 1979): 10.5 (19.3 K, 5 non-K). Female mean age at marriage (1970–78): 20; women age 15–49 in union (1970–78): 73.8%; 10.2% of total marriages were polygynous (1979). Marriages are usually arranged, often between cousins to keep property within the family. Kuwaiti women rarely marry non-Kuwaiti men, and may not marry non-Moslems, although Kuwaiti men may marry non-Kuwaiti women, including non-Arabs and non-Moslems. Dowry is obligatory; the cost has risen with the increased wealth of the country. Most married Kuwaiti women employ domestic servants. **Divorce.** *Policy:* Husbands can divorce wives through *talaq* (renunciation). Wives can seek a divorce on grounds of cruelty, desertion, impotence, incurable insanity, or chronic disease, or if the right to divorce is stipulated in the marriage contract. *Practice:* Divorces (per 1000 pop. age 15 and older, 1979): 2.4 (4.4 K, 1.1 non-K). The divorce rate is rising. More women are demanding that their right to divorce be included in a premarital agreement.

Family. *Policy:* The Constitution states, "National laws should preserve the family structure, strengthen family ties, and protect motherhood and childhood under the family." Women with family responsibilities are legally restricted from night employment. The government sponsors maternity benefits (1 month at full pay), 2-month maternity leave, and childcare for children age 3–6. *Practice:* In 1981 there were 73 free, government-run kindergartens serving 19,762 children. Most Kuwaitis depend on domestic workers for childcare. A modern maternity hospital (opened 1961) and 13 "motherhood centers" offer pre- and post-natal care and delivery; services are free to K and non-K women. **Welfare.** *Policy:* State policy is to distribute the new oil wealth among the citizens. Health services and education, including uniforms, books, and school meals, are free to everyone; stipends are paid to families of students who might otherwise be needed to contribute to the family income. University students (predominantly men) who are sent abroad on scholarships receive generous living stipends and annual round-trip tickets home. The government funds public assistance programs for needy individuals, the aged, disabled, orphans, widows, single women over 18, and prisoners' families; it also maintains orphanages, seniorcare facilities, libraries, theaters, and recreational facilities. The government offers low-interest automatic loans to Kuwaitis to encourage them to buy their own homes, sponsors large-scale low- and middle-income housing construction, and gives rent subsidies to all Kuwaiti families living in leased housing. *Practice:* In 1981, 8675 families received welfare.

Contraception. *Policy:* Legal, although the government is pro-natalist. Familyplanning services are restricted, but in the late 1960's the government opened a center offering sex-education and familyplanning information to those considering marriage. *Practice:* No statistics obtainable. Contraceptives are available without prescription, but public awareness of them is very low. There is no sexeducation in schools. **Abortion.** *Policy:* Legal if pregnancy is not beyond 4 months, if approved by a gynecologist and 2 other doctors, if the woman's life is in danger, or if fetus has brain damage "beyond hope of treatment"; must be performed in a government hospital. Kuwait was the first Arab nation in the Gulf to legalize abortion (1982). An attempt to induce abortion without "justifiable cause" is considered a "grave sin" and a criminal act. *Practice:* No statistics obtainable. Since legal abortion is permitted only in restricted circumstances, most women with the financial means to do so leave the country to obtain legal abortions elsewhere. Illegal abortions are performed in secrecy and at great cost. **Illegitimacy.** *Policy:* Premarital sexual relations and adultery are considered criminal acts. No further data obtainable. *Practice:* No statistics obtainable. Women who become pregnant "illegally" are secluded in government hospitals. Details of their relationships are investigated by police and social workers. Police frequently threaten imprisonment to force the man to marry the pregnant woman; such marriages often end in hasty divorce

after the child is born. If the woman does not marry, she may be forced to give up her child, who is placed in a State institution. The law is rarely applied to any but the poorest Kuwaiti women. Unmarried pregnant non-Kuwaiti women are deported. **Homosexuality.** *Policy:* Illegal, considered a sex crime, and punishable as a felony under the Penal Code. *Practice:* No data obtainable. **Incest.** *Policy:* Illegal, considered a sex crime, and punishable as a felony under the Penal Code. *Practice:* No statistics obtainable. In a 1979 study of 260 women who were pregnant out of wedlock, 5 had been victims of incest. **Sexual Harassment.** *Policy:* No data obtainable. *Practice:* No statistics obtainable. Women are often harassed when not wearing veils. Immigrant women dependent on male employers are subject to sexual pressure and exploitation. **Rape.** *Policy:* Illegal, considered a sex crime, and punishable as a felony under the Penal Code. *Practice:* No data obtainable. **Battery.** *Policy:* No specific data obtainable (see following article). *Practice:* No data obtainable. **Prostitution.** *Policy:* Illegal, considered a sex crime, and punishable as a felony under the Penal Code. *Practice:* No statistics obtainable. Prostitution is a highly organized industry in expensive suburban retreats. Some wealthy Kuwaiti men maintain Western women as mistresses, and many immigrant domestic workers have been forced into prostitution by male employers (see **Sexual Harassment**). **Traditional/Cultural Practices:** No data obtainable. **Crisis Centers:** No data obtainable.

HERSTORY. Archeological finds indicate that Failaka Island and the port of Kuwait were trading centers dating back to 3000 B.C.E. Early settlement in what is now Kuwait began in the 18th century C.E. when small groups emigrated there from Central Arabia. The Al-Sabah Dynasty was founded in 1756, and continues to rule today. The Shaikh concluded a treaty with Britain (1899), making Kuwait a British Protectorate and preventing a Turkish take-over.

Kuwait was recognized as an independent government in 1914, but continued under British protection, gaining full independence in 1961. A Constitution adopted in 1962 established Kuwait as a sovereign Arab State.

See following article on lack of information about women in the region. A girls' elementary school was opened in 1937. The first 6 Kuwaiti women college graduates received their degrees (from Cairo University) in 1960; the first woman received a graduate degree (in nuclear physics) in 1970. When women graduates first sought government jobs they were required to wear veils—a practice they had worked to end while in school—and consequently they refused the job offers. However, the Minister of Foreign Affairs (and royal heir) permitted women to work in his ministry without veils, and subsequently other ministries followed this policy. In 1970, 99% of women college graduates were employed; 50% held jobs in the Ministry of Education as teachers. That year, 215 Kuwaiti women held college degrees, and 5 held graduate degrees.

Ms. al-Qattami, a pioneer of women's rights, founded (1963) what is today the most prominent women's organization in Kuwait. The Arab Women's Conference was held in Kuwait in 1972; it issued a unanimous call for a minimum marriage age of 16, equal rights, the vote, and abolition of bridewealth.

In 1977–78 women demonstrated against and defeated a proposed bill which would have prevented women from working in offices. In 1980 the General Union of Trade Unions passed a resolution during its first annual conference, calling for Kuwait to grant full political and social rights to women.

A Women and Development conference organized by the Kuwaiti Women's Cultural and Social Assoc. (1980) hosted 16 delegations and many individuals from the Arabian Gulf nations and Arab world. A group was formed to organize a follow-up conference (1983–84) to establish a Gulf Women's Federation. In 1981 the Prime Minister "promised" that Kuwaiti women would soon be allowed to vote in parliamentary elections but not to run for office. However, in Jan. 1982, a bill to grant Kuwaiti women the vote came out of committee with a recommendation that it be rejected because "the time is not opportune for receiving the idea in the light of well-established traditions"; it was defeated by a vote of 27–7. A week later, 10,000 women demonstrated for enfranchisement, sent messages to the Assembly, and organized delegations to confront members who had voted against the bill. Women's groups were active in bringing about the 1982 legalization of abortion rights. An active women's suffrage movement, including the Kuwait Women's Social and Educational Society, lobbies for the right to vote and in 1984 planned a legal battle using the Constitution as a basis for winning women's suffrage.

MYTHOGRAPHY. In the region now known as Kuwait, matriarchal religion flourished for millennia. In Sumer (later Babylon) the major goddesses included Inana (who tamed nature and ruled fertility), Ninhursag ("The Lady of the Mountains and Mother of All," also known as Nintue, Ninmah, and Aruru), and the Great Goddess Nammu (Mother Sea) who gave birth to heaven and earth. To the ancient Arab population the sun was female, a goddess named Atthar, and Allat was the evening star. The Koreishites worshipped the goddess El-Ozza.

KUWAIT: God's Will—and the Process of Socialization
by Noura Al-Falah

This article will describe—rather than explain—women's position in this part of the world, with special focus on the present situation of women within the social institutions that constitute, in turn, the social structure.

My main sources of information in this descriptive study are the 1975 census[1] and the *Koran*—since the Constitution of Kuwait states in Article 2, "The Islamic Shari'a [code of law] shall be a main source of legislation."

Social studies on women in pre-Islamic society are rare. What is known about women's roles and status in that time is vague and mostly contradictory. About Islamic society, of course, we know much more. We know that Moslems believe males are superior to females. The *Koran* says, "men have a degree over them [women],"[2] "men are the protectors and maintainers of women,"[3] "get two witnesses . . . if there are not two men, then a man and two women . . . if one of them errs the other can remind her . . . ,"[4] and "God [thus] directs you as regards your children's [inheritance]: to the male, a portion equal to that of two females."[5]

Both sexes learn in the process of socialization that it is God's will that the female is created weak and emotional and the male is created strong, wise, and brave. The stronger sex must protect the weaker sex. Within the family, the female (whether she is mother, wife, sister, or daughter) has to depend on the male (whether he is father, husband, brother, or even son). The extension of his responsibilities increases his rights—at the expense of hers. In fact, she cannot enjoy any of her rights without his approval. Thus, in some cases, laws that are concerned with a woman's rights are boldly violated by the father or the woman's guardian.

Census data on marital status by age show that marriage occurs at an early age.[6] Some girls marry before they reach eighteen. It is very difficult for a female (or a male) to select a spouse, because of the segregation of opposite sexes: "Believing women . . . should . . . not display their beauty except to their husbands, their husbands' sons, their brothers and their brothers' sons or their sisters' sons, or their women, or slaves . . . or male servants free of physical needs, or small children who have no sense of the shame of sex. . . ."[7] Consequently, arranged marriage in this society excludes the participation of the female in the choice of her future husband. A woman cannot marry without the approval of her father or guardian even if she is *over* twenty-one years of age. And despite religious instructions that a woman has to be consulted in her marriage and must be free to accept or refuse the person chosen by her family, some girls are forced to marry even

---

[1] The figures of the 1980 Kuwait census are still (1983) considered by the Central Statistical Office as preliminary results which have to be revised.

[2] The *Koran*, translation and commentary by A. Yusaf Ali, American Trust Publication, 2nd ed., N. 228, Sūra II Al-Baqara.

[3] The *Koran*, N. 34, Sūra IV Al-Nisāa.

[4] The *Koran*, N. 282, Sūra II Al-Baqara.

[5] The *Koran*, N. 11, Sūra IV Al-Nisāa.

[6] In Kuwait there is no law which prescribes a minimum age for marriage.

[7] The *Koran*, N. 31, Sūra XXIV Al-Nur.

in the face of their own refusal. In this case, it is easy to violate the law as long as one does not have to register the marriage.

A Moslem female cannot marry a non-Moslem, while a Moslem male *can* marry "[not only] chaste women who are believers, but chaste women among the people of the book. . . ."[8] A Moslem man can marry up to four wives at a time: "Marry women of your choice, two or three or four; but if ye fear that ye shall not be able to deal justly [with them] then only one. . . ."[9] Data on marriage by number of wives indicate that out of 7595 marriages in Kuwait in 1979, 746 were polygamous.[10] *"Al-mahr,"* or dowry, is obligatory: "Give the women [on marriage] their dower as a free gift. . . ."[11] The wife, according to religious instructions, has to obey her husband. If she refuses, she must be punished by him: "As to those women on whose part ye fear disloyalty and ill conduct, admonish them [first], [next] refuse to share their beds, and [last] beat them. . . ."[12]

The husband has the right to divorce his wife: "A divorce is only permissible twice: after that, the parties should either hold together on equitable terms or separate with kindness. . . . If a husband divorces his wife [irrevocably], he cannot after that remarry her until after she has married another husband and he also divorces her. . . ."[13] The wife can obtain the right to divorce—*if* her husband agrees to have it stipulated in the marriage contract. (But she knows that her husband will disagree and this "right" is still regarded by the society as something unusual and unfair to the husband!) No female, until very recently, dared ask for the right to divorce. Every woman whose marriage is terminated by divorce or by the death of the husband must seclude herself for three months (in case of divorce) and four months and ten days (in case of death): "If any of you die and leave widows behind, they shall wait concerning themselves four months and ten days."[14]

According to the Nationality Law, a Kuwaiti female married to a foreign husband can retain her Kuwaiti citizenship, but her husband cannot acquire her nationality. A foreign wife of a Kuwaiti man can, however, acquire her husband's nationality.[15]

Data on education indicate that the rate of *illiteracy* in this society is *28.5 percent for males and 45.8 percent for females.* The illiteracy rate among Kuwaiti females is *higher* than among non-Kuwaiti females: 59.1 percent and 31.3 percent respectively. The rate of illiteracy for Kuwaiti females age ten to fourteen is 9 percent. This means that not all females of compulsory school age have been allowed by their families to attend school (education in Kuwait is free at all levels and supposedly compulsory until the end of the intermediate level).[16] According to the 1975 census, 2328 women out of 131,705 illiterate persons were enrolled in adult-education centers, where education is also free.[17] Data in Table 1 show that the majority of graduate women specialized in humanities and social sciences. This means that a woman's choice of areas of specialization is restricted by traditional ideas about educational areas suitable for what is called the "nature of the

[8.] The *Koran,* N. 6, Sūra V Al-Maida.

[9.] The *Koran,* N. 3, Sūra IV Al-Nisāa.

[10.] *Annual Bulletin of Vital Statistics, Marriage and Divorce 1979.* Ministry of Planning, Central Statistical Office, Kuwait (in Arabic), Table 9, p. 13.

[11.] The *Koran,* N. 4, Sūra IV Al-Nisāa.

[12.] The *Koran,* N. 3, Sūra IV Al-Nisāa.

[13.] The *Koran,* N. 230–32, Sūra II Al-Baqara.

[14.] The *Koran,* N. 239, Sūra II Al-Baqara.

[15.] Articles 8, 10, Nationality Law of 1959.

[16.] Article 40 of the Constitution states, "Education is a right for Kuwaitis, guaranteed by the State . . . [and] in its preliminary stages shall be compulsory and free in accordance with law."

[17.] *Annual Statistical Abstract,* Tables 39, 329.

female" (social sciences and arts) and about areas suitable for males (engineering, geology, medicine, etc.).

TABLE 1

Females Holding University Degrees by
Specialization and Nationality, 1975

Specialization	Kuwaiti	non-Kuwaiti	Total
Human sciences	521	2,011	2,532
Education	52	437	489
Fine arts	15	381	396
Law	37	135	172
Social sciences	297	1,441	1,738
Natural sciences	229	817	1,046
Engineering	5	121	126
Medical sciences	56	521	577
Agriculture	4	89	93
Unspecified specializations	8	—	8
Total	1,224	5,953	7,177

Source: Annual Statistical Abstract, Table 38, p. 44.

The participation of females in the labor force has increased since the 1950's: from 3 percent of the total labor force in 1957 to 7.3 percent in 1975. However, the participation of the female non-Kuwaiti in the labor force is *higher* than that of the Kuwaiti female: 12.9 percent, 3.2 percent respectively. (These percentages are based on female workers age twelve and over.) Article 41 of the Constitution of Kuwait states: "Every Kuwaiti has the right to work. . . ." But according to tradition, the female who intends to work outside the home must ask permission from the males—"the maintainers" of the family —who traditionally have the right to forbid female relatives to work. Many females (some with university degrees) have not been allowed to work outside the home. The Constitution states that every Kuwaiti has the right to choose the type of his *[sic]* work (Art. 41). Yet most females are not really free to choose the kind of job they like, because they must search for jobs where the sexes are segregated. Thus they mostly work for the government as teachers or administrators in girls' public schools. Furthermore, these days the traditionalists are waging a campaign against integration of the sexes, demanding further segregation and re-veiling of women: "Believing [devout] women . . . should draw their veils over their bosoms. . . ."[18] This campaign now has been extended to a direct attack on working women, reminding them of the Koranic *àya:* "Stay quietly in your houses. . . ."[19] The most difficult problem employed mothers face is the nonexistence of centers with proper standards of childcare, where mothers can leave their preschool children while they are working.

The Constitution assures the principle of equality between males and females. In respect to a woman's political rights it states, "All people are equal . . . in public rights and duties before the law without distinction as to sex, origin, language, or religion" (Art.

[18] The *Koran,* N. 31, Sūra XXIV Al-Nur.
[19] The *Koran,* N. 33, Sūra XXIII Al-Ahzab.

29). Yet the election law ignored the principle of equality and deprived women of their right to vote and to be elected.*

Females in Kuwaiti society suffer from the same problem encountered by females all over the world: the problem of sex discrimination. But this discrimination in itself—and the awareness of it by men or women, their attitudes, and the struggle against it—differs from one society to another.

Any social problem has to be examined within the social structure that forms its own culture and creates its own problems. In underdeveloped countries, people are preoccupied with the problems of underdevelopment—which makes it very difficult for women to conceive the specifics of their own situation. An illiterate female is unable to realize her subordination fully; she is not aware of her rights, she does not know how to enjoy the rights which the law does guarantee, and she is incapable of understanding the danger of being economically dependent on males.

In this society, women as well as men are victims of underdevelopment. Thus, Kuwait women who are conscious, willing, and able to help other women raise their consciousness have to take into consideration other social problems that should be eliminated, or at least reduced. The effects of these other problems have been, after all, perpetuating sex discrimination. In Kuwait, institutions and associations themselves reflect the general backwardness; most women's associations, for instance, are traditional or religious in their goals. And last but far from least, women in Kuwait have to learn from the experiences of women in various other societies, women who have been struggling to ensure equality between the sexes. Then, Kuwait women will be able to create in this country the first movement to liberate women and in the process, at the same time, develop their entire society.

Suggested Further Reading
[Contributor regretfully cannot recommend any books on women in Kuwait.]

Noura Al-Falah was born in Kuwait and educated at Cairo University in Egypt. She took her master's and doctoral degrees in sociology at New York University. She currently teaches sociology at Kuwait University, focusing on the problems facing women, the distribution of the national income and the Kuwait social structure, the social environment, and the concept of the public job.

---

* In Jan. 1982, ten thousand women marched through the streets of the capital city of Kuwait in protest of once again having been denied the vote.—Ed.

LEBANON
(Republic of Lebanon)

Located in southwest Asia, bordered by Syria to the north and east, Israel to the south, and the Mediterranean Sea to the west. **Area:** 10,400 sq. km. (4,015 sq. mi.). **Population** (1980): 3,161,000; female 49.7%. **Capital:** Beirut.

DEMOGRAPHY. Languages: Arabic (official), French, Armenian, English. **Races or Ethnic Groups:** Arab 93%, Armenian 6%, other. **Religions:** Islam and Christianity predominantly, Druze,* Judaism; there are more than 15 recognized religious communities in Lebanon. Among the Islamic pop.: Sunni (orthodox/traditionalist), whose 4 main branches are Hanafites, Malikites, Shafi'ites, and Hanabalites, and Shi'ite (sectarian), whose branches include Alaouites, Ismailites, and such "deviationist" sects as Assassins and Fatimites; among the Christian pop.: Maronite, Greek Orthodox, Greek Catholic, Armenian Orthodox or Gregorian, Armenian Catholic, Syrian Orthodox, Syrian Catholic, Assyrian Chaldean (Nestorian), Chaldean, Latine, Evangeline (Protestant), Israelite (see GOVERNMENT for an explanation of the political system based on religious diversity). **Education** (% enrolled in school, 1975): Age 6–11— of all girls 85%, of all boys 93%; age 12–17—of all girls 55%, of all boys 70%; higher education—no statistics obtainable; women began attending universities (primarily French and American) in the 1920's; today, women students are entering the fields of science, medicine, engineering, etc., in addition to "traditional women's areas" (teaching, nursing, etc.). **Literacy** (1977): Women 58%, men 78%. **Birth Rate** (per 1000 pop., 1975–80): 34. **Death Rate** (per 1000 pop., 1975–80): 10. **Infant Mortality** (per 1000 live births, 1975–80): Female 61, male 68. **Life Expectancy** (1975–80): Female 67 yrs., male 63 yrs.

GOVERNMENT. An independent republic was declared in 1943; a constitution was established in 1926 (since amended) while Lebanon was under French mandate. A unicameral parliamentary system reflects the representative religious groups through proportional representation in the elected 99-member Chamber of Deputies. Traditionally, the president (elected by parliament) is a Christian and the prime minister is a Moslem. The president appoints a cabinet (also composed by proportional representation, as is the civil service). Each religious group has drawn up a Personal Status Code, making the law conform to religious doctrine for its community. **Women's Suffrage:** 1952, but restricted to women who had completed primary education. All women were granted full suffrage in 1953, but voting was optional for women and compulsory for men. In 1957 women won the right to vote on the same terms as men. **Equal Rights:** The Constitution (Art. 7) stipulates that all Lebanese are equal before the law. **Women in Government:** No statistics obtainable. The first woman ambassador, Sameera Al-Daher, was appointed in 1983. Because of the structure of parliament, the participation of women is in effect limited because numerous sects may disagree on the right of a woman to serve at all.

ECONOMY. Currency: Lebanese Pound (May 1983: 4.2 = $1 US). **Gross National Product** (1981): $4 billion. **Per Capita Income** (1981): $1200. **Women's Wages as a Percentage of Men's:** No general statistics obtainable. Most women are concentrated in the lowest-paying jobs; 90% of women textile workers received below minimum wage (1979). **Equal Pay Policy:** No data obtainable. **Production** (Agricultural/Industrial): Fruits, olives, tobacco, grapes, vegetables, grains; food products, textiles, cement, oil products. **Women as a Percentage of Labor Force** (1981): 25%; **of agricultural**

---

* The Druzes have a distinct religious system relating to the Fatimids but are not in a strict sense part of Islam as generally practiced.

force—no general statistics obtainable (11% of women workers were employed in agriculture, 1975); **of industrial force** —no data obtainable; **of military**—no data obtainable. **(Employed) Women's Occupational Indicators:** Of skilled and semi-skilled workers 14%, of professional workers 20%, of service workers 23%, of administrative workers 33%, of the commercial sector 33% (1979–80); in the professions, most women were teachers (of elementary school 93%, of secondary school 67%); in the commercial sector, most women worked as salespersons, 11% were retail owners or managers, almost 90% were employed in the lowest-paid sector. Employers tend to hire young women; in 1979–80, single women made up at least 70% of the female work force in all the above sectors (98% in service, 93% in personnel) except commercial, in which 49% (primarily in sales) were married. **Unemployment:** No data obtainable.

GYNOGRAPHY. Marriage: *Policy:* Separate Personal Status Codes have been set up by the 15 Ecclesiastical Courts which represent the various religious communities in Lebanon. There are 11 Moslem courts, 3 Christian courts, and 1 Rabbinical Court. In Islamic communities, Personal Status Codes are based on the Shari'a, which is interpreted differently by the various Moslem communities and which governs marriage and divorce, among other matters. In addition, while the laws governing Lebanese Moslems are similar to those governing other Moslems, the laws affecting some Shi'ite sects and the Druze pop. are different. In the majority of Moslem communities, Personal Status Codes follow traditional Islamic marriage codes, in which the husband is the legal head of household in charge of family matters, children's education, property, and travel. Islamic jurisprudence stipulates general practice regarding the payment of *mahar* and women's right to only ½ the inheritance of men. Polygyny is legal for most Moslem men; a man is allowed 4 wives (the exceptions are the Druze and Shi'ite Ismailis, who abolished polygyny for their members). Civil marriage for Moslems is prohibited; marriage be-

tween Moslems and non-Moslems generally is prohibited unless 1 party converts; marriage between a Moslem man and a Christian woman is allowed, but the reverse is prohibited, except in certain rare cases. A woman who marries a man outside of her religion loses her inheritance rights. For all Lebanese, except men in legal polygynous marriages, bigamy is illegal and is punishable by imprisonment. Adultery is also illegal, punishable by imprisonment, and grounds for divorce in some communities. Art. 562 of the Penal Code stipulates that any man who surprises his wife, sister, daughter, or other kinswoman in adultery and kills her "benefits from alleviating circumstances," limiting punishment to a few weeks' imprisonment.

Practice: Female mean age at marriage (1970–78): 23; women age 15–49 in union (1970–78): 58%. While religious customs vary, many young girls are forced into arranged marriages by their families. Islamic jurisprudence stipulates equal treatment of wives in polygynous relationships, but this is not legally controlled. Polygyny is a source of conflict and economic insecurity for many wives (see **Divorce**). Frequent attempts to institute uniform civil laws regarding marriage, inheritance, divorce, etc., have been unsuccessful (see HERSTORY and following article).

Divorce. *Policy:* Legal in some communities; based on Personal Status Codes (see **Marriage**). For some Moslem groups, *talaq* (verbal repudiation) is legal. A Moslem woman can divorce her husband but must do so through the courts and she loses her right to her dowry; Shi'ites in Lebanon do not allow women to initiate divorce. Husbands are frequently granted custody of children over age 7. The Druze code permits divorce only by judicial process. For most Christians, divorce is difficult to obtain; it is illegal for Christian Maronites, but annulment of a marriage can be granted in some cases. In Greek Orthodox Christian communities, a husband can divorce a wife if she uses contraception without his knowledge, if he finds out that she was not a virgin upon marriage, or if she frequents "suspicious" places without his permission; a woman can divorce a husband if he falsely accuses her of adultery, if he leads her into prostitution, if he does not have marital relations with her for 3 yrs., or if he commits adultery in the marital home and "refuses to reform." For Rabbinical Court procedure, see ISRAEL. In some communities, divorce is permitted on grounds of mutual consent, adultery, bigamy, abandonment of the marital home, or prolonged absence, among other reasons; application of the law varies according to respective religious Personal Status Codes. In case of divorce by mutual consent, child custody may be given to either parent, but the husband is required to support a wife and child. *Practice:* No statistics obtainable. For some Islamic men, repudiative divorce is common and allows them to bypass the limit of 4 wives. In all communities, divorce is accompanied by economic hardship for women, who own little property, can inherit little property, and are often rejected by their families because of being "dishonored." Divorced women still bear a strong stigma in some orthodox religious communities.

Family. *Policy:* Family insurance and maternity leave are stipulated for all Lebanese workers. A woman who is not employed in the labor force and is the "legitimate" wife of an insured worker or the first wife of a man in a polygynous marriage is eligible for insurance benefits, as are "legitimate" dependent children and single females up to age 25. Maternity leave is available to women who register 10 *[sic]* months in advance of the presumed date of delivery. No data obtainable on childcare. *Practice:* No data obtainable. **Welfare.** *Policy:* National Social Security provides employees with sickness benefits and health care, insurance against accidents, and indemnity for termination of service (see **Family** for eligibility status). Medical insurance covers 26 weeks of care; persons must have had insurance for 3 months within the 6 months preceding the sickness to be covered; dental and eye care are also provided. Unemployment benefits are available to employees with a 20-yr. job record. Retirement is at age 55 for women, 60 for men. *Practice:* No statistics obtainable; second, third, and fourth wives of a man in a polygynous marriage are not covered by Social Security; divorced and single women over age 25 are not eligible for coverage under their own families' insurance. Workers who are in the "informal" labor market are not eligible for national insurance coverage. In addition, the death of many men through war has left a high number of female-headed households; often the women are nonliterate and unskilled and have never worked in the official labor force, and consequently fall outside of the regulations governing family and Social Security policies. **Contraception.** *Policy:* Illegal; no statements of population policy are known to have been made since 1979. *Practice:* Women age 15–49 in union using contraception (1970–80): 53%, of which traditional methods 58.5%, modern 39.6%, sterilization 1.9%. Although contraception is illegal, it is a socially accepted practice among members of the upper and middle class. Reports indicate that the Ministry of Labour and Social Welfare as well as the Lebanese Army provide family-planning services in their welfare clinics, with the goal of improving maternal and child health. Voluntary female sterilization is provided through nongovernmental organizations. Most poor and rural women are unaware of family-planning methods, although the Lebanon Family Planning Assoc. (founded 1969) has been active in providing services, especially for villages. **Abortion.** *Policy:* Legal only to save the woman's life; all other abortions are punishable by imprisonment; no further data obtainable. *Practice:* No data obtainable.

Illegitimacy. *Policy:* The legal status of a child is based on paternity. Following interpretation of Islamic jurisprudence, a "natural" child is given the mother's family name at birth and can be recognized later by the father. In the case of a child born to a single mother, legal legitimacy can occur if marriage takes place after childbirth. In all of the above cases, the child assumes the father's name and is given equal status to children born within wedlock. A child of incestuous relations cannot be legally recognized by the father. A Moslem man can legally repudiate his child *(la'am)*. Under Islamic jurisprudence, a man can challenge his paternity in court if he "suspects" his wife of adultery, or in cases of rape or of wife-kidnapping. An out-of-wedlock child has inferior legal status and inheritance rights. *Practice:* No data obtainable. **Homosexuality.** *Policy:* Illegal; punishable by a fine of L£.10–100 and 1 month–1 yr. imprisonment. Under the laws governing prostitution, homosexual acts in brothels are forbidden and, in addition to the penalties for prostitution, the brothel is forced to close for 1 week–6 months (see **Prostitution**). *Practice:* No statistics obtainable; there are strong cultural tabus against homosexuality in most of the religious communities.

Incest. *Policy:* It is illegal and punishable by not less than 1 yr. imprisonment for a father to have sexual relations with a daughter; no further data obtainable. *Practice:* No data obtainable. **Sexual Harassment.** *Policy:* No data obtainable. *Practice:* No data obtainable. **Rape.** *Policy:* Illegal; "seduction" of a female under age 18 is punishable by 3 months–2 yrs. imprisonment. Marital rape is not recognized by law. No further data obtainable. *Practice:* No statistics obtainable. Women bear the burden of proof in cases of rape. A woman who is raped has little measure of grievance and is often repudiated by her "dishonored" husband as well as her family. **Battery.** *Policy:* No specific legislation, but general laws governing assault may be applied in some cases. *Practice:* No statistics obtainable, but reports indicate that wife-beating is common and a socially tolerated practice in some communities.

Prostitution. *Policy:* Legal for an identified caste of registered prostitutes; illegal for "secret" prostitutes or "streetwalkers." Under legal prostitution, brothels may not be operated by males, may be opened only in areas specified by the authorities, must be completely separated from all neighboring buildings, and must comply with health regulations and sanitary conditions. A brothel owner who wants to leave her brothel must notify the police 15 days in advance; brothel owners must be over age 25 and may operate only 1 establishment for prostitution. Prostitutes must be over age 21, have legal identification, and fill out applications for police inspection and registration. Virgins may not become legal

prostitutes, and male clients under age 18 are not permitted. Prostitutes are legally allowed to leave their brothels from 9 A.M. to 4 P.M. but cannot leave on Sundays or holidays, or frequent such public gathering places as cafés, public gardens, etc.; they must be veiled in public and undergo free bimonthly medical inspections which are conducted by health officials appointed by the Ministry of Health. Singing and music are forbidden in brothels; a *Code des Moeurs* (Code of Morals or Manners) must be placed in every brothel sitting room. Vice squads may inspect the brothels at any time. Under the Penal Code covering illegal prostitution, female prostitutes are subject to a fine or imprisonment; pimps and solicitors are subject to imprisonment; male prostitutes may be sentenced to 2–6 months imprisonment. *Practice:* No statistics obtainable. Prostitution is prevalent in the urban areas of Lebanon and reports indicate that the incidence of illegal prostitution is high as well, particularly among immigrant women who are not legal residents of Lebanon and are not permitted to perform legal work.

Traditional/Cultural Practices. *Policy:* No data obtainable. *Practice:* Islamic customs (depending on the group, school of practice, and interpretation of legal code) include inspections to ensure a bride's virginity; such practices as female genital excision (see Glossary) are sometimes observed as well. **Crisis Centers:** No data obtainable.

HERSTORY. The Phoenicians established colonies and commercial seaports along the shores of present-day Lebanon in the 9th century B.C.E.; Alexander the Great conquered the area (333–332 B.C.E.). In 64 B.C.E. the Romans took control, and by the 7th century C.E., when the Arab conquest began, the Christian Maronites were already established in the region. The gradual disruption of the Arab Abbasid Empire began in the 9th century, when it broke into independent States created by Turkish, Persian, or Arab dynasties. Ottoman Turkish domination lasted from 1517–1918 when the French Mandate over Lebanon and Syria was established; that lasted until 1943.

In 1834 missionaries established in Beirut the first secondary school for girls in the Ottoman Empire; in the second half of the century, more religious groups established foreign schools for girls. The Women's School of Nursing was founded at the American University of Beirut in 1908, and in 1921 the first female students were admitted to the American and French universities. In 1926 Greater Lebanon (Lebanon and surrounding Moslem areas) gained a republican constitution. Lebanon won Independence in 1943.

An Armenian poet, writer, and journalist, Siran Seza, published a magazine, *Young Armenian Women* in 1948; other ethnic and religious women's groups founded journals, and were active in promoting health care, literacy, and social reforms that affected women.

Throughout centuries of conflict, Lebanese women have shared in the active resistance of their countrymen against foreign intervention or internal dissension. In the current war (since 1975) women have borne the brunt of suffering; there are no reliable statistics on the number of war widows in Lebanon, but survey estimates of women-headed households in the southern regions place the figure around 35% or higher.

Since 1969, intermittent hostile incidents have occurred on the frontier between Israel and Lebanon, caused by frequent clashes between Israeli and Lebanon-based Palestinians who, since 1948, had migrated to Lebanon in large numbers and, in 1970, attained 600,000. This led to civil war in Lebanon. Syrian troops were sent to Lebanon in 1976 with the aim of ending fighting between Palestinians and Lebanese, but in 1979 war broke out between Syrians and Lebanese militias. On June 6, 1982, Israel launched a full-scale air, land, and sea attack on Palestinian strongholds in Lebanon. Thousands of Palestinian and Lebanese civilians were killed in the cross-fire. The exodus of the PLO forces was begun. In Sept., hundreds of Palestinian civilians (mostly women and children) were massacred in the refugee camps of Sabra and Shatila near Beirut (see ISRAEL; PALESTINE). In late 1983, PLO factions led by Yassir Arafat were evacuated from Tripoli.

Women's associations in Lebanon have flourished persistently since the late 19th century and today constitute more than 100. Many are benevolent organizations focusing on social work and/or peace efforts. Each belongs to the Lebanese Women's Union (LWU), which is in turn affiliated with the Arab Women's Union.

The Beirut-based Institute for Women's Studies in the Arab World is a major research and resource center for all women. In 1981 the Ninth Conference of the Committee for Lebanese Women's Rights was held in Beirut. The National Alliance of Lebanese Women held its second conference in 1982. Feminist groups and associations have been pressing for a uniform system of personal status laws and the abolition of all laws that disadvantage women, such as Art. 562 of the Penal Code (see **Marriage).**

MYTHOGRAPHY. Among the goddesses who were revered in ancient Phoenicia, Ashtart (Astarte, Ishtar, Astaroth) was referred to as Queen of Heaven with the Crescent Horns (also sometimes called Urania). Astarte was said to have descended as a fiery sphere over Mount Lebanon. The Phoenicians, being sailors, had many myths that referred to the power of the goddess over water. They worshipped the Serpent Goddess and Asherah, the Holy Queen; in the cities of Sidon and Tyre there are still ruins of shrines built to Asherah.

LEBANON: The Harem Window
by Rose Ghurayyib

The Lebanese woman, like her sisters all over the world, suffers the burdens of the patriarchal system. Her treatment as an object of exploitation is reflected in the Lebanese proverbs "My husband loved me when I was young; my parents loved me when I was strong," and "Worry about a girl's future persists until death"—which means worry about her ability to keep intact the family "honor," her ability to win a husband who will be a source of pride to her family, and her ability to find favor in the eyes of her husband and in-laws by giving them a male heir.

The condition of the Lebanese woman began to change, however, during the last century, when opportunities opened up for her to receive a modern education and to seek economic independence. Lebanon came in contact with other modern cultures earlier than most Arab countries, and as a consequence, its women benefited from this contact earlier than other Arab women.

The central geographic position of Lebanon, its small size, and its limited natural resources made it a spot open to free trade and foreign influence, a refuge for racial and religious minorities, and a crossroads of cultures. On an area of 10,000 square kilometers, 3 million inhabitants are crowded, making it the most densely populated country in the region. That population represents seventeen religious communities, the bulk of which reside in villages scattered over the mountain slopes.

Since Phoenician times (3000 B.C.E.) emigration of the Lebanese westward and elsewhere has followed a steady stream. In the sixteenth–seventeenth centuries C.E., Fakhreddin II, a local governor under Ottoman rule (which lasted from 1517 to 1918), established commercial and cultural relations with Italy and France. Thus the way was paved for the spread of foreign schools founded by French and American missionaries, who flocked to Lebanon during the nineteenth century and contributed to its development as an early center of Arab awakening. Lebanese women who, in addition to household duties, shared with their husbands farming activities, silkworm raising, and domestic crafts, now had the chance to learn foreign languages and to acquire skills in refined types of arts and crafts, including sewing, embroidery, and needlework. During the first half of the nineteenth century, many of them set out to neighboring Arab countries—Egypt, Palestine, and Iraq—where they took part in the establishment of girls' schools and the development of female education. As an example, we may mention May Ziadeh, who emigrated with her parents to Egypt, where she worked as magazine correspondent, author, public speaker, and salon director. Other Lebanese women writers flourished in Egypt: Jeanne Arcache, Aimée Kheir, and Andrée Chédid, the well-known poet and novelist who, after a debut in Egypt and Lebanon, settled in Paris, where she published her voluminous literary works.

Influenced by spreading foreign ideas (and even backed by some male journalists and writers), a few intellectual women began to form voluntary associations and create women's magazines. Those early women writers and journalists were moved by the traditional ideal that a woman's value rests on her ability to benefit her family and her people, and so they identified their own needs with those of their country; they preached modern ideas of social justice, nationalism, woman's emancipation, romantic love, educational reform, and prison reform. Women's organizations flourished in the twentieth century, revolving around child welfare, village welfare, Red Cross services, and the establishment of child-care centers and old-age homes.

Two important achievements owed their existence to women's efforts and leadership. The first was the founding in the early 1930's of the Artisans' Association (Artisanat) by Marie Eddé, wife of the President of the Republic, assisted by other women; the Association helped to revive embroidery and lace-work skills and created work centers all over the country. The second achievement was the creation, around 1955, of the International Baalbeck Festival by a group of voluntary women leaders, including the wife of the then President of the Republic, Zalpha Chamoun, and other women representing various Lebanese communities. This enterprise gave impetus to local folkloric music, dances, and songs, and attracted a large number of international art groups, musicians, actors, dancers, and so forth.

Women succeeded in other fields as well. In addition to educational activity outside Lebanon, they also founded local girls' schools in their own country. Higher education for women started between 1920 and 1925, when the two universities of Beirut, the American and the French, admitted women to their professional schools and (in 1924) the American Junior College, now Beirut University College, started a two-year program preparing women students for further study at university level.

Progress and expansion have continued. Recent statistics show the growing interest of women students in science as a major, and the decision of many to enter a profession. In addition to the traditional careers of teaching, nursing, and secretarial work, new professions are now open to women: medicine, engineering, architecture, pharmacy, and law. (Of university professors however, only 14 percent are women.)[1]

The percentage of Lebanese women's participation in the total labor force has risen from 17 percent in 1972 to 25 percent in 1981. Women's work outside the home is not limited to the professions. There are those who do rural work and receive little or no compensation, and those who do paid work in industrial plants. A study on women and work in Lebanon, recently prepared by the Institute for Women's Studies in the Arab World, shows that in spite of the growing need for women's participation in development and their increasing interest in work for economic reasons, working conditions in the industrial sector still do not encourage women to seek permanent employment. Most women leave work upon marriage, not only because housework absorbs so much of their time but also because they have little opportunity for promotion and for occupying leadership positions. Working women in rural and industrial sectors need more training and more encouraging conditions so that they may like their work and persist in it. They deserve special attention from the authorities and from women's organizations in Lebanon.

The relatively large number of schools and institutes of higher education has, on the other hand, allowed women to achieve distinction in at least three fields.

First, in journalism, for which Lebanese women were prepared in the early part of the century, when they founded and edited magazines in Lebanon and Egypt. Right before World War II, they participated intensely in the publication of French papers and magazines published in the country and then extended their participation to Arabic and English print media. According to recent statistics, women constitute about 25 percent of all journalists in Lebanon. It is true that the majority of them do not occupy leadership positions, yet all are highly educated, and many have distinguished themselves as poets or novelists. "They have proved to be so efficient in the journalistic field that it will not be long before they gain admission to the upper echelons," prophesies Denise Ammoun, editing secretary of *L'Orient-Le-Jour* (a daily paper).

[1.] Report by Dr. J. Abu Nasr, presented at a Far Eastern conference, 1978.

A second field in which women have shown their competence is the literary one—particularly poetry. While in the early part of the century Lebanese women achieved distinction as prose writers and founders of women's magazines, during the second half of the century they have provided at least twenty poets out of the seventy well-known contemporary women poets in the Arab world. A relatively large number of these women wrote their poems in French or English as well as in Arabic. It is important to note that this poetry is nontraditional in both structure and content. Most of it takes the form of prose poems (influenced by Western forms, including the post-romantic and surrealist styles). In content this poetry is largely personal, depicting tension, longing, or escape; love in its various forms—romantic, mystical, erotic—plays an important role. There is also "committed poetry" which attacks social evils, injustice, corruption, war, fanaticism; some of it pleads for the Palestinian cause or reveals Leftist influence. As a whole, it is a poetry of defiance, implying revolt against the traditional socialization of women, which turns them into automatons whose only concerns revolve around their bodies and the desire to please the male—he who looms as the deity "with multiple presences," as Samia Tutunji says in a poem.

A third field in which Lebanese women have been showing their emancipation and creativity is the artistic one—painting, sculpture, and ceramics. In an unpublished 1975 study about contemporary Lebanese women artists done by Helen El-Khal (herself an artist), the author says, "Today the proportion of widely recognized women artists in Lebanon is greater than in most other countries in the Arab world or in the West. Of the twelve leading artists of Lebanon, four are women."[2] Art has been to them a form of self-expression and assertion. In their harem, it is a window to the outside.

It is clear that the Lebanese woman, since the period of awakening in the early nineteenth century and especially since Independence of the French Mandate in 1943, has been active outside the home, and as a result has acquired a certain amount of personal freedom and financial independence. What about her political freedom? What about the personal-status laws which define women's rights in the family and her share in inheritance? How far has she progressed in these important fields?

She was granted the right to vote in 1953. Since then, a few women have run for parliamentary elections, but they failed to win seats—a phenomenon generally attributed to sectarian rivalry and the inability of the numerous sects and parties to agree on a woman candidate. Though Lebanese women have a representative National Council which joins together their associations, they still face sectarian dissension that impedes their political activity.

As to the personal-status laws, here too sectarianism plays a role in preventing legal reform. Each of the religious sects has its own personal-status laws and courts which act independently of international agreements. However, obstacles that block change in this direction did not prevent a few Lebanese women's groups, encouraged by a number of men lawyers, from putting forward claims on several occasions for the establishment of civil marriage and the unification of the personal-status laws. One occasion was the seminar held in Beirut by the National Council of Lebanese Women in 1974, attended by delegates from other Arab countries and from various international councils of women. The Lebanese Democratic Party presented a paper which was read by lawyer Laure Mughayzil, deputy president of the International Women's Council, in which the Party proposed the adoption of a civil law applying to all citizens without differentiation due to religious beliefs and in conformity with the Universal Declaration of Human Rights. The war which followed in 1975 prevented any further action for the study and execution of the proposed plan. Political struggle superseded all other activity, and war served to

[2.] *Al-Raida*, No. 2, Beirut, Sept. 1977, p. 2.

revive religious fanaticism and division. Yet it did not deter the president of the Women's Democratic League, Linda Matar, from presenting (in 1980) a charter of women's rights claiming complete equality of women with men in family status, inheritance, civil, and penal laws.

Strongly related to sectarian division are feudal practices inherited from the past which give certain families a monopoly of political leadership in their own districts or communities. Tribal laws and clan loyalties are perpetuated by the family, which tries to bind its members in a solid union and to impose on them its political views and social concepts, including nepotism and dependence. In order to protect its power and prerogatives, the family becomes the guardian of entrenched traditions which stand against change and evolution. This in turn confirms beliefs in woman's inferiority and reinforces her subjugation to an oppressive double standard by restricting her function to reproduction. Such a condition was shown in a study made in 1972 by Dr. Mounir Chamoun, a well-known psychologist who came to the following conclusion: "The Lebanese woman approaches life with the undeclared desire to repeat her mother's image, i.e., to be a mother. Because of a precocious experience and through sociocultural influences, all her sexuality is oriented toward her function of reproduction and feeding. This polarization makes of her an asexual being, having no alternative but to live in an eternal motherhood."[3]

Thus the reasons which stand against national unity—sectarian division and clannish family structure—are the same as those which stand behind women's enslavement (specifically by preventing agreement on a unified personal-status law). Consequently, a woman who seeks liberation has to struggle on two fronts: the personal and the national. Because of this interdependence between personal and national freedom, the progress made in terms of education and work has failed to help the Lebanese woman build a new, independent personality, one free from the influence of oppressive traditions *and* free from mere imitation of Western models.

Education and work may have given her economic independence—but they have also subjected her to the authority of the boss. In many cases she has found herself using her job as bait for attracting suitors, thus continuing the dowry tradition. In her family she is not always free to dispose of the money she earns. The social influences that surround her remain largely traditional and have prevented her from accepting the wave which upholds sexual freedom (as publicized by Western films and magazines). However, her reserve in this respect has not necessarily prevented her blind imitation of foreign patterns and her adherence to foreign ideologies to the point of losing her own personality. The same woman who has been imbued with foreign culture may still be consciously or unconsciously attached to such harmful traits in her local heritage as morbid enslavement to a husband, to a son, or to an employer. On the whole, the average educated Lebanese woman still lacks the self-confidence to claim her rights and assert herself. Torn between contradictory influences, obliged to juggle education, work, and marriage, or to renounce one of them for the sake of the others, she is prey to worry and instability. The traditional fear of living alone often leads her to accept a compromise and sacrifice her ambition for the sake of complying with public opinion. What she says in her writing or in her poems is not always what she puts into practice. She needs honest support, validation, and further experience.

Feminism in Lebanon at this point requires dedicated women who believe in freedom and self-realization—and who act accordingly. These women will have to wage a lifelong struggle to achieve their aims and lead other women to follow their example.

The Lebanese feminist movement is still young. But what it has accomplished so far gives us high expectations of—and commitment to—its further progress.

[3] *Travaux et Jours,* No. 44, 1972, pp. 107–14.

Suggested Further Reading

Accad, Evelyne. *Contemporary Women Novelists in the Arab World;* a monograph to be published by the Institute for Women's Studies in the Arab World, Beirut.

Arab Women and Education, No. 2, 1980; monographs of the Institute for Women's Studies in the Arab World, Beirut.

Barakat, Halim. *Lebanon in Strife.* Austin and London: Univ. of Texas Press, 1977.

Ghurayyib, Rose. *Contemporary Women Poets in the Arab World;* a monograph to be published by the Institute for Women's Studies in the Arab World, Beirut.

Hamady, Samia. *Temperament and Character of the Arabs.* New York: Twayne Publishers, 1960.

The Status of Women in Arab Laws, in the Light of UN International Conventions, issued at the seminar of the National Council of Lebanese Women, Beirut, 1974.

Rose Ghurayyib is a Lebanese who after high school worked her way through college —at what is now Beirut University College, then at the American University of Beirut, where she obtained a B.A. and then an M.A. in Arabic literature. She has taught at several schools, including the French Protestant College in Beirut and Beirut University College, and written and published a series of Arabic books for children and young people, including poems, songs, stories, and plays. She also published textbooks of Arabic composition, books on literary criticism, literary studies about Gibran, May Ziadeh, and contemporary Arab women poets. She currently edits *Al-Raida,* the newsletter of the Institute for Women's Studies in the Arab World.

LIBYA
(Socialist People's Libyan Arab Jamahiriya)

Located in northern Africa, bordered by Egypt to the east, the Sudan to the southeast, Chad and Nigeria to the south, Algeria to the west, Tunisia to the northwest, and the Mediterranean Sea to the north. **Area:** 1,759,998 sq. km. (679,536 sq. mi.). **Population** (1980): 2,690,000, female 48%. **Capital:** Tripoli.

DEMOGRAPHY. Languages: Arabic (official). **Races or Ethnic Groups:** Arab-Berber 97%, Italian 1.4%, nomad, black-African origin, other. **Religions:** Islam (predominantly Sunni). **Education** (% enrolled in school, 1975): Age 6–11—of all girls 72%, of all boys 100%; age 12–17—of all girls 22%, of all boys 64%; in 1980–81 females made up 49.3% of primary-school enrollment, 46.4% of preparatory school, and 44.6% of secondary school; higher education—in 1980 women comprised 17% of university enrollment, compared to 9.9% in 1969–70. Most vocational schools train women in "domestic science" and health services. In 1982 the government initiated a campaign to increase the number of women in public teacher-training courses to 2500 annually while limiting male student enrollment, and to send 2000 female students annually to private teacher-training schools to become teachers at the preparatory level in all-girls' schools. Legislation (1977) prohibits women who graduate from teacher-training colleges from working in any field but teaching. Education is free and compulsory for both sexes through preparatory level; government stipends are available to both sexes for university education; however, since women are tracked into occupations "suitable for females," they commonly receive grants for studies in such traditionally female fields as teaching and social services [see (Employed) **Women's Occupational Indicators**]. **Literacy** (1977): Women 4%, men 38%; special government departments have been established to teach women to read. **Birth Rate** (per 1000 pop., 1975–80): 47. **Death Rate** (per 1000 pop., 1975–80): 13. **Infant Mortality** (per 1000 live births, 1975–80): Female 123, male 137; between the first and fifth yrs., female children's mortality rate rises precipitously to equal or surpass that of males, because of malnutrition and inadequate medical care. **Life Expectancy** (1975–80): Female 57 yrs., male 54 yrs.

GOVERNMENT. A 1969 military coup led by Col. Muammar el-Qaddafi deposed King Idris, who had ruled since Independence in 1951. In 1977 the Jamahiriya (State of the masses) was established as a form of "direct democracy." At the local level, 186 Basic and 46 Municipal People's Congresses appoint Popular Committees to carry out local policy. Officials from these groups constitute the 1000-member General People's Congress, the highest policymaking body; this Congress appoints its own General Secretariat and the General People's Committee to carry out national policy. The Secretary of the General People's Committee has functions comparable to those of a prime minister. Col. Muammar el-Qaddafi is the official leader of the Revolution and authority of the State, but does not hold a position in the "formal" administration. **Women's Suffrage:** 1963. **Equal Rights:** The 1969 Constitution considers all Libyans equal before the law, but women's inferior status is upheld in legislation based on Col. Qaddafi's belief in the biological "feebleness" (particularly during menstruation) of females, as outlined in *The Green Book* by Qaddafi (see **Marriage and Family**). **Women in Government:** No data obtainable.

ECONOMY. Currency: Libyan Dinar (May 1983: 0.296 = $1 US). **Gross National Product** (1980): $25.7 billion. **Per Capita Income** (1980): $8640. **Women's Wages as a Percentage of Men's:** No data obtainable. **Equal Pay Policy:** Law 58 (1970) stipulates equal wages with men under the same circumstances and for the same work, but prohibits women from employment in work considered "dangerous or toilsome," from employment between 7 P.M.–7 A.M. "except in such situations or occasions as are determined by decree," or for more than 48 hours per week including overtime. **Production (Agricultural/Industrial):** Dates, olives, citrus, grapes, tobacco; carpets, textiles, shoes, oil and petroleum products. **Women as a Percentage of Labor Force (1980):** 5.7% (see following article); **of agricultural force** (1977) 13.4% (approx. 90% of whom are unpaid family workers); **of industrial force**—no general statistics obtainable (of manufacturing 7.2%, 1977); **of military**—no statistics obtainable; military service is compulsory for all women before marriage. **(Employed) Women's Occupational Indicators:** Of construction 0.25%, of trade 0.65%, of petroleum industry 1%, of public administration 4.17%, of financial services 10%, of educational services 20%, of health services 30% (1977); of all employed women, 5.3% were in non-agricultural activities (mining, manufacturing, electricity, construction, transport), 32% were in agriculture, and 62% were in such services as education, health, public administration, finance and insurance, and trade (1979). **Unemployment:** No statistics obtainable; a large imported skilled labor force affects the employment of unskilled rural migrants to urban areas.

GYNOGRAPHY. Marriage. *Policy:* The 1969 Constitution stipulates that the State shall protect and endorse marriage. Legal marriage age is 16 for females and 18 for males.* The 1972 Law 176 ("Protecting Some Rights of Women in Marriage, Divorce for Prejudice and Consensual Divorce"—also see **Divorce**) governs personal status and makes a woman's consent to marriage mandatory; although a male guardian has no right to force a woman to marry against her will, she cannot marry without his permission. A man must pay *mahar* and is responsible for maintenance of a wife and children. A wife is entitled to ownership of the house she occupies, because of Col. Qaddafi's belief that a "maternity shelter" is a necessary condition for women because they

"menstruate, give birth, and care for their offspring." Although polygyny is legal (except for a man who marries a non-Libyan woman), in 1978 Col. Qaddafi stated that polygynous marriage was mentioned only in 1 verse of the *Koran* and was permitted only in exceptional circumstances. Law 58 (1970), which regulates women's employment, entitles an employed woman to a "pay bonus" upon marriage. Nubility for Bedouin females is set at age 15. *Mahar* is part of the formal marriage contract and is paid in the form of camels, carpets, mats or bedding, and a length of cloth to separate a wife's quarters from her husband's in their marital tent. Women cannot own their own tents. Bedouin women cannot inherit from their husbands. Although a widow cannot inherit her husband's tent, she is allowed to live in it by herself.

Practice: Female mean age at marriage (1970–78): 17; women age 15–49 in union (1970–78): 85%; according to the 1973 Census, 3.3% of marriages were polygynous. The practice of child marriage still exists in some regions. Reportedly, in some areas a bride's father will stand behind the door of the newly wedded couple's bedroom waiting to kill his daughter if she does not bleed during the act of consummation, as proof of virginity. The average dowry varies from $20,000–$60,000 and can take the form of gold, clothes, and other objects. Among Bedouins, a woman from a wealthy family typically commands a dowry of 20 camels in addition to other clothes and gifts. While a Bedouin woman cannot inherit property, she can lay claim to what is considered her husband's inheritable property for her sons. **Divorce.** *Policy:* 1972 Law 176 (see **Marriage**) gives the right to unilateral repudiation *(talaq)* for men only, to divorce by judicial decree for both women and men, and to divorce by mutual consent. After *talaq,* a husband must pay maintenance (generally for 3 months) and any unpaid *mahar.* In the case of divorce for prejudice, the court will appoint 2 or more arbitrators from among the couple's relatives (generally men) in order to deter-

---

* This age limit is calculated in Hegira years, based on the Moslem lunar calendar, and translates into age 15½ and 17½ respectively in the Western calendar.

mine which party is at fault. If the fault is determined to be the wife's, the court issues a divorce with "appropriate compensation" to be paid by her, and the husband does not have to pay maintenance. If the husband is at fault, he is required to pay maintenance for a given period. Under divorce by mutual consent *(khul')* a woman is allowed to pay her husband to obtain a divorce or to forfeit the remaining payments in the case of a deferred *mahar;* the court also may issue divorce by mutual consent without compensation to either party or may compensate both equally. Judicial dissolution of marriage on behalf of a wife is irrevocable; however, dissolution on behalf of a husband is considered revocable by him (as is *talaq*). *Practice:* In 1976 there was approx. 1 divorce for every 3.8 marriages performed. According to reports, the divorce rate decreased during 1972–76; however, many divorces are not recorded.

Family. *Policy:* The 1969 Constitution (Art. 3) states that the family is the basis of society. The status of male and female family members is based on what Col. Qaddafi calls "natural differences." The father is the legal head of the family. In inheritance, if a father has no son, his daughter receives ½ his estate; if he leaves more than 1 daughter but no son, the daughters share ⅔ of his estate. If he leaves both daughters and sons, the daughters' shares are ½ that of the sons'. Daughters from Bedouin families cannot inherit property; if a woman is a non-Moslem, her children cannot inherit her property. Law 72 (1973) provides a family allowance which equals D. 4 a month for 1 wife, D. 2 a month for each male child under age 18 and for single daughters; an employed woman may receive a grant of D. 3 a month from the fourth month of pregnancy to childbirth and a D. 25 bonus at the birth of her first child. Law 58 (1970) established a 50-day pre- and post-delivery maternity leave at ½ pay for pregnant women with 6 months of continuous employment; leave can be extended by 30 days if medically certified complications occur. Women who have worked less than 6 months may receive annual leave provisions provided by Social Security and labor laws that equal

the sum of wages over the preceding 3 months. Under Law 58, employed women are also entitled to 2 nursing breaks a day for 18 months after childbirth without a reduction in wages. Employers of 50 or more female workers are required to create day-care centers, despite Qaddafi's stated opposition to nurseries, which he defined in *The Green Book* as being "similar to a poultry breeding farm."

Practice: The average family size was 5.8 persons in 1978, and 51% of the pop. was under age 15. The government has established 1 children's home each in Tripoli, Benghazi, and Musrata for orphaned or abandoned children up to age 6. In 1977–78, 15 nurseries provided day-care services for 1010 children of employed mothers; the government's 1976–80 Transformation Plan called for the establishment of an additional 20 nurseries and 4 children's homes. **Welfare.** *Policy:* The 1957 Social Security Act provides insurance coverage for sickness, disability, unemployment, employment accidents, maternity benefits (see **Family),** and pensions for retired persons, widows, and orphans. Social Security Law 72 (1973) set the retirement age for women at 55 and provides for monthly pensions of at least D. 30 a month for widows, mothers of children whose fathers are unknown, divorced women over age 40, or under age 40 if they have children (in other cases, a social investigation is required). *Practice:* No statistics obtainable. The Ministry of Social Affairs and Social Security has established centers that provide medical care and public-health services for mothers and infants and disburse Social Security funds. A 1978 report indicated that Social Security benefits were "generous," as were widows' benefits, but that they served to encourage women to stay in the home rather than seek employment in the labor force.

Contraception. *Policy:* As of 1982 there was no government program of family planning, and the government encouraged maintenance of the present level of fertility. *Practice:* No data obtainable. **Abortion.** *Policy:* Legal only in cases of risk to the woman's life, and 2 gynecologists must agree on the necessity for the procedure; all other abortions are punishable by a minimum 6 months imprisonment for both the woman and the practitioner. *Practice:* No data obtainable. **Illegitimacy.** *Policy:* Laws against murder include specific categories concerning killing an "illegitimate" infant or the child's mother to save the family "honor," but consider these "lesser offenses" with lighter penalties than other murders. No further data obtainable. *Practice:* No statistics obtainable, but there are indications that murders of out-of-wedlock children and their mothers are extremely underreported. **Homosexuality.** *Policy:* No data obtainable. *Practice:* No specific data obtainable (but see **Crisis Centers).** **Incest.** *Policy:* No specific data obtainable, but Islamic Shari'a jurisprudence condemns incest. *Practice:* No data obtainable. **Sexual Harassment.** *Policy:* No data obtainable. *Practice:* No data obtainable. **Rape.** *Policy:* Illegal; the law makes a distinction between rape (by a man not her husband) of a married woman and rape of a single woman; the latter carries a heavier penalty. Rape of a single woman is considered a crime against her family's "honor" and an "illegitimate loss of virginity," while rape of a married woman is considered a crime against her husband. Marital rape is not recognized by law. *Practice:* There are indications that rape is a major problem and extremely underreported. The husband of a woman who is raped may invoke *talaq* to "save his honor" (see **Divorce** and **Crisis Centers).** **Battery.** *Policy:* No specific data obtainable; under Islamic Shari'a jurisprudence, a woman can bring charges against her husband for "personal injuries." Battery may constitute grounds for divorce if the court judges the grievance as proof of incompatibility. *Practice:* No statistics obtainable, but reports suggest that wife-beating is common.

Prostitution. *Policy:* No data obtainable. *Practice:* Prostitution is prevalent, particularly in major urban centers. Prostitutes are socially ostracized. Reports indicate that poor, rural, uneducated women who migrate to urban centers commonly turn to prostitution as a means of economic survival (see **Crisis Centers). Traditional/Cultural Practices.** *Policy:* No data obtainable. *Practice:*

Among many Bedouin families, females are separated from males after puberty and until marriage; during this time a female wears a silk shawl which she draws to the side of her face (leaving an eye visible) when in the presence of men who are not family members. It is customary to slaughter an animal and feast only at the birth of a boy. A couple without a son may "borrow" a male child from a brother or sister in exchange for livestock. **Crisis Centers.** *Policy:* The government passed a 1971 decree for the formation of women's "rehabilitation centers." The Ministry of Social Affairs and Social Security stated that its purpose was to shelter those "who are exposed to deviance, in order to guide them socially, psychologically, and religiously. The aim is to improve their behavior and enable them to return to a good family life and to adjust to the society"; 3 such centers were opened by 1977. *Practice:* 213 women were at 1 of the "rehabilitation centers" in Tripoli during some part of 1975; of these women, 56 were there because of out-of-wedlock pregnancies, 46 had been raped, 27 had been assaulted, 14 were prostitutes, 11 were divorced with no support, 10 had been kidnapped with the intention of forced marriage, and the remainder were there for other reasons. The centers have been criticized by some for several reasons: no distinction is made between those who have committed crimes and those who are victims, there are no physicians, nurses, or psychiatrists at the centers, and the main assistance and "rehabilitation" offered is training in sewing, knitting, cooking, cleaning, etc.

HERSTORY. The inhabitants of Libya are mostly of Arab ancestry, the descendants of people who came from Arabia in the 9th–11th centuries C.E. There also were and still are Berbers living in communities throughout Libya.

There is little record of the role of Libyan women prior to the 1900's, but both historical and mythological references to the Amazons, women-warriors in ancient Libya (see MYTHOGRAPHY), imply that Libyan women were powerful leaders.

In the Jahilia period before the age of

Islam, female infanticide was practiced among some peoples in the area—justified for economic reasons by poor families, and for "loss of prestige" reasons by wealthier families; the ancient saying "The grave is the best bridegroom" originated during this period.

As in other countries, women in Libya suffered at the hands of successive waves of invaders, among them the Ottoman Turks in the 16th century and the pirates who controlled trade in the 1700's. During the Italian occupation (early 1900's through WW II), many Libyan women were tortured and raped by Italian soldiers. After the Allied victory, Libya fell under Anglo-French control until 1949, when the United Nations was given jurisdiction. The United Kingdom of Libya was declared Independent in 1951.

Middle-class urban women formed women's organizations in the early 1960's; their work focused on women's education and increased participation in the public domain. In Sept. 1969, 27-year-old Col. Muammar el-Qaddafi led a successful coup d'état, overthrowing the King, nullifying the Constitution, and setting up the Revolutionary Command Council, which he still heads. According to Amnesty International, at least 14 Libyan women and men have been killed or wounded in assassination attempts outside their country since Feb. 1980, when the Third Congress of the Libyan Revolutionary Committees issued a declaration calling for the "physical liquidation" of "enemies of the Revolution" living abroad, a position which was seconded by the 1983 General People's Congress of Libya.

Current women's organizations include the General Women's Federation (in Tripoli), whose campaigns focus on literacy and domestic training for women, and the General Union of Women's Associations, an umbrella organization formed in 1972 (and made up of 58 women's groups by 1982) whose "awareness campaigns" target such issues as dowry. In 1982 there were 34 women's organizations and 43 "revolutionary committees" registered in Libya, but all were under direct or indirect State control. The General Union of the Women of Libya, formed by Libyan women abroad, in opposition to the current regime's repression, is attempting to call world attention to the human-rights violations occurring in Libya.

MYTHOGRAPHY. In ancient Libya** (approx. 1000 B.C.E.) powerful female armies known as Amazons were feared by other nations. The Libyan Amazons fought on horseback and established military training for all girls. The women controlled political life, leaving childrearing to the men. Under their leader Myrine, 30,000 Libyan Amazons defeated the Gorgons, another powerful women's army, killing many Gorgons and capturing and torturing others. The Gorgon prisoners rose up against the Libyans in a retaliatory massacre. The Libyan Amazons then waged a successful war campaign throughout Arabia, eventually controlling the entire area bordering the seacoast to the Caicus River. Shipwrecked, they colonized the island of Samothrace, naming it for the mother of the gods. Strabo (c. 63 B.C.E.–C.E. 21), Greek philosopher and historian, wrote that "there have been generations of belligerent women in Libya" (also see MOROCCO).

** Ancient Libya is thought to have comprised all of North Africa except Egypt.

LIBYA: The Wave of Consciousness Cannot Be Reversed
by Farida Allaghi

Writing a brief, informative, and realistic analysis of Libyan women's lives is a challenge, for the following reasons:

—The complex, dynamic, contradictory and at times vague conditions of reality in which Libyan women live make any superficial analysis or general description of their over-all status weak and not informative—if it is divorced from what is happening to the society in general.

—Any succinct, objective analysis of Libyan women should be made along the following classifications: a) nomadic Bedouin women, b) traditional rural women, c) women in changing rural settings, d) women in villages, e) women in newly urbanized settings, f) urban, educated, middle-class women, g) urban, rich, upper-class women, and h) poor, urban, working-class women.

—There is a web of intricate variables—political, economic, sociocultural, and religious—to be defined and analyzed, and these respective impacts (positive or negative) on the various groups of women should be assessed.

—The basic, cutting-edge issue of paramount importance to the majority of Libyan women today is not feminism and sexual liberation alone but humanism and national liberation as well. Consequently, it will be quite difficult to draw the lines between sexual and human liberation, psychological and social liberation, and political and economic liberation. There are no priorities in the list of liberations, because total liberation cannot be segmented.

—An analysis of the lives of Libyan women should be tied not only to what is happening internally in Libya, but also to what is happening in the Arab Moslem world and the Third World in general—politically, economically, and socially.

There will be a modest attempt in this article to incorporate some of the above-mentioned points; however, it is beyond the scope of this essay to provide a detailed discussion of all of them.

Unanswered Questions

The following specific, fundamental questions continue to dominate the thinking of thousands of not only Libyan but Arab women:

1) Is the present state of confusion, frustration, unsettled visions, and mixed views a natural state during the process in which women strive to change their status from total subordination and domination by the patriarchal society to a more egalitarian and liberated one?

2) Can we specifically define what exactly is happening to women in Libya today? Are women speaking out? And if they are, are they heard?

3) Are the Libyan women's problems, demands, aspirations, fears, and hopes visible to the society at large?

4) Is there indeed a silent, quiet, underground or overground feminist revolution taking place among Libyan women?

5) When we talk about the resistance of women to inequality, do we blame the men alone, certain political institutions, traditions, or other women as well?

6) What have the few educated Libyan women offered so far for their unfortunate, illiterate, and poor sisters living in both rural and urban areas?

7) Is it true that the ivory towers in which newly educated Libyan women are locking themselves are becoming a scary fact more than an imaginary reality?

8) What is the message, if any, that Libyan women could spread to other women around the world?

9) Do we really know what Libyan women need or want, or do they themselves know what they want? Is it only education and employment, or something more?

Needless to say, clear-cut answers to all the above questions cannot be provided. But I will attempt to shed some light on some of the questions.

A General Overview

At the time of its independence in 1951, barely more than thirty years ago, Libya was one of the poorest countries of the world. The income per head in 1952 was only $30 to $40 (US) per annum. The health standard was also very low. The rural sector of the economy comprised 90 percent of the active population and wages were paid in kind, by barter or money or mixtures of both. Equally disheartening was the high rate of illiteracy. And Libya had—and still has—one of the highest population-growth rates in the world.

The discovery of oil in the early 1960's has led to a higher investment in such areas as education and the introduction of new technologies, and has contributed to the emergence of large-scale industry, enticing strong migration from the rural areas to the cities. Such structural changes have also encouraged Libyan women to seek education and employment and to play a larger role in public life.

The Libyan Working Woman

Women in Libya account for 48 percent of the total population. The number of working-age women in 1980 was estimated at about 558,830, while the number of those who actually work is 42,950—which means there is still an available pool of 92.3 percent in the remaining population. Yet there has been a constant increase of women's participation in the labor force in the last fifteen years: a result of the various economic, technological, and social changes. In 1964 that rate was 4 percent; by 1973 it had increased to 5 percent; to 5.7 percent in 1980; and it is expected to reach 7.2 percent in 1985. Women have been recruited mainly in the teaching profession, and in nursing, clerical positions (such as secretaries), housekeeping services, and some industries (clothing and textile). There is a clear trend in women's employment in such new sectors as medicine, engineering, and law. (It should be strongly emphasized, however, that all figures reflecting trends in the employment of Libyan women should be used with some reservations.)

Until the early 1960's, agriculture was the main source of livelihood for the majority of the Libyan population. Libyan women, too, contributed substantially in the past, and still do—working part time, fulltime, or seasonally. However, like their rural sisters in many parts of the Arab world and the Third World, they are almost never paid for their work, and their contribution to the agricultural sector of the economy is rarely reflected in the official statistics.

In spite of the fact that there are over 200,000 females over the age of ten in the rural areas of Libya, the 1976 census reports that there were only 13,761 economically active females in the category of agriculture, forestry, hunting, and fishing. A recent study reports that the figure of 86,019 is closer to the reality concerning the actual female rural work force, a closer match to the male work force in rural areas—96,184. In other words, according to these calculations, females may comprise up to 45.7 percent of the total economically active population in the rural regions of Libya and 20.6 percent of the economically active Libyan population.

Bedouin women, although (like their rural sisters) not formally employed, are weaving baskets, rugs, and carpets in their homes, herding the sheep, collecting the wood, fetching the water, and helping their husbands in various other activities in order to survive the harsh desert conditions.

In brief, despite the inaccuracy of most statistics reflecting the participation of women in the labor force, Libyan women are increasingly seeking employment for several reasons; self-actualization, economic independence, and future security are undoubtedly major among them.

It should also be pointed out that negative and rigid attitudes concerning women's work are changing. There is no discrimination by law between men and women so far as wages. However, there are more jobs and opportunities provided to men than to women —and there are very few women in decision-making or high-level positions.

The Education of Women in Libya

Education is the field in which Libyan women have gained their most significant achievement. In 1951, 100 percent of Libyan women were illiterate (and only 10 percent of the adult male population had ever attended school). Later statistics reveal women's illiteracy to be 65 percent, men's 55 percent. In terms of major characteristics of women's education in Libya, one can make these summarizing observations:

Considering the younger generation, statistics indicate that girls' education is steadily progressing at all levels—although there is still a wide gap between girls and boys. In 1960 girls comprised 21 percent of the total primary-school enrollment; in 1969 this had improved to 34 percent, and in 1979 to 47 percent. There are, however, indications that there is a high drop-out rate among females after primary education.

Female enrollment in secondary and higher education is, surprisingly, increasing. In Libya, one out of every five secondary-school students is a woman.

The female proportion at university level has risen from 2 percent in 1960 to 11 percent in 1970 and 17 percent in 1980.

Although compulsory education for both males and females has been government policy since the early 1960's, it is not enforced, especially in rural areas where the female half of the population is least likely to be educated. However, rural women's development centers have been opened in almost twenty-five rural areas in different regions of Libya. These centers aim to train both young and old women in various home-economics skills.

Education, like work, is indeed helping thousands of Libyan women to leave a world of seclusion and ignorance and enter a more enlightened and modern world in which they not only are fulfilling their roles as contributors to their country's national development but also enhancing their own over-all status in the society. But education and employment—if not coupled with major institutional, structural, and attitudinal changes—will never help Libyan women achieve their ultimate goals of emancipation, equality, and human dignity.

A History of Libyan Women's Organizations

Libyan women began forming their own organizations in the early 1960's. In their first phase of activities, the women's organizations identified two major problems of Libyan women: *illiteracy* and *seclusion*. Promotion of women's educational rights and getting women out of seclusion—these were the two basic, debatable questions up to the early 1970's. Few Libyan men have been very supportive of women's demands, but governmental policies did encourage women's education, because it was realized that women are needed for the country's development.

Since their inception, women's organizations have traditionally been dominated by urban, educated, middle- and upper-class women. The interest and ideologies of this class have shaped the activities, outlook, and policies of these organizations. The women's organizations of the early 1970's were limited to urban centers and big towns and were identified as social-welfare organizations whose basic goals were to help women learn sewing, knitting, childcare, and cooking. Literacy and typing classes have been added to these activities. The branches of the Libyan Women's Union proliferated in the mid-1970's (related to an increase in female enrollment in schools).

Although today there are thirty-four women's organizations and forty-three "revolutionary committees," all the leaders of these organizations and committees are nominated by the government. Since the mid-1970's, both the women's organizations and the women's committees have been heavily used to propagate the ideology of the present military regime. Consequently, they have not been effective in building genuine local support, or in mobilizing public opinion concerning women's policies.

The Basic Situation of Libyan Women

The optimistic signals which reflect Libyan women's achievements, both in the labor force and in educational fields, cannot lead us to conclude that Libyan society is no longer male-dominated or that women are increasingly constituting a social force that can no longer be ignored. Attitudes and perceptions about women's roles, unfortunately, have not paralleled the achievements women have managed to make. The over-all societal attitude—especially in rural areas and among conservatives in urban areas—still considers women to be less than men, viewing their primary (if not only) roles to be those of good mothers and obedient wives or daughters or sisters, with no rights to make decisions, be given choices or control, or have any power.

The majority of Libyan women, however, in both rural and urban areas—educated and uneducated, young and old, rich and poor—are increasingly becoming aware of their inferior status and subordinate position. *Awareness of injustice and motivations for change do not wait for education and do not exist only among young women.* The frustration exemplified by the following quotations from two women who lived all their lives in an oasis in the Libyan desert and settled recently in a new agricultural project is a real indicator that Libyan women, even in the most conservative areas, are no longer accepting an inferior status which has stripped them of their human dignity.

The beautiful, intelligent, and energetic old woman told me in an angry tone what she did when her husband and eldest son prohibited her four daughters (two divorced and two unmarried) from joining the new women's development and training center:

I have been married to my husband for thirty years and I have always been an obedient wife. But when my husband and son prohibited my daughters from joining the center I became very angry and threatened to leave the home. I insisted very hard that all my four daughters should be educated, and thank God I won. If I were still young, I myself would have joined the center. Educated women are more respected by their husbands and families. Their husbands will not divorce them and will no longer treat them as they treat their animals on the farm. All young women in this village should no longer spend their lives cooking *Eish* [a local dish] every day and giving birth to children every year. They should learn a skill and secure some income. We, the old generation, suffered a lot from poverty, ignorance, and injustice, and we do not want to see our daughters live the way we did.

A newly married young woman also expressed her dissatisfaction with her life:

I am not happy in my life. I was forced to marry my husband, whom I had never seen or known before. Our parents and relatives control our lives, they determine everything for us. Young women in this village are never allowed to give their opinion about anything. I have seen on the television women in the cities of Tripoli and Benghazi driving cars, working in different jobs, and attending the university. I wish I could be educated. I could have a paid job and could have some control over my life.

What should be pointed out, however, is that—despite the fact that the majority of Libyan women are increasingly dissatisfied with their subordinate position—only a very few of these women are sure about the *aspects* of equality they are demanding as much as they are certain about their *difference* from men. This is a natural state of confusion in a country where one finds highly educated women who are imprisoned because of their political views and, at the same time, illiterate women who are imprisoned in their families' homes and forced to marry while still very young.

The fact remains true, however, that the wave of Libyan women's consciousness about their rights, individuality, capacities, and humanness can no longer be reversed. It might not yet be moving quickly forward, but it is undoubtedly becoming a reality.

The Future of Libyan Women

Forecasting the future of women in Libya is as complex and vague a task as describing their present status. On the one hand we could paint a rosy, optimistic picture, especially if we want to focus on their improving education, work, and health status. No one can deny that future generations of Libyan women will be healthier, free from the darkness of ignorance and total economic dependence on men. They will also be more equipped to play a larger role in their country's national development, to have more opportunities of choice, and to control more resources.

On the other hand, however, it is neither education nor work alone which enhances women's position in their societies, but many more factors, which include: men's willingness to change their stereotyped thinking about women's roles, moderate religious interpretations, strong support by political systems for women's rights (on both the *de jure* and the *de facto* levels), and, most important of all, genuine desire by the masses of women to fight all forms of discrimination and injustice.

Liberation cannot be segmented; therefore, the future of feminism in Libya goes hand in hand with the future of humanism. Once a democratic, progressive, and nationalistic regime begins to run the country, we could hope to see a somewhat brighter future for Libyan women. Needless to say, freedom, equality, and democracy will not necessarily "trickle down" to the masses of women, as development theorists hoped (e.g., the benefits that the masses of poor people supposedly will get from different development projects). However, under a liberal political system, Libyan women would at least have more opportunities to raise their voices, state their demands, and organize themselves freely.

As to the other major preconditions that should exist, not only in Libya but in the Arab world, if women are to achieve human dignity and sexual liberation:

—The model of liberation which Libyan, Arab, and Moslem women should seek to implement in their respective countries should not be an imported, alien model which has no roots in their own religion, history, culture, and civilization, and which does not fit the reality in which they live.

—Many Arab men are also victims of centuries of psychological complexities; accordingly, Arab women should strive to cooperate and work with those Arab men who are enlightened and progressive in order to achieve human dignity for all.

—Islam has been and will continue to be the strongest religious, social, and political force shaping the everyday life of the masses of people throughout the Arab and Moslem world, women among them. There are various interpretations of Islamic religion—fundamentalist, moderate, liberal. Moslem women scholars and enlightened religious leaders should exert a dedicated effort to reflect the status and over-all lifestyle of early Moslem women—which undoubtedly was much more liberated than what the orthodox Moslem fundamentalists are trying to portray today. Authorized progressive religious Moslem leaders also should play a larger role in advocating the fundamental rights which Islam gave to women, such as those of education, work, ownership of property, and their rights to choose their husbands and to ask for divorce if they meet the preconditions which have been set by the *Koran*.

Libyan and Arab women should be mobilized and organized to create a political force and play a larger political role—one which will eventually ensure the emergence of more progressive, democratic, political systems and which will, in turn, prepare women to play a larger political role in the future.

—A large number of Arab women social scientists and researchers are writing and publishing their research studies on various issues related to Arab women either in French or in English, more than in the Arabic language. There is an urgent need for translating these studies into Arabic, and for undertaking new studies which deal with various social, economic, and political problems related to different groups of women.

—There is a wide gap separating educated and professional Libyan and Arab women from their illiterate and less fortunate sisters. There is a desperate need for increased direct communication and cooperation between these two groups of women. This communication is needed in order to identify the interests, concerns, and priorities of this large, neglected, but extremely important pool of human resource, and in order to propose policies which reflect the interest of the majority of women and not that of a tiny, educated (and at times alienated) minority.

—In spite of the fact that the women's movement in the Arab world was founded in the early 1940's, there is not yet a strong, nongovernmental, coherent, and powerful feminist movement which defends the rights of Arab women. Closer networking and cooperation should be an urgent priority.

—Women's organizations and unions in Libya and in several other Arab countries are under the direct control of the Arab governments. Their policies, activities, and interests are all determined by the central governments. Libyan and Arab women should dedicate their future efforts (since it is quite impossible in the present) to create independent and free *non*governmental organizations whose basic interest is the creation of a powerful and autonomous women's movement, and not the perpetuation of ideologies and special interests of the political status quo.

—The struggle of Libyan and Arab women should not be a separatist and selfish one. It should go hand in hand with the struggle to help the masses of their people, women and men alike, to be free from a world of ignorance and underdevelopment.

—As part of humanity, Libyan and Arab women cannot isolate themselves from what is happening internationally to the millions of other women around the world. Libyan and Arab women should build bridges of dialogue and communication with these other women, in order to support each other's struggle for the achievement of global feminism —and in order to play more significant roles in shaping the future of humanity, a humanity which is increasingly threatened by hatred, wars, and destruction. A humanity which women everywhere are now claiming as our own—and which, in the process, we will "humanize" and transform.

Suggested Further Reading

Alfahum, Siba. *The Libyan Woman 1965–1975.* Beirut: Lebanese Section, Women's International League for Peace and Freedom, 1977.

Al-Huni, Ali Mohamed. "Determinants of Female Labour Force Participation: The Case of Libya." Diss., Univ. of Pittsburgh, 1979.

Allaghi, Farida. "The Libyan Woman in Transition." M.A. Thesis, Colorado State Univ., 1973.

——. "Rural Women and Decision-Making: The Case of the Kufra Settlement Project in Libya." Diss., Colorado State Univ., 1980.

First, Ruth. *Libya: The Elusive Revolution.* New York: African Publishing Co., 1975.

International Labour Organisation Experts Group. *Integration of Libyan Women in Economic and Social Development.* Tripoli: Ministry of Planning and Scientific Demography and Manpower Planning Section, 1975; booklet.

Mason, John P. "Sex and Symbol in the Treatment of Women in the Wedding Rite in a Libyan Oasis Community." *American Ethnologist,* Vol. 2, No. 4, Nov. 1975.

Farida Allaghi was born May 5, 1947, in Tripoli, Libya. She graduated from the Libyan University in 1970 (B.A., philosophy and sociology) with honors; M.A., 1973, and Ph.D., 1980 (sociology) from Colorado State University. She has lectured on various topics related to Arab and Moslem women, worked in 1979 as a consultant on Arab women at the UN Secretariat for the UN Women World Conference, held the position of vice-chairperson in 1977 at the UN Committee on the Status of Women, and was the committee representative to the meetings of the Subcommittee on Human Rights in Geneva in 1978. She has attended international and national conferences, both as a professional sociologist focusing on the areas of social planning, modernization, and development, and as a dedicated advocate for women's rights in the Arab world and Third World. A member of the African Women's Association for Research and Development, she is also an active member of the preparatory committee for the Foundation of the Association of Arab Women Social Scientists. She currently works as program and planning officer with UNICEF in Riyadh, Saudi Arabia, is married, and has two children.

MEXICO
(United Mexican States)

Located on the southern part of the North American continent, bordered by the Gulf of Mexico and the Caribbean Sea to the east, Guatemala and Belize to the south, the Pacific Ocean to the west, and the United States to the north. **Area:** 1,972,547 sq. km. (761,600 sq. mi.). **Population** (1980): 68,190,000, female 50%. **Capital:** Mexico City.

DEMOGRAPHY. Languages: Spanish (official), Native Indian languages (Mayan, Náhuatl, Zapotec, other). **Races or Ethnic Groups:** Mestizo 55%, Native Indian 29%, European 10%, other. **Religions:** Roman Catholicism 89%, Protestant 3.6%, other. **Education** (% enrolled in school, 1975): Age 6–11—of all girls 89%, of all boys 91%; age 12–17—of all girls 47%, of all boys 62%; higher education—in 1982 women were 27% of all students. In 1978, 1.3% of women age 15–49, ever-in-union, received higher education; 3% of rural women of that group had secondary and higher education, while 37% had no education. **Literacy** (1977): Women 70%, men 78%. **Birth Rate** (per 1000 pop., 1975–80): 37. **Death Rate** (per 1000 pop., 1975–80): 6. **Infant Mortality** (per 1000 live births, 1975–80): Female 66, male 74. **Life Expectancy** (1975–80): Female 67 yrs., male 64 yrs.

GOVERNMENT. The 1917 Constitution created a Federal Republic of 31 states and the Federal District. Executive power is held by the president. The bicameral congress consists of an elected Senate and elected and appointed Chamber of Deputies. **Women's Suffrage:** 1953 in national elections; 1947 in municipal elections. **Equal Rights:** Art. 4 of the 1917 Constitution (reformed 1974) stipulates equality of women and men. **Women in Government:** In the parliament there are 350 deputies, of which 67 are women, and 57 senators, 1 of which is female (1983); Griselda Alvarez Ponce de León is the 1 woman state governor (of Colima), 1983.

ECONOMY. Currency: Mexican Peso (May 1983: 148.5 = $1 US). **Gross National Product** (1980): $144 billion. **Per Capita Income** (1980): $2130. **Women's Wages as a Percentage of Men's:** No data obtainable. **Equal Pay Policy:** The 1970 Federal Labor Law established the principle of equal pay for equal work and stipulated equal rights and obligations at employment. **Production** (Agricultural/Industrial): Corn, cotton, coffee; metal products, textiles, chemicals, petroleum. **Women as a Percentage of Labor Force** (1979): 24.5%; **of agricultural force** 9%; **of industrial force**—no general statistics obtainable (of manufacturing 28.2%, 1979; of border-industry force [primarily electronics, textiles and garments, and light assembly] 75–90%, 1983); **of military**—no statistics obtainable; women are not permitted in combat but serve in clerical, medical, and support roles. **(Employed) Women's Occupational Indicators:** In 1982, 36% of employed women were in the textile industry, 25% of rural women were in handicraft and cottage industries. In 1975, 69.6% of employed women were in the service sector (of whom 25% were in domestic service). Women are employed in the lowest-skilled and lowest-paid jobs in factories; in border factories wages are often under $1 US per hour. Rural women generally work as paid or unpaid seasonal agricultural labor or migrate to cities to work as domestic servants or street vendors. **Unemployment:** 10% (unofficial, 1982); in border industries 67% (est., 1981); no rates by sex obtainable.

GYNOGRAPHY. Marriage. *Policy:* Reforms in the Civil Code (1974) accorded women legal equality in marriage. The minimum age for marriage without parental consent is 18 for both sexes. Both spouses are obliged to contribute to the marriage and provide mutual assistance (Art. 168). Property is administered jointly, but spouses have exclusive rights over individually owned property and any income it generates. A woman may own her own domicile, and both spouses choose the place of residence (Art. 163). *Practice:* Female mean age at marriage (1970–78): 21; women age 15–49 in union (1970–78): 62%. **Divorce.** *Policy:* Possible since 1931; a 1974 law reform accords women equal rights in divorce and separation. There are 17 grounds for divorce, including adultery and neglect of maintenance. A judge determines necessary means of separation, permitting spouses to live apart while divorce is pending. Alimony is awarded to the "innocent" spouse, and child custody is determined by a judge. *Practice:* Divorces (per 1000 pop., 1977): 0.29. No further data obtainable.

Family. *Policy:* The 1974 Family Law reforms removed discriminatory features and established the principle of equality within the family. A woman of legal age has equal status with a man and can dispose of individually owned property and conclude contracts, regardless of her marital status. Both spouses must contribute economically, according to their means, toward maintenance of the home and children (including education). Both spouses have the unconditional right to work outside the home, provided the activity "does not molest the morale and structure of the family." A fully paid maternity leave of 6 weeks both pre- and post-delivery is provided by law and financed by the Mexican Institute of Social Security (IMSS) and employers; the new Federal Labor Law (Art. 170) safeguards a woman's return to the same job. According to the Constitution (Art. 123), women have a right to childcare services. Under the new Federal Labor Law (Art. 171), IMSS began a program to establish childcare centers for insured employees' children in all municipalities; employers pay 1% of employees' salaries to finance the centers. *Practice:* From 1970 to 1980, 1.5 million women became heads of households; 20% of urban households were headed by women (1982). An increase in male migration to northern cities or the US in search of work in the 1970's has resulted in many abandoned families with no, or little, means of support. Sixty-five percent of women over age 18 are mothers (1983). Day-care centers are limited, and too costly for many employed women; bureaucratic proce-

dures also limit access. In 1974 IMSS operated 115 centers, providing places for 70,000 children, but in 1976 it had not reached its goal of 506 centers nationwide. Employers in border industries often give pre-hiring pregnancy tests to women applicants to avoid paying maternity benefits and day-care expenses.

Welfare. *Policy:* The Mexican Institute of Social Security, operating under the 1973 Social Security Law, provides services for sickness, disability, unemployment, and old age to all employees in the State, private, and military sectors; it is funded by employer, employee, and government revenue. Full-pay unemployment compensation is provided for 3 months, with an additional 20 days for each yr. of employment. Pensions are paid at age 60, or after 25 yrs. employment. Free medicine and hospital care are available to all insured employees; domestic workers have been covered by IMSS since 1972. *Practice:* No statistics obtainable. Generally, domestic workers, street vendors, and other women in marginal employment have no insurance, minimum wage, or pension protection. Employers in border industries and agro-export businesses frequently violate minimum-wage and Social Security requirements. **Contraception.** *Policy:* The Constitution (Art. 4) provides for "carrying out family-planning programs . . . in order to rationally regulate and stabilize the country's population growth." The government promotes family planning through government hospitals and clinics which offer birth-control counseling and devices. *Practice:* Women age 15–49 in union using contraception (1976): 35%; methods used (1976) pill 36%, IUD 19%, withdrawal 12%, rhythm 10%, female sterilization 9%, injectables 6%, diaphragm 5%, condom 3%, male sterilization 1%, other methods 5%; using inefficient methods 25%. The government's campaign has been effective in urban areas, but less so in rural areas, where family-planning services are still insufficient.

Abortion. *Policy:* The 1931 Penal Code permits abortion only in cases of rape or endangerment of the woman's life; the physician performing an abortion must consult another physician unless an emergency exists; consent of the woman is required. Other abortions are punishable by 1–3 yrs. imprisonment for the practitioner and 6 months–5 yrs. imprisonment for the woman; if abortion was performed "to save the woman's honor," the maximum imprisonment is 3 yrs. Although abortion in all but the above-mentioned specific cases is illegal, infanticide—if carried out for reasons of "family honor" and before the infant is formally registered—can be considered "attenuated homicide" and can receive a more lenient sentence. *Practice:* The IMSS estimates 1.6 million abortions annually, only 8% of which are performed under sanitary conditions. The majority of women cannot afford the abortions available in private hospitals or clinics but must resort to procedures performed in unsanitary conditions with inadequate techniques; an est. 100,000 women die each yr. from these improperly performed procedures. Women are rarely prosecuted for illegal abortions. Most women who have abortions are married and already have at least 3 children; primary reasons given for seeking abortion are financial difficulties, physically abusive or deserting husbands, and husbands who deny paternity. The Roman Catholic Church campaigns against the procedure. A "Voluntary Maternity" bill to legalize abortion and provide free, safe contraceptives was drafted by feminist groups and unsuccessfully introduced into the legislature in 1979. A proposal to include the legalization of abortion and assistance to rape victims in the National Development Plan was introduced by Dr. Diana Vidaste (1983). **Illegitimacy.** *Policy:* Under the Family Law, women and men can legally recognize their children born before marriage, but they cannot bring them to live in the conjugal home without spousal permission. *Practice:* No data obtainable. **Homosexuality.** *Policy:* Interpretation of the Criminal Code section "Offenses Against Public Morals" can permit prosecution of lesbian women and homosexual men. *Practice:* No statistics obtainable. Several groups have organized for the rights of same-sex lovers. The lesbian-feminist groups Lesbos, Oikabeth, and Akratas developed within the women's movement in the 1970's. The Homosexual Liberation Movement was also organized in the 1970's as a coalition of lesbian women's and homosexual men's groups. In 1979 the Homosexual Front of Revolutionary Action organized the first Gay Pride march in Mexico City; marches also were held in 1980 and 1981. A lesbian woman and a homosexual man were candidates of the Revolutionary Party for Workers in 2 different districts of Mexico City (1982).

Incest. *Policy:* Incest between ascendant and descendant relatives or between siblings is punishable under the Criminal Code by 6 months–3 yrs. imprisonment. *Practice:* Father-daughter incest, often accompanied by violence, is not uncommon. **Sexual Harassment.** *Policy:* None. *Practice:* No statistics obtainable (see following article). **Rape.** *Policy:* Sexual intercourse through force or violence is punishable by a fine and 2–8 yrs. imprisonment; if the victim has not attained puberty, the penalty is 4–10 yrs. imprisonment. A man cannot be accused of raping his wife, since he is considered to be exercising his connubial right. Rape committed by a public official or a professional who abuses his position is punishable by the above sentences plus dismissal from the profession for 5 yrs. In Apr. 1983, Mireya Toto and other feminist lawyers organized to present a proposal to amend the Penal Code; it would raise the penalty for rape to 13 yrs. imprisonment, and the issue itself would be moved from the section on sexual crimes to the section on crimes against freedom. Feminists also noted the urgent need for regional centers throughout the country, to study the issue and to aid rape victims. *Practice:* An est. 80,000 rapes were committed nationally, with 10,000 in Mexico City, where there is 1 rape every 10 minutes (est., 1982). In 1980, 973 rapes were reported in Mexico City. The Support Center of Raped Women estimates the national number of rapes at 160,000 per yr. Women who do prosecute are frequently exposed to humiliation and abuse by the authorities. **Battery.** *Policy:* No specific legislation, but general assault laws could apply. *Practice:* No statistics obtainable. Wife abuse is common and linked with a high rate of male alcoholism.

Prostitution. *Policy:* Under the Criminal Code section "Crimes Against Public Morals and Good Customs," one who invites another to a sexual exchange "in a scandalous manner" is subject to a fine and 6 months–5 yrs. imprisonment; pimping is punishable by a fine and 6 months–8 yrs. imprisonment. *Practice:* No statistics obtainable; female and male prostitution are both prevalent, especially in border cities, where unemployment is high. **Traditional/Cultural Practices.** *Policy:* No data obtainable. *Practice:* In rural areas, kidnapping-rapes of young girls persist, although less frequently than in previous periods. The motive is supposedly marriage—once raped, a woman who had refused a suitor would have to consent to marry him, and her family would be forced to grant approval as well. **Crisis Centers.** *Policy:* None. *Practice:* The first center in Mexico City (offering counseling and information for women in distress) opened in 1980; it was organized by feminists and a civil-rights group (see **Rape**). The MLM— Movimiento de Liberación de las Mujeres (Women's Liberation Movement)—operates a rape hot-line in Mexico City.

HERSTORY. High civilizations of the Maya, Aztec, Toltec, Mixtec, Zapotec, and Olmec Indians developed in precolonial Mexico. The Mayans occupied the Yucatán and much of Central America (approx. 1500 B.C.E.), and had conceived advanced mathematical, calendar, and writing systems as well as imposing architecture. The Aztec civilization was at its zenith in 1519 when Spanish conquistador Hernán Cortés captured the ruler Montezuma and conquered the Aztec Empire. The most notorious woman of precolonial Mexico is La Malinche, or Doña Marina, as she was known by the Spanish conquistadores. A brilliant Aztec woman of remarkable language abilities, she was sold into slavery, learned Spanish in a few weeks, and became the interpreter, adviser, and eventually mistress of Cortés during his expeditions and the ultimate conquest of Tenochtitlán. Although she has been maligned by some historians as a collabo-

rator, Hispanic feminist historians have been resurrecting La Malinche, noting that she deliberately used the influence she came to wield over Cortés to save the lives of thousands of Native Indians. She was only 25 years old when she died.

María de Zayas y Sotomayor, an early feminist in the 1600's, rebelled against the traditional Spanish image of women as submissive. Juana Inés de la Cruz, or Sor Juana (1651–95), was the outstanding poet of the colonial period. She joined a convent at age 16 but continued to study and write great lyric poetry; one of her most famous works is an argument for the education of women.

In the 18th century, Indian and Mestizo (mixed Indian and European ancestry) women were employed as market vendors, domestics, wet-nurses, cooks, and peddlers, while European women were primarily employed as teachers and seamstresses. Female slaves (usually Indian) were used in the sugar mills, and in mining camps women worked as domestic servants and prostitutes. Factories began to employ women in the mid-1700's in silk and cigar production. A reform by Charles III of Spain to permit women into more occupations became effective in what was termed New Spain in 1798.

In the 18th and 19th centuries, female textile and tobacco workers staged strikes over such issues as the reduction of the workday—which averaged 14–18 hours. Mexico won Independence in 1821, and 2 years later proclaimed itself a republic. In 1870 the teacher and poet Rita Cetina Gutiérrez started the feminist group La Siempreviva, which published a newspaper; feminists in Mexico City published the magazine *La Mujer Mexicana* (1904– 08). The governor of Yucatán, Salvador Alvarado, was influenced by socialist and feminist ideas of the period; from 1915– 18, he improved conditions for domestic workers, established vocational education for women, permitted women into public administration jobs, and gave women equal legal status with men at age 21. The first feminist congresses were held in Mérida in Jan. and Nov. 1915. Delegates passed resolutions to increase women's employment rights, obtain a secular education, and gain equality in marriage. Pres. Carranza passed the Law of Domestic Relations in 1917, according married women legal rights in the home and in business.

During the Revolutions of 1867–1917, women were integral to the struggle as soldiers, nurses, and underground activists; they participated in the Red Battalions and many attained the rank of colonel in Carranza's army. Ramona Flores was head of staff to a general. In the town of Puente de Ixtla, a woman called La China led a battalion of women against government troops to revenge the deaths of their relatives. Rosa Torres participated in the feminist congress and became the first woman elected to office, as president of the Municipal Council of Mérida in 1922. Frida Kahlo became a major figure in Mexican art (as a painter and also as the wife of Diego Rivera), and was a feminist and political activist. In 1920 María Ríos Cárdenas started the feminist journal *Mujer;* she attacked the patriarchal ethos in general and the physical and sexual abuse of women in particular, urging her readers to organize a feminist coalition. Elvia Carillo Puerto and Felipe Carillo Puerto, her brother and a powerful Yucatán politician, formed feminist leagues throughout the state. They focused on problems of alcohol, prostitution, and drugs. When Felipe became governor in 1922, he published Margaret Sanger's pamphlet on birth control, and invited one of Sanger's colleagues to set up birth-control clinics in Mérida.

At the second National Women's Congress of Workers and Peasants (1931), women demanded equality of rights, land grants, expansion of adult education, and equality in unions. Since the introduction of export industry (Border Industrialization Program, 1965), women have become a growing part of the labor force, comprising up to 85% of employees in assembly plants.

In 1970, Women in Solidarity organized consciousness-raising sessions. The Women's Liberation Movement later evolved (1974) from this group to work in a broad international context. The National Women's Movement formed in 1971 to fight for legalized abortion and against sexism in the media and in textbooks. The first lesbian-feminist groups also organized (see **Homosexuality**). In 1977 diverse feminist groups united as the Coalition of Feminist Women to support a woman who had killed her rapist; 1 year later the Autonomous Group of University Women organized to address sexual violence, labor discrimination, and abortion rights. *Fem,* a major feminist journal, was begun in 1976. It was guided by Margarita García Flores and Alaíde Foppa, a Guatemalan national who was kidnapped in 1981 during a visit home (see **GUATEMALA**). In 1983, Dr. María del Socorro Saghi led a campaign for the inclusion of approx. 20 million marginal workers in the Social Security system.

MYTHOGRAPHY. The Aztec pantheon included powerful goddesses. Coatlicue, Lady of the Serpent Skirt, lived on a mountain surrounded by water and was the creatrix of life. The goddess Chicomecoatl made the corn crops flourish and also guarded the souls of women who had died in childbirth. Tlacotleutl was the goddess of successful childbirth, and of mothers and their young. Teteoinan was the goddess of healing and prophet of the future. Chalchihuitlicue, goddess of water, caused a great flood; only the righteous were saved by a bridge she built to bring them safely to land.

MEXICO: Pioneers and Promoters of Women
by Carmen Lugo
(Translated by Magda Bogin and Lisa Kollisch)

Mexico is a country of conflicting realities: wealth and misery, sophistication and ignorance, austerity and waste.

With all its petroleum, Mexico produces more hydrocarbons than any other Latin American country. But it is also among the ten countries in the area that have the highest rate of infant mortality and malnutrition, while 5 percent of the richest families earn fifty times more than 10 percent of the poorest families. In spite of its wealth, Mexico lives off what it borrows. Its foreign debt, the highest in the world, could be paid off with 2 percent of the value of its petroleum reserves, but that also represents one third of its bureaucratic costs.

There are still 6 million Mexicans who cannot read or write in an educational system that includes 75,000 schools at all levels. Of these, 58 percent are women. Day-care centers are available (418 of them)—but 33,000 more are needed. According to the 1980 census, 4 million Mexican children did not eat meat, milk, or eggs, But yes, Mexico holds first place in the world in the consumption of soft drinks and one of the first in the consumption of "junk food." The social conditions are closely related to economic circumstances. Thus, the current devaluation of the currency causes the deterioration of the purchasing power of wages and the impoverishment of the majority of the population. It is estimated that one peso now buys ten times less food than it did ten years ago and that about one third of the population subsists on an income which is less than the minimum cost of a balanced diet.

Inequality is also evident in the housing situation. The possibility of owning a house is limited to the classes whose income is ten times more than the minimum. According to the 1980 census, only 30 percent of all houses are privately owned. There is a housing shortage of 6 million homes in Mexico.

Health conditions are also precarious. According to the World Health Organization, Mexico has one of the highest homicide rates in the world and one of the highest rates of cirrhosis of the liver in Latin America.

The economic crisis that the country is facing will undoubtedly take its toll in employment, production, and the political system. In times of crisis, the economic dependence of women makes them more vulnerable to sexual exploitation and more dependent on their families, and further weakens their social and economic position. The disadvantage of living in a sexist, *macho*, racist, and unjust society is complemented by the narrowing of opportunities for personal development and judicial and economic security—all of which is reserved for the dominant classes.

Generally speaking, women are guaranteed full equality with men, and the Constitution assures them the right to work, maternity leaves, the right to unionize, social security, pensions, and medical insurance. Since 1953 women have enjoyed the right to vote and run for office, and divorce has been possible since 1931. However, neither the civil nor the labor rights of women are fully respected. The attitudes of the judges and judicial officers responsible for family cases and divorce proceedings make the laws inapplicable. Women who have been raped lack legal protection. In the majority of cases, the victims are exposed to the aggression of their social environment.

Undoubtedly, the biggest obstacle that Mexican women face is their economic and social marginalization and their inability to participate in the processes that could help transform the reality described above. The oppression they suffer is a result of such ideological attitudes as *machismo* that is internalized in most Mexican men, and which has prevented women from enjoying a full and free existence.

Important changes in sexuality have occurred in recent years. The sexual revolution left its mark on the behavior of the younger generations, who express their sexuality in a much freer way than their predecessors of just a few decades ago. The appearance of organized lesbian groups, the growing number of women who choose motherhood without marriage, and the fact that less importance is given to virginity are all indicative of the recent changes. However, the scarcity of research, publications, and inquiries makes it difficult to analyze the changes and advances that have occurred in the labor, social, and political spheres.

In the 1960's, the State began to focus its attention on women. Family-planning campaigns succeeded in reducing the birth rate from 3.2 percent to 2.7 percent. However, these campaigns were directed only toward women.

Another recent advance is the reform legislation of 1974, which eliminated all discriminatory laws from Mexican legislation. But the gap between theory and daily reality still exists for a large sector of the female workers who have no access to nurseries, maternity leave, opportunities for specialization or promotion, or any of the other benefits of social security. These women represent approximately 60 percent of the economically active female population and earn a salary less than the legal minimum wage. They are the objects of super-exploitation, the marginal working force that subsists in the most wretched conditions while the multinational corporations multiply enormous profits. On a smaller scale, the financial firms, banks, and insurance companies also infringe on the rights of female workers, especially concerning motherhood—since they hire only single women. Some companies and even public schools require a certificate of nonpregnancy from their candidates. Such legislative anachronisms as inquiries into fatherhood still exist, disregarding the rights of single mothers and "concubines" and only protecting women as conduits of private property.

Nevertheless, thanks to the women's movement, research on themes related to women is now developing in almost all the universities and higher-education centers in Mexico. The impact of the movement also has led the way to new modes of communicating ideas to the masses of women and has publicized sexual and political questions. The magazine *Fem,* dedicated to feminism, has assumed the responsibility of promoting the main ideas of the movement. On the editorial pages of the major newspapers, in small specialized movie theaters, at seminars, round-table discussions, and conferences, themes related to women are discussed daily.

One essential condition for the growth of the spectrum of the women's movement is its alliance with such other popular movements as the "squatters" (working-class women fighting for marginal urban housing) and women workers who have been laid off and whose labor rights have been violated (operators, factory-assembly workers, subway-ticket agents, etc.). An alliance with political parties is also fundamental for the expansion of the women's movement. Active militancy in political parties can promote and accelerate the process of social consciousness-raising of women. It can also contribute to the struggle for emancipation that generates and maintains the self-esteem of women as well as their future occupational, family, educational, and sexual victories. The essential connection between the women's movement and other revolutionary movements will be possible when certain prior conditions are fulfilled:

—The development and consolidation of an *autonomous* feminist movement that is nevertheless *linked* to common aspects of other movements in the fight against capitalism and the patriarchy.

—The full dedication within every party and each individual political activist to the programming objectives and specific tactics of a revolutionary feminist movement.

One of the focuses of this movement could be the fight for abortion, which is of great importance in Mexico because of its social implications. Abortions are virtually illegal, performed in a clandestine and unsanitary manner, and are one of the main causes of female mortality.[1] Another common cause would be the denunciation of and fight against sexual crimes, from which women of all ages and social classes suffer. This would interest female union members and could be enlarged into a program that denounces the sexual harassment common among various sectors of female workers, students, and professionals.

Until now, movements with different tendencies have not run into big problems in joining in the common fight for the decriminalization of abortion, the battles against rape and sexual harassment. But as long as society is polarized and the problems of the social classes that suffer most from the economic crisis predominate, Mexican feminists will also have to define their position on class.

As for the traditional/electoral politics, the legislative reforms of 1976 have led to a broadening of the spectrum of political parties, which (according to law) are the arenas where politics should be conducted. In the last presidential election, eight political parties and six candidates competed, one of whom was a woman. Rosario Ibarra de Piedra, the candidate for a Leftist party that promotes feminist demands, did not however succeed in attaining the consensus and support of the whole feminist movement on election day.

At the moment, the Mexican women's movement has two alternatives: it can join political parties and promote feminist ideals from within, or it can become the pioneer and promoter of the organization of women for the defense of their human, labor, political, and economic rights.

Suggested Further Reading

Fem. Seven years of regularly published issues covering abortion, work, sexuality, the international women's movement, the family, sexist language, children, mother-daughter relationships, women's history, science, housework, men, women and the Church, marriage as an institution, etc.; available ($24 US for 1-yr. subscription): Av. México 76, Tizapár 01090, D.F. México.

García-Flores, Margarita. "Cosas de Mujeres" (Women's Things). Editado por Radio Universidad, Universidad Nacional Autónoma de México, México, 1979.

"Memorias del Seminario Feminism, Política y Movimientos Feministas" (Memories of the Feminist Seminar). CEESTEM (el Centro de Estudios Económicos y Sociales del Tercer Mundo), D.F. México, Mar. 1–3, 1982.

Rascón, Antonieta and Carmen Lugo. *Feminismo y Partidos Políticos en México* (Feminism and Mexico's Political Parties). Paris: UNESCO, 1981.

Urrutia, Elena, ed. *Imagen y Realidad de la Mujer* (Image and Reality of Women). D.F. México: Editorial Diana, 1981; anthology.

Carmen Lugo, born in 1945, is a feminist lawyer and university professor. She is a member of the collective management of the Mexican feminist magazine *Fem,* has worked in the area of technical cooperation since 1972, and has published various works on the situation of women in Mexico.

[1.] The Mexican Institute for Social Security *(IMSS: Instituto Mexicano del Seguro Social)* recently published the following statistics: it is estimated that 1.6 million abortions are performed annually, of which only 8 percent are performed under safe conditions; the rest take place under unsanitary conditions using methods that could be fatal to the woman.

MOROCCO
(Kingdom of Morocco)

Located in northwestern Africa, bounded to the east and south by Algeria, to the south by the Western Sahara, to the west by the Atlantic Ocean, to the north by the Mediterranean Sea, and separated from Spain by the Strait of Gibraltar. **Area:** 445,358 sq. km. (171,953 sq. mi.); Morocco also claims part of the Western Sahara. **Population** (1980): 20,959,000, female 50%. **Capital:** Rabat.

DEMOGRAPHY. Languages: Arabic, Berber (indigenous), French, Spanish. **Races or Ethnic Groups:** Arab 65%, Berber 33%, European 1%, other. **Religions:** Islam (Maliki school of Sunni Islam) 99%, Judaism. **Education** (% enrolled in school, 1975): Age 6–11—of all girls 30%, of all boys 50%; age 12–17—of all girls 20%, of all boys 36%; higher education—in 1982 women were 26.3% of university students. A training project, begun in 1979 by the Moroccan Ministry of Work, now permits women to study electricity, electronics, industrial art, architectural design, and commercial studies. **Literacy** (1977): Women 10%, men 34%; by 1981 the urban literacy rate was 27% for women, 44% for men. **Birth Rate** (per 1000 pop., 1975–80): 43. **Death Rate** (per 1000 pop., 1975–80): 14. **Infant Mortality** (per 1000 live births, 1975–80): Female 126, male 140. **Life Expectancy** (1975–80): Female 57 yrs., male 54 yrs.

GOVERNMENT. Constitutional monarchy with an (appointed and elected) 264-member Chamber of Deputies. **Women's Suffrage:** 1959. **Equal Rights:** According to the Constitution, women and men have political, legal, and economic equality. **Women in Government:** Princess Lalla Aicha, sister of King Hassan, was ambassador to London (1965–69). No women in the Chamber of Deputies as of 1982. In the local councils elections of June 1983, a great number of women in both large and small cities and villages ran for office; the gesture itself is viewed as even more relevant than the comparatively meager results.

ECONOMY. Currency: Dirham (May 1983: 6.55 = $1 US). **Gross National Product** (1980): $17.4 billion. **Per Capita Income** (1980): $860. **Women's Wages as a Percentage of Men's** (1981): 25% in certain industries. **Equal Pay Policy:** None. **Production** (Agricultural/Industrial): Grains, citrus fruits, dates, wool; textiles, chemicals, tourism. **Women as a Percentage of Labor Force** (1980): 16%; of agricultural force (1981) 25.3%; of industrial force 28.5%; of military—no data obtainable. **(Employed) Women's Occupational Indicators** (1981): Of administration employees 14.9%, of scientific professions 30%, of textile production 69%, of domestic-service workers 90.6% (29% of whom were under age 15 in 1975). Poor rural women comprise 50% of migrants to urban areas, working as cooks, domestic servants, or washerwomen. **Unemployment** (1979): 35%; no rates by sex obtainable.

GYNOGRAPHY. Marriage. *Policy:* Laws based on the Shari'a (Islamic legal code). A man may take up to 4 wives and unlimited concubines. A woman is given in marriage by a male guardian and cannot choose her husband or marry a non-Moslem. The husband pays a dowry before marriage. Under Family Law, "every human being is responsible for providing for his needs by his own powers except the wife, whose needs will be taken care of by the husband." A wife's "rights" are support, food, clothing, medical care, equal treatment with other wives, control over her own property, and authorization to visit her parents. A husband's "rights" are fidelity, obedience, his wife's breast-feeding of their children, supervision of the household, and respect to his relatives. A woman may stipulate in the marriage contract that the husband cannot take a second wife (Personal Code, Art. 31). Under the Penal Code, any sexual act between a man and a woman outside of marriage is punishable by 1 month–1 yr. imprisonment for each person. Virginity is required of women at marriage. Among the

448

Berbers, pre-Islamic codes often give women rights that are nonexistent in the Shari'a. In certain areas, Berber culture has retained its own traditions; sexual mores tend to be more relaxed and women seem to enjoy more freedom of movement (the Middle Atlas, with its capital, Khenifra, is known for the active participation of women in social events and rituals). *Practice:* Female mean age at marriage (1970–78): 19; in the countryside age 14.5 (1978); women age 15–49 in union (1970–78): 69%. Child marriages are common, in part because of emphasis on female virginity, which also brings a higher dowry. Polygyny is diminishing, especially in urban areas.

Divorce. *Policy:* Legal; 3 types of Moslem divorce are practiced: *talaq,* or repudiation by the husband; *khul',* divorce initiated by the wife in which she pays the husband an amount equal to the dowry she received on marriage; and judicial divorce, which is used almost exclusively by women in cases of cruelty, nonfulfillment of marital responsibilities, absence for 1 yr., sexual inabilities, or if the husband contracted a disease or defect unknown to the wife before marriage. A woman may have her marriage annulled if her husband violates a prenuptial agreement to take no other wives. *Practice:* No general statistics obtainable, but reportedly the divorce rate for younger women is extremely high. Rate is highest among the urban poor and rural migrant women. Divorced women outnumber divorced men 2–1. Divorcees comprise 53% of employed women, and 83% of female-headed households—a group which has increased 33% between 1960 and 1971.

Family. *Policy:* The Family Law was passed the day after Independence was gained (1957) and is based on the Shari'a. Family property is divided, with the son getting twice the share of the daughter. A husband has the authority in the household; a wife must obtain his permission to leave the house or work outside the home. Maternity leave for employed mothers is 2 months with pay; nursing mothers are entitled to 2 daily breaks during the first 8 months after childbirth. Childcare centers are supported by the State or private sources.

Practice: The traditional extended family is giving way, under the pressure of urbanization, to smaller conjugal units, threatening women's security by depriving them of the usual support group of relatives if widowed or divorced; rural women are especially vulnerable. The breakdown of women's segregation in the home is a result of more women being employed, and modernization. The State is taking over traditional functions of the husband by providing economic and educational services for family members. State-financed childcare centers have limited places, lack qualified teachers and equipment, and are often in substandard buildings. **Welfare.** *Policy:* Federal employees are covered under a special pension plan. Other employees receive social-insurance benefits, including unemployment, medical, and old-age pensions under a plan paid for by the government, employees, and employers. Pensions are paid at age 60. Social Security Law states that if husband and wife are both eligible for benefits, they are paid to the husband only. *Practice:* No data obtainable.

Contraception. *Policy:* Legal. Government favors family planning to slow population growth and plans (as of 1983) to increase the number of health centers to 300 and establish a family-planning reference center in each province. *Practice:* Women age 15–49 in union using contraception (1970–80): 7%, of which modern methods 100%. The pill and IUD are the most commonly distributed methods. **Abortion.** *Policy:* Legal, only if the woman's life or health are endangered, but with consent of spouse. Illegal abortions are punishable by a fine and 1–5 yrs. imprisonment for the practitioner (double penalty if habitual practice), and a fine and 6 months–2 yrs. imprisonment for the woman. *Practice:* No statistics obtainable. Traditional abortion methods are still used, especially by rural women; these include cramp-inducing herbal mixtures. However, more modern medicinal abortifacients are being used more commonly. **Illegitimacy.** *Policy:* Pregnancy and childbirth outside of marriage is forbidden, under interpretation of the Shari'a. *Practice:* No statistics obtainable. In such areas as the Middle Atlas, male migration to the cities is high, family instability is great, and the rate of out-of-wedlock births is reportedly high. In Assafi, the sardine-industry town where there is a concentration of the female industrial labor force and a greater number of women are heads of households, the rate of out-of-wedlock births is est. as high. **Homosexuality.** *Policy:* Forbidden by the Shari'a. *Practice:* No statistics obtainable. Reportedly, there is acceptance of lesbian women and homosexual men. There is greater concern, supposedly, about heterosexual relations between unmarried young people (in the new mode of sexual desegregation) than about same-sex relations.

Incest. *Policy:* Endogamy—marriage between cousins (especially paternal cousins)—was preferred and is still often the preferred match between two families. Sexual relations between other close relatives is tabu. *Practice:* No data obtainable. **Sexual Harassment.** *Policy:* None. *Practice:* No statistics obtainable. Women who do not wear the veil in public as well as those who do are sometimes subject to verbal and physical harassment. Domestic workers are often subject to sexual abuse by males of the employer's household. **Rape.** *Policy:* Illegal under the Penal Code as a "crime and offense against family order and public morality," punishable by 5–10 yrs. imprisonment; if the victim was a virgin, the penalty is 10–20 yrs. *Practice:* No data obtainable. **Battery.** *Policy:* Interpretation of Islamic law gives a husband the right to chastise his wife if she disobeys him, including hitting her "in such a way as to cause her no harm." If she remains unyielding, he is to divorce her rather than harm her. A mistreated wife may legally seek court intervention but must have physical evidence of an unbearable situation. The Penal Code is lenient toward a husband who harms a wife found in an adulterous situation. *Practice:* No statistics obtainable, but battery is reportedly common and few women have the means to seek court action. **Prostitution.** *Policy:* Illegal; no further data obtainable. *Practice:* Women's labor is often based on seasonal employment in agriculture and its related industries, forcing some women to become prostitutes during long periods of unemployment. The instability of the family owing to, among other things, the practice of *talaq* (see **Divorce**), increases the risk of employment insecurity for women and in some cases makes prostitution the only economic alternative. The incidence of prostitution is rising, along with the expectable effect on health, e.g., the spread of venereal disease. **Traditional/Cultural Practices.** *Policy:* None. *Practice:* Because of the high priority placed on virginity, hymen-reconstruction operations are not uncommon. At a cost of DH. 500–1000, the operation is virtually inaccessible to women of few means. **Crisis Centers:** No data obtainable.

HERSTORY. In the territory which is now Morocco, Libyan Amazons roamed the area of the Atlas Mountains in approx. 1000–500 B.C.E. According to such early chroniclers as Herodotus, they wore red-leather armor (to this day red Morocco leather is prized) and snakeskin shoes and carried python-leather shields. They founded a city in the area of Lake Triton, practiced animal husbandry, and lived on meat and milk. The Libyan Amazons trained all girls in compulsory military service for several years, after which time they joined the ranks of reserves and were permitted to choose a mate and have children. The women controlled the government and society.

From the area of Lake Triton, the Amazons went on to rule much of Libya and Numidia, even battling other Amazon tribes. One battle was won (against the Gorgon Amazons) by 30,000 Libyan Amazon horsewomen under the leadership of Myrine. After the Gorgon battle, Syria, Phrygia, and all the territory along the coast to the Caicus River was conquered by Myrine and her women's army. They built cities and settled such islands as Samos, Lesbos, Pathmos, and Samothrace. When the Thracians and Scythians invaded the Amazons' territory, Myrine was killed in battle, and the surviving Amazon army relinquished their empire and returned to North Africa.

Among the Berbers of North Africa, women were generally respected and important members of the community before the advent of Islam in the 7th century C.E.; various kinship and marriage systems existed that gave women status and sexual freedom. Queen Zineb An Nefzouia (11th century) and Queen Knata Bint Bekka (17th century) both exercised power through influencing their husbands and their sons. Lalla Aziza was a powerful 15th-century tribal woman (see MYTHOGRAPHY). Sida Al El Horra (16th century) was a power in her own right in north Morocco; she had a fleet that harassed Portuguese and Spanish ships and, through her marriage to the King of Morocco, she acquired the title "Caliph of the Sultan." She was a skilled politician who played on the divisions and alliances of her adversaries. During the "Golden Age of Islam" that began in the 8th century, female slavery was not uncommon; *Jawari,* usually women and young girls captured in raids on non-Moslem peoples, were used as objects of pleasure and symbols of wealth, exchanged between caliphs to win favors. Female slavery in urban upper-class Morocco was practiced until the 19th century. Questions of women's freedom and equality under Islam arose at the same time as the Arab-Moslem nationalism of the late 19th and early 20th centuries.

The nationalists who raised issues of women's equality included men; one such man was the Egyptian Kacem Amin, who wrote *Liberation of Women* in the 1880's. In 1947 Princess Aicha, the daughter of King Mohammed V, un-veiled with her father's support before crowds of people and read a feminist speech that shocked the public. Women's equality again was an issue in the Moroccan nationalist movement led by Allal Al Fassi on the eve of Independence in 1956. In his book *Self-Criticism,* he proposed that women come out of seclusion to participate in teaching and clerical occupations in the government bureaucracy. Feminist attitudes were adopted by some educated women. Formal and informal feminist groups exist in the larger cities today; Casablanca witnessed the emergence of numerous women's study groups in the late 1970's.

MYTHOGRAPHY. Samothrace was dedicated by Myrine to the mother of gods, because it was a refuge for the Amazons (see HERSTORY) after a shipwreck. Myrine founded sacred ritual Mysteries in honor of the Great Goddess, and built altars there. In the Sufi tradition of popular Islam, saints play an important role, and female saints figure prominently. In the south of Morocco, Lalla Aziza is a prominent religious figure; her religious festival attracts thousands each July. (Historically, Lalla Aziza was a 15th-century personage and one of the rare women who directly exercised political power in their tribal settings.) Contemporary Moroccan women play vital roles as healers, and may transfer their powers through rituals.

MOROCCO: The Merchant's Daughter and the Son of the Sultan
By Fatima Mernissi

Revolution is to understand the other's unfamiliar and threatening languages.

"Feminism is not home-grown in Arab lands, it is an import from Western capitals." This often-heard statement is shared by two groups of people one would never think of as having anything in common: Conservative Religious Arab Male Leaders, and the Provincial Western Feminists. The implication of this statement is that the Arab woman is a semi-idiotic submissive subhuman who bathes happily in patriarchally organized degradation and institutionalized deprivation.

With the first group—the conservative religious Arab male leaders—one can immediately identify the interests lying behind such a vision of the Arab woman. The statement itself reflects a key ideological assumption necessary if patriarchal Islam is to exist and thrive at all. A rebellious Arab female has been identified since the dawn of Islam as a potent threat. Quotes from the prestigious Bukhari's *Hadith*, where women are equated with social disorder and with Satan, were piously repeated to me when I showed any dissenting initiative, even at age six.

In the *Koran* there are two concepts referring to female subversive drives and disruptive powers: *Nušuz* and *Qaid*. Both refer to woman's potential for being an uncooperative and unreliable citizen of the Moslem *Umma* (Community). *"Nušuz"* refers specifically to the wife's rebellious tendencies toward her husband in an area where female obedience is vital: sexuality. The *Koran* calls *Nušuz* the wife's decision not to comply with her husband's desire to have intercourse. *Qaid* is the key word in the *Sūra of Joseph*, where the handsome prophet was harassed by an unscrupulous and persevering adulterous wife. Despite the sacred stamp the *Koran* itself branded on female subversive potential in the seventh century, contemporary male Arab leaders open big eyes and scream about Western destructive imported ideas whenever they sense any rebellion on the part of Arab women. The attitude of these men is understandable: if they acknowledge that women's resistance to patriarchal Islam is an *indigenous* phenomenon, they will have to face the fact that aggression against their system has come not only from Washington and Paris but also from the women they embrace every night. Who wants to live with such a thought?

The *Koran*—like the sacred texts of the two other great monotheistic religions Islam claims as reference and source (Judaism and Christianity)—proffers models of hierarchial relationships and sexual inequality. These models have been underscored for fourteen centuries by various additional elements, including the Moslem Golden Age of triumph and of political/economic power, during which time the concept of the *Jawari* (or highly accomplished, learned, exquisite female pleasure slaves) came into being. This is the fabricated archetype that Arab and Moslem women must confront. The *Jawari*, who actually were given as gifts (and bribes and rewards) between powerful men, were the secular aspect of what the *Koran* describes as the *houri*, the eternally virgin, loving, and beautiful female creature offered as a reward in paradise to devout believers—devout *male* believers, that is. These sacred and secular models of woman have had enormous influence on the creation and maintenance of sex roles in Moslem civilization. Why *wouldn't* women rebel?

The reality of the Arab woman's life is not, after all, out of *Arabian Nights*, much as many Arab men and most Western tourists would like to believe. The reality of most Moroccan women's lives, for instance, consists of enormous and vital (but often unacknowledged) labor: carpet-weaving, bead-setting, leather embroidery, sewing, field-work in agriculture, jobs in the massive bureaucratic administration, in light industry, and—of course—in the service sector and in housework, cooking, and childcare.

Colonization, to be sure, devalued women's labor even further than the indigenous patriarchal systems had, and with a double effect: the downgrading of manual labor in contrast to technical expertise, and the specific downgrading of *domestic* labor within the capitalist concept that defines domestic labor as nonproductive and therefore doesn't stoop to integrate it into national accounts.

Nationalization—for all its tragic and repeated historical betrayals of women (as in Algeria)—is nonetheless a strong determining factor in shaping women's expectations. For example, the North African woman of today usually dreams of having a steady, wage-paying job with social security and health and retirement benefits, at a State institution; these women don't look to a man any longer for their survival, but to the State. While perhaps not ideal, this is nevertheless a breakthrough, an erosion of tradition. It also partly explains Moroccan women's active participation in the urbanization process:

they are leaving rural areas in numbers equaling men's migrations, for a "better life" in the cities—and in *European* cities, as well. The rate of women's participation in activities outside of the Kingdom's territory is 40 percent, according to a recent employment survey.[1]

Furthermore, women's participation in various professions is growing,[2] surprisingly high, even, if one considers that until World War II Moroccan women were kept secluded and prevented from attending schools or competing for diplomas and jobs in both private and public sectors. Their contributions to agriculture, crafts, and services were limited to traditional spaces and were masked behind their domestic identity. They contributed as wives, mothers, daughters, aunts . . . but not as women *per se.*

But if Moroccan women in the 1940's and 1950's accepted domestic work as fate, younger women aspire to education and jobs. And it is still very difficult for them. In bureaucratic and industrial employment areas, it is only the woman with two or more years of secondary education who has a chance, and then only after obtaining secretarial skills. Only 37.4% of primary-school enrollments in 1982 were female, only 38.1% in secondary school, and only 26.3% of university students.

At the time of this writing, Morocco is preparing for a highly irregular event: elections. At the last elections (1977), women voters numbered 3 million. Among 906 candidates for parliament, eight were women—and none were elected. Our actual parliament is all male. But today women constitute almost half of the electorate—and that's what matters to the political parties, who are currently outdoing each other in trying to manipulate female voters and win them over. For these brief weeks, we Moroccan women are living in an incredible time-space, where male politicians who are usually oblivious to women's needs are trying to find a convincing language for actually talking to women. They will have to accomplish miracles to find the right tone, because they will have to renounce their centuries-old prejudices. They will have to overcome their stereotypes of femininity/ passivity and open their eyes to the reality of Moroccan women, whose main worries are not, after all, make-up, veiling, and belly dancing, but having equal opportunities in education, employment, promotion, etc.

In light of all this, the belief on the part of some Western feminists that Arab women are subservient, obedient slaves who discovered consciousness-raising and illuminating revolutionary ideas only when fed such goodies by the most liberated of all women (New York, Paris, and London feminists), is less understandable at first sight than the utterance of such sentiments by Arab patriarchs. But if you carefully ask yourself (as I often have) why an American or French feminist will think that I am less clever than she in grasping patriarchal degradation schemes, you realize that it gives her an immediate control of the situation; she is the leader and I the follower. She, in spite of her claimed desire to change the system and make it more egalitarian for women, retains (lurking deep down in her subliminal ideological genes) the racist and imperialist Western *male* distorting drives. Even when faced with an Arab woman who has similar diplomas, knowledge, and experience, she unconsciously reproduces the supremacist colonial pattern. Every time I come across a Western feminist who thinks that I am indebted to her for my own development on feminist issues, I worry not so much about the prospects of an international sisterhood, but about the possibility of Western feminism's transforming itself into popular

[1.] Direction de la Statistique, 1979, Rabat.

[2.] Aside from trade and business, Moroccan women have managed to set foot in practically all spheres, including the previously highly masculine world of *"professions liberales et scientifiques."* They constitute 30 percent of that body; 16.9 percent of university teachers, one quarter of secondary-school teachers, and one third of primary-school teachers are women. [See Statistical Preface preceding this article for further data.—Ed.]

social movements able to produce structural change in the world centers of industrialized empires. The basic question for each woman who thinks herself a feminist, is not how far ahead she is in her consciousness compared to women from other cultures, but how much she *shares* in that consciousness with women from different social classes in her *own* society. Sisterhood will be global when it cuts through both class and culture.

One of the necessary steps for intellectual women to share their privileged access to knowledge and higher consciousness is to try to decipher women's refutation of patriarchy when voiced in languages other than their own. One such endeavor is to grasp and decode illiterate women's rebellion, whether voiced in oral culture or in specifically dissenting practices considered marginal, criminal, or erratic. One of my greatest humility lessons is the one I received from listening closely to folk tales told by my illiterate Aunt Aziza, who is now seventy-nine years old. One of them goes as follows:

The Merchant's Daughter and the Son of the Sultan*

A rich merchant was possessed of a daughter named Aicha, as lovely as the moon. (Sing praises to God who created such a beautiful image.) One evening, while she was taking a stroll on her roof-top terrace, as was her custom, her nurse presented her with a bowl of soup of *Mhamça*. In drinking her soup, she let spill on her breast a small pastry ball which she proceeded to bring again to her mouth. On the adjoining terrace, the son of the Sultan saw her and said,

"O Lalla who tends basil and waters her crop on her terrace, I beg you to tell me how many leaves there are to your plant."

"O Son of the Sultan," she replied, "you who reign over vast lands, O learned one, you a doctor who reads the *Koran,* tell me how many fish there are in the sea, stars in the heavens, dots in the *Koran.*"[3]

"Be quiet greedy one," he mocked. "You have taken the *Mhamça* spilled on your breast and have eaten it."

The young girl descended from the terrace very displeased and asked her nurse to accompany her to the sanctuary of Moulay Idrise so that she might be entertained there and clear her mind. In making her way, she once again came upon the son of the Sultan. This time he was seated close by a vendor of fruits, eating a pomegranate. One seed from this pomegranate fell to the ground between his *balghas*[4] and he picked it up again and ate it. The young woman was gleeful to have witnessed this surprise gesture on his part and returned to her home in very fine spirits indeed.

Early the next morning, as usual, she mounted to her terrace and watered her pot of basil and worked on her embroidery. Later, they engaged in the same dialogue that had taken place the night before:

"O Lalla who tends her basil, how many leaves are there to your plant?"

"O son of the Sultan, you who reign over vast lands, O learned one, you a doctor who reads the *Koran,* tell me how many fish there are in the sea, stars in the heavens, and dots in the Koran."

"Go along with you, O covetous one, you who took the *Mhamça* spilled on your breast and have eaten it again."

But this time, on hearing these words, the young woman triumphantly replied, "Go along with you, O covetous one, who reclaimed the pomegranate seed that fell to the mud between your *balghas* and ate it again."

---

* Based on a translation by Lila Heron—Ed..

[3] The *Koran* is written in the Arabic alphabet, which includes many letters which have dots as a constitutive component.

[4] Loose trousers.

This turn of events prompted the prince to leave in a very vexed state. He purchased clothing to disguise himself as a traveling vendor of women's wares. Hooded in black, with black *balghas,* and carrying ladies' wares, he went through the streets crying out all the way to the residence of the daughter of the merchant. "Perfume!" he shouted, "Mirrors! Towels! Combs! Rings!" So good was his imitation that she took him to be a true vendor and sent her Dada to buy her some perfume. Seeing that his ruse was working, the disguised prince said to the Dada,

"Choose and take all that you desire. For all that I have, all I ask is for a kiss on the cheek from your mistress." The merchant's daughter consented to this and kissed the sooty merchant on the cheek. He then departed wholly satisfied at his success.

The next day, he went up to his terrace and found her watering her basil. Their usual dialogue took place. But this time, the prince triumphed with a retort:

"I posed as a street vendor and dallied with the cheek of the daughter of a merchant." Covered with confusion, Lalla Aicha angrily descended from the terrace.

"Dada," as she called her nurse, "I wish to go right away to visit with my aunt. Will you come with me?"

"Willingly," replied the Dada.

Lalla Aicha recounted to her aunt all that had taken place and asked for help in being skillfully disguised so that she might appear as a slave. Changed for all appearance' sake, she was led to the slave market by her aunt and sold. The slave trader found the girl so beautiful that he offered her to the son of the Sultan and sent her to him. Lalla Aicha brought with her a razor, a cucumber, rouge, and a very strong sleeping potion. She gave the prince this potion and when he had fallen asleep, she shaved off his beard and moustache, made him up to be a woman, hung a mirror around his neck, stuck a cucumber up his anus, and ran off. On returning home, she carefully washed herself and dressed in her own garments, while the prince was awakening to find himself in totally humiliating circumstances.

The next morning, on the roof-top terrace, the usual dialogue took place between the young woman and the prince (now wearing the silky skin of a woman). This time, she was able to end the conversation victoriously:

"I posed as a slave and played many a deceitful trick on a prince."

Furious and humiliated, the son of the Sultan swore that he would marry this opinionated young creature and force her to acknowledge that man is more cunning than woman. He asked for her hand in marriage, and this was granted by her father. Once she was in his possession, he incarcerated her in an underground cell, giving her only large, baggy garments to wear and barley bread once daily with a pitcher of Wad water[5] to drink.

But the sly young woman dug an underground tunnel allowing her to be in touch with her parents' household. There she would go every day to eat and drink, taking care to return to the cell for those times when her husband appeared to replenish her supplies. In handing her the black bread and pitcher, he would say:

"Lalla Aicha, the sorry inhabitant of the cell, who is the shrewdest, man or woman?"

"A woman, my Lord," was her reply. He was unable to make her surrender.

Days passed in this fashion. The Sultan died and his son succeeded him. At the beginning of spring, the young Sultan decided to spend some time in the country, as was his usual custom, and he went first to visit his wife in the cell.

"In eight days," he told her, "at five in the morning, I am leaving for Sour, where I will stay for about fifteen days."

"Enjoy yourself!" replied the young woman. "May you have luck." And she eagerly

---

[5.] Unprocessed river water not fit for drinking.

went by the underground tunnel to her father's, where she asked that she be provided with more sumptuous provisions and trappings than the Sultan himself would have at Sour. She wished to be comfortably settled there before he was to arrive.

The night before his departure, the Sultan went to bid his wife farewell, and the following day at dawn he started on his journey. When he arrived at Sour, he noticed tents of a much finer velvet than his own. Positioned at one of the tents was a young slave, beautifully attired. Very surprised, he made inquiries and learned that an exquisite young woman had come that same morning for a stay of several days. Full of curiosity, he told the slave to ask her mistress if she would receive him. She replied that her mistress said no one could see her who had not spent three previous days in the town as a *farnatchi,* collecting horse-dung.

The Sultan agreed and returned three days later. Water was heated so that he might bathe and dress finely, and he was now allowed into the tent of the mysterious woman.

"I will not talk with you," stated Lalla Aicha, "unless you agree to a contract of marriage. And as a dowry, that I may have your sword and belt." Touched by the sweetness of this voice, the Sultan agreed. Without realizing how much time was passing, he passed twenty full days with his beloved without recognizing her. On the twentieth day, they came and told him that if he did not return a revolution would unleash itself. So he left. His wife had become pregnant.

By the time the Sultan returned, Lalla Aicha had already reentered the cell. The first thing he did in going to see her was to persuade her to acknowledge the superiority of man's cleverness over woman's.

"I stayed," he told her, "twenty delicious and delightful days with a woman with your eyes, your hands, your figure, and a voice like your own."

"In truth, your fortune is large and you are not short on good luck coming your way. Joy and pleasure be with you!" she replied contentedly.

And all continued as it had before. In her fifth month of pregnancy, Lalla Aicha began preparations for the birth of her child. In the ninth month, she brought a boy into the world, whom she named Sour.

The following spring, the Sultan went again to the country, choosing to erect his tents in a place called Dour. Lalla Aicha preceded his arrival as she had the year before, and all passed in similar fashion. This time she demanded that the Sultan spend three days as a vendor of condiments, and give her as dowry his sheath with its silk cord. Later, she gave birth to a second child, whom she named Dour.

The third year, events passed in the same fashion at El Qcour. On this occasion the Sultan had to spend three days cleaning the tent that housed the beautiful woman's horse and give her his ring as dowry. The child born this time was a girl, who received the name of Lalla Hamamel El Qcour, the dove of palaces.

Each time he came by the cell, Lalla Aicha refused to acknowledge to her husband the superiority of men over women. The Sultan reached the point where he had enough of this obstinate woman. He told her that he intended to take a new wife, who would be his favorite. She acquiesced, unmoved.

"To Allah, may you triumph and strengthen your reign!" she said. "When are they going to prepare the chamber for the new spouse?"

"On such a day as this," he replied.

"Very good. I wish you good luck."

On the designated day, she dressed her children in their best clothes. She led them to the palace and ordered them to help with the nuptials. The children carried out this task marvelously, ransacking everything. When they were chased out they cried:

"This house is the home of our father and the sons of dogs are those who chase us!" They cried out the loudest that they were able:

"Come my brother Sour! Come my brother Dour! Come my sister Lalla Hamamel El Qcour!

The Sultan thus learned that they were his children, and he had to acknowledge that woman is much cleverer than man. He dismissed the idea of marrying any other woman, and it was in Lalla Aicha's honor the celebrations were carried out.

If they have not yet done feasting, they must be at it still.

Suggested Further Reading

Accad, Evelyne. *Veil of Shame.* Sherbrooke, Quebec: Editions Naaman, 1978.

Boullata, K., ed. *Women of the Fertile Crescent: An Anthology of Modern Poetry by Arab Women.* Washington, D.C.: Three Continents Press, 1978.

Mernissi, Fatima. *Le Maroc raconté par ses femmes.* Rabat: Editions SMER, 1983.

———. "Women and the Impact of Capitalist Development in Morocco," 2 parts. *Feminist Issues,* Fall 1982 and Spring 1983.

———. "Zhor's World: A Moroccan Domestic Worker Speaks Out." *Feminist Issues,* Spring 1982.

Walther, W., ed. *Femmes en Islam.* Paris: Sindbad, 1981.

Fatima Mernissi was born in 1940 in Fez, Morocco. She writes of herself: "In their yearning to change society, Nationalists opened schools for traditionally veiled and se-cluded city women. That allowed Mernissi to escape illiteracy. Later, the independent Moroccan State underwrote her university and living expenses." She studied political science and then sociology at Mohammad V University, where she taught from 1974 to 1980. She is currently a Researcher at the Centre Universitaire de Recherche Scientifique in Rabat. Her publications include *Women in Political Space in a Moslem Society: Mo-rocco* published by UNESCO in 1983, and her own early book—now a feminist classic—*Beyond the Veil* (available in English; Schenkman, Cambridge, Mass.) One way to recover from stress in Rabat, she recommends, is to "eat a huge orange very slowly on your sunny balcony between two and three (if you are not taking your nap) and never phone up in fits of anger when the event is futile."

NEPAL
(Kingdom of Nepal)

Located in south Asia, bordered to the east by Sikkim (an Indian border state), to the south and west by India, and to the north by the Himalayas and China's Tibetan Autonomous Region. **Area:** 140,797 sq. km. (54,362 sq. mi.). **Population** (1981): 15,000,000; female 48.9%; 94% of the total pop. lives in rural areas. **Capital:** Kathmandu.

DEMOGRAPHY. Languages: Nepali 52.54% (official), Maithili 11.49%, Bhojpuri 6.98%, Tamang 4.8%, Tharu 4.29%, Newari 3.94%, Abadhi 2.74%, Magar 2.49%, Rai 2.01%, Gurung 1.48%, Limbu 1.48%, other 5.84%. **Races or Ethnic Groups:** Newar, Bhotia, Sherpa, Gurkha, other. **Religions:** Hinduism (official) 89%, Buddhism (Tibetan and Newari) 8%, Christianity. Forms differ from the orthodox Pabatiya, more liberal Newari, and loosely Hindu-oriented hill peoples. It is illegal to convert from Hinduism or Buddhism to another religion. Caste and ethnic distinctions are extremely important and complex (see following article). **Education** (% enrolled in school, 1975): Age 6–11—of all girls 10%, of all boys 44%; age 12–17—of all girls 4%, of all boys 17%; higher education—in 1976 females were 17.7% of lower secondary students, 16.9% of higher secondary, 21% of university (including 29 out of 34 colleges). The government's Sixth Development Plan (1980–85) includes the goal of 38% female enrollment in primary school, 30% in lower middle school, and 20% in middle school; education is free for boys through grade 5 and for girls through grade 8 (middle school), including free board and scholarships in remote areas, and scholarships are also provided to females in higher-level trade schools and technical disciplines. School-related expenses and time lost from work continue to prevent most girls from attending school. **Literacy** (1975): Women 5%, men 33% (the 5% est. for women is considered high, and a 1978 survey found that only 3.8% of women were literate). **Birth Rate** (per 1000 pop., 1978): 45.

Death Rate (per 1000 pop., 1978): 20. **Infant Mortality** (per 1000 live births, 1976): Female 137.9 (140.6 rural, 50.2 urban), male 128.4 (130.7 rural, 55.3 urban). **Life Expectancy** (1976): Female 41.1 yrs., male 43.4 yrs.

GOVERNMENT. Partyless Democratic Panchayat System under the active leadership of King Birenda. A 1980 amendment to the Constitution provides for direct election (via village and district panchayats) of most of the 140-member unicameral National Panchayat (legislature), and for the National Panchayat to choose the prime minister. The king can declare a state of emergency and suspend the Constitution and civil rights (Art. 81). Political parties are illegal, but candidates represent opposing groups. **Women's Suffrage:** 1951, along with rights to stand for election. **Equal Rights:** The Constitution does not specify equal rights as a principle of the law but stipulates equal application of the law without regard to sex (Art. 10.2). Sex discrimination is prohibited in appointments to government jobs. The constitutional right to religion results in an ambiguous situation regarding equal rights for women, since certain religious traditions preclude such legislation. "Restrictions on the exercise of fundamental rights for protection of the interests of minors and women" is permitted (Art. 17.2). **Women in Government:** 7 women are in the National Panchayat, 4 women in the Raj Sabha (Privy Council)—1 in standing committee, 3 in general committee; Bidhya Devi Devkota is Asst. Health Minister (1983). Women were 10% of village and town panchayats, and 7.1% of district panchayats; in areas where the law does not require at least 1 woman member, women comprised 0.4% of village and 0.7% of district panchayats (1980). In a 1978 survey, only 1.3% of women were familiar with the name of any national political personality, excluding the king.

ECONOMY. Currency: Nepali Rupee (May 1983: 14.2 = $1 US). **Gross Na-**

tional Product (1980): $2 billion. **Per Capita Income** (1980): $140; 52% of the total pop. lived below the subsistence level of $0.19 per day (1981); 10% of the pop. controls 60% of the land. **Women's Wages as a Percentage of Men's** (1971): No national data obtainable; of sales managers 31% (Terai, Biratnagar), 29% (Hills, Ilam), 27% (Kathmandu); of textile workers 50% (Terai, Biratnagar), 54% (Hills, Hetauda), 24% (Kathmandu); of farmers and farm helpers 109% *[sic]* and 41% (Terai, Bhairhwa), 43% and 92% (Hills, Ilam), 24% and 70% (Kathmandu). **Equal Pay Policy:** The 1976 Minimum Wages for Industrial Workers Act stipulates "equal pay for equal work"; this Act, in conjunction with Art. 10.2 (see **Equal Rights),** can be interpreted as a policy of equal pay. Many contend that equal pay is not guaranteed by these provisions. Wage differentials are maintained in most sectors. Agricultural wages are paid to household heads for all family members. **Production** (Agricultural/Industrial): Rice, maize, wheat, millet, jute, sugar cane, oil seed, potatoes; cigarettes, bricks, sugar, lumber, jute products, hydroelectric power, cement. Approx. 66% of the national income is provided by agriculture, and tourism is a major source of foreign exchange income.

Women as a Percentage of Labor Force (1980): 39%; **of agricultural force** (1976) 38.8% (27.9% of whom are unpaid family workers and 65.9% are employers or self-employed; 92.9% of all "economically active" women are in agriculture); **of industrial force**—no general statistics obtainable (of manufacturing 21.6%, 1976); **of military**—no data obtainable. In 1971 the non-monetized sector constituted 40% of the total economy, and the vast majority of this work was done by women. In 1978 Hindu women in the hill region did 50–70% of agricultural work. **(Employed) Women's Occupational Indicators:** Of civil service clerical positions 2.37%, of civil service administrative 3.23%, of government and semi-governmental jobs (in specified

categories—financial, trading, industrial, public-service, and cultural institutions) 8.9% (1978); of engineers 0.95%, of agronomists 1.84%, of scientific and technical workers 8%, of physicians 13.33%, of nurses 75% (1977); of agricultural managers 4.36%, of schoolteachers 6.6% (1971); 0.14% of employed women were teachers or professionals (1971). An increase in imports and mechanization has resulted in a decline in village and cottage industries, and thus a displacement of many women from the monetized sector. Between 1952–54 and 1971 the rate of employed women declined from 3.75% to 1.83% in the nonagricultural sector, 34% to 13% in the industrial labor force, and 59.4% to 35.1% in the total labor force. Skills-training programs are part of the government's goal for women to comprise 50% of the labor force; 5000 women had been trained by 1982. Trained women are given knitting and sewing machines and looms on credit until they can establish a business. Women with masters' degrees as well as girls supporting themselves through middle school seek places in such programs. The 1959 Nepal Factories and Factory Workers Act prohibits women from night employment (6 P.M.–6 A.M.), and from heavy lifting. Unions are illegal, but some *de facto* organizations exist and have achieved limited gains. **Unemployment** (1977): 5.6%, female 5%, male 5.3%. In 1982, 63% of the rural population was underemployed during some part of the yr.

GYNOGRAPHY. Marriage. *Policy:* All marriages performed "according to any religious, communal, or family traditions" are valid unless both parties do not consent or 1 person is physically or mentally unsound (1971 Marriage Registration Act). Requirements for marriage registration include mutual consent, minimum ages, that neither person has a living spouse, and that no more than a 20-yr. age difference exists*; a marriage does not have to be registered. Minimum marriage age is 16 for females and 18 for

---

* The 20-yr. age-difference stipulation exists because girls who are married to older men become widows at a young age, and strong social/religious prohibitions prevent most widows from remarrying; consequently, there are a great many young widows.

males, with a guardian's consent, and 18 for females, 21 for males, without a guardian's consent; since 1975, parents or guardians who permit underage children to marry are subject to punishment. Polygyny is legal only if the first wife has leprosy or venereal disease, is incurably insane, has no living children after 10 yrs. of marriage, becomes lame or blind, or lives apart with her share of family property; all other polygamous unions are illegal. The 1976 Social Ceremonies (Reform) Act limited the *daijo* (bridewealth) that can be given by a family to a bride, and prohibited bride-price and payment to the groom. A married woman has full rights to own, manage, and dispose of gifts from her father and maternal grandfather upon marriage, gifts *(pewa)* from her husband and his family, and any income earned from work outside the home. The 1974 Evidence Act, however, requires a woman to prove that money or property in her name is acquired from these sources; otherwise, it is considered "family property," and her husband and his relatives can claim a share of it. A wife is entitled to a share of her husband's portion of joint family property but cannot use it as collateral. When family property is divided, a woman can dispose of only 50% of her share without the consent of her husband (or sons, if she is a widow). A widow is entitled to maintenance until age 30, at which time she receives a share of her husband's family property; if she remarries or has sexual relations she loses her right to family property.

Practice: Female mean age at marriage (1970–78): 17; women age 15–49 in union (1970–78): 84%; women in union (1971) age 6–9—2.4%, age 10–14—13.4%, age 15–19—60.7%, age 20–24—92%. The average marriage age for females is lower among the Hindu pop. in the Terai region. Although the minimum-age law is rarely enforced, child marriage is decreasing. Polyandry is practiced among some groups in the north mountains. Women of the Limbus, Khan Magar, Rai, and Tibetan-speaking groups of Baragaon have a higher status and more economic independence than most women in Hindu marriages. High-caste Hindu widows are forbidden to remarry and seldom do so.

Divorce. *Policy:* Legal divorce can be granted in cases of mutual consent. Lacking consent, grounds for divorce are desertion for 3 yrs. or plotting to kill or disable a spouse; a woman also can obtain a divorce if a husband becomes impotent, drives her from his house, does not provide her with food and clothes, or takes a second wife. Upon divorce, a woman loses her share in her husband's property; she can claim maintenance for 5 yrs. if she does not remarry. The grounds for automatic dissolution of a marriage include lack of consent to the marriage by either party, adultery by the woman, or concealment by her that she is a widow or has another husband. Since 1975 a married woman and the man with whom she commits adultery may be sentenced to a fine of up to 2000 Rupees and/or 2 months in prison if her husband files suit (which he may not do if he himself is polygynous). If either party was married before age 16, the marriage can be voided if both agree to the dissolution upon reaching age 16. A woman loses her right to both property and maintenance if a marriage is dissolved. Legal separation can be granted if a woman has been married 15 yrs., has reached age 35, is denied maintenance, is driven from her husband's house, is frequently beaten or abused, or if a husband marries a second wife. If a husband has received his share of family property, a wife may take her share of it upon separation; otherwise she is entitled to maintenance only if she remains unmarried and celibate. A woman can assume custody rights of children under age 16; the father is liable for child support including food, clothes, education, and medical care. If a woman chooses otherwise, a father is obliged to assume custody and maintenance. A mother loses custody rights to children over age 5 if she remarries. *Practice:* 0.24% of females over age 6 were divorced (1971); the rate by area was mountains 0.38%, hills 0.26%, Terai 0.14%, Kathmandu valley 0.33%. The rate of divorce is lowest (and polygyny rate highest) in the predominantly Hindu Terai. Divorce is more casual among hill and mountain ethnic groups. It is extremely difficult for a woman to obtain maintenance payments. Traditionally, Hindu fathers have sole rights to custody of their children. Many women are not yet aware of their new custody rights.

Family. *Policy:* If a man has no sons, he can designate his daughter as a *dolaji* daughter, making her heir to his ancestral property. A father divides his property among his sons, unmarried daughters over age 35, and wife, and retains a small *jiuni* share for his own subsistence. A son or daughter who cares for elderly parents inherits the *jiuni* share. Employees covered by the Nepal Factory and Factory Workers Act (Sec. 30) are entitled to 1½ months maternity leave for 2 different pregnancies each, and a half-hour nursing break every 4 hrs. The 1965 Nepal Factories and Factory Workers' Rules stipulate that workplaces must provide nurseries, milk, beds, toys, and a trained nurse for children under age 6 (Secs. 29, 34). A maternal- and child-health project has been operating since 1968.

Practice: Varies among groups. In Hindu families the status of daughters and sisters is generally higher than that of wives and daughters-in-law. A woman's status increases within the family when she has children. In some parts of Nepal, female infants and children are deliberately neglected in a form of passive female infanticide; in 1976 the child death rate (per 1000 live births) age 1–4 —girls 25.4, boys 11.9 (urban), girls 37.6, boys 33.2 (rural). Less than 5% of births occurred in health facilities, and the maternal death rate was 85 per 10,000 live births (1982). Most deliveries are assisted by midwives *(sudeni)* in unsanitary conditions; there is a high incidence of tetanus and sepsis among both mothers and infants. Mothers are responsible for childcare, and daughters often begin to do household work before age 8. In 1979 there were 505 Family Planning and Maternal and Child Health Centers and 3 training centers. Maternity leave applies to only a limited number of women in government jobs and private enterprises. Nursery facilities are insufficient, and the Women's Services Coordination Committee is working for enforcement of the law. Women are responsible for domestic chores including water portage, fuel collection, flour grinding, food processing, cooking and childcare, weaving, and making baskets. **Welfare.** *Policy:* The Sixth Development Plan (1980–85) is directed toward developing basic health and social services, education, agriculture, and small-scale industry. The government's goal includes 1 hospital in each district and 1 health worker in each village by 1985. *Practice:* The extended family provides care for the young, elderly, sick, and disabled. Less than 7% of the total pop. (5% rural, 81% urban) had access to pure water, and only 3% had electricity (1980). In 1982, 22 of 75 districts had hospitals, and there were 698 stationary and 2071 mobile clinics (up from 284 stationary clinics in 1975). Of the total pop., 80% suffers from roundworm, 15% from dysentery, and malnutrition is common, especially among children (1982).

Contraception. *Policy:* Legal. Pills and condoms are distributed free or for a minimal fee. Contraceptives can be administered by paramedical personnel. Government incentives, offered for those accepting sterilization after a second child is age 3, include bonds, free education in government schools for (the first 2) children through grade 8, and a bonus of 100 Rupees; government employees with only 2 children have 20% added to their pensions. The government includes family-planning education in schools, employment, and women's and rural development programs. *Practice:* Women age 15–49 in union using contraception (1976): 3%; methods used (1976) male sterilization 67%, pill 16%, condom 9%, female sterilization 3%, IUD 2%, abstinence 2%. Women using contraception (by ethnic/caste groups, 1978 Social Network Survey): Brahmans and Newari 13%, Chetri 6.4%, Tamang 4.9%, "untouchable" 2.9%, Moslem and Tharu 0%. According to the 1976 survey, only 21% of women were aware of 1 or more efficient contraceptive methods, of whom 67% knew where to obtain them, but the 1978 survey (which was administered by women) reported 70% awareness of 1 or more efficient methods, and 60% awareness of where to obtain contraceptives. One partner in each of 39,000 couples had been sterilized as of 1977. The Nepal Planning Family Assoc. was founded in 1958, and almost 2000 family-planning workers had been trained by the government by 1979. The government must reduce the infant mortality rate to 50/1000 and increase contraceptive use to 50% to meet its population goals by the year 2000. The program is currently underfunded and inaccessible to most of the population. **Abortion.** *Policy:* Permitted only if the woman's life is endangered, if the fetus is severely deformed, or if the woman is "mentally unbalanced"; these conditions must be certified by 2 physicians (National Code, and Medical Council Rules, 1967). All other abortions are punishable by 1 yr. imprisonment for the practitioner and the woman, or 1 1/2 yrs. if performed after the second trimester. If an abortion is performed without the woman's consent, the practitioner is punishable by 2–3 yrs. imprisonment, depending on the stage of pregnancy (National Code, Sec. "On Homicide"). A draft of a new Penal Code submitted to the National Panchayat would legalize abortion on expanded medical grounds. *Practice:* No statistics obtainable. Illegal abortions are not uncommon and have a high risk factor owing to primitive methods.

Illegitimacy. *Policy:* A single woman and her out-of-wedlock child have no rights to property from the father (National Code, Ch. 13, Sec. 8). *Practice:* No statistics obtainable. The social tabu against out-of-wedlock children and single mothers is strong among the Hindu population, less so among polyandrous groups. **Homosexuality.** *Policy:* No data obtainable. *Practice:* No data obtainable. **Incest.** *Policy:* No data obtainable. *Practice:* No data obtainable. **Sexual Harassment.** *Policy:* No data obtainable. *Practice:* No data obtainable. **Rape.** *Policy:* Under the National Code (Secs. 1–11), any person who has sexual intercourse with a female under age 14, with or without her consent, is punishable by 6–10 yrs. imprisonment. Any person who has sexual intercourse with a female older than age 14 through force, threat, intimidation, or undue influence is punishable by 3–5 yrs. imprisonment. Rape of a prostitute is punishable by a fine and

1 yr. imprisonment. Marital rape is not illegal. An accomplice to rape is punishable by 1 yr. imprisonment; attempted rape is punishable by 1/2 the penalty for rape. If a woman kills a man who has raped or attempted to rape her within 1 hour of the attack, she is not liable for punishment; if she kills him more than 1 hour later, she is punishable by a fine or a maximum 10-yr. imprisonment. A married woman who has been raped does not lose rights to her share of her husband's or former husband's property; 1/2 of the convicted rapist's property is confiscated and given to his victim. *Practice:* The law is rarely enforced (see **Crisis Centers**); no further data obtainable. **Battery.** *Policy:* Battered or harassed wives can obtain legal separations from their husbands (see **Divorce** and **Crisis Centers**). *Practice:* No data obtainable.

Prostitution. *Policy:* No specific data obtainable (see **Rape**). *Practice:* No data obtainable (see INDIA regarding traffick in Nepalese women). **Traditional/Cultural Practices.** *Policy:* No data obtainable. *Practice:* There were reports of "dowry murders" (see INDIA) in some of the Hindu communities until dowry was outlawed (see **Marriage**); there has been no evidence of the practice since. Hundreds of little girls age 2–3 are worshipped as the living form of the goddess in the mother/virgin cult of Kumari. In parts of the northwest region there is a tradition of dedicating 1 daughter to the service of a deity. There also are many women religious ascetics *(saivas)*. **Crisis Centers.** *Policy:* Since 1964, the Nepal Women's Organization has run the Women's Legal Aid Services Project, which offers free counseling to battered, neglected, or abandoned wives, and to rape victims (see HERSTORY). *Practice:* The services of the Legal Aid Services Project are insufficient to the need.

HERSTORY. The confluence of Indian Hinduism and Tibetan Buddhism has resulted in a mixed cultural heritage in Nepal since before the 4th century C.E., when the Newar people presided over the region. There was a large influx of Indian Buddhists, fleeing invading Moslems (8th–11th centuries). During this period the Hindu Gurkha principality was established west of the Kathmandu valley; the Newar Mallas Dynasty ruled the Kathmandu valley (14th–18th centuries). Local conflicts were exploited by the Gurkhas, who in 1768 conquered the valley. In 1846 Jung Bahadur Rana established the rule of his family as hereditary prime ministers and the Shah kings were reduced to public functionaries.

The first formal women's organization, the Mahila Samiti Women's Committee, was founded (1917–18) by Dibya Koirala, Yogmaya Devi, Mohan Kumari Koirala, and Purna Kumari Adhikari—all of them wives, daughters, or mothers of prominent Congress Party activists who were organizing against the Rana regime. The Committee had 30–40 members and focused on the plight of poor women. It encouraged handloom industries and sent a package of torn clothing to the Prime Minister's wife to stress the poverty of the populace. In 1919 Dibya Koirala's family was exiled to India because of her husband's political activities, and the Women's Committee was disbanded. Britain acknowledged Nepal's full Independence in 1923.

Rebanta Kumari Acharya founded the Adharsa Mahila Sangh (Model Women's Organization) in 1947 with the support of the Congress Party in Jainagar. The organization's general goals were to raise the sociopolitical consciousness of women; its specific aims were to oppose child marriage and the ban on remarriage for child widows. It was also deeply involved in underground activities against the government, with members acting as communication links between their imprisoned male relatives and the other Congress Party leaders in exile in India. During this period the Nepal Mahila Sangh (Woman's Organization), dedicated to women's suffrage, was founded by Mangla Devi, Punya Prava Dhungana, Shanta Shrestha, Sahana Pradhan, and Pushpalata. Through their continuing efforts, women's suffrage was won in 1951, following the overthrow of the Rana regime. Nari Jagriti (Consciousness of Women) was another group formed during the late 1940's in Biratnagar; it worked for education rights, and later founded the Model School for Girls.

In 1950 the Nepal Women's Organization split and the All Nepal Women's Organization was formed under the leadership of Punya Prava Dhungana. This group also supported the Congress Party and women's right to education; the first women's college was opened. The first Advisory Assembly was formed to work with the King in 1951; there were no women among its 35 members, and the Nepal Women's Organization and All Nepal Women's Organization conducted *satyagraha* (nonviolent) civil disobedience protests. A second Assembly was formed in 1954, and this time there were 4 women among its 113 members—Punya Prava Dhungana, Mangla Devi, Maya Devi Shah, and Prativa Jha. In 1952 the Women's Voluntary Services was founded by the Princesses Princep Shah and Helen Shah and Queen Rajya Laxmi Rana. It was a social-service organization, although the Queen was an advocate of expanded social and political rights for women. In 1957–58 various organizations formed the Women's United Front under the leadership of Punya Prava Dhungana. Membership reached 500, but the split between pro-Congress and pro-Communist organizations brought about the destruction of the Front after only 1 year. In 1960, following the disbanding of the Congress and formation of the panchayat system by King Mahendra, all women's organizations were merged into the All Nepal Women's Organization (NWO). Bimala Maskey was elected chair in 1962.

From 1960 to 1976 the NWO was largely autonomous with national leadership and grass-roots support. By 1976 it had over 1000 primary organizations and 60,000 members, mostly concerned with legislative reform and delivery of social services to women (see following article). Meanwhile, in 1963, the National Code made advances in terms of women's rights. It outlawed child marriage and forced marriage, and restricted polygamy, but legislation had little effect on actual practices. Shilu Singh, the first practicing woman attorney in Nepal, founded the Women's Legal Aid Services Project under the auspices of the NWO (1963). In 1967 the NWO published a legal-rights handbook for women, which was updated in 1975—International

Women's Year, and the year that the National Code was amended to expand women's inheritance rights. Special education projects for women were announced.

In 1976 the NWO was reorganized and put under the supervision of the Back to the Village National Campaign. It was recognized as 1 of 6 "class organizations," and a law was adopted requiring female representation on local and district panchayats. This brought approx. 4000 women into local governments—but the provision was repealed in 1978. The NWO lost much of its autonomy in the reorganization and currently functions mainly as a conduit for government literacy, hygiene, family-planning, and skills-training programs, although it has not entirely lost its advocacy role. Other government organizations for women include the Women's Service Coordination Committee, the Women's Affairs Training and Extension Center (which trains "barefoot lawyers" in the basic legal rights of women), the Equal Access of Women to Education project, Mothers' Clubs (concerned with family planning and mother and child health care), and the Business and Professional Women's Club.

MYTHOGRAPHY. (See Traditional/ Cultural Practices.) The mountain which the British called Everest is known as Chomo-Lungma ("God-Mother of the Country") and Chomo-Uri ("Mother of the Turquoise Peak") to the Nepalese. Women among the Gurung are thought to be powerful witches; they have permanent eating and sleeping associations which exclude men. Among many non-Hindu groups there are popular and important women's festivals and dances. Near Sanku, the fierce blue Buddhist goddess Tara, who bears a sword, is worshipped. Hindu men honor the warrior goddess Durga, but women are excluded from these rituals (for more information on Hindu female deities, see INDIA).

NEPAL: Women as a Caste
by Manjula Giri

Primarily a rural society, Nepal understandably does not yet have a strong feminist movement. Almost no Asian country has. The age-old patriarchy has seen to it that the female personality is thoroughly submerged in the male. When a woman asserts herself, she is assumed to be a fanciful "Westernized freak" not worthy of attention.

The Sexual Caste System

The Hindu tradition relegated women to secondary place—so much so that an independent, self-reliant Hindu woman is a contradiction in terms. The sacred laws are categorical in their demands for female submission. Hindu culture abounds with legends of a Sita or a Savitri, whose singular claim to distinction and divinity was her devotion to her husband; the husband is the raison-d'être of an ideal woman. Consistent with this thinking was the infamous practice of self-immolation by a widow as a demonstration of eternal fidelity to her dead husband. The immolated female was called Sati. Although such literal self-sacrifice was apparently a voluntary act, coercion always played a role if the need arose—and the need invariably would arise if the deceased husband left any considerable estate.

Hindu culture has given rise to a number of eerie rites and customs, including the "Sati system," the corollary fetish about female virginity, and the tradition that every woman is untouchable during her menstrual period, irrespective of her class and caste. *It is impor-*

tant to understand that women are clearly treated as a separate caste in themselves, whether acknowledged as such or not.

A caste system, after all, establishes a place into which certain members of a society have no choice but to fit, just because of a coincidence of birth: a certain sex, skin color, or parenthood. Segregation by sex, color, and birth thrive in interdependence; "untouchability" of one kind or another is the inevitable outcome. Women have the home as their ghetto; the *harijan,* or "untouchables," have their secluded habitation.

One not born into the context of a caste system is apt to miss the accompanying agony of being an untouchable. Psychologically it is much worse than being a slave. A slave of ancient Rome at least did not necessarily differ racially from the enslaving group. A slave could be freed and made equal under certain circumstances. The working conditions of the average Asian woman, unbelievable though it may sound, are probably more miserable than those of outright slaves.

As one fact-finding seminar paper[1] reveals:

Rural Nepalese women not only contribute more time but also generate more income than men for the total household economy. When only outside income from wages, salaries, or trading profits is considered we find that men contribute 72 percent of the household income while women and children contribute 27 percent and one percent, respectively. However, outside earnings accounted for only 18.6 percent of the total income of the households in our sample. *The remaining 81.4 percent of the household income came from home-production.* . . . It is not too surprising to find that women are responsible for 86 percent of the time-input into domestic activities. Housework, after all, is traditionally viewed as a female task. Nor is it particularly startling to find that women's input accounts for 74 percent of the time spent in expanded economic activities. What is significant, however, is the fact that women do all this in addition to contributing 49 percent of the total time-input to conventional economic activities.

But no social-research paper can do justice to the magnitude of the female ordeal. The working conditions of Nepalese women would put a Charles Dickens to shame: the dark den euphemistically called the kitchen is filled with smoke and dirt. While the mother cooks, children crawl about, crying. Sanitary facilities are virtually unheard of.[2] Women must wait for the darkness of night to relieve themselves.

The Hindu "Sati system," Chinese foot-binding, and the Moslem veil are all customs which fit like tiles into a mosaic. The Asian woman endures as a living example of the abyss into which the human self may be forced to descend.

And if she is an "exception," an intellectual, an artist? Goma, our first recognized Nepalese female poet, still recalls the difficulties she encountered in her endeavor to publish her early poems. Fifty years ago, all a woman poet could expect was ridicule. Editors rejected her poems because of the sex of their author. Goma was almost ostracized for the apparently amorous, romantic, and assertive content of her poems. She did persevere, however. Her polygamist husband, who was a source of constant harassment

[1] Paper prepared by Bina Pradhan and Lynn Bennett on Rural Women's Participation in the Nepali Household Economy for the seminar, Appropriate Technology for the Hill Farming Systems, June 1981.

[2] A recent survey of least developed countries conducted by the UN Conference on the Least Developed Countries (June 1981) reveals: "40 percent of Nepali rural households are estimated to be below the subsistence level, i.e., to have income less than $0.17 US per person per day."

to her, finally abandoned her. But the abandonment carried with it the stigma of blame—on *her*. In the circumstances she decided to call herself a widow.

Goma the poet symbolizes how some women have coped with the pain.

Royalty, Patriarchy, and "Official Feminism"

Most Asian countries today are reeling under despotism. The patriarchal family—always the backbone of tyranny—has strengthened contemporary, sophisticated authoritarianism all the more. The upsurge of national liberation movements has not been able, after all, to usher in open societies. In Nepal, people have been deprived of such basic civil rights as free speech, free association, and even free movement since the royal takeover in 1960. A few women participated in the struggle for civil liberties; some suffered prison terms. The late 1970's saw a number of strikes and skirmishes led chiefly by students and workers, forcing the King to call for a referendum to determine the nature of State and policy. Consequently, the Constitution was reformed—but with a considerable broadening of the power base of the ruler. A great advancement has been made, however, in the form of universal adult suffrage.

The State adheres to a strange ideology of "national unity" and "class coordination." Political parties are castigated as divisive forces. Even nonpolitical organizations require prior government consent to function legally. Otherwise, participation in such an organization is a punishable offense; there is an express law to this effect. The women's movement, or for that matter any popular movement, has great difficulty putting down roots in such circumstances. Various political groups are agitating for the lifting of this ban, and clearly feminist activists cannot help confronting the government on this issue.

But meanwhile there are *official* organizations of women directed and financed *by* the government. Indeed, the authoritarian attitude of the State has circumscribed the activities of many otherwise energetic and genuine leaders of the women's movement.

Mangla Devi is a good example. Vocal, ebullient Mangla Devi may claim the distinction of being one of the pioneer Nepalese women to speak up in her own right. She is a founding member of Nepal Mahila Sangh, the first noteworthy women's organization, begun almost thirty-five years ago. An activist in the civil-liberties movement, she has been jailed a number of times. Meeting her is an exhilarating experience. Nonetheless, the organization that she founded and led is banned in Nepal today.

Understandably, Mangla Devi is quite critical of the current "official" Nepal Women's Organization. She does not see any possibilities for an independent feminist movement in the near future unless civil liberties are restored; without the right to organize, women cannot hope to fight our battle meaningfully, she fears.

Although Mangla Devi refuses to have anything to do with the existing Nepal Women's Organization, there are a few others who hope to subvert the official organization by feminist infiltration from *within*. (There is no chance of setting up a rival organization; that would be illegal.) After all, in theory—though it has never had any relationship in this case with practice—the Nepal Women's Organization (and other such official institutions concerned with women) is committed to reforms of such traditional (mal)practices as polygamy, child marriage, bride sale, etc. The law of the land also prohibits these practices—in principle. The official women's organizations may have to look into legal violations in spite of themselves.

The Civil Code Act, for example, was introduced nearly two decades ago and supposedly protects women against polygamy, child marriage, and forced marriage. It also gives women property rights—but unfortunately it has not been very effective, owing to a lack of public education and to traditional social constructs.

Women, even in educated families, are still subject to maltreatment from their "superiors." Once a woman is married, she is expected to remain in that marriage for the rest of her life, even if she is ill treated by family members. The Civil Code Act does allow her a divorce should such a situation arise—but society looks down upon divorce. She still finds herself trapped between the abstract law and the concrete reality. The same is true of women's property rights. In her childhood, a woman lives under the father's guardianship. Later, her husband becomes her guardian—and finally, when she reaches old age, her son becomes her guardian. Thus women actually have very little say in decision-making.

As yet another example, the government and its associate bodies are concerned about checking the growth of population. Yet it is not unusual to find a woman bearing as many as ten children—to the detriment of her physical and spiritual health. At times, the Nepal Women's Organization undertakes certain constructive humanitarian projects: literacy campaigns, skill-development projects, family-planning programs, etc. Such projects may reach a tiny audience of some sort, and it is encouraging that occasional encounters with real issues and real atrocities do crop up on the premises of the Nepal Women's Organization now and then. But it is tragically true that the Nepal Women's Organization is inherently incapable of confronting even a fraction of the real challenge.

Enormous, Quiet, Patient Labor . . .

In the circumstances, it is not an easy job for women to organize along militant lines. The weight of patriarchal tradition is stupendous. The sway of male hegemony is almost complete. The primitive economy displays no signs of changing in the near future. In other words, the objective conditions that gave rise to the enslavement of the Nepalese woman appear as if they will remain intact for the foreseeable future.

A few women activists may dare to act as torch bearers. But without masses of women behind them, their programs will perforce remain at a standstill. All that an individual feminist activist can hope to accomplish right now resides in her *fight for the right to be heard.* This she may be able to do by working in concert with other groups as allies. The movement for civil liberties and the growing unrest among the *harijans* are two such important forces on the insurgent side of the barricades. The feminist movement must forge strong links with these and other progressive groups.

In the meantime, Nepalese feminist activists have a great deal of basic organizing to do. Theoretical work is necessary if anything meaningful is to come of our efforts; after all, it is chiefly in the cultural and social realms that we have to do battle, today as well as tomorrow. Enormous, quiet, patient labor has to be carried on, with the goal of raising our collective consciousness. It will be a protracted struggle.

Publication of a feminist journal may well serve as the first concrete step toward that desired goal. The journal would assimilate and publicize the ideas of feminist movements all over the world, serve as a forum for discussion and clarification of facts and strategy, and, perhaps most important, function as the nucleus and catalyst for nascent organizational activity.

Feminist ideas may seem to have arisen chiefly in the context of the industrialized West, but the universal significance of those ideas has been recognized immediately and seized upon by women all over the world.

The characteristics and problems faced by women of Third World cultures have yet to be taken fully into account by any of us. But this is a task that could be accomplished most fruitfully if pursued in a spirit of international feminist cooperation. The global sisterhood can serve as a fountain of inspiration for women everywhere.

Suggested Further Reading

Acharya, Meena. "The Maithili Women of Sirsia."

Acharya, Meena, and Lynn Bennett. "The Rural Women of Nepal: An Aggregate Analysis and Summary of 8 Village Studies."

Bennett, Lynn. "The Parbatiya Women of Bakundol."

Molnar, Augusta. "The Kham Magar Women of Thabang."

Pradhan, Bina. "The Newar Women of Bulu."

Rajure, Drone. "Tharu Women of Sukhrwar."

Schular, Sidney. "The Women of Baragaon."

[The above are all 1981–82 publications of the Status of Women Volume II Project funded by a grant from the US Agency for International Development (AID/PPC/WID, Washington, D.C. 20523, USA). They are excellent, and I prefer them to other publications on Nepalese women.—M.G.]

Manjula Giri was born in 1950 in Bastipur, Sirha District, Sagarmatha Zone, Nepal. She took her master of arts degree in political science from Banaras Hindu University (India) in 1974. She was awarded a World Press Institute fellowship for 1978–79 and has been a working journalist for six years. She has interviewed Prime Minister Indira Gandhi of India and former Portuguese Prime Minister Maria de Lourdes Pintasilgo,* among others. She has attended national Nepalese and international conferences on the status of women, has written many articles on Asian women and indigenous Asian feminist movements, and has worked as a reporter for the national news agency of Nepal. In 1983 she became founding editor and publisher of *Gargi,* a national monthly women's magazine named for a Hindu figure frequently cited as an example of women's intellectual achievement.

---

* See Maria de Lourdes Pintasilgo's contribution on women in Portugal, p. 571.—Ed.

THE NETHERLANDS
(Kingdom of the Netherlands)

Located in northwestern Europe, bordered by West Germany to the east, Belgium to the south, and the North Sea to the west and north. **Area:** 36,175 sq. km. (13,967 sq. mi.). **Population** (1980): 14,091,000, female 50.4%. **Capital:** Amsterdam. **Head of State:** Queen Beatrix.

DEMOGRAPHY. Languages: Dutch. **Races or Ethnic Groups:** Dutch 95%, immigrant pop. (mostly from Suriname and the Mediterranean region) 5%. **Religions:** Roman Catholicism 40%, Dutch Reformed 24%, Judaism, other, unaffiliated 24%. **Education** (% enrolled in school, 1975): Age 6–11—of all girls 94%, of all boys 92%; age 12–17—of all girls 88%, of all boys 90%; higher education—in 1982–83 women comprised 43% of students in higher vocational schools and 33% of university students; in 1977 women were 23.7% of medical school graduates, 22% of law graduates, and 22% of all social science graduates. **Literacy** (1977): Women 100%, men 100% (but government sources estimate that 1–4% of the pop. is nonliterate). **Birth Rate** (per 1000 pop., 1982): 12. **Death Rate** (per 1000 pop., 1982): 8. **Infant Mortality** (per 1000 live births, 1977): Female 10, male 12. **Life Expectancy** (1975–80): Female 78 yrs., male 72 yrs.

GOVERNMENT. Constitutional monarchy with an elected bicameral legislative parliament composed of a 75-member Upper Chamber and a 150-member Lower Chamber. The prime minister, council of ministers, and State secretaries are appointed by royal decree. The Christian Democratic Party, the Labour Party, and the People's Party for Freedom and Democracy are the main political parties. A new constitution was adopted in 1983. **Women's Suffrage:** 1919, 2 yrs. after male suffrage. **Equal Rights:** 1983 Constitution (Art. 1) states that all persons shall be treated equally under equal circumstances; discrimination on the grounds of religion, belief, political opinion, race, sex, or any other grounds whatsoever shall not be permitted. The 1980 Equal Treatment of Men and Women Act prohibits discrimination in hiring, promotion, and training. In 1982 a draft bill against discrimination on grounds of sex, marital status, or sexual preference was introduced. **Women in Government:** Women constitute 17% of the Upper Chamber and 18% of the Lower Chamber, Ms. Smit-Kroes is Minister of Transportation and Public Works and Ms. E. M. Schoo is Minister for Development Cooperation (1983). Since 1977 there has been a Secretary of State who coordinates Emancipation Policy; Ms. Kraayeveld-Woufers, Ms. d'Ancona, and Ms. Kappeyne van de Coppello held the post successively. Women comprised 16.5% of provincial parliaments, 5% of deputies, 12.5% of municipal councilors, 6.1% of aldermen, and 9.9% of the judiciary (1978).

ECONOMY. Currency: Dutch Guilder (May 1983: 2.8 = $1 US). **Gross National Product** (1980): $161.4 billion. **Per Capita Income** (1980): $11,470. **Women's Wages as a Percentage of Men's:** 23.5% of women earn the minimum income, compared to 5.7% of men (1982); 77.9% of the hourly wage in nonagricultural jobs (1980); 77.8% in agriculture (1975). **Equal Pay Policy:** The 1975 Equal Pay Act established the principle of equal pay for equal work, although this is not always practiced. **Production** (Agricultural/Industrial): Grains, potatoes, sugar, beets, flowers; metals, machinery, textiles, electronics. **Women as a Percentage of Labor Force** (1980): 30.4%; **of agricultural force** (1977) 16.4% (63% of whom were unpaid family workers); **of industrial force** (1977) 12.4% (of manufacturing 14.3%, of food, drink, and tobacco industries 21.8%, of textiles, clothing, leather, and footwear industries 40.8%); **of military**—no statistics obtainable; since 1979 women can enlist in all branches of the armed forces, with "equal status and duties" to men. The special women's corps in each branch is being disbanded to effect integration, but military combat for women is not under consideration. **(Employed) Women's Occupational Indicators:** Of barristers and solicitors 16.1% (1979); of senior civil servants 5.1%, of doctors 18.3%, of pharmacists 29.5% (1978); of administrative/managerial workers 6.8%, of professional/technical workers 34.5%, of sales workers 36.5%, of clerical workers 43.3%, of the service sector 64.7% (1977); 84% of employed women are in the service sector (1981). **Unemployment** (mid-yr. 1982): 11.26%, female 12.9%, male 10.7%.

GYNOGRAPHY. Marriage. *Policy:* Marriage age with parental consent is 16 for females, 18 for males, or age 21 for both without consent. Only a civil ceremony is legal and it must precede a religious ceremony. Marital property is held jointly unless otherwise specified in a premarital contract. *Practice:* Female mean age at marriage (1970–78): 22; women age 15–49 in union (1970–78) 66.9%. The mean age at marriage is rising and an increasing number of young couples are living together out of wedlock. **Divorce.** *Policy:* Legal; a 1971 bill amended the law to permit divorce 1 yr. after marriage if the marital relationship is "durably disturbed." When both spouses consent to divorce, their petition is granted automatically by the court. Separation—which eliminates the marital domicile and property arrangement but leaves the bond intact—is obtained on the same grounds as divorce. After a 3-yr. separation, divorce is granted when either spouse files a petition. *Practice:* The divorce rate has tripled since 1960. In 1980, 1 in 4 marriages ended in divorce; in large cities, 1 in 3. Divorced women face severe economic difficulties; since 1975, divorced women with 1 child have lost 12.5% of their purchasing power.

Family. *Policy:* The government considers the family the basic unit of society but acknowledges that an increasing number of people are choosing alternatives to the nuclear pattern. Both parents are responsible for raising children. A fully paid maternity leave for 6 weeks before and 6 weeks after childbirth is available to employed women under the Sickness Benefits Act of the Social Security System. Family allowances are available for children under age 16, under certain conditions. Childcare is available at day nurseries for children of employed parents and students; the State pays 60% of costs, and municipalities and parents (on a sliding-scale basis) pay the balance. Day-care centers sometimes offer supervised playtime for children after school and for pre-school-age children. *Practice:* Family size has decreased as contraceptive use has increased during the 1970's; the fertility rate (per woman) has fallen from 2.6 (1970) to 1.6 (1978); 30% of marriages remain childless (see **Contraception**). There is a growing number of women heads of households, including never-married women and their children. In 1982, 2.7% of families were headed by a single parent. The government subsidized 130 day-care centers in 1981 and 3000 playrooms for a few mornings a week, but approx. 20,000 children are on waiting lists. **Welfare.** *Policy:* The Social Security System is composed of national insurance which provides pensions to persons over age 65 based on compulsory wage deduction, family allowances (see **Family**), sickness benefits for all wage earners (paying 80% of wage) except public employees who are covered under separate plans, unemployment insurance for 90 days, and health insurance, which is either compulsory for employees earning Fls. 30,900 or less, or voluntary for others, and funded by wage deduction. The Health Insurance Act entitles members to free medical, dental, and hospital care, and medicines. The 1963 National Assistance Act provides financial aid to citizens in need. *Practice:* In 1980, 60% of divorced women with children received financial aid from the government. No further data obtainable.

Contraception. *Policy:* Legal; contraceptive services have been available free of charge since 1971 through the National Health Insurance Plan. No-cost sterilization has been available since 1973. *Practice:* Women under age 45 in union using contraception (1975): 75%; methods used (1975) pill 66%, condom 14%, IUD 6%, rhythm 4%, female sterilization 3%, male sterilization 3%, withdrawal 3%, diaphragm 1%, other methods 1%; using inefficient methods 8%. The introduction of the pill in 1964 revolutionized family planning; in 4 yrs., 4 out of 10 women age 21–34 were using it. By 1980, 10% of women and 11% of men age 25–59 had chosen sterilization (see **Family**). **Abortion.** *Policy:* Legal under 1981 Law 257; abortion is nonetheless still listed in the Penal Code. The procedure is permitted during the first 2 trimesters of pregnancy, after a 5-day waiting period and with the approval of 2 physicians, in hospitals and nonprofit clinics only. Procedures can be paid for under the National Health Service. *Practice:* During the 1970's abortions were available in nonprofit clinics and permitted by the government and the medical establishment despite their technical illegality. Foreign women and women of ethnic minorities used the services more than Dutch women. In 1979, 20 clinics performed 57,600 abortions; 72% of those obtaining abortions were nonresidents, the rate for residents in 1979 was 85 per 1000 known pregnancies or 5.3 per 1000 women age 15–44. Feminist groups have protested restrictions of the new law that require a waiting period and physicians' approval.

Illegitimacy. *Policy:* The 1982 Civil Code reform established equal inheritance rights for children born out of wedlock. The mother is the legal guardian of "illegitimate" children if she is an adult, but fathers are obliged to provide support to children until they are age 21. *Practice:* The number of children born out of wedlock has been increasing since 1973 and constituted 4% of all births in 1980. **Homosexuality.** *Policy:* There is no law regarding homosexuality. A 1982 proposed anti-discrimination bill (see **Equal Rights**) has met opposition from conservatives. Government officials claim that the article on equal rights in the new (1983) Constitution is meant to include nondiscrimination on the basis of sexual preference. *Practice:* Lesbian and male homosexual-rights groups are numerous and politically active. The COC, an umbrella group of 70 organizations, is the largest and includes 20 lesbian groups. There are 5 lesbian archives, radical-lesbian-feminist groups, and same-sex-preference sections of political parties. Evelien Eshuis, a member of parliament since 1982, wears a pink triangle badge

"for all those women who can't—who can then at least know that there are lesbians in political circles." The Pink Front organizes Pink Week yearly to celebrate international homosexual-rights actions in June. There are a lesbian teachers' section of the Teachers Union and a national lesbian/gay radio program.

Incest. *Policy:* Illegal under the Penal Code (Art. 249), which prohibits sexual relations between a father, guardian, or stepfather and his child under age 21; punishable by 6 yrs. imprisonment. *Practice:* No specific data obtainable (see **Crisis Centers**). **Sexual Harassment.** *Policy:* None. In 1983 a government interim report on sexual violence was published. *Practice:* A 1980 women's magazine survey found that 90% of 400 women respondents had experienced sexual harassment on the job. **Rape.** *Policy:* It is illegal under the Penal Code to have sexual intercourse with a woman against her will and is punishable by up to 12 yrs. imprisonment. There is no legal recognition of marital rape. (See **Sexual Harassment.**) *Practice:* There are approx. 150 convictions for rape every yr.; 40–50% of all rape charges are dismissed. **Battery.** *Policy:* The Penal Code makes assault and battery of another person a crime punishable by 2 yrs. imprisonment; combined with grievous bodily harm, 3 yrs.; with malice of forethought, 4 yrs. Battery against one's mother, father, wife, or children is punishable by a sentence increased by 1/3. *Practice:* No statistics obtainable (see **Crisis Centers**). **Prostitution.** *Policy:* The Penal Code does not criminalize prostitution, but each municipal government is empowered to issue local ordinances restricting or prohibiting the activities of prostitutes. The Penal Code forbids pimping and running a brothel (punishable by a fine or up to 1 yr. imprisonment) and trafficking in women (punishable by 5 yrs. imprisonment). *Practice:* No statistics obtainable. Prostitution is extremely common in most large urban areas. The "red-light district" of Amsterdam is notorious for the prostitutes who are put on display in windows, bathed in red light, waiting for customers. Prostitution is generally tolerated by officials when confined to certain areas.

Traditional/Cultural Practices: No data obtainable. **Crisis Centers.** *Policy:* In 1980 the government offered funding to approx. 30 centers founded by women's groups which aid rape and battery victims. In 1972 the government began an experimental program of assistance from confidential medical advisers in cases of child abuse; by 1978 there were 10 bureaus providing assistance in emergency cases. *Practice:* The Blijf van Mijn Lijf (Hands off My Body) movement was started in 1974 by 6 Amsterdam women. They opened a battered-wives shelter and now have sister groups in Rotterdam and many other Dutch cities. In 1980 more than 3000 women and 5000 children were aided, including a relatively high percentage of women and children from ethnic minorities (Suriname, Turkey, etc.). In 1974, 823 cases of child abuse were reported to the confidential bureaus. Feminist telephone hot-lines provide support and information to women in crisis. Some of the feminist shelters were established as part of the women's squatters movement *(kraak* actions)—women seizing and occupying vacant buildings, a movement caused in part by severe urban housing shortages and in part by the urgent need for women's crisis shelters.

HERSTORY. As one of the Low Countries, the Netherlands achieved unification only in the 16th century C.E., although the country of Holland was founded as early as the 10th century C.E. and governed by a powerful nobility. Flanders, Holland, Brabant, Gelderland, and Zeeland came under control of the dukes of Burgundy in the 15th century.

Mary of Burgundy (1457–82) succeeded her father, Charles the Bold, to the Burgundian throne in 1477, averted a French take-over of the Low Countries and her other inherited lands, and won assistance to do so from Holland, Brabant, Flanders, and Hainaut by restoring provincial privileges her predecessors had revoked. She rejected marriage to the French dauphin and wed Maximilian I of Austria (later Holy Roman Emperor) in 1477, thus joining the Low Countries with the Hapsburg house. Spain gained control of the Low Countries in 1555, but religious friction with Spain added fuel to an independence struggle which erupted in 1568 and persisted intermittently until 1648, after which the Netherlands was established through the Peace of Westphalia.

The Dutch 17th century was a culturally rich period, known especially for the art of Rembrandt and other Dutch masters, but recent feminist scholarship has revived interest in the many great women painters of the period, including Levina Teerlinc (1520–76), Caterina van Hemessen (1528–c.87), Clara Peeters (1594–c.1657), Judith Leyster (1609–60), Maria van Oosterwyck (1630–93), and Rachel Ruysch (1664–1750). Margaretha van Eyck (1370–?) and Susanna Horebout (1503–45) were acknowledged for their painting mastery but treated secondarily in comparison to their more celebrated brothers (Jan and Hubert van Eyck) and father (Gerard Horebout) respectively. Anna Maria van Schuurmann (1607–78) was a true Renaissance woman—a painter, engraver, sculptor, poet, musician, and linguist.

The roots of the first Dutch feminist movement were entwined with the Protestant struggle for individuation through schools and political parties which would promulgate their philosophy (mid-1800's). Protestant women expressed their religious sentiments in working to improve education for girls and the social conditions of the poor, and for the opening of nursing and teaching careers to women, but they did not consider suffrage or the right to employment appropriate issues for women. The earliest feminists who evolved from that group were intellectuals who sought education, employment, and political opportunities for women, later establishing De Vereniging voor Vrouwenkiesrecht (Assoc. for Women's Suffrage) in 1884.

One woman especially stands out as an active feminist of her time: Wilhelmina (Mina) Elisabeth Drucker was born in 1848, an out-of-wedlock child from a poor family. She embraced socialism and women's rights, founding De Vrije Vrouwenbeweging (Assoc. of Free Women) in 1889, and 4 years later founded and edited *Evolution,* the group's magazine. She was nicknamed

"Dolle Mina" (Mad Mina) because of her zealous devotion to women's rights.

The Industrial Revolution and trade unionism grew after the 1860's and Queen Wilhelmina began her almost 60-year reign in 1890. Aletta Jacobs (1854–1929) was another early feminist, the country's first woman university student and first woman doctor. She was also the first Dutch woman to claim the right to vote, and co-founded the Dutch Women's Suffrage Society in 1883 and the International Women's Suffrage Alliance in 1902. She was active in the international peace movement, fought against State-regulated prostitution, and in 1882 opened the first birth-control clinic in Europe. Women's groups, including the Committee for the Amelioration of the Social and Legal Position of Women, worked to change the law on married women's rights. Mina Drucker protested that the law kept married women from employment; in 1899 she organized a movement that (11 years later) crushed a bill to bar women under age 40 from teaching or civil service jobs. In 1915 Aletta Jacobs, together with other women, initiated a "Call to the Women of All Nations" for an International Women's Congress on peace which was held that same year at The Hague. In 1919 women won the vote.

The Netherlands remained neutral in WW I, but Germany invaded in WW II, forcing the government into exile; approx. 104,000 of the 112,000 Dutch Jews were sent to concentration camps in Poland and killed. Many Dutch women were active in the Resistance, especially as couriers and in providing shelter for fugitive Jews. Queen Wilhelmina and the government returned in 1945, after Germany's defeat. Juliana took the throne in 1948 when her mother Wilhelmina abdicated, and her daughter, Beatrix, ascended in turn in 1980, making to date almost a century of unbroken female (constitutional) monarchy. For contemporary women's HERSTORY, see following article.

MYTHOGRAPHY. Among the Frisians, the ancient inhabitants of the region, women were considered semi-divine beings revered as prophets and sibyls; they were consulted by chieftains and warriors and often presided over the great assemblies held at the foot of sacred oak or ash trees. The Roman historian Tacitus mentioned the famous Veleda, to whom many made pilgrimages in search of wise advice.

THE NETHERLANDS: In the Unions, the Parties, the Streets, and the Bedrooms
by Corrine Oudijk

The first feminist wave in the Netherlands, at the beginning of this century, brought about suffrage for women in 1919. It was thought that equality for women had been achieved. It took fifty years before a second feminist wave hit the country to show that inequality still existed. This inequality still is spread over many areas of Dutch social life. It is most clearly shown in the strict division of labor: men earn the family's living and women take care of husbands and children. The Netherlands, along with Italy and Ireland, always have been among those European countries where a relatively small amount of women have paid jobs.

More and more women do work after their youngest child has reached age four, although they work part time. Between 1960 and 1980 the number of women working outside the home has doubled.* However, this growth doesn't imply a change in the traditional division of male and female jobs. More than 80 percent of employed women are in the medical and social services, in education, and in the lowest-salaried functions. Research also shows that the chances for women to get a job commensurate with their education are smaller than for men. The number of male-dominated jobs in the Netherlands is greater than in other Western European countries. Furthermore, the hourly wage of women is unfavorable compared to that of men—*and* compared to *women* in most other Western European countries. Why this difference?

One of the reasons is that the Netherlands has a very solid social security system. The arrangements for unemployment benefits are good, as are the benefits for those unable to earn their own living. The benefits and the legal minimum income are the same. These arrangements start from the principle that a man has to support his family; therefore, it is not thought necessary for women to work outside the home. But the drawback is that married women are made totally dependent on their husbands for their livelihood. Still another factor is that the Dutch attach great importance to family ties: the most important thing in life is a "happy marriage," which means a tender, careful wife and a husband who comes home directly from work and doesn't drink too much. Most activities outside the workplace take place in the home. Homemaking and the upbringing of children are regarded as very important. (My mother still prides herself on the fact that she was almost always there, waiting, when I came home from school.)

The Church and the Labour Movement both had great influence on the evolution of these standards: "My wife doesn't need to work." As a consequence, the provision of adequate childcare centers for those comparatively few women who do work came about very slowly. Nevertheless, things are changing. A growing percentage of people (in 1980 almost 20 percent) doesn't live so traditionally as described above. Young people and the aged live for a longer period of time on their own. A woman alone isn't necessarily considered an "old spinster" anymore. The number of divorces used to be rather low in the Netherlands, but has increased enormously during the last ten years, and the number of women living alone with their children is increasing. Added to these women there is another small but growing group that wants to have children but no husbands. They call themselves Purposely Unmarried Mothers (BOM: Bewust Ongehuwde Moeder).

Despite all these developments, education and the choice of a profession are still considered less important for a girl than for a boy. It is true that girls nowadays stay longer at school and obtain a higher education than they used to, but they still leave school earlier and end up with a lower education than boys, often choosing an education which can be considered an extention of the still-existing sex-role division, and which has no prospects for an interesting professional career. The subjects chosen by boys have more possibilities on the labor market. In 1980, 37 percent of the boys chose science compared to 15 percent of the girls. This leads to a dangerous situation wherein girls and women are falling more and more behind with regard to technology, which is playing an increasingly important role in our society.

The storm which caused the second feminist wave in the Netherlands in the 1970's was raised by two action groups. The first group (1968), Man-Vrouw-Maatschappij (Man-Woman-Society), aimed at an equal division of tasks in housekeeping and income-earning between men and women, and directed their actions to the government and the Parliament. The other group, Dolle Mina (1970, Mad Mina—named after Wilhelmina Drucker, a pioneer of women's emancipation in the Netherlands in the early twentieth century), specialized in distinctive publicity campaigns designed to raise consciousness about women's oppression. They organized actions for the legalization of abortion, for

* See Statistical Preface preceding this article for details.—Ed.

enrollment of women at an exclusive business school, and for public urinals for women and children. It worked! The press and the media paid a lot of attention to the Dolle Mina actions, and a lot of women joined Dolle Mina.

Within a few years every woman who said anything in connection with feminism was called a "Dolle Mina." Women began to come together in smaller consciousness-raising groups to talk about their common situation. In addition to Man-Vrouw-Maatschappij and Dolle Mina, other action groups were born, aiming at specific issues: legalizing abortion, creating halfway houses for maltreated and battered women, forming feminist health-care and therapy groups, and raising public consciousness about such subjects as paid work, menopause, sexual violence, unequal education, etc. To support the movement, homes and cafés for women were established and, in the big cities, women's bookshops and publishing firms.

The active women who were part of the movement from the beginning (in Dolle Mina and Man-Vrouw-Maatschappij) played a central role in this development. A lot of them took the initiative to start new feminist groups. The result was that, although the original action groups lost their pioneer status, they now formed part of a total women's liberation movement. Theory and strategy expanded accordingly.

Equality can exist only if work outside the home and work inside the home is fairly divided. This is why the redivision-of-labor issue is an important one for the Dutch feminist movement. To achieve this goal, we are striving for a five-hour working day for everyone. Man-Vrouw-Maatschappij delineated ten advantages of the five-hour working day in a pamphlet in 1976.[1] The Dutch women's movement is also fighting for the right of every person to be covered equally under the social security system, regardless of their living arrangements.

Another important campaign during the 1970's was the struggle to legalize abortion. In 1967 abortion teams started operating in some hospitals with the cooperation of private-service institutions and aid societies. In 1971 the first out-patient abortion clinics were founded. Many bills to (more or less) legalize abortion failed in Parliament. The government harassed abortion services. There was one attempt to close an abortion clinic (Bloemenhove), but hundreds of women occupied the clinic and saved it. In 1980, after a lot of fuss between the Christian-Democrats and the Conservative Liberal Party, a new abortion law was accepted—allowing abortion on social indication, provided that two doctors agreed and after "a time for consideration" of five days for the woman. These conditions were unacceptable for the women's movement, since we felt that they showed disrespect for women.

To protest this bill, the committee Wij Vrouwen Eisen (We Women Demand Legalized Abortion) organized a women's strike on March 31, 1981, urging women all over the country to strike—women in paid jobs as well as housewives. About 130 committees organized local actions, and about twenty thousand women took part. As a *strike* the action had little success, because of the fact that the strike funds of unions were not made available to striking (paid) workers. There was no need for most firms and government services to close down. However, many women didn't cook supper. Never before had so many women in the Netherlands discussed oppression and opposition—and never had so

---

[1.] "On a five-hour working day more can be done and less has to be done; freedom and equality have more of a chance; the redivision of paid and unpaid labor is possible for all of us who are able to work; more people can participate in the labor-process; men and women both have a better chance to earn their own income; the motivation to work increases and therefore so does productivity; children can get much more attention; single persons, especially those who are in charge of the care of others, will no longer get so overburdened; there is more time left for social contacts and self-realization."

many women been united in a demonstration! In all, this day was a great success. Still, the abortion law was accepted, although the new law didn't change abortion practices (yet); the clinics continued with their operations.

The fight to legalize abortion made clear that many changes can be achieved only in politics. Under the influence of the feminist movement, the women's groups of the political parties became radicalized. In 1975 the women's organization of the Labour Party went through a fundamental change. At first they supported women's groups in the Third World and organized discussions and such recreation activities as "bingo parties." Then the Red Women (Rooie Vrouwen) started to act as a pressure group inside *and* outside the party, fighting for women and changing the political game, so that more women would become interested in politics. Over a period of time, the influence of the Red Women and other women's organizations in party politics has increased. This influence is reflected in the election platforms of the parties. However, campaign promises don't always translate into practice.

The same kind of development has taken place within the unions, especially in the union for teachers and the union for government employees. Groups of active feminists have fought with success to put the demand for legalized abortion in the program of these unions. One phenomenon which is unique in the world is the recognition of the Women's Union as a full-valued member of the Federation of Trade Unions in the Netherlands (FNV: Federatie van Nederlandese Vak Verenigingen). The Women's Union organizes the wives of the union members, and has been working on the position of housewives, the meaning of unpaid work in our society, and the conditions of women working at home. All women doing unpaid work can join the union, which has the same status as any regular trade union.

During the last years, the women's movement in the Netherlands has entered a new phase. It has become quite clear that socioeconomic changes are not enough; it is a change in *mentality* we need. We want a society that appreciates the showing of emotions, in which it is completely natural that men look after themselves and women give leadership. Therefore, power should be severed from personal relationships.

Feminism doesn't stop at the front door anymore. The so-called sexual revolution that took place in the 1960's made it *more* difficult for women to refuse undesired sexual intimacies and led to a new kind of sexual oppression. Now we ask ourselves: "Do we still make love with our oppressor?" What's important now is the fight for the recognition of our own sexuality apart from heterosexual standards and conventions—a fight which is even more threatening because it takes place in private, often in our own beds. One consequence of this is the struggle against sexual violence, street intimidations, and pornography. Assault, rape, and pornography are being targeted as expressions of men's power over women. (The actions of the Dutch women's movement delayed the liberalization of the Public Morality Act, which would have made it easier to show porn.)

Contrasts within the movement have increased. The smaller, more radical groups refuse to try for power within existing social and political structures. They consider themselves "autonomous." Some groups are more, others less radical. Every group works on its own issues and actions. The contacts are informal. This situation sometimes leads to denunciations of one group by the other: "Who is the right feminist?" (the wielding of the feminist measuring staff). Because of strategical differences, cooperation between the "autonomous" and the "political" women is often bad. Which is unfortunate, because the main difference lies not in whether one works within or without male-dominated organizations, but in how radical one is in one's demands.

Recently, there is a new phenomenon surfacing: women's groups within social movements—Women for Peace, Women Against Nuclear Power, Women Squatters Collectives, etc. Women in these groups want to break through the male models of leadership and action. This development has made the discussion about strategy differences flare up again: "Does this mean a loss of strength in the women's movement? Must we cooperate with male-dominated organizations in our struggle?"

All of which still remains a question.

It's my opinion that real changes in the feminist sense can be brought about only if women gain influence and power in places where decisions are being *made:* within the trade unions, in political parties, in business, and in government. No matter how difficult this struggle is, we cannot win a feminist revolution by being dependent on men in positions of authority. Women's interests and party interests undoubtedly do clash once in a while. It happened, for instance, with an abortion demonstration in which the Red Women were asked not to participate so as not to endanger (with their presence) a draft government agreement between the Labour Party and the Christian-Democrats. The government agreement didn't happen after all and the women were left with a bad taste in their mouths.

In the Labour Party there are about 350 Red Women groups, active over the country. Every division board is obliged to have a woman on the board to stimulate women's activities. Because of this kind of arrangement, the input of women in the Labour Party has been rather important. The party has taken up a number of demands of the Red Women: legalization of abortion, the right to an individual income and an individual unemployment benefit, the five-hour working day, etc. To ensure that men give up at least a part of their power to the other approximately 51 percent of the population, "reverse discrimination" is necessary. The domestic regulations of the Labour Party say that in all political bodies, in town councils as in government, 25 percent of the members must be women. This is not much (it *ought* to be *50* percent), but even this number is sometimes hard to attain. "There are not enough women with sufficient qualifications to run a big city" was the excuse at the nomination of candidates for the city council in Rotterdam. Among the qualifications asked for, not *one* had to do with "emancipation qualities." Nobody talked about stimulating women to go into politics. But by attending all meetings and writing protest letters, the Red Women got more women's names placed on the candidate list. In order to prevent the same struggle from taking place every four years, groups have been set up to support women who are active in local politics or neighborhood activities.

Women belonging to different political parties can come to understand that they have more in common with each other than with the men in their own party; they can coalesce their strengths. If the feminist women in Parliament had been in caucus with each other at the time the abortion law was being discussed, it might have been possible to change the bill. Since 1981, however, women of different political parties do consult each other. Once in a while some group or a person revives the discussion about a Woman's Party. Up until now, with little success.

Women in the labor unions have had the same experiences. Ever since they put pressure on the union congress they got some resolutions accepted on shorter working days, legalized abortion (paid for by the National Health Services), redivision of paid and unpaid labor, and the right to an individual income. But in practice the unions don't fight for these demands. Some union leaders don't like working women, who "take jobs from men." Others find it ridiculous to talk about abortion: "What do labor unions have to do with that?" Male trade-union leaders nearly exploded with rage at a union congress when women repeatedly showed their emotions talking about abortion in front of an auditorium full of men. The women founded a Platform of Trade-Union Women in order to turn the unions into organizations which defend women's interests. In this Platform alliance, women's groups from different unions cooperate as intensively as possible. The Platform also organizes independent actions.

The women's liberation movement has created a change in Dutch society so fundamental that it's impossible to turn it back. The number of activities and groups have increased tremendously. Feminist ideas have reached parts of the population never before interested, including housewives with a minimum of education. Traditional women's organizations have also begun occupying themselves with emancipation topics, and women in higher job positions organized themselves into a women's network to support each other. The consciousness has taken root in almost all parts of the population. This is shown clearly by changes in public-opinion polls. Contrary to ten years ago, a majority of the Dutch are in favor of an equal distribution of paid and unpaid work between the sexes. It has become quite acceptable for married women to do professional work. (The approval, however, is less if it means that a child has to stay in a day-care center.)

In 1975 a National Emancipation Board was set up to advise the government on how to improve the position of women in the Netherlands. In 1977 (rather late), the government began a Direction for Emancipation Affairs Department, with a Secretary of State specially entrusted with all affairs related to women's emancipation. The Dutch official policy to strengthen women's legal position evolves along two lines: removing or amending clauses in current legislation in which an unjustified distinction is made between the sexes, and adopting new rules to ensure the principle of equal pay and treatment (1975 Equal Pay for Men and Women Act; 1980 Equal Treatment of Men and Women Act). In 1982 a draft bill against discrimination on grounds of sex, marital status, and homosexuality was published. And another action undertaken by the government is the stimulation of part-time work on a large scale.

It is a beginning—but it is not at all enough. Most of the demands of the movement have not been met. Now, with the economic recession, there is a stagnation in childcare facilities, job opportunities for women, and changes in the social security system. As the power of the women's movement increases, so does the resistance. One of the common ways men fight back is with ridicule; another is denial. A Dutch writer wrote a book about feminists called: *The Woman Doesn't Exist.* Many young girls who still have the illusion of being free and independent consider feminism "extreme."

We don't believe in quick changes anymore. You can't break traditional patterns and a patriarchal mentality of centuries in fifteen years. But we *have* caused a general understanding of the fact that the way women traditionally participated in society was the result neither of "nature" nor of "personal preference," but of an unequal power structure that reproduces itself by countless mechanisms.

To strengthen and comfort ourselves we need support and inspiration not only from feminists in our own country but also from women in other countries. International publicity can be powerful and effective. We may learn from the experiences, the successes, *and* the bottlenecks of the movement in other countries. Even though the situation of women differs in each nation, the unequal power structure we reject is international.

Women of the world unite!

Suggested Further Reading

"Emancipation of Women, a Process of Change and Growth." Memorandum to the Parliament 1976–1977; the next memorandum will be published in 1983/1984. Publications available from Ministry of Social Affairs and Employment, Postbus 20801, 2500 EV 's-Gravenhage.

"Fact Sheet on the Emancipation of Women in the Netherlands." Ministry of Social Affairs, 1979; gives a brief synopsis of the history and recent initiatives, and includes some figures; written for the World Conference of the UN Decade of Women, Copenhagen, 1980.

Siegers, J. J., and R. Zandanell. "Simultaneous Analyses of the Labour Force Participation of Married Women and the Presence of Young Children in the Family." *The Economist,* Vol. 29, No. 2, 1981.

"A View of the Social Distribution of Paid and Unpaid Work Between Men and Women." National Advisory Commission on Women's Emancipation in the Netherlands, 1980; contains proposals for concrete policies and is available from Lutherse Burgwal 10, 2512 CB 's-Gravenhage.

"Women in the European Community." European Committee, 1980; information, research, and facts concerning women, available from B.E.R. 02/68 Wetstraat 200, 1049 Brussels.

Corrine Oudijk is a Dutch social scientist and socialist-feminist. She graduated from Erasmus University in Rotterdam, taught at the Catholic College of Social and Cultural Welfare in the Hague, and worked as an adviser on Cultural Affairs of the Province "Zuid-Holland." Since 1980, she has worked at the National Social and Cultural Planning Office. She was involved in the student movement of the 1960's and is a political activist in Red Women, the feminist organization in the Labour Party. Her report on the status of women in the Netherlands, called *Social Atlas of the Woman 1983,* was published in Nov. of that year, and she has written articles and a musical play (with Sybrich de Kramer) about feminism in the Dutch Socialist Movement from 1906 to 1980.

NEW ZEALAND
(Dominion of New Zealand)

New Zealand is composed of 3 large and several smaller islands, located in the Pacific Ocean approx. 1250 miles southeast of Australia. **Area:** 268,676 sq. km. (103,736 sq. mi.). **Population** (1980): 3,153,000, female 50%. **Capital:** Wellington. **Titular Head of State:** Queen Elizabeth II.

DEMOGRAPHY. Languages: English, Maori. **Races or Ethnic Groups:** European descent 89%, Maori 8%, other. **Religions:** Church of England 25.6%, Presbyterian 16.5%, Roman Catholicism 14.4%, indigenous faiths, other. **Education** (% enrolled in school, 1975): Age 6–11—of all girls 100%, of all boys 100%; age 12–17—of all girls 83%, of all boys 84%; higher education—in 1982 women were 80% of teacher trainees; in 1982 women comprised 44% of university students. **Literacy** (1977): Women 99%, men 99%; reportedly lower in the Maori pop. **Birth Rate** (per 1000 pop., 1982): 15.69. **Death Rate** (per 1000 pop., 1982): 8.02. **Infant Mortality** (per 1000 live births, 1981): Female 10.02, male 13.01; in 1981 the infant mortality rate in the Maori pop. was 15.44 as compared with 11.65 in the total pop. **Life Expectancy** (1978): Female (European descent) 75 yrs., (Maori descent) 68 yrs., male (European descent) 69 yrs., (Maori descent) 63–64 yrs.

GOVERNMENT. A unicameral 92-member elected House of Representatives, headed by a prime minister and a cabinet, comprises the government. **Women's Suffrage:** New Zealand was the first country in the world to grant women (of both Maori and European descent) suffrage, in 1893; women won the right to stand for parliament in 1919. **Equal Rights:** No comprehensive law establishing women's equality in all areas, but the 1977 Human Rights Commission Act made it illegal to discriminate on grounds of sex in the areas of employment, housing, and finance. **Women in Government:** 8 female members of parliament (1983). No female cabinet members. In 1980 women comprised 12% of all candidates elected to local government office.

ECONOMY. Currency: New Zealand Dollar (May 1983: 1.51 = $1 US). **Gross National Product** (1980): $23.2 billion. **Per Capita Income** (1980): $7090. **Women's Wages as a Percentage of Men's** (1981): 75%. **Equal Pay Policy:** The 1972 Equal Pay Act stipulates equal pay for equal work or for work of equal value. The Working Women's Charter, devised by women active in the trade-union movement, delineates both issues and means for equality for employed women; it was passed overwhelmingly in May 1980 by The Federation of Labour. **Production** (Agricultural/Industrial): Meat, dairy products, wool, timber; processed foods, textiles, machinery, transport. **Women as a Percentage of Labor Force** (1981): 24.2%; **of agricultural force** 20.7%; **of industrial force**—no general statistics obtainable (of manufacturing 20%, 1981); **of military** (1982) 8.55% (army 5.9%, navy 9.64%, air force 11.26%), noncombat roles only. **(Employed) Women's Occupational Indicators:** Of engineers 5.5%, of administrative/managerial workers 8.48%, of sales workers 39.3%, of professional/technical workers 43%, of service workers 58%, of clerical workers 68.75% (1981); women fill 78% of all part-time jobs (1981). In 1982 New Zealand revoked all restrictions on women's right to night employment. **Unemployment** (1980): 2.9%, female 3.3%, male 2.6%.

GYNOGRAPHY. Marriage. *Policy:* Legal marriage age is 16 for females and males with parental consent, and 20 for both without parental consent. Marriage is governed by the 1955 Marriage Act. The Citizenship Act of 1977 gives all citizens equal rights regarding foreign spouses and children. *Practice:* Female mean age at marriage (1970–78): 21; women age 15–49 in union (1970–78): 67%. **Divorce.** *Policy:* The Family Proceedings Act (1980) cites irreconcilable breakdown of marriage as the only grounds for divorce; the persons must live apart for 2 yrs. and submit to counseling for possible reconciliation. The Matrimonial Property Act (1976) allows for equal division of property on dissolution of marriage (with exceptions). The 1980 Family Proceedings Act stipulates that (with exceptions) former spouses have an obligation to support themselves and that maintenance provisions relate solely to the children of a marriage. *Practice:* Divorces (per 100 marriages, 1981): 48.5.

Family. *Policy:* The 1980 Maternity Leave and Employment Protection Act guarantees job security and 6 months unpaid leave for any woman in the private sector who has been employed 15 hours per week for a minimum of 18 months; 2 weeks paternity leave (unpaid) is available. The Child Care Regulations (1960) delegate the responsibility for childcare centers to the Social Welfare Dept. A single mother can claim the same "sickness benefit" as a married mother; the allowance lasts until 13 weeks after delivery or until the mother is fit to return to her job. Thereafter, she can claim a "domestic purposes" benefit from the Social Welfare Dept., provided she agrees to claim maintenance from the father (see **Welfare**). *Practice:* Part-time female workers (the majority of all part-time workers) are ineligible for maternity benefits. In 1981 there were 229 childcare centers, accommodating 5929 children. From Mar. 1981 to Mar. 1982, NZ$1.1 million was paid by the government in childcare subsidy. **Welfare.** *Policy:* Comprehensive social-welfare system includes benefits for invalids, widows, single parents, students, and the unemployed. Since 1979, married women have received unemployment compensation at the same rate as married men. The Domestic Purposes Benefit subsidizes single parents with dependent children who have no other income or support. The Family Benefit provides a weekly payment for each child while s/he is in school. All New Zealanders over age 60 receive National Superannuation; the rate for married persons is 80% of the average time wage; single persons receive 60% of the married rate; rates are adjusted every 6 months. Benefits are paid on the death of a spouse, and widows are eligible for government subsidy if they meet certain conditions (see **Family**). *Practice:* As of 1983 the Domestic Purposes Benefit provided NZ$143.4 per week for 1 child and an additional NZ$6 for each subsequent child; in 1981, 1.8% of women and 1% of men received this benefit. Family Benefit of NZ$6 per week per child was received by 39.7% of women and 0.8% of men (1981); 418,901 people received superannuation; 1.7% of women received the Widows Benefit of NZ$89.64 per week in 1983.

Contraception. *Policy:* Legal; the government subsidizes family-planning centers. Free contraceptives and pregnancy tests are available either on medical grounds or in circumstances where a patient cannot pay. *Practice:* In 1977 NZ women age 15–45 had the highest usage rate of contraceptive pills in the world; in 1975, 44.4% of that age group used the pill. Sterilizations for both women and men have increased during the 1970's. Contraceptives are available from more than 40 State-subsidized Family Planning Assoc. clinics. **Abortion.** *Policy:* Legal with qualifications. Under the 1977 Contraception, Sterilisation, and Abortion Act, pregnancies may be terminated during the first 20 weeks if a woman's life or health (physical or mental) is at serious risk, if the pregnancy is a result of incest, if there is a substantial risk that a child will be born with a severe physical or mental abnormality, or if the woman is severely abnormal; 2 specially appointed physicians must determine whether the necessary circumstances for an abortion are present. After 20 weeks, an abortion may be performed only to save a woman's life or to prevent serious injury to mental or physical health. Illegal abortions are punishable by a fine for the woman and up to 14 yrs. imprisonment for the practitioner. *Practice:* Abortions (per 1000 women age 15–44, 1982): 9.6. In 1982 there were 6903 legal abortions performed, a 2.1% increase over 1981. **Illegitimacy.** *Policy:* Out-of-wedlock births have been officially renamed "ex-nuptial" births. Registration can be in the name of mother and father if both agree (in which case the child takes the father's name), or solely in the mother's name. An ex-nuptial child has the same right to share in both parents' property (if paternity is established) as a nuptial child, although a man can exclude any of his children from his will. The Liable Parent Contribution Scheme introduced in 1981 ensures that the noncustodial parent contributes to the financial support of the children (see **Family**). *Practice:* There were 11,386 exnuptial births in 1982; over 25% were registered by the father. **Homosexuality.** *Policy:* Male homosexuality is punishable by a maximum of 5 yrs. imprisonment under the 1961 Crimes Act. Lesbianism is not mentioned. *Practice:* In 1982 there were 141 reported "offenses" of homosexuality and lesbianism, and 120 prosecutions. It is est. that in 1977 there were 150,000 same-sex-preference New Zealanders. Homosexual relationships of both sexes are not legally recognized—homosexuals cannot marry, adopt children, claim each other as dependents, or receive government allowances available to heterosexual couples. Active gay-rights groups in urban centers are lobbying for an end to discrimination based on sexual preference.

Incest. *Policy:* Illegal; under the 1961 Crimes Act incest is defined as sexual intercourse between parent and child, (full or half) siblings, or grandparent and grandchild, and is punishable by a maximum 10 yrs. imprisonment for anyone over age 16. *Practice:* In 1982, 36 cases of incest were reported, and 25 persons were prosecuted.

Sexual Harassment. *Policy:* "Serious" sexual harassment in the workplace is considered a form of sex discrimination and is unlawful under the 1977 Human Rights Commission Act. A woman dismissed by her employer after sexual harassment may file a personal grievance at the Arbitration Court under the 1973 Industrial Relations Act. *Practice:* In 1981 the Advisory Committee on Women's Affairs concluded that sexual harassment affects 4 out of 5 women in the labor force. **Rape.** *Policy:* Illegal, and punishable by a prison term not exceeding 14 yrs. Rape is defined as intercourse without the woman's consent, with consent obtained by threat of grievous bodily injury or death, by impersonation of the woman's husband, or with consent obtained by fraud; 2 additions to the Evi-

dence Amendment Act required a judge's consent before using evidence pertaining to the victim's past sexual experience (1977) and prohibited publication of the victim's name (1980). Marital rape is legal unless the couple is legally separated. As of 1984 a rape law reform bill was pending in Parliament; it would broaden the definition of rape. *Practice:* There were 1001 sexual attacks reported and 392 persons prosecuted in 1982; approx. 18% of rape victims reported their cases to the police, and 59% of those who did considered the treatment they received unsympathetic. **Battery.** *Policy:* The 1983 Domestic Violence Act broadened protection of a battered woman. The 1961 Crimes Act includes penalties for wounding or injuring with intent, assault by a male on a female, common assault, or cruelty to a child. *Practice:* There were 996 reported assaults by males on females and 621 persons prosecuted in 1982. The majority of offenses go unreported (see **Crisis Centers**).

Prostitution. *Policy:* Taking money for sexual services is not illegal; soliciting, living off the earnings of a prostitute, and brothel-keeping are illegal. Only women can be charged with soliciting; male prostitutes cannot be charged, nor can men who suggest paid sexual activity to women. Soliciting is punishable by a maximum NZ$100 fine or a maximum 1-month imprisonment. The remaining offenses are punishable by up to 5 yrs. imprisonment under the 1961 Crimes Act (Sec. 147). *Practice:* There were 152 reported offenses of brothel-keeping and prostitution in 1982 and 142 persons prosecuted. **Traditional/Cultural Practices:** No data obtainable. **Crisis Centers.** *Policy:* Some government support for certain centers. *Practice:* Approx. 20 centers in different cities provide emergency care (for rape, battery, child abuse, etc.); all are outgrowths of the women's movement.

HERSTORY. New Zealand was inhabited by Polynesian Maoris who had possibly emigrated from other Pacific islands, until Dutch explorers arrived in the 17th century C.E. In 1769, Captain James Cook claimed New Zealand for the British Empire. After several unsuccessful attempts at colonization, the British finally founded a permanent settlement in 1840.

Early Maori herstory has been obliterated by colonization and lack of written records. The first Pakeha (European) women settlers came to New Zealand as missionaries and missionaries' wives in 1814. Mother Mary Joseph Aubert formed an order of Roman Catholic nuns to help prostitutes and their children in the 1880's. New Zealand's first all-women's labor union was founded in 1889 under the leadership of Harriet Morison. Other women's labor unions soon emerged, but all were short-lived. Meanwhile, the women's suffrage movement was growing. In 1892 the Women's Christian Temperance Union, headed by Kate Shepherd, was instrumental in the formation of a women's franchise league. Suffrage was achieved for both Pakeha and Maori women (despite opposition by both Pakeha and Maori men) in 1893— the year Kate Edgar became New Zealand's first woman university graduate.

A newspaper addressing women's issues appeared in 1895, inspiring the 1896 formation of the National Council of Women, headed by Kate Shepherd. In 1893 Grace Neill became the first female inspector of factories, and later the assistant inspector of hospitals. Her concern over women's health brought about legislative reform: the Nurses' Registration Act (1901), the Midwives' Registration Act (1904), and the establishment of maternity hospitals (1905).

When WW I broke out, Ettie Rout, a free-lance journalist, recruited a group of women called the Volunteer Sisters; they were forbidden by the government to join New Zealand's troops in Egypt. In 1915 many women went despite the prohibition. In 1931 New Zealand was granted Independence, but not until 1947 did the country have management of its own for-

eign policy. Katherine Mansfield emigrated to England but wrote out of a New Zealand (and feminist) sensibility. During WW II women replaced men in the domestic labor force, but after the war they were ejected from their jobs.

In the 1970's a feminist movement again emerged; women have organized on such issues as rape, pornography, sexual harassment, domestic violence, equality in the labor force, women's studies, lesbian rights, nonsexist child-raising, reproductive rights, world peace, and female spirituality. The New Zealand Women's Health Network is a nationwide feminist alternative to the medical establishment. *Broadsheet* is a national feminist (monthly) magazine. There are childcare collectives, arts and theater collectives, and women's self-defense classes. Maori women organized within activist indigenous groups; they experienced sexism within those groups and created separate committees to address issues which relate specifically to Maori women. In 1980 the first National Black Women's Conference was held in Otara with over 70 black women from New Zealand and the Pacific Islands. The *hui,* as it was called, addressed itself to feminism, racism, and economic issues. In Mar. 1981, 12 Maori women were arrested during a protest against government seizure of Maori lands.

MYTHOGRAPHY. Among the Polynesian Maoris, the legend of a First Mother or Goddess is associated with caves and volcanoes—revered images. Mahuea is the goddess credited with having discovered fire. She bore a daughter, Hina, deep in the volcanic cave that was her home. Hina continued the tradition of her mother by teaching people how to build ovens and cook food.

NEW ZEALAND: Foreigners in Our Own Land
by Ngahuia Te Awekotuku
and Marilyn J. Waring

New Zealand women are without liberty. We are the chattel, the property of men. Some may well be contented, but we are, nonetheless, slaves.

Out of distinctly different cultural backgrounds, legal systems, and religious and spiritual hierarchies, the male species has evolved a complicated mixture of insidious and subtle, treacherous and brazen machineries of oppression to keep the female species subordinate.

To judge a New Zealand woman a slave is not to appraise the value of her way of life or to say that her way of life is not worthy of respect. It *is* to say that she does not possess the central right not to be treated as a chattel. Men are regarded as complete persons with potentials and rights, but women are defined by the functions they serve *in relation* to men.

Fourth World Women

To most Maori women, the proverb *"He wahine he whenua—i ngaro ai te tangata"* ("For women, and for land, people perish") means only their oppression, their persistent association with property—as objects of beauty, as bearers of chiefs, as conservators of reconstructed convention. For decades, even since the final gunfire of British subjugation faded, the Maori woman has been colonized. To deny her own awareness of this is to insult her, but ultimately she has remained powerless. Images of strong female warriors, shamans, and leaders rise—to be swiftly reduced to a more mundane, less national, and certainly relatively unthreatening status by the ethnographers, the historians, and, much more recently, the male Maori academics.

As a universally colonized people, all women have had their stories robbed by the clever scrawl of a male pen. While many continue to accept such patriarchal narratives, others—conscious of how half our history was unrecorded and undervalued—question them, and in their quest, reclaim the female forebearers so skillfully erased.

Like so many other Fourth World women,[1] Maori women's myths and the meaning of their world have been ignored or, even more dangerous, misrepresented. The profusion of Maori ethnography reflects a white, Christian, male, and often Victorian perspective, reinforced by contemporary writing. And from this hazardous material, Maori male leaders, ever hungry for that stolen heritage, validate these lies and reconstruct their own versions of our ethnic history and inheritance. Predictably, women are featured but little.

Law Versus Justice

One of the weapons instrumental in effecting the oppression of *all* New Zealand women has been the law. A British colony, New Zealand inherited English Common Law, and with it the doctrine of servitude defining a married woman's status: "The very being or legal existence of the woman is suspended during the marriage, or at least is

---

[1] We are using the phrase "Fourth World women" to denote an oppressed group *within* an oppressed group, as women suffer sexual oppression *within* "Third World" oppression.

incorporated and consolidated." By custom, we surrender our father's name to our husband's, and until recently domicile was still determined by the husband.

The vicarious status of New Zealand women is further demonstrated in two recent so-called liberal legal changes:

—The rural New Zealand woman makes a contribution which is unquantified, unpaid, and invisible. In addition to the three to four thousand hours of housework she does each year (and modern conveniences have not noticeably reduced the burden), she is also unremunerated family-farm labor. If she is injured, there is no compensation payable to her in the terms of the "universal" Accident Compensation Scheme.

—The Matrimonial Property Act, much lauded as enshrining a "value" for childbearing and the maintenance of the home, only perpetuates a status dependent on the principle income earner—still overwhelmingly the husband. After fifteen years of marriage and three children, the work of a pauper's wife is worth nothing; after fifteen years of marriage and three children, the work of a millionaire's wife is worth half a million dollars. The work of a widow is still worthless.

What form of legal system or social control did the English Common Law replace? Understanding that we work from the colonial ethnographic record, considerable querulous reconstruction, and a conservative tribal sector in which these beliefs and practices have survived (robust and resilient), four basic principles pervade Maori life:

Tapu—the forbidden quality, the sacrosanct—was a powerful controller, regulating property as well as human relationships. Landmarks, weapons, burial places, artifacts, are all imbued with *tapu*. Males, too, are *tapu*—all of them. But women, except for a few individuals of aristocratic lineage, are *noa:* unclean, contaminating, vile. Women were nevertheless necessary in certain rituals, such as the removing of *tapu* itself from a newly built house, or from a battle-fresh, recently returned war party. By her status as *noa,* a Maori woman has the power to reinvest people or places with the facility to reenter normal life. Because of this supposedly less exalted status, she is prohibited many privileges in most tribes: the arts of oratory and carving, for example, and training in the martial arts. (However, we believe that much of this bombastic reinforcement of female inferiority is pointedly post-Christian and post-colonial. Before colonization, Maori women assumed a relatively complementary role, albeit one quiet in the public sphere. In recent times, Maori male leadership—at its most insecure—has cast women as subordinate, and then worked hard to reinterpret, invent, and manipulate tradition to keep our gender down.) The other basic Maori principles are *rahui* and *utu. Rahui* involves conservation of natural resources: waterfowl, shellfish, and food supplies. *Utu* means revenge—the ancient patriarchal game of "getting even"—and *muru* is one way of achieving this: by violence and repossession of property. One form of *muru* was the public penalty for adultery: the family of a cuckolded spouse could attack and plunder the wayward spouse's family and the lover's family too. This was especially pertinent where the affected marriage had been arranged by both sets of parents to confirm peace or create strong land alliances. Although not common today, these practices allegedly continue in extremely isolated areas. And predictably, most of the earlier documented *and* current anecdotal records concern the female wrongdoer, the woman as lover and straying wife.

Family Servitude

"Natural" law has proven an equally effective tool of oppression. The universal experience of woman is to be mother and worker, producer and reproducer. Though the economic system may change, for women everywhere this experience does not change. But within the institution of the patriarchal family that serfdom is most complete. In the Maori situation, for instance, childrearing responsibilities often pass to the eldest female sibling, "as good training," and the role of the sister/daughter/daughter-in-law entrenches itself within the endless cycle of thanklessly nurturing others, because it is "right," and "traditional."

Housework has no capital value in any country. This fact means that women do not even own their own labor; they cannot sell it, hence they do not possess it. A woman must find employment as a wife. She must in effect sell herself as chattel and not just as labor power, in order to live and to let her children live.

Chattels do not have choices: the chattel relationship is established very quickly by way of sexual obligation. The law against rape was introduced as a way of protecting the violation of one man's property from another (and universally, it is still regarded so). Since you cannot violate your own property, the New Zealand brotherhood may rape their wives with impunity. People only take what belongs to them, but as the worldwide experience of sexual harassment tells us, women are common property.

Not content with individual ownership of women perpetuated through marriage, the patriarchal state has taken it upon itself to socialize the means of reproduction, to take governorship of the womb and its contents. Controlled by contraception, sterilization, and abortion legislation which "provides for the circumstances and procedures under which abortions may or may not be authorised after having full regard to the rights of the unborn child" the government decides *if* a woman may have an abortion, *when* a woman may have an abortion, who may *perform* that abortion, who may *recommend* or *not recommend* that the abortion take place, *where* that abortion will take place, that a woman *may not* procure her own miscarriage, and that women *may not* teach young girls about contraception, other than in particular circumstances.

Like most other Fourth World societies in which the women enjoyed a more segregated mode, the precontact Maori had a rich lore of almost exclusively female knowledge of the reproductive machinations of her body. Birth-control techniques, although primitive, were effective, and abortion—despite the mellifluous rantings of latter-day white experts —was practiced. (In a warrior society, and in some tribal groups which often endured lean times, a small but healthy population was essential.) Today these closely guarded secrets are still shared by a few wise women, although abortion itself is decried and abhorred as unnatural and *un*Maori. The Victorian fathers indoctrinated the elders well, and Christianity has suppressed, and thus effectively annihilated, that knowledge. In order to believe in a woman's right to an abortion, most Maori women today face the callously bewildering accusation of being "not a real Maori"—a form of heresy that few survivors of a fighting but fragmented people choose to carry.

Workplace Servitude

As elsewhere under patriarchy, the tenets of "natural law" and sexual slavery unite in New Zealand in that sphere of "for her own good"—which we are most familiar with as "protective legislation." This has been used to exclude us from equal participatory opportunities (e.g., night work shifts), but it has not been used to keep us from our "natural" duties (e.g., nursing at night). The same effort has been made when "allowing" women into paid work—to ensure that they stay with the domestic and nurturant professions. For instance, there are restrictions placed on women's right to work with lead oxide. New regulations will require all workers to have blood tests periodically, and women of child-bearing age or those who are pregnant will be removed from the lead work—*if* their blood count becomes too high.[2] As another example, the Mining Act of 1971, the Quar-

---

[2.] Protection of women's reproductive function is one of the primary motives behind much protective legislation for women, and the pregnant worker does indeed present a special case. But the temporary circumstance of pregnancy is not treated as such. The reaction of employers, unions, and governments alike has been to treat all women as if they were pregnant all the time.

ries Amendment Act of 1977, and the Coal Mines Act of 1979 all carry the same provision that no woman or girl shall be employed below-ground in a tunnel, mine, or dredge —*except* to do occasionally any "class of work" that she "usually" does above ground.

The Human Rights Commission Act of 1977 states that an employer cannot discriminate on grounds of sex, marital status, religion, or ethical belief. But nothing in this Act applies to requirements which concern the height or weight of members of the armed forces or the police, traffic officers, or officers of penal institutions. And nothing prevents preferential treatment based on sex being given *within* the armed forces to anyone who is or is intended to be a crew member on an aircraft or ship crewed by those forces, or who has the duty of serving in an active combat role. In sum, the *practice* of the legal provisions for equal opportunity in employment is minimal.

"For Women, and for Land . . ."

In the Maori world as well, woman persists as a threatening reality. She is discouraged in many tribal areas from running for political or tribal office or attaining higher education. She can never be considered a full human being because she bleeds—and therefore may rot the sweet potato, perish the flax, lay waste the fishing grounds, distract the carvers, and destroy the shellfish.* Seldom is the adolescent female told *why,* yet many of these menstrual restrictions had practical value in an ancient context (menstrual blood in the sea draws sharks and stingrays; to weave flax one squats above one's work, and the menstruating woman risks damage to her own work by an accidental drop of blood). In modern times, Maori women must learn to accept without question, duped by male mystification of their own healthy body functions.

A history of land disenfranchisement in English Common Law further adds to the enslavement of New Zealand women. Because property can be inherited through one's mother as well as one's father, Maori women enjoy seemingly equal land ownership. *Administration* of lands, however, may be quite another matter in contemporary Maori society, where development of lands is vested in the State, or in a number of elected tribal authorities. Where election depends on land ownership, women may be present on Trust Boards, but more often they defer to "tradition"—and their husbands, sons, or brothers take their place. (Actual possession of what little land there is left is determined primarily by genealogical rank and inherited status, and on these points, many women qualify indisputably.)

Rich in Our Differences

We are still finding our tongues to speak of our ills. We are still searching for our own words, searching through patriarchal languages which circumscribe our experiences. Doing this, however, requires the discipline to dream: to rediscover, reinvest the female strengths from within ourselves. For we *are* all women, and many of us are Maori, and lesbians, and workers and disabled, and jobless and rural. We share a common oppressor, but we are rich in our differences. Our woman-knowledge, or woman-strength, comes from different cultural and visionary sources.

Ironically, as their grandfathers colonized the Maori people as a whole, so do some feminists attempt to indoctrinate Maori women, disallowing cultural differences, challenging the struggles for land, culture, and language at a brother's side, silencing a unique contribution by seeing stunned muteness as implied agreement. (Similarly, the urban feminist, absorbed by issues of childcare, abortion, and affirmative action, can ignore the urgent needs of the isolated rural woman—for roading and communication services.)

---

* See Manjula Giri's article on Nepalese women (p. 460) for an analysis of women as a separate, literally "untouchable" caste.—Ed.

Woman-focused, woman-initiated political action groups have existed in Aotearoa for many decades, often sprung from the rich earth of tribal leadership. Still flourishing, they have conceived their own vigorous feminism, though it may not be so according to the Western definition, the *pakeha* word.** Failure to acknowledge this on the part of Western feminist thinkers and activists—some of whom may even be Maori—creates pain and fragmentation. And the rhetoric of feminist revolution curls bitter on the breath of women to whom "women's liberation" has been sold in the image of a Caucasian female executive demanding the ultimate privilege of a child-free home.

We women are—all of us—foreigners in our own land. Concepts of equality and liberty are not permitted us. Our work has no value. We are invisible except to each other. Kurangaituku, Ethel Benjamin, Wairaka, Francis Hodgkins, Te Aokapurangi, Katherine Mansfield, Te Puea, Kate Shepherd, Mihikotukutuku, Emily Siedeberg, Rangitiria, Jill Tremaine, Maggie Papakura. *Kia whawhai tonu tatou ake, ake ake:* We will fight on forever and ever and ever.

Suggested Further Reading

Ashton-Warner, Sylvia. *Spinster.* London: Penguin in assoc. with Secker and Warburg, 1961.

Bunkle, Phillida, and Beryl Hughes, eds. *Women in New Zealand Society.* Sydney: Allen & Unwin, 1980.

Makeriti, M. P. *The Old Time Maori.* London: Victor Gollancz, 1938.

Stirling, Amiria Manutahi. *Amiria.* Wellington: Reed, 1976; the life of a Maori woman, as told by Anne Salmond.

Ngahuia Te Awekotuku was born May 1949 in Rotorua, New Zealand. Raised in the traditional Maori community of Ohinemutu, she spent several years in a more metropolitan environment, studying English literature and anthropology. From this, she acquired three university degrees, including a Ph.D. in social sciences (her dissertation was on the impact of tourism on her tribal culture and society). She remains deeply involved in the political, cultural, and social concerns of the Maori world. She has also been active in contemporary feminism in Aotearoa (New Zealand) since its 1970 beginnings, and continues to discuss, write, "and dream." Since her return from four years of study and research in the United States and the Pacific, she has worked in Continuing Education and Re-entry Education Programs for Mature Women, focusing on Maori women and self-esteem. Currently, she is based at the University of Waikato, Hamilton. She describes herself as being "a writer, academic, and visionary."

Marilyn Waring was born October 1952 in Ngaruawahia, New Zealand. She studied music at Victoria University, Wellington, but took her degree in political science. In 1976 she was elected a Member of Parliament from Raglan at age twenty-three and is currently in her third term as the MP from Waipa; she was a member of the NZ Delegation to the UN Mid-Decade Conference on Women (Copenhagen, 1980) and the UN Commission on the Status of Women (Vienna, 1980). She was director of the First New Zealand Training School for Potential Women Candidates for Public Office and an executive member of the NZ Women's Studies Assoc. She has written widely on the subject of women and development, has attended numerous international conferences on the subject, and was a fellow *[sic]* at the John F. Kennedy School of Government Institute of Politics at Harvard. She is also learning how to pilot a plane. She describes herself economically as: "Thirty, M.P.; I am not my job." In June 1984, using a one-vote margin, Waring brought down her own party—and the government—by refusing to permit nuclear submarines the privilege of refueling in New Zealand ports; the ensuing elections swept the Labour Party into power and thus kept the country nuclear-free.

** Maori for a New Zealander of European ancestry.—Ed.

NICARAGUA
(Republic of Nicaragua)

Central American country bounded by the Caribbean Sea to the east, Costa Rica to the south, the Pacific Ocean to the west, and Honduras to the north. **Area:** 148,000 sq. km. (57,143 sq. mi.). **Population** (1980): 2,569,000, female 50.3%. **Capital:** Managua.

DEMOGRAPHY. Languages: Spanish (official), English, Amerindian languages (Miskito, Sumo, Rama). **Races or Ethnic Groups:** Mestizo 70%, European descent 17%, Creole (African origin) 9%, indigenous Indian (Miskito, Sumo, Rama, Garifuno) 4%. **Religions:** Roman Catholicism 90%, Protestant, indigenous faiths. **Education** (% enrolled in school, 1975): Age 6–11—of all girls 57%, of all boys 54%; age 12–17—of all girls 48%, of all boys 47%; higher education—no data obtainable. Primary education is free and compulsory; other levels are free. **Literacy** (1977): Women 57%, men 58%. Before 1980, nearly 2/3 of the rural pop. was nonliterate, and nearly 2/3 of nonliterates were women. By 1980 the government's literacy campaign (60% of which was waged by women) had reduced nonliteracy from 50% (1978) to under 15%. **Birth Rate** (per 1000 pop., 1975–80): 47. **Death Rate** (per 1000 pop., 1975–80): 12. **Infant Mortality** (per 1000 live births, 1975–80): Female 115, male 128; before 1980, almost 50% of registered deaths were of children under age 5. **Life Expectancy** (1975–80): Female 57 yrs., male 54 yrs.

GOVERNMENT. The 5-member Government Junta for Reconstruction that seized power from Pres. Anastasio Somoza Debayle (July 19, 1979) has been replaced by a 9-member directorate of the Sandinista Front for National Liberation (FSLN), coordinated by Daniel Ortega Saavedra. Each directorate member oversees 1 of the country's 6 regions and 3 special zones. A 51-member Council of State, representing 32 political, social, trade union, and people's organizations (political parties *per se* are defined as security risks), functions as a co-legis- lative body with the directorate. Judicial authority is exercised by the Supreme Court (appointed by the Junta) and by People's Tribunals. **Voting:** There have been no elections since the 1979 coup; the FSLN directorate has reiterated a promise for elections in 1985, but not "bourgeois democratic elections." **Women's Suffrage:** 1955. **Equal Rights:** Equal rights are stipulated in the 1950 Constitution (Art. 36). **Women in Government:** María Lourdes Vargas is Minister of Social Welfare (1983), succeeding Lea Guido (1979–80); 48% of government officials are women, Gloria Carrión is head of AMNLAE—the Assoc. of Nicaraguan Women Luisa Amanda Espinoza, the official State women's organization (see following article)—which has representatives on the Council of State, and Lieut. Nelba Blandón is Chief Press Censor (1983); 4 women were in the ruling junta, 2 women were Supreme Court judges (1982). Dora María Tallez was in charge of the FSLN's political sector, and Mónica Baltodana was head of the FSLN Mass Organization of the Secretariat (1980). Rosario Murillo, the wife of Directorate Coordinator Daniel Ortega Saavedra, is General Secretary of the Sandinista Cultural Workers' Assoc. Olga Aviles is the Nicaraguan Commissioner for Peace; in the Ministry of Interior, Nadine Lacayo is the Political Secretary of the regions of Boaco and Chontales, and Marta Cranshaw is the Political Secretary of the Department of León (also see following article).

ECONOMY. Currency: Córdoba (May 1983: 10. = $1 US). **Gross National Product** (1980): $1.9 billion. **Per Capita Income** (1980): $720. **Women's Wages as a Percentage of Men's:** No statistics obtainable; 1982 reports indicate that women earn less than their male counterparts in the same jobs and that most women are concentrated in low-paying, female-intensive sectors of the labor force (see **HERSTORY**). **Equal Pay Policy:** The principle of "equal salary for work performed with equal efficiency" is stipulated in the 1974 Constitution (Art. 105). **Production** (Agricultural/Industrial): Cotton, coffee, sugar cane, rice, corn, beans, cattle; processed foods, chemicals, metal products, clothing, textiles, timber.

Women as a Percentage of Labor Force (1980): 22%; **of agricultural force** —no general statistics obtainable (5% of women workers were employed in agriculture, 1975); **of industrial force**—no data obtainable; **of military**—as of 1983 women comprise 47% of the militia, with 70% of them in the health campaign; there are both mixed battalions and women's companies. In Aug. 1983, the Nicaraguan government initiated compulsory military service for men but not women. Sandinista women's groups criticized this as discrimination, but Commander Doris Tijeriano, the highest-ranking woman in the Sandinista army, responded by citing women's "well-known biological and organic limitations." Women were top-ranked commanders in the 1979 battles against Somoza, and by 1981 nearly 30% of the Popular Sandinista Army were women; in 1982 over 90% of the political instructors at the Carlos Aguero Military School were women. **(Employed) Women's Occupational Indicators:** No general statistics obtainable; women are concentrated in the service sector (comprising 57.7% of service-sector workers, 1982), in teaching (a low-paid profession), as domestic workers, and as market vendors. "Protective" legislation prohibits women and minors from work considered physically harmful or dangerous (Art. 105). AMNLAE, working with the International Metalworkers Federation and the ILO, has initiated production schemes to teach skills to women, and also is working with trade unions in the free-trade zones of Managua, organizing women employees concentrated in labor-intensive industries. The FUNDE program provides savings-and-loans cooperatives to women market vendors. **Unemployment:** No data obtainable.

GYNOGRAPHY. Marriage. *Policy:* The 1974 Constitution bases marriage on mutual consent and spousal equality. The legal marriage age is 14 for females and 15 for males with parental consent. Only civil marriage is recognized. A married woman is required to reside in her husband's domicile (Art. 270, 1950 Civil Code). Bigamy is illegal and punishable by 1–5 yrs. imprisonment. The law of Testamentary Disposition requires a married person to leave 1/4 of an estate to her/his spouse, as well as maintenance payments. *Practice:* Female mean age at marriage (1970–78): 20; women age 15–49 in union (1970–78): 58.8%. Among poor or rural women, it is common to live with a man without marrying or to wait until middle or old age to marry. The government promotes the concept of men's participation in household labor and childcare but women still have inferior status within marriage. **Divorce.** *Policy:* Legal in cases of mutual consent, or if there is justifiable cause, including "grave insults," bigamy, and adultery (1904 Civil Code). Any act of adultery by a woman is grounds for divorce, but a man must commit adultery inside the marital home or cohabit with another woman in the marital home or elsewhere for his act to be considered grounds; adultery is punishable by 2–3 yrs. imprisonment (1974 Penal Code). A man must pay child support if his child is registered and if he is employed; payments are a percentage of the father's salary. *Practice:* No statistics obtainable. Most men pay little or no support, and existing laws are difficult to enforce.

Family. *Policy:* In 1980 the law of Patria Potestas, which gave a father sole authority over the family and children, was abolished. The new Mother-Father and Child Relations Act gives both parents equal authority in decisions regarding children (Decree No. 1065, 1982). If the couple is separated, the spouse who is supporting the children has sole authority. The 1974 Constitution placed "the family and motherhood" under the protection of the State (Art. 96). Special subsidies are given to families with numerous children (Art. 99). Employed women are entitled to a paid maternity leave of 20 days pre- and 40 days post-delivery, if they have worked at least 6 months prior to giving birth (Art. 5). Maternity legislation permits employed mothers to take nursing breaks until a child is 6 months old. Government-sponsored day-care services have been established to assist employed mothers. AMNLAE is working to create more Child Development Centers. In intestate succession, children take first place; if there are heirs born both in and out of wedlock, the former inherit 3/4, the latter 1/4 of the estate. *Practice:* The average family included 6 children in 1980. The weak job market has resulted in a high rate of rural-to-urban male migration; in 1975, 48% of families were female-headed households, and in 1980, 50% of households were "abandoned" families—single women with children. AMNLAE, working with the Ministry of Social Welfare, set up over 12 day-care centers during 1980, with an attempt to hire both men and women as caretakers. Despite new laws, men still are *de facto* heads of households.

Welfare. *Policy:* The 1974 Constitution (Art. 107) provides Social Security to members of the labor force and includes benefits for illness, maternity, disability, old age, death, widowhood, orphanhood, and occupational hazards. The National Health system extends special social security to victims of war (Decree 55), miners (Decree 33), and cadets who participated in the literacy campaign of 1980 (Decree 468). Decree 595 covers Sandinista army members and relatives; Decree 555 gives them job security and wages. A 1982 law extended coverage to domestic workers; agricultural workers are also eligible. Under Art. 102 of the Social Security Act a (male) worker's life companion is given the same eligibility status as a wife. *Practice:* Although Social Security was established by Somoza in 1955, only a few urban centers (less than 10% of the pop.) were covered in 1980. Reports indicate that social welfare today (1983) favors workers earning less than $3000 annual salary.

Contraception. *Policy:* Government policies are pro-natalist, although some government sources have stated support for family planning. Certain contraceptives require medical prescriptions. *Practice:* Women age 15–49 in union using contraception (1970–80): 9%, of which modern methods 88.8%, sterilization 11.1%. A 1980 report stated that AMNLAE was planning to organize family-planning centers. Dec. 1980 reports revealed that women were hoarding the pill for fear that the government would issue a pro-natalist ban on sales. The government responded that while it would not ban contraceptives, it would not permit publicizing of them. Reports indicate that rural women unaware of modern contraceptive methods frequently resort to abortion. The Roman Catholic Church maintains a strong position against birth control. **Abortion.** *Policy:* Legal only in the case of proven danger to the woman's life (1974 Penal Code). Therapeutic abortion is granted only if determined necessary by a minimum of 3 doctors and with the consent of spouse or guardian. The penalty for the practitioner, lacking the consent of the woman, is 3–6 yrs. imprisonment; with consent, the penalty is 1–4 yrs. for both the practitioner and the woman. If force or threat is used, the maximum penalty is applied. The penalty is lessened for both woman and practitioner if the abortion was performed "to save the woman's honor." If a woman dies as a result of an improperly performed abortion, the practitioner is punishable by 6–10 yrs. imprisonment; doctors, druggists, surgeons, and midwives who regularly perform abortions can be punished by 5–10 yrs. at hard labor. *Practice:* No statistics obtainable; 1980 reports indicate that illegal abortions are common. The Roman Catholic Church's strong anti-abortion position has influenced social policies. An AMNLAE spokeswoman (1980) stated that free and legal abortion was not a primary goal of AMNLAE but that some feminists supported the idea. (see footnote p. 493). **Illegitimacy.** *Policy:* The 1974 Constitution (Art. 100) states that parents of out-of-wedlock children have the same obligations toward their children as parents of children born in wedlock (but see **Family**). *Practice:* No statistics obtainable; many children are born out of wedlock because of the large percentage of common-law unions. **Homosexuality.** *Policy:* Homosexuality is punishable under the section regarding sodomy in Offenses Against the Public Morality (Art. 205), as are acts that "disrupt public order and cause scandal." The penalty is 1–3 yrs. imprisonment, or 2–4 yrs. if a person forces another to commit sodomy. There is no specific law governing lesbianism, which generally falls under the same category of Offenses Against the Public Morality. *Practice:* No statistics obtainable; there is a strong social tabu against same-sex preference.

Incest. *Policy:* Illegal under the 1974 Penal Code (Art. 210). If a male minor commits incest, punishment is postponed until he reaches age 21, at which time he is subject to 2–4 yrs. imprisonment. Under the 1974 Penal Code, rape of a sister or female descendant is punishable by 3–6 yrs. imprisonment (Art. 196). *Practice:* No data obtainable. **Sexual Harassment.** *Policy:* None. *Practice:* No data obtainable. **Rape.** *Policy:* Illegal under the 1974 Penal Code and punishable by 8–12 yrs. imprisonment if rape has occurred "without the victim's consent, if force or threat of force was used, or if a woman was deprived of her ability to reason." If the victim is under age 12 and none of the above circumstances apply, when a rapist has convinced a married woman that he is her husband, or when 2 or more persons commit the crime (gang rape), the penalty is 12–15 yrs. imprisonment. Rape of a female age 12–18 is punishable by 2–4 yrs. (Art. 196); if the rape is by a teacher or guardian, the penalty is 3–6 yrs. Marital rape is not legally recognized. *Practice:* No statistics obtainable; reports indicate that rape is a major problem but is rarely reported or prosecuted. There have been many cases of women and girls raped by both government soldiers and insurgents fighting the government. On Dec. 29, 1981, 2 women —a doctor and a nurse in Leymus—were kidnapped by "counterrevolutionary forces" and taken to Honduran territory where they were gang-raped and then released. **Battery.** *Policy:* No specific laws regarding wife-beating. *Practice:* No data obtainable. **Prostitution.** *Policy:* Under the 1974 Penal Code, it is illegal to induce a female into prostitution and is punishable by 4–10 yrs. imprisonment if the female is a child, and 1–5 yrs. if she is over age 18. It is illegal to induce a woman to enter a brothel in order to exploit her body or to make a "general inducement" to a woman with offers to sell her body; the penalty is 6 months–3 yrs. imprisonment. A client who carnally

abuses a person of either sex is subject to 9 months–3 yrs. imprisonment (1974 Penal Code, Art. 195). A prostitute is subject to a fine. *Practice:* No statistics obtainable; 1980 reports indicate a high rate of prostitution by women and children in urban centers, owing in part to unemployment. AMNLAE is helping to establish a training program to teach technical skills to prostitutes. **Traditional/Cultural Practices:** No data obtainable. **Crisis Centers:** No data obtainable.

HERSTORY. The original inhabitants of Nicaragua were several indigenous groups, including the Bawikhas, whose descendants include Miskitos, Sumos, Manques, Ramas, and Garifunos. The country's name is thought to have derived from the Indian chief Nicarao, who was defeated by the Spanish conqueror Gil González de Ávila in 1522. The Spanish conquest resulted in the massacre of most of the indigenous population. During the 17th century, British explorers settled on the east coast of Nicaragua. Popular opposition (including female participation) to Spanish domination led to Independence in 1821 (see following article).

A long period of political instability brought American filibuster William Walker to power (1855–57). Conservatives gained and held control until José Santos Zelaya, a liberal, became president in 1894. But the US helped topple Zelaya in 1909, set up Adolfo Díaz as provisional president, and sent in US marines in 1912 to help Díaz put down a rebellion in which many women were active. In 1926 Emiliano Chamorro failed to oust the government; US marines returned to Nicaragua, and Augusto César Sandino became a nationalist guerrilla leader.

In 1937 Anastasio Somoza, backed by US support, became president; his dictatorship was enforced by the feared National Guard, who silenced political opponents and waged a campaign of terror on the population. Somoza was assassinated in 1956, and one of his sons became president, while another controlled the military. Somoza-backed rulers assumed power until 1967, when Anastasio Somoza Debayle was elected president.

As dissent grew, he suspended the 1950 Constitution and resigned the presidency, but remained head of the armed forces.

As a consequence of the earthquake of 1972, in which 12,000 people died and 60,000 houses were destroyed, investment grew, partly due to the diversion of aid relief and loans received. Somoza became Director of Relief Operations, initiating a reconstruction program which opened the way for land speculation in which he personally participated. He resigned from the army in 1974 and became president. A new constitution was passed and a 100-member National Congress established. From 1975–79, as popular opposition grew, he instigated a wave of repression. One tactic was the burning of entire areas of land in the north and east to drive out the rural (largely Native Indian) population and create "free-fire" zones, which Somoza then purchased. By 1978 there were only 60,000 industrial jobs; 54% of houses lacked safe drinking water; 59% lacked electricity; 74% lacked sewage facilities.

Reports indicate that 40,000 persons out of 2.5 million died in the war with Somoza. On May 29, 1979, anti-Somoza forces, including many women, invaded Nicaragua, taking control of Managua in July, and 2 months later the Sandinista Front for National Liberation (FSLN) declared itself the new government.

A "mixed economy" system (private and public ownership) was established, and a comprehensive agrarian reform program initiated, as well as major literacy and health programs organized and staffed largely by women (see **Literacy** and **Military**). In 1981 the government directorate declared a state of emergency due to reports that anti-FSLN forces were being trained by the US military in Florida. International criticism was leveled at the FSLN over the closure of 2 newspapers and the arrest of 2 prominent businessmen and 30 Communist Party followers. The government also was accused of human-rights violations over the forced transfer of indigenous Miskitos from their homelands to "resettlement" on open-system prison farms.

In Mar. 1982 another state of emergency was declared, restricting certain human rights, including *habeas corpus*. As of Aug. 1983, it is still in effect. The Nicaraguan Permanent Committee for Human Rights estimates that there have been 70 "disappearances" during 1983 of persons under suspicion for "counterrevolutionary dissent"; other estimates claim that 2500 people are in prison on political charges. Women are involved in the human rights organization, and have founded a loose association similar to the Mothers of the Plaza de Mayo (see ARGENTINA) to investigate disappearances of family members.

Women also are active in the Sandinista Defense Committees—block organizations which encourage political education, moniter "divergence," and manage the rationing system.

In Apr. 1983 *Barricada,* the Sandinista newspaper, reported that at the First National Encounter of Women Agricultural Workers, organized by AMNLAE and the Assoc. of Rural Workers, women cotton-pickers complained that they are still paid less than men after 4 years of revolutionary government, still discriminated against in the labor unions and in technical training, and still fired first during slow periods.

MYTHOGRAPHY. Among the Native Indian peoples, there was a belief that the goddess Zipaltonal took Tamagostad as her consort, and thus created the earth. Masaya was the goddess of volcanoes and a giver of oracles.

NICARAGUA: To My Compañeras on the Planet Earth
by María Lourdes Centeño de Zelaya
(Translated by Annette Fuentes)

> Dora María,
> the warrior woman
> whose fury blasted
> the heart of the tyrant.
>
> —fragment from "La Violenta Espuma"
> by Daisy Zamora

The massive participation of Nicaraguan women, their sacrifice and heroism, made possible our national liberation on July 19, 1979.

But it was not the first time. Women have marked the calendar of Nicaraguan history with brilliant accounts again and again, all of which have helped form the national character of our country.

In colonial times, women confronted the Spanish conquistadores. Women intervened in the struggle to abolish slavery, and in 1543 were rewarded with success, slavery being abolished. During the first fifty years of the Spanish conquest, an unusual strategy was tried by women in Nicaragua. In 1530, because of the slave trade established by the Spanish governor, Pedrarius Dávila, Nicaraguan women decided not to sleep with their husbands—so that their children would not be born slaves: the first "strike of the uterus" in the world.

In 1762, a woman prevented the invasion of Nicaragua by twelve thousand men and more than fifty ships of the English fleet. Rafaela Herrera lived with her father in the Fortress of the Conception at the mouth of the Río San Juan, which flows into the Atlantic Ocean. The English fleet sailed up the river and attacked the fortress. Hours before the battle began, Rafaela's father died, leaving her to assume command of the fortress defenses and, in effect, of the nation. The nineteen-year-old girl maintained a cannon battle with the English fleet for five days, bottling them up and killing the English commander. In the darkness of night, Rafaela Herrera couldn't make out the enemy positions, so she soaked sheets in alcohol and sent them blazing into the current on dry branches. The English thought they were dealing with the mythical Greek fire, and not being able to explain how the flame balls were carried by the current, panicked and fled. The Spanish King issued a proclamation recognizing the exploits of Rafaela Herrera.

Later, in 1890, women organized guilds and associations for mutual activities. Still later, the Nicaraguan woman transcended her confines, writing poems and articles dealing with politics and feminism. Most notable were Josefa Toledo de Aguerri and María Cristina Zapata (who interpreted her people's pain engendered by the North American intervention in our country), writing: ". . . that my cry of justice resounds from the most distant corner not only of America but of the whole world!"

The "Army of Free Men" *[sic]* of General Agosto César Sandino, composed of workers and peasants, repelled North American imperialism during the years 1927 through 1934. Many women participated in the campaigns, although it is not known if they bore weapons. Their acts of heroism were always recognized by General Sandino. One woman who stands out is María de Altamirano, commander of a guerrilla camp in Las Segovias. Also,

Blanca Aráuz, the wife of General Sandino, who was a telegrapher, sending coded messages to the guerrillas in the mountains. Among the historic photographs from this period are those of Angelita Aráuz, gun in hand, and Tiburcia García, who lost all of her sons to the invading troops. The list of women who took part in that army is long, and some died for their efforts.

When, in September of 1956, the tyrant Anastasio Somoza García was killed by the poet and patriot Rigoberto López Pérez, hundreds of us became the victims of a despotic reaction from the government. The suspects were taken to torture chambers for interrogation in the hours before dawn. They were beaten, shocked with electric rods, and raped, death being the frequent result. I myself remember vividly when they lined a group of us up to be shot on that October night. While the guards were pointing their rifles at us, one of the *compañeras*—an old woman—fell into a state of amnesia, forgetting her own name. Another member of that line was Doña Soledad López, mother of Rigoberto López Pérez.

With the death of Somoza García, his son, Luis Somoza Debayle, succeeded him in power. The chief of the armed forces was his other son, Anastasio, who continued the dynasty when his brother died in 1967. At that point, the people rose in protest and the genocidal *guardia* of Somoza launched repressions, jailings, collective assassinations, confinements, and exiles. In the city of León, the *guardia* machine-gunned a peaceful demonstration of students. Dozens of women participants were injured.

From 1956 to 1961, the dictatorship worsened, massacring and exploiting the people—principally the peasant sector, where women earned a salary of hunger, on occasion working solely for their food. In 1961, opposition groups proliferated, united by the ideology of General Sandino, in the Sandinista Front for National Liberation (FSLN). They continued the struggle initiated by General Sandino in 1926, who had died at the hands of Somoza in 1934. Around 1963, the Organization of Democratic Women was founded. Meanwhile, the syndicalist Lidia Maradiaga was assassinated by the National Guard after organizing a meeting for women's rights.

At the National University, the Revolutionary Student Front (forerunner of the FSLN), was formed by students of both sexes. They organized circles of clandestine study groups, strengthening the revolutionary theory of the Sandinista movement. They also organized meetings, hunger strikes, and demonstrations against the dictatorial government of Somoza, fought for freedom of the press, human rights, and the minimum wage for women domestic workers.

Violence broke out again in the rural areas. Supporters of the Sandinistas saw their ranches being burned. On the night of her capture, Amada Pineida was raped seventeen times by Somoza's army. Some women disappeared, and others died defending their rights: Arlen Síu, Martha Angélica Quezada, Verónica Lacayo, Angelita Morales, Claudia Chamorro.

In Nicaragua it became a crime to say the name "Sandino."

It is difficult to explain the cruelty of the dictatorship. Difficult because it is to remember a half century of agony, to relive the red rivers flowing in the streets, to remember the death of youth—because to be between fifteen and twenty-five years old might as well have been a crime.

Between 1967 and 1970, women participated in the struggle belligerently despite social prejudice, family opposition, and parental fears. Many became guerrillas and went to the mountains. Among the first were Gladys Báez, Doris Tijerino, and Leticia Herrera. Clandestine feminist groups were formed in the cities. An event of major importance occurred in 1973, when Red Cross mothers went on a hunger strike in solidarity with their jailed sons, who were refusing food to protest the isolation of fellow prisoners Tomás Borge Martínez and Marcio Jáen.

The first success of the FSLN was the assault on the house of José María Castillo Quant, on December 27, 1974. Brave participants were Leticia Herrera, Olga López Avilez, and Eleonora Rocha. They held hostage a group of Somocistas and obtained $1 million from the government, plus the release of political prisoners. For the first time, revolutionary Sandinista material was read over radio and television.

Another action in which women were central was the assault on the National Palace, where the members of the Executive Committee for the FSLN—all of them facing twenty to thirty years in prison—were freed. In the assault, a young woman of twenty-one, Dora María Téllez (known as Comandante 2), was the political director.

Later, the Association of Women Confronting the National Problem (AMPRONAC) was founded by Gloria Carrión, Lea Guido, and other FSLN militants. This group became AMNLAE, Association of Nicaraguan Women Luisa Amanda Espinoza, in honor of the first woman to fall in combat on April 3, 1970.

One phenomenon in the liberation struggle was the great participation of Christians, who began to practice a more authentic evangelism in service to the people. Distinguished religious women were Sisters Dorothea, Rosa, Guerry, Dolores, Martha, and still others. They functioned as a mail system between the mountains and the exterior, transported medicines, and staffed infirmaries.

In Nicaragua we advanced for years between shadows of blood and rumors of death. To see the sun rise and set, with your life still intact, was a privilege. We learned that we could no longer fight with poetry, music, and paintbrushes. The people united in a single force, with the Sandinista Front for National Liberation in the vanguard, to confront the monster supported by North American imperialism.

Everywhere in the war, women participated in the front lines, principally in León, Managua, Masaya, and Estelí. Commander Mónica Baltadano was one of the three members who directed the Revolutionary Army in the capital city of Managua.

León was the first area liberated—on June 17, 1979. In this university city, the liberating army was commanded by heroic *compañeras:* Dora María Téllez, Leticia Herrera, María Lourdes Jirón, and Ana Isabel Morales. The bloody war of liberation was over. Sovereignty had been bought with the blood and suffering of fifty thousand brothers and sisters, heroes and martyrs: women like Idalia Fernández, Areceli Pérez, Arlen Síu, Verónica Lacayo, Angelita Morales, María Angélica Quezada, Bertha Calderón, Martha Navarro, Herlinda López, Gloria Fernández, Claudia Chamorro, Martha Conrado, and others, in whose memory we Nicaraguans have raised monuments. Also bearing their names are centers for health and culture, centers for the protection of children, schools and institutes, libraries, streets and avenues, parks, hospitals, centers of military instruction, and residential universities.

AMNLAE has become a great movement that works for women's incorporation into all different spheres of society—at the educational, cultural, economic, and political levels. Organically, AMNLAE is structured in small groups located in the community or at job centers. There are women directors in the provinces as well as at the national levels.

As part of their program, this association is elevating the cultural level of women and of the people in general. Our revolution occurred with duties shared by men and women; in this period of reconstruction, we nevertheless still have problems with men sharing familial tasks. But this is also part of our social struggle.*

* In a 1979 interview published in *ISIS* (#19), the international feminist bulletin, Gloria Carrión, an AMNLAE Executive Committee member, was quoted as saying: "The aims of AMNLAE include a plan to set up production schemes linked to skill-training centers: a poultry-rearing unit, clothing workshops (to make army and school uniforms among other things). We would like to see the large

The Revolution has launched a second Battle of Liberation—this time against illiteracy —which has been nicknamed the "Crusade of Love," because the people, full of love, taught the people. Women were 60 percent of the literacy force. They reduced the illiteracy rate from 53 to 12 percent. Women also distinguished themselves in the mountains, working with the health brigades. (It is fitting to note the work of our Minister of Health, Lea Guido, a combatant woman, who in 1982 was named president of the Pan-American Health Organization. This organization has not had a woman president in eighty years.)

The fact of having participated in a guerrilla war and of having transformed the world of ignominy in which we lived obliges us, as Nicaraguan women, to transmit our experience to the worldwide feminist movement. *Compañeras* everywhere on Planet Earth—we must remember that the struggle of women everywhere, like every popular movement, is the same struggle. The liberation of women will come about when women succeed in liberating themselves—and all society!

Selected Further Reading

Murillo, Rosario. *Un Deber de Cantar.* Managua: Ministry of Culture, 1981.

Nicaraguan Women and the Revolution. A packet of materials that includes articles, poetry and graphics; available from Women's International Resource Service (W.I.R.E.), 2700 Broadway, Room 7, New York, NY 10025.

Poesía Libre. Managua: Ministry of Culture, 1982; poetry review.

Randall, Margaret. *Sandino's Daughters.* Vancouver/Toronto: New Star Books, 1981.

Zamora, Daisy. *La Violenta Espuma (Poemas, 1968–78).* Managua: Ministry of Culture, 1982.

María Lourdes Centeño de Zelaya was born March 9, 1932, in León, Nicaragua. She is a painter, "Promoter of Culture," and professor at Santa Rosa College. A founding member of the School of Fine Arts of the Autonomous National University of Nicaragua in 1968, she has taught drawing and painting there (1972–73). In 1979, with a group of intellectuals, she founded the Popular Cultural Center of León, serving as director for the Department of León for Painting. In 1980, she was departmental director for León for documentation and museums in the National Crusade for Literacy. She has produced, directed, and acted in documentary films, and is currently assistant to the private secretary of the Nicaraguan Minister of Education.

---

number of domestic servants bequeathed to us by the preceeding regime integrated into more productive work—secretarial and the like. We also want women to be able to learn, develop politically, and cultivate their minds. Divorce is a frequent occurrence. But the law is unjust. The man can take the children away without the woman's consent. Men pay no alimony, or hardly any. The man can have his wife put in prison for adultery. In short, it's still a case of 'irresponsible paternity.' There is a lot of prostitution in the towns, and above all the parts like Corinto, but it is not the same situation as in prerevolutionary Cuba. There is no open discussion of abortion. The struggle for education and free health care is more significant, is seen as more of a priority, for the first problem is to ensure that children survive. Of course there are clandestine abortions. The right to abortion is a legitimate struggle, but at the moment it doesn't represent the concerns of the majority of women. So far we haven't instituted a law. The Association's plan is to organize family planning, free contraception without restrictions under medical control."—Ed.

NIGERIA
(Federal Republic of Nigeria)

Located in west Africa and bordered by Niger to the north, Chad to the northeast, Cameroon to the east, the Gulf of Guinea to the south, and Benin to the west. **Area:** 923,853 sq. km. (356,700 sq. mi.). **Population** (1980): 77,082,000, female 50.6%. **Capital:** Abuja.

DEMOGRAPHY. Languages: English, Hausa, Ibo, Yoruba (all official), Ibibio, Orobo, Edo, other. **Races or Ethnic Groups:** 250 ethnic groups, including Hausa 21%, Yoruba 20%, Ibo 17%, Fulani 9%. **Religions:** Islam (Maliki school of Sunni Islam) 47%, Christianity 34%, indigenous faiths. **Education** (% enrolled in school, 1975): Age 6–11—of all girls 32%, of all boys 45%; age 12–17—of all girls 14%, of all boys 24%; higher education—no statistics obtainable; women were first admitted to universities only within recent decades and enrollment rates are still low. **Literacy** (1977): Women 6%, men 25%. **Birth Rate** (per 1000 pop., 1975–80): 50. **Death Rate** (per 1000 pop., 1975–80): 18. **Infant Mortality** (per 1000 live births, 1975–80): Female 144, male 170. **Life Expectancy** (1975–80): Female 49 yrs., male 46 yrs.

GOVERNMENT. In late 1983, Mohammed Buhari led a coup which overthrew the elected government and established a military government in its place. Nigeria gained Independence in 1960; the 1979 Constitution followed 12 yrs. previous of military rule and established a federation of 19 states and the Federal Capital. Executive power was vested in an elected president; an elected bicameral National Assembly consisted of a 92-member Senate and a 445-member House of Representatives. State governments consisted of governors and elected Assemblies. The legal system encompasses statutory law, Islamic jurisprudence (Shari'a courts in Northern Region), and customary law. **Women's Suffrage:** 1977. Under the 1960 Federal Constitution women in Northern Nigeria were denied the vote and the right to be elected to the House of Assembly; in 1954 women of the Eastern Region won the vote in regional elections for federal legislature; in the Western Region, tax-paying women won the same right. **Equal Rights:** The 1979 Constitution (Sec. 9) stipulates that discrimination on the grounds of religion, sex, status, ethnic or linguistic association, place of origin or ties shall be prohibited. **Women in Government:** 12 women are in the federal government, including 5 ministers; there were 1 woman member of the House of Representatives and 2 women members of the Senate (1983).

ECONOMY. Currency: Naira (May 1983: 0.69 = $1 US). **Gross National Product** (1980): $85.5 billion. **Per Capita Income** (1980): $1010. **Women's Wages as a Percentage of Men's:** No general statistics obtainable; according to a 1978 study, rural women earned 66% of men's wages. **Equal Pay Policy:** Equal pay for equal work is a labor policy for federal employees, although no sanctions exist to enforce it. **Production** (Agricultural/Industrial): Cocoa, peanuts, cotton; crude oil, processed foods, woods, rubber products. **Women as a Percentage of Labor Force** (1980): 40%; **of agricultural force** (1979) 22% of employed farmers, and a high % of unpaid family workers; **of industrial force**—no statistics obtainable; 1974 Labor Decree prohibitions against women's night employment restricts them from many factory jobs and contributes to a low % of women in industry; **of military**—no data obtainable. **(Employed) Women's Occupational Indicators:** Of all employed women, 0.5% are clerical workers, 1.5% are professional and technical workers, 6% are administrative, executive, and managerial workers, 12% are crafts and production process workers, 39% are sales workers (1979); of university teachers 10%, of secondary-school teachers 19%, of elementary-school teachers 23% (1978). Rates of activity vary among different ethnic groups, though generally women's economic activity is an established cultural fact. Yoruba women are traditionally in trade or other self-employed enterprises or crafts. The Constitution (Sec. 28) allows employers to establish criteria for hiring which permit discrimination against women. **Unemployment** (1982): 6%; no rates by sex obtainable.

GYNOGRAPHY. Marriage. *Policy:* The dualistic (statutory and customary) legal system recognizes both statutory marriages and customary marriages, which vary among different ethnic communities. Statutory marriages are governed by the 1914 Marriage Act and the 1970 Matrimonial Causes Decree. Marriage age is 12 for females and 14 for males; mutual consent and consent of parents for minors under 21 are required. A woman owns and controls property brought into marriage and income earned during marriage. Customary marriages are governed by laws of various communities; generally polygyny is legal. Marriage age is usually puberty, though some states have specific age limits. Consent of the bride, traditionally not necessary, is now required by law in some areas; parental consent is also necessary. Bride-price must be paid by the groom's family to the bride's family and is limited by statutes in the former Eastern, Western, and Mid-Western Regions. Marriage registration is not required in the Eastern Region; in Western and Mid-Western states a 1958 law requires a husband to register a marriage on penalty of fine. A woman must change her birth-name to her husband's name. If a husband has more than 1 wife he is obligated to treat them equally and provide separate living quarters. Property rights vary among groups. The property a Hausa woman brings to marriage belongs to both spouses; among the Yoruba, such property generally belongs to the husband. In Islamic communities dowry accompanies marriage and a man is permitted up to 4 wives; a wife is considered legally incapable of managing property and cannot dispose of more than 1/3 of it without her husband's consent. *Practice:* No statistics obtainable. Polygyny is still common in much of Nigeria. **Divorce.** *Policy:* In statutory marriage, divorce may not be filed before 2 yrs. of marriage (except in extreme cases). Divorces may be granted in cases of mutual consent and a 2-yr. sepa-

ration; lacking consent, grounds include irretrievable breakdown resulting from adultery, nonconsummation, 1-yr. desertion, or 3-yr. separation. Either spouse can claim damages in cases of adultery; prior to the 1970 Matrimonial Causes Act only the husband had this right. The court awards maintenance to the spouse in financial need, and custody on the basis of the child's best interests. Customary divorce can be nonjudicial (in which case the wife leaves the home voluntarily or at the husband's orders) or can be judicially decreed by customary courts. Bride-price must be returned to the husband. A father generally receives custody of the children; if he dies, his family assumes custody. *Practice:* No statistics obtainable. In customary judicial divorce, it is harder for women to lodge suit in that they must prove mental or physical cruelty to win the divorce case.

Family. *Policy:* Family laws are a combination of customary and statutory policies. Parental duties are shared jointly. Customary law had given a father control over unmarried children, but the 1873 Infants Act and the 1886 Guardianship of Infants Act established a mother's equal right to custody. Daughters are frequently denied inheritance rights over a father's property because they are not considered "permanent members of his family." Among the Hausa, who are Moslem, women inherit 1/2 of male descendants' shares. Among the matrilineal groups, Afikpo and Ohafia, women have legal rights to own land and to will their property. A fully paid maternity leave of 6 weeks both pre- and post-delivery is available to women, regardless of marital status, if they are employed in the public sector or in certain jobs in the private sector. An informal policy in the public sector allows women 1 hour per day to return home to care for children. There is no government childcare policy. *Practice:* The traditional extended-family system is breaking down under "modernization." Inadequate day-care facilities prevent many women from employment or force them to take frequent sick leave. **Welfare.** *Policy:* There is no national insurance or welfare system. Old-age pensions for retired workers are paid by employers in both the private and the public sectors.

The government operates several homes for the elderly, to which family members must contribute. *Practice:* No statistics obtainable. Extended families have traditionally provided the majority of support during sickness, disability, and old age.

Contraception. *Policy:* Legal; the government recognizes the need for family planning. The first family-planning clinic opened in 1958. In 1964 the National Council of Women's Societies sponsored family-planning services through the Family Planning Council of Nigeria; branches were established primarily in urban areas. A 1960 law permits physicians to perform (voluntary) sterilization. *Practice:* No statistics obtainable. The majority of women have limited information on or access to modern contraceptive methods and must rely on such traditional methods as abstinence and the hope that prolonged breast feeding will deter another pregnancy. The pill is the most frequently used modern contraceptive method. In 1974, 1 Nigerian woman died every 45 minutes from pregnancy or related causes.

Abortion. *Policy:* Legal only in cases of danger to the woman's life (in the Northern provinces), and under court authority (in other provinces); all areas require the approval of 2 physicians. All other abortions are illegal under the 1958 Criminal Code; the woman is punishable by 7–14 yrs. imprisonment, the practitioner by up to 14 yrs., and the supplier (of any abortifacient device) by up to 3 yrs. A 1981 bill sponsored by the Society of Gynecology and Obstetrics of Nigeria would have made all abortions legal in cases of danger to the woman's life or risk of fetal defect, but the bill was defeated by strong opposition from religious groups. *Practice:* Abortion, used as a method of birth control, is prevalent. In 1974, 5 out of every 1000 women died from illegal abortions in Western Nigeria. **Illegitimacy.** *Policy:* The 1979 Constitution accords children born in or out of wedlock equal rights and "legitimate" status. *Practice:* No data obtainable. **Homosexuality.** *Policy:* Under the Criminal Code Section "Offences Against Morality," carnal knowledge of any person "against the or-

der of nature" is considered a felony punishable by up to 14 yrs. imprisonment. *Practice:* No data obtainable.

Incest. *Policy:* Illegal; a person who has custody, charge, or care of a female under age 16 (age 13 outside the area of Lagos) and is proven guilty of seduction, unlawful carnal knowledge, or indecent assault is liable to 2 yrs. imprisonment. *Practice:* No data obtainable. **Sexual Harassment.** *Policy:* The 1956 Sexual Offences Act and the 1861 Persons Act contain sections which cover offenses against women in public places; no further data obtainable. *Practice:* No data obtainable. **Rape.** *Policy:* Illegal under the Criminal Code; carnal knowledge by a man of a woman who is not his wife is considered rape if the woman does not consent and/or force or threat of harm is used; punishable by life imprisonment, attempted rape by 14 yrs. A husband is prohibited from using force or violence against a wife to have sexual intercourse, but he cannot be charged with rape; he may be prosecuted, however, for assault and causing grievous harm. *Practice:* No data obtainable. **Battery.** *Policy:* Certain customary laws and some interpretations of Islamic jurisprudence permit a husband's use of corporal punishment to "discipline" his wife (but see **Rape**). *Practice:* No statistics obtainable. Reportedly, wife abuse is a major problem. **Prostitution.** *Policy:* Illegal; all forms of soliciting are prohibited. A person found guilty of soliciting, living off a prostitute's earnings, or inducing a woman or girl to become a prostitute or live in a brothel for the purposes of prostitution is subject to 2 yrs. imprisonment. *Practice:* No statistics obtainable. Reportedly, the laws are ineffective and prostitution is not uncommon. In certain areas, prostitution is considered a legitimate employment for women, and prostitutes have their own union. In 1950 prostitutes formed 2 civil-rights groups. **Traditional/ Cultural Practices.** *Policy:* None. *Practice:* Clitoridectomy* is practiced by several ethnic groups, including the Yoruba, the Ibo, and the Hausa; the Hausa and the Fulani practice uvulectomy as well. Practice is reportedly decreasing. Nutri-

* See Glossary.

tional tabus are observed in some areas: customary protein restriction means that girls and women, even when pregnant, exist on a diet without meat, eggs, beans, or milk. **Crisis Centers:** No data obtainable.

HERSTORY. The Nok people inhabited the region from 800 B.C.E. to 200 C.E. Kanem-Bornu, the first major state, developed in the 8th century, extending south from Lake Chad into present-day Nigeria by the 11th century. During this period Hausa city-states were established (in the north) and Islam was introduced into the region. Yoruba states evolved by the 14th century, the most outstanding being Oyo and Benin. Portuguese traders entered the area in the 15th century and began to propagate the kidnapping and buying of slaves. Ibo and Ibibio city-states were built with wealth acquired from the slave trade.

Amina, Queen of Zaria, a 15th-century Hausa Kingdom, succeeded her father as ruler, conquered the surrounding regions, and maintained control for 34 years; she originated the use of fortifications in Hausaland. A "holy war" led by the Fulani Moslem, Usuman dan Fodio, conquered the Hausa states (1804). His son, Muhammed Bello, founded Sokoto, the ruling state until the British colonization. Islam became established in the early 1800's (after Fulbe peoples conquered the Northern Region) and introduced segregation of the sexes, male authority in choosing domicile, and deprivation of women's traditional economic pursuits. *Purdah* was practiced in cities and spread to the rural areas. By 1906 Britain controlled the country and divided it into 2 protectorates under "indirect rule."

Before British colonization, Yoruba women of the Oyo kingdom held high political rank. The "ladies of the palace" were defined as 8 priestesses and 8 titled women, including *Iya Oba* (mother of the king), *Iya Kere* (royal treasurer), *Iyalagbon* (the crown prince's mother), and *Iyamode* (guardian of royal graves and medium for royal spirits). Madame Tinubu was a Yoruba woman who became the power behind Oba Akitoye, ruler of Lagos in the 1860's. Her power

eventually threatened the chiefs, who persuaded the British to exile her to Egba where she again became a political force. She helped defend Egbaland against attacks from Dahomey in the mid 1860's.

Ibo women had a role in traditional politics as well. The *Omu* was in charge of women in the village with her chosen *ilogo* (cabinet), which included an *awo* (policewoman) who kept order in the marketplace. Women also were organized in the institutions of the *Inyemedi* (wives of a lineage), and *Umuada* (daughters of a lineage) that acted as pressure groups. The *Inyemedi* gathered regularly for *mikiri,* a forum for women's issues. During the *mikiri,* rules were made about farming, livestock, and the market, and women discussed their problems about men; strategies for solving them—which might include sexual, housework, or childcare strikes—were arrived at collectively. The British established judicial systems that circumvented the Ibo women's arbitration courts and recognized only male power structures. Igboland was split into Native Court areas administered by British officers or Ibo men designated as warrant chiefs.

The usurpation of women's functions was the main cause of *Ogu Umunwanyi,* the Women's War of 1929, called the Aba Riots by British historians. The war was triggered by a census and property count in the Owenri Province. The previous census had resulted in taxes for men, and women organized to prevent taxation of their property. Ikonnia, Nwannedie, and Nwugo women leaders in Oloko held meetings at which women decided not to comply with the count and to raise an alarm if an official demanded information. On Nov. 23, when an Ibo warrant officer attempted to count the goats and sheep of Nwanyerunwa, women from all over the province protested at the district office. They obtained guarantees that they would not be taxed and forced the arrest and conviction of the official who had spread alarm and assaulted some women. When news spread, tens of thousands of women descended on their local Native Administration Centers. Their indigenous form of protest—dancing, chanting, singing songs of derision and ridicule—and their demands for the warrant chiefs' caps of office overwhelmed the British. The women demolished or burned 16 Native Courts and released prisoners in several jails. In 2 cases police and soldiers fired on them, killing over 50 women and wounding another 50.

Christian missionary influence intensified during the 1930's. The missionaries banned participation in traditional rituals and associations, such as the *mikiri*. In 1959 women again revolted against discriminatory colonial policies. Kon women of Eastern Nigeria protested when Fulani sheep trampled the women's crops. Further angered by rumors that the colonial government wanted to sell their lands to the Ibo, 2000 Kon women marched on a nearby town and burned down the marketplace. They demanded the closing of all foreign schools, courts, and other institutions, and the expulsion of all non-Kon peoples from the area.

On Oct. 1, 1960, Nigeria gained Independence. The role of the *Omu* has had a rebirth since 1960, as have the *Inyemedi* and *Umuada,* though their power and functions are greatly reduced. Ibo women were victims in the Hausa-Ibo hostilities of the early 1960's, and many Ibo women were massacred. Women in Northern Nigeria were the targets of religious fundamentalism in 1973; during a severe drought that burned West Africa, the emirs who dominated the government of the Northern Region decreed that single women must marry or leave the area, blaming the drought on the "immorality and prostitution of single women." In some towns, landlords evicted or refused to rent to single women; in Maiduguri, crowds attacked their residences; thousands of women were forced to flee their homes.

Women in the Northern Region, where Islamic peoples are concentrated, appear to enjoy fewer rights; *purdah* is still practiced in some of these areas. Southern women have more influence, largely because of relatively powerful market-women's associations.

Flora Nwapa (see following article), Nigeria's first published woman novelist, also became her country's first woman publisher when, in 1976, she founded her own book-publishing company as an outlet for African writers.

MYTHOGRAPHY. Ala, the goddess of the Ibo, is the life-giver and the one who oversees the transition to death. She is also the law-giver and, as such, the purveyor of morality. Ibo homes often display statues of Ala at their entrance. Oya was the mother goddess of the Yoruba, and shared in the magic power of Shango. Oshun and Oba are both river goddesses revered for their bounteous generosity.

NIGERIA: Not Spinning on the Axis of Maleness
by 'Molara Ogundipe-Leslie

On the Globality of Sisterhood

This article will begin with excerpts from a poem by a distinguished male poet friend of mine who is a professor of English literature. His poem sprang from many arguments and discussions we have had on women, feminism, and politics in Africa. Although he is Malawian, his poem reflects some of the basic attitudes of men in Nigeria and throughout Africa.

Letter to a Feminist Friend

My world has been raped
looted
and squeezed

                by Europe and America . . .
AND NOW
                the women of Europe and America
                after drinking and carousing
                on my sweat
                rise up to castigate
                      and castrate
                their menfolk
                from the cushions of a world
                I have built!

                Why should they be allowed
                to come between us?
                You and I were slaves together
                uprooted and humiliated together
                Rapes and lynchings . . .

                do your friends "in the movement"
                understand these things? . . .

                No, no, my sister,
                      my love,
                first things first!
                Too many gangsters
                still stalk this continent . . .

                When Africa
                at home and across the seas
                is truly free
                there will be time for me
                and time for you
                to share the cooking
                and change the nappies—
                till then,
                first things first![1]

Notice the use of the first person. It is *his* world that has been raped. The Promethean person who endured slavery and the slave trade, colonialism, imperialism, and neocolonialism does not have time for women's rights yet. The world has been built by *him* and *he* must attend to those pressing issues.

But the oppression of women is not solely a radical confrontation—although the oppression of black women is deeply tied to the variable of race in the history of imperialism. In addition, the study of women must be done from class perspectives, taking cognizance of class differences in all societies, Africa in particular. Such an inclusive approach would yield a truer picture of women's place in society. The white women in the poem— as wives of colonizers and collaborators with colonialism, imperialism, and neocolonialism—cannot be sisters, just as black women in the same roles in independent and neocolonial Africa and the United States are not sisters. We need to keep our minds firmly fixed on what is meant by the globality of sisterhood.

My friend's poem ends on a final note irritatingly typical of male supremacists every-

---

[1] Felix Mnthali, "Letter to a Feminist Friend." The poem will appear in an as yet unpublished volume entitled *Beyond the Echoes*.

where: to wit, that other issues abound which are more urgent than the liberation of women. Somehow, miraculously, you can liberate a country and later turn your attention to the women of that country—first things first! But such liberators of nations as Lenin, Mao, Machel, Neto, and Cabral, among others, knew that no basic and effective change can occur in a society without the synchronic liberation of its women. Note also that in the poem the liberation of women is conceived as women's desire to reduce men to housekeepers, to "feminize" men—that is, degrade them.[2] In middle-class capitalist societies, mental labor is more respected than physical labor; in feudal society, the great man works not at all but makes others work for him. Hence, women's work is never respected. No, women's liberation is not only about cooking and nappies. Women's liberation is about the fundamental human rights of women in all areas of life, public and private.

Women in Nigeria: Problems and Realities

Most middle-class Nigerian women will agree that the basic situation of women in Nigeria is not intolerable or appalling because of the economic opportunities women have within the system. And these economic opportunities are not recent or postcolonial but *pre*colonial. In fact, colonialism *eroded* many of these economic avenues for women.[3] Women had been able to engage in farming, fishing, herding, commerce, and such industrial labor as pottery, cloth-making, and craftswork, among other activities alongside their men. They had the right to keep the financial proceeds from their work. The economic position, rights, and gains of *aristocratic* African women in precapitalist societies is less known to this writer. But even in *purdah,* in Islamic Northern Nigeria where, in the early nineteenth century, Islam took away many established social rights of the Hausa woman by driving her indoors into seclusion—even there, women in *purdah* work and sell their products through emissaries. Thus, the economic opportunities for which the middle-class woman may be fighting in other societies and in some pockets of postcolonial and post-Christianized Nigeria have, in fact, always existed for some women.

All women in contemporary Nigeria are under the stress of living in a Third World, neocolonial nation ruled by an indifferent, oppressive, and wasteful black bourgeoisie. The reactions of women differ from class to class. Women of the urban working class, the urban poor, and the peasantry insist more on their right to work, as they very often have to live within polygynous systems, both Islamic and traditional. They tend to ignore the biological and emotional oppressions they endure, feeling that men are incorrigibly polygynous and women socially impotent to correct them. They insist only on the right to have their children fathered, sexually and financially, while they expect little from men in terms of companionship, personal care, and fidelity. Their only objection *within* polygyny is to the rupture or distortion of the system—for example, the older wife being relegated to the background by an uncaring husband or the younger wife not keeping her lower, deferential place.

It is within marriage, however, that the Nigerian woman suffers the most oppression. The issue of illegitimacy was dealt with in the 1979 Constitution, making all children born inside *and* outside marriage legal. But the oppression of a married woman takes various forms. First, she loses status by being married, because in the traditional system

---

[2] Other reasons can be adduced to explain the fear by men of women's liberation, a basic one of which is their fear of the loss of their property rights over their women and wives.

[3] See N. Sudarkasa, *Where Women Work: A Study of Yoruba Women in the Marketplace and the Home* (Ann Arbor: Anthropological Paper No. 53, Museum of Anthropology, Univ. of Michigan, 1973).

—which is still at the base of the society[4]—the woman as daughter or sister has greater status and more rights in her own lineage. Married, she becomes a possession, voiceless and often rightless in her husband's family, except for what accrues to her through her children. She also loses much of her personal freedom, which she can only regain at prices expensive to herself: the admittance of other wives or publicly acknowledged girl-friends of her husband. She has to submit to dominance by her husband or face blame from the total society. She can, however, win by "stooping to conquer" as the generally held cliché goes. (This means accepting concrete subjection in order to "conquer" abstractly.) There is also peer-group pressure on the husband—pressure which encourages even would-be gentle and just husbands in the direction of male supremacy.

The subordination of women within marriage has yet another reality: women are over-worked. Generally, men do no housework or childcare of any sort, so the woman struggles at two fronts, the home and the workplace. Traditional support systems—grand-mothers, siblings, younger relatives, and co-wives—have been withdrawn by such new social developments as compulsory education, urbanization, and capitalist atomization of the family.

Not least of the biological oppressions women endure within marriage is the compulsion to have children. Childless marriages are blamed on women; it is never admitted that men can be sterile. The anguish of childless women is recorded in many a Nigerian literary narrative, traditional and modern.[5] A childless woman is considered a monstrosity—as is an unmarried woman (spinster or divorcee), who becomes the butt of jokes and scandal and the quarry of every passing man, married or not. She is often seen by males as an unclaimed and degenerating commodity to be exploited in all ways, including emotionally and sexually, financially and intellectually.

It can be said that the main areas where women in Nigeria need to struggle now are national development and political representation. Abortion is not likely to be legalized soon. (When the issue arose in 1981, the greatest opponents were in fact middle-class women who expressed very moralistic and unscientific attitudes. Men proved more progressive about the issue.) The issue of genital mutilation has not received attention yet in Nigeria. This is probably because not enough is known about its occurrence and the frequency of its incidence. Certainly, basic research needs to be done on genital mutilation in Nigeria—for information *and* action.

In modern politics, the role of women is negligible, although traditional avenues did exist (and persist) for the political participation of women.[6] Very often, dual-sexual politi-

---

[4.] Personal communication during an interview with Professor (Mrs.) Bolanle Awe, professor of history at the University of Ibadan, activist leader in many Nigerian women's societies, former Commissioner for Education in Oyo State. Ibo businesswomen express the same views in Flora Nwapa's latest novel, *One Is Enough* (Enugu: Tana Press, 1981).

[5.] See, for instance, Flora Nwapa, *Efuru* (London: Heinemann, 1966), *Idu* (London, Heinemann, 1979), *One Is Enough* (Enugu: Tana Press, 1981); Buchi Emecheta, *The Joys of Motherhood* (London: Heinemann, 1979); and Chuma Ifedi, *Behind the Clouds* (London: Longman, 1981).

[6.] See D. Paulme, *Women of Tropical Africa* (Berkeley: Univ. of California Press, 1971), in particular A. M. D. Lebeuf, "The Role of Women in the Political Organisation of African Societies"; Samuel Johnson, *The History of the Yorubas from the Earliest Times to the Beginning of the British Protectorate* (1966 ed., Lagos, C.M.S. Bookshops, 1921); Bolanle Awe, "The Position of the Iyalode in the Traditional Political System," *Sexual Stratification*, ed. A. Schlegel (New York: Columbia Univ. Press, 1977); and Nina Mba, "Women in Southern Nigeria Political History (1900–1965)," Ph.D. Diss. Univ. of Ibadan 1978 (her impressive bibliography will be extremely useful).

cal systems existed in precolonial societies[7]: women's voices were heard, their opinions consulted, their participation guaranteed, from familial households to councils. Today, we behave as if it were new for women to have political power.

In the current presidential system,* a woman's visibility and leadership opportunities are negligible, though women's political liberties are theoretically guaranteed in the 1979 Constitution. Women are pre-empted from leading political roles by the attitude of men who cannot see women in leadership roles over them. Women were not considered fit to sit among the fifty and later forty-nine "wise men" who drafted the 1979 Constitution, despite the large number of qualified professional women in the country. Political parties are alleged to be unwilling to field women candidates, and women lack capital to conduct campaigns on their own if not fielded by their male-dominated parties. Women are additionally disadvantaged by their own unwillingness, as mothers within a polygynous society, to commit themselves to the vagaries of public life without the assurance that their children will be supported.

Some women would argue that women withdraw from politics because they are shy of public criticism and wish to avoid the rough-and-tumble of politics.[8] Others put it down to women's lack of dynamism and inability to pull together and exploit their own potential.[9] These observations, whatever their truth, must have their causes sought in societal institutions, in particular the structures of oppression—including the effective subjection of women's minds, a phenomenon typical of the psychology of servitude: the constant desire and anxiety to please the master until continual failure produces a dialectical and revolutionary change in the servant. Women typically engage in self-flagellation, blaming their own oppression on themselves. *Mea culpa!* So effective has male domination and patriarchal ideology been within Nigeria.

Can women be organized against the structures of oppression here? Are there organized women's movements in the country? Various women's societies exist: the Movement for Muslim Women, the Women's Improvement Society, the Nigerian Association of University Women, among others—some of which come under the umbrella of the National Council of Women's Societies (a government-recognized body) and some of which do not.[10] In addition, there are the women's wings of political parties, frequently

---

[7] See, for instance: K. Okonjo, "The Dual-Sex Political System in Operation: Igbo Women and Community Politics in Midwestern Nigeria," *Women in Africa,* ed. Nancy J. Hafkin and Edna G. Bay (Stanford, CA: Stanford Univ. Press, 1976).

* See Statistical Preface preceding this article for governmental system update.—Ed.

[8] Interview with Chief (Mrs.) G. T. Ogundipe (mother of this writer). (A word about my mother: she is a retired teacher of trigonometry, elementary mathematics, and literature, wife of a retired Bishop, himself now a traditional chief of agricultural life in his native town of Ago-Iwoye. Lay president of the Ibadan Diocese of the Methodist Church of Nigeria, Chief [Mrs.] G. T. Ogundipe has called for the ordination of women and has written a booklet to that effect entitled *The Ordination of Women,* Ibadan: Methodist Literature Dept., 1977. She has been deputy national president of the National Council of Women's Societies and co-founder of her own group, the Women's Improvement Society; she is a major figure and sometime president of the Nigerian branch of the International Women's Alliance; she toured Nigeria in the 1960's as a woman leader within the women's wing of a political party. A traditional chief of all women in economic life, in particular the markets, she sits and deliberates on the king's councils in her town and her husband's town. To keep herself busy and in touch with contemporary ideas, she runs a children's day-care center in her home. She is seventy-six years old.)

[9] Interview with Professor (Mrs.) Bolanle Awe, cited earlier.

[10] Interview with Mrs. Adeola Ayoola, current national social secretary of the Nigerian Assoc. of University Women (NAUW) Mar. 26, 1982. She reports how supportive government bodies are of her group and planned women's activities in general. Her view is that women members of some organizations need to be more committed and consistent.

used only as party workers without compensation or political recognition. The most lasting and effective bodies are organized around economic interests with immediate, concrete, material, and social benefits: market-women's associations, credit cooperatives, religious representation (for instance, churchwomen's societies which provide administrative power and emotional support in times of crisis to women who find themselves in urban situations far from their own families). Not negligible also are the ethnic groups and peer-group associations which attempt to maintain cultural continuity in the city among their members.[11] Middle-class unions, such as those of university women or "old girls'" associations, seem the most unstable—perhaps because they appear to have no concrete objective or strategies. Some of the difficulty in organizing women, I believe, springs from the lack of time and the overworked nature of women's lives, particularly of married mothers. Such behavior should not be explained by any self-blaming theory. Nigerian women are tired, emotionally neglected, socially stressed, but brave women! The reason should be sought in its objective causes—societal structures which breed various forms of personal, emotional, psychological, and *institutionalized* oppressions, some of which are so integrated as to be almost unrecognizable, even by their victims.

Prospects

The future of feminism in Nigeria depends on raising the consciousness of women to a greater awareness of their human rights in general *and* in relation to men, followed by a keener desire to know and act on the various possible modes of ensuring these rights. The greatest strength of Nigerian women lies in their right and ability to work, in addition to their resourcefulness and great capacity for emotional survival. The extended African family probably guarantees this or contributes enormously. A certain fatalism, even masochism, about male dominance still prevails here in women of every class. All of them, however, believe in education as a way out of their differing oppressions, a way of providing the social and economic basis and security from which they can resist subjection and indignities.

It would seem that I am arguing that men are the enemy. No, men are not the enemy. The enemy is the total societal system, which is a jumble of neocolonial and feudalistic, even slave-holding, structures and social attitudes. As women's liberation is but an aspect of the need to liberate the total society from dehumanization, it is the social system which must change. But men do become enemies when they seek to retard or even block these necessary historical changes; when for selfish power-interests, they claim as their excuse "culture and heritage"—as if human societies are not constructed by human beings; when they plead and laugh about the natural and enduring inferiority of women; when they argue that change is impossible because history is static—which it is not.

I shall end with a stanza from one of *my* poems, which says:

> How long shall we speak to them
> Of the goldness of mother, of difference
>   without bane
> How long shall we say another world lives
> Not spinned on the axis of maleness
> But rounded and wholed, charting through
> Its many runnels its justice distributive.[12]

[11.] Interview with Professor (Mrs.) Bolanle Awe, cited earlier.
[12.] Omolara Ogundipe-Leslie, "On Reading an Archaeological Article on Nefertiti's Reign and Ancient Egyptian Society," from *Sew the Old Days and Other Poems* (London and Ibadan: Evans Brothers Publishers, forthcoming).

Suggested Further Reading

Adekanye-Adeyokunnu, T. "Women in Nigerian Agriculture." Unpublished Monogram, Dept. of Agricultural Economics, Univ. of Ibadan, Nigeria, 1982.

Akande, J. *Law and Status of the Nigerian Woman.* UNESCO Commissioned Monogram, 1979.

Ardener, S., ed. *Perceiving Women.* New York: John Wiley & Sons, 1975; revealing essays on Ibo women.

Hafkin, Nancy J., and Edna G. Bay, eds. *Women in Africa.* Stanford, CA: Stanford Univ. Press, 1976; important essays on the political position of women in some Nigerian groups.

Hill, P. *Rural Hausa.* Cambridge: Cambridge Univ. Press, 1972.

Smith, M. *Baba of Karo.* London: Faber and Faber, 1954; on the socioeconomic role of the Northern Nigerian woman.

Sudarkasa, N. *Where Women Work: A Study of Yoruba Women in the Marketplace and the Home.* Anthropological Paper No. 53, Museum of Anthropology, Univ. of Michigan, Ann Arbor, 1973.

'Molara Ogundipe-Leslie was born in Lagos, Nigeria, of Yoruba parentage. A graduate of the University of Ibadan, she was the first student in the history of the university (then a college of London University) to take a first-class honours in the Faculty of Arts. She has taught English and African literature, was a visiting fellow *[sic]* and lecturer to the universities of Columbia, Berkeley, and Harvard in the US, and was assistant professor at Northwestern University for three years. She has published critical articles and poetry in many journals and magazines, lives in Ibadan, and teaches in the department of English, where she is senior lecturer. She has been active in several women's organizations and has been writing and lecturing on women in the US and Africa since the middle 1960's. She was a founding member of AAWORD/AFARD (Association of African Women for Research and Development) based in Dakar, Senegal, is on the editorial board of the AAWORD/AFARD newsletter, and is secretary of the steering committee of the University of Ibadan branch. She has two daughters, Titilayo and Isis Leslie.

NORWAY
(Kingdom of Norway)

Located on the western Scandinavian peninsula, with the Barents Sea to the north, Finland and the USSR to the northeast, Sweden to the east, the Skagerrak Straits to the south, and the Norwegian Sea to the west. **Area:** 324,219 sq. km. (125,182 sq. mi.). **Population** (1980): 4,087,000, female 50.4%. **Capital:** Oslo.

DEMOGRAPHY. Languages: Norwegian, Lapp, New-Norwegian. **Races or Ethnic Groups:** Scandinavian, Germanic, Lapp. **Religions:** Lutheran (official), small % Roman Catholicism, other. **Education** (% enrolled in school, 1975): Age 6–11—of all girls 84%, of all boys 84%; age 12–17—of all girls 89%, of all boys 88%; higher education—in 1978–79 women were enrolled almost equally in advanced colleges/universities but received only 22% of degrees. Women students are concentrated in health, social work, teaching, and liberal arts, and are rarely enrolled in technical schools. **Literacy** (1977): Women 99%, men 99%. **Birth Rate** (per 1000 pop., 1977–78): 13. **Death Rate** (per 1000 pop., 1977–78): 10. **Infant Mortality** (per 1000 live births, 1977): Female 10, male 11. **Life Expectancy** (1975–80): Female 78 yrs., male 72 yrs.

GOVERNMENT. Constitutional monarchy with executive power shared by the sovereign, the cabinet, and the prime minister; legislative power held by an elected unicameral 155-member Storting (parliament). **Women's Suffrage:** 1913 in national elections; equal voting in municipal elections won in 1910 (see HERSTORY). **Equal Rights:** Equal Status Act (1978) stipulates equality between the sexes and prohibits discrimination in all sectors with the exception of "internal conditions in religious communities." **Women in Government:** Women are 25.8% of the Storting and 4 of the 17 ministers (1983). Dr. Gro Harlem Brundtland was the first Norwegian woman prime minister (1981); 23% of municipal council members were women in 1980.

ECONOMY. Currency: Norwegian Krone (May 1983: 7.1 = $1 US). **Gross National Product** (1980): $51.6 billion. **Per Capita Income** (1980): $12,650. **Women's Wages as a Percentage of Men's** (1980): 82% in manufacturing; in general, women earn 10–15% less than men, and are concentrated in the lowest-paid occupations [see **(Employed) Women's Occupational Indicators**]. **Equal Pay Policy:** Under the 1978 Equal Status Act, "women and men employed by the same employer shall have equal pay for work of equal value." **Production** (Agricultural/Industrial): Dairy products, grains, fruits, potatoes; lumber, paper and pulp products, ships, fishing, oil and gas, chemicals, metals, hydroelectric power. **Women as a Percentage of Labor Force** (mid-yr. 1982): 41.6%; **of agricultural force** (1980) 29.8% (of whom 68.7% are unpaid family workers); **of industrial force**—no general statistics obtainable (of manufacturing, mining, quarrying, electric, gas and water workers 23.3%, of textile and apparel industry 66%, 1980); **of military**—no statistics obtainable; women serve in civilian jobs (secretarial and medical) and since 1975 as reserve officers, in mobilization forces, and officer candidate courses; women are barred from combat. **(Employed) Women's Occupational Indicators** (1980–81): Of administrative and managerial workers 18%, of sales workers 56%, of nursing, clerical, and service workers 66%. Approx. 50% of employed women hold part-time jobs. **Unemployment** (mid-1982): 2.4%, female 2.8%, male 2.1%.

GYNOGRAPHY. Marriage. *Policy:* Under the Marriage Acts (1918 and 1927), women and men have equal rights in marriage. A woman may keep her birthname. Property is jointly held unless otherwise contracted. *Practice:* Female mean age at marriage (1979): 23; women age 15–49 in union (1970–78): 64.6%; marriages (per 1000 pop., 1979): 5.6. Since the late 1970's, common-law marriages have been increasing while the marriage rate and number of existing marriages

have been declining. **Divorce.** *Policy:*
Separation and divorce are granted on 2
grounds: mutual consent, in which case
divorce automatically is granted after a
1-yr. separation; or misconduct of 1
spouse, including neglect of financial responsibilities or neglect of duty toward
children or spouse. Lacking consent, mediation and a 2-yr. separation are required. If misconduct includes adultery,
or a serious offense against children or
spouse, or long-term imprisonment, a divorce may be granted without a separation. Property jointly owned during marriage is divided equally after debts are
paid. Alimony is based on income and is
paid to the spouse whose employment
opportunities were reduced during marriage. The mother usually receives custody of children unless the court decides
otherwise. Child maintenance is paid by
noncustodial parent up to age 18 of child.
Practice: In 1982, 30% of marriages
ended in divorce; women initiate the majority of divorces. Alimony and child
maintenance are often paid late or not at
all, despite strict regulations.

Family. *Policy:* Under Family Law,
men and women have equal rights and
responsibilities regarding their children.
Both parents must contribute to the
"livelihood" of the family, according to
ability, through "contributions of money,
activity in the home, or in other ways."
The National Insurance Act (1967) covers expenses for hospital and/or midwife
deliveries among other benefits. A lump-
sum maternity allowance of NKr. 3040 is
paid to unemployed women. The Working Environment Act (1977) provides a
12-month leave of absence in connection
with pregnancy and childbirth for employed men and women. Of this 12
months, 18 weeks are fully paid—6 of
which the mother must take post-delivery; the remaining 12 paid weeks can be
divided between the parents, as can the
balance of the yr's. leave. The Act stipulates protection against dismissal of pregnant women, or for employees exercising
their right to the leave, and the right to
10 days absence per yr. to care for ill
children under age 10. A 1946 Act (since
amended) instituted a family allowance
payable to any person supporting children under age 16; benefits increase with

each child. A 1971 Act provides a
monthly allowance (NKr. 1770) to divorced and separated family providers
(both men and women) who are alone in
caring for children. Mother and Child
Health Centers (MCH Centers Act,
1972) are run by voluntary health organizations and municipalities and provide
free gynecological and pediatric exams.
Day-care centers are regulated by local
authorities and the Ministry for Family
Affairs and operated by private organizations. Costs are paid by municipalities
(50%), federal government (30%), and
sliding-scale fees paid by parents (20%).
Some privately supervised day care is
available. *Practice:* The Ministry of Foreign Affairs reported (1980) that employed women's "working" hours were
unfairly curtailed because they bear a disproportionate burden of family responsibility; studies revealed that men spent little time on childcare and the home
whether or not the woman was employed
and regardless of the number of children.
By 1978, 1313 MCH Centers were established. In 1981 there were 78,189 places
in day-care centers, accommodating 25%
of children under age 7. The shortage of
available spaces is partially a result of an
increase in both-parent-employed families.

Welfare. *Policy:* The National Insurance Act (1967) covers all residents and
includes benefits for sickness, pregnancy
and birth (see **Family**), unemployment
(40 weeks maximum per yr.), disability,
old age, death, and loss of supporter; hospitalization is free for everyone. The system also includes benefits for single
mothers (see **Illegitimacy**). All persons
over age 70 receive a basic old-age pension; employed workers are entitled to a
supplementary pension, based on income
and yrs. of employment, at age 67. The
system is financed by contributions from
members, employers, and the government; membership is compulsory for all
citizens. *Practice:* In 1979 public-assis-
tance spending was 23% of the GNP.
Contraception. *Policy:* Legal; government considers family planning "necessary and desirable." Public and voluntary
health clinics offer instruction and information on contraceptives, which are
widely available. *Practice:* Women under

age 45 in union using contraception (1977): 71%; methods used (1977) IUD 39%, condom 23%, pill 18%, female sterilization 6%, withdrawal 5%, rhythm 4%, diaphragm 3%, male sterilization 3%; using inefficient methods 9%. A 1934 law made sterilization accessible to anyone with "decent cause" and is increasingly used by women and men since 1970. **Abortion.** *Policy:* A law effective 1979 made abortion available on request within the first 12 weeks of pregnancy. *Practice:* Abortions (per 1000 women age 15–44, 1981): 16.4. Statistics (1979) show a slight decrease in abortion requests due to the increased availability of contraceptive devices.

Illegitimacy. *Policy:* Norway was the first country in the world to grant children born out of wedlock equal inheritance rights with "legitimate" children in regards to the mother, and to the father if paternity is legally established. A woman is required to name the father of an out-of-wedlock child during pregnancy; she is subject to punishment if she doesn't report such a birth or supplies false information regarding the father. Generally, the mother has parental authority. If father's legal paternity is established, both parents are responsible for the care, maintenance, and education of children; noncustodial parent is required to pay allowance until child is age 18. A single mother who does not live with the father of the child is entitled to a 1-time maternity grant at the birth, a benefit for 2 months before the birth if she is unable to work, and for a limited period after if she cannot support herself. *Practice:* In 1979, 13.1% of all births were out of wedlock, reflecting the increase of common-law marriages and single parents.

Homosexuality. *Policy:* Penal Code amended in 1981 to prohibit persecution and discrimination against consenting adult homosexual persons of either sex. *Practice:* Discrimination against lesbian women in Norway still exists; protection by the 1981 amendment has not been thoroughly tested. There are several lesbian organizations and support groups including Lesbik Bevegelse (the Lesbian Movement, founded in Oslo in 1975), Leirgruppa, and the Feminist Panthers.

Incest. *Policy:* Illegal. Penal Code (1902) prohibits sexual relations with any relative of the next generation, punishable by 5 yrs. imprisonment or, if intercourse occurs, 8 yrs. imprisonment. *Practice:* No statistics obtainable. Feminists have begun organizing on the issue. **Sexual Harassment.** *Policy:* No specific law, but Equal Status Act (1978) prohibits "treatment which in fact acts in such a manner that one sex is placed at an unreasonable disadvantage as compared with the other." *Practice:* No statistics obtainable, but reports indicate that the Act is ineffective in this area. **Rape.** *Policy:* Illegal; 1902 Penal Code stipulates that sexual intercourse by threat is punishable by 5 yrs. imprisonment. Victim no longer needs to prove her "morality" when prosecuting the rapist. *Practice:* In 1980 reported rapes were 4.6 per 100,000 pop., the lowest of all Scandinavian countries. In 1982, 2 men were convicted of marital rape. **Battery.** *Policy:* Punishable only under general laws of assault and battery, none specific to spouse abuse. *Practice:* No statistics obtainable, but convictions of abusive husbands are increasing. The issue has recently gained the attention of the public, media, and lawmakers (see **Crisis Centers**). **Prostitution.** *Policy:* Not illegal for prostitutes or clients, but pimping is a crime punishable by fine and/or imprisonment. There are government-supported programs to aid and rehabilitate women who work as prostitutes. *Practice:* No statistics obtainable; exists openly in cities. Rehabilitation programs for prostitutes stress individual counseling.

Traditional/Cultural Practices: No data obtainable. **Crisis Centers.** *Policy:* The Ministry of Health and Social Affairs allocates funds for centers on a basis of matching contributions from municipalities where services exist or are planned. *Practice:* In 1976 women's groups in Oslo organized a hot-line for rape and battery victims and later established a center offering refuge. In 1982, 21 crisis centers and 26 telephone hot-lines were being operated by women's groups across the country. Funding is supplied by municipalities, private sources, and the State; in 1982 the Storting allocated NKr. 8 million for this purpose, which the Ministry of Health and Social Affairs has distributed.

HERSTORY. The early story of Norway, like that of the other Scandinavian countries, is a record of the Nordic peoples who inhabited the Scandinavian peninsula since approx. the 11th millennia B.C.E. The recorded history begins with nobles and petty kings who ruled the area in the 9th century C.E. until their defeat by Harold I (c. 900 C.E.). Many nobles fled to Iceland, France, and Western Europe (the Norse or Viking raids) over the next 200 years. Christianity was established during the reign of Olaf II (1015–28).

Margaret, "Maid of Norway" (1283–90), daughter of Eric II of Norway and granddaughter of Alexander III of Scotland, became Queen of Scotland (1286–90) under a regency but died en route to Scotland before she could assume rule. In 1363 Queen Margrethe I of Denmark (see DENMARK) married Haakon VI of Norway. Margrethe became regent for her son, Olaf V, when Haakon died (1380), maintained her regency after Olaf's death (1387), and was elected queen jointly by Denmark, Norway, and Sweden in 1397; the 3 kingdoms were united by the Kalmar Union. The tripartite union later dissolved (1523) but the union between Denmark and Norway continued. Denmark transferred rule of Norway to Sweden by the Treaty of Kiel (1814). Early Norwegian nationalist activity was halted when Norway was forced to accept the Swedish king, Charles VIII (1748–1818). An act of union in 1814, however, succeeded in establishing Norway as a separate kingdom "in personal union with Sweden," with a parliament and constitution. Full Independence finally was achieved in 1905.

Several women's organizations, mainly with social and religious focuses, were active in the 1840's. In 1863 single women gained "legal majority"; married women did not receive this right until 1888, when they could control their earnings and own separate property (though the husband maintained legal control of jointly held property until 1927).

Women were permitted to take examinations for secondary schools in the 1870's, and for higher levels and universities in the 1880's.

After the first performance of Henrik Ibsen's *A Doll's House* (completed in 1879), the issue of women's status became even more of a controversial subject. Women so identified with Ibsen's heroine, Nora, that informal "Nora Groups" sprang up, and on Ibsen's return from abroad sometime later, a crowd of hundreds of women spontaneously assembled beneath the windows of his house to pay tribute to him. To their disillusion, Ibsen appeared on a balcony of the house and told them to return home to their husbands and families "where women belonged."

The Norwegian Assoc. for the Rights of Women was the first organization to work solely in the interests of women. It was created in 1884 and moved to improve women's education and the legal rights of married women. Suffrage became the crucial issue in the 1880's and the Assoc. for Women's Suffrage was founded in 1885. More militant women split from this group and formed the National Assoc. for Women's Suffrage (1898), building a membership base of thousands. Domestic servants tried to organize for better working conditions in the 1890's.

Women achieved limited suffrage, based on income, for parliamentary elections in 1907, and universal female suffrage in 1913; Norway was the second country in Europe to extend this right. Women also organized groups within trade unions and the Labour Party; between 1890–1900, 20 women's unions were formed. In 1912 women nurses and teachers established organizations separate from male colleagues.

Beginning in the 1920's, women started local housewives' groups whose concerns included health, legislation regarding the family, and social change. The election of women to parliament also became a central focus after suffrage was achieved. Katti Anker Moller led a movement for contraception and abortion rights and the rights of out-of-wedlock children. She established health centers for contraceptive advice in 1924. By 1930 only 2–3% of married women were employed, while 60% of single women performed paid work.

Women's groups continued to work for a vast spectrum of issues, and an attempt at a united women's front was halted by the German occupation in WW II (Norway had remained neutral in WW I and early WW II). After the war women entered the labor force in increasing numbers. The contemporary feminist movement in Norway began in the late 1960's and early 1970's. Nyfeministene (New Feminists, 1970), Kvinnefronten (Women's Front), Lesbisk Bevegelse (the Lesbian Movement, 1975), and Brod og Roser (Bread and Roses, 1976) were among the organizations formed which embraced the wide-ranging issues of women's employment and election to political office, lesbian rights, and connections between class and sex oppression. The Equal Status Council was formed in 1972. The issue of abortion united many women's groups in 1974, and a bill passed the Storting in 1978 (with a 1-vote majority) which gave women the right to terminate an unwanted pregnancy within the first 12 weeks. In the late 1970's women's organizations launched a campaign against pornography. In 1983 the Women's Front and feminist activist Bente Volder won a landmark court case against pornographer Leif Hagen for slandering women as a class and Volder as an individual; Hagen had published editorials deriding women politicians and feminists against pornography. Feminists have also started refuges for battered women and for other women in emergency situations. The Labour Party, in power almost continuously since 1936, designated Dr. Gro Harlem Brundtland as the first Norwegian woman prime minister in Feb. 1981. Kaare Willoch of the Conservative Party became prime minister in Oct. 1981. Attempts at a coalition government failed because of Christian Democratic party opposition to abortion.

MYTHOGRAPHY. *Poetic Edda,* a collection of ancient Norse beliefs from the 10th century C.E., includes an epic called *Wise Woman's Prophecy,* or *The Sibyl's Vision.* The poem is the *volva's* (prophet's) predictions, as well as her account of history from creation. Other images from the collection are of Audhumla, a cow goddess whose udder feeds 4 rivers and who created the first human. Jarnved is the land of Giant Women, mentioned in the *Voluspa,* an epic poem that also talks of Heitha, the witch with magical powers, and Gollveig, a victim of the first earthly war, who survived burning and spear wounds to live forever. The goddess Frigga was queen of all deities, living in a palace called Fensalir surrounded by such goddesses as Gefjon, guardian of women who lived without husbands.

NORWAY: More Power to Women!
by Berit Ås

Norway has been perceived, as have the other Nordic countries, as an egalitarian society. Finland and Norway were the second and third countries in the world to grant women suffrage (in 1909 and 1913, respectively),[1] and these countries, similar to Sweden and Denmark, today have more than 25 percent women in their parliaments. In 1981 the

[1.] After New Zealand, in 1893.

Regent of Denmark, the President of Iceland, and the Prime Minister of Norway were all women.[2]

This does not mean, however, that women's status in the Nordic countries is very different from that of their sisters in almost every other country. In Norway *the conditions of men have improved more than those of women.* Women are victims of institutional rules of discrimination which affect them economically and politically. For example, husbands do not participate more in household and childcare activities when an increasing number of women enter the paid labor force. It is much more difficult for women to obtain paid work than for men, and, when hired, women get lower salaries. Women with education equal to that of men are promoted less often and fired at an earlier stage when crises occur. Quota systems, demanded as affirmative action to improve women's positions in the educational system, have been used to a greater extent to guarantee less-qualified *men* educational opportunities within traditionally *women's* areas. Divorce rates have increased from 11.7 percent in 1970 to 25.4 percent in 1979, and almost to 30 percent as of today.[3] The majority of divorces are initiated by women. And women have understood that mere "equal opportunity" rights are unjust—because they favor those groups which already have the greatest resources, and increase the gaps between weak and strong, poor and rich—in plain text, between women and men.

It is not only in the developing countries that women's conditions are worsening when more aid and/or money is available to male political leaders. Structural changes in the industrialized world, centralization measures, the development of suburbias, and the destruction of family networks put new burdens on women during the 1960's. In spite of the Scandinavian Labour parties' successful welfare policy after World War II, members of women's voluntary welfare organizations had their hands full taking care of elderly and sick persons for whom the welfare state had no adequate provisions. The Norwegian Council of Women's Associations (NKN), an umbrella organization for most of the women's organizations in Norway, became aware early on of these conditions. The leader of this organization, together with some of the most well known women from the political parties, as well as the Minister of Family Affairs and a judge, all decided that an increase of women in local community and city councils was a necessity. They went to the Prime Minister, who at that time was the leader of the Labour Party, and asked him to intervene so that more women would be nominated for the 1967 council election. At first he responded positively, as did other male party leaders.

The average percentage of women representatives rose from less than 5 to almost 10 percent during this election. Expectations about what the elected women could do for women's issues rose accordingly. But after a few years, it became apparent that this was still too few women to make an impact and that politics in the 454 community or municipality councils had not changed much owing to this slight increase. Some of the elected women became quite rapidly co-opted by male leaders. Others were indeed too isolated to resist group pressure from an established male majority.

The elections for local community councils (including city councils) take place every fourth year. There were elections to come in 1971, 1975, and 1979. Prior to the 1971 election NKN's leaders approached the party chairs once more. They asked them to nominate still more women for the election. This time they were turned down. The clear-cut message of the patriarchs was: "Enough is enough." This reaction made the women search for ways in which the election laws themselves could be used to gain a more just representation of the sexes. And the women found a way.

[2] Queen Margrethe II of Denmark, President Vigdis Finbogadottir of Iceland, and Prime Minister Dr. Gro Harlem Brundtland of Norway.
[3] Divorce rates are calculated from divorces in percentage of the number of marriages per year.

Norwegian election laws for community-council elections are very democratic. Despite the fact that the parties most often construct the ballots and so include the names of their own party members only, the law gives a voter substantial power. In my own community, for instance, where six parties competed for forty-seven seats, each of the parties had forty-seven names on their ballots—as if they expected to win all the seats. Only a certain number, however, counted from the top of the list, could win.

The voters could, according to the law, rearrange names to change each candidate's chances to be elected. The law also gave the following opportunities: If there was a woman's name on a ballot, and a woman voter wanted her to be elected, she could remove a man's name and replace it with a woman's, giving her one extra vote. If there were more women on a ballot (the women's names were often at the bottom of the list, giving the ballot some advertising effects!), each of the women's chances of being elected could be increased 100 percent by exchanging a man's name for a woman's. In addition, there were other ways of using the ballot: if another party's ballot carried women's names, their names might be moved from their original ballots to the one which the woman voter had decided to use. A woman from another party's ballot could be given an extra vote too, if women voters were willing to take away a man from the party that she supported in other ways. The total procedure asked for a crossing of party lines to increase women's representation. It meant that party solidarity became weakened.

In spite of threats and appeals from party leadership, women all over the country printed and distributed instructions on how to proceed legitimately to change the ballots. The new feminist groups in Oslo, and the Housewives' Association in my own community, Asker, gave instructions with enthusiasm and optimism.

Old documented stories about how men had used electoral "manipulations" on earlier occasions were well known. In a little Norwegian town in the far north, football players had used the method to increase their membership in the community council—and thereby increase funding for building football fields. In a community which produced aquavit, teetotalers had won a majority to take measures against increasing alcoholism. And women had, in fact, become the majority in a council far out on the little island of Utsira in 1925. There, a few men had been so opposed to the male council that they had elected most of the men's wives to govern their society for a four-year period. On all these occasions, people in Norway mostly had laughed. The Utsira story on how *men* elected women in revenge over other men was considered a good practical joke.

But in 1971, when women used these same procedures to increase women's representation on the average from 10 to 15 percent in community and city councils, men did not laugh. Some token women supported the male powers in telling those of us who had participated in the campaign that we were undemocratic, selfish, and irresponsible. The "dangers" of this "unfortunate" system suddenly became such a theme that a proposal to change these election laws was submitted to our parliament, the Storting. Apparently the system seemed especially dangerous because the city council of the capital of Norway, Oslo itself, now had a majority of women. In another large town in the north, Trondheim, the same "catastrophe" took place, and then again in the Oslo suburban community of Asker, where a woman vice-mayor[4] was elected.

New laws were adopted in the Storting. Some of the women members voted against the change. The major intention—to make women feel guilty—became obvious when, in 1978, the Storting quite silently changed the laws back to almost the equivalent of what they had been in the first place.

The *third* community election took place in 1975, International Women's Year. While elected delegations went to Mexico, and many fine words were uttered about the "World

[4.] The writer of this article.

Plan of Action," the increase of women representatives in Norwegian community councils rose only on the average of 0.8 percent. This was a serious backlash—not only because the new law functioned well but because women parliamentarians observed that now a series of other laws and regulations were being adopted which would *worsen* the conditions of women in our country.

We *had* experienced two successes, in 1967 and 1971. Now we could not afford to risk depression and pessimism in those women's groups which had become politically conscious. Fortunately, positive changes had also occurred after 1971. A new left-wing party had been formed. I had been elected the first woman party leader in the country and then the Liberal Party had elected their woman leader. These two small parties had adopted by-laws saying that no fewer than 40 percent women should be elected to all party committees, including the central committees of the parties.

In the parliamentary elections of 1973 (these elections take place in the middle of community-council periods) 16 percent of the 155 elected parliamentarians were women. These women could observe directly the detrimental effects from new laws and regulations during the following years, in spite of the fact that they were often not allowed by the male majorities to vote against their passage. In the case of military programs, requiring new huge sums for the armament race, women from three other parties told me (while we met in the women's lavatory), that they would have voted like me had they not been vetoed down by the male majorities in their parties.

What had now taken place with respect to election laws and other issues, made it obvious to many of us that more women had to take parliamentary seats.

In the summer of 1976, when women began to get disillusioned, a group of women who had learned to work together in their professional capacities as politicians in Oslo and Asker, came together. They formed a secret underground organization of twenty-five workshops, each containing women from many parties as well as women from grass-roots levels. They developed a structured campaign to attack party programs and to influence the nomination procedures for the parliamentary election of 1977.[5] One of their demands was that all parties install quotas of 50 percent women at all levels, and that the goal for the elections should be 50 percent women in Parliament.

The strength of the campaign was that women—including members of five political parties' central committees—would rather take their parties' punishment for working together with women from other parties than to have women's issues voted down. When the increase of women representatives in Parliament rose from 16 to 24 percent, the action group of the organization calculated that at least half the increase could be accounted for by the strength of the secret action.

I was a member of Parliament from 1973 until 1977. One of the reasons I was not re-elected might be the fact that I told the election committee of my party that I would—while of course following the party's program—make women's issues and peace policy my main focus. After the election I became an alternate,[6] who fortunately could make arrangements with the elected man in my party to take his place in Parliament whenever important women's issues came up.

But I foresaw that I would not be re-elected to the Storting for the next period. Consequently, in June 1976, together with three other women parliamentarians, I submitted a proposal to change the Norwegian Constitution: that at least 50 percent of parliamentary seats should be guaranteed for women.

At first ridiculed, the proposal was discussed in Parliament on February 12, 1980.

---

[5] Election to the Storting follows more stringent rules than election to community councils.

[6] An alternate functions as a stand-in for an ordinarily elected member, should that member become sick or have to leave Parliament for legitimate reasons.

Confronted with hundreds of women listeners and women's organizations supporting the proposal, representatives of all parties had to say that equal representation of the sexes in all political bodies was (of course) every party's goal. Swedish and Danish media covered the discussion. People who had laughed earlier stopped smiling.

In addition, quotas have been demanded by women of other Norwegian parties. One Danish party has adopted by-laws similar to those of the two above-mentioned Norwegian parties. The city council of Oslo has decided that at least 30 percent of committee members must be women. In Sweden, a proposal has been submitted to the Swedish Parliament to change their country's election laws. In Norway, women soon realized that a change of community election laws back to the earlier version meant that they were again free to use them for their own legal purpose. In the community elections of 1979, women encouraged women to vote for women. The NKN applied for government funds to inform women voters about the last changes in the election laws—and received more than 100,000 crowns for that purpose.

Representation rose again, on the average from 15 to 22.2 percent in the community councils. Never has any group or party achieved such an increase during a single election. But none of the political scientists, historians, or media commented upon or reported these successes. Swedish feminists wrote a song in 1971 about the women in Norway which had the refrain: *"Why is it called strategy when men perform it, but labeled 'coup' when women do it?"* They could now have written: "Why is history made when men have success, but nothing reported when women progress?"

Norway's women can look back on four electoral successes—three for the community and city councils, and one for the Storting. We can see clearly that political action is induced as a result of what happened in previous elections. So: *politics is a process.*

The Viking women were very strong. Later, the Norwegian farms were extremely independent units fostering cooperation between women and men. Norway was practically without nobility throughout the Middle Ages, and consequently most of the population never experienced a feudal state. In Norway, witch-hunting never reached the dimensions it did in Central Europe. Furthermore, women and men experienced Danish rule for more than four hundred years, as well as union with the much stronger Swedes (which terminated as late as 1905), and then German occupation for five years during World War II. Suppression of freedom has been the common experience of both our men and our women, and during such periods women have behaved courageously. This is in the historical memory of the people. Despite the fact that history, as a male-made science, always forgets to tell us about strong women, Norwegian literature is full of them. Not only does Henrik Ibsen have his Nora, described as a woman whose legitimate motives make her leave her family to enter society, but other Norwegian authors have written plays and fiction picturing political women. Sigrid Undset did it before the last war, and currently the author Vera Henriksen has rediscovered famous women from the Viking sagas and written their stories. During the last 150 years Norway has not experienced such fierce class struggles as have Denmark, Sweden, and Finland—a precondition which might account for the greater women's solidarity across party lines. Finally, when women still had no legal opportunity to vote, in 1905 they gathered 244,755 signatures to support the male majority vote (368,208 against 194) to become free from Sweden. So politics and the individual's struggle for freedom might be our historical heritage, and as such, a special precondition for women to try to achieve power within political parties.

Norwegian women have developed a clear understanding that without a strong, independent, feminist movement—in the unions, in the peace movements, in the crisis centers —no change will take place in party policy. Still, there are problems: to change token women into real women; to tear apart the veil of illusion that women have "become more equal to men"; to reveal the fact that violence against women increases as the patriarchy grows stronger; to understand that a patriarchal State is one which is either rehabilitating from war, is presently at war, or is preparing for war.

This means that there is enough work to do for women everywhere: from working within parties and unions to working in strong separate feminists' organizations. Why? Because our world is facing too many disasters, from problems of ecology and population to total war and techno-fascism. It is my opinion that if the world is to be saved from a holocaust, only women can do it.

Suggested Further Reading

Hernes, Helga. "Women's Research in Norway." *The International Supplement to the Women's Studies Quarterly,* No. 2, 1982.

Holter, Harriet. *Sex Roles and Social Structure.* Oslo: Universitets-Forlaget (The Univ. of Oslo Press), 1970.

Ibsen, Henrik. *A Doll's House.* London: Rupert Heart-Davis, 1965.

Ramsøy, Natalie Rogoff, ed. *The Norwegian Society.* Trans. Susan Høivik. Oslo: Universitets-Forlaget (The Univ. of Oslo Press), 1974; the chapter on "Women's Conditions" is recommended.

Sandel, Cora (Sara Fabricius). *Alberta Alone.* London: Peter Owen, 1965; fiction.

———. *Krane's Café.* London: Peter Owen, 1968; fiction.

Undset, Sigrid. *Kristin Lavransdatter.* London: Cassels, 1953, reprint 1969; fiction—an essential literary classic by a Nobel Prize winner.

Berit Ås was born in 1928, in Asker, Norway. She combines her work as an assistant professor at the University of Oslo, teaching methodology and feminist perspectives in social psychology, with vigorous political activity. She has served as vice-mayor of Asker, as a Member and an Alternate Member of Parliament, as chair of the Democratic Socialist Party (AIK) and of the Socialist Left, as a Norwegian representative at the United Nations, and as a consultant to WHO. Founder of a Norwegian Peace Organization early in the 1960's, she is known as an ardent feminist and a campaigner for nuclear disarmament. Author of *Women of All Countries: A Handbook in Liberation,* which has been translated into Swedish and Danish, she has developed a theory, "On Female Culture," has traveled and lectured internationally, and has written other books and articles, on consumer economics, accident research, adult education, and preventive health. She is chair of the Norwegian chapter of the International Federation of University Women. She has four children between the ages of twenty-five and thirty-one, and her present research focuses on the construction of feminist societies.

THE PACIFIC ISLANDS
(Oceania)

Editor's Note: Because the Pacific Islands consist of approx. 20,000 islands (many with individual national status) located between the Tropic of Cancer and the Tropic of Capricorn, it was impossible to assemble the type of Statistical Preface offered elsewhere in this book. The range in races and ethnic groups, cultures, languages and dialects, and religions is enormous. Some of the islands have won full independence from former colonizing powers; others are semi-independent; still others are actively seeking independence. For most of the information categories in our Statistical Prefaces, there are little (or conflicting, or unrepresentative) data obtainable on the majority of the islands—or no data yet obtainable at all.*

Such a huge and richly diverse area is virtually a world in itself: matrilineal and patrilineal cultures coexist with bilateral ones; civil law stands juxtaposed with customary jurisprudence (which in turn varies from area to area); exogamy and endogamy, monogamy and polygamy, all are represented—and within the latter, polyandry as well as polygyny is practiced, although less frequently; definitions of marriage, family, sexuality, work, government, and society itself, differ. The mythography itself would fill volumes. The complexity of the Pacific Islands can make even the most painstaking research seem simplistic.

Yet just as it would have been a disservice not to include the too-often overlooked women's movement in this area, so it would be a disservice to the reader—and certainly to the peoples of this region —to attempt a general and thus extremely superficial statistical background, or a limited and thus unrepresentative one (by focusing on only a few of the islands). Consequently, we have been forced to restrict this preface to a cursory presentation.

What is most important is the article which follows—and which movingly delineates the vision, courage, and solidarity of women in the region. Ironically, the same factors which obstructed the compilation of a satisfactory preface illumine the article itself with depth, diversity, and the excitement of a staggering challenge being met. Across barriers of space, culture, communication, and stages of colonization, neocolonization, and decolonization, Pacific women are uniting in new and creative ways—from demanding a "nuclear-free" Pacific to the economic, civil, reproductive, and sexual rights of women.

More than any statistics, it is this gathering force of women which can affect the world's perceptions of the region, and which can transform the reality itself.

HERSTORY. The original inhabitants of the region known as the Pacific Islands emigrated from parts of Asia as early as 1000 B.C.E. Marco Polo, Balboa, Magellan, Captain James Cook, and other Europeans explored the islands and variously claimed them for their respective countries. In the 16th century C.E., Spain and Portugal controlled trade in the region; the Dutch and English moved into the area in the 17th century; Christian missionaries had arrived by the 18th century.

In the late 1800's, Indian, Chinese, Vietnamese, and South Sea Islands "contract laborers" were brought to many of the islands. Indian women comprised 4% of the required indentured laborers in the late 1800's. In 1878 the kidnapping of a Kanak woman in New Caledonia set off the Kanak uprising against the French. In the 19th century, Australia, New Zealand, Germany, Japan, France, and the United States took an interest in the region, and many of the islands fell under successive occupations by the major powers. In WW II, decisive battles were fought between the Japanese, who occupied certain islands, and the Allied powers. The Marshall Islands—especially Bikini—were used by the US to test atomic bombs, and they remain a military base

* For readings on this region, see Pacific Islands in Bibliography.

today; germ warfare took place in Eniewtok Island.

Two major political movements have affected the region. One is the struggle of indigenous populations for national liberation; the other is the regional Nuclear-Free Pacific movement. The Marshall Islands, the Federated States of Micronesia, and the Republic of Belau are negotiating for "free association" status with the US; indigenous independence movements also exist in French Polynesia, New Caledonia, West Irian (West Papua New Guinea), and other islands. The Nuclear-Free Pacific movement began in the 1970's, after the environmental and health dangers of French nuclear testing were noted by scientists. Women, as bearers of children, have been particularly concerned with the genetic dangers of radiation. The incidence of stillborn or abnormal births, miscarriages, cancer, and radiation sickness among the inhabitants of certain islands had risen dramatically following nuclear testing.

In 1971 Fiji joined Western Samoa, Tonga, Nauru, and the self-governing segments of the Cook Islands to create the South Pacific Forum. Tonga is the only surviving kingdom of the South Pacific; Western Samoa was declared independent in 1962; Fiji and Tonga in 1970; Papua New Guinea in 1975; Tuvalu and the Solomon Islands in 1978; Kiribati in 1979; Vanuatu in 1980; New Caledonia and French Polynesia are French overseas territories.

Women in the Pacific traditionally have played important roles. In some cultures, women hold control over inheritance and use of land. Although "behind the scenes" in village meetings, the views of women—particularly older women—still have great influence. Women in the Cook Islands hold chieftain positions; in 1975, 7 out of a total of 23 Paramount Chiefs were women. (At the First Regional Pacific Women's Conference in 1975, women felt that colonialism and Western culture had reduced their traditional power in many ways.) Women also have played a vital role in the economic life of the islands, as gatherers of seafood and as agriculturalists; women's crafts often produced valuable items for exchange: shell money and tapa cloth and mats.

Pacific women also have been active in politics. In Samoa, the wives and sisters of indigenous chiefs took part in a 1926–29 resistance campaign against the New Zealand government. Queen Salote Tupou III ruled Tonga from 1918 to 1965. Women have been deeply involved in anticolonial movements in the New Hebrides (now Vanuatu), New Caledonia, Tahiti, East Timor, and West Irian; in 1974, Dewe Gorodey of New Caledonia was sentenced to 4 years imprisonment for protesting against French rule. The National Island Women's Assoc. in Tahiti protested the dumping of radioactive waste in the Pacific, and women blocked roads used to transport waste materials.

Thousands of women were affected by the 1950's US test bombings in the Marshall Islands; women coined the term "jellyfish babies" to describe the children being born without eyes, arms, or legs. Traditional women's groups and church groups have been active since the 1950's in social work, and in encouraging women's involvement in civic affairs. The National Council for Women was formed in Samoa in 1966; Adi Losalini Dovi was the first Fijian woman member of Parliament that year.

The contemporary Pacific feminist movement began in the 1970's. In 1975 the First Pacific Regional Women's Conference was held, and the Pacific Women's Resource Center was founded in 1976. In Papua New Guinea, the National Council of Women has created provincial councils made up of over 1000 women from village organizations, church groups, etc. In Fiji, the YWCA, under the guidance of Amelia Rokotuivuna, was a key organization in the 1970's Fijian Nuclear-Free Pacific campaigns. The Pacific Women's Bureau recently has been set up in New Caledonia to facilitate women's projects and activities. Pacific women continue to be leaders in the independence and antinuclear movements of the 1980's as well as in building a women's movement that spans both distance and diversity.

THE PACIFIC ISLANDS: All It Requires Is Ourselves
by Vanessa Griffen

The Pacific Ocean does not simply begin with the coast of California and Chile and end against the shores of Japan, the Philippines, and Australia. In that wide expanse exist the island countries of the Pacific, some of whose names are familiar and some less so: Tahiti, the Cook Islands, Kiribati, Tuvalu, Western Samoa and American Samoa, Tonga, Fiji, New Caledonia, Vanuatu, the Solomon Islands, Papua New Guinea, Micronesia to the north, and the smaller island countries of Niue and Nauru. (Australia and New Zealand are included in the Pacific but because of their larger size and the dominance of a white-settler population, they are less the image of the Pacific island state than the others.)*

The Pacific island countries are separated by the sea, and also by the different political status of some of the countries. Colonialism still exists and is one of the political issues still being fought. Nickel-rich New Caledonia, Tahiti (or French Polynesia, as it is some-times called), Wallis, and Futuna, are still under French rule. West Papua, the other half of the island of Papua New Guinea, is fighting a more than ten-year-old battle against a take-over by Indonesia in 1969. East Timor, also in the Pacific but rarely involved in Pacific affairs, gets annual mention in the United Nations asserting the right of its people to self-determination, but still suffers the decimation of an Indonesian military takeover.

Almost everywhere in the Pacific, an important issue is land. There's too little of it (in such atoll countries as Kiribati and Tuvalu), and for the colonial territories, it is *the* issue: they want their own land back; even in independent nations, large tracts of land still belong to white plantation owners and governments have to legislate or negotiate to regain the land.

The early 1980's have been important years for Pacific women, who have been examin-ing themselves and their position, particularly in relation to the participation of women in development. They are also beginning to organize and relate to the women's movement generally.

Emerging Women's Consciousness In The Pacific

Pacific women have always met together in their countries. The Pacific has a prolifera-tion of women's groups, an introduced phenomenon partly missionary/church organized, partly a social or administrative convenience for organizing community activities or dis-pensing government services. Traditionally, in some societies, women were separated from the men and spent much of their time working together.

The women's groups of the present exist in almost every village and, depending on their degree of contact with outside influences, are involved in what are now considered "traditional" women's activities: sewing, cooking, handicrafts. Women's groups raise a lot of money and are often called upon for fund-raising activities for the community or the church. It is rare that women put the money back into an activity for themselves. Most national women's organizations that exist are a point for affiliation of these women's groups and clubs, but (with perhaps one or two exceptions) do not direct women's con-

* Because both the Australian and New Zealand women's movements are represented elsewhere in this anthology, they will not be dealt with here; this article focuses on the other, smaller Pacific island nations.—Ed.

cerns along any new lines. It has been left to individual women, meeting at regional or international conferences, to coalesce around what is emerging as a Pacific women's consciousness and participation in the women's movement. This consciousness is regional in focus (it concerns itself with issues affecting women in the Pacific as a whole) and is national in intent (how women in their own countries can work to improve their conditions).

It is difficult to look back and trace the origins of a developing women's consciousness in the Pacific. I can only speak from my own experience and that of friends, of our first early awareness of the women's movement that was developing in other countries of the world.

We were students at our own regional University of the South Pacific (USP), in the early 1970's. The university was new and we were some of the first women students. This didn't particularly impress us at the time, since we saw no reason why we should *not* be there: we were unaware of sexism in the sense that no one had told us a situation existed in which women were unequal, downtrodden, trained to be wives and mothers, and that exceptions would be to the contrary rather than the rule. Somehow, it filtered down to us, by way of books, articles, items in the press, that women in some parts of the world were saying that this was—and did not have to be—so.

It all made sense. The issues that particularly stood out were the unpaid labor of women in the home, the dual roles of wife and working mother, unequal pay for equal work (we had women in the banks who clearly fell into this category), and socialization into sex roles that stay with us all our lives.

We ran an issue of the student paper on the position of women, covering generally the conditioning and economic exploitation of women and featuring two specific articles related to the position of women in Fiji. One was titled "Call It Indian Male Chauvinism,"[1] the other, "Can the Fijian Woman Be Liberated?" The articles drew some response and we defended them. We have been defending ever since, our basic argument being that women in the Pacific have an unfair and unequal position, low status, and are oppressed by society's expectations of them.

Similar questions were being raised by women at the university in Papua New Guinea. Nahau Rooney, attending a development seminar in Fiji in 1973, raised the issue of how women are forgotten in planning, and the importance of relating particularly to village women who are the backbone of traditional agricultural production.

For those of us beginning to pick up the issues of the women's movement, feminist events in other countries, as reported (with amusement) in the media, were not helpful. The label "women's liberation" was especially suspect among older, more established women's groups. However, the publicity could not be escaped. By 1975, when the United Nations declared International Women's Year, there was an awareness that something related to women was going on in the world, but *what* it was was hazy or misconceived. Some groups of women thought the Year was an acknowledgment by governments of women's contribution to the home and the nation. Others were aware that it was a meeting on an international stage of the struggle which had been gaining momentum in the previous years. We still thought then that it was "someone else's movement," a Western movement—but something in the world was happening related to women and we wanted to be there.

---

[1] Indian immigrants were brought in by the British to work on sugar plantations. Their descendants make up half the population of Fiji.

1975—International Women's Year

International Women's Year brought the women's movement to the Pacific, whether countries liked it or not. Governments were forced by the UN system to make statements, prepare papers, and send a delegation to the Conference. Most Pacific governments did this with an easy conscience, since until then there had been little pressure from women. At the official UN Conference, delegations had some women representatives, but they were from establishment women's organizations, or were women with civil service or political standing in their own right. Some Pacific women had no official representation because their countries were still colonies.

Where women did go, at great effort and cost, was to the NGO (Non-Governmental Organizations) Tribune meeting that was being held at the same time as the official UN Conference, in Mexico City, June–July 1975. Mexico City was important, not so much for the consciousness it raised as for the increased awareness it gave Pacific women of the multiplicity of interests that made up the international women's movement. It also revealed to Pacific women that their individual voices were inadequate if they wished to raise issues; they found that they must present their views *as a region.*

This was an important and unifying point. After some preparation and working together, Pacific women toward the end of the meeting were able to make statements concerning two issues uniquely important in the Pacific: French nuclear testing and independence for colonial territories.[2]

What Mexico revealed to Pacific women, and to women generally, was the movement itself. There *was* a women's movement, and it was worldwide; it wasn't just American, or British, or white, as the media had painted it. Mexico was an experience, a meeting on an international scale, of women.

First Pacific Women's Regional Conference, October/November 1975

This was the first meeting where women in the region came together to talk about and assess the position of women in society. Some women's organizations which have also had regional meetings dispute that was the first meeting of this kind. However, the fact remains that it was the first meeting where women in the Pacific came specifically to talk about *themselves* and look at the institutions which defined women: the family and traditional culture, religion, education, the media, the law, and politics. The organizers were for the most part young, were based in Suva, Fiji, and worked by correspondence with Pacific women in all the island countries of the region, including Micronesia to the north, and with indigenous women in Australia and New Zealand. What occurred was a meeting of some eighty Pacific women, representing women's organizations or there on the basis of their individual work for women in their own countries. Sixteen Pacific countries were represented.

What came out of the conference was a range of views on the position of women and some disagreement over what exactly were "women's issues": the traditional role of women in the home, how women were not represented in decision-making, how colonialism had removed many of the traditional rights of women and was a system of daily oppression. Most women—conservative or wavering or committed—went away with a broader perspective of what women's issues in the Pacific would involve, and an awareness of the need to retain regional links. With this in mind, the conference resolved to set up a Pacific Women's Resource Centre where women could remain in contact, share

---

[2.] Women attending the Tribune meeting were from Fiji, New Caledonia (French colony), New Hebrides (British and French condominium, now independent Vanuatu), Papua New Guinea.

information and skills, and present a stronger Pacific women's perspective in regional and international forums.

The Pacific Women's Resource Centre was set up at the end of 1976. It was nongovernmental and sought funds from outside the region. It consisted of an office in Suva with two full-time staff workers, who were responsible to an executive committee representing the different regions in the Pacific.[3]

The Centre was to coordinate regional activities, collect and communicate information, do research after identifying areas of need, and, later, initiate types of training not already being done. After some time, the Centre was faced with the difficulty of communication in the region, a structure that did not allow staff autonomy, lack of active support from women, and dwindling funds. In 1978, at a second Pacific women's meeting, the Centre was suspended until such time as Pacific women were freed from national organizing to be able to use such a Centre. It would be tempting to gloss over this failure, but that would be to ignore the fact that it was unique as a first effort by Pacific women to respond to a growing regional awareness.

Women maintained contacts during the following year through use of the satellite link-up at the University of the South Pacific. Communication is one of the main obstacles of a Pacific women's movement. Unless women meet and talk at regional gatherings, little can be done to build up momentum. The satellite sessions at the university link women in other countries and are a way of solving problems on the spot.

Copenhagen—1980

At the UN Mid-Decade conference on women held in Copenhagen, Pacific women were much better prepared. Representatives from Tahiti, Fiji, and Vanuatu (now independent), Samoa, Tonga, and Papua New Guinea, attended the NGO Forum meeting as a Pacific *delegation*. This time, Pacific women immediately met to discuss how they would raise issues of concern to them. They also arranged a liaison with members of their official delegations to present these issues at the official conference. Among the issues that remained the same was an end to French nuclear tests in the Pacific.[4] Since 1966, France has conducted its nuclear program from the island of Mururoa, near Tahiti. The tests were at first atmospheric and have now gone underground. This is no comfort; there is a danger that the small island atoll will crack and leak radioactive substances into the ocean. Reports now reach us that the island is splitting up.

The Pacific is also being set aside as an area for the dumping of nuclear wastes from industrialized countries. (Japan is currently lobbying Pacific island governments to gain approval to dump wastes in the Northern Pacific.) To Pacific women, these issues will never die. They affect us all. Women in Micronesia and in Tahiti suffer miscarriages and give birth to deformed babies as a result of US and French nuclear tests. Pacific women as a whole have the potential to suffer similar effects long term.

Another issue raised at Copenhagen was a call for independence for the colonial Pacific territories. The list is long: New Caledonia, French Polynesia, West Papua, Wallis and Futuna, Easter Island (under Chile).

In Copenhagen, Pacific women were not lost, as they had been in Mexico. They knew what they wanted and how to go about it.

After Copenhagen, a regional meeting was held to inform other women of what had

---

[3.] The Pacific is sometimes divided up into Micronesia, Polynesia, and Melanesia, on the basis of sociocultural distinctions as defined by anthropologists. As a matter of principle, I have not used these divisive categories here.

[4.] A resolution on nuclear testing and dumping in the Pacific was watered down by male delegates at the official UN conference.

happened, to review progress in implementing the World Plan of Action, and to discuss the issues affecting women. Organized by the UN Economic and Social Commission for Asia and the Pacific (ESCAP), it was attended by many UN and other agencies working with, or interested in, women's projects in the Pacific.

Women agreed that progress had been made in the areas of education, health, nutrition, and small business enterprises. However, they still had unequal access to employment and education, did not participate in decision-making, and were not found in leadership roles. Women wanted more representation on government delegations and an end to economic exploitation and financial dependence in the Pacific: "We shall not allow aid to divide women from men, forcing women to remain as in the picture postcards of the Pacific Islands while the men are trained to enter the modern technological world.[5]

The nuclear issue and colonialism came up again. In addition, women were concerned about the lack of information on drugs and contraceptives used in the Pacific, particularly condemning as racist and sexist the use of the injectable Depo-Provera, after it had been banned for use in its country of origin, the United States. Other issues that arose were the displacement of traditional medicine and its role in health, the increasing alcoholism that was leading to more crimes of violence against women, and the spread of venereal disease.

The talking among women was beginning to have results. A meeting of the South Pacific Commission[6] was held in Port Moresby, Papua New Guinea, in October of 1980. Though one of the main themes of the conference was women, few governments bothered to prepare anything. Worse, they did not include women representatives in their delegations. As the conference progressed, it was clear that the much-heralded item was not going to get anything more than perfunctory discussion and had been included as token reference rather than a serious starting point. The National Council of Women and other women's groups in Papua New Guinea were not going to let this pass. To the surprise of the conference, they were invaded by protesting women, who disrupted their meeting to protest the lack of representation of women on the delegations and the fact that the conference did not intend listening to women at all. Kila Amini of Papua New Guinea did not mince words in dealing with the conferees: "The offices of your governments are full of documents calling for the recognition of the work of women. But governments have not taken any notice of them." The women demanded support for the Pacific Women's Resource Centre to be set up again, and for the South Pacific Commission to include more management and leadership training in its Community Education and Training Centre. The Commission rescued itself from this onslaught by offering to hold a conference for Pacific women.

The South Pacific Commission regional women's meeting was held in Tahiti in July of 1981. The purpose was to suggest ways and means whereby the SPC could serve the needs of women in its program. Not a bad prospect—except that the South Pacific Commission is something of an anachronism in the Pacific, representing as it does the leftover colonial powers, mainly France. It does research, runs training programs, and has a Community Education and Training Centre which for years has trained Pacific women in community development skills, including simple technology, cooking, budgeting, etc. This work is not to be discounted, but the SPC has been very slow in making any changes which might broaden women's perspectives and roles.

The Tahiti meeting poses the question of just where Pacific women should draw the line. They are beginning to respond to the demands of agencies rather than to initiate their own responses to their problems. In the case of SPC, to support a program which

---

[5.] Report of ESCAP Sub-regional Meeting for Pacific Women.

[6.] A regional organization left over from colonial times, with government representatives, including France, Australia, and New Zealand as main supporters.

will help women may be somewhat contradictory if the programs are subject to direction by one of the remaining colonial powers in the Pacific, France.

At the conference, women were accused by the organizers of "deliberately" raising the issue of French nuclear testing, though this had been an issue for a long time. The women did go ahead and discuss their views on the position of women. In a sense, it was perfect that these assessments be made in Tahiti, whose image of women appears around the world to represent the Pacific generally and Pacific women in particular:

> "The usual image of the Tahitian woman is one of a beautiful flower-adorned girl, dressed in a very low tied *pareu,* to show her perfect proportions, performing a hula dance in the sun, on a white sand beach, under a waving coconut tree. . . ."
>
> —Marie Therese Danielsson

But the Gauguin or Michener fantasy of the Pacific is not correct. The tourist industry exploits the swaying hips of Tahitian or Cook Island women on its posters (not all Pacific islanders look or dance that way), while the reality of tourism is the commercialization of the Pacific—and of its women. New demands are coming from women, especially concerning their need to have their own income. More women are so-called career women, but they fill their traditional roles as well: women oppressed by culture, custom, traditional roles; decision-making in the hands of men; the obligation to marry and have children making it "unthinkable" for a mature woman to be without a family; women's groups still involved in activities that reinforce women's traditional role: they sew, cook, crochet, or make handicrafts together, but when will all this energy go toward *themselves?* And when will someone tell them that there are other things they can do, other women they can be?

The recommendations set down by the women in the Tahiti meeting, including the setting up of a Pacific Women's Bureau, were approved at the annual South Pacific Conference held in Vila, Vanuatu, in October 1981.

The adoption of this program could be regarded as a success for Pacific women. But I don't think this is all. In a sense we have come a long way from the redefinitions and assessment of 1975, but is it a real progression for women?

Internationally and regionally, Pacific women have learned to press for their issues and to demand greater representation. The whole "women and development" theme has been taken up by the many international aid agencies working in the Pacific, and they are seeking views from Pacific women and suggesting projects. Women are finding it easier to be funded for their projects. (In many cases the money and the projects are being put to them before they can even think about it themselves.) All this clearly aids Pacific women and involves more of them in projects which they might otherwise not conceive of, or have the means of initiating, using local sources. However, in all this activity, I feel the momentum has slipped away from us. How much thinking are we actually doing for ourselves? What we have not done enough of is help the Pacific woman "in her head." We have not continued to deal with issues of women's culture and tradition. And we have not yet come up with a Pacific ideology of women's liberation (and I use this term deliberately) which will help our women to extricate themselves from the obligations, roles, prejudices, and fears that hold them back.

There are still too many women who will not be able to use contraceptives because their husbands have told them not to, too many girls who will not finish school because they are pregnant, too many women who will go back to men who beat them, too many women who cannot conceive of leaving bad marriages because it is simply not done. We have not dealt with the *personal powerlessness* that many women face.

Culture, Custom

The "culture" argument was raised first and will continue to be raised in opposition to women doing anything to improve their status in society. The traditional role of women exerts its strongest influence because women reinforce it in other women also. In some cases, women cannot speak in the traditional meeting house. In the Solomon Islands, the life expectancy of women is *lower* (forty-three years) than that of men (fifty-nine years) simply because women have too much work to do and too many pregnancies. Culture, or custom, is the commonest argument used against any call for a new image of women in the Pacific. Even aware women are confused about this question because in the postcolonial period, cultural identity is an important part of national rehabilitation and pride. We as women need to deal with this question and present a clear statement of custom and tradition in relation to the liberation of women. Vanuatu, in a country paper presented at the SPC conference, summarized the argument succinctly:

"Cultural activities have a potentially freeing effect on women. However, the confusion between these rich historical traditions of culture and the social convenience (to men) of custom practices has led to the retention of attitudes which ensure that women find it difficult to escape from their traditional roles."

We need more thinking like this.

Men are clearly the biggest obstacle to the progress of women in the Pacific. They are in power, make decisions, and control women through the assertion of customs and traditions which give them this right. Pacific women have been reluctant to take the position of considering men their enemies. While there is in fact no need to adopt this position, Pacific women *do* need to consider what their approach will be to the opposition they receive from men. Representation of women in delegations, the adoption of women's projects, even the setting up of a Pacific Women's Bureau, all are easier than forcing a change in *attitudes.*

Many women are in fact making feminist choices for themselves, but on their own; there is little support from other women for the woman who is stuck, with the ability, interests, and ambition to move, but who stays where she is or moves only so far, until she feels the pressures of public disapproval and somehow redirects herself so that she also satisfies the traditional role expected of her. I do not mean only educated, urban, career women, but village women too. How many of them must fall back into the fold because they are too successful and cannot face disapproval and pressure—from other women, particularly from men, and from their community?

We have done too little work on the question of choice for women. Women's meetings in the Pacific have moved more toward "development" remedies, particularly as publicized and supported by the United Nations and the aid agencies in the Pacific. All this will help to involve women more in the development processes presently being adopted by Pacific countries, but it of course does not change the unbalanced economic priorities, the unequal distribution, the dependency and linkage with the international capitalist system of the development processes themselves. It is perhaps too much to expect Pacific women to deal with this issue on a regional basis—but an interesting thought is that they could spearhead it! There is no reason why Pacific women cannot critically examine the economic choices being made by their countries. Women need to be able to demand a greater degree of power, at least in their personal lives, and *to be able to hold on to it,* in the face of opposition.

Pacific women have been successful in making changes at the organizational level. What we need is to have a *feminist* perspective that is regional, Pacific, and convincing, which will help women face the criticism, ostracism, and "custom" arguments they will always meet once they truly try to break sexist barriers. Only when women think this way collectively can they begin to bring about a real change in attitudes.

The women's movement must begin with women being able to see their oppression and, separate from what is being offered them, define their *own* solutions. In this sense we in the Pacific do not yet have a women's movement, but we must develop one. It does not require funds. It requires ourselves.

Suggested Further Reading

Griffen, Vanessa. *Women Speak Out.* Report of the Pacific Women's Conference. Oct. 27– Nov. 2, 1975. Suva, Fiji: Pacific Women's Conference, 1976.

Molisa, Grace. "The Traditional Status of Women in the New Hebrides." *Vanuaaku Viewpoints.* Vila: Vanuaaku Pati, 1978.

———. "Women." In *Vanuatu: Twenti Wan Tingting Long Taim Blong Independens.* Suva: Institute of Pacific Studies, 1980.

Report and Papers of the Sub-regional Follow-up Meeting for Pacific Women on the World Conference of the UN Decade for Women. Oct. 29–Nov. 3, 1980. Suva: ESCAP, n.d.

Papers of the Seminar of South Pacific Women, Papeete, Tahiti, French Polynesia. July 20–24, 1981. Noumea: South Pacific Commission, 1981.

Women in Development: The Role of Women in Church and Society. Report of the first Pacific Conference of Churches Women's Consulation. Suva: Lotu Pasifika, 1979.

Vanessa Griffen was born in Suva, Fiji, in 1952. She has been active in women's issues since 1970 and was on the organizing committee of the first Pacific Women's Conference in 1975. She was among a small group of Pacific women who attended the Tribune meeting in Mexico in 1975, and she has followed women's developments in the Pacific since then. She has acted as a consultant for the Asian and Pacific Centre for Women and Development, based with the Pacific Women's Resource Centre, in 1978; is presently working on a Pacific Women's Resource Book, as part of the Women's Programme of the Centre for Applied Studies in Development at USP; and is producing a series of manuals for Pacific women with information on simple technology, health, nutrition, and better methods of food production. She is also a writer of short stories which have appeared in Pacific anthologies and in English curriculum books used in Fiji schools, and has been active in support of nuclear-free Pacific and independence movements in the region. She is a member of the Action Centre for Women in Need, in Fiji.

PAKISTAN
(Islamic Republic of Pakistan)

Located in South Asia, bordered by India to the east, the Arabian Sea to the south, Afghanistan and Iran to the west, and (in disputed territory) the USSR and China to the north. **Area:** 877,723 sq. km. (342,750 sq. mi.). **Population** (1980): 86,462,000, female 48.4%. **Capital:** Islamabad.

DEMOGRAPHY. Languages: Urdu, English, Punjabi, Sindhi, Pashto, Baluchi, Brahvi, other. **Races or Ethnic Groups:** Punjabi 66%, Sindhi 13%, Iranian 8.15%, Urdu 7.6%, Baluchi 2.5%, Afghan (see HERSTORY), other. **Religions:** Islam 97%, Christianity 1.4%, Hinduism 1.5%, Buddhism, Parsi. **Education** (% enrolled in school, 1975): Age 6–11—of all girls 26%, of all boys 58%; age 12–17—of all girls 6%, of all boys 18%; higher education—in 1973 women comprised 14.5% of professional college students; in 1972 women were 21% of university students. Coeducational schools are being closed under current (1984) influence of Islamic fundamentalism, and there is a campaign to decrease or deny female admission to medical schools. **Literacy** (1977): Women 6%, men 24%. **Birth Rate** (per 1000 pop., 1975–80): 44. **Death Rate** (per 1000 pop., 1975–80): 16. **Infant Mortality** (per 1000 live births, 1975–80): Female 139, male 145. **Life Expectancy** (1975–80): Female 52 yrs., male 52 yrs.

GOVERNMENT. A 1977 military coup by the chiefs of army staff installed a junta under Gen. Mohammed Zia ul-Haq, who was declared head of a 4-man council. State assemblies were dissolved, the 1973 Constitution suspended, and political parties outlawed; martial law and suspension of such civil rights as *habeas corpus* has been in effect since 1978. **Voting:** As of Dec. 1983, no national elections had been held since the coup. **Women's Suffrage:** A limited number of women had suffrage in colonial, undivided India/Pakistan in 1935. The 1947 Constitution (at Independence) granted women the vote in provincial elections.

Women won full suffrage in 1956. **Equal Rights:** The 1973 Constitution (Art. 25), now suspended, stipulated equality of all citizens, prohibited discrimination on the basis of sex, caste, creed, or race, and stated that at least 1 member of the Islamic Ideology Council, which proposes legislation, must be a woman (see HERSTORY). **Women in Government:** There are no full cabinet ministers and only 1 woman junior cabinet member; Afifa Mamdot holds the portfolio of Social Welfare but has no ministry under her authority; Attiya Inayatullah is National Adviser on Population Planning; Viqar-un-nisa-Noon is National Adviser on Tourism. Out of 50,000 local representatives, approx. several thousand are women (1982). A 1983 proposal seeks to prevent unmarried women in the diplomatic corps from being posted outside the country.

ECONOMY. Currency: Pakistan Rupee (May 1983: 12.8 = $1 US). **Gross National Product** (1980): $24.9 billion. **Per Capita Income** (1980): $300 (International Monetary Fund est. is $360; government figure is $200). **Women's Wages as a Percentage of Men's:** No data obtainable. **Equal Pay Policy:** None. **Production** (Agricultural/Industrial): Rice, wheat, livestock, cotton; footwear, textiles, chemicals, food processing. **Women as a Percentage of Labor Force** (1980): 11%; **of agricultural force**—no general statistics obtainable (70% of women workers were employed in agriculture, 1975); **of industrial force**—no general statistics obtainable (30% of employed women worked in nonagricultural labor, 1964); **of military**—no statistics obtainable; women are not permitted in combat roles but serve as civilian medical personnel. **(Employed) Women's Occupational Indicators** (1982): Of managerial, administrative, and clerical workers 1.42%, of medical-profession workers 25%, of teachers 30%. In urban areas 10% of employed women were in professional jobs, in rural areas 1%. **Unemployment** (1980): 6%; no rates by sex obtainable.

GYNOGRAPHY. Marriage. *Policy:* Laws are based on interpretation of Islamic jurisprudence. Polygyny is legal for Moslem and Hindu men; up to 4 wives is permissible. However, according to the Moslem Family Laws Ordinance (1961), a husband must obtain a wife's permission before marrying another wife. The legal marriage age is 16 for females and 18 for males. The Married Woman's Property Act makes a married woman's wages and remunerations her separate property. The 1974 Dowry Prohibition Act abolished *jahez* (dowry paid by the bride's family to the groom's). Zina (adultery) Ordinances, passed during the late 1970's, make sexual relations between a woman and a man not legally married a crime punishable by whipping and/or imprisonment. *Practice:* Female mean age at marriage (1970–78): 20; women age 15–49 in union (1970–78): 75%. The rate of polygynous marriages is reportedly low, but the custom of dowry persists despite the law. Marriages are often arranged between families. With the rising tide of Islamic fundamentalism, police are empowered to check couples in the street for violations of Zina Ordinances, forcing them to explain their relationship. In Sept. 1981 a Shariat (religious) court in Karachi sentenced a 21-yr.-old woman to 100 lashes and her husband to death by stoning for the crime of a "love marriage" elopement (the sentence was commuted). Adultery may be severely punished, as in the case of 2 people in Islamabad who were convicted of adultery and sentenced to 20 lashes in public and 5 yrs. imprisonment (1982). Gen. Zia's Council has moved to prove in the Supreme Court that the "proper Islamic punishment" for adultery is death by stoning. While married women have rights to obtain and control certain forms of property, husbands frequently manage their wives' property.

Divorce. *Policy:* Divorces are under the jurisdiction of Family Courts, where an official must make 2 attempts at reconciling the spouses. A Moslem woman may seek a court divorce on grounds of her husband's impotence, insanity, or battery (Dissolution of Marriage Act). Under the 1961 Moslem Family Laws Ordinance, a man may divorce his wife by a modified form of *talaq;* he is required to notify her of his intentions in writing, register with the local authority, and wait 90 days for the divorce to become final; a wife is entitled to support payments during the 90-day period. If Christian, a husband is allowed to petition the court for divorce on grounds of a wife's adultery; a Christian woman may seek a divorce if her husband is guilty of bigamy, adultery with his wife's close relative, rape, sodomy, bestiality, or adultery combined with cruelty or desertion. *Practice:* No statistics obtainable. Men frequently do not return the *jahez* at divorce, as custom dictates they should. Women who initiate divorce actions may be socially ostracized. As of 1983 there is a still-pending legislative attempt to amend conservatively the Moslem Family Laws Ordinance of 1961; the proposed amendments include changing *talaq* divorce back to a simpler form (to allow a husband to repudiate a wife verbally and without restrictions), less stringent marriage-registration requirements, elimination of the need for a first wife's permission for a man to take a second wife, and reduction of the marriage age for females. The women's movement has staged demonstrations in opposition to these amendments.

Family. *Policy:* Under some fundamentalist interpretations of Islamic law women must be segregated within the home *(purdah),* must be veiled in public, and are not permitted to socialize with men who are not family members. Women have full title over inherited property, but if the property has been left intestate they are entitled to less than men. If both daughters and sons are heirs, sons inherit twice that of daughters. Childcare must be provided at factories with 50 or more women workers (1934 Factories Act). A paid maternity leave for employed women is available both 6 weeks pre- and post-delivery (1958 Maternity Benefit Ordinance). *Practice:* Reportedly, factories do not provide childcare, despite the law. No further data obtainable. **Welfare.** *Policy:* There is no national social insurance. A recently initiated tax, *zakaat* (charity), has provided the government with a welfare fund for the extremely poor which is disbursed by voluntary agencies at the local level. Government employees and employees of some private companies are covered by pension plans. There is no national old-age pension plan. The government allots $5 per person per month to registered refugees in the camps (see HERSTORY). *Practice:* The majority of people have no insurance coverage for old age or retirement. Of a total 10.5 million families, only 220,000 individuals are privately insured (1981).

Contraception. *Policy:* Legal; voluntary population control has been a concern of the government since 1948; the Family Planning Assoc. was formed in 1953, and in 1965 the government began family-planning programs. In 1976 the family-planning program was federalized. Current policy is to reduce population growth to 2.5% by 1982–83. Sterilization is legal only with conditions. *Practice:* Women age 15–49 in union using contraception (1975): 7%; methods used (1975) abstinence 22%, condom 19%, pill 18%, female sterilization 18%, IUD 12%, diaphragm 3%, rhythm 2%, withdrawal 2%, male sterilization 1%, other methods 2%; using inefficient methods 28%. **Abortion.** *Policy:* Legal only if a woman's life is medically certified to be endangered by pregnancy. Illegal abortion is punishable by a fine and 3–7 yrs. imprisonment. As of 1983, a proposed law (Law of Qisas and Diyat) would make all abortions illegal. *Practice:* No statistics obtainable; reports indicate illegal abortions are common. **Illegitimacy.** *Policy:* Children born out of wedlock cannot be legal heirs. By law (Zina Ordinance), single pregnant women are subject to whipping and imprisonment. *Practice:* No statistics obtainable. One recent case involved a single pregnant woman who was sentenced to 100 lashes and 2 yrs. imprisonment applicable after she gave birth; the father was found innocent of any crime, owing to "lack of evidence"; the case was later withdrawn. In Karachi in 1983, mullahs stoned a newborn child to death on the suspicion of its being "illegitimate." **Homosexuality.** *Policy:* The Penal Code (Sec. 377) defines "unnatural offenses" as sodomy, buggery, and bestiality; relations between men are punishable by up to 10

yrs. in prison. No specific wording on lesbianism. *Practice:* No data obtainable.
Incest. *Policy:* Sexual relations with a close blood relative are illegal; no further data obtainable. *Practice:* No data obtainable. **Sexual Harassment.** *Policy:* The Penal Code (Sec. 354) defines "outraging the modesty of a woman" as an offense punishable by a fine and up to 2 yrs. imprisonment. *Practice:* No data obtainable. **Rape.** *Policy:* Penal Code (Secs. 375–76) defines rape as an act of sexual penetration against a woman's will or without her consent, or if she is incapable of consent, or with her consent obtained by threat of hurt or death, or in case of fraud or impersonating her husband, and is punishable by a fine and up to 10 yrs. imprisonment; if the victim is the rapist's under-age-13 wife, his punishment is a fine and imprisonment up to 2 yrs. The law specifically excludes marital rape unless wife is under age 13. For conviction it is necessary to prove penetration and "to have 4 adult male Moslem witnesses to the crime" (see HERSTORY). *Practice:* No statistics obtainable. Rape is prevalent. Reportedly there have been cases where rape is adjudged the same as adultery and the victim as well as the rapist has been sentenced to public flogging "for having incited rape." **Battery.** *Policy:* A woman can seek court intervention and annulment of her marriage in case of assault by her husband (Moslem Family Laws Ordinance, 1961); she may also seek divorce (see **Divorce**). *Practice:* No data obtainable. **Prostitution.** *Policy:* The 1973 Constitution states that "prostitution shall be prevented." It is illegal under the Penal Code to employ women under age 18 for the purposes of prostitution or illicit intercourse; no further data obtainable. *Practice:* No statistics obtainable. Some licensed singing-and-dancing houses, which operate in sectors of large cities, are known to be fronts for prostitution.

Traditional/Cultural Practices. *Policy:* The tradition of secluding women in the domestic sphere is being expanded by "Islamization" practices of Moslem fundamentalists in the government (see HERSTORY). The 1870 Female Infanticide Act made murder of female children punishable by a fine and 6 months imprisonment. *Practice:* There are scattered reports that female infanticide persists in some rural areas. **Crisis Centers.** *Policy:* None. *Practice:* There are no crisis centers for women who are raped or battered; institutions for homeless women and orphans do exist.

HERSTORY. Women in the region have been politically active in the distant as well as the recent past. In 1230 C.E. Razia Sultana was a famous stateswoman who commanded her own armies in battle. Noor Jehan, who died in 1638 at age 72, was the Queen Regent of the Moghul Emperor Jehangir; she was renowned for her statecraft, and the Emperor deferred to her rulings in, among other matters, the outlawing of *sati.* Another 16th-century leader was Chand Bibi, the Princess of Deccan, who became legendary for her bravery in leading armies against the Moghuls. Queen Habba Khatoon of Kashmir was a poet as well as a ruler beloved by her people for her battles on their behalf against injustice (also see INDIA).

British colonial power took control of the region by defeating various indigenous groups in the late 18th century C.E., but the northeast sector remained unsubdued. Conflicts between Hindus and Moslems and the creation of the Moslem League in 1906 precipitated a movement for Moslem statehood, led by the lawyer Mohammad Ali Jinnah.

The participation of women in the Independence movement was intense. Abadi Begum ("Bi Amma") was a founder of the 1917 Khilafat movement and mother of its two leaders, the Jauher brothers. In 1917 she addressed an all-male meeting of the Moslem League (a political party); she spoke from behind her veil but was the first Moslem woman to address any political meeting. She toured the entire region helping to unite Hindus and Moslems against their common adversary, the British colonialists. In 1921, 3 years before her death, she publicly unveiled while speaking to a mass meeting. Attiya Faizi of Bombay disrupted the Mohammedan Education Conference of 1925, to protest their having banned the entry of women; the presiding officer was forced to let her speak

from the podium, and thereafter the rules were changed so that women were permitted entry. Nishat un Nissa Hasrat was a major 1920's literary figure—a poet, journalist, and political activist. Dr. Rashid Jehan, another writer, founded the Anjuman Taraqi Pasand Musanifeen progressive writers' association and, through her innovative writing, fought poverty and disease.

India's Moslem women were active supporters of the All India Moslem League, the party of Mohammad Ali Jinnah (see INDIA). He believed in women's full participation in society and was often accompanied by his unveiled sister, Fatima Jinnah.

In 1937 a Women's Section of the Moslem League was formed, with subcommittees in the provinces and districts of India. Its purpose was to raise the political and social consciousness of women secluded at home. The 1940 Khaksar movement met with bans and arrests, yet despite this, a small group of Moslem women for the first time organized a procession for freedom on June 16, 1940; they formed under the leadership of 11-year-old Saeeda Bano, who inspired them with her fiery eloquence. In 1944 Mohammad Ali Jinnah stated, "It is a crime against humanity that our women are shut up within the 4 walls of the houses as prisoners." Noor un Nissa (also known as Noor Inayat Khan) was a young Indian Moslem woman who was the first British secret agent to enter the Nazi Reich during WW II; she became known as the heroic "Madeleine" of the French Resistance and was the only woman to receive both the George Cross and the Croix de Guerre (posthumously). At her appointment by the British she declared openly that she would fight with them against the Nazis but fight against them when it came to the independence of her own country. Arrested and tortured by the Gestapo, she refused to divulge a secret code and was shot on Sept. 13, 1944. Fatima Sughra, a student during the 1947 civil-disobedience movement for Independence, broke through the police cordon and climbed the Punjab Secretariat building in Lahore. She pulled down the British Union Jack and replaced it with a Pakistani flag which she had fashioned out of her *dopatta* (a long scarf-like material used as a head covering); she was the first to raise the flag of Pakistan.

After WW II, support for the creation of a separate Moslem State had become overwhelming, and on Aug. 14, 1947, the Islamic Republic of Pakistan was declared in the 2 areas to the north and west of India. When Pakistan was declared independent, 14 million Moslems migrated from India to the new homeland. Ra'ana Liaqat Ali Khan (wife of Pakistan's first Prime Minister) organized women in the rehabilitation of the refugees. In 1949 she formed the All-Pakistan Women's Assoc. (APWA). The main focus of women's organizations was the revision of laws on the family and marriage, and a committee was created to investigate them. The committee published a report in 1956 that recommended restrictions on *talaq* divorce and polygyny, and the establishment of family courts. Their efforts resulted in maternity legislation for employed women in 1958, and the 1961 Family Laws Ordinance (see **Marriage**).

Conflicts between east and west Pakistan erupted in civil war in 1970, eventually resulting in the new State of Bangladesh (Mar. 1971). Zulfigar Ali Bhutto assumed the prime ministry of Pakistan and recognized Bangladesh.

In 1972 women were elected to participate on the drafting committee of the new constitution, but in 1973 the committee reportedly excluded women from the process, saying that Islam forbade their involvement. The 1973 Constitution nonetheless claimed to guarantee women equality, provided for 1 woman to sit on the Islamic Ideology Council, and reserved 10 seats for women in the National Assembly. Educational and professional opportunities for women increased. In 1975 the International Women's Year National Organizing and Coordinating Committee set up conferences and workshops; they established a number of local neighborhood councils aimed at improving women's literacy and setting up childcare centers.

Elections in 1977 failed when a military take-over was instituted, led by Gen. Mohammed Zia ul-Haq; in Apr. 1979

Bhutto was tried and executed. His widow, Begum Nusrat Bhutto, has remained under house arrest since the coup, but is at present (1984) abroad for medical treatment. Bhutto's daughter, Benazir Bhutto, is considered a leader of the (banned) opposition party and has been under steady house arrest since the coup; she was recently permitted to leave the country on medical grounds. Martial law remains in effect, and Gen. Zia, backed by Islamic fundamentalists, has embarked on a campaign of "Islamization" of the country's legal and social systems. The aging Begum Liqat Ali Khan has challenged Gen. Zia to a meeting between himself as "head of state" and herself "as a leader of Pakistani women"—to oppose the rise in religious fundamentalism and the suppression of democratic processes.

In 1979 Afghan refugees, largely women and children, began their flight into Pakistan (see AFGHANISTAN). As of 1983 there are more than 2½ million Afghan refugees largely concentrated in 300 camps in the North-West Frontier Province and in Baluchistan.

In 1979 the government promulgated the Hadood Ordinance: that the evidence of a woman would not be permissible at all in judgment for the maximum sentences regarding such crimes as theft, adultery, rape, or murder; the Law of Evidence (see below) could extend this testimonial incapacity of women to all cases whether they require the maximum penalty or not.

A new feminist movement—including housewives, students, lawyers, and professional women—was galvanized in the early 1980's in reaction to the discriminatory measures pushed by religious fundamentalists in the name of "Islamization." In Mar. 1982 Israr Ahmed, a television evangelist of Moslem fundamentalism and then a member of the Federal Council and the Islamic Ideology Council, advocated complete seclusion of women and total veiling, since "women were responsible for all sex crimes." His comments provoked an outcry from women all over the country; feminists demonstrated at the television station where he appeared. In Aug. 1982 the Islamic Ideology Council proposed the Law of Evidence, which would require 2 female witnesses to equal the testimony of 1 male witness in court cases, and advocated that the *diyat* (compensation) paid to the family of a woman victim of murder or injury be half that paid to the family of a male victim (if a woman is found guilty of a crime, however, she will receive the same punishment as a man). The government pressed for separate universities for women, and a fundamentalist lobby proposed abolishing women's right to vote, to drive, to seek paid employment, and to appear in radio and television news programs. The Federal Council placed heavy restrictions on women athletes in spectator sports, claiming that it was "un-Islamic" for women to appear before a mixed audience. Women were barred from the National Games for the first time on the grounds that women should not play sports in front of men.

Women organized to counter the moves of the fundamentalists. In Mar. 1981 Tehrik-e-Niswan (Women's Movement) was created, with a women's center that offers skills courses, literacy classes, and courses and lectures on feminist issues. The Women's Action Forum (WAF) began in 1981 as a coalition pressure group to protect women's rights and to work against proposed discriminatory changes in law. APWA, endorsed by WAF and other organizations, revived a repeated demand that the government establish a National Commission on the Status of Women with majority representation from the private (nongovernmental) sector; under feminist-movement pressure, the regime has appointed an advisory committee to set up this commission, but some feminists claim that the advisory committee, which has women members who are in the government, is virtually under State control and gives blanket support to government policies. One of the tactics employed by the Women's Action Forum and other feminist groups has been to quote *Koranic* injunctions to prove the basis of women's equality, as they feel that the text has been interpreted incorrectly to justify discrimination and suit the purposes of male politicians and religious fundamentalists. Tehriki Khawteen, a women's group, organized a protest in Nov. 1982 at the Lahore airport to protest the exclusion of women athletes from the Asian Games in New Delhi, India. The Women's Forum organized or participated in mass marches for women's rights during the spring and summer of 1983. In protest against the imminent passage of the Law of Evidence (see following article) women staged mass demonstrations in Lahore and in Karachi; the protesters were beaten and tear-gassed, and 33 were arrested in Lahore. In the autumn of 1983, Gen. Zia's nominated Federal Council *(Shoora)* formally approved the Law of Evidence, which cannot come into force, however, until the General gives his own formal assent.

MYTHOGRAPHY. No data obtainable.

PAKISTAN: Women—A Fractured Profile
by Miriam Habib

In 1946, lawyer-statesman Mohammad Ali Jinnah, the founder of Pakistan, said, "No nation achieves anything unless the women go side by side with the men . . . even to the battlefield." There was to be no ambiguity about the future position of women in the modern Moslem state which achieved Independence one year later, in August of 1947. Today, thirty-six years later—after periods of democratic rule alternating with military take-overs—the Pakistani citizen is enmeshed in a bewildering web of conflicting forces. Pakistani women dwell all the more in a perpetual social dualism which reflects the ambivalent attitudes of major groups describable in simplistic terms as "orthodox" and "modern." The counterpoint theme is not peculiar to Pakistan; it can be found all over the Islamic world, and can be attributed to several historical factors: male domination, narrow interpretation of scriptures, colonialism, feudalism, exploitation, and class polarization. Pakistan, when it emerged on the world map, found itself carrying a legacy of these negative influences along with the burdensome task of absorbing millions of Moslem refugees—all the while struggling to establish a stable government and national economy.

Over the almost four decades of independent existence, ambivalent thinking on women's rights and roles in society is exemplified by the Moslem Family Laws Ordinance (1961). A mild reform to place curbs on polygamy and unilateral divorce (pronounced by the husband), it was promulgated after much lobbying by women activists and nongovernmental organizations. Considered a landmark in Pakistani women's struggle for justice, this law's enactment has drawn constant criticism from the male clergy, who brand it repugnant to *Koranic* injunction. Other elements, however—which include enlightened men and women, and progressive scholars and students—are in favor of the Ordinance and regard it as only a stepping-stone toward codifying laws that should ensure justice to every member of the family. Even now, periodically, the reactionary chorus demands repeal of these Family Laws. At the time of this writing, a new feminist group (the Women's Action Forum), broadly coordinating existing women's organizations and committed individuals, has formed to raise a voice against any attempts to erode women's limited and hard-won legal and social status. A signature-on-petitions campaign in the big urban areas has been under way since October 1981, demanding safeguarding of the Family Laws.

This women's lobby decries a noticeable new trend to discourage women from spectator sports and from cultural activities. A move to segregate university education is also being opposed, as is the introduction of certain recent harsh laws in the name of Islam. Women's vulnerability to police brutality and abuse have been noted in this fresh struggle against ignorance, oppression, and intolerance—forces inimical to the emancipation of women everywhere.

The economic and political structure of a country conditions the life aspirations of its women. Like most developing countries, Pakistan is predominently agrarian; three quarters of the population lives in 45,000 villages in the four provinces, spanning a varied terrain and climate. The great majority of women exist in this rural setting without benefit of formal education or the basic amenities of life. Running water and electricity are still lacking in most villages, and opportunities for girls' education are scarce. I accompanied a group of journalists on a field visit to a particularly backward village where the one rich family, aspirants to political office, were eager to parade their "welfare" activities. The women had planned a demonstration: dramatically breaking empty earthen pitchers to protest the chronic absence of water. (The single well in the locality yields brackish water quite unsuitable for domestic use; sweet water for drinking and washing had to be fetched from a distant point and this was the task of the girls in that community of two thousand people.) "Give us a water pipe. Then we will send our girls to school," said one peasant. Most of the boys already were in the rudimentary village school, older ones walked a few miles away for high school, and some aspired to the junior college yet farther away. But the females typically had been trapped into a traditional treadmill as maintainers of the simple one- or two-room dwellings, tenders of animals, and auxiliary farm workers.

Meanwhile, as development rhetoric resounds during seminars in the capital, the sturdy, good-natured rural women of Pakistan, only 6 percent of them literate, continue to fulfill a vital function through domestic and field labor in supporting an agricultural system which is the mainstay of the country's economy. Rice and cotton, the two important export crops, depend heavily on female labor. Pakistan's land-owning structure must be one of the most inequitable in the world. Approximately half the 20 million hectares of arable land is held by fewer than 10 percent of all owners. Cosmetic land reforms have permitted loopholes through which the hereditary landlords managed to retain control of their vast estates, thus perpetuating a system where the small proprietors and landless sharecroppers remain in bondage to them as captive labor and voters when election time comes.

Rural women are subject to various forms of exploitation as unpaid drudges and child-bearers by their own men, and as sexual quarry by the rural aristocracy. The daily press carries frequent stories of violations and abductions of women. Unfortunately, it is government by feudal lords in collusion with other vested-interest groups that brought the democratic process into disrepute, repeatedly paving the way for military action.

About one third of the people live below the poverty line on annual Per Capita Incomes around $360 (US).* Their calorie intake is below the nutritionally acceptable minimum. It is often asserted, although not documentarily proved, that women and girls get the leftovers since men and boys by right and function should be better fed. The village mentioned earlier certainly showed an unhealthy pallor in all the women and children, who had prematurely lined skins. In another village, in the rich fruit-growing farmland, I called on a peasant family whose menfolk worked on the absentee feudal lord's land. One of them, however, preferred employment as a messenger in nearby Lahore in my newspaper office, a bicycle ride of about twenty-five kilometers each way. All around that humble home, as far as the horizon's edge, lush orchards hung with ripening fruit forbidden to the anemic young wives and babies of the local laborers. The landlord, vacationing in Europe, had sold the crop to a contractor for millions of rupees.

In view of the highly visible malnutrition among the poor, a society aimed at improving standards of nutrition through dissemination of knowledge and other means has recently been formed. It is in the largest city, Karachi, and is a voluntary association of several women's welfare groups and interested organizations. (Like all other volunteer welfare associations in Pakistan, this new organization is urban-based, endeavoring to alleviate distress within the existing system rather than attempting to do away with the exploitative structures themselves.) In a highly stratified, unequal society, hunger coexists with sumptuous, glittering banquets in the urban mansions of fabulously rich industrialists and absentee landlords—particularly when these families celebrate a marriage, a religious festival, or the birth of a son.

A floating reservoir of unorganized, cheap domestic and industrial female labor—some of it child labor—is available owing to urban migration as the dispossessed rural poor move toward the twenty-odd major urban centers to settle down in the hideous shanty towns which number about eight hundred all over Pakistan. The women supplement family incomes by working as domestic servants or unskilled factory hands; terms are more or less at the mercy of the employer. At a May 1 labor-day meeting I heard an illiterate woman laborer speak of her manual work in a bone-crushing factory where she works eight hours a day—following which she fulfills the usual routine tasks of a low-income housewife. She even had a word of praise for the proprietor, whom she described as good to his employees. (He owns three homes in Lahore!) The affluent middle class never tire of complaining about servants, male and female—their laziness and irregularity, their constant pilfering and requests for used clothes, bonuses, extra holidays, and free medical aid.

* $360 is the International Monetary Fund estimate; the (June 1981) government figure is $200.—Ed.

In the absence of social services and social security, poor widows and deserted women are reduced to near-destitution. A friend took me to meet one young woman whose vigorous young husband had suddenly died, leaving her propertyless with three small children. A relative allowed her the use of a typical village mud-walled home with a small courtyard, preferable in many ways to city tenements where whole families crowd into one room. Such untutored women are often artists with the needle; this young widow took to embroidering velvet uppers for evening shoes at the rate of three rupees a pair, earnings that could hardly sustain her if she sewed all day and all night. A tremendous amount of piece-work is done at home, between chores, by women who do not or cannot seek jobs. The markets ooze with articles produced by these women: embroidered Kashmir shawls, crocheted tablecloths and bedspreads, gold and silver threadwork, and hand-knitted garments. The famous Baluchi mirror-work, the poetic *rilli* or floral patchwork appliqué from the Sind province, and the *phulkari* satin-stitch of the Frontier Province— all are the creations of anonymous urban and rural women. Craftswomen all over the country weave fabric mats and baskets. Their work is a delight for the local buyer and the tourist, but except for a few government-controlled institutions, it is the middleman who reaps the profits.

The majority of Pakistan's women live on the edge of poverty in a male-dominated environment where the average number of surviving children is seven per family. According to the current Population Welfare Plan only 7 percent of fertile couples practice family planning. Taken together, all these factors hardly provide an ambience for self-realization. It is a measure of women's resilience and stoicism that they retain a modicum of cheerfulness and dignity.

Generally speaking, whatever her station in life, the Pakistani woman derives identity in the family circle as mother, wife, daughter, and sister. The stability and sanctity of family life, kinship ties and loyalties, the fabric of religious observance and custom—all these are maintained largely through women who are looked upon as preservers and upholders of social virtues. Traditional values and the Moslem ethic both honor the domestic role: a much-quoted saying of the Prophet Mohammad runs, "Paradise lies beneath the feet of the mother." Moslem modernists claim that Islam as a faith and a system has been the greatest liberator of women. The conservatives, on the other hand, use the scriptures to argue for a subservient position for women. Much energy and ink continues to be expended on the rightful status of women in an Islamic society. The great majority of these interpreters of God's law at policy level are men.

Now in its sixth year, the military regime has pledged to complete a process of "Islamization" before transfer of power to a representative government. This envisages a truly Islamic Republic where all laws and institutions are in conformity with Koranic tenets. Among financial measures is an effort to eliminate usury from the banking system and also a compulsory levy on wealth (the Islamic *Zakaat,* or alms) for redistribution among the needy. Some of these funds are to be channeled into women's programs. A recommendatory body nominated by the head of state and designated the Council of Islamic Ideology is charged with the duty of reviewing existing laws in order to "Islamize" them. A one-hundred-year-old statute, the Law of Evidence, came under scrutiny, and its replacement has been recommended, causing consternation among jurists and a section of women. The latter have taken exception to certain clauses which render a woman's testimony inadmissible. The CII draft does not become law until promulgated by the president;** however, it has caused controversy and raised apprehensions regarding attitudes of the orthodox elements who have gained ascendancy under an authoritarian regime.

** See Statistical Preface preceding this article.—Ed.

Women have failed so far, outside of their own circles, to make their mark as recognized authorities on the *Koran* and Islamic jurisprudence. Historically, the seclusion of Moslem women in the sub-continent stemmed to some extent from the desire for protection against the ways of alien rulers. A generation of women born since Independence have to feel this tug-of-war between hardened patterns of thought and the pull of present realities. Male supremacy, often in the name of protection, is still regarded as very much a natural condition of society, though feminists may argue themselves hoarse that this was not the case in early Islam when the faith was expressed individually and collectively in its pristine purity.

Successive governments, democratic or military, have acknowledged in principle the equality of women, both domestically and internationally. But women activists are impatient to see their rights *operating* in the social, educational, cultural, and political institutions of the country. And over the years, women's organizations have played a crucial role in bringing women into economic and public life.

The All-Pakistan Women's Association (APWA), founded in 1949, is the single national women's body to take up the whole spectrum of issues affecting women's position. Starting as a welfare-oriented association, it has become increasingly vocal in the sphere of women's legal and professional rights. The Moslem Family Laws Ordinance was a direct outcome of APWA's lobbying. Again, in the early 1970's, when a new constitution was to be adopted, APWA, along with representatives of other women's groups, sent members (among whom I was included) to meet with ministers and parliamentarians still basking in electoral victory. Our task was to ensure the inclusion of constitutional articles that would safeguard the position of women. Pakistani women are covered by a nondiscrimination clause as follows:

Article 25. 1) All citizens are equal before law and are entitled to equal protection of law.

2) There shall be no discrimination on the basis of sex alone.

3) Nothing in this Article shall prevent the State from making any special provision for the protection of women and children.

Women's professional groups can be given credit for opening the doors for women in government service. In 1973 a career women's delegation (I was again happy to be among them) called on the then Prime Minister to point out the discrepancy between constitutional provisions and actual practice in recruitment to State service. Until then, women had been eligible only for accounts services in various departments of government. Soon after the meeting, all services—including the much-coveted diplomatic service—were opened to women. Pakistan now has two full-fledged women career ambassadors and several women in other diplomatic positions,*** plus a sprinkling of new recruits in the administrative and foreign services each year. Teaching, nursing, and medicine remain the most popular fields, although women are venturing in larger numbers into other paid work in business and media, in engineering and architecture and also trade. The low over-all participation in education and employment is a reflection of the neglect women have suffered. The almost worldwide disadvantage regarding women's access to education is quite apparent in Pakistan from school enrollment figures, which reveal a ratio of four boys to one girl. A girl drops out early, especially in villages; she is needed as an extra hand around the house and as a little nursemaid for younger children. Education is not yet universal or compulsory. Each government advances the timetable for such measures further into the future.

Within the voluntary women's organizations in which I work, I seem to have drafted more resolutions and memoranda than I care to recall. Our collective demands, with

*** See Preface.—Ed.

APWA in the lead, finally resulted in the establishment of a Women's Division at the federal level. Headed by a woman career civil servant of the rank of Federal Secretary and set up in January 1979, it has a broad mandate to support, oversee, and coordinate all activity for the progress of Pakistan's women. Starting with a budget of 2 million rupees, the Division has had a progressively increased allocation, with 8 million rupees to spend on behalf of women for the financial year 1981–82. The Division has held several national women's conferences, the last being a gathering of about eighty women scientists. (With its resources, a government can do much to project women's problems and to increase educational and earning opportunities for them.) The Women's Division and such non-governmental organizations as APWA have demanded higher budgetary allocations for women in all sectors for the forthcoming Five Year Development Plan of the government.

The few distinguished women parliamentarians are regarded with respect for their contribution and for giving a political profile to women in an almost exclusively masculine picture of government. At the time of this writing, the military regime rules with the help of a nominated cabinet containing three junior (in rank) women ministers. By their own admission, military dictatorship is not the proper framework within which to strive for the egalitarian goals enunciated by the country's early leaders. As a first step toward untrammeled democracy, the caretaker army regime has held three-tier local government elections which have brought in over 50,000 local representatives. Of these, about four thousand are women—selected rather than elected. This experiment should prove a good training ground for subsequent political involvement.

The story of Pakistan's women is yet to be written. We are a community in transition within a young nation still seeking to define its personality. It seems to me that a twofold process of emancipation is required: the country's economy must be freed from economic neocolonialism—and the minds of its women must be decolonized from the start.

Suggested Further Reading

Chaudhary, Muhammad Anwar. *Muslim Family Laws.* Lahore: Lahore Law Times Publications, 1971.

Hafeez, Sabiha. *Metropolitan Women in Pakistan.* Karachi: Asia Printers and Publishers, 1981.

Mayo, Molly. *Women's Organisations in Pakistan: A Preliminary Identification.* Islamabad: Ford Foundation, 1976.

Mirza, Sarfaraz Hussain. *Muslim Women's Role in the Pakistan Movement.* Lahore: Research Society of Pakistan, 1969.

Pakistan Population Welfare Plan 1980–83. Islamabad: Population Division, Ministry of Planning and Development, Government of Pakistan, n.d.

Swynnerton, Charles. *Romantic Tales from the Panjab.* Lahore: Qausain, 1976.

Miriam Habib is a leading member of the All Pakistan Women's Association (APWA) and of the Business and Professional Women's Club, among other women's organizations. She was a member of the Pakistan Women's Rights Committee set up by the federal government and is on the Advisory Committee of the Pakistan Women's Institute. As delegate, consultant, and adviser, she has participated in numerous conferences and seminars on women, both abroad and in Pakistan. Among Pakistan's leading women journalists, she has been with the Pakistan *Times* (Lahore), the country's national English daily, for over eighteen years. As a senior staffer and women's editor, she edits a weekly Women's Page, writes features and art, music, and cultural reviews, and general editorials for the Leader Page. Two collections of her articles have been published: *Population Planning Through Development* (1974) and *Half the World* (1975). She has lectured in art and journalism, and as a painter has exhibited in group exhibitions in the 1950's. She is married and has two grown children.

PALESTINE*

Located on the eastern shore of the Mediterranean Sea, Palestine is an historic region that was divided in 1948 into the Gaza Strip (under Egyptian control), the West Bank (under Jordanian control), and Israel.** **Population:** In 1948 the population of Palestine was 65.2% Palestinians and 34.8% (primarily Sephardic) Jews. In 1980 the Palestinian population was: Jordan (East Bank) 1,127,000; West Bank 722,000; Gaza Strip 416,000; Lebanon 336,000; Kuwait 259,000; Syria 209,000; Saudi Arabia (est.) 180,000; United Arab Emirates, Qatar, and other Gulf states (est.) 115,000; US 100,000; other Western nations (est.) 90,000 (in 1975, there were 15,000 Palestinians in West Germany and 5000 in Latin America); Egypt (est.) 47,000; Iraq 19,000; Libya 19,000. The Palestinian Liberation Organization (PLO) defines Palestinians as "citizens in Palestine before 1947 and children born to Palestinian fathers after 1947 whether in or around Palestine or any other part of the world." **Population** (total, 1979): 4,250,000, female 49.7%. In 1975, 36% of the Palestinians lived in United Nations refugee camps; prior to Sept. 1982 there were 13 refugee camps in Lebanon housing approx. 400,000 Palestinians. After the Sept. 1982 Palestinian-Israeli war in Beirut (see LEBANON), the majority of Palestinians were transferred or fled to other countries, particularly Tunisia, Algeria, Syria, and Yemen (see HERSTORY and following article). **Capital:** Jerusalem was the capital of Palestine before 1948.

DEMOGRAPHY. Languages: Arabic (Hebrew was spoken by the pre-1948 Jewish population in Palestine). **Races or**

Ethnic Groups: Arab peoples, including some Bedouins and Druzes; Jews (pre-1948), including both Sephardic (Semitic) and Ashkenazic (East and Central Europeans). **Religions:** Islam (predominantly Sunni), Christianity (and in pre-1948 Palestine, Judaism). **Education:** The majority of Palestinian students attend schools operated by the United Nations Relief Works Agency (UNRWA) or schools operated by host governments for the refugee Palestinians. In the West Bank the curriculum in UNRWA schools is Jordanian; in the Gaza Strip it is Egyptian. In 1979–80 the total Palestinian elementary and preparatory student population in 627 UNRWA schools was 314,164 (in Lebanon, Jordan, West Bank, Gaza Strip); another 87,641 Palestinian refugee pupils attended government and private elementary, preparatory, and secondary schools in the same areas.

The Palestinian Red Crescent Society (PRCS) operates vocational centers for girls after 9th grade, offering training in sewing, languages, and typing; students pay $60 per month to attend. The PRCS schools in Beirut were destroyed in the 1982 war. In 1978 Palestinian students made up 40% of the total student population at Birzit University and 45% at Al-Nagah University in the Gaza Strip. The PLO provides student scholarships for education after 9th grade. In the Israeli-occupied West Bank, Palestinian teachers are prohibited from teaching Palestinian history or culture. As of June 1980, West Bank schools were subject to control by the military authorities; a Palestinian student who is arrested or imprisoned in the occupied territories cannot be re-admitted to school without the

---

* Because of the dispersion of the Palestinian peoples and their current lack of a formal landed State, it is impossible to present our standard Statistical Preface here. Although we have attempted to assemble what data exists, many statistics simply are not obtainable.

** In the 1967 war, Israel occupied territories formerly under the hegemony of Egypt and Syria (see EGYPT and ISRAEL).

approval of the governor of the area; the 2 universities, Birzit and Al-Nagah, are periodically closed down by authorities. **Literacy:** No general statistics obtainable. A 1979 report indicated that 31% of the Palestinian women in refugee camps were nonliterate. In 1982 there were 125 literacy centers in refugee camps in West Bank and Gaza Strip. **Birth Rate:** No general statistics obtainable. Reports indicate that the present birth rate for Palestinians is high; the average Palestinian family has 8–10 children. **Death Rate:** No data obtainable. **Infant Mortality:** No data obtainable. **Life Expectancy:** No data obtainable.

GOVERNMENT. In 1964 representatives from the various Palestinian communities established the Palestinian National Covenant and the General Principles of Fundamental Law, the Palestinian Constitution; the Palestinian National Council or first Congress was founded. That same yr. the Palestinian Liberation Organization also was established; by 1974 it had become the representative body for the Palestinian people. It functions independently from host governments and has its own conventional army, the Palestinian Liberation Army. After the 1967 Israeli occupation of territories formerly under Egyptian or Syrian control, the PLO became a guerrilla organization (1969) which acted as the umbrella for several guerrilla groups. By 1980 the National Council included 94 members of the 8 major guerrilla movements (Al Fatah, Saiga, Popular Front, Democratic Front, Arab Liberation Front, Popular Front–General Command, Palestinian Popular Struggle Front, and Palestinian Liberation Front). The Council also consisted of 51 members of the 10 General Unions—including the General Union of Palestinian Women (GUPW), the second largest group next to General Union of Workers —and 62 members from the Palestinian communities. The Executive Committee (similar to a cabinet) is made up of 15 members, each with a portfolio (health, foreign affairs, etc.). Yassir Arafat is chairman of the National Council (June 1983), but faces rebellion from various insurgent factions in the PLO. **Women's Suffrage:** Palestinian women can vote for a (pre-chosen) slate of officers of the General Union of Palestinian Women (but see following article). **Equal Rights:** The Palestinians fall under the sovereignty of the country in which they are living and must comply with the laws of that host country. For discriminatory clauses in the Palestinian Constitution, see following article. **Women in Government:** 1 out of 10 members of the PLO Central Council is a woman; there are 27 women (out of a total 315 members) on the National Council, 8 of whom are General Union of Palestinian Women representatives.

ECONOMY. No data obtainable on **Currency, Gross National Product,** or **Per Capita Income. Women's Wages as a Percentage of Men's:** No general statistics obtainable, but 1982 reports indicate that Palestinian women workers in the occupied territories not only earn much less than Israeli men and women workers, but also much less than their Palestinian male colleagues. In Palestinian revolutionary organizations, women receive 60% of men's pay (see following article). **Equal Pay Policy:** No policy data obtainable. The Palestinian Martyrs Works Society (SAMED), which was established in Jordan in 1970 and then transferred to Lebanon in 1971, operated factories employing both female and male Palestinian workers who were discriminated against in the Lebanese industrial sector. **Production:** SAMED factories produce textiles, clothing, and handicrafts (embroidered rugs, pillows, and clothing in traditional Palestinian designs). In 1982 there were 4 SAMED factories in Lebanon (destroyed in the Sept. 1982 war) and 5 in Syria. **Women as a Percentage of Labor Force:** No general statistics obtainable on Palestinian women's participation in the various countries in which they are living; a 1982 report indicated that women comprised 55–60% of SAMED factories' work force. The number of Palestinian women working in agriculture has declined as a result of their lack of access to land in the occupied territories; women work at home (cottage industry) or enter the industrial labor market. From 1967–72, there were

7000 Palestinian women in the Israeli industrial market; **of agricultural force**— see above; **of industrial force**—see above; **of military**—no statistics obtainable; women are active in the various guerrilla forces (see following article). **(Employed) Women's Occupational Indicators:** No general statistics obtainable. Palestinian women employed in the Gaza Strip in 1982 worked up to 14 hours per day under difficult conditions with low pay and no worker benefits or social insurance. In 1981 there were 20,000 illegally employed Palestinians in Israel. **Unemployment:** No data obtainable.

GYNOGRAPHY. Marriage. *Policy:* Palestinians are subject to the laws of the particular country in which they are refugees (and see following article). *Practice:* No data obtainable. **Divorce.** *Policy:* Palestinians are subject to the laws of the particular country in which they are refugees. *Practice:* No statistics obtainable, but 1978 reports indicate divorce is common. **Family.** *Policy:* The PLO prohibits the adoption of a Palestinian child by non-Palestinians. Few Palestinian women working outside the home are eligible for national insurance or maternity coverage in the respective countries they occupy. Married SAMED workers are given monthly payments for their spouses and a monthly allowance for each child. Upon the death of the worker, his or her full salary is paid to the family for a given period which varies. The GUPW has a program of day care and nursery care for employed mothers with children. The PRCS provides day care for children of PRCS employees. Other PLO branches give assistance to widowed and divorced women with children. *Practice:* The GUPW has established 15 day-care centers as well as nurseries for employed mothers in various refugee camps. **Welfare.** *Policy:* Palestinians are not eligible for national welfare as foreigners (official status) in most countries where they live. Various PLO branches provide health and medical care and established clinics in Jordan in 1968, transferring them to Lebanon after most independent PLO activity was banned in Jordan. Health care is either free or provided at a low cost. *Practice:* 1978 reports indicated that 36% of Palestinian women in the West Jordan area and 24.3% in the Gaza Strip gave birth to their children in hospitals or clinics, a figure similar to 1983 PLO figures indicating that over 70% of deliveries occur at home with the assistance of PRCS-trained midwives. **Contraception.** *Policy:* Pro-natalist. The PLO discourages the use of contraceptives and encourages large families. The PRCS hospitals and clinics do not offer contraceptive services. *Practice:* No data obtainable.

Abortion. *Policy:* The PLO discourages abortion and no procedures are obtainable through the PRCS hospitals or clinics. *Practice:* No data obtainable. **Illegitimacy.** *Policy:* No data obtainable on PLO policy. In general, Islamic Shari'a jurisprudence establishes legitimacy on proof of consummation. *Practice:* No data obtainable. **Homosexuality.** *Policy:* No data obtainable. *Practice:* No data obtainable. **Incest.** *Policy:* No data obtainable. *Practice:* No data obtainable. **Sexual Harassment.** *Policy:* No data obtainable. *Practice:* No data obtainable. **Rape.** *Policy:* No data obtainable. *Practice:* No statistics obtainable. Palestinian women, particularly those in the refugee camps, are vulnerable to rape not only by Palestinian men but also by soldiers of the host country or the occupying power. **Battery.** *Policy:* No data obtainable. *Practice:* No data obtainable. **Prostitution.** *Policy:* No data obtainable. *Practice:* No data obtainable. **Traditional/Cultural Practices:** No data obtainable. **Crisis Centers:** No data obtainable.

HERSTORY. There is little record of Palestinian women, although their participation in the struggle against invading forces has been constant throughout history. The area of Canaan, or Palestine, as the region later was called, was inhabited by various Neanderthal-stock peoples until the Canaanites settled there. In the 2nd millennium B.C.E. both the Egyptians and the Hyksos (a northwestern Semitic Canaanite or Amorite people) ruled the area. At the end of the 2nd millennium, Moses led the Heberu (Hebrew) people across the Sinai desert from Egypt into Canaan. The Philistines entered the area in 1200 B.C.E. and settled Philistia, or Palestine. In the ensuing centuries the

Palestinians fought conquest by the Hebrew kingdom (see ISRAEL), the Assyrians (720 B.C.E.), the Babylonians (586), the Persians (536), Alexander the Great of Macedonia (333), the Romans (312), the Moslem Arab Caliphate (640 C.E.), the North African Fatamid Dynasty (9th century), the Crusades (1099–1187), and the Mamelukes (1291), followed by 400 years of Turkish rule, and decades of 20th-century British hegemony.

In 1921 Arab women protested the increasing European immigration into Palestine. On Oct. 26, 1929, 300 Moslem and Christian women attended the first Palestinian Arab Women's Congress in Jerusalem. Women have been in the labor force in Palestine in large numbers since before 1948, working in textiles, food processing, and agriculture.

In 1969 the General Union of Palestinian Women, an official section of the PLO, was created as a forum for women to promote the Palestinian nationalist cause. By 1983 there were 11 GUPW branches in host countries and approx. 20,000 members in both Syria and Lebanon; the Union, although banned in the occupied Gaza Strip, was active in literacy and vocational training, as well as martial arts and military training, for women in over 90 refugee camps.

The Assoc. of Palestinian Working Women in the West Bank and Gaza Strip is active in organizing Palestinian women into "cottage industries"—the home production of traditional embroidered products, etc. Many younger women joined the PLO guerrilla forces during the 1970–80 period, and were active against Israeli forces. Fatma Barrnawi and the late Dala-Almukrabi are two military heroines.

In Sept. 1982, women and children were the principal victims of the massacres at the Shatila and Sabra refugee camps in Lebanon, a massacre in which hundreds were killed, reportedly by Christian militiamen under the protection of Israeli forces; world outrage forced a full investigation by the Israeli government, which found that Israeli military forces had been indirectly responsible. Thousands of Palestinian women were jailed in Lebanon following the Israeli invasion (see LEBANON and ISRAEL).

On Mar. 28, 1983, official reports indicated that at least 250 Palestinian schoolgirls in 5 West Bank schools were suffering from illnesses believed to be caused by gas poisoning; PLO sources claim that the poisoning was done purposely. The UN Security Council requested an investigation into the issue. Throughout 1983, thousands of Palestinian women were wounded or killed in the cross-fire between various warring groups in Lebanon, including battles between different PLO factions. In May 1983, 26 Palestinian women political prisoners in Neveh-Tirtsa prison went on a strike when ordered to cook food for the guards; they were supported by a coalition of Israeli and Palestinian women who demonstrated in East Jerusalem (see ISRAEL).

MYTHOGRAPHY. The Canaanites (see HERSTORY) worshipped many goddesses, as shown by the Ras Shamrat tablets. Ashtart (Ashtoreth, Astarte) was Queen of the Heavens, a goddess whose image was a horned heifer armed with a bow and arrows. Asherah's image, like that of Ashtart, was Holy Mother, or Mother of All Wisdom. Anat, a goddess of Semitic Canaanite devotion, was a warrior goddess; her companion, Shapasa, was a sun goddess. It was Anat who resurrected the god Baal from death, brought rain, and made the earth fruitful. The goddess Atargatis was the fish-tailed goddess who controlled the sea; the temple of Ascalon on the Mediterranean coast is thought to have been built to her. Some evidence suggests that the Philistines revered the snake goddess, and contemporary scholarship has discovered the pre-Mosaic female deity beliefs of the earliest Hebrews (see ISRAEL). Before the advent of monotheism in the Palestine region (through the 3 major religions of Judaism, Christianity, and Islam), it appears that the pre-patriarchal peoples in the area lived in relative harmony.

PALESTINE: Women and the Revolution
by Fawzia Fawzia

This brief essay is written at a time when the Palestinian revolution is at a critical stage and there is a need for all Palestinians to take new steps in our attitudes and actions. It is true that the dilemma of Palestinian women is extremely complicated as a result of the special political situation of Palestinian people. However, this article will concentrate on Palestinian women and *our* revolution.

The Palestinian woman of the 1980's finds that she must struggle against different forms of oppression: patriarchy, sexism, classism, and zionism. This means that there are several levels of struggle which she must engage daily, in order to survive—much less reform—her present status.

The Ideology of Priorities

The main ideology which most Palestinians—including the so-called radicals—adopt with regard to "the question of women" sets the priority as follows: "to liberate the land, *then* the women." The belief is that there is not enough time right now to develop a pattern for the solution of the Palestinian "women's question," although no one has developed any target date for when doing so *would* be feasible. Samira Salah, the director of the Palestinian Popular Front women's office in Beirut, mentioned in a panel discussion that one of the obstacles facing Palestinian women in Lebanon is "the lack of a target —for the Unions and Institutes which deal with woman's work and improve her status— from *the Palestinian revolution leaders.*"[1]

Even the radicals among the leadership—themselves Marxist, Leninist, etc., on "political" issues—never practically apply their models to the realm of "women's issues." They divide the two matters and thus try to legitimize their own sexism. At the same time, they embarrass women who seek seriously to discuss their rights by telling them that they should focus "first" on how to liberate Palestine. A woman who questions such a directive is labeled a "Westernized woman" who has imitated foreign models without consideration for her own cause, culture, and religion (Islam). Moreover, it is said that if a woman is a good Palestinian, she must never speak of the real situation of Palestinian women to "strangers."

The men who hold this ideology could be categorized as follows: 1) the men who are sexist but deny it (and there is, consequently, no possibility of convincing them otherwise); 2) the men who are sexist and recognize it (and who have, therefore, the potential to improve); and 3) the men who are sexist and recognize it—but blatantly refuse to change. These three categories include most of the men who are active politically and who hold positions of power. The majority of men who have held official positions in the revolution have practiced an ideology which excluded women's participation in all decision-making.

Since women are not admitted to the center of power, they are unable to establish a policy for women and thus further their own and other women's capacities for making real contributions. For example, in the Palestine National Council and in the PLO Central Council, it is men who decide how many women will be allowed in as representatives

[1] *Al Hourria,* No. 1054, Beirut, Mar. 8, 1982, p. 40.

—and who they are to be. Virtually all of the few women who *are* selected are bourgeois and petit bourgeois and/or the appendages of particular men. Such "representatives" constitute an ineffective, powerless, and *un*representative voice vis à vis the masses of women who are their constituency. Consequently, many women among the masses become alienated and withdraw from the GUPW (General Union of Palestinian Women) or other political activities. In a panel evaluating Palestinian women's activities, Amnah, a member of the GUPW, said:

> It was necessary to invite [here] the sisters who are working directly in the camps. . . . These sisters *have first-hand knowledge of the obstacles which are facing them.* . . . Some have mentioned that the GUPW is ineffective and lacks the ability to reach the women in the camps. . . . I am speaking about the union experience of 1973 in the Shatila camps, where some sisters worked and obtained great experiences in this field *but they didn't continue and pulled out.* . . . Thus, we lack experienced cadres.[2]

At the top of the political pyramid, in the PLO Central Council, there is only one woman out of ten members[3]—and she is the wife of one of the Palestinian leaders. At the next level, the Palestine National Council, there are 27 women out of a body of 315.[4] Again, most are bourgeois or petit bourgeois. The third level of power consists of representatives and directors of the PLO missions. There are 74 such offices all over the world —and none have women as key representatives or directors.[5]

With regard to the Palestinian Constitution,[6] one finds that if any woman who is non-Palestinian marries a Palestinian man, she automatically becomes Palestinian, that she then has all the Palestinian rights for membership in any union (such as the General Union for Palestinian Students, etc.), and that the children of such a marriage are considered Palestinian. However, if a Palestinian woman marries a non-Palestinian man, he doesn't gain these rights, and their children are not considered Palestinian. This double standard reinforces the continuation of male supremacy through an archaic identification of generations with the male lineage and patriarchal structure.

"Woman Against Woman"

To escape criticism and retain power, men have used the age-old tactic of divide-and-conquer, the pitting of woman against woman. Petit bourgeois and bourgeois women have been positioned against a coalition of educated, radical, and poor women. The former have been given some token power within the patriarchal structure; most of these women are related—as either wife, daughter, or sister—to a man who holds a position of power in the revolution, and a few may advance if they come from what are traditionally considered major Palestinian families (the Al-Aila system).

This process of appointment by nepotism—which existed in traditional Palestinian society—has actually increased despite the appearance of substituting a revolutionary society for the traditional one. The problems become even sharper and more damaging as nepotism continues within the newly emerging structures and especially within the revolution. It has created a new class of women defined according to their families' status and through the sponsorship of men. The opposite should be the case: women's represen-

[2] *Al Hourria,* Mar. 8, 1982.
[3] The General Union for Palestinian Women Yearly Report, 1980, p. 3.
[4] The General Report for Palestine National Council, 1981, pp. 215–26.
[5] General Report for Palestine National Council.
[6] The Constitution of the PLO, Beirut, Lebanon.

tatives should be *elected by the women,* and, most importantly, *by women of the camps;* if this were so, then one could expect that the representatives would come *from* the camps, especially since most of the population lives *in* the camps.

Of the women in the camps, 31 percent are illiterate.[7] Among these, many are housewives or work in small factories; some work in the Palestinian organization SAMED in Lebanon. Others have what are considered low-level jobs as teachers, nurses, clerical workers, etc. These women sometimes vote for "elite" women whose names they don't even know, rather than voting for a woman who might genuinely represent them. They vote this way because the elite women represent a particular party which their *men* support. Radical and educated women don't even have a chance to run, since the bourgeois women have the full political and economic support and blessing of the men. The result is that though the system may *appear* democratic, it actually legitimizes the power elites and aggravates the domination of men over women. For the majority of Palestinian women to become truly involved in their own political process would require the risk of daring to engage certain questions: Who should hold power? Where should women be in the revolution? To what extent should they share power? Should their role be reduced to a minority in the military, as is now the case, or should they participate as the full half of the society which they are? What *kind* of power should they have? Is it to be on the decision-making level or merely as a superficial presence in the system until Palestine is liberated? Are political decisions to be the privilege of an elite, even in a revolution?

The Need for Women's Mobilization

Women comprise 49.7 percent of the total Palestinian population. How can we allow for the alienation from political struggle of almost one half of the Palestinian population? The ratio of women to men in the camps is almost two to one. The alienation of women from the struggle therefore decreases the capability of the Palestinian people to succeed.

The distribution by sex among the Palestinian people on the West Bank and in Gaza is 51 percent female to 49 percent male. Among Palestinians in the East Bank (Jordan) the distribution is outlined in Table 1.[8] This shows that the percentage of Palestinian women who are at an age (15–59-year range) which allows them to be part of the struggle as military cadres or active supporters is 44.4 percent. Some 51.3 percent of the females are less than 14 years of age, while elderly women (those above 59 years) represent 4.2 percent of the population. From this we can conclude that 55.5 percent of the female sex among Palestinians cannot be part of the struggle because of their age. Rather, they require protection and care, especially in any political crisis.

TABLE 1. **The Distribution of Palestinians by Sex and Age East Bank (1979)**

Age Group	Male	Female
0–14	52.0	51.3
15–59	43.8	44.4
60+	4.3	4.2

[7.] *Al Hourria,* Mar. 8, 1982, p. 41.

[8.] The numbers are drawn from the basic demographic and socioeconomic characteristics of women in Jordan (the Hashemite Kingdom of Jordan, Dept. of Statistics, Sept. 1981, p. 7); they are based on the Central Office of Palestinian Statistics, "The Palestinian Census 1979," from a brief report published in *Middle East* newspaper, London, June 2, 1980, p. 3.

In addition to this percentage, we have the percentage of the males who are in the same status: 52 percent of them are less than 14 years of age, 4.3 percent of the males are above 59 years of age. As such, 56.3 percent of the males are not likely to be part of the struggle. Thus, 56.3 percent of the male and 55.5 percent of the female Palestinian population need to be taken care of.

The other part of the population—namely those between age 15 and 59—are capable of being mobilized by the revolution. In fact, it is upon them that the revolution must rely; they are the backbone, the core of the struggle. The percentage of women from 15 to 59 years of age is 44.4 percent; among the men 43.8 percent. Since a very limited number of Palestinian women are mobilizable, especially as military cadres, we can estimate that only 5 percent of these women are using their full capacity for the revolution. As such, we have 39.4 percent whose capacity for struggle is not used and who continue to need protection since they are unable to defend themselves. We have witnessed this in the Palestinian-Israeli conflict in Lebanon (June 5, 1982) and in the September 1982 massacres at the Lebanese camps. Other figures, for Iraq and the camps in Lebanon, support this thesis.[9]

Consequently, the revolution relies on (part of) the male youth not just to carry out the Palestinian struggle but also to protect the majority of Palestinians who are not mobilized, not prepared to defend themselves. A mobilization of Palestinian women could indeed *increase* the capacity of the struggle. It would help to prepare women to be good protectors of the children and elderly, instead of leaving this job to the male military cadres who must also struggle in outright war.

One of the objectives of this article is thus to point out the fallacious idea of the male-defined "priorities" mentioned earlier. Women's full participation and mobilization is needed *during* the Palestinian struggle and *not after* "liberation."

Meanwhile, What Are Palestinian Women Doing Now?

Palestinian women have shown a superior ability to be good military cadres. The late Dala-Almukrabi, and Fatma Barrnawi, among others, represent women who have been heroic in combat. Throughout the revolution women's role as military cadres in commando bases has been very limited, but no one can question the ability—or willingness—of Palestinian women in this regard. In a report on a training center for Palestinian women in Syria, one such woman pointed out in an interview: "I am receiving training here as a typist, but I don't feel that this is what I should be doing. Palestinian women still aren't permitted to take a serious role in the revolution."[10]

They do play a serious role, of course—and not only one of suffering. But their participation is not *recognized* or respected *as* serious by men. In the camps, for example, Palestinian women have played a major role in meeting the needs of the Palestinian communities, especially in Lebanon. They have been active in handicraft workshops, sewing, and popular Palestinian embroidery which has been sold all over the world. Some have worked in childcare centers which in turn free Palestinian mothers to enter the labor force. They have been active in health-care programs, literacy classes, political and social education programs to raise awareness. They have worked with the Red Cross, especially during the continuous and devastating bombings in Lebanon, and have played a major role in meeting the needs of the wounded. In other words, Palestinian women *are* work-

[9.] Palestine National Fund, Central Bureau of Statistics. The general demographic characteristics of the Palestinian in Syria and Iraq, Dec. 1, 1979, Syria-Damascus; and Palestine National Fund, Central Bureau of Statistics Socio-Economic Arabs in Lebanon-Naher Elbared Camp, Nov. 1980, Syria-Damascus.

[10.] *Falastein Althoura*, No. 304, Beirut, Oct. 29, 1979, p. 32.

ing in most Palestinian revolutionary institutions, but under unfortunate circumstances: the women are paid only 60 percent of the men's pay. There are no rules for leave for pregnancy and delivery.[11]

Sexual Oppression

The oppression of a Palestinian woman is not limited to the traditionally defined political one. She also suffers from sexual oppression, whatever her marital status—single, married, widowed, or divorced. Palestinian society, like any other Arab Islamic society, considers sexual relationships acceptable only between a married couple. The standard of course may be relaxed for men, but the single woman is supposed to be a virgin until she marries. In fact, part of the marriage ritual is the man presenting "testimony" for his and the wife's families—proof of her virginity. (This means, to be sure, that the woman must accept his sexual demands; she may feel that her husband is a stranger but she must accept being, in effect, raped.) Even now, among many so-called educated and progressive men—who most probably had pre-marital sexual relationships—virginity of a prospective wife is an important matter.

After marriage, expectation of the woman's sexual availability to her husband at all times continues. She has no right to initiate lovemaking herself; that would imply that she has sexual desires of her own, which in turn would imply that she had had previous sexual experience—which is tantamount to defining her as impure. Though the woman is merely a sexual object, she isn't permitted to participate actively in lovemaking, and it's unlikely that she ever has an orgasm. In interviews with young married Palestinian women,[12] one woman said, "What are you talking about? He makes love for himself. As a matter of fact, I hate the night because of that. I am his bondmaid." This woman's day starts at 5 A.M., preparing her children for school and her husband for work. Then, after organizing the house, she leaves to go to work. She spends the rest of the day working to increase the family income; then, in the afternoon, she prepares food for the family, cleans the house, supervises the children, and puts them to bed. After all that she is supposed to be attractive, relaxed, happy, and eager for making love with her husband.

The expectation of the "good" widow is then deplorably consistent: she must be faithful to her dead husband and not remarry, especially if she has children. She must raise her children and live a very limited social life (if she has any social life at all). Of course, it is forbidden for her to have any sexual relationships. The same is true for the divorced woman—but the divorced woman has even more problems: she wasn't good enough to make a proper wife (or at least she wasn't patient enough to hear all of her husband's problems, though society blames *her*). Her social life is strictly observed. In an interview,[13] one young divorcee said, "I must forbid myself to socially receive not only a man but even any woman accompanied by her husband. Otherwise people will think that I wanted a divorce in order to have several sexual relationships." This woman is in her early forties, educated, working, and from a middle-class background! The restrictions practiced on widowed and divorced women are parallel to constraints on the single woman—as if the society believed that a state of required virginity would protect a single woman from practicing sex out of marriage (most unlikely).[14]

[11.] *Al Hourria,* No. 1054, Beirut, Mar. 8, 1982, p. 41.

[12.] Interviews held in Jordan as part of the author's research on Palestinian women, Nov. 1982.

[13.] Jordanian interviews conducted by author, Nov. 1982.

[14.] This attitude naturally manages to overlook rape—whether in the "normal" course of things, by some Palestinian men, or as a specific act of political-sexual aggression, as when certain Israeli soldiers would rape Palestinian women during raids, or while the women were under arrest, in an attempt to vanquish the women *and* their society.

Obvious Conclusions to Difficult Questions

It is clear that Palestinian women are capable of full participation in the Palestinian cause—if only they were allowed to struggle in their full capacity. The Palestinian woman is a fighter, a wage earner, a housewife; in addition to bearing and raising children, she also "serves" her "revolutionary" husband.

Nonetheless, the Palestinian woman is also a human being, and a sexual being. It is she who is giving birth to the much-admired fighters, she who raises them, marries them, gives support to them, and often must bury and mourn for them. But she has yet to gain recognition and respect from them or to become an equal participant in the decision-making process and the centers of power, which remain controlled by men.

Until she gains the full status of her humanity, liberation will be a hollow word—in Palestine or anywhere else on the planet.

Suggested Further Reading

Bonds, Joy, Jimmy Emerman, Linda John, Penny Johnson, and Paul Rupert (Palestinian Book Project). *Our Roots Are Still Alive.* New York: Peoples Press, 1977.

Langer, Felicia. *With My Own Eyes.* London: Ithaca Press, 1975.

Said, Edward. *The Question of Palestine.* New York: Vintage Books, 1980.

Sayigh, Rosemary. *Palestinians: from Peasants to Revolutionaries.* London: Zed Press, 1980.

Fawzia Fawzia was born and grew up in the West Bank. She is currently working on two books: *Women in Kuwait* and *Palestinian Women and the Revolution.*

PERU
(Republic of Peru)

Located in western South America, bordered by Brazil and Bolivia to the east, Chile to the south, the Pacific Ocean to the west, and Ecuador and Colombia to the north. **Area:** 1,285,216 sq. km. (496,222 sq. mi.). **Population** (1981): 17,005,210, female 50.3%. **Capital:** Lima.

DEMOGRAPHY. Languages: Spanish, Quechua (first and second official, respectively), Aymará. **Races or Ethnic Groups:** Native Indian 45% (approx. 100 different indigenous groups), Mestizo 37%, European descent 15%, African descent, Asian. **Religions:** Roman Catholicism 90%. **Education** (% enrolled in school, 1975): Age 6–11—of all girls 78%, of all boys 81%; age 12–17—of all girls 67%, of all boys 80%; higher education—in 1980 women were 30% of matriculated university students, 6% of engineering and architecture, 30% of medicine (including nursing, pharmacology), 46% of education. A 1977 report estimates that 40% of married women age 40 have no education, and 2.6% of women age 15–49 in union have university education. **Literacy** (1977): Women 62%, men 83% (30% of the entire pop. is nonliterate, 70% of which is female). **Birth Rate** (per 1000 pop., 1975–80): 40. **Death Rate** (per 1000 pop., 1975–80): 12. **Infant Mortality** (per 1000 live births, 1975–80): Female 87, male 97. **Life Expectancy** (1975–80): Female 58 yrs., male 55 yrs.

GOVERNMENT. The 1979 Constitution, which became effective after the 1980 elections, provides for a bicameral legislature with an elected 60-member Senate, 180-member Chamber of Deputies, and a president; the executive branch comprises the president and a presidentially appointed council of ministers. Current Pres. Fernando Belaúnde Terry heads the Acción Popular party. Partido Popular Cristiano and the Partido Aprista Peruano are other main political parties. A national State of Emergency is in effect (1983), suspending certain civil liberties. **Women's Suffrage:** 1933 in municipal elections and 1955 in all elections (literate women only); 1979 all women. **Equal Rights:** Civil Code (Art. 5) states that "men and women enjoy the same civil rights, except for the restrictions imposed on married women." The 1979 Constitution (Art. 2) prohibits discrimination with respect to sex, race, religion, opinion, or language. **Women in Government:** There are 12 women in the legislature (1983); women were 2.3% of top-level public administrators, 2.1% of mayors, and 3.9% of municipal council members in 1974. No woman has held a cabinet position.

ECONOMY. Currency: Sol (May 1983: 1450. = $1 US). **Gross National Product** (1980): $16.5 billion. **Per Capita Income** (1980): $930. **Women's Wages as a Percentage of Men's** (1980): 50%; women who complete secondary schooling improve their incomes by an est. 99%. **Equal Pay Policy:** Civil Code (1936) established equal pay for equal work without regard to sex. **Production** (Agricultural/Industrial): Cotton, corn, sugar, coffee; processed minerals, fish meal, textiles. **Women as a Percentage of Labor Force** (1981): 28.5%; **of agricultural force** (1973) 10% (a 1981 study found that 60% of rural women worked full-time on small farms); **of industrial force** —no statistics obtainable; women's employment in industry reportedly is declining, owing in part to "protective" legislation that limits night employment and types of jobs open to women; women's maximum workday is 8 hours, with a 2-hour mid-day rest, and they are prohibited from work deemed "health or morally endangering" (1981 Civil Code, Law 2851); **of military**—no statistics obtainable; virtually none, although a 1974 decree stipulates that military service is a responsibility of all citizens, and the mandatory conscription of women age 18 was initiated onto the service register in 1975. **(Employed) Women's Occupational Indicators:** Of professionals (medicine, engineering, architecture) 8.4%; 2/3 of 75,000 street vendors were rural women, and 54% were women with their children (1982); in Lima 42% of employed women worked in the services, 30.9% in commerce (1978). More women work as domestic servants than in any other employment. In rural areas women's agricultural activities include raising and selling livestock, eggs, or surplus crops, herding sheep and alpacas, and making woolen cloth. **Unemployment** (1980): 7%; no rates by sex obtainable.

GYNOGRAPHY. Marriage. *Policy:* Civil Code establishes marriage based on mutual consent; marriage age is 21 for both sexes, or 14 for females and 16 for men with parental consent. The wife adds the husband's name to her own (Civil Code, Art. 171); the husband has authority to choose the domicile and the wife is obliged to follow (Art. 162). He must provide her and their children with all necessities; she may not work outside the home without his authorization (Art. 173), and he is their legal representative (1936 Civil Code, Art. 168). Each retains individual ownership rights over property brought to marriage, but profit or property acquired during marriage falls under the husband's control (Arts. 177–78); Art. 180 stipulates that if the wife does not contribute economically to the matrimonial duties, the husband can request that his wife's property go under his administration. "Concubinage," or union between 2 single people who are in a permanent and constant sexual relationship which is publicly acknowledged, is the only extra-marital union legally recognized. Property acquired during such unions is not considered joint, and neither partner is covered by common-property laws. *Practice:* Female mean age at marriage (1970–78): 22; women age 15–49 in union (1970–78): 59.2%. Concubinage unions, an Incan legacy, is found in the Andes coastal region and the *pueblos jóvenes,* or newly developed towns on the outskirts of Lima.

Divorce. *Policy:* The Civil Code permits divorce on 10 grounds, including adultery by either spouse, mutual consent, and 2 yrs. absence without just cause. A woman may be eligible for maintenance payments of up to ⅓ husband's income if he was responsible for the divorce and she is without property; or she may be responsible for maintenance if he has no property and she was the guilty party (as in adultery). Each is equally responsible for the education of their children. A woman may cease using her ex-husband's name upon divorce. Separations can be obtained on the same grounds as divorce. *Practice:* The divorce rate is reportedly growing, particularly among urban couples. The Women's Rights Movement within the Revisory Commission for the Civil Code proposed changes in 1982 that would permit divorce after a 3-yr. continual separation of spouses (5 yrs. if there are children). The high number of men with paternal responsibilities in different homes, and the inability of the legal wife to end marriages easily in practice, are the feminist motivations.

Family. *Policy:* The 1931 Civil Code gives parents "equal" rights over children, but the father's authority prevails in conflicts, and he is the children's legal representative (Arts. 391–92). Both parents exercise Patria Potestad and both are responsible for maintaining and educating the children. Maternity leave for employed women is 42 days pre- and post-delivery with a subsidy of 30% of earnings for salaried employees or 36 days pre- and post-delivery for waged workers. Pre- and post-natal health care for the woman and her child is provided free by the Ministry of Health. Law 2851 also stipulates that workplaces employing women over age 18 must have a room for employees' children under age 1, and that the mother is entitled to 2 hours for nursing each day (1918 Civil Code). *Practice:* In parts of northern Peru up to 50% of all households are "second families" of men who are legally married to other women; 43% of all children live in homes with 1 parent (1982). A major problem women face is collecting child support from negligent fathers. There are few childcare services in poor neighborhoods or in factories. **Welfare.** *Policy:* Current contributory Social Security system, which was formed in 1973 by merging 2 older systems and adding a National System of Pensions, covers business and government employees. It provides illness, infirmity, and maternity insurance (see **Family**), subsidies for health and dental care, hospitalization, and medicine. Pensions equal to 50% of salary are granted at age 55 for women (after 13 yrs. employment) and 60 for men (after 15 yrs. employment). *Practice:* Reports indicate that over 85% of those covered are men. The majority of women are self- or marginally employed in family agriculture, vending, or domestic services, or are housewives, not covered; reportedly, wives and newborn children of insured workers recently attained coverage.

Contraception. *Policy:* Fertility rate is not considered a major problem. There is no official family-planning program; in 1979 State-supported contraceptive services in public hospitals were ended; in 1977 sterilization-as-contraception, family-planning, and fertility-control groups were prohibited and family planning was merged with other health services. *Practice:* Women age 15–49 in union using contraception (1977): 36%; methods used (1977) rhythm 35%, pill 13%, douche 11%, withdrawal 11%, female sterilization 9%, abstinence 7%, IUD 4%, diaphragm 3%, injectables 3%, condom 3%, other methods 2%; using inefficient methods 66%; 82% of women know of 1 or more contraceptive methods. Low usage rate is reportedly because of strong Roman Catholic influence, lack of information and devices (especially in rural areas), and the high cost of modern contraceptives in Peru. **Abortion.** *Policy:* Illegal, but may be authorized in cases of danger to the life of the woman or damage to the fetus, with the consent of 2 physicians (1964 law). The penalty for illegal abortion is up to 4 yrs. imprisonment for the woman, up to 2 yrs. for the accomplice (midwife), and no more than 5 yrs. for a doctor. *Practice:* Official statistics place the number of illegal abortions at 27,000 annually; unofficial estimates indicate 127,000 abortions annually. Of every 10,000 women, 50 die from complications arising from births or illegal abortions, compared to 5 out of 10,000 in highly industrialized countries (1982). In one Lima house of correction, 60% of the women were convicted of having or performing illegal abortions. A 1982 report estimated 10–15% of all

women in prisons are there for having obtained or performed an abortion.

Illegitimacy. *Policy:* Children of concubinage unions are guaranteed food allowances and certain filial rights. The Law of Family states that the father who recognizes his out-of-wedlock children has custody and rights over their property, while the mother has legal rights only through court action and will receive limited custody (Art. 394). The Law of Succession stipulates that in inheritance, an "illegitimate" child will receive 1/2 the share of each "legitimate" child. The former cannot be legitimized through mother's marriage. *Practice:* In urban areas an estimated 1/2 of all children are born out of wedlock to mothers abandoned by the fathers (1980). Women have little legal protection and the chances of receiving court-ordered maintenance from the father are few. **Homosexuality.** *Policy:* Confined to the private sphere, without "disrupting the public order," sexual relations between same-sex lovers are not illegal. *Practice:* No statistics obtainable. There is no visible lesbian-rights movement, either separate from or within the feminist movement. **Incest.** *Policy:* No data obtainable. *Practice:* No data obtainable. **Sexual Harassment.** *Policy:* None. *Practice:* No statistics obtainable. Reportedly, police harassment of women out alone at night is common under the guise of checking prostitutes' registration.

Rape. *Policy:* Illegal, defined in Penal Code as forcing a person by violence or serious threat to have sexual intercourse outside of marriage. Rape by 2 or more attackers is punishable by 10 yrs. imprisonment. Also illegal are "abusive sexual acts" performed by those in authority. Marital rape is not a legal concept. *Practice:* No statistics obtainable. Domestic workers are commonly raped by the *patrón* or his sons, as it is expected that such women are sexually available. **Battery.** *Policy:* No data obtainable. *Practice:* Reportedly common. According to 1980–81 medical reports, 80% of injuries reported daily are a result of husbands battering wives. Police assistance is limited, with such complaints given low priority (see following article).

Prostitution. *Policy:* Legal, with brothels licensed and regulated by the Ministry of the Interior. Prostitutes must be registered with the government, carry ID cards, and submit to check-ups every 15 days. In the 1972 Census, prostitution was categorized as one of women's possible activities under "other services." *Practice:* 3100 prostitutes were registered in Lima and an est. additional 3000 worked illegally in 1972; the figures have risen drastically since then (see following article). The government receives income from licensing brothels (see HERSTORY). **Traditional/Cultural Practices:** No data obtainable. **Crisis Centers.** *Policy:* None. *Practice:* There are no crisis centers yet (1983), but women's groups plan to create them in the near future.

HERSTORY. Ancient Peru was inhabited by the Chavin, Chimu, Nazca, and Aymará Indians. The Incans conquered the Cuzco Valley, building a vast empire which by the time of the Spanish Conquest (1533) held power over the Andes from Ecuador to Chile—a militaristic state with an absolute monarchy and high technical skill in architecture and metallurgy.

Matriarchal systems existed in pre-Inca Peru and women retained power and influence in certain areas after the ascendance of the Incans in the 13th century C.E. On the coast, the *capullanas* (wives of the governors and chiefs) played an important political role. Mana Ocllo was a founder of the Incan Empire, together with her 3 sisters and 4 brothers, who conquered the tribes of the Cuzco Valley. She married her brother, Manco Copac, and together they founded the line of Incan rulers. Patriarchy was established under the Incans and included the practices of polygyny and *cobada* (bride-price). Virgins of the Sun were women consecrated to the service of the sun god, the supreme deity of the Incans.

Under 16th-century Spanish colonial rule, a new tribute system strained the resources of old and widowed women, who were forced to supply the majority of the corn and cloth collected by the Spaniards. Women's services as domestic workers were in great demand, causing many to migrate from the rural villages to towns starting in the late 1500's. Slav-

ery placed women at the Spaniards' disposal, and Roman Catholic mores were imposed.

José de San Martín and Simón Bolívar led the independence struggle against Spain (1820–24), ending with the defeat of Spanish forces at Júnin and Ayacucho. A constitution was promulgated in 1860. Spain acknowledged Peru's independence in 1879.

The first glimmerings of a women's movement began in the early 1900's. María Jesús Alvarado Rivera was the driving force behind the early suffrage movement for 14 years. She dropped out of school after primary level, but continued her own education, becoming a teacher and sociologist and opening a free school for workers' daughters. In 1911 she gave a public lecture on women's rights that shocked many people. She founded Evolución Femenina (1916) as the first women's organization, which won the right of women to serve on public-welfare committees, and she headed the suffrage battle in 1923. Alvarado Rivera became secretary of the Peru National Council of Women, an arm of the International Women's Suffrage Assoc., in 1924. She published pamphlets which supported Indians' and women's rights and an 8-hour workday, and which criticized the repressive government. When she proposed a Civil Code reform to give women equality, she was imprisoned as a political troublemaker in Dec. 1924 for 3 months of solitary confinement. Subsequently, she was exiled and lived in Argentina for 12 years.

Women joined various social movement organizations in the 1930's, including the Popular Revolutionary Alliance of America (APRA); Magda Portal, a novelist and poet, was a leader in APRA. Portal, reflecting her party's stance, came out against women's suffrage, believing that only privileged women would qualify as voters; many women deserted APRA when it ignored women's rights. Suffrage was finally granted by Pres. Manuel A. Odría in 1955 in a bid for re-election votes.

Peasant women were active in the uprisings that spread through the highlands in the 1960's, and young educated women joined social-change movements.

Feminist groups formed in the 1970's as women became disillusioned with male-dominated political groups. The Flora Tristan group was started by intellectuals in 1971. The Alliance for the Liberation of Peruvian Women (ALIMUPER) was created in 1973; 2 years later, for International Women's Year, the government set up the National Commission for Peruvian Women, an umbrella for professional, community, and union groups.

Feminism came to major public attention in 1977 as women organized a drive for abortion on demand; the campaign included television debates. The issue split the feminist ranks, with more moderate women choosing other priorities. Women's groups multiplied from the late 1970's on, as independents or as affiliates of political parties. Women participated in strikes by teachers and government employees; Leftist women became dissatisfied with their roles in Left groups, and created such organizations as the Manuela Ramos Movement, which incorporated Leftist and feminist theory to work with poor urban women. The Flora Tristan Center, successor to its earlier namesake, was formed in 1979 to do outreach to working-class and poor women and publish information on sexuality and contraceptives. The same year, Asociación Perú-Mujer, a feminist collective, was founded to work with women in the new developments on the outskirts of Lima; one of their first projects trained women in community management and leadership.

The Feminist Militancy (MIFE) proposed changes in the Family Code for the new 1979 Constitution. The Coordinating Committee of Feminist Organizations formed in that year, bringing together ALIMUPER, Flora Tristan, Manuela Ramos, Women in Struggle, and the Socialist Women's Front. The first women's center opened in Lima with Creativity and Change (a publishing and information center) on the first floor, ALIMUPER on the second, and Flora Tristan Center on the third.

A march to protest violence against women and pornography was held in Nov. 1981. The Lima Woman's Bookstore opened and feminist publications appeared: *La Tortuga,* a monthly magazine, and *Mujer y Sociedad* (Woman and Society). Feb. 1982 was a month of intense feminist activity, with 12 women's groups organizing against the government's hosting of the Miss Universe contest in Lima. Prostitutes in the port city of Callao organized demonstrations against the abusive treatment, violence, and exploitation to which they are subjected by officials and crime syndicates; they announced plans for a union. The first women's-studies course was launched that year in Lima at the Catholic University. In 1983 the Second Feminist Conference of Latin America and the Caribbean was held in Lima.

MYTHOGRAPHY. Pachamama was the Incan goddess of the crops, revered by the farming population. People of the coastal region had their own goddess, Mamacocha, who ruled the sea in the shape of a great whale. The moon was revered as Mamaquila (Golden Mother).

PERU: "Not Even with a Rose Petal . . ."
by Ana María Portugal
(Translated by Magda Bogin)

In Lima—founded in 1535 by Pizarro's *conquistadores* and capital of the once thriving vice-royalty of Peru—the vice-regal spirit has persisted in the gestures and expressions of a culture unable to shape or reaffirm its own identity, its own roots. The image of the vice-royalty, a sort of "colonial Arcadia," affects not only economics but also the political and cultural life of the country.

"Not even with a rose petal (strike a woman)" is the essence of an attitude that can be termed collective to the degree that it represents one of the values in the canon of accepted social behavior of the dominant class. It makes explicit the idea which in (good) Spanish we call *caballerosidad:* chivalry. This is the inheritance of the Spanish *conquistadores* who, despite their rape of Native Indian women, took their place in history as knights errant. It is in this feudal-patriarchal world that the lives of Peruvian women unfold.

The word "woman" in Peru is linked directly to the image that the middle class holds of its own women. This is why no one is surprised when it is affirmed that Peruvian women have no need of liberation "because they have the same rights as men." Most incredible is the fact that many women agree. But who are these women? Generally those few who managed to escape the four walls of their homes to find work among males: the executive secretary who speaks three languages, has been to Europe, and reads *Cosmopolitan;* the television model who warns: "We don't need to liberate ourselves from anything, we've been liberated for ages." Also in this category are the token women who have succeeded: the banker, the jurist, the ambassador.

But how many women are actually in the work force? According to the 1972 census, out of a total of 6,753,678 women in the country, 3,831,147 are over fifteen years old. Of these, 2,564,842 are housewives and only 763,150 work outside the home, while 506,175 are unemployed. According to these figures, there are four men working for every woman. As to the type of work women do, 27 percent of all working women in the country are secretaries, cashiers, and saleswomen; 8.3 percent work in factories and shops; 29.9 percent are street vendors; and 18.4 percent work as maids. We should also mention professional women—still a minority; in the highest-paying professions (naturally considered "masculine") such as medicine, law, engineering, and architecture, there are eleven men for every woman.

A Multiple Woman

Only a realistic analysis—one capable of situating the problem in an economic, social, and political context—can give full dimension to the issues. This analysis will show that the word "woman" in Peru is multiple. There is no one Peruvian Woman, because there are many Peruvian women who belong to different social classes. The peasant woman or the woman factory worker rarely contemplates her lack of equality by calling upon abstract rights. (Many do not even know that such rights exist.)

Peasant women suffer the double oppression of being female and of belonging to a social group that has been exploited for centuries. In general, peasant women in Peru are illiterate and/or do not speak Spanish, which is officially the first language of the country despite the fact that Peru is a multilingual nation. (There are no fewer than twelve large linguistic groups spread over Peru's three regions. In the jungle alone there are approximately nine. The most widely spoken vernaculars are Quechua and Aymará, both of which are spoken mainly in the Sierras.)

According to census data from 1972 there is a combined Quechua- and Aymará-speaking monolingual population of 1,608,183. Of these, 1,013,325 are women. (The same figures show 594,858 men who are unable to communicate in Spanish.) But for the past three decades there has been an intense urban expansion directly linked to the level of economic development. Of every 100 Peruvians, 65 now live in the cities; the population as a whole has thus ceased to be predominantly Andean and has moved toward the coast. In 1981, almost one in three Peruvians was living in Lima.

The unequal growth of urban and rural areas can be explained by the flow of migrants seeking improved living conditions. Particularly in the last decade, there has been an increase in the number of peasant women who have moved to Lima from the mountains.

These women enter urban culture either as street vendors or peddlers or as maids *(sirvientas);* this in the best of cases, because many become trapped in prostitution when they are unable to obtain a steady job. It is estimated that three or four women become prostitutes every day in Lima (at least two of whom are peasants from the provinces). As to legalized prostitution, in Lima alone—a city of 5 million inhabitants—there are 70,000 women "employed" as prostitutes.

Laws and Abuses

If we wanted to speak of advances in women's status, we would have to point to Article 2 of the Constitution: "Each person is equal before the law, with no discrimination because of race, religion, opinion, or language. Men and women have the same rights, opportunities, and responsibilities. The law does not grant women any fewer rights than men." In political terms, women have been considered "full citizens with the right to vote" since 1955.[1] The Constitution also prohibits any distinction between legitimate and illegitimate children and establishes the right of mothers to protection from the State in case of need. Furthermore, there is labor legislation that is favorable to women workers.[2] In marked contrast to all this, the Código Civil (Civil Code) of 1936[3] is still in effect and formally considers women inferior to men. Article 5 states that "men and women shall enjoy the same civil rights with the exception of the restrictions established regarding married women." It also stipulates that the husband holds power in a marriage.

Of course, for feminists it is not simply a question of improving certain laws or eliminating obsolete ones. The central issues lie in the daily life of a society whose highest and most sacred values are "God, Country, and Family." The sanctifying of the family has played a determining role in shaping the characteristics of Peruvian *machismo.* (Article 162 of the Civil Code: "The husband shall choose the domicile of the family, as well as make all decisions relating to its economic well-being." Article 173: "The wife may work in any profession or employment, as well as perform any job outside the common domicile, *with the express or tacit consent of her husband.")* It is not infrequent for Peruvian husbands, therefore, to resort to violence to make their authority felt. This is important to know: *between 70 and 80 percent of crimes reported daily to the Peruvian police are cases of women who have been beaten by their husbands.* This brutal, commonplace reality strips the mask from "Peruvian chivalry," whose real face smiles in perverse delight at the Sierra folklore phrase, "The more you hit me the more I love you." This attitude is responsible for numerous contributions to our national literature, more than one caricature, many jokes, and, yes, innumerable beatings. And these beatings, which Sierra men are particularly inclined to lavish on their women, are known poetically as "Sierra love" *(amor Serrano).*

[1] The new Constitution of 1979 grants illiterate Peruvians (approximately 2 million) the right to vote. However, only a small percentage of these newly eligible voters took part in the general elections of 1980, owing to the government's lack of interest in promoting their participation; particularly high was the absenteeism of illiterate women voters, whose number was 1,444,225 in the 1972 census.

[2] Law Decree 22183 from 1978 establishes that all women workers—factory workers and office or shop workers—will receive daily maternity benefits for forty-two days before and after delivery, on the condition they do not do any remunerative work during that period. There is also a provision that requires all businesses with more than twenty-five women to set up a day-care center.

[3] In 1981 the government of Fernando Belaúnde Terry named a commission to elaborate proposed changes of the new Civil Code. In 1978 the feminists of ALIMUPER [see text] had waged a campaign to bring about changes in the Code.

The Mask of Class Oppression

Peru is an underdeveloped country that is dependent on imperialism. Within this framework, the forms of oppression are many and specific, because not only such vast portions of the population as workers and peasants are oppressed, but also women and the various ethnic and linguistic national groups, which are oppressed in terms of sex, race, nationality, *and* language. *Thus, class oppression, which is the most widely recognized form of oppression, frequently masks other forms of oppression.* In the case of women, the male-female relationship transcends the concept of class. This means that women as a sex are oppressed and exploited. However, women of economically oppressed classes are doubly exploited: as sex *and* as class. This is why class struggle and feminist struggle are two currents that converge in a single historical objective: changing the system. . . .[4]

Ten years have passed since the founding of ALIMUPER—Acción para la Liberación de la Mujer Peruana.[5] This period has seen the rise of such new groups as the Centro de la Mujer Peruana Flora Tristán (Flora Tristan Peruvian Women's Center), the Frente Socialista de Mujeres (Socialist Women's Front), the Movimiento Manuela Ramos (Manuela Ramos Movement) and Mujeres en Lucha (Women in Struggle). What all these groups have in common is their definition as socialist-feminists, balanced by their belief in the need to fight for the autonomy of the women's movement. With the creation of the Coordinadora de Organizaciones Feministas (Coordinating Committee of Feminist Organizations) in 1979, their joint objective was reaffirmed: to unify the struggle and gain strength.

The class origin of the Peruvian feminist movement is, to use Marxist terminology, "petit bourgeois" (as are all the various Marxist groups themselves). Feminism has gained recruits mainly from the universities and professional circles, including party members, intellectuals, artists, sociologists, and writers. But feminist groups do involve themselves in attracting women from the poorer classes, particularly housewives from the slums and women factory workers. This is an arduous task in a depoliticized country with practically no tradition of social organizing.

The feminist message comes up against the rejection of the very women to whom it is addressed, who have been raised with the traditional expectation (aggravated by the Iberian-Judeo-Islamic-Catholic-Counter-Reform heritage) that a woman's primary mission on earth is to procreate "all the children that God sends her."[6] On the other hand, feminism also meets up with an economic and social reality so dramatic that, ironically, it does not allow women from the poorer classes to recognize that they are also oppressed *as women.*

At present, such issues as the legalization of free abortion on demand, the right to contraception, and the campaign against male violence have turned out to be minority struggles to the degree that they are not considered "legitimate" either by the Left or by those women who see feminism as something "exotic," "imported," or "unnecessary." In

---

[4.] "Hacia un Feminismo Socialista" (Toward a Socialist Feminism), ALIMUPER pamphlet, Lima, Nov. 1979.

[5.] ". . . ALIMUPER as a Socialist Feminist Movement does not claim to be a messianic mass organization controlling the 'correct line.' It seeks only to be a catalyst in raising consciousness, especially that of our most oppressed sisters, so that each sector can develop its own methods of work and action, autonomously and creatively, through its own organizations."

[6.] That is, a woman should produce an average of six live births during her reproductive years. The use of contraceptives is still limited, and despite government interest in population control, the Church is of course strongly opposed.

this context it is difficult to imagine a single movement that could bring together great masses of women. A plurality of feminist organizations seems more possible, each addressing the needs and realities of a different sector. For the moment the challenge is to raise consciousness about the need to organize ourselves.

Suggested Further Reading

Andradi, Esther, and Ana María Portugal. *Ser Mujer en el Perú* (To Be a Woman in Peru). Lima: Ediciónes Mujer y Autonomía, 1979.

Barrig, Maruja. *Cinturón de Castidad* (Chastity Belt). Lima: Editorial Mosca Azul, 1979.

———. *Convivir: La Pareja en la Pobreza* (Living Together: The Couple in Poverty). Lima: Editorial Mosca Azul, 1981.

Burga, Teresa, and France Cathelat. *Perfil de la Mujer Peruana* (Profile of the Peruvian Woman). Lima: Ediciones ISA y Fondo del Libro del Banco Industrial del Perú, 1981.

Ana María Portugal is an active feminist, a writer and journalist, and is author of two books of poems: *Poemas* (Poems), 1964, and *Las Celebraciones* (The Celebrations), 1969. She also co-authored, with Esther Andradi, *Ser Mujer en el Perú* (To Be a Woman in Peru). She is currently working on a book on the history of beauty contests in Peru during the past fifty years.

POLAND
(Polish People's Republic)

Located in east central Europe, bounded by the USSR to the east, Czechoslovakia to the south, the GDR (East Germany) to the west, and the Baltic Sea to the north. **Area:** 311,730 sq. km. (120,359 sq. mi.). **Population** (1980): 35,525,000, female 51.1%. **Capital:** Warsaw.

DEMOGRAPHY. Languages: Polish (official) 90%, German, Russian, other. **Races or Ethnic Groups:** Polish 98%, German, Ukrainian, Byelorussian, Slovak. **Religions:** Roman Catholicism (majority), Greek Orthodox Church, Protestant, Judaism (approx. 12,000 Jews in Apr. 1983; before WW II an est. 3.5 million). **Education** (% enrolled in school, 1975): Age 6–11—of all girls 87%, of all boys 90%; age 12–17—of all girls 78%, of all boys 73%; higher education—women as graduates, 25.1% of technology, 48.4% of agriculture, 55.7% of economics, law, and administration, 68.2% of medical studies, 73.2% of humanities, math, natural science, and pedagogies (1974). Education (including university) is free and is compulsory for students age 7–17. Reports indicate that it is easier for male students to gain admission to study in art, film, agriculture, and medicine. In Jan. 1979 the unofficial "People's University" was organized by the Farmers' Self-Defense Committee and well-known intellectuals as a center for the study of subjects not taught in the State university system. Labor legislation (1975) allows employed women to receive paid leave to take educational examinations; employed women who have taken an unpaid maternity leave of 3 yrs. may enroll in schools to further their education. **Literacy** (1977): Women 97%, men 99%. **Birth Rate** (per 1000 pop., 1977): 19.5. **Death Rate** (per 1000 pop., 1977): 9. **Infant Mortality** (per 1000 live births, 1977): Female 20, male 27. **Life Expectancy** (1975–80): Female 75 yrs., male 67 yrs.

GOVERNMENT. The Politburo of the Polish United Workers' Party (Communist Party) holds supreme *de facto* power and is led by First Secretary Gen. Wojciech Jaruzelski (who is also Prime Minister, 1983). The 1952 Constitution established a unicameral Sejm (parliament) with legislative power whose 460 members are elected by universal suffrage every 4 yrs.; the Sejm elects a Council of Ministers and a Council of State, comprised of a Chair (Henryk Jablonski, 1983), Secretary, and 14 members. Local government consists of People's Councils, elected by communities and *voivod*ship (administrative regions). The People's Council Chair is Secretary of the regional Polish United Workers' Party for the area. The United Peasants' Party and the Democratic Party are the other official political parties which together with the Polish United Workers' Party and social and professional organizations make up the National Unity Front, which acts as a political platform.* **Women's Suffrage:** 1919. **Equal Rights:** The 1952 Constitution stipulates equality on the basis of sex; other legislation stipulates women's equal rights in labor, education, marriage, and family life. Equality of civil rights was granted in 1918; in the 1970's the Law of Opportunities was passed to counter discrimination against women entering universities (see **Education**). In practice, women report discrimination in the areas of government, labor, education, social, and cultural life. **Women in Government:** In 1980 there was 1 woman minister, 1 committee chair, and 1 deputy speaker, and women held 3 vice-ministry posts as well as 8 *voivod*ship offices; there were 10 women out of 102 judges of the Supreme Court. There were 106 women members (23%) in the Sejm in the late 1970's, women were approx. 1/4 of the Polish United Workers' Party members. In 1978 women were 40% of total official trade-union membership; in the late 1970's, women

---

* The first congress of the Patriotic Movement of National Rebirth was held in spring 1983; it is expected that it will replace the National Unity Front.

were 35% of union membership at lower levels and 25% at upper levels (see following article).

ECONOMY. Currency: Zloty (May 1983: 88. = $1 US). **Gross National Product** (1980): $139.8 billion. **Per Capita Income** (1980): $3900. **Women's Wages as a Percentage of Men's** (1979): Women earn an average 30% less than men in the areas of sales, clerical work, services. **Equal Pay Policy:** "Equal pay for equal work" is referred to in the 1952 Constitution (Art. 48). As of 1983, there have been no court cases challenging discrimination in salaries, although reports indicate the principle of equal pay for equal work is not applied; women teachers earned an average 30% less than men in 1975; 1981 reports showed that women factory and pharmaceutical workers were paid less than men in the same positions (see following article). **Production** (Agricultural/Industrial): Grains, potatoes, sugar beets, tobacco; ships, textiles, chemicals, wood products, metal, autos, aircraft. **Women as a Percentage of Labor Force** (1980): 46%; **of agricultural force** (1978) 49.1% (62% of whom are unpaid family workers); **of industrial force** (1978) 39.2%; **of military** —no statistics obtainable; women are not permitted to serve in the military but are allowed to work as civilians in service jobs; the only exceptions are female medical students who undergo military training (the same as male students) in the course of their studies. **(Employed) Women's Occupational Indicators** (1979): 60% of all employed women work in services, clerical work, and sales; 70% of all teachers are women, but only 10 out of 100 are in executive positions. The 1974 Labor Code prohibits female employment in jobs listed by the Council of Ministers (amended 1979), deemed "especially difficult or dangerous to health" (see **Family**). **Unemployment:** None; there is a shortage of workers in industry, agriculture, and jobs which don't require skilled labor. Persons with higher education (esp. in the humanities) may have problems finding jobs, as do those banned from their professions for political reasons.

GYNOGRAPHY. Marriage. *Policy:* The 1964 Family and Custodian Code stipulates spouses' equal rights, equality of all children, and equal cooperation between spouses for the good of the family. Legal marriage age for women is 18, for men 21. *Practice:* Female mean age at marriage (1970–78): 22; women age 15–49 in union (1970–78): 64.7%. Reports indicate that women are still relegated to traditional and often subordinate positions in marriage. **Divorce.** *Policy:* Legal; governed by the 1964 Family and Custodian Code (Art. 56); grounds include "a complete and lasting decomposition of marriage," and battery. The 1975 Alimony Fund regulates maintenance of spouses after divorce; alimony laws are stipulated in the 1964 Code—parents are obliged to pay support to children unable to maintain themselves (Art. 133), 1 spouse is obliged to provide sustenance for the other after cessation of marriage (Art. 130), and alimony obligations of fathers not married to the mothers of their children are stipulated in Arts. 141–42. The Alimony Fund is allocated to support allowances for children and other persons living in difficult material conditions due to inability to execute their rights to alimony allowances. *Practice:* Registered divorces (per 1000 pop., 1979): 1.1. A 1974 survey estimated that 66.6% of all women age 15 and over were divorced or separated, out of whom 62.7% were rural women. In 1980 the number of persons entitled to allowances from the Alimony Fund totaled 86,715.

Family. *Policy:* The 1964 Family and Custodian Code reflects constitutional principles which hold the nuclear family to be the basic, "natural" social unit. The Council for Family Affairs (created 1978) coordinates all family-support institutions. Social security system (see **Welfare**) pays family allowances and maternity benefits. In 1971 and 1974 there were increases in family allowances, giving priority to families with several children and to single mothers.

Legislation (1977) extended family allowances to unemployed wives caring for a "student-child"; in 1978 to persons employed in State-controlled industries, to craftspersons, and to self-employed persons. All women are entitled to a 1-time birth-allowance of Zl.2000, regardless of employment or income (1978). By a 1982 Regulation of the Council of Ministers, employed single mothers receive special benefits—a maternity-leave allowance double that of married mothers, and if they give birth to more than 1 (or to a sick) child, a 36-month allowance, as opposed to that of employed married mothers who are entitled to 16 weeks fully paid maternity leave after the first childbirth, 18 weeks for each successive childbirth, and 26 weeks in case of multiple birth. Maternity leave may begin 1 month prior to the estimated birth date. Women who have been employed at least 1 yr. may also take a 3-yr. unpaid leave to care for children up to age 4 (see following article for information on parental leave). Women on unpaid leave may work part time, at home, or on contract, and may enroll in school without losing their jobs (see **Education**).

All pregnant women are entitled to free pre-delivery health care. In 1978 social security benefits were extended to farmers, giving them a lump-sum maternity grant of Zl.500 at childbirth. Employed women may take paid sick leave when their children are ill; the leave was extended to fathers (1975) under limited circumstances. The 1974 Labor Code prohibits female employment in jobs deemed difficult or physically dangerous to health, and pregnant women from night employment, overtime work, and assignments distant from their permanent place of employment. If a pregnant employed woman is transferred to a lower-paying job for this reason, she is entitled to compensation allowance. If a woman's work contract ends during pregnancy and maternity leave, she is entitled to receive the maternity allowance until childbirth. State nurseries for children under age 3, kindergartens for children age 3–6, and school clubs for school-age children are available to children of employed women and men. Weekday nurseries exist for children of single women who have "difficult housing conditions from a morally neglected environment" and for families where parents or guardians work in shifts. Nurseries are organized to aid parents whose work is affected by the agricultural calendar (harvest periods, etc.). Families are entitled to a quota for rationed goods; in 1983 coffee, cigarettes, soaps, shoes, alcohol, butter, and candy were removed from the rationed list. In the spring of 1983, the government issued an edict to curtail the black market and "free market" in goods, household items, and books.

Practice: In 1974 the total number of families registered was approx. 8.8 million, of which 66.4% had children, 20.5% had no children, 10.8% were single women with children, and 1.3% single men with children. A 1967 survey indicated that only 32% of Polish married women stopped working for maternity reasons, of whom blue-collar women workers were 40%, and white-collar and professional women workers 20%. In 1969–70 only 9000 employed women took an unpaid 3-yr. maternity leave; 8.3% of all child-bearing employed women took unpaid leave in 1969. The sick leave granted to fathers was repealed when women protested that their husbands used the leave to drink and go fishing (but see following article for new feminist-backed reform proposals); Polish authorities acknowledge that alcoholism is a serious problem in Polish family life. Reports (1977) indicated that employed women spent an average of 4 hours a day doing housework in addition to paid work; only 60% of their husbands gave them "occasional" help. Women spend several hours each day standing in lines to receive their quota of rationed products. Out of the total 75% of married women who work in the labor force, 5.4% of their children under age 3, and 34% of their children age 3–7, are admitted to State-operated nurseries and kindergartens (1981).

Welfare. *Policy:* A comprehensive National Insurance System includes the following: superannuation pensions are received by State-sector employees and their families, individual farmholders, production co-op employees, the military, public militia, disabled war veterans, concentration-camp and POW victims, craftspersons, and members of artists' unions; disability pensions are available (also see Alimony Fund, above). Social Welfare Assistance covers permanent fiscal allowances (for mothers, the handicapped, etc.). Pension eligibility qualifications vary according to benefits and pensions; a person employed less than 10 yrs. is eligible for an old-age pension, but not a retirement pension (which is based on earnings). Retirement age for farmers is 65 for men, 60 for women; to be pension-eligible, men must have worked 25 yrs., women 20 yrs. (continuous work), including the 5-yr. period before retirement. A non-inheriting spouse is entitled to ½ the amount of the farmers' old-age pension and to the entire amount upon the partner's death. An orphan's pension is equal to 70% of the average old-age and disability pensions. *Practice:* No data obtainable.

Contraception. *Policy:* State family-planning campaigns began in the late 1920's to counter a high rate of illegal abortion. In 1959 a law was passed requiring doctors to give contraceptives to women who had just delivered or had abortions. National Insurance covers approx. 70% of the cost of contraceptives. *Practice:* Women age 15–49 in union using contraception (1970–80): 57%, of which traditional methods 77%, modern 23%. The first family-planning clinic began in 1928 but was closed due to opposition by both the Roman Catholic Church and the State, which pursued pro-natalist policies after the world wars. In 1957 the privately run Family Planning Assoc. began; in 1980 it was changed to the Family Development Assoc., reflecting a shift in social policies that Polish feminists view as pro-natalist. The pill and the IUD require a doctor's prescription, but other devices are sold at newspaper kiosks and stores. A 1972 survey of 16,160 married women showed that women with higher education used contraceptives twice as much as women with elementary education; the former used modern methods, the latter more traditional ones. Other reports indicated that a large % of urban women relied on the rhythm method (the only method approved by the Roman Catholic Church); twice as many urban as rural women depended on the condom method. Reports (1978) indicated that the distribution of contraceptives was scarce because over-all production was down for economic reasons.

Abortion. *Policy:* Legalized in 1956, liberalized in 1960; available on request during the first trimester; later, permitted during the second trimester exclusively for "medical indications" and called "induced delivery." Abortions performed in official government institutions are fully subsidized by the State, with a 3-day medical leave from work provided. Females age 18 or younger need parental consent. Legislation (1981) backed by the Roman Catholic Church allows a doctor to refuse to perform an abortion on "moral grounds" and requires all doctors to give abortion counseling before performing the procedure. *Practice:* Abortions (per 1000 live births, 1978): 230, the lowest rate in Eastern Europe, owing to strong Roman Catholic influence (although 1982 saw a precipitous rise, because of economic factors). From 1972 to 1978, the number of spontaneous, induced, and therapeutic abortions was approx. 300,000 annually, with ⅓ to ½ induced. Recent (1983) unofficial estimates put the figure between 800,000 and 1 million abortions annually. Women reportedly prefer to obtain abortions in private institutions (even though the fee ranges from $25–$50 per procedure), because those performed in government institutions are reported to officials. Feminists have described Polish abortion clinics as "mincemeat machines," referring to poor standards of health care and unsanitary conditions. **Illegitimacy.** *Policy:* The 1964 Family and Custodian Code stipulates protection of the "interests" of out-of-wedlock children and removes them from a separate legal category (see **Divorce**). *Practice:* In 1975 every 20th birth was out of wedlock. **Homosexuality.** *Policy:* Homosexuality is not punishable by Polish law (1980). *Practice:* No statistics obtainable. Lesbian women are "invisible," with no representative organizations, publications, etc.

Incest. *Policy:* Illegal (1964 Penal Code, Art. 175), and punishable by 6 months–5 yrs. imprisonment. *Practice:* There were 11 court cases each yr. in 1980, 1981, and 1982. **Sexual Harassment.** *Policy:* None. *Practice:* No data obtainable. **Rape.** *Policy:* 1964 Penal Code (Art. 168) stipulates penalties of 1–10 yrs. imprisonment. An accomplice in gang-rape is liable for no less than 3 yrs. imprisonment. Marital rape does not exist as a concept in the law. *Practice:* There were 1060 rape cases tried by the courts in 1979. No further data obtainable. **Battery.** *Policy:* Wife-beating is not referred to separately in the Penal Code, although Art. 184 covers general battery laws regarding family members. Penalties can range from 6 months–5 yrs. imprisonment, and battery can be grounds for divorce. *Practice:* No data obtainable. **Prostitution.** *Policy:* Not a legal offense in itself. The Penal Code (Art. 174) posits a penalty of 1–10 yrs. imprisonment for soliciting and profiting from someone else's prostitution. *Practice:* Prostitution is practiced in Warsaw and other urban centers. Records on prostitution are kept by the police, but there are no statistics obtainable on the current number of women working as prostitutes. Neither feminist groups nor women working as prostitutes are yet organizing on the issue of prostitutes' rights. **Traditional/Cultural Practices:** No data obtainable. **Crisis Centers:** No data obtainable.

HERSTORY. There is little recorded information on Polish women prior to the 20th century, but there were powerful queens such as Jadwiga (reigned 1384–99 C.E.), who ruled in Poland while her sister was Queen of Hungary. Jadwiga, today revered as a saint, married Ladislaus II of Lithuania in 1386; they reigned jointly, starting the Jagiello Dynasty, which held sway into the 16th century, considered the Golden Age of arts and culture in Poland. Polish women suffered during successive waves of invaders, including Hungarians and Ottoman Turks in the 15th and 16th centuries, and Cossacks, Russians, Swedes, and Prussians in the 17th and 18th centuries. In 1787 Poland abolished witch-trials, but the last execution for witchcraft in Europe took place in Poland in 1793. Partitioned for over 100 years, it was owing in no small part to the influence of the Countess Maria Walewska that Napoleon temporarily reconstituted the country as the duchy of Warsaw.

Emilia Plater (1806–31) was a Polish aristocrat and volunteer in the 1831 October Uprising against Russia; a famous soldier, she became a symbol of the heroism of Polish women fighting for national independence. Marie Sklodowska-Curie (1867–1934), a Polish physicist, discovered radium and polonium; together with her husband and scientific colleague, Pierre Curie, she won the Nobel Prize in 1903, and again in 1911, this time alone. (She was the first woman to receive the Nobel, and the first person to receive it twice.)

Rosa Luxemburg, born in Russian Poland in 1871, was a revolutionary and feminist who helped found the Polish Socialist Party in 1892 and another faction in 1894 (Social Democratic Party of Poland) which was allied to Russia; she became leader of the German branch of that party after 1898 (see GERMANY/EAST), and in 1905 was a leader of the Second International. A brilliant orator and writer, Luxemburg started the Sparticist Party in 1918 and was killed in 1919 for her activities. Women also were active in the Polish Resistance against the Nazis during WW II. Niuta Tietelboim, Mira Fuchrer, Dvorah Baron, Regina Fudin, Pola Elster, and Zivia Lubetkin were among the Polish Jewish leaders of the Warsaw Ghetto Uprising (Apr.–Sept. 1943). The Nazis killed over 6 million Poles and set up concentration camps (including the infamous Auschwitz) to exterminate Polish Jews. In the death camps, many women fought back: Rosa Robota and 3 other women were hanged for their role in the Auschwitz resistance.

Still later, in 1968, Polish Jewish women were among those expelled during the anti-Semitic purges. Many women were active in the student revolts of 1968, including Ursula Wislanka, a feminist writer. But the Women's League became the only official women's organization (see following article).

In 1970 Anna Walentynowicz, a crane operator at the Gdansk shipyard, led strikes protesting food-price increases; she triggered the creation of the free trade union Solidarity after she was arrested for laying a wreath at the Gdansk shipyard gates to honor workers killed in the 1970 uprising. The workers struck to get her reinstated; women workers called for "solidarity" strikes across the country.

After revolts and more strikes in 1976, Helena Lucywo, Ludwika Wujec, and Irena Woycicka wrote and edited *Robotnik,* a magazine that was banned by the government. In 1978 peasant women in Gorney and Osterwek brandished sickles to protest a new retirement tax for farmers, then organized a milk strike, refusing to deliver milk to State collection points. On Aug. 3, 1980, workers won a curb on censorship and the right to organize independent trade unions; Solidarity became a free trade union, and its demands included those of women workers —day care, kindergartens, a 3-yr. paid maternity leave. Women continue to be active in the underground Solidarity movement in the 1980's: in Katowice, women were attacked and their arms and legs broken by police when they blocked the entrance to a worker-occupied steel mill; at the Wujek mine in Silesia, women threw tear gas and lay in front of advancing trucks to prevent police from arresting the miners. At Gdansk in 1980, 3000 women handed out flowers and Solidarity bulletins while facing tanks ready to crush the shipyard gates. In Dec. 1980 Halina Bortnowska led workers in a general strike at the Lenin steelworkers' plant in Cracow. Krystyna Kowalewska was one of the founders of SIGMA, a feminist student organization with approx. 100 members in late 1980. That same year the Neofeminists' Assoc. was founded (see following article). Women comprise 50% of Solidarity, although as of 1982, only 1 member of Solidarity's national council was female; 7.8% of the delegates to Solidarity's national conference were women.

In 1981 over 10,000 women and children in Lodz staged mass demonstrations to protest martial law, carrying the banner "Hungry Women of the World Unite." In Oct. of that year, a similar strike was held in Zyradow, where women textile workers struck for 4 weeks, refusing to elect representatives but instead acting *en masse.* In July 1982 Anna Walentynowicz was released from the Goldap camp where she had been since her 1981 arrest, but she was picked up again 6 weeks later and held in custody. Other underground labor activists include Alina Pienkowska and Joanna Duda-Gwazda, both leaders in the Gdansk strikes.

In early 1983 the government drew criticism from women for publishing "for profit" a calendar of nude women; 20,000 copies were sold before it was recalled. In May 1983 a Franciscan convent in Warsaw was broken into by government troops, who beat and arrested some of the nuns accused of hiding the families of certain jailed Solidarity activists. As of July 1983 the issue at stake for Poles remains articulated by a women-originated but now general popular slogan: "Bread and Freedom."

MYTHOGRAPHY. The Celtic and Teutonic undercurrent of goddess worship has persisted in Polish iconography up to the present, with the figure of Mary holding a particularly powerful place of veneration in contemporary Roman Catholic Poland.

POLAND: "Let's Pull Down the Bastilles Before They Are Built"[1]
by Anna Titkow

I am by profession a sociologist—and that undoubtedly determines the style of my article. However, I hope that this professional approach turns out to be helpful in presenting

[1] The title has been taken from the collection *Myśli nieuczesane nowe,* Jerzy Stanislaw LEC (Kraków: Wydawnictwo Literackie, 1964).

the specifics of the situation of Polish women. This specificity resolves itself into the bald fact that in 1981, equality of the sexes in Poland is only a trite platitude—although it does exist "formally."

It has been legally guaranteed in the Constitution and in other legislation of my country. Moreover, particular indicators are visible: similar average levels of education achieved by men and women (measured by the numbers of completed school grades, it is 8.8 percent for women and 9 percent for men), a similar ratio of both sexes in the labor market (46 percent of employees in the State-controlled enterprises are women). In my 1979 research I found that the average occupational prestige of working men and women is approximately the same. Women have been formally guaranteed the opportunity to combine occupational and family roles. In 1948 both blue- and white-collar mothers were granted a twelve-week paid maternity leave. In 1972 the length of the leave was extended to sixteen weeks for the first child and eighteen weeks for those that followed. *Un*paid one-year-long maternity leaves came into force in 1968 and were extended to three years in 1972. (Unpaid maternity leaves can be taken *after* the paid leaves.)

At the same time, however, no women are present in the government, or in the groups of decision makers, or in the authorities of the Polish Workers' Party, or in the leadership of the free trade-union movement, Solidarity. Women do not dominate in low-prestige occupations, but sex equality in occupational prestige in Poland seems to be rather vacuous; power and income are not its correlates. Women's employment does prevail in the worst-paid branches of the national economy: education, health care, administration, and various services. In 1979 women comprised the majority of workers in the service sector (90 percent)—among clerks (76 percent) and salespeople (90.4 percent). About 60 percent of all working women are employed in the above-mentioned branches, and they earn 30 percent less than men. Occupational promotion of women is much more difficult than that of men, even in such "feminized" occupations as, for example, teaching—where women comprise 70 percent of the employees, but only 10 in 100 women hold executive posts.

The all-Polish surveys on time-budget show that professionally working women are four times more burdened with housework than men. On the average, men spend about one hour and thirteen minutes daily on housework, while women spend four hours and forty-five minutes. This includes women's twelvefold-more-frequent meals (cooking and cleaning), and twentyfold-more-often washing and ironing. One must not forget that 75 percent of Polish married women work professionally. In such a context it is needless to comment on how these women are affected by the fact that only 5.4 percent of children up to three years old and 34 percent of children aged three to seven years of professionally working women are admitted to kindergartens.

Why does it happen so? What stands in the way of carrying into effect real sex equality? We do have legal guarantees for it; the more-than-a-century-old tradition of a campaign for women's equal rights (men also participated in the campaign); for thirty-five years we have assumed the ideology of total sex equality in a socialist country. (I might add that these assumptions get strong support from very noisy propaganda.) Then why?

In my opinion, several factors cooperate in contributing to such a situation. The main ones would be: historical and cultural traditions, the character of post-World War II socioeconomic changes, the influence of the Roman Catholic Church, and the inertia and "passivity" of women.

In the history of Poland, our statehood did not exist for over 120 years (1795–1918) since the country was partitioned by three world powers. Circumstances demanded courage, caution, devotion, and prowess from women. With men fighting, imprisoned, and killed, women had to become family heads, pursue businesses, and take care of their children's future. Women safeguarded Polish nationality and religion; they worked in conspiracy, conducted the underground teaching of the Polish language, promoted agriculture and health education in the villages. One legacy from that period is the (stereotypical) cultural pattern which casts a woman as a heroic person capable of coping with all the duties burdening her—and still retaining her "feminine charm." Right now, when I am writing these words, Poland is passing through a deep sociopolitical and economic crisis. Women bear the direct consequences of the crisis. After finishing their jobs they queue for hours to buy food; they take responsibility in extremely difficult present conditions for the organization of family life and the satisfaction of its needs. While men, as before, struggle with other men—either for preserving the previous state of affairs or for its democratic change. (In spite of all claims to modernity, this resembles a rather feudal pattern of social relations.)

Women Workers as an Economic Variable

After 1945, one more important element was added to the above-outlined multi-roled, heroic pattern of Polish women: professional work. Equality in civil rights for the sexes had been granted in 1918, just after Poland had regained its statehood and independence. However, such equality did not provide sufficient stimulus for women's activism, owing mainly to economic depression and unemployment. After World War II the situation changed. A significant role was played by the economic advancement of postwar Poland, its two dimensions in particular: industrialization and urbanization. In the first years of our second independence, as many women as possible were recruited for all branches of the national economy. The second essential factor responsible for the rapid occupational activity of women was the low level of average salaries: many families required two salaries monthly to satisfy their basic needs.

This raises the question as to whether such an occupational "activation" helps women define their identity, test their own capabilities, and enrich aspirations. We can assume that, as the sociologist Ludwik Krzywicki wrote at the turn of the nineteenth century: "Economic conditions do not ask about likes and dislikes. They detach woman from her home and, placing her in new circumstances, sometimes develop in her new tastes. . . ." But there is another factor which is an even bigger hindrance to women's making use of opportunities beyond a family circle. In the course of the last three decades, the declared model of the position of women in Polish society was switched from one extreme to another. Whether women's work was needed or not depended mainly on the economic situation, the requirements of the labor market, and the accepted ideology of a given period. In the years 1945–54, when all hands were needed for labor, the streets were full of posters with joyfully smiling women tractor drivers, women streetcar drivers. But about 1958 "the homecoming" of women was promoted. From then until the late 1960's these two attitudes were combined into one "feminine issue." The 1970's in turn, were a period of intensive pronatal policy and of shifting the responsibility for medical and educational institutions onto families (and for "families" read "women").

Can anyone feel like a seriously treated partner or develop new definitions of self-identity in such a climate? One must not forget that in a sociopolitical system like Poland's every decision or ideological trend is of a macrosocial value; everything takes place on a mass scale. No wonder that urging women to take jobs outside the house is not enough for a social change on the individual level to occur. It should also be noted that the professionally working woman and the fulltime homemaker both perceive the institution of marriage in an identical way: marriage is seen as insurance for life—and this is not a comforting fact. Equally little comfort comes from another fact: that working women are more prone to claim that having children is worthwhile "because children are the main goal of life."

A Conspiracy of Church and State

A climate so unfavorable for women's rights has been supported all this time by the Catholic Church. This, in addition to the political authorities, is of course another monopolistically acting social power. The Church is not in authority in the literal meaning of the word, but it enjoys unvaryingly great respect in Polish society. Consequently, we have two centers of power influencing the formation of patterns of behavior. In spite of the fact that the ideological assumptions of these two centers are radically different, *their actions cause similar results vis à vis women.* The effect of this unintended cooperation between Party bureaucrats and Church clerks is the exploitation of women—accompanied, to be sure, by appearances of equality, respect, and even mawkish gallantry.

The Church's influence on defining women's position in Polish society, where 75 percent of women are faithful and practicing Catholics, hardly has to be proven—especially when we constantly hear how woman's domain is home and family while man's world is his job, politics, and all activites outside the family circle. It seems to me that Poland's greater tolerance for the premarital sexual life of men than for that of women can also be attributed to the Church's influence.

Passivity? Or Powerlessness?

I hope that a question arises now in the minds of my readers, a question about the attitudes of women themselves, or even the impression that they were and still are rather passive. Historical epochs and political systems changed, while women continued to function according to the "norm" that they are brave, resourceful, capable of coping with all requirements, and selfless. Such an attitude is visible in all serious issues, even those concerning them directly. Just one example: at the turn of the 1920's there were constant attempts (initiated by men, by the way) to draft and pass a bill that would legalize the right to abortion. Without success. But when the campaign was being carried on to pass the bill and establish centers of Planned Parenthood, the primary concern of women's magazines was to enlighten their readers on such various issues as homemade marmalades, fish soups, and crocheting braids. The bill was not passed until 1956, and this happened without any initiative or participation on the part of women. That legal act was the core of the policy to laicize our society.

The word "inertia" has a strong emotional coloring. I have no right, I think, to write about Polish women's inertia as regards the struggle for their rights after 1945. There is not much freedom left in our sociopolitical system for active, non-official organizations to function and fill the social vacuum between family and State. There does still exist one official women's organization, the Women's League. The scope of its activity has been limited to financial matters: welfare benefits, allowances, and aid to women in difficult situations (for example, wives of alcoholics). It has been unable, however, to strive for real equal rights because of its clumsiness and its hierarchical, strongly bureaucratic character which leaves no place for individual initiative. It was organized and managed by authorities and clerks, and therefore it has never truly represented women's interests; for example, it did not realize the importance of so vital an issue as easy access to reliable contraceptives for women, and that issue has not been settled to this very day.

What I have written here proves, I hope, that it would be a simplification to maintain that we Polish women are discriminated against solely by men or by our enemies. Men constitute but one element in the configuration of tradition, the undertaking of professional careers by women, the specificity of a political system which prefers monopolistic solutions, and erroneous social policy which hardly ever had any strategy in the fight for women's equal rights. Names of a great number of men might be cited here, from both past and present times, as women's-rights supporters; particularly worth mentioning is

Tadeusz Boy-Zelenski, a physician and translator of French literature, who in the 1930's launched a campaign against "the hell endured by women."

Solidarity—and Feminist Rumblings

Where, then, are the potentials which allow us to cherish some hope that equal rights between the sexes will ever become a reality?

One such potential may be found, in my opinion, in ever-spreading education on a hitherto unachieved level, and in providing gainful employment for women. This will enable further improvement of the society's average level of education, increase change in the polarization of its attitudes, facilitate the formation of new patterns of behavior and, finally, bring about an enriched perception of one's individual relations to the outer world. Just two examples:

Simplifying a little, it may be said that in Poland the degree of sex rigorism reveals an individual's way of thinking, which can be either traditional or modern. Furthermore, research proves that women's occupational careers release the corset of their restrictive norms; it is well known that those women who perceive themselves in the roles of both mother and wife as well as of a person realizing herself through work (and this is the opinion of 42 percent of Polish women) have emotionally richer attitudes toward their children than those women who identify themselves only with the roles of mother and wife.

If we define radical feminism as a search for the root causes of our suffering, then the above-characterized kind of hope will enable us to eradicate these roots in the future. I do not think, however, that this will happen very soon. Social processes follow their own rules and require time; they transform social consciousness slowly but in a profound way. Seventy percent of our society are of peasant origin, a social class where the patriarchal model of family life prevails. So it will take time for Poles to adopt other, new ways of living, all the more so if actual social policy does not undergo any change.

Another potential lies behind the processes and changes that have been taking place in my country since August of 1980. The mass movement which conceived the Independent Self-Governed Trade Union Solidarity has activated the whole society. The movement is democratic, is open to new ideas and initiatives, and inspires the whole society—*except* for us, the women. It is we who are burdened with the results of the economic crisis which, together with other factors, gave rise to the people's protest in August 1980. How to feed our families is our everyday worry. But we do have some satisfaction, since it was in defense of a fired woman worker that the Gdańsk 1980 strike broke out in the first place, and at the most critical moment it was a young female nurse who encouraged the workers to continue the strike.*

The August outburst has not produced any women's movement, so far. But it is quite obvious why this is so. We have had some bad experiences with mass women's organizations, the country's situation is really grave, and the so-called feminine issue can be made to appear rather unserious at the present moment. Nevertheless, the over-all animation generated by August of 1980—which can be described as this society's struggle for socialism with a human face—has made some changes possible. Here are two examples closely connected with the situation of women:

Until July of 1980 it was only a mother who was entitled to a maternity leave. Under pressure from women *(and* women's magazines, a suddenly revolutionized Women's League, and the Neofeminists' Association, founded in 1980), the government, though reluctant, did give in—and now parental leave is granted to fathers as well. This was a great success.

* See Statistical Preface preceding this article.—Ed.

Poland boasts of having introduced a reform on abortion rights as early as 1956. For the last few years a group of the reform's opponents, closely connected with Catholic circles, has been very active, advocating "the protection of life." But the reform has its supporters, among both women and men. Letters keep pouring in to editors (not only of women's magazines), presenting all the pros and cons of these two attitudes. The Minister of Health and Welfare was provoked into discussing this problem at the editorial office of the leading women's magazine. I am presently trying to collect arguments in favor of abortion rights by conducting an all-Poland survey of women's opinions on this question. For the time being, it seems that the abortion reform will resist the attack.

Neofeminism—and Hope

Let us consider the most suitable formula for a feminist movement in Poland. I have already mentioned our reluctance to join mass women's movements; a mass women's organization has proven a poor advocate of our interests. The same opinion was held by a group of women who established the Neofeminists' University Association in 1980. They receive no salaries, have no office or telephones; informality seems to be their strength. They are exerting pressure on all those who decide about a broadly understood policy toward family and women. For example, Neofeminists collaborated with the Women's League to extend maternity leave to parental leave. They alert the League's activists to new problems and new perspectives—and they find acceptance. Who are these young women and men (the latter are granted the status of supporters) who have decided to come up with some action on their own? They are mainly students, with a sprinkling of (university-educated) professionally working people. There are thirty of them and they range in age from twenty to sixty years. Their main goal is to endow the sexes with equal social and economic status. They want to propagate the idea of the personal development of a woman as an individual, and their ambition is to so deeply transform women's consciousness that women no longer yield to stereotypes and social pressure. They want women to realize and live up to their own needs. As to practical matters, their program includes, among other things: social benefits for women not working professionally (pensions first of all), the right for a *father* to take a day off if a child is ill, and general improvement of services with reference to women's needs. All of these reforms are to be put into practice by various pressure groups influenced by the feminists.

It is very difficult to make any predictions about the future of the feminist movement in my country when the future of the country itself is uncertain. But one thing I know. There are many Bastilles, the building of which women can obviate. Because it is not only men who build them for us; women sometimes erect Bastilles on our own. But we can pull them down—before *and* after they are built.

Suggested Further Reading

Sokolowska, Magdalena. "Poland: Women's Experience Under Socialism." *Roles and Status in Eight Countries.* Ed. J. Zollinger Giele and A. Chapman Smock. New York: Wiley, 1977.

———. "Women in Decision Making Elites: The Case of Poland." *Access to Power: Cross-National Studies of Women and Elites.* Eds. Cynthia F. Epstein and Rose L. Coser. London: Allen & Unwin, 1981.

Szczepanski, Jan. *Polish Society.* New York: Random House, 1970.

Anna Titkow was born in Poland 42 years ago. She graduated from the University of Warsaw and took her Ph.D. in sociology; she works at the Institute of Philosophy and

Sociology, Polish Academy of Sciences, her focuses being the sociology of medicine, family planning, and sex roles. She is the chairperson of the Medical Sociology Section of the Polish Sociological Association, and she lives in Warsaw with her husband, Andrzej Titkow, a movie director, and her fifteen-year-old son, Tomasz.

PORTUGAL
(Republic of Portugal)

Portugal lies in the west of the Iberian Peninsula, bordered by Spain to the north and east, the Strait of Gibraltar to the south, and the Atlantic Ocean to the west. **Area:** 91,531 sq. km. (35,340 sq. mi.). **Population** (1980): 9,936,000, female 53%. **Capital:** Lisbon.

DEMOGRAPHY. Languages: Portuguese. **Races or Ethnic Groups:** Portuguese, African minority. **Religions:** Roman Catholicism 98% (by baptism; 30% practicing). **Education** (% enrolled in school, 1975): Age 6–11—of all girls 97%, of all boys 98%; age 12–17—of all girls 54%, of all boys 57%; higher education—in 1982 women were 43.7% of all students. **Literacy** (1977): Women 65%, men 78%. **Birth Rate** (per 1000 pop., 1975–80): 17. **Death Rate** (per 1000 pop., 1975–80): 10. **Infant Mortality** (per 1000 live births, 1975–80): Female 35, male 43. **Life Expectancy** (1975–80): Female 72 yrs., male 66 yrs.

GOVERNMENT. The 1976 Constitution provides for the popular election of a president and of the 250-seat unicameral Assembly of the Republic. As of Apr. 1983, power was held by a coalition government of the Socialist and Social Democratic parties. **Women's Suffrage:** 1976 —full political rights. In 1931 women could vote only if they had a university degree or secondary-school qualifications; in 1946 there were different requirements for women than for men running for election to the National Assembly; in 1968 women won equal political rights but only "heads of families" could run for or elect local councils. **Equal Rights:** Equal duties, rights, privileges, and equality before the law are stipulated by Art. 13 of the 1976 Constitution to all citizens regardless of sex. In 1980 a Committee on Women's Status (at work on an exploratory basis since 1970) was established. **Women in Government:** Maria de Lourdes Pintasilgo became the first woman Minister of Social Affairs in 1974 and the first woman Prime Minister in 1979. In 1981 women were named to 4 of the 60 posts in the new government; Mariana Calhau became civil governor of Evora; and 8.8% of the National Assembly deputies were women. A diplomatic career was not open to women until 1975; women constituted 9% of the diplomatic service in 1983. As of June 1, 1983, women comprised 7.2% of the National Assembly; of 305 municipal offices, 6 women were elected (Dec. 1982); there are no women in the cabinet of the new government elected Apr. 1983.

ECONOMY. Currency. Escudo (May 1983: 99. = $1 US). **Gross National Product** (1980): $23.1 billion. **Per Capita Income** (1980): $2350. **Women's Wages as a Percentage of Men's** (1981 average): 76% (not including agriculture, public administration, defense, cultural activities, and service sector); in 1982 women earned 35.7% of men's wages in agriculture, 52.8% in industry. **Equal Pay Policy:** The 1976 Constitution (Art. 53) guarantees equal salaries for equal or comparable work. In practice, wage discrimination against women continues. **Production** (Agricultural/Industrial): Grains, potatoes, olives, wine, grapes; textiles, footwear, wood pulp, paper, cork, metal, refined oil, chemicals, canned fish. **Women as a Percentage of Labor Force** (1980): 40.5%; **of agricultural force** 51% (70% of whom are unpaid family workers); **of industrial force** —no general statistics obtainable (of manufacturing 38.8%); in 1970 women were only a small % of the total industrial work force (of which 64.4% were concentrated in the textile industries, while 2/3 of the work force in the food, drink, and tobacco industries was female); **of military**—no statistics obtainable; women have not been permitted to serve, although the first woman naval cadet was admitted to the academy in 1982. **(Employed) Women's Occupational Indicators** (1980): Of science and liberal professions 7.7%, of clerical work 11.9%, of nonagricultural manual workers 22%; female manual workers represent 60.7% of the total employed female labor force, and are concentrated largely in domestic service; 74% of unpaid family helpers and other unpaid workers are women (28% of the female work force). **Unemployment** (2nd semester, 1981): 7.9%, female 12.3%, male 4%.

GYNOGRAPHY. Marriage. *Policy:* Prior to 1976, married women owed their husbands "obedience" by law. Today husbands and wives have equal rights and obligations (political, civil, social, and with regard to child maintenance) under the 1976 Constitution. In 1977 the Civil Code was amended to raise the marriage age for females to 16, the same as for males, and the amended Code recognized the value of housework and childcare as equivalent to paid employment. Law 37 (1981) made transmission of citizenship equal for Portuguese women marrying foreign nationals to that for Portuguese men. In a 1978 revision of the Civil Code, the term "head of household" was obliterated. Either marriage partner may add the other's name to her/his own. *Practice:* Female mean age at marriage (1970–78): 23; women age 15–49 in union (1970–78): 60%; husbands are generally regarded as "heads of household" by society.

Divorce. *Policy:* The first law legalizing divorce was passed in 1910. In 1949 the signing of the "Concordat" made divorce illegal for couples married in the Church, but in 1975 divorce was extended to cover Church marriages. There are 2 types of divorce allowed: by mutual consent and (if contested) by court order —on grounds of misconduct or on "no-fault" irretrievable breakdown of marriage if the couple has been separated 6 yrs., if 1 partner has deserted for at least 4 yrs., or if 1 has deteriorated mental faculties for over 6 yrs. *Practice:* Divorces (per 1000 pop., 1975): 0.16; in 1979 there were 5866 divorces (not counting separations). Separations are common and divorce is reportedly on the rise.

Family. *Policy:* All economically active women (including household servants) receive 90 days paid maternity leave; they may not be dismissed during leave or for 1 yr. after childbirth. A woman has the right to 2 half-hour nursing periods per workday. There is no paternity leave.

Provisions have been made by the Constitution for optional and free pre-school education for children age 3 and older. No legal provisions are made for younger children. *Practice:* In 1982 government childcare covered 50,000 children; private centers covered 120,000 children. There were 946 primary-school classes accommodating 23,000 children in 1980–81, an insufficient number of spaces to meet the need. **Welfare.** *Policy:* State Social Security grants family allowances for children and young disabled people, childbirth benefits, milk allowances, allowances for attendance of special schools, marriage allowances, and funeral allowances. Old-age and death-of-a-spouse benefits cover employees in the public and private sector (domestic service and rural workers included). *Practice:* No statistics obtainable, but the programs reportedly are insufficient to the need.

Contraception. *Policy:* In accord with the 1976 Constitution, the government supports "responsible parenthood" and promotes family planning and contraception education; there were 250 advice centers in 1979. *Practice:* Women age 15–49 in union using contraception (1982): 77%, of which reversible methods 53%, traditional 45%, sterilization 2%; there were 320 family-planning centers and 163,762 consultations given in 1980. **Abortion.** *Policy:* Until 1984, illegal (Criminal Code, Art. 358), punishable by 2–8 yrs. imprisonment for person "committing" abortion (doctor, midwife, and the woman herself). In Jan. 1984 Parliament passed new legislation legalizing the procedure under limited conditions: in case of danger to the life of the woman, pregnancy resulting from rape (only if a formal rape complaint is filed), or fetal defect; the procedure may be performed only in the first trimester and only with the authorization of 3 physicians. *Practice:* Incidence of illegal abortions has been very high. In 1982 a pro-choice group estimated the number of illegal abortions, which cost an average of $200, at 200,000 annually; government sources put the figure closer to 100,000. Before legalization, approx. 2000 women died each yr. from complications following abortion attempts; fewer than 8 abortion cases are heard in court per yr. Some feminist groups had begun a program of illegal abortion services, and feminists are now pressing for more liberalized abortion laws. **Illegitimacy.** *Policy:* The 1976 Constitution grants equal status in all matters to children born in or out of wedlock. *Practice:* No data obtainable. **Homosexuality.** *Policy:* Legal between consenting adults in private. *Practice:* No statistics obtainable. Reports say that homosexuals are harassed due to a strong social tabu against homosexuality reinforced by Roman Catholic mores. Lesbian women and homosexual men are beginning to voice their demands for equal treatment.

Incest. *Policy:* Illegal; seduction of a minor is punishable under the rape laws by 2–8 yrs. imprisonment. All penalties for rape are more severe if the acts are committed between persons related in ascendant or descendant relationships, between cousins, or with a ward. *Practice:* In 1979 there were 132 charges of seduction of a minor and 72 prison sentences handed down. Most incest cases go unreported, although in the early 1980's reports increased, due partly to family crowding in the housing crisis. **Sexual Harassment.** *Policy:* The Criminal Code (Art. 208C) specifies the illegality of sexual abuse or pressure by superiors (economic, religious, parental, or educational). A woman who complains of sexual discrimination cannot be fired or have sanctions applied against her by her employer for a 1-yr. period after she files a complaint; if the employer does, she has a right to compensation. *Practice:* No statistics obtainable, but sexual harassment is reportedly prevalent and women actually have few grievance measures, bearing the burden of proof in legal complaints; women are now beginning to organize on the issue. **Rape.** *Policy:* Illegal, and punishable by 2–5 yrs. imprisonment, or 6 months–3 yrs. if in the form of seduction with the fraudulent promise of marriage. Marital rape is not recognized by law. *Practice:* In 1980 there were 150 charges of rape and 94 convictions; most cases go unreported.

Battery. *Policy:* No specific laws governing spouse abuse, but general laws for assault and battery can be applied, and all sexual crimes against women can draw more severe sentences if aggravated by violence. *Practice:* No statistics obtainable, but wife-beating is reportedly widespread. Few battery cases are heard in court. **Prostitution.** *Policy:* The Criminal Code stipulates that the fostering or facilitating of prostitution, when a minor or mentally impaired person is involved, or when a person's economic or social condition is exploited, constitutes a crime punishable by 100 days–2 yrs. imprisonment; supporting oneself wholly or partially by earnings acquired through prostitution of another or trafficking in persons is punishable by 2–8 yrs. imprisonment. *Practice:* No statistics obtainable, but reportedly prostitution is common. **Traditional/Cultural Practices:** No data obtainable. **Crisis Centers:** No data obtainable.

HERSTORY. Portuguese today consider themselves descendants of the Lusitanians, a Celtic people who came to the Peninsula after 1000 B.C.E. Following the Roman conquest (4th century B.C.E.–2nd century B.C.E.), Roman customs and the Latin language were adopted. At the start of the 5th century C.E. Germanic invaders overran the area; the Visigoths ruled until 711, when the Moors conquered almost all of the Peninsula. During the 6th–7th centuries, what is now Algarve was under the control of the Byzantine Empire. In the 8th century the long Christian Reconquest began, and it was during this period that the Portuguese nation was established. In 1143 Spain recognized Portugal's independence, as did the Pope in 1179.

In the 12th century, Queen Isabel was named the "Holy Queen" and was a popular ruler, as was 14th–century Queen Philippa of Lancaster, who married João I in 1387 and whose great-granddaughter Queen Leonor (married to João II) installed a national welfare plan that continues today. Inêz de Castro (d. 1355) was a tragic romantic figure who became the lover of Dom Pedro (heir to the throne of Alfonso IV), was murdered with Alfonso's permission, and was revenged by a father-son war and a tomb which Dom Pedro had built at Alcobaça. During that period, *Christina's Mirror* appeared as a translated version of French writer Christine de Pisan's feminist tract (see FRANCE). By the climax of its era of maritime expansion and colonization in the 14th and 15th centuries, Portugal had a world empire stretching to Asia, Africa, and the Americas. The "Padeira" (Baker) of Aljubarrota was a woman whose 14th-century militance against the Spaniards won her almost legendary status. In the 15th century, the Infanta D. Maria established a court for women poets, humanists, and musicians. In 1577 the feminist book *Privileges and Prerogatives of Women* was published. Maria I reigned 1777–1816, and Maria II reigned 1826–53 (see BRAZIL). The latter's reign was marked by coups and countercoups, yet she made progress in building roads, the first railroad, and schools.

From the 15th-19th centuries, the "Ordençaoes" (compilations of legislation) gave men complete legal authority over women. In 1822 the first political constitution was passed giving equality to "all" but not referring to women. In 1891 Amelia Cardia became the first female doctor; 18 years later, the Republican League of Portuguese Women was founded. In 1910 the fall of the monarchy brought about a republic and legal improvements in women's status, including a divorce law, improved rights in marriage, and, with the 1911 Constitution, the right to work in the civil service. Carolina Beatriz Angelo voted in a local election (1911) as "head" of her family, but the law was later changed to allow only "male heads of household" the vote. Women made gains in education: Carolina Michaelis de Vasconçelos was the first to be appointed to a university chair and Regina Quintanilha was the first law graduate, in 1913.

Two books were published at the turn of the century: *A Vida da Mulher* (The Life of a Woman) which supported women's education, and *A Mulher em Portugal* (Women in Portugal). In 1914 the National Council of Portuguese Women was formed by Dra. Adelaide Cabete (founder of the Republican League). Well-known writers who favored women's rights were essayist and historian Maria Amalia de Carvalho and novelist Ana de Castro Osorio. Osorio led the Crusade of Portuguese Women, an educational and welfare group that supported Portugal's intervention on the Allied side in WW I. Aurora de Castro became the first woman notary in the world, girls entered previously all-male secondary schools (1920), and in 1924 the First Feminist Congress was held by the Council of Portuguese Women, who also published a journal, *Woman's Soul.*

In 1926 a military coup overthrew the government. Antonio de Oliviera Salazar became prime minister in 1932 and dominated Portugal until 1968. Under Salazar, women were stopped from organizing a Portuguese branch of the International Federation of University Women. In 1931 university and secondary-school-educated women won the right to vote; in 1933 a new constitution specifically denied women equal rights with men, based on "differences resulting from their nature and from the interest of the family." The country remained neutral in WW II. The electoral law was changed in 1946 to provide different political rights for men and women. Two years later, the government banned the National Council of Portuguese Women, and Maria Lamas, a journalist, published the book *As Mulheres do meu Pais* (The Women of My Country), creating a breakthrough for feminist thought and activism in contemporary Portugal; she was the first modern Portuguese feminist to see woman's status as inextricably linked with all general social issues.

In 1967 a new Civil Code named husbands as the "heads of the family" in all matters relating to marital life and children; a ruling a year later that proclaimed equal political rights for men and women regardless of status failed to remove the inequalities of the Civil Code, making husbands the only qualified electors for local councils.

The 1960's and 1970's brought numerous reforms for women, among them the principle of equal pay for equal work and changes in marriage laws. In 1973 the "Three Marias" (Maria Teresa Horta, Maria Isabel Barreño, and Maria Velho da Costa) published *New Portuguese Letters,* which exposed the plight of Portuguese women. The book was soon banned and its 3 authors tried in court for "offending public decency." After a national and international feminist campaign of protest on their behalf, they were released.

Women were active in the Revolution and in pressing for the policy of decolonization which followed. The Revolution of Apr. 25, 1974, truly propelled women's entry *en masse* into political and economic life. In 1979 Maria de Lourdes Pintasilgo became the first woman Prime Minister, and women were admitted to the magistracy, the diplomatic service, and all posts in local administrations. After the "Three Marias" trial, a feminist campaign for abortion and contraception began, and some feminists established links with women's groups in Leftist political parties and women active in the trade-union movement. Women in Sogantal took control of a textile factory and were attacked by the local population; another women's strike was held at the Via Longa brewery. Feminist lawyer Lia Viegas published *The Constitution and the Status of Women*. In

1979 journalist Maria Antonia Palla was acquitted—after feminist protest—of the charge of "outrage against public morals" and "incitement to crime" for her production of a documentary television film which discussed abortion. In 1981 a new law prohibited the use of a female image as an advertising object. Current women's publications include *Boletim Informação* (Information Bulletin), *Documentação das Mulheres* (Documentation of Women), and the work of a women's press, Edition das Mulheres (Women's Edition).

MYTHOGRAPHY. Deuladeu Martins is a woman folk-hero dating from the 12th century; she is thought of as a hugely tall and strong woman whose actions were so feared by invaders that, because of her, the country of Portugal itself came into being. Portugal was a center of Mariolatry during the 14th and 15th centuries, with adoration of Mary often superseding worship of Jesus Christ.

PORTUGAL: Daring to Be Different
by Maria de Lourdes Pintasilgo

I can no longer count the number of times I have been asked: "How do you explain that a country like Portugal has had a woman Prime Minister?"

Usually I react with a great outburst of indignation: women in Portugal are not like the image which has been put forth to portray us! If statistics say that women are only 28 percent of the "economically active population," then what is wrong is the statistics—*and* the definition of being active!

What about, for instance, the 32 percent of the rural population, more than half of whom are women? Aren't they working? What about the activities carried on by so many women which are (or have been until recently) totally unpaid? What about the women writers who represent, in the last thirty years, a most astounding cultural phenomenon in Portugal, since most of them are in the forefront of literature, portraying in extremely perceptive ways the deep shifts and trends which agitate our society beneath the surface? And what about the women in technical professions—a higher percentage than in any other Western country? (In my own field, chemical engineering, we have moved from a 20 percent women's presence when I graduated a quarter of a century ago to more than 50 percent in 1981.)

Of course, I could also argue the case by pointing out the enormous leap made in the law since April of 1974. The Portuguese Constitution is a unique example of the integration of the principle of equality in the basic text of a country. The sheer quantity of new legislation passed in recent years has drastically changed the identity of women, their image, and their status in society.*

Statistics and laws reassure certain souls. But the question I am asked—about the general situation of women and a female Prime Minister—belongs to another realm. In 1979, the appointment of a woman Prime Minister created a strong reaction in my country. Many expressed support and solidarity, speaking of new hope, a "fresh breeze," another style and concept of politics. But many others rejected the idea in the most violent way. I will never forget the undisguised loss of control of most members of the conservative parties when, in the Parliament, I denounced the lies they had used to attack the program of my government. It went so far that some of the house-desks cracked under the fury of their fists! Neither the enthusiasm nor the rage was connected, though, with the personality of the Prime Minister (I think). Rather, they were responses to what was obviously still a *revolutionary act,* belonging to the "new tradition" of the April 25th process. Through the appointment of a woman Prime Minister it was clearly demonstrated that such a tradition would no longer be an exclusively male heritage. It was one of the few situations when men and women transcended their conflictual relationship and worked together in full equality toward a new future. Seen from that perspective, the fact of a woman as Prime Minister was a totally logical result of the participation of women on equal footing with men in the revolution.

How did we get there? Let me briefly review the paths we had covered in the preceding years.

Women's Struggle and Political Change

Before the political change in 1974, the situation of Portuguese women was deeply affected by the closed, horizonless society in which we lived. War with the colonies in Africa drained us of money, dignity, hope—and people. Unrest among women had already begun to be expressed, through denunciations of the war's effect on women's lives —uncertainty about their families, the loneliness of those women left behind by men serving in Africa or who had fled elsewhere in Europe running away from the war, the weight of so many burdens carried alone, and the very fact of many women's being for the first time independent from men.

In the early 1970's, women journalists (who had managed to acquire a high status in their profession) started several newspaper-article series about women's lives and concerns. They denounced sexual discrimination but always put it into the general context of injustice in Portuguese society. It was during that period (in 1972) that the *New Portuguese Letters* appeared—for a moment—in the bookshops.** The book was of paramount significance for all Portugal. It was, in fact, the first Portuguese public act denouncing the global system of patriarchal oppression, and it would be central to the revolutionary movement that would have its climax and triumph on April 25th. Rebellion against the political status quo took, in my country, the form of a liberation cry from *women* and about *women:*

> . . . We will make our way back to the root of our own anguish,
> all by ourselves, until we can say "Our sons are sons, they are
> people and not phalluses of our males." We will call children chil-

* See Statistical Preface preceding this article for details of legislation.—Ed.
** See HERSTORY section of the Preface preceding this article.—Ed.

dren, women women, and men men. We will call upon a poet to
govern The City.[1]

This is why, when the military coup of April 25, 1974, burst out, people's power
became, to a large extent, women's power. Women were active in claiming fundamental
rights for workers, in asking for better living and housing conditions, in shaping action
committees at the neighborhood level, in denouncing the fraud that the capital owners
from Portugal and abroad were ready to make in order to "save" their profits. Women
themselves made their specific struggle a point of concern for the whole society: family
law changed drastically, different forms of childcare centers and old-age day-homes were
created to alleviate women's tasks, motherhood was assumed to have a social function
(and thus part of the responsibility of the whole community), measures to attain equal
work status were begun in all fields.

For almost two years, women and men were side by side in struggle on many fronts in
order to shape a more just society. We can say that in Portugal women's struggle has been
part and parcel of the whole process of change. It organized itself and changed modes,
patterns, scope, and intensity according to the events and moods of the revolution. This
experience tells us that there really is no theoretical question about priorities; women's
struggle and the global process in society are two aspects of the same front. For the
women's movement to emerge and make a significant contribution there must be some
signs of a breakthrough in society. Otherwise, a women's movement seems to represent
some kind of peculiar "sideline" goals, and its ideas can easily be taken up, mollified, and
co-opted by the establishment. On the other hand, in order for the general political
process to go beyond a mere game of superstructure, the women's movement is vital as a
link to reality, to the new needs of a society in the process of creating itself.

But if the Portuguese women's struggle found in our Revolution its *reinforcement,* it is
equally true that it also found its *limitations.* Women's issues had been regarded by the
Right as dangerous, evil, political stands; therefore these issues could never be discussed
on their own. Yet the limitation showed up as well in that the general enthusiasm of the
Revolution disguised deep layers of subtle discrimination against women. As time went
by and society entered the postrevolutionary period, women discovered that—beyond the
structural and legal changes—there are concepts and values which are not so easily wiped
out. Old attitudes keep coming up and shaping behavior at all levels.

The greatest limitation can be seen clearly in the question most central today to the
Portuguese women's movement: when political evolution comes to a deadlock, when so-
called democratic institutions get stifled (if not outright corrupt and contrary to the
interests of the people), is women's struggle possible? Doesn't it become an isolated effort
re-creating the pattern of earlier feminisms? Or does it in itself carry such potential that,
together with other social forces, it may evoke a new turn in the sociopolitical picture as a
whole?

Sex and Politics

While I was thinking about writing this article, I met (separately) with several groups
of adult women and young women in their late teens. I asked them, "What is the worst
obstacle for Portuguese women?" Adult women gave a unanimous answer: the theme of
violence built around sexual life. Young women, on the contrary, felt that they have no
specific obstacle! How to juxtapose these two contradictory reactions? What do they
mean?

It is a fact that the changes of April 1974 brought with them all kinds of freedom. The

[1] *New Portuguese Letters* (US ed., Garden City, NY: Doubleday, 1974), p. 70.

permissiveness of society appears to be all but total in the sexual area. But adult women today are challenging the values *underlying* that "permissiveness." They are convinced that this is creating in younger generations the conviction that the end of tabus can be equated with full dignity for women—while their own experience as adult women has taught them that the old forms of sexual repression and abuse re-seized their lives as soon as the Revolution had ceased to mobilize the energies of the people. These women say that they still are viewed and treated primarily as objects of men's sexual lives, that violence is exercised on them, that they are required to behave according to men's modes and desires. They say that even when there is full equality between man and woman, the demands of sex according to the man's rule defines them as slaves—a feeling that cuts across all social classes and all distinctions between urban and rural women. Portuguese women feel that what is at stake is the introjection of a patriarchal model imposed on women under the label of "sexual liberation." They say that such a model is shaped by the competitive style of society and is charged with individualistic overtones which manipulate and employ the satisfaction of the "ego" in order to make the machinery of society run smoothly. (In other words, if you are too busy with yourself, you never get deeply and actively concerned with society around you; you relativize it, you see it in a mist, you imagine that you can "save" yourself alone, you become alienated through the very instrument that ought to free you.) For these women, such widespread slogans as "Women must be owners of their own bodies" are an ambiguous cry of freedom, since such ideas convey the concept of a society geared by "ownership of property" as the supreme value and sign of status.

From their experience, older Portuguese women strongly resent the path of "sexual liberation" which has been prevailing. They feel oppressed by the masculine mode of expressing sexuality as well as by values coming from alien and dominant cultures. Because they want to reinforce the cultural identity of the people to which they belong, they cannot accept a path of sexual liberation through which, in their view, foreign domination is imposed upon local lifestyles and choices.

What are women asking, then?

First of all, in a sudden transition like the one which took place in 1974 in Portugal, they plead for crystal-clear lucidity when sexual questions are analyzed. For them, sex and revolution must be seen together in the sense that the most personal experience is interwoven with the values, aspirations, and failures of the collective experience. In Portugal, sex has become for many the ultimate revolution, the other side of politics in a strange mixture of "the peace after the battle" and "the search for a place beyond all battles." Most of all, sex in practice has become the last bastion of the powerless revolutionaries—as well as the victory shout of the professional politicians. For the former, sex is what can be done when nothing else can; for the latter, sex is the exaltation, the paroxysm of politics. In such a situation, women not only are victims and objects but are even trapped as subjects, swept up in the same tide as men and repeating what men have always done.

Second, Portuguese women are clamoring for broader understanding of sexuality. They are very much aware of the sexual overtones of *all* human activity. They don't deny sexuality but are convinced that their own sexuality so far hasn't had any chance to be expressed. They cry out for the possibility of expressing a whole gamut of feelings, sensations, affections, and tenderness which they sense as inherent elements of their own sexuality. Even when these women are dismissed as "fusional" or utopian—because for them "to think of a flower is to see it and to smell its perfume"—they persist in exploring this path. They are convinced that a less Cartesian and rationalistic approach to societal questions is inextricably connected to the rediscovery of a much broader expression of human sexuality. For them, sexuality equated with mere genitality and commercialized into the consumerism of the producer-owner-buyer is to be fought as a fatal cycle of a society led by the paradigm of "progress" and by linear reasoning. For them, the shaping of a new society is interwoven with the articulation—and the living out—of new modes of women's sexuality.

This awareness and experience is the greatest strength women in Portugal already possess. They know that they are—and can become even more—a real force in Portuguese society. They know, too, that the evolution of women in this country has a lot to do with women elsewhere.

For my part, I believe deeply that women can change society. I feel that what we must say to one another is based on encouraging each of us to be true to herself: "Now that we are equal, let us dare to be different!"

Suggested Further Reading

Belleza, Leonor. "O Estatuto da Mulher na Constituição" (The Status of Women in the Constitution). *Estudos sobre a Constituição* (Studies on the Constitution). Ed. Miranda Jorge. Lisbon: Ed. Livraria Petrony, 1977.

Gersão, Teolinda. *O Silencio* (The Silence). Lisbon: Bertrand, 1980.

Palla, Maria Antonia. *So Acontece Aos Outros* (It Only Happens to Others). Lisbon: Bertrand, 1979.

Silva, Manuela. *Mulher Eo Trabalho* (Women and Work); publication available in Portuguese and French from any European Economic Commission Information Center.

The Three Marias (collective book). *New Portuguese Letters.* US ed., Garden City, NY: Doubleday, 1974; New York: Bantam Books, 1976.

Viegas, Lia. *A Constituição e a condição da mulher.* (The Constitution and the Condition of Women). Lisbon: Diabril, 1977.

Maria de Lourdes Pintasilgo was born in 1930 in Abrantes, Portugal. An engineer in industrial chemistry, she took her degree at the Superior Technological Institute in Lisbon, also doing autodidactic studies in anthropology, sociology, and theology. She served as researcher in the National Nuclear Energy Commission, is a member of "The Grail" international movement, and has been a member of the women's liaison group between the Roman Catholic Church and the Ecumenical Council of Churches. She was president of the Interministerial Commission dealing with the Condition of the Status of Women (1970–74). She has also served as State Secretary for Social Security (First Provisional Government), Minister of Social Affairs (Second and Third Provisional Governments), Portuguese Ambassador at UNESCO, a member of the Executive Council of UNESCO, and the Prime Minister of the Fifth Constitutional Government of Portugal (1979)—the first woman Prime Minister in Portugal. A member of the Portuguese delegation to the UN General Assembly in 1971 and 1972, she is currently Special Adviser to the President of the Republic of Portugal. Her books include *Les nouveaux féminismes* (The New Feminisms), Paris: Cerf, 1980, *Imaginar a igreja* (To Think the Church Anew), Lisbon: Multinova, 1979, and *Sulcos do nosso querer comum* (Roads for Our Joint Efforts), Porto: Afrontamento, 1980.

RUMANIA
(Socialist Republic of Rumania)

Located in southeastern Europe and bordered by the USSR to the north and east, the Black Sea to the east, Bulgaria to the south, Yugoslavia to the southwest, and Hungary to the northwest. **Area:** 237,500 sq. km. (91,700 sq. mi.). **Population** (1980): 22,201,000, female 50.7%. **Capital:** Bucharest.

DEMOGRAPHY. Languages: Rumanian (official), Hungarian, German, Serbian, Turkish. **Races or Ethnic Groups:** Rumanian 88.1%, Hungarian 7.9%, German 1.8%, other. **Religions:** Rumanian Orthodox 80%, Roman Catholicism 9%, Serbian Orthodox, Calvinism, Lutheranism, Judaism, Islam, Uniate (Greek Catholic) Church. There are 14 recognized religious communities; the Uniate Church was suppressed in 1948 and is not recognized by the State. **Education** (% enrolled in school, 1975): Age 6–11—of all girls 84%, of all boys 89%; age 12–17—of all girls 95%, of all boys 99%; higher education—in 1983 women were 42% of all students. **Literacy** (1977): Women 84%, men 94%. **Birth Rate** (per 1000 pop., 1982): 18. **Death Rate** (per 1000 pop., 1982): 10. **Infant Mortality** (per 1000 live births, 1977): Female 27, male 47. **Life Expectancy** (1975–80): Female 73 yrs., male 68 yrs.

GOVERNMENT. An elected 465-member Grand National Assembly meets for 2 sessions a yr., delegating its legislative authority to the State Council, comprising a president and 28 members. A 61-member government, composed solely of ministers, is in charge of all executive matters. The sole political party is the Rumanian Communist Party (RCP), whose Congress elects the General Secretary and whose 385-member Central Committee elects a 40-member Executive Political Committee and a 44-member Permanent Bureau (or Politburo). *De facto* power is concentrated in the President, the General Secretary, and the RCP Politburo. The 40 counties are administered by elected People's Councils. More than 1 candidate is allowed to stand for office in each constituency. **Women's Suffrage:** 1946 (full suffrage); right to vote in municipal elections granted in 1929. **Equal Rights:** The 1965 Constitution (Art. 23) states, "Women shall have equal rights with men." **Women in Government:** Of the Grand National Assembly 33%, State Council 17.2%, with Maria Ciocan as a vice-chair, and an additional 11 women as deputy ministers to the State Council, government members 10%, RCP members 33%, RCP Central Committee 24.7%, RCP Executive Political Committee 23%, Politburo 22.7%; Elena Ceauşescu (wife of President and General Secretary Ceauşescu) is a member of the Politburo and the Executive Political Committee, and is the first woman First Vice-Prime Minister. Maria Groza is a deputy foreign minister, and Ana Muresan is president of the National Council of Women. Women are 35% of People's Council deputies (1983).

ECONOMY. Currency: Lei (May 1983: 12.5 = $1 US). **Gross National Product** (1980): $52 billion. **Per Capita Income** (1980): $2340. **Women's Wages as a Percentage of Men's:** No data obtainable. **Equal Pay Policy:** The Constitution stipulates equal pay for equal work for men and women. Wages are regulated by the State; the ratio of maximum to minimum wages is 6:1, with a government goal of reducing the gap to 5.5:1. Pay scales are based on training, skills, seniority, and "difficulty of work." Monthly minimum wages were 1406 Lei for skilled work, 1200 for unskilled work, and 1000–1500 for agricultural/co-op work (1980). The concentration of women employees in agriculture and unskilled jobs, and in service-sector jobs which are not ranked as "difficult," results in lower wages for women. **Production** (Agricultural/Industrial): Corn, wheat, sugar beets, grapes, fruits; steel, metals, coal, oil products, machinery, chemicals, textiles, shoes, wine. **Women as a Percentage of Labor Force** (1980): 45%; **of agricultural force** (official est.) 50% (in 1975, 69% of women workers were employed in agriculture); in 1979, 99.88% of the entire agricultural labor force was female [as derived from ILO statistics]; **of industrial force** (1980) 40.3%; **of military**—no data obtainable. **(Employed) Women's Occupational Indicators:** Of machine-building and metal-working 26%, of physicians 40%, of textile industry 78% (1983); of telecommunications 50.7%, of commerce 57.6%, of education, arts, and culture 64.8%, of health care 74.5% (1980). Despite rapid industrialization resulting in an increased participation of women in the labor force, the machine-building, chemical, and energy industries were almost entirely closed to women until 1973, and women remain concentrated in agriculture and the service sector. The Constitution (Art. 18.2) supports the principle of "protective" labor legislation for women and young workers; night employment is restricted for all women and prohibited for those more than 6 months pregnant or nursing children. **Unemployment:** Officially there is full employment; reports indicate chronic underemployment, especially in the agricultural sector.

GYNOGRAPHY. Marriage. *Policy:* The Family Code (Art. 1) states, "Marriage with the full consent of the spouses shall be the basis of family life. . . . Men and women shall have equal rights in relations between the spouses and with regard to children." If a married person must relocate to meet the work requirements of a spouse, employment seniority is not considered to have been interrupted. *Practice:* Female mean age at marriage (1970–78): 20; women age 15–49 in union (1970–78): 74.5%. **Divorce.** *Policy:* Legal; no data obtainable on grounds for divorce. The Family Code (Art. 42) stipulates that the courts shall decide custody in the interests of the children and can require child-support payments from either or both parents. *Practice:* Divorces (per 1000 pop., 1980): 1.54. **Family.** *Policy:* The Constitution stipulates, "The State shall protect marriage and the family and shall defend the interests of mothers and children." Decisions about children and their property must be made jointly by spouses; parents are responsible for supporting and educating

their children (Family Code). The State is pro-natalist and encourages women to have 4 or more children, awarding the Order of Heroine Mothers or the Maternity Medal to women with large families (Decree 190, 1977); beginning with her third birth, a woman is entitled to a 1000-Lei birth grant. Women who care for their children up to age 18 are entitled to a monthly allowance which increases with each child.

Family allowances are paid to employees (including members of agricultural co-ops) for each child (Decree 241, 1977); "confinement grants" are paid to women with 3 or more children (Decree 197, 1977); additional aid is given to women with 8 or more children (Decree 411, 1972). Employed pregnant women are entitled to be transferred to lighter work at their regular wages; they are also entitled to a partially paid maternity leave of 52 days pre- and 60 days post-delivery; amount increases with length of employment, or after the third child. Employed mothers are entitled to fully paid 1/2-hour nursing breaks every 3 hours for a maximum of 2 hours per day; travel time is permitted if no creche is available at the workplace. A woman can choose to work 2 hours less each day until her child is age 9 months (12 months if special care is required) instead of taking nursing breaks. A woman with an ill child under age 3 is entitled to a paid leave. If a nursery or kindergarten is not available, a woman with a child under age 6 can work half-time and receive credit for fulltime employment. Women cannot be fired for pregnancy or during maternity leave, nursing leave, or sick-child leave (Labor Code, Arts. 46, 152–58). Pregnant women are entitled to 8 pre-natal check-ups from the fourth month until delivery, and to post-natal mother and infant care. Priority is given to young married couples in housing loans, and to large families in State-subsidized rental housing. The government program to increase both the birth rate and women's participation in the work force included a 1974 plan to provide childcare facilities for 200,000 children by 1980. *Practice:* In most families where a husband is present he is *de facto* head of household. Women bear the primary responsibility for childcare and domestic work. In 1980, 77.5% of pre-school children were enrolled in kindergarten.

Welfare. *Policy:* The government provides free education, medical care, and vocational training, guaranteed jobs, orphanages, workers' compensation, and pensions. Official retirement age is 55–57 for women and 62 for men; a woman's retirement age may be reduced by 1–3 yrs. if she gave birth to and cared for over 3 children until they reached age 10. *Practice:* Expenditures for education, health, social assistance, family allocations, pensions, and social security accounted for 23.5% of the 1980 budget. Average pensions were 950 Lei per month in 1980.

Contraception. *Policy:* The pro-natalist government discourages contraceptive use and restricts sales. The pill, IUDs, and diaphragms are not available (it is illegal to import the pill). Voluntary sterilization is not practiced. *Practice:* Women under age 45 in union using contraception (1978): 58%; methods used (1978) withdrawal 44%, rhythm 41%, condom 6%, diaphragm and foam 2%, pill 1%, other methods 6%; using inefficient methods 91%. Condoms and traditional methods have been the main means of contraception available since 1966. **Abortion.** *Policy:* Abortions were illegal until 1957 and then were legal upon request until 1966, when restrictions limited the procedure to saving the life or physical health of the woman, in cases of rape or incest, or if a parent has a congenital disease likely to affect the fetus; in addition, since 1972 the procedure has been legal on request for women over age 40 and women with 4 or more children. All abortions must be approved by a medical board and are permitted only until the end of the third month (or the sixth month in rare cases necessary to save the woman's life). For all other abortions, a woman and a practitioner both are punishable under the Criminal Law (Secs. 185–88). The woman may be sentenced to 3 yrs. imprisonment. *Practice:* Abortions (per 1000 women age 15–44, 1965): 252.3, with an estimated 80% of all conceptions ending in abortion. Abortions (per 1000 women age 15–44, 1979): 88.1 (1979 data include women admitted to hospitals for care after illegal abortions). The number of abortion-related deaths increased by 600% after 1966. Illegal abortions cost approx. 3000–5000 Lei in 1979. Doctors are required to report all abortion-related injuries to the police; however, some may attempt to induce illegal abortion by administering hormone shots, by repeatedly irradiating the abdominal area, or by inducing internal bleeding so that a legal abortion can then be performed on health grounds. Women are reportedly checked for pregnancy when they leave and re-enter the country, to ensure that they do not have abortions while abroad. **Illegitimacy.** *Policy:* The Family Code (Art. 97.1) states, "Parents shall have the same rights and obligations with respect to their minor children irrespective of whether the children were born in or out of wedlock. . . ." *Practice:* No data obtainable. **Homosexuality.** *Policy:* Reportedly illegal; no further data obtainable. *Practice:* No data obtainable.

Incest. *Policy:* According to the Family Code (Art. 104), if the physical, moral, or intellectual development of a child is in jeopardy in the parental home, the State may assume guardianship or assign the child to another home; the ruling is not specific to incest but includes it. *Practice:* No data obtainable. **Sexual Harassment.** *Policy:* No data obtainable. *Practice:* No data obtainable. **Rape.** *Policy:* Illegal; no further data obtainable. *Practice:* No data obtainable. **Battery.** *Policy:* No data obtainable. *Practice:* No data obtainable. **Prostitution.** *Policy:* Reportedly illegal; no further data obtainable. *Practice:* Prostitution reportedly exists in urban centers and is linked with the black market in consumer goods and foreign currencies. No further data obtainable. **Traditional/Cultural Practices:** No data obtainable. **Crisis Centers:** No data obtainable.

HERSTORY. The Thracians and Scythians occupied the region north of the Danube before it became a Roman province, Dacia, in approx. 100–275 C.E.; Christianity made its first converts during this period. Successive invasions, including those by the Goths and Huns, ended with a period of Mongol rule in the 13th century. Walachia and Moldavia became vassal states of the Ottoman Empire in 1417 and the mid-1500's respectively. Michael the Brave united Moldavia, Walachia, and Transylvania, formerly a Hungarian dependency, for a period before his death in 1601. From 1711 until 1821 the Turks dominated the region. In 1859 Alexander John Cuza was elected prince of both Moldavia and Walachia, and the two were united officially as Rumania. Cuza partially freed the serfs and redistributed some land but was deposed by a coup and replaced by Carol I in 1866. Rumania was declared a kingdom in 1881.

Queen Elisabeth (1843–1916), married King Carol I in 1869. Of German birth, she devoted herself to the Rumanian people and culture. She wrote profusely (novels, diaries, children's books) in German, French, English, and Rumanian, under the pseudonym Carmen Sylva, sometimes collaborating with Mite Kremnitz, her lady-in-waiting.

Queen Marie (1875–1938), wife of Ferdinand I, was an important influence in the decision to join the Allies in WW I. She followed the Rumanian army as a Red Cross nurse and wrote fiction and an autobiography. Her son, Carol, renounced his right to the throne because of his relationship with a Jewish Rumanian woman, Elena Lupescu. Ferdinand died in 1927 and Carol's son Michael became king under a regency. In 1930 Carol reclaimed the throne as Carol II, making Elena his "official mistress." The King's party was opposed by the Liberal Party, the Peasant Party, and the anti-Semitic National Christian Party. Fascist elements rose to power, and Rumania became a neutral partner of the Axis in 1940, but under Axis pressure lost most

of the territories it had gained after WW I. In 1944 Rumania joined the Allied powers, and recovered some lost territories, but became more dependent on the Soviet Union after the war.

A Communist coalition government was elected in 1946. The King abdicated in 1947, and the People's Republic of Rumania was declared.

Women first won political rights in the 1945 Constitution. In 1948, 11% of the RCP's Central Committee was female, but the percentage had dropped to 4% by 1969, 4 years after Nicholas Ceauşescu came to power. The Communist Party launched its biggest campaign to promote women's rights in 1973. Elena Ceauşescu and Lina Ciobanu were elected to the Politburo as full members, and Magdalena Filipas and Aurelia Danila were elected alternate members. By 1974, 11% of the Central Committee was once again women—but women who were the wives, daughters, and friends of male officials.

Women are, however, active in the civil-rights and religious-rights movements (see following article). Silvia Tarniceru and Elena Boghian were among the prisoners of conscience released in an amnesty declared in Aug. 1982.

MYTHOGRAPHY. The Scythians revered a goddess of the hunt whose image has been found on gold plaques and bronze buckles; she was similar to the Greek goddess Artemis and was depicted with hounds.

Much like the neighboring Slavic peoples, the Rumanians have a folklore of forest spirits, sun and moon, and Mother Earth personification; this last was conjured as such and addressed directly by the peasantry, who still maintain certain seasonal rituals of devotion.

RUMANIA: The "Right" to Be Persecuted
by Elena Chiriac
(Translated by Edite Kroll)

After World War II, the Socialist Republic of Rumania, which had fought on the side of the Allied Forces but which had had to deal with remnants of pro-fascist elements in the government, came under the influence of yet another foreign power: the USSR.

Since then, the Rumanian woman has been a victim of a totalitarian regime which was appointed by Moscow against the will of the Rumanian people and which is governed today by a puppet-government "clan" that places its own interests above those of the people. The Rumanian woman—as mother, wife, worker, and citizen—suffers under the constraints imposed by that government, constraints which are carried into all areas of political, social, and economic life. Her fate, like that of all 22 million inhabitants of Rumania, is dependent on the head of state and party chief N. Ceauşescu and his family. Because of the economic hardship endured by Rumanians in general—which is the direct responsibility of this clan—women in particular are forced to exert themselves in ways which only contribute to the destruction of their lives.

According to law, a Rumanian woman has the same rights as a man. Consequently, she has to *work* as a man, but without any allowances being made for her other roles. For example, she has the additional "right" *(and* the duty) to bring four children into the world before she is forty years old. Abortions have been, in effect, illegal since 1966, and the situation is further exacerbated by the fact that Rumanian women are given no help in fulfilling their functions as mothers, wives, workers, and citizens.

Despite the government's claims to the contrary, there are virtually no available kindergarten openings in Rumania. A woman is therefore forced to stay home and bring up her children with no governmental support. Her husband's salary is their only means of survival, since the governmental child subsidy is a ridiculous 125 LEI—which doesn't come *close* to feeding a child for a month. In addition, the shortage of food and consumer goods, which is steadily worsening in Rumania, contributes to the fact that Rumania has the lowest Per Capita Income in Europe. Naturally, this affects the condition of Rumanian women. The Rumanian government's only solution to the shortage of food has been to ration some, to remove other products from the market, and to devise a law whereby certain foods are distributed in different amounts according to sex, profession, weight, and age. This solution has no precedent in the history of the misery that has developed because of the current regime.

The Rumanian woman has to take care of her family and stand in shopping lines so as to be able to feed them. Her time is totally swallowed between her job, her shopping time, and her housewifely "duties." She has *no* free time for herself—despite her so-called equality with men.

She may have the same rights as a man, but can she hold her own in the job market after having brought a second, third, or even fourth child into the world? Perhaps after many years she would like to re-enter her profession (most likely because economic conditions in her family demand it), but she is forced to accept lower compensation than a man for the same job—although she has the same qualifications. This discrimination is justified by the excuse that she has "interrupted her working life."

On the other hand, because Rumanian men and women supposedly have the same "rights to establish a family," to "life in freedom," and to support "principles" that are internationally recognized—women *are* politically persecuted and convicted on an equal basis with men. The IGFM[1] cites cases that clearly show how Rumanian women are subjected to torture: Tekla Haplea from Bucharest was sentenced to many years in prison because she wanted to join her husband, George, who lives in Munich; her one son, age eight, was sent to a reform school. Carmen Popescu, also from Bucharest, was sentenced to six years in prison because she took part in demonstrations on behalf of human rights and free trade-unions. The sisters Maria and Sibia Delapeta from Cimpuri in the district of Hunedoara each were sentenced to six years in prison and fined 67,000 LEI for no other reason than that they stood up for their religious beliefs. Dr. Silviu Cioata from Ploiesti was in effect condemned to die of starvation together with her three children, because her husband was sentenced to six years in prison on religious grounds. Ana Georgescu from Ploiesti and her two children suffer the same fate, since her husband George, an engineer, was also sentenced to six years in prison.

And I? I am an exile. A woman and an exile. Who thinks about Rumania today, in this busy world? Who thinks about—least of all—a Rumanian woman? But this is a Rumanian voice, a woman's voice, a human voice, crying out to women all over: Help me. Help us. Help.

Suggested Further Reading
Caranfil, Constantza. *The Life from the Morning to the Evening.* 1979.
Groza, Maria. *Woman in the Contemporary Life of Roumania.* 1979.
Ioanid, Ana. *Way for Beginning.* 1970.
Nestor, Elena. *The Warm Rains.* 1976.
Oproiu, Catrinel. *3 x 8.* 1980.
Vulpescu, Ileana. *The Craft of Conversation.* 1980.
(All the above books are published by the State Publishing House, Bucharest, Rumania.
—E.C.)

Elena Chiriac was born in Rumania in 1943. She took her postgraduate degree in architecture and worked in Rumania for fifteen years as an architect. In 1981 she sought political asylum in West Germany, and she has become involved in the civil-rights movement as a political activist with IGFM/Frankfurt/Main, and in the Rumanian-German Democratic Circle, where she is the secretary of *Dialog,* the publication of the R-G Democratic Circle. She is married and has a sixteen-year-old son.

[1] International Society for Human Rights (Kaiserstrasse 72, D-6000 Frankfurt-am-Main, FRD).

SAUDI ARABIA
(Kingdom of Saudi Arabia)

Located on the Arabian Peninsula, bordered by the Persian Gulf and Qatar to the east, the 2 Yemens, Oman, and the United Arab Emirates to the south, the Red Sea and the Gulf of Aqaba to the west, and Jordan, Iraq, and Kuwait to the north. **Area:** 2,261,070 sq. km. (873,000 sq. mi.). **Population** (1980): 4,500,000,* female 49.4%. **Capital:** Riyadh.

DEMOGRAPHY. Languages: Arabic. **Races or Ethnic Groups:** Arab, other. **Religions:** Islam 99% (predominantly Sunni); Mecca, the center of the Moslem world, is in Saudi Arabia. **Education** (% enrolled in school, 1975): Age 6–11—of all girls 24%, of all boys 46%; age 12–17 —of all girls 20%, of all boys 32%; higher education—in 1982 women were 25% of students at Riyadh University; in 1980 a total of 12,655 women comprised 27% of students at 5 universities. Education is sex-segregated from age 6. The first girls' schools opened in 1960, and Saudi women were first admitted to universities in 1962. Only 15% of appropriations for educational and technical training in the First Five-Year Development Plan (1970–75) was directed toward females. In 1970 there were 395 schools for females and 1652 for males. In some universities, women students are taught by male instructors via closed-circuit television, and female students may use libraries 1 day a week (when males are prohibited). Women are not permitted to study engineering in any Saudi university. **Literacy** (est., 1977): Women less than 1%, men 5%; a 1979 study reported an increase in female literacy to 19%, male to 48%. **Birth Rate** (per 1000 pop., 1975–80): 49. **Death Rate** (per 1000 pop., 1975–80): 18. **Infant Mortality** (per 1000 live births, 1975–80): Female 142, male 158. **Life Expectancy** (1975–80): Female 49 yrs., male 47 yrs.

GOVERNMENT. Saudi Arabia is governed by the absolute monarchy of the Saud family. Jurisprudence is based on the Islamic Shari'a. A 21-member council of ministers advises King Fahd Bin Abdul-Aziz, who is also the Imam. There are no political parties. In the judicial system the Islamic Law of Evidence is strictly interpreted: the testimony of 1 man equals that of 2 women, and women are not permitted to serve as judges. **Voting:** There are no elections in Saudi Arabia. **Women's Suffrage:** There is no vote for women or men. **Equal Rights:** No legislation. **Women in Government:** None.

ECONOMY. Currency: Riyal (May 1983: 3.43 = $1 US). **Gross National Product** (1980): $100.9 billion. **Per Capita Income** (1980): $11,260. **Women's Wages as a Percentage of Men's:** No data obtainable. **Equal Pay Policy:** Women in the public sector [see **(Employed) Women's Occupational Indicators**] are to receive equal pay for equal work. **Production** (Agricultural/Industrial): Dates, wheat, barley; petroleum and petroleum products, cement, plastic products. **Women as a Percentage of Labor Force** (1980): 5%; **of agricultural force** (1974) 33% (of whom 96% are nonwaged labor) of total force, including permanent, temporary, and seasonal workers, but excluding herding communities; **of industrial force**—no data obtainable; **of military**—women are prohibited from military service. **(Employed) Women's Occupational Indicators:** No general statistics obtainable. In 1983 approx. 3000 women worked for ARAMCO (Arab American Oil Co.), the only private corporation permitted to employ women—but only 200 of these were Saudi women; in 1980, 90.8% of the over 2800 female employees at ARAMCO were in secretarial training or grades 5–10 (primarily clerical jobs), and only 12 women were in the professional grades 15–88 (primarily doctors). Following Saudi custom, when a woman

---

* Official and unofficial pop. statistics vary widely (from 4 million to 8 million), in part because of the nomadic peoples in the region; consequently, all the subsequent statistics are also estimates.

and her husband both are ARAMCO employees, the woman is forced to leave her job when her husband ceases to be employed by the company. In 1982, 25,000 women were in public-sector jobs, mostly in health, education, and social services. In 1980, 11,847 women were teachers in government schools. The Directorate of Girls' Schools is the main employer of women. Labor laws prohibit women from working with men, although this is not always strictly enforced. Women are not permitted to operate a professional private practice (e.g., law) with the exception of medicine. Bedouin women often are traders or vendors in the women's *souq* (marketplace). The exclusion of women from most jobs has caused a severe labor shortage; foreign nationals comprised approx. 65% of the work force in 1982. **Unemployment:** No data obtainable.

GYNOGRAPHY. Marriage. *Policy:* Marriage, divorce, and family laws have not been re-codified but are based strictly on the Islamic Shari'a. A man may marry up to 4 wives. Marriages are arranged by families, frequently between first cousins. Marriage of a young female without her consent is permitted. A 1980 Royal Decree required that a bride and groom be permitted to meet each other before marriage. Saudis may marry only Saudis unless they receive permission to do otherwise. A bride-price *(mahar)* is paid to the bride's family by the groom. After marriage, the husband is supposed to provide all wives with separate rooms and with material necessities. Property brought into marriage is individually owned; a woman may administer possessions acquired during marriage. *Practice:* No statistics obtainable, but nuptiality rates are reportedly very high, and there is pressure for females to marry no later than age 16. Polygyny is decreasing; in reality, multiple wives are not always provided with their own rooms. Mothers usually arrange marriages, while fathers, uncles, or brothers approve them. A bride who is not a virgin is shamed, as is her family, who may send her away. The price of *mahar* has risen sharply and is sometimes as high as $30,000–$40,000, forcing many men to postpone marriage

until they are older, which in turn creates more young-bride–older-groom pairings. Despite the 1980 decree, many couples never meet until the marriage ceremony.

Divorce. *Policy:* Legal. A woman can divorce her husband because of rights stipulated in the Shari'a, but these rights are interpreted/adjudged by the Qadi (Islamic religious judge). A man can divorce a wife by *talaq.* A woman who is divorced must wait 4 months and 10 days before remarrying. *Practice:* No statistics obtainable; reportedly, the rate of divorce is increasing. Despite a man's right to an unlimited number of divorces, it is not acceptable to divorce a woman without cause. If a woman does not bear children a man frequently takes a second wife instead of divorcing the first wife. Traditionally, a divorced woman will return to her father's home.

Family. *Policy:* The family is the focus of social life, and family responsibilities are considered a primary obligation. Women's and men's living areas in the home are segregated. A woman may socialize only with males who are her relatives prior to marriage, and only with males who are her or her husband's relatives after marriage. An employed woman is entitled to a fully paid maternity leave 4 weeks pre- and 6 weeks post-delivery, and to job reinstatement. Childcare centers are subsidized by the government. A woman may inherit only 1/2 the amount of a man's share. *Practice:* A father is considered the supreme authority in the family. Male children are prized over females; a woman who doesn't bear a male heir is considered a failure. Childcare facilities are insufficient; in 1983 there were approx. 200 day-care centers (including both public and private) in the country.

Welfare. *Policy:* The welfare system consists of several branches. Social Security provides income supplements to the disabled and the deprived and poverty relief for persons unable to work. Social Care provides financial and rehabilitation aid for persons in physical or social distress and includes assistance to orphanages and homes for the elderly and the handicapped. The General Organization for Social Insurance, a government agency, has a compulsory insurance system for employees in the private sector and in State-owned corporations; it provides health insurance, workers' compensation, and disability and old-age pensions. The Ministry of Health, along with 13 other government agencies, offers free health-care services to all citizens through State-supported hospitals and health centers. *Practice:* As of 1980, 700,000 employees were enrolled in the Social Insurance system. In 1972–73, 32,100 women in need and 2600 orphaned females were covered under the Social Security System; in 1971–72, 36,100 partially or completely disabled females, 24,500 widows, 2400 divorced females, 2200 orphaned females, 200 homeless women, and 200 single women were covered.

Contraception. *Policy:* Contraceptives were banned by Royal Decree in Apr. 1975 after a campaign by the World Moslem League. Importing pills or contraceptive devices is punishable by 6 months imprisonment. Sterilization is legal with extremely restrictive conditions. *Practice:* No statistics obtainable. Contraceptive information and some devices are available by strictly limited prescription. **Abortion.** *Policy:* Legal only to save the life of the woman; no further data obtainable. *Practice:* No data obtainable. **Illegitimacy.** *Policy:* Under orthodox interpretation of Islamic law, a woman who gives birth to a child out of wedlock is subject to public flogging. *Practice:* No statistics obtainable. A hospitalized woman who gives birth to an out-of-wedlock child may be reported to the police by hospital authorities. **Homosexuality.** *Policy:* Illegal as an "offense against nature," according to the Shari'a. No further data obtainable. *Practice:* No statistics obtainable, but reportedly not uncommon for both women and men (see Saudi proverb on p. 757). **Incest.** *Policy:* Marriages between cousins is accepted and even desired, but sexual relations between other close relatives is prohibited by Islamic law. *Practice:* No data obtainable. **Sexual Harassment.** *Policy:* None. *Practice:* Women who disregard *purdah*

or do not wear the *abaya* (veil) are frequently subjected to physical and verbal abuse. Western women who are employed in Saudi Arabia are also vulnerable to harassment since they often do not observe Saudi cultural practices regarding women. At one Riyadh hospital where Scandinavian and other European women worked as nurses, there were 40 incidents of sexual assault within 6 weeks (1977). **Rape.** *Policy:* Illegal; punishable by beheading. *Practice:* No statistics obtainable. Rape is reportedly rare because of strict segregation of the sexes; rapes which do occur are rarely reported. **Battery.** *Policy:* According to some interpretations of the Islamic Shari'a, a husband is permitted to "discipline" his wife "by hand" but not to employ objects that might cause severe harm. *Practice:* No statistics obtainable. Wife-beating is a major problem on the west coast; in the central region wife-beating is considered a sign of weakness.

Prostitution. *Policy:* Illegal and generally punishable by 6 months imprisonment for both woman and client. *Practice:* No statistics obtainable. Prostitution is not uncommon. Following the 1962 Anti-Slavery Decree, many women who had been enslaved had no means of support or training and were forced to resort to prostitution. **Traditional/Cultural Practices.** *Policy:* According to strict interpretation of Islamic law, a woman is required to wear the *abaya* upon reaching puberty and to observe other restrictions of *purdah*—segregation from the public sphere and from interactions with men who are not family members. A woman may not drive, travel without a male relative, or eat alone in a restaurant. *Practice:* As a result of *purdah,* many women are rarely permitted to leave the home except to go to marketplaces; they must rely on men to procure most necessities from outside. An increasing number of women are discarding the face veil entirely. Partial excision** and infibulation*** is practiced by certain groups in the western border region. **Crisis Centers.** *Policy:* None. *Practice:* No data obtainable.

** See Glossary.
*** See Glossary.

HERSTORY. The Arabian Peninsula was inhabited by Semitic peoples of the separate political entities of Stieba, Ma'in, and Himyarite in 1000 B.C.E. Rome attempted conquest of the north in 24 B.C.E. but was unsuccessful. The prophet Mohammed founded the Islamic religion in Mecca in the 7th century C.E. and unified the tribes of Arabia.

The Gahelia (pre-Islamic) period of the Arabian Peninsula was dominated by both nomadic and sedentary tribal cultures. Such matriarchal systems of lineage as the Gadiki and Khanda were not uncommon and contributed to women's relatively high status and vital role in society. Kings were sometimes named for their mothers; the prophet Mohammed traced his descent through his mother, El Awalek, and her female relatives. Polyandry, with women taking as many as 10 husbands, was practiced. *Zawag el mosharaka* (marriage of sharing) allowed a woman to choose which of her husbands would be father of her child. A Bedouin woman could divorce a husband by merely changing the position of her tent. The *Istibdaa* form of polyandry allowed a woman to have sexual relations and children with men other than her legal husband; the husband would chose the man and then claim the children as his own. *Zawag el mutaa* was a marriage of pleasure that lasted for a few days, after which the man would pay the woman remuneration.

Women often chose their husbands. Khadija was a widow who chose her young employee and the future prophet Mohammed as her husband; a wealthy merchant in Mecca, she supported him in the founding of Islam during their 25-yr. marriage. Among the desert nomads, women performed the invaluable chores of herding, making cheese and yogurt, and shearing wool.

In the 7th century C.E. urban areas developed, and matrilineal nomadic communities decreased. Patrilineal descent became dominant and women's independence and the economic protection offered by tribal kinship diminished. Many principles proposed by Mohammed concerned marriage and the family and offered women economic security—dowries, the right to manage property and income, and the right to inherit part of a husband's and other relatives' property. Female infanticide, which was practiced frequently among some nomadic peoples, was outlawed by Islamic jurisprudence. Polyandry, however, was replaced by polygyny. Adultery by a woman, which included taking more than 1 husband as well as extra-marital relations, became punishable. The practice of women's seclusion in a harem, and the wearing of the veil *(abaya)* when appearing in public were instituted—customs thought to be of Persian and Byzantine origin.

Nonetheless, some women exercised great influence in political and religious matters. Another of Mohammed's wives, Aisha, was only age 7 when she married him. The daughter of the premier caliph of Mecca, she wielded much power even as an adolescent and became a scholar of the Hadith. After Mohammed's death, Aisha used her knowledge of Islamic principles to direct the caliphs. When she condemned the machinations of Ali, who murdered to attain a caliphate, a civil war ensued between the newly formed factions of Shi'ite and Sunni Moslems. Aisha led soldiers against Ali in the Battle of the Camel (656). Despite her defeat by Ali, Aisha was a political force until her death at age 64.

Sukaina (b. c. 671) was the granddaughter of the caliph Ali and staged her *nuchuz* (rebellion) in Medina and Mecca. She had 4–6 equally aristocratic husbands and stipulated in her marriage contract to her husband Zayd that he must never take a second wife, prevent her from acting as she chose, or prevent her from living near her close woman friend Ummmu Manchouz. When he displeased her by visiting a concubine, she took him to court. She went unveiled and became so famous for her fiery beauty that men as well as women copied her style of dressing her hair; her home was a salon for poets and intellectuals.

Many women fought in the early battles of Islam, including Umm Umarah, one of Mohammed's first disciples, and Safiya, a 70-year-old aunt of the prophet, who was a guard during an attack against the Moslems in Medina and who killed an enemy attempting to infiltrate the fortifications. Soon after Mohammed's death, women were excluded from all political and religious functions. In contravention of the prophet's orders, women were prohibited from worshipping in mosques and from making pilgrimages alone to Mecca, and they were forced into seclusion in the home.

Arab Moslem unity lessened after the religious and political center moved to Damascus, and Syria and independent emirates emerged. Portuguese traders conquered Oman in 1508, but were expelled in 1650 by the Ottoman Turks, who maintained a presence throughout Arabia. A conservative reform movement, founded by Muhammed Abdul Wahab in the late 18th century, became powerful across the peninsula, and by 1811 the Wahabi fundamentalist movement dominated Arabia (with the exception of Yemen). Driven to the desert by the Egyptians (1818), the Wahabis reclaimed the Gulf Coast from 1821 to 1833 but lost territory by the end of the century. Ibn Saud, in coalition with the Wahabis, initiated a revival before the outbreak of WW I and in 1925 created the State of Saudi Arabia. The Nejd region was added (1932) to form the Kingdom of Saudi Arabia with Ibn Saud as the first king.

Islamic jurisprudence and the traditions of *purdah* continue to dominate the lives of most women in Saudi Arabia. Marriage is still considered a woman's ultimate goal and she is still subject to the father's will. In 1977 Princess Misha of the royal family tried to marry a man of her choice. She wed secretly and the couple attempted to leave the country in disguise. They were caught and sent to her grandfather, Prince Muhammad, who wanted them tried under Islamic jurisprudence. A religious court refused on the grounds that they had broken no law. Prince Muhammad had the couple executed in public for defying his will.

Foreign women employed in non-Saudi companies are subject to severe harassment if they do not adapt to the role expected of women. In 1980 a British woman was sentenced to 80 lashes for serving alcoholic drinks (which are prohibited by Islam) at a private party. The British Embassy intervened to prevent the carrying out of the sentence.

In contemporary Saudi Arabia, women are essential producers of goods and services which sustain their families, yet their participation in the paid labor force is one of the lowest in the world. Since the entrance of women into primary and higher educational institutions in the 1960's—due in part to the influence of the Amirah Iffat, wife of the late King Faisal—women's role in Saudi society has undergone major changes. A women's-rights movement for broader opportunities in education and employment—and on such issues as the right to drive a car—is growing. The need for a trained labor force is an incentive for women's increased economic activity beyond teaching and the social services. The government formed a committee in 1980 to formulate a policy on women's employment "within the framework of Islam." Conservative Moslems oppose women's employment outside the home as being detrimental to the family; they accuse the large numbers of foreign domestic workers in Saudi families of being a negative influence. Other obstacles to women's employment include male disapproval and noncooperation, lack of childcare facilities, the law against women driving, and lack of public transportation. However, in 1981 a transportation company initiated a policy of reserving 1 section on their buses for women working in Jiddah, Mecca, Riyadh, and other urban centers. In 1980 the Al-Rajihi money exchange company of Riyadh opened the first women's branch, run by and for women, since Saudi women control an est. 30–40% of Saudi Arabia's wealth; by 1982 there were 13 such bank branches (4 in Jiddah) with women directors and staff.

MYTHOGRAPHY. Female deities were prevalent in the Gahelia era of Arabia; each tribe claimed its own goddess would aid them in war. Allat was the supreme female goddess, "Mother of All." Al Uzza was worshipped by pilgrims to Mecca; she was thought to be a personification of the planet Venus. Manat was a sibyl, a shaper of fortunes who was consulted for visions of the future. Idols and paintings of Allat and Al Uzza were carried to battle by the Koraish to strengthen them against the Moslems. When Islam prevailed in Arabia, the god- desses of tribal cultures were declared demonic, and their shrines were destroyed.

SAUDI ARABIA: An Emerging Social Force
by Aisha Almana

Saudi Arabian women are emerging as a major social force, demanding an increase in their participation in the economic and social life of the country and calling for the recognition of their active and necessary roles in the development process. As a result, a controversy has heightened between two major groups.

The liberals are calling for an increase in women's economic and social participation and the improvement of their conditions, plus the necessity of recognizing that women constitute half the population—a half which should be utilized in relieving the country's shortage of "manpower" and its dependence on foreign labor (which presently constitutes more than 50 percent of the total labor force).

The conservatives, on the other hand, view women's role as virtually singular: mainly as mother-and-wife. They insist that a woman's participation in the labor market should be limited, and that jobs which may require (or expose) women "to mingle" with men in the workplace are objectionable and abhorrent.

But Saudi women have high hopes, based in part on the increase in educational and training opportunities which began in 1962. Women now constitute more than 35 percent of the total students in Saudi Arabia—and more than 14,000 of them are enrolled in teachers' colleges and higher education. Furthermore, the numbers are increasing, and the projected number of female enrollment in colleges is expected to reach more than 40,000 by the late 1980's. At present, women are enrolled mainly in the social sciences, in medical schools, and teachers' preparation colleges—all of which prepare them for jobs in the traditional female sector.

This reflects the current trend: women in Saudi Arabia work mainly in female services —female education, social welfare, and medical services. This separation has, however, contributed to women's holding *higher positions* in the work structure, albeit in running the female sectors. Consequently, we find that there are females occupying such jobs as deans of women's colleges, directors of different female institutions and social welfare agencies, and principals of female schools. Nonetheless, women still comprise less than 4 percent of the total labor force and work opportunities *are* limited to the female sectors. Yet even this work remains the major avenue for women to get out of their homes.

The economic gains resulting from the oil revenues have affected different aspects of Saudi society, and women are gradually finding themselves having more freedom. Modern conveniences make housework less time-consuming, and there is greater access to more efficient modes of transportation and communication. Still, all these changes which have affected the fabric of the society and contributed to changes in family ties and living conditions have failed to change the basic perception of women's position in the family and in the society. A woman's status remains marginal, not even equal to the position enjoyed by her sisters in the Gulf area, other Arab countries, or the rest of the world. This injustice has contributed to growing feelings of frustration among Saudi women in all economic groups, in the urban as well as in the rural areas.

Women are calling for more economic opportunities and for social justice. For example, in one of the workshops conducted in a remote rural area of southern Saudi Arabia (a workshop on women in rural development), the female participants voiced their frustration and discontent with their marital and family status and insisted on discussing these means of social injustice—which they felt were more important than what the conductors of the workshop considered important.

The new trend is that Saudi women are seeking employment or starting their own businesses, even with all the legal and cultural limitations that restrict women's work to the female services sector. There are women involved in real estate, construction, and commerce, plus those who work in animal husbandry, farming, and different crafts. Starting a business is not limited to the wealthy; there are many wage workers who are taking this step. One example is a nomadic woman who came to the city with seven children and an elderly ailing husband. She opened a small shop in her shack, catering to the neighbors. She would work as a janitor in the morning from 7 A.M. to 2 P.M., then continue with her store in the afternoons and evenings. She now owns her own home and has two grocery stores. She sells (to the *new* neighbors), continues to work as a janitor, *and* goes to a literacy program two hours every day.

Even with all these changes in Saudi women's attitudes toward work outside the home, the Saudi woman still suffers from social and economic injustices. Whatever benefits women *have* gained have been tied to the consent, cooperation, and permission of their male guardian(s). Yet the Saudi woman recognizes that she alone cannot challenge cultural values or bring change with the same speed as that of the economic progress her country is experiencing, that there are certain givens she must for the moment accept and work within, and that she needs understanding and support to do so.

Suggested Further Reading

Abd Al-Hay, Abdalkahaleh. "Contemporary Women's Participation in Public Activities: Differences Between Ideal Islam and Muslim Interpretation with Emphasis on Saudi Arabia." Diss., Univ. of Denver, 1983.

Almana, Aisha. "Economic Development and Its Impact on the Status of Women in Saudi Arabia." Diss., Colorado Univ., 1981.

Al-Torki, Soraya. "Family Organization and Women's Power in Urban Saudi Arabia." *Anthropological Research,* Fall 1977.

Gadi, Adnan. "Utilization of Human Resources: The Case of Women in Saudi Arabia." Thesis, California State Univ. (Sacramento), 1979.

Shaker, Fatin A. "Modernization of the Developing Nations: The Case of Saudi Arabia." Diss., Purdue Univ., 1972.

Aisha M. Almana is a sociologist and Director of the Women's Social Bureau, Eastern Province of Saudi Arabia. Her field-work has included studies on women's work conditions and the differential in wages based on national origin: the case of ARAMCO in Saudi Arabia, and economic development and its impact on rural, nomadic, and urban women.

SENEGAL
(Republic of Senegal)

Located in western Africa, bordered by Mali to the east, Guinea and Guinea-Bissau to the south, the Atlantic Ocean to the west, and Mauritania to the north; Gambia is surrounded by Senegal on 3 sides. **Area:** 197,161 sq. km. (76,124 sq. mi.). **Population** (1981): 5,892,940, female 50.8%. **Capital:** Dakar.

DEMOGRAPHY. Languages: French (official), indigenous African languages including Wolof, Serer, Pular, Mandingue, Diola, Sarakole. **Races or Ethnic Groups:** Wolof, Serer, Fulani, Peuhl, Toucouleur, Leboue, Niominka, Diola, European descent. **Religions:** Islam 80%, indigenous faiths 9%, Christianity (predominantly Roman Catholicism) 5%, Hinduism. **Education** (% enrolled in school, 1975): Age 6–11—of all girls 24%, of all boys 33%; age 12–17—of all girls 21%, of all boys 35%; higher education—no data obtainable. **Literacy** (1977): Women 1%, men 10%. **Birth Rate** (per 1000 pop., 1975–80): 48. **Death Rate** (per 1000 pop., 1975–80): 22. **Infant Mortality** (per 1000 live births, 1975–80): Female 147, male 170. **Life Expectancy** (1975–80): Female 44 yrs., male 41 yrs.

GOVERNMENT. Unicameral parliamentary system with an elected 100-member National Assembly, an elected president who appoints a prime minister, a 7-member council of ministers, 2 secretaries of state, and 8 other ministers. **Women's Suffrage:** 1956; constitutionally confirmed at Independence in 1960. **Equal Rights:** The 1960 Constitution stipulates equality for all; no specific legislation governing equality for women. **Women in Government:** In 1983 women were 8% of the National Assembly; the Secretary of State for Human Development and 1 cabinet minister were women.

ECONOMY. Currency: CFA Franc (May 1983: 370. = $1 US). **Gross National Product** (1980): $2.6 billion. **Per Capita Income** (1980): $450. **Women's**

Wages as a Percentage of Men's: No data obtainable. **Equal Pay Policy:** No data obtainable. **Production** (Agricultural/Industrial): Peanuts, millet, rice, cotton, sorghum; processed foods and fish, peanut oil, fertilizer, cement, phosphate, refined petroleum. **Women as a Percentage of Labor Force** (1980): 38%; **of agricultural force**—no general statistics obtainable but est. at more than 60% (87% of women workers were employed in agriculture, 1975); **of industrial force**—no statistics obtainable (see following article); **of military**—no statistics obtainable; as of 1983, women may apply to the military-status Polytechnic School to train as civil engineers, and to the military School of Health. Nine women became the first female police officers and inspectors in the 1983 National Police School promotions. **(Employed) Women's Occupational Indicators:** No statistics obtainable (see following article). **Unemployment:** No data obtainable.

GYNOGRAPHY. Marriage. *Policy:* The Constitution (Art. 10) states that marriage is the basis of the community and shall be protected by the State. Marriage laws differ for various ethnic and religious communities—Islamic, Christian, Hindu, and customary law. According to the 1973 Family Code, minimum marriage age is 16 for females, 20 for males, and consent of both is required; marriages must be recorded with the civil registrar. Dowry is paid in Islamic, Hindu, some Christian, and some customary marriages. In Islamic marriages, the husband is the legal head of household with complete authority over the wife, and is in charge of the family's common interests, children and their education, and choice of domicile, and all objects within it are legally considered to be his property. Polygyny is legal, and a man may have up to 4 wives; however, the 1973 Family Code requires that a man decide at the time of marriage whether he will have a monogamous or polygynous marriage, and his decision is legally binding. The law stipulates equal treatment of wives in a polygynous marriage. A woman must obtain her husband's consent to work outside the home, but if he opposes her decision she may take the matter to court. A wife cannot own land or inherit property but may keep and control property she owned prior to marriage. She may keep her birth-name or take her husband's name. In other than legal polygynous marriages bigamy is punishable by a fine of CFAF 20,000–100,000 and 6 months–3 yrs. imprisonment. Adultery is punishable by CFAF 20,000–100,000 and imprisonment (also see **Divorce**). Under the law, murder in the case of adultery is not illegal if a spouse finds the other spouse and the third party in the illegal sexual act. A wife who abandons the marital home can be fined CFAF 20,000–100,000. Among Hindus, strict observance of the caste system would require persons to marry within their caste; interpretation of religious doctrine varies, but a fundamentalist reading demands that a wife be defined in relation to her husband, who is considered her superior. Customary marriage laws reflect the patrilineal or matrilineal traditions of various respective groups (see following article).

Practice: Female mean age at marriage (1970-79): 19; females age 15–19 in union (1970-79): 42%. Reports indicate that the majority of women are married and that they marry young. The minimum marriage age limit is frequently not enforced. Many marriages are arranged by families who view the unions as economic arrangements; second (or parallel) cousins are generally the preferred mates, as that will assure that the dowry remains within the family. Although a wife is entitled to keep and control her dowry, families commonly take possession of it. Young women generally have limited social contact with men before marriage because of the considerable emphasis placed on virginity. A blood-stained sheet is sometimes displayed in public on the wedding night as proof of virginity; some women who have not bled have been murdered by their "dishonored" husbands. While Islamic jurisprudence stipulates equal treatment of wives under polygyny and separate living areas for multiple wives, there are no measures to enforce the code. Women who are not virgins or who have been divorced command a lower dowry. Polygyny is not uncommon, and some men use the "suspicion of adultery" divorce clause (see **Divorce**) to by-pass the 4-wife limit of polygyny.

Divorce. *Policy:* Legal; under the 1973 Family Code there are 10 grounds for contested divorce, and divorce by mutual consent. Adultery (must be proven in accusing a husband; can be proven or merely "suspected" in accusing a wife) is grounds for divorce. The new Family Code eliminates *talaq* (repudiation) and stipulates the legality of annulment if either spouse has not consented to the marriage. A wife may divorce her husband, but she forfeits her dowry; if a husband divorces a wife, he is obliged to maintain her and their children, and she may keep her dowry and any objects belonging to her; however, a husband who is granted a divorce on the grounds of his wife's incompatibility or sickness can have his obligation of maintenance reduced to a bare minimum. A woman who divorces by mutual consent and keeps her dowry may lose it if she remarries. Child custody in the case of divorce by mutual consent is granted to either parent. *Practice:* No statistics obtainable. Men often use divorce to circumvent the limits on polygyny, and thus they divorce frequently despite social pressures against it. For women, divorce is generally an economic disaster, since most females marry young, lack education and job skills, and may face rejection by their families after divorce.

Family. *Policy:* Family legislation includes health and nutritional care for mothers with several children. A paid maternity leave for 6 weeks pre- and 8 weeks post-delivery (which can be prolonged for a maximum of 3 weeks in certain cases) is available to employed women. Under the Social Security Code (Sec. 18), women married to workers, single women workers, or women workers whose husbands are not employed are entitled to maternity allowances until a child is age 2. Family allowances are payable to males as "heads of households" and to single women in some circumstances. No further data obtainable. *Practice:* In 1978 the average family had

7 children. No further data obtainable. **Welfare.** *Policy:* Under National Insurance, most employees, including domestic workers, are eligible for health and medical care, retirement pensions, and disability benefits (also see **Family**). *Practice:* No data obtainable.

Contraception. *Policy:* Although the sale of contraceptives is technically illegal, they can be obtained from pharmacies, clinics, and some private doctors. Government support of family-planning measures includes a plan of condom distribution to men, the opening of 10 hospitals and 25 health clinics in the Dakar–Cap Vert region, and a program of annual 1-day orientations for 800 midwives and 800 nurses. *Practice:* Women age 15–49 in union using contraception (1978): 4%; methods used (1978) abstinence 67%, rhythm 10%, pill 8%, IUD 4%, condom 2%, other methods 8%; using inefficient methods 86%. The government has stated its support of the activities of international family-planning agencies, but there are strong religious tabus (especially among Moslems and Roman Catholics) against any method of birth control other than abstinence or the "rhythm" method. Emphasis is placed on educating couples to space births rather than directly limiting or reducing them (see **Family**). **Abortion.** *Policy:* Legal only in case of danger to the woman's life; the physician performing the procedure must have the written certification of 2 other doctors. It is illegal to help a woman procure an abortion and to supply or use drugs to induce abortion. Illegal procedures are punishable by a fine of CFAF 20,000–100,000 and 6 months–2 yrs. imprisonment for the woman, and a fine of CFAF 20,000–100,000 and 1–5 yrs. imprisonment for the practitioner (whether or not the woman gave her consent). A person found guilty of performing numerous illegal abortions may be given a harsher penalty; doctors performing the procedure can be suspended from medical practice for up to 5 yrs. In 1977 the Ministry of Health proposed that laws regarding abortion be liberalized, but (as of 1983) the government has not acted on this recommendation. *Practice:* No statistics obtainable; reports indicate that illegal abortions are common. There is a strong religious (both Islamic and Roman Catholic) tabu against abortion. A woman who aborts without her husband's knowledge risks divorce and rejection by her family.

Illegitimacy. *Policy:* An out-of-wedlock child is given the mother's family name at birth and can be recognized later by the father, but to be considered "legitimate," a child must be formally recognized by a man whether the child is his or not; in the above cases, the child assumes the man's name and is given equal status with children born in wedlock. The child of an incestuous relationship cannot be legally recognized by the father. A man may legally repudiate a child if he can prove through blood tests that he is not the father. Under Islamic jurisprudence, a father can exercise the right of *la'am* and repudiate even his own child if he suspects his wife of adultery (see **Marriage** and **Divorce**). An out-of-wedlock child who is not recognized by the father or any other man has inferior legal status and rights. *Practice:* No statistics obtainable. Reports indicate that some polygynous husbands "suspect" their wives of adultery, thereby repudiating a child, to avoid paying child support. **Homosexuality.** *Policy:* Illegal; no further data obtainable. *Practice:* No data obtainable.

Incest. *Policy:* Illegal; punishable by a fine and imprisonment. No further data obtainable. *Practice:* No statistics obtainable. Father-daughter incest is reportedly common, especially in rural areas. The high value placed on virginity at marriage makes a female victim especially vulnerable to repercussions beyond the incest itself; reportedly, there have been cases in which such a young woman has been murdered by family members who wanted to avoid being "dishonored" at her wedding. **Sexual Harassment.** *Policy:* No data obtainable. *Practice:* No statistics obtainable, but reports indicate that sexual harassment is common.

Rape. *Policy:* Both rape and attempted rape are illegal. Rape of a minor under age 13 is punishable by the (undefined) maximum penalty; rape of a person over age 13 is punishable by 5–10 yrs. imprisonment. Marital rape is in effect condoned by law, as a husband's right to sexual relations is included in the marriage contract. Attempted rape of a minor of either sex under age 13 is punishable by 2–5 yrs. imprisonment or 5–10 yrs. "if violence is used"; attempted rape of a minor over age 13 by a guardian or person in authority is punishable by the maximum penalty. Castration, usually a crime punishable by 10–20 yrs. imprisonment, is regarded differently in a proven case of self-defense against rape (sentence is then reduced to 2–5 yrs.) or against attempted rape. (For gang rape, see **Prostitution.**) *Practice:* No statistics obtainable. Reports indicate that rape is common. Single women who are rape victims may be disowned or killed by their families because as non-virgins they can no longer command a high dowry; a married woman who is raped may be repudiated or killed by her "dishonored" husband.

Battery. *Policy:* There is no specific law prohibiting wife-beating, but general laws against battery and assault may be applied in extreme cases. *Practice:* No statistics obtainable; reports indicate that wife-beating is a common practice that is tolerated in some regions. Generally, a battered woman who attempts to leave her husband faces economic privation, in addition to being subject to legal charges of abandoning her marriage (see **Marriage**). A battered woman may find little protection from her own family, which has economic and social interests in the continuance of her marriage. **Prostitution.** *Policy:* Prostitution itself is not illegal. It is illegal to aid or abet a woman to enter prostitution, live off the earnings of a prostitute, or run a hotel for purposes of prostitution; these acts are punishable by a fine of CFAF 250,000–2.5 million and 1–3 yrs. imprisonment. Prostitutes must be registered with the State, undergo regular health examinations, and carry health cards. If minors are involved, if force is used, if acts occur outside the national boundaries, and "in cases of gang rape," the penalty is a fine of CFAF 300,000–4 million and 3–5 yrs. imprisonment. *Practice:* No statistics obtainable. Prostitution exists predominantly in the urban centers, affecting es-

pecially young Serer and Wolof women (see following article); it is common for young, unskilled, noneducated rural women who migrate to the cities for jobs to turn to prostitution as their only means of survival. In addition, women who have been rejected by their husbands or families may turn to prostitution. Prostitutes are considered social outcasts and have no measure of protection from harassment, beatings, and other forms of mistreatment by male clients, pimps, and the police. **Traditional/Cultural Practices.** *Policy:* None. *Practice:* Young girls of the Toucouleur, Diola, and Mandingue cultures are usually excised*; the Toucouleurs also practice infibulation.** In some communities, female facial and body tattooing and scarification are practiced (see following article). **Crisis Centers.** *Policy:* None. *Practice:* None.

HERSTORY. Evidence of Paleolithic and Neolithic civilizations has been found in the area which is now Senegal. The Wolof and Serers first settled in the region in the first millennium C.E. In the 9th century, the Toucouleur arrived, and from the 10th–14th centuries they established the powerful state of Tekrur. The Toucouleur were converted to Islam, and in the 14th century Tekrur was conquered by the Mali Empire. In the 15th century, the Wolof founded the Jolof Empire. In 1445 Portuguese sailors established settlements on the Senegal River and began trading in African slaves.

There are few records of Senegalese women before the arrival of the Portuguese in the 15th century C.E., but there were female chieftains and warriors who fought against the influx of Europeans. Along the upper Gambia River, the Bainounka queens were powerful. In 1639 French settlers arrived at St. Louisiane, along with Dutch and British settlers in the 17th century. The British gained temporary control over all the French posts and set up Senegambia, the first British colony in Africa, but by 1840 the French had regained possession of the area.

In the 17th century, the tradition of female traders continued as African

* See Glossary.
** See Glossary.

women controlled European access to trade along what is now the Senegambia River and the Upper Guinea Coast. On the coast, in Rufisque, notable women traders were Senhora Philippa ("Dame Portugaise"), Senhora Catti, and Marie Mar, an Afro-European who aided shipwrecked sailors. Biblana Vaz built a vast trading empire between the Gambia and Sierra Leone Rivers in the 1670's and 1680's.

In the 18th century, there were many notable women *signares* (or entrepreneurs); in the Portuguese settlements south of Gambia, Rosa de Carvalho Alvarenga was one of the most powerful traders in West Africa and acted as an arbitrator between the Portuguese and African peoples. Leading Afro-European women traders along the Nunez and Pongo Rivers were Mae Avrelia Correia, Eliza Proctor, Mary Faber, and Isabella Lightburn.

Throughout the 19th century, Senegalese women participated in indigenous protest against the entrenched colonial administration. Women were active in the labor and student strikes of the 1950's and 1960's, and the percentage of women in the National Labor Union (CNTS) increased steadily and continues to do so. In July 1960 Senegal was declared an In-dependent Republic. Since the 1950's, women's organizations have formed to work on such issues as education, health, and labor rights for women. The Federation of Senegalese Women is an umbrella organization of 40 such groups. The Centre Social des Femmes in Dakar, under the direction of Awa Dia Thiam, organizes women's courses in literacy, hygiene, childcare, and skills training. AAWORD (Assoc. of African Women for Research and Development) is a pan-African women's federation based in Dakar; AAWORD (French acronym AFARD) publishes a journal, does research and networking, and organizes for women's rights continent-wide.

MYTHOGRAPHY. Long before Islamic or Christian influence arrived in the Sene-Gambia region, Asia, goddess of the earth, shared the devotion of the indigenous peoples with Nyamia, the god of the sky. The Serers revered the spirits of the dead, and their myths followed the pattern of other sun-moon worshippers. One such myth explains that the reason one can look at the moon without straining one's eyes is that the moon muted her own light so that her daughter might watch, without being blinded, her mother the moon bathing naked.

SENEGAL: Elegance Amid the Phallocracy
by Marie-Angélique Savané
(Translated by Anne-christine d'Adesky)

Senegalese women are famous for their elegance. It is true that the *grand boubou,*[1] the national costume, gives Senegalese women a certain majestic presence. But this seeming uniformity of dress and mannerism, owing to strong influence by the Wolof culture and Islam, must not mask the diversity of their behavior, based on their respective environments and specific cultures.

The Diola woman of the rice paddies—robust and independent—is very different from the St. Louisiane, graceful and jaunty in her walk.

The Leboue trader who pays for the services of her own fisherman husband contrasts with the quasi-reclusive Toucouleur woman.

[1] Big turban.

The animist Serer woman maintains a relationship with the earth and her work not found in the Islamic Wolof woman, who is burdened by domestic chores.

These women, despite the vital role they play in the economy, remain under masculine authority until old age, when they acquire independent status. Marriage marks the most important event of their lives and gives them social status as adults. This is why, from childhood on, women are prepared for this event by learning domestic work, initiation into the games of love and the art of marriage, and also prepared for the pain of child-birth (and of married life).

Thus, whatever their culture may be, the women submit with the same resignation: multiple childbirths, polygyny, repudiation, excision and infibulation,* tattooing and scarring, forced marriages, physical and moral violence. But they also develop forms of resistance to male power through the means offered them by tradition: sexuality, magic, madness, etc. This reaction can take violent forms when it involves what is most precious to them—their children.[2] It is this culture of resistance that made them oppose foreign domination. Just as the NDer women of the Waalo in the last decade preferred collective suicide to slavery under the invading Maures of Trarza. Just as the Diolas organized against the colonialist French administration in the 1940's.

In the Countryside

Senegal is essentially an agricultural country, peanuts being the main cash crop. The country also produces cereals (meal, sorghum, rice, corn), as well as cotton, sugar cane, manioc, and the market vendors' produce. The agriculture, largely exported, is affected by fluctuations in the world market, by climatic factors (mainly drought), and by the situation in the Sahelo-Sudanian zone.

Women play a decisive role in agricultural production. They participate in the peanut and cereal industries and are solely in charge of the production of condiments, as well as of harvesting and processing food. Domestic labor falls completely on their shoulders. Yet statistics undervalue the impact of women's work in the rural sector, estimated at over 60 percent since women carry out certain tasks critical to the cash-crop industry, as well as almost half of the necessary services for their families' food—*and* they reproduce and maintain the work force itself.

In the rural sector, all women participate in agricultural production. Furthermore, the activities of women (artisan/craftwork, small farming, small commerce) are indispensable for balancing the family budget. But it is also in the countryside, where tradition still dominates social norms, that women suffer most from male oppression, without much hope of freedom.

The Rice-Cultivating Societies in Casamance

It is in Casamance, the southernmost region of Senegal, that the rice country is found. It is a land of mangroves, savannahs, and forest. The Diolas and Mandingues are the main ethnic groups. The animist Diola society presents a certain homogeneity, because it is not vertically structured. Diola women, despite their submission to male authority, enjoy certain choices: they benefit from relative economic autonomy, they freely manage their harvest and feed their children from their personal granary. Their status is due to the important role they occupy in rice production, an economic product with religious significance. Fecundity is the focus of a special cult, so the Diola woman also gains status

---

* See Glossary.—Ed.

[2] This explains the celebrated march of the Thies women during the Chaminots strike in 1957 and that of the women of Casamance during the student strikes in Jan. 1981, after the assassination of a student by the police.

through her fertility. Diola women pluck oil palms all along the river-banks and transform the nut into a red oil that is important in food production. They also sell palm wine and other by-products. Yet the Diola woman remains subordinate to the man, whose decisions are unquestioned. She never inherits land, even if she is given rice lands when she marries.

Mandingue women, by contrast, do not have this even relative autonomy. They rarely appear in public. Mandingues are broken down into castes and are a very ancient Islamic people. Mandingue women are excised and sometimes infibulated. Polygyny is prevalent. Women take part in the most difficult, skilled work of the rice-gathering process, while men work the crops on the dry plateaus.

In the Wolof and Serer Peanut Basin

This region is located in the western center of Senegal, a forest zone buffeted by the Sudano-Sahelian climate. The Wolof and Serers are the basic ethnic groups. Agriculture is dominated by the peanut. Modernization of agricultural techniques has introduced a new sexual division of labor in the peanut and meal industry. Wolof and Serer women process their husbands' cereals; they themselves are in charge of condiments and other proteins.

At the same time, the overpopulation of the peanut basin, the deterioration of overworked earth, and traditional rigid social structures are also causes for the rural exodus of women, especially among the Serers, who leave their villages during the dead season to work in the city as maids. This relative mobility can be explained by the fact that the society is a mix of animist, Catholic, and (recently) Islamic faiths. The lineage is matrilinear—the maternal uncle being the moral authority for the woman and her children, even when she is under her husband's rule.

The productive efforts of Serer women are very high. They participate in the collective production of meal and peanuts. More and more, Serer women cultivate their individual crops, which they themselves sell. (One must say that the production of cash crops is a means of emancipation for women, while the collective cultivation of meal by all the workers does not allow for individual gain.)

The Wolof society, on the contrary, is vertically structured and based on the caste system. A family is composed of a male chief with authority, free men, and captives but also *sourgas,* or dependent males. The Wolof are strongly Islamic. Yet Wolof women are also affirming, more and more, their economic independence through peanut production. But the importance of domestic tasks (particularly well-digging), limits the possibility of individual women's peanut production. Also, Wolof women take part in the collective field-work of the chief's land or of sorghum.

In these two groups, polygyny is prevalent, owing to the constraints of the agricultural calendar, since the rotation of domestic tasks in the polygynous system liberates a large part of the women's work force for production tasks, while in monogamous households the woman remains a prisoner of domestic work. In the absence of advanced technology, women remain a source of manual labor.

The River Region

This territory includes the middle valley, or Fouta-Toro, of the Delta or Waalo. The climate is Sahelian. The river's activity determines agricultural activity and human occupation. Husbandry is an important activity. The Toucouleurs and the Peuhls [or Fulani] are the large ethnic groups. In the river region, male migration is high because of deteriorating economic conditions in the valley, and because the participation of women in agricultural labor is growing. In the area of hydroagriculture (irrigation farming), women and children are an important source of familial manual labor. Among the Peuhls, women milk the animals and make derived products (milk curd, butter, etc.), or trade it for meal.

The life of the Toucouleur woman is marked by the continuation of patriarchal structures and a belief in a strict Islamic code. It is a hierarchical society, with castes. Women exist only in relation to men. They are excised and given in marriage as soon as they are nubile, and their primary function is to reproduce. The matrimonial system is dictated by exogamy, which calls for the exchange of women outside the caste boundaries of the husband.

Polygyny is a common practice. But the prolonged absence of husbands creates new problems for abandoned women: illegitimate pregnancies and induced abortions. In this context, there is some demand for modern birth-control methods.

On the Coast and the Saloum Islands

The presence of a long coastline has permitted vital development of a local fishing industry and related activities.

The Serer, Leboue, and Niominka women fish with nets in the shallow waters. But their principal activity is the transformation by hand of sea products over which they exercise a monopoly: they salt or smoke the fish and then dry them, they pick oysters and mussels which they process into spices used in Senegalese cooking, and they are very active in the selling of fish in the markets and on the beaches. Considering the importance of distribution in the fishing industry, one can say that women occupy an important role in local fishing. Yet they are increasingly in competition with men, who are more independent and more mobile and can relocate in search of new markets.

In the Cities

In Senegal, the city is a colonial creation. The activities found there are a reflection of an extroverted economy: a plethora of banks, businesses, and small local industries. These activities, given the massive rural exodus and the natural population growth, can no longer offer jobs to everyone. A vast informal sector has developed where women can find low-income but rarely steady jobs. The ethnic mix in the cities creates a certain cosmopolitanism that emphasizes social boundaries.

Industry does not offer diverse jobs to women, who are generally hired on a daily or seasonal basis. Women are found in food and textile industries where the turnover of workers is high and valid statistics are hard to find. These workers have neither job security nor the social advantages given to salaried workers. They are confronted daily with problems of employment, transportation, and childcare. The women workers are generally married to other workers (or unemployed workers) and are in constant conflict with traditional values versus their need to work outside the home. Confronted by the rhythm of machines and the hard conditions of life and work, they reject traditional customs but are still unable to assume the model prescribed by elite urban women. They recognize the need to harness their fertility and develop new styles of living, and—when they are well organized—they are militant activists in trade-union struggles.

The greatest number of city women are employed in the service sector, in areas deemed traditionally female: secretarial, health, social services, etc. Some university-educated women occupy administrative posts in ministries, banks, and private businesses. Despite their education, these women are still victims of such traditional models as multiple pregnancies, arranged marriages, polygyny, dowries, etc. They are pulled by two worlds, the traditional and the modern. They want a liberation that represents the adoption of basic Western consumerism and bourgeois taste while maintaining traditional structures and roles which offer psychological security. They are the great defenders of African cultural values—even though many of these practices are an affront to the individual rights of women. These educated women are also the ones who benefit most from the 1973 Family Code regulating marriage, divorce, inheritance, family relations, and personal status.

In the business sector, women have traditionally been small traders in the markets, where they sell vegetables, fish, and other foodstuffs. At present, they are developing new forms of business—first on the regional level for subsistence products; then (in such neighboring countries as Mauritania, Gambia, and Mali) for textile and other manufactured goods that are taxed at a lower rate than in Senegal; finally, they have discovered markets in America and Europe for luxury articles (gold, precious stones, perfumes, etc.). This uncontrolled trade constitutes disguised black-market contraband. Some women traders offer their articles on a credit basis to middle-class women, whose demand for consumer goods rises steadily. Credit corresponds to their financial means. This informal trade hurts women who own boutiques and must pay high taxes that put the price of goods out of the range of the local population.

The rural exodus of females and the development of tourism have increased two activities for women: domestic work and prostitution. Young girls coming from the countryside without training or professional qualifications present themselves as "household workers." They live in a precarious situation, despite legislation protecting domestic work. The number of young girls seeking work is so high that they are forced to accept very low wages and arduous working conditions. These young migrants, alone in a hostile city, are easy bait: illegal abortions, nervous depressions, single motherhood, exploitation —this is their daily lot.

Prostitution is relatively developed in the cities and surrounding tourist areas. It affects in particular the young Serer and Wolof women who, far from their homes, take up prostitution without immediate social repercussions. Legal statutes regulate this practice, which is tolerated but controlled. Public patrolling and enticement is forbidden, and prostitutes must possess a health card from the Institute of Social Hygiene requiring them to have regular medical check-ups.

Prostitutes are the victims of rackets by pimp intermediaries and also by the police. They suffer ostracism from their neighbors and are forced to pay a high price for lodging and educating their children. In the absence of a liberal policy of contraception, they have multiple pregnancies, multiple induced abortions, etc. Over the last years, a form of high-class prostitution has developed which touches on that part of the middle-class female population with a newly acquired taste for luxury goods.

Women's Organizations

There are many traditional and modern women's organizations. The first are social-aid-type associations that organize women in neighborhoods around the *tontines*** and *caisses populaires,* *** or by age and peer group. The modern associations are made up of middle-class women who come together on a professional (or confessional) basis: the Zonta Club, the Soroptimist Club, etc. These associations, forty of which belong to the Federation of Women's Associations of Senegal (Fédération des Associations Féminines Sénégal, FAFS), do not focus on the question of the status of women in a broad sense. Their actions are limited to preserving economic privileges and improving legal conditions. They have a "voluntary charity" attitude toward less privileged women.

The struggle against the subordination of women in the economy and the culture is still relatively new and fragile. Senegalese feminists are considered "inauthentic" in that femi-

---

** A *tontine* is an informal savings/credit union maintained by deposits of women in a compound, village, office, etc.—Ed.

*** A *caisse populaire* is a loan against security with a small rate of interest.—Ed.

nism is perceived as being about the problems, hopes, and struggles of Western women. This poses the question of the nationalist aspect of feminism.

Such consciously maintained confusion is explained by the absence of a clear political vision of the "women's question." It must be said that the participation of women in the political sphere is marginal in that the women's groups of the various political parties are mostly perceived as masses to be maneuvered, or possibly as an electoral constituency— and yet the representation of women in these political institutions is still very weak: two ministers, eight parliament members.

At the moment, therefore, the absence of women's activism does not favor the emergence of a theoretical debate on the question. But glimmers of such a debate *are* appearing, as young professional women daily confront the phallocracy of their colleagues at work and also domination by their partners at home.

Conclusion

The description of Senegalese women in their work and culture(s) may give the impression that they are resigned or that their situation is not evolving. Yet women, individually and as a group, transgress certain norms. They revolt; they organize around income-generating projects; they risk confronting the anger of men to express needs that conflict with those of their spouses; some of them become militant in the labor unions or in political parties.

These acts are not theoretical ones, but they express tendencies which more and more will be affirmed in order to create a coherent vision capable of mobilizing and organizing women for their rights and for a radical transformation of their status. And that will be the dawn of a new era.

Suggested Further Reading

Ba, Mariama. *Une Si Longue Lettre* (Such a Long Letter). Dakar-Abidjan: Nouvelles Editions Africaines, 1980.

Fall, Aminata Sow. *Le Revenant* (The Returning One). Dakar-Abidjan: Nouvelles Editions Africaines, 1975.

Famille et développement (Family and Development), No. 9, Dakar; article on polygamy.

Famille et développement (Family and Development), No. 13, Dakar; article on prostitution.

Le Code Sénégalais de la famille (The Senegalese Family Code). Dakar: Librairie Clairafrique, 1973.

Loquay, Annie. *La Main d'oeuvre Feminine dans le Secteur Industriel en Afrique de L'Ouest—le Cas du Sénégal* (Female Labor in the Industrial Sector of West Africa— The Case of Senegal). Dakar: ENDA (Environment et Développement en Afrique), 1977.

Plan d'action de la femme Sénégalaise (Plan of Action of Senegalese Women). Secrétariat d'Etat à la Promotion Humaine (Senegal), Mar. 1982.

Savané, Marie-Angélique. *Femmes et Développement au Sénégal* (Women and Development in Senegal). Addis Ababa: CEA (Comission Economique pour l'Afrique); annotated bibliography, to be published.

———, et Mamadou H. Idy Niane. *Attitudes des femmes face à la fécondité et à la contraception* (Attitudes of Women on Fertility and Contraception). Dakar: CONAPOP (Comission Nationale de la Population), Oct. 1982; mimeo.

Vidal-Crouzet, Claude. "Les Femmes Wolofs dans un Milieu Rural en Mutation: Marginalisation ou intégration?" (Wolof Women in a Changing Rural Area: Marginalization or Integration?). Thèse de 3è Cycle, EHESS (Ecole des Hautes Etudes en Sciences Sociales), Paris, 1981.

Marie-Angélique Savané is a Senegalese sociologist. She currently directs the UN Research Program on Nutritional Systems for Social Development (UNRISD). Earlier, at the same institute, she coordinated a research program on the incidence of socioeconomic transformation of the role and status of African women south of the Sahara. For four years, she was editor-in-chief of the African review *Family and Development*. She is married, has two children, is president of the Association of African Women for Research and Development (AAWORD), and is "a militant feminist who has participated in many international women's meetings."

SOUTH AFRICA
(Republic of South Africa)

Located on the southern tip of Africa, bordered by Mozambique, Swaziland, and the Indian Ocean to the east, the Atlantic Ocean to the south and west, and Namibia (South-West Africa), Botswana, and Zimbabwe to the north; Lesotho forms an enclave within South Africa. **Area:** 1,140,519 sq. km. (440,355 sq. mi.); this figure includes the provinces of the Cape of Good Hope, Natal, Transvaal, Orange Free State, and nonindependent "homelands"* of Gazankulu, KwaZulu, Lebowa, Qwaqwa, Ndebele, and KaNgwane, but excludes Walvis Bay and the allegedly independent "homelands" of Transkei, Bophuthatswana, Ciskei, and Venda. The "White area" constitutes approx. 87% of the country. **Population** (1980): Total 27,886,270; African 20,084,319, White 4,453,273, Coloured 2,554,039, Indian 794,639; female out of total pop.—50%. According to 1980 official figures, 52% of the African pop. (including migrant workers) resides in the "homelands"; however, other estimates indicate the African pop. is divided evenly between the 2 areas when Afri-

cans living "illegally" in White areas are included (see HERSTORY). **Capital:** Cape Town (legislative), Pretoria (administrative), Bloemfontein (judicial); in independent "homelands": Umtata (Transkei), Mmabatho (Bophuthatswana), Bisho (Ciskei), and Thohoyandou (Venda).

DEMOGRAPHY. Languages: English, Afrikaans (both official), indigenous African languages (Zulu, Xhosa, Setswana, Sepedi, Sesotho, other), Indian (Urdu, Gujarati), other. **Races or Ethnic Groups** (Official Categories): African (Zulu, Xhosa, Tswana, Sepedi, Swazi, other), Asian (Indian, Chinese minority), Coloured (can include Indian, Cape Malays, etc.), White (Dutch, British, and other European descents). **Religions:** Christianity (Dutch Reformist majority), Hinduism, Islam, Anglican, Judaism, indigenous faiths, other. (Among Indians: Hindu 70%, Moslem 20%, Christian 8%.) **Education:** Based on official policy of segregation under which National Education applies to Whites only; primary

---

* With the exception of Qwaqwa, each "homeland" consists of numerous discontiguous pieces of land which vary greatly in size; the "homelands" make up approx. 13% of the total South African area and, although independent "homelands" have considerable control over internal affairs, all "homelands"—nonindependent, semi-dependent, and even independent—fall under varying degrees of White South African control (in such areas as economics, foreign policy, registration and passbooks, etc.). South Africa is the only country to claim recognition of the independence of the above-mentioned 4 "homelands"; other nations have stated that this promotion of alleged independence and the "homeland" policy itself are simply devices to further apartheid (see HERSTORY). The majority of the African pop.—including those living in both independent and nonindependent "homelands" as well as in "White areas"—favor a racially integrated State, although there are many Africans who despair of such integration taking place and consequently defend the idea of independent "homelands" as regions of relative African autonomy and of incipient true independence from White rule. However, even for this group, a more equitable distribution of land and a legitimate choice of citizenship in SA or the "homeland" are goals.

** The 1950 Population Registration Act officially established the racial classification of African, Coloured (which includes Asian), and White, and requires the assignment of every person into 1 of these categories. In general usage and under some laws the pop. is divided into 4 groups: African, Asian (predominantly Indian), Coloured, and White. Consequently, for this Preface only, in order to depict accurately the extremity of the South African system of racial categorization, we have capitalized the different racial "color" group names, as do the government's laws, acts, and policies. To further complicate this rigid compartmentalization system, popular usage (and even some official documentation) often makes reference to Black (for all peoples of color) and White. In this Preface, when we use that terminology, we are reflecting the terminology of the sources from which that particular datum was drawn.

and secondary education are segregated along official race indicators and there is strained token integration at universities (if no ethnic university offers specialized courses in such disciplines as medicine or architecture, a "White university" may admit Blacks). (Enrolled in school, Whites only, 1975): Age 6–11—of all girls 86%, of all boys 84%; age 12–17— of all girls 72%, of all boys 76% (the rates are considerably lower for Blacks; no specific statistics obtainable); higher education—in 1979, 7000 Africans and 80,000 Whites were enrolled in universities as fulltime residential students. In 1970 there were 1400 African university graduates and 104,500 White university graduates. In 1976, 216 Blacks and 3516 Whites graduated from White universities in specialized fields (medicine, engineering, law, architecture, etc.). In 1976 there were 27,000 White students in advanced technical training; in 1977 African technical colleges had 541 students. Only 15% of African students who entered primary school in 1967 reached the last yr. of high school. In 1978–79 government expenditures for education per child were $90 African, $290 Coloured, $940 White. In 1978, 15% of teachers in the African educational system and 68% of teachers in the White system had matric or senior certificates and teacher's diplomas. In 1981 there was an official est. shortage of 7000–8000 classrooms in "Black areas"; a greater shortage exists in the African "homelands."

The 1953 Bantu*** Education Act, which required education in mother-tongue languages for Africans through much of early schooling, has been replaced by the 1979 Education and Training Act, which requires mother-tongue education only through the fourth grade; Africans had protested the earlier policy as a discriminatory measure designed to inhibit the study of modern scientific ideas and limit their participation in the world. In defiance of government orders, some religious private schools recently opened their doors to African and Coloured students, although at high private-school fees. Female African and Col-

oured students generally attend school only for a few yrs. and are trained in traditional fields relating to household work—sewing, cooking, etc. Despite the obstacles, the number of female African university professors and technical assistants doubled over the period 1969–81. **Literacy** (1977): Women 57%, men 57%. **Birth Rate** (comparative rates per 1000 pop., 1977–78): African 28, Asian 18.7, Coloured 16.2, White 8.9. **Death Rate** (per 1000 pop., 1975–80): 10; the death rate is reportedly much higher among Blacks than Whites, and higher for persons living in the "homelands" than in urban industrial centers. **Infant Mortality** (per 1000 live births, 1975–80): Female 88, male 106; comparative rates (per 1000 live births, 1981) rural Black 240, urban Black 64, White 12; recent est. put the infant mortality rate in the African "homelands" at 300; 50% of deaths among Africans and Coloureds are of children under age 5. **Life Expectancy** (1975–80): Female 62 yrs., male 59 yrs.; comparative rates (1981) African 58 yrs., Coloured 56 yrs., White 72 yrs.

GOVERNMENT. The 1961 Constitution (amended 1980) established an independent republic. A unicameral parliamentary system consists of an all-White 177-member House of Assembly, a prime minister (leader of the majority party in Parliament) who appoints a cabinet, a president (elected by Parliament), and an appointed 61-member President's Council (for which Coloureds but not Africans are eligible). A new (1983) Constitution put forward by "moderates" includes a provision for the addition to Parliament of a Coloured House of Representatives and an Asian House of Deputies, but no House for Africans (the government, reportedly, has stated that a fourth House for Africans will never be included). The White House of Assembly continues to maintain primary control of Parliament and the presidency is given increased authority. Each official racial group has a representative council (see **Voting**). After the 1976 Soweto uprising (see HERSTORY), the elected Urban Bantu Coun-

*** The word Bantu, which had been used regarding the African pop., was dropped from official government usage in 1976 as a result of African students' demands (see following articles).

cils were replaced by Community Councils that oversee rental regulations, building permits, etc., but have no legislative power; the President's Council currently oversees Coloured political rights (the Coloured Persons' Representative Council dissolved following clashes between elected and appointed members); the elected and appointed 30-member South African Indian Council also has no legislative power. All "homelands" (including independent ones) have unicameral legislatures. The main political parties are the all-White National Party and the all-White Progressive Federal Party. The 1968 Prohibition of Political Interference Act prohibits racially mixed political parties and makes distinctions between African, Asian, Coloured, and White, thereby preventing a member of 1 group from joining a party of any other group. The 1976 Internal Security Act, the 1974 Affected Organizations Act, the 1967 Terrorism Act, the 1960 Unlawful Organizations Act, etc., have been used to ban such organizations as the African National Congress, the Pan-Africanist Congress, Black women's organizations, and Black writers' groups, and prevented almost all African political organizations from open existence or participation in the system.

Voting: Only Whites are allowed to vote for or be members of the central government. African men had but were stripped of their right to vote (for central government) in 1936, Coloured men in 1956 (for central government). African men and women can vote for their representative community council members and internal "homeland" representatives; Coloureds (male and female) can vote for their representative council members. **Women's Suffrage:** White women gained the right to vote for central government in 1930; African and Coloured women can vote only for their representative council members (see **Voting**). Large voter boycotts (over 90%) have been a means of protesting the system.

Equal Rights: No general law of equal rights based on sex. In 1920 the Principle of Political Equality for White Men and Women was passed. Most African women have the legal status of permanent minors; all other women are legal minors under the guardianship of a father or other male and remain so even after marriage, unless they have drawn up a special contract for legal majority. "Influx Control" regulations under the 1952 Section 10 amendment to the 1945 Black Urban Areas Consolidation Act forbids African women and men to be in urban areas for more than 72 hours unless they have been continuous residents in the area since birth, had continuous work in the area for the same employer for 10 yrs., or had lawful residence in the area for at least 15 yrs.; a wife, single daughter, or minor son of a male who qualifies under 1 of the above categories is also permitted to remain in urban areas; special permission to remain for more than 72 hours may sometimes be granted by a labor bureau if an African meets certain requirements. A person accused under Sec. 10 is considered to be in urban areas illegally until proven otherwise, and if convicted is subject to a fine, imprisonment, and resettlement (see HERSTORY for other discriminatory legislation affecting women). **Women in Government** (1983): African and Coloured women sit on their representative councils (no statistics obtainable); there are 2 White women in the House of Assembly, and White women are on provincial councils.

ECONOMY. Currency: Rand (May 1983: 1.08 = $1 US). **Gross National Product** (1980): $67 billion; in 1980 the GNP in the "homelands" was est. at less than 5% of the total South African GNP. **Per Capita Income** (1980): $2290. In 1975 per capita gross domestic product in the "homelands" ranged from R.49 in KaNgwane to R.108 in Bophuthatswana, with an average of R.73 (however, it was closer to R.300 when the earnings of migrant workers were included). In 1970, the PCI of Africans equaled 19% of the total for South Africa, and the PCI of 15 Africans equaled the PCI of 1 White. **Women's Wages as a Percentage of Men's:** In 1982 African women generally earned 50% of African males' wages and 8% of White males' wages. In 1980 the average monthly wages in manufacturing were $308 for African, $355 Coloured, $399

Indian, $1273 White; in 1974 the average annual cash earnings in agriculture were $268 for African, $502 Coloured, $1309 Indian, $4987 White; no rates by sex obtainable. In 1970 African female nurses earned R.18 per month with a Standard 8 certificate and R.27 with a matric compared to R.100 and R.120, respectively, for White female nurses. Minimum wage labor legislation does not cover agricultural workers, domestic workers, or workers in "border industries" (outside African "homelands"). In 1981 the (frequently 70-hour) weekly wages for domestic workers averaged $21 in large urban centers, $13 in smaller cities, and $9 or less in rural areas; a minimum wage of $24 per week for domestic workers has been recommended by the South African Institute of Race Relations.

Equal Pay Policy: Discriminatory wage rates are calculated *(de facto)* on the basis of race and sex in most categories. Recent legislation entitles Black workers to take part in statutory bargaining but does not accord them genuine trade-union rights; virtually all strikes are illegal under legislation which considers strikes ill suited to the workers' needs; the incidence of (primarily illegal) strikes rose 65% between 1980–81. **Production** (Agricultural/Industrial): Corn, wool, dairy products, grain, tobacco, sugar, peanuts; largest world production of gold, diamonds and other minerals, steel, tires, motors, textiles, plastics.

Women as a Percentage of Labor Force (1980): 35%; **of agricultural force** (1970) 35.8% (38% of women workers were employed in agriculture, 1975); **of industrial force**—no general statistics obtainable (of manufacturing 3.8%, 1970); **of military**—no statistics obtainable; the South African Defense Force is recruiting more White women in attempts to strengthen the forces; some African women are guerrilla fighters in the outlawed South-West African People's Organization (SWAPO) and other military units of groups fighting against apartheid and for national liberation.

(Employed) Women's Occupational Indicators: Of administrative/managerial workers 6%, of sales workers 30.3%, of professional/technical workers 42.7%, of clerical workers 47%, of service workers 68.5% (1970); only 4.2% of women employed in the clerical sector held high-level supervisory positions (1970); 55.9% of employed White women are in the clerical and professional sectors, 37.9% of employed African women are in the service sector and 34.7% are in agriculture, 43.8% of all employed Coloured women are in the service sector (1970); the majority of employed Indian women are in industry. Women in the industrial sector are concentrated in clothing, textile, food processing, and canning plants; women in the professional sector generally work as teachers, nurses, and medical aides (in 1977, 90% of the African work force classified as professional/technical were teachers and nurses). In 1982 African women comprised 1/3 of the Black work force; in 1977, 82% of Africans were in unskilled or semi-skilled jobs. Registration at labor bureaus is compulsory for African women and men (as part of "influx control"); contract (migrant) laborers must renew their registration in the "homelands" every yr.; labor bureaus cannot recruit African "homeland" workers unless no "qualified" labor is available, and they cannot place Africans registered as farm laborers in urban employment. Of the total "homeland" work force, 1/3 are migrants, 1/3 are (daily) commuters, and 1/3 are employed in the "homeland" or are jobless. Domestic service is one of the few areas of contract employment available to African women; in 1981 there were an est. 800,000–1 million domestic workers in South Africa. In 1981, 35% of African women employed in White urban centers were migrant workers or daily commuters. Women who go to urban centers "illegally" in search of employment are forced into low-paying work as unlicensed peddlers, handicraft artisans, beer brewers, etc., and risk prosecution under Sec. 10 (see **Equal Rights**). An African woman who refuses work offered by a labor bureau 3 times "without good cause," loses employment twice within 6 months "through her own fault," or is fired more than 3 times in 1 yr. for "her own misconduct" becomes an "idle Bantu" and risks resettlement to the "homelands"; the labor office and the employer determine whether a particular category applies. African women who have participated in "actions or strikes" deemed "detrimental to the maintenance of peace and order" or joined such groups as the South African Domestic Workers Assoc. have been fired; the Minister of Labour has made public statements referring to African women and children as "superfluous appendages to the male unit of labor."

Unemployment: No general statistics obtainable. In 1980 the Minister of Manpower *[sic]* estimated that over 1 million Africans were unemployed; several unofficial 1980 estimates placed the figure at almost 2 million (approx. 25%). In 1981 unemployment in the "homelands" was est. at 20–30% higher than in urban areas; approx. 70% of African women in the "homelands" are unemployed. Reportedly, there is a shortage of White (and sometimes Coloured) labor for many jobs. As of 1981, 80% of the total South African work force was Black (85% African, 11% Coloured, 3% Asian).

GYNOGRAPHY. Marriage. *Policy:* Marriages are governed by civil, customary, and religious laws. The 1949 Prohibition of Mixed Marriages Act prohibits marriages between Europeans and Non-Europeans; the 1950 and 1957 Immorality Acts outlaw sexual intercourse and any "immoral or indecent act" between Blacks and Whites. In many provinces and "homelands" an African woman is legally considered a perpetual minor under the guardianship of her husband or other male. Marriages are sometimes arranged and accompanied by a dowry. An African woman can rarely own land. In most "homelands," if a woman does own land, she needs a male's consent to dispose of it. In some cases, on the death of a husband, the land reverts to the State's control, although a wife is allowed to live on it (unless she must move in search of employment, in which case she forfeits this right).

A 1978 policy permits Africans who are "qualified" under Sec. 10 (see **Equal Rights**) for urban rights to own a home in specified areas on land leased from the State for 99 yrs.; generally women, even if "qualified," employed, and married to a "qualified" man, are unable to purchase homes through this system since they cannot receive loans because they are legal minors and prevented from taking on "financial responsibilities." In 1981 a reform of the Code of Zulu Law (formerly the Natal Native Code) had passed the KwaZulu Legislative Assembly and was under consideration of the president. Under the old code a woman had no independent powers; a husband legally controlled a wife's movement, right to employment and earnings, custody of children, etc. The proposed revision accords a woman majority status at age 21 with the right to establish her own home and marriage outside of community of property unless she signs an agreement otherwise. Moslem marriages generally are arranged, and accompanied by a dowry. Polygyny is legal for certain Moslems; a man is permitted up to 4 wives. *Practice:* Female mean age at marriage (1970–79): 23; women age 15–44 in union (1970–79): 57%. A commission has been set up to study the possibility of legislation to decriminalize sexual relations between Blacks and Whites. Many women remain near their husbands in urban areas by living in illegal "squatter" settlements or refusing to leave land that has been rezoned and forbidden to African occupation (also see **Divorce** and **Family**).

Divorce. *Policy:* Legal; no further data obtainable. *Practice:* No statistics obtainable. Many African couples, in which the husband is a migrant worker but the wife cannot obtain employment or other legal permission to be in urban areas, have chosen to divorce in order to remain together; once divorced, the woman can qualify as the single daughter of a family member already qualified under Sec. 10 (see **Equal Rights**) and remain in an urban area. Some couples have been forced to divorce under the Immorality Acts when 1 spouse has been reclassified by the government into a different racial group.

Family. *Policy:* A husband or other male family member is the legal head of household. Maternity leave is granted to some female workers, but domestic workers, among others, are not entitled to maternity leave or other benefits. A White employer who permits a Black servant to have a husband or child in her quarters is subject to a stiff fine. If an African woman is unable to care for her child (who was born in an urban area) and sends the child to live with a relative in the "homelands," the child loses Sec. 10 rights to live in the urban area. No government program of childcare exists. *Practice:* In 1980 an est. 75% of rural African families lived under the minimum household income considered necessary for subsistence. A high percentage of African women suffer from malnutrition and lack of medical care during pregnancy (see **Infant Mortality**). The majority pop. in the "homelands" is women, children, and the elderly, many of whom have been forcibly resettled under the government's policy of apartheid, resulting in a high number of female-headed households. From 1960 to 1980 over 3 million Africans were "resettled"; by 1981, 600,000 Indians and other Coloureds had been forced to move under the Group Areas Act.

In 1982 the Minister of Cooperation and Development stated that 75 additional "Black spots" were designated to become "White areas" (and consequently would necessitate forced removal of the Black pop.). The migrant labor system, under which workers return to the "homelands" only a few weeks a yr. to renew their contracts, creates tremendous hardships for separated African families. All urban Africans are required by law to live in designated townships outside of the White urban centers (see HERSTORY). In Soweto (outside of Johannesburg), the largest township and considered by many the most "privileged," a standard 4-room house (approx. 520 sq. ft.) was occupied by an average of 9 and up to 20 people; a 1979 survey revealed that 5.8% of the houses had inside baths, 12.8% had inside toilets, fewer than 20% had electricity, and 21% had running (cold) water. Migrant workers live in single-sex barracks-type dwellings which usually contain 50 or more bunks in 2 levels, and 1 sink and tap. In defiance of government orders, women have established illegal "squatters'" settlements (composed of tin shanties without electricity, heat, sewage, etc.) located outside of urban areas, where they live

with their children and sometimes husbands who have left hostels or also are in urban areas illegally. (In 1980 approx. 1 million Africans and Coloureds lived in squatters' settlements and faced a constant threat of fine, imprisonment, or forced resettlement. In the past, several squatters' settlements have been razed by government bulldozers; however, in late 1980 the government stated that without "condoning the phenomenon" they were preparing for a "controlled" amount of squatting.)

According to 1983 UN reports, medical experiments have been performed on healthy Black children; schoolchildren admitted to Baragwanath Hospital had various organs removed or grafts performed to test tissue rejection. The same UN report noted that child labor is prevalent (although illegal), especially in the agricultural sector; allegations of Black child slavery in the Cape Province were revealed in 1982. African women provide 75% of the public and private childcare for (primarily White) children (1981). The Charlotte Maxeke (see HERSTORY) creches and nursery schools were created to help African employed mothers. In 1955 the National Council of Women in South Africa issued a demand for better labor laws for all women, including 4 months maternity leave with full pay, childcare, etc. At present, the majority of international "border industries" (i.e., along *internal* "homeland" borders) and foreign companies operating in South Africa have been negligent about providing adequate childcare facilities and maintain an informal policy of hiring women on a part-time or seasonal basis in order to avoid providing maternity leave and other benefits. **Welfare.** *Policy:* Social insurance, welfare, unemployment compensation, and old-age and widow's pensions are granted to certain workers. Workers' compensation, unemployment compensation, and many other benefits are not granted to domestic, part-time, and agricultural workers. *Practice:* No general statistics obtainable. The complex system of requirements effectively limits the number of workers eligible for benefits. In 1974, 94% of private health care was obtained by Whites; the majority of Blacks rely on government-subsidized public health care. Hospitals are either totally segregated or segregated by wards. In 1973 there were 69 African doctors in South Africa; only 2.8% of all registered doctors work in the "homelands."

Contraception. *Policy:* Legal. Government family-planning agencies have instituted a program of birth control for African women which includes such methods as the controversial Depo-Provera injectable drug and forced sterilization. *Practice:* No statistics obtainable. The government is forcibly administering birth control to African and many Coloured women; Depo-Provera is administered regularly to many African women. Others are forcibly sterilized (non-reversible method) without their knowledge or consent. Recent government attempts to issue House Fertility Surveys in order to monitor the activities of African women were unsuccessful. In terms of voluntary contraceptive use, devices are more available to White urban women than to rural. **Abortion.** *Policy:* Under the 1975 Abortion and Sterilization Act, legal only in cases of danger to the woman's mental/physical health, fetal defect, imbecility, pregnancy resulting from rape (if reported within 72 hours; see **Rape**) or incest; the certification of 3 physicians is required. Illegal procedures are punishable by a fine and up to 5 yrs. imprisonment. *Practice:* In 1977 there were 539 legal abortions for all causes (399 for Whites, 78 Coloureds, 46 Africans, 16 Asians). It is difficult for any woman to get an abortion. Reportedly, 1 hospital (Baragwanath) handles approx. 5000 cases of septic abortions each yr. The Abortion Reform Action Group (ARAG) is a multi-racial organization working to reform the law (see **Crisis Centers**).

Illegitimacy. *Policy:* Legal status of a child is determined by the father. Out-of-wedlock children have inferior legal status and rights regarding inheritance, education, etc. In the indigenous African tradition the concept of "illegitimacy" does not exist; all children belong to the family/clan/tribe and have full membership rights (see following articles). *Practice:* No statistics obtainable. An out-of-wedlock child cannot inherit the father's

land or other property. Under Islamic jurisprudence, a father can repudiate even his own (acknowledged) child by the practice of *la'am.* **Homosexuality.** *Policy:* Male homosexuality is illegal; lesbianism is not mentioned in the law. *Practice:* No statistics obtainable. Homosexuals face severe oppression and so conduct their lives in secrecy; there are no homosexual-rights groups.

Incest. *Policy:* Illegal; no further data obtainable. *Practice:* No statistics obtainable. Incest is tabu in most South African societies and is a ground for legal abortion; no further data obtainable. **Sexual Harassment.** *Policy:* No data obtainable. *Practice:* No data obtainable. **Rape.** *Policy:* Illegal; punishable by a fine and imprisonment in most cases; rape of a White woman by a Black man is considered an "aggravated offense," because of the "special suffering" caused the victim, and is punishable by death; rape of a Black woman by a White man is considered a "normal offense" (see below). *Practice:* 16,000 rapes were reported in 1982. The National Institute for Crime Prevention and the Rehabilitation of Offenders estimates that 1 out of every 20–30 rapes is reported, which indicates an actual occurrence of at least 320,000 rapes per yr.; 95% of rapes occur within the same color (race) groups. There are an est. average of 8 cases of White-on-Black rape to 1 case of Black-on-White rape. From 1969–78, 20 African men were executed for rape; no White rapist has been sentenced to death and most are given minor prison sentences. Many African women have reportedly been raped by police during detention. Rape-crisis centers have stated that many women who had been raped and needed legal abortions could not obtain them; in 1980, 16 women were granted abortions on rape grounds.

Battery. *Policy:* No data obtainable. *Practice:* No statistics obtainable. Wife-battering is prevalent and a commonly tolerated practice. The problem is a "hidden" crime and is rarely reported. **Prostitution.** *Policy:* It is illegal to solicit for purposes of prostitution, to aid or abet a woman to enter prostitution, or to live off the earnings of a prostitute; punishable by a fine or imprisonment. *Practice:* No statistics obtainable. Prostitution is common, especially around urban and border industry areas; it is more often a forced means of survival among African women than Coloured or White women. **Traditional/Cultural Practices.** *Policy:* No data obtainable. *Practice:* Genital mutilation† of female children still is practiced in some areas, such as the northern Transvaal (see following articles). **Crisis Centers.** *Policy:* No government centers aid female victims of rape, battery, or incest. *Practice:* Women have established rape-crisis centers (see **Rape**) in several cities, including Cape Town, Johannesburg, and Durban (in 1967–77), and have plans for battered-women's shelters.

HERSTORY. Such indigenous African peoples as the Khoikhoi and the San, who migrated to southern Africa in approx. 1000 B.C.E., had matrilineal cultures. By the 17th century C.E., Zulu, Xhosa, Swazi, and Sothos were the principal African tribes in the region. In 1652 the Dutch East India Trading Company brought the first wave of Dutch and other European settlers, who established a colony at the Cape of Good Hope; a small group of French Huguenots arrived in 1688–89. The first South African marriage ceremony was between Jan Wouter and Catherine, a freed slave woman; the second was between Pieter van Meerhof and Eva, a Hottentot woman who worked as a translator for the Dutch. Such interracial marriages were common during the ensuing century, generating the unique South African caste of Cape Coloureds.

In 1795 the Dutch Boers, or Afrikaners, failed in their attempt to establish an independent republic, and the British took control of the colony in 1806. The slave trade was abolished in 1807, halting the import of slaves from tropical Africa and Madagascar, Ceylon, Indonesia, and India by the Dutch East India Trading Company. Many African female chieftains waged battles against the invading colonialists. In 1820 (and 1902), thousands of British women and men were given free passage and land grants in the colony. The influx of the British and the halt of the slave trade caused many Boers to begin the "Great Trek" north and east, where they established the republic of Transvaal and the Orange Free State. Slavery was abolished in the colony in 1834, but a system of white supremacy called *baaskaap* (bossdom) was maintained by the Dutch and the English. From 1860 to 1911, Indians were brought to South Africa to work as "contract laborers" on sugar plantations in Natal. After the discovery of diamonds (1867) and gold (1876), White immigration increased, and struggle for control of the area incited the Anglo-Boer War in 1899; the British defeated the Boers in 1902. African women began organized resistance to the Dutch and English administrations in the early 1900's. The National Council of Women in South Africa (NCWSA) was formed in 1909.

In 1910 the Union of South Africa was declared with British Commonwealth status. Africans formed the African National Congress (ANC) in 1912 in response to the White-ruled Union and to fight racial segregation policies by nonviolent methods. Charlotte Maxeke, the first Black woman doctor, became a national executive member of the ANC that year. In 1913 the government attempted to extend the existing pass laws already governing African men to African women in the Orange Free State. Women marched (600 in Bloemfontein and 800 in Windburg and Jaggersbontein) in protest and refused to carry the passes in one of the first known acts of resistance to segregationist policy. When hundreds of women were imprisoned and almost filled the jails, the government relinquished its position (and did not establish women's pass laws until 40 years later). The system of *baaskaap* was central to the goals of the Afrikaner National Party, which called for "separate development" of the races. Land laws were enacted (1913 and 1936) which established boundaries for African "reserves" (present-day "homelands" or "bantustans") of fragmented pieces of land which had few resources and received little rainfall. Other legislation severely restricted Africans' employment, and established compulsory resi-

† See Glossary.

dence of urban Africans in designated townships; ethnic advisory boards were set up to give Blacks strictly limited legislative power.

In 1920 the principle of political equality (see **Equal Rights)** was passed for White women only. White women organized the Women's Enfranchisement Union, to enforce their newly won right to vote in 1930, and protested the 1931 Women's Jurors Act which prevented them from serving on juries on the same terms as men. Black women in Johannesburg went on a 19-mile-a-day 9-day march in 1934 to protest rising bus fares. African women began forming squatter camps in the 1930's in reaction to the "homeland" policy and forced resettlement programs.

In 1948 the racial policy of "apartheid" (apartness) was officially established, with "separate development" for Africans, Asians, Coloureds, and Whites. The 1950 Group Areas Act (since amended) required segregated areas for all racial groups for "residential and business purposes," necessitated further resettlement, and limited ownership in and occupation of certain areas (e.g., public restaurants). The 1950 Suppression of Communism Act was a landmark piece of legislation since it became the forerunner of later Internal Security Acts. The 1950 Population Registration Act divided the population into official categories of African, Coloured (including Asian), and White; African and Col-

oured groups were further categorized into numerous subdivisions under some laws. The 1951 Bantu Authorities Act and the 1959 Bantu Self-Government Act laid out a structure for internal self-rule by Africans in the "homelands," identified and defined Africans in terms of separate tribal groups, and further limited their role in political life; all Africans, regardless of where they live, are considered citizens of a particular "homeland."

In 1952 the Blacks Abolition of Passes and Coordination of Documents Act replaced previous passes with "reference books" and for the first time required African women to possess them also; the law requires that every African over age 16 be fingerprinted and supplied with a "reference book" containing an identity card and information on employment and tax and family status. The police may demand to see a reference book at any time, and failure to have one is punishable by a fine or imprisonment. A 1975 judicial decision interpreted the law as giving persons a "reasonable opportunity" to locate passes not with them—but this opportunity is rarely acknowledged in practice. Until recently, Indians were required to obtain permits to travel between provinces and prohibited from being in certain areas for more than a short time; now Coloureds and Whites have unrestricted travel rights except that they must receive permission to enter African "homelands," townships, or locations.††

†† Some additional measures of government control instituted under apartheid:

The 1956 Riotous Assembly Act extends State control to public or private meetings of 2 or more persons.

The 1974 Publications Act authorizes committees to ban books, films, records, etc., which it considers "undesirable"; a person can be prosecuted for producing, distributing, and sometimes possessing such material.

The 1982 Internal Security Act (replacing the 1967 Terrorism Act) permits detention without charge for an indefinite period (frequently in isolation) if a person is suspected of acts that endanger the maintenance of public order, encourage further feelings of hostility between Blacks and Whites, or are designed to bring about social, economic, or political change, etc.; the act permits withholding of information about a detained person; potential witnesses in trials may also be subject to detention.

The recent legislation, Orderly Movement and Settlement of Black Persons Bill, increased the penalty for being in White areas without permission.

Banning orders, which have been used extensively, can be instituted randomly against individuals, organizations, and newspapers; the government is not required to offer explanation for such an order, it cannot be contested, and the courts are prohibited from intervening in the procedure. A banned person is generally prohibited from leaving a specified area, communicating with

These laws and numerous other legislative acts are elements of "petty apartheid," intended to implement complete racial segregation, and the "grand apartheid" system of separate, independent African states ("homelands") under which, eventually, there would be no African citizens in South Africa.

The African and Coloured populations responded in protest to the intensified policies of racial segregation. The ANC, formally inaugurated in 1948, assumed a more militant role. Charlotte Maxeke helped form the African Women's League (1948), and Ida Mntwana became its leader. Women participated in the 1949 ANC campaign of labor strikes. In 1950 the ANC, and several Coloured, Indian, and White organizations, adopted the 1950 Freedom Charter which demanded the vote and full political rights for every woman and man. Women participated in the massive nonviolent civil-disobedience movement, the 1952 Defiance Campaign, against apartheid. The government responded by mass arrests under repressive legislation and the enactment of further laws to limit gatherings, prohibit protest or incitement of protest, etc., and added whipping as a punishment in an attempt to eliminate the civil-disobedience movement.

The Federation of South African Women united many women's groups in 1954 under an umbrella organization that fought for African women's equality. In 1955 White women formed the Black Sash organization (so named because of the black mourning sashes they wore during demonstrations), which protested the government's racial policies and founded legal-advice centers for Africans. When the government began to implement the 1952 "pass law" extension in 1955, women responded with protests against them, and for improved labor legislation and political rights; 2000 women of all races marched on Pretoria, and thousands marched in Durban and Cape

Town. In 1956 women burned their passes in an act of civil disobedience, and Helen Joseph was the first woman arrested, along with Lilian Ngoyi, Dorothy Nyembe, and many others; 400 domestic workers went on strike in Johannesburg; 4000 women in Pretoria blocked city streets; 500 women in Venterpost presented a petition against apartheid signed by 10,000 women; 2000 women in Evaron marched for 7 miles to the Native Commissioner's office. In Aug. 1956, 20,000 women assembled in Pretoria to meet with the Prime Minister; the formal procession was banned so the women walked for hours in groups of 3 to the capitol, but the Prime Minister refused to see them. The women stood in silence for a half hour, singing Zulu freedom songs, and then left. Many women were eventually forced to accept the passes; they were not permitted to register the births of children and were fired from employment when they did not have passes. Protests continued, however, and hundreds of women were beaten and imprisoned; 1 jail intended to hold 155 people held 482 women.

The Pan-Africanist Congress (PAC), formed in 1959, called for armed resistance to the government. The 1960 Sharpeville massacre occurred when police opened fire on a peaceful crowd of African demonstrators; women and children were among the 67 dead and 186 wounded. Among the 150 leaders arrested, 19 were women. The ANC and PAC were banned in 1960, and the Republic of South Africa was declared independent in 1961. The All-African Women's Conference (1962) was set up by the (banned) PAC. The NWCSA put forth a resolution in 1968 supporting the entry of Indian women into the teaching profession and lobbied Indian leaders to accord Indian women equal pay for equal work. In the late 1960's the Black Consciousness movement, consisting of Africans, Coloureds, and Indians, emerged.

---

another banned person, attending educational institutions, etc., and publications are not permitted to quote anything a banned person has ever written or said; the most severe form amounts to virtual house arrest; banning orders typically last 3–5 yrs.

Torture under interrogation, "accidental" hangings, and sexual assault are among the methods of repression security police have been accused of using.

Women were among the more than 200,000 who participated in strikes during 1973–76. Many women living in illegal squatters' camps in the early 1970's were arrested and their homes were destroyed by bulldozers. In 1974 the government's claim to Namibia (South-West Africa) prompted the UN Security Council to bar South Africa from a seat in the General Assembly; the South African government has instituted apartheid in Namibia and reportedly has displaced civilians, destroyed homes, and instituted "security measures," and South African military men have raped and tortured many in the population. In the mid-1970's and early 1980's, the "homelands" of Transkei, Bophuthatswana, Venda, and Ciskei were declared "independent"; the residents of these homelands no longer have South African citizenship. The government's policy of apartheid drew worldwide criticism, and under public pressure many countries refused to trade with South Africa. In June 1976, uprisings occurred in Soweto as tens of thousands of Black and White anti-apartheid demonstrators and over 200,000 students and 600 teachers boycotted schools in rebellion against discriminatory education; the government arrested more than 2000 persons from June to Sept. The government instituted even more severe repression after the Soweto uprisings; Steve Biko, a leader in the South African Students Organization (SASO), died in 1977 while in police custody; he was the forty-fourth Black South African to die in police custody since 1963. In 1977 Helen Joseph, Ilana Kleinschmidt, Jacqueline Bosman, and Barbara Waite were arrested and sentenced for refusing to testify against Winnie Mandela, an ANC activist; (in Dec. 1981 Winnie Mandela was put under her fifth banning order; in all, she has been banned for over 19 yrs.).

Rape-crisis centers were started in Cape Town in 1977. In 1980 African women demonstrated against rent increases, and Coloured students in Cape Town were active in school and consumer boycotts; at least 30 persons in Cape Town were killed by police during a 3-day period. In 1981 the South African Domestic Workers' Assoc. began organizing (mostly African) domestic workers; Ellen Molapo, a PAC activist, is leader of the garment workers' organization. In 1981, 6 leading women trade-union activists were arrested and detained. Ruth First, a major South African writer and activist who left South Africa after her release from prison, was killed (in Mozambique) by a letter bomb in 1982.

According to a 1983 report, an increasing number of Black children (including those of primary-school age) have become victims of detention, interrogation, torture, and "disappearance"; the majority are held for participating in boycotts against discriminatory legislation; the International Defense and Aid Fund estimates that approx. 700 young people were held between 1977 and mid-1981 under "security" laws.

In 1983 a court ruled that migrant workers who have been employed for 10 years by the same employer qualify for (Sec. 10) urban rights status and can remain as permanent residents; this overturns the previous policy which considered the required yearly renewal of a migrant contract as an interruption in employment. The Minister of Cooperation and Development *[sic]* said he would request Parliament to pass legislation to nullify the decision. Black Sash predicted that labor bureaus would simply overlook the decision, causing each person to go to court to acquire this right; this last course was taken after a court ruled in 1980 that the wife and children of an African male who lived legally in an urban center could live with him without obtaining a special permit.

Active women's organizations and journals include the United Women's Organization (UWO), Women's Legal Status Committee (WLSC), People Opposed to Woman Abuse (POWA), Union of Jewish Women and other religious women's groups, Action (a Durban women's group that teaches African women trade skills), various active women's groups at the White and Asian universities, the ANC Women's Section's (banned) *Voice of Women* newspaper, the journal *From Women,* and *Girl's Voice* (a high-school feminist newspaper). Women are active in the struggle for national liberation in the Azanian People's Organization (AZAPO) and other groups.†††

MYTHOGRAPHY. The early inhabitants of Southern Africa believed they were ruled by a goddess who had both female and male priests in charge of carrying out her orders. Lovedu was the Rain Queen of the Azanian people. Among the Zulu, Mbaba Mwana Walesa, the rain goddess, lived in a small house with an eternal rainbow over the roof. The goddesses and female spirits of the many tribal and clan groups are too numerous to list here, but the pantheon is rich and varied.

SOUTHERN AFRICA: Going up the Mountain
by Motlalepula Chabaku

I was born and brought up on the outskirts of Johannesburg. (In Johannesburg, the indigenous people to whom I belong, the Africans, are forbidden by law to live in the city. We are forcibly housed outside the city.) I am one of seven children, from a very poor family. My parents were able to educate us only up to the sixth grade. As I was the second eldest daughter there were more difficulties for me; there was preference for educating a boy over a girl. I now also realize the pressures my mother faced. There was pressure on her to give birth to a boy to retain the lineage, as daughters cannot carry on the family name. Even before that, there was hostility toward her marriage because it was a marriage of choice instead of one arranged by their parents. And, too, they did not have a dowry as expected, and they were poor—so when my mother gave birth to another girl, that was an added problem.

I am a product of multiple detribalizations. My parents and many generations before me have been practitioners of miscegenation and detribalization. (This does not negate the existence of tribes; I see having tribes as a beautiful enrichment, but I have problems with tribal*ism*). For instance, my last name is supposed to be a Swazi name, yet I cannot speak one word of Swazi. But my parents do acknowledge that there have been Swazi strains in our lineage, and also Nguni, a separate ethnic grouping. On my passbook, it says "Motswana," a tribal group and also the name of a nation. There is also an independent kingdom of Botswana, which is next to South Africa; the language is called Setswana and is spoken across those colonialist geographical borders. We spoke Setswana, Sepedi, Sesotho, and Zulu. At school we were taught in our native languages up to the second grade. My parents chose Setswana because the teacher was Setswana-speaking and my mother came from a predominantly Setswana background. But in our classrooms, we had children of different ethnic backgrounds; they would be taught in the native languages they spoke, the basic idea being to recognize the alphabets and numerals. The next language we were taught was English—mostly salutations and a few remarks. Then we'd begin to read—negative publications written by whites for us which

††† As a result of domestic protest and worldwide pressure, in July 1983, all but 11 banning orders were lifted by the government (1 woman, Winnie Mandela, remained banned); however, arrests, detention, and imprisonment of previously banned persons and other political activists were increased. In 1984, 68-year-old Albertina Sisulu, an executive member of the Federation of South African Women and the mother of 5 children, was sentenced to 4 years imprisonment for supporting the ANC and singing freedom songs at the funerals of South African activists.

still boggle my mind. Then the teachers would gradually go into teaching almost solely in English because it was the medium of communication within the business and education worlds and we were part of the British Commonwealth. We also were taught the white South African tribal language called Afrikaans. Education for whites is called National Education; they are "the nation." All other people have Coloured Education, or Indian Education, or Bantu Education.

Bantu is the pure, unadulterated, indigenous, plural word for "people." But the oppressors used it derogatively to label the indigenous African, and anthropologists have perpetuated that misuse.*

The demarcation of Southern Africa was done by colonialists. Even though we indigenous peoples may have had geographic areas with a preponderance of one ethnic group, still there was a relationship between the tribes; the conflict was mostly over land boundaries and not so much on conquering one another. When it comes to marriage, many of the indigenous ethnic groups would prefer to marry within their classes, because every community of people has a class system; the royalty, the elderly, and the ordinary. Royalty marries royalty from another tribe; that way their tribes become related. So tribalism was not deeply rooted; it is exaggerated by the oppressor.

The attitude of "race" actually is a borrowed one, because when you look at our *own* history, you find that we have always preferred to care for people over property, and it did not matter who the people were. In the rural areas, if you are a stranger stopping at a house to ask for directions, tradition has it that they shall open the gate, give you a place to sit and water to drink and to wash your hands, provide you with a meal—and only when you have eaten will the head of the family greet you. And then before you mention what you need, they will want to find out who you are, where you come from, relationship-identification. If there is any remote connection, even by a first name, maybe via a nineteenth cousin, you automatically become a cousin for life. Our families are extended families. But the oppressors put down our traditions and forced us to despise our own ancestry.

The pass laws, in one form or another, have been in existence in South Africa for over a hundred years, so at my youthful age of fifty-one, I have never known life without them. The pass laws came with the Dutch from the Netherlands as early as the seventeenth century. And then the British also came in through colonization after they defeated the Boers. The people who have historically resisted—openly, violently, and visibly—have always been the women. The authorities stayed clear of issuing passbooks to African women working in the cities because they knew what kind of opposition they would face. So in 1952, they passed a law called the Abolition of Passes and the Coordination of Documents Act (implemented in 1955) in which they deceived the African people by saying that they were getting rid of the passes. They now have "reference books," which are far *more* restrictive than the passes.

I went to an Anglican school (although we were not Anglicans), an all-black school in the black ghetto of Johannesburg. It was a mission school with a black teacher—not trained to the same level as a white teacher—teaching a syllabus specifically designed for blacks. We were in a class of ninety children, taught by one teacher. We had one blackboard, and we would sit outside; this was a small church in which they would cram about eight or ten classes. During the summer we would all be scattered around the church building; in the winter we took turns alternating inside and out. We had no food at school

---

* As a result of black student demands and the rebellion in Soweto in 1976, the word "Bantu" was eliminated from official use by the Education and Training Act of 1979. Nonetheless, primary and secondary education in South Africa remains segregated, although there is now a kind of token integration at the universities (see Statistical Preface preceding this article).—Ed.

because only white children get school feeding in South Africa. Later on, they did start what was claimed to be school feeding—unpalatable soup with rejects of vegetables and a slice of brown bread—but we had to pay for it. If you didn't have pennies to buy the soup or bread, you would not get it. But we were the privileged few that could *have* some morsel.

Where we lived was originally a trash and night-soil dump. At that time they didn't have a drainage system, so there was a pail system of collecting night-soil from the different outhouses' toilets every evening, and it was dumped there. Before the present government came into power, there were a number of places in the city that had been black-owned. These were taken over by whites and laws were passed that blacks could not own or rent property in the cities; that's when my parents were forcibly moved out to the dump at the city outskirts, where I was born.

There are other slum areas, predominantly Asian and African, in Johannesburg. Where I grew up were only black folks. We lived in a two-room house, each room about nine by ten feet—seven children with Mom and Dad. There were walls with used bricks, the mortar still bulging in between, no plaster. There was no ceiling whatsoever; it was just a corrugated iron roof, and there was no door between the two rooms, and no electricity. Every night Mom and Dad would use dirt and water to plaster the walls. My mother put up a ceiling by taking burlap and nailing it to the roof. Then she would take ordinary lime, which she mixed herself, and cover her head with a scarf and take a rough old broom and splash this onto the burlap. She had to be careful because a little speckle of white was so strong that it would blind you if it got into your eyes. So she had a piece of glass that she wrapped cloth around and put over her face so she could still see as the specks dropped on her eyes. And it would get on the table where she was standing—clean it up, get up again. That's how my mother made our ceiling.

Both my parents went to school as far as the sixth grade because the missionaries of that time (of the Lutheran Church), allowed African children to go to school only up to that level, and then they had to spend a year or two taking confirmation classes in order to be confirmed in the Church as full members. And after that, they had to go out and work for the local white farmer for twelve months, seven days a week, throughout the year—doing everything from domestic work to field work, only to get a calf at the end of the year as payment. My father used to tell me many things. For instance, as a very poor black Christian child on a Lutheran-German mission station, he had to collect money for orphans in Germany. He used to ask, "Why can't we collect for orphans in South Africa and for our own families?" The churches have been involved actively in robbing us of our basic human rights and property in South Africa—and in many other parts of the world.

My father worked for over twenty-five years as a clerk. It was the Union Gramophone Saloon of South Africa, where they used to sell gramophones. He was also a messenger; he was everything; he used to make tea for his employers. It was very humiliating but he stuck it out for twenty-five years and never got a pension. My mother had to take in laundry. She would go into the city, take up the laundry of whites, and come home and wash it and iron it and return it. I used to say, "Mom, look how much you pay for transport to go collect the things, how much it costs you—the soap, the blue to dye the water for the last rinse to give it whiteness—how much time you take ironing, and how much do you get?" She barely made back her expenses.

We used to buy one small loaf of brown bread a day. We children could have one slice each in the morning for breakfast with a cup of hot water with sugar (not tea). We could only afford one pint of milk a day, and it wasn't for us, the children. We'd buy milk in the afternoon and boil it so it wouldn't turn sour (this was before pasteurization, and we had no refrigeration). It was to make sure that when my father came back from work he and Mom could have white tea together or white coffee. And the remainder of the pint was there in case a visitor or a stranger came. Or in the morning it would be used for my father's bottle of coffee that he took to work. We used to go out into the fields to collect weeds that we cooked to supplement our food. Staple food was corn porridge. We would supplement it with pumpkin leaves or carrot tops, tops of red beets—those were things we lived on. We would go to the stores where they sell vegetables and root around in the garbage tins for leaves.

My parents always used to tell us how we were loved, how special we were, how we were meant to be greater than what we were. My father used to take a tennis ball and say, "You are like a tennis ball. People can squeeze you, but always bounce back as who you are. They will even try to bounce you down, but the *harder* they hit, the higher up you should go."

And I never forgot that. We used to pay school fees in our black mission school. Many missionaries would collect money in our name overseas, and we would be forced to write a letter of thanks—not knowing who the benefactors were and never having seen the money. Sometimes we would not be able to pay the school fees at all but my parents would always dress us up and say, "Go." And I would go and remain outside the schoolyard for the whole day because if you pay no school fees you can't enter the schoolyard. But after school I'd go back home as if I'd gone to school. We did this so that our neighbors wouldn't know that we couldn't pay the fees that month. It was very humiliating. In black schools we could not afford to have a janitor. We, the kids, cleaned our own classrooms. Many of the kids hated collecting the dirt from their own classrooms to put in the local trash box. The most humiliating thing for me was to go and collect dirt from classrooms where I couldn't even attend class. They used to jeer at me— *but I did it to get two pennies to pay my school fees.* And I used to search for ink pen nibs. Sometimes the nib would fall out of the pen and some of the kids wouldn't see them, or sometimes the pen would be pressed too hard during writing and the nib would be bent, so I used to repair them myself. My teeth are serrated to this day because I used to try to pull the nibs straight with my teeth. And after the nibs could write again, I'd sell them for a penny each. In the white schools they used to get free exercise books and I would come in on Friday and find a half-way-used one they had thrown away (they would get a new one on Monday). I took a razor blade to cut off the unused pages. Then I would take the money I had collected from the pen nibs and buy wheat flour to make paste, and one yard of brown paper. From there I would go to the trash dump and search for thrown-away magazines. I used the wheat paste in two or three layers with the brown paper to make a firm cover, measuring it to the pages and cutting with a razor blade and a ruler. Sometimes I didn't have a ruler but any straight plank would be my guideline. All the empty tins of condensed milk—Nestlé's and the rest—I'd take and scrape the remains and use it to glue the pages together in the middle. Then the magazine pictures would be pasted on the outside and I would draw lines at the top where the children could write their names. I would sell the exercise books for the same price as these from the store: five pennies. I could sell at the same price because I had the advantage that mine already looked covered, decorated. The teachers wanted the kids' books to look clean and tidy. That's how I raised money to pay for my school fees.

Even though I didn't have much in the way of food and clothing, I still remember that I grew up with three dresses a year: one gymnasium dress—navy blue—with two white shirts and two navy blue warm knickers. My mother was a meticulously clean woman. And we always had white shirts. When one was dirty, it was washed by the following day. (And if it got torn she would patch it up and you got hell.) I never had shoes. In Johannesburg, we have below-zero Fahrenheit temperatures in winter.

I remember there was a culvert for water where I used to walk in the wintertime; I'd put my toes there to warm up because they would get so numb I would walk on rocks and stones without feeling. Then I would run until I got to another culvert and warm them up again and then run until I got to school. One day, when I was about twelve years old, I arrived late and was standing outside the school's church door. I had battered my toes, and where I was standing there was a pool of blood. One of the white nuns, who was coming to the church service (which always preceded the first class), saw this pool of blood and picked me up and took me in the car to the clinic and I was bandaged on both feet. They also gave me a Scottish maroon dress, like the Scottish patterned material they use for their kilts. It was a nice dress—the best dress I'd ever had. They drove me home, which was quite a distance. They also brought a food parcel. But as soon as they left, my mother accused me of having gone begging. Did I think we were beggars that I had gone and begged for food? I tried to deny this but she didn't believe it. She took that dress of mine, put it in the stove—and burned it. I still remember the pain of watching it burn— that beautiful dress. Those things happened, they're hurtful. I have forgiven my mother even though I don't forget the incident. Now I understand. She had her pride.

Because I excelled in athletics (I was the state champion of high jump for over eight years) and because I studied hard, the Anglican church offered me a scholarship. So I went through high school and was able to go on to a teacher-training school founded by the African Methodist Episcopal Church, the Wilberforce Training Institute, named after the English anti-slavery crusader. It was run by blacks, for blacks. On some weekends, those students who had relatives who had a car would come pick them up. I would remain alone and work for my plate of food by cleaning up the whole hostel. The worst times were the two major vacations. They would go home; I would remain in the empty school, hearing creaking doors and strange noises, having no one to call.

I think how different it already is for my daughter. She is eighteen years old now. She was an abandoned baby I picked up in the Johannesburg ghetto. She suffered from acute malnutrition. I gave her the name Mamolemo, which means mother of kindness. The first day *she* went to school, when she went to the bathroom, she went to the nearest one—and of course it was the *boys'* bathroom. The boys tried to stop her at the door, and she just pushed them aside and went in. The boys dashed to tell their teacher. So when she came back she was asked, "Why did you do that?" She answered, "I did nothing wrong. At home we have one bathroom for all people; how come these boys have a bathroom for themselves alone?" That was the first time she encountered sexism—in a bathroom. She broke the rules the very first day she went to school. She is tough and very loving, with a definite mind of her own. I've brought her up with a lot of independence, and sometimes, when she exercises her uniqueness, even I can't take it!

When I was growing up, I got a lot of encouragement from women. Women are so resourceful, all over the world. They are the ones who keep the family together, who augment salaries, who absorb and tolerate pain and suffering and humiliation. I'm *not* saying absorbing pain is the answer, the ideal. But it *is* an inspiration. Women have always resisted injustice. Even in our own ancestral heritage, women played very prominent roles. To this day, outside Pretoria in an area called Hammamskraal, there is an African woman, Esther Kekana, who is a chieftain in her own right over men *and* women. (Almost all of our chiefs—male and female—got their position by heredity because they were of royal blood, but the South African government appointed chieftains themselves, so chiefs who do not obey the white man's law are robbed of their chieftainhood and those who are willing to be tools of the system can have this title conferred on them, much to our chagrin.)

It is a Western idea that women have always been subservient in an African context. Yes, we have had sexism within our own African heritage—where women become mere vessels of men, where women don't have equal opportunities to positions of leadership— but it was not as rigid as the present white government enforces it. For example, in the northern Transvaal there is a hereditary chief, a woman who has ruled the entire area and is known as Modjadji; she is a rainmaker. This is often a matriarchal, hereditary position for women in an indigenous African society. In initiation ceremonies for girls, there were also women specially appointed by the community to give sex education—which unfortunately included the mutilation of the genitalia of the girls.** (This awful practice is dying out but it still seems to be very much practiced by the Bavenda tribe in the northern Transvaal and in quite a few other areas.)

Sex is seen as a personal, private matter. Women who never married in our traditional African culture were not seen as abnormal. They could own land, build their houses, stay with kids—because the greatest sin in the African community is selfishness, which is considered worse than murder. (You and I can live together as neighbors, you can have a fridge and I not have it; no problem. But if I have a guest and it's hot and I ask for ice cubes and you don't give them to me when you have them—even if you make amends afterward—I will never forget that selfishness.) As for myself, well, I forgot to get married.

There were women around me who never married; some had children. Either they had been jilted by their boyfriends who had denied paternity of their children or they had two or three kids with one man who promised to marry but never married. Or in some cases they had dowry problems, or there were others who never married because they were "too smart." There is still that fear in men all over the world about women who are bright, or articulate, or educated, or skilled. Men see it as a threat.

Those women were a source of inspiration for me, although I confess that many times I did not want "a role model." I wanted to be *me*, to find my own unique path. For example, I studied to be a minister and yet I still maintain my vision of what the churches did and continue to do, so hideously, in my country and around the world.

But the Christian church was originally not Caucasian or European. It was predominately African-Asian. The *Torah* was written in Africa. You didn't get that kind of knowledge in missionary schools. I had to see it and understand it for myself. When I looked at it, I found that the Africanness of the Gospel had been ignored, rejected, or excluded completely. I began to teach our own people from what I analyzed to be a correct understanding of the text. Of course, this means that I have been knocking on doors from one denomination to the other without success; I couldn't get ordained because the Johannesburg (white) Anglican bishop is opposed to the ordination of women: bureaucracy and patriarchism. We need matriarchism and *matriotism* (a word I've made up myself). It's still awfully difficult for women anywhere to be ordained, although there are breakthroughs. We have to work ten times harder than the men. It probably hasn't helped much that I question; many of us are afraid to question how and why the Christian faith is involved with oppression.

I am still a South African, although I am now without citizenship by decree of the white South African government. I still love Southern Africa. We are going through a very painful but exciting moment. We are people at the bottom of the mountain struggling to go up, and saying to those in power who are on top, "Come down, meet us halfway so that we can live and share and be together." And the longer they delay coming down . . . well, we *are* coming up, and the harder they will fall when they finally tumble down.

Our lives have been violent. Many of our people have tried peaceful ways to survive, only to be pushed into a corner where they have to take on counter-survival, counter-violence. But one way or the other, the people are going to win. And when I say "the

** See Glossary.—Ed.

people," I mean not only the indigenous African and the Asian, but also those whites who are for justice.

The system is trying to split the people, following divide-and-rule techniques. The oppressor wants to create a class system as the most effective way of delaying a change—creating a black middle class that will be a buffer zone between the oppressor and the oppressed. They are the ones who will make us "hurry up slowly." Most of the time the system divides not only on the basis of race and color but also via a class system within whiteism. And—of course—sexism.

The impact of apartheid on all our lives creates pressure to relegate "women's issues" to a remote priority. But I strongly believe that feminist issues must be dealt with *concurrently*, as a major area of injustice, because after the "political" struggles are over, the women tend to be forgotten.

The struggle is not only an individual struggle: it's a national, mass, liberating movement. Many have been in detention and many have fled the country. The support comes from inside and outside. The movement is outlawed by whiteman's law, but we carry our membership cards in the heart. Now the violence is accelerating, is unavoidable. I strive for peaceful ways of making change, but I understand and support those who are in an armed struggle. And we women have a central part to play both for ourselves and for humanity, because we tend to be more sensitive to human needs, more open to compassion. We are also the source of reconciliation, far more than men. I'm not putting down men, but this is a fact of life. We women are the pioneers of peace.

And, finally, *we are more than three fifths of the world's population, in all sectors of life.* I believe that only women can reduce the coming blood bath. Therefore the solidarity of all women everywhere is essential for the survival of all people. That's what women give me: guts, and the will to keep on. That's what I live for.

[For Suggested Further Reading, see p. 620.]

Motlalepula Chabaku was born in Johannesburg in November 1933. She is a "South African without citizenship by decree of the white South African government." She graduated in May 1979 from the Lancaster Theological Seminary after three years of study in the master of divinity program, and has been a schoolteacher, social worker, executive member of the Moroka School and the Molapo Secondary School boards, a member of the Christian Institute of South Africa (now outlawed) and a founding member of the Black Women's Federation of South Africa (now outlawed). She is the national president of VOW (Voice of Women—an outlawed multiracial women's organization), was a member of the African National Congress (ANC), and held offices as national secretary and fulltime organizer for the ANC Women's League before it was declared illegal. She has conducted workshops on human relations for religious conferences in various cities in South Africa as well as in Kenya, Namibia, Zimbabwe, Mozambique, Swaziland, and Lesotho, and was a keynote speaker at the UN Women's Conference on the Mid-Decade for Women in Copenhagen.

SOUTH AFRICA: A Bulletin from Within
by Anonymous White South African Feminists
of both Dutch and British Ancestry

South Africa is governed by a patriarchal, fascistic, white regime that stays in power by completely controlling the lives of all its citizens.

It is not only the daily violence that people fear, but also the immense and complicated system of government departments that have the power to determine who should be allowed to seek work, where they may seek it, and what rights they have. It is almost impossible to fight the all-powerful bureaucracy.

There are four classifications of race in South Africa—White, so-called Coloured, Asian, and Black African. Each group is controlled by a different puppet government and by different laws. And in each group, women have even fewer rights than men.

It suits the capitalists to allow only black men to come to the cities to work since they have to pay them just enough to survive without worrying about the welfare of their families. It is very difficult for black women to get permission to seek work in the cities, and there is hardly any industry in the "homeland" areas. Black women in rural areas have to exist by scratching a living from barren, overgrazed, and often drought-stricken land. Most of the men work in the cities or in the mines while women, children, and the old people live in the rural areas. When women *do* work in the cities or rural areas it is usually as domestic or farm labor. Neither of these jobs has any minimum wage or legal protection. Women also do not have the right to organize a trade union. It is becoming a common sight to see women working in road gangs.

Many African women are forced to make a living doing illegal work: prostitution and making and selling alcohol. Because African families are so often separated, women are frequently the main breadwinners. Even when they do live with their husbands, the responsibility for keeping the home, buying and cooking the food, and raising the children falls on them. There are hardly any childcare facilities and most women do not have a safe place to leave their children when they go to work.

Women from the Asian and so-called Coloured groups have more rights but are in a similar position. The majority live in the cities. While white women obviously have more privileges on every level, they too are still subject to a sexist education, sexist laws, and the sexism of all men in the society.

Black women are considered legal minors all their lives. Women of other racial groups become legal minors when they marry—unless they draw up a special contract. There are very few laws protecting women against violence, desertion, and financial exploitation by their husbands, and all women are generally still considered to be the property of their husbands.

Women have little control over their reproduction. Abortion is virtually illegal and backstreet abortions are common. *Eighty percent of all deaths in the gynecological wards of the major black hospitals in Soweto—the largest black township—were caused by septic abortions in 1978.* The government encourages the use of contraceptives for black women, but the most common form of contraception used in the black state clinics is Depo-

Provera, which has very dangerous side effects.* White women in South Africa are discouraged from using it and the drug has recently been banned in the newly independent neighboring state of Zimbabwe.

Black women are often forcibly sterilized after having children in State hospitals and clinics, whereas white women are encouraged to have more than two children.

Lesbianism is not illegal; that is, there are no laws on the books against it. Male homosexuality *is* illegal, and has to remain underground. At this stage there are no gay or lesbian civil-rights organizations.

Education is not free and most African women go to school for only a few years. So few people complete high school that teachers themselves often don't hold qualifications higher than junior high—about eight years of schooling. Women who do get higher education are still pushed into such service occupations as secretarial jobs, nursing, social work, and teaching. They are paid less than their male counterparts of equal training and expertise.

South Africa has one of the highest violent crime rates in the Western world, and much of this violence is directed against women. There are an estimated three hundred thousand rapes every year; one in every forty women is a rape victim. Wife-battering is common and socially accepted, even though it is still very much a hidden crime. There are no facilities for battered women, and it is not even recognized as a problem.

The South African defense force is fighting a war in Namibia, a neighboring territory that it occupies illegally. Stories of atrocities in the war zones are becoming more and more common. Many of these brutal acts involve the rape, torture, and murder of women and children. This in turn affects the rest of society, since all white men must serve in the army and the government puts out a great deal of propaganda to foster militaristic and "he-man" attitudes in men.

Changes are happening in South Africa—but they affect only the "black bourgeoisie." It is easier now for some Africans to get into managerial positions, to play sports with whites, and to share theaters and luxury hotels with whites. The government is pushing for more skilled women of all races to remain in the labor market. Every minor change inside South Africa is hailed as a major breakthrough. In reality the basic living conditions of the people have not changed at all.

There is no doubt that radical change will come to South Africa. Resistance to the system is stronger now than ever. Black trade unions work against great odds but still manage to organize hundreds of strikes (which are illegal). Communities are organizing and fighting for short- and long-term changes. Women are playing an even greater role than before in community action. The early 1980's saw a dramatic increase in successful acts of sabotage against both strategic and symbolic targets. Black high schools have started playing a major part in resistance. During 1980, most African schools and universities closed down for three months in protest over inferior educations. On the borders of South Africa, the government army is fighting a war against South African and Namibian liberation movements; it is a war that the government can never win. At the moment all white men over eighteen spend more than two years in the army—and shortly white women will be conscripted. International pressure on the government is mounting and South Africa can expect less military and economic aid from its Western allies.

Southern Africa is a dynamic sub-continent. In the past decade, Angola, Zimbabwe, and Mozambique have had revolutions that changed the basic structures of their societies. It is inevitable that the same kind of social change will come to South Africa—but it

* This is a US-produced and manufactured drug that by law may not be used in the US but is exported in great quantities to the Third World—with the approval of the World Health Organization.—Ed.

will not come easily. The government uses everything in its power to repress whatever threatens the system. At the time of this writing, hundreds of trade unionists and political activists are in detention without trial for unlimited periods. People are being banned, placed under house arrest, jailed for life, and executed for political acts. Torture is a common practice in the jails and since 1964 more than fifty people are known to have died while being interrogated by security police. Funerals of people who have died in the struggle are becoming everyday occurrences.

That struggle is one for basic human rights against poverty and starvation. The oppression of women is still seen (if recognized at all) as secondary. We have a much longer battle ahead. Women have always been oppressed here; precolonial societies offered them not much more freedom than postcolonial ones. At the moment women are not well represented in political organizations and we have no powerful voice of our own.

In Zimbabwe and Mozambique women fought alongside men for their freedom and were promised equality after the revolution. Encouraging changes have taken place, but in both countries women felt they had to build strong women's organizations to continue to fight for women's rights. In South Africa more and more women's organizations are springing up within the Left. There is a long herstory of resistance by women in South Africa, but for the first time women's issues *per se* are being given some small attention.

As early as 1956, twenty thousand women marched on the government buildings in the capital singing:

> Now you have tampered with the women
> You have struck against rock
> You have dislodged a boulder
> You will be crushed.

And that song was prophetic.

The above article was of necessity written anonymously by white South African radical feminist women of both Dutch (Afrikaaner) and British ancestry, transformed descendants of the colonizers, women who are today still living in South Africa at daily risk, organizing underground for women's freedom and for a just society.

Suggested Further Reading

Bernstein, H. *For Their Triumphs and Their Tears;* available through IDAF (International Defence and Aid Fund), London, England.

Cock, Jacklyn. *Maids and Madams.* Johannesburg: Ravan Press, 1980.

Simons, H. J. *The Legal Status of African Women.* London: C. Hurst, 1968.

South Africa: Time Running Out. Berkeley and Los Angeles: Univ. of California Press, 1981; the Report of the Study Commission on US Policy Toward Southern Africa.

Walker, C. "Suffrage and Passes: Two South African Women's Campaigns"; available through IDAF, London, England.

SPAIN
(Spanish State)

A southern European country on the Iberian Peninsula bordered to the north by France and the Atlantic Ocean, to the east and south by the Mediterranean Sea and Strait of Gibraltar, to the west by Portugal and the Atlantic. **Area:** 504,750 sq. km. (194,885 sq. mi.) including the Canary and Balearic Islands. **Population** (1980): 37,806,000, female 51.1%. **Capital:** Madrid.

DEMOGRAPHY. Languages: Spanish (Castilian), Basque, Catalán, Galician. **Races or Ethnic Groups:** Spanish (Castilian, Valencian, Andalusian, Asturian) 72.8%, Catalań 16.4%, Galician 8.2%, Basque 2.3%. **Religions:** Roman Catholicism (official), Protestant, Judaism. **Education** (% enrolled in school, 1975): Age 6–11—of all girls 100%, of all boys 100%; age 12–17—of all girls 61%, of all boys 67%; higher education—in 1979–80, women were 52% of matriculating university students; in 1977–78, 38% of medical students, 19% of economics, 5% of technical college, 65% of teacher college; in 1981, 38% of vocational training students; 25% of women graduates are unemployed (1981). **Literacy** (1977): Women 86%, men 94%. **Birth Rate** (per 1000 pop., 1977–78): 17. **Death Rate** (per 1000 pop., 1977–78): 8. **Infant Mortality** (per 1000 live births, 1977): Female 12, male 23. **Life Expectancy** (1975–80): Female 76 yrs., male 70 yrs.

GOVERNMENT. Juan Carlos I is king and formal head of state; the head of government is Prime Minister Felipe González (elected 1982; see HERSTORY). The elected Cortes (bicameral parliament) consists of a 350-member Chamber of Deputies and a 207-member Senate (the 1978 Constitution abolished the system of an appointed Cortes); major parties include the Socialist Party, the Union of the Democratic Center, Socialist Workers, Communist, and Popular Alliance. Provincial governments consist of their own assemblies. **Women's Suffrage:** 1931, granted with the establishment of the Second Republic. **Equal Rights:** The

1931 Constitution, reaffirmed by the 1978 Constitution (Art. 14), prohibits all discrimination on the basis of sex and affirms equality between the sexes. **Women in Government:** In 1979 women constituted 4.8% of the Cortes. In 1981 there was 1 woman minister (of Culture), Soledad Becerril; in 1983 there were no highly placed women in national government, but there were 2 women provincial governors.

ECONOMY. Currency: Peseta (May 1983: 139. = $1 US). **Gross National Product** (1980): $199.8 billion. **Per Capita Income** (1980): $5350. **Women's Wages as a Percentage of Men's** (1980): 50–70%. **Equal Pay Policy:** None. **Production** (Agricultural/Industrial): Grains, olives and oil, fruits, wines; textiles, footwear, autos, machinery. **Women as a Percentage of Labor Force:** (1982) 29%; **of agricultural force** (1979) 28% (61% of whom are unpaid family workers); **of industrial force**—no general statistics obtainable (of manufacturing 22.5%, 1980); **of military**—women prohibited from service. In 1975, 65% of women workers were age 16–24, and 16.1% of married women and 44% of separated or widowed women were in the labor force. **(Employed) Women's Occupational Indicators:** Of scientists 4.6%, of high-level public sector 5%, of lawyers 6%, of health workers 46.5% (1980); 59.6% of employed women are in the service sector—of whom 4.4% are in domestic service (1980); of administration and management 3%, of professional, technical (and related) workers 36%, of clerical 38% (1979). Home-working, usually on garments, is common, especially in the south. **Unemployment** (1980): 11.7%, female 13.1%, male 11.1%.

GYNOGRAPHY. Marriage. *Policy:* The 1978 Constitution (Art. 32) stipulates equal rights in marriage; both spouses are responsible for administering property, which is jointly owned unless spouses contract to retain individual ownership at marriage. A 1975 civil law abolished legislation that stipulated a husband's duty was to protect his wife and hers was to obey and to live in his chosen residence. Women no longer must be represented by their husband in legal matters. The 1976 labor law gives a woman the right to work without her husband's consent. A 1978 reform law decriminalized adultery, which had been a crime solely for women. Only civil marriage is recognized, and religious ceremonies must be seconded by civil ones. *Practice.* Female mean age at marriage (1970–78): 24; women age 15–49 in union (1970–78): 60%. In urban areas women usually marry later and are more likely to work outside the home.

Divorce. *Policy:* 1981 law legalizes divorce and annulment of civil marriages; previously, only religious marriages could be annulled. In cases of mutual consent, a 2-yr. separation or a 1-yr. court-decreed separation is required for divorce; in cases of nonagreement, a 5-yr. separation is necessary. The couple may determine child custody, maintenance payments, and division of property, or the court will decide. Domestic work is considered a financial contribution that must be counted at divorce in terms of property division. *Practice:* As of 1982, 10,000 divorces had been filed. Despite the new law, divorce is still difficult for women because of their economic status. Maternal child custody generally is granted, but a woman's sexual behavior and employment may be taken into account. Child-support payments by fathers frequently are defaulted.

Family. *Policy:* Family law regarding property and inheritance is determined regionally. Under reform civil law (1975) both spouses must respect and protect each other and act in the family interest. A 1981 law makes both parents jointly responsible for children; previously, the father had greater authority. A woman can be deemed guilty of abandoning the marital home if she leaves for a few days; a man must stop financial support to be considered comparably guilty. Under the national social insurance system, families with more than 2 children under age 14 receive a monthly allowance varying with family size; additional allowances and tax deductions are given per child to families with more than 12 children. Additional benefits include monthly allowances for homemakers, husbands who are dependents of employed women, a once-only marriage grant, and additional payments at birth of each child. Maternity leave for employed women is 6 weeks pre- and 6 weeks post-delivery, with 75% of the basic social security allowance and guaranteed reinstatement, as well as unpaid leave up to 3 yrs. by either parent without guaranteed reinstatement. National health insurance covers maternity health care for employed women and wives of insured workers. The Civil Code abolished an article that forbade a woman under age 25 to leave home without parental consent (1960's). The Ministry of Labor subsidizes the cost of establishing/maintaining nonprofit day-care centers; parents often pay sliding-scale fees. *Practice:* In rural areas, women and children are frequently still considered husbands' property. Women generally bear full weight of childcare and housework. Employers often fire women during pregnancy and sometimes pay compensation or "dowries" to female employees as inducements to quit when they marry. A 1978 study showed that 75.9% of employed women found day care costly and insufficient. There were 694 day-care centers in 1975; in 1980 the government subsidized 619.

Welfare. *Policy:* A national social insurance system based on employees' and employers' mandated contributions provides national health insurance (which includes maternity benefits), family allowances (see **Family**), and limited pensions for employed workers and their spouses. Partial pension is paid at age 60; full pension at 65. Widows over 45 who care for an insured person may receive a pension if they have no other resources. An employed woman cannot pass her pension on to her husband if she dies, unless he was her dependent. *Practice:* In rural areas, extended families frequently provide the only old-age security, since pensions are inadequate for men and virtually nonexistent for women who work in agricultural and domestic labor.

Contraception. *Policy:* Legal as of 1978. Contraceptives are not obtainable through the national health service but are available from some private physicians and urban counseling centers sponsored by municipal governments. *Practice:* Women under age 45 in union using contraception (1977): 51%; methods used (1977) withdrawal 44%, pill 26%, rhythm 12%, condom 10%, abstinence 3%, diaphragm 2%, IUD 1%, other methods 2%; using inefficient methods 58%. Counseling centers opened since 1978 are increasing in number but are generally ineffective due to lack of funds and information. Women's groups run centers for cancer screening, sex/pregnancy/childbirth counseling, and contraceptive dispensation. **Abortion. Policy:** Illegal under the Penal Code and punishable by 6 yrs. imprisonment for the woman and her "accomplice"; a woman who claims her abortion was to "save her honor" may receive a reduced sentence of 6 months. The new (1982) government announced plans to legalize abortion in cases of rape, malformed fetus, or threat to the life or health of the woman; severe penalties for abortions performed for other reasons would remain. Feminist groups have criticized the government bill for being too narrow in its grounds, but the Roman Catholic Church and the conservative Popular Alliance Party have been campaigning strongly against any attempts to liberalize the law. In Oct. 1983 the Parliament voted in favor of the liberalized bill, but the opposition immediately challenged the reform in the Constitutional Tribunal, which in the past has bottled up legislation for as long as 18 months. In 1983 the Church and the Socialist government came into conflict over a government ban on parochial school textbooks which list abortion—together with terrorism, torture, concentration camps, and nuclear war—as a major act of violence. *Practice:* A 1974 Supreme Court study estimated abortions at 300,000 per yr. In 1981, 20,500 Spanish women obtained abortions in Great Britain. In Bilbao in 1982, 9 women were prosecuted for having abortions and 2 women for performing them; major feminist protests ensued (see HERSTORY).

Illegitimacy. *Policy:* The 1978 Constitution established equal parental responsibilities toward all children. Paternity of out-of-wedlock children is regulated by civil law. A 1981 law prohibits discrimination against "illegitimate" children. *Practice:* No statistics obtainable. Strong Roman Catholic influence places a stigma on single mothers and their children, especially in rural areas. **Homosexuality.** *Policy:* Sexual relations between same-sex consenting adults is legal. *Practice:* While legal discrimination is not practiced, strong prejudices persist. The Gay Liberation Front (FLG) is a political party; Institute Lambda, a homosexual-rights group, has a lesbian caucus.

Incest. *Policy:* No law specifically prohibits sexual relations between direct blood relatives, but sexual abuse or corruption of minors is illegal. No further data obtainable. *Practice:* No statistics obtainable, but incest is estimated to be prevalent, with fathers, uncles, and elder brothers as the major perpetrators (see **Rape**). **Sexual Harassment.** *Policy:* None. *Practice:* Reportedly common, but incidents are rarely challenged for fear of job dismissal. In 1979 a woman successfully prosecuted her boss for attempting to abuse her sexually; he was fined 15,000 pesetas and jailed 5 days. **Rape.** *Policy:* Sexual intercourse with a woman against her will is punishable by 12–20 yrs. imprisonment. A rape victim may legally pardon a convicted rapist, thus allowing him to go free. *Practice:* A total of 235 rapes were reported in all of Spain for the yrs. 1977–81; of those, 27 victims had died, 111 had been gang-raped, 14 had been raped by their fathers, 8 by the police, and 14 by male minors. There are an est. 40 rapes each day—15,000 per yr. (1981). The criteria used legally to classify sexual assault as rape are so strict that the majority of reported incidents are classified as "dishonest abuses," which include oral and anal rape. Few rape victims report the crime; those who do often face pressure or threats from the rapist and his family, and so "pardon" him, as allowed by law. There are no government or voluntary organizations to assist rape victims. **Battery.** *Policy:* Legislation does not specify wife abuse as illegal, although it can be considered included in general physical assault. *Practice:* No statistics obtainable. Battery is a major problem but there is no official system to aid victims (see **Crisis Centers**). **Prostitution.** *Policy:* Prostitution itself is not illegal; but it is illegal to exploit a prostitute, i.e., live off her earnings. *Practice:* An est. 500,000 Spanish prostitutes (1981) generate revenues of 547.5 billion pesetas annually. In Barcelona there are approx. 60,000 prostitutes, with comparably high numbers in the Mediterranean port cities. **Traditional/Cultural Practices.** *Policy:* No data obtainable. *Practice:* In some rural areas, remnants of such practices as bride-kidnapping and "crime of honor" jealousy murders of women persist. **Crisis Centers.** *Policy:* None. *Practice:* The first refuge for victims of spouse abuse opened in Barcelona in 1982; sponsored by the women's movement, it receives some municipal funding.

HERSTORY. Spain has been inhabited since the Stone Age, and the cave paintings at Altamira are among the earliest known examples of human esthetic-religious expression; some theories posit the artists to have been women, because the "signature" hand-prints are small. Basques, Celts, and Iberians lived on the Spanish peninsula even before the Phoenicians established colonies (9th century B.C.E.) in Andalusia. Carthaginian and Greek colonies followed and the Punic Wars ended with the Roman conquest in 201 B.C.E. Christianity was introduced by the 1st century C.E. From 409–711 (with an interim of Byzantine rule), Germanic invaders held control. Moslem Berbers from north Africa (the Moors) conquered in 711. In 1094 Rodrigo Díaz de Vivar ("El Cid") conquered the kingdom of Valencia, after having fought against both Moors and Christians.

In the 11th century, the Albigensian "heresy," which was so strong in the south of France (see FRANCE), was also active in northern Spain, and Peter II of Aragón was one of the influential defenders and patrons of this Catharist wave— which itself had many dynamic women leaders and which interacted with the great (and *de facto* feminist) Provençal culture. The 12th century saw the flowering and expansion of the Beguines, sometimes religious, sometimes intellectual and activist communities of women who also were later accused of heretical tendencies; the Beguines flourished throughout France, Belgium, and parts of Germany, as well as in northern Spain.

In 1479 the modern Spanish State was created with the marriage of Isabella I of Castile and Ferdinand II of Aragón. In 1492 Columbus sailed to the Americas with ships supplied by Isabella, and the last Moslem state, Granada, fell to Isabella and Ferdinand. Roman Catholicism solidified its position as the dominant religion and Spain's colonial power grew. Two major intellects of the 15th century were Beatrix Galindo, professor at the University of Salamanca, and Francisca de Lebrixa, of the University of Alcalá. In the Catholic Reformation, the activist and mystic (St.) Teresa of Ávila (1515–82) was a major figure; she founded 17 Carmelite convents, wrote major theological works, survived being suspected of heresy, and became, after her death, 1 of the only 2 women ever to be made a Doctor of the Church, along with (St.) Katherine of Siena. Joanna of Castile and León (reigned 1504–55), daughter of Isabella and Ferdinand, succeeded to the throne but was replaced by her father's regency, and the regencies of her husband Philip I and her son Charles (later Holy Roman Emperor); she was proclaimed insane ("Joanna the Mad") and sequestered in the fortress of Tordesillas.

In the 1500's, Spain became the wealthiest monarchy in Europe with huge fortunes of gold and jewels taken from the Americas. Virtually all of South and Central America, as well as the Philippines and Southern North America, became part of the Spanish Empire. Spain lost some power when the Armada sent by Philip II was defeated by England (1588). The 1600's were marked by a series of territorial wars with France, by the Spanish Inquisition, and by the Catholic Reformation. Jews, Moslems, and women accused of witchcraft were the primary victims of the Spanish Inquisition, but it also became a political tool of the monarchy and the Church for undoing one's enemies of any rank.

Women have distinguished themselves in military action for centuries in Spain. One of the earliest recorded examples, Doña Urraca, defended Zamora against her own brother, Alfonso VI, in the 12th century. Catalina de Erauzo (16th century) fled the convent at age 14, dressed as a man, and joined the army, fighting in Flanders, Italy, and the New World and earning the title "La Monja Alférez" (Lieutenant-General). In the 17th century María Pita fought against Drake's pirates, and in the 18th century Agustina de Aragón drove off Napoleon's troops, defending Zaragosa alone with a cannon. In 1833 Isabella II ascended the throne with her mother, María Cristina, as regent (María had persuaded Isabella's father, Ferdinand VII, to revoke the Salic Law, thus permitting female succession to the throne). Isabella II had support from liberal factions in the Carlist Wars. The First Republic lasted only from 1873–74. Women were active in the Carlist Wars: Mariana Pineda, who was hanged for being part of a conspiracy against Ferdinand VII, became the subject of one of Federico García Lorca's plays. The 20th century saw women participate in active combat in the Spanish Civil War, among them Lina Odena and Caridad Mercader, and there were also groups of Anarchist militia women. The well-known Dolores Ibarruri ("La Pasionaria") was an official in the Communist Party.

Spanish women also have been important literary figures. In the 17th century, María Zaya wrote the first Spanish feminist novels. Rosalia de Castro (1837–85) was an important novelist and poet who wrote the first major verse in Galician since the 1200's. Other significant women of letters in the 19th and early 20th centuries include Concepción Arenal, Emilia Pardo Bazán, Cuban-born Gertrudis Gómez de Avellaneda, Cecilia Böll de Faber, and Fernán Caballero (who wrote under a male pseudonym).

In the early 1900's, Spanish women began to organize on the issue of women's civil rights. In 1923 Primo de Rivera became dictator, but an antimonarchist, republican movement later forced him to resign (1930) and expelled King Alfonso XIII in 1931 (the Second Republic). In 1920 various women's associations had been founded: the Woman of the Future, the Progressive Female in Barcelona, and the National Assoc. of Spanish Women, which had branches throughout the country. At the conference of Women's Social Action (1920) women denounced their low status and pledged to improve it; 3 years later, because of pressure from women's groups, Primo de Rivera appointed 15 women to the National Assembly.

After the birth of the Second Republic, women gained important civil rights regarding family and work (see following article). Several journals on women's emancipation developed. Women activists addressed issues of abortion, day care, and equal pay and employment opportunities. Women's situation improved with the rights to divorce, suffrage, education, and better health care. Catalonia, having some autonomy, passed a liberal bill on abortion and contraception.

Following the 1936 elections, General Francisco Franco led a military rebellion of the conservative insurgents, including the fascist Falange, ending the Second Republic and precipitating a 3-year civil war. Mussolini and Hitler supported Franco, while international volunteers, including those from the USSR and a US contingent (the Abraham Lincoln Brigade), supported the Loyalists. Franco's forces won in 1939 and he assumed control. After the Civil War and the rise of Franco and the Falange, women's rights and freedoms gained under the Second Republic were revoked. The 1889 Civil Code was restored, banning divorce, making the husband the administrator of marriage property, and restoring Roman Catholic marriages to a position equal to civil ceremonies. The Law on Work (1938) barred women from certain jobs, permitted husbands to forbid their wives to work, and allowed men to collect their wives' wages. During WW II women were active in the anti-fascist resistance (see following article).

In 1962 popular discontent with the Franco regime erupted with student demonstrations and strikes by miners in Asturias. During Franco's 36-year regime, the various popular struggles of workers, women, students, and intellectuals achieved some improvements in freedom of expression, religion, civil rights, and trade-union activism. Franco died in 1975 and Juan Carlos became king. Free elections were held in June 1976. The contemporary feminist movement had begun in 1970 with groups in Barcelona and Madrid. Because Franco denied legal status to democratic organizations, the women met secretly. After International Women's Year (1975), women acted more openly. On Mar. 8, 1975, a women's-rights demonstration was held without government authorization, and women were arrested. In Dec. 1975 the first National Days for Women's Liberation brought together 400 women in a clandestine meeting sponsored by the Democratic Movement of Women, a section of the Spanish Communist Party; the meeting stimulated the growth of 200 groups throughout the country. In Catalonia, in May 1976, the Catalán Women's Days were attended by 4000 women. The movement began to focus on divorce, abortion, equal pay, decriminalizing adultery, and equal rights for children born out of wedlock.

In 1976 the journal *Vindicación Feminista* (Feminist Vindication), was first published in Barcelona, and *Donnes en Lluita* (Women in Struggle) was begun by the Feminist Coordinate of Barcelona. La Sal, a feminist publishing house in Barcelona, was founded in 1978. Lesbian-feminist groups developed in the larger cities. In 1977 political repression eased, as opposition political parties were legalized and some elections held. The Feminist Party was created (1979) to fight for women's interests; it publishes *Poder y Libertad* (Power and Liberty), a journal of feminist theory. A reproductive-freedom campaign began in 1979, with thousands of women from all social classes and professions publicly declaring that they had had abortions. In 1980 the birth-control clinic in Valencia was raided by the police and more than a dozen people were prosecuted for having had or performed abortions. That same year in Seville, more than 400 women were arrested on the same charges when the Los Naranjos clinic was raided. Eleven women were tried in Bilbao in 1982, 9 for having had abortions a decade earlier and 2 for having performed them; thousands of women all across Spain staged sit-ins to protest the trial, and international feminist support was mobilized. Ten women were acquitted and 1 was sentenced to 10 years in jail. As of 1983, the case still was being appealed.

In Oct. 1982, 80% of Spain's population voted in national elections; the Socialist Party won with 10,000,000 votes, and the new government has pledged legal reforms regarding women's rights.

MYTHOGRAPHY. In the 9th–8th centuries B.C.E. during the period of intense trade activity in the Mediterranean basin, it is theorized that gynocratic Cretan settlements were established in Spain, and the stone bulls at Guisando (near Ávila), as well as the still-popular bullfights, are said to be evidence. In Castellar de San Esteban and Despeñaperros, both in the Sierra Morena, more than 5000 small statues have been found in the pre-Roman ruins—primarily figures of women and sacred animals. Two of the most famous are "La Dama del Cerro de los Santos" and "La Dama del Elche," thought to be ritualized representatives of queen or goddess figures. Mariolatry has been stronger in Spain than in perhaps any other Roman Catholic country.

SPAIN: Women Are the Conscience of Our Country
by *Lidia Falcón*
(Translated by Gloria Feiman Waldman)

To write about the Spanish feminist movement is to write about a revolution betrayed. The fascism that triumphed in Spain for forty years—after the longest civil war of our time—not only crushed the male proletariat and peasants, destroyed culture, censored literature, ended theater, and exiled the Spanish intelligentsia and the university class for two generations; in addition, and I would say above all, it savagely exploited women, oppressed and humiliated them as only fascist *machismo* can do.

Historical facts often conceal history. While today, for example, women fight daily to obtain the legalization of abortion, everyone has forgotten that Spain was one of the first countries in the world to legalize abortion; in 1937, in the middle of the Civil War, even contradicting the interests of those who advocated many children to compensate for the dead and wounded, a Catalan woman, Federica Montseny, the first female Minister to the Department of Health, approved the law that allowed women to exercise control over their bodies—and with the support of the State hospitals.

One can add many other, similar examples in the history of Spanish women to this significant and representative one. From 1931, when the Second Spanish Republic gave women the vote, until 1939, when the war ended with the defeat of democracy, Spanish women saw their suffering alleviated by the approval of civil marriage, divorce, equality in marriage, shared *patria potestad* (custody), removal of legal discriminations against unwed mothers, and the legislated right of a woman to administer her own property. In 1932, Concha Espina, a writer, was the first Spanish woman to be named consul in France. Three women were members of the Spanish Parliament: Victoria Kent, Dolores Ibarruri ("La Pasionaria"), and Margarita Nelken. The war was to thwart these first feminist achievements and destroy all hope.

For forty years Spanish women worked in the countryside, abandoned by men who were exiled, imprisoned, or dead. They reconstructed and enlarged the industries destroyed by the war. The price was their broken, overburdened shoulders—and their exhausted wombs, ever producing. It was they who achieved the demographic miracle of this century: nearly doubling the Spanish population in only forty years. In 1939 Spain had only 20 million inhabitants; in 1980 it had a population of 37 million.

This reconstruction of the country, which allowed Spain to enter the realm of industrialized nations with a brilliant number ten ranking, is owed to women: the anonymous heroines who for half the salary of any man sewed and wove, dug ditches for highways and quarries, dragged themselves through mines (where they were injured by explosive substances and burned by chemical products), and manufactured shoes, tools, optics, and jewelry. In addition, they were reproducing, always without remuneration, in order to make the male world richer, more powerful, and more efficient.

In exchange, they suffered humiliation, scorn, and repression. With the new fascist state, legislation reverted to what it had been in the nineteenth century. The Civil Code of 1889 and the Commercial Code of 1829 were resurrected in all their purity. They proclaimed that a woman must obey her husband in all areas, that she could not manage her own wealth (not even the salary she might earn from work), that she required the permission of her husband to engage in business, get a job, have a career, or go to court concerning her own property and possessions. Prison awaited her, as a prize for her efforts, if she rebelled in the slightest way: if she abandoned the conjugal residence and her legitimate master, if she committed adultery (a crime in no way similarly punished when committed by the male), or if she attempted to practice birth control. Any action in this direction was punished by a prison sentence for the woman, for the pharmacist who sold the product, for the doctor who prescribed it, for the friend who recommended it, for the journalist who wrote in favor of it, and for the editor who published the article.

Divorce disappeared from the Spanish panorama and the Roman Catholic Church reentered, with its court of obscurantism and prejudice, to rule the destiny of Spanish women. The ecclesiastical tribunals were the only ones that could make decisions for Spanish couples about marital separation, child custody, love, and sexuality. Endless court cases dragging on for three, five, and even ten years ended in negative verdicts, despite the fact that these couples might have been living apart during all those years. Women were condemned to lose their children, their homes, and all financial support for any suspicion of living a "dishonest" life. Abortion was severely punished by dozens of years in prison for the midwives who performed the procedures and the women who anxiously sought them. Some sentences even reached ninety years in prison for doctors and midwives who dared challenge the law. The ghost of the Inquisition moved through the lives of many unfortunate women.

It is no surprise that with the death of the tyrant Franco, women arose from every corner of Spain to form the most aggressive, explosive, and brilliant feminist movement in all of Europe. Even in 1975, months before the end of so much horror, it was possible to take advantage of the United Nations declaration of International Women's Year, and to organize some conferences and work groups with the (very grudging) permission of the government. The triumph of the movement, however, was achieved in 1976. It was then that women's desperation, their never-abandoned vitality, and their yearning to fight overflowed into dynamic activity.

It's true that this was achieved with the reluctant permission of the political parties, whose role in Spanish life and politics is definitive. During the years of the dictatorship, the entire anti-fascist struggle was led by the Communist Party—which gave its best men and women to the battle for democracy, but not, evidently, for feminism. During that same period, the term "feminist" was identified by the Spanish Left as a synonym for "bourgeois," and the women who defined themselves as feminists were labeled *"señoritas"* from good families who claimed to do charity with the women workers or obtain privileges for themselves from this kind of work.

Therefore, in the first moments of the organization of contemporary feminism, the political parties of the Left played a decisive role. They were shocked by the scope of the movement, the number of women participating in it, the lively aggressiveness of its components, and the vanguard nature of its goals and proposals. For the Communist Party, the Socialist Party, the National Confederation of Workers (Anarchists), and other parties of the moderate Left, capitalizing on the feminist struggle was absolutely indispensable for achieving future success. And they dedicated themselves to it.

In Madrid in December of 1975, in Barcelona in May of 1976, and later in Bilbao, Galicia, and Granada, conferences were held on all facets of "the woman question," generated by women in the political parties and supported by men in the parties' executive committees. On various occasions there were 4000 people overflowing university auditoriums to debate such issues as women and work, birth control, and abortion.

From those beginnings came the first work groups, all with diverse objectives and ideologies. Apropos of this, in Barcelona in July of 1976, the magazine *Vindicación Feminista* (Feminist Vindication) was born, and marked an important achievement for Spanish feminism. For three years it was the principal vehicle for the expression of feminist ideas and a forum for national and international political analyses from a feminist perspective. (All this while maintaining the schizophrenic distinction between politics and feminism.) In the pages of *Vindicación Feminista* we published the beginnings of the crucial polemic of Spanish feminism: that women are a social and economic class in themselves and are the mode of domestic production. Meanwhile, we were organizing the first Feminist Party. Originally we had an assembly-type structure which was later forced to become more hierarchical so that we could achieve the efficiency for which we were striving. It was absolutely necessary for women to have their own party, their own class organization that would defend their interests and fight actively in their defense—without trusting any longer in men or in political party redeemers. Only we women—as a class sharing the same interests—can elaborate feminist theory that can develop the discourse of oppression and imagine its antithesis: liberation. Only we can invent the tactics and strategy of the struggle against the oppressor. When *Vindicación Feminista* could no longer survive because of financial problems resulting from our ambitious project and the reluctance of other sectors of the movement to help us financially, the Feminist Party was founded to fill the vacuum, and has continued to do so since June of 1979.

At that time, we felt sure of our proposals. For two years we had elaborated the theses of the Feminist Party, and we had a strategy for daily struggle with simple, short-term objectives. The immediate goal was getting the Party legalized by the government. (The period of transition toward democracy had begun but, as usual, without the women. Or, more precisely, against the women.) Little did any of us know how long it would take to get through the tunnel that would lead to democracy in Spain. Our struggle had only just begun.

For two years I devoted myself to writing, arguing, drafting memos and documents, making visits, and soliciting recommendations to achieve the legalization of the Feminist Party—the first party of its kind in the country, the first party made up of women, and therefore suspect, hated, ridiculed, persecuted. This time, as on so many other occasions, international feminist solidarity saved us. The telegrams and letters from many countries —France, Australia, Latin America, Canada among them—piled up on the desk of the Secretary of the Interior, expressing disgust over the long and unprecedented delay in legalization. On March 4, 1981, an official from the Department of the Interior informed us of the legalization and gave us a number in the Register of Political Parties. From then on, our work consisted of getting our internal organization up to date, calling the First Feminist Party Congress to organize ourselves for the daily work of attending to the grave everyday problems of the women, and continuing to study the causes of and solutions for our oppression.

While other feminist institutions were closing (bars, women's centers, and feminist collectives—for lack of spirit, economic aid, or active members), we opened our first feminist club, called Vindicación Feminista, of course. There we established a center for family planning with legal and psychological counseling, group therapy for women, and courses on sexuality, reproduction, and various political themes. At the same time the Feminist Party further elaborated the theories that we were publishing in our magazine, *Poder y Libertad* (Power and Liberty)—the first theoretical magazine about feminism, of the first feminist party in Spain.

In the meanwhile, what had happened to the rest of the Spanish women's movement? The movement that in the previous five years had achieved, through the vehemence of its demonstrations, the aggressiveness of its militants, and the constancy of its work, the abolition of the majority of discriminatory laws against women that still had existed at the time of the dictator's death? It had taken two years of struggle to eliminate the adultery law which sent only women to prison; three years to legalize contraception; six years to obtain a divorce law with equality of spouses regarding child custody, family rights, and responsibilities. Now we were faced with the greatest challenge of all: securing the legalization of abortion.

But it was at that moment that the women seemed tired. Some felt that they had worked very hard and wanted to rest; others thought that they had not done anything and that the feminist revolution was a too-distant goal. In 1980 the Feminist Platform of Madrid disappeared, as did the Feminist Coordinatorship of Barcelona. And when the groups that comprised them dissolved, so too did the Front for the Liberation of the Woman, the Union for the Liberation of the Woman, the Women's University Associations, all in Madrid. In Barcelona, small groups were formed and then dissolved, following that city's more anarchist and libertarian tradition. And even though more women joined in the struggle to free women accused of having had abortions in Bilbao, Sevilla, Valencia, and Zaragoza,* the older organizations languished.

But it is no miracle that the Feminist Party still is advancing in the face of the general malaise. Our work has been done on the margin, and at times against the political parties; therefore it is not controlled by anyone. We have delved deeply into theory, and also worked at everyday tasks. We have studied, but not distanced ourselves from the majority of the women who are homemakers, wives, and mothers. We know how we must focus their problems without becoming a group of elitists who do nothing but constantly debate the sex of the angels. We are the only ones who have posed the thesis of woman as a social class.

Nowadays it is no longer possible to separate the world economy from domestic work, industrial production from human reproduction, income from work (including the work of a housewife). Sexual exploitation may be the topic that provokes the most aggressive responses from men, but it is also the one which provokes the deepest level of understanding from women. The denunciation of the work conditions of women; the emphasis on the gratuitous task of reproduction and on exploited sexuality; the emphasis on the servile nature of domestic work which most women realize in exchange for bed and board (without any social security, vacations, weekly rest, or retirement rights); the sexual aggression that women endure in marriage; the slavery of daughters; the abandonment of the elderly; all that which conspires to make women the largest exploited class in all countries, at all times—that is what comprises the theoretical foundation of our Feminist Party and what has made it attractive to women of all economic and cultural conditions. To deny the condition of women as a class is to deny the evidence.

Without a doubt, the struggle continues to be difficult, especially now that a sector of the original women's movement rejects its roots. Certain groups of women—writers, professionals, academics—are denying their former involvement in feminism. They want to maintain their economic and professional status, to be thought well of in male circles, to obtain the crumbs that those who control society allow them. The women who are active in the political parties follow the mandates of their male-controlled central committees. The ones who want a government job on the local or national level indignantly reject even the word "feminism."

The political parties of the Left, the mass media, the universities, all launched a serious offensive against the movement once they believed that its forces were "domesticated." They had already capitalized upon the strength and energy of the women during the first and second national elections, in 1977 and in 1979. With the triumph of the Socialist Party in the 1982 elections, a few reforms are being realized, but at the same time some sectors of the movement are being better domesticated and will be snuffed out forever. Abortion will be legalized, albeit with great limitations, and some family-planning centers will be created. But little more. The great majority of women will remain outside of the social advantages of a salary, health insurance, old-age and retirement pensions. Rape victims, battered wives, abandoned wives, divorced women without support, and children without schools, vacations, and social resources—all will continue waiting for help not forthcoming.

Spain is still a country without academic scholarships for older women or support for working wives, with an insufficient system of day-care centers, schools, clinics, facilities for the handicapped, reformatories for juvenile delinquents, and old-age homes. So it is that Spanish women (in addition to being the producers of human beings and the sustainers of the country through its foundation, the family) also are the free labor force that the State counts on to care for the sick, the retarded, the mentally ill, the elderly, and the

* See Statistical Preface preceding this article for details.—Ed.

delinquents. The economic statistics in a masculine society which exhaustively exploits its women are incredible, although they are still hidden. When all is said and done—so everyone thinks—that's what women are for anyway. And as the *Bible* prescribed, they were born to suffer. Because they were born to reproduce, they should be exploited in all aspects of their lives.

The reproductive capacity that constitutes the first line of the work force, the origin of life and human society, is the one that condemns women to suffering and death in order to sustain the social body through life. It is that capacity that man exploits relentlessly, whose product he appropriates, whose output he becomes master of, and over whose work he asserts his dominion in the world. This is just as true of the men of the Left as of the men of the Right, of those who govern and those who attack the government. Taking advantage of the female womb, controlling its activity, demanding its tribute, imposing his will by force and persuasion, threats and punishment, man dominates the female labor force. With women's double-job burden he builds his State, advances his economy, and makes his policy.

For that reason we are the conscience of the country, the incitement to rebellion, the political organization, and the elaborators of the theory that women are a social class. For that reason, it will never again be said that in Spain the women did not know how to organize themselves, that they did not know how to fight, that they did not win their place in the country and their place in history.

Today, among us, we are writing it.

Suggested Further Reading

Alcalde, Carmen. *La Mujer en la Guerra Civil Española* (Women in the Spanish Civil War). Madrid: Editorial Cambio 16, 1976.

Arias, María José Ragué. *Procedo a la Familia* (Indictment Against the Family). Barcelona: Editorial Granica, 1977.

Falcón, Lidia. *En el Infierno—Ser Mujer en las cárceles de España* (In Hell—To Be a Woman in the Spanish Prisons). Barcelona: Ediciones de Feminismo, 1976.

———. *Los Hijos de los Vencidos* (The Children of the Vanquished). Barcelona: Editorial Pomaire, 1978.

———. *Mujer y Sociedad* (Women and Society). Barcelona: Editorial Fontanella, 1969.

Waldman, Gloria F., and Linda Gould Levine. *Feminismo Ante el Franquismo* (Feminism During the Franco Years). Miami, FL: Ediciones Universal, 1979.

Lidia Falcón was born on December 13, 1935, in Madrid. She earned her law degree from the University of Barcelona in 1960 and her journalism degree from the School of Journalism of Madrid in 1961. She was jailed during the Franco years, has been a practicing lawyer since 1960 (specializing in family law), was the founder of the monthly review *Vindicación Feminista* and of the Spanish Feminist Party. She has lectured widely in Spain and other countries, attended world gatherings of women, and written articles for periodicals around the globe. She is also the author of fourteen books of fiction, nonfiction, and social criticism, including her major four-volume work *La Razón Feminista* (The Reason for Feminism). She is divorced, and has two grown children.

SRI LANKA
(Democratic Socialist Republic of Sri Lanka)

An island in the Indian Ocean off the southeast tip of India. **Area:** 65,610 sq. km. (25,332 sq. mi.). **Population** (1982): 15,250,000, female 48.6%. **Capital:** Sri Jayewardenapura Kotte (Colombo).

DEMOGRAPHY. Languages: Sinhala (official), Tamil, English. **Races or Ethnic Groups:** Sinhalese (and/or Kandyan)* 72%, Tamil 19%, Moor 7%, Burgher (Dutch descent), Eurasian, Malay. **Religions:** Buddhism 63%, Hinduism 18%, Christianity 8%, Islam 7%. **Education** (% enrolled in school, 1975): Age 6–11—of all girls 63%, of all boys 61%; age 12–17—of all girls 54%, of all boys 54%; higher education—in 1978 women were 37.7% of all students, 9.5% of engineering students, 9.5% of architecture, 20% of agriculture, 45% of liberal arts, 45% of medical students, 46% of dentistry, 50% of veterinary medicine. All carpentry and masonry students in 130 centers were men, and all students in the single mat-weaving center and 5 lace-making centers were women (1978). **Literacy** (1977): Female 68%, male 86%; only 48% of women plantation workers were literate. **Birth Rate** (per 1000 pop., 1975–80): 28. **Death Rate** (per 1000 pop., 1975–80): 7; malnutrition- and anemia-related deaths (per 1000 pop., 1976)—female 4.6, male 3.2. **Infant Mortality** (per 1000 live births, 1975–80): Female 36, male 47 (see **Family**). **Life Expectancy** (1975–80): Female 65 yrs., male 62 yrs.

GOVERNMENT. In 1972 a republican constitution came into effect, establishing an elected unicameral 168-member National Assembly with legislative and ex-

ecutive powers. A president appoints the prime minister, who heads a Council of Ministers. In 1977 the constitution was amended to grant extensive executive powers to the president. A new constitution for the Democratic Socialist Republic of Sri Lanka was passed in 1978. Major parties include the (ruling) United National Party, the Sri Lanka Freedom Party, and the Lanka Sama Samaja and Communist parties. **Women's Suffrage:** The 1931 Constitution granted all women over age 21 the right to vote and stand for election; at Independence, the Tamil pop. (male and female) was disenfranchised, then partly re-enfranchised in 1964, although their citizenship status remains in question (1983). In 1970 the voting age was lowered to 18. **Equal Rights:** The 1978 Constitution prohibits sex-discrimination, permits passage of affirmative-action legislation on behalf of women, and omits job-reserving for men. The Cabinet decided not to enforce the 25% quota system (a section of the 1972 Constitution which said that women could not occupy more than 25% of jobs in the government's administrative, accounting, and clerical services), but the regulation remains and in practice still operates (see ECONOMY). Single adult women have property rights equal to those of men. Lower-class and -caste women and girls have a greater degree of freedom to travel alone, swim with boys, and participate in public life.

Women in Government: In 1960 Sirimavo R. D. Bandaranaike became the first woman in modern world history to be elected a head of state by popular vote; from 1947 to 1970 there were only 15

---

* During the 18th-century Dutch occupation (see HERSTORY), the indigenous Sinhalese were in effect separated into 2 groups: those in the coastal areas came under direct Dutch rule and cultural influence, while those in the interior (especially the central highlands) constituted the independent Kandyan Kingdom for 300 yrs. and were more able to pursue their own traditions. By 1815, when the Kandyan Kingdom was ceded to the British, there were considerable cultural differences between the 2 (coastal and interior/Kandyan) Sinhalese groups. The complex laws of Sri Lanka reflect this variance in customs, as well as those of other religious/ethnic citizens, and are further complicated by the overarching "general law" (based on Dutch-Roman jurisprudence mixed with British law) which has limited application when in conflict with certain customary laws of the various groups.

women elected to the (then) Parliament and 54 to local governing bodies. In 1977, 4 women were in the Assembly; the Minister of Health is a woman, Ms. Ranasinghe, as is the Minister of Rural Development, Ms. Kanangara (1983). Women constituted 35% of local party membership in 1977, but only 10% of the ruling United National Party decision makers in 1980.

ECONOMY. Currency: Sri Lankan Rupee (May 1983: 22.9 = $1 US). Gross National Product (1980): $4 billion. Per Capita Income (1980): $270. Approx. 80% of the pop. earns less than $30 per month, and 40% earns less than $16 per month (1982). Women's Wages as a Percentage of Men's: No general statistics obtainable. Minimum wages (set by government Wage Boards) for women averaged 65% of men's (1980); in agriculture, women's wages ranged from 38% to 80% of men's (1981). Equal Pay Policy: None. Wage Boards fix wages in 31 sectors; there are often 3 pay rates (for men, for women, and for young workers, or for skilled, semi-skilled, and unskilled jobs; women employees are excluded de facto from the skilled category). No minimum wage is set for plantation or domestic work. Women's groups are lobbying for equal pay laws. Production (Agricultural/Industrial): Tea, coconuts, rice, cacao, cinnamon, tobacco; rubber, plywood, paper, textiles, glassware, ceramics, chemicals, cement. Women as a Percentage of Labor Force (1980): 25%; of agricultural force (1979) 49.5% (65% of women workers are employed in agriculture, 1975); of industrial force—no general statistics obtainable (of manufacturing 28.9%, 1979); of military—no statistics obtainable, but women serve in clerical, nursing, etc., capacities. In a 1975 survey of almost 7000 women, 66.2% of married urban women and 43.6% of married rural women had never worked outside the home, and 36.5% of married women age 15–49 were in the labor force.

(Employed) Women's Occupational Indicators: Of tea pickers 90% (1980); of professors 2.5%, of administrative service workers 7.6% (with only 1.8% of the top level), of certified teachers 70.1% (1979); of supervisors 9.9%, of unskilled workers 39.8% (1976); 42% of all employed women work on plantations. Tea pickers—predominantly low-caste Tamil women—work 10 hours a day and are paid 4.7 Rupees per day (1976). Plantation workers have double the national infant mortality and maternal death rates and suffer widespread malnutrition. Women agricultural workers do the most onerous jobs—transplanting, weeding, picking, and harvesting. Spinners and weavers, carpet, rug, and matting makers, beedi (cigarette) makers, and textile and garment workers are almost all women. More than 100,000 rural women are employed in these handicraft industries, or work in sweatshops. Women textile workers in the Free Economic Zone earn $1–1.10 for a 10-hour day with mandatory overtime, no sick leave, no unions, and no right to strike. In national unions with overwhelmingly female membership (nurses 95%, typists 70%) the leadership and officers are almost entirely male. In recent yrs., a large number of Sri Lankan women have been recruited as domestics in oil-producing Middle Eastern countries; women's organizations in Sri Lanka are seeking government regulations, minimum wages, and employment conditions to safeguard these workers. Unemployment (1980–81): 15.3%, female 23%, male 12.4%. Unemployment became a problem among women college graduates in the 1960's, and the Unemployed Women's Arts Graduates Project was formed (1980) to network jobs.

GYNOGRAPHY. Marriage: Policy: Under the General Marriage Ordinance (1917), legal marriage age is 14 for females and 16 for males. Under the Kandyan Marriage Ordinance (1859), it is 12 for females and 16 for males. According to the Moslem Marriage and Divorce Act (1951), marriage of a girl under 12 is legal but must be approved by a religious judge. Polyandrous marriages (usually between 2 or more brothers and 1 wife) were common among Kandyans until 1859, when all polygamy—except for polygyny among Moslems—was banned. Women assume the legal domicile of their husbands except in Kandyan Binna (uxerical and matrifocal) marriages. Married women control their own property except in Kandyan *Diga* (patrifocal) marriages, where the husband manages and can sell joint property without consent of the wife, and in Thesawalamai law** under which women can make no contracts or suits without their husbands' written consent. Dowry was prohibited under Roman-Dutch law but legalized by the Matrimonial Rights and Inheritance Ordinance (1876). In Sinhalese and Tamil customary laws, a dowered daughter forfeits her ancestral inheritance rights. Under general law, spouses are legally responsible for mutual financial support. Under both Moslem and Kandyan *Diga* marriage laws, husbands must support their wives; in Kandyan law women can sell or mortgage their husbands' property if they fail to provide support. Married women's property and inheritance rights are determined by the laws applicable to their husbands' nationality and ethnic group.

Practice: Female mean age at marriage (1970–78): 24; women age 15–49 in union (1970–78): 59.6%. Approx. 1/2 of all marriages are arranged by parents or matchmakers, frequently between cross-cousins (see **Incest**). There are few polygynous marriages in the Moslem community. Dowry—in the form of jewelry, clothes, furniture, and housing—is prevalent in all communities but more popular in traditional areas. In Sinhalese custom, the dowry is intended and accepted as the bride's own property and is to remain as her personal estate. Tamil women have less control over the dowry, which is also titularly their property but which is under their husbands' control. In the Moslem community, both *mahar* (dowry money given by the husband to the wife) and *kaikuli* (dowry money given by the bride's father to the bride) remain under the husband's control. Women's groups have been working to ban dowry and to raise the minimum age for marriage to 18, regardless of sex and ethnic group.

Divorce. *Policy:* Differs in religious, regional, and civil codes. Under interpretations of Islamic law, husband can divorce wife by renunciation *(talag);* wife can divorce husband for failure of support, cruelty, insanity, impotence, or incurable disease; the father is guardian and awarded custody of boys over age 7 and girls past puberty. In Kandyan divorce law (1952), husband's grounds are adultery; wife can divorce on proof of adultery coupled with cruelty or incest; either can divorce for desertion substantiated by a 1-yr separation, or by mutual consent. In *Binna* marriages, fathers have no claim to custody of the children (matrilineal descent) and in *Diga* marriages custody is awarded depending on who is at fault in the divorce. No data obtainable regarding divorce among the Tamils, who are governed, reportedly, under general law regarding divorce. Dutch-Roman law allows divorce for adultery, impotence, or desertion, with the same terms for women and men; father has primary rights to guardianship, but custody is awarded "in the best interests of the children" and mothers usually retain custody of minor children; alimony can be required of either men or women, depending on financial circumstance and need. *Practice:* Divorces (per 1000 pop.— excluding the Moslem pop.—1975): 0.14. Legal divorces are rare, most are *de facto* by desertion. Sinhalese divorced women are not always stigmatized because prior to colonization it was not unusual for women in certain areas of the country to leave their husbands and support themselves.

Family. *Policy:* Office employees are entitled to 14 working days paid maternity leave pre-delivery and 28 working days paid leave post-delivery, regardless of length of employment. Factory workers who are permanent employees on a monthly wage plan receive 42 days paid leave, and reinstatement is stipulated. Nursing mothers are entitled to 2 half-hour nursing breaks in addition to regular daily breaks (Maternity Benefits Ordinance). Plantation, agricultural, small-shop, and domestic-service employees are not eligible for maternity benefits; plantations are legally obligated to supply food

** Law based on the customary laws of the Tamil population (descendants of early invaders from India who settled largely in the Jaffna area), but applied with differing application to Jaffna-Tamils and to Tamils dwelling elsewhere in Sri Lanka.

and shelter to a woman for 1 month after childbirth and to provide creches for children under age 5. Creches are also required in most factories. Daughters have equal inheritance rights, except those governed by Moslem law (who inherit 1/2 the share of sons) and dowried Kandyan daughters in *Diga* (patrilineal) marriages. Dowried Tamil women forfeit inheritance rights to their parents' property, and they cannot be widow-beneficiaries although they can have a life interest in husbands' estates.

Practice: Factories avoid paying maternity benefits by hiring women as temporary employees for long periods and by hiring single women (88% female employees in the Free Trade Zone are single). Plantation employees sometimes give birth in the midst of work. There were 1500 creches on plantation estates (1979), but many areas lack them. The inspection system to enforce creche requirements is infrequent and ineffective; a "creche" can consist of 1 woman who is supposed to care for all the workers' children. In 1980, 194 day-care centers enrolling 600 children were operated by nongovernmental organizations receiving State aid. The Sarvodaya movement organizes village Mothers' Clubs (active in 3000 villages, 1979), which often start cooperative childcare groups. The wealthy depend on domestic workers for childcare. It is considered a great shame in some areas to let men participate in domestic work. Rural women (78% of the 1978 population lived in rural areas) often rise at 3 A.M. to draw water, cook, and gather fuel before going to their jobs, then continue housework from 7 P.M. until late at night. Girls age 1–9 have a higher mortality rate than boys owing to neglect and inferior nutrition and medical care (1976). Such high-protein foods as fish, meat, and eggs are considered tabu for women when they are menstruating, pregnant, or nursing. In a 1976 study of 464 pregnant women, 28.89% were moderately anemic and 5% were severely anemic. Women's groups are calling for extended maternity benefits, enforcement of creche provisions, work leaves (to study, raise small children, or travel with a husband who must study or

work abroad), and male participation in housework.

Welfare. *Policy:* Free national health plan is available to all; free education through university. Destitutes without income or family support receive a small monthly allowance; there is aid to leprosy and tuberculosis patients and their families, to flood and famine victims, and to some fisherfolk in the event of storms, etc. There are government-run homes for the aged and grants to voluntary organizations which run orphanages, creches, and nursing homes. A workers' compensation law has been in effect since 1934. *Practice:* No data obtainable.

Contraception. *Policy:* Government supports family planning for demographic reasons and provides financial incentives to favor small families. The Family Planning Assoc. was founded in 1953, and the government began to promote contraception nationally in 1965. Currently, the Family Planning Assoc. pays 500 Rupees to adults volunteering to be sterilized in its mobile units. The cost to the country is expected to be 50 million Rupees (1982). Men and women with 3 or more children can be sterilized; women need written permission of husbands. *Practice:* Women age 15–49 in union using contraception (1982): 55%, of which traditional methods 45%, modern 38%, sterilization 17%; over 90% aware of 1 or more efficient methods; 7% unaware of any method. In a 1974 sample study, 28.2% of births were unwanted; 61% of women wanted no more children. A USAID experimental Operations Research Project subjected 120,000 women to the controversial injectable Depo Provera (1981). Contraceptives are difficult to obtain in rural areas, where supplies of pills and condoms are irregular. **Abortion.** *Policy:* Legal only if the woman's life is endangered. Penalties for illegal abortion range up to 3 yrs. imprisonment or to 7 yrs. if the procedure is done in advanced stages of pregnancy (Penal Code, Sec. 303). *Practice:* No statistics obtainable. The law is interpreted liberally by doctors; nevertheless, illegal abortions are common, and it is a lucrative field. **Illegitimacy.** *Policy:* Under Roman-Dutch law, mothers have full custody of children born out of wedlock.

Practice: No data obtainable. **Homosexuality.** *Policy:* No specific laws pertaining to homosexual behavior, although homosexual acts can be punishable as "unnatural offenses" (10 yrs. maximum imprisonment) or specifically as "gross indecency between males" (2 yrs. maximum imprisonment and/or fine and/or whipping,*** 1966 Penal Code). *Practice:* No data obtainable.

Incest. *Policy:* Under general law, marriage or cohabitation between ascendant and descendant relatives, and between collaterals within third-degree relationships, are illegal and punishable as incest; the marriage of parallel-cousins is legal. No further data obtainable. *Practice:* No statistics obtainable. Marriage between cross-cousins is common among the Sinhalese. **Sexual Harassment.** *Policy:* Illegal under the 1966 Penal Code as "outraging a woman's modesty." The maximum penalty is 2 yrs. imprisonment plus a fine and possible whipping. *Practice:* Sexual harassment is cited as a reason for restricting women from night employment. Men who harass and follow factory-worker women home at night are known colloquially as "tigers." **Rape.** *Policy:* Illegal under 1966 Penal Code and punishable by 20 yrs. maximum imprisonment plus a fine. There is a law of "Right of Private Defense" under which a woman may justify killing an attacker who had the "intention to cause rape or gratify unnatural lust." Sexual intercourse with a girl younger than 12 is also considered rape, regardless of her consent or marital status. *Practice:* No data obtainable. **Battery.** *Policy:* No data obtainable. *Practice:* Battery is reported to be common practice. Women are considered to be under their husbands' authority, so interference is rare. Alcoholism is associated with battery; women who have killed their drunken violent husbands in self-defense have been incarcerated.

Prostitution. *Policy:* Soliciting generally comes under magistrates' rulings; common penalty is 6 months–1 yr. imprisonment. Procuring a girl or woman for prostitution is punishable by 2 yrs. maximum imprisonment plus whipping (1966 Penal Code). *Practice:* As Sri Lanka became a more popular tourist resort, prostitution, especially in Colombo, has increased. **Traditional/Cultural Practices.** *Policy:* Kidnapping or abduction of a woman to compel marriage, seduction, or illicit intercourse is punishable by 7 yrs. maximum imprisonment (1966 Penal Code). *Practice:* Some nutritional tabus (see **Family**) are still observed. **Crisis Centers:** No data obtainable.

HERSTORY. According to the Mahawansa chronicle, Vijaya, an Indian prince from the Ganges valley, became the first king of the Sinhalese in the 6th century B.C.E. The monarchal form of government continued until the arrival of the Dutch in the 18th century, C.E., and persisted in the Kandyan (interior) Kingdom until the British conquest in the early 19th century. Portuguese settlements in the west and south, established in 1505, were taken by the Dutch in the 1600's. In 1796 the British annexed the settlements to their rule in Madras, and in 1802 Ceylon (now Sri Lanka) was constituted as a separate colony.

The Dutch started a small number of coeducational primary schools, which were taken over by the British in 1796. Lady Brownrigg (wife of the then British Governor) founded an English girls' school in Colombo in the early 1800's. During the 1820's a number of girls' missionary schools were opened, and in the 1840's the British government started 5 Girls' Superior Schools in Colombo, Kandy, Galle, and Jaffna. These were elite schools; in 1868, 87% of the students were European, Eurasian, or Burgher. By that year the government had opened 12 Sinhalese and Tamil girls' schools, called vernacular schools. Toward the end of the 19th century the government closed the Girls' Superior Schools and followed a policy of providing grants to missions to start schools, resulting in the opening of a number of secondary schools. To meet the need for teachers, a Normal School opened in 1870 (but closed in 1884). The Cambridge exams were introduced in Sri Lanka and formed the basis for the curricula of all English schools. The first

---

*** Women are exempt from whipping as a legal punishment in Sri Lanka.

woman sat for the senior exam in 1881, and the first woman entered medical school in 1884. A new teacher-training college opened in 1902.

The first formal women's organization founded was the YWCA (Young Women's Christian Association) of Colombo (1852). The Young Women's Christian Temperance Union of Ceylon was founded in 1886. This was followed by others, including the Sri Lanka Tamil Women's Union (1909), the Mallika Niwasa Samithiya (1921), the Sri Lanka Women's Society (1930), the Ceylon Moor Ladies' Union (1936), the Sri Lanka Federation of University Women (1941), the Sri Lanka Women's Conference (an umbrella organization, 1944), and the Women's International League for Peace and Freedom, Sri Lanka (1974). Professional women's organizations include the Sri Lanka Nurses Assoc. (1928), the Women Lawyers Assoc. (1962), the Medical Women's Assoc. (1968), and the Sri Lanka Women's Administrative Service Assoc. (1978).

Sirimavo R.D. Bandaranaike, widow of the previous prime minister, was herself elected prime minister in 1960. In 1962 she nationalized oil and other businesses, and became involved in a controversy over compensation with the US and Britain; in the 1965 elections, Ms. Bandaranaike's Freedom Party was defeated by the conservative United National Party, which agreed to pay compensation. Ms. Bandaranaike again became prime minister in 1970. Ceylon became the Republic of Sri Lanka in 1972.

The government had sponsored the formation of rural women's organizations, called Kantha Samitis, in 1952; in the mid-1970's there were 579 such groups in 22 administrative districts.

They developed handicraft co-ops and health, sanitation, gardening, and child-care groups. In 1978 the government disbanded these women's organizations and replaced them with Rural Development Societies, mixed-sex organizations which are now male-dominated.

Women workers have a history of labor activism, which still continues: they were active during labor strikes in the 1920's and the 1940's; Isabella Hamy was an outstanding labor leader in Colombo in the 1920's. Recently, women have been attacked and beaten by hired strikebreakers for participating in union activities. In 1971 soldiers raped a number of women detainees and murdered Prema Manamperi, a prisoner.

In 1980 Moslem women's organizations held a national conference to discuss problems specific to them. In 1983 Nirmala Nithiyananthan, a Tamil feminist, dramatist, and literary critic, was arrested under the Prevention of Terrorism Act, which enables the government to hold any person in detention for 18 months without trial (as of 1983 hostilities persist between the minority Tamil and majority Sinhalese pops.). In response to pressure from women's groups beginning in 1975, the government established a Women's Bureau. The main areas of concern are women on plantations and in poor rural areas, the Mahaweli resettlement area, urban slums, and the Free Trade Zone.

MYTHOGRAPHY. Lakshmi (the goddess of wealth) and Sarasvati (the goddess of learning) are popular Hindu deities. The goddess Pattini also has a large following, and a particular Buddhist holiday requires preparing Food for The Seven Grandmothers.

SRI LANKA: The Voice of Women
by Hema Goonatilake

The role of women in Sri Lanka must be viewed within the context of the country's economic, political, social, and cultural heritages—a 2500-year-old civilization. Sri Lanka was subject to nearly 500 years of foreign domination by the Portuguese, Dutch, and British, until it gained independence in 1948.

The rural economy in ancient Sri Lanka was based on paddy cultivation, and the sociocultural values that guided the ordinary people's lives stemmed from this agrarian economy. The royalty and the nobility had their own social and cultural institutions that centered around the royal palace. (Women of this elite group were confined to their palatial homes surrounded by a retinue of male and female attendants.) Among the ordinary people, on the other hand, women were co-producers with men in the field as well as in cottage industries. Yet there was a family division of labor defined by custom: plowing was mainly man's work, while weeding and transplanting were woman's. The children were cared for by father *and* mother and the members of the extended family. Decisions were made together.

Yet the status ascribed to women in society by the sociocultural and ideological system was low. Sri Lankan poets saw women only as ornaments whose purpose was to bring entertainment to men, fragile and delicate creatures who could not do hard work.

> A face like the full moon,
> A waist that can be clasped with both hands,
> Hips as wide as a chariot wheel,
> Breasts like swans, golden skinned,
> She is a celestial maiden, but for the fluttering of her eyelids.[1]

These sentiments were voiced by court poets in the "legitimized" literature, while the hard reality of the majority of women was reflected in the folk literature, two examples of which appear below.

> Drops of sweat drip down her forehead,
> Like a string of pearls.[2]

> The baby cries and howls,
> The tiny throat is dry.
> Mother is reaping paddy in the blazing sun.
> Stop that reaping,
> And fondle your child.[3]

With the advent of imperialism, the plantation economy was introduced (in what was then called Ceylon) after the 1830's and was based on wage labor, factory-type operation of large estates, and production for a foreign market. (Women and children were employed as a source of cheap industrial labor in nineteenth-century Britain, and this method of exploitation was introduced into the Sri Lankan tea estates, where the majority of the workers were women.)

Before the growth of the tea plantations, there was mass-scale employment of women in the European-owned coffee mills in Colombo, where the coffee peeling, sorting, and packing was all done by women. Women were also employed in construction and road work by the colonial authorities. Women were employed for sorting and cleaning of plumbago in large plumbago mines—and so were exploited by the local capitalists, too. Thus, women entered the labor market as wage workers for less pay than men, forming the more oppressed of the oppressed working class.

The (colonially derived) behavior of upper-class women required subjugation to Victorian values, which were propagated as part of the modern Western educational package at

[1] Fragment from the 15th-century *Salalihini Sandesaya*.
[2] and [3] Old folk-poems.

the time. The code of conduct for these women was "lady-like" behavior: polite, feminine, innocent, shy, timid, passive, and self-effacing.

Arranged marriage and the dowry system (for the upper strata), both remnants of feudal society, took different forms during colonial times. Earlier, marriage between cross-cousins was considered ideal and marriages between families of the same or neighboring villages were common; the dowry was more a gift given to the daughter in the form of jewelry, cattle, or property. Under the influence of commercialism based on trade, the marriage and dowry system assumed new dimensions. Arranging marriage through a *Kapuva* (matchmaker) became the accepted norm, particularly among the middle classes. Such traditional feudal characteristics as caste, family, religion, place of birth (whether low-country or up-country), horoscopes, and dowry were considered, while at the same time such modern capitalistic attributes as the class background of respective parties—including occupation, educational qualifications, wealth, dress (whether European garb or not)—played an equally important role.

The plantation-based economy in Sri Lanka gave way after Independence to an import-substitution phase in 1956 which continued for about a twenty-year period, supported both by the national private sector and by government-sector involvement. This has been followed in the last five years by a sharp reorientation away from a nationalist import-substitution phase to a new dependent capitalist economy, now being forged under the hegemony of Western domination, especially the International Monetary Fund. This strategy has yet to bear fruit and yield the economic growth that was expected by its designers. Because of several concessionary loans and grants, an import-led growth (whose main beneficiaries are the trading classes and the intermediaries between Western interests and the locals) has emerged at the expense of the producing classes. These deep socioeconomic changes are reflected today, traders and the intermediary strata forming the dominant (although dependent) class.

The Position of Women Today

The introduction of free elementary and tertiary education (1945) and the change in instruction from English to the mother tongue in the 1950's have led to a significant increase in enrollment in schools and the university. It is significant that the statistics reveal that girls participate almost equally with boys in the formal school system, as well as in the university. The number of female students admitted to the medical, dental, and veterinary sciences, and the law faculties, have reached near-parity. Engineering and architecture faculties still remain male preserves, however, with only 9.5 percent female presence.

There is a strong imbalance between women's access to education and to employment. It is significant that women constitute only 26 percent of the total labor force, despite the fact that almost half the student population is female. This low proportion of economically active women is the result of computations based on the definition of working women as those engaged in "gainful" occupations measured in terms not related to household duties or to home-based and part-time work. In a labor-force survey (1973) which *included* housewives as a component of the labor force, the proportion of women was 44.9 percent.

Women are concentrated, as usual, in the lower levels of the occupational pyramid and so continue to be a source of cheap labor. Although there is equal remuneration in high- and middle-level occupations, sex disparities in wages with regard to skilled, semi-skilled, and unskilled workers are almost "legalized." The Labour Gazette of the Department of Labour regularly lays down minimum wages with respect to thirty-one trades, of which sixteen have male and female wages stipulated. The wage difference is approximately 15 percent of the male wage. Twelve of these trades are agricultural and agrobased (for example, tea, rubber, coconut, and allied trades), largely linked with the export economy. It is significant that over half the employed female population in Sri Lanka is blatantly discriminated against in wages.

The latest exploitation of women stems from the newly established Free Trade Zone which operates through foreign collaborative ventures or multinational corporations. Approximately 87 percent of the labor force in the Free Trade Zone is composed of women, who receive low wages for long hours of monotonous work.

Ironically, the new form of "propaganda" about women—once performed by religious and secular literature produced at the ancient monastic centers and disseminated through the village temples—is today disseminated via modern mass communication: the press, radio, cinema, school textbooks, and magazines perpetuate the views that women are dependent, subservient, inferior, physically fragile, have less brains than men, and generally are fit only to be wives and mothers. The hidden message is that the woman's place is in the home and that women who work outside the home lose their "femininity"; this provides the rationale for discrimination in wages and for unequal participation permitted in political, economic, and social activities.

The Growth of an Incipient Women's Movement

In the early 1970's, sporadic news items on the Western women's liberation movement had appeared in the Sri Lankan English media. The coverage tended to sensationalize and ridicule the issue without focusing attention on the deprivation and discriminations which inspired these protests in the West. The Western women's movement was portrayed as an example to be avoided by Sri Lankan women, thus evoking an unfavorable reaction against women's issues from the English-newspaper readership in the country. This reaction was all the more distinct among the middle classes, who were tied on the one hand to a feudal view of women and on the other to a view of social reality derived from colonial and neocolonial relationships.

In the wake of the International Women's Year (1975), the "women's question" came to the fore and for the first time national-language newspapers and the national radio began discussing the position of Sri Lankan women. The Sri Lanka National Committee for International Women's Year was formed, consisting of representatives from the political parties of the then Left-oriented coalition government and from national women's organizations. The Committee, whose main objective was creating an awareness of the issue, organized public meetings and workshops in Colombo and other districts. Photographic and art exhibitions were held. Trade unions and women's organizations followed suit. The first-ever academic seminar on the "women's question" was sponsored by the Social Science Section of the Sri Lanka Association for the Advancement of Science in 1976. (The flippant editorial response of an English daily was, "We suggest as their motto the stirring call: Women of Sri Lanka unite. You have nothing to lose but your husbands.") The *Status of Women* study undertaken in 1978 by a team of faculty members remains the major study done on Sri Lankan women to this day, and the interest on the women's issue which began with the International Women's Year has continued.

Weekly women's newspapers and women's columns (in addition to covering such "feminine activities" as cooking and fashion) continue to publish an article or two in each issue on the women's question, highlighting discrimination against women in the economic sphere, or the dowry system. General discussions touching on a sociocultural overview, however, reflect the lack of a clear ideology. For example, the president of the Sri Lanka Women's Administrative Service Association—a woman who has made it to the top—advocates the access of more and more women to professions but at the same time believes that children are entirely the mother's responsibility and the mother is to blame if the children go astray. Another example is that of a well-known female novelist and the head of a leading girls' school who believes that chastity should be a man's as well as a woman's virtue, but also declares that women should not demand or fight for their rights but be patient and suffer in silence, hoping for some eventual success to follow.

In spite of the contradictions, these articles in the mainstream media (whose circulation is extremely high) perform a very useful function, in that large sections of women in the country get exposed to the fact that women's issues do have direct relevance to their lives.

The discussions on the women's question in the English-language newspapers sometimes came down to a ludicrous and frivolous level with such responses as "In Sri Lanka, every year is a women's year." Debates in national-language papers often centered on such issues as "Should the wife be subservient to the husband?" But the major criticism leveled was that the concept was a Western import and only a problem among certain immoral Western women who disliked their roles as mothers and wives and took to drinks and drugs—and that feminism had become a "fad" only among some sectors of bourgeois Sri Lankan women.

It is interesting to note that *the whole issue has been criticized by both conservative and progressive elements.* The conservatives advanced the view that equality in terms of race, caste, creed, and sex is guaranteed in the Constitution and women in Sri Lanka could thus hold the highest posts. (An often-quoted example was that Sri Lanka had produced the first woman Prime Minister in the world.) They also pointed out that there is no need in Sri Lanka for a women's movement, since women got emancipated 2500 years ago when Buddha allowed women to enter the Buddhist Order and aspire to the highest intellectual attainments. Furthermore, they added, women in Asian societies have always been most respected as mothers and venerated as goddesses. The progressives—and even the left-wing radicals—continue to argue that the women's movement is a "diversion tactic of the bourgeoisie" to draw attention away from class struggle; when socialism is achieved, they claim, women will be liberated anyway. It is important to note that no left-wing political party in Sri Lanka so far has attempted to make a theoretical analysis of "the women's issue." Neither are there any women in the top rungs of the Left political parties.

The Concept of Women and Development

Funds from international development agencies on women's projects were pouring into the country by 1978, and the newly set up Women's Bureau began several projects to train women in different skills and income-generating activities. The social-service-oriented women's organizations, whose leadership has remained urban and relatively elite to this day, turned to focus on women's projects as well.

"Integrating women into development" has been the spirit, no doubt inspired also by the wishes of the aid donors, that pervaded the development plan. Women are being trained in "feminine skills"—sewing, knitting, and weaving—which are made use of in textile industries or agrobusiness often linked to transnational corporations. Low wages, long hours of work, and discriminatory ease in hiring and firing practices are characteristic of most of the exercises of "integrating women into development."

It has been believed that equal participation in the development process can be achieved by education and income generation. But it should be noted that educational systems in developing countries with a colonial heritage have no relevance to the needs of the people, and also prevent people from understanding the social, political, and economic structures that oppress them—and the very nature of that oppression. This is evident from the fact that it is largely educated people who don't question the oppressive system and who perpetuate the status quo. Government-sponsored institutions and voluntary organizations engaged in the promotion of income-generating activities (which can be defined as reformist measures) do not question the root cause of oppression at large, or of women in particular. Nevertheless, their efforts are genuine and altruistic and certainly contribute to the improvement of the situation, although they will not ultimately solve the problem.

The Voice of Women

As a reaction to the approach described above, a small group of women in 1978 formed Kantha Handa (Voice of Women) and began to meet regularly to discuss such oppressive structures as patriarchy and capitalism that keep women in a subordinate position, and to launch consciousness-raising campaigns. The group consisted of university faculty members, teachers, clerks, factory workers, farmers, and fisherwomen. The Kantha Handa considers women's economic and social emancipation as a part of the general struggle for emancipation and not a conflict between men and women, and has been publishing a quarterly journal in three languages, Sinhala, Tamil, and English. Meetings, seminars, and workshops are held in all parts of Sri Lanka. Research and studies on women's issues have been undertaken and the findings are being disseminated among the urban, rural, and plantation sectors of the country.

The Kantha Handa cannot, however, be called a national women's movement, although an attempt is being made to reach all women, cutting across various sectors, classes, religions, and ethnic groups through the three-language journal. The Women's Liberation Movement (Sri Lanka), The Katha Shakthi, Devasarana Farm Women's Group, and the Tamil Women's Liberation Movement, Vavuniya, are the other groups which have a structural approach.

Social-service-oriented women's organizations (which now do more and more education and income-generating projects with foreign aid) and structural-approach-oriented groups having consciousness-raising as their major objective will continue in parallel fashion for some years to come. In this context, it is best to encourage both categories independently. However, in order to promote a broader women's movement, already existing groups of the latter category—as well as the link between the two categories—have to be strengthened.

Then the true voice of women in Sri Lanka will begin to be heard.

Suggested Further Reading

Economic Review, issues of June 1975, Sept. 1976, Jan.–Feb. 1981, Colombo: People's Bank.

Samarasuriya, Shireen. *Who Needs Tourism? Employment for Women in the Holiday Industry of Sudugama, Sri Lanka.* Colombo: Leiden, 1982.

Status of Women. Colombo: Univ. of Colombo, 1979.

Voice of Women: Sri Lankan Journal for Women's Emancipation, Colombo; available at 18/9 Chitra Lane, Colombo 5, Sri Lanka.

Women Workers in the Free Trade Zone of Sri Lanka: A Survey. Voice of Women Publication Series, No. 1, Colombo, 1983.

Born and raised in a village seventeen miles from Colombo, Hema Goonatilake specialized in Oriental languages for her first degree; she obtained her doctorate in 1974 in a field related to sociology of religion at the School of Oriental and African Studies, University of London. At present, she is a senior lecturer in Sinhala at the University of Kelaniya, Sri Lanka. She was a co-researcher on the first comprehensive study of the status of women in Sri Lanka. She has given lectures at several universities and institutions in Asia, Europe, and America, and has been a free-lance broadcaster of cultural and women's programs for over fifteen years. She is a founding member of the Voice of Women, an activist group committed to the emancipation of Sri Lankan women. She is also a co-editor of the *Voice of Women*, the Sri Lankan Journal for women's emancipation.

SUDAN
(Democratic Republic of the Sudan)

The largest nation on the African continent, bordered to the north by Egypt, to the northeast by the Red Sea, to the east by Eritrea and Ethiopia, to the south by Kenya, Uganda, and Zaire, to the west by the Central African Republic and Chad, and to the northwest by Libya. **Area:** 2,505,802 sq. km. (967,491 sq. mi.). **Population** (1982): 18,752,000, female 49.3%. **Capital:** Khartoum.

DEMOGRAPHY. Languages: Arabic (official), English, Nilotic, and indigenous languages. **Races or Ethnic Groups:** Arab, Nubian, and 31 different indigenous groups including Nilotic, Dinka, Nuer, Shilluk, Bari, Azandi. **Religions:** Islam (predominantly Sunni) 66%, indigenous faiths 29%, Christian (including Greek Orthodox and Coptic Christian) 4%, Judaism. **Education** (% enrolled in school, 1975): Age 6–11—of all girls 20%, of all boys 38%; age 12–17—of all girls 12%, of all boys 25% (in 1978 approx. 1/2 of boys and 1/3 of girls age 7–12 were enrolled in primary schools); higher education—in 1977 women comprised 20% of post-secondary students; (University of Khartoum only) women were 3.9% of engineering and architecture students, 11% of economics students, 16.4% of medical students, 17.1% of law, 19.4% of art, 20.76% of education; women were also 13.4% of students at Shambat Agricultural Institute, and there were no women students at Engineering College in Atbara. In 1981 girls were 40.4% of elementary-school students, 38.1% of intermediate-school students, and 36.7% of secondary- and post-secondary-school students. **Literacy** (1977): Women 4%, men 25%. The first literacy programs which included women began in 1949; now there is a national effort to increase women's literacy. **Birth Rate** (per 1000 pop., 1975–80): 48. **Death Rate** (per 1000 pop., 1975–80): 18. **Infant Mortality** (per 1000 live births, 1975–80): Female 133, male 148. **Life Expectancy** (1975–80): Female 48 yrs., male 46 yrs.

GOVERNMENT. The 1973 Constitution, amended in 1975, provides for a president elected by popular vote for a 6-yr. term, and a People's Assembly (replacing the Parliament) of 368 members, 136 of which are elected from geographical constituencies and 196 from such groups as the Sudan Women's Union (see HERSTORY), national youth organizations, workers' organizations, local councils and cooperatives. The president appoints members to the remaining 36 seats. The Sudan consists of 15 provinces; the southern 3 have considerable autonomy, including an elected 60-member People's Assembly and a High Executive Council to administer the area. The Sudan Socialist Union (SSU) is the only legal political party, but almost 1/2 the members of the People's Assembly are members of banned political parties, which are also represented in the Cabinet and the SSU Central Committee. **Women's Suffrage:** 1964 (see HERSTORY). **Equal Rights:** Constitution prohibits discrimination on the basis of sex and stipulates equal rights for all citizens before the law.

Women in Government: In 1964 Fatma Ahmed Ibrahim was the first woman elected to Parliament; in 1980, 10 women were elected to the National People's Assembly. In 1983 there were 7 women in the 60-member Politburo of the SSU, Umm Salima Said was president of the Higher Council for Youth Welfare, and the Under-Secretary for Social Affairs was Rashida Abdul Mutalb. There is a 25% minimum quota for women in all government councils (no statistics obtainable on practice). The National Commission on the Status of Women was established in 1974 to coordinate government planning for the integration of women in development programs. A Women's Affairs Section was established within the Dept. of Social Welfare to implement the policies of the Women's Commission. The Women's Secretariat functions as an intermediary organization between the Central Committee of the SSU and the Sudanese Women's Union.

ECONOMY. Currency: Sudanese Pound (May 1983: 1.3 = $1 US). **Gross National Product** (1980): $8.6 billion. **Per Capita Income** (1980): $470. In 1980, 20% of the pop. earned 50% of the national income; 80% of the pop. relies on agriculture for a living. **Women's Wages as a Percentage of Men's:** No data obtainable. **Equal Pay Policy:** Constitution stipulates equal pay for equal work regardless of sex, but fields with a high concentration of women workers are less well salaried than male occupations. Rural women, although their work is essential to agricultural production, are not covered by some labor laws. **Production** (Agricultural/Industrial): Cotton, gum arabic, sorghum, sesame, tobacco, wheat, dates, rice, coffee, sugar cane; textiles, sugar refining, food processing. **Women as a Percentage of Labor Force** (1980): 11%; **of agricultural force**—no general statistics obtainable (77% of women workers are employed in agriculture, 1975); **of industrial force**—no data obtainable; **of military**—no statistics obtainable, but women can be trained for combat although they are concentrated in support and service sectors. In 1973, 10.4% of urban women and 27% of rural women in northern provinces were in the labor force; the highest participation rate was in Darfur Province, where 21.9% of urban and 56.3% of rural women were active; in 1972, 47% of the migrant labor force in the Khartoum-Omdurman area was female.

(Employed) **Women's Occupational Indicators:** Of all economically active women, 7.14% were in animal husbandry, 7.52% were in handicraft activities, 81.02% were in agriculture, and 4.32% were in all other fields (1979). Women comprise 40% of government-service employees (1981); the government is the biggest single employer of women, hiring them as primary-school teachers, midwives, and health-care workers. Women are rarely given public-contact jobs or supervisory positions with male subordinates. In the north, where most of the population is Moslem, it is usually not considered respectable for women to work outside the home. Domestic workers are mostly from indigenous southern groups or refugee popula-

tions. In the huge cotton-growing Gazira Scheme (northern Sudan development project) women usually work only during peak labor seasons, picking cotton by hand, while most men's jobs are mechanized. Traditional female employment areas have been transferred to men through mechanization. In pastoral groups females begin to work at age 7, tending cattle, making handicrafts, moving tents, processing milk products, and cultivating millet. Among the Dinka and the Nuer peoples, milking is women's work and a man invites supernatural penalties by milking for himself. In the east, women market their produce and spend the money for the family; in the south, women grind grain, brew beer, locate water and wood, and produce more than 1/2 their families' food, retaining certain ownership rights over the produce. In general, women exercise greater economic control in cultivating areas than they do in cattle-keeping regions. Attitudes toward women working are caught in conflict between Moslem *purdah* and a long indigenous history of women doing the bulk of labor required in a subsistence economy. **Unemployment** (1979): 6,616,000, females are 14.9% of the unemployed.

GYNOGRAPHY. Marriage. *Policy:* The Civil Justice Ordinance (Sec. 5) states that marriage, divorce, and family relations are governed by customary/religious law of the individuals when "not contrary to justice, equity, or good conscience," and that Islamic law be applied to the pop. at large where other customary practices do not take precedence. Civil courts have no jurisdiction over Islamic marriage, divorce, and family matters and cannot amend Islamic law. Marriage laws vary among Moslems, Jews, different categories of Christians, and 31 distinct indigenous groups, and become more complex when mixed marriages occur between different communities, or with foreigners. Polygyny is legal for Moslems, Jews, and indigenous groups; illegal for Christians. Since 1960 (Shari'a Court Circular 54) mutual consent has been required for a valid marriage in all communities (Non-Mohammadan Marriage Ordinance, 1926). Minimum marriage age for women is 14–18 in Christian sects, puberty in southern indigenous groups, 13 in civil law, and 10—with the consent of a *kadi* (religious judge) or *feki* (Koranic teacher)—in Islamic law (but marriage cannot be legally consummated until the bride has reached puberty). Islamic *mahar* (dowry) is paid directly to the bride by the groom, and other gifts are made to her family; a portion of *mahar* is paid at marriage, and a further portion paid in case of divorce or her husband's death. Payment of bridewealth by the groom's family concludes marriage in many indigenous groups; it is in the form of cows, sheep, spears, hoes, or cloth, depending on the group, and is paid to various members of the bride's family.

Among almost all the groups of Darfur Province a partial payment is made to the bride's mother. In Greek Orthodox groups dowry is paid by the bride's father to the bride and groom. Under Islamic law, widows are entitled to up to 1 yr. support from their husbands' families. In most indigenous groups a woman remains legally married to her dead husband and becomes the responsibility of his nearest living male relative; to remarry she must first obtain a divorce from the dead husband. Among the Nuer, the Dinka, and some other groups, woman-woman marriage is legal, and any single woman who can afford bridewealth can obtain a wife (or wives). Shilluk princesses (in the south), who would lose royalty rights if they married common men, can marry common women and raise the women's status; some of these marriages are for the purpose of inheritance or gaining (foster) children, but some are love marriages.

The Penal Code makes punishable abducting a woman to force her into a marriage (Sec. 307) and bigamy when illegal (Sec. 429). In Sept. 1983 Pres. Numeiri decreed that a new Penal Code based on Islamic Shari'a law would immediately replace the secular Penal Code. Under the new Code the penalty for adultery is execution by stoning for a married person and flogging for an unmarried person; punishments are to be carried out in public. Legal domicile is determined by the husband. For Moslems, a clause may be inserted into the marriage contract giving the woman the right to remain in her native town or country; married women also retain full rights to their own property under Islamic and civil laws. *Practice:* Female mean age at marriage (1978): 21.3; women age 15–44 in union (1970–79): 76%. In the south, marriage age usually is between age 13–15 for girls. Almost all marriages are arranged (sometimes at birth, as among the Azande), and despite the theoretical right of veto, most women accept their parents' choice. A woman from an indigenous group can subvert arranged marriage by eloping with the man of her choice, who then will usually be accepted. A customary marriage is completed in stages, with ceremonies lasting up to 40 days; the bride often resides in her parents' home until her first child is born. Polygyny is widespread, but few men have more than 2 wives, except for chiefs of indigenous groups who may have as many as 100. Bridewealth may amount to as much as 100 cattle, and an entire family will pool resources to buy a bride for a male family member. Married indigenous women in the south appear to have greater autonomy than Moslem wives.

Divorce. *Policy:* In Sudanese Islamic legal interpretation, a husband who is not drunk or under duress can divorce a wife by *talaq* (verbal renunciation) for any reason, if there are 2 adult male Moslem witnesses.* A wife can divorce her husband if it is written into her marriage contract; she may also obtain a divorce by *khula* (mutual consent), in which she gives up her right to *mahar* and pays an additional sum to her husband to be released from the marriage. A woman is entitled to a divorce by a religious court if her husband fails to support her, is guilty of cruelty, deserts her for over 1 yr., is insane, or has a disease (e.g., T.B. or leprosy). Divorce customs vary among indigenous groups. In some, husbands can divorce wives at will but must go to court to secure return of the bridewealth; in others, divorce by mutual consent is

---

* In 1972 there were 8004 such divorces; in 1976 there were 7332.

possible. Maban women can obtain divorces for their husbands' "laziness." Civil marriages may end in divorce if either party is guilty of adultery, desertion, cruelty, or incurable insanity, or if the husband is guilty of rape, sodomy, or bestiality. Reforms passed in 1969 entitle a divorced woman to 1/2 her husband's salary as support for herself and her children. Sudanese laws allow courts to award custody "in the best interests" of children. *Practice:* No statistics obtainable. The requirement that *mahar* must be paid and bridewealth forfeited restrains men from lightly divorcing their wives. Instead, a man may make marriage so unbearable that the woman agrees to *khula* divorce and relinquishes *mahar* rights or pays ransom to free herself from the marriage. Women from indigenous groups, who are often economically independent of their husbands, are more likely to divorce. Primary causes for divorce include sexual and psychological problems resulting from genital mutilation (see **Traditional/Cultural Practices**). Incidence of remarriage is fairly high.

Family. *Policy:* No data obtainable. *Practice:* Breastfeeding is almost universally practiced, and is prolonged in the belief that it acts as a constraint on fertility. In 1979 there were 789 kindergartens serving 35,281 children age 3–6. In the south, children are cared for by mothers and grandmothers until puberty, when girls are married and boys are transferred to the authority and instruction of their fathers. In many groups it is the daughters and not the sons who support aging parents. Clan loyalty persists as the major kinship system. In the Moslem community, court testimony by 1 man equals that of 2 women (Islamic Law of Evidence), and the customary bloodwealth paid to a family as compensation for the death of 1 of its members is twice as much for a man as for a woman; in Islamic property inheritance, women are entitled to 1/2 the share of men. Only a few groups—the Krongo and Talodi groups of Nuba in southern Kordofan, retain traditional matrilineal descent.

Welfare. *Policy:* The Constitution stipulates free education and medical care. The Sudan has a refugee population of over 400,000 from Ethiopia, Chad, and Uganda; the government does not turn away refugees and tries to provide them with land and a means of livelihood. *Practice:* Major medical facilities are concentrated in Khartoum. Due to inadequate infrastructure and lack of trained personnel, services are poor elsewhere. In the south in 1976, there was 1 midwife per 18,251 people; 90% of the population suffered from malaria, and 97% of the women were anemic. In 1981 midwives could cover only 20% of the nation, but a new program to train women from villages aims to extend care to 85% of the pop. Nurse-midwives have traditionally been older women, but the new recruits are young. The Soba Center, the Abu Halima Center, and the Amadi Center (serving Moru women in Equatoria Province) are among those centers which provide women with skills-training, childcare, and classes in nutrition, literacy, hygiene, and home economics.

Contraception. *Policy:* All forms legal. Government supports family-planning for "health and human rights" reasons, not demographic reasons. *Practice:* Women age 15–49 in union using contraception (north only, 1978): 5%; methods used (1978) pill 67%, rhythm 10%, female sterilization 6%, injectables 3%, condom 3%, IUD 2%, diaphragm 2%, withdrawal 2%, abstinence 2%, male sterilization 1%; using inefficient methods 14%; 49% of married women were unaware of any method. Culturally, women are encouraged to have many children because of the high infant mortality rate. In 1974 there were 10 family-planning centers in and near Khartoum; in 1977 there were no family-planning programs in the south. In 1979 contraceptives were available through government clinics and the Family Planning Assoc. Over-the-counter contraceptives are very expensive and not always available (see **Family**). **Abortion.** *Policy:* Legal only to save the life of the woman (Criminal Code). Anyone performing an illegal abortion is subject to a fine and/or up to 3 yrs. imprisonment. Government-trained midwives are instructed in ways to prevent abortion and premarital sex. *Practice:* No statistics obtainable. In a 1976 study of the 3 main hospitals in

Khartoum, "incomplete" abortion was the main cause of gynecological admissions.

Illegitimacy. *Policy:* Under laws governing non-Moslem and nonindigenous groups, children born after the celebration of a marriage (regardless of when conceived) or after divorce or death of the father (if conceived during the marriage) are considered "legitimate." In Islamic jurisprudence, a child conceived after marriage or born within 1 yr. after the marriage's termination is "legitimate." In southern customary laws, children are the legal offspring of their mother's husband, regardless of their biological father. A "father" may be long dead or may be the woman married to the mother in a woman-woman marriage. A child born to a single woman will become the "legitimate" child of anyone who marries the mother and in the few remaining matrilineal societies children are members of their mother's clan whether she is married or not. The government supports Child Welfare Homes for illegitimate, orphaned, and destitute children. *Practice:* No general statistics obtainable. In the Child Welfare Homes, 1 out of every 5 children has a foster mother; owing to lack of food and medical care many children die. **Homosexuality.** *Policy:* No data obtainable. *Practice:* No statistics obtainable (see **Marriage**).

Incest. *Policy:* Incest with close relatives, a niece, or a nephew is punishable except in cases where permitted by customary laws (Penal Code, Sec. 435). *Practice:* No data obtainable. **Sexual Harassment.** *Policy:* No data obtainable. *Practice:* No statistics obtainable; there are reports of male government employers requiring sexual concessions of female employees (1976). **Rape.** *Policy:* Illegal. Marital rape is not recognized unless the wife has not yet reached puberty (Penal Code, Sec. 316). No further data obtainable. *Practice:* No data obtainable. **Battery.** *Policy:* The locally interpreted Islamic right of the husband to "chastise" his wife with a small switch is recog-

nized; any other physical abuse is illegal. In 1969, *Bat etaha*—the right of a Moslem husband to enlist the police in forcibly retrieving a wife who had fled his house—was abolished. *Practice:* No statistics obtainable; reportedly not uncommon in the Islamic community. Among indigenous groups, the Azande have a reputation for harsh treatment of wives. Among most Neolitic peoples physical coercion is rare. Wife battery is reportedly an expected practice among many groups of indigenous southern peoples.

Prostitution. *Policy:* No data obtainable. *Practice:* No statistics obtainable, but women going out alone or talking freely with men not their relatives are often considered the equivalent of prostitutes. **Traditional/Cultural Practices.** *Policy:* Infibulation** was made illegal in 1946, punishable by a fine and/or 5 yrs. imprisonment. It is not an offense under Art. 284 of the Penal Code (1974) to remove "the free and projective part of the clitoris" (see MYTHOGRAPHY and following article). *Practice:* Infibulation is still practiced in many communities, across racial, class, regional, and religious differences. It is not practiced by the Fur, most of the Baggara, and some other indigenous groups in the south. Reportedly it is being newly adopted by some groups in the process of "Islamicization." Some Sudanese women believe that infibulation is not practiced to protect chastity or for "cleanliness," as claimed, but is primarily for men's pleasure.*** The government places less emphasis on enforcing the 1946 law than on conducting educational campaigns about the health hazards of genital mutilation, educating midwives, and attempting to separate the issue from religious debate. In 1979 the Sudan hosted the World Health Conference on Traditional Practices Affecting the Health of Women and Children, which formulated a plan of action to address the practice of genital mutilation. In a 1983 northern Sudan survey, 82% of females and 87.7% of males approved of female "circumcision"; of

---

** See Glossary.

*** One woman in the Gazira area said: "It is not so much for virginity, it is for the pleasure of the man. He enjoys it, and after 1 or 2 years he will help you go and rearrange yourself—have it sewn again so that you are tight for him" (1976).

those who approved, 43% of the women and 4.2% of the men approved the "intermediate" form (of infibulation), 28.2% women and 18.5% men approved the extreme Pharaonic form (full infibulation), and 23.5% women and 73.1% men approved the less drastic Sunna form (clitoridectomy). Women approved because of "tradition," "religious demand," and "cleanliness," and they usually favored the form which had been performed on them (except for those women with Pharaonic experience, who preferred the intermediate form); women who preferred the Sunna form cited as their reason that it was "less harmful" than Pharaonic or intermediate.

Those opposing female excision were generally younger and better educated; the 2 main reasons cited for rejecting the practices altogether were: complications during marriage and childbirth (37%) and difficulties personally experienced (16%); other reasons were religious prohibition (15%), failure to achieve sexual satisfaction (12%), and that the practices were detrimental to "the human rights and dignity of women" (12%). Among men, those opposing the practice entirely or favoring the Sunna form were generally younger and better educated; many men who supported the Sunna practice claimed that it enhanced the pleasure of the husband. Men who opposed it did so because of failure to achieve sexual satisfaction (30%), religious prohibition (26%), and for the human rights and dignity of women (20%). Most fathers (75%) did not interfere with their daughters' excisions because "it is women's business." The primary over-all reasons cited for the continuation of these practices were fear of social criticism, ignorance of after-effects, the ignorance of mothers, and the strong influence of grandmothers; men felt insufficient health education was an additional factor. Various methods for eradicating the practices were suggested: enforcing legislation which would punish parents and/or practitioners, better health education for women, and an education program for fathers. Facial scarification of girls for "esthetic purposes" is still practiced by some groups north of Khartoum, although this is discouraged by the govern-

ment. In certain communities, nutritional tabus mean that women are denied fish, chicken, eggs, and camel meat, in a protein-restricting tradition. **Crisis Centers:** No data obtainable.

HERSTORY. Around 2000 B.C.E. Nubia (northeast Sudan) was colonized by Egypt. From 800 B.C.E. to 400 C.E. the area was ruled by the Cush Kingdom and the city of Meroe was a trade center. Most Nubians were converted to Coptic Christianity around 500. Two independent states arose by 700, then fell between 1200–1400 as the area was converted to Islam by invaders from the north.

There is a tradition of great queens in ancient Nubia, one of whom was Amani-Shakhti. Many of the southern groups were matrilineal and largely egalitarian before northern influence and conversion to Islam.

The Moslem Funj State ruled from 1500 to 1821, when it was conquered by Egypt. British and Egyptian intervention provoked a successful Moslem rebellion in 1881; in 1899 an Anglo-Egyptian "condominium government" was formed, but the British had de facto control. In 1948 an elected national assembly was created and in 1956 a parliamentary republic was declared.

The first modern women's group, the Sudanese Women's League, was formed in 1946 by women members of the Communist Party, which was the first Sudanese political party to open its membership to women and to make equal rights for women one of its party goals. The League was composed mostly of highly educated women; in 1951 it was disbanded and replaced by the Sudanese Women's Union, which had a broader membership. In 1955 the Union began to publish the progressive magazine The Women's Voice, which spoke out against colonialism, facial scarification, genital mutilation, Moslem divorce-law inequity, and polygyny, and in favor of equal pay, maternity benefits, and equal rights. During the period of independence (1950's) more women's groups began to organize, and women's magazines Al-Manar, Al-Qafila, and Sawt-ul-Mara'a were published. The parliamentary republic was terminated in 1958 by a military coup staged by Gen. Ibrahim Abboud. Abboud was unable to solve the country's economic problems or end the north-south civil war which had been raging since 1955, and he was ousted by popular rebellion in 1964. During the Abboud regime the Sudanese Women's Union (SWU) was banned and an "official" organization for women created in its stead. In the 1964 popular revolt, women demonstrated, fought, and died along with men. Fatma Ahmed Ibrahim, one of the founders of the SWU, led the first demonstration of several hundred women. Women's participation in the revolt hastened female suffrage in 1964.

From 1965 to 1969 the SWU was again active in promoting women's education and women's rights. In 1969 the SWU supported the initially progressive regime, but in the 1971 attempted Communist coup and subsequent anti-Communist purge Fatma Ahmed Ibrahim's husband was executed, and she was imprisoned. The north-south civil war ended with the (1972) Addis Ababa agreement, which granted the south considerable autonomy, and in 1973 a new constitution with a 1-party parliamentary structure was adopted. In 1971 the "official" Sudan Women's Union was formed by the government; it has a membership of 750,000 (1977) in all provinces and works with voluntary organizations. It is affiliated with the SSU (see GOVERNMENT) and undertakes projects on literacy, family welfare and childcare, price controls, women's work co-ops, savings unions, handicraft skills training, and market development. It publishes a monthly women's magazine and maintains contacts with local and international women's organizations. The previous women's organization has been forced underground but is still active despite harassment.

MYTHOGRAPHY. There is a rich and varied mythography among the different peoples of the Sudan region. It was thought that Amma, the supreme god of the Dogon, created Earth and copulated with her—but her clitoris rose against his penis, and Amma, afraid, cut off the clitoris before raping Earth. The Bambara believed that Pemba, a god in the form of a tree, molded the first woman out of dust and that she, in turn, created all animal and plant life. Pemba's wife, Mussokuroni, planted her husband so that his tree-life would have roots, but he began to demand blood sacrifices to survive; Mussokuroni went mad with grief and left in a great rage, circumcising males and excising† females wherever she went. The Songhoi believed that a spirit woman revealed the art of magic to humans.

SUDAN: Women's Studies—and a New Village Stove
by Amna Elsadik Badri

Historically, the Sudanese movement for the emancipation of women started in 1907 when Sheikh Babiker Bedri opened the first school for girls in Rufa'à, in the central region. This was followed by the establishment of the women teachers' college in 1921 and the midwifery school in the Khartoum province. It was not until 1945, however, that Sudanese women were admitted to Khartoum University.

Female education has always been the initial struggle—the one which precedes the struggle for women's emancipation. Accordingly, organized activity of Sudanese women began in 1947, when the Girls' Cultural Union was founded. In 1949 the Society of Women's Modernization was started by the late revolutionary leader Abdel Rahman El

† See Glossary.

Mahdi, and that same year the female elementary-school teachers organized themselves into a union. The midwives' trade union was organized in 1950. In 1951 the first national Sudanese Women's Union was founded. (However, in 1971 it was dissolved by the government and the "official" Sudan Women's Union was formed in its place.)

Prior to that era, back in 1882–1908, women shared in the revolution against foreign invaders. For example, Mihaira Bint Aboud distinguished herself in the battle against the invasion of the Sudan by Turks and Egyptians, and Rabia El Kinania's work as an informal intelligence agent was the cause of success in one of the Mahdis' encounters with enemies in the Rashid Battle.

The Present Situation

Women and Education

The illiteracy rate in the Sudan is very high. According to the 1973 census, it was 83 percent. The illiteracy rate for females alone was 94 percent, while for males it was 72 percent.

Although the Sudan has made considerable strides in the field of education since Independence in 1956, the education of women is still lagging behind that of men; for example, the percentage of female students in schools has increased, but females still constitute only one third of the total population of the schools.

With the increase in women's education, however, more and more women are entering the labor force. Traditionally, their occupations were teaching and the medical services. (It is interesting to note that the first women to graduate from the University of Khartoum were graduates of the school of medicine.) But during the last decade women students have increasingly entered such other fields of study as engineering, agriculture, and law. There seems to be a steady growth of the number of women students in previously male-dominated professions.

Women and the Economy

According to the International Labour Organisation 1975 report, there is a low rate of participation of women in the labor force. The *urban* female labor-force-participation rate is about 9 percent. First, because women are far behind men in education and training; second, the scarcity of day-care centers makes it very difficult for those mothers who *are* trained and educated to join the labor force in the modern sector. In the *rural* areas female labor-force participation is reported to be 10 percent. This low rate may be attributed to the problem of defining "economic activity." There is no clear reference as to whether water and fuel portage and food processing and preservation are considered housework or "productive activity."

In the modern rural economy (agricultural) the impact of women is limited (see Table 1).

Table 1. GEZIRA SCHEME

SEASON	TOTAL NO. OF TENANTS	FEMALE TENANTS
1969/70	89,911	9,569
1970/71	92,873	10,218
1971/72	93,473	10,311
1972/73	94,218	10,635
1973/74	94,677	11,048

In the case of the Gezira Scheme, even though the over-all percentage of female tenants reaches up to 10 percent, this does not mean that females are directly involved in operation of the land. In most cases, women hire other people to operate it on their behalf. In some situations, however—such as in both the Suki and the Rahad Schemes—10 percent of the tenant population is also female, *but* production is highly mechanized, which keeps the direct involvement of all the tenants in the operation to a minimum. (It should be mentioned that most of the female tenants in both the Rahad and the Suki *are* operating their own tenancies and are treated by the scheme on an equal basis as the male tenants.)

Unlike the modern rural agricultural activities, the modern rural agro-industries show a greater presence of women. In the spinning and weaving industries women were employed in a wide range of jobs from simple observation to highly technical quality control. In the Wad Medani Spinning and Weaving Company, for example, 48 percent of the skilled labor force is female. In the spinning and weaving sections (the most important sections of this industry), the number of females exceeds the number of males. According to the management of the factories, female workers are more efficient and punctual and, "if the government permits their involvement in night shifts, the future is for them." In the same area of the Blue Nile province, female workers are also the majority at the Aspro and Tobacco factories.

In the traditional economic sector, women in the Darfur region participate to the extent of 35–43 percent in such major agricultural operations as cleaning the fields, turning the soil, sowing, planting, weeding, and harvesting.

In petty trading, women are known as the sellers of their own or others' products. In the Nuba mountains (Kordofan region) about 40 percent of the women participate in the market, and in the southern region women also participate in many different kinds of market activity.

In most Sudanese villages, market days are organized once or twice a week. Elderly women occupy huts or tree shades in these marketplaces, displaying their agricultural products and homemade handicrafts. (In a study done in the Omdurman women's handicrafts market, it was found that most of the women who engage in trade are old women or middle-age widows.)

Women's Studies Programs

Beginning in 1973, governmental as well as nongovernmental bodies began to show an interest in developing women's studies programs.

That year, the Ahfad University College for Women started to offer a required course in "Rural Extension." The course has been introduced as an implementation of the Ahfad policy to involve university students in the community at large, with special emphasis on the role of rural women in development. The course is a unique idea. The fact that the students in this college are women in a society where women have been traditionally "sheltered" is a breakthrough from an educational point of view. The course was initiated in response to the need to improve the quality of life for families in rural and poor urban settlements. In addition, the course attempts to interest students in rural life and problems so as to give them an increased awareness of and sensitivity to the situation of more than 80 percent of the Sudan's population (hopefully, to motivate them to work in rural areas). As part of their training, students have the opportunity to practice what they have learned by a field-trip to some of the villages. For example, family-science students were especially appalled by the inefficient use of energy in local stoves and so were motivated to work on a modification of the traditional stove. The modified stoves were then taken into the villages by students who worked on them with rural women and obtained feedback. At this writing, the experiment is still going on—and everyone is very enthusiastic.

Another practical effect of the field-work is the training of rural women and rural women *leaders,* training which consists of home-economics subjects as well as income-generating skills, both vocational and administrative.

In February of 1979, the Ahfad University College for Women convened a symposium, the Changing Status of Sudanese Women. One of the results of that symposium was the formation of the first Scientific Women's Association in the Sudan—the Babiker Bedri Scientific Association for Women's Studies. It is a voluntary organization open to educated Sudanese women, and its main function is to mobilize the social awareness of women in the Sudan. This association is the means by which educated women can operate honestly, objectively, and scientifically. For its initial program, the association is undertaking two projects.

The first is an integrated rural welfare program in selected villages in the White Nile and Red Sea provinces, a program embracing such issues as women's and children's health, trade skills, the forming of cooperatives, and leadership training for women.

The second is a functional program designed to bring the practice of female circumcision to complete cessation. It is a custom which causes hazards to the health of mothers *and* female children.

In 1980, the Development and Research Center at the University of Khartoum formed a women's studies program. The program, mirroring the center's activities generally, has five elements: research, documentation, open seminars, training, and publications.

Other Women's Voluntary Groups

There are five women's voluntary associations registered with the Department of Social Welfare: the Save the Children and Mothers Society, the Women's Charity Society, the Diplomats' Wives Society, the Moslem Women's Society—and the Babiker Bedri Scientific Association for Women's Studies. In addition, there are four groups which soon may be officially "recognized": Women Students' and Graduates' Association of Darfur, the Women Doctors' Association, the University Women's Association, and the Women's Rights Association at the University of Khartoum.

Suggestions for "Feminist Foreign Aid"

There are specific ways in which women from the rest of the world—in particular from the Western developed countries—can help their sisters of the Sudan. These include:

1) Financial support of research and studies that deal with women, particularly with learning about the status of rural women.

2) Financial support of the implementation of integrated programs that help raise the status of rural women—programs that are planned according to a scientific and realistic study of the status of rural women and their environment.

3) Financial support and technical assistance for programs and projects which aim at the *training* of *women trainers* in the following fields:

—Improving traditional technology;

—Food production, processing, and preservation;

—Administrative and managerial skills of women's cooperatives or other women's productive groups;

—Income-generating activities.

The Sudan is the largest country in Africa, and 50 percent of our population is under the age of twenty—and is female. We women have only just begun the business of freedom—but nothing can stop us now.

Suggested Further Reading

Badri, Amna. *Integrated Welfare Programmes for Rural Women: A Suggested Approach to the Sudan.* Second Population Conference. Khartoum, 1982.

Badri, Humodi, and Belghis and Amna. *Women in Development.* Second Population Conference. Khartoum, 1982.

Growth, Employment and Equity: A Comprehensive Strategy for the Sudan. Geneva: International Labour Organisation, 1975.

Papers on the Symposium of the Changing Status of Sudanese Women. Ahfad Univ. College for Women, Omdurman, 1979.

Sudan, D. R. *National Literacy Programme.* Khartoum: The National Council for Literacy and Adult Functional Education, 1975–79.

Sudan Guide. Planning and Management Consultancy Report. Khartoum, 1980–81.

Women and the Environment. Workshop Report papers, Institute of Environmental Studies, Khartoum Univ., 1981.

Amna Elsadik Badri was born in 1950. Educated in the Sudan, she graduated with a degree in business administration from the University of Khartoum, and in 1978 took her master's degree in economics from the University of California at Santa Barbara. She is a lecturer in economics and management at the Ahfad University College for Women in Omdurman, her native town. She has participated in national and international conferences on women, and has been working on an integrated training program for rural women (in the White Nile province) which is implemented by the Babiker Bedri Scientific Association for Women's Studies and funded by Swedish Save the Children. She is also involved with the population education program at the Ministry of Education and is developing a training manual on population education for rural women.

SWEDEN
(Kingdom of Sweden)

Located on the east of the Scandinavian peninsula, bordered by Finland and the Gulf of Böthnia to the east, Denmark and the Baltic Sea to the south, Norway to the north and west, and Finland to the north. **Area:** 449,792 sq. km. (173,665 sq. mi.). **Population** (1980): 8,313,000, female 50.4%. **Capital:** Stockholm.

DEMOGRAPHY. Languages: Swedish, Finnish, Lapp. **Races or Ethnic Groups:** Swedish 93%, Finnish 3%, Lapp, Yugoslav, Danish, other. **Religions:** Swedish Lutheran (official) 95%, other Protestant 3.4%, Roman Catholicism 1.1%, Orthodox Catholicism 0.42%, Judaism 0.18%. **Education** (% enrolled in school, 1975): Age 6–11—of all girls 82%, of all boys 80%; age 12–17—of all girls 87%, of all boys 86%; higher education—in 1981 women comprised 55% of university students, and in 1977, 25% of post-graduate students; in 1979, of first-yr. students, women were 6.2% of mechanical engineering, 7.6% of computer technology, 38.5% of medicine, 48.5% of law, 73.9% of library science, 87.2% of nursing. Education is compulsory from age 6 to 16 and free up through university and professional college; nonsexist educational policy requires all students to take courses in home economics, industrial shop, sex-education (see **Contraception**), the equality of the sexes, and children's rights. (see **Incest**). **Literacy** (1977): Women 99%, men 99%. **Birth Rate** (per 1000 pop., 1977–78): 11. **Death Rate** (per 1000 pop., 1977–78): 11. **Infant Mortality** (per 1000 live births, 1977): Female 7, male 9. **Life Expectancy** (1975–80): Female 78 yrs., male 72 yrs.

GOVERNMENT. Constitutional monarchy with King Carl XVI Gustaf as nominal head of state. New Constitution (1975) provides for the central legislative body to be a unicameral 349-member elected parliament (Riksdag). Executive power is held by the prime minister. There are 5 major political parties: Conservative, Center, Liberal, Social Democrat, and Communist. Government is largely decentralized; 24 counties and 279 municipalities decide local priorities and policy. **Women's Suffrage:** 1919 (in national elections). Single tax-paying women could vote in municipal elections in 1862; married tax-paying women in 1908; equal voting rights in municipal elections in 1918. **Equal Rights:** Government's policy is for full equality between men and women, which includes integrating men into childrearing and housework roles. Advisory Council to the Prime Minister on Equality Between Men and Women was appointed in 1972; a Committee on Equality under the Ministry of Labour (appointed 1976) presented recommendations adopted in the 1980 Act Concerning Equality Between Women and Men at Work, which bans discrimination in hiring, training, wages, promotions, and working conditions, and requires that employers actively promote equality in all jobs and at all levels [see **(Employed) Women's Occupational Indicators**]. The Equal Opportunity Ombudsman is appointed by the government to monitor enforcement. Major unions include sex-equality issues in their action programs.

Women in Government: Women comprised 27.5% of the Riksdag (1982) and won an average of 30% of local council seats (1979). Female party membership (as % of members, 1979): Conservative 50%, Center, Liberal, and Social Democrat 40–50%, Communist 34%. The Ministers of Social and Health Services, Education and Cultural Affairs, Immigrant and Equality Affairs, Energy, and Labour were women (5 out of 15 ministers) in 1983. The first woman appointed to the 24-member Supreme Court, Ingrid Gärde Widemar (served 1968–80), was succeeded by the second, Berit Palme. The Act of Succession was amended in 1980 so that the monarch's first-born child of either sex succeeds to the throne, making the then-2-yr.-old Princess Victoria heir.

ECONOMY. Currency: Swedish Kronor (May 1983: 7.5 = $1 US). **Gross Na-**

tional **Product** (1980): $111.9 billion. **Per Capita Income** (1980): $13,520. **Women's Wages as a Percentage of Men's** (1977): average, 58.75% [see **(Employed) Women's Occupational Indicators**]. In 1982 women earned 72.7% of men's earnings in industry, 73.7% in trade, and 68.9% in construction; in general, women earn 30% less than men. **Equal Pay Policy:** Labor unions and the Swedish Employers Assoc. concluded an agreement (1970) for equal pay for equal work; 1980 Equality Between Women and Men at Work Act made wage discrimination illegal (see **Equal Rights**). In practice, wage differentials still persist and women work in female-intensive job sectors. **Production** (Agricultural/Industrial): Dairy products, grains, sugar beets, potatoes, wood; machinery, instruments, metal products, automobiles. **Women as a Percentage of Labor Force** (mid-1982): 46%; **of agricultural force** (1980) 25.1% (24.4% of whom are unpaid family workers); **of industrial force**—no general statistics obtainable (of manufacturing 26.9%, 1980); **of military**—no statistics obtainable; women were first admitted into the military in 1978, and may become officers but are not allowed in combat. Seventy-five percent of married women are wage earners, as are 75.3% of mothers with children under age 7. In 1980, 90% of part-time employees were women.

(Employed) Women's Occupational Indicators: Of mechanical engineers 2%, of architects 3%, of administrative, executive, and managerial workers 16.4%, of employers and self-employed 24.1%, of teachers 79%, of clerical workers 87% (1980); 80% of employed women are concentrated in 1/4 of existing occupations, the lowest-paying ones (1980); 78% of women work in the service sector (1978). The labor market is sex-segregated although the government encourages training/hiring to combat traditional segregation through "equality grants" which subsidize the wages of the "nontraditional worker" for approx. 6 months; "industrial location subsidies," which are provided to enterprises that agree to hire 40% nontraditional workers in a new or expanded facility; and "labor market grants" (to the worker), which subsidize training for job sex-integration. However, only a limited number of occupations qualify for equality grants and a nontraditional worker cannot qualify if any workers of the "traditional sex" are already unemployed in that field. Consequently, only 291 firms (affecting 883 workers) qualified for grants in 1980. In general, many more men enter traditionally female occupations (e.g. nursing, childcare) than vice versa. Only 2.6% of appointees to executive boards and other decision-making positions in State-owned businesses were women (1977). **Unemployment** (mid-1983): 3.5%, female 3.9%, male 3.2%.

GYNOGRAPHY. Marriage. *Policy:* Marriage is legally considered only "1 form of voluntary cohabitation" (Marriage Code, amended 1973); State policy is that legal marriage should not be supported more or less than any other style of family or household. Spouses have equal property rights in marriage (1920 Marriage Code). Married people are taxed separately (1971) and are equally obliged to support each other and their children through salaried work or housework (1979). Property can be independently owned and managed but certain "community property" cannot be sold or mortgaged without mutual consent. Each partner is responsible for individually incurred debts (except household debts) and contractual agreements. A woman's name is automatically changed to her husband's upon marriage, but since 1983 the woman and/or man can apply to keep and/or take the wife's birth-name. Widows and surviving female partners of cohabitation relationships both receive State pensions, but the latter do not receive widow's pensions based on their partner's earnings. Bigamy is an offense punishable by 2 yrs. maximum imprisonment (1962 Criminal Code); adultery has not been an offense since 1937. Minimum marriage age for both sexes is 18 (1969). Legislation permitting same-sex legal marriage is being considered (1983). *Practice:* Female mean age at marriage (1970–78): 26; women age 15–49 in union (1970–78): 56.34%. Owing to increased incidence of cohabitation, the marriage rate fell 40–50% from 1966 to

1973. Sweden has one of the highest co-habitation rates in the world. Of all persons age 20–24, 21.7% were married, and 28.6% were cohabiting (1975). Almost all couples live together before they marry.

Divorce. *Policy:* Divorce is considered the dissolution of a voluntary contract and is granted upon request, except to parents of children under 16 or when 1 partner contests. In these instances there must be a 6-month "consideration period," when the couple is encouraged to take advantage of free counseling (1973 Family Law Reform). Free legal aid is available. Laws are designed to be sex-neutral; both partners are responsible for maintaining a dependent after divorce, if necessary, and both are liable for child support. If a parent fails to pay child support, the government will pay instead. Child custody is awarded in the interests of the child and may be shared. When cohabiting couples separate, custody is awarded to the mother unless the parents agree to joint custody or the mother is proven "unfit"; each person takes her/his personal property only. Community property is divided equally. *Practice:* Divorces (per 1000 pop., 1978): 2.46. Half of all marriages end in divorce (1981). Only 50% of divorced men and women remarry (1975). Sex-neutral divorce laws assume women's economic equality, and alimony is rarely awarded for longer than a short adjustment period, and then it is mostly paid by men; in practice, however, women rarely achieve economic equality with their husbands.

Family. *Policy:* Men and women have equal responsibility for childcare and housework. Parenthood Insurance Benefits (under national insurance) include a 7-month leave at 90% of salary (100% for government workers), which may be taken by either parent (married or cohabiting), or split between them, after the birth of a child (legislation on joint parental leave is pending, 1983); 3 months of the leave may be saved and taken anytime before the child is 8 (since 1974). Parents split an allowance of 60 days per yr. to care for a sick child under age 10 and may work a 6-hour day (at pro-rated wages) until the child is 8; parents keep job security, pension rights, and pro-tected seniority even if they extend their leave (unpaid) until a baby is 18 months old. Women are entitled to 60 days paid leave before expected delivery date, and nursing breaks as necessary. Pre-natal and post-natal care as well as delivery are free. As of 1980, families received a child benefit of SKr. 2800 per child per yr. until a child was 18 (or 21 if still in school). The State subsidizes day-care facilities; 11% of day-care costs are paid by parents, who do so on a sliding scale. Priority is given to single parents, students, children with special needs, and immigrants. Children's rights are a priority; it has been illegal to physically punish or spank children, or to subject them to humiliating treatment, since 1979, the same yr. that war toys were banned. *Practice:* Childcare and housework remain primarily women's responsibility. Of 585,000 fulltime homemakers, 99% were women, and 90% of these women expressed a desire to work outside the home (1979). Among couples where both partners worked fulltime, 50% of women, as opposed to 18% of men, did more than 20 hours per week of housework (1979). Most employed mothers work only part time. Fathers take limited advantage of Parenthood Insurance Benefits; 1/3 of benefits claimed for child-related sick leave were paid to fathers, and only 10–12% of fathers took any leave to care for newborns; average leave was 41 days (1977). There is a great shortage of childcare facilities. Only 33% of eligible children could be enrolled in day-care facilities, and 5% of children age 7–12 could be enrolled in after-school centers (1981).

Welfare. *Policy:* The comprehensive welfare system is based on the principle that society has responsibility for the well-being of its members; the system is financed by heavy taxation (50–85% of income). National Health Insurance provides low-cost medical and dental care and covers all citizens, including homemakers. Social security covers part-time workers (over 17 hours per week). Basic Pensions are the same for all workers, but additional payments are determined by income and number of yrs. worked. Food-staple prices and housing construction are government-subsidized. Unemployment benefits and paid training programs are available to those out of work. Fulltime workers get 5 weeks paid vacation and unlimited paid sick leave. *Practice:* In 1978 the average pension for women was 1/3 that of men's, owing to interruptions in work (yrs. of child-raising, etc.), lower pay, and part-time work. From 1960 to 1976, 33% of all women age 60 had not earned a single "pension year."

Contraception. *Policy:* The ban on contraceptives and sex-education was lifted in 1938 (see HERSTORY). It is considered the government's responsibility to provide counseling and contraceptive services. National Health Insurance covers related costs and doctors' fees. Voluntary sterilization is legal and free on request for citizens over age 25 and with the approval of the National Board of Health for those age 18–25 (1976 Sterilization Act). Midwives are authorized to insert IUDs (1975) and prescribe oral contraceptives (1978). Comprehensive sex-education is mandatory through all school levels, beginning at age 7 (1955). *Practice:* In 1977, 1 million women and/or their partners used contraceptives. In 1981, of those using contraceptives, the distribution by method was: barrier methods 33%, pill 32%, IUD 26%, natural methods 9%; sterilizations (Jan.–June 1980): women 3400, men 1500. In 1978 midwives handled 1/2 of the 460,000 consultations on contraceptives. The campaign to make contraceptive information and services completely accessible was enhanced with passage of the 1975 Abortion Act. Services are available in clinics, schools, and youth centers.

Abortion. *Policy.* Free on request (in consultation with a doctor) until end of first trimester; in consultation with a doctor and a social worker until the end of the 18th week; weeks 18–28 only with approval of National Board of Health; after 28th week only to save the woman's life (1975 Abortion Act). *Practice:* Abortions (per 1000 women age 15–44, 1981): 19.4. In 1978, 89% of abortions were performed before the end of the first trimester, and only 1% after the 18th week. Abortions were legalized under limited circumstances in 1938, and the law was further liberalized in 1946, 1963, and 1975. Since 1977 there has been a decrease in the abortion rate among young women, indicating increased use of contraceptives.

Illegitimacy. *Policy:* All children have the same rights, including rights to support from both parents. In 1917 the term "illegitimate" was changed to "born out of wedlock" in all relevant laws. As of 1970 children born out of wedlock could take their fathers' names and inherit equally from paternal families. In 1977 all distinctions, including the phrases "child born out of wedlock" and "child born in wedlock" were struck from Swedish law. *Practice:* In 1979, 33% of all births were to cohabiting or single women. A 1969 public-opinion survey showed 99% in favor of equal rights for all children; 98% in favor of equal treatment for married and single mothers. If there is difficulty in establishing paternity or reaching a child-support agreement, a single mother is entitled to financial and legal assistance from the State. Usually men acknowledge paternity. **Homosexuality.** *Policy:* Decriminalized since 1944. In the 1950's the High Court ruled that sexual preference was not a relevant consideration in determining parental fitness. In 1977 the Riksdag decreed that "2 persons of the same sex living together shall be fully accepted by Swedish society." In 1978 the minimum age for same-sex intercourse was lowered from age 18 to age 15, the same as for heterosexual intercourse. The Committee Concerning the Situation of Homosexuals (appointed 1977) will make recommendations in 1984 for legislation to end discrimination and make available all benefits afforded heterosexual couples (see **Marriage**). *Practice:* In 1981 there were approx. 650,000 lesbian women and homosexual men in Sweden, or 10% of the pop. over age 15. The lesbian/homosexual rights movement, led by the Swedish Union for Sexual Equality, is demanding full acceptance, including the right to legal same-sex marriage and adoption of children by same-sex couples. The government Committee Concerning the Situation of Homosexuals is expected to recommend the inclusion of sexual-preference rights in the constitutional nondiscrimination clause.

Incest. *Policy:* Sexual abuse of children

by parents or siblings is a criminal act punishable by 2 yrs. maximum imprisonment and 1 yr. maximum imprisonment respectively (Penal Code, 1972). The office of the government-appointed Advocate for Children (established 1973) designs educational campaigns and handles reports of child abuse. Emphasis is on parental counseling, not punishment. Since 1980, ninth-graders have been required to take a weekly course about child abuse. *Practice:* Approx. 10 children per yr. are killed by parents, and approx. 1000 are violently or sexually abused; there are an est. 4000 unreported cases annually. **Sexual Harassment.** *Policy:* Offense through indecent words or actions is a criminal act punishable by a maximum 1 yr. imprisonment. Sexual harassment is not specifically covered by the 1980 Act Concerning Equality Between Women and Men at Work. *Practice:* No data obtainable.

Rape. *Policy:* Using threat or violence to force a woman's submission to sexual penetration is punishable by 2–10 yrs. imprisonment. Sexual assault is punishable by 4 yrs. maximum imprisonment. Marital rape is illegal. Prior conduct of the woman is not considered relevant evidence. *Practice:* In 1980, 885 rapes were reported to the police (15.8 per 100,000 pop.), the highest incidence in any Scandinavian country (1980). In 1976 only 12% of reported rapists were tried in court. Convicted rapists usually receive the minimum 2-yr. sentence and serve an average of 2–3 months in prison. The RFSU (Swedish Association for Sex Information) opened the country's first rape-crisis center in Stockholm (1977), sponsoring clinics for rape victims, seminars for police, lawyers, and hospital staff, and therapy for rapists. **Battery.** *Policy:* Spouse battery is covered under general assault provisions. A law allowing for automatic prosecution of violent spouses (without complaint by the abused) was passed by the Riksdag in 1982. Government-sponsored awareness campaigns encourage neighbors and passers-by to report domestic violence. *Practice:* 2500–3000 cases are reported to police each yr. (1981); an est. 99% of cases go unreported. Approx. 50 women

are killed by their spouses each yr. (see **Crisis Centers**).

Prostitution. *Policy:* Not a criminal offense (for the person working as a prostitute) since 1917. It is illegal to promote or profit from prostitution, and pimping is punishable by sentences ranging from a fine up to 4 yrs. imprisonment. In 1983 the Commission on Sexual Abuse was considering recommending the prosecution of clients of prostitutes. *Practice:* A 1981 national study on prostitution found that the practice has decreased since the mid-1970's (street prostitution down by 40%, massage institutes and nude modeling studios by 60%, and sex club prostitution by as much as 80%). The practice still persists, however; each yr. approx. 100,000 men are active as clients, approx. 2000 women as vendors, and an est. 2000 persons as procurers; an est. 1000 of the women involved work as street prostitutes, some 500 at massage parlors, approx. 100 at sex clubs, and approx. 300 as "call girls" in an elite bracket. The study also showed that allegations made about prostitution progressively affecting lower age groups were groundless: less than 5% of street prostitutes and practically none in any other categories are under age 18. However, the number of women who have at 1 time or another practiced prostitution is relatively large: 2% of women born in the Stockholm area in the mid-1950's have worked as prostitutes, although many for only a short time. Street prostitution is common in such urban areas as Stockholm, Gothenburg, Malmö, Norrköping, and other cities, and there is a considerable correlative between prostitution and drug addiction. Prostitution gross earnings in Sweden in 1980 were est. at SKr. 120 million, with massage parlor and studio prostitution accounting for the largest share. The Swedish study also noted the strong connections between prostitution and pornography, mainstream "pin-up" materials, and other such propaganda which perpetuate images of women in sexually objectifying ways, and openly acknowledged the work done by feminist organizations in educating the public about these connections. **Traditional/Cultural Practices:** No data obtainable. **Crisis Centers.** *Policy:* A 1981 bill made government funds available for women's shelters. *Practice:* The All Women's House in Stockholm has accommodations for 16 women and their children seeking shelter; it runs discussions on rape, battery, and other forms of violence against women and helps women in other cities start shelters. There are shelters in Gothenburg, Lund, and some other cities (see **Rape**).

HERSTORY. Sweden shares with other Scandinavian countries a legacy of Celtic, Brigante, and Norse women warriors, chieftains, and rulers in the centuries B.C.E. In the late 1st century C.E., the Svear people warred with their southern neighbors in Gotaland. By the 6th century they conquered and merged with the Gotar. The Swedes were introduced to Christianity in 829, and had fully converted by the 12th century. Swedes were among other Scandinavian groups who participated in the Viking raids. In Russia the Vikings were called Varangians (see USSR); they gained control of areas extending to the Black Sea (10th century), and conquered Finland (12th century).

St. Bridget (or Birgitta) of Sweden (1303?–1373) was a noblewoman and mother of 8 children who later founded the Order of the Holy Savior ("Bridgettines") for religious and learned women. Her diplomatic journeys to Rome, outspoken (and sometimes unwelcome) advice to the Pope, and her controversial writings about political and religious ideas provoked Church criticism. Her daughter, Katharine of Vadstena, also is venerated as a saint, although never formally canonized; she continued her mother's work after Birgitta's death, by obtaining official approval for the Bridgettine Order at Rome. In 1397 Queen Margarethe I (1353–1412) united Sweden, Denmark, and Norway under the Kalmar Union; she forged one of the largest empires of her time through military conquest and political machinations. Queen Christina (1626–89, reigned 1632–54) came into full power at age 18, was devoted to State affairs, and fostered a literary and artistic court. She was a supporter of philosophy and the arts, refused to marry, and upon abdication in favor of

her cousin, left Sweden in male attire and joined the Roman Catholic Church.

The first formal girls' school was founded in 1632. Ulrika Eleonora succeeded her brother (1718) to the throne, but abdicated in favor of her husband. A 1720 Constitution strengthened the power of the Riksdag. Power shifted back and forth between the sovereign and Riksdag until a constitutional monarchy was established (1809). Fredrika Bremer, the feminist writer, was first published in 1828. An equal-inheritance law was passed in 1845. In 1873 universities were opened to women (except in theology and advanced law), and the Society for Married Women's Rights was formed. The following year Marriage Law reform gave married women the right to dispose of their own property and wages.

In 1884 single women were declared to be of legal age at 21, no longer perpetual minors subject to paternal authority. That same year the Fredrika Bremer League was founded to fight for women's rights. The publication of Ellen Key's *The Abuse of Women's Energy* (1896) fostered debate over feminist and "free love" ideals. A concerted effort to win the vote began in 1902.

In 1909 a law prohibiting women's night employment passed and was not repealed until 1963. No-fault divorce laws were enacted in 1915, and in 1919 a constitutional amendment gave women the vote in national elections. The 1920 Marriage Code ended a husband's guardianship of a wife, declared married women to be of legal age at 21, and established equal responsibility for mutual support in marriage. Women were allowed to enter most civil service jobs in 1923, and 4 years later girls were first admitted to public high schools.

Elise Ottesen-Jensen established the (still active) Swedish National Assoc. for Sex Information and Education (RFSU, 1933); her work led to the introduction of sex-education in the public schools, and to legislative reform about contraception and abortion. In 1938 State maternity benefits were enacted, a therapeutic abortion law was passed, and the ban on contraception and sex-education was lifted; by 1939 a woman could not be fired upon engagement or marriage. Ulla Lindstrom became minister without portfolio in 1953 and dealt with family welfare. In 1958 women were permitted ordination as ministers in the Swedish Lutheran Church. Feminist and anti-militarist activist Alva Myrdal was appointed to the cabinet as the Minister of Disarmament (1966); she later won the Nobel Peace Prize (1982) and is largely responsible for Sweden's rejection of nuclear, biological, and chemical weapons.

The modern feminist movement began in the late 1960's and the early 1970's when Group 8, an independent socialist-feminist organization, was formed. By the late 1970s there was significant development of "women's culture," shelters, and women's studies programs. Major feminist organizing brought about the enactment of model legislation on rape. Currently, the Swedish Women's Left Federation works toward peace and on

feminist issues. The Fredrika Bremer League publishes *Hertha,* the oldest feminist magazine in the country, and serves as a network and resource center. The Woman's House in Stockholm runs a bookstore, a coffeehouse, discussions, and self-defense classes. The First International Feminist Congress Against Incest was held in Sweden in Aug. 1983.

MYTHOGRAPHY. The influence of Nordic and Celtic peoples had an effect on the early inhabitants of Sweden, and various local forms of Celtic or Teutonic goddess figures were revered (see DENMARK, FINLAND, NORWAY). Lucia, sometimes thought of as the deity of the Northern Lights, persists as an image: Winter Solstice festivals are still celebrated, with processions led by young women wearing crowns of lighted candles.

SWEDEN: Similarity, Singularity, and Sisterhood
by Rita Liljeström

To understand what's happening in the Swedish feminist movement, we must outline some history first.

The division of labor in yesteryear's agrarian society in Sweden was by sex. Marriage rested on an economic basis, and the spouses did not form any island of "twoness." On the contrary, ethnologists describe how Swedish women and men comported themselves in separate collectives. Such segregation held true of day-to-day work in the farmyard or out in the fields, of meetings by the well or on the village street, of merrymaking at festive gatherings, of attendance at church and journeys to market. The women felt strong bonds of mutual sympathy that sprang from the need to help each other, both at work and in minding the children.

Around 1900 a new conjugal pattern (based on bourgeois marriages) began to take root among the broad masses of people. With the entry of "the new couple" into the social arena, single-sex collectives and women's former solidarity were weakened.

The tradition of reserving church pews on different sides of the aisle for women and men was broken during the nineteenth century. Persons of higher social strata started the change by sitting in pairs. Many an eyebrow was raised in a rural congregation when the first woman left the female side of the aisle to sit next to her husband. The first ones to break with tradition were "nice people," members of the higher classes and social climbers; the rest followed later. As it happened, the act itself was heavily charged with symbolism, publicly marking as it did the new meaning of twoness or duality.[1] Not only

---

[1.] Berndt Gustafsson, *Manligt-kvinnligt-kyrkligt i 1800-talets svenska foklive* (Male-Female-Clerical in Swedish Nineteenth Century Folk-life), Lund: n.p., 1956.

that, but this twoness was introduced at the very time when the household separated into workplace and dwelling place. The old division of labor in the self-contained household had come to an end.

The male and female members of the new pair came into a wholly different relationship with their own same-sex collectives. Whereas the men joined forces to organize themselves as wage earners and citizens, the women experienced a diminishing sense of community. The four walls of home, the offspring, the modern nuclear family, all served to shut the women off into their private worlds. Because of the time put in by fathers (on the job and getting to work and back), men became more mobile and less "homebodies"— which only increased *maternal* ties to the dwelling place.

The old division of labor had drawn strict distinctions between male and female norms. Men and women did not compete on the same tracks but were rated along different performance scales. Women were compared with one another in the context of "female attributes." A woman who ranked high on the female scale would enjoy the esteem of society, but that didn't help her advance outside the world of women. A different yardstick was in use for measuring the men.

Changes in society tear the rug out from under people. Unless outdated rating criteria are replaced by a new female yardstick, nothing remains for women but to start fighting for their own self-confidence on men's terms. And that is precisely what happened. Women oscillated between attempts to achieve parity with men and attempts to uphold their singularity as women. But during that same period, the animus of political ideologies and legislation was to disregard sex. The free individuals and citizens of liberalism, as well as the workers and comrades of socialism, lack gender. Rhetoric, legal passages, and the texts of political ideologies supposedly do away with sex. In practice, however, this means that the yardstick used for *men* was extended to *women*. In times past, women in Sweden had been subordinate to male authority, but now that they came into possession of "equal entitlement" they stopped existing in their own right.

All of these developments must be kept in mind in order to understand what happened in June of 1982, when two hundred women convened to open Sweden's first women's university at Umeå, our northernmost seat of learning. The hedgeberries were in bloom and snow was falling. Over the course of four days, women representing different academic disciplines sought answers to this question: What does a feminist perspective mean for my subject? The women's university grew into a serious and intense manifestation of sisterhood among women researchers. It was a unique experience in a country where official policy has gone in vigorously for equality—in a spirit of (fraternal) sex neutrality.

One theme ran like a red thread through several women's speeches: the issue of similarity and singularity. The introductory lectures, given by two historians, brought us straight to the intersecting point of feminist debate.

One historian described antagonisms in feminist history as an undulation between periods when women put forward their interests as *individuals* and periods when they appealed to their singularity as *mothers;* at one point, the struggle would be concerned with a woman's right to develop just like other (read: "male") individuals, and at another there would be the preoccupation with defense of her special experiences. Irrespective of whether these experiences are attributed to different upbringings of girls and boys, to different functions in reproduction, or to the division of labor between the sexes, the defenders of singularity have contended that women's insights and attitudes are socially valuable. Women should not renounce them: on the contrary, as many argue, experiences that are specific to women must govern society to a greater extent. When the first speaker illumined the dialectics of the struggle for woman as individual and woman as mother, she portrayed a conflict that cannot be resolved either by repudiating women's individuation—i.e., their right to personal development—or by denying specific experiences that are typical for women.

The other speaker went on record as being decidedly skeptical about women's singularity. A woman could choose from only two alternatives: either she becomes a "working creature" or she stays a "female." It is in exactly this fashion that women have constantly been maimed, now from one direction, now from the other: cut off your own development or truncate your sex. Shut in the individual and let out the mother—or vice versa. The freedom of paid work has been opposed to the slavery of unpaid work—or the reverse.

These antagonisms are as old as time. The historian of religion looked to the visual arts as a source of women's *Weltanschauung.* Her words made it evident that our search for identity has deep roots in classical antiquity. Aphrodite and Artemis were both objects of women's cults. Although women admittedly paid homage to Aphrodite as the goddess of love, they donated most of the small doll-offerings to Artemis, Amazon of the woodlands, asking her for a merciful dispatch by bow and arrow in case their labor pains were too severe. Artemis, virgin and huntress, the merciful liberator: forever locked away are her private musings that the great men of antiquity didn't put in print, or perhaps never dared to. For me, at any rate, Aphrodite is a cherished masculine dream, while Artemis still appeals to women's double being of similarity and singularity.

What are the origins of the historical undulation we know of, where feminist movements press down on each other, now in the name of similarity, now in the name of singularity? Whoever hit on the notion that individuality, paid work, and parenthood are irreconcilable *a priori?* The premises are manifest givens of a male society. It is remarkable that women have leveled so much criticism at other women. But women have been preoccupied with pleasing men so as to gain access to public life or to get married. In the process they have been willing to cut off their big toe to make the foot fit the prince's shoe; in any event, we have adhered to the behavior of our sisters as told to us in the fairy tale.

To help me in my self-reflections, I have tried to capture four positions in the following table. It distinguishes on the one hand between those who believe in *fundamental similarity between the sexes* and those who uphold *woman's singularity* (I shall have more to say about man's singularity later on), and on the other hand between *integration* and *segregation* as strategies for bringing influence to bear on a male-dominated culture. The point I want to make is that the various positions must be put in relation to male power structures. They should be seen in their historical context. Women's endeavors have been constantly enveloped by a patriarchal culture, which has taken a benign view of the quest for emancipation—whenever this coincided with sufficiently weighty male interests.[2] Decision-making assemblies of men flexibly have adapted their gender policy to priorities that fall in line with the Grand Development Utopia, with the techno-scientific future-oriented projects in which Western male elites have invested during the most recent centuries.

	SIMILARITY	SINGULARITY
Together with men	1. Swedish policy of equality in a spirit of sex neutrality	2. Defensive complementarity, "niches for women"
Women by themselves	3. Women's wings of political parties	4. Offensive women's culture, feminist research

2. Gunnar Qvist, *Konsten att blifva en god flicka* (The Art of Becoming a Good Girl). Stockholm: LiberFörlag, 1978.

The perspective I adopt to interpret the four positions starts out with the 1960's. I've sharpened and abstracted the different standpoints to chisel out the basic issues in dispute. Position 1 assumes that women and men are basically alike and best serve the cause of equality when they work together. This stance has characterized Swedish equality policy since the 1960's. The basis of fairness and justice is similarity; sex is irrelevant, consisting of no more than prejudice and superstition. Since equality is regarded as a matter of "fair shares," the similarity line does not recognize any conflicts between the sexes. Nor do its advocates want to hear of any quotas. How on earth do you assign quotas between equals? You choose the best comrade; you give the job to the best qualified individual; in our capacity as wage earners and citizens, we have interests in common. But in a spirit of would-be sex neutrality, men in all countries accord priority to other issues: class struggle, free rivalry, war on poverty, anti-imperialism and anti-Westernization.[3] Whenever women take up the subject of intersexual inequities, whenever they single out the marginalization of women in modern economies and women's sexual vulnerability, they are reproached for making common cause with the adversary, for sowing discord and betrayal. *Thus the dogma on similarity functions as protection from all crosswise contacts.*

Although position 3 is for similarity between the sexes, it still wants to keep them a bit separate. How is that possible? Well, it is possible if you declare women incapable of managing their own affairs. The discrete activities are acceptable only so long as women upgrade their skills to reach the male level. During the 1960's and 1970's, the *raison d'être* of political organizations for women often came under fire. Wasn't it about time to dissolve them and integrate them with the parties? According to the supporters of women in politics, that time had not yet come. Women were not accustomed to speaking in public, they lacked savoir faire and self-confidence. It was important to let them practice the art of argumentation, become sure of themselves, and get training in substantive issues to enable them to appear before mixed audiences.

In grappling with the question of singularity, I am aware of the various meanings that can attach to it and of the associations it arouses in different directions.

—Singularity can induce one to think of conservatively romantic ideas about complementarity between the sexes under the man's leadership and protection.

—Our (patriarchal) teachers have sought in their sciences to trace woman's singularity to genetic dispositions, to evolution's sociobiology, and to hormonal undercurrents in our psyche. They have construed their findings to square with male-dominated culture's notions of woman as puerpera and mother.

—In today's economic crisis all talk of female singularity is hushed up as a threat to women's right to remunerated work. Similarity pays off. Singularity can be a trap.

But who sets the trap? Similarity's advocates have learned only too well the historical lesson that every concession to singularity will be turned against women themselves—as a retreat to economic dependence. And when the winds have blown from the Right, the crucial task has been not to make any concessions, not even to pretend that women and men derive different experiences from their work—as though it would be embarrassing to have to admit that women are more knowledgeable than men in their own walks of life. That is how the supporters of similarity keep the prevailing male dominance secret to themselves. They turn a blind eye to the usual meaning of "together with men," which is, really, simply agreement on men's terms. So for tactical reasons women have cooperated

[3] Anita Jacobson, *Landsbygdskvinnan i Kenya och Tanzania* (The Rural Woman in Kenya and Tanzania). Ulandskvinnor: SIDA (Swedish International Development Authority), 1974.

in rendering their sisters invisible. All along, similarity and singularity take on their meanings *in negotiations with the dominant party.*

The crucial factor, however, is *who decides* over the singularity: whether it is thrust upon women from without or whether women themselves define it as their willful choice of self-understanding. *Whoever decides gets to draw the boundary line between defensive and offensive singularity.*

—Seen tangibly, singularity may allude to the various experiences which a gendered division of labor gives women and men, both in a segregated labor market and one in which women have acquired special competence.

—Singularity contains an archaic echo of childhood's triangle drama, plus all the imprints that maternal presences and paternal absences leave on the children's future sexual relations. As long as the theories of sex and sexuality ascribed hysteria, they gave female singularity little to affirm. But once feminist researchers began to purge the theories of these androcentric biases, the female sex has been freed from its discriminatory purport. Instead, we have to elaborate what we know about the early maiming of young girls as well as boys.

—Singularity can mark a degree of reservation, a distrust of a male-dominated culture whose focus on the forces of production and on the big "development project" that hurtles ahead on evolution's nomothetic tracks monitored by technoscience's remote controls, has alienated it from the values closest to women, from daily living as a meaningful life form, from the sphere of reproduction with its human needs and qualities.

—Singularity can express itself in symbols of women's gendered perceptions, e.g., of the womb as imagery for all the lunations of bleedings, the months of waiting, the triumph of giving birth, the emptiness felt after miscarriage or abortion, and the relief of the menopause years. Both the phallic culture *and* many advocates of similarity become easily provoked by the "uterine cult." But why should women's sexual organs be either tabu as message-carrying symbols or reduced to the graffiti of public toilets?

The difference between positions 2 and 4 in the table is one of *who decides.* Position 2 upholds female singularity together with men. In practice this signified either a pact between the sexes to preserve the status quo or an appeal to confer "minority rights" on women. In the first case women and men agree that the social and material world in which they were born, brought up, and had their being is good enough for them; in the second case, they defend a niche in society for womanly values. It is also in this sense that singularity can become a blind alley, a place set apart for virtues and ideals without influence on the greater run of public life, a form of solitary confinement that shuts women off from rewards that accrue to men and their equals.

What do women themselves have to say about female singularity? Advocates of position 4 question the merits of the similarity ideology for equality. What good does it do, they ask, to treat women and men alike if the whole system is permeated by a male culture? If all of society's prioritized values rest on a collective male consciousness, then what is equality but assimilation in the dominant culture?

If female singularity has so many meanings, then wherein lies the man's singularity? That question cannot be put because the very word "singularity" marks a deviation from the general norm. That which is male is no deviation. It *is* the norm. Male singularity stands out *as* similarity. The male-dominated culture has answered for the "joint" exegesis of the world. It has told us how everything is composed.

Sweden has long enjoyed considerable international esteem for its progressive sex-equality policies. Central government agencies have tried to promote equal terms between women and men in a spirit of total community of interests. It took a long time before we discovered the bias that was built into the Swedish model, its scattered "woman's side" and hushed-up feminist culture. We have begun to regain mastery over ourselves. Women gravitate toward one another to inspect the men's big "development projects" at the seams and to build up a corpus of knowledge seen from a female perspective.

We no longer ask whether a woman's culture exists. Indeed, we are creating it.

Suggested Further Reading

Berg, K. Westman, ed. *Cheri Register on Swedish Women Authors.* Uppsala: Univ. of Uppsala, 1983; research project on Swedish women authors 1830–1940.

Kälvemark, Ann Sofie. *More Children of Better Quality? Aspects on Swedish Population Policy in the 1930s.* Uppsala: Studia Historica Upsaliensis 115, 1980.

Dahlström, Edmund, and Rita Liljeström. *Working-Class Women and Human Production.* Forskningsrapport No. 70, Dept. of Sociology, Univ. of Gothenburg, 1982.

Liljeström, Rita, Gillan Liljeström Svensson, och Gunilla Fürst Mellström. *Roller i omvandling.* SOU (Swedish Official Investigation) 1976:71, Stockholm: LiberFörlag; English trans., *Sex Roles in Transition* available from the Swedish Institute, Stockholm.

Mellström, Gunilla Fürst, and Mariann Sterner. *Improving Working Conditions and Advancement Opportunities of Women.* Dept. of Sociology, Univ. of Gothenburg, 1980; the State administration taken as an example. A comparative study in the US, Sweden, and the FRG.

Wistrand, Birgitta. *Swedish Women on the Move.* Stockholm: Swedish Institute, 1981.

Dr. Rita Liljeström was born in 1928 and works with the department of sociology, University of Gothenburg, Sweden. She has written several books on gender, sexuality, and childhood in changing societies, of which the latest are *Det erotiska kriget* (The Erotic Warfare), Stockholm: LiberFörlag, 1981; and, together with Edmund Dahlström, *Arbetarkvinnor i hem-, arbets- och samhallsliv* (Working-Class Women in the Home, on the Job, and in Society), Stockholm: Tidens Förlag, 1981.

THAILAND
(Kingdom of Thailand)

Southeast Asian country that stretches from the Indochinese Peninsula to the Malay Peninsula, bordered by Laos and Kampuchea to the east, the Gulf of Thailand and Malaysia to the south, and the Andaman Sea and Burma to the west and north. **Area:** 514,000 sq. km. (198,455 sq. mi.). **Population** (1980): 47,347,000, female 50.2%. **Capital:** Bangkok.

DEMOGRAPHY. Languages: Thai, Chinese, English. **Races or Ethnic Groups:** Thai 75%, Chinese 14%, Malay 3%, Khmer, Soai, Karen, Indian, plus a sizable group of refugees from Laos and Vietnam (see **Rape**). **Religions:** Buddhism 94%, Islam 4%, Christianity, Hinduism, other 2%. **Education** (% enrolled in school, 1975): Age 6–11—of all girls 76%, of all boys 80%; age 12–17—of all girls 29%, of all boys 39%; higher education—in 1971–78 women were 87.5% of humanities students, 56.4% of education, 49% of medicine, 15.8% of law. **Literacy** (1977): Women 70%, men 87%. **Birth Rate** (per 1000 pop., 1975–80): 32. **Death Rate** (per 1000 pop., 1975–80): 9. **Infant Mortality** (per 1000 live births, 1975–80): Female 61, male 75. **Life Expectancy** (1975–80): Female 63 yrs., male 58 yrs.

GOVERNMENT. King Bhumibol Adulyadej (Rama IX) is the monarch of a government controlled by the military. A bicameral National Assembly consists of an elected 500-member House of Representatives (which chooses a prime minister) and a 250-member Senate (appointed by a cabinet chosen by the prime minister). Political parties have limited freedom and elections are held infrequently. **Women's Suffrage:** 1932. **Equal Rights:** 1976 Civil and Commercial Code Amendment stipulates equal legal rights for women and men. **Women in Government:** 13 women are members of the House; there are no women cabinet ministers; there has been an increase of women on town councils and in district judgeships (1984).

ECONOMY. Currency: Baht (May 1983: 22.96 = $1 US). **Gross National Product** (1980): $31.1 billion. **Per Capita Income** (1980): $670. **Women's Wages as a Percentage of Men's** (1974): 67% in industry; children earn 36% (see below). **Equal Pay Policy:** Labor law stipulates equal pay for equal work. **Production** (Agricultural/Industrial): Rice, rubber, corn, tapioca; textiles, auto assembly, processed foods, wood. **Women as a Percentage of Labor Force** (1978): 47%; **of agricultural force** 49% (82% of whom are unpaid family workers); **of industrial force** 45.6%; **of military**—no statistics obtainable, but women are not permitted in military schools, general ranks, or combat duty; some women technicians have achieved high rank within the military. **(Employed) Women's Occupational Indicators:** Of managerial and administrative workers 16.5%, of clerical workers 43.6%, of service workers 43.6%, of technical, professional, and related workers 46%, of sales workers 60% (1978); of judges 2%, of lawyers 2%, of doctors 16.9% (1975); 3 times as many women as men were owners of businesses and worked as market sellers (1975). Women are the majority of workers in tobacco, textile, and chemical manufacturing; 82% of all women are economically active. In 1969 children under age 15 constituted 31% (58% of whom were female) of the labor force. **Unemployment** (1978): 0.9%, female 0.7%, male 1%.

GYNOGRAPHY. Marriage. *Policy:* Marriage is governed by the 1976 Civil and Commercial Code (Book V). Minimum marriage age is 17 for females and males with the consent of both parents, and 20 without consent. *Khongman,* given by the man to the woman on the day of engagement, becomes her property (dowry) upon marriage. Marriage is legal upon registration. A husband and wife are required to maintain each other according to their abilities. Property bought after marriage by either spouse is considered *Sin Somros* (common property) and both spouses have equal rights over it, unless an agreement otherwise is signed by both prior to marriage; property owned individually before marriage is considered *Sin Suan Tua* (separate property) and can be disposed of without the consent of the other spouse. A widow must wait 310 days before remarrying unless she gives birth during this time or obtains a court order. Moslems are governed by Islamic jurisprudence regarding family and property, except in matters of inheritance. *Practice:* Female mean age at marriage (1970–78): 22; women age 15–49 in union (1970–78): 62.5%. Minimum marriage-age requirements are sometimes not followed. Jurists have debated the legality of *khongman,* but the custom is still practiced widely. Many marriages, performed through religious (primarily Buddhist) ceremonies, are not registered with the government. Polygyny still is practiced, with men taking additional "minor wives" who are generally acknowledged by custom but not by law. Many women are unaware of their legal rights regarding property, divorce, etc. In northern Thailand there is a strong tendency toward matrifocality.

Divorce. *Policy:* Legal; divorce is obtainable by mutual consent or by either spouse on certain grounds, including adultery by the wife, maintenance by the husband of another woman as a wife, gross misconduct or bodily harm, imprisonment of 1 spouse for over 3 yrs., desertion for 1 yr. or more, and neglect of support. Before the passage of the Civil and Commercial Code Amendment (see **Equal Rights),** women could sue only on grounds of husband's adultery. If a spouse must change domicile because of employment and the other spouse refuses to move, desertion is not considered to have taken place. A marriage can also be voided if it took place against the will of either party, if either was under age 17, or if parental consent was not obtained, among other reasons, unless 6 months have passed, the woman has become pregnant, or the underage party has reached age 20. The court decides child custody, support payments, and division of property in cases of dispute. A woman must wait 310 days following divorce before remarriage unless she remarries her former spouse, gives birth to a child, or

receives court permission. *Practice:* No statistics obtainable. The actual rate of divorce is difficult to determine because of the frequency of *de facto* divorce (when 1 spouse simply abandons the relationship) and the high number of unregistered marriages; however, divorce and remarriage are common and bear no religious or social stigma. Child-custody battles are rare, and children usually stay with the mother. Payment of maintenance is generally practiced only by the wealthy. Marital disputes are often mediated by village leaders and district officials in attempts to obtain reconciliation. Dissolution of a marriage and subsequent division of property and payment of support can be complicated by the question of the rights of "minor wives."

Family. *Policy:* The Family Law is formed in part by Buddhist ideas of reciprocal support between parents and their children. Parental authority rests with the father unless the mother has custody of children or the court has ordered otherwise. Some female employees are entitled to a 60-day maternity leave with 30 days pay from the employer and guaranteed reinstatement. Daughters and sons share inheritances equally; a woman may will her property to a daughter or son without her husband's consent. There is no State-funded day care. *Practice:* Many Thai women, especially in the northern region, control family affairs and finances (see following article). Sons generally do field-work and daughters work in the home and have the responsibility of caring for parents in old age and sickness. The extended family is predominant, sometimes including the children of secondary wives. In 1976 in Chiengmai Province, 72% of women contributed more to household income than did men. In 1978, 18% of all households were headed by women (not including single mothers). Employers are often reluctant to hire married women, preferring single women to avoid paying maternity benefits. **Welfare.** *Policy:* No national insurance system, but federal employees participate in a retirement plan at age 60. The State supports maternal/child health programs and places an emphasis on preventive medicine and the provision of potable water and health services in rural areas. *Practice:* No statistics obtainable. The extended family is the traditional source of support.

Contraception. *Policy:* Legal; the State aims to lower fertility and birth rates. The government provides direct support, sponsors family-planning education in schools and adult literacy classes, and receives aid from international agencies for research on and distribution of contraceptives, including the controversial injectable Depo-Provera. *Practice:* Women age 15–49 in union using contraception (1975): 40%; methods used (1975) pill 41%, female sterilization 19%, IUD 18%, male sterilization 6%, injectables 6%, withdrawal 3%, rhythm 3%, abstinence 2%, condom 1%, other methods 2%; using inefficient methods 9%. **Abortion.** *Policy:* Under the Criminal Code, legal only in cases where pregnancy and childbirth pose a severe threat to the woman's life or health, or if pregnancy resulted from rape. Illegal procedures are punishable by a fine or up to 3 yrs. imprisonment for the woman and a fine or up to 5 yrs. for the practitioner or anyone who aids the woman. A proposed bill to liberalize abortion passed the lower house of Parliament in 1982 but was stalled, and came up again in 1983. If passed, Thailand would become the only Southeast Asian country where abortion is legal on request. There is strong religious (Buddhist) opposition to the bill. *Practice:* According to 1983 reports, the incidence of illegal abortion is increasing; as of 1982, each yr. an est. 1 million women seek illegal abortions and approx. 10,000 women die from the procedures.

Illegitimacy. *Policy:* A child born out of wedlock is considered the "legitimate" child of the mother and takes her name. Only children of a registered wife, not a "minor wife" or a single woman, are considered the legal offspring of both parents unless a father legally acknowledges paternity of the child. An out-of-wedlock child can be "legitimized" if the parents marry, through registration by the father, or by court action; the mother or child can refuse to consent to such paternal registration only on the grounds that the man is not the real father. A child born during the 310-day waiting period following divorce or death of a husband is considered the "legitimate" child of the former husband unless the woman has remarried. Under the Civil and Commercial Code (Arts. 1520–21, 1536), a husband can repudiate a child (up to 1 yr. after he knows of the birth until the child is age 10) if he did not cohabit with the mother during the time of conception, or if the child was born less than 180 days after marriage; however, if an engaged man is known to have had sexual intercourse with the mother before marriage during the presumed time of conception he is considered the father. Only the "legitimate" child of a man can take his name or inherit from him. *Practice:* No statistics obtainable. Children of a secondary wife or a single woman take the mother's name unless the father acknowledges paternity. Such children are generally considered part of the extended family and live with the principal wife and her children. **Homosexuality.** *Policy:* Legal. *Practice:* No statistics obtainable. Lesbian and homosexual relationships are accepted; same-sex marriages are not uncommon and may have a Buddhist monk's blessing.

Incest. *Policy:* Illegal. Under the Criminal Code (Sec. 285) the punishment for rape (see **Rape**) is increased by 1/3 if the offense is committed by a parent on a descendant. In addition, the Criminal Code makes any "indecent act" committed by violence, threat, fraudulent means, or while the person is unable to resist, punishable by a fine or up to 3 yrs. imprisonment, or a fine or up to 5 yrs. if a female is under age 13 (Secs. 278–79); punishment for this offense is also increased by 1/3 if committed by a parent on a descendant. *Practice:* No data obtainable. **Sexual Harassment.** *Policy:* None. *Practice:* Reportedly common in the workplace, but not acknowledged by officials as a problem.

Rape. *Policy:* Illegal; under the Criminal Code (Sec. 276), "whoever has sexual intercourse with any woman, she not being his wife," by violence, threat, while she is unable to resist, or by misrepresenting his identity, is punishable by a fine and 1–10 yrs. imprisonment. If "severe bodily harm" is caused, or if the victim is under age 13 (regardless of consent), the penalty increases to 2–15 yrs.

(Secs. 277, 280); if the woman dies, punishment is a fine and 12–20 yrs. or life imprisonment. *Practice:* No general statistics obtainable. If an engaged woman is raped, her fiancé may demand financial compensation from the rapist. A 1983 report from the Overseas Education Fund indicates that many women among the thousands of Indochinese refugees (largely from Vietnam, Kampuchea, and Laos) landing in Thailand have been brutally raped, and sometimes abducted and sold by pirates who attack arriving boats; in 1 incident 7 women were assaulted by 70 men. Women rarely report the attacks for fear of reprisals or problems in resettlement. A Thai government anti-piracy program reportedly has resulted in limited deterence but no arrests or convictions. **Battery.** *Policy:* No specific legislation; may be prosecuted under general laws against assault (also see **Divorce**). *Practice:* No statistics obtainable. Wife abuse is common and generally dealt with by members of the extended family. However, Thai women frequently assert their own sense of justice, and there have been cases of women who have shot their abusive husbands.

Prostitution. *Policy:* It is illegal under the Criminal Code to work as a prostitute or to live off the earnings of a prostitute; punishable by a fine or imprisonment. *Practice:* Prostitution, brothels, and massage parlors became institutionalized during the Vietnam War when US troops were stationed in Thailand. After the troops left, tourism took over as the mainstay of prostitution. The authorities unofficially approve, since sex tourism, promoted by travel agents and catalogues in Europe and Japan as well as in Thailand, generates large revenue. A 1981 report estimated that 300,000 women worked in approx. 1157 places offering sex services in Bangkok alone; many earn an average of $40 per month, while sex-tour guides and hotel/bar (brothel) owners keep the profits. Approx. 70% of Thai prostitutes have venereal disease. Prostitution is one of the few means of survival for young women from rural areas who migrate to cities and are unable to find other work; approx. 40% of women working in the Bangkok region are prostitutes (1980). **Traditional/Cultural Practices:** No data obtainable. **Crisis Centers.** *Policy:* None. *Practice:* The first shelter for victims of domestic abuse was founded in 1981 by Kanitha Wichiencharoen. She turned her home into a women's refuge and has since expanded the center into another building.

HERSTORY. The Thai people migrated from southern China into the region of present-day Thailand. Siam, as the country was formerly known, was ruled by monarchies from 1238 C.E. to the present: the Sukhathai, Ayutthaya, Thonburi, and Chakri. In the Ayutthaya period, Queen Sri Suriyothai saved the lives of her husband and their loyal armies by running her elephant between the fighting forces.

During the Burmese wars (14th–18th centuries) several women led armies: Thao Thepsatri, Thao Shri Sunthon, and Thao Suranari. Khun Ying Chandra and her sister led forces which defended a southern province. In 1827 Khun Ying Mo, while captured by a Laotian prince, organized an army of female prisoners to rise up against the invading forces from Laos. During the reign of King Mongkut, Amdang Munan refused to marry the man her parents chose; she petitioned the King in 1868, and he changed the law to give all women the freedom to choose their spouses. That same year, another woman, Amdang Char, refused to be sold by her husband, and King Mongkut enacted a law that prohibited a husband from selling his wife without her consent.

Despite the intrusion of British and French colonizers in the region, Thailand remained the only Southeast Asian country to maintain its independence. King Mongkut and his son King Chulalonkorn, who were in power from 1851–1910, signed accords with the colonial powers that guaranteed Thailand's autonomy. In the early 19th century, Chaoying Khampq, a princess from the northern province of Lamphun, was known for her legal skills and courtroom wisdom in disputes. In 1921, the Elementary Education Act made primary education compulsory for children of both sexes, giving Thai females the opportunity for schooling. The absolute monarchy fell in a 1932 bloodless coup that in-stituted a constitutional representative government. The military emerged as a central part of the government, a role it maintains.

Despite restricted rights, Thai women have historically played a major eco-nomic role in society, especially in the north. The 1935 Monogamy Law was passed under pressure from the British, making bigamy or polygyny a crime and requiring husbands to register only 1 wife. The Civil and Commercial Code of 1935, however, restricted married women, making husbands legal house-hold heads, prohibiting women from es-tablishing a business or career without their consent and requiring written au-thorization from husbands to obtain passports or conclude a business matter. Wives had the legal status of chattel. The tripartite power structure which defines the social system—monastery, military, and monarchy—is closed to women.

Several women's organizations are generating a feminist consciousness in contemporary Thailand (see following ar-ticle).

MYTHOGRAPHY. See following arti-cle.

THAILAND: We Superwomen Must Allow the Men to Grow Up
by Mallica Vajrathon

Before we can analyze the situation of Thai women today, it is important to look back into the history of the more than 44 million Thai people. Thai culture and ways in the family and the community have been for generations influenced by Mon, Khmer, Chi-nese, and Indian culture. The Thai people have inherited Indian ideas about royalty, religion, literature, languages, and mythology—and business and finance from the Chi-nese. Most of all, we have inherited concepts of the differences between male and female and differences between the roles and behavior of women of different classes. For exam-ple, there have been vast differences between the way of life of Thai women from royal families and that of Thai women who work on farms. And between these two poles, there exists a large majority of business or market-women.

In Indian culture, no matter from what class the women come, they have gone through similar teachings, which were passed on from one generation to another by stories and songs, then later through formal education in schools. For instance, we believe in the strong power possessed by women from what we learn about such goddesses as: Maya-Sakti Devi, a world-protecting supreme power that generates and animates the display of cosmic energy; Padma Devi, the lotus goddess exhibiting her breast with a familiar maternal gesture, ruling over all the waters of the earth; Ganga Devi, the powerful goddess of the river Ganga, who possesses a magic effect that transforms the nature of those devotees who touch her.

Thai theater and folk music have focused for generations on the story of Mekhala Devi, the goddess who saved Bodhisattva (one of the incarnations of Buddha) from a shipwreck, and also on the story of Lord Vishnu's two queens, Shri Lakshmi, who per-sonified earth welfare, and Shri Sravati, who personified wisdom in making speeches and composing songs.

Many Thai girls are named after these goddesses. For instance, my first name, Mallica,

[Note: The view expressed in this article is a personal view of the author and does not represent the view of the United Nations Organization in which she works.]

which in Sanskrit means Jasmine Flower, is also the name of one of the Burmese queens who killed over fifty military elephants when leading an army in a tribal war. My last name, Vajrathon, is the name of another mythological figure, one who controls thunder and lightning, from a Buddhist doctrine called Vajrayana (the vehicle of the irresistible thunderbolt), symbolized by a figure sitting on a lotus throne which itself was originally the sign of the vehicle of the goddess Padma—mother, or *yoni* (the Indian word for the female sex/reproductive organ, opposite to the male organ *lingam)* of the universe.

Strong female figures have been recognized even in the formal Thai history we studied in school. We honored women who led armies during the Thai-Burmese war: Thao Thepsatri, and Thao Shri Sunthon, and Thao Suranari. We also recognized the importance of the women who performed important ceremonies in peacetime—marriage arrangements by "Mae Sue" (an elderly female go-between) and the mothers of the grooms and brides. Engagement money and the marriage ceremony were and still are arranged totally by them. In a favorite sixteenth-century Thai story, "Khun Chang Khun Paen," when a marriage was arranged, it was the mothers who did the negotiating. The groom's mother called on the bride's mother and asked her consent with the following words: "I have come to ask you for the seeds of melon, marrow, and gourd, so that I may plant my fields. I have no silver to offer you, so I will give my son to serve you; please use him as you would use your sandals, and I will answer for him." After marriage, the common practice in Thailand is that the groom moves in with the bride's family.

In Thailand, all important things—such as rice, trees, and rivers—always have a protecting, powerful goddess or female ghost: for example, Mae Phra Prasop (the goddess of the rice), Nang Tani (the female ghost who protects the banana trees), and Maenam (the mother of water, guardian of rivers). This is why Thai society is often called a matriarchy, even to this day.

But in modern-day Thailand, I would say that the society is a mixture between matriarchy and patriarchy. The majority of Thai women are economically independent. They work in agriculture or industrial factories; they do not wait for the men. Money-making and money management have traditionally been roles performed by Thai women. The buying and selling in local markets, in both cities and provinces, are in the hands of women. Even educated middle-class women don't stay home doing household chores; they go out to earn incomes as teachers, nurses, government officials, and businesswomen in such modern market sectors as wholesale-retail, banking and accounting, export-import, or tourist businesses. When married couples set up house, the woman normally provides the land and the man builds the house on it. This arrangement is considered best for the woman's security, for if the marriage dissolves, the man can leave but the house remains for the woman and children—on *her* land.

The Thai extended-family structure assigns great power to mothers and mothers-in-law, and there is a strong support system among female family members. For example, when a husband and a wife quarrel, the female members of *both* sides of the extended family will normally join forces in taking the woman's side. This female support system also exists in the marketplace. When women get together and talk about the men in their lives, they almost invariably discuss them as though they were all fragile beings, behaving like children, needing to be looked after and cared for, and how impossible it would be for women to rely on them financially. Because of this attitude, the market-women have formed among themselves a mutual self-help financial system for lending and borrowing totally outside the banking system.

Women in Thailand have been taught by their mothers and grandmothers not to leave important things in life—earning money and providing food—to men. This special sense of responsibility is drummed into the ears of young girls. Considering "what is important in life" differently from men, Thai women in general leave the affairs of community and national politics to men—because traditionally they have thought that politics is not a matter of life or death, therefore it can be left to men to talk and make speeches in parliament and in government offices—while women are busy making money. That is why, at present, government management and the judicial system are mainly in the hands of men. Now, however, we women are realizing that we cannot afford to leave government or parliament to men either. But this adds another job to what is already a double work-load.

When society trains women to be more responsible than men, a situation is created wherein women carry the burden of a heavy double work-load, inside and outside of the home. A large number of Thai women over the years have willingly accepted these loads as the fate of being born female. A middle- or upper-class woman will rush home from work just to be able to welcome her husband when *he* comes home from work, and to help the children with their homework and look after their needs. Pleasing people is the basic traditional training for Thai women; it is considered next in importance only to keeping a tidy physical appearance. We women are supposed to be *riabroi* (a combination of polite demeanor and calm body movement), while men are free to be clumsy and unruly. This is why Thailand is often called a land of superwomen. Perhaps even more than women in other countries, Thai women try extremely hard to be as pleasing as possible—*and* to be in control of everything.

But the future doesn't look encouraging for Thai women who wish to continue being in control of their own life conditions. Land in Thailand is coming more and more under the control of big business, such as agribusiness, and its farm use for export to foreign markets. In the rural areas, where women used to be able to grow food in the family plot of land and take it to sell in the local market, growing numbers of women farmers find that they have no land on which to grow anything independently and that in order to feed the family they must work as employees of big agribusiness companies whose policy of seeking high profit from cheap and "docile" female labor is infamous all over the world.

It seems to me, however, that men of government and men in the management of international business enterprise are determined to keep the situation as it is—because they profit from it. Thus, to make female workers "happy" in what they do, male managers find ingenious (and sexist) ways to keep women busy with sports competitions and beauty contests; they work closely with advertising and cosmetic firms who rely on these activities to advertise their products.

Recent statistics from Thailand show a large migration of rural women into such big cities as Bangkok, Chiengmai, Haadyai, and Korat—women clearly hoping to find urban work, since they lost their land in the rural areas. The younger ones turn to the service sector—and become bar-girls, coffee-shop girls, massage-parlor girls, hotel receptionists, and quite often prostitutes. It is estimated that nearly 500,000 women in Thailand are employed in these service industries. The tourist industry works closely with the sex-related industry, providing the country with up to 11 or 12 percent of foreign earnings. Advertising firms have been using women as a key attraction for male tourists from rich industrialized countries. The "reputation" of Thai "girls" is notorious in capitals of neighboring countries and in rich industrialized countries, a fact which most Thai women resent intensely.

To bring about a change in this alarming situation would require an attitude shift in the government and in big corporations. Women have to join and work with these two structures in large numbers in order to transform the situation from within.

Feminist consciousness-raising is also very much needed in my country. Many feminists in Thailand have already organized activities to try to get women out of these exploitative conditions which in many cases have been brought about by outside forces. Members of the Women Lawyers' Association, the Women Doctors' Association, the

National Council of Women, and the Association for the Promotion of the Status of Women in Thailand, have launched several campaigns to alert the public and the government to the grave conditions of women.

Such individuals as Kanitha Wichiencharoen, an active member of the Women Lawyers' Association, have recently created an Emergency Home for Distressed Women, providing care and counseling to women who suffer harassment and violence at home. Her sister, Kanok Samsenvil, also is active in organizing seminars on the situation of women in Thailand. Prathoomporn Vajrasathira, a university professor and a well-known novelist under the pen name Duangchai, has written several essays and novels exposing the dilemmas of Thai women. And Prateep Unsongtham, a young teacher who has devoted her life to improve the education of girls at the Klongthoey harbor slum, has also set an example to many young Thai women as to how they can contribute to improving the status of women in the country.

Despite these challenges, we Thai women do not see ourselves as the helpless victims of male domination, simply because we do not look on men as having much power over our lives; we see them as less responsible and less mature beings than we are, because of how they were brought up. On the other hand, it is not easy for us to get organized and take action as a group—because we are influenced by Buddhism, which taught each of us to be self-reliant and to look after herself as an individual.

The other difficulty we face is that to date most Thai women prefer negotiations, prefer to manipulate the weakness of male opposition to our advantage, rather than to engage in confrontation with the male establishment and structure, whose sexist attitudes will take a long time to change. (For example, if some leading—widely noted—Thai women still respond to the polygynist tendencies of their men by *choosing* the minor wife—or wives— does this resolve or merely perpetuate the root problem?)

The main strategy that must be formulated by feminists in Thailand is one to eliminate the political and business exploitation of women by local and international firms and by the commercial sex industry. But any strategy would have to aim not only at men but also at women, in that a large number of us must change our own attitudes about ourselves—about trying to be superwomen taking care of everything in life to please the men.

It's time we allowed the men to grow up.

Suggested Further Reading

Aspects of Thai Women Today. Bangkok: Thailand National Commission on Women's Affairs, 1980.

Study of the Status of Women in Thailand. National Economic and Social Development Board. Government of Thailand (prepared with assistance from UNICEF), 1978.

Vajrasathira, Prathoomporn. *Woman Cabinet Minister.* Bangkok: Central Express Suksa Printing, 1976 (B.E. 2519).

Mallica Vajrathon was born in Thailand and studied political science at Chulalongkorn University in Bangkok, French literature at the Sorbonne in Paris, and sociology at Southern Illinois University in the US, where she received her master's degree. She worked for twelve years with UNICEF and UNDP in the Development Support Communication Service for Asia, based in Bangkok. She has written professional papers for the UN and for various journals on the subjects of population and women's development in the new international economic order, women and the media, and development support communication; she was special adviser to the Secretary-General of the World Conference of the United Nations Decade for Women (Copenhagen, 1980), and is Research and Technical Cooperation Among Developing Countries liaison officer in the office of the executive director of UNFPA. She was a vice-president of the Ad Hoc Group on Equal Rights for Women in the UN, is married to Erskine B. Childers, and has one son.

THE UNION OF SOVIET SOCIALIST REPUBLICS
(Soviet Union)

The USSR covers one-seventh of the world's land mass, stretching from eastern Europe across northern Asia to the Pacific Ocean. **Area:** 22,402,200 sq. km. (8,649,489 sq. mi.). **Population** (1980): 265,712,000, female 53%. **Capital:** Moscow.

DEMOGRAPHY. **Languages:** Slavic (Russian, Ukrainian, Byelorussian, Polish), Altaic (Turkish, etc.), other Indo-European, Uralian, Caucasian. **Races or Ethnic Groups:** Russian 52%, Ukrainian 17%, Uzbek 5%, Byelorussian 4%, Kazak 3%, Tatar 2%, other. **Religions:** Official policy of the State is atheism. Russian Orthodox 18% (approx.), Islam (predominantly Sunni) 9% (approx.), other Orthodox, Protestant, Roman Catholicism, Judaism, Buddhism. **Education** (% enrolled in school, 1975): Age 6–11—of all girls 99%, of all boys 99%; age 12–17—of all girls 95%, of all boys 95%; higher education—in 1981–82 women comprised 52.2% of all students and were concentrated in humanities and biological sciences; in 1975 women were approx. 40% of engineering students, 33% of agricultural students, 62% of economics and law. In 1983 the government began pilot programs of sex education in secondary schools, to combat a rise in teenage pregnancies. **Literacy** (age 9–49 only, 1977): Female 100%, male 100%; reportedly lower among the older pop. **Birth Rate** (per 1000 pop., 1977–78): 18. **Death Rate** (per 1000 pop., 1978): 9.7. **Infant Mortality** (per 1000 live births, 1977): (est.) 35 (Soviet definition). **Life Expectancy** (1975–80): Female 74 yrs., male 63 yrs. (approx.).

GOVERNMENT. The USSR consists of 15 Union Republics, 20 Autonomous Republics, 8 Autonomous Regions, and 10 Autonomous Areas. The national government formally operates on a 3-branch, 1-party system. The Supreme Soviet (assembly) holds legislative authority and consists of 2 chambers: the 750-member Soviet of the Union and the 750-member Soviet of Nationalities are elected by citizens for 5-yr. terms. A conference of nominating organizations selects a single candidate; voting is mandatory. The Supreme Soviet elects a Presidium to preside over matters of State when the full Soviet is not in session; the chair is also known as the president. A Council of Ministers (appointed by the Supreme Soviet) exercises executive authority; its chair is the premier. Judicial authority is held by the Supreme Court, whose members are elected to 5-yr. terms by the Supreme Soviet. The Communist Party is the highest authority and the only legal party. The central organ of the Party is the Party Congress which is scheduled to meet once in 5 yrs. The Congress elects a Central Committee (consisting of 320 full and 151 candidate members), which in turn selects a Political Bureau (Politburo) and Secretariat to function between full sessions; the Secretariat is headed by the General Secretary, which is the pre-eminent position of actual power.

Women's Suffrage: Universal suffrage granted in 1917. Previous suffrage, even male, had been severely limited. Early Soviet policies based the franchise upon social class and contribution, thus extending fuller citizenship to some women while effectively disenfranchising others, including many middle-class women who had been politically active (the "bourgeois feminists"). **Equal Rights:** 1977 Constitution (Art. 35) states, "Women and men in the USSR have equal rights." **Women in Government:** Only 1 woman, E. A. Furtseva, has ever served (1957–61) on the Politburo. In 1981, 26.6% of 5002 delegates to the Party Congress and 3.1% of the Central Committee were women. Women are present in government primarily on local/regional levels, and in such areas as health, public welfare, education, and culture. Party membership is 24.7% female; there are no female ministers or ambassadors (1977).

ECONOMY. **Currency:** Ruble (May 1983: 0.72 = $1 US). **Gross National Product** (1980): $1212 billion. **Per Capita**

Income (1980): $4550. **Women's Wages as a Percentage of Men's** (1959–73): 65–70%. **Equal Pay Policy:** Labor Code (1918) and 1977 Constitution stipulated equal remuneration and established a system for labor classification of skills, qualifications, and wages. However, women are concentrated in low-prestige, low-paying sections of the work force. Professions in which females are concentrated are underclassified within the labor classification system. "Protective" labor legislation (1932, revised 1980) bars women from 460 occupations. **Production** (Agricultural/Industrial): Wheat, rye, corn, oats, potatoes, sugar beets, cotton, flax, cattle, pigs, sheep; metals, fuels, power, building materials, chemicals, machinery. **Women as a Percentage of Labor Force** (1980): 51%; **of agricultural force** 44%; **of industrial force** 49%; **of military**—no statistics obtainable, but women are present in combat and noncombat roles. **(Employed) Women's Occupational Indicators:** In a 1975 urban study, 40% of women with higher or secondary specialized education occupied "low-skilled" positions, compared to 6% of men; 1973 figures for a typical industrial city revealed that 66% of employed women held jobs classified as "low-skilled," 30% as "average," and 4% as "highly skilled." Women are 70% of doctors and 90% of pediatricians, but 6% of surgeons (1973). In 1961 women were almost 1/2 the agricultural labor force but held fewer than 2% of directorships of farms. **Unemployment:** No data obtainable.

GYNOGRAPHY. Marriage. *Policy:* Marriages must be registered with the State; *de facto* marriages were recognized legally only from 1926 to 1944. National family legislation (1968) added a 1-month waiting period to the marriage requirements and regulated marriage applications somewhat, owing to high incidence of marriages of convenience and fictitious marriages.* Minimum marriage age is 18 but may vary by 1–2 yrs. between republics. Marriage does not enti-

tle either spouse to economic support from the other unless disabled or unable to work; parents share child-support responsibility. Women were declared equal partners in marriage in 1917. Married women may keep their birth-name. Obstruction of a wife's choice of work or education is illegal. In 1983, Nikolaeva Tatiana, a USSR spokeswoman at the UN, said that equality in housework was a matter to be resolved at home "under the blankets"; she declared that due to biological inequality, a woman had to be feminine, a good housewife, and a mother, and that "husbands have to be cuddled. If people look to the forest, they will see [the inequality]: the female elks are lying down while the male elks are out looking for food." *Practice:* Women generally marry at approx. age 23. Despite some Party statements (but no legislation) on the advisability of dividing housework between spouses, women carry the double burden of employment and household duties, devoting 28 hours a week to housework compared to 12 hours by men.

Divorce. *Policy:* Freedom of divorce granted by decree (1917), written into republic family codes (1918), and further liberalized in 1965. Divorce is available by mutual consent without court suit (in the absence of minor children) with a 50-Ruble fee and a 3-month waiting period. Divorce by court requires a 10-Ruble filing fee, 2 reconciliation stages, a court hearing, and a second (registration) fee of 50–200 Rubles. Spouses split fees, and property is divided equally except when unequal division is in the interests of children or particular need of 1 spouse (e.g., disabled). A husband may not sue for divorce without wife's permission if she is pregnant or within 1 yr. after she gives birth. *Practice:* Registered divorces (per 1000 pop., 1976): 3.4 (for country as a whole; regional nationalities differ widely). An equal number of "divorces" exist *de facto* to avoid paying a fee unless necessary (e.g., when 1 partner wishes to remarry). Unofficial figures for 1981 put

* Marriages of convenience are entered into to obtain benefits (i.e., housing, residence permits, pensions) and are legal but frowned upon. Fictitious marriages (which are illegal) are enacted only in form, for much the same reasons of convenience, but the couple has no intention of having sexual relations or creating a family.

the divorce rate at 1 out of 3 marriages. Rates are highest in cities. More than half of all divorce actions are brought by women; husbands' alcoholism, adultery, and poor fathering/indifference to children are primary reasons cited.

Family. *Policy:* Childcare is supported partially by private and public funding; parents pay 15–25% of the cost. The Family Allowance Program provides State subsidies to families. Women in need receive monthly stipends until their children reach age 8 (as of 1974). Families with 4 or more children receive stipends (increasing per child) from the child's birth to age 5. Single mothers are entitled to this stipend for the first child (age 0–12). By a national decree (1981) lump-sum allowances are paid to women on the birth of first, second, and third children. Women are granted 112 days paid maternity leave (with an additional 14 days for abnormal pregnancies or multiple or difficult births), plus (as of 1981) 1 yr. with partial pay and 18 months–2 yrs. unpaid leave; leave counts as no interruption of employment and no loss of seniority. Nursing mothers are entitled to a shorter day with regular nursing breaks. A married woman with a sick child under age 14 may take 7 days leave per illness; a single mother may take 10 days per illness. Women who bear and raise 5 or more children are now entitled to retirement pensions even if they lack a complete work record, and to titles and medals as "Mother Heroines." *Practice:* As of 1976, creches, nursery schools, and kindergartens enrolled 12 million children (37% of pre-schoolers); 5 million were enrolled in seasonal day care, and extended day school for older children is growing. There are long waiting lists and only about 40% of all children under age 7 are currently placed. Facilities are frequently understaffed, with unsanitary conditions, illness, and insufficient food. Group day care and private babysitters are rare and expensive. The rights of pregnant women and new mothers are commonly violated and rarely protected by unions. Maternity leave is not available to graduate or post-graduate students.

Welfare. *Policy:* A comprehensive, State-sponsored, national insurance system provides income supplements, medical services, and retirement pensions (the last administered through trade unions). Women can officially retire at age 55, men at 60. *Practice:* Stipends are small. Retired women have severe financial problems owing to their longer life expectancy and to insufficient payments; this accounts for the high % of women over age 60 involved in crime (petty theft and especially the selling of home-brewed liquor) to supplement their incomes.

Contraception. *Policy:* Legal, although government policy is pro-natalist. *Practice:* No statistics obtainable. Contraception is almost unavailable; abortion is the *de facto* primary method of birth control (see **Education, Abortion,** and following article). **Abortion.** *Policy:* The USSR was the first country in the world with formally legalized abortion on request (1920). Made virtually illegal with severely limited grounds under Stalin (1936), it was re-liberalized in 1955 and is currently legal only in licensed State clinics through the first trimester, after which discretion rests with hospital staffs. Fees are low and may be waived in cases of need. Current rules (1983) authorize no more than 1 abortion every 6 months. Policy requires women to be counseled against abortion before being permitted the procedure. *Practice:* Official abortion rates (per 1000 women age 15–44, 1981): 80; abortions (per 1000 known pregnancies, 1981): over 500. International population-monitoring sources put the rates for 1970 at 180 per 1000 women age 15-44, and 700 per 1000 known pregnancies. Soviet women report that the average woman in the USSR has 6–8 abortions in her lifetime; the number can go as high as 20. State abortion clinics are known popularly as "butcheries"; the system is open to abuse by doctors and staff (see following article).

Illegitimacy. *Policy:* Family legislation of 1968 ties rights and responsibilities of children to certified descent rather than registered marriage. Men may acknowledge paternity or be court-declared legal fathers on proof of *de facto* marriage. Women can press paternity suits and claim child support until child reaches age 18. Limited State support for single mothers is available (see **Family**). *Prac-*

tice: In 1980 out-of-wedlock children accounted for 9–10 in every 100 live births. The social attitude toward out-of-wedlock children and their mothers remains discriminatory. **Homosexuality.** *Policy:* All laws abolished in 1917. In 1928 male homosexuality was reclassified as a "social danger"; in 1934 the Soviet Penal Code (Art. 134) established 5-yr. prison terms for men accused of homosexuality, 8 yrs. if act included violence, abuse of power, or pederasty. There are no laws on lesbianism. *Practice:* Strong social tabus against same-sex preference still exist. Women have been confined to psychiatric hospitals on the suspicion of lesbianism by neighbors or co-workers.

Incest. *Policy:* No specific laws, but punishable under Penal Code (Art. 120) as "depraved conduct." *Practice:* No data obtainable. **Sexual Harassment.** *Policy:* See **Rape.** *Practice:* No data obtainable. **Rape.** *Policy:* Illegal, punishable by 3–7 yrs. imprisonment. Rape "with violence" or threat of murder, rape of a minor, gang rape, and rape committed by a previously convicted rapist all bring heavier sentences. Taking advantage of a woman who is "dependent economically or occupationally" to compel her to have sexual relations is a crime punishable by 3 yrs. maximum imprisonment (Penal Code, Art. 118). If the rapist marries his victim, it may mitigate his punishment. Aid to a rapist (help in restraining or subduing a victim) is considered the equivalent of physical rape. The woman's prior sexual history and "moral character" are admissible in a rape case. The Penal Code makes no mention of marital rape. *Practice:* Only 10% of rape cases involved robbery; 75–80% of case defendants acted in groups averaging 3 or more men; 64–84% of cases involved defendants under the influence of alcohol (1976). It is est. that fewer than 2% of rapes committed are ever reported and that most Soviet women are victims of at least 1 rape or attempted rape in their lifetimes (1971). Rape accounted for 75–95% of all sex-crime cases (1968). Rape victims may elect for a closed courtroom. Social attitudes inhibit bringing charges; cases

rarely come to court and convictions are rarer. Judges seldom apply maximum sentences and often assign even less than the minimum sentence. **Battery.** *Policy:* No specific laws on spouse abuse. *Practice:* No statistics obtainable. Battery is a serious problem in the Soviet Union, closely related to the high incidence of male alcoholism. In cases of extreme abuse, a husband may be brought before local police and given a severe warning by the Procuracy, but prosecution is very rare.

Prostitution. *Policy:* Not illegal, but punishable under "parasitism laws" (see following article) by 1–2 yrs. imprisonment, or under the charge of other illegal acts (theft, etc.). Prostitutes also risk violating a law against spreading venereal disease, punishable by a severe fine or 1 yr. imprisonment. *Practice:* No statistics obtainable. In port cities, women working as prostitutes are often arrested, charged with theft, released, and frequently used by police as informers (see following article). **Traditional/Cultural Practices.** *Policy:* Polygyny, bride-stealing, bride-price/dowry, wife murder, and female sexual slavery have been illegal in the USSR since the Revolution. *Practice:* Strict legal enforcement is sporadic and these practices still occur in the largely rural areas of the Eastern Republics. Both *kalym* (bride-price) and *kaitarma* (reclaiming and holding the bride until *kalym* is paid) occur frequently under the cover of "Komsomol weddings"** with the complicity of village residents and officials. Although government campaigns are conducted to eliminate these practices, reports of female slave markets, private wife exchanges, and wife murder persist. In the Western Republics, particularly in the cities, incidence of tranquilizer-prescription abuse is on the rise, as is female alcoholism. **Crisis Centers:** *Policy:* No data obtainable. *Practice:* None.

HERSTORY. The earliest recorded Stone Age inhabitants of Russia were matriarchal river cultures. During the Iron Age the Amazons, female warrior tribes, lived among the Scythian and Sar-

---

** Elaborate "New Socialist Rites" conducted at Palaces of Festive Events and devised to combat and replace the power of religious rituals with secular ceremonies.

matian peoples of the northern Black Sea region. Even after patriarchal culture was established, some Slavic peoples still worshipped a sun goddess. During the Kievan period (10th century C.E.) Olga, regent for Sviatoslav, became the first Christian among the Kievan nobility. She later converted her grandson, Vladimir I, who established Christianity among his subjects.

Under Tatar/Mongol rule, the custom of *terem* (separate quarters and isolation from public view) for women came into practice. Queen Thamar ruled (1184–1212) the region of Georgia, which enjoyed its greatest expansion (including all of Transcaucasia) and a period of high culture under her hegemony. In the medieval period the Russian church expanded; the only woman recorded as having held a position of power during this period was Marfa Boretstraia, who was mayor of Novgorod.

At the onset of the Imperial period (17th century) Sophia, elder sister of Peter "the Great" (reigned 1682–1725), served as regent for her brother. Peter commanded the end of *terem,* brought women into court life, crowned his wife Catherine tsarina, and named her his successor. Catherine I was followed by a number of ruling tsarinas: Anna (reigned 1730–40), Elizabeth (reigned 1741–62), and Catherine II, "the Great" (reigned 1762–96), who introduced French culture to the court, extended Russia's territories to the south and west, increased opportunities for women's education, and named a woman, Princess Catherine Dashkova, head of the Academy of Sciences in 1782 and head of the Academy of Letters in 1783. Catherine's successor, Paul, established male primogeniture, precluding the possibility of another regnant tsarina and ending almost 70 years of female rule.

Elena Pavlovna (sister-in-law of the Tsar) and Nikolai Pirogov (a surgeon and educator) organized the first women's medical unit, which functioned successfully throughout the Crimean War (1853–56). Women's rights and serf emancipation emerged as political issues. Such women as Mariya Venadskaya began to link women's education with the need for women's work and independence.

The emancipation of the serfs (Emancipation Proclamation, 1861) inspired women to fight for their own liberation. Women from families formerly based on the serf economy sought employment; decrees of 1858 and 1860 established secondary education for girls. In the 1860's feminists began to articulate a program for improving the status of women. Their leaders (including A. Filosofova and N. Stasova) were educated women; their focus was economic and educational concerns, and they were partly responsible for women being admitted (1861) to universities. In 1863 the government revoked this right and many women went to Paris or Zürich to complete their education—among them Russia's first woman doctor, Nadezhda Suslova.

After the Emancipation Proclamation, when large numbers of women migrated to the cities but could find no work, feminists turned their energies to services for them. The Nihilist women, who had become active in the late 1850's, were part of a general movement composed less of organized political programs than of an ethos; the Nihilists insisted on personal usefulness, and experimented with communes and cooperative work ventures.

Women participated in student upheavals at the universities, and in propagandizing. The first radical literature to deal with women's issues was *Young Russia* in 1862; the first revolutionary manifesto addressed to women was issued by the Russian Revolutionary Society in Geneva in 1870. Many Jewish women and intellectual women became active in the populist movement both in the Russian colony in Zürich and in Russian propaganda circles (e.g., the Chaikovsty in St. Petersburg); the best known of the Zürich women was Vera Figner, and of the Chaikovsty women, Sofia Perovskaya. In 1872, after years of struggle, a medical school and a few women's universities were established. In 1873 a tsarist decree ordered the women studying in Zürich back to Russia and gave impetus to populist activities of the following year, which led to large-scale arrests. In 1877–78 the government mounted political trials in which these women leaders, contrary to government plans, won still more support. Beginning in the late 1870's terrorist circles came into action. Among their members was Sofia Perovskaya, who became the "first woman political" in Russia to be executed (for assassinating Tsar Alexander II in 1881).

In the early 1880's, under Alexander III, most radical activities were crushed. Later in the decade a few women became involved in Social Democratic circles and through the 1890's a new group of radicals, including Nadezhda Krupskaya (who married the Bolshevik leader V. I. Lenin), were active. In 1905 the first birth-control literature appeared. After the 1905 Revolution, with the promise of suffrage and democratic assembly, women's activism increased. While the older feminist groups largely continued to stress reforms, the new generation initiated the women's suffrage movement. The Russian Women's Mutual Philanthropic Society, inaugurated by A. Shabanova and A. Filosofova, was the chief organization of the original feminists and later joined the suffrage movement. The Moscow suffragists founded the All Russian Union for Women's Equality, followed by the League for Women's Equality, which petitioned the Duma and local councils for voting rights. Within the same year the Union had branches throughout Russia with its center in St. Petersburg, where, on Apr. 10, 1905, it called the first major political meeting for women in Russian history. In May the Union established its program of "seven-tailed" suffrage (equal, direct, secret, universal, without distinction of religion, nationality, or sex), winning endorsement from professional and trade unions and acceptance into the Union of Unions. The Women's Progressive Party joined the struggle in Dec. 1905. On Dec. 11, the government announced that the electorate for the Duma would not include women. Government suppression of radical movements intensified and the Women's Union was eliminated (1908). That same year, however, the Mutual Philanthropic Society organized the first All Russian Women's Congress.

Krupskaya had published *The Woman Worker* in 1900; by 1905 Alexandra Kollontai began speaking about feminism and in 1907 won support in the textile workers' union. At the 1908 Women's Congress, Kollontai led a Social Democratic delegation of workers, and later that year published *The Social Basis of the Woman Question*. In 1910 Inessa Armand and Nadezhda Krupskaya, along with Clara Zetkin (see GERMANY/ EAST), established an International Women's Day, first observed in Russia in 1913, and Kollontai drafted a maternity-welfare bill for the Mensheviks in the Duma. With the onset of WW I, women were again divided. The liberals and many Mensheviks supported the war, some feminists hoping that expressed patriotism would lead to women's suffrage. Kollontai joined with Lenin and the Bolsheviks in calling for peace and in 1914 published her pamphlet *Who Needs War?* By 1917 the desperate economic situation caused by the war had escalated; the food strikes of 1915–16 had multiplied.

In 1917 in Petrograd (on International Women's Day) women textile workers' strikes and bread riots actually initiated the Revolution. Women's suffrage was granted by the Provisional Government. A women's battalion was formed in May and other local women's battalions joined; some 5000 women had enrolled by the fall of 1917, and the battalion fought in WW I. In 1917 Tsar Nicholas was forced to abdicate; Lenin was driven into hiding and his former colleague Leon Trotsky was arrested. In Sept.–Oct. 1917, the Bolsheviks, with their land-reform programs and peace policies, gained support and won a majority in the soviets; Lenin returned to Petrograd (St. Petersburg), and on Oct. 25 Bolshevik forces arrested the Provisional Government. The Second All Russian Congress of Soviets was convened with a Bolshevik majority and Lenin as leader, and the new government declared itself a Communist State.

After the Second Revolution of 1917 (Oct.) and during the civil war, women again served in the military, holding high posts in Military Revolutionary Committees and Political Departments of the Red (Bolshevik) Army. Elena Stasova became Secretary of the Communist Party, Kollontai became Commissar of Public Welfare. Early legislation eliminated many remaining civil, legal, economic, and social injustices faced by women, particularly with regard to family status. Marriage and divorce laws were separated from religious jurisdiction. In 1919 the Zhenotdel (Women's Dept.) was formed, headed by Inessa Armand; it elaborated women's concerns to the new government and conducted massive education campaigns throughout the country. Mass unveilings by/of Islamic women were met with murders of women organizers, which became punishable counterrevolutionary offenses.

In the early 1920's in Bryansk province, women staged a sexual strike to resist husbands' brutality. Abortion was legalized (1920) and the Family Code (1926) extended recognition and protection to *de facto* marriages. Drought, famine, and the consequent introduction of the New Economic Plan (1921–22) led to high female unemployment and migration of women to urban areas. In 1932 the first "protective" labor legislation excluded women from a wide variety of jobs.

Under the (Stalinist) 1936 Constitution, equal rights were stipulated for women, but Stalinist policy and family legislation stressed women's role as child bearer. Abortion was made illegal except in cases of medical emergency. In literature, the dissident and feminist voices of Anna Akhmatova and Nadezhda Mandelstam articulated the political/personal conditions of women.

During WW II women entered many previously closed fields. Legislation of 1943, however, established sex-segregated education programs. The Family Edict (1944) made divorce difficult and expensive, ended recognition of unregistered marriages, and eliminated paternity suits, leaving women to bear full responsibility for children suddenly declared illegitimate. With the return of soldiers at the end of WW II, the number of women in positions of economic, social, and political authority was reduced drastically. Family codes were reformed under Nikita Khrushchev (who came to power in 1953), liberalizing abortion laws, easing divorce procedures, and re-establishing paternity suits. Nationally notable women of the period were few and included Valentina Tereshkova, the first woman cosmonaut in space (1963); Tereshkova is head of the Women's Federation (1983). Censorship, under Khrushchev and even more under Leonid Brezhnev, (in power 1964–82) inhibited dissident (including feminist) activities. In 1979 a few Leningrad women put out a *samizdat* publication, *Almanac, Woman and Russia,* launching the new Soviet feminist movement (see following article).

Following the forced exile in 1980 of 4 of the *samizdat* founders, pressure continued on those feminists still known to be organizing, particularly in Moscow and Leningrad. Natalya Lazareva and Natalya Maltseva were arrested (see following article). In 1982, feminist poet Kari Unksova, who contributed to the suppressed feminist publication, was run down by an automobile while preparing to emigrate. In Mar. 1983 the poet Irina Ratushinskaya was sentenced to 7 years imprisonment and 5 years internal exile for her writings.

MYTHOGRAPHY. Representative figurines of the female torso est. as dating back to Stone Age origin have been found in the Soviet Union, primarily along the banks of the Don River. The Don, the Dnieper, and the Kniestr are among the major world rivers (including the Danube and the Thames) with names based on that of the goddess Dona (or, variably, Dana, Danu, Tana, Thama, or Tiamet). This deity was one of the most widely worshipped forms of the Great Goddess. Vesua, from whose name the contemporary Russian word "spring" derives, was the goddess of spring among Slavic peoples. In the southeastern USSR, along the Turkish border (ancient Anatolia), evidence of a prehistoric and possibly matriarchal civilization has been found not unlike that in the famous site of Catal Huyuk in Turkey. The figure of Sophia (St. Sophia, or Haggia Sophia—

which means holy wisdom) persists from
its Byzantine origins as influence in the

Eastern Orthodox Churches, as does a
strong tendency toward Mariolatry.

THE USSR: It's Time We Began with Ourselves
by Tatyana Mamonova
(Translated by Rebecca Park)

Since childhood, the idea that we Russian women are the most fortunate women on earth
has been drummed into us: "You have been provided with everything. The Revolution
has eliminated all forms of oppression. Equality between the sexes has been achieved." I
was quite young when I understood these claims to be false. My understanding began
during the World War II evacuation. I was surrounded by women who, in the absence of
men, had been obliged to take over all male responsibilities. I saw what an arbitrary
distinction the usual division of labor was, and that women were perfectly capable of
assuming the responsibilities of men. But I soon learned that this crossover of duties
didn't work both ways: women might perform male tasks but men did not perform female
tasks. I noted, for example, that while I could be sent out to chop wood with my brother,
he would not be sent to wash dishes with me. The Revolution had not managed to
eradicate patriarchy.

In some ways women in the Soviet Union are plagued by the same problems which
plague women everywhere. We get little or no help from men with the housework and
childcare. We are not adequately represented in the political arena (women comprise 25
percent of Party membership; there are no women in the Politburo). We need safe,
effective, and readily available contraceptives, more day-care centers, better conditions in
maternity wards and abortion clinics, protection from domestic violence (there are no
rape or battery shelters, although rape is common and battery is at epidemic proportions), more effective enforcement of rape laws, more access to well-paying jobs, better
pensions for older women, financial assistance for single mothers, better conditions in
women's prisons, an end to prostitution,[1] etc.

In other ways, though, our problems are either uniquely Soviet or pertain only to
women in countries with totalitarian regimes (of the Right *or* the Left). At this stage our
biggest problem is one of information—both gathering it and disseminating it. We need
access to the media. The USSR is a huge country and the printed word is, for the time
being, the most effective way to communicate information. But all organs of the media
are controlled by the State, so we are forced to print and distribute feminist literature
clandestinely. We achieve this (though by no means easily) through an elaborate and
risky network, tapping the services of women who travel on business, in order to distribute literature, and using our own typewriters at home to print our materials with
multiple carbon copies. (The use of a photocopying machine for unofficial documents is a
criminal offense.) The other side of the coin is that we need access to information from

---

[1] Prostitution is officially nonexistent, yet prevalent. There are women who actually live in railway
stations, who take three rubles to have sexual intercourse with men. This is a very small amount of
money—worth one meal. They have nowhere to go. These women are not always accused of
"parasitism"—vagrancy or being without an acceptable job—because the State needs them to be
prostitutes. And also, of course, they try not to be caught by the police. [See Statistical Preface
preceding this article.—Ed.]

abroad and from other so-called socialist countries. It is our first priority to tear down this wall of silence.

Another major problem is KGB[2] harassment of women working in the feminist movement. Methods range from interception of mail and interruption of telephone calls to surveillance of apartments, searches, confiscation of typewriters and manuscripts, interrogations, threats, arrests, prison sentences, and exile. In this atmosphere, meetings, exchanges, and interviews can be risky, forcing women to meet secretly on the streets, in parks, and in cafés. Communications within the country and with contacts from outside are hindered considerably.

On the domestic front, women have to contend with hard-drinking husbands. Alcoholism is an extremely widespread problem among Soviet men.* Male alcoholism contributes significantly to domestic violence and is also a factor in the majority of rape cases. For the working mother, just the daily business of getting by is a constant struggle. Even obtaining food to put on the table can be a frustrating, time-consuming task, involving endless queuing in the stores. (Men are rarely seen in these queues.) Especially in the big cities, where housing is at a premium, families often have to live in very close quarters, frequently sharing a bathroom and kitchen with several other families. Rare is the household that has such luxuries as a washing machine, and many families manage without minimal conveniences like hot water. It is left almost entirely to women to contend with these day-to-day difficulties and to keep the family fed and clothed and the home clean.

Yet it must be acknowledged that women in the Soviet Union are better off in some ways than women in other countries. The goal of the Revolution was to make Russia an egalitarian society, and certainly women have gained more rights since the days of tsarist Russia. Soviet women have the right to abortion and divorce and to practice birth control. We have the right to an education equal to men's. We have entered every professional sector and receive the same pay as men (though ways are found to wiggle around this). We have clauses in the Constitution guaranteeing our equal rights. At least in theory, the State provides for its citizens—and in certain limited ways it has. It acknowledges its responsibility to provide housing and medical treatment, day-care centers, contraceptive devices, maternity homes, and abortion clinics.

The trouble is that the State fails to live up to its claims. For every example of gains made by women, a qualifying statement must accompany it. What good is the right to practice birth control if effective contraceptive devices are not available? What good are day-care centers if there aren't enough of them or if the childcare there is inferior or if the parent can't qualify to use them? What good is equal pay if the higher-paying jobs are reserved for men? What good is an equal-rights clause in the Constitution if women are excluded from the real arenas of power? What good are five- to seven-year prison sentences for rapists when women are made to feel so ashamed of being raped that only 1 percent of victims report the crime? And what good are legalized abortions if they are performed under inhumane and dangerous conditions? Because effective contraceptive devices are so difficult to obtain, there are many unwanted pregnancies. I have known women who have had up to fifteen abortions.

Abortions are performed in the State clinics, often on several women at a time, and frequently without anesthesia. In some clinics women are tied to the operating table. Effective contraceptives are almost unavailable in the USSR: diaphragms can seldom be obtained, there are no IUDs, and the pill is not manufactured. The contraceptives that are available (but even in Moscow and Leningrad cannot be found in drugstores) are vaginal suppositories, plus prophylactics for men, which the men don't like to use. The

[2.] Committee for State Security.

* Alcoholism is now a growing problem among Soviet women, as of 1983.—Ed.

scarcity of contraceptives is due to the Soviet Union's not considering women's needs an industrial priority; furthermore, the government wants (white) Russians to have more children, because of its racist concern about the greater growth of the ethnic populations in the other Soviet republics. An abortion by a private doctor, with anesthetics and antiseptics, is illegal, difficult to find, and very expensive (between 50 and 100 rubles). Sick pay is given to a woman who falls ill, but not to a woman in the hospital for an abortion. Many women terminate pregnancy by going to midwives, who perform simple curettage at an early stage or a full abortion later—but who do it with any instrument available, on a couch, and without anesthetics. Some midwives pour vodka into the uterus: this brings on a heavy hemorrhage and disinfects at the same time, but burns the uterus. Another widely used method is for a woman to drink all kinds of dangerous liquids—solutions of soap and manganese, or solutions of saffron and tobacco elixir—or sometimes a woman may get an intravenous injection of Synestrol to contract the uterus. Usually, there are severe complications. When the women goes to the hospital, she must face doctors who are trained to refuse her medical attention until she tells them who performed the illegal abortion. She is tortured, in a way. Many women die in such a situation.

Conditions in maternity wards also leave much to be desired. It was partly my own experience giving birth in a Leningrad clinic which moved me to propose the establishment of a free women's press so that women could at least air their grievances. I remember my stay at the clinic like a nightmare. Labor was difficult and protracted but they refused to give me any anesthesia. They wouldn't let my husband see me nor would they let me talk to him by phone. In ten days at the clinic I was not permitted to take a shower. The underpaid, overworked staff was cold and irritable. Such treatment traumatizes both mother and child. And my experience was not unique.

The idea of creating a free women's press had occurred to me as early as the 1960's, and I even naïvely mentioned the necessity for it to the KGB in 1968, when I was called in for questioning regarding participation in protests over the Soviet invasion of Czechoslovakia. I returned to the idea in 1975, the year my son was born. But it was not until 1979 that it was finally possible to gather together a women's editorial staff. That year the first issue of the *Almanac, Woman and Russia* came out—and the contemporary women's movement in the Soviet Union was launched.

Like all dissident material, the *Almanac* was circulated in *samizdat* (self-published) form. In the introductory remarks written by the editorial staff, we shattered the myth of the emancipated woman, and in the closing pages we appealed to women to send in stories and articles about their concerns and complaints. From the letters and statements we received, it was obvious that women were eager to express themselves about the pervasive sexism in the USSR.

From the beginning, the *Almanac* tried to address the needs of women from the widest possible range of backgrounds. We wanted to create a pluralistic, democratic movement. (The Soviet Union boasts a great deal about the progress of women, especially in its Islamic areas. They're always citing some woman who was born into the veil and was going to be sold into marriage—but along came the Young Communist League and then suddenly she became a member of the Presidium. Unfortunately, these women usually are just following the orders of men. The authorities like to put up one woman of a minority group to show off.) Not surprisingly, it didn't take the KGB long to react to this potential threat. I was the first to be summoned. (We hadn't indicated any of the editors' names in the *samizdat* but evidently the KGB had not forgotten my suggestions about a free women's press because they knew just where to come looking when the first issue made its appearance.) They tried to talk me out of continuing my work, saying it was bourgeois, divisive, irrelevant; I asked them why there were no women in the Politburo, why Valentina Tereshkova was the only token "known" woman in the USSR, why you have to be a "specialist" to gain access to the archives where Alexandra Kollontai's writings are kept (they did reprint one collection of her articles but it was enough to have written "party political and social journalists" on the title page to ensure that no one would read it). Then they tried to frighten me: they warned that I could be sent to prison or a work camp, that my husband could be punitively drafted, that my then-four-year-old son could be taken from us and sent to a juvenile-delinquency institution for "difficult children of difficult parents," that I could be forced into exile. I was very frightened, but by then more women had joined the editorial staff and that gave us all a renewed sense of strength.

At that point the KGB decided to take more radical measures. On December 10, 1979 (Human Rights Day and, coincidently, my birthday), I received a present from the KGB, an official warning: should a second volume of *Woman and Russia* appear, I would be arrested. But by then our *samizdat* feminist journal—copies of which had been smuggled all over the country and out to the West—had received considerable publicity in other countries, and we thought this ensured us some protection. In addition, we gave the next issue a different name, *Rossyanka,* hoping to mislead the KGB—but the KGB embarked on a series of repressive measures. A surveillance car was dispatched to follow me. My husband was summoned by the draft board and warned that he might be sent to Afghanistan. We were both called in by the police and attempts were made to accuse us of "parasitism" and "private enterprise." The KGB recruited neighbors in the communal apartment to intercept our mail and prevent us from using the telephone. Still, our underground editorial staff continued to function.

In our first issue we had published articles by Russian women and women of the neighboring republics of Estonia and the Ukraine. In the second volume we were able to expand our circle of contributors to include articles by women of Kamchatka, Central Asia, and the Urals. In March 1980, we produced the third volume, *Woman and Russia,* under its original title. It contained articles from women of Kamchatka, Central Asia, the Caucasus, and the Baltic republics. On July 20, 1980, two other feminists working on the *samizdat* (Natalya Malakovskaya and Tatyana Goricheva) and I were stripped of our citizenship papers and expelled from the Soviet Union.** I was flown with my young son and husband to Vienna. Since then, with the support of the women's movement in various countries all over the world, I have continued to act as editor-in-chief from abroad. Various volumes of the *Almanac* have been or are being published in seventy languages, some in their entirety and others only in parts.***

The welcome I have received abroad has been extremely encouraging. I have had the chance to travel to countries all over Europe, to Japan, Scandinavia, India, Africa, Canada, and the United States; everywhere I have met with support and friendship. None of us inside the USSR had any idea of the vast scope of the international feminist movement —yet the help from outside has been invaluable in sustaining the publication, and hence in sustaining the women's movement. Many people have helped get materials in and out of the Soviet Union.

The KGB, of course, hasn't been idle either. After having exiled what they thought were the "troublemaker ringleaders," they were furious to find that feminist *samizdats* continued appearing in the USSR. They went on a rampage to crush the feminist movement. Remaining members of the editorial staff were ferreted out and subjected to

** A fourth co-editor, the poet Yulya Voznesenskaya, who had previously tried to leave the USSR unsuccessfully, had accepted "voluntary exile" in May of that same year.—Ed.

*** French-, German-, and English-language editions have appeared, and others are in progress (see Suggested Further Reading at the end of this article for information about the US edition).—Ed.

searches and harassments. Books, typewriters, and manuscripts of the fourth issue were confiscated. The only feminist library in the entire Soviet Union was seized. One elderly woman who had worked for twenty-five years as a radio-communication technician had been helping us by keeping our journals, photographs, and correspondence in her home. Early one morning, KGB agents came and seized all our materials, as well as her own personal books. Far worse things have happened to others: two women (Natalya Lazareva and Natalya Maltseva) were arrested because of their work on the *Almanac.* Through the efforts of a huge international feminist campaign (letters, cables, demonstrations at Soviet embassies and consulates in many countries), they have since been released, but others have not been so fortunate. Space prevents a comprehensive listing of all the women and the many forms of harassment they have endured. Their stories are numerous and frightening.

In the fall of 1980, women in Leningrad put together the fourth issue under severe conditions of surveillance and repression. From my exile in France, I have been able to expand that issue to include material from other "socialist" countries, notably Czechoslovakia and Poland. At this point, enough material has been collected so that we can start to produce two separate publications, one to be dedicated to the creative arts *(Almanac, Woman and Russia)* and the other to concentrate on social and political problems *(International Bulletin, Woman and Russia).*

The feminist movement in the Soviet Union is a complex phenomenon. Because it is such a big country, encompassing so wide a range of ethnic, educational, and religious backgrounds, it is only natural that women bring to the movement a most diverse range of interests, values, and problems. The *Almanac* set out to embrace the widest possible set of needs, striving to create a pluralistic movement which would stress the common bonds women have with one another. But inevitably disagreements arose within the editorial staff as to what the priorities for the women's movement should be. After the first issue came out, three women (Natalya Malakovskaya, Tatyana Goricheva, and Yulya Voznesenskaya) left the co-editorship of the *Almanac* and the former two formed a group called Club Maria. Since their exile they have published a collection of writings called *Maria.* The members of Club Maria see the Russian women's movement as being in some ways related to the Russian Orthodox Church—which indeed may share a common adversary (the government) with women, but is hardly the solution to women's problems. Club Maria is especially preoccupied with religious freedom. We're all for religious freedom, but I fail to see how the act of unfettering the Russian Orthodox Church is going to significantly improve the lives of Soviet women. With its conservative stances on birth control, abortion, and homosexuality, the Church is just another patriarchy. The coupling of a specific religion and feminism also limits the scope of the movement and alienates women of other religious backgrounds and women who are atheists. Since the women of Club Maria hold views which are strongly nationalistic, the Russian émigré press was quick to champion their cause; they recognized an ally, i.e., a group which, however bravely it challenges the totalitarian regime in the USSR, does not pose a threat to the *patriarchy.*

Sadly, most Soviet women don't realize there was once a strong feminist movement in our country. It dates back as far as the 1860's, but it was the period just following the Revolution which looked especially promising. It was a heady time of experimentation and radical proposals; there were discussions about pay for housework, abortion was legalized, and "women's departments" were established to address the specific needs of women. Then, in the late 1930's, the dark period of Stalinism and the cult of personality began. The "women's departments" were shut down and abortion was again made illegal. The gains that had been made were wiped out and the whole subject of women's rights was branded "petit bourgeois" and dropped from discussion.

Ironically, it was World War II which opened up possibilities again. With the war raging, all able-bodied people were mobilized into action; women were called upon to assume every conceivable role previously reserved for men. (Incidentally, this partly explains why we have such a strong representation of women in the field of medicine.[3]) In the 1960's, there was a thaw under Khrushchev, when abortion was legalized again. But this period of liberalization didn't last long, and the 1970's saw a return to repression, persecution, and strict censorship.

The needs and rights of women have always been subordinated to one cause or another. First we were told that once the Revolution had been realized, women would automatically become the equals of men. When that failed to happen, a new rallying cry was heard: "Everything must be subordinate to the goal of collectivization." Then came World War II: "Make every sacrifice for the fatherland." And so it went—a history of sacrifice and unrealized dreams. The weakness of Marxism is that it counted on an automatic solution to "the woman question" and when this did not occur, the Party tried to sweep the problem under the rug by declaring the problem resolved and deeming any further discussion of it "petit bourgeois."

In truth, however, our emancipation is false. We were allowed into previously male-dominated professions (actually we were prevailed upon to do this work because it needed doing), but none of the *traditional* demands made of women were eliminated. Thus the Soviet Superwoman—a heroine at the factory, a model mother (preferably of several children) and housewife, and through it all, a beautiful and obedient wife.

Many people in the West look to the general dissident movement in the Soviet Union as a sign of hope for change. Unfortunately, women cannot take much heart from this movement. Like the revolutionaries before them, these dissidents see the women's movement as a mere distraction on their march to "more important" changes. With the exception of Andrei Sakharov, who has supported our feminist movement, the male-dominated dissident community either feels that our demands should be subordinated to their "greater" fight or else dismisses the idea of feminism out of hand altogether. So ardent are these dissidents in their pursuit of freedom that they can't even see the slavery in their own homes. (I myself suffered at the hands of the so-called nonconformist underground artists—who may be nonconformist in relation to their art, but when it comes to women, are very conformist indeed.) In our so-called classless society, women are the most oppressed class.

The roots of patriarchal thinking in Russian society go very deep. What feminists are fighting for first is a psychological revolution where men stop taking for granted the round-the-clock support system provided by women. Since women cannot expect help from either the State or the dissident movement, we must rely on ourselves. The first step in this process is to draw women out of isolation. This is a long and difficult process, but the *Almanac* has already broken the ground and the movement can only continue to grow from there. We rely heavily on feminists all over the world to help us spread the word, both inside and outside the country. Our circles and networks are expanding. As feminism gains support in other nations, so interest in Soviet feminism increases. We consider

[3] The Soviet Union frequently boasts about the statistic that approximately 70 percent of its doctors are women. But what they do not explain is that the medical system is structured around polyclinics; the average doctor in the USSR must see about thirty patients a day, and earns only 80 to 100 rubles a month—which means that no doctor can afford to work at only one job but must take patients at night (plus house calls). These doctors are women. The profession is no longer regarded as a prestigious one; on the contrary, the prestige and the good salaries are attached to the doctor-administrators and directors who *run* the polyclinics, and to work in the area of medical research —and these jobs are of course held by men.

the creation of an International Feminist Union (possibly attached to the United Nations or some other world body) to be essential for the monitoring of the position of women in the Soviet Union. We are also encouraged by the blossoming of feminist movements in other Eastern European countries. In women lies the real hope for the democratization of totalitarian countries and, eventually, for the elimination of war. The process has begun and there's no turning back now.

We will save humanity—but it's time we began with ourselves.

Suggested Further Reading

Goldberg, Rochelle Lois. "The Russian Women's Movement: 1859–1917." Diss., Univ. of Rochester, 1976.

Lapidus, Gail Warshofsky. *Women in Soviet Society—Equality, Development and Social Change.* Berkeley and Los Angeles: Univ. of California Press, 1978.

———, ed. and with an Introduction. *Women, Work, and Family in the Soviet Union.* Armonk, NY: M. E. Sharpe, 1982.

Mamonova, Tatyana, ed. *Women and Russia.* Boston: Beacon Press, 1984.

Tatyana Mamonova was born in 1943. She studied to be a pharmacist but was drawn to the arts—especially poetry and painting. She became involved with the "nonconformist painters" movement in Leningrad but eventually left because of the sexism in those groups. Since her forced exile in 1980, as punishment for having edited the first feminist *samizdat* journal in the USSR, she has been living in Paris with her husband, Genady, and their young son, Phillipe.

THE UNITED NATIONS

Editor's Note: One of the first-line defensive arguments thrown at feminists by male-controlled governments of individual nations is that such-and-such specific country has so many crushing problems it is "unreasonable" to expect the rights of half its citizens (women) to be a priority; for the present, feminists must look to international organizations, goes the argument, because there we will find a more idealistic structure less burdened by imperative crises, one that can afford to have a more open attitude. And, we are told, such global organizations have resources to enact change as a model for individual States.

It is for this reason that the following article is important, and that the United Nations is included in this book: this largest, most venerable, and most powerful of all international organizations, although not a patriarchal *country,* does share patriarchal attitudes.

These attitudes are exposed not only in the composition of diplomatic delegations, but in the over-all functioning of the General Assembly, the Security Council, the other Councils, the Judiciary, the Commissions, the Secretariat, and the Specialized Agencies—in other words, throughout the entire UN System. It is not coincidental that there is (as of 1983) not 1 woman among the 15 lawyers at the International Court of Justice, the 25 members of the International Law Commission, or the Human Rights Commission; there *is* 1 woman (out of 15 members) on the International Civil Service Commission.

Diplomats come and go, appointed by the changing governments of their respective countries. But the consistent, ongoing work of the UN is done via the Specialized Agencies, the Regional Commissions—and the Secretariat.

There has never been a woman Secretary-General.

As this book goes to press, then, the statistical preface on the United Nations Secretariat (all duty stations—New York, Geneva, Vienna, and Regional Commissions) must reflect the following dismal facts*:

Out of 26 Under-Secretaries-General, 1 is a woman.

Out of 22 Assistant Secretaries-General, 3 are women.

Out of 316 Division Directors (first and second level included), 16 are women.

Out of a total of 2582 persons in the Professional category (including levels 1 through 5), 959 are women.

In the General Service category, however, the numbers reverse interestingly. There are only 3450 men to 4591 women. The General Service category covers secretarial and clerical work.

In the Field Service, Security Service, Manual Workers, Dispatchers, Guides, and other such categories, male employees constitute 89.2%, females 10.8%. (Women are concentrated in "female-intensive" jobs—as Visitor Guides.)

The UN does stipulate equal pay for equal work. But since the majority of women hold lower-paid jobs, there is a salary differential in practice: at UN Headquarters, for instance, the average male salary (Professional and General Service categories) is $44,000 per yr.; the average female salary for those same categories is $27,000.

The economic inequity isn't the whole of the problem, though. The UN System reflects androcentric thinking in other ways: sexual harassment is a major issue which for years has been repeatedly raised by the Ad Hoc Group on Equal Rights for Women at the UN. Despite a poll that showed 80% of all employees strongly favoring adequate on-site child-care facilities, it was not until 1982 that the General Assembly allotted $100,000 toward the creation of such facilities—out of an annual budget that runs close to $700 million. And perhaps most distressing of all, the *de facto* policies in hiring and promotion, examined so incisively in the following article, have an obvious ef-

---

* These statistics are from materials made available by the Ad Hoc Group for Equal Rights for Women at the United Nations, on Mar. 8, 1983.

fect: women very rarely gain access to decision-making positions and therefore are unable to influence the System toward reform on all the above-mentioned issues—much less have access to influence UN Member-State government programs and to transform the world itself.

Fortunately, UN women have been raising these issues, daring to break the silence of bureaucracy and diplomacy by naming "impolite" realities.** Yet only when not just "the first" but many women Secretaries-General have been permitted to serve, when more than half (reflecting the global majority of women) of all Under- and Assistant Secretaries-General and Directors, Commissioners, and other policy-makers are women, when many women represent many countries as full ambassadorial delegates and not as beauty-pageant contestants,*** will there be a truly nondiscriminatory United Nations—*and* a truly effective one.

Feminists in the international women's movement have fantasized about women demanding Member-State admission to the United Nations—as a worldwide people, albeit a dispersed one. (It's a lovely, tempting thought. Women, after all, could claim Developing Nation status; we are emerging from male colonization everywhere.) But perhaps a more concrete "fantasy" would be for the United Nations to sign its own Convention on the Elimination of All Forms of Discrimination Against Women—and really implement it.

** Indeed, by doing so, these women challenge another UN "traditional/cultural practice"—a shockingly archaic one: United Nations Regulation 1.9 requires that all international civil servants (female and male) employed by the UN System swear a loyalty oath; in addition, they are bound by rules and regulations to avoid "any public pronouncement of a controversial nature" (ST/AI/190/Rev.1), to request permission before performing "acts relating to the purpose, activities, or interests of the United Nations" (Rule 101.6e, which can cover everything, including attending non-UN seminars, conferences, or any public gatherings), and to submit for advance clearance any and all writings (including even fiction) which might be published. To disobey any of these regulations is to risk disciplinary action, dismissal, and loss of livelihood (Regulation 10.2, Rule 110.3). True, the UN is supposed to be "above politics"; yet one might wonder at the peculiar double standard that permits diplomats, Member States, and power blocs to engage in politicking about hiring, firing, and promotion procedures, but prohibits an individual employee from attending a demonstration or press conference—or even publishing a poem—without prior clearance. One might also question how the issues of free speech, freedom of assembly, and freedom of the press came to be so muddied in a world organization that purports a commitment to human rights.

*** In 1983, plans to hold a Miss Nations United Beauty Pageant were obstructed by protests from women working at the UN; the pageant, to be held in New York, called for applicants "age 18–30, single, and citizens of the eligible countries," and announced that its search "for beautiful women from all over the world to represent their countries" would be a benefit project with part of the proceeds going to UNHCR, UNRWA, and UNDRO as UN refugee relief organizations. Only after intense objections from the Ad Hoc Group for Equal Rights for Women at the UN were plans for the pageant cancelled.

THE UNITED NATIONS: "Good Grief, There Are Women Here!"*
By Claire de Hedervary

In a world of hunger and misery, one can wonder why bother with the problems of relatively few women who are fortunate to work in secretariats of international organizations. As one high-ranking official recently told me in New York—and she seems to have said it quite seriously—"How can you worry about women in the United Nations; you are so much better off than your sisters in the poor countries!"

This, I feel, is a most pernicious argument. Obviously women officials should want their disadvantaged sisters to fare better, but can you imagine an official of the male persuasion being told: forget your career as long as your brothers in the poor countries are hungry—or, how can you think of a promotion when your brothers kill each other off in Afghanistan or El Salvador?

The situation of women in international secretariats can obviously be compared usefully to that of their *male* counterparts only, and this is indeed a worthwhile subject for investigation—not simply from the point of view of the individuals concerned but most important for the moral standing of the United Nations, for the image it projects to the world, its credibility, and the example it sets.

The situation of women in the UN in the 1960's had deteriorated to such a point that we were an endangered species. We were *fewer* in number than we had been in earlier years. Well-trained women with equal or even better education than their male counterparts were systematically kept out not only of the decision-making process but also at the working level of both the so-called Professional and General Service categories. This led to an increased consciousness—and considerable unrest—among the remaining women in the early 1970's.

Unfortunately, the initiative for greater equality did not come from the Administration of that time but from a small number of women and men who were forced to act on their own by the *in*action of those whose job it should have been to apply Article 8 of the UN Charter—which expressly forbids discrimination on the grounds of sex. The male leadership of the time behaved not unlike the great folk-hero Siegfried, who cavorts in nature, talks to the birds, befriends animals, vanquishes his enemies, and saunters through life with insouciance until he comes upon a sleeping form in battle dress. Thinking he has met one of his own kind, he leans over the reclining form (which turns out to be Brunhilde), straightens up, and states in total bewilderment—and to the accompaniment of appropriate orchestration—*"Das ist kein Mann,"* which roughly translated into modern UNese would be "Good grief, there are women here."

But the UN male establishment of the 1960's, just like Siegfried, got lured away from Brunhilde and continued in its total disregard of women as equal partners.

Accordingly, women had little choice but to band together and, with the help of a few enlightened men, start to agitate, publicize, make statistical and analytical surveys, hold panels and even rallies, bring pressure on the Secretary-General and delegations, and thus lay the groundwork for improving their lot.

* This article is an expansion of remarks presented by its author at the March 8, 1982, International Women's Day Roundtable Panel sponsored by the Ad Hoc Group for Equal Rights for Women and the UNIDO Staff Union of the UN Vienna International Center, Vienna.

In the 1970's the situation changed. Thanks to a number of pressure groups, and mostly the Ad Hoc Group for Equal Rights for Women at the United Nations,[1] women became "fashionable." It can safely be said that never has a subject been more legislated than the equality of women in international organizations. In addition to Article 8 of the UN Charter—which explicitly calls for equal opportunity in employment for women and men—numerous resolutions have been passed by the General Assembly, the Economic and Social Council, the Commission on the Status of Women, as well as reports by the Joint Inspection Unit and several UNITAR seminars. All these efforts culminated in the Bulletin of the Secretary-General (ST/SGB.154 of 8 March 1977), which, had it been implemented, would have eliminated much of the inequality and certainly the necessity of my writing these remarks. It is true that some of the reforms we worked for in the 1970's have in fact been realized: extension of maternity leave, changes in androcentric language in staff rules and regulations, an administrative circular on the permitted employment of both spouses—this last measure being equally advantageous to husbands. But even now, as we near the end of the UN Decade for Women, very little has actually happened *in* the United Nations System to improve women's situation, namely their recruitment and their placement into policy-making positions. The ingenuity of men in finding excuses for not recruiting and promoting women is truly impressive and is not unlike that of a child who can give a hundred reasons for not eating spinach.

In the 1970's the reasons (to cite only a few) were that women could not be found in certain professions and were not presented as candidates by their governments. As to the first excuse, they could not find women because they were not looking hard or intelligently enough, and as to the second reason, it was true that women were not presented by governments—but then the overwhelming majority of men occupying important posts in the Secretariat and the UN Specialized Agencies (WHO, FAO, ILO, UNESCO, UNICEF, UNIDO, etc.) had not been presented by governments either, but had walked in and applied for a job or been brought in by their cronies. Women, it was also said, were not mobile but tied down by families. This excuse however had to be abandoned, in view of the considerable number of men explaining why they could not move their families. Finally, it was said that "attitudes had to be changed": men were not ready to accept women as their colleagues on equal terms.

Nowadays, I believe nobody would seriously advance these arguments. Attitudes *have* changed. There is an awful lot of talk about career possibilities for women at the UN. There is a great deal of activity—on the surface—and much bustling: exchanges of views, interviews, recruiting trips. All this has actually resulted in the occasional recruitment of a woman. There also is a change of attitudes in managers of programs. Nowadays they continue not to recruit—but they at least have an intermittent pang of conscience in doing so.

But now in the 1980's, new and powerful obstacles have arisen: they have to do with the linkage of women's career opportunities to the question of geographic distribution. Those who are less familiar with the UN system should be informed that there are quotas for each Member State in the Secretariat. We have reached the stage at the United Nations where women are at least considered a part of the geographic distribution, a kind of 158th Member State. You recruit a Guatemalan, a Belgian, someone from Singapore— and then you also recruit a woman. There is at this time a considerable push to recruit from countries that are underrepresented in the United Nations, which of course is the right thing to do. But then the argument goes: "Let us recruit women from those countries that are underrepresented." This is called killing two birds with one stone. Great efforts are deployed to find women from Belize or the Maldive Islands (and these are only

[1.] Founded in 1971.

a few extreme examples), and should this by chance prove impossible then the argument is, of course, that women cannot be found. The reverse side of this coin is to refuse to recruit women in even junior grades, however highly qualified they may be, on the grounds that they are from an *over*represented country, while at the same time recruiting men at a high grade from the same overrepresented country on the grounds that their political savvy, their experience, or their personalities are so exceptional that they cannot be found anywhere else. Translated, this means that these men are in trouble with their governments, or simply that their governments want to unload them on the UN.

The writer Maurice Maeterlinck observed that "woman is mysterious—like everyone else." To women in the United Nations nobody is more mysterious than those who have to implement the legislated policies set down by various bodies. Although the necessary guidelines, philosophy, and apparatus already exist to bring the problem to a solution, there seems to be a blockage when it comes to implementation.

Women can improve their lot in a limited way by working simultaneously through different organs: The Staff Union, the administration, and through bodies that contain both—such as the Joint Advisory Committee, which deals with personnel policies of the UN itself, and the Staff Management Coordinating Committee, which does the same thing System-wide. The primary responsibility of these two bodies is, however, much broader than the issue of women working at the UN and Specialized Agencies, and therefore women's status often becomes a marginal issue or a political football. Working through the Union is a cumbersome procedure since their Council is often paralyzed by bloc politics and has become a kind of poor man's Security Council. The Administration is weak, has little or no influence on program managers, and has shirked its responsibility toward women by throwing the ball into the court of the General Assembly—which then passes one more resolution. Women's status, therefore, is only one example of the managerial problems which should be solved internally instead of being dumped into the lap of the General Assembly. After all, the Secretariat is supposed to be an independent entity "above politics"; its work force was meant to be based on skill, not political appointments; it was not intended to function as if it were a delegation—or a pawn for delegations. Nor should it be the reflection of the least enlightened governments' policies toward women. If improvements need to be brought about in the functioning of the organization in general, or in the conditions of women in particular, it is the organization that should give the good example to the governments. It is an essential contradiction to ask instructions from governments on problems that should be solved internally, and then fail to implement the recommendations of these same governments. The mandate of the Secretary-General is clear. He has all the powers necessary to implement Article 8 of the Charter, and as Chief Administrative Officer he has the right to see that his subordinates implement his directives. Yet there is a Byzantine quality to the system which allows subordinates to ignore his directives. Bringing pressure to bear sometimes helps. The Ad Hoc Group is one example of such pressure, and political expediency is another. In any case, it is a sad commentary that so far as women are concerned, progress is not based on constitutional provisions, logic, efficiency, and fairness.

As a delegate to the General Assembly in the Fifth Committee, I came across blatant discriminatory practices against women staff members by program managers, and I acquired a new insight into such managers' attitudes and practices. Women, I discovered, are generally placed in peripheral areas of the United Nations, often put in extra-budgetary posts which provide no security, no tenure, and no career development. One also discovers that some of the managers have not the slightest idea of the number of women on their staff and that some have totally blocked out of their minds the contents of the directives of the Secretary-General on equal opportunities for women and men. Some admit to never having heard of these directives at all.

But things *are* looking up. Each new Secretary-General brings fresh hope. A positive and simple step would be to pressure or even directly instruct program managers to *implement* Article 8 of the Charter, because the bottleneck is at their level. At the top levels, recently, a few appointments have been made—into impossible jobs where the visibility is high and the chances of failure even greater. It is openly stated that a certain job of this sort must go to a woman, "because it will look good in the statistics, and we absolutely need it." This is hardly giving much of a chance to women.

To those men who still wonder "What is it that women want?"—a word of reassurance. Women at the United Nations want not confrontation with men but cooperation. We do not want polarization but a sense of balance. We want not tokenism but an equal opportunity to contribute to the work of the Organization. Instead of reflecting the world's existing inequalities we would like to see the United Nations set an example of the highest order in observing the principles of its own Charter.

What we hope men will understand is that women colleagues are neither a threat to them nor a carbon copy of them, and that failure to involve women in the increasingly complex tasks of the United Nations is not only inequitable but a shameful waste of human resources.

Suggested Further Reading

Equal Times, periodical published by the Ad Hoc Group for Equal Rights for Women at the UN; available from the Secretary of the Ad Hoc Group for Women, United Nations, New York.

Nicol, Davidson, and Margaret Croke. *The United Nations and Decision-Making: The Role of Women,* 2 vols. New York: UNITAR, 1978.

Claire de Hedervary, a Belgian, was a staff member at the United Nations, New York —most recently as assistant director of the Political Affairs Division. She was chairperson of the UN Ad Hoc Group for Equal Rights for Women, of the Joint Advisory Committee, and of the Staff Management Coordination Committee. At present she is a member of the Belgian delegation to the General Assembly of the UN, where she represents Belgium at the Administrative and Budgetary Committee.

THE UNITED STATES
(The United States of America)

Comprised of 50 states; 48 are located on the North American continent, bordered by the Atlantic Ocean to the east, the Gulf of Mexico and Mexico to the south, the Pacific Ocean to the west, Canada to the north; Hawaii is in the North Pacific Ocean, and Alaska is on the northwestern part of the continent with Canada to the east, the Gulf of Alaska and the North Pacific Ocean to the south, the Bering Sea and Strait to the west, and the Arctic Ocean to the north.* **Area:** 9,363,353 sq. km. (3,615,191 sq. mi.). **Population** (July 1983): 234,193,000, female 51.3%. **Capital:** Washington, District of Columbia (D.C.).

DEMOGRAPHY. Languages (1980): English 89%, Spanish 5.3%, Italian 0.75%, German 0.74%, French 0.73%, Polish 0.38%, Chinese 0.3%, Greek 0.19%, Japanese 0.16%, Korean 0.13%, other (over 20 additional languages including Native American, Middle Eastern, and African languages). **Races or Ethnic Groups**** (1980): Euroamerican (white) 79.6%, Afroamerican (black) 11.5%, Hispanic surnames 6.4%, Asian and Pacific Islander 1.5%, Indian, Eskimo, and Aleut 0.6%, other 0.4%. **Religions** (1978): Protestant 54.7%, Roman Catholicism 37.2%, Judaism 4.3%, Eastern Churches 2.7%, Old Catholic, Polish National Catholic, Armenian 0.6%, Buddhism 0.04%, other 0.12%; approx. 40% of the pop. was not affiliated with a religious institution.

Education (% enrolled in school, 1981): Age 5-6—of all girls 93.8%, of all boys 94.2%; age 7-13—of all girls 99%, of all boys 99%; age 13-17—of all girls 94%, of all boys 94.3%; higher education —in 1982 women were 55% of 2-yr. college students, 53% of 4-yr. college and university students, and 39% of graduate students, and received 50.3% of B.A. degrees, 50.8% of M.A. degrees, and 32% of Ph.D. degrees; women were 94% of home-economics students, 84% of all health professions (but only 25% of medicine), 76% of education, 63% of (applied) fine arts, 45% of biology, 26% of physical sciences, 11% of engineering. In 1980, 40% of female students were age 25 or older. Education is free through 12th grade and compulsory for age 7-16. A 1972 amendment to the Education Act, Title IX, prohibits sex discrimination in hiring, educational programs, or activities at schools and universities which receive federal funding. The current (1983) administration (under Pres. Ronald Reagan) proposed rescission of all 1983 allocations ($5.78 million) to the Women's Educational Equity Act Grant Program, which promotes compliance with Title IX regulations. An Affirmative Action program promotes equal education opportunities, but in 1978 the Supreme Court ruled that strict numerical quotas (although not Affirmative Action itself) were illegal. **Literacy** (1977): Female 99%, male 99%; functional illiteracy (1975) 20%, female 23%, male 17%; white 16%, black 44%, Hispanic surname 56%, other 26%.

Birth Rate (per 1000 pop., 1982 est.): 16. **Death Rate** (per 1000 pop., 1982 est.): 8.6. **Infant Mortality** (per 1000 live births, 1980): Female 11.2, male 13.9; white 11, all other (including black) 19.1, black (only) 21.4. In 1981 infant mortality rates rose significantly (e.g., 33 per 1000 live births in Detroit, MI) in 34 urban areas among the poorest sector of the pop. **Life Expectancy** (1982 est.): Female 78.2 yrs., male 70.8 yrs.; (1980) white female 78 yrs., white male 70.6 yrs., women of color 74.5 yrs., men of color 65.6 yrs.

GOVERNMENT. Based on the 1787 Constitution. An elected bicameral Congress (a 100-member Senate and a 435-

---

* US noncontiguous territories include the Commonwealth of Puerto Rico, the US Virgin Islands, the Panama Canal Zone, Guam, and American Samoa.

** Statistics regarding racial and ethnic groups are cited here reflecting the terminology and categories in government statistics (e.g. "black," "white," "Hispanic surname," etc.).

member House of Representatives) holds legislative power. An elected president heads the executive branch and appoints a 13-member cabinet. Each state is governed by an elected bicameral legislature (except Nebraska, which has a unicameral legislature) and an elected governor; the 2 major political parties are the Democratic and the Republican. **Women's Suffrage:** 1919; after a 70-yr. fight, women won voting rights with the 19th Amendment to the Constitution (with the exception of those Native American women who, along with Native American men of federally recognized tribes, were not enfranchised until 1924); Afroamerican men had won suffrage in 1868. Women had first won local suffrage rights in 1869 (Wyoming Territory), and in 1893 Colorado was the first of 8 states to allow women to vote before 1919.

Equal Rights: No general legislation. The proposed Equal Rights Amendment (ERA) to the Constitution (see p. 706) was first introduced into Congress in 1923, gained approval in Congress in 1972, and failed to achieve ratification by 3 of the necessary 38 states by 1982; it was reintroduced into Congress in 1983; 1983 national polls showed that 62–69% of the pop. support the ERA. The pending Economic Equity Act was introduced into Congress in Mar. 1983; it would make it easier for women to become fully vested in private pension plans, make it impossible for 1 spouse to sign away an option for survivor's benefits without the other's consent, allow homemakers to open tax-exempt IRA accounts equal to those of employed spouses, provide tax credits to employers who hire recently divorced or widowed homemakers, allow the same zero-tax bracket amount for single heads of households as for jointly taxed couples, increase tax deductions for expenses for dependent care, create a clearinghouse for childcare information, prohibit all discrimination in insurance plans on the basis of sex, race, color, religion, and national origin, require federal depts. and agencies to identify all laws and policies which result in different treatment based on gender, strengthen mechanisms for collecting overdue child-support payments. **Women in Government** (1983): Women

hold 4% of all elected posts and are 2% of the Senate, 5% of the House of Representatives, 13% of state legislators, 8.7% of mayors of major cities; there are 1 woman governor, 3 lieutenant governors, and 3 cabinet members, Elizabeth Dole (Secretary of Transportation), Margaret Heckler (Secretary of Health and Human Services), and Jeane Kirkpatrick (Ambassador to the UN). In 1981 Sandra Day O'Connor became the first woman Supreme Court justice; women comprise 9% of the federal judiciary (1983). The National Women's Political Caucus is a bipartisan nongovernmental organization focusing on women running for office and on electoral issues; the Congressional Women's Caucus (Senate and House, also bipartisan) focuses on legislative issues.

ECONOMY. Currency: US Dollar. **Gross National Product** (1983, 3rd quarter): $3360.3 billion. In 1980, 52.7 million women participated in volunteer work valued at $18 billion which was not calculated into the GNP; in 1975 the est. value of unpaid housework would have increased the GNP by 48%. **Per Capita Income** (1983, 3rd quarter): $10,075; in 1980 more than 30 million people lived below the poverty level ($9320 per yr. for a family of 4); 77.7% of the poor are women and children. **Women's Wages as a Percentage of Men's** (1983, 3rd quarter): Women employed fulltime earned 64.7% of the median weekly income for male fulltime workers age 16 and older (but 30% of employed women work part time, 1981); 65% for white women, 60.3% for black women, 54.6% for Hispanic women; in 1981, for elementary-school teachers 82%, for lawyers 71%, for engineers 68%, for clerical workers 67%, for sales workers 52%. As of 1983, the female median income was $12,000 (compared to $20,260 for males). **Equal Pay Policy:** 1963 Federal Equal Pay Act stipulated equal pay for equal work, and Title VII of the 1964 Civil Rights Act made it illegal for employers and unions to discriminate in "terms, conditions, and privileges of employment" on the basis of sex; however, 80% of employed women are in sex-segregated, low-paying, low-status, low-benefit, "pink-collar" jobs, and 2/3 of all part-time workers are female. The National Institute of Women Working "9 to 5," has won equal-pay suits totaling more than $3 million in back pay and pay raises for women. **Production** (Agricultural/Industrial): Grains, cotton, tobacco, fruits and vegetables, dairy products, livestock; heavy and light machinery, steel, shipping, aviation, automobiles, appliances, packaged food products, textiles, clothing, electronics.

Women as a Percentage of Labor Force (1982): 43%; **of agricultural force** 19.9%; **of industrial force**—no general statistics obtainable (of manufacturing 33%); **of military** 9% (active duty); army 9.4% (12% of whom are officers, including 2 out of 199 brigadier generals); navy 7.22% (13.3% of whom are officers, including 2 out of 130 rear admirals); air force 10% (15.4% of whom are officers, including 2 out of 172 brigadier generals); marines 4.2% (6.6% of whom are officers, but no women are among the 33 top-ranked officers); women are not permitted in combat roles but serve mainly as clerical, communications, and medical personnel. In 1983, Sally Ride became the first US woman astronaut in space (see USSR). In 1982, 62% of women age 18–64 were in the work force; in 1981 almost 50% of mothers with children under age 6 and 66% of mothers with children age 6–17 were employed; in 1981, 45% of employed women were single (divorced, widowed, never married) and self-supporting with dependent children.

(Employed) Women's Occupational Indicators: Of physicians and dentists 14.6%, of lawyers 15.5%, of non-farm managers and administrators 28%, of sales workers 45%, of service workers 62% (health services 90%, protective services [police, fire] 11%), of clerical workers 80.7%—of secretaries 99%, of bank tellers 92%, of telephone operators 92% (1982); of blue-collar workers 18.6%, of college and university professors 35.2%, of reporters and editors 50.2% (1981); only 1% of employed women held managerial positions (1982). An Affirmative Action program for women and minorities applying to companies with federal contracts was established by the 1965 Executive Order 11246 (amended 1968); the current

(1983) administration has weakened wage-discrimination and sex-segregation guidelines substantially. **Unemployment** (official civilian rates, all workers age 20 and older, 1983): 8.9%, female 8.1%, male 9.6%; white 7.9% (female 6.9%, male 8.4%), black 18.1% (female 16.5%, male 19.5%), Hispanic 13.8% (no rates by sex obtainable).

GYNOGRAPHY. Marriage. *Policy:* State laws govern marriage. Minimum marriage age without parental consent is 18 in 47 states and Washington, D.C., 19 in Nebraska and Wyoming, and 21 in Mississippi and Puerto Rico; parental consent is not required in Delaware and Georgia if the woman is pregnant or the applicants are the parents of a child. Marriage age with parental consent is the same for females and males in 35 states and Washington, D.C. (ranging from 14 to 18); in KY and WV there is no minimum age; it is 13 for females in NH, and 14 in AL, NY, and SC. The Married Women's Property Acts passed during the 19th century established varying degrees of property rights. Currently, property and legal domicile rights vary by state; married women generally have rights to own and dispose of their own property and to sue and contract independently; however, in some states, the husband's permission is still required. After marriage, a woman can keep her birth-name or add/adopt her husband's. The 1974 Federal Equal Credit Opportunity Act, as amended, prohibits discrimination in access to credit on the basis of sex or marital status. Title VII of the 1964 Civil Rights Act prohibits discrimination in employment on the basis of marital status; the 1978 Pregnancy Discrimination Act, on the basis of pregnancy. *Practice:* Female median age at first marriage (1982): 22.3; women age 15–44 in union (1982): 56%. As of 1982 an est. 10% of women never marry (an increase of 100% since 1970); in 1980, 3% of all households were composed of heterosexual cohabiting (nonmarried) couples (a 400% increase since 1970).

Divorce. *Policy:* Legal. In 1981, 48 states, Washington, D.C., and Puerto Rico had no-fault-divorce provisions in addition to such grounds as adultery, desertion, cruelty, bigamy, refusal of sexual relations, etc., which vary by state. In 1981 courts in 34 states and Washington, D.C. had the authority to divide marital property upon divorce; in the "community property" states (AZ, CA, ID, LA, NV, NM, TX, WA) and Puerto Rico, each partner is assumed to own 1/2 of all property, but courts must make a "just and equitable" division. In 1983 courts in 31 states were required to consider the value of a homemaker's labor as a contribution; 30 states had specific laws supporting joint custody of children if in the child's interest. In joint legal custody arrangements the child lives with 1 parent but the other has an equal voice in decisions affecting the child, and required child-support payments are often reduced. In joint physical custody arrangements, both parents are responsible for care of the child and support payments are further reduced. Alimony payments are court-determined, according to need and the ability to pay; in 1977 alimony was awardable to husbands as well as wives in 29 states. The 1971 Uniform Marriage and Divorce Act suggests alimony based on the need for training to enter the work force. State agencies are empowered to collect overdue child support. *Practice:* Divorces (per 1000 pop., 1980): 5.2; in 1980 there was 1 divorce for every 2 marriages; in 1982, 8% of females over age 15 were divorced; the divorce rate doubled between 1970–80. In 1981, of the over 8 million women raising children alone, only 59% had been awarded any child support (of these, 72% actually received payment, and only 47% received the full amount). Average payments totaled $2106 per yr. but 60% received less than $1500 (often to be used for more than 1 child). After 1 yr. of divorce, an average woman's income drops 73% and a man's rises 42% (1982). Ninety percent of children are in their mothers' custody; 90% of joint custody cases are awarded for legal and not physical joint custody, and therefore can permit the spouse without physical custody (primarily fathers) to interfere, cut support payments, etc., but assume no real responsibility. Fathers who genuinely seek custody rights are awarded sole or joint physical custody in 2/3 of all cases.

Family. *Policy:* Title VII of the 1964 Civil Rights Act (through the 1978 Pregnancy Discrimination Act) requires employers to apply the same standards to pregnancy as to any other temporary "disability"; e.g., a worker is not fired and is reinstated with continuing seniority and benefits. As of 1981, Massachusetts and Montana laws mandated that employers grant maternity leave (8 weeks in MA and a "reasonable" period in MT); 5 states (CA, HI, NJ, NY, RI) plus Puerto Rico have temporary disability insurance laws which cover pregnancy. A section of the pending Economic Equity Act (see **Equal Rights**) would guarantee the right of mothers and fathers to a 1-yr. employer-approved leave to have a child and a 5-yr. general leave to raise a child or attend school without losing most pension benefits. Some federal funding (Title XX Block Grants) for childcare is available to low-income families. *Practice:* In 1982 the average family size was 3.25; white 3.19, black 3.65, Hispanic 3.89. In 1982, 20% of all households were people living alone, 25% were composed of nonrelated members, 27% were maintained by women either alone or as partners in marriage, 15% of all families and 90% of single-parent families were headed by women, 55% of all children had employed mothers; in 1980 only 28% of all families were composed of an employed father and a fulltime homemaker mother, yet women still did 70% of housework. In 1982, 40% of children with employed mothers were in home day care with a sitter and 40% were in family day care with 4–6 other children in a sitter's home; there are a small number of workplace childcare facilities. Title XX Block Grants were cut by 21% in 1981, and 32 states were providing less childcare to the poor in 1983 than in 1981. There are some company-sponsored maternity-leave programs, but few are paid. Women's-movement co-op childcare centers exist with no federal or state aid.

Welfare. *Policy:* Federal programs include Social Security Insurance (benefits based on wages earned and length of employment to those over age 65, widows over age 60 or with young children, disability insurance, and a death benefit),

Supplemental Security Income (SSI, benefits for the very poor, disabled, blind, and elderly not receiving Social Security —approx. $122 per month), Aid for Families with Dependent Children (AFDC, "welfare" to low/no income families with children), Food Stamps (food subsidy to low-income persons), Special Supplemental Food Program for Women, Infants and Children (WIC, food supplements and medical care to pregnant and nursing poor women and children under age 5), child nutrition programs, Low Income Energy Assistance (heating cost subsidies), Medicare (medical insurance for the elderly), Medicaid (medical insurance for low-income persons), federally subsidized housing for low-income families, Legal Services Corp. (free and low-cost legal services to the poor), Social Services Block Grants (may be used by states to fund social services), Unemployment Insurance, and Job Training programs. Private and public employers may also provide pension, health insurance, disability, and life insurance plans.

Practice: Social Security pays much lower benefits to women, who work in low-paying, high-turnover jobs and who leave the job market to have and raise children and care for sick or elderly family members; in 1983, 60% of the elderly (over age 65) and 74% of the elderly poor were women; the poverty rate is 18.6% for elderly women and 10.5% for elderly men; women are 85% of elderly poor living alone. In 1982 avg. Social Security payments were $355 per month for retired women employees and $438 per month for retired male employees; the 1979 poverty level was $3472 for a single elderly person and median income for black women was $2671, for Hispanic women $2655. Only 10% of women and 27% of men over age 65 received any private pension and the avg. income from pensions and annuities was $2186 for women and $3657 for men (1979); in 1981 the median income from all sources for women over 65 was $4757, for men $8173. Women comprise 73% of the 1.7 million elderly poor receiving SSI (1981). In 1983 over 10 million families were headed by women; in 1982, 36% of all female-headed households and 56.2% of

black female-headed households were at or below the poverty level. In 1983, 20% of all children and 50% of black children were living in poverty; 1/2 of all black children live in female-headed families (over 66% of whom—3 million children —live in poverty).

Of all 11 million AFDC recipients, 94% are women and children (1983); AFDC awards to a family of 4 est. at $0.43 per person per meal; the program has been cut in funding by 24% from 1981 to 1984. Skills-training programs for AFDC mothers have been replaced by work requirements. In 1983, 66% of 22 million Medicaid recipients are AFDC women and their children; in 30 states children in 2-parent poor families are not eligible for Medicaid, and 2-parent poor families can qualify for AFDC in only a few states. Food-stamp recipients are 85% women and children; the program has terminated over 1 million recipients from 1981 to 1983 and reduced aid to several million more; emergency food services (soup kitchens, etc.) experienced a 50% greater demand in 1982–83 largely because of the cut in food stamps. In 1983 approx. 2.34 million women are served by the WIC nutritional and medical program; an additional 7 million who meet the low-income and high health-risk requirements cannot be helped because WIC funding was cut 30% in 1981–82; as of Jan. 1983, 480,000 women and children had lost health services. Funding for immunization of children against dread diseases was cut 50% (1981–82). School Lunch funds were cut 35% in fiscal 1982, eliminating 3 million children. In federally subsidized housing, 68% were female-headed households (1981); 50% of public housing and 40% of assisted units were occupied by the elderly, 75% of whom lived in female-headed households (1983). There were more than 2 million households on waiting lists for public housing (1982); budget appropriations have been cut 80% (1980–83). Low Income Energy Assistance recipients are 85% elderly or female-headed households; in the 1984 budget the Reagan administration proposed including the program in the Social Service Block Grant at 1/3 lower funding level. The administration has proposed elimination of all funding for legal services to the poor in every yr. (1981–84). In 1981 at its highest funding level, the Legal Services Corp. could not meet 80–85% of the legal needs of the poor; 67% of clients are women seeking help with housing, child support, divorce, battery, termination of AFDC or Food Stamps, etc.

Medicare covers 25.7 million elderly people (60% of whom are women) for 60% of their medical costs, not including many essentials (e.g. dentures, glasses). Hospital costs are high; in 1981, $287 billion was spent on health care (avg. $1225 per person). As of 1983 various insurance industry practices caused a woman to pay $17,372 more for life, health, disability, and auto insurance than a man. In 1982, although programs for the poor amounted to 18% of non-defense spending, 44% of budget cuts were from these programs. (If one spent $1 million a day for 2000 yrs. it would equal ½ of the administration's proposed defense budget of $1.5 trillion for 1983 to 1988.) In 1982 the National Advisory Council on Economic Opportunity projected that if current trends continue, the entire poverty pop. will be composed of women and children by the yr. 2000. **Contraception.** *Policy:* Legal. The Food and Drug Administration (FDA) approved use of the pill in 1960. Voluntary sterilization is legal and is funded for low-income women by Medicaid at 90% of cost. In Dec. 1983, the FDA was reconsidering approval of the use of the controversial injectable Depo-Provera. *Practice:* Women age 15–49 using contraception (1982): 92%; methods used (1982) pill 29.9%, female sterilization 20.2%, male sterilization 14.6%, condom 13.5%, IUD 6.9%, diaphragm 5.7%, vaginal spermicide 4.5%, withdrawal 2.7%, rhythm 1.8%, douche and other methods 0.6%. A 1982 national study showed that low-income women are more likely to be sterilized, Afroamerican women are more likely to use the pill and less likely to choose sterilization than Euroamerican women, and religious beliefs have very little impact on contraceptive practices. By 1979, 37.9% of Puerto Rican women of child-bearing age had been sterilized in US government programs and clinics, and by 1982, 41%

of Native American women had been sterilized, often without their consent.

Abortion. *Policy:* In 1973 the Supreme Court legalized abortion on request when performed by a licensed physician during the first trimester of pregnancy; states may enact regulations in the second trimester to protect the woman's life/health; in the third trimester, states may regulate or prohibit abortions except when the woman's life/health is in danger. In 1976 Congress limited Medicaid funding for all abortions not necessary to save the life of the woman or in cases of pregnancy resulting from rape or incest (upheld in 1980); in 1981 Congress eliminated federal Medicaid funding in cases of rape and incest (only AL, CA, CO, HI, MI, NY, NC, OR, WA, and Washington, D.C. continued to fund Medicaid abortions on request; CT, MA, NJ, and PA fund those Medicaid abortions deemed "medically necessary," 1984). In June 1983 proposed legislation which would have resulted in the recriminalization of abortion failed to gain ⅔ Senate approval. In Nov. 1983 Congress voted not to cover abortion in health-insurance plans for federal employees; unions are contesting the law. *Practice:* Abortions (per 1000 women age 15–44, 1980): 29.3; white 24.3, all others 56.8; in 1983 approx. 30% of known pregnancies were terminated by abortions. In 1980, 1,553,890 abortions were reportedly performed; 30% involved women under age 20 and 79% involved single women; 91% were performed during the first trimester; 18–23% of women eligible for Medicaid who wanted abortions were unable to obtain them because of lack of funds. Before 1973, over 1 million abortions were performed illegally each yr. A highly organized anti-choice movement continuously presses for restrictive legislation at federal and state levels and has vandalized clinics providing the procedure. The National Women's Health Network is 1 of many activist groups working to further liberalize laws on reproductive freedom.

Illegitimacy. *Policy:* In 1973 the Supreme Court ruled that all children have the same rights to support by their parents regardless of the parents' marital status, but mothers must file and win paternity suits (usually through blood-test results) to gain child support from fathers. State-imposed time limits on when a mother or child could sue were overturned by the Supreme Court in 1983. In many states inheritance rights depend on prior legal recognition of the child by the father. *Practice:* In 1980, 18.4% (665,747) of all births were out of wedlock; 40.8% were born to females under age 20; out-of-wedlock births to teenagers rose 26.5% between 1970–80. The number of never-married mothers heading families rose by 367% from 1970–82 (1.09 million families in 1982). Women can rarely afford to file paternity suits and receive very little support from the fathers. A small but growing number of single women are choosing to have children out of wedlock. Some lesbian couples also are choosing to have children through artificial insemination (est. 1500 births per yr., 1980).

Homosexuality. *Policy:* As of 1983, 26 states had no restrictions on adult consensual sexual acts; in other states, sodomy, oral-genital sex, and/or "unnatural sex acts" are illegal; sodomy is considered a felony in some states. As of 1982, 40 municipalities, 9 counties, and 5 states protect some civil rights of homosexuals (public employment, public accommodations, private employment, housing, education, real-estate practices, credit, etc.). Wisconsin passed the first comprehensive statewide same-sex-rights bill in 1982. A national gay civil-rights bill was introduced into Congress in 1976; although it has gained support, it has not yet (as of Jan. 1984) been brought to a vote. The military considers same-sex acts grounds for "less than honorable" discharge and loss of benefits. *Practice:* An est. 10% of the pop. exercises same-sex preference (1982); in 1978 there were an est. 1.5 million lesbian mothers with children in their homes (also see **Illegitimacy**); however, lesbian mothers lose 80% of custody battles in lower courts, and few have the resources to appeal their cases. Greater acceptance exists where there are large lesbian/gay communities, but antihomosexual violence and harassment are common. The National Gay Task Force, the National Coalition of Lesbian Women, the Lesbian Mothers' National Defense Fund, Custody Action for Lesbian Mothers, etc., are active civil-rights advocates.

Incest. *Policy:* Parent-child and brother-sister sexual relations are illegal in all states; in some states incest laws extend to uncle-niece and aunt-nephew sexual relations. Penalties range up to 15 yrs. imprisonment. The Child Abuse Prevention and Treatment Act provides federal funding for programs at the state level. *Practice:* In 1982 there were 953,120 reports of child neglect and abuse; 7% of substantiated cases in 1981 involved incest, rape, molestation, or sexual exploitation, but an est. 75–90% of cases are unreported. An est. 25% of women have experienced an unwanted sexual encounter with a male adult before age 13, and 40–50% of schoolchildren experience such an encounter with an adult (1983). In 1978, approx. 70% of young prostitutes and 80% of all female drug abusers were incest victims. It is est. that 80% of child sexual assaults are committed by a family member or family friend, that 80–90% of assailants are male, and that 87% of victims are female (1980). There is a lack of treatment centers and alternative placement centers, and courts and adults often discredit the testimony of children. The National Center for Child Abuse and Neglect and the Children's Defense Fund are information and action resources. Feminists have established refuges and promoted public education. **Sexual Harassment.** *Policy:* Illegal (Title VII, 1964 Civil Rights Act); the 1980 Equal Employment Opportunity Commission guidelines state, "Unwelcome sexual advances, requests for sexual favors, and other verbal or physical conduct of a sexual nature constitute sexual harassment." All employers are liable to be sued for sexual harassment committed by employees. Unions are required to represent sexual harassment grievances of any 2 workers protesting unfair working conditions. Victims can sue for back pay and damages if they are fired or not promoted, and they are eligible for unemployment benefits if the harassment has forced them to quit. *Practice:* Incidence of sexual harassment (depending on how defined) ranges from 42–90% of employed women; in 90% of cases a male harasses a female (although EEOC guidelines recognize female-male and same-sex harassment). Settlements have been as high as $100,000, but the majority of women suffer in silence, afraid to lose jobs or promotions. A 1981 government study revealed that the cost of sexual harassment in the federal work force (owing to low productivity, low morale, sick time, and turnover costs) is $95 million per yr. Working Women's Institute in NY is the national information clearinghouse on sexual harassment.

Rape. *Policy:* Illegal in every state, but definitions and penalties vary. In 1974 Michigan passed a model law which removed the need for witness corroboration and the requirement or necessity to prove force or "resistance to the utmost"; in addition, it included a "rape shield" measure prohibiting the use of a victim's sexual history not directly involving the accused rapist. Minnesota and California also have model rape laws and such laws are pending in some other states. Legislative reforms are shifting the burden of proof from the victim. In 1977 Oregon became the first US state to make marital rape illegal. In 1981 husbands and cohabitors could be charged with rape of their partners in 10 states without restrictions, and in an additional 27 states if they were living apart or legal proceedings for divorce/separation were under way; in 9 states husbands could never be charged with rape of their wives. By 1983 in 19 states a husband could be prosecuted under the same laws as any other man (AR, CA, CT, FL, GA, IA, KS, MA, MN, MS, NE, NH, NJ, ND, OR, VA, WA, WI, WY).

Practice: In 1982 there were an est. 65 reported rapes per 100,000 women; in 1981, 81,536 rapes were reported. The actual incidence is est. at 10–35 times the number reported. The feminist network of rape-crisis centers estimates that 1 out of every 3 women will be raped and that a woman is raped every 3 seconds; Federal Bureau of Investigation findings (1980) reported 1 rape every 6 minutes, adding that only 60% of all rapes are reported; they did not factor marital rape into their statistics. Arrests were made in 38% of reported rape cases (1980). At least 50% of all rapes are committed by acquaintances of the victims. By extremely conservative estimates 14% of wives are raped by their husbands (1978), and from 2 million to 40 million such rapes occur each yr. (figures depend on definition). In California, where marital rape has been illegal since 1980, husbands were convicted in 43 of the 56 cases which went to court. Rape is also a serious problem in prisons and psychiatric hospitals. Since the early 1970's feminists have campaigned to expose the prevalence of rape, to reform hospital, court, and social services, and to educate the public. Because of women's-movement pressure, many urban police departments have special rape sections staffed by female officers, so as to create a less intimidating atmosphere for a victim. Annual anti-rape "Take Back the Night" marches are now common in many cities.

Battery. *Policy:* Wife battery was first outlawed in Alabama and Massachusetts in 1871. As of 1983, specific legislation against wife-beating exists in 10 states. Unless extreme, it is usually classified as a misdemeanor. In 43 states and Washington, D.C., a woman can get a civil protection order independent of family court proceedings; in 41 states, protection-order laws permit courts to evict an abuser from a residence shared with the victim; in 41 states an abuser who violates a protection order is guilty of committing a misdemeanor or contempt of court; 16 states allow courts to impose penalties of 6 months or more for violation of a protection order; in 33 states police authority has been expanded to permit arrest without a warrant if the officer has probable cause to believe the abuser is in violation of a protection order or has committed a misdemeanor (6 of these states [DE, ME, MN, NC, PA, UT] impose a duty to arrest the abuser when probable cause exists); 28 states require agencies to keep records of all cases. A Presidential Task Force on Family Violence was appointed in Sept. 1983 to investigate child and spouse abuse and maltreatment of the elderly. *Practice:* Approx. 2 million–6 million women each yr. are beaten by the men they live with or are married to; 50–70% of wives experience battery during their marriages;

2000–4000 women are beaten to death by husbands each yr.; in 1979, 40% of all women who were killed were murdered by their partners (10% of men who were killed were murdered by partners often acting in self-defense); 25% of women's suicide attempts follow a history of battery; wife battery injures more US women than auto accidents, rape, or muggings; every 18 seconds a woman is beaten by her husband severely enough to require hospitalization (1983). Police spend 1/3–1/2 of their time responding to domestic violence calls; 97% of spouse abuse is directed against wives. Battery is a cross-class, cross-race problem.

Prostitution. *Policy:* Legal only in Nevada; in other states, illegal and punishable as a misdemeanor by a fine and/or imprisonment. Laws prohibit sexual acts for money, soliciting, loitering with the intent to engage in prostitution, etc., and vary by state. *Practice:* In 1980, 88,900 arrests were made on charges of prostitution (8.5% of all arrests), and an est. 500,000 women worked as legal and illegal prostitutes. As of 1970, 1.2 million children under age 16 were involved in prostitution or pornography every yr. In 1980 child pornography was a $2.5-billion-per-yr. industry; pornography as a whole was an $8-billion-per-yr. industry as of 1981; new bias-free studies conducted in the late 1970's and early 1980's showed direct causal correlation between the proliferation of pornography, prostitution, and the rising rate of violence against women. Such prostitutes' civil-rights groups as COYOTE lobby for decriminalization and legal protection against physical abuse by clients and police. The vast majority of arrests involve only prostitutes and not clients (who are also in violation of laws).

Traditional/Cultural Practices. *Policy:* None. *Practice:* 30 million US women regularly take stimulant and depressant drugs prescribed by their doctors; in 1975, 80% of amphetamines, 67% of tranquilizers, and 60% of barbiturates were prescribed for women. One third of the 800,000 annual hysterectomies performed have been judged medically unnecessary; a high proportion of cesarean-section deliveries also are performed unnecessarily. Thousands of women annu-

ally develop breast and uterine cancer from estrogen pills prescribed during menopause. (Also see "genital mutilation" in Glossary.) **Crisis Centers.** *Policy:* Federal funds allocated in block grants may be used at the discretion of the states for various programs; 29 states have appropriated funds for battery shelters and prevention services, 21 derive some funds from a surcharge on marriage licenses, and 3 have surcharges on both marriage licenses and divorce actions. The Family Violence Prevention and Services Act, which would provide federal funds for shelters, police training, and a clearing-house for coordination/compilation of national research efforts, is pending (Dec. 1983). The Law Enforcement Assistance Administration funds some rape-crisis centers and battered women's shelters. *Practice:* The first battered-women's shelter was opened in 1964 in Pasadena, CA, and by 1983 there were an est. 500–800 shelters and safe-home networks for abused women and their children, many founded and staffed by feminist activists. There are approx. 50 programs to counsel abusive husbands. The National Coalition Against Domestic Violence held its first conference in 1980; NCADV had 123 active member groups and 167 supportive groups in 1980, but the needs of battered women are grossly under-met. In 1981 New York City shelters were forced to refuse 85% of women seeking shelter; from 1978–80, the YWCA ran 210 shelters in 30 states which sheltered 46,100 women and children and counseled another 50,000 women; the YWCA cannot help 80% of women seeking shelter. Despite this situation, in 1983, 95% of shelters responding to a National Center for Women Policy Studies survey reported that federal support was either reduced or eliminated. In 1983 approx. 700 rape-crisis programs (founded and still largely sustained by feminists) provided services (see following article). The National Center for Women and Family Law (NY), the Marital Rape Clearing-house (CA), and the Center for Prevention and Control of Rape (Washington, D.C.) are other national resources.

HERSTORY. Three factors—the international emphasis of *Sisterhood Is*

Global, space limitations in these pages, and the considerable monographic literature which exists for US women—have made it both necessary and possible for us to drastically curtail the HERSTORY section of this Preface. Fortunately, this does not deprive a reader, since such an abundant amount of this information is already available in published form (see the Contributor's Suggested Further Reading list, the US section of the Bibliography, and Jane Williamson's *New Feminist Scholarship: A Guide to Bibliographies,* The Feminist Press, 1979, for a minute sampling).

This available information includes historical, biographical, analytical, and literary works, which reveal the uniquely multiracial and multiethnic profile(s) of US women (see DEMOGRAPHY, GOVERNMENT, ECONOMY, and GYNOGRAPHY), and which explore women's lives, struggles, and accomplishments throughout US history—from the original indigenous Native societies (see following article) to colonial times, through the Revolution, Westward expansion, the institution and abolition of slavery, the Civil War and Reconstruction, immigrant populations, the labor movement, and two World Wars. Native American, Afroamerican, Asian-American, Hispanic-American, and Euroamerican women; women in the arts, sciences, and politics; lesbian, heterosexual, and bisexual women; older women militants and schoolgirl activists; and the hundreds of feminist issues and thousands of feminist groups in the US—all are covered variously and in depth by this available literature and are, in fact, summarized in the following article by the US Contributor.***

In all, the lives of US women, like those of women in every other nation, are best understood in context of long-term historical trends. The literature which exists for US women has indicated that, in addition to the achievements of individual women and women's groups, female life in the US has been affected by certain major developments: the diminishing size of the family; industrialization (which separated women's work from that of men's as men went to the factories); the involvement of women in what was (and still is) a sex-segregated labor market and women's attempts to unionize; the profound impact women have had on religious development beginning with the early revival movement; women's slow and painful entrance into the educational system; the emergence of women into the professions in the late 19th and early 20th centuries; the fight for reproductive freedom; the continuing female influence in both domestic and foreign reform movements; and women's battle to become full citizens with equal rights under the Constitution.

For MYTHOGRAPHY, see following article.

THE UNITED STATES: Honoring the Vision of 'Changing Woman'
by Rayna Green

"We are here," the Declaration of American Women stated in 1977, "to move history forward." As a Native American feminist, I support the sentiment of that Declaration for the present and the future. But I enjoin American women and men to look back to this country's Native roots to find the feminist landmarks that will guide us in moving history forward.

*** Much of contemporary US feminist organizing has been done by women deliberately working collectively; for the names of some of these dedicated feminists who forged the contemporary movement in the US, see the Acknowledgments section of this book.

According to the sacred tales of many Native peoples of North America, the earth and its beings were born of woman. Her names are many—Changing Woman, Spider Woman, Earth Mother, Corn Mother, Turtle Grandmother—but her first importance as Giver of Life remains unchallenged. So, in this America, the idea of woman's importance (even primacy) is old, fundamental to the beginning of all that is.

As a Native American woman, a Cherokee whose tribe was once justly governed by Beloved Women, our Clan Mothers, I now sit on this promontory in North America and ask what happened to the visions our grandmothers dreamed for us so long ago; for First Mother's vision demanded much of women and men: cooperation and community, mutual dependence and individual strength, mutual respect and honor. The world she brought into being was meant to be in balance with all living things—old and young, tribes of people, humans, animals and nature, men and women. First Woman's dream offers the feminist challenge to American history, insisting on the delightful paradox that *a feminist revolution here would simply honor American tradition, not overthrow it.* That revolution would restore to my people an equality between men and women robbed from them by those bent on conquering everything in the New World (humans *and* nature) and offer equality to those who have never enjoyed it. To accomplish this, we must honor the vision of Changing Woman.

Failure Is Impossible

American women of the nineteenth and twentieth centuries reactivated the vision, the struggle for equality. That cause, so intertwined with attempts to achieve equal status of the races before the law, remains ironically vital in a country founded on principles of equality, democratic freedom, and respect for diversity of belief and action. Still, in 1984, women of *all* races stand unequal to men before US law. The proposed Equal Rights Amendment to the Constitution, which states, "Equality of rights under the law shall not be denied or abridged by the United States or any State on account of sex," remains yet unratified. In a Constitution modeled after that of the great tribal Iroquois Confederacy which overtly guaranteed the social and political power of women, no legal respect for women's status exists. Well may women ask what US democracy holds for them.

American Indian people remember that, on many occasions, white women captured in battle by Native peoples refused to return to their own communities when offered the opportunity. If "civilization" meant a return to European patriarchal bondage, could not "savagery"—where social and political equality with men was common—be preferable? Well too our people remember that, unsatisfied with dominion over African slaves and European women, European men undermined the authority and decision-making process of Native peoples—for many essentially a female-centered process—by negotiating treaties and agreements with males unauthorized to make them. And would such European men not carefully control a written history so as to discredit systems which offered alternative sociopolitical behavior? Yet women, believing with Susan B. Anthony that "failure is impossible," continue to challenge American mythological equality, refusing to accept pallid versions of what that equality might be.

Call me Ms., not Mrs. "Him"

In the decade and a half since *Sisterhood Is Powerful* documented the rise of feminist voices in the United States, the US women's movement has spoken clearly—in slogans, in small and large gatherings, in humor, in rage and passion—addressing every aspect of human activity. Its success in creating change has been at least as great as its failures. From the most basic of concerns for the importance of language, the "she/he" debate moved to other forums, in political campaigns where women have run for and won elective office, in legislative action and judicial suit brought to rectify discriminatory laws, in the marketplace where work and income security remained unequally distributed and available, and in education where bias robbed women of equal access *and* of knowledge about female achievements.

Those years made feminism a public issue. Since the 1972 inaugural publication of *Ms.* magazine, a symbolic and real change has pervaded the American media. In so-called women's magazines and newspaper "women's pages," recipes and household hints began to share space with articles on job discrimination, nontraditional work, and the Equal Rights Amendment. Female television and radio reporters began to report on world and national news, not just on matters of supposed interest to women. And overtly feminist magazines and newspapers filled subscriber mailboxes and the shelves of commercial and women's bookstores across the country (and these publications exist for virtually every kind of feminist—lesbian, middle-class, homemaker, factory and clerical worker, executive, black, Chicana, Asian-American, Native American, academic, Marxist, Jewish, Catholic . . .). Even when a major city newspaper forbade the use of the title "Ms."* and when some parents and school officials objected to the appearance of feminist publications in school libraries the issue made a public point. Today, few US citizens can plead ignorance of what feminists believe and do, and though a major battle over recent right-wing attempts at censorship persists, the agenda of the US women's movement will continue to be aired publicly.

Biology Is Not Destiny

A generic category on the feminist agenda is sex discrimination—in education, work, law, health care, and human services—and the focus of attention has fallen primarily on regulatory, legislative, judicial, and institutional remedies. In education, feminists attacked sex stereotyping in training, employment, and scholarship itself. In 1972, they won passage of Title IX to the Educational Amendments Act, which required that all educational programs be equally available to men and women. (My own people, the Cherokees, had guaranteed an equal education to boys and girls long before their tragic removal to Oklahoma in 1832, and one of their first acts on removal was to set up seminaries for men and women alike.) Title IX, backed up by the Women's Educational Equity Act of 1978, offered a remedy for unequal treatment in curriculum and in sports activities. Education began to reflect real change, so much so that in 1981, most professional schools of law, medicine, theology, and business (alas, not engineering) show a 35 percent or better enrollment of women. Women insisted that the corollary of training for real change lay in the amendment of scholarship itself, to reflect women's real and substantial achievements, to support women scholars, and to revise basic curriculum to reflect women's needs and interests. Our success might simply be measured by the enlarged amount of bookshelf space now allotted to women in bookstores and libraries. Women's scholarship has become a major industry. Women's presses, women's studies programs and departments, and academic journals devoted to the publication of material on and by women attests to the respectability and importance of research and scholarship on women. And yet, as I write this, Title IX enforcement has been gutted by an Executive Order of a conservative President,** and federal programs designed to effect educational equity for women are targeted for budgetary extinction. General academic retrenchment threatens the fragile tenure of women in academe. Academic rank and pay shows no improvement, in terms of percentages for women, from forty years ago. And the recent crop of female doctorates will find slim chance of employment when they graduate. Too

* As of 1984, *The New York Times* still refused to use this appellation.—Ed.
** Ronald Reagan.—Ed.

much has changed to revert back to the older system, but gains and losses appear in greater balance than we might wish in this new decade.

Equal Pay for Equal Work

Improved access to training in nontraditional fields and in the professions, statutory equal opportunity, and affirmative action in employment, training, work security, equal pay for work of comparable value,*** and an end to occupation segregation—all proved major arenas for feminist activism. Major successes lay in breaking down barriers in the prestigious higher-paying professions, and a host of women donned the three-piece suits of lawyers and businessmen, the white coats of physicians, the clerical collars of (non-Roman Catholic) clergy, and the hard hats of engineers. Women abandoned health-care, clerical, and domestic work by the thousands—leaving a genuine crisis in nursing and clerical employment—to demand access to formerly male domains in the trades (construction, transportation, industry) and public service (law enforcement, fire departments, military service). Women's push for equality even opened up traditionally *female* jobs for *men*. The pursuit of economic justice breached other barriers of unequal treatment—in securing credit, insurance, retirement, and disability income. (Here, as in other areas, feminist demands created opportunities even for men and women who oppose feminist goals and tactics.)

Still, in 1983, women's income only equaled approximately 61 cents for every dollar made by a male.† Strong seniority and "old boy" network systems for apprenticeships in the unions, plus economic collapse in construction and industry, the cancellation of federally funded subsidies for training women and minorities, and continuing "reverse discrimination" suits against employers by white males—all erode women's economic gains. Women of color and disabled and elderly women still live at the margin, in exploitative jobs with occupational and safety hazards that threaten their fertility and general health, or with no jobs and ever-diminishing hopes. More women do earn more money in different jobs than ever before, but the over-all economic picture offers little for those not already upwardly mobile.

Welfare Is a Women's Issue

Through research, legislation, and social action the women's movement addressed the problems of poor, displaced, elderly, and disabled women, female-headed households with dependent children, victims of sexual assault and family violence, and convicted female offenders. We demanded (and usually initiated) rape-crisis centers, shelters, legal aid and counseling programs for displaced homemakers and abused women and children, and childcare for low-income women and women in the work force, though the number of programs never met the demand or the need. Some (not enough) federal monies were expended to remedy the severe problems of hunger, poverty, lack of adequate housing, and violence against women, but the social and economic roles of women changed faster than the services provided for them. More importantly, their needs were greater than those the society was willing to fill. The high percentage of minority, disabled, elderly, and offender women needing services tied in to a history of race, age, and social discrimi-

---

*** Feminists' replacement of the phrase "for equal work" with the phrase "for *comparable* work" was a recognition of the fact that many job areas are still closed to women—and also that the "pink-collar ghetto" of service jobs, as well as homemaking and motherhood, should be regarded (and remunerated) with the respect due them as being vital to society (e.g., 1978 government job classification pay scales listed wages for a secretary at less than for a parking-lot attendant and those of a childcare worker the same as of a dog-pound attendant).—Ed.

† See Statistical Preface preceding this article for detailed information.—Ed.

nation irremediable by public assistance alone. Conflicting regulations often pay women more to stay on public assistance than to find even low-paying employment. Yet recent federal and state budgets severely cut back public assistance while encouraging unemployment as a means of reducing inflation. How will these women and children survive, and can feminist action do more than call attention to their dilemma? (I recall what the elders of one American Indian tribe said to a group of white religious leaders horrified at the number of "illegitimate" children on one reservation. "But," said an elder, "we love *all* our children.") In the human-services arena, the intractability of US attitudes and values toward women can be most profoundly and sadly observed, and it is here that feminists must act for the future.

If Men Got Pregnant, Abortion Would Become a Sacrament

Action in the area of women's health deserves special mention for the real advances brought about by the US women's movement. With the landmark 1973 Supreme Court decision to legalize first-trimester abortion, women believed that their call for control over their own bodies might be heard. Feminists everywhere took subsequent action in reducing the number of unnecessary sterilizations, especially on Native American and other minority women, in changing outmoded and harmful obstetrical practices (gratuitous episiotomies, or sedating women in labor, for example), in exposing the dangers of commonly over-prescribed drugs (estrogens, tranquilizers), and in alerting women to their need for more sensible knowledge about their own bodies. Women's health-care organizations, local and national, and such publications as *Our Bodies, Ourselves* (now widely translated) convinced women of their rights to better and nonsexist health-care delivery, research into women's health and contraceptive techniques, health education, and an increase of women in health policy-making positions. Moreover, they convinced large numbers of women of the importance of taking some health care into their own hands (the self-help movement).

Still, threats to these gains remain as substantial as the gains themselves. A well-funded political and religious opposition to abortion continues to put forward one legislative and judicial block after another, the most recent victory a cut-off of federal funds for abortion. Federal funds for control (through abortion and contraception) of spiraling adolescent pregnancy rates have been diminished, and a conservative government's negative attitude toward government regulation means that research and regulation of potentially harmful drugs again threatens the health of US women *and* men. I ask whether I and other American women are better off now, deprived of the knowledge of our grandmothers—more than midwives and herbalists—declared unfit by a male medical "scientific" establishment which still regards women as objects of experimentation. The women's health movement has gone far in restoring them to us, but that struggle will continue as long as health is a function of the marketplace.

Many Voices, Many Rooms

Within the US women's movement, themes and sub-themes abound, and the movement's diversity remains complex. Voices raised for one part of the cause do not always speak for another part; even organized groups divide up "turf" so as not to draw away potential constituents and workers. Over five hundred *formally* organized feminist groups and literally thousands of informal ones—working on issues as diverse as business, scholarship, politics, children, the elderly, science, labor, the disabled, ethnic and minority affairs, medical ethics, education, the home and family, pornography, religion, sexual preference, sports, and such international issues as peace and nuclear power—speak to women's concerns. Whether large or small, national or local, general- or special-interest, these groups and organizations act on behalf of women's interests; inevitably, too, they dissent. As often over methods to achieve broad goals as between which goals deserve priority, these divisions of thought and feeling remain arguments about class, culture, economics, and basic life philosophies, no more easily resolved by feminism than by other forms of revolution. Moments of trust between homosexual and heterosexual women, women of color and "Anglo" women, rich, poor, marginal, middle-class, disabled, old, and "successful" women are still too few. Those who want access to "work within the system" believe in it and want success in it, while others for whom the system does not work do not want to be part of it or believe it will never work for them. For some, the success of the women's movement in gaining even a little access to political and economic power is really its failure.

Women-Identified Women

For lesbian women, whether they are separatists†† or not, true feminists are those who love women, and discrimination against lesbians is a primal form of hatred against women. For some, who believe that a wholly distinct form of culture—"women's culture"—exists, refusal to interact and "collaborate" with a male-centered world remains the only solution for the future. For others, not inclined to separatism, respect for and a defense of their right to love and live with women—both legally and socially—constitutes the minimum demand.

Without question, the social and political option lesbians pose to US society and most particularly to US feminism exposes a divided house. While the delegates to the National Women's Conference in Houston (1977) did vote for a resolution barring discrimination on the basis of sexual preference, many US feminists still feel that the issue of sexual preference is irrelevant to basic issues of women's rights and that it will divert some women and men from support of other items on the feminist agenda. I long again for a truly Native solution, for most tribes simply accepted homosexuality as one category of human behavior, made room for it in the social system, and either ignored or paid attention to homosexual individuals as *individual* behavior dictated—as with any other human behavior. But this issue will not be resolved easily, largely because of its relevance to painfully felt questions about the nature of the family and relationships between men and women.

Viva la Mujer: It's Our Movement Now

As dramatic (and sometimes rancorous) as the gay-straight split, but with more international implications, exists that division between ethnic and minority women and "Anglo/European" women. Related really to issues of class as well as race, this apparent lack of sympathy between First and Third World women rests in long-standing wars between men and nations as well as between different individuals. For women of color (and for poor women), the needs for food, shelter, and freedom from enslavement and imprisonment and from physical violence and exploitation are so basic that frequently expressed feminist concerns for political power or professional advancement seem trivial. These

†† "Separatism" can have different meanings to different people. Its political etymology goes back to US black civil-rights activists in the 1960's claiming their movement for themselves without further white participation. In the late 1960's and early 1970's, many radical feminists called themselves separatist in that, although they might be heterosexual women, they refused to work with men politically. In the ensuing years, and *within* the US women's movement itself, the word has been used variously in terms of class, age, marital status, whether a mother or not, etc. By the mid-1970's, it was mostly being used (subjectively or objectively) to describe a lesbian woman who would not associate with men and/or with heterosexual women and/or with lesbian mothers of male children.—Ed.

women, says Joy Harjo, a Native American poet, "are grinding the mortar of their houses through straw-thin teeth." For such women to join with non-tribal, non-poor, non-colored women and rebuke the very cultures and male relations historically subjugated and repressed *by* those women's cultures and male relations, is to deny their own lives. And yet they know quite deeply that the domination of women is signal to the domination of all peoples and that as various categories of dominated peoples are freed, so shall we all be freer. Like all feminists, Third World feminists hope that the women's revolution can force men, all of whom have a female referent of some kind (mother, sister, lover), to confront the inequities of race and class through the inequities forced on women because of gender. Yet the diversity that our democracy proposes will not easily be proffered by US feminism so long as perceptions remain as far apart as they often do for First and Third World women.

Make the Air Force Hold a Bake Sale to Buy a Bomber

As intractable as issues of race, class, and sexual preference—and just as amenable to a feminist analysis—are those surrounding militarism, pacifism, the nuclear-arms race, and Western and multinational corporate imperialism. For many, feminism and opposition to nuclear power and arms buildup, to multinational corporate control of arms and resources, to militarism and war, constitute logical corollaries. But for some, the essential goals of equality for feminists produced yet another paradox, for as women gained access to jobs in the military, law enforcement, and corporate power, they perform work that many feminists regard as nonfeminist, even immoral. Have they become the instruments of oppression and of destruction? "We don't want 50 percent of the fingers on the nuclear button to be women's," a poster said at a recent National Organization for Women meeting. The women's movement struggle for equal status in the military now produces a debate about whether women should be in combat roles. I recall the tales of Blackfeet and Sioux women, called "brave-hearted" when they bore their dead male relatives' bodies from the field and fought in their stead. Were they wrong to fight the US armies? And I think too of the Iroquois and Cherokee women whose responsibility it was to decide when to make war *and* when to make peace. No easy resolution here either, except to note that feminist debate interlocking with these important issues offers a more massive forum than ever before.

Equality Begins at Home

One final debate brought about by the US women's movement rages over the nature of the family. What constitutes the family and its component parts, appropriate male and female roles, and the implications of single-parent, nonrelational, extended, and communal families? Antifeminists contend that feminists (and homosexuals) are bent on destroying the family, while most feminists either contend that families as we know them need revising or that "the family" always has been a transmutable entity in constant flux. Some try to demonstrate that one can be "Pro-God, Pro-Family, and Pro-ERA," as one poster read. Perhaps the movement only highlighted changes already in progress; perhaps it actually engineered new options. For American Indians and other traditional peoples in the United States, for example, the extended family was *the* family until European middle-class values forced migration, urbanization, and other factors that disrupted traditional patterns. For poor women everywhere, single-parent families are the rule, not the exception. But for some, the changes—visible and profound—disturb and challenge. In some instances, the debate strengthened men's demands for equality before the law in such areas as child custody and payment of alimony in divorce settlements. As one Navajo tribal man who supported the ERA said in an Arizona meeting, "I come from a matriarchy, and I want my equal rights, too." Even nonfeminist women challenged the unfair distribution of Social Security eligibility and payment. And still others responded to options never dreamed of back when a nuclear family seemed the only option. Yet an ingrained homophobia, a fear of too many options, and a great confusion pervades the social relations of US women and men, and that confusion inspires attack and regression by a radical right. This too, feminists must continue to address, with considerable effort and personal pain.

And so the movement marches on, each part not always in step with another. The enormous resistance to this revolution gives me nightmares, and in the worst of them a male metaphor of battle invades my sleep. We are all assembled on a great plain, ready to do battle. Each part of the movement forms an independent brigade, each with a separate command and battle cry. Arrayed below us stands the enemy, led by the Pope, congressmen, senators, the elders of the Mormon Church and the so-called Moral Majority,††† antiabortionists and pornographers—each in a different uniform, but with only one battle cry: "Down with Feminism!" Variously and at different moments, they cry out in unison "Baby killers!" "Anti-Christ!" "Man haters!" "Family destroyers!"—and as they fire on us with these slogans we fall back unable to muster the unity to fight them. Our briefcases and posters are not strong enough weapons. Our forces are weakened from too many internal battles. But are we truly so fragmented that we cannot work for a common cause? I think not. Our gains in this decade prove that the cause is just and "failure *is* impossible." However uneasily, alliances do join and work together, and that is what revolution can be about.

A Woman's Place Is in the House . . . and the Senate

One thing is certain. We cannot go back.

Change is inevitable, and some of that change will take the form of what we have demanded. We may lose even the revived fight for the Equal Rights Amendment. We may lose the fight for abortion. And we may win. But these are not the only issues which drive us or need feminist organization. Poverty, racism, the threat of nuclear holocaust, violence—*all* of these are our issues, and we just may be the Americans who can raise them because of the past we've shared together.

Three scenes remain in my mind and give me hope. I think of that day in 1978 when a hundred thousand women marched down Constitution Avenue in Washington, in a rally for passage of the ERA. I look back at their faces, and I see all American women represented. If that was possible, even more is possible. I remember, too, the traditional shawl Native women gave Gloria Steinem for her assistance to them in hammering out language for the minority women's plank at the National Women's Conference. If women as different as those women can work together for a while, even more can happen in the long run. And I think of the young Cherokee woman who came into my office on her first day of college and announced that her goal was to restore a female chiefdom to the Cherokee Nation. We have come a long way indeed if we've made her aims possible. In the future we will have to take courage in our diversity *and* our unity. As Bella Abzug said at the National Women's Conference in Houston when women bearing the torch of equality ran into the arena: "Some of us run with a torch. Some of us run for office. Some of us run for equality. But none of us runs for cover."

Women Hold Up Half the Sky

It is odd to write this article as an "American." Sometimes I think of myself as anything *but* that—and yet an American is what I am. I was shaped and bred in this country and formed by the myth and reality of the US experience. In some way too, I

††† An ultra-Right fundamentalist Christian group.—Ed.

know that this experience was shaped and formed by *me,* and by my sisters and brothers, and by those who came here after us, often unwillingly, to share in its transformation. So no matter how painful my alliance with the United States and no matter how strongly I feel a part of the experience of other worlds, I belong to this place. As a Native American feminist, that belonging translates into a continuing struggle to make this country live up to its own mythos, its own real heritage, and to comprehend what that heritage might mean for its future.

So I, and other Native women with me, sit on this promontory in North America and wait for American women and men to come home. We sing Changing Woman's song and dance the women's dance for all to see. We sing for our men, praying they have ears to hear and eyes to see. We sing for the women who've lost the capacity to hear, whose eyes have been taken from them, who cannot see visions that would give true power. We sing for the women who do have visions, who have eyes and ears to let them know what they must know. We sing to restore the balance of living things.

On Turtle Grandmother's back sits the world, and we also sit on her back, listening to the stories she has to tell us. Who will hear her voice?

Suggested Further Reading

Edwards, Lee R., and Arlyn Diamond, eds. *American Voices, American Women.* New York: Avon Books, 1973.

Fisher, Dexter. *The Third Woman: Minority Women Writers of the United States.* Boston: Houghton Mifflin, 1979.

Flexnor, Eleanor. *Century of Struggle: The Woman's Rights Movement in the United States.* Cambridge, MA: Harvard Univ. Press, 1975.

Lerner, Gerda, ed. *The Female Experience: An American Documentary.* Indianapolis: Bobbs-Merrill, 1977.

Lorde, Audre. *Zami: A New Spelling of My Name.* Watertown, MA: Persephone Press, 1983.

Morgan, Robin. *Going Too Far: The Personal Chronicle of a Feminist.* New York: Random House and Vintage Books, 1978.

Rayna Green is a writer, scholar, and political activist, currently a visiting scholar at the Smithsonian Institution. An American Indian from the Cherokee Nation of Oklahoma, she works with tribes and Third World countries in development. A folklorist, she writes on Native women, American culture, indigenous science, technology, and medicine, and works in museum and media production. She has taught folklore, Native American studies, and women's studies at the Universities of Arkansas, Massachusetts, and Maryland, as well as at George Washington University, Yale, and Dartmouth College. Her work has most recently appeared in two books from Indiana University Press, *Native American Women: A Contextual Bibliography* and *That's What She Said: A Collection of Contemporary Fiction and Poetry by Native American Women* (1984).

VENEZUELA
(Republic of Venezuela)

Located in northern South America, bordered by Guyana to the east, Brazil to the south, Colombia to the west, and the Caribbean Sea to the north. **Area:** 912,050 sq. km. (352,143 sq. mi.). **Population** (1980): 13,930,000, female 49.7%. **Capital:** Caracas.

DEMOGRAPHY. Languages: Spanish, various Native Indian languages and dialects. **Races or Ethnic Groups:** Mestizo 69%, European descent 20%, African descent 9%, Native Indian 2%. **Religions:** Predominantly Roman Catholicism, Protestant, other. **Education** (% enrolled in school, 1975): Age 6–11—of all girls 74%, of all boys 75%; age 12–17 —of all girls 58%, of all boys 53%; higher education—in 1979–80 women comprised 50% of students entering university. In 1982, of all employed women over age 15, 12% were nonliterate, 43% had only primary education, 37% had secondary education, and 8% had university education. **Literacy** (1977): Women 73%, men 80%. **Birth Rate** (per 1000 pop., 1975–80): 36. **Death Rate** (per 1000 pop., 1975–80): 6. **Infant Mortality** (per 1000 live births, 1975–80): Female 40, male 50. **Life Expectancy** (1975–80): Female 68 yrs., male 65 yrs.

GOVERNMENT. A bicameral parliamentary system consists of an elected National Congress, composed of a 52-member Senate and a 213-member Chamber of Deputies, and an elected president. The major political parties are the Democratic Action Party, the Social Christian Party, the People's Electoral Movement, the Democratic Republican Union, the Socialist Movement Party, and the Radical Cause Party. **Women's Suffrage:** A 1946 decree by the ruling junta established equal voting rights and the provision was included in the 1947 Constitution; 1945 in municipal elections. **Equal Rights:** The 1961 Constitution (Art. 61) stipulates equality regardless of race, sex, creed, or social condition. **Women in Government:** There are 4 women cabinet ministers: Mercedes Pu-

lido de Briceño, Minister of State for Women's Participation in Development; Nidia Villegas, Minister of Agriculture; Maritza Izaguirre Borras, Minister of State and Chief of Coordination and Planning; and Leonor Marabal, Minister of State for Parliamentary Coordination (1983); women comprise 29 members and 2 substitute members in the Senate, 43 deputies and 8 substitutes in the Chamber of Deputies, and 207 of 1477 councillors in municipal councils (1982).

ECONOMY. Currency: Bolívar (May 1983: 10. = $1 US). **Gross National Product** (1980): $54.2 billion. **Per Capita Income** (1980): $3630. **Women's Wages as a Percentage of Men's** (1978): 79.1% of average monthly earnings for a 30–40-hour work week; 67.7% for more than a 40-hour work week. **Equal Pay Policy:** The Constitution (Art. 87) includes the principle of equal pay for equal work without discrimination; 1936 Labor Law also stipulates equal pay for equal work. **Production** (Agricultural/Industrial): Coffee, rice, sugar; petroleum, steel, textiles, paper. **Women as a Percentage of Labor Force** (1982): 30%; **of agricultural force** (1980) 6%; **of industrial force**—no general statistics obtainable (of manufacturing 28.1%, 1980); **of military**—no statistics obtainable; under the 1979 Law of Conscription women must register for military service at age 18 and may enter all branches on the same terms as men. "Protective" legislation prohibits women from employment at night, underground work, or work which might be "morally damaging" (Labor Law, Arts. 111–13). **(Employed) Women's Occupational Indicators:** Of all employed women, 50% work in the service sector, 21% in commerce, 16.1% in industry, and 12.9% in other economic activities (1979–80); of administrative/managerial workers 11.5%, of sales workers 14.2%, of clerical workers 45%, of professional/technical workers 48.4%, of service workers 60% (1971). **Unemployment** (first semester, 1980): 6.2%, female 4.6%, male 6.7%.

GYNOGRAPHY. Marriage. *Policy:* A major Civil Code reform in 1982 radically altered the legal relationship of women and men in marriage and family life. Minimum marriage age is 16 for females and males with parental consent and 18 for both without consent. All decisions regarding marital life are to be made jointly by the spouses; in cases of conflicts, a judge decides. Women have the right to work outside the home without first obtaining their husbands' consent. Property is administered jointly by spouses unless they contract for separate ownership prior to marriage. The legal domicile is the conjugal residence established by mutual accord; a wife need not reside at her husband's domicile. *Practice:* Female mean age at marriage (1970–78): 20; women age 15–49 in union (1970–78): 48.2%. **Divorce.** *Policy:* The 1982 Civil Code (Art. 31) established equal spousal rights in divorce. Grounds include voluntary desertion, excesses, grave injury, adultery by either spouse, corruption of children, imprisonment of either spouse, alcohol or drug dependency, insanity, and 1-yr. separation without reconciliation. *Practice:* In 1977, 6.4% of all marriages ended in divorce; the average duration of those marriages was 5–9 yrs.

Family. *Policy:* The 1982 Civil Code established the principle of parental equality. The 1975 Labor Code stipulates a maternity leave of 6 weeks pre- and 6 weeks post-delivery with full salary or wages (Art. 116); a female employee cannot be fired for pregnancy (Art. 218); workplaces employing more than 30 women are required to provide childcare rooms (Art. 118). *Practice:* An est. 500,000 households were headed by women in 1982, and the number reportedly is increasing with the rise in male migration to the cities for employment. There is a growing need for day care. In 1979, 48.3% of homes were formed by married couples, 22.8% by common-law couples, 19.3% by female heads of households, and 9.16% by male heads of households. **Welfare.** *Policy:* The 1966 Social Security Law established a system which pays employed persons pensions (to women at age 55, to men at 60), and benefits for sickness, accidents, maternity

(see **Family** and below) and old age. The wives or common-law spouses of employed men are eligible for benefits, whereas the husbands or common-law spouses of employed women are not. The National Nutrition Institute provides food allowances to low-income families. The Ministry of Health and Social Assistance and the Venezuelan Institute of Social Security provide free pre- and postnatal care at maternal/infant centers and hospitals. *Practice:* No data obtainable.

Contraception. *Policy:* Legal. Government directly supports family-planning services within the national health services system. According to a 1971 law, sterilization is permissible for medical/eugenic reasons only. *Practice:* Women age 15–49 in union using contraception (1977): 52%; methods used (1977) pill 31%, IUD 17%, female sterilization 16%, withdrawal 10%, condom 10%, rhythm 8%, douche 5%, diaphragm 2%, other methods 1%; using inefficient methods 24%. As of 1977 the National Family Planning Program operated 507 clinics that served approx. 7% of women of reproductive age; family-planning facilities are insufficient in number to meet the need. **Abortion.** *Policy:* Under the Criminal Code, abortion is permitted in cases of severe risk to the woman's life or fetal abnormality. Illegal abortions are punishable by 6 months–2 yrs. imprisonment for the woman, and 12–30 months imprisonment for the practitioner. *Practice:* No statistics obtainable. Illegal abortions are the leading cause of female deaths in Caracas, and the fourth major cause of female deaths in the countryside (see following article). The feminist group La Conjura in Caracas is pressuring to reform the law (1982). **Illegitimacy.** *Policy:* Under the 1982 Civil Code, children born out of wedlock have the same rights to maintenance by both parents as do children born within marriage. Patria Potestad is exercised by the first parent who legally recognizes the child; if both do, joint authority is established. *Practice:* More than 1/2 of all live births (an est. 52%) are out of wedlock; approx. 3 million children are paternally unacknowledged and unsupported (see following article). Fathers of out-of-wedlock children rarely pay maintenance.

Homosexuality. *Policy:* There are no laws specifically prohibiting homosexuality. *Practice:* No data obtainable. **Incest.** *Policy:* Under the 1964 Penal Code, rape of a person under age 16 by an older relative, guardian, or instructor is punishable by 5–10 yrs. imprisonment (Art. 375); a person who abuses authority, confidence, or domestic relations, and commits a lascivious act with a person of either sex, by threats or violence, is subject to 1–5 yrs. imprisonment (Art. 377); incestuous relations with an ascendant or descendant relative, or with a brother or sister, in circumstances that cause public scandal, are punishable by 3–6 yrs. imprisonment (Art. 381). *Practice:* No data obtainable. **Sexual Harassment.** *Policy:* None. *Practice:* No data obtainable. **Rape.** *Policy:* Under the 1964 Penal Code (Art. 375), anyone who, through violence or threats, forces a person of either sex to perform a carnal act is subject to 5–10 yrs. imprisonment; the penalty is the same if the act is performed with a person under age 12, or with a person unable to resist because of physical or mental infirmity or the influence of drugs; leniency is given to convicted rapists in cases where the victim is a woman working in prostitution (Art. 393). Art. 379 of the 1926 Penal Code

(revised in 1958 and 1964) makes it a crime to "seduce with the promise of marriage" a female age 16–21. *Practice:* Reports indicate that in Caracas approx. 1 rape is reported per day (see following article); no further data obtainable. **Battery.** *Policy:* No specific spouse-abuse laws, but the crime could be prosecuted under general assault laws. *Practice:* No data obtainable. **Prostitution.** *Policy:* There is no law prohibiting the act of prostitution itself. The Penal Code (Arts. 396–97) defines pimping as a "crime against the family"; inducing another person into prostitution or corruption with the purpose of profit, or to satisfy the desires of another person, is punishable by 1–6 yrs. imprisonment; if the victim is a minor, the penalty is between the minimum and the maximum; if the offender is a relative, spouse, or guardian, the penalty is 1–4 yrs.; if violence or threats are used, 4–6 yrs. (Penal Code, Arts. 382, 388). *Practice:* No data obtainable. **Traditional/Cultural Practices:** No data obtainable. **Crisis Centers.** *Policy:* None. *Practice:* No data obtainable.

HERSTORY. See the following article.

MYTHOGRAPHY. No data obtainable.

VENEZUELA: For As Long As It Takes
by Giovanna Merola R.
(Translated by Magda Bogin)

If we examine the history of sociopolitical events in Venezuela beginning with the discovery of the Americas by Europeans and the inaugurating of the colonial period, we find a paucity of information relating to significant activities by women. Through certain chronicles of the Spanish Conquest, we know of the wretched acts to which indigenous women were subjected, and we know that in defiance they practiced infanticide to spare their children fates similar to their own.

The chronicles do show, however, that in 1524 Venezuela became the first country to have a female governor—on the island of Margarita. Her name was Aldonza Manrique and she inherited the position from her father. She held the post for approximately sixty years. It is also known that women took part in the fight for independence from Spanish rule, and that their participation was evident from the first uprisings. Only a few names have been rescued to leave a record of their bravery: Juana Ramírez, Ana María Campos,

La India María, Josefa Camejo, Asunción Silva, Eulalia Ramos, and Dominga Ortiz. More than two hundred women accompanied Bolívar's army in the battle of Carabobo.

Shortly after the Declaration of Independence (1813), an event deserving of special mention took place: according to Miguel Colombet,[1] the first known strike in Venezuela was that of the laundresses in the hospitals of Valencia, who stopped work in February of 1818 to demand back pay for work they had already done.

Aside from these few above-mentioned facts, following Independence women's lives were spent essentially within the four walls of their homes and were dedicated to the traditional roles society demanded of them. At that time, Venezuela's main activity was agricultural and pastoral, its economy noted for the exportation of agricultural products prized on the international market (cocoa, coffee, spices, etc.). With the establishment of the dictatorship of General Juan Vicente Gómez (who ruled the country from 1909 until his death in 1935), the first steps toward oil production were taken, and in the same period Venezuelan women began to work outside the home and the farm for the first time. Initially they went into tobacco factories—where they earned rock-bottom salaries. Meanwhile, in 1915, Virginia Pereira Alvarez and Luisa Martínez faced down insults and jokes and became the first women to enter the University of Caracas medical school, which had been an exclusively male preserve until that date.

In the 1920's, with the expansion of the oil industry, the few jobs open to women continued to be in the service sector—as maids, telephone operators, primary-school teachers, cashiers, and file clerks. Yet it was still not considered appropriate for women to leave their homes to work, and only financial desperation was deemed justification. Despite the boredom of lives locked in the house, women did not fail to act against the tenacious dictatorship that gripped the country. In 1926 the Junta Patriótica Femenina (Women's Patriotic Front) was created, and its members wrote to the Associated Press in New York and to US President Hoover to explain the terrible situation of their imprisoned husbands. They were also brave enough to write to the national government at home, denouncing the physical mistreatment of political prisoners. In 1928 many of these same women joined the student movement that rose up against the iron rule of Juan Vicente Gómez.

But it was not until Gómez's death in 1935 that the Venezuelan women's movement really took form. Olga Luzardo and Luisa del Valle Silva, both members of the Venezuelan Communist Party (PCV), along with other women, founded the Agrupación Cultural Femenina (Women's Cultural Group). This group dedicated itself to founding schools for working women, created the Casa Obrera (Women Worker's House), and began preparation for the First Congress of Women. On December 30, 1935, along with the Sociedad Protectora de la Infancia (Childhood Protection Society) they sent a petition with over a hundred signatures to President Eleázar López Contreras. For the first time, distinct women's demands were set forth: social protection for women and children; fresh milk; pure water; air and sun in special parks for children; and day-care centers for the children of women factory and office workers.

In 1936 such groups as the Asociación Venezolana de la Mujer (Venezuelan Women's Association), the Unión de Mujeres Americanas (Union of American Women), and the Asociación Cultural Interamericana (Inter-American Cultural Association) were founded—all of which were fighting for equal rights for working women and for child-protection laws. In that same year the first Venezuelan woman doctor, Lya Imber, received her degree, and the first Venezuelan woman journalist, Carmen Clemente Travieso

---

[1.] Miguel Colombet, *Carabobo, Histórico y Pintoresco* (Picturesque and Historic Carabobo). Biblioteca de Autores y Temas Caraboboños. Valencia, Ediciones del Ejecutivo del Edo. Carabobo, 1968.

of the Agrupación Cultural Femenina, began to write cultural columns addressed to women in the pages of the newspapers *Ahora, El Naçional,* and *La Esfera.* As a result of the political, cultural, and syndicalist activity of the above groups, the Ley del Trabajo (Work Law) granted working women social security coverage for maternity along with six weeks pre- and post-maternity leave, plus affirmation of the right to equal pay for equal work.

In 1936, women's organizations participated in the first strike of oil-industry workers in Zulia, running collective kitchens and taking the children of striking workers into their own homes. The forty-two-day strike grew into a nationwide movement for the rights of working people. In 1940 the Agrupación Cultural Femenina held a Preparatory Conference for the First Women's Congress, at which time such issues as reforming the Código Civil (Civil Code), the right to vote, the facilitation of divorce, and the elimination of discrimination against illegitimate children were discussed. That same year, the Asociación Cultural Interamericana founded the Biblioteca Femenina Venezolana (Venezuelan Women's Library), and the Unión Nacional de Mujeres (National Women's Union) set up the Biblioteca "Trina Larralde" (the Trina Larralde Library), two important institutions for women's advancement.

In 1942 the Congreso Nacional (National Congress) approved the first reform of the Civil Code in response to pressure from the Agrupación Cultural Femenina and the Asociación de Mujeres. In cases of separation, women were granted custody of children under three years of age; joint rights to the common property of a couple living together were recognized; and, along with other reforms of the articles governing marriage, the phrase "the wife's duty to obey her husband" was eliminated. For the first time women put forth their right to be considered persons under the law. In the same year the Commercial Code was reformed, permitting women to engage in commerce independent of their husbands.

From 1943 to 1947 women fought to obtain the right to vote. In 1944 International Women's Day was celebrated in Venezuela for the first time. A petition signed by more than eleven thousand women was presented to the Congress, demanding women's enfranchisement. The Agrupación Cultural Femenina, organizer of the March 8 Celebration, held an assembly, and a "Message to Venezuelan Women" was published, with a call for unity among women and a greeting to the women of Europe and Asia who were fighting to defeat fascism. On May 1, the Asociación de Amas de Casa (Housewives' Association) was formed to fight for lower food prices and rents.

In 1945, under the government of Isaías Medina Angarita, women won the right to vote in municipal elections. In that year the group Acción Femenina (Feminine Action) was founded and on March 8 the Second Preparatory Conference for a Women's Congress was held to demand equal responsibility with men, the breaking off of diplomatic relations with Spain's Franco, protection of mothers and children, and improved conditions in the workplace. The First Women's Congress was set for 1946 but did not take place. In that year twelve women appeared before the constituent assembly to demand the *full* right to vote. On March 15, 1946, a decree issued by the Ruling Junta presided over by Rómulo Betancourt granted women the right to vote and run for office in elections for the constituent assembly. The following year Venezuelan women voted for the first time.

After the overthrow of Rómulo Gallegos in 1948, there was a succession of *de facto* governments in Venezuela, and the Agrupación Cultural Femenina became a semi-clandestine organization, disappearing altogether during the dictatorship of General M. Pérez Jiménez (1948–58). During this period women in the underground fought alongside men against the authoritarian government. These years saw the founding of the Unión de Muchachas Venezolanas (Union of Venezuelan Girls) by the Juventud Comunista (Communist Youth), while the Organización de Mujeres Comunistas continued to function and the Democratic Action Party founded, clandestinely, the Asociación Juvenil Femenina de AD (the Young Women's Association of the Democratic Action Party). In 1953 the Junta Patriótica Femenina resurfaced. The goal of all these women's organizations was the return of democracy to Venezuela.

Shortly after the fall of Pérez Jiménez (January 1958), the Primer Mitin Femenino (First Women's Meeting) was held in Caracas. Women from the Venezuelan Communist Party, the Democratic Republican Union, and the Democratic Action Party were among the participants. The group issued a call to the entire nation to work for their newly won freedom. With the accession of Rómulo Betancourt (Democratic Action Party) a new political era began. Women divided along party lines. Class struggle and each party's desire to win control of the country became priorities, and women's demands once again gave way to other issues, although women were active on a variety of political fronts: as guerrillas—both in rural and urban areas—or as members of the women's organizations of traditional parliamentary parties.

While 1967 and 1968 were key years in the resurgence of the European and US feminist movements, by 1969 all existing women's groups in Venezuela had disappeared. During this period, Venezuelan women were strongly involved in political parties, and they defined the women's issues only within the context of class struggle. Nevertheless, in 1969 the Federación Venezolana de Abogadas, or FEVA (Venezuelan Federation of Women Lawyers), was created to fight for the legal rights of women and to draft reforms of the Civil Code.

The influence of the international women's movement was spreading, so that by the end of 1969 the first truly feminist group appeared in Venezuela. This was the Movimiento de Liberación de la Mujer (Women's Liberation Movement) which began meeting in the homes of its members, initially in the form of study groups which led to discussions broadening the perspectives of struggle beyond previously set limits. The feminist movements in Europe and the US, the French "May Rebellion," and the process of development in Venezuela—with the massive absorption of women into the work force and the universities—brought us into the 1970's with a number of groups of independent women.

In 1970 the group Planteamiento de la Mujer de Hoy (Strategy for Today's Woman) held a meeting to demand that the government conduct a full evaluation of the status of women. The Liga de Mujeres (Women's League) was formed at the university in 1972, participating in the boycott of the Miss Venezuela contest and publishing pamphlets. In 1973 Mujeres Socialistas (Socialist Women) was formed as part of the Movimiento al Socialismo (Movement Toward Socialism), and published various bulletins as well as holding meetings and printing a variety of feminist literature. The first Liga de Mujeres divided in 1974 and the group that kept the name published a newspaper called *Juana la Avanzadora* (Juana the Advancer—i.e., the improver), with a political analysis grounded in class struggle. The other group took the name Movimiento Hacia la Nueva Mujer (Movement for a New Woman) and dedicated itself to studying the situation of women, holding work sessions, doing translations of feminist works, and publishing pamphlets and articles in Caracas papers.

In 1975 (International Women's Year), President Carlos Andrés Pérez created the Comisión Femenina Asesora de la Presidencia de la República (Women's Presidential Advisory Commission), which organized the First Women's Congress that had been planned and postponed so many times during the 1940's. More than two thousand women from all over the country and all walks of life were delegates, arriving at resolutions similar to those that women had already been demanding for twenty years.

Nineteen seventy-eight was perhaps the year of the greatest Venezuelan feminist activity thus far. Movimiento Hacia la Nueva Mujer folded but new groups appeared: La Conjura (Conspiracy), focusing on denouncing the virtual illegality of abortion and on publication of the bulletin *Una Mujer Cualquiera;* Persona, which held a major women's exhibition; Miércoles (Wednesday), which makes movies about Venezuelan women; and the anarchist group Mujeres Libres (Free Women). All the groups were based in Caracas, but 1978 saw the formation of feminist groups in the major cities of the country's interior, including Liga de Mujeres de Maracaibo (Women's League of Maracaibo), which has published a bulletin called *Voz Feminista* (Feminist Voice) since 1978; and the Liga Feminista de Maracaibo, whose publication is called *Luisa Cáceres.* Women's groups also formed in Valencia, Mérida, and San Cristobal.

In 1979 Luis Herrera Campins' Social Christian government created the State Ministry for the Participation of Women in Development, incorporating some of the demands of the country's women, but within the ideological limits of the government. And, too, in 1979 the Comisión Nacional Pro-Derechos de la Mujer (National Commission for the Rights of Women) was created to ensure implementation of the resolutions of the First Women's Congress. The First Feminist Meeting of Venezuela was held in Maracaibo that November, at the urging of the group La Conjura. Organized by the Liga Feminista de Maracaibo, the meeting brought together women of Miércoles, Persona, Movimiento de Liberación de la Mujer, and groups from Táchira, Mérida, Aragua, Bolívar, Falcón, and Barinas.

In 1980 La Conjura issued an international call to the Primer Encuentro Feminista Latinoamericano (First Latin American Feminist Conference) and did initial organizing on the conference until a site for the meeting could be chosen. Bogotá was the choice, and Colombian feminists from many different groups made it possible for feminists of all Latin American countries to meet there in July of 1981 to discuss women's struggles and strategies on a continental level [see COLOMBIA—Ed.].

The years 1981 and 1982 saw continuing activism: the Venezuelan Federation of Women Lawyers (along with women from the political parties) presented congress with a proposal for civil-code reform; women marched and demonstrated; the first conference on the Work and Productivity of the Female Work Force took place, jointly sponsored by the State Ministry for Women, the Ministry of Labor, and the Central Office of Coordination and Planning. The data presented on this occasion give us an evaluation and a panorama of the situation of Venezuelan women.

More than half the live births in Venezuela are of "illegitimate" children; an estimated 3 million children are paternally unacknowledged and unsupported. Job discrimination and a high rate of female illiteracy persist. There is a lack of childcare centers, family-planning programs, and sex education (the Roman Catholic Church is still very powerful); some 10,000 women die each year of illegal abortions; 98 percent of rape victims do not report the crime out of fear and shame. Women workers suffer from the classic double work burden—on the job and at home. There is excessive manipulation of women via advertising and the mass media. Women's participation in political parties is still limited.

In short, the Movimiento de las Mujeres in Venezuela still has a long and arduous struggle ahead, in order to overcome all the obstacles to freedom for Venezuelan women. But we are committed to that cause—for as long as it takes.

Suggested Further Reading

Clemente Travieso, Carmen. *Las mujeres en el pasado y en el presente* (Women of the Past and Present). Caracas: Publicación de la Agrupación Cultural Femenina, 1977.

———. *Mujeres de la Independencia* (Women and National Struggle). México: Talleres Gráficos México, 1964.

"Día Internacional de la Mujer. Tradición de luchas heroicas existe en el movimiento femenino venezolano" (International Women's Day. A Tradition of Heroic Struggle Lives in the Venezuelan Women's Movement), *El Nacional,* Mar. 8, 1977.

"Documentos de La Jornada sobre el Trabajo y la Productividad de la Mano de Obra Femenina" (Documents on the Proceedings of a Meeting on Work and Productivity of Women's Manual Labor). Caracas, Feb. 16–19, 1982 (Parque Central).

Laya, Argelia. *Nuestra Causa* (Our Cause). Caracas: Equipo Ed. C.A., 1979.

Petzoldt, Fania and Jacinta Bevilacqua. *Nosotras también nos jugamos la vida—Testimonios de la mujer venezolana en la lucha clandestina, 1948–1958* (We Also Risk Our Lives—Testimonies of Venezuelan Women and the Underground). Caracas: Ed. Ateneo, 1979.

Revista *Educación,* Nos. 155–56, Caracas, June 1975. Número dedicado al Año de la Mujer Venezolana (issue dedicated to the Year of the Venezuelan Woman).

Revista *Al Oído,* No. 2, Vol. 3, Caracas, Mar. 1978. Número especial dedicado a la Mujer (issue dedicated to women).

Giovanna Merola R. is a Venezuelan biologist who has done post-graduate studies in ecology and the management of natural resources. She has a master's degree in the sociology of development, and is currently professor on the faculty of architecture and urban studies of the Universidad Central de Venezuela in Caracas. She was a member of the Movimiento Hacia la Nueva Mujer, a founding member of La Conjura (1978–present), and a founding member of Miércoles. Her articles on women's rights have appeared in numerous reviews and newspapers, and her book *En Defensa del Aborto en Venezuela* (In Defense of Abortion in Venezuela) was published by Ediciones Ateneo in Caracas in 1979.

VIETNAM
(Socialist Republic of Vietnam)

Located in Southeast Asia on the east coast of the Indochinese Peninsula, bordered by the South China Sea to the east and south, Laos and Kampuchea to the west, and China to the north. **Area:** 327,469 sq. km. (126,436 sq. mi.). **Population** (1980): 53,302,000, female 49.8%. **Capital:** Hanoi.

DEMOGRAPHY. Languages: Vietnamese, Chinese, French, English. **Races or Ethnic Groups:** Kinh (Vietnamese) 84%, Hoa (ethnic Chinese) 3%, Tay 1.6%, Khmer 1.4%, Thai 1.3%, Muong 1.3%, Nung 1%, Meo 0.7%, Dao 0.6%, other. **Religions:** Taoism-(Mahayana) Buddhism 70–80%, Roman Catholicism 11%, Caodaism (synthesis of Christianity, Buddhism, Confucianism) 4.2%, other. **Education:** In 1981 females were 50% of primary- and general-school students, 45% of secondary and vocational school, 30–40% of technical school and university, 33% of university, 50% of math-teacher trainees; in 1980 women were 60% of medical students and 8.1% of those holding master's and doctoral degrees; in 1982 women were 50% of agricultural students. **Literacy** (1978): 78%; no rates by sex obtainable. Officially, illiteracy was eliminated in the North by 1958 and in the South by 1977. **Birth Rate** (per 1000 pop., 1975–80): 41. **Death Rate** (per 1000 pop., 1975–80): 18. **Infant Mortality** (per 1000 live births, 1975–80): Female 103, male 127; the total infant mortality rate had been reduced to 70 by 1980. **Life Expectancy** (1975–80): Female 49 yrs., male 46 yrs.

GOVERNMENT. An elected 496-member National Assembly holds legislative power and elects a Standing Committee, which in turn elects a chair and appoints ministers of state. The leading role of the Vietnam Communist Party (VCP) is recognized in the Constitution. Indirectly elected delegates to the National Party Congress elect the Central Committee, and the Politburo of the Central Committee holds *de facto* authority. The Socialist and Democratic Parties exist under the leadership of the VCP. Approx. 1.5% of the pop. are VCP members. Local government consists of People's Councils elected at district, county, and village levels. **Voting:** Universal suffrage for adults over age 18; however, in the first national election, one must have voted to have one's ration card validated. Voting rights are denied citizens undergoing "re-education" (approx. 16,000, 1982). **Women's Suffrage:** 1945, including the right to hold office. These rights were re-issued by the Diem regime in 1956 in the South, and are currently stipulated by the 1980 Constitution. **Equal Rights:** The 1980 Constitution (Art. 62) specifies equal rights (political, economic, cultural, social, and within the family). **Women in Government:** Of National Assembly deputies 26.8% (1976); of ministers, deputy ministers or leaders of State functions 23% (1981); of VCP members 17% (1979); of deputies to the 1982 Party Congress 14%. Nguyen Thi Binh is Minister of Education, and Nguyen Thi Dinh, as president of the Vietnam Women's Union, is a cabinet minister (1983). Le Phuong Hang is 1 of 2 women Supreme Court justices (1982). Ngo Ba Thanh was a co-author of the 1980 Constitution. Ha Thi Que and Nguyen Thi Thap are members of the Central Committee. There are no female Politburo members. In 1980 there were 8000 women in Party committees, 200 secretaries of village Party committees, secretaries or deputy secretaries on district or provincial committees, 421 heads or deputy heads of provincial branches, 2563 heads or deputy heads at the precinct or district level.

ECONOMY. Currency: Dong (May 1983: 11.65 = $1 US). **Gross National Product** (1978): $8.9 billion. **Per Capita Income** (1978): $150. **Women's Wages as a Percentage of Men's:** No data obtainable. **Equal Pay Policy:** The 1980 Constitution stipulates equal pay for equal work. Wages are scaled according to skill level, difficulty, productivity, and seniority; however, sex-segregation in the labor force results in lower wages for women, and traditionally female-intensive labor is undervalued. A machinist (usually male) earns 30% more than a childcare worker (all of whom are women); plowing, traditionally a man's job, is rated as more difficult than rice transplanting, onerous work traditionally done by women. **Production** (Agricultural/Industrial): Rice, rubber, sugar cane, corn, fruits, vegetables, fish; processed foods, textiles, chemical fertilizers, cement, tires, glass, coal, machinery. **Women as a Percentage of Labor Force** (1982): 45%; **of agricultural force** (1981) 61% (75% of women workers were employed in agriculture, 1975); **of industrial force** (1982) 40%; **of military**—no statistics obtainable. Women are not drafted but serve in local militias; most women are given combat training. **(Employed) Women's Occupational Indicators:** Of health-care workers 63% (1982); of agricultural co-op presidents 5.1%, of university professors 25%, of scientists, engineers, and technical personnel 35%, of co-op workers 70%, of crop cultivators and animal breeders 80% (1981); of childcare workers 100% (1980). "Protective" labor laws prohibit work considered dangerous or heavy for women, and stipulate paid menstrual leave. **Unemployment:** No data obtainable.

GYNOGRAPHY. Marriage. *Policy:* Governed by the 1960 Marriage and Family Law and based on mutual consent. Spouses have equal rights to own and dispose of property, to inherit each other's property, to study and work outside the home, and equal obligations to support the family and each other through productive and domestic labor. *Practice:* No statistics obtainable. Most women marry in their mid-20's. Marriage is considered "natural" for women, but an alternative is to join the Buddhist nuns who serve many social welfare functions in rural communities. Bride-price is still paid in some areas, and polygyny is still practiced sporadically, as are forced marriages. Adultery is considered a much more serious social offense for a woman than for a man. There are a great number of widows, the result of continuous warfare, and most choose not to re-

marry although they are legally allowed to do so. The Marriage Law is not as well enforced in the South as in the North. Marriage is generally patrilocal, but is matrilocal among some ethnic groups (Ede, Jarai, Hre). **Divorce.** *Policy:* Legal; women and men have equal rights to a court divorce; a man cannot divorce a woman who is pregnant, without her consent, until 1 yr. after she has given birth. Grounds for divorce include adultery, bigamy, and violations of the provisions for respect and equality specified in the Marriage Law, but only after reconciliation is attempted. A homemaker's work is considered equal to wage contributions in property division. Child custody is to be awarded in the best interests of the child. Judges in divorce cases are usually women. *Practice:* No national statistics obtainable. In a 1979 survey in the Red River Delta area (North) 7 people out of 6000 were divorced. Divorces are generally granted quickly to persons subjected to forced or child marriage. Women's Union cadres (see **Women in Government** and HERSTORY) often work as members of reconciliation teams.

Family. *Policy:* The 1980 Constitution (Art. 63) declares that the family is the cell of society, that the State protects marriage and the family; that it is the parents' duty to raise and educate children and the duty of children to care for sick or elderly parents; that decisions regarding children must be made by both parents and in the best interests of the children. It also gives the State responsibility for creating and supporting creches, kindergartens, maternity homes, community dining halls, and other facilities to aid women's participation in employment and study. Maternity leave has been stipulated as a constitutional right since 1945. Female government and formal sector workers are entitled to 60–75 days fully paid maternity leave, 1 hour per day paid nursing breaks for 1 yr., and relief from night-shift and overtime work for 2 months pre- and 6 months post-delivery. Female agricultural co-op members receive only what maternity benefits the co-op's social welfare fund can afford, as well as help with domestic work, provided by mutual-aid teams. Milk and meat rationing may be suspended for all pregnant women, who may also be entitled to cash subsidies for food and medicine and are scheduled for 3 pre-natal health exams. Women with children under age 7 are entitled to 15–20 days paid leave to tend sick children. The Central Committee for Mother and Child Welfare, chaired by Dinh Thi Can, has been responsible for developing maternity and childcare facilities since 1971. The national Movement to Build the New Cultural Family encourages men to share housework, women to enter production, and daughters and sons to be educated and treated equally.

Practice: The number of rural maternity clinics increased from 6565 in 1975 to 9034 in 1980; 90% of births take place in clinics (1982), and the maternal death rate has fallen from 40% in 1945 to 1% in 1982. The Tu Du Hospital, the largest hospital in Ho Chi Minh City (formerly Saigon), reports an increased rate of miscarriages after 2 months of pregnancy from 1% in the 1950's to 20% in 1976, and a 500% rise in incidence of cervical cancer from 1952 to 1980, attributed to wartime spraying of toxic defoliants. In 1982 there were creche facilities for 26.5% of children age 0–3, and kindergartens for 32% of those age 3–6. Women still bear primary responsibility for childcare, as well as for carrying water and fuel, shopping, cooking, sewing, and animal care. The Women's Union and the Party uphold women's role as primary-care parent. Traditional preference for sons continues. There are many female-headed households, as a result of past wars and continuing mass conscription; a 1980 survey in the Red River Delta area found 60% of families headed by women, and 76% with finances controlled by women.

Welfare. *Policy:* A Welfare Fund provides old-age, war-widow, and war-wounded pensions, maternity (see **Family**) and orphans' benefits, free education and health care, and food-price subsidies. The retirement age is 55 for women and 60 for men, with employees pensioned at 80% of salary. Government-run social-welfare committees are responsible for care of those elderly who are without family or pensions; 10% of a co-op or factory's earnings are allotted to the wel-

fare fund. *Practice:* From 1976 to 1980 the State spent 735 million Dong on pensions to the families of war dead, war wounded, and orphans. The government cares for tens of thousands of orphans, many of whom (in the South) are Amerasian children, although reportedly there is racial discrimination against them, especially against the children of Afroamerican fathers. From 1975 to 1980, 1000 new hospitals were built in the South; there are mass inoculation campaigns against disease. Persons not associated with the State agricultural co-ops or factories may not be allowed access to health care in government hospitals; ethnic Chinese and former South Vietnamese government officials and their families are most affected; the families of army deserters or emigrants may be removed from ration-distribution lists.

Contraception. *Policy:* Legal; the 1980 Constitution states that the government shall campaign for family planning (Art. 47). Urban couples are encouraged to have only 2 children; couples in the countryside, 3. Use of the pill is discouraged, but condoms are distributed free, and women are entitled to a 2-week paid leave and extra food rations as incentives for the insertion of IUDs. Sex-education for young people over age 18, regardless of marital status, is provided by the Youth and Women's Unions. Female government workers are entitled to a bonus if they have only 2 children and space them 5 yrs. apart. *Practice:* No general statistics obtainable; in 1978, 27% of women of child-bearing age were using IUDs, 2000 women were using the pill, and the Committee for the Protection of Mothers and Children was distributing 7 million free condoms per yr. Sterilization usually is not permitted for women under age 35 who have fewer than 3 children. **Abortion.** *Policy:* Free and legal on request in the entire country since 1975. *Practice:* An est. 50,000 abortions are performed annually, almost none of which are unauthorized (1982). **Illegitimacy.** *Policy:* 1980 Constitution (Art. 63) recognizes equal rights for all children, regardless of their parents' marital status. *Practice:* No statistics obtainable. Traditionally, single pregnant women were a source of shame to their family and village; they were forced to undergo illegal abortions, and their families had to pay fines to the village. Now, the co-op will generally try to arrange a marriage or force the father to share child maintenance. **Homosexuality.** *Policy:* No laws prohibit homosexuality, but it is officially considered "deviant social behavior." *Practice:* No data obtainable.

Incest. *Policy:* No data obtainable. *Practice:* No data obtainable. **Sexual Harassment.** *Policy:* No data obtainable. *Practice:* No data obtainable. **Rape.** *Policy:* Illegal; no further data obtainable. *Practice:* No statistics obtainable. The Women's Union attempts to fight the stigma of shame attached to victims of rape in war (see THAILAND). **Battery.** *Policy:* Illegal under the 1960 Law on Marriage and the Family; no further data obtainable. *Practice:* No statistics obtainable. Battery is not uncommon. The Reconciliation Teams of the Women's Union are supposed to intercede. **Prostitution.** *Policy:* Illegal; no further data obtainable. *Practice:* In 1982 there were 30,000 prostitutes, 15% of whom had become prostitutes since 1975. During the US presence in South Vietnam, there were over 500,000 prostitutes in Saigon alone, and prostitution was promoted by both the American military and the Thieu regime, as it had been during French colonial days (see HERSTORY). Prostitutes were paid $1 per client and 80% of their earnings went to the central (South) government. In 1976 the (new national) government's Program for the Restoration of Women's Dignity began treating prostitutes for venereal diseases and drug addiction and teaching them to read and write. **Traditional/Cultural Practices.** *Policy:* Dowry, forced marriage, child marriage, and polygyny are illegal since 1960. *Practice:* Incidents of dowry, forced marriage, child marriage, and polygyny still occur. Women are generally prohibited from devotions at Buddhist altars while menstruating. **Crisis Centers:** No data obtainable.

HERSTORY. The earliest known people of Vietnam were the Dong Son culture, dating from approx. 5000 B.C.E. Hung kings overthrew the traditional matrifocal civilization in 300–200 B.C.E. Viet-nam was conquered by the Chinese Han Dynasty in 111 B.C.E. and was named Annam (Pacified South) by the Chinese; Confucian values were imposed and an imperial educational and court system were developed.

When the Chinese conquered Vietnam they noted that their subjects knew their mothers' names, but not their fathers'. Women proposed marriage and acted as judges, chiefs, and traders. Despite the imposition of Confucianism, vestiges of matrifocality remained into the 15th century C.E. In 40 C.E., 2 sisters, Trung Trai the strategist and Trung Nhi the military leader, trained 36 female generals who led 80,000 troops in a successful war against the Chinese. The sisters co-ruled for 3 years and, upon re-conquest by China, committed suicide. In 240 C.E. another woman, Trieu Thi Trinh, led more than 30 battles against the Chinese, driving them from the country for 6 months. Confucian philosophy considered education wasted on women and instituted strict female obedience (see CHINA), but a few daughters of wealthy officials managed to enter the Chinese imperial educational system by disguising themselves as men. Women were not allowed to own land. Many women became Buddhist nuns but were confronted with status subordinate to that of monks. The Chinese were finally expelled in 939, and Buddhism was adopted as the State religion, but China reoccupied the country in 1407 and was driven out by Le Loi, who founded the Le Dynasty in 1428. The Le Dynasty Law Code (1428), which allowed women to inherit equally and to own property, became the basis of customary law. The 15th–18th centuries were fraught with North-South hostilities, warring dynasties, and Buddhist-Confucian conflict.

At the end of the 18th century, Bui Thi Xuan, a general in the peasant rebellion to establish the Tay Son Dynasty, fought until she was killed by the first Gia-Long Emperor, Nguyen Anh. Under the Gia-Long Code, women again lost inheritance and property rights. Single women suspected of sexual activity were punished by 100 lashes, and accused adulteresses sometimes were trampled by elephants or had their heads shaved and plastered with lime. In the 1850's Ho Xuan Huang wrote poems attacking the Confucian view of women.

In 1862 part of southern Vietnam (Cochin-China) was ceded as a French colony. Treaties in 1874 and 1884 forced central Vietnam (Annam) and the north (Tonkin) into the status of a French protectorate. During the French colonial period, women were victimized by poverty and landlessness; daughters were often killed at birth, sold in times of famine, or given as concubines and slaves to pay debts to landlords. Democratic movements arose in the early 1900's. The Indochinese Communist Party (ICP) was founded in 1930 by Ho Chi Minh, with the goals of fighting both French colonialism and feudalism and with a platform including equal rights for women. Ho Chi Minh's first article, in 1922, was written in protest of the rape of several women and an 8-year-old girl by French Legionnaires.

In 1924 only 12% of all children were in school, and only 14% of these students were girls. In 1926 Dam Phuong and other women formed the Women's Labor Study Assoc. in Hue. At that time 60% of rubber plantation workers were women. Minh Khai, among other women, founded the Women's Union of Vietnam to mobilize women to fight for both independence and equal rights. During the tumultuous 1930's women organized mass demonstrations against the French. The Women's Union was legal from 1936 to 1939, and at other times operated secretly.

In 1938 Nguyen Thi Kim Anh, a leader of the ICP, wrote a book, *The Woman Question,* on the status of women under feudalism and colonialism. This activist era was followed by Japanese occupation in 1940. The pro-Vichy French administration cooperated with the Japanese, forcing farmers to plant jute for export instead of rice, burning rice as fuel, and raising taxes. As a result, 2 million people died of starvation from 1943 to 1945. In 1941 the ICP formed a coalition of democratic and nationalist groups, called the Viet-Minh, which carried on extensive covert action against the French and Japanese; the Women's Assoc. for National Salvation was formed

covertly, to work with the Viet-Minh. Over 1 million women joined the national resistance, acting as spies, weapons procurers, and transporters. In 1944, 3 of the 34 members of the first armed Liberation Brigade were women. The first all-woman brigade was organized by Ha Thi Que in 1945.

On Mar. 9, 1945, the Japanese imprisoned the French administration and proclaimed the independence of Indochina. However, the "August Insurrection" left the Viet-Minh in control of Hanoi. The Emperor, Bao Dai, was forced to abdicate, and on Sept. 2, 1945, Ho Chi Minh declared Independence for all Vietnam, including Cochin-China, Annam, and Tonkin. At that time, 1/3 of all female deaths occurred in connection with childbirth; the infant mortality rate was 300–400 per 1000 births, and 90–95% of all women were illiterate. The 1946 Constitution of the DRV (Democratic Republic of Vietnam) granted women equal rights, equal pay, and paid maternity leave. The First Congress of the Women's Union was held in 1946. During the ensuing war, when the French tried to reassert control, the Women's Union grew to several million members, conducted literacy campaigns, gave women military training, and conducted education campaigns against polygyny, forced marriage, and child marriage. Some notable women of the era were Nguyen Thi Ngai, who seized power from the French in Sedec; Vo Thi Sau, the youngest woman executed by the French; and Anh Tho, who became a well-known writer. The 30,000 prostitutes who "serviced" the French army were skilled in intelligence-gathering and sabotage and are credited with the destruction of 1/3 of all French posts destroyed by the Viet-Minh. Women comprised 2/3 of all supply porters during the long assault on French-held Dien Bien Phu.

In 1954 the French were defeated, and the Geneva Accords recognized Vietnam as a unified, independent nation. The 17th parallel was designated a temporary boundary to facilitate troop demobilization. Bao Dai temporarily was to administer the South and Ho Chi Minh the North until national elections could be held in 1956. However, following the Accords, the South-East Asia Treaty Organization unilaterally placed the South under its "protection." In 1955 Prime Minister Ngo Dinh Diem ousted Bao Dai and declared the Republic of Vietnam. The US backed the Diem regime.

From 1954 to 1960 women made gains in the North through the land-reform programs and "speak bitterness" meetings denouncing the crimes of the French and the feudal landlords. In 1960 a school was established to train women cadres in an attempt to increase their numbers in the Party, and the Women's Union in the North began the "3 Responsibilities Campaign." Women were responsible for home production and the family, supporting the front, and fighting if necessary. During the Vietnam–US War, women in the North had to assume control of village agriculture; they served in the militia and became expert at shooting down enemy planes.

In the South, the PLAF (People's Liberation Armed Forces) had 40% women commanders. In 1960 the NLF (National Liberation Front) was formed, and women fighters led by Nguyen Thi Dinh (see following article) ousted Diem officials from the Mo Cay district. Dinh rose to become a general and the second in command of all PLAF soldiers. In 1960 the Union of Women for the Liberation of South Vietnam was formed to work with the NLF. Dubbed the "Long-Haired Army," women led a campaign against first the Diem and then the Thieu regimes; they held rallies of 20,000 women and children to distract troop and police attention from guerrilla movements and actions. From 1969 to 1975, 25% of PRG (Provisional Revolutionary Government) ministers and deputy ministers were women. These included Bui Thi Me (Minister of Health) and Nguyen Thi Binh (Foreign Minister), who represented the PRG at the Paris peace talks, which began in 1968. That year was also marked by the massacre of 504 civilians —mostly women and children—by South Vietnamese and US troops in My Son.

In the early 1970's, the Women's Committee to Defend the Right to Live formed in Saigon to protest the rape and torture to which many women were being subjected. The Committee, in coali-tion with the Women's Union and many Buddhist nuns, led demonstrations demanding Thieu's resignation. A peace agreement finally was achieved in Jan. 1973; the US withdrew more troops but fighting continued until the spring of 1975, when NLF forces finally gained control of Saigon.

Between 1965–75, 2 million Vietnamese were killed, 3 million wounded, 1 million women widowed, and 800,000 children orphaned; the US dropped 14.3 million tons of bombs (the equivalent of 2 Hiroshima-strength bombs per week), devastating most of the cultivable land. Half of all bombs dropped were anti-personnel bombs.

In 1975, the 5-million-member Women's Union in the North and the 2-million-member Women's Union for the Liberation of South Vietnam merged into one organization. It adopted the New Women Build and Defend the Homeland movement, which had been formulated at the 4th National Congress of the Women's Union in 1974.

In July 1976 the country was formally reunited as the Socialist Republic of Vietnam. Since 1976 the Women's Union has led literacy campaigns, organized women into small collective labor groups to promote production, and published *Women of Vietnam,* a weekly magazine. It holds local magazine-reading circles, drafts and submits legislation to the National Assembly on behalf of women, and is the advocate for women at village and national levels. It has had to struggle to promote women into leadership positions.

Attacks and counterattacks between Vietnam and the Chinese-backed Pol Pot regime in Kampuchea resulted in the Vietnamese invasion of Kampuchea in 1979. In retaliation, China invaded 6 northern border provinces of Vietnam. In 1980 a new constitution was adopted. In 1982 the 5th National Congress of the Women's Union was held and set as its first priority mobilizing women for production, but it criticized itself for not paying attention to the specific discrimination which still affects women. Although every National Party Congress since 1930 has supported the policy of equal rights for women, the Party has not provided material support for implementation.

There is no autonomous women's movement outside of the official Women's Union.

MYTHOGRAPHY. There are many Vietnamese legends of giant women, stronger and more capable than men. One is the story of Nu Oa, who challenged Tu Tuang, a suitor, to a mountain-building contest; after she won, she kicked over his mountain, laughing. Au Co, a fairy who ruled the mountains, and her dragon husband, who ruled the sea, are the legendary founders of Vietnam; when they decided to end their marriage they did so with mutual respect. Lady Sao Cai is credited with the introduction of rice cultivation, irrigation, fire, and cooked food. Lady Dau (Mulberry) invented silkworm farming. There are many goddesses, including Lady Fire and the goddess of carpentry, who taught people how to build houses and canoes, and legends still proliferate about a great warrior general, Lady Tuong.

VIETNAM: "The Braided Army"
by Nguyen Thi Dinh

The history of Vietnamese women is closely linked with the thousand-year history of the construction and defense of the country.

At the beginning of the twentieth century, at a time when the Vietnamese people were exploited to the limit under the domination of the French colonialists and feudal lords, women suffered indescribable humiliation, both in the family and in society. As they were no longer willing to endure this, the majority of Vietnamese women joined the patriotic movement. The Vietnamese Women's Union (founded in 1930) reached out to large circles of women very quickly and opened up new prospects for them in the conscious struggle at the national level.

In manifold and untraditional ways—in associations of women sowers and reapers, in mutual-help groups and other associations corresponding to the peculiarities of the various stages of the struggle (the Union of Women for Liberation, the Union of Democratic Women, the Union of Anti-imperialist Women, etc.)—our organization brought women together and continuously made efforts to encourage and educate them for active participation in the struggle of the working class in the factories and in the farmers' movements in the country, in the mountains, and in the valleys.

In 1941 the women's organization joined the Viet-Minh Front. Under the slogan "Women's League for National Well-Being" it devoted itself to the task of mobilizing the women of the whole country in preparation for the general uprising. Women worked in the propaganda departments of the army of liberation, contributed to the establishment of revolutionary bases, supported the fighters, and collected money for buying weapons for the Viet-Minh Front. In many areas women led the revolt. The women's movement made a significant contribution to the victory of the Revolution.

The victory of the August 1945 Revolution paved the way for an era of independence and freedom for the whole people. It led to a radical change in the life of Vietnamese women. They became active co-founders of society.

At that time they were still prey to internal and external enemies. They had to fight against starvation, illiteracy, and foreign aggression. Together with the whole people, they waged a long and difficult resistance struggle against the French colonialists. Among these women were the partisans Me Linh, Minh Khai, and Binh Thi Thien.

The historic victory of the Vietnamese People's Army at Dien Bien Phu on May 7, 1954, was the final defeat for the French colonialists. The Vietnamese Revolution entered a new phase after the 1954 Geneva Conference and took on two strategic tasks: the construction of socialism in the North and the continuation and final attainment of the national and democratic revolution in the South.

The South Vietnamese women struggled heroically in the front lines under legal, semi-legal, and illegal conditions. They were active in villages, cultivated the fields, cared for the liberation troops, concealed functionaries, inspired their husbands and sons to join the revolutionary struggle, in 1968 joined the Tet Mau Than revolt, and in 1975 joined the historic Ho Chi Minh campaigns. At the same time they devoted themselves to raising the children and to social tasks. The heroic deeds of the "braided army" will go down in the history of the country.

Hundreds of thousands of women were arrested, thrown into jail, and subjected to barbarous torture. Many of them were killed. The heroic deeds and unspeakable sacrifices of Nguyen Thi Ut Tich, Le Thi Hong Gam, and the thousands of nameless heroines will be forever remembered.

In the North, women actively strengthened the Movement of the Three Responsibilities under the slogan "Everything for production, everything for victory against the American imperialists." For decades, mothers, wives, and sisters were separated from their sons, husbands, and brothers who were fighting at the front. Thousands of girls and women freely joined the youth raiding parties and were active in the "front-line battles" so that "Ho Chi Minh Street" could finally connect North and South Vietnam.

Immediately after the liberation of South Vietnam and the reunification of the country, when the wounds of war had not yet healed, we had to meet new reactionary forces: the Chinese expansionists and the Pol Pot/Ien Sary Clique. In the border provinces women, side by side with their husbands, defended every inch of the soil of our country. Together with the whole people, women warded off China's war of invasion on our southeastern and northern borders. Once again, there were innumerable examples of female heroism: Ho Thi San, Hoan Thi Hong Chiem. . . .

With the reunification of the country, Vietnam is now progressing on the path toward socialism. In view of the resolutions of the Fourth Party Congress of the Communist Party of Vietnam, women have raised the slogan "To distinguish oneself in the affairs of the State, to prove oneself able in the family, to implement equality between men and women." In the past five years women have participated actively in the reconstruction of the country. The women of South Vietnam have energetically devoted themselves to the establishment and defense of the revolutionary power, the maintenance of order and security, the overcoming of social difficulties, the construction of socialist production relationships, and the development of a new people and a new society. Socialist Vietnam is making efforts to create conditions which will make it possible for women to fulfill their task as mothers and to help them bring up their children as good citizens. The Vietnamese Women's Union, whose first concern is problems concerning the family and upbringing of children, is playing a major role in this. Our President Ho Chi Minh once said about Vietnamese mothers: "Our people owe their thanks to the mothers in both regions of our country, in the North and South, for having borne and raised a whole generation of heroes."

The fifty years of our revolutionary struggle is not a very long time, but it is a stage of profound revolutionary change which is characteristic of the life of our women.

Suggested Further Reading

Eisen, Arlene. *Women and Revolution in Vietnam.* London: Zed Press, 1984.

Mai Thi Thu, and Le Thi Nham Tuyet. *Women in Vietnam.* Hanoi: Foreign Languages Publishing House, 1978.

Ngo Dinh Long, and Nguyen Hoi Chan. *Vietnamese Women in Society and Revolution: 1. The French Colonial Period.* Cambridge, MA: Vietnam Resource Center, 1974.

Werner, Jayne. "Women and Socialism in the Economy of Vietnam, 1960–1975." *Studies in Comparative Communism,* Vol. 14, Nos. 2 and 3, Summer-Autumn 1981, pp. 165–90.

Nguyen Thi Dinh is president of the Vietnam Women's Union. She was a guerrilla in the South, active with "the Long-Haired Army," and served as a general, deputy commander of the People's Liberation Forces. The above article is excerpted from her longer article, which appeared in the Women's International Democratic Federation's journal *Women of the Whole World* (March 1981), published in Berlin, GDR.

YUGOSLAVIA
(Socialist Federated Republic of Yugoslavia)

Yugoslavia is located on the Balkan Peninsula in southeastern Europe and is bordered by Rumania and Bulgaria to the east, Greece and Albania to the south, the Adriatic Sea to the west, and Italy, Austria, and Hungary to the north. **Area:** 255,804 sq. km. (98,766 sq. mi.). **Population** (1980): 22,364,000, female 50.7%. **Capital:** Belgrade. **Head of State:** Prime Minister Milka Planinc.

DEMOGRAPHY. Languages: Serbo-Croat, Slovene, Macedonian (all official), Albanian, Hungarian, other. **Races or Ethnic Groups:** Serbian 39.7%, Croatian 22.1%, Arab 8.4%, Slovene 8.2%, Albanian 6.9%, Macedonian 5.8%, Montenegrin 2.5%, Hungarian 2.3%, Turk 1%, other. **Religions:** Greek Orthodox 50%, Roman Catholicism 30%, Islam 10%, Protestant 1%, other. **Education** (% enrolled in school, 1975): Age 6–11—of all girls 70%, of all boys 69%; age 12–17—of all girls 79%, of all boys 90%; higher education—in 1980 women were approx. 44.6% of university students. **Literacy** (1977): Women 76%, men 92%. **Birth Rate** (per 1000 pop., 1977–78): 17. **Death Rate** (per 1000 pop., 1977–78): 8.69. **Infant Mortality** (per 1000 live births, 1977): Female 35, male 43. **Life Expectancy** (1978): Female 78.2 yrs., male 65.4 yrs.

GOVERNMENT. Yugoslavia is a Socialist Federated Republic consisting of 6 Socialist Republics: Serbia (including the Autonomous Provinces of Vojvodina and Kosovo), Croatia, Slovenia, Bosnia and Herzegovina, Macedonia, and Montenegro. The country is administered by the Federal Executive Council and the Presidency. The highest government posts rotate at regular intervals between Autonomous Provinces and Republics. Major parties are the League of Communists and the Socialist Alliance of Working People. **Women's Suffrage:** 1945. **Equal Rights:** The 1946 Constitution (Art. 24) stipulated equal rights for men and women. The 1974 Constitution (Art. 188) elaborated protection of mother and child. **Women in Government:** The Prime Minister, Milka Planinc, is the first woman to hold that post (1983). In 1978–82, there were 53 women out of 308 members of the SFRY National Assembly, 273 women out of 1480 members of the 6 Socialist Republics' Assemblies, and 101 women out of 435 members of the Provincial Assemblies.

ECONOMY. Currency: Yugoslav Dinar (May 1983: 82.85 = $1 US). **Gross National Product** (1980): $58.6 billion. **Per Capita Income** (1980): $2620. **Women's Wages as a Percentage of Men's:** No data obtainable. **Equal Pay Policy:** The 1946 Constitution (Art. 24) stated, "Women shall have equal pay for the same work as men," but illiteracy limits opportunities for women and in cases of limited employment, men are preferentially hired. Women are concentrated in lower-paying service, education, and cultural areas. **Production** (Agricultural/Industrial): Grain, corn, tobacco, sugar beets; steel, chemicals, wood products, cement, textiles, tourism. **Women as a Percentage of Labor Force** (1980): 36%; **of agricultural force** (1980) 22.7%; **of industrial force**—no general statistics obtainable (of industry and mining 34.5%, of trade 46.8%, of financial and other services 50%, of tourism 60.1%, 1980); **of military**—no statistics obtainable; a recently passed law permits women to volunteer for military service, and women have reportedly been enlisting in large numbers. **(Employed) Women's Occupational Indicators:** No data obtainable. **Unemployment** (1980): 11.9%; 57.8% of the total unemployed are women.

GYNOGRAPHY. Marriage. *Policy:* Marriage is recognized as a secular practice under protection of the State (1946 Constitution). The Marriage Act (1949) posits marriage as the basis of the family and recognizes the social and economic equality of the spouses, equal property rights, right to choice of job/occupation of each spouse, and rights and duties toward children. Since 1965 both husband

and wife have had the right to a choice of surname. *Practice:* Female mean age at marriage (1970–78): 21; women age 15–49 in union (1970–78): 69.7%. Marriage remains traditional in most of the country. Many opt for a religious service, and women generally take the man's surname; his employment and place of residence take precedence. Traditional division of labor predominates in most households, although some change is observed among the younger generation. **Divorce.** *Policy:* Legal; both spouses are equally entitled to divorce. The 1974 Constitution and family legislation created mutual-consent divorce and eliminated most "guilty party" suits. Property, if acquired during marriage, is divided on basis of contribution, need, and child support. Preference for custody of a child over age 10 must be considered by the court. Further legislation varies between the different Republics. *Practice:* No statistics obtainable, but divorce is on the rise. Custody is generally granted to the woman, who frequently must go to court for increased child support.

Family. *Policy:* The 1974 Constitution recognized the need to eliminate discrimination on the basis of maternity and to implement legislation directed toward the elimination of *de facto* inequalities between men and women. Maternity legislation provides for medical and dental care through the Public Health Service, as well as a 105–210-day parental leave from work (for women or men) and reduction from an 8- to a 4-hour workday, both while maintaining full pay from the Health Insurance Fund. Women or men may request additional paid leave to care for children. Children are increasingly covered by preventive and curative health protection including both medical and educational programs. Family allowances are received until the child reaches age 15 and may continue through age 26 if schooling continues. Day-care, preschool, and educational institutions are increasing, and more mothers now are able to seek fulltime employment. *Practice:* With high unemployment, men are hired preferentially so that employers avoid paying maternity costs and scheduling leaves. Childcare is inadequate. In 1979 only 8% of children age 0–7 were accommodated by day-care facilities. **Welfare.** *Policy:* Yugoslavia and its various Republics support a system of social insurance covering social security and care for disabled and elderly persons. Work-related benefits are provided through insurance in the labor and health sectors. *Practice:* No statistics obtainable. Amounts of benefits are small and insufficient, although legislation is comprehensive.

Contraception. *Policy:* Legal; covered under the health-care system; hormonal contraceptives are obtainable through prescription, and spiral copper-T, diaphragms, and spermicides can be purchased over the counter. *Practice:* Women age 15–49 in union using contraception (1970–80): 59%, of which traditional methods 83%, modern 17%. Contraceptives are hard to obtain (because of general shortage of drugs) and not advertised. **Abortion.** *Policy:* Legal on request through the 10th week of pregnancy; after the 10th week, for health and social reasons, fetal defect, and if pregnancy resulted from rape or incest—if committee-approved. The 1974 Constitution (Art. 191) made family planning a right, and thus legalized abortion. The different Federal Republics have various regulatory laws concerning this, but always under the umbrella of the national Constitution. *Practice:* Abortions (per 1000 women age 15–44, 1979 est.): 70; abortions (per 1000 known pregnancies, 1979 est.): 500; a total est. of 350,000 legal abortions were performed in 1979. Most abortions are performed legally and under the 10-week limit, and often are covered under national health insurance. Abortion is frequently used as a method of contraception. **Illegitimacy.** *Policy:* The 1974 Constitution (Art. 190) states, "Children born out of wedlock shall have the same rights and duties as children born in wedlock." *Practice:* No statistics obtainable. The law is enforced in property rights, but in many areas social stigmas for mother and child prevail. Mothers of out-of-wedlock children are entitled to family allowances. **Homosexuality.** *Policy:* No data obtainable. *Practice:* No statistics obtainable. Homosexuality (both male and female) is socially unacceptable. While a few bars for lesbian women and homosexual men exist in Belgrade and other urban areas, most citizens of same-sex preference remain extremely covert in their activities and associations. **Incest.** *Policy:* Illegal under Chapter XVII of the Penal Code. Imprisonment up to 3 yrs. is usually required. *Practice:* No data obtainable.

Sexual Harassment. *Policy:* No data obtainable. *Practice:* No statistics obtainable. Sexual harassment is reported present to a high degree in Yugoslav society. **Rape.** *Policy:* Illegal, and punishable by a maximum of 10 yrs. imprisonment; with "serious injury" or death, a term of 15 yrs. (maximum prison term in Yugoslavia) may be invoked. *Practice:* No statistics obtainable. The burden of proof, as in all criminal cases, rests with the prosecution. Enforcement is strict but social pressures prevent many cases from reaching court. The maximum penalty for rape is hardly ever applied. The aggressor (especially if he is the victim's husband) comes off with symbolic punishment. **Battery.** *Policy:* No data obtainable. *Practice:* No data obtainable. **Prostitution.** *Policy:* The Criminal Code does not define prostitution as a crime; however, in the individual Republics, sentences may include imprisonment, banishment, and, in cases of venereal disease, compulsory medical treatment. Pimping or otherwise exploiting prostitution or "traffick in persons" is a federal crime. Offenses become more serious when involving minors. *Practice:* No data obtainable. **Traditional/Cultural Practices:** No data obtainable. **Crisis Centers:** *Policy:* No data obtainable. *Practice:* None.

HERSTORY. Macedonia comprises approx. the same territory as ancient Macedon. Slovenia, in ancient history, was inhabited by tribes of Illyrians and Celts, among whom women held high status. Serbs and Croats arrived in the Balkan Peninsula in the 6th and 7th centuries C.E.; Christianity was accepted in the 9th century. Bosnia, which was located partially in the former Roman province of Illyricum, was taken by the Serbs in the 7th century, but by the 12th century it became an autonomous country, overcome by the Ottoman Turks in 1463. The status of women declined under Turkish rule. The Croats established a kingdom in the 10th century but in the 11th century were conquered by Hungary, remaining connected to the Magyars for 800 years, thereafter in liaison with the Turks (1526) and the Austrians (1527). Autonomy has been a major theme for Croation women and men, since the 19th century. The Montenegrins fought off the Turks for 500 years (beginning in the 14th century); battling the Turks, the Venetians, and the Russians was, for half a millennium, the main Montenegrin activity. In 1878, at the Congress of Berlin, Montenegro was given official independence.

One of the causes of WW I was the drive for unification of the 6 Republics (Pan-Slavism). Only Serbia and Montenegro were independent in 1914 (the others belonged to Austro-Hungary), when a Serbian nationalist assassinated Archduke Francis Ferdinand in Sarajevo, an act which symbolically triggered WW I.

The "Kingdom of the Serbs, Croats, and Slovenes" was established by the unification of the South Slavic peoples under the Serbian King Peter I in 1918; only in 1929 was the name of the country changed to Yugoslavia, and the new State was given official recognition at the Paris Peace Conference.

In 1919, at the Founding Congress of the Communist Party of Yugoslavia, demands for equal rights for women were voiced; 1 year later the question of equal pay for equal work was raised, and both issues were included in the Party program, although the Communist Party was not yet a legal party in the country. During this period a Conference of Socialist Women was held.

During WW II, in 1941, German troops occupied Yugoslavia, together with troops from Bulgaria, Hungary, and Italy. Organized resistance struggled against the German-led take-over; one faction was headed by Josip Broz Tito, a partisan backed by the USSR and Great Britain. Tito's army was victorious, and when the Germans had been repulsed, he became premier. In 1945 elections put an unopposed Tito at the head of a Federal Republic consisting of the 6 Republics. The Serbs remain distinct from the

Croats and Slovenes, still adhere to the Orthodox Eastern Church, and use the Cyrillic alphabet. The new Republics were organized on a federal basis, and the power remained with the Communist Party.

During the WW II German occupation and the following periods of liberation and socialist revolution, Yugoslav women played major military and organizational roles. Women constituted a high percentage of Partisans and underground fighters in occupied cities, and in 1942 joined together to form the Anti-Fascist Women's Front. For large numbers of rural women this was the first avenue into political involvement.

Beginning in 1944 the Party's Central Committee found itself at odds with autonomous women's organizations, accusing them of being closed groups cut off from Party-defined mass issues and needs. Current official treatment of women's issues is delegated to "Conferences for Women's Social Activities," which include men and women voluntarily associated to work on women's issues and needs. In 1978 the first feminist conference was held in Belgrade. Pressure from these groups has brought women's issues to the fore, and in 1980 a political-scientific conference and a session of the Central Committee on women's social, political, and economic positions were held to discuss these issues. Current Yugoslav feminists work both within and outside of the "conference" system.

MYTHOGRAPHY. No data obtainable.

YUGOSLAVIA: Neofeminism—and Its "Six Mortal Sins"
by Rada Iveković and Slavenka Drakulić-Ilić

Yugoslav Neofeminism
(by Rada Iveković)

The women's movement has a pre-war tradition in Yugoslavia—but, as elsewhere, women's history has been obliterated and each new generation must rediscover it. Women's demands surface at each new political, social, cultural, and economic crisis, with more or less quiet periods in between. A new wave of feminist activity appeared in the late 1970's in several big centers. But it had not emerged out of nowhere.

During the period immediately preceding World War II, the Yugoslav Communist Party placed a major emphasis on work among women (an up-to-then neglected subject); women were to be the main force preparing the resistance and revolution, since most Communists (men) had been imprisoned or otherwise immobilized by the then-bourgeois Rightist regime. During this period, many active women who had previously belonged solely to feminist organizations (mostly focusing on women's suffrage, civil rights, the right to work, equal pay, etc.) joined the Party. The antifeminist propaganda—which had artificially sustained the notion that "feminists" and "women of the working class" had supposedly contrary interests—was temporarily hushed. Working women did indeed have a long trade-union experience, but largely by the side of their men; they had no organizations of their own. With hindsight, it does seem more probable that women workers and women from the middle and upper classes who called themselves feminists had more problems in common than is usually admitted by a rigid analysis which refuses to see the "women's question" as anything but a sub-category of the "class question." After all, elementary civil rights and a minimum of "bourgeois democracy" do appear to be elementary preconditions for and not impediments to the possible development of socialism.

A very high proportion of Yugoslav women fought with the Partisans during World

War II or helped them in other ways—some in traditional female roles (as nurses, etc.) but many with guns. Their presence was still great in political life a few years after the war ended, and it seemed for a while that a breakthrough in the patriarchal Balkan mentality had occurred. But this turned out to be a premature conjecture, because as the years went by, women were confined again to their private lives, with less and less impact on politics.

It was said that the law had given them equal rights, and that many women were in the work force. Indeed, most women worked, but they were and still are expected to perform household duties as well. In politics or in workers' self-management control of their enterprises, women are usually found in posts of low and local responsibility. Patriarchal mentality remains widespread in Yugoslavia and fosters confusion by repeating a sophism: "Women have all rights *by law,* so they already *are* equal."

The official women's organization (since the Anti-Fascist Front of Women has been abolished) is the Conference for the Social Role of Woman, now part of the Socialist Alliance and called a Council. Working along the lines of the League of Communists and the Socialist Alliance, it has adopted a realistic style of step-by-step *reformist* and grassroots activity among (mostly employed) women, rejecting any proposal of "feminist excess," but nevertheless accepting, supporting, and pushing through many a helpful reform regarding women's condition. The language and ideological framework of this organization, although Marxist, is antiquated and reluctant to accept or even take note of the new sensibility which emerged during the 1970's and became highly visible in 1978 at the first neofeminist conference in Belgrade.

Thereafter, several groups were formed, joined by women (and by a few men as well), each with its own emphasis: research on women's studies, or dealing with women's practical problems, or the concerns of women writers and artists. Homosexuals, both women and men, also joined to analyze the problems of oppression they face.

One of the differences between this kind of neofeminism in Yugoslavia and its counterparts in Western countries is that no big legal issue had to be fought (though many smaller ones would deserve it). Divorce, abortion, equal rights, etc., were all there as acceptable—though merely legal—possibilities. Furthermore, the impact of the Church in Yugoslavia is probably less than in some other countries with a strong feminist movement (Italy, for example).

But practically everything else is open to feminist criticism and activity, which is of course countered by a relentless and aggressive opposition from different sectors. Neofeminist groups have promoted public discussions and lectures on many previously unquestionable matters. Many of their members have written articles for newspapers and magazines and statements for the radio and TV, thus helping to raise the consciousness of women and men. This has proven to be a very important and fruitful activity. Many new groups have been formed (with no hierarchical interrelationship), sometimes coalescing spontaneously. The contributions of various authors to women's studies[1] is also important (in different disciplines—sociology, philosophy, theory of literature, political theory of workers' control, etc.) and bears an interesting stamp of Yugoslav political and historical character.

Publishing in the existing media is the best possibility available for communicating ideas. Neofeminists have no papers or book publishers, but the traditional women's organization, which is cooperative to some extent, does. There are also "women's magazines," mainly conservative, but with some occasional opening for neofeminist ideas.

[1.] Most of these writers' work is in Serbo-Croatian, but some of it is available in French or English. Almost all of the authors have been working in loose or tight collaboration with the group Women and Society of the Sociological Assoc. of Croatia (address: Amruseva 8, 4100—Zagreb).

Neofeminism in Yugoslavia has no university backing and no funds, and it is not yet a mass organization. There are no such feminist institutions as refuges for battered women (although the problem of violence against women is as great here as everywhere else). The problems being faced by Yugoslav neofeminists are not only those regarding women but in addition the more general problems of development. Theory is so far confined to the work of a few serious authors—plus the slight but constant awakening of a feminist sensibility in women's awareness—and still is far more prominent than practice or political activity. *As yet.*

"Six Mortal Sins" of Yugoslav Feminism
(by Slavenka Drakulić-Ilić)

Immediately after the 1982 Twelfth Congress of the Central Committee of the Yugoslav Communist League (the highest political forum in the country), all ideas, theses, and programs were publicly commented on in the media—except one: the speech of Branka Lazić, the new president of the Conference for the Social Role of Woman of Yugoslavia. Speaking about the general position of women in our society, the president had said something (in passing) about feminism: "Such ideas as are foreign to our socialist, self-management society, especially the feminist ones which are imported from developed capitalist countries . . . demand an organized fight for suppression and elimination in daily actions by our subjective forces, especially the League of Communists."

This judgment, from the highest and most authoritative platform in Yugoslavia, certainly gives us pause—and a good motive for thinking.

First of all, again it is only Party *women* who speak, however superficially, about women's problems, ironically overturning even their own thesis that "there is no separate women's question outside the destiny of the working class." If this is so, then why did no one else at the conference find the subject important enough to raise?

Of course, the new president and her statement are not at all new. Rather, we could say that her words represent a culmination of the attitudes of our politicians toward the phenomenon of feminism—or neofeminism—in Yugoslavia. We must also note that this is one of the few issues, outside of the traditional ones, to which the conference reacted at all. Not reacting to prostitution, rape, beaten women, the unpaid labor of housewives, sexism, etc., they quickly launched, however, an ideological battle against "imported ideas." We could summarize their rigid official opinion: "There is no separate women's question, or there is one only in some practical but not theoretical aspect; in any event, it is merely a part of the class question, and solving class means solving women—so it is only a matter of time." What do these feminist women want? asked the conference. Public workers, politicians, cultural workers, publicists, and newspapermen hurried to reply with their opinions about this "enemy action." They even quite seriously posed the question, "Who gives them (feminists) a right to speak?" Then followed the different attacks on feminism, from vulgar and comic accusations about feminists always wearing silk underwear to more dangerous ones about feminist negation of the leadership of the working class—which would be tantamount to a counterrevolutionary deed.

A large part of all these attacks, naturally, spring from stubborn ignorance resulting in dogmatism. All of these critics repeatedly intone the following "Six Mortal Sins of Feminism" as their proof of the need to eliminate it:

1) *Imported Ideology.* The mere fact that feminism appears to have originated in "developed capitalistic countries" is taken as a main argument against it. It seems that certain ideas are good only because they came from certain parts of the world. (It also seems that they forget that Marxism didn't come from the East. To tell the truth, I and many others of my generation truly and deeply believed—up until we were about age fourteen—that Marx and Engels were Russians.) It is also interesting that in those "de-

veloped capitalist countries" the women's movement is considered revolutionary, progressive, and bound with the Left, the workers' movement, Marxism, and socialism. In
Yugoslavia, it suddenly becomes something suspicious and conservative. How is it possible that ideas of a very progressive movement, when transported to this country, suddenly become so rotten? It is *not* possible to look at women's problems separated from
their local social, economical, cultural, and political background; it is also impossible to
look at them separated from the international situation, especially considering feminism's
international character (and how central it has been to all workers' movements at their
inception, too).

2) *Love for Power.* This is one of the dearest refrains of the authorities: women only
want to substitute female power for male power; their aim is not to change the structure
of power itself. According to this simplification, after the "battle of the sexes," only a
change of hierarchy will follow. From this kind of thinking it is really easy (maybe too
easy) to conclude that feminism is a "kind of conservative consciousness" which must be
fought. An example of such reasoning comes from the already cited B. Lazić: "There is
only one question I would like to ask our feminists: do they want woman above society or
inside our self-management socialist society?"[2]

3) *Elitism.* Is feminism considering the basic questions of women's position today in
Yugoslavia? The answer of the establishment is that feminism is an artificial invention
alien to the organism of our healthy society; only a few unoccupied intellectuals are
interested in it. Therefore, the nature of feminism in Yugoslavia is "intellectualized"—
which automatically disqualifies it. These "intellectuals" don't understand the real problems of working-class women (obviously intellectual activities are not considered work)
and they are interested only in their careers, so feminism is merely a means for the
realization of their selfish aims.

4) *Uninstitutional Activity.* Every spontaneous uninstitutional activity is dangerous,
because it cannot be controlled (which means that it is free). Outside of institutions, all
critics are considered incompetent, illegal, and malicious.

5) *Apoliticization* (apolitical activity). This accusation is based upon the thesis that the
feminist movement ("movement" is a strong word for our condition) is leading the majority of women directly into political inertia, if not something even worse. We can quote
the words of a well-known functionary: "Insisting on 'the women's question' and organizing women into women's organizations or independent movements in itself brings a
danger of separating women from the whole. It means the weakening of women as
potential builders of contemporary socialist society." And another functionary added:
"These movements are, in a way, negating the leading role of the working class and the
Communist League."[3] Here we can witness how a nonexistent "movement" becomes
"movements," and so strong in fact that it can influence millions of women in Yugoslavia,
making them passive. It is an excellent example of how a little fly becomes an elephant.
Does the speaker ever ask himself what Yugoslav feminism has to *gain* from such passive
followers? It would be the most unique feminist movement in the world with such an
absurd aim—especially if we keep in mind that right-wing parties in the West are currently accusing feminism of mobilization of the masses.

6) *The Relation of Class to the Women's Question.* This is a theoretical objection which
interprets feminist theory as excluding women's issues from those of class. Solving the
general class question, it is proclaimed, will also solve all specific problems, including
those of women. But this relationship in fact is much more complicated. Sex discrimination is much deeper than we dare to believe. It is at the *base* of the class system; in fact, it

---

[2.] *Večernji list,* May 1982.
[3.] *Danas,* July 1982.

makes the class system possible. This fabricated dilemma (class versus women) often presents feminism as being opposed to Marxism—which can only be viewed as a deliberate misrepresentation, since Marx and Engels were among the first critics of women's position in society throughout history.

The Conference for the Social Role of Woman, as the only legal institution dealing specifically with women's problems in Yugoslavia, dooms itself to a marginal position in society; it is closed within a circle of ideological phraseology meaning nothing, and unable to conduct a lively dialogue with the elements of change. A stubborn refusal to understand one of the most important world phenomena only confirms that phenomenon. The women's movement does not mean a separation from socialist forces. On the contrary, it means *contribution* to socialist transformation of society, from a specifically *woman's* perspective. . . .

We may eventually win the war, but meanwhile there are still quite a few battles ahead: in school, at work, on the street, in the family. Women in Yugoslavia need self-consciousness so that they can *use* the rights they supposedly have. And therein lies the unavoidable necessity for a new women's sensibility—call it feminism or not.

Suggested Further Reading

Despot, Blaženka. "Woman and Self-Management." *QAS (Questions Actuelles du Socialisme),* No. 3, Belgrade, 1981; available in English, French, German, Italian, Russian, and Spanish.

Društveni položaj žene i razvoj porodice u socijalističkom samoupravnom društvu (The Social Position of Woman and the Development of the Family Within the Socialist Self-Managed Society). Ljubljana: *Komunist,* 1979; documents from an official conference in Portorož, 1976—summaries in English.

Faits et tendances, Nos. 15–16, Belgrade, 1978 (available in English and French: "Les Femmes et le développement," Oct. 1978, Bled); documents from a conference organized by the Conference for the Social Role of Woman of Yugoslavia.

Kecman, Jovanka. *Žene Jugoslavije u radničkom pokretu i ženskim organizacijama 1918–1941* (Yugoslav Women Within the Workers' Movement and Women's Organizations, 1918–1941). Belgrade: Narodna Knjiga, 1978.

Ženski svijet (The Feminine World), Zagreb, 1979; reprint of a women's magazine issued during the years 1939–41 in Zagreb.

In preparation:

Despot, Blaženka. *Žena i socijalističko samoupravljanje* (Woman and Socialist Self-Management). Belgrade: Radnička Stampa.

Drugarica-žena (Comrade-Woman); an anthology to be issued by the group Women and Society of the Sociological Assoc. of Croatia, Izdavački Centar, Rijeka.

Katunarić, Vjeran. *Žena i sistem* (Woman and the System). Zagreb: Naprijed.

Rada Iveković was born in 1945 and attended school in Belgrade and Zagreb. She joined the arts faculty of Zagreb University in 1964, reading Indian studies, with English literature and language as auxiliary subjects. She published her first articles, and in 1970 left for India, where she obtained a Ph.D. degree from Delhi University in Buddhist philosophy. She published her first books on Indian philosophy on her return to Yugoslavia and also dedicated herself to the study of Western philosophy, Third World culture and politics, and the subject of Gypsies in Yugoslavia. She is still engaged in Indian philosophy, but also in women's studies, and says that her ambition is "to reread and rewrite the history of philosophy (Eastern *and* Western) from a feminist perspective."

Slavenka Drakulić-Ilić is a sociologist, a newspaperwoman, and the mother of a teen-age daughter. Her section of the above article is a short version of her major defense of feminism which was "published in a big political review and raised much dust."

ZAMBIA
(Republic of Zambia)

Zambia is located in southeast Africa, bounded by Zaire to the north, Tanzania to the northeast, Malawi to the east, Mozambique, Zimbabwe, Botswana, and Namibia to the south, and Angola to the west. **Area:** 752,975 sq. km. (290,724 sq. mi.). **Population** (1980): 5,828,000, female 50.3%. **Capital:** Lusaka.

DEMOGRAPHY: Languages: English (official), 73 Bantu dialects. **Races or Ethnic Groups:** Bantu (Bemba, Cewa, Lozi, Tonga, other) 99%, European and Asian 1%. **Religions:** Indigenous faiths, Roman Catholicism, Protestant, Hinduism, Islam. **Education** (% enrolled in school, 1975): Age 6–11—of all girls 70%, of all boys 75%; age 12–17—of all girls 42%, of all boys 64%; higher education—in 1971 women comprised 16.3% of university students. **Literacy** (1977): Women 34%, men 61%. **Birth Rate** (per 1000 pop., 1975–80): 49. **Death Rate** (per 1000 pop., 1975–80): 17. **Infant Mortality** (per 1000 live births, 1975–80): Female 132, male 156. **Life Expectancy** (1975–80): Female 50 yrs., male 47 yrs.

GOVERNMENT. The president is head of state and the prime minister is head of government; legislative power is held by the 125-member elected (with 10 additional appointed members) National Assembly. The 1972 Constitution (enacted 1973) established 1-party rule by the United National Independence Party, whose 25-member Central Committee maintains precedence over the National Assembly. **Women's Suffrage:** African women and men age 21 won the vote in 1964 at Independence (European women and men had been enfranchised earlier); the voting age was lowered to 18 in 1969. Under the British colonial government Africans had to fulfill educational and property requirements in order to vote. **Equal Rights:** Constitution stipulates fundamental rights for all people regardless of race, color, sex, creed. **Women in Government:** 6 women are in the National Assembly; 5 are ministers of State; 2 are in the Central Committee (1983).

ECONOMY. Currency: Kwacha (May 1983: 5.82 = $1 US). **Gross National Product** (1980): $3.2 billion. **Per Capita Income** (1980): $560. **Women's Wages as a Percentage of Men's:** No data obtainable. **Equal Pay Policy:** The principle of equal pay for equal work was adopted at Independence (1964) for both government and private-sector employees. **Production** (Agricultural/Industrial): Corn, tobacco, sugar, cotton; copper, cobalt, chemicals, textiles. **Women as a Percentage of Labor Force** (1980): 32%; **of agricultural force**—no general statistics obtainable (64% of women workers are employed in agriculture, 1975); **of industrial force**—no data obtainable; **of military**—no statistics obtainable; women are permitted in the military on an equal basis with men in all sectors, including combat, and a few serve as commissioned officers. **(Employed) Women's Occupational Indicators:** 30 women are lawyers (1980); of service workers 10.4%, of administrative and managerial workers 10.5%, of professional, technical and related workers 21% (1969). Noneducated women are generally limited to such unskilled or semi-skilled employment as traders or domestic servants. **Unemployment:** No data obtainable.

GYNOGRAPHY. Marriage. *Policy:* Both customary and statutory marriages are recognized. The former is governed by the various customary laws of different groups. Generally, the minimum marriage age is determined by puberty. Parental consent, particularly for the female, is required, and a bride-price is paid to the bride's family. Marriage often is arranged between kinship groups, and polygyny is permitted. Statutory marriage is governed by the Marriage Act (1963). Minimum age for marriage is 16 with parental consent, 21 without parental consent. The woman is entitled to support, and property is individually owned. Couples married under the Marriage Act are not permitted to then marry under customary law, although a nonpolygynous customary marriage can be converted to a statutory marriage. *Practice:* Female mean age at marriage (1970–78): 18; women age 15–49 in union (1970–78): 72%. Polygyny is decreasing. The government is attempting to "modernize" customary marriages. (See **Traditional/Cultural Practices.**) **Divorce.** *Policy:* Under customary law, grounds for divorce vary between different groups. Generally, a woman's parents must consent to a divorce, and repayment of the bride-price is required. Grounds for divorce for marriages contracted under the Marriage Act include mutual consent and irretrievable breakdown of the marriage, of which adultery can be a cause. *Practice:* No statistics obtainable. Since parental consent and repayment of the bride-price are required under most customary divorce laws, a woman often must wait for a long period before obtaining a divorce and the right to remarry.

Family. *Policy:* The Employment Act entitles women to a 1-day absence from work per month without a doctor's certificate. Employees in government and some other industries are entitled to a fully paid 3-month maternity leave. Childcare is limited and provided at privately owned childcare and pre-school centers. *Practice:* Both matrilineal and patrilineal kinships systems exist. The extended-family system is breaking down in urban areas. Widows and children are more vulnerable without the family network. Childcare facilities are limited and too expensive for the majority of women. **Welfare.** *Policy:* The Zambia National Provident Fund was established in 1969 as a compulsory system for all employed people. Monthly deductions are taken from members' salaries and paid back at retirement. Employed pregnant women are entitled to a grant which does not affect their pension. Government employees contribute to a separate civil service pension plan; retirement for male and female government employees is age 55. Health services are free for all. *Practice:* Though the Provident Fund is compulsory, many employees do not register in order to avoid monthly deductions. The government initiated a media campaign in the early 1980's to inform people of the need to contribute. The limited welfare system and the absence of State welfare agencies forces most people to rely on the family for security.

Contraception. *Policy:* Legal. Contraceptives are available from government health centers. Birth-control pills are distributed only with a doctor's prescription. *Practice:* Women age 15–49 in union using contraception (1970–80): 1%. **Abortion.** *Policy:* A 1972 law permits abortion in cases of extreme risk to a woman's life or health, risk of physical/mental impairment of fetus, or if physical/mental injury would result to existing children. Unless an emergency exists, 3 medical practitioners must agree that 1 of these conditions pertains, and the procedure must be performed in a government or other approved hospital. Other abortions are illegal and punishable by a maximum of 14 yrs. imprisonment for the practitioner; a woman who induces her own miscarriage is subject to a maximum of 7 yrs. imprisonment. *Practice:* No statistics obtainable; the incidence of illegal abortion is very high, particularly in expanding urban areas. Lack of facilities and trained medical personnel limits implementation of the law. **Illegitimacy.** *Policy:* Customary law opposes pregnancy out of wedlock; a man who impregnates a single woman must pay "damages" to her guardian. Under the Births and Deaths Registration Act (1972), the mother of an out-of-wedlock child is required to register the birth, while the father is not required to acknowledge paternity, but may do so voluntarily in writing to a registrar. *Practice:* No data obtainable.

Homosexuality. *Policy:* Male homosexual acts are illegal. Lesbianism is not specifically mentioned under the Penal Code, although Sec. 155 states that "any person who has carnal knowledge of any person against the order of nature" is considered guilty of a felony and is subject to a maximum of 14 yrs. imprisonment. *Practice:* No data obtainable. **Incest.** *Policy:* A male who has carnal knowledge of a granddaughter, daughter, sister, or mother is considered guilty of a felony and subject to a maximum of 5 yrs. imprisonment; if the female is under age 12, the maximum penalty is life imprisonment. A female age 16 or older who "with consent permits her grandfather, father, brother, or son to have carnal knowledge of her" is considered guilty of a felony and subject to a maximum of 5 yrs. imprisonment (Penal Code). *Practice:* No data obtainable. **Sexual Harassment.** *Policy:* None. *Practice:* No data obtainable. **Rape.** *Policy:* Under the Penal Code, carnal knowledge of a woman or girl, without her consent, or with her "consent" if it is obtained by force, threats, intimidation, or fear of bodily harm, is punishable by life imprisonment, as is attempted rape. *Practice:* No data obtainable. **Battery.** *Policy:* No data obtainable. *Practice:* No data obtainable. **Prostitution.** *Policy:* Under the Penal Code, traffick in women or young persons for immoral purposes, living off the earnings of prostitutes, and keeping a brothel are considered misdemeanors. *Practice:* No data obtainable. **Traditional/Cultural Practices.** *Policy:* No data obtainable. *Practice:* Wife-lending *(rusena)* still occurs in some areas. **Crisis Centers.** *Policy:* None. *Practice:* No data obtainable.

HERSTORY. Peoples inhabited the area now known as Zambia approx. 1 million years ago. They developed both Stone and Iron Age cultures. By 1200 C.E. peoples who spoke Bantu arrived in the region, and later, groups from the areas of Zaire and Angola arrived (16th–18th centuries). The Lozi of western Zambia (who established a kingdom in the 18th and 19th centuries) traced kinship through bilateral descent. Their oral tradition reveals the shift from female to male chieftains in their past Iron Age cultures, and the origin of patriarchy.

Women's status deteriorated in 19th and 20th century British colonial Northern Rhodesia, now Zambia. Women were forbidden to migrate to towns, while men left to work in the cities or mines. Employment opportunities for women were virtually nonexistent and many urban women were forced to turn to prostitution. Inferior education contributed to women's diminished status.

In the 1960's rural women did migrate to the cities, though job opportunities remained limited. African women were barred from certain jobs reserved for European women, were not allowed to "loiter" in towns or work as drivers, secretaries, or as nurses in European hospitals.

Three quarters of Zambia's women participated in the nationalist movement for Independence, starting as far back as the 1920's. Women cut down trees, blocking roads against government soldiers who were searching for African saboteurs. The Women's League staged demonstrations at the Lusaka airport against the arrival of the British Colonial Secretary. Julia Chikamoneka, known as Mama UNIP (United National Independence Party), led many of these nationalist actions. Women organized another demonstration at Ndola airport and blocked the road to prevent the Colonial Secretary's car from passing. The Women's League led civil-disobedience movements and boycotts. Women burned marriage certificates to protest discriminatory pass laws while men burned *situpas* (identity cards).

Since Independence (1964), the Women's League has struggled for paid maternity leaves. The Women's Section of the African National Congress publishes *Voice of Women,* a quarterly magazine on women's movement activities. During International Women's Year in 1975, women organized against beauty contests.

In 1982 the Zambian Alliance of Women, the UNIP Women's League, and other women's groups formulated a 3-year plan of action aimed toward the end of the UN Decade for Women. The plan contains comprehensive guidelines for establishing or furthering women's equality in the areas of appropriate technology, education (formal and nonformal) and skills training, health, employment, trade-union activity, nondiscriminatory taxation, education as to existing legal rights, and protection of widows against maltreatment by their in-laws. The guidelines also call for legal reforms, including those which would give a customary wife the same rights at separation and divorce as those of a wife under statutory law.

MYTHOGRAPHY. The Lozi believe that a group of men plotted to overthrow the original female chieftain,

Mbuywamwambwa, because they claimed she could not control the various groups in the village. However, the coup was exposed and reported. Mbuywamwambwa prevented a revolt by proposing her son, Mboo, as chieftain and herself as adviser to the throne. This role became traditional for women of the royal family. Mbuywamwambwa, mother of the first male chief, became a mythological character among the Lozi. She was believed to live in the Zambezi River in the form of a great white cow, Liombekalala, who could create kings and transmit power. Oral tradition also includes the story of Notulu, daughter of the chief Ngombala; Notulu captured the royal drums from peoples in the southern region and became Litunga-la-Mboela, first woman chieftain of the south.

ZAMBIA: Feminist Progress—More Difficult Than Decolonization
by Gwendoline Konie

Having gone to a boarding school at the age of eight, I learned to be responsible for myself at an early age. Both my parents were educators and served in ten different parts of Zambia, which necessitated boarding school for the children. School was a girls' Methodist school and therefore strict; one had to fend for oneself. I was forced to learn leadership quite early—class captain, house captain, and school captain. My formative years were spent in this female environment.

After school, however, I was pitched into a world where men also existed. Fortunately, at home both of my parents had given us all equal treatment. There was not special work for boys and special work for girls. Everybody cleaned and cooked. I therefore did not grow up with an awe of men.

When I went to college, my idea was to have an all-round education. I was not gunning for a distinction but I was certainly working to avoid a failure. Even at that time, I remember doing it for my country, because of the growing awareness of the politics of independence in Africa. When the major struggle for independence was raging, I was abroad at university in Swansea, Wales. I saw the need for doing well as a duty I owed to the emerging nation. My father had impressed upon me the concept that the new country was going to need qualified people to help in its administration. In fact, it was such ideas of his that were responsible for my choosing in the end to do social science against my natural inclination—which was to do music.

I came back from college a year and a half before Independence. Although I was qualified to be a social worker, the colonial politics of the day were such that, as an African, I could not go by that title—whereas a colleague, a young white woman with a degree in French, was right away designated assistant social welfare officer! The scene was set for my first major battleground—and as a person who thrives on controversy, I took up the struggle with ferocity until it reached the Chief Secretary.

One working day, I received a telephone call from the Governor's office. Everyone in the office (including me) believed that I was going to be sacked. A chauffeur-driven car, which to me at the time looked like the height of luxury, came to pick me up, drove me to

This article is based on an essay of Gwendoline Konie's, originally written for the UNITAR Seminar Creative Women in Changing Societies, July 9–13, 1980, and is printed in *Creative Women in Changing Societies: A Quest for Alternatives* (Dobbs Ferry, NY: Transnational Publishers). Copyright © 1982 by UNITAR. Reprinted by permission.

the Secretariat, and with the greatest of speed I found myself in the Governor's waiting room. When I was called in I steeled myself against any fears I had, and after some discussion with the Governor, I distinctly remember him saying to me that he liked my guts! I will never forget that discussion because at the end of it he asked me how I would like to serve in the Legislative Council (which was the precursor of the present National Assembly). I was thoroughly taken aback. I asked the Governor to give me an opportunity to think about it for a month. I took that time to consult with my family and with President Kenneth Kaunda. Kaunda was then the leader of the coalition government during the transitional period and, coincidentally, was the Minister dealing with what was then termed "Native Affairs," which covered welfare matters. He was therefore my Minister. He encouraged me to accept the appointment. Consequently, I became not only the first woman but also the youngest member of the Legislative Council. From then onward, I found myself catapulted into the world of men—professionally, politically, and socially. About a year later I was the only woman among the people who were picked to train for the Foreign Service of the independent country of Zambia. I served in the Foreign Service and rose to ambassador level. I left the Foreign Service in January 1979, on appointment to the post of Permanent Secretary in the newly created Ministry of Tourism.

Women, like men, are just ordinary human beings subject to the same temptations when in the position of power. Nonetheless, every profession experiencing an influx of women tends to become transformed—at least in a change of attitudes. This is not because women have brought about the change, necessarily, but because men who are already in the field begin to respond to the presence of women and the peculiar pressures this situation brings with it. In the main, the tendency is for women to try to work more than fulltime, in order to make sure that they do a good job. Not only that: women always appear to be under pressure to prove that they can do just as good a job as their male colleagues, *if not better*. The point of friction always comes when a man realizes that a woman is his intellectual superior. Then, extracurricular considerations are brought to bear. Postures of superiority are assumed when (strictly speaking) they are manifestations of feelings of *inferiority*.

However, generally it can be said that when women are introduced to a predominantly male group, there is a tendency for the men to be on their best behavior and vice versa. (This phenomenon is better observed at the club level.) But this observation can be misleading if extended wholesale to the work situation, which, because of the heightened competitive atmosphere, introduces the survival instinct and consequently the jockeying for positions in a vicious game for promotion. The assertion that women change the ethics and attitudes of a given profession upon entering it must therefore be viewed with all these aspects in mind.

There is no gainsaying the fact that the demands of a home, husband, and children impinge on the time that a woman can put aside. Creativity calls for time and quiet. These are more often than not a luxury where wives and mothers are concerned, especially if the children are very young. This problem is not as great, however, where there are no children, or no children yet, or in cases where the children are grown, or in the rare cases where the husband/father really does more than "help out" at home.

Throughout the years, I have found that I have, perhaps unconsciously, developed for myself certain attitudes for survival. The first attitude I adopted was never to feel that any problem or assignment was beyond me. Each time I am given a new assignment, I completely blank out any other assignment and/or achievements I have made and concentrate on the problem at hand. I try to work out not only one strategy but alternatives too. I never give up unless and until I have tried all alternatives. And more often than not, at least one of the alternatives does tend to work.

Furthermore, whenever I approach a problem, I never consider the question of either sex or color. I have discovered that people give you what they think you deserve; thus, if one is being apologetic because of being a woman, then the chances are that those responding will treat one "as a woman." When one is confronted with sexist attitudes at work, the only solution seems to be direct challenge, and in many cases the response to challenge is withdrawal, because the majority of professional men and women in Zambia do not want to be branded as conservatives where these issues are concerned.

In the Zambian Civil Service, the principle of equal pay for equal work is fundamental and was adopted at Independence. I therefore have not had to struggle for economic survival any more than would a man in my position. In the Foreign Service, the ratio of women to men is infinitesimal. Being an ambassador, for example, is looked upon with awe and envy even when the ambassador is a man. It is therefore even more so when the ambassador is a woman. In the main, the glamour is mistaken for reality. A woman is trusted less because people find it difficult to believe that she can keep her hat on and not let her head be turned by all this "glamour." It often happens therefore that instead of accepting the entertaining that goes on for lobbying purposes for what it is, there is a tendency to believe that perhaps personal feelings of the woman ambassador are involved. Although this attitude is also applied to male ambassadors, it is much more common where women ambassadors are involved.

However, a point has to be made that to some extent, at least in Zambia, supportive attitudes do also exist. In the main, it is a source of pride for governments and individuals to prove in concrete terms that women do not have a raw deal after all—and one often finds oneself as the personification of this "proof." For other women, this is a matter of pride and also inspiration. In my present position of Permanent Secretary of a Ministry, I happen to be the only woman and in a sense therefore a pioneer. On the whole, the same arguments as in the ambassador situation above apply.

The international community in general and individual nations in particular have a long way to go yet to integrate women. The struggle for equal rights between the sexes is going to prove even more difficult than that of de-colonization because in essence it is a struggle between husband and wife, brother and sister, and father and mother. We live in a world in which aptitude, skill, and intellect are all measured in masculine terms. Hence the expressions "She works as hard as a man," "She has the nerve of a man," "She drives as hard a bargain as a man," "She thinks like a man," etc. The day when a different measurement for achievement and ability is adopted will mark the day when meaningful change in the advancement of women will have begun in earnest.

This change will not come of its own bidding. It's up to all of us—the international family, national governments, and individual human beings—women *and* men.

Suggested Further Reading

Basins, J. A. *Marriage in a Changing Society.* Lusaka: n.p.: The Rhodes Livingston Press, No. 20, 1951.

Mitchell, Dr. J. Clyde. *African Marriage in a Changing Society.* Report of the Annual Conference on Marriage and Family. Northern Rhodesia Council of Social Services. Lusaka: Government Printer, 1961.

Ndulo, Prof. M. *African Marriage and Social Change.* N.p.: n.p., 1953.

Radcliff-Brown, Alfred, ed. *African System of Kinship and Marriage.* Oxford: Oxford Univ. Press, 1950.

Report of the Annual Conference on Marriage and Family. Northern Rhodesia Council of Social Services. Lusaka: Government Printer, 1961.

The Report on Women's Rights in Zambia. N.p.: Mindola Ecumenical Foundation, 1970.

Gwendoline Chomga Konie was born in 1938, in Lusaka. She has diplomas in social studies, international relations, and public administration, and a law degree from the University of Zambia. She has served as a member of the Legislative Council, and as an Assistant Secretary in the Ministry of Foreign Affairs. She was appointed Zambia's Ambassador Extraordinary and Plenipotentiary to Sweden, Denmark, Norway, and Finland (1974–77), was Zambia's Permanent Representative to the United Nations (1977–79), President of the UN Council for Namibia, and since 1979 has been Permanent Secretary of the Zambian Ministry of Tourism. She was chair of the Zambian Delegation to the All African Women's Conference seminar, Dar-es-Salaam, Tanzania, 1972, has been president of the National YWCA, and is chair of the Interim Committee of the William Konie Memorial School, Lusaka. She is also founder and publisher of the magazine *Woman's Exclusive.*

ZIMBABWE
(Republic of Zimbabwe)

Located in southern Africa and bordered by Mozambique to the east, South Africa to the south, Botswana to the west, and Zambia to the north. **Area:** 389,362 sq. km. (150,333 sq. mi.). **Population** (1980): 7,431,000, female 50.3%. **Capital:** Harare.

DEMOGRAPHY. Languages: English (official), Shona, Sindebele, other. **Races or Ethnic Groups:** Shona 77%, Ndebele 19%, European (predominantly British) 3%, Coloured (official category) 0.1%, Asian 0.4%, Tonga, other indigenous groups 0.5%.* **Religions:** Indigenous faiths 80%, Christianity (Anglican, Presbyterian, Methodist, Roman Catholicism) 20%. **Education** (% enrolled in school, 1975): Age 6–11—of all girls 61%, of all boys 73%; age 12–17—of all girls 19%, of all boys 30%; higher education (1981)—age 18 (form VI, jr. high school)—of all girls 2.64%, of all boys 3.64%; age 19 (form VII, sr. high school) —of all girls 0.54%, of all boys 1.01%. In 1983, 61.6% of fulltime university students were black; 13.8% of the total enrollment were black females. A mid-1970's study showed that 32% of women received less than 3 yrs. of education; a 1978 study of urban black women found 8% had no education, 66% had primary school, 20% had 2–3 yrs. of secondary school; in 1980 only 1% of rural black women had been to secondary school. Prior to 1980, education was free and compulsory for whites, and expensive and voluntary for blacks. Chibero Agricultural College, the only college below university level open to black men before 1980, admitted black women in 1981. Since Liberation, the government has made public education racially integrated and noncompulsory at all levels, and free at the primary level. **Literacy** (1977): Women 31%, men 48%; black 30%, white 99% (1981); 60% of nonliterates were women (1982). **Birth Rate** (per 1000 pop., 1980): 49; black 52, white 12.

Death Rate (per 1000 pop., 1980): 15; black 16, white 9. **Infant Mortality** (per 1000 live births, 1975–80): Female (black) 124, male (black) 134; white (total) 14 (1979). **Life Expectancy** (1975–80): Female 55 yrs., male 52 yrs.

GOVERNMENT. Zimbabwe was established as a full republic in 1980. The prime minister and cabinet hold executive power; the president is head of state. Legislative power is held by a 100-member House of Assembly (80 seats elected by black voters, 20 by white voters) and a 40-member Senate (to which the black Assembly members elect 14 members, white Assembly members elect 10; 5 tribal chiefs from Mashonaland and 5 from Matabeleland are elected by their peers, and 6 members are appointed by the president). There are 5 provinces with local administrative governments; tribal chiefs and councils exercise authority at the village level. Major political parties are the (ruling, and primarily Shona) Zimbabwe African National Union (ZANU)—57 seats, the (primarily Ndebele) Zimbabwe African People's Union (ZAPU), headed by Joshua Nkomo—20 seats, the United African National Council (ANC)—3 seats, and the Republican Front—17 of the 20 white seats.

Women's Suffrage: 1979, for black women and men; white women already had voting rights under the previous colonial government.

Equal Rights: Equal rights are stipulated in the Constitution; however, the clause comes into direct conflict with some equally binding sex-biased customary laws. Black women over age 18 were granted rights as independent adults in 1982; previously, they remained legal minors under the guardianship of a father, husband, or other male relative, and traditionally, only divorced and widowed women could choose to become "emancipated" (independent adults). **Women in**

* In this Preface, when we refer to racial "color" classifications (black, coloured, white), we do so as a reflection of the terminology of the particular sources from which the data was drawn.

Government: There are 8 women Assembly members, 3 women senators, and 3 women ministers including Teurai Ropa Nhongo (Minister of Community Development and Women's Affairs) and Victoria Chitepo (Minister of Natural Resources and Tourism). Only 15 of 55 district councils have women members, and women constitute only 5% of the 1204 total members (1982). Women do not sit on tribal councils, but often older women are influential in village decision-making. Recently, rural black women have boycotted decisions made unilaterally by men.

ECONOMY. Currency: Zimbabwe Dollar (May 1983: 0.96 = $1 US). **Gross National Product** (1980): $4.6 billion. **Per Capita Income** (1980): $630. In 1979 the estimated PCI was $8000 for whites and $240–$500 for blacks; in 1981, 6% of the pop. received 80% of the national income. **Women's Wages as a Percentage of Men's:** No general statistics obtainable. Most agreements under the Industrial Conciliation Act regulated female wages at 56–67% of men's wages for the same job (1981); women teachers received 82–87% of the wages of male teachers with the same experience and qualifications (1979). **Equal Pay Policy:** An equal pay law was passed in 1982 but is rarely enforced. The government has also set minimum wages of 70 Zimbabwe Dollars per month for agricultural work and Zim. $105 per month for industrial work. Pay scales and job opportunities are stratified by both race and sex. The monthly income for many rural women has risen from Zim. $10 to Zim. $50 since Liberation. **Production** (Agricultural/Industrial): Tobacco, maize, wheat, coffee, tea, soyabeans, cotton, sugar, vegetables, wood, cattle, goats, sheep; clothing, chemicals, light industries, steel, coal, gold and other metals. **Women as a Percentage of Labor Force** (1980): 29%; **of agricultural force** (1979) 26% (65% of employed black women work in agriculture); **of industrial force**—no general statistics obtainable (of manufacturing 10.4%, 1980); in 1979 women were 4.9% of the black industrial labor force and in 1981 were 6.9% of the total work force in nonagricultural activities; **of military**—

no statistics obtainable. Approx. 1/2 of the women soldiers in the liberation armies have been integrated into the national army.

(Employed) Women's Occupational Indicators: In 1979 black women comprised 1% of agricultural officers, 3.75% of public administration, 16.72% of domestic service, 23.41% of education, and 42.26% of health services. Very few jobs are open to black women in formal urban employment; clerical and service jobs are held by white, Coloured and Asian women, and by black men. In 1978, 48% of women in urban areas were homemakers economically dependent on their husbands; an additional 36% were engaged in such forms of self-employment as vegetable marketing and handicrafts. Rural black women comprise up to 80% of the peasant pop. in some areas; they generally work from 4 A.M.–9 P.M., carrying water, finding fuel, cooking, cultivating, and caring for young, old, and sick family members. In 1978, 57% of black women who lived in urban areas migrated to rural areas during farming seasons. The male migration to urban employment has necessitated the entry of women into such traditionally male agricultural occupations as plowing and cattle-tending. The Ministry of Community Development and Women's Affairs has been proposing incentives and a quota system to promote the hiring of black women.

Unemployment (1981): 20%; no rates by sex obtainable.

GYNOGRAPHY. Marriage. *Policy:* Traditional (customary) marriages are recognized when *lobola* (bride-price) has been paid by the husband to the wife's family, and after marriage registration. Unregistered customary marriages, when part of the *lobola* has been paid, are also recognized, but with less weight of law. *Mapoto* (traditional unregistered) marriages entail no family arrangements or bridewealth. Black women no longer need the permission of their legal guardians to marry (Age of Majority Act, 1982). All whites, and blacks who choose to do so, are married under the Civil Marriage Act (Ch. 37). Registered traditional marriages can be polygynous; a husband may take additional wives if a circumstance arises in which he may previously have been entitled to divorce his first wife. Unregistered marriages can also be polygynous but with no such restraints. Civil marriages are monogamous. Wives can now own property but have difficulty acquiring it. According to colonial interpretation of tribal law, a husband is entitled to a wife's income, and the salary of a married woman often is still paid directly to her husband; a high tax is placed on married women's wages. A widow is traditionally entitled to 1 yr. support before the distribution of her husband's property, which is then usually inherited by his male relatives, although a woman can be left property in her husband's will. She may choose to be "inherited" (see below) as a wife by her husband's male relative, to return to her family, or to live independently in the village. The husband's family can assume custody of her children over age 7. Traditionally, she has property rights to her clothes, kitchen utensils, and property acquired through professional services (midwife, potter, etc.). She also has the right to collect the "mother's cow" as part of the bride-price paid for her daughters.

Practice: Female mean age at marriage (1970–78): 22; women age 15–49 in union (1970–78): 60%; in 1982, 41% of all marriages were traditional unregistered, 34% were traditional registered, and 25% were civil. The cost of a bride has risen; consequently, it may take a long time for a young man to pay. It is difficult for a wife to return to her family because the bride-price (in cattle and cash) would have to be returned, and a husband generally expects a wife to work hard and bear many children to "justify" bride-price. Polygyny has increased since 1980. Some men refuse to complete bride-price payment so that a woman's father will not allow the marriage to be registered; this permits the groom to marry additional wives. Men sometimes use income earned by their wives as bride-price for additional wives. In *mapoto* marriage, protected by neither law nor family, a woman can be made to leave at any time and must support her own children. Widows lose land-use

rights, and single women and widows are allotted the least cultivable and smallest pieces of land in the Communal Areas (formerly Tribal Trust Lands). Widows, but not divorced women, are entitled to land in government resettlement areas, but they receive only ½ the amount of male heads of households. Many widows are not given a choice of how they will live after a husband's death but are themselves forced to be "inherited" by his family in order to keep property within the family's control.

Divorce. *Policy:* Legal. In unregistered marriages, divorces are obtained through an agreement between the men of the 2 families; grounds include a wife's adultery, her inability to have children (Shona only), her failure to perform domestic duties, or her being thought a witch; insanity is not grounds to divorce a woman under Ndebele law, but is under Shona law. A man can be divorced for desertion, cruelty (see **Battery**), impotence, sterility, or insanity. Partners in traditional marriages which are registered can seek divorce on the same grounds from a village court. Civil divorces are granted to either spouse on grounds of malicious desertion, cruelty, incurable insanity, adultery, and imprisonment for more than 5 yrs. Generally only the father has custody of children over age 7, but he forfeits these rights if the *lobola* is returned to him. Women are entitled to maintenance and child-support payments from an ex-husband who is employed in the formal sector. *Practice:* In 1982, 74% of all divorces were of unregistered marriages, 19% were of registered traditional marriages, and 7% were of civil marriages. Divorce is strongly disapproved of among the Shona and Ndebele, and usually partners simply separate, or a husband will desert his wife. Few women are aware of their rights to maintenance and child support, and those who try to obtain payment are sometimes hindered by petty male officials, who frequently protect the husband. Some divorced and deserted women are forced to support their families by petty trading, prostitution, or brewing beer illegally.

Family. *Policy:* The new government is trying to re-stabilize the family and raise the status of wives, but some customs still consider women to be "property" of their husbands. A law providing unpaid maternity leave was passed after Liberation. The government recognizes the need for pre-school childcare facilities. It has begun a 3-yr. project (1981–84) in coordination with UNICEF to build day-care facilities. *Practice:* The status of a married woman increases with the number of children she has. Sons are preferred, although daughters bring in bridewealth. Women perform all housework and husbands who help are thought "bewitched." In 1980, at least 30% of families were separated because of men's migrant working patterns; in 1982, 9% of women were heads of households and the sole supporters of their children (see following article). In some areas as many as 77–78% of families have members employed as migrant workers; many male workers send no money back to the family. In 1981 there were 1000 pre-school centers run by voluntary and women's organizations. The need for childcare facilities has increased, since free primary education has occupied many children who traditionally would have cared for younger siblings.

Welfare. *Policy:* A workers' compensation program and pensions are provided in the formal sector; there is no social security or pension system in the rural sector. Limited short-term war relief and homes for thousands of children orphaned during the liberation war (see HERSTORY) are provided. Free health care is available for the aged and the very poor. An emphasis is placed on rural development and preventative medicine. *Practice:* In 1980 there were 269 rural clinics serving a pop. of 5 million. These services are inaccessible to most people because transportation is unreliable and expensive. In 1981, 250 village health workers, 246 of whom were female, were trained in preventative medicine, nutrition, hygiene, and traditional herbal medicine. Eighty percent of water is drawn from wells and rivers, of which 50% is unsafe. Reportedly, 47% of women are in ill health.

Contraception. *Policy:* Legal; Depo-Provera, the controversial injectable, was banned in 1981 as a health hazard. The pill and IUDs are available at government and private clinics. Village health workers are trained in family-planning methods. The Ministry of Community Development and Women's Affairs is promoting modern methods of "child-spacing." *Practice:* Women age 15–49 in union using contraceptives (1970–80): 5%. Over 100,000 women were affected by the ban on Depo-Provera, which had been credited with reducing the pop. growth rate from 3.7% to 3.2%; blacks perceived the family-planning policies of the former white government as racist and genocidal. Zimbabwean women fear the side effects of Western birth-control methods; in 1982, 38.5% of all women in poor health complained of abdominal pains and bleeding, and attributed these largely to certain birth-control methods and to venereal disease. Most women prefer attempting to space births by long periods of nursing. Many men oppose contraceptives, fearing infidelity by their wives. **Abortion.** *Policy:* Legal since 1978 if the woman's health is endangered, if the fetus is deformed, or if the pregnancy resulted from rape; legal procedures must be performed in a hospital. *Practice:* From Jan. to June 1981 only 10 authorized abortions were performed; most were permitted on the grounds of poor health resulting from malnutrition. Many in the black population strongly oppose abortion, and folk practitioners (generally female) perform the procedure clandestinely. **Illegitimacy.** *Policy:* Under traditional law, if the mother is "emancipated" (see **Equal Rights**), she has legal rights to her out-of-wedlock child and the right to support from the child's father; otherwise, the mother's guardian has custody rights. If a woman's father is her guardian, he may maintain custody or agree to accept a compensation payment from the child's father, who then assumes custody rights. A husband can also assume custody of a wife's out-of-wedlock child or transfer custody rights to the child's natural father after payment. *Practice:* No statistics obtainable. There are many women supporting children born out of wedlock. They are not severely stigmatized but are not fully accepted. **Homosexuality.** *Policy:* No data obtainable. *Practice:* No data obtainable.

Incest. *Policy:* No data obtainable. *Practice:* No data obtainable. **Sexual Harassment.** *Policy:* No data obtainable. *Practice:* No data obtainable. **Rape.** *Policy:* No data obtainable. *Practice:* No data obtainable. **Battery.** *Policy:* Traditionally, husbands have the right to beat their wives. If abuse is "excessive" the woman may sue for assault. *Practice:* No statistics obtainable. Wife-beating is a major problem. Police rarely interfere. It is difficult to obtain a divorce on the grounds of cruelty unless abuse is constant and extreme. **Prostitution.** *Policy:* No data obtainable. *Practice:* No statistics obtainable. Prostitution is prevalent and provides one of the few avenues of support for displaced or single urban women supporting families. Prostitutes face constant harassment from police (see HERSTORY). There has been a decline in prostitution since the establishment of the minimum wage. **Traditional/Cultural Practices:** No data obtainable. **Crisis Centers:** No data obtainable.

HERSTORY. A number of early Iron Age sites, among these the ruins at Great Zimbabwe, have been found in the country. An advanced local civilization also inhabited the area in the 3rd century C.E. Early cultures were supplanted by migrating Bantu-speaking groups. Great Zimbabwe, once thought to be the biblical Ophir where King Solomon's mines were located, was re-inhabited in the 10th century. In the early 16th century, the Portuguese developed a gold trade with the Shona. In the 1830's the Shona were forced to pay tribute to the invading Ndebele; British and Boer traders began to arrive.

In 1889 the British South Africa Company, under Cecil Rhodes, gained a charter to colonize the area, and British settlers founded Ft. Salisbury (1890). The Ndebele were defeated in 1893 and lost control of their territory to the British. The legacy of women-warriors in the area includes a women's army in the old kingdom of Monomotapa, which had the final voice in the election of kings, and the Shaman woman warrior Ambuya Nehanda, who led the Shona in a war for liberation in 1896–97; she was executed by the British in 1897, and the war was

lost. In 1922 European settlers rejected incorporation into South Africa and became the self-governing colony of Southern Rhodesia, under the British Crown (1923). Arable land was appropriated from African inhabitants, who were relocated in Tribal Trust Lands. Since these areas had poor soil and were not suitable for agriculture, the African economy became impoverished. Black men were forced to migrate to cities and mines to work; women and children supported themselves by subsistence farming.

In precolonial times women had had certain guarantees of security. They were entitled to use of special plots of family land and to any property earned from work as midwives, potters, spiritual mediums, and traders. With the introduction of cash crops, women lost their land-use rights, and colonial law revoked their property rights.

In 1953 Southern Rhodesia, Northern Rhodesia, and Nyasaland formed the Federation of Rhodesia and Nyasaland, with a capital in Salisbury. Blacks protested the consolidation of white minority rule. A 1961 Constitution, which contained voting provisions to ensure white rule, caused large demonstrations. The Federation dissolved in 1963; Southern Rhodesia refused to permit majority rule and remained a colony.

In 1965 Rhodesian Prime Minister Ian Smith declared unilateral independence from Britain. The UN imposed economic sanctions, but South Africa and Mozambique refused to participate and supported Rhodesia. At this time, the banned black nationalist ZAPU and ZANU parties (see GOVERNMENT) turned from tactics of civil disobedience to armed resistance, and in 1966 the second *Chimurenga* (liberation war) began. There were 2 women in the African National Council delegation at the 1976 negotiations in Geneva. Women had to fight for even this degree of representation. In Nov. 1978 Smith and 3 black moderate leaders, Muzorewa, Sithole, and Chief Chirau, agreed to the transfer of rule to blacks, and the 4 formed an Executive Council. In 1980 Robert Mugabe of ZANU was elected prime minister, and the Republic of Zimbabwe was established.

African women were discouraged from participation in the nationalist movement of the early 1960's. Nevertheless, in 1962 the first mass women's demonstration against discrimination and detention of political prisoners took place; 2000 women were arrested, along with their children. They refused to pay fines, and during their imprisonment staged sit-ins, destroyed prison property, and disrupted order by singing, shouting, and politicizing other women prisoners.

Despite women's courage and involvement, when guerrilla units were organized, women were barred from combat roles. Eventually, women's activity in noncombat areas and demands for further participation gained them inclusion in combat; women soon comprised 25–30% of active fighters. Teurai Ropa Nhongo, who joined ZANLA (Zimbabwe African National Liberation Army) at age 17, eventually became the commander of the Women's Detachment; she led battles even during her last trimester of pregnancy. At age 25 she became the Minister of Youth, Sports, and Recreation in the new government, and later Minister of Community Development and Women's Affairs. By the end of the liberation war there were more than 10,000 women soldiers. Many women who were not in the military supported the soldiers by cooking, spying, hiding munitions, sewing clothes, and raising funds. Women were targets for political instruction, and in some areas attempts were made to break down traditional sex roles in both work and social relations. Women's committees were established at local and district levels.

No women were involved in drafting the 1979 Constitution. In the 1979 elections 3 women were elected to Parliament; these women were frequently subjected to harassment by male peers who thought women should be content with the newly won right to vote.

Robert Mugabe's current (1983) government has been more supportive of women's rights by appointing women to the Senate, House, and Cabinet, creating an advocacy department in the Ministry of Community Development and Women's Affairs, and passing legislation granting majority status to all women. Sally Mugabe has been quoted as saying, "Personally, I see no fundamental differences between African and Western feminism." The YWCA, the Assoc. of University Women, the Assoc. of Business and Professional Women, the Federation of African Women's Clubs, Girl Guides, the Zimbabwe African Women's Assoc., the Zimbabwe Women's Bureau (nongovernmental), the National Federation of Women's Institutes, savings clubs, and church and grass-roots women's organizations have been reoriented to provide more skills-training activities, in addition to their usual social welfare programs.

In Nov. 1983 a government crackdown on "urban squatters, beggars, and prostitutes" resulted in indiscriminate roundups of thousands of women across the country, including women students, homemakers, professionals, etc., who happened to be alone in public places. The women were detained in football stadiums in major cities. Outcry from women's groups and the media brought about police denial of "random harassment," but most of the women were subsequently released. The government claimed that those women who were working in prostitution would be sent to skills-training centers to learn another trade.

MYTHOGRAPHY. Notambu, High Priestess of the moon goddess Jezanna, is said to have ended the annual practice of a child sacrifice to ensure favor for the coming year. Mella, a young woman in Buhera Ba Rowzi legend, saved her sick father's life through her own strength, honesty, and courage; on the advice of the moon goddess, Bomu Rambi, she sought the aid of the feared Python Healer. In indigenous religious practices, women are often spiritual mediums and are associated with both healing and retaliatory witchcraft.

ZIMBABWE: It Can Only Be Handled by Women
By Olivia N. Muchena

Semadzimai emu Zimbabwe	As women of Zimbabwe
Takamirira zvakaoma	We symbolize toughness
Kurema kwazvo	It's so tough
Kunoda madzimai	It can only be handled by women
Hazvina mhoswa nyange zvorema	It does not matter how hard or tough it becomes;
Takamirira zvakaoma	We ourselves as women symbolize toughness.

This is one of the songs of the liberation struggle of Zimbabwe. Women sang it in villages, at the well, at church meetings and political rallies and just about everywhere during the war. During that struggle the song had specific reference to the political battles. Today, in the 1980's, it remains very popular; the words remain the same but now they refer to women's struggles for emancipation from social and economic subordination, from our marginal position in society.

The Basic Situation of Women in Zimbabwe

The position of the overwhelming majority of women in Zimbabwe, rural and urban, can be described as being socially subordinate to and economically dependent on men—men representing father or brother, husband or his relatives. The reasons are partly cultural and partly historical.

Culturally the position of women in traditional society was typical of most patriarchal systems: factors that account for women's subordinate position include *lobola* (so-called bride-price), virilocal marriage system, men's ownership and control of means of production (land, agricultural tools, etc.), limited legal rights for women, and little or no participation by women in the political or religious institutions of society.

In Zimbabwe, however, through age, marriage, reproduction, and agricultural production women's social status and ability to influence decisions within the family and community gradually increased. According to one writer, "There is little doubt that behind the scenes the elderly married women call the tune in the household and the village."[1] If one were to grade the social visibility of women on a low-medium-high visibility scale, the traditional Shona and Ndebele women could be rated medium to high for their economic and social contributions to the family.

Historically, the dual economy and racially segregated land policies of the colonial era affected the situation of women in various ways. The dual economy heavily relied on the cheap labor supplied by the neglected subsistence sector of the African reserves, later called the Tribal Trust Lands and now known as the Communal Areas. This political-economic system resulted in a split-family survival strategy which has become almost a way of life for the majority of Zimbabweans. The men, young and middle-aged, migrated to towns, mines, and commercial farms for wage employment at very low earning rates

[1.] J. F. Holleman, *The Shona Customary Law* (New York: Oxford Univ. Press, 1952).

with no or limited family provisions such as housing, family allowances, pension, or social security provisions. The women, children, and old men remained in the villages, involved in subsistence agriculture under difficult agro-ecological conditions and very limited extension services. The black majority-rule government has begun the mammoth task of redressing the imbalances of the system it inherited. However, the situation of split family is still applicable to such a great extent that in some areas up to 80 percent of the able-bodied men are away from their villages. The wife of a labor migrant becomes a *de facto* household head. She is responsible for managing the small family farm on a day-to-day basis, in consultation with the older male relative of the husband (if there is one), and in consultation with the husband through occasional visits (by either spouse) or by correspondence.

This system results in an ambivalent position for the woman who on the one hand is capable of holding the fort while the husband is away, but on the other hand has to play the subordinate wife on the occasion of the husband's visit. The question of how much decision-making power rural women married to labor migrants in Zimbabwe have has not yet been thoroughly investigated. But from limited investigations it appears that while many wives of labor migrants enjoy some decision-making power, that power is not commensurate with their roles of manager-*cum*-laborer. Ultimately, because the man owns and controls land and other means of production, he has the final say. However, there are a substantial number of women who have gained much more knowledge and agricultural experience than their husbands. In many of these cases the husbands merely endorse their decisions or suggestions with regard to how much of what crop has to be produced. What is not yet clear is how much say women in general have in the disposal of the *cash* from the surplus produced. Our observations are that a woman's voice in these matters is still limited.

Another closely related salient feature resulting from exogenous factors is the increased dependence on men economically both in rural and urban areas. This was specially true toward the end of the colonial era as subsistence agriculture declined in production, or women fled to the city and became totally dependent on husbands' wages. In the words of one unemployed housewife, "It is very un-African and dehumanizing to be so dependent that one has to ask for money for salt from a husband."

In 1979, black women constituted only 6.9 percent of the total labor force of Zimbabwe, excluding the agricultural sector. The reasons for women's high rates of unemployment include lack of education, lack of adequate childcare facilities, and men's negative attitudes toward women in the workplace.

A further characteristic of the rural woman's situation is the time demand on her because of her dual role as homemaker and agricultural worker. The situation has been exacerbated by free primary education (occupying even the little children who would previously have tended other children or herded the cattle) and is further aggravated by distant water supply and very limited health services. Fortunately, the present government is beginning to address itself to some of these issues.

One could thus summarize the basic situation of the majority of women in Zimbabwe, resulting from cultural and historical factors, as being still largely subordinate and many times subservient to men at home, at work, and in society. The worst obstacles seem to be women's own internalized negative self-image and men's negative attitudes toward women's emancipation—usually couched in defense of "culture."

Women's Gains in Post-Independence Zimbabwe

The struggle for political liberation involved women in various ways at the front line, inside the country, and in the villages in particular. It would not be an exaggeration to say that rural women—perhaps much more than any other category of people—bore the brunt of the war, as for them it was a day-to-day thing faced from many angles. Through their involvement in the struggle and through the politicization process by the cadres, rural women gained a political consciousness that has pervaded other aspects of their lives. In fact, women gained such confidence that it has manifested itself in the increased awareness of their situation by expressions of a desire to change—not just improve—their basic position.

Perhaps the biggest gain in the recent past for Zimbabwe women is having a government with a leadership fully committed to the emancipation of women and the achievement of equal status with men. This commitment is not only expressed in numerous official public statements, but also through the establishment of the Ministry of Community Development and Women's Affairs. In addition there are three women in ministerial positions and eleven women members of Parliament. Although these figures are small when the proportion of women in the country population is considered, it is not such a bad beginning. What women of Zimbabwe have to guard against is tokenism and complacency.

In real terms, some of the benefits women have derived from Independence include equal pay for the same jobs held by men, forty-five days (unpaid) maternity leave, and the recent passing of the Age of Majority Act, which for the first time makes black women majors in law. Although the practical implications of majority status still have to be tested vis à vis other laws that negatively affect women (Customary Law, African Marriages Act, Property and Inheritance laws, custody of children), the Majority Act was hailed by many women as a positive first step toward full emancipation.

Zimbabwe women in general, both rural and urban, are quite aware that legislation alone cannot change their basic situation. A lot still has to be done to address some of the cutting-edge issues. At the top of the list of priorities is economic power. Owing to several factors already mentioned, the majority of women have little or no economic power base in the home and the community. Second, the educational gap between men and women needs to be narrowed through the formal and non-formal education system. Third, the burden of women's work, particularly in rural areas, remains a major obstacle to what women can or cannot do in terms of developing themselves as individuals *or* as a group. Fourth, women's participation in decision-making bodies is still extremely limited, in both the private and the public sectors, because of lack of education, time, means, and negative cultural attitudes about women in public life.

Women Organized and United?

Zimbabwe has numerous women's organizations, some indigenous and others with international ties, political and nonpolitical organizations catering to various groups or classes of women. What seems to be a common weakness of most of these organizations —a weakness inherited and perpetuated by the colonial mentality—is a program-orientation which relegates women to the home through so-called home craft (alias home economics). There has been very little emphasis on women's economic roles such as agriculture production. Recent efforts toward strengthening women's economic power base have taken various forms of income-generating activities which include crochet work, poultry breeding, and gardening—but on a very small scale. Because of inadequate pre-planning or feasibility studies, lack of basic business know-how, and other factors, such projects at best provide irregular small incomes and at worst entertain women while perpetuating their marginal economic situation.

What, then, seem to be the best ways of organizing and uniting women in Zimbabwe? This is a difficult question to answer at the moment. An attempt is currently under way to form an umbrella organization which would at least coordinate the various women's groups. Such an organization, together with the Ministry of Community Development and Women's Affairs, would need to have clearly defined objectives. This would help mobilize the group efforts of all women working for the attainment of specified objectives. Such objectives would include affirmative action in the fields of education and employment, eradication of all legal disabilities from which women suffer, and lessening the burden of rural women's work, to mention just a few.

It would be unrealistic to give a time estimate of when these objectives would be achieved. Zimbabwe women have two factors in their favor: experiences from the liberation struggle and a government with an egalitarian ethos. Rural women in many areas of Zimbabwe are, for example, responding to the government's cooperative approach toward work and production much more than the men because women stand to benefit more from cooperative efforts than do men.

It is difficult to write about the situation of women in Zimbabwe in the short space available. The foregoing is a very broad descriptive overview of a rapidly changing and dynamic situation. The reader is advised to investigate the few available literature sources on women in Zimbabwe for a better understanding. In the meanwhile, the struggle for women's emancipation in Zimbabwe continues. Perhaps, as the liberation lyric proclaims, "It can only be handled by women."

Suggested Further Reading

Chizengeni, Siphikelelo. *Customary Law and Family Predicaments.* Harare: Centre for Applied Social Sciences, Univ. of Zimbabwe, 1979.

Holleman, J. F. *The Shona Customary Law.* New York: Oxford Univ. Press, 1952.

May, Joan. "Social Aspects of the Legal Position of Women in Zimbabwe-Rhodesia." Thesis, Univ. of Rhodesia, 1980.

Muchena, Olivia N. "Women, Subsistence Farming and Extension Services in the Tribal Trust Lands of Rhodesia." Thesis, Cornell Univ., 1977.

————. *Women in Town.* Harare: Centre for Applied Social Sciences, Univ. of Zimbabwe, 1980.

————. *Women's Organisations in Zimbabwe: An Assessment of Their Needs, Achievement, and Potential.* Harare: Centre for Applied Social Sciences, Univ. of Zimbabwe, 1980.

————. *Zimbabwe Women: A Socio-Economic Overview.* Addis Ababa: ARTCW, (UN)ECA, 1982.

Weinrich, A.K.H. *Women and Racial Discrimination in Rhodesia.* Paris: UNESCO, 1979.

Zimbabwe Ministry of Community Development and Women's Affairs. *Report on the Situation of Women in Zimbabwe,* Feb. 1982; obtainable from the Ministry, Harare.

Olivia N. Muchena, *née* Mukuna, was born in Mutoko, Zimbabwe. She earned her bachelor's degree in Zimbabwe, her diploma of adult education in Edinburgh, and her master's degree at Cornell University in the US. She has done extensive research and published many works on women and rural development within Zimbabwe. In addition, she has worked with Zimbabwe women at grass-roots and national levels. At present, she is the president of the YWCA of Zimbabwe, past president of the Zimbabwe Association of University Women, a member of AAWORD (Association of African Women for Research and Development), and a lecturer in research methods and philosophical foundations of adult education (at the University of Zimbabwe in Harare)—as well as being "the mother of two boys, and wife."

CROSS-CULTURAL REBELLION
A Sampling of Feminist Proverbs from Around the World

Men are mountains and women are the levers which move them.
—Afghanistan (Pushtu)

Now you have offended women; now you have touched rock; now you will be crushed.
—Africa (Zulu women warrior song)

Work is the liberator of women.   —Algeria (feminist slogan)

Where women are honored the gods are pleased.   —Arab

Remember the dignity of your womanhood. Do not appeal, do not beg, do not grovel. Take courage, join hands, stand beside us, fight with us.
—Britain (Christabel Pankhurst)

She must do twice as well as a man to be thought of as half as good. Fortunately, it's not too hard for a woman to be twice as good as a man.
—Canada (Charlotte Whittier, Mayor of Ottawa,
speaking of women in public life)

When a woman loves a woman, it is the blood of the mothers speaking.
—The Caribbean

A man thinks he knows but a woman knows better.   —China

A rich widow's tears soon dry.   —Denmark

A poor woman has many troubles: weeping children, wet firewood, a leaking kettle, and a cross man.
—Finland

Men are the reason for women disliking each other.   —France

A woman is not a fiddle to be hung on the wall after being played with.—Germany

Womanhood is awakening—*"Jag Rahi Hai."*
—India (chant by women demonstrators in Delhi, 1979)

Wherever you go, have a woman friend.   —Ireland

Men should leave women alone and go study mathematics.   —Italy

A man who betrays a woman had best sleep with one eye open.   —Japan

A brilliant daughter makes a cranky wife.   —The Netherlands

A woman is more crafty than a king.   —Nigeria (Hausa)

Quick-loving a woman means quick not-loving a woman.   —Nigeria (Yoruba)

A rich widow weeps with one eye and laughs with the other.   —Portugal

If a woman is cold, it is her husband's fault.   —Russia (Ukrainian)

Trusting a man is like trusting a sieve to hold water.   —Saudi Arabia

When a woman loves another woman, it brings no shame to her father's head and no swelling to her own belly.

—Saudi Arabia

The women will get there but the men won't.   —Samoa

Who speaks ill of his wife dishonors himself.   —Scotland

A wife's advice may seem of little value—but he who does not take it is a fool.
—Spain

She recognizes the reality of the society around her. She dedicates herself to its future. She sets alight the world with her talent. She acts with firmness and resolve. She works for the well-being of society. These truly are the five qualities of beauty that will make a new *pancha kalyani* [beautiful woman].

—Sri Lanka

A woman's heart sees more than ten men's eyes.   —Sweden

Women are all one nation.   —Turkey

If particular care and attention is not paid to the ladies we are determined to foment a rebellion, and will not hold ourselves bound by any laws in which we have no voice or representation.

—United States (Abigail Adams)

My dream is to ride the tempest, tame the waves, kill the sharks. I want to drive the enemy away to save our people. I will not accept the usual fate of women who bow their heads and become concubines.

—Vietnam (Trieu Thi Trinh, 240 C.E.)

You need double strength if you quarrel with an independent woman.
—Zimbabwe (Shona)

Afghanistan	*khwahar* (Dari), *khore* (Pushtu)
Algeria	*ukht* (Arabic), *soeur* (French)
Argentina	*hermana* (Spanish)
Australia	*caathee, yabboine* (Aboriginal), *sister* (English)
Brazil	*irmá* (Portuguese)
Britain	*sister* (English), *sister* (Scottish), *chwaer* (Welsh)
Canada	*sister* (English), *soeur* (French)
Caribbean	*'tisoeur* (Creole), *zuster* (Dutch), *sister* (English), *soeur* (French), *hermana* (Spanish)
Chile	*hermana* (Spanish)
China	*jiemei* (Mandarin)
Colombia	*hermana* (Spanish)
Cuba	*hermana* (Spanish)
Denmark	*søster*
Ecuador	*turi* (Quechua), *hermana* (Spanish)
Egypt	*ukht* (Arabic)
El Salvador	*hermana* (Spanish)
Finland	*sisar*
France	*soeur*
Germany	*Schwester*
Ghana	*onuabea* (Akan and Brong), *sister* (English), *novinye nyonu* (Ewe), *nyemiyo* (Ga), *danwa* (Hausa)
Greece	*adelf'*
Guatemala	*chak-ues* (Mam), *nuanapp* (Quiche), *hermana* (Spanish)
Hungary	*növér*
India	*bōn* (Bengali), *sister* (English), *ben* (Gujarti), *bahan* (Hindi), *beni* (Kashmiri), *anujathy* (Malaualam), *penn* (Punjabi), *sahidari* (Tamil and Kannada)
Indonesia	*saudara perempuan*
Iran	*khwahar* (Farsi)
Ireland(s)	*deirsiúr* (Gaelic), *sister* (English)
Israel	*achot* (Hebrew), *schvester* (Yiddish)
Italy	*sorella*
Japan	*shimai*
Kenya	*sister* (English), *dada* (Swahili)
Korea	*nui*
Kuwait	*ukht* (Arabic)
Lebanon	*ukht* (Arabic)
Libya	*ukht* (Arabic)
Mexico	*hermana* (Spanish)
Morocco	*ukht* (Arabic), *soeur* (French)
Nepal	*didi* (older sister, Nepali), *bahini* (younger sister, Nepali)
The Netherlands	*zuster*
New Zealand	*tuahine* (Maori), *sister* (English)
Nicaragua	*hermana* (Spanish)

Nigeria	*oterelohu* (Edo), *eyen-eke-anwan* (Efik), *sister* (English), *nwanne nwanyi* (Igbo), *yaaya* (older sister, Hausa), *kenwa* (younger sister, Hausa), *egbon obirin* (older sister, Yoruba), *aburo obirin* (younger sister, Yoruba)*
Norway	*søster*
Pacific Islands	*tama'ita'i* (woman, Samoan), *tei* (younger sister, Samoan)**
Pakistan	*bahan* (Urdu), *sister* (English)
Palestine	*ukht* (Arabic)
Peru	*turi* (Quechua), *hermana* (Spanish)
Poland	*siostra*
Portugal	*irmá*
Rumania	*soră*
Saudi Arabia	*ukht* (Arabic)
Senegal	*a tion ani faa nawu* (older sister, Diola), *a tion* (younger sister, Diola), *soeur* (French), *nkoto maa musoo* (older sister, Mandingues), *ndoko maa musoo* (younger sister, Mandingues), *o maages o teew* (older sister, Serer), *o ndebes o ndew* (younger sister, Serer), *maw nam debbo* (older sister, Toucouleur), *mi nam debbo* (younger sister, Toucouleur), *mak diou dgijueni* (older sister, Wolof), *rak diou dgijueni* (younger sister, Wolof)***
Southern Africa	*kgaitsedi* (Sepedi, Sesotho, Setswana), *dade, sisi* (Swazi, Xhosa, Zulu), *suster* (Afrikaans), *sister* (English)
Spain	*hermana*
Sri Lanka	*savodariya* (Sinhalese)
Sudan	*ukht* (Arabic)
Sweden	*syster*
Thailand	*peesao* (older sister, Thai), *nongsaoo* (younger sister, Thai)
The United States	*a-gi-lv-gi* (Cherokee), *shádí* (older sister, Navajo), *nimesa* (Ojibwa), *sister* (English), *hermana* (Spanish)†
The USSR	*sestrá* (Russian)
Venezuela	*hermana* (Spanish)
Vietnam	*chi* (older sister), *mem* (younger sister)
Yugoslavia	*sestra* (Serbo-Croatian)

* There are more than 200 dialects and 12 languages spoken in Nigeria. The above-listed ones are intended as samples, not as an inclusive representative listing.—Ed.

** Samoan is only one of hundreds of languages and dialects in the Pacific Islands.—Ed.

*** The Leboue are Wolof-speaking.—Ed.

† Since virtually every language group is represented in some generational way in the US, the above are only samples of 3 of the numerous native Nations, and 2 of the major ethnic-immigrant groups.—Ed.

Zambia   *inkashi* (Bemba and Bisa), *mucizye* (Ila), *kaizeli*
                (Lozi), *kalongozi* (Nyanja), *mwanakwesu musimbi*
                (Tonga),†† *sister* (English)
Zimbabwe   *sisi* (Ndebele), *hanzvadzi* (Shona), *sister* (English)

†† These are only a sampling of the many indigenous languages and dialects in Zambia.—Ed.

GLOSSARY

abaya: the veil, as referred to in Saudi Arabia and neighboring regions.

ascendant relationship: direct blood-relation predecessor (mother or father, grandparents).

B.C.E.: Before Common Era; an alternative dating terminology to B.C., and one less based on Christian religious ethnocentricism.

bilateral kinship system: kinship and descent defined through both the matrilineal (mother's) and patrilineal (father's) lines.

bride-price: money and/or material items given by the groom's family to the family of the bride at marriage, in acknowledged exchange for rights and privileges over the woman and any children she eventually may bear.

bridewealth: money and/or material items, livestock, etc., given by the bride's family through the medium of the woman to the groom and his kin, to accompany the woman's entrance into marriage. Ostensibly, bridewealth is a protective measure to ensure a woman's financial independence, but in practice, control of the bridewealth often passes into the hands of the husband or his family.

burqa: the veil, as referred to in Pakistan and neighboring regions.

"The Burning Time": 300–400-year period in Europe (primarily the 15th, 16th, and 17th centuries), during which approx. 9 million women were killed as witches after accusation, torture, and trial by Christian authorities.

C.E.: Common Era; an alternative to A.D.; see B.C.E., above.

chador: Iranian term for the veil (complete body veiling of a woman in black cloth, with only the face or, in strict observance, one eye, exposed).

clitoridectomy: the practice of excising the clitoris. "Sunna circumcision" is the removal of the prepuce and/or tip of the clitoris; full clitoridectomy consists of the removal of the entire organ (both prepuce and glans) plus adjacent parts of the labia minora. Clitoridectomy is practiced in more than 26 countries from the Horn of Africa and the Red Sea across to the Atlantic coast of the African continent, and from Egypt in the north to Mozambique in the south, also including Botswana and Lesotho. According to Awa Thiam, the Senegalese writer, the practice of clitoridectomy can also be found in the two Yemens, Saudi Arabia, Iraq, Jordan, Syria, and southern Algeria. Some researchers cite evidence of the practice in such diverse areas as Indonesia, Malaysia, Australia, Brazil, El Salvador, Pakistan, and among the Skoptsi Christian sect in the Soviet Union (see genital mutilation).

creche: nursery or childcare center for infants or very young children.

descendant relationship: direct blood-relation descendant (daughter or son, grandchild).

dowry: material items (sometimes including money) exchanged between the families of new marriage partners; depending on the country and culture, dowry may be contingent on the bride's virginity and may be payable by the groom's family to that of the bride (see bride-price), or by the bride's relatives to those of the groom (see bridewealth); it may also consist of a mutual exchange of such gifts between the families.

ECA: (UN) Economic Commission for Africa.

ECAFE: (UN) Economic Commission for Asia and the Far East.

ECE: (UN) Economic Commission for Europe.

ECLA: (UN) Economic Commission for Latin America.

ECWA: (UN) Economic Commission for Western Asia.

ECOSOC: (UN) Economic and Social Council.

ESCAP: (UN) Economic and Social Commission for Asia and the Pacific.

excision: see clitoridectomy; genital mutilation.

FAO: (UN) Food and Agriculture Organization.

"female circumcision": a euphemistic term for clitoridectomy or excision; the degree of damage is far more severe than that resulting from male circumcision. Although the two cultural practices are related—especially insofar as both are widely practiced with no medical necessity and, in fact, with deleterious side effects to health—clitoridectomy is more analogous to total penisectomy than to circumcision (see clitoridectomy; genital mutilation).

genital mutilation: Although female genital mutilation in its various forms is erroneously thought by many to be an Islamic practice, the procedure pre-dates Mohammed, who himself counseled reform and moderation of the operation. In the 5th century B.C.E., Herodotus mentioned it as a practice of the Phoenicians, Hittites, Egyptians, and Ethiopians. Furthermore, in addition to being performed by some Islamic peoples, clitoridectomy and/or infibulation is practiced by some Coptic Christians, members of various indigenous tribal religions, some Catholics and Protestants, and some Fellasha (an ancient Jewish sect living in Ethiopia). In addition, the procedure is not unknown in the so-called developed world: clitoridectomy was practiced in 19th-century London (as a cure for the "epilepsy" it was thought would result from female orgasm), and as late as the 1940's in the United States (as a cure for female masturbation); during the 1970's in the US, an Ohio gynecologist offered an operation involving vaginal reconstruction "to make the clitoris more accessible to direct penile stimulation." In addition, the psychic clitoridectomy legitimized by Freud (who wrote that "the elimination of clitoral sexuality is a necessary precondition for the development of femininity") has caused inestimable female suffering in the West. As of 1984, estimates differ on the number of women alive today enduring various forms of physical genital mutilation: the figure ranges from 65 million to 75 million. Clitoridectomy is usually performed by midwives, and the age of the female child varies—between 9 and 40 days after the child's birth (Ethiopia), between age 4 and 6 (Egypt), and near puberty (the Sudan); the severe health consequences include primary fatalities owing to shock, hemorrhage, or septicemia, and such later complications as incontinence, calcification deposits in the vaginal walls, recto-vaginal fistulas, vulval abscesses, recurrent urinary retention and infection, keloid formation, infertility, and an array of grave obstetric, sexual, and psychological complications. Overt justifications include such contradictory explanations as custom, religion, family honor, cleanliness, initiation, insurance of virginity at marriage, and prevention of female promiscuity. Yet such courageous women as Nawal El Saadawi, Marie Angélique Savané, Edna Adan Ismail, Marie Bassili Assad, Esther Ogunmodede, Fawzia Assad, and many others in the regions directly concerned have for years been doing studies on the effects of this custom and pressuring governments and international agencies to oppose the practice. Some governments have taken a stand (the Sudan outlawed infibulation in 1946, Egypt passed legislation against clitoridectomy in the 1970's, and in 1982 Pres. Daniel arap Moi of Kenya publicly denounced the practice and Kenyan medical authorities forbade it); some nongovernmental organizations (including the Assoc. of African Women in Research and Development, the Voltaic Women's Federation, the Somali Women's Democratic Organization, the International Commission for the Abolition of Sexual Mutilations, and the Coalition of African, Arab, and Western women who formed the Women's Action Group on Female Excision and Infibulation), and some United Nations agencies (notably UNICEF and WHO) have organized conferences and seminars to develop creative educational and/or legislative strategies which would effectively combat the practice of female genital mutilation.* (Also see clitoridectomy; infibulation.)

hajib (or *hejab):* literally "modest dress" for a woman in the Moslem world; usually the wearing of a headscarf or other head covering, long sleeves, and a (long-hemmed) skirt, although it can also mean more complete forms of veiling, as in *chador.*

Halacha: religious legal code of Judaism; the basis of law in Rabbinical courts.

hejab: see *hajib.*

home-working: piecework (usually sewing or other needlework) done on assignment at home for wage pay, but without contract or benefits.

idda: under Islamic jurisprudence, the period of seclusion for a woman following the end of a marriage; in the case of repudiation (see *talaq)* or revocable divorce (see *radji),* a woman must remain secluded and cannot remarry for 3 months (or until delivery if she is pregnant) following the final divorce pronouncement; in the case of a husband's death, the *idda* for a widow is 4 months and 10 days. In Coptic Christian divorces, the wife's period of *idda* is 10 months.

ILO: (UN) International Labour Organisation.

IMF: (UN) International Monetary Fund.

infibulation (from the Latin *fibula,* or clasp): the removal of the entire clitoris, the labia majora, and the labia minora—and the joining of the scraped sides of the vulva across the vagina, where they are secured with thorns or sewn with thread or catgut; a small opening is maintained by inserting a sliver of wood (commonly a matchstick) into the wound during the healing process, to permit passage of urine and menstrual blood. An infibulated woman must be cut open to permit intercourse and cut further to permit childbirth; often, she is closed up again after delivery, and so may be subject to such procedures repeatedly during her reproductive life. The practice of infibulation still exists (sometimes despite legal proscription against it) in certain areas of the Sudan, Somali Republic, Ethiopia, Nigeria, Upper Volta, the Ivory Coast, Kenya, and Mali. The Sudanese name for infibulation credits its origin to Egypt ("Pharaonic circumcision"); the Egyptians call the same operation "Sudanese circumcision" (see genital mutilation).

INSTRAW: (UN) International Research and Training Institute for the Advancement of Women.

kadi (or *qadi):* a judge in Islamic religious courts.

khul' (or *khula* or *khole)*: in Islamic jurisprudence, the right of a wife to obtain a divorce from her husband by paying him a sum of money (amount negotiable) in compensation; sometimes called "divorce by mutual consent."

la'am: a man's right to repudiate his already acknowledged child (under certain interpretation of Islamic Shari'a law) by verbal pronouncement; a father may exercise this right by repeating "I repudiate thee" 3 times, before witnesses (see *Shari'a; talaq).*

mahar (or *mah'r):* in the Islamic world, an "obligatory gift" (form of dowry) which accompanies the marriage contract and is paid (in full when the contract is drawn or in part at that time and in deferred payments) by the fiancé's/groom's family to the fiancée/bride. Under most interpretations of Shari'a jurisprudence (see *Shari'a),* the *mahar* belongs to the woman herself to control and dispose of as she wishes—but

---

* See *Traditional Practices Affecting the Health of Women and Children,* WHO/EMRO Technical Publication No. 2 Vol. 2, World Health Organization Regional Office for the Eastern Mediterranean, 1981; *The Hidden Face of Eve* by Nawal El Saadawi, Beacon Press, Boston, 1982; "Female Circumcision, Excision, and Infibulation: Facts and Proposals for Change," Report No. 47, Minority Rights Group, London; "The International Crime of Genital Mutilation," by Robin Morgan and Gloria Steinem, *Ms.,* Vol. VIII, No. 9, Mar. 1980, among other sources.

this right comes to her only by the act of marriage. In practice, her natal family is often the recipient. If the engagement has not been solemnized in marriage, the entire *mahar* must be returned to the man (in case of full payment at engagement), no matter who is at fault; if the marriage has been solemnized but not consummated, half the *mahar* must be returned to the groom. In case of either spouse's death, the wife (or her family) keeps the entire *mahar.* For Coptic Christians in Egypt, the *mahar* is also observed as part of the legal marriage contract. In practice, the *mahar* sometimes is used as the *khul'* (see above) payment, e.g., returned by a woman in order to obtain a divorce from her husband.

matrifocal (or matrilocal): the practice of a male spouse living with his wife's family or in her ancestral region.

matrilineal kinship system: kinship and descent defined through the matrilineal (mother's) line, sometimes traced back generations to a common female ancestor.

mikvah: orthodox Jewish ritual bath of total immersion required of women in order to purge themselves of the "unclean" state following a menstrual period or childbirth.

monogamy: the practice of one person (of either sex) being married to one spouse (of either sex).

mullah: Islamic religious authority and functionary.

mut'a (or *mout'a): in Islamic jurisprudence, an agreed-on remuneration (male to female) in exchange for a marriage which has been contracted on a temporary basis for reasons of the groom's pleasure.

OAS: Organization of American States.

Patria Potestad (or Patria Potestas or Patrio Poder): a legal concept from Roman law, literally "power of the father"; sometimes more generally defined as parental and/or guardianship powers, rights, and responsibilities. In many countries, this concept is encoded in law and specifically declares the husband/father head of the household and family, with full power to determine place of residence, children's education, etc. (in Brazil, for example, Patrio Poder defines the husband as "head of the marital union"). Women's movements, particularly those in Latin America, have been focusing on the issue and attempting to bring about reforms in family laws that would stipulate parental guardianship and authority as shared between a mother and a father.

patrifocal (or patrilocal): the practice of a female spouse living with her husband's family or in his ancestral region.

patrilineal kinship system: kinship and descent defined through the patrilineal (father's) line and/or traced back to a common male ancestor.

patrimony: inheritance from one's father.

polyandry: the practice of one woman being married concurrently to more than one husband; a (rare) form of polygamy.

polygamy: the practice of one person (of either sex) being married concurrently to multiple spouses (of the opposite sex).

polygyny: the practice of one man being married concurrently to more than one wife; the most common form of polygamy.

purdah: the practice of female seclusion; sometimes taken to mean separate women's quarters, women dining separately from male family members, women not permitted to travel or appear in public (or to do so only in the company of a guardian, usually male).

qadi: see *kadi.*

radji: an Islamic legal concept of revocable divorce as a man's option (see *talaq).*

Salic Law: in many European countries, the rule of succession which forbade a woman (or anyone in a female line of royal descent) from ascending the throne or claiming a noble title in her own right.

sati (or *suttee)*: the practice in which a widow is voluntarily or forcibly killed, usually by being burned alive on her husband's funeral pyre. Despite repeated legislation against this practice, it still persists in parts of India and some other countries on the Asian sub-continent, and is thought (in fundamentalist Hindu religious observance) to further the progress of the dead husband's soul, notwithstanding the fact that the practice is nowhere mentioned in major Hindu holy texts, including the *Sastras* and the *Laws of Manu*, and that this tradition may actually pre-date Aryan invasions into ancient India and surrounding regions. In many cases, the widow is driven to suicide by intense pressure from her in-laws, or she is killed by them, ostensibly for religious reasons but often with the motive of repossessing her inheritance portion and/or gaining full control over her children.

sex-tourism: pre-packaged tours in Asia patronized by businessmen, which include the sexual services of women in the country or countries visited. (See esp. the Statistical Prefaces on Japan, Thailand, Korea.)

Shari'a: Islamic legal code; interpreted differently by the two major branches of Islam (the majority Sunni, and the minority Shi'ite); also interpreted differently within the four primary Sunni legal schools of thought (Hanafi, Maliki, Shafite, and Hanbalite), and within the numerous sectarian subdivisions of the Shi'ite branch as well (see *Shi'ite* and *Sunni).* Influence of the Shari'a on secular law varies: in many countries with a majority Moslem population, the Shari'a affects secular law (e.g., Egyptian secular law is based on Hanafi interpretation of the Shari'a); in Iran, the Shi'ite majority has affirmed fundamentalist interpretation in a virtual theocracy.

sheitl: wig worn to cover the shorn head of a married woman (so that her hair will not tempt men to sin); an orthodox Jewish practice.

Shi'ite: minority branch of Islam (largely Persian) comprising sects believing in Mohammed's cousin Ali and the Imams as his only rightful successors, and in the messianic return of the last recognized Imam; Shi'ite sects are many, and include the Hassassin, the Fatimid, and the mystical Sufi.

Sunni: majority branch of Islam claiming adherence to the orthodox tradition; acknowledges the first four caliphs as rightful successors of Mohammed.

suttee: see *sati.*

talaq: in some interpretation of Islamic jurisprudence, a man's right to repudiate or renounce his wife by verbal divorce; under *talaq,* a man repeats "I divorce thee" three times (depending on the interpretation, he must do so in front of male witnesses and/or let lapse a period of time between pronouncements); a woman has no parallel right and, in strict Islamic interpretation, no right to divorce, unless prespecified in the marriage contract. Until the third and final pronouncement, the divorce is revocable *(radji)* and a man can decide to reclaim his wife with or without her consent. Despite the fact that the majority of Moslems today do not practice (and even oppose) *talaq,* and that the *Koran* itself defines wife-repudiation as "the most hateful to God of all the permitted acts," the practice still persists and is even encoded in the law as a male prerogative in some Islamic countries; Moslem religious fundamentalists defend it as tradition, Moslem theological moderates, liberals, and reformers contest it, and feminists in the Islamic world are vocal in their own opposition (also see *la'am).*

UNDP: United Nations Development Program.

UNESCO: United Nations Educational, Scientific, and Cultural Organization.

UNFPA: United Nations Fund for Population Activities.

UNHCR: Office of the United Nations High Commissioner for Refugees.

UNICEF: United Nations Children's Fund.

UNIDO: United Nations Industrial Development Organization.

UNITAR: United Nations Institute for Training and Research.

UNRWA: United Nations Relief and Works Agency for Palestine Refugees in the Near East.

virilocal: a synonym for patrilocal or patrifocal (see the latter).

WFP: (UN) World Food Program.

WHO: (UN) World Health Organization.

BIBLIOGRAPHY
General*

Amnesty International Report 1982 and *1983*. London: Amnesty International Publications, 1982 and 1983.

Attwater, Donald. *The Penguin Dictionary of Saints*. Middlesex, England: Penguin Books, 1965.

Barry, Kathleen. *Female Sexual Slavery*. Englewood Cliffs, NJ: Prentice-Hall, 1979.

Boserup, Ester. *Woman's Role in Economic Development*. New York: St. Martin's Press, 1970.

————, and Christina Liljencrantz. *Integration and Women in Development: Why, When, How*. New York: UNDP, May 1975.

Boulding, Elise. *Handbook on International Data on Women*. Beverly Hills, CA: Sage Publications, 1976.

Brownmiller, Susan. *Against Our Will: Men, Women, and Rape*. New York: Bantam Books, 1976.

Bulletin of Labour Statistics 1982–83. Geneva: ILO, 1982.

Chaney, Elsa M. *Supermadre: Women in Politics in Latin America*. Austin: Univ. of Texas Press, 1979.

Comisión Interaméricana de Mujeres. *Estudio Comparativo de la Legislación de los Países Americanos Respecto a la Mujer*. Washington, D.C.: Organización de los Estados Americanos, 1982.

————. *Situación de la Mujer en la Legislación de los Países de América*. Documento presentado a la XIX Asamblea de la CIM. Washington, D.C.: Organización de los Estados Americanos, 1978.

Curtin, Leslie B. *Status of Women: A Comprehensive Analysis of Twenty Developing Countries—Reports on the World Fertility Survey*, No. 5. Washington, D.C.: Population Reference Bureau, June 1982.

Dames, Michael. *The Silbury Treasure: The Great Goddess Rediscovered*. London: Thames and Hudson, 1976.

Davis, Elizabeth Gould. *The First Sex*. New York: Putnam, 1971.

Diehl, Charles. *Byzantine Empresses*. New York: Knopf, 1963.

Diner, Helen. *Mothers and Amazons*. Ed. and trans. John Philip Lundin. Garden City, NY: Anchor Press/Doubleday, 1973.

Encyclopaedia Britannica: Macropaedia. 1977 ed.

Esposito, John L. *Women in Muslim Family Law*. Syracuse, NY: Syracuse Univ. Press, 1982.

Evaluation Study No. 3: Rural Women's Participation in Development. New York: UNDP, June 1980.

de Figueroa, Teresa Orrego. "A Critical Analysis of Latin American Programs to Integrate Women in Development." *Women and World Development*. Eds. Irene Tinker, Michele Bo Bramsen, and Mayra Buvinić. New York: Praeger, 1976.

Flynn, Patricia, Aracelly Santana, and Helen Shapiro. "Latin American Women: One Myth, Many Realities." *NACLA Report on the Americas*, Vol. XIV, No. 5, Sept.–Oct., 1980.

Giorgis, Belkis Wolde. *Female Circumcision in Africa*. Addis Ababa, Ethiopia: (UN)ECA, 1981.

Graves, Robert. *The Greek Myths*, 2 vols. Baltimore: Penguin Books, 1955.

---

* This Bibliography is in 2 major sections: General and Specific. General sources include those used for many or, in some cases, all countries in this book; Specific sources are those used specifically for the country under which they are listed and begin on p. 770. Whenever foreign sources cited a city of publication, we have given this citation. No cities are listed for periodicals published in the United States, as these sources are easily found through *Reader's Guide to Periodical Literature*.

Grimal, Pierre, ed. *Larousse World Mythology.* London and New York: Hamlyn, 1973; *New Larousse Encyclopedia of Mythography.* London and New York: Hamlyn, 1968.

Hafkin, Nancy J., ed. *Women and Development in Africa: An Annotated Bibliography.* Addis Ababa, Ethiopia: (UN)ECA, 1977.

————, and Edna G. Bay, eds. *Women in Africa.* Stanford: Stanford Univ. Press, 1976.

Hahner, June. *Women in Latin American History: Their Lives and Views.* Los Angeles: UCLA Latin American Center Publications, 1976.

Harris, William H., and Judith S. Levey, eds. *The New Columbia Encyclopedia.* New York: Columbia Univ. Press, 1975.

Haub, Carl, and Douglas Heisler. *1980 World Population Data Sheet.* Washington, D.C.: Population Reference Bureau, 1980.

Haub, Carl, Douglas Heisler, and Margaret Condron. *World's Women Data Sheet.* Washington, D.C.: Population Reference Bureau, 1980.

al-Hibri, Azizah, ed. *Women and Islam.* Oxford: Pergamon Press, 1982.

Huston, Perdita. *Message from the Village.* New York: Epoch B. Foundation, 1978.

Information Please Almanac, Atlas and Yearbook, 1982. New York: Simon & Schuster, 1981.

Information Please Almanac, Atlas, and Yearbook, 1983. New York: A&W Publishers, 1982.

International Bank for Reconstruction and Development. *1981 World Bank Atlas: Gross National Product, Population and Growth Rates.* Washington, D.C.: The World Bank, 1982.

Inventory of Population Projects in Developing Countries Around the World 1978/79. New York: UNFPA, 1980.

Jayawardena, Kumari. *Feminism and Nationalism in the Third World.* The Hague: Institute of Social Studies, 1982.

Kidron, Michael, and Ronald Segal. *The State of the World Atlas.* New York: Simon & Schuster with Pluto Press, 1981.

Knapp, Victor, ed. *International Encyclopedia of Comparative Law,* 2 Vols.: *National Reports.* The Hague: J. C. B. Mohr (Paul Siebeck), 1973.

Lane, Hana Umlauf, ed. *The World Almanac and Book of Facts 1983.* New York: Newspaper Enterprise Assoc., 1981.

Larson, Ann. *Fertility and the Status of Women.* Washington, D.C.: Population Reference Bureau, 1981.

Latin American and Caribbean Women's Collective. *Slave of Slaves: The Challenge of Latin American Women.* Trans. Michael Pallis. London: Zed Press, 1980.

Leghorn, Lisa, and Katherine Parker. *Women's Worth: Sexual Economics and the World of Women.* Boston, London, and Henley: Routledge & Kegan Paul, 1981.

Lightbourne, Robert, Jr., Susheela Singh, and Cynthia P. Green. *The World Fertility Survey: Charting Global Childbearing, Population Bulletin,* Vol. 37, No. 1. Washington, D.C.: Population Reference Bureau, Mar. 1982.

Lindsay, Beverly. *Comparative Perspectives of Third World Women: The Impact of Race, Sex, and Class.* New York: Praeger, 1980.

"Maternity Protection Laws Around the World." *ISIS,* No. 23, Geneva, June 1982.

Mernissi, Fatima. *Beyond the Veil: Male-Female Dynamics in a Modern Muslim Society.* New York: Schenkman with John Wiley & Sons, 1975.

Minai, Naila. *Women in Islam.* New York: Seaview Books, 1981.

"Mujer y Legislación." *Mujer* (Número Especial), México City, 1983.

Murray, Margaret A. *The God of the Witches.* Oxford: Oxford Univ. Press paperback, 1970.

————. *The Witch-Cult in Western Eu-*

rope. Oxford: Oxford Paperbacks, 1962.

The New International Atlas. New York: Rand McNally, 1981.

Newland, Kathleen. *The Sisterhood of Man.* New York: W. W. Norton, 1979.

Nordic Statistical Secretariat, ed. *Yearbooks of Nordic Statistics 1977, 1980, and 1981.* Stockholm: Nordic Council and the Nordic Statistical Secretariat 1978, 1981, and 1982.

O'Neill, Lois Decker, ed. *The Women's Book of World Records and Achievements.* Garden City, NY: Anchor Press/Doubleday, 1979.

Paxman, John M. *Law and Planned Parenthood.* London: International Planned Parenthood Federation, 1980.

Paxton, John, ed. *The Statesman's Year-Book, 1981–1982.* London: Macmillan, 1981.

Reimer, Eleanor S., and John C. Fout. *European Women: A Documentary History, 1789–1945.* New York: Schocken Books, 1980.

Rush, Florence. *The Best Kept Secret: Sexual Abuse of Children.* New York: McGraw-Hill, 1980.

Russell, Diana E. H., and Nicole Van de Ven, eds. *The Proceedings of the International Tribunal on Crimes Against Women.* Millbrae, CA: Les Femmes, 1976.

el Saadawi, Nawal. *The Hidden Face of Eve: Women in the Arab World.* Boston: Beacon Press, 1982.

Steady, Filomina Chioma, ed. *The Black Woman Cross-Culturally.* Cambridge: Schenkman, 1981.

Steiner, W. A. *Index to Foreign Legal Periodicals 1977–1979.* London: Univ. of London, 1980.

Stone, Merlin. *Ancient Mirrors of Womanhood,* 2 vols. New York: New Sibylline Books, 1979.

———. *When God Was a Woman.* New York: Dial Press, 1976.

Survey of Laws on Fertility Control. New York: UNFPA, 1979.

Tadesse, Zenebeworke. "Women and Technology in Peripheral Countries:

An Overview." *Scientific-Technological Change and the Role of Women in Development.* Eds. Pamela M. D'Onofrio-Flores and Sheila M. Pfafflin. A UNITAR Book. Boulder, CO: Westview Press, 1982.

Tietze, Christopher. *Induced Abortion: A World Review 1981* (4th ed.) and *1983* (5th ed.). New York: The Population Council, 1981 and 1983.

Traditional Practices Affecting the Health of Women and Children. WHO/EMRO Technical Publication, No. 2, 2 Vols. Alexandria, Egypt: WHO Regional Office for the Eastern Mediterranean, 1981 and 1982.

Trevor-Roper, H. R. *The European Witch-Craze of the Sixteenth and Seventeenth Centuries and Other Essays.* New York: Harper & Row (Harper Torchbooks), 1969.

(UN)ECOSOC. *Civic and Political Education of Women.* New York: United Nations, 1964.

———. *1979 Demographic Yearbook.* New York: United Nations, 1980.

———. *World Population Trends and Policies—1981 Monitoring Report: Population Policies,* 2 vols. New York: United Nations, 1982.

(UN)INSTRAW. *National Machineries for the Advancement of Women: Selected Case Studies.* New York: United Nations, 1980.

Veenhoven, Willem A., ed. *Case Studies on Human Rights and Fundamental Freedoms: A World Survey,* 5 vols. The Hague: Martinus Nijhoff, 1976.

Visaria, Leela. *Family Planning and Marriage 1970–1980.* Washington, D.C.: Population Reference Bureau, 1980.

Watson, Justice Ray, ed. *Lawasia,* 2 vols. Singapore: Singapore Univ. Press, 1979.

Williamson, Jane. *New Feminist Scholarship: A Guide to Bibliographies.* Old Westbury, NY: The Feminist Press, 1979.

Women and Literature: An Annotated Bibliography of Women Writers, 3rd ed.

Cambridge, MA: Women and Literature Collective, 1976.

Yearbook of Labour Statistics 1981. Geneva: ILO, 1981.

Specific

AFGHANISTAN
"Afghan Women Speak." *New World Review,* July–Aug. 1980.

Christensen, Hanne. *Sustaining Afghan Refugees in Pakistan.* Geneva: UN Research Institute for Social Development, 1983.

Delloye, Isabelle. *Des Femmes d'Afghanistan.* Paris: Editions des Femmes, 1980.

Dupree, Louis. *Afghanistan.* Princeton: Princeton Univ. Press, 1973.

Dupree, Nancy Hatch. "Revolutionary Rhetoric and Afghan Women Summary." American Anthropological Assoc. Meeting, Washington, D.C. Dec. 5, 1980.

Knabe, Erika. "Afghan Women: Does Their Role Change?" *Afghanistan in the 1970's.* Eds. Louis Dupree and Linette Albert. New York: Praeger, 1974.

Newell, R. S. and N. P. *The Struggle for Afghanistan.* Ithaca, NY: Cornell Univ. Press, 1981.

Poullada, Leon. *Reform and Rebellion in Afghanistan 1919–1929.* Ithaca, NY: Cornell Univ. Press, 1973.

"Women in the Afghan Resistance." *Labor: Monthly Review on Trade Union Information and Training,* No. 3. Brussels: World Confederation of Labor, Mar. 1983.

ALGERIA
"Algerian Women in Their Apartments." *Al-Raida,* Vol. V, No. 20, Beirut, 1982.

"Algerian Women: Myths of Liberation." *Connexions,* No. 2, Fall 1981.

Barber, Ben. "Algeria: Women's Status May Fall Behind the Veil." *Chicago Tribune,* Apr. 14, 1982.

Dearden, Ann. "Arab Women." *Minority Rights Group,* Report No. 27, London, 1976.

"The Dowry in Algeria." *Al-Raida,* Vol. IV, No. 17, Beirut, 1981.

Isis: Bulletin of the Research Group on Algerian Women, No. 3. Oran: Center of Documentation of Human Sciences, June 1982.

Minces, Juliette. "Women in Algeria." *Women in the Muslim World.* Eds. Lois Beck and Nikki Keddie. Cambridge, MA: Harvard Univ. Press, 1978.

M'rabet, Fadéla. "Excerpts from *Les Algériennes.*" *Middle Eastern Muslim Women Speak.* Eds. Elizabeth Warnock Fernea and Basima Qattan Bezirgan. Austin: Univ. of Texas Press, 1977.

Smith, Jane, ed. *Women in Contemporary Muslim Societies.* Lewisburg, PA: Bucknell Univ. Press, 1980.

ARGENTINA
Buvnik, Mayra, Nadia Youssef, and Barbara Voneln, eds. *Women-Headed Households: The Ignored Factor in Family Planning.* Washington, D.C.: International Center for Research on Women, Mar. 1978.

"Changing Roles of Latin American Women." *Journal of Inter-American Studies and World Affairs,* Vol. XVII, Nov. 1975.

Hollander, Nancy Caro. "Women: The Forgotten Half of Argentine History." *Female and Male in Latin America.* Ed. Ann Pescatello. Pittsburgh: Univ. of Pittsburgh Press, 1973.

Kinzer, Nora Scott. "Women Professionals in Buenos Aires." *Female and Male in Latin America.* Ed. Ann Pescatello. Pittsburgh: Univ. of Pittsburgh Press, 1973.

"Latin American Women: Varieties of Oppression." *Off Our Backs,* Vol. XI, No. 3, Mar. 1981.

"Lita de Lazzaris . . . Estamos velando

al no te metás *(Somos,* Argentina)."
Mujer, No. 14, México City, Sept.
1982.

Little, Cynthia Jeffress. "Education, Philanthropy, and Feminism: Components
of Argentine Womanhood, 1860–
1926." *Latin American Women.* Ed.
Asunción Lavrin. Westport, CT:
Greenwood Press, 1978.

Marini, Ana María. "Women in Contemporary Argentina." *Latin American
Perspectives,* Vol. IV, No. 4, 1977.

"Media as Manipulation." *ISIS,* No. 18,
Geneva, 1981.

"The Problem of Power in the Family
(Mujeres, Argentina)." *Mujer,* No. 11,
México City, June 1983.

"Shrouded in Silence." *Connexions,* No.
3, Winter 1982.

"A Silent Weapon." *Connexions,* No. 1,
Summer 1981.

AUSTRALIA

"Australia." *New Directions for Women,*
Vol. II, No. 2, Mar. 4, 1982.

"Australia Addendum" to the *Initial Reports of States Parties* due in 1981 on
the International Covenant on Civil
and Political Rights (CCPR/C/1 Add.
17). New York: UN Human Rights
Committee, Dec. 11, 1981.

Australia Information Service. *Women in
Australia.* Canberra: Government Publishing Service, 1979.

Australian Bureau of Labor Statistics.
Labor. Canberra, 1980.

Bell, Diane. "Desert Politics: Choices in
the Marriage Market." *Women and
Colonization.* Eds. Mona Etienne and
Eleanor Leacock. New York: Praeger,
1980.

Bernstein, Richard. "Labor Party Wins
Australian Voting." *New York Times,*
Mar. 6, 1983.

Jones, Adrienne. *Women in Australia,* 2
Parts. Canberra: Australia Information
Service, 1982.

Kaufman, Barbara. "My Mother, the
Land." *Women of the Whole World,*
No. 2, Berlin, GDR, 1982.

Mackinolty, Judy, and Heather Radi. *In
Pursuit of Justice: Australian Women*
and the Law 1788–1979. Sydney: Hale
Iremonger, 1979.

Mann, Judy. "Women Gain Foothold in
Australian Race." *Washington Post,*
Oct. 3, 1980.

"Matilda and the Mates." *Newsweek,*
May 24, 1976.

National Women's Advisory Council.
Migrant Women Speak. Canberra,
1979.

New South Wales Women's Advisory
Council. *Reform of NSW Rape Legislation.* New South Wales, Aug. 1980.

———. *Sexual Harassment.* New South
Wales, Aug. 1981.

———. *Women and Family Law: Being
Single Again.* New South Wales, 1981.

"Outworkers: The Forgotten Workforce." *ISIS,* No. 14, Geneva, 1980.

Summers, Anne. *Damned Whores and
God's Police: The Colonization of
Women in Australia.* New York: Penguin Books, 1975.

Women's Bureau, Dept. of Employment
and Youth. *Facts on Women at Work in
Australia 1980.* Canberra, n.d.

———. *Women and Work Newsletter,* issues Vol. 2, No. 4, Dec. 1979, and Vol.
3, No. 1, Apr. 1980.

AUSTRIA

Austrian Federal Ministry of Social Affairs. *The Status of Women in Austria.*
Vienna, 1976.

Douer, Rosemarie, and Irmtraut Leirer,
eds. *Mid-Decade 1980: Review and
Evaluation of Progress.* Vienna: Eigentümer, Verleger, & Herausgeber, n.d.

Federal Press Service. *Austria Documentation: Austria in Figures.* Vienna,
1982.

———. *Austria Documentation: Women
in Austria.* Vienna, 1980.

———. *Austria Elaborates New Family
Law,* NE 0008/0001. Vienna, n.d.

———. *Austria: Facts and Figures.* Vienna, 1979.

Report from Austria to (UN)ECOSOC.
"Implementation of the International
Covenant on Economic, Social and
Cultural Rights." July 31, 1980. New
York: United Nations, Oct. 15, 1980.

Women's Division, Federal Ministry of Social Affairs. *Equal Opportunities for Women in Technical Vocations.* Vienna, n.d.

BRAZIL

Acosta, Odacy. "Contraception." *International Press Service,* Rio de Janeiro, Apr. 22, 1982.

Jones, Clayton, and Ward Morehouse, III. "Amazon Indians Still Fight Battle of the Sexes." *Christian Science Monitor,* Aug. 1977.

Barroso, Carmen (Coordinator). *Mulher, Sociedade e Estado no Brasil.* São Paulo: Ed. Brasiliense in conjunction with UNICEF, 1982.

Blay, Eva A. "The Political Participation of Women in Brazil: Female Mayors." Trans. Susan A. Soeiro. *Signs,* Vol. 5, No. 1, Autumn 1979.

"Brazil: Men's Crimes 'of Passion.' " *Spare Rib,* Issue 114, London, Jan. 1982.

Bruschini, Maria Cristina, and Fulvia Rosenberg. *Trabalhadoras do Brasil.* São Paulo: Ed. Brasiliense under the sponsorship of Fundacão Carlos Chagas, 1982.

"Don't Label Me, I Label Myself." *Connexions,* No. 3, Winter 1982.

Economic Dept., Central Bank of Brazil. *Information Mensal* (Monthly Information Bulletin), Brasilia, Feb. 1983.

Foppe, Alaíde. "The First Feminist Congress in Mexico, 1916." Trans. Helene F. de Aguilar. *Signs,* Vol. 5, No. 1, Autumn 1979.

Hahner, June E. "The Beginnings of the Women's Suffrage Movement in Brazil." *Signs,* Vol. 5, No. 1, Autumn 1979.

———. "The Nineteenth-Century Feminist Press and Women's Rights in Brazil." *Latin American Women.* Ed. Asunción Lavrin. Westport, CT: Greenwood Press, 1978.

Hoge, Warren. "Machismo Murder Case: Women Bitter in Brazil." *New York Times,* May 23, 1983.

"Inovado Na Forma e Na Forca." *Mulher,* México City, Aug. 1982.

"Lifeboats for Brazil." *New York Times,* Apr. 15, 1983.

Madeiros, Dr. Romy. "Law and the Condition of Women in Brazil." *Law and the Status of Women.* Ed. *Columbia Human Rights Law Review.* New York: Centre for Social Development and Humanitarian Affairs, United Nations, 1977.

Morgan, Robin, and Gloria Steinem. "The International Crime of Genital Mutilation." *Ms.,* Vol. VIII, No. 9, Mar. 1980.

Nova Diconário Aurélio da Lingua Portuguesa, 1975 ed. N.p.: Ed. Nova Fronteira, 1975.

"Participants: Brazil." *ISIS,* No. 22, Geneva, 1982.

Pimental, Sylvia. "The Necessary Political Participation of Women." São Paulo: Pontifica Universidade, Frente de Mulheres Feministas, 1981.

"Report on Women's Festival." *Mujer,* México City, Sept. 1982.

Russell-Wood, A. J. R. "Female and Family in the Economy and Society of Colonial Brazil." *Latin American Women.* Ed. Asunción Lavrin. Westport, CT: Greenwood Press, 1978.

Safa, Helen K. "The Changing Class Composition of the Female Labor Force in Latin America." *Latin American Perspectives,* Vol. IV, No. 15, Fall 1977.

Soeiro, Susan A. "The Feminine Orders in Colonial Bahia, Brazil: Economic, Social, and Demographic Implications, 1677–1800." *Latin American Women.* Ed. Asunción Lavrin. Westport, CT: Greenwood Press, 1978.

BRITAIN

"Britain: Organization of Women of Asian and African Descent—1st National Conference." *Off Our Backs,* Vol. X, No. 1, Jan. 1980.

Britain's Divorce Laws. London: Central Office of Information, Sept. 1982.

"British Women Decry Rape Penalties." *New Women's Times,* Vol. VIII, No. 5, May 1982.

Central Office of Information. *Britain in Brief.* London: Maybank Press, 1981.

———. *Social Welfare in Britain.* London: Maybank Press, 1980.

"England." *New Directions for Women,* Vol. 12, No. 1, Jan. 1983.

"England." *Women's Information Resource and Exchange Services,* No. 74, London, n.d.

"English Parliament Reform in Rape Laws." *The Longest Revolution,* Vol. 7, No. 3, Feb.–Mar. 1983.

"First Divorce, Then Deportation." *Manchester Guardian,* Manchester, Dec. 2, 1982.

Gepsman, Gail. "National Women's Aid Federation: Feminist Solution to Woman Abuse in England." Bloomington, IN, Mar. 1979.

Graves, Robert. *The White Goddess.* New York: Vintage Books, 1959.

"Harassment on the Job." *New Women's Times,* Vol. IX, No. 1, Jan. 1983.

Jenkins, Elizabeth. *Elizabeth the Great.* New York: Berkeley Medallion Books, 1972.

"Lesbian Custody Victory." *ILIS,* No. 10, Helsinki, May 1983.

MacKenzie, Midge. *Shoulder to Shoulder.* New York: Knopf, 1975.

McDowell, Kaye B. A., ed. *Halbury's Statutes of England,* 3rd ed. London: Butterworth, 1982.

Meade, Marion. *Eleanor of Aquitaine: A Biography.* New York: Hawthorn, 1977.

Owen, Lyn. "England." *The Observer,* London, Apr. 5, 1981.

The Public General Acts and Measures of 1956. London: Her Majesty's Stationery Office, 1957.

"Rape and the Law." *Spare Rib,* Issue 113, London, Dec. 1981.

Report from the United Kingdom of Great Britain and Northern Ireland to (UN)ECOSOC. "Implementation of the International Covenant on Economic, Social and Cultural Rights." Apr. 15, 1980. New York: United Nations, Sept. 3, 1980.

"Sex Harassment Survey." *New Women's Times,* Vol. IX, No. 3, Mar. 1983.

Statistical Service. "Health and Personal Social Services." *Statistics for England.* London: Her Majesty's Stationery Office, 1979.

———. "Social Trends." *Statistics for England.* London: Her Majesty's Stationery Office, 1981.

———. "United Kingdom in Figures." *Statistics for England.* London: Her Majesty's Stationery Office, 1981.

"United Kingdom of Great Britain and Northern Ireland Addenda" to the *Initial Reports of States Parties* due in 1977 on the International Covenant on Civil and Political Rights (CCPR/C/1/Add. 17). New York: UN Human Rights Committee, Sept. 21, 1977.

"Whatever Became of Shirley?" *The Observer,* London, Oct. 10, 1982.

Whitaker's Almanack. London: Whitaker, 1983.

Women in Statistics: Supplement No. 10 to Women of Europe. Brussels: Commission of the European Communities, 1982.

Women of Europe. Brussels: Commission of the European Communities, Jan.–Feb. 1981.

CANADA

"Across Canada." *Kinesis,* Vancouver, Feb. 1982.

Armstrong, Pat and Hugh. *A Working Majority: What Women Must Do for Pay.* Ottawa: Canadian Advisory Council on the Status of Women, 1983.

Canadian Advisory Council on the Status of Women. *The Person Papers: Regarding Rape.* Ottawa, 1976.

———. *The Royal Commission Report: Ten Years Later.* Ottawa, 1979.

Cleverdon, Catherine. *The Women's Suffrage Movement in Canada.* Toronto: Univ. of Toronto Press, 1974.

Communiqu'elles, issues of Vol. 7, No. 5, June 1981, and Vol. 7, No. 6, July 1981, Montreal.

Conseil de Statut de la Femme. *Pour les Québécoises: Egalité et Indépendance.*

Québec: Gouvernement de Québec, 1978.

———. *Essai sur la santé de la femme.* Québec: Gouvernement du Québec, June 1981.

"Incest Survivors Speak." *Kinesis,* Vancouver, Dec. 1981–Jan. 1982.

Jackman, Nancy. "Bill C-53: Law Reflects Values." *Canadian Women's Studies,* n.p., Summer 1982.

Jamieson, Kathleen. *Indian Women and the Law in Canada: Citizens Minus.* Ottawa: Canadian Advisory Council on the Status of Women, 1978.

"Kit of the Mail." *Content; Canada's National News Media Magazine,* n.p., May 1978.

Mallory, Naomi. *About Face: Toward a Positive Image of Women and Health.* Toronto: Ontario Status of Women Council, 1978.

McKie, D. C., B. Prentice, and B. Reed. *Divorce: La Loi et la Famille au Canada.* Ottawa: Statistics Canada, 1983.

McLeod, Linda. *Wife Battering in Canada: The Vicious Circle.* Ottawa: Canadian Advisory Council on the Status of Women, 1980.

Minister of Supply and Services. *Education in Canada: Statistical Review for 1980–81.* Ottawa: Statistics Canada, 1981.

Nova Scotia Task Force on the Status of Women. *Herself.* Nova Scotia, Mar. 1976.

Statistics Canada. *Canadian Statistical Review, September 1982.* Ottawa, Oct. 1982.

Topical Law Reports, Vol. I: Family Law Guide. Toronto: CCH Canadian, Ltd., 1978.

"Toward Equality for Women." *Status of Women in Canada.* Ottawa, 1979.

Vallee, Evelyne. "Sexual Harassment Survey" (from *Communiqu'elles). New Women's Times,* Vol. XIII, No. 3, Mar. 1983.

Van Praagh, Pat. "Family Planning: A Rationale for Federal Funding." Paper prepared for Planned Parenthood Federation of Canada, n.p., Dec. 1982.

"Women Become Persons." *Calgary Women's Newspaper,* Vol. 5, No. 9, Calgary, Sept. 1979.

Women's Bureau, Labour Canada. *Canadian Women and Job Related Laws 1981.* Ottawa, 1982.

CARIBBEAN

Antrobus, Peggy. "Women and Development: A Caribbean Perspective." Barbados: Women and Development Extra-Mural Dept., Mar. 1979.

Apandeye, Sis Einjou. "The Caribbean Woman as Writer." *Black Woman,* Vol. 1, No. 1, Trinidad and Tobago, Nov. 1975.

Bell, Ian. *The Dominican Republic.* Boulder, CO: Westview Press, 1981.

Civil Code of the Dominican Republic. Santo Domingo: Editora Taller, 1980.

Dominican Republic: Population Policy Compendium. New York: A joint publication of (UN)ECOSOC and UNFPA, Sept. 1979.

Hartog, Dr. J. *From Colonial Dependence to Slavery.* Aruba: Dewit, 1968.

Hawkins, Irene. *The Changing Face of the Caribbean.* Barbados: Cedar Press, 1976.

"Images of Women in Calypso in the Caribbean." *The Tribune,* No. 14. New York: International Women's Tribune Center, 1981.

Joseph, Gloria I. "Caribbean Women: The Impact of Race, Sex and Class." *Comparative Perspectives of Third World Women.* Ed. Beverly Lindsay. New York: Praeger, 1980.

Laws of Jamaica: A Revised Edition, Vol. VI. Kingston: Government Printers, 1953.

Moses, Yolanda T. "Female Status, the Family, and Male Dominance in a West Indian Community." *Signs,* Vol. III, No. 1, Autumn 1977.

National Joint Action Committee. *Black Woman,* issues of Nov. 1975, and June 1977, Trinidad and Tobago.

de Paredes, Querubina Henríquez, Maritza Izaquirre P., and Inés Vargas Delaunay. *Participación de la Mujer en el*

Desarrollo de América Latina y el Caribe. Santiago, Chile: UNICEF, 1975.

Pilgrim, Grace, and Marlene Cuthbert. "The Changing Caribbean." *New World Outlook,* Apr. 1971.

Price, Richard. *The Guyana Maroons.* Baltimore: Johns Hopkins Press, 1976.

"Sistren: Street Theater in Jamaica." *Connexions,* No. 4, Spring 1982.

Revolution and Counterrevolution in Suriname, 1983; available from the Suriname Consulate, New York.

Tancer, Shoshana B. "La Quisqueyana: The Dominican Woman, 1940–1970." *Female and Male in Latin America.* Ed. Ann Pescatello. Pittsburgh: Univ. of Pittsburgh Press, 1973.

UNDP. *Rural Women's Participation in Government.* No. 3. New York, June 1980.

UNESCO. *Women and Development: Indicators of Their Changing Role.* Paris, 1981.

CHILE

"Abortion Epidemic in Latin America." *Development Forum,* May 1983.

Adriesola, Claudia, María Eugenia Aguirre, Rosa Bravo, María Isabel Cruzet, María Soledad Lago, and Elena Serrano. *Algunas Ideas Respecto a la Condición de la Mujer.* Santiago: Academia de Humanismo Cristiano, May 1979.

Banco Central de Chile. *Boletín Mensual,* No. 653, Santiago, July 1982.

"Chilean Exile: Seven Fat Years." *Connexions,* No. 2, Fall 1981.

"Chile." *ILIS,* Helsinki, Apr. 1983.

Chile: Population Policy Compendium. New York: A joint publication of (UN)ECOSOC and UNFPA, Mar. 1981.

Creses, Santiago, July 1982.

Especial-Mujer: Maternidad y Aborto, México City, 1982.

Flora, Cornelia Butler. "Socialist Feminism in Latin America." Working Paper No. 14. Dept. of Sociology, Anthropology, and Social Work, Kansas State Univ., Nov. 1982.

Instituto Nacional de Estadísticos. *Compendio Estadístico 1982.* Santiago, 1982.

"Media as Manipulation." *ISIS,* No. 18, Geneva, 1981.

"One Myth, Many Realities." *NACLA Report: Latin American Women,* Vol. XIV, No. 5, Sept.–Oct. 1980.

Prochile-Chilean Government Trade and Investment Bureau. *The Chilean Economy: A General Survey.* Santiago, 1979.

Report from Chile to (UN)ECOSOC. "Implementation of the International Convenant on Economic, Social and Cultural Rights." Sept. 26, 1979. New York: United Nations, Dec. 1979.

Schumacher, Edward. "Full Stores and Empty Pockets Tell Chile's Story." *New York Times,* May 2, 1983.

Séptima Edición Oficial de Código Penal. Santiago: Editorial Jurídica de Chile, 1975.

Shearer, Lloyd. "Lady Vigilante." *Boston Globe,* Apr. 4, 1982.

"They Have Lost Their Fear. . . ." *Women of the Whole World,* No. 3, Berlin, GDR, 1981.

UNICEF. *Chile: Mujer y Sociedad.* Eds. Paz Covarrubias and Rolando Franco. Santiago: Alfabeta, 1978.

"Women and Work." *ISIS,* No. 22, Geneva, 1982.

CHINA

Andors, Phyllis. "Politics of Chinese Development: The Case of Women, 1960–1966." *Signs,* Vol. 2, No. 1, Autumn 1976.

Baldursson, Ragnar. "Chinese Women: From Enslavement to Equality." *Feminist International: Asian Women '80,* No. 2, Tokyo, June 1980.

Birke, Linda. "Women's Health in China." *Spare Rib,* Issue 84, London, July 1979.

Butterfield, Fox. "Another Dissident on Trial in Peking." *New York Times,* Nov. 18, 1981.

———. "Mao's Wife Is Reported Under Attack." *New York Times,* Nov. 27, 1975.

"Census Results, 1982." *Beijing Review,* No. 45, Beijing, Nov. 8, 1982.

"China: Concern over Killing of Baby Girls." *International Children's Rights Monitor,* Pilot Issue. Geneva: Defence for Children International, Spring 1983.

"China Still Fighting an Old Abuse: Women for Sale." *New York Times,* Jan. 6, 1983.

"Chinese Break Up an Abduction Ring." *Manushi,* New Delhi, Aug.–Sept. 1983.

Chinese Documents: Resolution on CPC History (1949–1981). Beijing: Foreign Language Press, 1981.

Chinese Documents: The Twelfth National Congress of the CPC. Beijing: Foreign Language Press, 1982.

"Committee on Elimination of Discrimination Against Women Concludes Reports of Hungary and China." Apr. 22, 1984. UN Press Release.

"Constitution of the People's Republic of China." *Beijing Review,* No. 52, Beijing, Dec. 27, 1982.

Croll, Elisabeth. *Feminism and Socialism in China.* New York: Schocken Books, 1978.

Dickson, Mary. "From No Name to Full Status: How Long for Chinese Women?" *Network,* Dec. 1982.

Ding Ling: Purged Feminist. Tokyo: Femintern Press, 1974.

"For the Healthy Growth of China's 300 Million Children." *Beijing Review,* No. 22, Beijing, May 31, 1982.

Kristeva, Julia. *About Chinese Women.* New York: Urizen Books, 1981.

Li, Jianguo, and Zhang Xiaoying. "Infanticide in China." *New York Times,* Apr. 11, 1983.

Liu Zheng, Song Jian, *et al. China's Population: Problems and Prospects.* Beijing: New World Press, 1981.

Loi, Michelle. "Chinese Women and the Fourth Rope." *Feminist Issues,* Vol. 1, No. 3, Summer 1981.

Moudud, Hasna Jasimuddin. *Women in China.* New Delhi: Vikas Publishing House (Pvt.), 1980.

O'Sullivan, Sue. "China: Fines Are Not Enough." *Spare Rib,* Issue 112, London, Nov. 1981.

"A Peking Scene: Pimps and Prostitutes at the Peace Cafe." *New York Times,* Oct. 12, 1979.

Reischauer, Edwin O., and John K. Fairbank. *East Asia: The Great Tradition.* Winchester, MA: Allen & Unwin, 1960.

Ropp, Paul S. "The Seeds of Change: Reflections on the Condition of Women in the Early and Mid Ch'ing." *Signs,* Vol. 2, No. 1, Autumn 1976.

Sheridan, Mary. "Young Women Leaders in China." *Signs,* Vol. 2, No. 1, Autumn 1976.

Sidel, Ruth. *Women and Childcare in China.* Baltimore: Penguin Books, 1972.

Studies in Family Planning, Vol. 13, No. 6–7. New York: Population Council, June–July 1982.

Su Wenming, ed. *From Youth to Retirement.* Beijing: Beijing Review, 1982.

———, ed. *Population and Other Problems.* Beijing: Beijing Review, 1981.

Wen, Qi. *China: A General Survey.* Eds. (English text) Zhao Shuhan and Yang Lixing. Beijing: Foreign Language Press, 1981.

Wieger, Dr. L. *Chinese Characters.* New York: Dover, 1915.

Women of China, issues of June, Oct., and Nov. 1982, Beijing.

Women of Europe. Brussels: Commission of the European Communities, Sept.–Oct. 1980.

COLOMBIA

Arango, Marta. "The Chocó Woman: Agent For Change." *Latin American Woman: The Meek Speak Out.* Ed. Jane H. Turner. Silver Springs, MD: International Development Corp., 1980.

Cárdenas, Marta Cecilia Osorno. *La Mujer Colombiana y Latino Américana,* n.p., 1974.

Cherpak, Evelyn. "The Participation of Women in the Independence Movement in Gran Colombia, 1750–1830."

Latin American Women. Ed. Asunción Lavrin. Westport, CT: Greenwood Press, 1978.

"Colombian Maids: Work for Room and Board." *Secondclass, Workingclass.* Oakland, CA: Newsfront International, Nov. 1979.

"Film: New Images for Women." *The Tribune,* No. 14. New York: International Women's Tribune Center, 1981.

Harkness, Shirley J. "The Pursuit of an Ideal: Migration, Social Class, and Women's Role in Bogotá, Colombia." *Female and Male in Latin America.* Ed. Ann Pescatello. Pittsburgh: Univ. of Pittsburgh Press, 1973.

Jones, Clayton, and Ward Morehouse, III. "Amazon Indians Still Fight Battle of the Sexes." *Christian Science Monitor,* Aug. 3, 1977.

CUBA

Anuario de Estadísticas de Cuba. Havana: Comité Estatal de Estadísticas, 1980.

"Committee on Elimination of Discrimination Against Women Hears Cuba's Response to Questions on its Report." Aug. 11, 1983. UN Press Release.

Cuba: Population Policy Compendium. New York: A joint publication of (UN)ECOSOC and UNFPA, Sept. 1979.

Federation of Cuban Women. *Memories, Second Congress.* Nov. 25–29, 1975. Havana: Editorial Orbe, 1975.

———. *The News Bulletin: Third Congress of the Federation of Cuban Women.* Mar. 5–8, 1980. Havana, 1980.

"Mariel." *New York Times,* Oct. 29, 1980.

"Cuban Women, 1975–1979." *Official Government Submission to the UN World Conference on Women,* Copenhagen. July 1980. Havana: Ministry of Foreign Affairs, 1980.

Ministry of Justice. *Family Code.* Havana: Cuban Book Institute, 1975.

Woman Maternity Law and Regulations. Havana: Editorial Orbe, 1979.

Monografía Nacional Presentada por Cuba. Conferencia Mundial del Decenio de las Naciones Unidas para la Mujer, Copenhagen. July 1980. New York: United Nations, May 1980.

Randall, Margaret. *Cuban Women Now.* Toronto: The Women's Press, 1974.

Stone, Elizabeth, ed. *Women and the Cuban Revolution.* New York: Pathfinder Press, 1981.

DENMARK

"Copenhagen's Refuge for Battered Women: A Fairy Tale Comes True." *Connexions,* No. 1, Summer 1981.

Dahlsgaard, Inga. *Women in Denmark: Yesterday and Today.* Copenhagen: Danish Institute for Information about Denmark and Cultural Cooperation with Other Nations, 1980.

Gammeltoff-Hansen, Hans, Bernard Gomard, and Allan Philip. *Danish Law: A General Survey.* Copenhagen: G. E. C. Gads, 1982.

Georg, Anders, and Thorkild Borre, eds. "Women in Denmark." *Danish Journal.* Copenhagen: Ministry of Foreign Affairs, 1980.

Gerlach-Nielsen, Merete. *New Trends in the Danish Women's Movement 1970–78.* Roskilde: Emmeline Press, 1980.

Haugsted, Ida. "The Status of Women." *Fact Sheet/Denmark.* Copenhagen: Press and Cultural Relations Dept. of the Ministry of Foreign Affairs, 1979.

Ministry for Economic Affairs. *Danish Economic Survey.* Copenhagen, Mar. 1982.

Ministry of Labor. *Women and Employment.* Report by the Press and Cultural Relations Dept. of the Ministry of Foreign Affairs for the UN Decade for Women World Conference, Copenhagen. July 1980.

Women in Statistics: Supplement No. 10 to Women of Europe. Brussels: Commission of the European Communities, 1982.

Women of Europe, issues of Jan.–Feb. 1981, and May–June–July 1982. Brussels: Commission of the European Communities.

ECUADOR

"Cables." *Mujer,* No. 15, México City, Oct. 1982.

"Ecuador." *International Press Service,* Quito, Mar. 10, 1982.

Ecuador: Population Policy Compendium. New York: A joint publication of (UN)ECOSOC and UNFPA, Sept. 1980.

Leroux, Ketty Romo. *The Legal and Social Situation of the Woman in Ecuador.* Guayaquil: Univ. of Guayaquil, 1975.

Nueva Mujer, No. 3, México City, Aug. 1982.

"Report of Ecuadorean Mission on Needs Assessment for Population Assistance." Report No. 26. New York: UNFPA, n.d.

"Women's Committee in Solidarity with Labor Conflicts." *Pachacama Journal,* Quito, Jan. 1975.

EGYPT

el Badawi, Zeinab el Fatih. *The Muslim Woman.* Khartoum: Khartoum Univ. Press, 1975.

"Ban on Female Circumcision." *Al-Raida,* Vol. V, No. 21, Beirut, Aug. 1, 1982.

"Development of 3- to 6-Year-Old Children and Their Environment." *Al-Raida,* Vol. IV, No. 17, Beirut, Aug. 1, 1981.

"Egypt." *Connexions,* No. 4, Spring 1982.

Fernea, Elizabeth Warnock, and Basima Qattan Bezirgan. "Huda Sh'arawi, Founder of the Egyptian Women's Movement." *Middle Eastern Muslim Women Speak.* Eds. Elizabeth Warnock Fernea and Basima Qattan Bezirgan. Austin: Univ. of Texas Press, 1977.

Giorgis, Belkis Wolde. *Female Circumcision in Africa.* Addis Ababa, Ethiopia: (UN)ECA, 1981.

Hamman, Mona. "Women and Industrial Work in Egypt." *Arab Studies Quarterly,* Winter 1980.

el-Kharboutly, Maitre Attiat, and Dr.

Aziza Hussein. "Law and the Status of Women in the Arab Republic of Egypt." *Law and the Status of Women.* Ed. *Columbia Human Rights Law Review.* New York: Centre for Social Development and Humanitarian Affairs, United Nations, 1977.

Marsot, Afaf Lutfi al-Sayyio. "The Revolutionary Gentlewomen in Egypt." *Women in the Muslim World.* Eds. Lois Beck and Nikki Keddie. Cambridge, MA: Harvard Univ. Press, 1978.

"A New Feminist Party in Cairo." *Al-Raida,* Vol. VI, No. 25, Beirut, Aug. 1, 1983.

Philipp, Thomas. "Feminism and Nationalist Politics in Egypt." *Women in the Muslim World.* Eds. Lois Beck and Nikki Keddie. Cambridge, MA: Harvard Univ. Press, 1978.

Raccagni, Michelle. "Ingi Efflatoun: Author, Artist, and Militant—A Brief Analysis of Her Life and Works." Diss., New York Univ., n.d.

Sproul, Christine. "Lifting the Veil: Hoda Sh'arawi." *Network News,* Sept. 1982.

el-Wan, Schwikar. *Status of Women in the Arab World.* Presented by the League of Arab States. New York: Arab Information Center, Mar. 22, 1974.

EL SALVADOR

American Friends Service Committee. *AFSC Women's Newsletter,* Summer 1981.

AMES. *Boletín Internacional,* No. 1, San Salvador, Sept. 1981.

———. *Posición de AMES por la Paz, Distención y desarme,* San Salvador, 1982.

"AMES: Women in El Salvador." *Off Our Backs,* Vol. XII, No. 1, Jan. 1982.

Women and War: El Salvador. New York: Women's International Resource Exchange, 1981.

"Women's Lives in El Salvador." *ISIS,* No. 19, Geneva, 1981.

FINLAND

Central Statistical Office of Finland. *Position of Women.* Helsinki, 1980.

————. *Statistical Yearbook of Finland.* Helsinki, 1980.

The Council for Equality Between Men and Women. *A Woman in Finland.* Helsinki, 1981.

"Finland." *ILIS,* No. 10, Helsinki, May 1980.

ILIS Conference Report. Proceedings from a Conference on the International Lesbian Movement, Lichtaart, Belgium. Dec. 30, 1981–Jan. 3, 1982.

Jousimaa, Kaarina. *Finland—A Scandinavian Modern Country.* Helsinki: Finnish-American Cultural Institute, 1978.

Leskinen, Jyrki, ed. *Finland Facts and Figures.* Helsinki: Otava Publishing Co., 1979.

FRANCE

Bogin, Meg. *The Women Troubadours.* London and New York: Paddington Press, 1976.

Bulletin de la Condition Féminine, No. 10. Paris: Mensuel-Ministère délégué à la condition féminine, Feb. 1980.

The Central Bureau of Statistics. *The Statistical Yearbook of France 1981.* Paris, 1981.

Delawasse, Lilian. "Women in Politics—No Longer on Suffrance." *The Guardian,* Apr. 11, 1982.

"France Gives Maman Equal Voice with Papa." *New York Times,* Oct. 16, 1969.

"France Minimizes Sexual Discrimination." *Al-Raida,* Vol. VI, No. 24, Beirut, May 1, 1983.

French Press Information Service. *France in 1982.* New York, 1981.

————. *Social Security and National Health Insurance in France.* New York, 1981.

————. *Women in France.* New York, 1981.

"Gadfly of French Cabinet." *New York Times,* Oct. 21, 1974.

Guichard, Marie-Thérèse, and Roselyne Bosch. "Féminisme: L'âge adulte." *Le Point,* Paris, Mar. 8, 1982.

"Law and Work." *ILIS,* Helsinki, Apr. 1983.

Meade, Marion. *Eleanor of Aquitaine: A Biography.* New York: Hawthorn, 1977.

————. *Stealing Heaven: The Story of Heloise and Abelard.* New York: William Morrow, 1979.

Ministry for Women's Rights Publication Service. *La population des femmes seule.* Paris, 1981.

Le Monde, Paris, Feb. 27, 1982.

Oldenburg, Zoé. *Massacre at Montsegur: A History of the Albigensian Crusade.* Paris: Gallimard, 1959; New York: Pantheon Books, 1961.

Prial, Frank J. "Birth Control Ads Make Debut on French TV." *New York Times,* Nov. 29, 1981.

"Protests Mark Decisions." *New Women's Times,* Vol. IX, No. 4, Apr. 1983.

Sojourner: The New England Women's Journal of News, Opinions and the Arts, Mar. 1979.

Weitz, Margaret Collins. "The Status of Women in France Today: A Reassessment." *Contemporary French Civilization,* Vol. VI, Nos. 1–2, Fall 1981.

Women in Statistics: Supplement No. 10 to Women of Europe. Brussels: Commission of the European Communities, 1982.

Women of Europe, issues of Sept.–Oct. 1980, Jan.–Feb., May–June–July 1981, Nov.–Dec. 1982, and Mar.–Apr. 1983. Brussels: Commission of the European Communities.

GERMANY (EAST/GDR)

"Consideration of Reports and Information Submitted by States Parties under Article 18 of the Convention on the Elimination of All Forms of Discrimination Against Women." New York: United Nations, Aug. 9, 1983.

Documentation: Social Security for All: The Laws and Their Application in the GDR. Berlin, GDR: Panorama DDR, n.d.

Evans, Richard J. *The Feminist Movement in Germany 1894–1933.* Beverly Hills, CA: Sage Publications, 1976.

Families in the GDR: Portraits, Facts, Opinions. Berlin, GDR: Panorama DDR, 1981.

GDR: Facts and Figures. Berlin, GDR: Panorama DDR, 1981.

Jung, Hertha. "Women and the Family in the GDR." *Women of the Whole World,* No. 3, Berlin, GDR, 1981.

Lauterer-Pirner, Heidi. "The Woman Who Married Luther: Katharina von Bora." *Women,* No. 21. N.p.: Lutheran World Federation, Mar. 1983.

"Love Through Letters." *Connexions,* No. 5, Summer 1982.

Niedzielska, Kyrstyna. "35 Years—Democratic Women's League of Germany." *Women of the Whole World,* No. 3, Berlin, GDR, 1982.

"Peace Campaigners Arrested." *Amnesty International Newsletter,* Vol. XIV, No. 2, Feb. 1984.

Questions and Answers: Life in the GDR. Berlin, GDR: Panorama DDR, 1981.

Report from the German Democratic Republic to the Convention on the Elimination of All Forms of Discrimination Against Women. "Initial Reports of States Parties." New York: United Nations, Nov. 12, 1982.

Report from the German Democratic Republic to (UN)ECOSOC. "Implementation of the International Covenant on Economic, Social and Cultural Rights." Oct. 16, 1979. New York: United Nations, Dec. 21, 1979.

Schrader, Richard J. *God's Handiwork: Images of Women in Early Germanic Literature.* Westport, CT: Greenwood Press, 1983.

Der Spiegel, No. 13, Berlin, FRD, 1979.

Statkowa, Susanne. *Firsthand Information: Women Under Socialism.* Berlin, GDR: Panorama DDR, 1974.

Steinem, Gloria. "The Nazi Connection." *Outrageous Acts and Everyday Rebellions.* New York: Holt, Rhinehart & Winston, 1983.

Sudau, Christel. "Women in the GDR." *New German Critique,* No. 13, Winter 1978.

"The Trade Union Commission of Women in Industry: A Dynamic Body for the Defense of Working Women's Interests." *Flashes from the Trade Unions,* No. 22, Prague, June 2, 1983.

GERMANY (WEST/FRD)

"Battered Women Need Refuges: The Women's Aid Movement in West Germany." *ISIS,* No. 21, Geneva, 1981.

Employment and Social Security in the Federal Republic of Germany, 3rd ed. Revised by Dr. Klaus Burchardt. Bonn: Federal Ministry for Labour and Social Order, 1980.

"German Women: How Liberated Are They?" *Meet Germany,* Hamburg, Nov. 1982.

"German Women's Congress *vs.* Church Polemic." *Off Our Backs,* Jan. 1980.

Inter Nationes. *Social Reports,* 5–77 ("Women's Affairs III-51"), 7–77 ("Marriage, Family III-50"), 9–81 ("Women—Thoughts of Security in Old Age III—51"), and 7–82 ("Women in Public Life in the Federal Republic of Germany III-52"); available from the West German Consulate, New York.

Press and Information Office. *Social Security for All.* Bonn, 1980.

———. *Women,* No. 13. Bonn, June 1978.

Report from the Federal Republic of Germany to (UN)ECOSOC. "Implementation of the International Covenant on Economic, Social and Cultural Rights." Dec. 21, 1979. New York: United Nations, Feb. 4, 1980.

Shanor, Donald R. "Red-Faced Greens." *World Press Review,* Vol. 30, No. 10, Oct. 1983.

Women in Statistics: Supplement No. 10 to Women in Europe. Brussels: Commission of the European Communities, 1982.

Women of Europe. Brussels: Commission of the European Communities, May–July 1982.

GHANA

"Background Paper." Accra, n.d.

Ghana National Council on Women and Development. *Annual Report.* Accra, 1977.

Information Services Dept. *Ghana 1977: An Official Handbook.* Accra, 1977.

Morgan, Robin, and Gloria Steinem. "The International Crime of Genital Mutilation." *Ms.,* Vol. VIII, No. 9, Mar. 1980.

Opoku, Kwame. *The Law of Marriage in Ghana: A Study in Legal Pluralism.* Hamburg: Univ. of Hamburg, 1976.

Pellow, Deborah. *Women in Accra: Options for Autonomy.* Algonac, MI: Reference Publications, 1977.

Valenga, Dorothy. "Ghana: Liberation." *New World Outlook,* Apr. 1971.

White Paper on Marriage, Divorce and Inheritance. Accra: Government Printer, 1961.

GREECE

The American Series for Foreign Penal Codes 18: The Greek Penal Code. Trans. Dr. Nicolas Lolis. South Hackensack, NJ: Fred B. Rothman, 1973.

Cobbs, Lica. "Women's Union of Greece." *The Longest Revolution,* Dec. 1978.

"Equal Rights: The Greek Case." *YWCA of Greece Newsletter,* Athens, n.d.

"Family Law in Greece." *ISIS,* No. 17, Geneva, 1980.

Fhoca, Angela, ed. *Nei Orizontes: The Greek Woman.* Athens: Athens YWCA, July–Aug.–Sept. 1982.

General Secretariat of Press and Information. *Greece Today.* Athens, Feb. 1983.

Howe, Marvine. "Greece Gives Wives Equal Voice in the Home." *New York Times,* Jan. 30, 1983.

Isnard, Jacques. "Femmes en uniforme." *Le Monde Dimanche,* Paris, Apr. 6, 1980.

Livas, Haris. "Breaking the Mold: An Interview with Margaret Papandreou." Athens News Agency (feature story, No. 62), Mar. 28, 1983.

National Report by Greece to the World Conference of the UN Decade for Women: Equality, Development and Peace. Copenhagen, July 1980.

Papandreou, Margaret C. "The Program for Women of the New Greek Government." Women's National Democratic Club, Washington, D.C., Feb. 25, 1982.

"Reformed Greek Civil and Family Laws." *New Women's Times,* Vol. XIII, No. 4, Apr. 1983.

"Women in Greece Join Military." *New York Times,* Jan. 12, 1979.

Women of Europe, issues of Nov.–Dec. 1980, Mar.–Apr., May–June–July, and Sept.–Oct. 1982. Brussels: Commission of the European Communities.

GUATEMALA

Bossen, Laurel. "Wives and Servants: Women in Middle Class Households, Guatemala City," Pittsburgh, PA, Oct. 1979; unpublished paper.

Chinchilla, Norma S. "Industrialization, Monopoly Capitalism, and Women's Work in Guatemala." *Signs,* Vol. 3, No. 1, Autumn 1977.

Colectivo de Solidaridad con el Pueblo de Guatemala. "Análisis de la Problemática de la Mujer Guatemalteca." Ponencia presentada en el Evento de Solidaridad con la Mujer Centroaméricana. San José, Costa Rica, 1981.

Concerned Guatemalan Scholars. *Guatemala: Dare to Struggle, Dare to Win.* Brooklyn, NY, Oct. 1981.

Constitution of the Republic of Guatemala. Washington, D.C.: Pan American Union, General Secretariat, OAS, 1965.

Frente Popular 31 de Enero. "La Mujer Guatemalteca en la Revolución," 1982; an unpublished document.

Moran, Betsy Crites. "The Sacred Affinity of Women's Roles in the Mayan Culture of Guatemala and Mexico," 1982; unpublished paper.

Paul, Lois. "The Mastery of Work and the Mystery of Sex: A Highland Maya Case." *Woman, Culture, and Society.* Eds. Michele Z. Rosaldo and Louise Lamphere. Stanford: Stanford Univ. Press, 1974.

Robles, Julio Gómez. *A Statement of the Laws of Guatemala in Matters Affecting Business,* 2nd ed. Washington, D.C.: Pan American Union, General Secretariat, OAS, 1959.

Santiso, Roberto, Jane T. Bertrand, and María Antonieta Pineda. "Voluntary Sterilization in Guatemala: A Comparison of Men and Women." *Studies in Family Planning,* Vol. 14, No. 3, Mar. 1983.

HUNGARY

Civil Code of the Hungarian People's Republic. Trans. Pál Hamberg. Budapest: Corvina Press, 1960.

Connexions, No. 5, Summer 1982.

Constitution of the Hungarian People's Republic. Trans. William Sóloyöm-fekete. Washington, D.C.: Library of Congress, 1973.

Criminal Code of the Hungarian People's Republic. Trans. Pál Hamberg. Budapest: Corvina Press, 1962.

Family Planning Perspectives, Vol. 12, No. 4, July–Aug. 1980.

Friendly, Alfred J. "Alcohol Called a Big Factor in Hungarian Suicides." *New York Times,* Aug. 1, 1971.

Hungarian Central Statistics Office, ed. *Statistical Pocket Book of Hungary.* Budapest: Statistical Publishing House, 1981.

Hungarian Lawyers Assoc. *Hungarian Law Review,* Nos. 1–2. Budapest, 1981.

"Hungary." *ILIS,* No. 9, Helsinki, Mar. 1983.

"Hungary: No Movement?—An Interview with Maria Markus." *Spare Rib,* London, Mar. 1979.

ILO News Bulletin: Women at Work, No. 2, Geneva, 1978.

"Influence of Social Developments on Treaties Relating to the Rights of Women." *Acta Juridica Scientiarum Hungaricarum,* Vol. 18 (3–4). Budapest: n.p., 1976.

Kamerman, Sheila B. "Work and Family in Industrialized Societies." *Signs,* Vol. 4, No. 4, Summer 1979.

National Council of Hungarian Women. *Women of Hungary.* Budapest, 1981.

INDIA

Ahmad, Karuna. "Educated Indian Women: A Privileged Minority?" *Feminist International: Asian Women '80,* No. 2, Tokyo, June 1980.

Bang, Rani. "Pregnancy and Childbirth in Developing Countries." *ISIS,* No. 20, Geneva, 1981.

Bhoite, Anurandha. "Deceptive Equality: An Analysis of the Present Status of Indian Women" and "Women in Asia: A Feminist Perspective." *Feminist International: Asian Women '80,* No. 2, Tokyo, June 1980.

Borders, William. "Divorce More Frequent in India as Women Increasingly Assert Their Rights." *New York Times,* May 24, 1976.

———. "Dowries in India Attacked as Degrading Women's Roles." *New York Times,* Jan. 12, 1977.

———. "India Disappointed in Birth Control by Persuasion." *New York Times,* Aug. 9, 1978.

"Bury Us Together." *Connexions,* No. 3, Winter 1982.

Chaman, Lal. "Emerging from Silence." *Manushi,* No. 2, New Delhi, Jan.–Feb. 1983.

Chandra, Prakash. "India's Newest Goddess Gains More Devotees." *Depthnews,* Manila, Apr. 20, 1983.

"Crimes Against Women Stir Protests in India." *New Women's Times,* Vol. VI, No. 19, Nov. 1980.

Data Services, Ltd., Dept. of Economics and Statistics, ed. *Statistical Outline of India 1978.* Bombay: D. R. Pendse, 1977.

"A Discussion on the Proposed Amendment to the Marriage and Divorce Laws." *Manushi,* No. 11, New Delhi, 1982.

"Dowry Murders Happen Every Day." *New Women's Times,* Vol. V, No. 16, Aug. 31–Sept. 13, 1979.

Farooqui, Vimla. "New Perspectives for a Better Life." *Women of the Whole World,* No. 3, Berlin, GDR, 1981.

Horowitz, B., and Madhu Kishwar. "Family Life—The Unequal Deal." *Manushi,* No. 11, New Delhi, 1982.

"India." *The Tribune,* No. 15. New York: International Women's Tribune Center, n.d.

"India: Devdasis Organise." *Manushi,* No. 7, New Delhi, 1981.

"India: Forum Against Rape." *ISIS,* No. 14, Geneva, 1980.

"Indian Women Fight Possession, Violence." *Off Our Backs,* Vol. X, No. 10, Nov. 1980.

"In India, Birth Control Focus Shifts to Women." *New York Times,* Mar. 7, 1982.

Jain, Devaki. "Women and Development." *Sixth Five Year Plan: 1980–85.* New Delhi: Planning Commission, Government of India, 1980.

Kelkar, Govind. "Women in Post-Liberation Societies: A Comparative Analysis of Indian and Chinese Experiences." *National Liberation and Women's Liberation.* Eds. Maria Mies and Rhoda Reddock. The Hague: Institute of Social Studies, 1982.

Malini, Vol. 1, No. 6, and Vol. 2, No. 1 [US], 1982.

Ministry of Information and Broadcasting. *India 1980.* New Delhi, 1980.

Ministry of Social Welfare. *Handbook on Social Welfare Statistics, 1981.* New Delhi: Government of India, 1981.

"New Rape Bill Passed." *Manushi,* New Delhi, Nov.–Dec. 1983.

Omvedt, Gail. *We Will Smash This Prison.* London: Zed Press, 1980.

Ranchhoddas, Ratanalal, and Dhirajlal Keshavlal Thakore, eds. *The Indian Penal Code.* Bombay: Law Reporter (Pvt.), 1967.

Roy, Shibani. "Status of Muslim Women in North India." *Manushi,* No. 1, New Delhi, Nov.–Dec. 1982.

Sarkar, Lotika. "Law and the Status of Women in India." *Law and the Status of Women.* Ed. *Columbia Human Rights Law Review.* New York: Centre for Social Development and Humanitarian Affairs, United Nations, 1977.

Singa, Gayatri, and Mira Savara. *A Case Study on Child Care Facilities in Metropolitan Bombay.* Bangkok: Asian and Pacific Centre for Women and Development, 1980.

Stevens, William K. "Rise in Dowry Deaths Alarms Indian Women." *New York Times,* Sept. 12, 1982.

————. "Sexual Repression in the Land of the Kama Sutra." *New York Times,* Apr. 22, 1983.

Women in the World: A Ford Foundation Position Paper. New York: Ford Foundation, Nov. 1980.

INDONESIA

Annual Review of Population Law, 1978. New York: UNFPA, 1978.

Canadian International Development Agency. *Integration of Women in Development: Fact Sheet for Indonesia.* Ottawa, 1982.

Carrean, Estela. "Java Rural Women Play Dual Role of Housewife and Worker." *Depthnews,* Manila, Dec. 16, 1982.

Country Report: Indonesia. Prepared for the Regional Conference for the UN Decade for Women. New Delhi, Nov. 5–9, 1979. Jakarta: (UN)ESCAP, 1979.

Dept. of Information. *Indonesia 1981.* Jakarta: Directorate for Foreign Information Services, 1981.

Jones, Clayton. "Key to Indonesia's Smaller Families: New Economic Role for Women." *Christian Science Monitor,* Apr. 30, 1981.

Milone, Pauline. *A Preliminary Study in Three Countries: Indonesia Report.* Washington, D.C.: Federation of Organizations for Professional Women, International Center for Research on Women, Sept. 1978.

Soewondo, Nani. "Law and the Status of Women in Indonesia." *Law and the Status of Women.* Ed. *Columbia Human Rights Law Review.* New York: Centre for Social Development and Humanitarian Affairs, United Nations, 1977.

Southwood, Julia. "Rape Is Legal—Love Is Not." *Spare Rib,* Issue 110, London, Sept. 1981.

"Trial and a Marriage." *Connexions,* No. 3, Winter 1982.

Ujang, Sharifah. "Capitalists Use Local Patriarchs to Control Women Factory

Workers." *Depthnews*, Manila, Feb. 18, 1983.

UNDP. *Evaluation Study No. 3: Rural Women's Participation in Development.* New York: United Nations, June 1980.

Zafra, Emma Ruth. "Mechanization Displaces Indonesian Rural Women." *Depthnews*, Manila, Jan. 23, 1983.

IRAN

Bayat-Philipp, Mangol. "Women and Revolution in Iran, 1905–1911." *Women in the Muslim World.* Eds. Lois Beck and Nikki Keddie. Cambridge, MA: Harvard Univ. Press, 1978.

Beck, Lois. "Women Among Qashqa'i Nomadic Pastoralists in Iran." *Women in the Muslim World.* Eds. Lois Beck and Nikki Keddie. Cambridge, MA: Harvard Univ. Press, 1978.

Benard, Cheryl. "Islam and Women: Some Reflections on the Experience of Iran." *Journal of South Asian and Middle Eastern Studies,* Vol. IV, No. 2, Winter 1980.

CAIFI [Committee for Artistic and Intellectual Freedom in Iran] *Newsletter,* issues of Vol. 3, No. 1, Mar. 1977, and Vol. 4, No. 3, Summer 1978.

Fallaci, Oriana. "An Interview with Khomeini." *New York Times Magazine,* Oct. 7, 1979.

"15,000 Teheran Women Protest for Fifth Day over Dress Code." *New York Times,* Mar. 13, 1979.

Fischer, Michael M. J. "On Changing the Concept and Position of Persian Women." *Women in the Muslim World.* Eds. Lois Beck and Nikki Keddie. Cambridge, MA: Harvard Univ. Press, 1978.

de Goulart, Claude. "Iran: The Next Power Struggle." *World Press Review,* Mar. 1982.

Hillmann, Michael C. "Furugh Farrukhzad, Modern Iranian Poet." *Middle Eastern Muslim Women Speak.* Eds. Elizabeth Warnock Fernea and Basima Qattan Bezirgan. Austin: Univ. of Texas Press, 1977.

"How the Revolution Betrayed Women."

Spare Rib, Issue 111, London, Oct. 1981.

Ibrahim, Youssef M. "Iranian Komiteh Has Final Say over Life, Oranges, Brothels." *New York Times,* Mar. 8, 1979.

"Iran." *New Directions for Women,* Vol. 12, No. 2, Mar.–Apr. 1982.

"Iranian Comeback." World Economy Section, *World Press Review,* Vol. 30, No. 10, Oct. 1983.

"Iranian Feminist Arrested." *Off Our Backs,* Vol. XII, No. 1, Jan. 1982.

"Iranian Women Betrayed." *Off Our Backs,* Vol. X, No. 5, May 1980.

"Iran: The Revolution That Failed." *Spare Rib,* Issue 128, London, Mar. 1983.

"Islamic Revolution." *ZIQA'AD 1400,* Vol. 2, No. 7. Falls Church, VA: Research and Publication, Sept. 1980.

Millett, Kate. "Message to Iranian Women." *Circle of Support Newsletter,* Mar. 26, 1979.

Mirahabi, Farin. "The Status of Women in Iran." *Journal of Family Law,* Vol. 14, No. 3. Louisville, MO: Univ. of Louisville School of Law, 1975–76.

"New Regime in Iran Harsh on Women." *Al-Raida,* Vol. VI, No. 24, Beirut, May 1, 1983.

Pakizegi, Behnaz. "Legal and Social Positions of Iranian Women." *Women in the Muslim World.* Eds. Lois Beck and Nikki Keddie. Cambridge, MA: Harvard Univ. Press, 1978.

"Question of the Violation of Human Rights and Fundamental Freedoms" (E/CN.4/1983/19). New York: (UN)ECOSOC, Commission on Human Rights, Feb. 22, 1983.

Ramazan, Nesta. "Beyond the Veil: Status of Women in Iran." *Journal of South Asian and Middle Eastern Studies,* Vol. IV, No. 2, Winter 1980.

Reid, Elizabeth. "Iran: An Inside View." *National Times,* Jan. 20, 1979.

"Report from Iran." *Manushi,* No. 12, New Delhi, 1982.

Tapper, Nancy. "The Women's Subsociety among the Shahsevan Nomads of Iran." *Women in the Muslim World.* Eds. Lois Beck and Nikki Keddie. Cambridge, MA: Harvard Univ. Press, 1978.

Vieille, Paul. "Iranian Women in Family Alliance and Sexual Politics." *Women in the Muslim World.* Eds. Lois Beck and Nikki Keddie. Cambridge, MA: Harvard Univ. Press, 1978.

"Women Against the Khomeini Regime." *New Women's Times,* Apr. 1983.

"Women Against the Shah." *Spare Rib,* Issue 91, London, Feb. 1979.

IRELAND(S)

Binchy, William. "Family Law Reform in Ireland: Some Comparative Aspects." *International and Comparative Quarterly,* Vol. 25. Ed. K. R. Simmonds. London: British Institute of International and Comparative Law, Oct. 1976.

"Cheap Divorce and Contraception for Ireland." *New Women's Times,* Vol. X, No. 1, Jan. 15–28, 1980.

Corea, Gena. "Northern Ireland: The Violence Isn't All in the Street." *Ms.,* Vol. VIII, No. 1, July 1979.

"A Decade of Struggle." *Spare Rib,* Issue 118, London, May 1982.

"Family Planning Act Fails." *Plexus,* Mar. 1981.

"15,000 Join Rally for Ulster Peace." *New York Times,* Nov. 28, 1977.

Government Statistical Service. "Census 1981 Preliminary Report England and Wales and Regional Trends." *Annual Abstract of Statistics 1982 Edition (AAS).* London: Her Majesty's Stationery Office, 1982.

———. *Digest of Statistics of Northern Ireland (June 1981).* Belfast: Her Majesty's Stationery Office, 1981.

———. *Ulster Yearbook of 1981.* Belfast: Her Majesty's Stationery Office, 1981.

"Ireland." *ISIS,* No. 14, Geneva, 1980.

"Ireland—The Contraceptive Corps." *Time,* June 7, 1971.

"Irish Women Offer Support." *Spare Rib,* Issue 111, London, Oct. 1981.

"Irish Women Organize." *Multiple Vision,* Vol. 1, No. 4, Mar. 1980.

Kelly, John Maurice. *Fundamental Rights in the Irish Law and Constitution.* Dublin: Allen Figgs, 1961.

Longcope, Kay. "Feminists in Ireland." *Boston Globe,* Oct. 7, 1982.

McCafferty, Nell. *The Armagh Women.* Dublin: Co-op Books, 1981.

Nordheimer, Jon. "Abortion Battle Catches Dublin Leader Unawares." *New York Times,* Apr. 27, 1983.

Reed, Roy. "Northern Ireland's Peace Movement Being Buffeted by Criticism from Inside and Out." *New York Times,* Apr. 29, 1977.

Report from the United Kingdom of Great Britain and Northern Ireland to (UN)ECOSOC. "Implementation of the International Covenant on Economic, Social and Cultural Rights." April 15, 1980. New York: United Nations, Sept. 3, 1980.

Servan-Schreiber, Claude. "Another Voice: Interview with Marie Drumm." *Ms.,* Vol. V, No. 6, Dec. 1976.

Shatter, Alan Joseph. *Family Law in the Republic of Ireland,* 2nd ed. Dublin: Wolfhound Press, 1981.

"Talking with Bernadette Devlin McAliskey." *Spare Rib,* Issue 108, London, July 1981.

"Why Belfast Is in Mourning." *New York Times,* Jan. 24, 1980.

"The Women in Armagh (Ireland)." *ISIS,* No. 17, Geneva, 1980.

Women in Statistics: Supplement No. 10 to Women of Europe. Brussels: Commission of the European Communities, 1982.

Women of Europe, issues of Jan.–Feb. 1981, May–June–July and Sept.–Oct. 1982. Brussels: Commission of the European Communities.

ISRAEL

Bureau of the Advisor to the Prime Minister on the Status of Women. "Participation of Women in Political and Social Life" (Israel National Statement). *The Status of Women,* No. 3. Bonn:

European Regional Seminar of UNESCO, Nov. 1982.

"Change in Israel—A World Press Report." *World Press Review,* Vol. 30, No. 7, July 1983.

"CHEN: The Women's Corps." *The Israeli Defense Forces Spokesman,* n.p., May 30, 1977.

Commission on the Status of Women, Office of the Prime Minister. *Recommendations of the Commission on the Status of Women.* Jerusalem: Government Printing Office, 1978.

Davis, Nina Yuval. "Israeli Women and Men: Divisions Behind the Unity." *Change International Reports.* London: International Reports, Women's Society, 1982.

Eldar-Avidar, Attaché for Women's Affairs. *Notes from Israel,* No. 1. Washington, D.C.: Embassy for Israel, Women's Affairs Dept., Feb. 1978.

"Group Battles Deaths of Unwed Pregnant Arabs." *Washington Post,* Jan. 7, 1981.

Hazelton, Lesley. *Israeli Women: The Reality Behind the Myth.* New York: Simon & Schuster, 1977.

Kaye, Melanie. "Some Notes on Jewish Lesbian Identity." *Nice Jewish Girls: A Lesbian Anthology.* Ed. Evelyn Torton Beck. Watertown, MA: Persephone Press, Inc., 1982.

Israel Information Center. *Women: A Brief Report on the Status of Women in Israel.* Jerusalem, May 1980.

Levavi, Lea. "All Things Being Equal." *Jerusalem Post,* Jerusalem, Jan. 19, 1983.

Ministry of Justice. *Laws of the State of Israel,* Special Volume on Penal Law. Jerusalem, 1977.

———. *Laws of the State of Israel,* No. 31. Jerusalem, 1976–77.

Patai, Raphael. *The Hebrew Goddess.* New York: Discus/Avon Books, 1978.

Pogrebin, Letty Cottin. "A Feminist Goes to Israel." *Ms.,* Vol. VI, No. 4, Oct. 1977.

"Rape Amendment." *New Women's Times,* Vol. XIII, No. 1, Jan. 1983.

"Report from Israel: Recognition of Media Abuse of Women." *Newspage* of Women Against Violence in Pornography and Media, Vol. VIII, No. 7, Aug.–Sept. 1983.

Shipler, David K. "In West Bank Humiliation Is an Israeli Weapon." *New York Times,* May 31, 1983.

———. "Israeli Furor over Accord." *New York Times,* May 10, 1983.

Society. Jerusalem: Keter Publishing House, 1974.

Statistical Abstract of Israel, 1981. Jerusalem: Central Bureau of Statistics, 1981.

"Women Against Occupation." *Connexions,* Winter 1984.

ITALY

de Bianchini, Angela. *Voce Donna.* Torino: Tascabili Bompiani, 1979.

Caldwell, Lesley. "Abortion in Italy." *Feminist Review,* No. 7, Spring 1981.

Corriere della sera, May 7 and May 15, 1976, and June 2, 1982.

"Divorce: Some Figures." *Women of Europe.* Brussels: Commission of the European Communities, Mar.–Apr. 1983.

Hoepli, Ulrico, ed. *Quatro Codici per le Udienze Civil e Penali.* Milan: Ranchi-Feroci-Ferrari, 1963.

Howard, Judith Jeffrey. "Patriot Mothers in the Post Risorgimento." *Women, War, and Revolution.* Eds. Carol R. Berkin and Clara M. Lovett. New York: Holmes & Meir, 1980.

"In Italy." *ISIS,* No. 3, Geneva, 1977.

"Italy." *ISIS,* No. 16, Geneva, 1980.

Presidenza del Consiglio dei Ministri. *Il Nuovo Dirito di Famiglia.* Rome, 1975.

Women in Statistics: Supplement No. 10 to Women of Europe. Brussels: Commission of the European Communities, 1982.

Women of Europe, issues of May–June–July and Sept.–Oct. 1982. Brussels: Commission of the European Communities.

"Workshop Reports." *ISIS,* No. 20, Geneva, 1981.

JAPAN

Agora. *The Low Status of Women in Japan, a Paradox.* Tokyo, 1979–80.

Baumgartner, Georges. "The Legacy of Nagasaki." *World Press Review,* Vol. 30, No. 10, Oct. 1983.

Bethel, Diana. "Visions of a Humane Society: Feminist Thought in Taisho Japan." *Feminist International: Asian Women '80,* No. 2, Tokyo, 1980.

Blasing, Anne. "The Lavender Kimono." *Connexions,* No. 3, Winter 1982.

Broderick, Catherine. "Kabuki by Foreigners: In the Spirit of the Feminine Kabuki Tradition." *Feminist International: Asian Women '80,* No. 2, Tokyo, 1980.

Bruin, Janet, and Stephen Salaff. "Never Again: The Organization of Women Atomic Bomb Victims in Osaka." *Feminist Studies,* Vol. 7, No. 1, Spring 1982.

Cook, Alice, and Hiroko Hayashi. *Working Women in Japan: Discrimination, Resistance, and Reform.* Ithaca: Cornell Univ. NY State School of Labor and Industrial Relations, 1980.

Criminal Statutes. Tokyo: Ministry of Justice, 1957.

"Employment Discrimination." *Plexus,* Mar. 1981.

Higuchi, Keiko. "Japan." *Creative Women in Changing Societies: A Quest for Alternatives.* Eds. Torill Stockland, Mallica Vajrathon, and Davidson Nicol. A UNITAR Book. Dobbs Ferry, NY: Transnational Publishers, 1982.

Ikuko, Atsumi. "Goals of Feminism in Modern Japan." *Feminist International: Asian Women '80,* No. 2, Tokyo, 1980.

International Women's Year Action Group, English Pamphlet Task Force. *Action Now in Japan,* Tokyo, 1980.

Japanese Ministry of Labor. *Facts of Women's Labor in Japan.* Tokyo, 1980.

"Japanese Women." *Report of the Mid-Decade National Conference for the UN Decade for Women.* Tokyo: Executive Committee of the National Conference of Nongovernmental Organizations of Japan, July 1980.

"Japanese Women Oppose Sexist Violence." *Women Against Violence in Pornography and Media,* 1982.

Koshi, George. *The Japanese Legal Advisor.* Rutland, VT, and Tokyo: Charles E. Tuttle, 1972.

Mackie, Vera, Diana Bethel, and Anne Blasing. "Women's Groups in Japan." *Feminist International: Asian Women '80,* No. 2, Tokyo, 1980.

Masanao, Kano. "Takamure Itsue: Pioneer in the Study of Women's History." *Feminist International: Asian Women '80,* No. 2, Tokyo, 1980.

Michiko, Naoi. "Report on Elderly Women." *Feminist International: Asian Women '80,* No. 2, Tokyo, 1980.

Mitsue, Mariko. " 'Dishonorable' Abortion Rights Threatened in Japan." *Womanews,* Feb. 1983.

Naftulin, Lois J. "Women's Status Under Japanese Laws." *Feminist International: Asian Women '80,* No. 2, Tokyo, 1980.

Newcomb, Amelia A. "Traditional Role of Japanese Women Changing in the '80's." *Christian Science Monitor,* Dec. 30, 1982.

Noriko, Sano. "Japanese Women's Movements During World War II." *Feminist International: Asian Women '80,* No. 2, Tokyo, 1980.

Nuita, Yoko. "Fusae Ichikawa: Japanese Woman Suffragist." *Frontiers: A Journal of Women's Studies,* Vol. III, No. 3, Fall 1978.

Prime Minister's Office. *Population and Household Finances of the Elderly in Japan.* Tokyo: Foreign Press Center, 1981.

———. *Women of Japan: Conditions and Policies Report on the National Plan of Action (2).* Tokyo, May 1980.

Public Information Bureau. "Government." *Facts About Japan,* No. 05201. Tokyo: Ministry of Foreign Affairs, July 1979.

———. "Social Security." *Facts About*

Japan, No. 05401. Tokyo: Ministry of Foreign Affairs, Mar. 1981.

————. "Status of Women." *Facts About Japan,* No. 05402. Tokyo: Ministry of Foreign Affairs, Nov. 1977.

"A Safe Place in Japan." *New Women's Times,* Vol. VII, No. 4, Apr. 1981.

Terue, Ohashi. "The Marriageable Age" and "The Reality of Female Labor." *Feminist International: Asian Women '80,* No. 2, Tokyo, 1980.

Vasiliades, Mary. "Sayonara, Male Chauvinism: Women's Liberation in Japan." *Womanews,* Dec.–Jan. 1983.

Watanabe, Haruko, and Yoko Nuita. "Japanese Women Pioneers." *Frontiers: A Journal of Women's Studies,* Vol. III, No. 3, Fall 1978.

"Why I Have Been Struggling All These Years." *Connexions,* No. 3, Winter 1982.

"Women Do Not Allow War." *Connexions,* No. 6, Fall 1982.

Women in the World: A Ford Foundation Position Paper. New York: Ford Foundation, Nov. 1980.

KENYA

"Child Marriage in Kenya." *Al-Raida,* Vol. VI, No. 24, Beirut, May 1, 1983.

Gügler, Josef. "The Second Sex in Town." *The Black Woman Cross-Culturally.* Ed. Filomina Chioma Steady. Cambridge, MA: Schenkman, 1981.

"Historic Ruling." *Viva,* Nairobi, May 1981.

Hollander, Roberta Beth. "Out of Tradition: The Position of Women in Kenya and Tanzania During the Pre-Colonial, Colonial and Post-Independence Eras." Diss., American Univ., 1979.

Huston, Perdita. "To Be Born a Woman Is a Sin." *Populi,* Vol. 4, No. 3. New York: UNFPA, 1977.

Kaufman, Michael T. "Tradition a Big Barrier in Kenya's Marriage-Reform Drive." *New York Times,* Oct. 23, 1978.

"Kenya Country Paper." Presented at the Second Regional Conference on Integration of Women in Development, Lusaka, Zambia. Dec. 3–7, 1979.

"A Kenyan Bank." *World Press Review,* Vol. 30, No. 9, Sept. 1983.

Lamb, David. "Africa Moves Ahead, but Its Women Lag." *New York Times,* Jan. 17, 1978.

Laws of Kenya: The Penal Code. Nairobi: Government Printer, 1970.

Lindsay, Beverly. "Issues Confronting Professional African Women: Illustrations from Kenya." *Comparative Perspectives of Third World Women.* Ed. Beverly Lindsay. New York: Praeger, 1980.

Maina, Rose, V. W. Muchai, and S. B. O. Gutto. "Law and the Status of Women in Kenya." *Law and the Status of Women.* Ed. *Columbia Human Rights Law Review.* New York: Centre for Social Development and Humanitarian Affairs, United Nations, 1977.

"Marriage Reform Fails: Wife Beating Upheld in Kenya." *New Women's Times,* Vol. 5, No. 9, Sept. 14, 1979.

Ministry of Finance and Planning. *Women in Kenya.* Nairobi: Central Bureau of Statistics, July 1978.

————. "Women in Kenya." *Social Perspectives,* Vol. 3, No. 3. Nairobi: Central Bureau of Statistics, Apr. 1978.

Omo-Fadaka, Jimoh. "Women's March Slow in Kenya." *New African,* Nov. 1981.

"Women in the Rural Areas of Kenya and Tanzania." *Women in Developing Countries: Case Studies of Six Countries.* Stockholm: Swedish International Development Authority Research Division, 1974.

Women in the World: A Ford Foundation Position Paper. New York: Ford Foundation, Nov. 1980.

Women's Bureau. *Kenya Country Report for the UN Mid-Decade for Women Review Conference.* July 1980. Nairobi: Ministry of Culture and Social Services, 1980.

KOREA (SOUTH)

Caldwell, Mildred. "The Economics of Sexual Exploitation in Korea." *Feminist International: Asian Women '80,* No. 2, Tokyo, 1980.

"Change Our Working Conditions." *Connexions*, No. 6, Fall 1982.

"Changing Roles of Korean Women." *Korea Newsreview*, Seoul, Nov. 27, 1982.

Fuentes, Annette, and Barbara Ehrenreich. *Women in the Global Factory*. Boston: South End Press, 1983.

Kim, Yung-Chung. *Women of Korea—A History from Ancient Times to 1945*. Seoul: EWHA Women's Univ. Press, 1976.

Korea Annual 1977. Seoul: Hapdong News Agency, 1977.

Korean National Council of Women. *The Woman*, Vol. 18, No. 2, Seoul, Nov. 1982.

Lee, Hoyo-Chai. "Women as Victims of the Dual Marriage System in Korea." *Feminist International: Asian Women '80*, No. 2, Tokyo, 1980.

Malcolm, Andrew H. "Pioneer Woman Runs Seoul Legal Aid Unit." *New York Times*, Sept. 4, 1977.

Ministry of Health and Social Affairs. *Women in Korea 1980*. Seoul, July 1980.

Mueller, Gerard, ed. *The Korean Criminal Code*. South Hackensack, NJ: Fred B. Rothman, 1960.

Noriko, Sano. "Japanese Women's Movements During World War II." *Feminist International: Asian Women '80*, No. 2, Tokyo, 1980.

"South Korea: Textile Workers Fighting for Their Rights." *ISIS*, No. 10, Geneva, Winter 1978–79.

"South Korea: Women's Groups Oppose Kisaeng Tourism." *ISIS*, No. 13, Geneva, 1979.

KUWAIT

Ahmad, Haider, ed. *The Kuwaiti Digest*, Vol. 10, No. 4. Ahmadi: Kuwait Oil Co., Oct.–Dec. 1982.

Central Statistical Office. *Annual Statistical Abstract 1982*, XIX ed. Kuwait: Ministry of Planning, 1982.

Hassouna, Fawzia. "The Forbidden Sex in Kuwait," n.d.; unpublished paper.

"Kuwait." *New Directions for Women*, Vol. 11, No. 2, Mar.–Apr. 1982.

"Kuwaiti Parliament Legalizes Some Abortions." *New York Times*, Jan. 31, 1982.

Kuwait Ministry of Information. *Kuwait's New Horizons*. Kuwait, n.d.

"Kuwait Rejects Proposal To Let Women Vote." *New York Times*, Jan. 21, 1982.

Nath, Kamla. "Education and Employment Among Kuwaiti Women." *Women in the Muslim World*. Eds. Lois Beck and Nikki Keddie. Cambridge, MA: Harvard Univ. Press, 1978.

"Role of the Kuwaiti Woman in Development Administration." *Al-Raida*, Vol. VI, No. 23, Beirut, Feb. 1, 1983.

Sapsted, David. *Modern Kuwait*. Kuwait: Ministry of Information, 1980.

A View of Kuwait. Washington, D.C.: Middle East Services, July 1979.

Weil, Barbara. "I Divorce Thee, I Divorce Thee, I Divorce Thee." *The Middle East*, No. 41, London, Mar. 1978.

"Women's Rights in Kuwait." *Al-Raida*, Vol. IV, No. 17, Beirut, Aug. 1, 1981.

LEBANON

"The Armenian Women in Lebanon." *Al-Raida*, Vol. IV, No. 18, Beirut, Nov. 1, 1981.

Chatty, Dawn. "Changing Sex Roles in Bedouin Society in Syria and Lebanon." *Women in the Muslim World*. Eds. Lois Beck and Nikki Keddie. Cambridge, MA: Harvard Univ. Press, 1978.

"Conference of the National Alliance of Lebanese Women." *Al-Raida*, Vol. V, No. 22, Beirut, Nov. 1, 1982.

"Daily Resistance." *Connexions*, No. 6, Fall 1982.

Dearden, Ann. "Arab Women." *Minority Rights Group*, Report No. 27, London, Dec. 1976.

The International Organization for the Elimination of all forms of Racial Discrimination, ed. *Witness of War Crimes in Lebanon* (Testimony given to the Nordic Commission, Oslo, Oct. 1982). London: Ithaca Press, 1983.

Joseph, Suad. "Women and the Neighborhood Street in Borj Hammoud,

Lebanon." *Women in the Muslim World.* Eds. Lois Beck and Nikki Keddie. Cambridge, MA: Harvard Univ. Press, 1978.

Khalaf, Semir. *Prostitution in a Changing Society.* Beirut: American Univ. of Beirut, 1965.

Lebanese Constitution—Reference Edition in English Translation. Beirut: Kayats Publishers, 1960.

"Miss Sameera Al-Daher, the First Lebanese Woman to Occupy the Post of Ambassador." *Al-Raida,* Vol. VI, No. 25, Beirut, Aug. 1, 1983.

"Ninth Conference of the Committee for Lebanese Women's Rights." *Al-Raida,* Vol. IV, No. 17, Beirut, Aug. 1, 1981.

Peters, Emrys L. "The Status of Women in Four Middle East Communities." *Women in the Muslim World.* Eds. Lois Beck and Nikki Keddie. Cambridge, MA: Harvard Univ. Press, 1978.

"Seminar on Social Problems of the Lebanese Working Woman: A Serious Effort for Her Promotion." *Al-Raida,* Vol. IV, No. 17, Beirut, Aug. 1, 1981.

Sharara, Yolla Polity. "Women and Politics in Lebanon." *Khamsin: The Journal of Revolutionary Socialists of the Middle East.* London: Pluto Press, 1978.

Social Security Law. Trans. S. Hakim and L. L. Lendon. Beirut: Arab Documentation Office, 1963.

"The Status and Role of the Aged in Lebanon." *Al Raida,* Vol. V, No. 2, Beirut, May 1, 1982.

Women and Work in Lebanon. Monograph Series. Beirut: Institute for Women's Studies in the Arab World, Beirut Univ. College, 1980.

LIBYA

Alfahum, Siba. *The Libyan Woman 1965–1975.* Beirut: Lebanese Section, Women's International League for Peace and Freedom, 1977.

Allaghi, Farida, and Zahiya El-Sahli. *On Libyan Women.* New York: Mission of the Libyan Arab Jamahiriya to the UN, 1977–78.

"Appeal Case." *Amnesty International Newsletter,* Vol. XIII, No. 4, London, Apr. 1983.

Benedict, Michael. *Labor Law and Practice in the Kingdom of Libya.* Washington, D.C.: US Dept. of Labor, 1966.

"Libyan Women Active for Equality." *Women of the Whole World,* No. 3, Berlin, GDR, 1982.

Mayer, Anne. "Developments in the Law of Marriage and Divorce in Libya Since the 1969 Revolution." *Journal of African Law,* Vol. 22, London, 1980.

Mernissi, Fatima. *Country Reports on Women in Libya, Morocco and Tunisia.* Addis Ababa, Ethiopia: (UN)ECA, 1978.

al-Quathafi, Muammar. *Letter to the World Conference at the UN Decade for Women.* July 1980.

———. *The Green Book.* Tripoli: Libyan Government, 1979.

Report from the Libyan Arab Jamahiriya to (UN)ECOSOC. "Implementation of the International Covenant on Economic, Social and Cultural Rights." New York: United Nations, Apr. 25, 1983.

Secretariat of Planning. *Role of Women in the Development of the Socialist People's Arab Jamahiriya with Special Reference to Their Employment, Health, and Education.* Tripoli: People's Libyan Arab Jamahiriya, Nov. 1979.

Wren, Christopher. "Qaddafi Green Book Charts Libyan Path." *New York Times,* Oct. 5, 1979.

———. "The Moslem World Rekindles Its Militancy." *New York Times,* June 18, 1978.

MEXICO

"Abortion in Mexico." *Plexus,* Feb. 1981.

Arizpe, Lourdes. "Women in the Informal Labor Sector: The Case of Mexico City." *Signs,* Vol. 3, No. 1, Autumn 1977.

———, and Josefina Aranda. "The Comparative Advantages of Women's Disadvantages: Women Workers in the Strawberry Export Agribusiness in

Mexico." *Signs,* Vol. 7, No. 2, Winter 1981.

Bialostosky de Chazén, Sara, Beatriz Bernal de Bugeda, *et al. Condición Jurídica de la Mujer en México.* México City: Universidad Nacional Autónoma de México, Facultad de Derecho, 1975.

Carranca y Trujillo, Raul, and Raul Carranca y Rivas. *Código Penal Anotado.* México City: Editorial Porrua, 1971.

"Comunicado de Disolución de FHAR." *Fem,* Vol. VI, No. 21, México City, Feb.–Mar. 1982.

"Crece la Desprotección de la Mujer." *Excelsior,* México City, Feb. 2, 1982.

Elmendorf, Mary. "The Dilemma of Peasant Women: A View from a Village in Yucatán." *Women and World Development.* Eds. Irene Tinker and Michele Bo Bramsen. Washington, D.C.: Overseas Development Council, 1976.

"El Femenino es el Sector más Golpeado por la Crisis Económica: Lourdes Arizpe." *El Día,* México City, Dec. 19, 1982.

Lavrin, Asunción. "In Search of the Colonial Woman in Mexico: The Seventeenth and Eighteenth Centuries." *Latin American Women.* Ed. Asunción Lavrin. Westport, CT: Greenwood Press, 1978.

Leyes y Códigos de México. *Código Penal para el Distrito Federal.* México City: Editorial Porrua, 1980.

López, Rogelio Hernández. "Dramática Marginación y Desigualdad de la Mujer." *Excelsior,* México City, Jan. 19, 1983.

Macias, Anna. "Felipe Carillo Puerto and Women's Liberation in Mexico." *Latin American Women.* Ed. Asunción Lavrin. Westport, CT: Greenwood Press, 1978.

"New Tactics for an Old Crime." *Connexions,* May 1, 1981.

Sanders, Thomas G. "Mexican Women." *North American Series,* Vol. III, No. 6. Hanover, NH: American Universities Field Staff Reports, 1975.

Srinivasan, Mangalam. "The Impact of Science and Technology and the Role of Women in Science in Mexico." *Scientific-Technological Change and the Role of Women in Development.* Eds. Pamela M. D'Onofrio-Flores and Sheila M. Pfafflin. A UNITAR Book. Boulder, CO: Westview Press, 1982.

"Trágico Saldo de la Violación." *Fem,* Vol. V, No. 20, México City, Aug. 1981–Jan. 1982.

Valdés, María Guadalupe. "El Trabajo Doméstico." *El Día,* México City, May 24, 1982.

Work Group No. 7. "Women in Mexico." *Punto Crítico,* México City, Sept. 1972.

MOROCCO

"A Glance into the Status of the Moroccan Woman." *Al-Raida,* Vol. IV, No. 17, Beirut, Aug. 1, 1981.

Mernissi, Fatima. *Country Reports on Women and Social Change in North Africa: Libya, Morocco, Tunisia.* Addis Ababa, Ethiopia: (UN)ECA, 1978.

———. "The Moslem World: Women Excluded from Development." *Women and World Development.* Eds. Irene Tinker and Michele B. Bramsen. Washington, D.C.: Overseas Development Council, 1976.

———. "Women and the Impact of Capitalist Development in Morocco." *Feminist Issues,* Vol. 2, No. 1, Spring 1983.

———. "Women, Saints, and Sanctuaries." *Signs,* Vol. 3, No. 1, Autumn 1977.

"Moroccan Women Take to Vocational Training." *Al Raida,* Vol. VI, No. 24, Beirut, May 1, 1983.

Women and Development: Indicators of Their Changing Role. Paris: UNESCO, 1981.

NEPAL

Acharya, Meena. *The Status of Women in Nepal: Statistical Profile of Nepalese Women—A Critical Review,* Vol. I, Part 1. Kathmandu: Center for Economic Development and Administration, Tribhuvan Univ., 1979.

Annual Review of Population Law, 1980. New York: UNFPA, 1980.

Bennett, Lynn. *The Status of Women in Nepal: Tradition and Change in the Legal Status of Nepalese Women,* Vol. I, Part 2, Kathmandu: Center for Economic Development and Administration, Tribhuvan Univ., 1979.

Country Reports on Human Rights Practices. Washington, D.C.: US Dept. of State, Feb. 1981.

Mair, Lucille. "The Rama Mehta Inaugural Lecture—Primary Force, Active Participants: Women in Third World Rural Development." *Second Century Radcliffe News,* Vol. II, No. 3, June 1981.

Panday, Meena. Articles in *Depthnews,* Manila, Feb. 24, Apr. 14, July 18, Aug. 6, Oct. 9, Nov. 11, and Dec. 27, 1982, and Feb. 4 and Mar. 27, 1983.

Pradhan, Bina. *The Status of Women in Nepal: Institutions Concerning Women in Nepal,* Vol. I, Part 3. Kathmandu: Center for Economic Development and Administration, Tribhuvan Univ., 1979.

Reejal, Pushkar Raj. *The Status of Women in Nepal: Integration of Women in Development, the Case of Nepal,* Vol. I, Part 5. Kathmandu: Center for Economic Development and Administration, Tribhuvan Univ., 1979.

"Selections from the 1963 Legal Code." *Nepal Law Translation Series,* Vol. 39. Kathmandu: Nepal Press Digest (Pvt.), Apr. 24, 1968.

Shrestha, Aditya Man. "Nepalese Women Facing Bleak Job Prospects." *Depthnews,* Manila, Jan. 3, 1983.

THE NETHERLANDS

van Buuren, Hanneke. *The Last Five Years of Women's Emancipation in the Netherlands.* The Hague: Man-Vrouw-Maatschappij, Mar. 1973.

Constitution of the Kingdom of the Netherlands. The Hague, 1983.

"Defence." *The Kingdom of the Netherlands: Facts and Figures.* The Hague: Ministry of Foreign Affairs, 1981.

Fine, Elsa Honig. *Women and Art.* Montclair and London: Allenheld & Schram/Prior, 1978.

Information Service. *Emancipation in the Netherlands.* Rijswijk: Ministry of Cultural Affairs, Recreation, and Social Welfare, July 1980.

Kettig, Evert. "Contraception and Fertility in the Netherlands." *Family Planning Perspectives,* Vol. 15, No. 1, Jan.–Feb. 1983.

Ministry of Cultural Affairs, Recreation, and Social Welfare. *Emancipation of Women in the Netherlands.* The Hague, 1979.

———. *General Family Policy in the Netherlands.* The Hague, 1978.

———. *National Assistance in the Netherlands.* The Hague, 1982.

———. *Social Provisions for Children and Parents in the Netherlands.* The Hague, 1981.

"Netherlands Liberalizes Abortion Law after 10 Years of Wide Availability, Low Abortion Rates." *Family Planning Perspectives,* Vol. 13, No. 3, May–June 1981.

Newton, Gerald. *The Netherlands: An Historical and Cultural Survey, 1795–1977.* Boulder, CO: Westview Press, 1978.

Rosalind. "Parliamentary Pink." *Connexions,* No. 10, Fall 1983.

Women in Statistics: Supplement No. 10 to *Women of Europe.* Brussels: Commission of the European Communities, 1982.

Women of Europe, issues of Mar.–Apr., May–June–July, and Sept.–Oct. 1982. Brussels: Commission of the European Communities.

"Women Squatters in Holland: A Two-Sided Battle." *Connexions,* No. 1, Summer 1981.

The Women's Emancipation in the Netherlands. Amsterdam: Nationwide Foundation, Information, Documentation Center for Women's Liberation, 1980.

NEW ZEALAND

Advisory Committee on Women's Affairs. *Report on Sexual Harassment.*

Wellington: State Services Commission, 1981.

Aitken, Judith. *A Woman's Place.* Auckland: Heinemann Educational Books, 1975.

Bank of New Zealand. *Bank of New Zealand Business Indicators,* 1982.

Broadsheet, issues of Dec. 1976, Jan., Mar., Apr., May, and July 1977, and Mar. 1981, Auckland.

Duncan, S. W. B. "Women's Employment—Progress and Prospects." Auckland and North Shore Business and Professional Women's Clubs Meeting. Feb. 16, 1982.

Government Research Unit. "Women Position Paper," No. 81/24, Wellington, June 1981.

Government Sources (Wellington): "Abortion Supervisory Committee Annual Report," for year ended Mar. 31, 1981; *Census,* 1976; "Early Childhood Care and Education: A Report of the SSC Working Group," June 1980; *Family Guide to New Zealand Law,* Reader's Digest, 1980; "New Zealand Budget," 1981; "New Zealand Dept. of Internal Affairs, Local Authority Election Statistics," 1980; "New Zealand Dept. of Social Welfare Annual Reports"; *New Zealand Official Yearbook,* 1981; "Police Report," 1980; "Policy Statement . . . on the Subject of Sexual Harassment," Apr. 21, 1982; "Report of the Dept. of Education," for year ended Mar. 31, 1982; "Statistics of Offences Calendar Year 1980"; "Update of New Zealand Country Report Prepared for the High Level Conference on the Employment of Women," 1981.

Grimshaw, Patricia. *Women's Suffrage in New Zealand.* Auckland: Auckland Univ. Press; Oxford: Oxford Univ. Press, 1972.

McLay, Hon. J. K. "Paper to the Legal Research Foundation Seminar on Sexual Violence." Auckland Univ., Aug. 27, 1982.

Military Balance 1980–81. London: International Institute for Strategic Studies, 1981.

New Zealand Statutes. Wellington: Government Printer, 1975.

Reprinted Statutes of New Zealand, Vol. 1. Wellington: Government Printer, 1979.

Royal Commission of Inquiry. *Contraception, Sterilisation and Abortion in New Zealand.* Wellington, 1977.

Spare Rib, Issue 127, London, Feb. 1983.

NICARAGUA

Bruce, Judith. "Market Women Cooperatives: Giving Women Credit." *Seeds.* New York: Carnegie Corporation and Population Council, 1980.

Chayoga, Janine. "Women in Nicaragua: The Movement Forward." *Plexus,* Apr. 1981.

Hernández, María Isabel. "The National Liberation Struggle and Women in Nicaragua." *National Liberation and Women's Liberation.* Eds. Maria Mies and Rhoda Reddock. The Hague: Institute for Social Studies, 1982.

Kinzer, Stephen. "Conscription for Young Nicaraguans." *New York Times,* Aug. 31, 1983.

———. "Nicaragua Loosens the Reins on Opposition Paper." *New York Times,* Nov. 21, 1983.

Hoge, Warren. "Nicaragua's Revolution Breaks the Mold." *New York Times,* Dec. 30, 1981.

"Nicaragua." *New Directions for Women,* Vol. 10, No. 2, Mar.–Apr. 1981.

"Nicaragua." *New Women's Times,* Vol. IX, No. 3, Mar. 1983.

"Nicaragua Addenda" to the *Initial Reports of States Parties* due in 1979 on the International Covenant on Civil and Political Rights (CCPR/C/14/Add. 3). New York: UN Human Rights Committee, Mar. 8, 1983.

"Nicaragua: Victory and After." *ISIS,* No. 19, Geneva, 1980.

"Nicaraguan Women and the Revolution." *Women's International Resource Exchange Service Bulletin,* 1980.

"Nicaraguan Women Making Changes."

NACLA Report, Vol. 14, No. 5, Sept.–Oct. 1980.

"The Pill Hoarded in Nicaragua." *New Women's Times,* Vol. VI, No. 2, Dec. 1980.

"Report on Women Agricultural Workers' Encounter." *Barricada,* Managua, Apr. 12, 1983.

Simons, Marlise. "Nicaragua Lists US Violations in Bitter Reply to Reagan Speech." *New York Times,* May 2, 1983.

Tolchin, Martin. "House Panel Bars Aid for the CIA Against Nicaragua." *New York Times,* May 5, 1983.

Vinocur, John. "Nicaragua: A Correspondent's Portrait." *New York Times,* Aug. 16, 1983.

NIGERIA

Adeyokunau, Tomilayo. *Women and Agriculture in Nigeria.* Addis Ababa, Ethiopia: (UN)ECA, 1981.

Akande, Dr. (Mrs.) J. O. Debo. *Law and the Status of Women in Nigeria.* Addis Ababa, Ethiopia: (UN)ECA, 1979.

"Bastard Bill Is Smashed by Women's Strong Protest." *New African,* Nov. 1981.

Federal Office of Statistics. *Annual Abstract of Statistics.* Lagos: Director of Statistics, 1981.

"Getting Things Done." Florence Nwapa." *World Press Review,* Vol. 30, No. 7, July 1983.

Kingdon, Sir Donald, ed. *Laws of the Federation of Nigeria and Lagos,* Vol. II. London: Eyre & Spottiswoode, 1959.

Lewis, Martha W. *Women in Development: Women, Migration and the Decline of Smallholder Agriculture.* Washington, D.C.: Office of Women in Development, Agency for International Development Cooperation, 1980.

Mere, Kisekka. "The Case of Nigeria and Uganda." *Women and Development: Indicators of Their Changing Role,* Socio-Economic Studies 3. Paris: UNESCO, 1981.

Okonjo, Kamene. "Women's Political Participation in Nigeria." *The Black Woman Cross-Culturally.* Ed. Filomina Chioma Steady. Cambridge, MA: Schenkman, 1981.

Traditional Practices Affecting the Health of Women and Children. WHO/EMRO Technical Publication, No. 2, 2 Vols. Alexandria, Egypt: WHO, 1981 and 1982.

NORWAY

Evang, Karl. *Health Services in Norway.* Oslo: Universitesforlaget, 1976.

Family Affairs and Dual Status Dept. *Family and Child Policy in Norway.* Oslo: Royal Norwegian Ministry of Consumer Affairs and Government Administration, 1978.

ILIS Conference Report. Proceedings from a Conference on the International Lesbian Movement. Lichtaart, Belgium, Dec. 30, 1981–Jan. 3, 1982.

National Insurance Institution. *Social Insurance in Norway.* Oslo, 1978.

Norway Information. *The Equal Status Act and the Equal Status Commissioner.* Oslo: Royal Norwegian Ministry of Foreign Affairs, 1980.

———. *Women's Status in Norway.* Oslo: Royal Ministry of Foreign Affairs, 1981.

Norwegian Ministry of Health and Social Affairs. *Voluntary Action in Social Development.* Oslo: NGO/Government Relation, 1982.

Report from Norway to (UN)ECOSOC. "Implementation of the International Covenant on Economic, Social and Cultural Rights." Oct. 12, 1979. New York: United Nations, Dec. 12, 1979.

Selid, Betty. *Women in Norway.* Oslo: Norwegian Joint Committee on International Social Policy, 1970.

Stromberg, Erling. *The Role of Women's Organization in Norway.* Oslo: Equal Status Council, June 1980.

PACIFIC ISLANDS

Amratlal, Jyoti, Eta Baro, Vanessa Griffen, and Geet Bala Singh. *Women's Role in Fiji.* Suva: South Pacific Social Sciences Assoc., 1975.

Cory, Jenny. *Rural Women's Access to*

Legal, Health and Education Services in Papua New Guinea. Port Moresby, Papua New Guinea: Dept. of Community and Family Services, July 1981.

The Far East and Australasia. London: Europa Publications, 1982.

Gokal, Sumitra. *Women of Fiji.* Suva: Lotu Pasifika Productions, 1978.

Griffen, Vanessa. *Women Speak Out.* Report of the Pacific Women's Conference. Oct. 27–Nov. 2, 1975. Suva: Pacific Women's Conference, 1976.

Johnson, Diane. "Aspects of the Legal Status of Women in Papua New Guinea, A Working Paper." Office of Home Affairs, n.d.

Meleisea, Penelope Schoeffel. *O Tama 'Ita 'I Samoa, The Women's Associations in Western Samoa.* Suva: Univ. of South Pacific, 1980.

"Present Status of Women in Papua New Guinea, Constraints and Goals of the Future." *Papua New Guinea Country Report for Regional Conference for UN Decade for Women.* Nov. 1979.

Schoeffel, Penelope. "Origin and Development of Women's Associations in Western Samoa, 1830–1977." *Journal of Pacific Studies III.* Suva: University of South Pacific, 1977.

——, and Eci Kikay. "Women's Work in Fiji: A Historical Perspective." *Review,* Vol. 1, No. 2. Suva: Univ. of South Pacific, May 1980.

"Shaping a New Pacific." *Connexions,* No. 6, Fall 1982.

Survey of Laws in Fertility Control. New York: UNFPA, 1979.

"UN Decade for Women." *National Report Submitted by Samoa to the UN Decade of Women World Conference.* Copenhagen, July 1980.

"Women for a Nuclear Free Pacific: A Nuclear Paradise." *Connexions,* No. 1, Summer 1981.

PAKISTAN

Azam, I. "Infant Stoning," *Muslim Magazine,* n.p., Mar. 11, 1983.

Claiborne, William. "Pakistani Women's Groups Oppose Zia's Drive for Islamic Rules." *Washington Post,* Mar. 28, 1983.

"Federal Advisory Council Adopts Law of Evidence." *Pakistan Times,* Lahore, Mar. 4, 1983.

"In the Male World of Islam, an Occasional Feminist War Cry." *New York Times,* Feb. 16, 1972.

Jethmalani, Rani. "We May Even Be Denied the Right to Vote—Interview with Attorney Asma Jilani." *Express Magazine,* New Delhi, Apr. 24, 1983.

Mazari, Shireen. " 'Islamisation' and the Status of Women in Pakistan: A Note." *South Asia Bulletin,* Vol. III, No. 1, n.p. Spring 1983.

Nagi, Husain. "Lahore Diary." *Viewpoint,* Nov. 18, 1981.

Nizam, Muhamad Miazhar Hassan, ed. *The Pakistan Penal Code.* Islamabad: The All Pakistan Legal Decisions, 1960.

"Pakistan: A Wave of Reaction." *Al-Raida,* Vol. VI, No. 24, Beirut, May 1, 1983.

"Pakistani Women Against Repression: An Interview with Sheema Kermani." *Manushi,* No. 12, New Delhi, 1982.

Women's Action Forum Lahore Newsletter, Nos. 1–3, Lahore, 1982.

PALESTINE

Abdul-Rahman, Dr. Asad, and Rashid Hamid. "The Palestinian Liberation Organization: Past, Present and Future." Proceedings from the UN Seminar on the Question of Palestine. Arusha, July 14–18, 1980.

Bendt, Ingela, and James Downing. *We Shall Return: Women of Palestine.* Trans. Ann Henning. London: Zed Press, 1982.

Committee on the Exercise of the Inalienable Rights of the Palestinian People. *Social, Economic and Political Institutions in the West Bank and the Gaza Strip.* New York: United Nations, 1982.

——. *International Status of the Palestinian People.* New York: United Nations, 1981.

"Fences, Laws and Border Controls

(Women of Palestine)." *Connexions,* No. 2, Fall 1981.

Hasan, Sadat. *Introducing the Palestine Liberation Organization.* New York: Palestine Liberation Organization, n.d.

Khamsin: Journal of Revolutionary Socialists of the Middle East, No. 6. London: Pluto Press, 1978.

"Letter Dated 30 March 1983 from the Chairman of the Committee on the Exercise of the Inalienable Rights of the Palestinian People to the Secretary-General." *United Nations Document No. s/15667,* New York, Mar. 31, 1983.

"Living Conditions of the Palestinian People in the Occupied Palestinian Territories" (A/38/278, E/1983/77). New York: (UN)ECOSOC, June 22, 1983.

Palestine, Vol. 9, No. 3. Brussels: Editions Palestine, Mar. 1–15, 1983.

Palestinian National Covenant. N.p.: Palestine Liberation Organization, June 1968.

Rubenberg, Cheryl. *The Palestine Liberation Organization: Its Institutional Infrastructure.* Palestine Studies, No. 1. Belmont, MA: Institute of Arab Studies, 1983.

Sayigh, Rosemary. "Daily Life in Palestinian Camps." *Spare Rib,* Issue 66, London, Jan. 1978.

Smith, Colin. "The Palestinians." *Minority Rights Group,* Report No. 24, London, May 1975.

"Women Against Occupation." *Connexions,* Winter 1984.

PERU

"A la Hora del Divorcio." *La Tortuga,* No. 5, Lima, 1983.

Barrig, Maruja. "Peru: Los Anti-Conceptivos o Como Aprender Amar la Píldora y no Usarla." *OIM-IPS,* Jan. 1982.

Burkett, Elinor C. "Indian Women and White Society: The Case of 16th Century Peru." *Latin American Women.* Ed. Asunción Lavrin. Westport, CT: Greenwood Press, 1978.

"Campaigns and News of Groups." *ISIS,* No. 14, Geneva, Mar. 1980.

Figueroa, Blanca, and Jeanine Anderson. "Women in Peru." *CHANGE International Reports: Women and Society.* London: CHANGE, Sept. 1981.

Flora, Cornelia Butler. "Socialist Feminism in Latin America." Working Paper No. 14. Dept. of Sociology, Anthropology, and Social Work, Kansas State Univ., Nov. 1982.

Hinojosa, María de Lourdes. "Vargas Speaks on Struggle of Poor Women in Peru." *Barnard Bulletin,* Feb. 23, 1983.

de Muñoz, Dr. Carmen Rodríguez, and Dr. Elsa Roca de Salomen. "Law and the Status of Women in Peru." *Law and the Status of Women.* Ed. *Columbia Human Rights Law Review.* New York: Centre for Social Development and Humanitarian Affairs, United Nations, 1977.

"Organizaciones Femeninas Demandan a FBT Cancelar Proyecto de Miss Universo." *El Diario,* Lima, Feb. 22, 1982.

"Peru in Crisis." *World Press Review,* Vol. 30, No. 7, July 1983.

"Polémica: Por el Aborto Libre y Gratuito." *Mujer y Sociedad,* Lima, July 15, 1982.

Price, Julia. "Women and Feminism in Peru." 2 Parts. *Off Our Backs,* Jan. and Feb. 1983.

Schumacher, Edward. "Peru Arrests Hundreds in an Effort to Stamp Out Growing Insurgency." *New York Times,* June 2, 1983.

Vargas, Virginia, and Armida Testino. "La Violencia Nuestra de Cada Día." *El Diario,* Lima, Nov. 25, 1982.

POLAND

"All the Nudes Fit to Print." *New York Daily News,* Jan. 4, 1983.

Central Statistical Office. *Statistics 1975.* Warsaw, 1975.

———. *Women and Family In Poland.* Warsaw, 1980.

Darnton, John. "Poles *vs.* Riot Police:

Ridicule Is Best Revenge." *New York Times,* Aug. 30, 1982.

"From Fields to Factories." *Connexions,* No. 5, Summer 1982.

"In Poland." *Connexions,* No. 5, Summer 1982.

Kifner, John. "Glemp Mass Marks Uprising in Ghetto." *New York Times,* Apr. 10, 1983.

———. "New Gdansk Street Rally Broken Up." *New York Times,* Mar. 14, 1983.

———. "One Death Reported Among Polish Marchers." *New York Times,* May 3, 1983.

———. "Poland's Parallel Economy Thriving." *New York Times,* Apr. 30, 1983.

———. "Seizing of Solidarity Activist Despite Suspension of Martial Law." *New York Times,* Jan. 10, 1983.

———. "Solidarity Now a Cause for Rebels." *New York Times,* Mar. 20, 1983.

———. "Solidarity Rallies Turn into Clashes with Polish Police." *New York Times,* May 2, 1983.

———. "2,000 Poles Attend Illegal Protest Rally at Gdansk Shipyard." *New York Times,* Mar. 14, 1983.

———. "Warsaw Secret Police Said to Break into a Convent." *New York Times,* May 5, 1983.

———. "Workers at Gdansk Shipyard Demand Restoration of Solidarity." *New York Times,* Mar. 11, 1983.

Lobodzińska, Barbara. "The Education and Employment of Women in Contemporary Poland." *Signs,* Vol. 3, No. 3, Spring 1978.

"Newsbrief." *Womanews,* June 1982.

"Partial Amnesty." *Amnesty International Bulletin,* Oct. 1983.

"Poland." *Annual Review of Population Law—1978.* New York: UNFPA, 1978.

"Polish Prisoners." *Womanews,* Feb. 1982.

"The Revolutionary Activity of Polish Women." *News and Letters,* Vol. 27, No. 2, Mar. 1982.

Wislanka, Ursula. "Polish Women in Forefront of Protest." *New Directions for Women,* Vol. 12, No. 2, Mar.–Apr. 1982.

"The Solidarity Movement: Women's Roles." *New Women's Times,* Vol. XII, No. 3, Mar. 1982.

"Yes, There Is a Women's Movement in Poland." *Connexions,* May 1, 1981.

PORTUGAL

Barreño, Maria Isabel, Maria Teresa Horta, and Maria Velho Da Costa. *New Portuguese Letters.* Trans. Helen R. Lane. Garden City, NY: Doubleday, 1974.

Darnton, John. "Socialists Are Favored to Win the Portuguese Election Today." *New York Times,* Apr. 25, 1983.

Guimarães, Elina. *Portuguese Women—Past and Present.* Lisbon: Comissão da Condição Feminina, 1978.

"Portugal." *New Directions for Women,* Vol. II, No. 6, Nov.–Dec. 1982.

Reynolds, Maria de Sousa, and Ana Vicente, eds. *Folder on the Status of Women in Portugal.* Lisbon: Prime Minister's Office, Commission on the Status of Women, 1981.

Women in Portugal: Supplement No. 11 to Women of Europe. Brussels: Commission of the European Communities, 1983.

RUMANIA

"Abortion: A Privilege?" *Connexions,* No. 5, Summer 1982.

"Campaign for Prisoners of the Month." *Amnesty International Newsletter,* Vol. XIII, No. 5, May 1983.

Country Reports on Human Rights Practices. Washington, D.C.: US Dept. of State, Feb. 1981.

"The Incongruous Shadow." *Connexions,* No. 5, Summer 1982.

Report from Romania to (UN)ECOSOC. "Implementation of the International Covenant on Economic, Social and Cultural Rights." May 30, 1979. New York: United Nations, Dec. 21, 1979.

"Romania Raises Birthrate by Restricting Abortion, Birth Control Access."

Family Planning Perspectives, Vol. 11, No. 5, 1979.

Romania Yearbook 1982. Bucharest: Government Publishing House, 1983.

"Situation Report: Romania, Women." *Radio Free Europe Research,* Vol. 7, No. 13, Apr. 2, 1982.

SAUDI ARABIA

Almana, Aisha. "Wage Differentials Based on National Origin," 1979; unpublished paper.

Avril, Catherine. "Purdah: A Feminist's Hell." *The Second Wave,* Spring–Summer 1977.

Bahry, Lou'ay. "The New Saudi Woman: Modernizing in an Islamic Framework." *The Middle East Journal,* Vol. 36, No. 4, Autumn 1982.

Census of the Agricultural Sector, 1973–74. Riyadh: Ministry of Agriculture and Water Resources, n.d.

Cockburn, Alexander. "A Saudi Romance." *Village Voice,* Jan. 30, 1978.

Dearden, Ann, ed. "Arab Women." *Minority Rights Group,* Report No. 27, London, 1976.

First Five-Year Development Plan, 1970–75. Riyadh: Ministry of Planning, 1970.

"Flogging Appealed." *New York Post,* Apr. 1, 1980.

Gerth, Jeff. "3 US Employees Ousted by ARAMCO." *New York Times,* Nov. 21, 1983.

House, Karen Elliot. "Saudi Marriage Mores Are Shaken as Women Seek a Stronger Voice." *Wall Street Journal,* June 8, 1981.

Martin, Douglas. "Saudi Banks for Women Thriving." *New York Times,* Jan. 27, 1982.

———. "Saudi Women Moving into Banking." *International Herald Tribune,* Feb. 4, 1982.

Mernissi, Fatima. "The Symbolics of Feminity Models: *Nuchuz* (Women's Rebellion) and the Issue of Freedom in 1980's Islam's Democracy Crisis." Paper delivered at the Harvard Conference on Women, Religion, and Social Change. Cambridge, MA, June 12–18, 1983.

Ministry of Planning. *Social Affairs: Third Development Plan, 1400–1405 A.H.—1980–1985 A.D.* Riyadh, 1980.

"Modern Arabia: Saudi Women Get More Education but Few Get Jobs." *Wall Street Journal,* June 4, 1981.

"The New Saudi Woman." *Al-Raida,* Vol. VI, No. 24, Beirut, May 1, 1983.

Preliminary Summary Statistics on Education in the Kingdom of Saudi Arabia, 1979–80. Riyadh: Ministry of Education Data Center, 1980.

"Saudi Arabia." *New York Times,* Jan. 31, 1982.

Saudi Arabia: Population Policy Compendium. New York: A joint publication of (UN)ECOSOC and UNFPA, Mar. 1980.

Statistical Yearbook, 1974. Riyadh: Ministry of Finance and Planning, 1974.

"University Education Segregated." *New Women's Times,* Vol. VIII, No. 7, July–Aug. 1982.

SENEGAL

Adams, Neale, and Dennis Bell. "Even Socialists are Chauvinists." *Vancouver Express,* Vancouver, Nov. 3, 1978.

"A Co-Action Project in Senegal." *International Women's News* (Journal of the International Alliance of Women), Vol. 78, 1983/1.

Diop, Kader. "The Senegalese: A Woman Set Adrift." *Agence France Presse,* Paris, n.d.

"Genital Mutilation: A Statement from Africa." *ISIS,* No. 14, Geneva, 1980.

Heinzerling, Larry. "New Code Stirs Up Senegal." *New York Post,* Oct. 25, 1972.

Report from Senegal to (UN)ECOSOC. "Implementation of the International Covenant on Economic, Social and Cultural Rights." Apr. 15, 1981. New York: United Nations, Apr. 15, 1981.

Senegal: Population Policy Compendium. New York: A joint publication of (UN)ECOSOC and UNFPA, Dec. 1980.

"Senegal Will Have Women in the Police

Corps." *Al-Raida,* Vol. VI, No. 25, Beirut, Aug. 1, 1983.

Senegalese Penal Code and Code of Contraventions. Rufisque: National Press Publications, 1972.

Thiam, Awa. *La parole aux négresses.* Paris: Editions Denoël/Gonthier, 1978.

SOUTH AFRICA

Africa Report, Feb., 1977.

African National Congress (South Africa), Women's Section. *Voice of Women,* issues of Fourth Quarter 1977, First Quarter 1978, and Fourth Quarter 1980, London.

American Friends Service Committee. *AFSC Women's Newsletter,* Summer 1981.

Amnesty International. *Programme of Action for Banned People in South Africa.* London: International Secretariat, Dec. 1979.

Cape Times, Cape Town, Nov. 3, 1978.

Carnegie Quarterly, Vol. XXIX, Nos. 1 and 2. New York: Carnegie Corporation, Winter and Spring 1980 and 1981.

Chabaku, Motlalepula. "Growing Up in the Era of Pass Laws." *Ms.,* Vol. XI, No. 5, Nov. 1982.

Clarke, Liz, and Jane Ngolese. *Women Without Men.* Durban: Institute for Black Research, 1975.

" 'Cruel, Inhuman and Degrading' Situation in South Africa." *UN Chronicle,* Vol. XX, No. 3. New York: UN Dept. of Public Information, 1983.

From Women, available from P.O. Box 11486, Vlaeberg, 8018, Cape Town, South Africa.

Howe, Marvine. "Under Apartheid It's Black Women Who Suffer Most." *New York Times,* Oct. 20, 1970.

"I Opened the Road for You . . ." *ISIS,* No. 21, Geneva, Nov. 1981.

Jawitz, Merle, Moira Maconachie, and Jenny Schreiner. "Special Issue on Women." *Africa Perspective,* Cape Town, July 1979.

Lapchik, Richard E. "The Role of Women in the Struggle Against Apartheid in South Africa." *The Black Woman Cross-Culturally.* Ed. Filomina Chioma Steady. Cambridge, MA: Schenkman, 1981.

Lelyveld, Joseph. "South African Maids Organize, but Fear Wrath of 'Madam.' " *New York Times,* Mar. 30, 1981.

Leonard, Richard. *South Africa Fact Sheet.* New York: Africa Fund, n.d.

Lombard, J. A., *et al. Employment through Education.* Johannesburg: Mercabank, 1980.

Monro, E. E., and E. B. Hall. *Resolutions Adopted by the National Council of Women in South Africa from 1909.* Johannesburg: NCWSA, Mar. 1981.

"Power-Sharing Bill Introduced in South Africa." *New York Times,* May 6, 1983.

Rennie, Susan. "Apartheid Day by Day —An Obsession with Difference." *Ms.,* Vol. XI, No. 5, Nov. 1982.

Rivkin, Elizabeth Thaele. "The Black Woman in South Africa: An Azanian Profile." *The Black Woman Cross-Culturally.* Ed. Filomina Chioma Steady. Cambridge, MA: Schenkman, 1981.

de Smidt, Lorna. "Sex Survey Scrapped." *Spare Rib,* Issue 110, London, Sept. 1981.

Sojourner: The New England Women's Journal of News, Opinion and the Arts, Vol. 8, No. 4, Dec. 1982.

"South Africa and Lesotho: Three Lesbian Conversations." *Connexions,* No. 3, Winter 1982.

"South African Court Eases Black Residency Rules." *New York Times,* June 1, 1983.

South African Institute of Race Relations. *Survey of Race Relations in South Africa.* Johannesburg: SAIRR, 1983.

"South African Rape: An Ignored Epidemic." *The Longest Revolution,* Feb.–Mar. 1982.

"South Africans to Review International Sex Laws." *New York Times,* Apr. 22, 1983.

Study Commission of US Policy Toward

Southern Africa. *South Africa: Time Running Out.* Berkeley and Los Angeles: Univ. of California Press, 1981.

Talbot, Shirley Mashiane. "South African Women." *Asian Women,* Vol. XII, No. XXII, Tokyo, Mar. 1982.

"This Makes Me a Child All My Life." *Johannesburg Star,* Johannesburg, Aug. 22, 1981.

Treen, Joseph, and Holger Jensen. "Apartheid's Harsh Grip." *Newsweek,* Mar. 28, 1983.

Tsolo, Gladys. "Azania (South Africa): My Experience in the National Liberation Struggle." *National Liberation and Women's Liberation.* Eds. Marie Mies and Rhoda Reddock. The Hague: Institute for Social Studies, 1982.

(UN)ECOSOC. "Human Rights: Allegations Regarding Infringements of Trade Union Rights" (E/1983/49). New York: United Nations, May 4, 1983.

SPAIN

Falcón, Lidia. "La Violación: Tortura para Mujeres." *Poder y Libertad,* No. 2. Barcelona: Partido Feminista de España, 1981.

———. *Mujer y Sociedad.* Barcelona: Editorial Fontanella, 1969.

Feminist Coordinate of Barcelona. *Donnes en Lluita.* Barcelona, Apr. 1979.

Powell, Amanda. "Spanish Women's Movement Advancing." *Sojourner: The New England Women's Journal of News, Opinions, and the Arts,* Mar. 1979.

Sojourner: The New England Women's Journal of News, Opinions, and the Arts, Mar. 1983.

"Spain Acquits Women of Abortion Charges, Despite Law." *The Longest Revolution,* Apr.–May 1982.

"Spain's Abortion Law Faces Court Challenge." *New York Times,* Oct. 9, 1983.

"Spain's Parliament Votes to Ease Abortion Law." *New York Times,* Oct. 7, 1983.

"Supporting Spanish Women." *Spare Rib,* Issue 104, London, Mar. 1981.

Reports from Spain to (UN)ECOSOC. "Implementation of the International Covenant on Economic, Social and Cultural Rights." New York: United Nations, Feb. 16 and Oct. 7, 1982.

Waldman, Gloria F., and Linda Gould Levine. *Feminismo Ante el Franquismo.* Miami: Ediciones Universal, 1979.

Women in Spain: Supplement No. 8 to Women of Europe. Brussels: Commission of the European Communities, 1981.

Women in Statistics: Supplement No. 10 to Women of Europe. Brussels: Commission of the European Communities, 1982.

SRI LANKA

"Free Nirmala." *Spare Rib,* Issue 128, London, Mar. 1983.

Gunawardhana, Hema. *Status of Women: Sri Lanka.* Colombo: Univ. of Colombo, 1979.

Investment Promotion Division. *Sri Lanka's Investment Promotion Zones.* Colombo: Greater Colombo Economic Commission, 1979.

Jayasinghe, Vinitha. *National Report Submitted by Sri Lanka to the World Conference on the UN Decade for Women, Copenhagen, 1980.* Colombo: Women's Bureau of Sri Lanka, 1980.

———. *Promotion of Equality of Opportunity and Treatment by Reinforcing the Social Infrastructure.* Colombo: Women's Bureau of Sri Lanka, Ministry of Plan Implementation, Feb. 1980.

Jayawardena, Kumari. "Some Aspects of the Status of Women in Sri Lanka." *Selected Country Papers Presented at the ACPWD Expert Group Meeting.* Teheran, Iran, Dec. 1977. Bangkok: Asian and Pacific Center for Women and Development, June 1980.

Policy Branch. *Integration of Women in Development: Fact Sheet for Sri Lanka.* Ottawa: Canadian International Development Agency, 1980.

Postel, Els, and Joke Schrijuers, *et al. A Woman's Mind Is Longer Than a Kitchen Spoon: Report on Women in Sri*

Lanka. Leiden: Women and Development Research Project, June 1980.

"Sri Lankan Violence." *World Press Review,* Vol. 30, No. 10, Oct. 1983.

Stegall, L. S. *Women's Organizations and Development: An Assessment of Capacities for Technical Assistance in Sri Lanka and Thailand.* Washington, D.C.: Women in Development, n.d.

Voice of Women: Sri Lankan Journal for Women's Emancipation, issues of No. 2, June 1980, No. 3, Mar. 1981, and No. 4, July 1982, Colombo.

Wanigasundra, Mallika. "Modern Contraceptive Methods Preferred by Most Sri Lankan Women." *Depthnews,* Manila, Sept. 12, 1982.

Wickremesinghe. *Civil Procedure in Ceylon.* Colombo: n.p., 1971.

SUDAN

"Amputations in the Sudan." *Amnesty International Newsletter,* Vol. XIV, No. 2, Feb. 1984.

Cookson, John A., *et al. Area Handbook for the Republic of the Sudan.* Washington, D.C.: Foreign Affairs Studies Division, American Univ., 1964.

Country Reports on Human Rights Practices. Washington, D.C.: US Dept. of State, Feb. 1981.

el Dareer, Asma. "Attitudes of Sudanese People to the Practice of Female Circumcision." *International Journal of Epidemiology,* Vol. 12, No. 2, Oxford, 1983.

Farran, C. D'Olivier. *Matrimonial Laws of the Sudan.* London: Butterworth, 1963.

"Female Genital Mutilation." *ISIS,* No. 25, Geneva, 1982.

Fluehr-Lobban, Coarlyn. "Sudan: Arab Women's Struggle." *The Second Wave,* Vol. 2, No. 2, 1972.

International Corporation Dossier: Sudan. New York: UNDP, 1981.

International Directory of Women's Development Organizations. Washington, D.C.: US Agency for International Development, 1977.

Ismail, Manar Mohd, and Mary Jervasc Yak. "Statement Presented by the Sudan Delegation at the Second Regional Conference on the Integration of Women in Development." Lusaka, Zambia, Dec. 1979.

Lootens, Tricia. "Women in the Sudan." *Off Our Backs,* Vol. XIII, No. 2, Feb. 1983.

Morgan, Robin, and Gloria Steinem. "The International Crime of Genital Mutilation." *Ms.,* Vol. VIII, No. 9, Mar. 1980.

Mustoba, Zaki. *The Common Law in the Sudan.* Oxford: Clarendon Press, 1971.

Naisho, Joyce. "Tradition and Other Constraints on Health Care for Women in the Sudan." *Health Needs of the World's Poor Women.* Ed. Patricia W. Blair. Washington, D.C.: Equity Policy Center, 1981.

"Report on the Administration of the Sudan for 1948." Presented by the Secretary of State for Foreign Affairs, n.p.

Rushwan, Hamid. "Health Issues of Abortion." *Health Needs of the World's Poor Women.* Ed. Patricia W. Blair. Washington, D.C.: Equity Policy Center, 1981.

"Sudan: Arab Women's Struggle." *The Second Wave,* Vol. 2, No. 2, 1977.

"Sudan: Future Food Basket of the Middle East." *US/Arab Commerce,* Apr. 1983.

"The Sudanese Woman in Mass Media." *Al-Raida,* Vol. V, No. 20, Beirut, May 1, 1982.

Weil, Barbara. "I Divorce Thee, I Divorce Thee, I Divorce Thee." *The Middle East,* No. 41, London, Mar. 1978.

Women of Africa Today and Tomorrow. Addis Ababa, Ethiopia: (UN)ECA, 1975.

SWEDEN

Almbladh, Ingrid. "New Proposed Amendments to Sweden's Penal Code Regulations on Sexual Misconduct." *Current Sweden,* No. 300. Stockholm: The Swedish Institute, Apr. 1983.

The American Series of Foreign Penal Codes. Trans. Thorsten Sellin. South

Hackensack, NJ: Fred B. Rothman, 1973.

"Committee on Elimination of Discrimination Against Women Considers Report of Sweden." Aug. 8, 1983. UN Press Release.

"Committee on Elimination of Discrimination Against Women Concludes Consideration of Reports of Soviet Union and Sweden." Aug. 8, 1983. UN Press Release.

Eduards, Maud. "The Swedish Woman in Political Life." *Political Life in Sweden,* No. 4. New York: Swedish Information Service, Swedish Consulate General, June 1980.

Employment Service Division. *Equality in the Labour Market: Statistics.* Stockholm: National Labour Market Board, 1981.

"Equality Between Women and Men in Sweden." *Fact Sheets on Sweden.* Stockholm: The Swedish Institute, July 1981.

Gustafsson, Siv. "Women and Work in Sweden." *Working Life in Sweden,* No. 15. New York: Swedish Information Service, Swedish Consulate General, Dec. 1979.

Hedlund, Eva, Birgitta Lundmark, and Gunilla Lundmark. "Meeting and Working with the Problem of Rape." *Social Change in Sweden,* No. 14. New York: Swedish Information Service, Swedish Consulate General, Nov. 1979.

"Legislation on Family Planning." *Fact Sheets on Sweden.* Stockholm: The Swedish Institute, Aug. 1982.

Liljeström, Rita. "Integration of Family Policy and Labor Market Policy in Sweden." *Social Change in Sweden,* No. 9. New York: Swedish Information Service, Swedish Consulate General, Dec. 1978.

Linner, Birgitta. "Status of Women and Law in Sweden." *Law and the Status of Women.* Ed. *The Columbia Human Rights Law Review.* New York: Centre for Social Development and Humanitarian Affairs, United Nations, 1977.

Ministry of Labour. *Act Concerning Equality Between Women and Men at Work.* Stockholm, 1980.

National Committee on Equality Between Men and Women. *Step by Step, National Plan of Action for Equality.* Stockholm: LiberFörlag, 1979.

Odmark, Ingegerd. *Swedish Report to the International Seminar on Women's Education, Training and Employment in Industrialized Countries.* Tokyo, Dec. 2–6, 1980. Stockholm: National Swedish Board of Education, Information Section, Dec. 1980.

Pogrebin, Letty Cottin. "A Feminist in Sweden: I Have Seen the Future and It (Almost) Works." *Ms.,* Vol. X, No. 10, Apr. 1982. [Data drawn from both the above published article and also from unpublished notes.]

"Prostitution i Sverige" (Prostitution in Sweden), Swedish National Study. Stockholm: Socialdepartmentet (Dept. of Social Affairs), 1981.

Report from Sweden to (UN)ECOSOC. "Implementation of the International Covenant on Economic, Social and Cultural Rights." Dec. 12, 1979. New York: United Nations, Jan. 4, 1980.

Rollen, Berit. "Gently Towards Equality." *Working Life in Sweden,* No. 5. New York: Swedish Information Service, Swedish Consulate General, May 1978.

———. *Report to the Conference on the Implementation of Equal Pay and Equal Opportunity Legislation for Women in the United States, Western Europe and Canada.* Center for Research on Women, Wellesley College. May 1–4, 1978. Stockholm: National Labour Market Board, 1978.

Sanders, Elizabeth, ed. *Equality Is the Goal.* Stockholm: The Swedish Institute, 1975.

Scott, Hilda. *Sweden's "Right to Be Human."* Armonk, NY: M. E. Sharpe, 1982.

Statistical Abstract of Sweden, 1982/83. Stockholm: Swedish Central Statistics Bureau, 1982.

"Swedish Succession to Girls." *New Women's Times,* Vol. VI, No. 3, Feb. 1–14, 1980.

Trost, Jan. "Unmarried Cohabitation in Sweden." *Social Change in Sweden,* No. 18. New York: Swedish Information Service, Swedish Consulate General, May 1980.

Vision, Reality, Activities. Stockholm: RFSU Swedish Assoc. for Sex Education, 1981.

Wistrand, Birgitta. *Swedish Women on the Move.* Stockholm: The Swedish Institute, 1981.

THAILAND

Alert: Pirate Attacks on Refugee Women in the Gulf of Thailand. Washington, D.C.: Overseas Education Fund, the Refugee Women in Development Project, 1983.

American Friends Service Committee. "Mobilization Against Sex Tourism in Asia." *AFSC Women's Newsletter,* Summer 1981.

Bunnag, Morut, ed. *Law Journal,* Vol. 6, No. 3. Bangkok: Morut Bunnag International Law Office, 1977.

The Criminal Code B.E. 2499. International Translation. Bangkok, n.d.

Engel, David M. *Code and Custom in a Thai Provincial Court.* Tucson: Univ. of Arizona Press, 1978.

National Commission on Women's Affairs. "Aspects of Thai Women Today." Paper presented at the UN Decade for Women Conference, Copenhagen. July 1980.

National Council of Women in Thailand. *Survey Report on the Status of Thai Women in Two Rural Areas.* Bangkok, 1977.

National Identity Board. *Thailand Towards the 80's.* Bangkok, 1981.

Proceedings of the Peace Corps Conference on Women and Development. Bangkok: US Peace Corps, 1979.

Rand, Heidi. "Controversy Awaits 'Depo-Provera' in FDA Hearing." *The Longest Revolution,* June–July 1982.

"Sex Tourism to Thailand," and "Tourism Prostitution in Asia." *ISIS,* No. 13, Geneva, 1979.

Thailand: Population Policy Compendium. New York: A joint publication of (UN)ECOSOC and UNFPA, Jan. 1979.

Thitsa, Khin. *Providence and Prostitution, Image and Reality for Women in Buddhist Thailand.* London: CHANGE International Reports, 1980.

UNDP. "Recommendation by the Executive Director: Assistance to the Government of Thailand—Support to the National Family Planning Programme, Phase IV." New York: United Nations, Mar. 22, 1983.

Vajrasthira, Prathoomporn. "Thailand." *Creative Women in Changing Societies: A Quest for Alternatives.* Eds. Torill Stokland, Mallica Vajrathon, and Davidson Nicol. A UNITAR Book. Dobbs Ferry, NY: Transnational Publishers, 1982.

Women in the World: A Ford Foundation Position Paper. New York: Ford Foundation, Nov. 1980.

THE UNION OF SOVIET SOCIALIST REPUBLICS

Addendum Report from the USSR to (UN)ECOSOC. "Implementation of the International Covenant on Economic, Social and Cultural Rights." June 5, 1980. New York: United Nations, Jan. 27, 1981.

Atkinson, Dorothy, Alexander Dallin, and Gail Warshofsky Lapidus, eds. *Women in Russia.* Stanford: Stanford Univ. Press, 1977.

Boulton, Ralph. "Soviets Force Gritty Women Laborers into More Conventional Roles." *Washington Post,* Jan. 5, 1981.

"Committee on Elimination of Discrimination Against Women Considers [the] Report[s] of USSR (Aug. 3, 1983), Byelorussia (Aug. 4 and 10, 1983), and the Ukraine (Aug. 5, 1983)." UN Press Releases.

"Committee on Elimination of Discrimination Against Women Concludes

Consideration of Reports of Soviet Union and Sweden." Aug. 3, 1983. UN Press Release.

Goldberg, Rochelle Lois. "The Russian Women's Movement: 1859–1917." Diss., Univ. of Rochester, 1976.

"In the USSR." *Connexions,* No. 5, Summer 1982; translated from *L'Alternative,* French-language bi-monthly about Eastern Europe, No. 3, Mar.–Apr. 1980.

Juviler, Peter H. "Forcible Rape and Soviet Responses." Prepared for the annual meeting of the Academy of Criminal Justice Sciences, Philadelphia. Mar. 12, 1981.

———. "Whom the State Has Joined: Conjugal Ties in Soviet Law." *Soviet Law After Stalin: Part I—The Citizen and the State in Contemporary Soviet Law.* Eds. Donald D. Barry, George Ginsburgs, and Peter B. Maggs. Layden: A. W. Sijthaff-Layden, Univ. of Layden, 1977.

Lapidus, Gail Warshofsky. *Women in Soviet Society—Equality, Development and Social Change.* Berkeley and Los Angeles: Univ. of California Press, 1978.

de Madariaga, Isabel. *Russia in the Age of Catherine the Great.* New Haven, CT: Yale Univ. Press, 1981.

Mamonova, Tatyana, ed. *Women and Russia.* Boston: Beacon Press, 1984.

Morgan, Robin. "First Feminist Exiles from the USSR." *Ms.,* Nov. 1980.

"New Soviet Rituals Seek to Replace Churches." *New York Times,* Mar. 15, 1983.

Rzhanitsyna, L. "Current Problems of Female Labor in the USSR." *Women, Work and the Family in the Soviet Union.* Ed. Gail Warshofsky Lapidus. Armonk, NY: M. E. Sharpe, 1982.

"Sex Education." Moscow Beat, *World Press Review,* Vol. 30, No. 5, May 1983.

Sheptulina, N. N. "Protection of Female Labor." *Women, Work and the Family in the Soviet Union.* Ed. Gail Warshof-sky Lapidus, Armonk, NY: M. E. Sharpe, 1982.

Stites, Richard. *The Women's Liberation Movement in Russia: Feminism, Nihilism amd Bolshevism 1860–1930.* Princeton, NJ: Princeton Univ. Press, 1978.

THE UNITED NATIONS
See Suggested Further Reading list after Contributor's article.

THE UNITED STATES
"Administration's Budget Proposals Spell Hardship for Women and Children." *New Women's Times,* Apr. 1983.

Anderson, Kurt. "Private Violence." *Time,* Sept. 5, 1983.

"Beware of the Small Print." *New Women's Times,* Jan. 1983.

Boggan, E. Carrington, Marilyn G. Haft, Charles Lister, and John P. Rupp. *The Rights of Gay People: The Basic ACLU Guide to a Gay Person's Rights.* New York: Discus/Avon, 1975.

Bureau of Statistics. *Employment and Earnings, April 1983.* Washington, D.C.: US Dept. of Labor, 1983.

Cocks, Jay. "How Long Till Equality?" *Time,* July 12, 1982.

Davis, Marianna W., ed. *Contributions of Black Women to America,* 2 vols. Columbia, SC: Kenday Press, 1982.

"A Decade of Choice." *CARASA* [Committee for Abortion Rights and Against Sterilization Abuse] *News,* Vol. IV, No. 8, Nov.–Dec. 1982.

De Pauw, Linda Grant, and Conover Hunt, with Miriam Schneir. *Remember the Ladies: Women in America 1750–1815.* New York: Viking Press in assoc. with the Pilgrim Society, 1976.

Dowd, Maureen, *et al.* "Rape: The Sexual Weapon." *Time,* Sept. 5, 1983.

"Economic Equity Act: What Is the Need?" *Women Today,* Vol. 13, No. 19, Sept. 23, 1983.

Ehrenreich, Barbara, and Karin Stallard. "The Nouveau Poor." *Ms.,* July–Aug. 1982.

"Employment Statistics Prove Irregularity." *New Women's Times,* Vol. XIII, No. 3, Mar. 1983.

The Equal Rights Amendment: A Bibliographic Study. Compiled by the Equal Rights Amendment Project. Westport, CT: Greenwood Press, 1976.

"Federal Budget Cuts Jeopardize Domestic Violence Programs: A National Survey Report." *Response to Violence in the Family,* Vol. 6, No. 3, May–June 1983.

Gay Rights Protection: US and Canada. New York: National Gay Task Force, Sept. 1982.

Government resources (1983): Bureau of Economic Analysis; Census Bureau; Dept. of Defense; Dept. of Educational Statistics; Dept. of Immigration; Dept. of Justice; Dept. of Labor; Food and Drug Administration; National Bureau of Health Statistics; National Center for Marriage and the Family; National Center for Mental Health.

Grumet, Robert Steven. "Sunksquaws, Shamans, and Tradeswomen: Middle Atlantic Coastal Algonkian Women During the 17th and 18th Centuries." *Women and Colonization.* Eds. Mona Etienne and Eleanor Leacock. New York: Praeger, 1980.

Gurko, Miriam. *The Ladies of Seneca Falls: The Birth of the Woman's Rights Movement.* New York: Macmillan, 1974.

Hymowitz, Carol, and Michaele Weissman. *A History of Women in America.* New York: Bantam Books, 1978.

Inequality of Sacrifice: The Impact of the Reagan Budget on Women. Washington, D.C.: Coalition on Women and the Budget, Mar. 16, 1983.

Lerman, Lisa G., and Franci Livingston. "State Legislation on Domestic Violence." *Response to Violence in the Family,* Vol. 4, No. 7, Sept.–Oct. 1983.

Lerner, Gerda, ed. *Black Women in White America: A Documentary History.* New York: Vintage Books, 1973.

———. *The Woman in American History.* Menlo Park, CA: Addison-Wesley, 1971.

Levine, Suzanne, and Harriet Lyons, eds. *The Decade of Women: A Ms. History of the Seventies in Words and Pictures.* New York: Paragon, 1980.

Lewin, Tamar. "Sex Differentials in Insurance." *New York Times,* May 2, 1983.

Magnuson, Ed, *et al.* "Child Abuse: The Ultimate Betrayal." *Time,* Sept. 5, 1983.

Mendelsohn, Ethel, and John H. Galvin. *The Legal Status of Women.* Washington, D.C.: US Dept. of Labor, Women's Bureau, 1983.

Millstein, Beth, and Jeanne Bodin. *We, the American Women: A Documentary History.* N.p.: Jerome S. Ozer, 1977.

Morgan, Robin. *The Anatomy of Freedom: Feminism, Physics, and Global Politics.* Garden City, NY: Anchor Press/Doubleday, 1982; paperback 1984.

Ms., special issue on the Family, Aug. 1978.

National Organization for Women Legal Defense and Education Fund. *The Myth of Equality.* Washington, D.C.: NOW, Jan. 1983.

National Women's History Week: Women's History Curriculum Guide. Santa Rosa, CA: National Women's History Week Project, 1979.

"New Study of Contraceptive Use Shows Most US Women Choose Sterilization or the Pill." New York: Alan Guttmacher Institute, Sept. 14, 1983; press release on findings published in *Family Planning Perspectives,* the institute's bi-monthly professional journal.

Off Our Backs, Vol. XIII, No. 5, May 1983; special issue on Women and the Law.

O'Reilly, Jane, *et al.* "Wife Beating: The Silent Crime." *Time,* Sept. 5, 1983.

Picker, Jane M. "Law and the Status of Women in the United States." *Law and the Status of Women.* Ed. *Columbia Human Rights Law Review.* New York: Centre for Social Development and Humanitarian Affairs, United Nations, 1977.

Pogrebin, Letty Cottin. *Family Politics: Love and Power on an Intimate Frontier.* New York: McGraw-Hill, 1983.

Pomroy, Martha. *What Every Woman Needs to Know About the Law.* Garden City, NY: Doubleday, 1980.

"Portrait of America." *Newsweek,* Jan. 17, 1983.

"Poverty Hits 20 Percent of All Children." *CDF* [Children's Defense Fund] *Reports,* Vol. 5, No. 8, Oct. 1983.

Rix, Sara E., and Anne J. Stone. *Reductions and Realities: How the Federal Budget Affects Women.* Washington, D.C.: Women's Research and Education Institute, 1983.

Russell, Diana E. H. *Rape in Marriage.* New York: Macmillan, 1982.

Sauvigné, Karen. *Digest of Leading Harassment Cases.* New York: Working Women's Institute, Sept. 1981.

———. *Sexual Harassment Is Against the Law.* New York: Working Women's Institute, 1982.

Schechter, Susan. *Women and Male Violence: The Visions and Struggles of the Battered Women's Movement.* Boston: South End Press, 1982.

Schneir, Miriam, ed. *Feminism: The Essential Historical Writings.* New York: Vintage Books, 1972.

Seligmann, Jean, and Rebecca Boren. "The Coupling of America." *Newsweek,* Sept. 19, 1983.

Sicherman, Barbara, and Carol Hurd Green, eds. *Notable American Women.* Cambridge, MA: Belknap Press of Harvard Univ. Press, 1980.

Sochen, June. *Herstory: A Woman's View of American History.* New York: Alfred, 1974.

Sojourner: The New England Women's Journal of News, Opinions, and the Arts, issues of Dec. 1981, and Mar. and May 1983.

The Spirit of Houston—The First National Women's Conference. An Official Report to the President, Congress and the People of the United States. Washington, D.C.: National Commission on the Observance of International Women's Year, 1978.

"Sterilization Study Confirms the Worst." *CARASA News,* Vol. 7, No. 2, Mar.–Apr. 1983.

"Supreme Court Gives Equal Rights to Support." *CDF Reports,* Vol. 5, No. 8, Oct. 1983.

Urbanska, Wanda. "The Status of Women in the United States." *Los Angeles Herald Examiner,* Jan. 23, 1983.

US Bureau of Census. "Money, Income of Households, Families and Persons in the US, 1981." *Current Population Report.* Washington, D.C., Mar. 1983.

US Dept. of Labor. *Employment and the Economy.* Washington, D.C., Jan. 1983.

Wallace, Michele. *Black Macho and the Myth of the Superwoman.* New York: Dial Press, 1979.

"WEAL'S Agenda for Women's Economic Equity." *Weal Washington Report,* Vol. 12, No. 3, June–July 1983.

"Who Are the Poor in the US?" *New Women's Times,* Vol. XIII, No. 4, Apr. 1983.

Williamson, Jane, Diane Winston, and Wanda Wooten, eds. *Women's Action Almanac: A Complete Resource Guide.* New York: William Morrow, 1979.

Women Growing Older. Washington, D.C.: Women's Equity Action League, Apr. 1983.

"Women's Issues Are American Issues." Editorial. *New York Times,* Apr. 29, 1983.

"WLDF Advocates for Child Support Enforcement." *WLDF* [Women's Legal Defense Fund] *News,* Fall 1983.

VENEZUELA

"Así Vivimos." *Acción Popular.* Caracas: Centro al Servicio de la Acción Popular, Oct.–Nov.–Dec. 1981.

"Backwards in Venezuela." *Off Our Backs,* Vol. XII, No. 3, Mar. 1982.

Código Penal Venezolano. Caracas: Editorial La Torre, 1964.

Falcón, Lidia. "La Violación: Tortura para las mujeres." *Poder y Libertad,*

No. 2. Barcelona, Spain: Partido Feminista de España, 1981.

Fuentes, Elizabeth. "La Democracia es Cosa de Hombres." *Suplemento al Diario El Nacional,* Caracas, Jan. 23, 1982.

González, Olga. "País Líder en Ministras de Estado." *OIM-IPS,* Mar. 1982.

Instituto Autónomo Biblioteca Nacional y de Servicios de Bibliotecas, ed. *Guía de la Mujer.* Caracas: Ministerio para la Participación de la Mujer en el Desarrollo, 1981.

Maldonado, Dra. Ana Lucina García. "Social-Juridical Situation of Women in Venezuela." Paper presented at the Mid-Decade Forum of the World Conference of the UN Decade for Women. Copenhagen, July 1980.

"La Participación de la Mujer." *Boletín Bimestral,* issues No. 1, Sept.–Oct., and No. 2, Nov.–Dec. 1980. Caracas: Despacho de la Ministro de Estado para Desarrollo.

Venezuela: Population Policy Compendium. New York: A joint publication of (UN)ECOSOC and UNFPA, Feb. 1982.

VIETNAM

Eisen, Arlene. *Women and Revolution in Vietnam.* London: Zed Press, 1984.

Eisen-Bergman, Arlene. *Women of Vietnam.* San Francisco: People's Press, 1975.

Haberman, Clyde. "Hong Kong Is Now a Chilly Port for 'Boat People.'" *New York Times,* Apr. 28, 1983.

"Long-term Detentions in Viet Nam." *Amnesty International Newsletter,* London, May 1983.

Ngo Dinh Long, and Nguyen Hoi Chan. *Vietnamese Women in Society and Revolution: 1. The French Colonial Period.* Cambridge, MA: Vietnam Resource Center, 1974.

"Report of the Central Committee of the Vietnam Women's Union to the Fifth Congress of Vietnamese Women." Hanoi. May 19, 1982; unpublished proceedings.

Research Division. *Women in Developing Countries: Case Studies of 6 Countries.* Stockholm: Swedish International Development Agency, 1974.

YUGOSLAVIA

First, Ruža. "The National Liberation Struggle and Women in Yugoslavia." *National Liberation and Women's Liberation.* Ed. Maria Mies and Rhoda Reddock. The Hague: Institute of Social Studies, 1982.

Kovačević, Dušanka. *Women of Yugoslavia in the National Liberation War.* Belgrade: Jugoslovenski Pregled, 1977.

Olga. "In Search of Yugoslav Lesbians." *Off Our Backs,* Vol. XII, No. 4, Apr. 1982.

Pick, Hella. "Belgrade's Woman at Top." *Manchester Guardian,* Manchester, Jan. 16, 1982.

Report from Yugoslavia to (UN)ECOSOC. "Implementation of the International Covenant on Economic, Social and Cultural Rights." June 18, 1982. New York: United Nations, Jan. 3, 1983.

"Sixth Report by the Committee of Experts on the Application of Conventions and Recommendations of the International Labour Organisation on Progress in Achieving Observance of the International Covenant on Economic, Social and Cultural Rights." New York: United Nations, Apr. 15, 1983.

Statistical Calendar of Yugoslavia 1979. Zagreb: N.p., n.d.

ZAMBIA

"Helsinki Follow-Up: Zambia." *International Women's News* (Journal of the International Alliance of Women), Vol. 78, 1983/1.

Kankassa, Mrs. B. C. *Report on the Development of the Status of Zambian Women.* Lusaka: Zambian Information Services and Freedom House, 1976.

Pellman, Jan. *Zambia: Security and Conflict.* New York: St. Martin's Press, 1974.

Prins, Gwyn. *The Hidden Hippopotamus.* Cambridge, England: Cambridge Univ. Press, 1980.

Republic of Zambia: Laws of Zambia—Marriage. Lusaka: Government Printer, 1918, as amended 1964.

Republic of Zambia: Penal Codes, Vol. 4. Lusaka: Government Printer, 1931.

Schuster, Ilsa. "Cycles of Dependence and Independence: Westernization and the African Heritage of Lusaka's Young Women." Working Paper No. 7. Ann Arbor: Women in International Development, Michigan State Univ., 1982.

Women Are the Strength of a Nation. Lusaka: Zambian Information Services and Freedom House, 1975.

ZIMBABWE

Africa, No. 117, London, May 1981.

Bare, Tendai. *Report on the Situation of Women in Zimbabwe.* Harare: Ministry of Community Development and Women's Affairs, Feb. 1982.

Country Reports on Human Rights Practices. Washington, D.C.: US Dept. of State, Feb. 1981.

DeVeaux, Alexis. "Zimbabwe: Women Fire!" *Essence,* July 1981.

Hadley, Janet. "Zimbabwe: Depo-Provera Out." *Spare Rib,* Issue 112, London, Nov. 1981.

"Hundreds Held in New Swoop on Prostitutes." *Sunday Mail,* Harare, Nov. 13, 1983.

Jones, J. D. F., and Michael Holman. "Zimbabwe Tries to Assuage Blacks' Land Hunger." *Financial Times,* Apr. 15, 1983.

Legum, Colin. "Zimbabwe's Uncertain Course." *World Press Review,* Vol. 30, No. 5, May 1983.

Liberation Through Participation, Women in the Zimbabwean Revolution: Writings and Documents from ZANU and the ZANU Women's League. New York: National Campaign in Solidarity with ZANU Women's League, n.d.

May, Joan. *The Women's Guide to Law Through Life.* Harare: Women and Development Research Unit, Center for Inter-Racial Studies, Univ. of Rhodesia, Apr. 1979.

McCalman, Kate. *We Carry a Heavy Load: Rural Women in Zimbabwe Speak Out.* Harare: Zimbabwe Women's Bureau, Dec. 1981.

Ministry of Economic Planning and Development. *Annual Economic Review of Zimbabwe.* Harare, Aug. 1981.

Muchena, Olivia N. "African Women in Town: A Socio-Economic Survey of Women in Highfield Township." Diss., Univ. of Rhodesia, 1978.

———. *Zimbabwe Women: A Socio-Economic Overview.* Addis Ababa, Ethiopia: ARTCW, (UN)ECA, 1982.

———. *Women's Organizations in Zimbabwe: An Assessment of Their Needs, Achievement and Potential.* Harare: Center for Applied Social Sciences, Univ. of Zimbabwe, 1980.

Mugabe, Sally, Tsitse Munyati, and Confidence Chengetayi. "Zimbabwe: My Experience in the National Liberation Struggle." *National Liberation and Women's Liberation.* Eds. Maria Mies and Rhoda Reddock. The Hague: Institute of Social Studies, 1982.

Nhariwa, Margaret. "Women and the Health System in Zimbabwe." *ISIS,* No. 20, Geneva, 1981.

"Overcoming Feudalism and Colonialism." *ISIS,* No. 3, Geneva, 1977.

"Zimbabwe: Against the Ideology of Power." *ISIS,* No. 19, Geneva, 1981.

Zimbabwe: Interview with Teurai Ropa Nhongo, Minister of Community Development and Women's Affairs, Secretary General of the ZANU Women's League. New York: Material Aid Campaign for ZANU-PF, Aug. 1982.

Zimbabwe Women's Bureau. *Black Women in Zimbabwe.* Harare, June 1980.

INDEX

Editor's Note: For the reader's convenience, we have compiled a deliberately focused Index, rather than attempting an all-inclusive one.

The entries listed are both specific and thematic. Such general overarching subjects as colonialism, imperialism, war and peace, poverty, hunger, racism, class differences, nationalism, development, and education are so omnipresent throughout the book as to make their indexing neither possible nor necessary. Space limitations required that the literally thousands of names (of persons, places, organizations, etc.) in *Sisterhood Is Global* not be indexed.

The following Index lists references and cross-references for the book's front matter, Contributor articles, and back matter only. The Statistical Prefaces have not been indexed, because they are structured in reference-book format, with clear headings and sub-headings (see the Prefatory Note and Methodology, pp. xvi–xxiii, for a detailed explanation of this format). In brief, and as a further aid to the reader, we restate that format here, including some sample sub-themes which can be found under certain headings in addition to the data one would normally expect to find there.

After the geographical data at the beginning of each Statistical Preface, the reader will encounter the **DEMOGRAPHY, GOVERNMENT,** and **ECONOMY** sections, followed by **GYNOGRAPHY,** which contains the subjects below, each with sub-headings of *Policy* and *Practice:*

Marriage (includes data on various forms of marriage, on dowry, property rights, spousal inheritance, adultery, widowhood, choice of domicile, wife-seclusion, etc.); **Divorce** (includes information on grounds and rights, child custody and support, property division, alimony, etc.); **Family** (covers data on varying family structures, single parents, pregnancy, childbirth, maternal death rates, maternity/paternity benefits, childcare centers, guardianship, child inheritance rights, and the elderly); **Welfare** (covers benefits and eligibility); **Contraception** (includes data on methods and use thereof, on sterilization, on incentives and disincentives, on male participation, and on sex education in schools); **Abortion** (covers conditions, methods, types of consent required, costs, penalties, and data on women's deaths due to illegality of the procedure); **Illegitimacy** (includes information on renunciation, single mothers, custody and surname, discrimination, paternal support, inheritance rights, "legitimization," and "honor murders"); **Homosexuality** (covers lack of and struggle for civil rights, data on lesbian mothers and custody rights, same-sex marriage, groups and publications); **Incest** (includes data on adult/consenting, marriage [endogamy], child rape, incest-survivor groups, etc.); **Sexual Harassment** (covers conditions of vulnerability to, activism against, and labor/employment legislation); **Rape** (includes marital rape, "honor murders," rape as political torture, distinction in status of victims [e.g., single women, married women, minors, women working in prostitution, etc.], court requirements for prosecution, and rates of arrest and conviction); **Battery** (data on the beating of women and of children, the lack or presence of police intervention, alcoholism-causality information, victim shelters, etc.); **Prostitution** (includes data on the abduction and sale of women and children, international sexual slave traffic in women and children, regulation of prostitution, customer liability or lack thereof, pimping and brothel-keeping, "holy" [temple] prostitution, venereal disease); **Traditional/Cultural Practices** (including dowry murder, bride-kidnapping, virginity strictures, genital mutilation, body scarification, hymen reconstruction, female infanticide, footbinding, gratuitous use of hysterectomy, shock treatment, tranquilizers, crimes of "honor," forced suicides [*sati,* etc.], menstrual or nutritional tabus, *purdah* and other forms of seclusion); **Crisis Centers** (provides information on refuges, shelters, and hotlines for victims of rape, battery, incest, child abuse, and abandonment). The **HERSTORY** and **MYTHOGRAPHY** sections, which close each Statistical Preface, are self-explanatory.

R.M.

Abortion, xx, xx n., xxii, 3, 6–8, 9, 24, 25, 28,
    34, 55, 56, 57, 72, 85, 86–87, 96, 100, 109,
    112, 118, 132, 136, 177, 188, 213, 236,
    279, 294, 295, 336–7, 339, 350, 353,
    354, 374–5, 376, 446, 446n., 473, 474–5,
    476, 485, 496n., 504, 556, 566, 568, 583,
    599, 600, 621, 630, 631, 632, 633, 668,
    686, 687–8, 690, 691, 712, 715, 723,
    738
    See also Contraception, Reproductive
    freedom
Adultery, 56, 336, 339, 365, 451, 484, 496n.,
    630, 632
    See also Crimes of (and offenses against)
    honor, Divorce, Illegitimacy, Marriage
Aging, xv, xxii, 1, 2, 3, 8, 9, 12, 13, 35, 41,
    132, 134, 141, 157, 165, 177, 186, 221,
    233n., 246, 252, 285, 386, 389, 389n., 390,
    407–8, 423, 435, 466, 473, 505n., 513,
    545, 546, 576, 597, 615, 621, 633, 655,
    686, 711, 712, 713, 713n., 755
    See also Family, Suicide, Widows
Alcoholism, 23, 95, 195, 293, 310–11, 514,
    524, 566, 687, 687n.
    See also Battery, Child, Rape, Violence
Anti-nuclear activism, 25, 67, 74, 95n., 98, 99,
    186, 254, 475, 515, 516, 522, 523, 523n.,
    524, 525, 714, 715
Apartheid, xv, 19, 614–23
Art, xv, xxii, 15, 25, 30, 31, 35, 73, 84, 86, 96,
    99, 110–11, 123, 127, 130, 141, 142, 143,
    165, 166, 179–80, 186, 188, 203, 204,
    237, 245, 246, 247, 251, 254, 262, 263n.,
    265–6, 309, 415, 422, 423, 424, 425,
    464, 484, 493, 495, 501, 504, 516, 520,
    525, 536, 546, 556, 574, 591, 597,
    629–30, 641, 643, 666, 674, 677, 690,
    691, 723, 738

Battery, xv, xvi, xxi, xxi n., xxiii, 3, 9 10, 10n.,
    13n., 20, 23, 33, 34, 67, 74, 95, 96, 109,
    123, 130, 132, 156, 157, 186, 195, 237,
    262, 264, 267, 278, 293, 311, 353, 414,
    474, 525, 553–4, 555, 622, 633, 677, 686,
    711, 739
    See also Alcoholism, Child, Crisis
    centers/hot-lines, Marriage, Violence
Bilateral family. *See* Family
Bisexuality. *See* Sexuality
Bride-kidnapping, 9, 10
    See also Marriage, Violence

Celibacy. *See* Sexuality
Child
    abuse, xx n., 1, 2, 3, 13n., 123, 711
    See also Alcoholism, Battery, Family,
        Genital mutilation, Incest, Pornography,
        Prostitution, Rape, Sex-tourism,
        Violence
    care, 12, 29, 48, 67, 85, 86, 101, 108, 155,
        175, 176, 177, 188, 205, 213, 221, 233n.,
        279, 294, 295, 335, 338n., 339, 366, 374,
        389n., 415, 423, 435, 444, 445, 451, 473,
        474n., 477, 486, 505n., 546, 555n., 564,
        576, 583, 599, 621, 633, 654, 686, 687,
        711, 711n., 720, 723, 756, 764. *See also*
        Family, Maternity leave/benefits,
        Paternity leave/benefits
    custody, 9, 10, 27, 206, 334, 336, 363, 496n.,
        630, 632, 714, 721, 757. *See also* Divorce,
        Patria Potestad
    health, 2, 131, 184, 308, 656. *See also*
        Health, Infant mortality
    marriage, 9, 13n., 323, 399, 413, 413n., 465,
        599. *See also* Marriage
    See also Family, Illegitimacy, Inheritance
Clitoridectomy. *See* Genital mutilation
Contraception, xv, xx, xx n., xxi, 2, 6–8, 9,
    20n., 25, 26, 34, 57, 86–87, 109, 122, 132,
    141, 158, 167, 177, 188, 208, 213, 246,
    256, 279, 294, 295, 322, 335, 337, 338n.,
    350, 351, 352–3, 354, 374, 375, 399, 445,
    466, 485, 496n., 524, 525, 536, 556, 556n.,
    566, 599, 600, 621–2, 630, 632, 633, 686,
    687–8, 712, 723
    See also Abortion, Depo-Provera,
    Reproductive freedom
Crafts. *See* Art
Crimes of (and offenses against) honor, 8, 20,
    21, 36, 84
    See also Abortion, Adultery, Illegitimacy,
    Infanticide, Rape, Violence, Virginity
Crisis centers/hot-lines, xxi, 13n., 23, 29, 65,
    67, 84, 96, 97, 109, 112, 237, 251, 474,
    516, 622, 677, 686, 711, 739
    See also Battery, Child, Incest, Migrants,
    Rape, Violence

Depo-Provera, 7, 524, 621–2, 622n.
    See also Contraception, Health,
    Reproductive freedom
Disablement, xxiii, 2, 206, 337, 376, 389n.,
    407, 413n., 486, 633, 711, 712, 713

Divorce, xx, 10, 11, 19, 26, 27, 74, 108, 157, 177, 186, 188, 193, 204, 205, 206, 208, 323, 334, 337, 350, 363, 364, 365, 376, 389, 414, 435, 437, 444, 466, 473, 496n., 504, 513, 513n., 547, 600, 630–31, 632, 633, 675, 687, 714, 721, 738, 766, 767, 768
   verbal (unilateral) repudiation/ renunciation (*talaq*), 10, 206, 323, 334, 414, 534, 597, 766, 767, 768
   See also Adultery, Child, Dowry, *Idda*
Dowry, 10–12, 28, 309–10, 373, 400, 414, 425, 455, 599, 614, 619, 642, 643, 764
   bride-price, 10, 400, 755, 764
   bridewealth, 10–11, 764
   lobola, 755
   mahar, 411, 766–7
   See also Divorce, Dowry murder, Marriage, Violence
Dowry murder, 11, 11n.–12n., 20
   See also Divorce, Marriage, Suicide, Violence

Excision. *See* Genital mutilation

Family
   bilateral, 12, 761
   general institution of, xx, xx n., 2, 3, 8, 9, 10, 12–13, 13n., 16, 24, 42, 57, 74, 97, 108, 110, 117, 118, 122, 125, 132, 135, 142, 155, 156–7, 158, 167, 173, 174, 177, 185, 188, 193, 205, 206, 214, 215, 216, 221, 222, 223, 225, 261, 262, 266, 294, 309, 321, 322, 323, 324, 325, 335, 336, 337, 339, 365, 376, 386, 389, 389n., 398, 413, 415, 422, 424, 425, 444, 445, 465, 473, 484–5, 504, 506, 513, 522, 525, 534, 536, 537, 544, 547, 555, 564, 565, 566, 567, 568, 575, 576, 583, 590, 591, 598, 600, 614, 615, 618, 621, 632, 633, 641, 655, 665, 674, 675, 687, 711, 712, 713, 714–15, 731, 732, 741, 755–6
   matrifocal systems, 12, 17, 119, 123, 675, 767
   matrilineal descent, 12, 14, 17, 598, 767
   single-parent, xx n., 2, 12, 13, 108, 120, 125, 263, 295, 351, 353, 445, 473, 600, 619, 630, 686, 714. *See also* Divorce, Illegitimacy, Migrants, Widows, Women-headed households, Women (single)

   See also Aging, Child, Incest, Inheritance, Maternity leave/benefits, Migrants, Paternity leave/benefits, Patria Potestad, *Purdah*, Violence
Family planning. *See* Contraception, Reproductive freedom
Female circumcision. *See* Genital mutilation

Gay rights. *See* Sexuality
Genital mutilation, xv, xxi, 4, 8, 13n., 20, 20n., 27–8, 28n., 29, 36, 237, 504, 597, 598, 599, 619, 656, 764, 765–6
   See also Health, Violence, Virginity

Hysterectomies. *See Health*
Health, xxi, 2, 2n., 3, 7, 20, 20n., 25, 67, 109, 112, 132, 166, 167, 175, 177, 178, 184, 188, 195, 213, 221, 262, 308, 321, 322, 323, 324, 398, 400, 433, 436, 444, 466, 474, 485, 485n, 495, 496, 496n., 523, 524, 526, 535, 546, 564, 565, 600, 656, 710, 711, 712, 756, 765
   gratuitous hysterectomies, xxi, 6, 36
   malnutrition, 2, 7, 20, 21, 123, 194, 195, 321, 444, 535, 618
   See also Abortion, Battery, Child, Depo-Provera, Genital mutilation, Infant mortality, Maternal death rates, Migrants, Prostitution, Rape, Violence
Heterosexuality. *See* Sexuality
Homosexuality. *See* Sexuality

Idda, 414, 766
   See also Divorce, Widows
Illiteracy. *See* Literacy
Illegitimacy, xx, xx n., 7, 8, 13, 126, 143, 350, 351, 352, 365, 386, 399, 503, 555, 599, 712, 721, 723
   See also Adultery, Child, Crimes of (and offenses against) honor, Family, Infanticide, Inheritance, Women (single)
Incest, xvi, xx, xx n., xxiii, 350
   See also Child, Crisis centers/hotlines, Family, Rape
Infanticide, xxi, 8, 20–21, 118, 156, 719
   See also Crimes of (and offenses against) honor, Illegitimacy, Violence
Infant mortality, xviii, xviii n., 109, 132, 195, 208, 308, 321, 444
   See also Child, Health
Infibulation. *See* Genital mutilation

Inheritance, 13, 14, 206, 214, 321, 336, 386, 389, 400, 408, 413, 424, 425, 486, 598, 600, 719, 757, 767, 768
  See also Family, Illegitimacy, Marriage, Widows

Law of Evidence, 36, 206, 413, 536
Lesbian mothers, 713
  See also Family, Women-headed households
Lesbian women. *See* Sexuality
Literacy, xviii, xviii n., 1, 2, 19, 20, 24–25, 27, 31–32, 122, 174, 178, 194, 205, 215, 308, 323–4, 335, 337, 338 n., 339, 400, 401, 414, 416, 433, 434, 435, 436, 437, 444, 453, 466, 496, 534, 545, 546, 554, 555n., 591, 654, 723, 731
  See also Migrants

Malnutrition. *See* Health
Marriage
  common-law, xxii, 123, 365
  "concubinage" unions, xxii, 56, 123, 124, 131, 445, 504
  customary, 323
  forced/arranged, 6, 8, 9, 13n., 156–7, 158, 323, 413–14, 435, 436, 437, 465, 484, 597, 599, 614, 642, 675, 688. *See also* Bride-kidnapping
  general institution of, xv, xx, xxii, 9n., 9–12, 11n.–12n., 14, 14n., 27, 31, 74, 81, 117, 123, 131, 132, 155, 156–7, 158, 177, 193, 204, 205, 206, 208, 222, 245–7, 262–3, 266, 279, 321, 322, 323, 334, 337, 351, 363, 364, 365–6, 386, 388, 389, 413–14, 423, 424, 425, 437, 451, 453–6, 463, 465–6, 473, 483–4, 485, 503–4, 525, 535, 544, 547, 555, 565, 591, 597, 599, 600, 614, 615, 621, 630, 642, 664–5, 666, 721, 755, 757, 767
  See also Adultery, Battery, Bride-kidnapping, Child, Dowry, Dowry murder, Inheritance, Migrants, Patria Potestad, Polygamy, *Purdah*, Rape, Sexuality, Violence, Virginity, Widows
Maternal death rates, xviii, xxii, 7, 20, 109
  See also Abortion, Health
Maternity leave/benefits, 9–10, 16, 85, 126, 134, 155, 164, 206, 294, 295, 338n., 444, 445, 547, 555n., 564, 567, 568, 696, 721, 757

  See also Child, Family, Paternity leave/benefits
Matrifocal systems. *See* Family
Matrilineal descent. *See* Family
Migrants, xxi, 2–3, 16, 18, 22, 74, 195, 398, 433, 451–2, 535, 554–5, 598, 599, 600, 676, 714, 755–6
  See also Family, Prostitution, Refugees, Unemployment, Women-headed households

Nušuz, 34, 451

Paternity leave/benefits, 16, 295, 567, 568
  See also Child, Family, Maternity leave/benefits
Patria Potestad, 9, 10, 13n., 56, 630, 767
  See also Child, Family, Marriage
Peace movements. *See* Anti-nuclear activism
Polyandry. *See* Polygamy
Polygamy, xxi, xxii, 6, 9, 10, 14, 27, 203, 311, 323, 334, 398, 399, 414, 464, 465, 503, 504, 505, 534, 597, 598, 599, 677, 767
  See also Marriage
Polygyny. *See* Polygamy
Pornography, 4, 14n., 22, 95–6, 100, 109, 175, 236, 236n., 475, 712, 715
  See also Violence
Prostitution, xxi, xxi n., 3, 8, 21, 21n., 22, 84, 99–100, 143, 167, 292, 311, 333, 336, 337–8, 339, 398, 496n., 555, 600, 621, 676, 677, 686, 686n., 739
  See also Migrants, Sex-tourism, Unemployment, Violence
Purdah, 4, 14, 434, 452, 503, 537, 767

Rape, xv, xvi, xx n., xxi, xxiii, 8, 20, 21, 21n., 25, 29, 33, 63–8, 95, 96, 100, 109–10, 132, 133, 134, 167, 175, 186, 236, 237, 251, 256, 267, 285, 308, 309–10, 350, 376, 444, 446, 475, 485, 494, 501, 502, 547n., 554, 622, 633, 686, 687, 711, 723, 739
  marital, 9, 10, 10n., 21, 485, 547. *See also* Marriage
  See also Alcoholism, Child, Crisis centers/hot-lines, Crimes of (and offenses against) honor, Incest, Violence
Refugees, 1, 2, 20, 24–5, 29, 41–4, 132, 133, 133n, 279, 286, 287, 534, 543–8, 768, 769
  See also Migrants, Prostitution, Unemployment, Violence

Reproductive freedom, xx n., 1, 6–8, 9, 13, 26, 29, 31, 57, 82, 86–87, 120, 166, 167, 177, 206, 208, 213, 233n., 323, 350, 353, 374, 375, 485, 565, 566, 599, 622, 631, 634, 690, 712
    See also Abortion, Contraception, Depo-Provera, Sexuality

Sati, xxi, 20, 28, 29, 463, 464, 768
    See also Marriage, Suicide, Violence, Widows
Seclusion. *See* Purdah
Sex-tourism, xiii, 8, 15, 22, 22n.– 23n., 35, 768
    See also Prostitution, Unemployment, Violence
Sexual assault. *See* Rape
Sexual harassment, xvi, xx, xxiii, 8, 84, 108, 125, 236, 446, 485
    See also Violence
Sexuality, xv, xvi, xxii, 1, 3, 8, 9, 13–14, 14n., 22, 28, 30, 49, 76, 86, 97, 156, 158, 165, 166, 167, 174, 177, 186, 188, 224, 233n., 253, 254, 256, 261, 309, 310, 311, 337, 376, 377, 425, 432, 436, 445, 451, 475, 547, 548, 566, 576–8, 597, 619, 630, 632, 633, 668, 712, 713, 714, 765
    bisexuality, 14
    celibacy, 13
    heterosexuality, 9n., 13, 55, 96, 112, 174, 186–7, 236, 377, 475, 713, 713n.
    same-sex preference (female), xx, xxiii, 9n., 13–14, 14n., 35n., 55, 76, 84, 86, 97, 107, 112, 175, 186–7, 236, 237, 238, 350, 351, 377, 445, 477, 486, 622, 690, 710, 713, 713n., 714, 715, 738, *See also* Marriage
    same-sex preference (male), xx, xxiii, 9n., 13–14, 175, 236, 350, 477, 622, 690, 713, 714, 715, 738. *See also* Marriage
    transsexuality, 97
    See also Virginity
Squatters, 3, 96, 312, 445, 475
Suicide, xxiii, 9, 10, 11, 12n., 118, 156, 175, 247, 390, 597, 768

    See also Aging, Dowry murder, *Sati*, Violence, Widows
Suttee. *See* Sati

Transsexuality. *See* Sexuality

Unemployment, xix, xix n., xx, 2, 15, 17–18, 95, 119, 122, 123, 125, 131, 143, 184, 185, 194, 195, 205, 207, 208, 215, 308, 351, 387, 473, 476, 554, 565, 712, 756
    See also Migrants, Prostitution, Refugees

Violence, xxi n., xxii, 1, 9, 11, 20–23, 34, 35, 43, 76, 84, 95, 96, 109–10, 112, 120, 142, 165, 166, 167, 233n., 236, 264, 265, 278, 285–8, 309, 336, 375, 390, 446, 474, 475, 494, 517, 524, 535, 555, 556, 576–7, 597, 621, 622, 633, 677, 686, 687, 711, 713, 715, 739
    See also Alcoholism, Battery, Bride-kidnapping, Child, Crimes of (and offenses against) honor, Dowry murder, Genital mutilation, Health, Incest, Infanticide, Pornography, Prostitution, Rape, *Sati*, Sex-tourism, Sexual harassment
Virginity, 8, 13, 20, 21, 134, 156, 377, 445, 451, 463, 547, 666, 764, 765
    See also Crimes of (and offenses against) honor, Genital mutilation, Marriage

Widows, 9, 20, 29, 108, 143, 255, 261, 277, 365–6, 389, 390, 414, 463, 465, 484, 536, 547, 655, 766, 768
    See also Aging, Family, *Idda*, Inheritance, Marriage, *Sati*, Suicide
Wife-beating. *See* Battery
Women, single, xxii, 2, 108, 109, 155, 188, 222, 223, 262–3, 267, 323, 351, 366, 445, 473, 474n., 504, 547, 619
    See also Aging, Divorce, Family, Migrants
Women-headed households, 1–2, 12, 18, 119, 120, 123, 125, 195, 295, 309, 398, 564, 621, 711, 756
    See also Divorce, Family, Lesbian mothers, Migrants, Women (single)